D1620937

Security Engineering
Third Edition

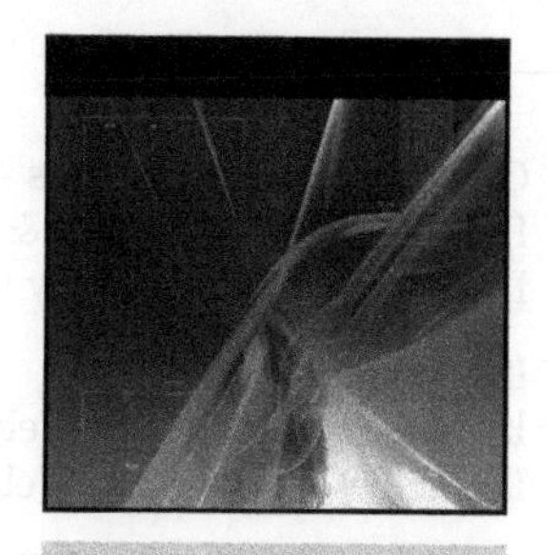

Security Engineering

A Guide to Building Dependable Distributed Systems
Third Edition

Ross Anderson

WILEY

Published by John Wiley & Sons, Inc., Indianapolis, Indiana
Published simultaneously in Canada

ISBN: 978-1-119-64278-7
ISBN: 978-1-119-64283-1 (ebk)
ISBN: 978-1-119-64281-7 (ebk)

Printed and bound by CPI Group (UK) Ltd, Croydon, CR0 4YY

For general information on our other products and services please contact our Customer Care Department within the United States at (877) 762-2974, outside the United States at (317) 572-3993 or fax (317) 572-4002.

Wiley publishes in a variety of print and electronic formats and by print-on-demand. Some material included with standard print versions of this book may not be included in e-books or in print-on-demand. If this book refers to media such as a CD or DVD that is not included in the version you purchased, you may download this material at `booksupport.wiley.com`. For more information about Wiley products, visit `www.wiley.com`.

Library of Congress Control Number: 2020948679

C9781119642787_181223

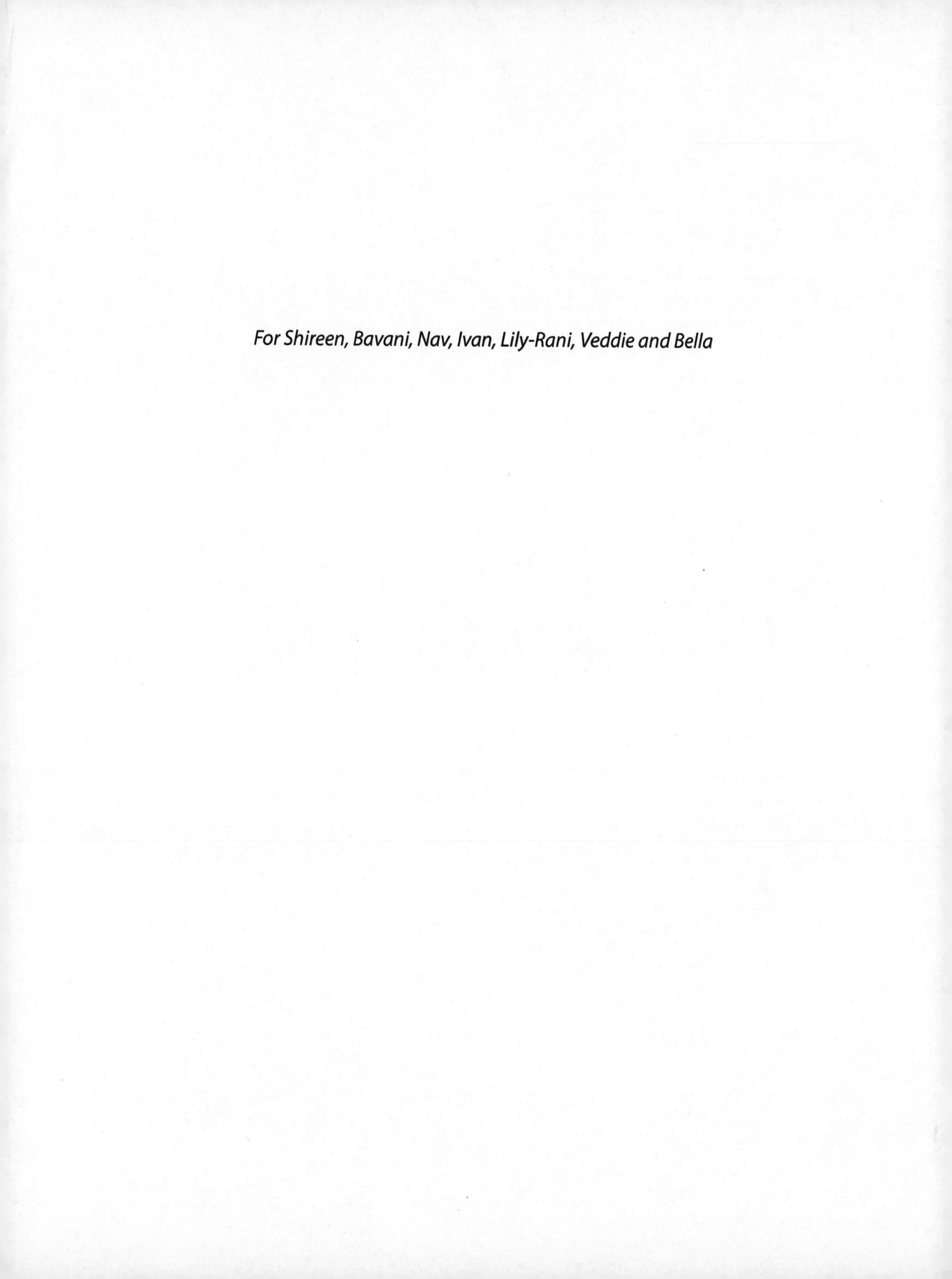

For Shireen, Bavani, Nav, Ivan, Lily-Rani, Veddie and Bella

About the Author

I've worked with systems for over forty years. I graduated in mathematics and natural science from Cambridge in the 1970s, and got a qualification in computer engineering; my first proper job was in avionics; and after getting interested in cryptology and computer security, I worked in the banking industry in the 1980s. I then started working for companies who designed equipment for banks, and then on related applications such as prepayment electricity meters.

I moved to academia in 1992 but continued to consult to industry on security technology. During the 1990s, the number of applications that used cryptology rose rapidly: burglar alarms, car door locks, road toll tags and satellite TV systems all made their appearance. The first legal disputes about these systems came along, and I was lucky enough to be an expert witness in some of the important cases. The research team I lead had the good fortune to be in the right place at the right time when technologies such as peer-to-peer systems, tamper-resistance and digital watermarking became hot topics.

After I'd taught security and cryptology to students for a few years, it became clear to me that the existing textbooks were too narrow and theoretical: the security textbooks focused on the access control mechanisms in operating systems, while the cryptology books developed the theory behind cryptographic algorithms and protocols. These topics are interesting, and important. But they're only part of the story. Most working engineers are not overly concerned with crypto or operating system internals, but with getting good tools and learning how to use them effectively. The inappropriate use of protection mechanisms is one of the main causes of security failure. I was encouraged by the positive reception of a number of articles I wrote on security engineering (starting with 'Why Cryptosystems Fail' in 1993).

Finally, in 1999, I got round to rewriting my class lecture notes and a number of real-world case studies into a book for a general technical audience.

The first edition of the book, which appeared in 2001, helped me consolidate my thinking on the economics of information security, as I found that when I pulled my experiences about some field together into a narrative, the backbone of the story was often the incentives that the various players had faced. As the first edition of this book established itself as the standard textbook in the field, I worked on establishing security economics as a discipline. In 2002, we started the Workshop on the Economics of Information Security to bring researchers and practitioners together.

By the time the second edition came out in 2008, it was clear we'd not paid enough attention to the psychology of security either. Although we'd worked on security usability from the 1990s, there's much more to it than that. We need to understand everything from the arts of deception to how people's perception of risk is manipulated. So in 2008 we started the Workshop on Security and Human Behaviour to get security engineers talking to psychologists, anthropologists, philosophers and even magicians.

A sabbatical in 2011, which I spent partly at Google and partly at Carnegie Mellon University, persuaded me to broaden our research group to hire psychologists and criminologists. Eventually in 2015 we set up the Cambridge Cybercrime Centre to collect lots of data on the bad things that happen online and make them available to over a hundred researchers worldwide. This hasn't stopped us doing research on technical security; in fact it's helped us pick more relevant technical research topics.

A medic needs to understand a whole series of subjects including anatomy, physiology, biochemistry, pharmacy and psychology, and then temper this knowledge with experience of working on hundreds of cases with experienced colleagues. So also a security engineer needs to understand technical subjects like crypto, access controls, protocols and side channels; but this knowledge also needs to be honed by studying real cases. My goal in my academic career has been to pull all this together. The result you now hold in your hands.

I have learned a lot in the process; writing down what you think you know is a good way of finding out what you don't. I have also had a lot of fun. I hope you have as much fun reading it!

Ross Anderson
Cambridge, November 2020

Acknowledgements

A great many people have helped in various ways with the third edition of this book. I put the chapters online for comment as I wrote them, and I owe thanks to the many people who read them and pointed out assorted errors and obscurities. They are: Mansoor Ahmed, Sam Ainsworth, Peter Allan, Amit Seal Ami, James Andrews, Tom Auger, Asokan, Maria Bada, Daniel Bates, Craig Bauer, Pilgrim Beart, Gerd Beuster, Johann Bezuidenhoudt, Fred Bone, Matt Brockman, Nick Bohm, Fred Bone, Phil Booth, Lorenzo Cavallaro, David Chaiken, Yi Ting Chua, Valerio Cini, Ben Collier, Hugo Connery, Lachlan Cooper, Franck Courbon, Christopher Cowan, Ot van Daalen, Ezra Darshan, Roman Dickmann, Saar Drimer, Charles Duffy, Marlena Erdos, Andy Farnell, Bob Fenichel, David Fernee, Alexis FitzGerald, Jean-Alain Fournier, Jordan Frank, Steve Friedl, Jerry Gamache, Alex Gantman, Ben Gardiner, Jon Geater, Stuart Gentry, Cam Gerlach, John Gilmore, Jan Goette, Ralph Gross, Cyril Guerin, Pedram Hayati, Chengying He, Matt Hermannson, Alex Hicks, Ross Hinds, Timothy Howell, Nick Humphrey, James Humphry, Duncan Hurwood, Gary Irvine, Erik Itland, Christian Jeschke, Gary Johnson, Doug Jones, Henrik Karlzen, Joud Khoury, Jon Kilian, Timm Korte, Ronny Kuckuck, Mart Kung, Jay Lala, Jack Lang, Susan Landau, Peter Landrock, Carl Landwehr, Peter Lansley, Jeff Leese, Jochen Leidner, Tom de Leon, Andrew Lewis, David Lewis, Steve Lipner, Jim Lippard, Liz Louis, Simon Luyten, Christian Mainka, Dhruv Malik, Ivan Marsa-Maestra, Phil Maud, Patrick McCorry, TJ McIntyre, Marco Mesturino, Luke Mewburn, Spencer Moss, Steven Murdoch, Arvind Narayanan, Lakshmi Narayanan, Kristi Nikolla, Greg Norcie, Stanislav Ochotnický, Andy Ozment, Deborah Peel, Stephen Perlmutter, Tony Plank, William Porquet, David Pottage, Mark Quevedo, Roderick Rees, Larry Reeves, Philipp Reisinger, Mark Richards, Niklas Rosencrantz, Andy Sayler, Philipp

Schaumann, Christian Schneider, Ben Scott, Jean-Pierre Seifert, Mark Shawyer, Adam Shostack, Ilia Shumailov, Barbara Simons, Sam Smith, Saija Sorsa, Michael Specter, Chris Tarnovski, Don Taylor, Andrew Thaeler, Kurt Thomas, Anthony Vance, Jonas Vautherin, Alex Vetterl, Jeffrey Walton, Andrew Watson, Debora Weber-Wulff, Nienke Weiland, David White, Blake Wiggs, Robin Wilton, Ron Woerner, Bruno Wolff, Stuart Wray, Jeff Yan, Tom Yates, Andrew Yeomans, Haaroon Yousaf, Tim Zander and Yiren Zhao. I am also grateful to my editors at Wiley, Tom Dinse, Jim Minatel and Pete Gaughan, and to my copyeditors Judy Flynn and Kim Wimpsett, who have all helped make the process run smoothly.

The people who contributed in various ways to the first and second editions included the late Anne Anderson, Adam Atkinson, Jean Bacon, Robin Ball, Andreas Bender, Alastair Beresford, Johann Bezuidenhoudt, Maximilian Blochberger, David Boddie, Kristof Boeynaems, Nick Bohm, Mike Bond, Richard Bondi, Robert Brady, Martin Brain, John Brazier, Ian Brown, Mike Brown, Nick Bohm, Richard Bondi, the late Caspar Bowden, Duncan Campbell, Piotr Carlson, Peter Chambers, Valerio Cini, Richard Clayton, Frank Clish, Jolyon Clulow, Richard Cox, Dan Cvrcek, George Danezis, James Davenport, Peter Dean, John Daugman, Whit Diffie, Roger Dingledine, Nick Drage, Austin Donnelly, Ben Dougall, Saar Drimer, Orr Dunkelman, Steve Early, Dan Eble, Mike Ellims, Jeremy Epstein, Rasit Eskicioğlu, Robert Fenichel, Fleur Fisher, Shawn Fitzgerald, Darren Foong, Shailendra Fuloria, Dan Geer, Gary Geldart, Paul Gillingwater, John Gilmore, Brian Gladman, Virgil Gligor, Bruce Godfrey, John Gordon, Gary Graunke, Rich Graveman, Wendy Grossman, Dan Hagon, Feng Hao, Tony Harminc, Pieter Hartel, David Håsäther, Bill Hey, Fay Hider, Konstantin Hyppönen, Ian Jackson, Neil Jenkins, Simon Jenkins, Roger Johnston, Oliver Jorns, Nikolaos Karapanos, the late Paul Karger, Ian Kelly, Grant Kelly, Alistair Kelman, Ronald De Keulenaer, Hyoung Joong Kim, Patrick Koeberl, Oliver Kömmerling, Simon Kramer, Markus Kuhn, Peter Landrock, Susan Landau, Jack Lang, Jong-Hyeon Lee, the late Owen Lewis, Stephen Lewis, Paul Leyland, Jim Lippard, Willie List, Dan Lough, John McHugh, the late David MacKay, Garry McKay, Udi Manber, John Martin, Nick Mathewson, Tyler Moore, the late Bob Morris, Ira Moskowitz, Steven Murdoch, Shishir Nagaraja, Roger Nebel, the late Roger Needham, Stephan Neuhaus, Andrew Odlyzko, Mark Oeltjenbruns, Joe Osborne, Andy Ozment, Alexandros Papadopoulos, Roy Paterson, Chris Pepper, Oscar Pereira, Fabien Petitcolas, Raphael Phan, Mike Roe, Mark Rotenberg, Avi Rubin, Jerry Saltzer, Marv Schaefer, Denise Schmandt-Besserat, Gus Simmons, Sam Simpson, Sergei Skorobogatov, Matthew Slyman, Rick Smith, Sijbrand Spannenburg, the late Karen Spärck Jones, Mark Staples, Frank Stajano, Philipp Steinmetz, Nik Sultana, Don Taylor, Martin Taylor, Peter Taylor, Daniel Thomas, Paul Thomas,

Vlasios Tsiatsis, Marc Tobias, Hal Varian, Nick Volenec, Daniel Wagner-Hall, Randall Walker, Robert Watson, Keith Willis, Simon Wiseman, Stuart Wray, Jeff Yan and the late Stefek Zaba. I also owe a lot to my first publisher, Carol Long.

Through the whole process I have been supported by my family, and especially by my long-suffering wife Shireen. Each edition of the book meant over a year when I was constantly distracted. Huge thanks to all for putting up with me!

Contents at a Glance

Contents

Preface to the Third Edition

The first edition of *Security Engineering* was published in 2001 and the second in 2008. Since then there have been huge changes.

The most obvious is that the smartphone has displaced the PC and laptop. Most of the world's population now walk around with a computer that's also a phone, a camera and a satnav; and the apps that run on these magic devices have displaced many of the things we were building ten years ago. Taxi rides are now charged by ride-hailing apps rather than by taxi meters. Banking has largely gone online, with phones starting to displace credit cards. Energy saving is no longer about your meter talking to your heating system but about both talking to your phone. Social networking has taken over many people's lives, driving everything from advertising to politics.

A related but less visible change is the move to large server farms. Sensitive data have moved from servers in schools, doctors' offices and law firms to cloud service providers. Many people no longer do their writing on word processing software on their laptop but on Google Docs or Office365 (I'm writing this book on Overleaf). This has consequences. Security breaches can happen at a scale no-one would have imagined twenty years ago. Compromises of tens of millions of passwords, or credit cards, have become almost routine. And in 2013, we discovered that fifteen years' worth of UK hospital medical records had been sold to 1200 organisations worldwide without the consent of the patients (who were still identifable via their postcodes and dates of birth).

A real game-changer of the last decade was the Snowden revelations, also in 2013, when over 50,000 Top Secret documents about the NSA's signals intelligence activities were leaked to the press. The scale and intrusiveness of government surveillance surprised even cynical security engineers. It followed on from Stuxnet, where America attacked Iran's nuclear weapons program using malware, and was followed by NotPetya, where a Russian cyberweapon, deployed against the Ukraine, inflicted hundreds of millions of dollars' worth of collateral damage on firms elsewhere. This brings us to the third big change, which is a much better understanding of nation-state security threats. In addition to understanding the capabilities and priorities of western intelligence agencies, we have a reasonably good idea of what the Chinese, the Russians and even the Syrians get up to.

And where the money is, the crooks follow too. The last decade has also seen the emergence of a cyber-crime ecosystem, with malware writers providing the tools to subvert millions of machines, many of which are used as criminal infrastructure while others are subverted in various ways into defrauding their users. We have a team at Cambridge that studies this, and so do dozens of other research groups worldwide. The rise of cybercrime is changing policing, and other state activity too: cryptocurrencies are not just making it easier to write ransomware, but undermining financial regulation. And then there are non-financial threats from cyber-bullying up through hate speech to election manipulation and videos of rape and murder.

So online harms now engage all sorts of people from teachers and the police to banks and the military. It is ever more important to measure the costs of these harms, and the effectiveness of the measures we deploy to mitigate them.

Some of the changes would have really surprised someone who read my book ten years ago and then spent a decade in solitary confinement. For example, the multilevel security industry is moribund, despite being the beneficiary of billions of dollars of US government funding over forty years; the Pentagon's entire information security philosophy – of mandating architectures to stop information flowing downward from Top Secret to Secret to Confidential to Unclassified – has been abandoned as unworkable. While architecture still matters, the emphasis has shifted to ecosystems. Given that bugs are ubiquitous and exploits inevitable, we had better be good at detecting exploits, fixing bugs and recovering from attacks. The game is no longer trusted systems but coordinated disclosure, DevSecOps and resilience.

What might the future hold? A likely game-changer is that as we put software into safety-critical systems like cars and medical devices, and connect them to the Internet, safety and security engineering are converging. This is leading to real strains; while security engineers fix bugs quickly, safety engineers like to test systems rigorously against standards that change slowly if at all. A wicked problem is how we will patch durable goods. At present, you might get security patches for your phone for three years and your laptop for five; you're expected to buy a new one after that. But cars last for fifteen years on average and if we're suddenly asked to scrap them after five the environmental costs won't be acceptable. So tell me, if you're writing navigation software today in 2020 for a car that will launch in 2023, how will you ensure that you can keep on shipping security patches in 2033, 2043 and 2053? What tools will you choose today?

Finally, there has been a sea change in the political environment. After decades in which political leaders considered technology policy to be for men in anoraks, and generally took the line of least resistance, the reports of Russian interference in the Brexit referendum and the Trump election got their attention. The prospect of losing your job can concentrate the mind wonderfully. The close attention of lawmakers is changing the game, first with tighter general rules such as Europe's General Data Protection Regulation; and second as products that are already regulated for safety, from cars and railway signals to children's toys acquire software and online connectivity, which has led to rules in Europe about how long software has to be maintained.

The questions the security engineer has to ask today are just the same as a decade ago: what are we seeking to prevent, and will the proposed mechanisms actually work? However, the canvas on which we work is now much broader. Almost all human life is there.

Ross Anderson
Cambridge, October 2020

Preface to the Second Edition

The first edition of *Security Engineering* was published in May 2001. Since then the world has changed.

System security was one of Microsoft's lowest priorities then; it's now one of the highest. The volume of malware continues to increase along with the nuisance that it causes. Although a lot of effort has gone into defence – we have seen Windows NT replaced by XP and then Vista, and occasional service packs replaced by monthly security patches – the effort put into attacks has increased far more. People who write viruses no longer do so for fun, but for profit; the last few years have seen the emergence of a criminal economy that supports diverse specialists. Spammers, virus writers, phishermen, money launderers and spies trade busily with each other.

Cryptography has also moved on. The Advanced Encryption Standard is being embedded into more and more products, and we have some interesting developments on the public-key side of things too. But just as our algorithm problems get solved, so we face a host of implementation issues. Side channels, poorly designed APIs and protocol failures continue to break systems. Applied cryptography is harder than ever to do well.

Pervasive computing also opens up new challenges. As computers and communications become embedded invisibly everywhere, so problems that used to only afflict 'proper computers' crop up in all sorts of other devices too. What does it mean for a thermometer to be secure, or an air-conditioner?

The great diversity of intelligent devices brings with it a great diversity of interests and actors. Security is not just about keeping the bad guys out, but increasingly concerned with tussles for power and control. DRM pits the content and platform industries against consumers, and against each other; accessory control is used to tie printers to their vendors' cartridges, but leads to antitrust lawsuits and government intervention. Security also interacts with safety in applications from cars through utilities to electronic healthcare. The security engineer needs to understand not just crypto and operating systems, but economics and human factors as well.

And the ubiquity of digital devices means that 'computer security' is no longer just a problem for a few systems specialists. Almost all white-collar crime (and much crime of the serious violent sort) now involves computers or mobile phones, so a detective needs to understand computer forensics just as she needs to know how to drive. More and more lawyers, accountants, managers and other people with no formal engineering training are going to have to understand system security in order to do their jobs well.

The rapid growth of online services, from Google and Facebook to massively multiplayer games, has also changed the world. Bugs in online applications can be fixed rapidly once they're noticed, but the applications get ever more complex and their side-effects harder to predict. We may have a reasonably good idea what it means for an operating system or even a banking service to be secure, but we can't make any such claims for online lifestyles that evolve all the time. We're entering a novel world of evolving socio-technical systems, and that raises profound questions about how the evolution is driven and who is in control.

The largest changes, however, may be those driven by the tragic events of September 2001 and by our reaction to them. These have altered perceptions and priorities in many ways, and changed the shape of the security industry. Terrorism is not just about risk, but about the perception of risk, and about the manipulation of perception. This adds psychology and politics to the mix. Security engineers also have a duty to contribute to the political debate. Where inappropriate reactions to terrorist crimes have led to major waste of resources and unforced policy errors, we have to keep on educating people to ask a few simple questions: what are we seeking to prevent, and will the proposed mechanisms actually work?

Ross Anderson
Cambridge, January 2008

Preface to the First Edition

For generations, people have defined and protected their property and their privacy using locks, fences, signatures, seals, account books, and meters. These have been supported by a host of social constructs ranging from international treaties through national laws to manners and customs.

This is changing, and quickly. Most records are now electronic, from bank accounts to registers of real property; and transactions are increasingly electronic, as shopping moves to the Internet. Just as important, but less obvious, are the many everyday systems that have been quietly automated. Burglar alarms no longer wake up the neighborhood, but send silent messages to the police; students no longer fill their dormitory washers and dryers with coins, but credit them using a smartcard they recharge at the college bookstore; locks are no longer simple mechanical affairs, but are operated by electronic remote controls or swipe cards; and instead of renting videocassettes, millions of people get their movies from satellite or cable channels. Even the humble banknote is no longer just ink on paper, but may contain digital watermarks that enable many forgeries to be detected by machine.

How good is all this new security technology? Unfortunately, the honest answer is 'nowhere near as good as it should be.' New systems are often rapidly broken, and the same elementary mistakes are repeated in one application after another. It often takes four or five attempts to get a security design right, and that is far too many.

The media regularly report security breaches on the Internet; banks fight their customers over 'phantom withdrawals' from cash machines; VISA reports huge increases in the number of disputed Internet credit card transactions; satellite TV companies hound pirates who copy their smartcards; and law enforcement agencies try to stake out territory in cyberspace with laws controlling the use of encryption. Worse still, features interact. A mobile phone that calls the last number again if one of the keys is pressed by accident may be just a minor nuisance – until someone invents a machine that dispenses a can of soft drink every time its phone number is called. When all of a sudden you find 50 cans of Coke on your phone bill, who is responsible, the phone company, the handset manufacturer, or the vending machine operator? Once almost every electronic device that affects your life is connected to the Internet – which Microsoft expects to happen by 2010 – what does 'Internet security' mean to you, and how do you cope with it?

As well as the systems that fail, many systems just don't work well enough. Medical record systems don't let doctors share personal health information as they would like, but still don't protect it against inquisitive private eyes. Zillion-dollar military systems prevent anyone without a "top secret" clearance from getting at intelligence data, but are often designed so that almost everyone needs this clearance to do any work. Passenger ticket systems are designed to prevent customers cheating, but when trustbusters break up the railroad, they cannot stop the new rail companies cheating each other. Many of these failures could have been foreseen if designers had just a little bit more knowledge of what had been tried, and had failed, elsewhere.

Security engineering is the new discipline that is starting to emerge out of all this chaos.

Although most of the underlying technologies (cryptology, software reliability, tamper resistance, security printing, auditing, etc.) are relatively well understood, the knowledge and experience of how to apply them effectively is much scarcer. And since the move from mechanical to digital mechanisms is happening everywhere at once, there just has not been time for the lessons learned to percolate through the engineering community. Time and again, we see the same old square wheels being reinvented.

The industries that have managed the transition most capably are often those that have been able to borrow an appropriate technology from another discipline. Examples include the reuse of technology designed for military identify-friend-or-foe equipment in bank cash machines and even prepayment gas meters. So even if a security designer has serious expertise in some particular speciality – whether as a mathematician working with ciphers or a chemist developing banknote inks – it is still prudent to have an overview of the whole subject. The essence of good security engineering is understanding the potential threats to a system, then applying an appropriate mix of protective measures – both technological and organizational – to control them. Knowing what has worked, and more importantly what has failed, in other applications is a great help in developing judgment. It can also save a lot of money.

The purpose of this book is to give a solid introduction to security engineering, as we understand it at the beginning of the twenty-first century. My goal is that it works at four different levels:

1. as a textbook that you can read from one end to the other over a few days as an introduction to the subject. The book is to be used mainly by the working IT professional who needs to learn about the subject, but it can also be used in a one-semester course in a university;
2. as a reference book to which you can come for an overview of the workings of some particular type of system (such as cash machines, taxi meters, radar jammers, anonymous medical record databases or whatever);
3. as an introduction to the underlying technologies, such as crypto, access control, inference control, tamper resistance, and seals. Space prevents me from going into great depth; but I provide a basic road map for each subject, plus a reading list for the curious (and a list of open research problems for the prospective graduate student);
4. as an original scientific contribution in which I have tried to draw out the common principles that underlie security engineering, and the lessons that people building one kind of system should have learned from others. In the many years I have been working in security, I keep coming across these. For example, a simple attack on stream ciphers wasn't known to the people who designed a common anti-aircraft fire control radar so it was easy to jam; while a trick well known to the radar community wasn't understood by banknote printers and people who design copyright marking schemes, which led to a quite general attack on most digital watermarks.

I have tried to keep this book resolutely mid-Atlantic. A security engineering book has to be, as many of the fundamental technologies are American, while many of the interesting applications are European. (This isn't surprising given the better funding of US universities and research labs, and the greater diversity of nations and markets in Europe.) What's more, many of the successful European innovations – from the smartcard to the GSM mobile phone to the pay-per-view TV service – have crossed the Atlantic and now thrive in the Americas. Both the science, and the case studies, are necessary.

This book grew out of the security engineering courses I teach at Cambridge University, but I have rewritten my notes to make them self-contained and added at least as much material again. It should be useful to the established professional security manager or consultant as a first-line reference; to the computer science professor doing research in cryptology; to the working police detective trying to figure out the latest computer scam; and to policy wonks struggling with the conflicts involved in regulating cryptography and anonymity. Above all, it is aimed at Dilbert. My main audience is the working programmer or engineer who is trying to design real systems that will keep on working despite the best efforts of customers, managers, and everybody else.

This book is divided into three parts.

- The first looks at basic concepts, starting with the central concept of a security protocol, and going on to the human-computer interface, access controls, cryptology and distributed system issues. It does not assume any particular technical background other than basic computer literacy. It is based on an 'Introduction to Security' course which we teach to second year undergraduates.
- The second part looks in much more detail at a number of important applications such as military communications, medical record systems, cash machines, mobile phones and pay-TV. These are used to introduce more of the advanced technologies and concepts. It also considers information security from the viewpoint of a number of different interest groups such as companies, consumers, criminals, the police and spies. This material is drawn from my senior course on security, from research work, and from experience consulting.
- The third part looks at the organizational and policy issues: how computer security interacts with law, with evidence, and with corporate politics; how we can gain confidence that a system will perform as intended; and how the whole business of security engineering can best be managed.

I believe that building systems which continue to perform robustly in the face of malice is one of the most important, interesting, and difficult tasks facing engineers in the twenty-first century.

Ross Anderson
Cambridge, January 2001

For my daughter, and other lawyers ...

The tricks taught in this book are intended only to enable you to build better systems. They are not in any way given as a means of helping you to break into systems or do anything else illegal. So where possible I have tried to give case histories at a level of detail that illustrates the underlying principles without giving a 'hacker's cookbook'.

Governments fought to restrict knowledge of cryptography until the turn of the century, and there may still be people who believe that the knowledge contained in this book should not be published.

Their fears were answered in the first book in English that discussed cryptology, a 1641 treatise on optical and acoustic telegraphy written by Oliver Cromwell's cryptographer and son-in-law John Wilkins [2025]. He traced scientific censorship back to the Egyptian priests who forbade the use of alphabetic writing on the grounds that it would spread literacy among the common people and thus foster dissent. As he said:

> *'It will not follow that everything must be suppresst which may be abused ... If all those useful inventions that are liable to abuse should therefore be concealed there is not any Art of Science which may be lawfully profest.'*

The question was raised again in the nineteenth century, when some well-meaning people wanted to ban books on locksmithing. In 1853, a contemporary writer replied [1899]:

> *'Many well-meaning persons suppose that the discussion respecting the means for baffling the supposed safety of locks offers a premium for dishonesty, by showing others how to be dishonest. This is a fallacy. Rogues are very keen in their profession, and already know much more than we can teach them respecting their several kinds of roguery. Rogues knew a good deal about lockpicking long before*

locksmiths discussed it among themselves ... if there be harm, it will be much more than counterbalanced by good.'

Thirty years later, in the first book on cryptographic engineering, Auguste Kerckhoffs explained that you must always assume that the other side knows the system, so security must reside in the choice of a key.

His wisdom has been borne out by long experience since. The relative benefits of 'Open' versus 'Closed' security systems have also been studied by researchers applying the tools of dependability analysis and security economics. We discuss their findings in this book.

In short, while some bad guys will benefit from a book such as this, they mostly know it already – and the good guys benefit much more.

Ross Anderson
Cambridge, November 2020

Foreword

In a paper he wrote with Roger Needham, Ross Anderson coined the phrase 'programming Satan's computer' to describe the problems faced by computer-security engineers. It's the sort of evocative image I've come to expect from Ross, and a phrase I've used ever since.

Programming a computer is straightforward: keep hammering away at the problem until the computer does what it's supposed to do. Large application programs and operating systems are a lot more complicated, but the methodology is basically the same. Writing a reliable computer program is much harder, because the program needs to work even in the face of random errors and mistakes: Murphy's computer, if you will. Significant research has gone into reliable software design, and there are many mission-critical software applications that are designed to withstand Murphy's Law.

Writing a secure computer program is another matter entirely. Security involves making sure things work, not in the presence of random faults, but in the face of an intelligent and malicious adversary trying to ensure that things fail in the worst possible way at the worst possible time ... again and again. It truly is programming Satan's computer.

Security engineering is different from any other kind of programming. It's a point I made over and over again: in my own book, Secrets and Lies, in my monthly newsletter Crypto-Gram, and in my other writings. And it's a point Ross makes in every chapter of this book. This is why, if you're doing any security engineering ... if you're even thinking of doing any security engineering, you need to read this book. It's the first, and only, end-to-end modern security design and engineering book ever written.

And it comes just in time. You can divide the history of the Internet into three waves. The first wave centered around mainframes and terminals. Computers were expensive and rare. The second wave, from about 1992 until now, centered around personal computers, browsers, and large application programs. And the third, starting now, will see the connection of all sorts of devices that are currently in proprietary networks, standalone, and non-computerized. By 2003, there will be more mobile phones connected to the Internet than computers. Within a few years we'll see many of the world's refrigerators, heart monitors, bus and train ticket dispensers, burglar alarms, and electricity meters talking IP. Personal computers will be a minority player on the Internet.

Security engineering, especially in this third wave, requires you to think differently. You need to figure out not how something works, but how something can be made to not work. You have to imagine an intelligent and malicious adversary inside your system (remember Satan's computer), constantly trying new ways to subvert it. You have to consider all the ways your system can fail, most of them having nothing to do with the design itself. You have to look at everything backwards, upside down, and sideways. You have to think like an alien.

As the late great science fiction editor John W. Campbell, said: "An alien thinks as well as a human, but not like a human." Computer security is a lot like that. Ross is one of those rare people who can think like an alien, and then explain that thinking to humans. Have fun reading.

Bruce Schneier
January 2001

PART I

In the first section of the book, I cover the basics. The first chapter sets out to clarify concepts and terminology by describing the secure distributed systems commonly found in four environments: a bank, an air force base, a hospital, and the home. The second chapter then plunges into the thick of things by describing the threat actors and how they operate. We look at state actors such as the US, Chinese and Russian intelligence communities, about which we now know quite a lot thanks to disclosures by Ed Snowden and others; we describe the cybercrime ecosystem, which we've been studying for some years now; and we also describe non-financial abuses from cyber-bullying and intimate partner abuse up to election manipulation and political radicalisation. This teaches that a wide range of attackers use similar techniques, not just at the technical level but increasingly to deceive and manipulate people.

In the third chapter we therefore turn to psychology. Phishing is a key technique for both online crime and national intelligence gathering; usability failures are exploited all the time, and are really important for safety as well as security. One of the most fruitful areas of security research in recent years has therefore been psychology. Security engineers need to understand how people can be deceived, so we can design systems that make deception harder. We also need to understand how risk perceptions and realities have drifted ever further apart.

The following chapters dig deeper into the technical meat. The fourth chapter is on security protocols, which specify how the players in a system – whether people, computers, phones or other electronic devices – establish and maintain trust. The fifth is on the 'duct tape' that underlies most of the protocols and holds distributed systems together: cryptography. This is the art (and science) of codes and ciphers; but it is much more than a clever means for keeping messages secret from an eavesdropper. Nowadays its job is taking trust from where it exists to where it's needed, maintaining the integrity of security contexts, and much more besides.

The sixth chapter is on access control: how can we keep apart the different apps on a phone, or the different virtual machines or containers on a server, and how can we control the data flows we want to permit between them. Sometimes this can be done cleanly, but often it's hard; web browsers deal with JavaScript code from multiple untrustworthy websites, while home assistants have to deal with multiple people.

The next chapter is on distributed systems. Systems that run on multiple devices have to deal with coordination problems such as concurrency control, fault tolerance, and naming. These take on subtle new meanings when systems must be made resilient against malice as well as against accidental failure. Many systems perform poorly or even fail because their designers don't think through these issues.

The final chapter in this part is on economics. Security economics has grown hugely since this book first appeared in 2001 and helped to launch it as a subject. We now know that many security failures are due to perverse incentives rather than to deficient technical protection mechanisms. (Indeed, the former often explain the latter.) The dependability of a system is increasingly an emergent property that depends on the self-interested striving of large numbers of players; in effect it's an equilibrium in a market. Security mechanisms are not just used to keep 'bad' people out of 'good' systems, but to enable one principal to exert power over another; they are often abused to capture or distort markets. If we want to understand such plays, or to design systems that resist strategic manipulation, we need some game theory and auction theory.

These chapters cover basic material, and largely follow what we teach first-year and second-year undergraduates at Cambridge. But I hope that even experts will find the case studies of interest and value.

CHAPTER

1

What Is Security Engineering?

Out of the crooked timber of humanity, no straight thing was ever made.
– IMMANUEL KANT

The world is never going to be perfect, either on- or offline; so let's not set impossibly high standards for online.
– ESTHER DYSON

1.1 Introduction

Security engineering is about building systems to remain dependable in the face of malice, error, or mischance. As a discipline, it focuses on the tools, processes, and methods needed to design, implement, and test complete systems, and to adapt existing systems as their environment evolves.

Security engineering requires cross-disciplinary expertise, ranging from cryptography and computer security through hardware tamper-resistance to a knowledge of economics, applied psychology, organisations and the law. System engineering skills, from business process analysis through software engineering to evaluation and testing, are also important; but they are not sufficient, as they deal only with error and mischance rather than malice. The security engineer also needs some skill at adversarial thinking, just like a chess player; you need to have studied lots of attacks that worked in the past, from their openings through their development to the outcomes.

Many systems have critical assurance requirements. Their failure may endanger human life and the environment (as with nuclear safety and control systems), do serious damage to major economic infrastructure (cash machines and online payment systems), endanger personal privacy (medical record systems), undermine the viability of whole business sectors (prepayment utility meters), and facilitate crime (burglar and car alarms). Security and safety are becoming ever more intertwined as we get software in everything.

Even the perception that a system is more vulnerable or less reliable than it really is can have real social costs.

The conventional view is that while software engineering is about ensuring that certain things happen ("John can read this file"), security is about ensuring that they don't ("The Chinese government can't read this file"). Reality is much more complex. Security requirements differ greatly from one system to another. You typically need some combination of user authentication, transaction integrity and accountability, fault-tolerance, message secrecy, and covertness. But many systems fail because their designers protect the wrong things, or protect the right things but in the wrong way.

Getting protection right thus depends on several different types of process. You have to figure out what needs protecting, and how to do it. You also need to ensure that the people who will guard the system and maintain it are properly motivated. In the next section, I'll set out a framework for thinking about this. Then, in order to illustrate the range of different things that security and safety systems have to do, I will take a quick look at four application areas: a bank, a military base, a hospital, and the home. Once we've given concrete examples of the stuff that security engineers have to understand and build, we will be in a position to attempt some definitions.

1.2 A framework

To build really dependable systems, you need four things to come together. There's policy: what you're supposed to achieve. There's mechanism: the ciphers, access controls, hardware tamper-resistance and other machinery that you use to implement the policy. There's assurance: the amount of reliance you can place on each particular mechanism, and how well they work together. Finally, there's incentive: the motive that the people guarding and maintaining the system have to do their job properly, and also the motive that the attackers have to try to defeat your policy. All of these interact (see Figure 1.1).

As an example, let's think of the 9/11 terrorist attacks. The hijackers' success in getting knives through airport security was not a mechanism failure but a policy one; the screeners did their job of keeping out guns and explosives, but at that time, knives with blades up to three inches were permitted. Policy changed quickly: first to prohibit all knives, then most weapons (baseball bats are now forbidden but whiskey bottles are OK); it's flip-flopped on many details (butane lighters forbidden then allowed again). Mechanism is weak, because of things like composite knives and explosives that don't contain nitrogen. Assurance is always poor; many tons of harmless passengers' possessions are consigned to the trash each month, while less than half of all the real weapons taken through screening (whether accidentally or for test purposes) are spotted and confiscated.

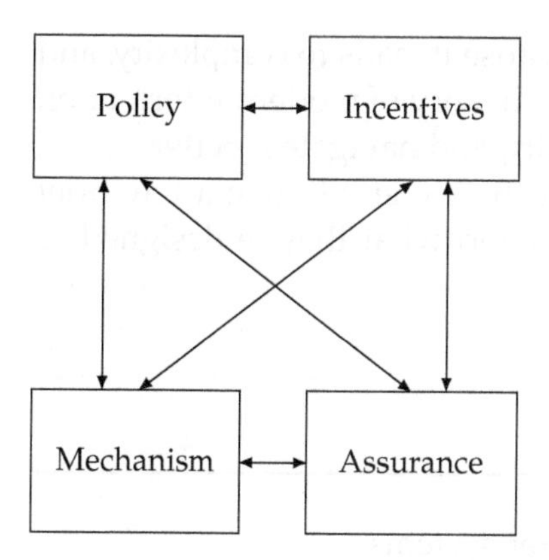

Figure 1.1: – Security Engineering Analysis Framework

Most governments have prioritised visible measures over effective ones. For example, the TSA has spent billions on passenger screening, which is fairly ineffective, while the $100m spent on reinforcing cockpit doors removed most of the risk [1526]. The President of the Airline Pilots Security Alliance noted that most ground staff aren't screened, and almost no care is taken to guard aircraft parked on the ground overnight. As most airliners don't have door locks, there's not much to stop a bad guy wheeling steps up to a plane and placing a bomb on board; if he had piloting skills and a bit of chutzpah, he could file a flight plan and make off with it [1204]. Yet screening staff and guarding planes are just not a priority.

Why are such policy choices made? Quite simply, the incentives on the decision makers favour visible controls over effective ones. The result is what Bruce Schneier calls 'security theatre' – measures designed to produce a feeling of security rather than the reality. Most players also have an incentive to exaggerate the threat from terrorism: politicians to 'scare up the vote' (as President Obama put it), journalists to sell more papers, companies to sell more equipment, government officials to build their empires, and security academics to get grants. The upshot is that most of the damage done by terrorists to democratic countries comes from the overreaction. Fortunately, electorates figure this out over time, and now – nineteen years after 9/11 – less money is wasted. Of course, we now know that much more of our society's resilience budget should have been spent on preparing for pandemic disease. It was at the top of Britain's risk register, but terrorism was politically more sexy. The countries that managed their priorities more rationally got much better outcomes.

Security engineers need to understand all this; we need to be able to put risks and threats in context, make realistic assessments of what might go wrong, and give our clients good advice. That depends on a wide understanding of what has gone wrong over time with various systems; what sort of attacks have worked, what their consequences were, and how they were stopped (if it was worthwhile to do so). History also matters because it leads to complexity, and complexity causes many failures. Knowing the history of modern information security enables us to understand its complexity, and navigate it better.

So this book is full of case histories. To set the scene, I'll give a few brief examples here of interesting security systems and what they're designed to prevent.

1.3 Example 1 – a bank

Banks operate a lot of security-critical computer systems.

1. A bank's operations rest on a core bookkeeping system. This keeps customer account master files plus a number of journals that record incoming and outgoing transactions. The main threat here is the bank's own staff; about one percent of bank branch staff are fired each year, mostly for petty dishonesty (the average theft is only a few thousand dollars). The traditional defence comes from bookkeeping procedures that have evolved over centuries. For example, each debit against one account must be matched by a credit against another; so money can only be moved within a bank, never created or destroyed. In addition, large transfers typically need two people to authorize them. There are also alarms that look for unusual volumes or patterns of transactions, and staff are required to take regular vacations with no access to the bank's systems.
2. One public face is the bank's automatic teller machines. Authenticating transactions based on a customer's card and personal identification number – so as to defend against both outside and inside attack – is harder than it looks! There have been many epidemics of 'phantom withdrawals' in various countries when local villains (or bank staff) have found and exploited loopholes in the system. Automatic teller machines are also interesting as they were the first large-scale commercial use of cryptography, and they helped establish a number of crypto standards. The mechanisms developed for ATMs have been extended to point-of-sale terminals in shops, where card payments have largely displaced cash; and they've been adapted for other applications such as prepayment utility meters.
3. Another public face is the bank's website and mobile phone app. Most customers now do their routine business, such as bill payments and transfers between savings and checking accounts, online rather than at a branch. Bank websites have come under heavy attack since 2005 from *phishing* – where customers are invited to enter their passwords

at bogus websites. The standard security mechanisms designed in the 1990s turned out to be less effective once criminals started attacking the customers rather than the bank, so many banks now send you a text message with an authentication code. The crooks' reaction is to go to a phone shop, pretend to be you, and buy a new phone that takes over your phone number. This arms race poses many fascinating security engineering problems mixing elements from authentication, usability, psychology, operations and economics.

4. Behind the scenes are high-value messaging systems, used to move large sums between banks; to trade in securities; to issue letters of credit and guarantees; and so on. An attack on such a system is the dream of the high-tech criminal – and we hear that the government of North Korea has stolen many millions by attacks on banks. The defence is a mixture of bookkeeping controls, access controls, and cryptography.
5. The bank's branches may seem large, solid and prosperous, reassuring customers that their money is safe. But the stone facade is theatre rather than reality. If you walk in with a gun, the tellers will give you all the cash you can see; and if you break in at night, you can cut into the safe in minutes with an abrasive wheel. The effective controls center on alarm systems, which are connected to a security company's control center, whose staff check things out by video and call the police if they have to. Cryptography is used to prevent a robber manipulating the communications and making the alarm appear to say 'all's well' when it isn't.

I'll look at these applications in later chapters. Banking computer security is important: until the early 2000s, banks were the main civilian market for many computer security products, so they had a huge influence on security standards.

1.4 Example 2 – a military base

Military systems were the other technology driver back in the 20th century, as they motivated much of the academic research that governments funded into computer security from the early 1980s onwards. As with banking, there's not one application but many.

1. Military communications drove the development of cryptography, going right back to ancient Egypt and Mesopotamia. But it is often not enough to just encipher messages: an enemy who sees traffic encrypted with somebody else's keys may simply locate and attack the transmitter. *Low-probability-of-intercept* (LPI) radio links are one answer; they use tricks that are now adopted in everyday communications such as Bluetooth.

2. Starting in the 1940s, governments spent a lot of money on electronic warfare systems. The arms race of trying to jam enemy radars while preventing the enemy from jamming yours has led to many sophisticated deception tricks, countermeasures, and counter-countermeasures – with a depth, subtlety and range of strategies that are still not found elsewhere. Spoofing and service-denial attacks were a reality there long before blackmailers started targeting the websites of bankers, bookmakers and gamers.
3. Military organisations need to hold some information close, such as intelligence sources and plans for future operations. These are typically labeled 'Top Secret' and handled on separate systems; they may be further restricted in compartments, so that the most sensitive information is known to only a handful of people. For years, attempts were made to enforce information flow rules, so you could copy a file from a *Secret* stores system to a *Top Secret* command system, but not vice versa. Managing multiple systems with information flow restrictions is a hard problem, and the billions that were spent on attempting to automate military security helped develop the access-control technology you now have in your mobile phone and laptop.
4. The problems of protecting nuclear weapons led to the invention of a lot of cool security technology, ranging from provably-secure authentication systems, through optical-fibre alarm sensors, to methods of identifying people using biometrics – including the iris patterns now used to identify all citizens of India.

The security engineer can still learn a lot from this. For example, the military was until recently one of the few customers for software systems that had to be maintained for decades. Now that software and Internet connectivity are finding their way into safety-critical consumer goods such as cars, software sustainability is becoming a much wider concern. In 2019, the European Union passed a law demanding that if you sell goods with digital components, you must maintain those components for two years, or for longer if that's a reasonable expectation of the customer – which will mean ten years for cars and white goods. If you're writing software for a car or fridge that will be on sale for seven years, you'll have to maintain it for almost twenty years. What tools should you use?

1.5 Example 3 – a hospital

From bankers and soldiers we move on to healthcare. Hospitals have a number of interesting protection requirements – mostly to do with patient safety and privacy.

1. Safety usability is important for medical equipment, and is by no means a solved problem. Safety usability failures are estimated to kill about as many people as road traffic accidents – a few tens of thousands a year in the USA, for example, and a few thousand in the UK. The biggest single problem is with the infusion pumps used to drip-feed patients with drugs; a typical hospital might have half-a-dozen makes, all with somewhat different controls, making fatal errors more likely. Safety usability interacts with security: unsafe devices that are also found to be hackable are much more likely to have product recalls ordered as regulators know that the public's appetite for risk is lower when hostile action becomes a possibility. So as more and more medical devices acquire not just software but radio communications, security sensitivities may lead to better safety.
2. Patient record systems should not let all the staff see every patient's record, or privacy violations can be expected. In fact, since the second edition of this book, the European Court has ruled that patients have a right to restrict their personal health information to the clinical staff involved in their care. That means that systems have to implement rules such as "nurses can see the records of any patient who has been cared for in their department at any time during the previous 90 days". This can be harder than it looks. (The US HIPAA legislation sets easier standards for compliance but is still a driver of information security investment.)
3. Patient records are often anonymized for use in research, but this is hard to do well. Simply encrypting patient names is not enough: an enquiry such as "show me all males born in 1953 who were treated for atrial fibrillation on October 19th 2003" should be enough to target former Prime Minister Tony Blair, who was rushed to hospital that day to be treated for an irregular heartbeat. Figuring out what data can be anonymized effectively is hard, and it's also a moving target as we get more and more social and contextual data – not to mention the genetic data of relatives near and far.
4. New technology can introduce poorly-understood risks. Hospital administrators understand the need for backup procedures to deal with outages of power; hospitals are supposed to be able to deal with casualties even if their mains electricity and water supplies fail. But after several hospitals in Britain had machines infected by the Wannacry malware in May 2017, they closed down their networks to limit further infection, and then found that they had to close their accident and emergency departments – as X-rays no longer travel from the X-ray machine to the operating theatre in an envelope, but via a server in a distant town. So a network failure can stop doctors operating when a power failure would not. There were standby generators, but no standby

network. Cloud services can make things more reliable on average, but the failures can be bigger, more complex, and correlated. An issue surfaced by the coronavirus pandemic is accessory control: some medical devices authenticate their spare parts, just as printers authenticate ink cartridges. Although the vendors claim this is for safety, it's actually so they can charge more money for spares. But it introduces fragility: when the supply chain gets interrupted, things are a lot harder to fix.

We'll look at medical system security (and safety too) in more detail later. This is a younger field than banking IT or military systems, but as healthcare accounts for a larger proportion of GNP than either of them in all developed countries, its importance is growing. It's also consistently the largest source of privacy breaches in countries with mandatory reporting.

1.6 Example 4 – the home

You might not think that the typical family operates any secure systems. But just stop and think.

1. You probably use some of the systems I've already described. You may use a web-based electronic banking system to pay bills, and you may have online access to your doctor's surgery so you can order repeat prescriptions. If you're diabetic then your insulin pump may communicate with a docking station at your bedside. Your home burglar alarm may send an encrypted 'all's well' signal to the security company every few minutes, rather than waking up the neighborhood when something happens.
2. Your car probably has an electronic immobilizer. If it was made before about 2015, the car unlocks when you press a button on the key, which sends an encrypted unlock command. If it's a more recent model, where you don't have to press any buttons but just have the key in your pocket, the car sends an encrypted challenge to the key and waits for the right response. But eliminating the button press meant that if you leave your key near the front door, a thief might use a radio relay to steal your car. Car thefts have shot up since this technology was introduced.
3. Your mobile phone authenticates itself to the network by a cryptographic challenge-response protocol similar to the ones used in car door locks and immobilizers, but the police can use a false base station (known in Europe as an IMSI-catcher, and in America as a Stingray) to listen in. And, as I mentioned above, many phone companies are relaxed about selling new SIM cards to people who claim their phones have been stolen; so a crook might steal your phone number and use this to raid your bank account.

4. In over 100 countries, households can get prepayment meters for electricity and gas, which they top up using a 20-digit code that they buy from an ATM or an online service. It even works off-grid; in Kenyan villages, people who can't afford $200 to buy a solar panel can get one for $2 a week and unlock the electricity it generates using codes they buy with their mobile phones.
5. Above all, the home provides a haven of physical security and seclusion. This is changing in a number of ways. Burglars aren't worried by locks as much as by occupants, so alarms and monitoring systems can help; but monitoring is also becoming pervasive, with many households buying systems like Alexa and Google Home that listen to what people say. All sorts of other gadgets now have microphones and cameras as voice and gesture interfaces become common, and the speech processing is typically done in the cloud to save battery life. By 2015, President Obama's council of advisers on science and technology was predicting that pretty soon every inhabited space on earth would have microphones that were connected to a small number of cloud service providers. (The USA and Europe have quite different views on how privacy law should deal with this.) One way or another, the security of your home may come to depend on remote systems over which you have little control.

Over the next few years, the number of such systems is going to increase rapidly. On past experience, many of them will be badly designed. For example, in 2019, Europe banned a children's watch that used unencrypted communications to the vendor's cloud service; a wiretapper could download any child's location history and cause their watch to phone any number in the world. When this was discovered, the EU ordered the immediate safety recall of all watches [903].

This book aims to help you avoid such outcomes. To design systems that are safe and secure, an engineer needs to know about what systems there are, how they work, and – at least as important – how they have failed in the past. Civil engineers learn far more from the one bridge that falls down than from the hundred that stay up; exactly the same holds in security engineering.

1.7 Definitions

Many of the terms used in security engineering are straightforward, but some are misleading or even controversial. There are more detailed definitions of technical terms in the relevant chapters, which you can find using the index. In this section, I'll try to point out where the main problems lie.

The first thing we need to clarify is what we mean by *system*. In practice, this can denote:

1. a product or component, such as a cryptographic protocol, a smartcard, or the hardware of a phone, a laptop or server;
2. one or more of the above plus an operating system, communications and other infrastructure;
3. the above plus one or more applications (banking app, health app, media player, browser, accounts/payroll package, and so on – including both client and cloud components);
4. any or all of the above plus IT staff;
5. any or all of the above plus internal users and management;
6. any or all of the above plus customers and other external users.

Confusion between the above definitions is a fertile source of errors and vulnerabilities. Broadly speaking, the vendor and evaluator communities focus on the first and (occasionally) the second of them, while a business will focus on the sixth (and occasionally the fifth). We will come across many examples of systems that were advertised or even certified as secure because the hardware was, but that broke badly when a particular application was run, or when the equipment was used in a way the designers didn't anticipate. Ignoring the human components, and thus neglecting usability issues, is one of the largest causes of security failure. So we will generally use definition 6; when we take a more restrictive view, it should be clear from the context.

The next set of problems comes from lack of clarity about who the players are and what they're trying to prove. In the literature on security and cryptology, it's a convention that principals in security protocols are identified by names chosen with (usually) successive initial letters – much like hurricanes, except that we use alternating genders. So we see lots of statements such as "Alice authenticates herself to Bob". This makes things much more readable, but can come at the expense of precision. Do we mean that Alice proves to Bob that her name actually is Alice, or that she proves she's got a particular credential? Do we mean that the authentication is done by Alice the human being, or by a smartcard or software tool acting as Alice's agent? In that case, are we sure it's Alice, and not perhaps Carol to whom Alice lent her card, or David who stole her phone, or Eve who hacked her laptop?

By a *subject* I will mean a physical person in any role including that of an operator, principal or victim. By a *person*, I will mean either a physical person or a legal person such as a company or government[1].

[1]The law around companies may come in handy when we start having to develop rules around AI. A company, like a robot, may be immortal and have some functional intelligence – but without consciousness. You can't jail a company but you can fine it.

A *principal* is an entity that participates in a security system. This entity can be a subject, a person, a role, or a piece of equipment such as a laptop, phone, smartcard, or card reader. A principal can also be a communications channel (which might be a port number, or a crypto key, depending on the circumstance). A principal can also be a compound of other principals; examples are a group (Alice or Bob), a conjunction (Alice and Bob acting together), a compound role (Alice acting as Bob's manager) and a delegation (Bob acting for Alice in her absence).

Beware that groups and roles are not the same. By a *group* I will mean a set of principals, while a *role* is a set of functions assumed by different persons in succession (such as 'the officer of the watch on the USS Nimitz' or 'the president for the time being of the Icelandic Medical Association'). A principal may be considered at more than one level of abstraction: e.g. 'Bob acting for Alice in her absence' might mean 'Bob's smartcard representing Bob who is acting for Alice in her absence' or even 'Bob operating Alice's smartcard in her absence'. When we have to consider more detail, I'll be more specific.

The meaning of the word *identity* is controversial. When we have to be careful, I will use it to mean a correspondence between the names of two principals signifying that they refer to the same person or equipment. For example, it may be important to know that the Bob in 'Alice acting as Bob's manager' is the same as the Bob in 'Bob acting as Charlie's manager' and in 'Bob as branch manager signing a bank draft jointly with David'. Often, identity is abused to mean simply 'name', an abuse entrenched by such phrases as 'user identity' and 'citizen identity card'.

The definitions of *trust* and *trustworthy* are often confused. The following example illustrates the difference: if an NSA employee is observed in a toilet stall at Baltimore Washington International airport selling key material to a Chinese diplomat, then (assuming his operation was not authorized) we can describe him as 'trusted but not trustworthy'. I use the NSA definition that a *trusted* system or component is one whose failure can break the security policy, while a *trustworthy* system or component is one that won't fail.

There are many alternative definitions of trust. In the corporate world, trusted system might be 'a system which won't get me fired if it gets hacked on my watch' or even 'a system which we can insure'. But when I mean an approved system, an insurable system or an insured system, I'll say so.

The definition of *confidentiality* versus *privacy* versus *secrecy* opens another can of worms. These terms overlap, but are not exactly the same. If my neighbor cuts down some ivy at our common fence with the result that his kids can look into my garden and tease my dogs, it's not my confidentiality that has been invaded. And the duty to keep quiet about the affairs of a former employer is a duty of confidence, not of privacy.

The way I'll use these words is as follows.

- *Secrecy* is an engineering term that refers to the effect of the mechanisms used to limit the number of principals who can access information, such as cryptography or computer access controls.
- *Confidentiality* involves an obligation to protect some other person's or organisation's secrets if you know them.
- *Privacy* is the ability and/or right to protect your personal information and extends to the ability and/or right to prevent invasions of your personal space (the exact definition of which varies from one country to another). Privacy can extend to families but not to legal persons such as corporations.

For example, hospital patients have a right to privacy, and in order to uphold this right the doctors, nurses and other staff have a duty of confidence towards their patients. The hospital has no right of privacy in respect of its business dealings but those employees who are privy to them may have a duty of confidence (unless they invoke a whistleblowing right to expose wrongdoing). Typically, privacy is secrecy for the benefit of the individual while confidentiality is secrecy for the benefit of the organisation.

There is a further complexity in that it's often not sufficient to protect data, such as the contents of messages; we also have to protect metadata, such as logs of who spoke to whom. For example, many countries have laws making the treatment of sexually transmitted diseases secret, and yet if a private eye could observe you exchanging encrypted messages with a sexually-transmitted disease clinic, he might infer that you were being treated there. In fact, a key privacy case in the UK turned on such a fact: a model in Britain won a privacy lawsuit against a tabloid newspaper which printed a photograph of her leaving a meeting of Narcotics Anonymous. So *anonymity* can be just as important a factor in privacy (or confidentiality) as secrecy. But anonymity is hard. It's difficult to be anonymous on your own; you usually need a crowd to hide in. Also, our legal codes are not designed to support anonymity: it's much easier for the police to get itemized billing information from the phone company, which tells them who called whom, than it is to get an actual wiretap. (And it's often more useful.)

The meanings of *authenticity* and *integrity* can also vary subtly. In the academic literature on security protocols, authenticity means integrity plus freshness: you have established that you are speaking to a genuine principal, not a replay of previous messages. We have a similar idea in banking protocols. If local banking laws state that checks are no longer valid after six months, a seven month old uncashed check has integrity (assuming it's not been altered) but is no longer valid. However, there are some strange edge cases. For example, a police crime scene officer will preserve the integrity of a forged check – by placing it in an evidence bag. (The meaning of integrity has changed in the new context to include not just the signature but any fingerprints.)

The things we don't want are often described as hacking. I'll follow Bruce Schneier and define a *hack* as something a system's rules permit, but which was unanticipated and unwanted by its designers [1682]. For example, tax attorneys study the tax code to find loopholes which they develop into tax avoidance strategies; in exactly the same way, black hats study software code to find loopholes which they develop into exploits. Hacks can target not just the tax system and computer systems, but the market economy, our systems for electing leaders and even our cognitive systems. They can happen at multiple layers: lawyers can hack the tax code, or move up the stack and hack the legislature, or even the media. In the same way, you might try to hack a cryptosystem by finding a mathematical weakness in the encryption algorithm, or you can go down a level and measure the power drawn by a device that implements it in order to work out the key, or up a level and deceive the device's custodian into using it when they shouldn't. This book contains many examples. In the broader context, hacking is sometimes a source of significant innovation. If a hack becomes popular, the rules may be changed to stop it; but it may also become normalised (examples range from libraries through the filibuster to search engines and social media).

The last matter I'll clarify here is the terminology that describes what we're trying to achieve. A *vulnerability* is a property of a system or its environment which, in conjunction with an internal or external *threat*, can lead to a *security failure*, which is a breach of the system's security policy. By *security policy* I will mean a succinct statement of a system's protection strategy (for example, "in each transaction, sums of credits and debits are equal, and all transactions over $1,000,000 must be authorized by two managers"). A *security target* is a more detailed specification which sets out the means by which a security policy will be implemented in a particular product – encryption and digital signature mechanisms, access controls, audit logs and so on – and which will be used as the yardstick to evaluate whether the engineers have done a proper job. Between these two levels you may find a *protection profile* which is like a security target, except written in a sufficiently device-independent way to allow comparative evaluations among different products and different versions of the same product. I'll elaborate on security policies, security targets and protection profiles in Part 3. In general, the word *protection* will mean a property such as confidentiality or integrity, defined in a sufficiently abstract way for us to reason about it in the context of general systems rather than specific implementations.

This somewhat mirrors the terminology we use for safety-critical systems, and as we are going to have to engineer security and safety together in ever more applications it is useful to keep thinking of the two side by side.

In the safety world, a *critical* system or component is one whose failure could lead to an accident, given a *hazard* – a set of internal conditions or external circumstances. *Danger* is the probability that a hazard will lead to an accident, and *risk* is the overall probability of an accident. Risk is thus hazard level combined with danger and *latency* – the hazard exposure and duration. *Uncertainty* is where the risk is not quantifiable, while *safety* is freedom from accidents. We then have a *safety policy* which gives us a succinct statement of how risks will be kept below an acceptable threshold (and this might range from succinct, such as "don't put explosives and detonators in the same truck", to the much more complex policies used in medicine and aviation); at the next level down, we might find a *safety case* having to be made for a particular component such as an aircraft, an aircraft engine or even the control software for an aircraft engine.

1.8 Summary

'Security' is a terribly overloaded word, which often means quite incompatible things to different people. To a corporation, it might mean the ability to monitor all employees' email and web browsing; to the employees, it might mean being able to use email and the web without being monitored.

As time goes on, and security mechanisms are used more and more by the people who control a system's design to gain some commercial advantage over the other people who use it, we can expect conflicts, confusion and the deceptive use of language to increase.

One is reminded of a passage from Lewis Carroll:

> *"When I use a word," Humpty Dumpty said, in a rather scornful tone, "it means just what I choose it to mean – neither more nor less." "The question is," said Alice, "whether you can make words mean so many different things." "The question is," said Humpty Dumpty, "which is to be master – that's all."*

The security engineer must be sensitive to the different nuances of meaning that words acquire in different applications, and be able to formalize what the security policy and target actually are. That may sometimes be inconvenient for clients who wish to get away with something, but, in general, robust security design requires that the protection goals are made explicit.

CHAPTER

2

Who Is the Opponent?

Going all the way back to early time-sharing systems we systems people regarded the users, and any code they wrote, as the mortal enemies of us and each other. We were like the police force in a violent slum.

– ROGER NEEDHAM

False face must hide what the false heart doth know.

– MACBETH

2.1 Introduction

Ideologues may deal with the world as they would wish it to be, but engineers deal with the world as it is. If you're going to defend systems against attack, you first need to know who your enemies are.

In the early days of computing, we mostly didn't have real enemies; while banks and the military had to protect their systems, most other people didn't really bother. The first computer systems were isolated, serving a single company or university. Students might try to hack the system to get more resources and sysadmins would try to stop them, but it was mostly a game. When dial-up connections started to appear, pranksters occasionally guessed passwords and left joke messages, as they'd done at university. The early Internet was a friendly place, inhabited by academics, engineers at tech companies, and a few hobbyists. We knew that malware was possible but almost nobody took it seriously until the late 1980s when PC viruses appeared, followed by the Internet worm in 1988. (Even that was a student experiment that escaped from the lab; I tell the story in section 21.3.2.)

Things changed once everyone started to get online. The mid-1990s saw the first spam, the late 1990s brought the first distributed denial-of-service attack, and the explosion of mail-order business in the dotcom boom introduced credit card fraud. To begin with, online fraud was a cottage industry; the same person would steal credit card numbers and use them to buy goods which he'd then sell, or make up forged cards to use in a store. Things changed in the mid-2000s with the emergence of underground markets. These let the bad guys specialise – one gang could write malware, another could harvest bank credentials, and yet others could devise ways of cashing out. This enabled them to get good at their jobs, to scale up and to globalise, just as manufacturing did in the late eighteenth century. The 2000s also saw the world's governments putting in the effort to 'Master the Internet' (as the NSA put it) – working out how to collect data at scale and index it, just as Google does, to make it available to analysts. It also saw the emergence of social networks, so that everyone could have a home online – not just geeks with the skills to create their own handcrafted web pages. And of course, once everyone is online, that includes not just spies and crooks but also jerks, creeps, racists and bullies.

Over the past decade, this threat landscape has stabilised. We also know quite a lot about it. Thanks to Ed Snowden and other whistleblowers, we know a lot about the capabilities and methods of Western intelligence services; we've also learned a lot about China, Russia and other nation-state threat actors. We know a lot about cybercrime; online crime now makes up about half of all crime, by volume and by value. There's a substantial criminal infrastructure based on malware and botnets with which we are constantly struggling; there's also a large ecosystem of scams. Many traditional crimes have gone online, and a typical firm has to worry not just about external fraudsters but also about dishonest insiders. Some firms have to worry about hostile governments, some about other firms, and some about activists. Many people have to deal with online hostility, from kids suffering cyber-bullying at school through harassment of elected politicians to people who are stalked by former partners. And our politics may become more polarised because of the dynamics of online extremism.

One of the first things the security engineer needs to do when tackling a new problem is to identify the likely opponents. Although you can design some specific system components (such as cryptography) to resist all reasonable adversaries, the same is much less true for a complex real-world system. You can't protect it against all possible threats and still expect it to do useful work at a reasonable cost. So what sort of capabilities will the adversaries have, and what motivation? How certain are you of this assessment, and how might it change over the system's lifetime? In this chapter I will classify online and electronic threats depending on motive. First, I'll discuss surveillance, intrusion and manipulation done by governments for reasons of state, ranging from cyber-intelligence to cyber-conflict operations. Second, I'll deal with criminals whose motive is mainly money. Third will be researchers who find vulnerabilities for fun or for money, or who report them out of social conscience – compelling firms to patch their software and clean up their operations. Finally, I'll discuss bad actors whose reasons are personal and who mainly commit crimes against the person, from cyber-bullies to stalkers.

The big service firms, such as Microsoft, Google and Facebook, have to worry about all four classes of threat. Most firms and most private individuals will only be concerned with some of them. But it's important for a security engineer to understand the big picture so you can help clients work out what their own threat model should be, and what sort of attacks they should plan to forestall.

2.2 Spies

Governments have a range of tools for both passive surveillance of networks and active attacks on computer systems. Hundreds of firms sell equipment for wiretapping, for radio intercept, and for using various vulnerabilities to take over computers, phones and other digital devices. However, there are significant differences among governments in scale, objectives and capabilities. We'll discuss four representative categories – the USA and its allies, China, Russia and the Arab world – from the viewpoint of potential opponents. Even if spies aren't in your threat model today, the tools they use will quite often end up in the hands of the crooks too, sooner or later.

2.2.1 The Five Eyes

Just as everyone in a certain age range remembers where they were when John Lennon was shot, everyone who's been in our trade since 2013 remembers where they were when they learned of the Snowden revelations on Friday 7th June of that year.

2.2.1.1 Prism

I was in a hotel in Palo Alto, California, reading the Guardian online before a scheduled visit to Google where I'd been as a scientific visitor in 2011, helping develop contactless payments for Android phones. The headline was 'NSA Prism program taps in to user data of Apple, Google and others'; the article, written by Glenn Greenwald and Ewen MacAskill, describes a system called Prism that collects the Gmail and other data of users who are not US citizens or permanent residents, and is carried out under an order from the FISA court [818]. After breakfast I drove to the Googleplex, and found that my former colleagues were just as perplexed as I was. They knew nothing about Prism. Neither did the mail team. How could such a wiretap have been built? Had an order been served on Eric Schmidt, and if so how could he have implemented it without the mail and security teams knowing? As the day went on, people stopped talking.

It turned out that Prism was an internal NSA codename for an access channel that had been provided to the FBI to conduct warranted wiretaps. US law permits US citizens to be wiretapped provided an agency convinces a court to issue a warrant, based on 'probable cause' that they were up to no good; but foreigners could be wiretapped freely. So for a foreign target like me, all an NSA intelligence analyst had to do was click on a tab saying they believed I was a non-US person. The inquiry would be routed automatically via the FBI infrastructure and pipe my Gmail to their workstation. According to the article, this program had started at Microsoft in 2007; Yahoo had fought it in court, but lost, joining in late 2008; Google and Facebook had been added in 2009 and Apple finally in 2012. A system that people thought was providing targeted, warranted wiretaps to law enforcement was providing access at scale for foreign intelligence purposes, and according to a slide deck leaked to the Guardian it was 'the SIGAD[1] most used in NSA reporting'.

The following day we learned that the source of the story was Edward Snowden, an NSA system administrator who'd decided to blow the whistle. The story was that he'd smuggled over 50,000 classified documents out of a facility in Hawaii on a memory stick and met Guardian journalists in Hong Kong [819]. He tried to fly to Latin America on June 21st to claim asylum, but after the US government cancelled his passport he got stuck in Moscow and eventually got asylum in Russia instead. A consortium of newspapers coordinated a series of stories describing the signals intelligence capabilities of the 'Five Eyes' countries – the USA, the UK, Canada, Australia and New Zealand – as well as how these capabilities were not just used but also abused.

The first story based on the leaked documents had actually appeared two days before the Prism story; it was about how the FISA court had ordered Verizon to hand over all call data records (CDRs) to the NSA in February that year [815]. This hadn't got much attention from security professionals as we knew the agencies did that anyway. But it certainly got the attention of lawyers and politicians, as it broke during the Privacy Law Scholars' Conference and showed that US Director of National Intelligence James Clapper had lied to Congress when he'd testified that the NSA collects Americans' domestic communications 'only inadvertently'. And what was to follow changed everything.

2.2.1.2 Tempora

On June 21st, the press ran stories about Tempora, a program to collect intelligence from international fibre optic cables [1201]. This wasn't a complete surprise; the journalist Duncan Campbell had described a system called Echelon in 1988 which tapped the Intelsat satellite network, keeping voice calls on tape while making metadata available for searching so that analysts could select

[1]Sigint (Signals Intelligence) Activity Designator

traffic to or from phone numbers of interest [375, 376] (I'll give more historical background in section 26.2.6). Snowden gave us an update on the technology. In Cornwall alone, 200 transatlantic fibres were tapped and 46 could be collected at any one time. As each of these carried 10Gb/s, the total data volume could be as high as 21Pb a day, so the incoming data feeds undergo *massive volume reduction*, discarding video, news and the like. Material was then selected using *selectors* – not just phone numbers but more general search terms such as IP addresses – and stored for 30 days in case it turns out to be of interest.

The Tempora program, like Echelon before it, has heavy UK involvement. Britain has physical access to about a quarter of the Internet's backbone, as modern cables tend to go where phone cables used to, and they were often laid between the same end stations as nineteenth-century telegraph cables. So one of the UK's major intelligence assets turns out to be the legacy of the communications infrastructure it built to control its nineteenth-century empire. And the asset is indeed significant: by 2012, 300 analysts from GCHQ, and 250 from the NSA, were sifting through the data, using 40,000 and 31,000 selectors respectively to sift 600m 'telephone events' each day.

2.2.1.3 Muscular

One of the applications running on top of Tempora was Muscular. Revealed on October 30th, this collected data as it flowed between the data centres of large service firms such as Yahoo and Google [2020]. Your mail may have been encrypted using SSL en route to the service's front end, but it then flowed in the clear between each company's data centres. After an NSA PowerPoint slide on 'Google Cloud Exploitation' was published in the Washington Post – see figure 2.1—the companies scrambled to encrypt everything on their networks. Executives and engineers at cloud service firms took the smiley as a personal affront. It reminded people in the industry that even if you comply with warrants, the agencies will also hack you if they can. It made people outside the industry stop and think: Google had accreted so much access to all our lives via search, mail, maps, calendars and other services that unrestricted intelligence-service access to its records (and to Facebook's and Microsoft's too) was a major privacy breach.

Two years later, at a meeting at Princeton which Snowden attended in the form of a telepresence robot, he pointed out that a lot of Internet communications that appear to be encrypted aren't really, as modern websites use *content delivery networks* (CDNs) such as Akamai and Cloudflare; while the web traffic is encrypted from the user's laptop or phone to the CDN's point of presence at their ISP, it isn't encrypted on the backhaul unless they pay extra – which most of them don't [87]. So the customer thinks the link is encrypted, and it's protected from casual snooping—but not from nation states or from firms who can read backbone traffic.

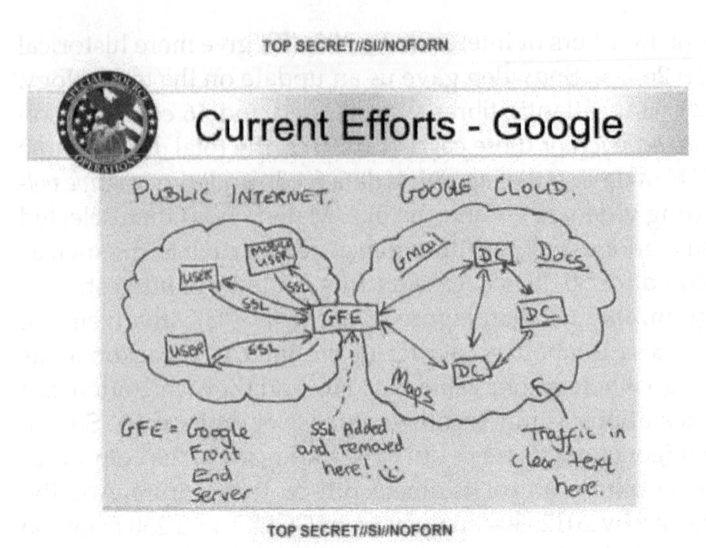

Figure 2.1: Muscular – the slide

2.2.1.4 *Special collection*

The NSA and CIA jointly operate the Special Collection Service (SCS) whose most visible activity may be the plastic panels near the roofs of US and allied embassies worldwide; these hide antennas for hoovering up cellular communication (a program known as 'Stateroom'). Beyond this, SCS implants collection equipment in foreign telcos, Internet exchanges and government facilities. This can involve classical spy tradecraft, from placing bugs that monitor speech or electronic communications, through recruiting moles in target organisations, to the covert deployment of antennas in target countries to tap internal microwave links. Such techniques are not restricted to state targets: Mexican drug cartel leader 'El Chapo' Guzman was caught after US agents suborned his system administrator.

Close-access operations include Tempest monitoring: the collection of information leaked by the electromagnetic emissions from computer monitors and other equipment, described in 19.3.2. The Snowden leaks disclose the collection of computer screen data and other electromagnetic emanations from a number of countries' embassies and UN missions including those of India, Japan, Slovakia and the EU[2].

2.2.1.5 *Bullrun and Edgehill*

Special collection increasingly involves supply-chain tampering. SCS routinely intercepts equipment such as routers being exported from the USA,

[2]If the NSA needs to use high-tech collection against you as they can't get a software implant into your computer, that may be a compliment!

adds surveillance implants, repackages them with factory seals and sends them onward to customers. And an extreme form of supply-chain tampering was when the NSA covertly bought Crypto AG, a Swiss firm that was the main supplier of cryptographic equipment to non-aligned countries during the Cold War; I tell the story in more detail later in section 26.2.7.1.

Bullrun is the NSA codename, and Edgehill the GCHQ one, for 'crypto enabling', a $100m-a-year program of tampering with supplies and suppliers at all levels of the stack. This starts off with attempts to direct, or misdirect, academic research[3]; it continued with placing trusted people on standards committees, and using NIST's influence to get weak standards adopted. One spectacular incident was the `Dual_EC_DRBG` debacle, where NIST standardised a random number generator based on elliptic curves that turned out to contain an NSA backdoor. Most of the actual damage, though, was done by restrictions on cryptographic key length, dovetailed with diplomatic pressure on allies to enforce export controls, so that firms needing export licenses could have their arms twisted to use an 'appropriate' standard, and was entangled with the Crypto Wars (which I discuss in section 26.2.7). The result was that many of the systems in use today were compelled to use weak cryptography, leading to vulnerabilities in everything from hotel and car door locks to VPNs. In addition to that, supply-chain attacks introduce covert vulnerabilities into widely-used software; many nation states play this game, along with some private actors [892]. We'll see vulnerabilities that result from surveillance and cryptography policies in one chapter after another, and return in Part 3 of the book to discuss the policy history in more detail.

2.2.1.6 Xkeyscore

With such a vast collection of data, you need good tools to search it. The Five Eyes search computer data using Xkeyscore, a distributed database that enables an analyst to search collected data remotely and assemble the results. Exposed on July 31 2013, NSA documents describe it as its "widest-reaching" system for developing intelligence; it enables an analyst to search emails, SMSes, chats, address book entries and browsing histories [816]. Examples in a 2008 training deck include "my target speaks German but is in Pakistan. How can I find him?" "Show me all the encrypted Word documents from Iran" and "Show me all PGP usage in Iran". By searching for anomalous behaviour, the analyst can find suspects and identify strong selectors (such

[3]In the 1990s, when I bid to run a research program in coding theory, cryptography and computer security at the Isaac Newton Institute at Cambridge University, a senior official from GCHQ offered the institute a £50,000 donation not to go ahead, saying "There's nothing interesting happening in cryptography, and Her Majesty's Government would like this state of affairs to continue". He was shown the door and my program went ahead.

as email addresses, phone numbers or IP addresses) for more conventional collection.

Xkeyscore is a federated system, where one query scans all sites. Its components buffer information at collection points – in 2008, 700 servers at 150 sites. Some appear to be hacked systems overseas from which the NSA malware can exfiltrate data matching a submitted query. The only judicial approval required is a prompt for the analyst to enter a reason why they believe that one of the parties to the conversation is not resident in the USA. The volumes are such that traffic data are kept for 30 days but content for only 3–5 days. Tasked items are extracted and sent on to whoever requested them, and there's a notification system (Trafficthief) for tipping off analysts when their targets do anything of interest. Extraction is based either on fingerprints or plugins – the latter allow analysts to respond quickly with detectors for new challenges like steganography and homebrew encryption.

Xkeyscore can also be used for target discovery: one of the training queries is "Show me all the exploitable machines in country X" (machine fingerprints are compiled by a crawler called Mugshot). For example, it came out in 2015 that GCHQ and the NSA hacked the world's leading provider of SIM cards, the Franco-Dutch company Gemalto, to compromise the keys needed to intercept (and if need be spoof) the traffic from hundreds of millions of mobile phones [1661]. The hack used Xkeyscore to identify the firm's sysadmins, who were then phished; agents were also able to compromise billing servers to suppress SMS billing and authentication servers to steal keys; another technique was to harvest keys in transit from Gemalto to mobile service providers. According to an interview with Snowden in 2014, Xkeyscore also lets an analyst build a fingerprint of any target's online activity so that they can be followed automatically round the world. The successes of this system are claimed to include the capture of over 300 terrorists; in one case, Al-Qaida's Sheikh Atiyatallah blew his cover by googling himself, his various aliases, an associate and the name of his book [1661].

There's a collection of decks on Xkeyscore with a survey by Morgan Marquis-Boire, Glenn Greenwald and Micah Lee [1232]; a careful reading of the decks can be a good starting point for exploring the Snowden hoard[4].

2.2.1.7 *Longhaul*

Bulk key theft and supply-chain tampering are not the only ways to defeat cryptography. The Xkeyscore training deck gives an example: "Show me all the VPN startups in country X, and give me the data so I can decrypt and discover the users". VPNs appear to be easily defeated; a decryption service

[4] There's also a search engine for the collection at `https://www.edwardsnowden.com`.

called Longhaul ingests ciphertext and returns plaintext. The detailed description of cryptanalytic techniques is held as *Extremely Compartmented Information* (ECI) and is not found in the Snowden papers, but some of them talk of recent breakthroughs in cryptanalysis. What might these be?

The leaks do show diligent collection of the protocol messages used to set up VPN encryption, so some cryptographers suggested in 2015 that some variant of the "Logjam attack" is feasible for a nation-state attacker against the 1024-bit prime used by most VPNs and many TLS connections with Diffie-Hellman key exchange [26]. Others pointed to the involvement of NSA cryptographers in the relevant standard, and a protocol flaw discovered later; yet others pointed out that even with advances in number theory or protocol exploits, the NSA has enough money to simply break 1024-bit Diffie-Hellman by brute force, and this would be easily justified if many people used the same small number of prime moduli – which they do [854]. I'll discuss cryptanalysis in more detail in Chapter 5.

2.2.1.8 Quantum

There is a long history of attacks on protocols, which can be spoofed, replayed and manipulated in various ways. (We'll discuss this topic in detail in Chapter 4.) The best-documented NSA attack on Internet traffic goes under the codename of Quantum and involves the dynamic exploitation of one of the communication end-points. Thus, to tap an encrypted SSL/TLS session to a webmail provider, the Quantum system fires a 'shot' that exploits the browser. There are various flavours; in 'Quantuminsert', an injected packet redirects the browser to a 'Foxacid' attack server. Other variants attack software updates and the advertising networks whose code runs in mobile phone apps [1999].

2.2.1.9 CNE

Computer and Network Exploitation (CNE) is the generic NSA term for hacking, and it can be used for more than just key theft or TLS session hijacking; it can be used to acquire access to traffic too. Operation Socialist was the GCHQ codename for a hack of Belgium's main telco Belgacom[5] in 2010–11. GCHQ attackers used Xkeyscore to identify three key Belgacom technical staff, then used Quantuminsert to take over their PCs when they visited sites like LinkedIn. The attackers then used their sysadmin privileges to install malware on dozens of servers, including authentication servers to leverage further access, billing servers so they could cover their tracks, and the company's core Cisco routers [734]. This gave them access to large quantities of mobile

[5]It is now called Proximus.

roaming traffic, as Belgacom provides service to many foreign providers when their subscribers roam in Europe. The idea that one NATO and EU member state would conduct a cyber-attack on the critical infrastructure of another took many by surprise. The attack also gave GCHQ access to the phone system in the European Commission and other European institutions. Given that these institutions make many of the laws for the UK and other member states, this was almost as if a US state governor had got his state troopers to hack AT&T so he could wiretap Congress and the White House.

Belgacom engineers started to suspect something was wrong in 2012, and realised they'd been hacked in the spring of 2013; an anti-virus company found sophisticated malware masquerading as Windows files. The story went public in September 2013, and the German news magazine Der Spiegel published Snowden documents showing that GCHQ was responsible. After the Belgian prosecutor reported in February 2018, we learned that the attack must have been authorised by then UK Foreign Secretary William Hague, but there was not enough evidence to prosecute anyone; the investigation had been hampered in all sorts of ways both technical and political; the software started deleting itself within minutes of discovery, and institutions such as Europol (whose head was British) refused to help. The Belgian minister responsible for telecomms, Alexander de Croo, even suggested that Belgium's own intelligence service might have informally given the operation a green light [735]. Europol later adopted a policy that it will help investigate hacks of 'suspected criminal origin'; it has nothing to say about hacks by governments.

A GCHQ slide deck on CNE explains that it's used to support conventional Sigint both by redirecting traffic and by "enabling" (breaking) cryptography; that it must always be "UK deniable"; and that it can also be used for "effects", such as degrading communications or "changing users' passwords on extremist website" [735]. Other papers show that the agencies frequently target admins of phone companies and ISPs in the Middle East, Africa and indeed worldwide – compromising a key technician is "generally the entry ticket to the network" [1141]. As one phone company executive explained, "The MNOs were clueless at the time about network security. Most networks were open to their suppliers for remote maintenance with an ID and password and the techie in China or India had no clue that their PC had been hacked".

The hacking tools and methods used by the NSA and its allies are now fairly well understood; some are shared with law enforcement. The Snowden papers reveal an internal store where analysts can get a variety of tools; a series of leaks in 2016–7 by the Shadow Brokers (thought to be Russian military intelligence, the GRU) disclosed a number of actual NSA malware samples, used by hackers at the NSA's Tailored Access Operations team to launch attacks [239]. (Some of these tools were repurposed by the Russians to launch the NotPetya worm and by the North Koreans in Wannacry, as I'll discuss later.) The best documentation of all is probably about a separate store of goodies used by the

CIA, disclosed in some detail to Wikileaks in the 'Vault 7' leaks in 2017. These include manuals for tools that can be used to install a remote access Trojan on your machine, with components to geolocate it and to exfiltrate files (including SSH credentials), audio and video; a tool to jump air gaps by infecting thumb drives; a tool for infecting wifi routers so they'll do man-in-the-middle attacks; and even a tool for watermarking documents so a whistleblower who leaks them could be tracked. Many of the tools are available not just for Windows but also for macOS and Android; some infect firmware, making them hard to remove. There are tools for hacking TVs and IoT devices too, and tools to hamper forensic investigations. The Vault 7 documents are useful reading if you're curious about the specifications and manuals for modern government malware [2023]. As an example of the law-enforcement use of such tools, in June 2020 it emerged that the French police in Lille had since 2018 installed malware on thousands of Android phones running EncroChat, an encrypted messaging system favoured by criminals, leading to the arrest of 800 criminal suspects in France, the Netherlands, the UK and elsewhere, as well as the arrest of several police officers for corruption and the seizure of several tons of drugs [1334].

2.2.1.10 *The analyst's viewpoint*

The intelligence analyst thus has a big bag of tools. If they're trying to find the key people in an organisation – whether the policymakers advising on a critical decision, or the lawyers involved in laundering an oligarch's profits – they can use the traffic data in Xkeyscore to map contact networks. There are various neat tools to help, such as 'Cotraveler' which flags up mobile phones that have traveled together. We have some insight into this process from our own research into cybercrime, where we scrape tens of millions of messages from underground forums and analyse them to understand crime types new and old. One might describe the process as 'adaptive message mining'. Just as you use adaptive text mining when you do a web search, and constantly refine your search terms based on samples of what you find, with message mining you also have metadata – so you can follow threads, trace actors across forums, do clustering analysis and use various other tricks to 'find more messages like this one'. The ability to switch back and forth between the detailed view you get from reading individual messages, and the statistical view you get from analysing bulk collections, is extremely powerful.

Once the analyst moves from the hunting phase to the gathering phase, they can use Prism to look at the targets' accounts at Facebook, Google and Microsoft, while Xkeyscore will let them see what websites they visit. Traffic data analysis gives still more: despite the growing use of encryption, the communications to and from a home reveal what app or device is used when and for how long[6]. The agencies are pushing for access to end-to-end messaging systems such as WhatsApp; in countries like the UK, Australia and China, legislators have already authorised this, though it's not at all clear which US companies might comply (I'll discuss policy in Chapter 26).

Given a high-value target, there's a big bag of tools the analyst can install on their laptop or cellphone directly. They can locate it physically, turn it into a room bug and even use it as a remote camera. They can download the target's address book and contact history and feed that into Xkeyscore to search recursively for their direct and indirect contacts. Meanwhile the analyst can bug messaging apps, beating the end-to-end encryption by collecting the call contents once they've been decrypted. They can set up an alarm to notify them whenever the target sends or receives messages of interest, or changes location. The coverage is pretty complete. And when it's time for the kill, the target's phone can be used to guide a bomb or a missile. Little wonder Ed Snowden insisted that journalists interviewing him put their phones in the fridge!

Finally, the analyst has also a proxy through which they can access the Internet surreptitiously – typically a machine on a botnet. It might even be the PC in your home office.

2.2.1.11 *Offensive operations*

The Director NSA also heads the US Cyber Command, which since 2009 has been one of ten unified commands of the United States Department of Defense. It is responsible for offensive cyber operations, of which the one that made a real difference was Stuxnet. This was a worm designed to damage Iran's uranium enrichment centrifuges by speeding them up and slowing them down in patterns designed to cause mechanical damage, and was developed jointly by the USA and Israel [326, 827]. It was technically sophisticated, using four zero-day exploits and two stolen code-signing certificates to spread promiscuously through Windows PCs, until it found Siemens programmable logic controllers of the type used at Iran's Natanz enrichment plant – where it would then install a rootkit that would issue the destructive commands, while the PC assured the operators that everything was fine. It was apparently introduced using USB drives to bridge the air gap to the Iranian systems, and came to light in 2010 after copies had somehow spread to central Asia and Indonesia. Two other varieties of malware (Flame and Duqu) were then discovered using similar tricks and common code, performing surveillance at a number of companies in the Middle East and South Asia; more recent code-analysis tools have traced a lineage of malware that goes back to 2002 (Flowershop) and continued to operate until 2016 (with the Equation Group tools) [2071].

[6]See for example Hill and Mattu who wiretapped a modern smart home to measure this [902].

Stuxnet acted as a wake-up call for other governments, which rushed to acquire 'cyber-weapons' and develop offensive cyber *doctrine* – a set of principles for what cyber warriors might do, developed with some thought given to rationale, strategy, tactics and legality. Oh, and the price of zero-day vulnerabilities rose sharply.

2.2.1.12 Attack scaling

Computer scientists know the importance of how algorithms scale, and exactly the same holds for attacks. Tapping a single mobile phone is hard. You have to drive around behind the suspect with radio and cryptanalysis gear in your car, risk being spotted, and hope that you manage to catch the suspect's signal as they roam from one cell to another. Or you can drive behind them with a false base station[7] and hope their phone will roam to it as the signal is louder than the genuine one; but then you risk electronic detection too. Both are highly skilled work and low-yield: you lose the signal maybe a quarter of the time. So if you want to wiretap someone in central Paris often enough, why not just wiretap everyone? Put antennas on your embassy roof, collect it all, write the decrypted calls and text messages into a database, and reconstruct the sessions electronically. If you want to hack everyone in France, hack the telco, perhaps by subverting the equipment it uses. At each stage the capital cost goes up but the marginal cost of each tap goes down. The Five Eyes strategy is essentially to collect everything in the world; it might cost billions to establish and maintain the infrastructure, but once it's there you have everything.

The same applies to offensive cyber operations, which are rather like sabotage. In wartime, you can send commandos to blow up an enemy radar station; but if you do it more than once or twice, your lads will start to run into a lot of sentries. So we scale kinetic attacks differently: by building hundreds of bomber aircraft, or artillery pieces, or (nowadays) thousands of drones. So how do you scale a cyber attack to take down not just one power station, but the opponent's whole power grid? The Five Eyes approach is this. Just as Google keeps a copy of the Internet on a few thousand servers, with all the content and links indexed, US Cyber Command keeps a copy of the Internet that indexes what version of software all the machines in the world are using – the Mugshot system mentioned above – so a Five Eyes cyber warrior can instantly see which targets can be taken over by which exploits.

A key question for competitor states, therefore, is not just to what extent they can create some electronic spaces that are generally off-limits to the Five Eyes. It's the extent to which they can scale up their own intelligence and offensive capabilities rather than having to rely on America. The number of scans and

[7]These devices are known in the USA as a Stingray and in Europe as an IMSI-catcher; they conduct a man-in-the-middle attack of the kind we'll discuss in detail in section 22.3.1.

probes that we see online indicates that the NSA are not alone in trying to build cyber weapons that scale. Not all of them might be nation states; some might simply be arms vendors or mercenaries. This raises a host of policy problems to which we'll return in Part 3. For now we'll continue to look at capabilities.

2.2.2 China

China is now the leading competitor to the USA, being second not just in terms of GDP but as a technology powerhouse. The Chinese lack the NSA's network of alliances and access to global infrastructure (although they're working hard at that). Within China itself, however, they demand unrestricted access to local data. Some US service firms used to operate there, but trouble followed. After Yahoo's systems were used to trap the dissident Wang Xiaoning in 2002, Alibaba took over Yahoo's China operation in 2005; but there was still a row when Wang's wife sued Yahoo in US courts in 2007, and showed that Yahoo had misled Congress over the matter [1764]. In 2008, it emerged that the version of Skype available in China had been modified so that messages were scanned for sensitive keywords and, if they were found, the user's texts were uploaded to a server in China [1963]. In December 2009, Google discovered a Chinese attack on its corporate infrastructure, which became known as Operation Aurora; Chinese agents had hacked into the Google systems used to do wiretaps for the FBI (see Prism above) in order to discover which of their own agents in the USA were under surveillance. Google had already suffered criticism for operating a censored version of their search engine for Chinese users, and a few months later, they pulled out of China. By this time, Facebook, Twitter and YouTube had already been blocked. A Chinese strategy was emerging of total domestic control, augmented by ever-more aggressive collection overseas.

From about 2002, there had been a series of hacking attacks on US and UK defence agencies and contractors, codenamed 'Titan Rain' and ascribed to the Chinese armed forces. According to a 2004 study by the US Foreign Military Studies Office (FMSO), Chinese military doctrine sees the country in a state of war with the West; we are continuing the Cold War by attacking China, trying to overthrow its communist regime by exporting subversive ideas to it over the Internet [1884]. Chinese leaders see US service firms, news websites and anonymity tools such as Tor (which the State Department funds so that Chinese and other people can defeat censorship) as being of one fabric with the US surveillance satellites and aircraft that observe their military defences. Yahoo and Google were thus seen as fair game, just like Lockheed Martin and BAe.

Our own group's first contact with the Chinese came in 2008. We were asked for help by the Dalai Lama, who had realised that the Chinese had hacked his office systems in the run-up to the Beijing Olympics that year. One of my research students, Shishir Nagaraja, happened to be in Delhi waiting for his UK visa to be renewed, so he volunteered to go up to the Tibetan HQ in Dharamsala and run some forensics. He found that about 35 of the 50 PCs in the office of the Tibetan government in exile had been hacked; information was being siphoned off to China, to IP addresses located near the three organs of Chinese state security charged with different aspects of Tibetan affairs. The attackers appear to have got in by sending one of the monks an email that seemed to come from a colleague; when he clicked on the attached PDF, it had a JavaScript buffer overflow that used a vulnerability in Adobe Reader to take over his machine. This technique is called *phishing*, as it works by offering a lure that someone bites on; when it's aimed at a specific individual (as in this case) it's called *spear phishing*. They then compromised the Tibetans' mail server, so that whenever one person in the office sent a .pdf file to another, it would arrive with an embedded attack. The mail server itself was in California.

This is pretty sobering, when you stop to think about it. You get an email from a colleague sitting ten feet away, you ask him if he just sent it – and when he says yes, you click on the attachment. And your machine is suddenly infected by a server that you rent ten thousand miles away in a friendly country. We wrote this up in a tech report on the 'Snooping Dragon' [1376]. After it came out, we had to deal for a while with attacks on our equipment, and heckling at conference talks by Chinese people who claimed we had no evidence to attribute the attacks to their government. Colleagues at the Open Net Initiative in Toronto followed through, and eventually found from analysis of the hacking tools' dashboard that the same espionage network had targeted 1,295 computers in 103 countries [1225] – ranging from the Indian embassy in Washington through Associated Press in New York to the ministries of foreign affairs in Thailand, Iran and Laos.

There followed a series of further reports of Chinese state hacking, from a complex dispute with Rio Tinto in 2009 over the price of iron ore and a hack of the Melbourne International Film festival in the same year when it showed a film about a Uighur leader [1902]. In 2011, the Chinese hacked the CIA's covert communications system, after the Iranians had traced it, and executed about 30 agents – though that did not become publicly known till later [578]. The first flashbulb moment was a leaked Pentagon report in 2013 that Chinese hackers had stolen some of the secrets of the F35 joint strike fighter, as well as a series of other weapon systems [1381]. Meanwhile China and Hong Kong were amounting for over 80% of all counterfeit goods seized at US ports. The Obama administration vowed to make investigations and prosecutions in the theft of trade secrets a top priority, and the following year five members of the People's Liberation Army were indicted in absentia.

The White House felt compelled to act once more after the June 2015 news that the Chinese had hacked the Office of Personnel Management (OPM), getting access to highly personal data on 22 million current and former federal employees, ranging from fingerprints to sensitive information from security clearance interviews. Staff applying for Top Secret clearances are ordered to divulge all information that could be used to blackmail them, from teenage drug use to closeted gay relationships. All sexual partners in the past five years have to be declared for a normal Top Secret clearance; for a Strap clearance (to deal with signals intelligence material) the candidate even has to report any foreigners they meet regularly at their church. So this leak affected more than just 22 million people. Officially, this invasive data collection is to mitigate the risk that intelligence agency staff can be blackmailed. (Cynics supposed it was also so that whistleblowers could be discredited.) Whatever the motives, putting all such information in one place was beyond stupid; it was a real 'database of ruin'. For the Chinese to get all the compromising information on every American with a sensitive government job was jaw-dropping. (Britain screwed up too; in 2008, a navy officer lost a laptop containing the personal data of 600,000 people who had joined the Royal Navy, or tried to [1074].) At a summit in September that year, Presidents Obama and Xi agreed to refrain from computer-enabled theft of intellectual property for commercial gain[8]. Nothing was said in public though about military secrets – or the sex lives of federal agents.

The Chinese attacks of the 2000s used smart people plus simple tools; the attacks on the Tibetans used Russian crimeware as the remote access Trojans. The state also co-opted groups of 'patriotic hackers', or perhaps used them for deniability; some analysts noted waves of naïve attacks on western firms that were correlated with Chinese university terms, and wondered whether students had been tasked to hack as coursework. The UK police and security service warned UK firms in 2007. By 2009, multiple Chinese probes had been reported on US electricity firms, and by 2010, Chinese spear-phishing attacks had been reported on government targets in the USA, Poland and Belgium [1306]. As with the Tibetan attacks, these typically used crude tools and had such poor operational security that it was fairly clear where they came from.

By 2020 the attacks had become more sophisticated, with a series of advanced persistent threats (APTs) tracked by threat intelligence firms. A campaign to hack the phones of Uighurs involved multiple zero-day attacks, even on iPhones, that were delivered via compromised Uighur websites [395]; this targeted not only Uighurs in China but the diaspora too. China also conducts industrial and commercial espionage, and Western agencies claim they exploit

[8]The Chinese have kept their promise; according to US firms doing business in China, IP is now sixth on the list of concerns, down from second in 2014 [704]. In any case, the phrase 'IP theft' was always a simplification, used to conflate the theft of classified information from defence contractors with the larger issue of compelled technology transfer by other firms who wanted access to Chinese markets and the side-issue of counterfeiting.

managed service providers[9]. Another approach was attacking software supply chains; a Chinese group variously called Wicked Panda or Barium compromised software updates from computer maker Asus, a PC cleanup tool and a Korean remote management tool, as well as three popular computer games, getting its malware installed on millions of machines; rather than launching banking trojans or ransomware, it was then used for spying [811]. Just as in GCHQ's Operation Socialist, such indirect strategies give a way to scale attacks in territory where you're not the sovereign. And China was also playing the Socialist game: it came out in 2019 that someone had hacked at least ten western mobile phone companies over the previous seven years and exfiltrated call data records – and that the perpetrators appeared to be the APT10 gang, linked to the Chinese military [2021].

Since 2018 there has been a political row over whether Chinese firms should be permitted to sell routers and 5G network hardware in NATO countries, with the Trump administration blacklisting Huawei in May 2019. There had been a previous spat over another Chinese firm, ZTE; in 2018 GCHQ warned that ZTE equipment "would present risk to UK national security that could not be mitigated effectively or practicably" [1477][10]. President Trump banned ZTE for breaking sanctions on North Korea and Iran, but relented and allowed its equipment back in the USA subject to security controls[11].

The security controls route had been tried with Huawei, which set up a centre in Oxfordshire in 2010 where GCHQ could study its software as a condition of the company's being allowed to sell in the UK. While the analysts did not find any backdoors, their 2019 report surfaced some scathing criticisms of Huawei's software engineering practices [933]. Huawei had copied a lot of code, couldn't patch what they didn't understand, and no progress was being made in tackling many problems despite years of promises. There was an unmanageable number of versions of OpenSSL, including versions that had known vulnerabilities and that were not supported: 70 full copies of 4 different OpenSSL versions, and 304 partial copies of 14 versions. Not only could the Chinese hack the Huawei systems; so could anybody. Their equipment had been excluded for some years from UK backbone routers and from systems used for wiretapping. The UK demanded "sustained evidence of improvement across multiple versions and multiple product ranges" before

[9]This became public in 2019 with the claim that they had hacked Wipro and used this to compromise their customers [1095]; but it later emerged that Wipro had been hacked by a crime gang operating for profit.

[10]The only router vendor to have actually been caught with a malicious backdoor in its code is the US company Juniper, which not only used the NSA's Dual-EC backdoor to make VPN traffic exploitable, but did it in such a clumsy way that others could exploit it too – and at least one other party did so [415].

[11]This was done as a favour to President Xi, according to former National Security Adviser John Bolton, who declared himself 'appalled' that the president would interfere in a criminal prosecution [157].

it will put any more trust in it. A number of countries, including Australia and New Zealand, then banned Huawei equipment outright, and in 2019 Canada arrested Huawei's CFO (who is also its founder's daughter) following a US request to extradite her for conspiring to defraud global banks about Huawei's relationship with a company operating in Iran. China retaliated by arresting two Canadians, one a diplomat on leave, on spurious espionage charges, and by sentencing two others to death on drugs charges. The USA hit back with a ban on US suppliers selling chips, software or support to Huawei. The UK banned the purchase of their telecomms equipment from the end of 2020 and said it would remove it from UK networks by 2027. Meanwhile, China is helping many less developed countries modernise their networks, and this access may help them rival the Five Eyes' scope in due course. Trade policy, industrial policy and cyber-defence strategy have become intertwined in a new Cold War.

Strategically, the question may not be just whether China could use Huawei routers to wiretap other countries at scale, so much as whether they could use it in time of tension to launch DDoS attacks that would break the Internet by subverting BGP routing. I discuss this in more detail in the section 21.2.1. For years, China's doctrine of 'Peaceful Rise' meant avoiding conflict with other major powers until they're strong enough. The overall posture is one of largely defensive information warfare, combining pervasive surveillance at home, a walled-garden domestic Internet that is better defended against cyber-attack than anyone else's, plus considerable and growing capabilities, which are mainly used for diligent intelligence-gathering in support of national strategic interests. They are starting to bully other countries in various ways that sometimes involve online operations. In 2016, during a dispute with Vietnam over some islands in the South China Sea, they hacked the airport systems in Hanoi and Ho Chi Minh City, displaying insulting messages and forcing manual check-in for passengers [1197]. In 2020, the EU has denounced China for spreading disruptive fake news about the coronavirus pandemic [1580], and Australia has denounced cyber-attacks that have happened since it called for an international inquiry into the pandemic's origins [937]. These information operations displayed a first-class overt and covert disinformation capability and followed previous more limited campaigns in Hong Kong and Taiwan [564]. Diplomatic commentators note that China's trade policy, although aggressive, is no different from Japan's in the 1970s and not as aggressive as America's; that the new Cold War is just as misguided and just as likely to be wasteful and dangerous as the last one; that China still upholds the international order more than it disrupts it; and that it upholds it more consistently than the USA has done since WWII [704]. China's external propaganda aim is to present itself as a positive socio-economic role model for the world, as it competes for access and influence and emerges as a peer competitor to the USA and Europe.

2.2.3 Russia

Russia, like China, lacks America's platform advantage and compensates with hacking teams that use spear-phishing and malware. Unlike China, it takes the low road, acting frequently as a spoiler, trying to disrupt the international order, and sometimes benefiting directly via a rise in the price of oil, its main export. The historian Timothy Snyder describes Putin's rise to power and his embrace of oligarchs, orthodox Christianity, homophobia and the fascist ideologue Ivan Ilyin, especially since rigged elections in 2012. This leaves the Russian state in need of perpetual struggle against external enemies who threaten the purity of the Russian people [1802]. Its strategic posture online is different from China's in four ways. First, it's a major centre for cybercrime; underground markets first emerged in Russia and Ukraine in 2003–5, as we'll discuss in the following section on cybercrime. Second, although Russia is trying to become more closed like China, its domestic Internet is relatively open and intertwined with the West's, including major service firms such as VK and Yandex [605]. Third, Russia's strategy of re-establishing itself as a regional power has been pursued much more aggressively than China's, with direct military interference in neighbours such as Georgia and Ukraine. These interventions have involved a mixed strategy of cyber-attacks plus 'little green men' – troops without Russian insignia on their uniforms – with a political strategy of denial. Fourth, Russia was humiliated by the USA and Europe when the USSR collapsed in 1989, and still feels encircled. Since about 2005 its goal has been to undermine the USA and the EU, and to promote authoritarianism and nationalism as an alternative to the rules-based international order. This has been pursued more forcefully since 2013; Snyder tells the history [1802]. With Brexit, and with the emergence of authoritarian governments in Hungary, Turkey and Poland, this strategy appears to be winning.

Russian cyber-attacks came to prominence in 2007, after Estonia moved a much-hated Soviet-era statue in Tallinn to a less prominent site, and the Russians felt insulted. DDoS attacks on government offices, banks and media companies forced Estonia to rate-limit its external Internet access for a few weeks [692]. Russia refused to extradite the perpetrators, most of whom were Russian, though one ethnic-Russian Estonian teenager was fined. Sceptics said that the attacks seemed the work of amateurs and worked because the Estonians hadn't hardened their systems the way US service providers do. Estonia nonetheless appealed to NATO for help, and one outcome was the Tallinn Manual, which sets out the law of cyber conflict [1667]. I'll discuss this in more detail in the chapter on electronic and information warfare, in section 23.8. The following year, after the outbreak of a brief war between Russia and Georgia, Russian hackers set up a website with a list of targets in Georgia for Russian patriots to attack [1994].

Estonia and Georgia were little more than warm-ups for the Ukraine invasion. Following demonstrations in Maidan Square in Kiev against pro-Russian President Yanukovich, and an intervention in February 2014 by Russian mercenaries who shot about a hundred demonstrators, Yanukovich fled. The Russians invaded Ukraine on February 24th, annexing Crimea and setting up two puppet states in the Donbass area of eastern Ukraine. Their tactics combined Russian special forces in plain uniforms, a welter of propaganda claims of an insurgency by Russian-speaking Ukrainians or of Russia helping defend the population against Ukrainian fascists or of defending Russian purity against homosexuals and Jews; all of this coordinated with a variety of cyber-attacks. For example, in May the Russians hacked the website of the Ukrainian election commission and rigged it to display a message that a nationalist who'd received less than 1% of the vote had won; this was spotted and blocked, but Russian media announced the bogus result anyway [1802].

The following year, as the conflict dragged on, Russia took down 30 electricity substations on three different distribution systems within half an hour of each other, leaving 230,000 people without electricity for several hours. They involved multiple different attack vectors that had been implanted over a period of months, and since they followed a Ukrainian attack on power distribution in Crimea – and switched equipment off when they could have destroyed it instead – seemed to have been intended as a warning [2070]. This attack was still tiny compared with the other effects of the conflict, which included the shooting down of a Malaysian Airlines airliner with the loss of all on board; but it was the first cyber-attack to disrupt mains electricity. Finally on June 27 2017 came the NotPetya attack – by far the most damaging cyber-attack to date [814].

The NotPetya worm was initially distributed using the update service for MeDoc, the accounting software used by the great majority of Ukrainian businesses. It then spread laterally in organisations across Windows file-shares using the EternalBlue vulnerability, an NSA exploit with an interesting history. From March 2016, a Chinese gang started using it against targets in Vietnam, Hong Kong and the Philippines, perhaps as a result of finding and reverse engineering it (it's said that you don't launch a cyberweapon; you share it). It was leaked by a gang called the 'Shadow Brokers' in April 2017, along with other NSA software that the Chinese didn't deploy, and then used by the Russians in June. The NotPetya worm used EternalBlue together with the Mimikatz tool that recovers passwords from Windows memory. The worm's payload pretended to be ransomware; it encrypted the infected computer's hard disk and demanded a ransom of $300 in bitcoin. But there was no mechanism to decrypt the files of computer owners who paid the ransom, so it was really a destructive service-denial worm. The only way to deal with it was to re-install the operating system and restore files from backup.

The NotPetya attack took down banks, telcos and even the radiation monitoring systems at the former Chernobyl nuclear plant. What's more, it spread from Ukraine to international firms who had offices there. The world's largest container shipping company, Maersk, had to replace most of its computers and compensate customers for late shipments, at a cost of $300m; FedEx also lost $300m, and Mondelez $100m. Mondelez' insurers refused to pay out on the ground that it was an 'Act of War', as the governments of Ukraine, the USA and the UK all attributed NotPetya to Russian military intelligence, the GRU [1234].

2016 was marked by the Brexit referendum in the UK and the election of President Trump in the USA, in both of which there was substantial Russian interference. In the former, the main intervention was financial support for the leave campaigns, which were later found to have broken the law by spending too much [1267]; this was backed by intensive campaigning on social media [365]. In the latter, Russian interference was denounced by President Obama during the campaign, leading to renewed economic sanctions, and by the US intelligence community afterwards. An inquiry by former FBI director Robert Mueller found that Russia interfered very widely via the disinformation and social media campaigns run by its Internet Research Agency 'troll farm', and by the GRU which hacked the emails of the Democratic national and campaign committees, most notably those of the Clinton campaign chair John Podesta. Some Trump associates went to jail for various offences.

As I'll discuss in section 26.4.2, it's hard to assess the effects of such interventions. On the one hand, a report to the US Senate's Committee on Foreign Relations sets out a story of a persistent Russian policy, since Putin came to power, to undermine the influence of democratic states and the rules-based international order, promoting authoritarian governments of both left and right, and causing trouble where it can. It notes that European countries use broad defensive measures including bipartisan agreements on electoral conduct and raising media literacy among voters; it recommends that these be adopted in the USA as well [387]. On the other hand, Yochai Benkler cautions Democrats against believing that Trump's election was all Russia's fault; the roots of popular disaffection with the political elite are much older and deeper [228]. Russia's information war with the West predates Putin; it continues the old USSR's strategy of weakening the West by fomenting conflict via a variety of national liberation movements and terrorist groups (I discuss the information-warfare aspects in section 23.8.3). Timothy Snyder places this all in the context of modern Russian history and politics [1802]; his analysis also outlines the playbook for disruptive information warfare against a democracy. It's not just about hacking substations, but about hacking voters' minds; about undermining trust in institutions and even in facts, exploiting social media and recasting politics as showbusiness. Putin is a judo player; judo's about using an opponent's strength and momentum to trip them up.

2.2.4 The rest

The rest of the world's governments have quite a range of cyber capabilities, but common themes, including the nature and source of their tools. Middle Eastern governments were badly shaken by the Arab Spring uprisings, and some even turned off the Internet for a while, such as Libya in April–July 2010, when rebels were using Google maps to generate target files for US, UK and French warplanes. Since then, Arab states have developed strategies that combine spyware and hacking against high-profile targets, through troll farms pumping out abusive comments in public fora, with physical coercion.

The operations of the United Arab Emirates were described in 2019 by a whistleblower, Lori Stroud [248]. An NSA analyst – and Ed Snowden's former boss – she was headhunted by a Maryland contractor in 2014 to work in Dubai as a mercenary, but left after the UAE's operations started to target Americans. The UAE's main technique was spear-phishing with Windows malware, but their most effective tool, called Karma, enabled them to hack the iPhones of foreign statesmen and local dissidents. They also targeted foreigners critical of the regime. In one case they social-engineered a UK grad student into installing spyware on his PC on the pretext that it would make his communications hard to trace. The intelligence team consisted of several dozen people, both mercenaries and Emiratis, in a large villa in Dubai. The use of iPhone malware by the UAE government was documented by independent observers [1221].

In 2018, the government of Saudi Arabia murdered the Washington Post journalist Jamal Khashoggi in its consulate in Istanbul. The Post campaigned to expose Saudi crown prince Mohammed bin Salman as the man who gave the order, and in January 2019 the National Enquirer published a special edition containing texts showing that the Post's owner Jeff Bezos was having an affair. Bezos pre-empted the Enquirer by announcing that he and his wife were divorcing, and hired an investigator to find the source of the leak. The Enquirer had attempted to blackmail Bezos over some photos it had also obtained; it wanted both him and the investigator to declare that the paper hadn't relied upon 'any form of electronic eavesdropping or hacking in their news-gathering process'. Bezos went public instead. According to the investigator, his iPhone had been hacked by the Saudi Arabian government [200]; the malicious WhatsApp message that did the damage was sent from the phone of the Crown Prince himself [1055]. The US Justice Department later charged two former Twitter employees with spying, by disclosing to the Saudis personal account information of people who criticised their government [1502].

An even more unpleasant example is Syria, where the industrialisation of brutality is a third approach to scaling information collection. Malware attacks on dissidents were reported from 2012, and initially used a variety of spear-phishing lures. As the civil war got underway, police who were arresting suspects would threaten female family members with rape on the spot unless the suspect disclosed his passwords for mail and social media. They would then spear-phish all his contacts while he was being taken away in the van to the torture chamber. This victim-based approach to attack scaling resulted in the compromise of many machines not just in Syria but in America and Europe. The campaigns became steadily more sophisticated as the war evolved, with false-flag attacks, yet retained a brutal edge with some tools displaying beheading videos [737].

Thanks to John Scott-Railton and colleagues at Toronto, we have many further documented examples of online surveillance, computer malware and phone exploits being used to target dissidents; many in Middle Eastern and African countries but also in Mexico and indeed in Hungary [1221]. The real issue here is the ecosystem of companies, mostly in the USA, Europe and Israel, that supply hacking tools to unsavoury states. These tools range from phone malware, through mass-surveillance tools you use on your own network against your own dissidents, to tools that enable you to track and eavesdrop on phones overseas by abusing the signaling system [489]. These tools are used by dictators to track and monitor their enemies in the USA and Europe.

NGOs have made attempts to push back on this cyber arms trade. In one case NGOs argued that the Syrian government's ability to purchase mass-surveillance equipment from the German subsidiary of a UK company should be subject to export control, but the UK authorities were unwilling to block it. GCHQ was determined that if there were going to be bulk surveillance devices on President Assad's network, they should be British devices rather than Ukrainian ones. (I describe this in more detail later in section 26.2.8.) So the ethical issues around conventional arms sales persist in the age of cyber; indeed they can be worse because these tools are used against Americans, Brits and others who are sitting at home but who are unlucky enough to be on the contact list of someone an unpleasant government doesn't like. In the old days, selling weapons to a far-off dictator didn't put your own residents in harm's way; but cyber weapons can have global effects.

Having been isolated for years by sanctions, Iran has developed an indigenous cyber capability, drawing on local hacker forums. Like Syria, its main focus is on intelligence operations, particularly against dissident Iranians, both at home and overseas. It has also been the target of US and other attacks of which the best known was Stuxnet, after which it traced the CIA's covert communications network and rounded up a number of agents [578]. It has launched both espionage operations and attacks of its own overseas. An example of the former was its hack of the Diginotar CA in the Netherlands which enabled it to monitor dissidents' Gmail; while its Shamoon malware damaged thousands of PCs at Aramco, Saudi Arabia's national oil company. The history of Iranian cyber capabilities is told by Collin Anderson and Karim Sadjadpour [50]. Most recently, it attacked Israeli water treatment plants in

April 2020; Israel responded the following month with an attack on the Iranian port of Bandar Abbas [230].

Finally, it's worth mentioning North Korea. In 2014, after Sony Pictures started working on a comedy about a plot to assassinate the North Korean leader, a hacker group trashed much of Sony's infrastructure, released embarrassing emails that caused its top film executive Amy Pascal to resign, and leaked some unreleased films. This was followed by threats of terrorist attacks on movie theatres if the comedy were put on general release. The company put the film on limited release, but when President Obama criticised them for giving in to North Korean blackmail, they put it on full release instead.

In 2017, North Korea again came to attention after their Wannacry worm infected over 200,000 computers worldwide, encrypting data and demanding a bitcoin ransom – though like NotPetya it didn't have a means of selective decryption, so was really just a destructive worm. It used the NSA EternalBlue vulnerability, like NotPetya, but was stopped when a malware researcher discovered a kill switch. In the meantime it had disrupted production at carmakers Nissan and Renault and at the Taiwanese chip foundry TSMC, and also caused several hospitals in Britain's National Health Service to close their accident and emergency units. In 2018, the US Department of Justice unsealed an indictment of a North Korean government hacker for both incidents, and also for a series of electronic bank robberies, including of $81m from the Bank of Bangladesh [1656]. In 2019, North Korean agents were further blamed, in a leaked United Nations report, for the theft of over $1bn from cryptocurrency exchanges [348].

2.2.5 Attribution

It's often said that cyber is different, because attribution is hard. As a general proposition this is untrue; anonymity online is much harder than you think. Even smart people make mistakes in operational security that give them away, and threat intelligence companies have compiled a lot of data that enable them to attribute even false-flag operations with reasonable probability in many cases [181]. Yet sometimes it may be true, and people still point to the Climategate affair. Several weeks before the 2009 Copenhagen summit on climate change, someone published over a thousand emails, mostly sent to or from four climate scientists at the University of East Anglia, England. Climate sceptics seized on some of them, which discussed how to best present evidence of global warming, as evidence of a global conspiracy. Official inquiries later established that the emails had been quoted out of context, but the damage had been done. People wonder whether the perpetrator could have been the Russians or the Saudis or even an energy company. However one of the more convincing analyses suggests that it was an internal leak, or even an accident;

only one archive file was leaked, and its filename (`FOIA2009.zip`) suggests it may have been prepared for a freedom-of-information disclosure in any case. The really interesting thing here may be how the emails were talked up into a conspiracy theory.

Another possible state action was the Equifax hack. The initial story was that on 8th March 2017, Apache warned of a vulnerability in Apache Struts and issued a patch; two days later, a gang started looking for vulnerable systems; on May 13th, they found that Equifax's dispute portal had not been patched, and got in. The later story, in litigation, was that Equifax had used the default username and password 'admin' for the portal [354]. Either way, the breach had been preventable; the intruders found a plaintext password file giving access to 51 internal database systems, and spent 76 days helping themselves to the personal information of at least 145.5 million Americans before the intrusion was reported on July 29th and access blocked the following day. Executives sold stock before they notified the public on September 7th; Congress was outraged, and the CEO Rick Smith was fired. So far, so ordinary. But no criminal use has been made of any of the stolen information, which led analysts at the time to suspect that the perpetrator was a nation-state actor seeking personal data on Americans at scale [1446]; in due course, four members of the Chinese military were indicted for it [552].

In any case, the worlds of intelligence and crime have long been entangled, and in the cyber age they seem to be getting more so. We turn to cybercrime next.

2.3 Crooks

Cybercrime is now about half of all crime, both by volume and by value, at least in developed countries. Whether it is slightly more or less than half depends on definitions (do you include tax fraud now that tax returns are filed online?) and on the questions you ask (do you count harassment and cyber-bullying?) – but even with narrow definitions, it's still almost half. Yet the world's law-enforcement agencies typically spend less than one percent of their budgets on fighting it. Until recently, police forces in most jurisdictions did their best to ignore it; in the USA, it was dismissed as 'identity theft' and counted separately, while in the UK victims were told to complain to their bank instead of the police from 2005–15. The result was that as crime went online, like everything else, the online component wasn't counted and crime appeared to fall. Eventually, though, the truth emerged in those countries that have started to ask about fraud in regular victimisation surveys[12].

[12]The USA, the UK, Australia, Belgium and France

Colleagues and I run the Cambridge Cybercrime Centre where we collect and curate data for other researchers to use, ranging from spam and phish through malware and botnet command-and-control traffic to collections of posts to underground crime forums. This section draws on a survey we did in 2019 of the costs of cybercrime and how they've been changing over time [92].

Computer fraud has been around since the 1960s, a notable early case being the Equity Funding insurance company which from 1964-72 created more than 60,000 bogus policies which it sold to reinsurers, creating a special computer system to keep track of them all. Electronic frauds against payment systems have been around since the 1980s, and spam arrived when the Internet was opened to all in the 1990s. Yet early scams were mostly a cottage industry, where individuals or small groups collected credit card numbers, then forged cards to use in shops, or used card numbers to get mail-order goods. Modern cybercrime can probably be dated to 2003–5 when underground markets emerged that enabled crooks to specialise and get good at their jobs, just as happened in the real economy with the Industrial Revolution.

To make sense of cybercrime, it's convenient to consider the shared infrastructure first, and then the main types of cybercrime that are conducted for profit. There is a significant overlap with the crimes committed by states that we considered in the last section, and those committed by individuals against other individuals that we'll consider in the next one; but the actors' motives are a useful primary filter.

2.3.1 Criminal infrastructure

Since about 2005, the emergence of underground markets has led to people specialising as providers of criminal infrastructure, most notably botnet herders, malware writers, spam senders and cashout operators. I will discuss the technology in much greater detail in section 21.3; in this section my focus is on the actors and the ecosystem in which they operate. Although this ecosystem consists of perhaps a few thousand people with revenues in the tens to low hundreds of millions, they impose costs of many billions on the industry and on society. Now that cybercrime has been industrialised, the majority of 'jobs' are now in boring roles such as customer support and system administration, including all the tedious setup work involved in evading law enforcement takedowns [456]. The 'firms' they work for specialise; the entrepreneurs and technical specialists can make real money. (What's more, the cybercrime industry has been booming during the coronavirus pandemic.)

2.3.1.1 Botnet herders

The first botnets – networks of compromised computers – may have been seen in 1996 with an attack on the ISP Panix in New York, using compromised Unix machines in hospitals to conduct a SYN flood attack [370]. The next use was spam, and by 2000 the Earthlink spammer sent over a million phishing emails; its author was sued by Earthlink. Once cyber-criminals started to get organised, there was a significant scale-up. We started to see professionally built and maintained botnets that could be rented out by bad guys, whether spammers, phishermen or others; by 2007 the Cutwail botnet was sending over 50 million spams a minute from over a million infected machines [1836]. Bots would initially contact a command-and-control server for instructions; these would be taken down, or taken over by threat intelligence companies for use as sinkholes to monitor infected machines, and to feed lists of them to ISPs and corporates.

The spammers' first response was peer-to-peer botnets. In 2007 Storm suddenly grew to account for 8% of all Windows malware; it infected machines mostly by malware in email attachments and had them use the eDonkey peer-to-peer network to find other infected machines. It was used not just for spam but for DDoS, for pump-and-dump stock scams and for harvesting bank credentials. Defenders got lots of peers to join this network to harvest lists of bot addresses, so the bots could be cleaned up, and by late 2008 Storm had been cut to a tenth of the size. It was followed by Kelihos, a similar botnet that also stole bitcoins; its creator, a Russian national, was arrested while on holiday in Spain in 2017 and extradited to the USA where he pled guilty in 2018 [661].

The next criminal innovation arrived with the Conficker botnet: the domain generation algorithm (DGA). Conficker was a worm that spread by exploiting a Windows network service vulnerability; it generated 250 domain names every day, and infected machines would try them all out in the hope that the botmaster had managed to rent one of them. Defenders started out by simply buying up the domains, but a later variant generated 50,000 domains a day and an industry working group made agreements with registrars that these domains would simply be put beyond use. By 2009 Conficker had grown so large, with maybe ten million machines, that it was felt to pose a threat to the largest websites and perhaps even to nation states. As with Storm, its use of randomisation proved to be a two-edged sword; defenders could sit on a subset of the domains and harvest feeds of infected machines. By 2015 the number of infected machines had fallen to under a million.

Regardless of whether something can be done to take out the command-and-control system, whether by arresting the botmaster or by technical tricks, the universal fix for botnet infections is to clean up infected machines. But this raises many issues of scale and incentives. While AV companies make tools available, and Microsoft supplies patches, many people don't use them. So long as your infected PC is merely sending occasional spam but works well enough otherwise, why should you go to the trouble of doing anything? But bandwidth costs ISPs money, so the next step was that some ISPs, particularly the cable companies like Comcast, would identify infected machines and confine their users to a 'walled garden' until they promised to clean up. By 2019 that has become less common as people now have all sorts of devices on their wifi, many of which have no user interface; communicating with human users has become harder.

In 2020, we find many botnets with a few tens of thousands of machines that are too small for most defenders to care about, plus some large ones that tend to be multilayer – typically with peer-to-peer mechanisms at the bottom that enable the footsoldier bots to communicate with a few control nodes, which in turn use a domain generation algorithm to find the botmaster. Fragmenting the footsoldiers into a number of small botnets makes it hard for defenders to infiltrate all of them, while the control nodes may be located in places that are hard for defenders to get at. The big money for such botnets in 2020 appears to be in clickfraud.

The latest innovation is Mirai, a family of botnets that exploit IoT devices. The first Mirai worm infected CCTV cameras that had been manufactured by Xiaomi and that had a known factory default password that couldn't be changed. Mirai botnets scan the Internet's IPv4 address space for other vulnerable devices which typically get infected within minutes of being powered up. The first major attack was on DynDNS and took down Twitter for six hours on the US eastern seaboard in October 2016. Since then there have been over a thousand variants, which researchers study to determine what's changed and to work out what countermeasures might be used.

At any one time, there may be half a dozen large botnet herders. The Mirai operators, for example, seem to be two or three groups that might have involved a few dozen people.

2.3.1.2 Malware devs

In addition to the several hundred software engineers who write malware for the world's intelligence agencies and their contractors, there may be hundreds of people writing malware for the criminal market; nobody really knows (though we can monitor traffic on hacker forums to guess the order of magnitude).

Within this community there are specialists. Some concentrate on turning vulnerabilities into exploits, a nontrivial task for modern operating systems that use stack canaries, ASLR and other techniques we'll discuss later in section 6.4.1. Others specialise in the remote access Trojans that the exploits install; others build the peer-to-peer and DGA software for resilient command-and-control communications; yet others design specialised payloads for bank fraud. The highest-value operations seem to be platforms that are maintained with constant upgrades to cope with the latest countermeasures from the anti-virus companies. Within each specialist market segment there are typically a handful of operators, so that when we arrest one of them it makes a difference for a while. Some of the providers are based in jurisdictions that don't extradite their nationals, like Russia, and Russian crimeware is used not just by Russian state actors but by others too.

As Android has taken over from Windows as the most frequently used operating system we've seen a rise in Android malware. In China and in countries with a lot of second-hand and older phones, this may be software that uses an unpatched vulnerability to root an Android phone; the USA and Europe have lots of unpatched phones (as many OEMs stop offering patches once a phone is no longer on sale) but it's often just apps that do bad things, such as stealing SMSes used to authenticate banking transactions.

2.3.1.3 Spam senders

Spamming arrived on a small scale when the Internet opened to the public in the mid-1990s, and by 2000 we saw the Earthlink spammer making millions from sending phishing lures. By 2010 spam was costing the world's ISPs and tech companies about $1bn a year in countermeasures, but it earned its operators perhaps one percent of that. The main beneficiaries may have been webmail services such as Yahoo, Hotmail and Gmail, which can operate better spam filters because of scale; during the 2010s, hundreds of millions of people switched to using their services.

Spam is now a highly specialised business, as getting past modern spam filters requires a whole toolbox of constantly-changing tricks. If you want to use spam to install ransomware, you're better off paying an existing service than trying to learn it all from scratch. Some spam involves industrial-scale email compromise, which can be expensive for the victim; some $350m was knocked off the $4.8bn price at which Yahoo was sold to Verizon after a bulk compromise [772].

2.3.1.4 Bulk account compromise

Some botnets are constantly trying to break into email and other online accounts by trying to guess passwords and password recovery questions. A large email service provider might be recovering several tens of thousands of accounts every day. There are peaks, typically when hackers compromise millions of email addresses and passwords at one website and then try them out at all the others. In 2019, this *credential stuffing* still accounts for the largest number of attempted account compromises by volume [1885]. Compromised accounts are sold on to people who exploit them in various ways. Primary email accounts often have recovery information for other accounts, including bank accounts if the attacker is lucky. They can also be used for scams such as the stranded traveler, where the victim emails all their friends saying they've been robbed in some foreign city and asking for urgent financial help to pay the hotel bill. If all else fails, compromised email accounts can be used to send spam.

A variant on the theme is the pay-per-install service, which implants malware on phones or PCs to order and at scale. This can involve a range of phishing lures in a variety of contexts, from free porn sites that ask you to install a special viewer, to sports paraphernalia offers and news about topical events. It can also use more technical means such as drive-by downloads. Such services are often offered by botnets which need them to maintain their own numbers; they might charge third party customers $10-15 per thousand machines infected in the USA and Europe, and perhaps $3 for Asia.

2.3.1.5 *Targeted attackers*

We've seen the emergence of hack-for-hire operators who will try to compromise a specific target account for a fee, of typically $750 [1885]. They will investigate the target, make multiple spear-phishing attempts, try password recovery procedures, and see if they can break in through related accounts. This continues a tradition of private eyes who traditionally helped in divorce cases and also stalked celebrities on behalf of red-top newspapers – though with even fewer ethical constraints now that services can be purchased anonymously online. John Scott-Railton and colleagues exposed the workings of Dark Basin, a hack-for-hire company that had targeted critics of ExxonMobil, and also net neutrality advocates, and traced it to a company in India [1695].

In recent years, targeted attacks have also been used at scale against small business owners and the finance staff of larger firms in order to carry out various kinds of payment fraud, as I'll discuss below in 2.3.2.

2.3.1.6 *Cashout gangs*

Back in the twentieth century, people who stole credit card numbers would have to go to the trouble of shopping for goods and then selling them to get money out. Nowadays there are specialists who buy compromised bank credentials on underground markets and exploit them. The prices reveal where the real value lies in the criminal chain; a combination of credit card number and expiry date sells for under a dollar, and to get into the single dollars you need a CVV, the cardholder's name and address, and more.

Cashout techniques change every few years, as paths are discovered through the world's money-laundering controls, and the regulations get tweaked to block them. Some cashout firms organise armies of *mules* to whom they transfer some of the risk. Back in the mid-2000s, mules could be drug users who would go to stores and buy goods with stolen credit cards; then there was a period when unwitting mules were recruited by ads promising large earnings to 'agents' to represent foreign companies but who were used to remit stolen funds through their personal bank accounts. The laundrymen next used Russian banks in Latvia, to which Russian mules would turn up to withdraw cash. Then Liberty Reserve, an unlicensed digital currency based in Costa Rica, was all the rage until it was closed down and its founder arrested in 2013. Bitcoin took over for a while but its popularity with the cybercrime community tailed off as its price became more volatile, as the US Department of the Treasury started arm-twisting bitcoin exchanges into identifying their customers.

As with spam, cashout is a constantly evolving attack-defence game. We monitor it and analyse the trends using CrimeBB, a database we've assembled of tens of millions of posts in underground hacker forums where cybercriminals buy and sell services including cashout [1501]. It also appears to favour gangs who can scale up, until they get big enough to attract serious law-enforcement attention: in 2020, one Sergey Medvedev pleaded guilty to inflicting more than $568 million in actual losses over the period 2010–15 [1932].

2.3.1.7 *Ransomware*

One reason for the decline in cryptocurrency may have been the growth of ransomware, and as the gangs involved in this switched to payment methods that are easier for victims to use. By 2016–17, 42% of ransomware encountered by US victims demanded prepaid vouchers such as Amazon gift cards; 14% demanded wire transfers and only 12% demanded cryptocurrency; a lot of the low-end ransomware aimed at consumers is now really scareware as it doesn't actually encrypt files at all [1746]. Since 2017, we've seen ransomware-as-a-service platforms; the operators who use these platforms are often amateurs and can't decrypt even if you're willing to pay.

Meanwhile a number of more professional gangs penetrate systems, install ransomware, wait until several days or weeks of backup data have been encrypted and demand substantial sums of bitcoin. This has grown rapidly over 2019–20, with the most high-profile ransomware victims in the USA being public-sector bodies; several hundred local government bodies and a handful of hospitals have suffered service failures [356]. During the pandemic, more hospitals have been targeted; the medical school at UCSF paid over $1m [1482]. It's an international phenomenon, though, and many private-sector firms fall victim too. Ransomware operators have also been threatening large-scale leaks of personal data to bully victims into paying.

2.3.2 Attacks on banking and payment systems

Attacks on card payment systems started with lost and stolen cards, with forgery at scale arriving in the 1980s; the dotcom boom ramped things up further in the 1990s as many businesses started selling online with little idea of how to detect fraud; and it was card fraud that spawned underground markets in the mid-2000s as criminals sought ways to buy and sell stolen card numbers as well as related equipment and services.

Another significant component is pre-issue fraud, known in the USA as *'identity theft'* [670], where criminals obtain credit cards, loans and other assets in your name and leave you to sort out the mess. I write 'identity theft' in quotes as it's really just the old-fashioned offence of impersonation. Back in the twentieth century, if someone went to a bank, pretended to be me, borrowed money from them and vanished, then that was the bank's problem, not mine. In the early twenty-first, banks took to claiming that it's your identity that's been stolen rather than their money [1730]. There is less of that liability dumping now, but the FBI still records much cybercrime as 'identity theft' which helps keep it out of the mainstream US crime statistics.

The card fraud ecosystem is now fairly stable. Surveys in 2011 and 2019 show that while card fraud doubled over the decade, the loss fell slightly as a percentage of transaction value [91, 92]; the system has been getting more efficient as it grows. Many card numbers are harvested in hacking attacks on retailers, which can be very expensive for them once they've paid to notify affected customers and reimburse banks for reissued cards. As with the criminal infrastructure, the total costs may be easily two orders of magnitude greater than anything the criminals actually get away with.

Attacks on online banking ramped up in 2005 with the arrival of large-scale phishing attacks; emails that seemed to come from banks drove customers to imitation bank websites that stole their passwords. The banks responded with techniques such as two-factor authentication, or the low-cost substitute of asking for only a few letters of the password at a time; the crooks' response, from about 2009, has been credential-stealing malware. Zeus and later Trojans lurk on a PC until the user logs on to a bank whose website they recognise; they then make payments to mule accounts and hide their activity from the user – the so-called 'man-in-the-browser attack'. (Some Trojans even connect in real time to a human operator.) The crooks behind the Zeus and later the Dridex banking malware were named and indicted by US investigators in December 2019, and accused of stealing some $100m, but they remain at liberty in Russia [796]. Other gangs have been broken up and people arrested for such scams, which continue to net in the hundreds of millions to low billions a year worldwide.

Firms also have to pay attention to business email compromise, where a crook compromises a business email account and tells a customer that their bank account number has changed; or where the crook impersonates the CEO and orders a financial controller to make a payment; and social engineering attacks by people pretending to be from your bank who talk you into releasing a code to authorise a payment. Most targeted attacks on company payment systems can in theory be prevented by the control procedures that most large firms already have, and so the typical target is a badly-run large firm, or a medium-sized firm with enough money to be worth stealing but not enough control to lock everything down.

I'll discuss the technicalities of such frauds in Chapter 12, along with a growing number of crimes that directly affect only banks, their regulators and their retail customers. I'll also discuss cryptocurrencies, which facilitate cybercrimes from ransomware to stock frauds, in Chapter 20.

2.3.3 Sectoral cybercrime ecosystems

A number of sectors other than banking have their own established cybercrime scenes. One example is travel fraud. There's a whole ecosystem of people who sell fraudulently obtained air tickets, which are sometimes simply bought with stolen credit card numbers, sometimes obtained directly by manipulating or hacking the systems of travel agents or airlines, sometimes booked by corrupt staff at these firms, and sometimes scammed from the public directly by stealing their air miles. The resulting cut-price tickets are sold directly using spam or through various affiliate marketing scams. Some of the passengers who use them to fly know they're dubious, while others are dupes – which makes it hard to deal with the problem just by arresting people at the boarding gate. (The scammers also supply tickets at the last minute, so that the alarms are usually too late.) For an account and analysis of travel fraud, see Hutchings [938]. An increasing number of other business sectors are acquiring their own dark side, and I will touch on some of them in later chapters.

2.3.4 Internal attacks

Fraud by insiders has been an issue since businesses started hiring people. Employees cheat the firm, partners cheat each other, and firms cheat their shareholders. The main defence is bookkeeping. The invention of double-entry bookkeeping, of which our earliest records are from the Cairo of a thousand years ago, enabled businesses to scale up beyond the family that owned them. This whole ecosystem is evolving as technology does, and its design is driven by the Big Four accounting firms who make demands on their audit clients that in turn drive the development of accounting software and the supporting security mechanisms. I discuss all this at length in Chapter 12. There are also inside attacks involving whistleblowing, which I discuss below.

2.3.5 CEO crimes

Companies attack each other, and their customers too. From the 1990s, printer vendors have used cryptography to lock their customers in to using proprietary ink cartridges, as I describe in section 24.6, while companies selling refills have been breaking the crypto. Games console makers have been playing exactly the same game with aftermarket vendors. The use of cryptography for accessory control is now pervasive, being found even on water filter cartridges in fridges [1073]. Many customers find this annoying and try to circumvent the controls. The US courts decided in the Lexmark v SCC case that this was fine: the printer vendor Lexmark sued SCC, a company that sold clones of its security chips to independent ink vendors, but lost. So the incumbent can now hire the best cryptographers they can find to lock their products, while the challenger can hire the best cryptanalysts they can find to unlock them – and customers can hack them any way they can. Here, the conflict is legal and open. As with state actors, corporates sometimes assemble teams with multiple PhDs, millions of dollars in funding, and capital assets such as electron microscopes[13]. We discuss this in greater detail later in section 24.6.

Not all corporate attacks are conducted as openly. Perhaps the best-known covert hack was by Volkswagen on the EU and US emissions testing schemes; diesel engines sold in cars were programmed to run cleanly if they detected the standard emission test conditions, and efficiently otherwise. For this, the CEO of VW was fired and indicted in the USA (to which Germany won't extradite him), while the CEO of Audi was fired and jailed in Germany [1086]. VW has set aside €25bn to cover criminal and civil fines and compensation. Other carmakers were cheating too; Daimler was fined €860m in Europe in 2019 [1468], and in 2020 reached a US settlement consisting of a fine of $1.5bn from four government agencies plus a class action of $700m [1859]. Settlements for other manufacturers and other countries are in the pipeline.

Sometimes products are designed to break whole classes of protection system, an example being the overlay SIM cards described later in Chapter 12. These are SIM cards with two sides and only 160 microns thick, which you stick on top of the SIM card in your phone to provide a second root of trust; they were designed to enable people in China to defeat the high roaming charges of the early 2010s. The overlay SIM essentially does a man-in-the-middle attack on the real SIM, and can be programmed in Javacard. A side-effect is that such SIMs make it really easy to do some types of bank fraud.

So when putting together the threat model for your system, stop and think what capable motivated opponents you might have among your competitors, or among firms competing with suppliers on which products you depend. The obvious attacks include industrial espionage, but nowadays it's much more complex than that.

2.3.6 Whistleblowers

Intelligence agencies, and secretive firms, can get obsessive about 'the insider threat'. But in 2018, Barclays Bank's CEO was fined £642,000 and ordered to

[13]Full disclosure: both our hardware lab and our NGO activities have on occasion received funding from such actors.

repay £500,000 of his bonus for attempting to trace a whistleblower in the bank [698]. So let's turn it round and look at it from the other perspective – that of the whistleblower. Many are trying to do the right thing, often at a fairly mundane level such as reporting a manager who's getting bribes from suppliers or who is sexually harassing staff. In regulated industries such as banking they may have a legal duty to report wrongdoing and legal immunity against claims of breach of confidence by their employer. Even then, they often lose because of the power imbalance; they get fired and the problem goes on. Many security engineers think the right countermeasure to leakers is technical, such as data loss prevention systems, but robust mechanisms for staff to report wrongdoing are usually more important. Some organisations, such as banks, police forces and online services, have mechanisms for reporting crimes by staff but no effective process for raising ethical concerns about management decisions[14].

But even basic whistleblowing mechanisms are often an afterthought; they typically lead the complainant to HR rather than to the board's audit committee. External mechanisms may be little better. One big service firm ran a "Whistle-blowing hotline" for its clients in 2019; but the web page code has trackers from LinkedIn, Facebook and Google, who could thus identify unhappy staff members, and also JavaScript from CDNs, littered with cookies and referrers from yet more IT companies. No technically savvy leaker would use such a service. At the top end of the ecosystem, some newspapers offer ways for whistleblowers to make contact using encrypted email. But the mechanisms tend to be clunky and the web pages that promote them do not always educate potential leakers about either the surveillance risks, or the operational security measures that might counter them. I discuss the usability and support issues around whistleblowing in more detail in section 25.4.

This is mostly a policy problem rather than a technical one. It's difficult to design a technical mechanism whereby honest staff can blow the whistle on abuses that have become ingrained in an organisation's culture, such as pervasive sexual harassment or financial misconduct. In most cases, it's immediately clear who the whistleblower is, so the critical factor is whether the whistleblower will get external support. For example, will they ever get another job? This isn't just a matter of formal legal protection but also of culture. For example, the rape conviction of Harvey Weinstein empowered many women to protest about sexual harassment and discrimination; hopefully the Black Lives Matter protests will similarly empower people of colour [32].

An example where anonymity did help, though, was the UK parliamentary expenses scandal of 2008–9. During a long court case about whether the public could get access to the expense claims of members of parliament, someone

[14]Google staff ended up going on strike in 2018 about the handling of sexual harassment scandals.

went to the PC where the records were kept, copied them to a DVD and sold the lot to the Daily Telegraph. The paper published the juicy bits in instalments all through May and June, when MPs gave up and published the lot on Parliament's website. Half-a-dozen ministers resigned; seven MPs and peers went to prison; dozens of MPs stood down or lost their seats at the following election; and there was both mirth and outrage at some of the things charged to the taxpayer. The whistleblower may have technically committed a crime, but their action was clearly in the public interest; now all parliamentary expenses are public, as they should have been all along. If a nation's lawmakers have their hands in the till, what else will clean up the system?

Even in the case of Ed Snowden, there should have been a robust way for him to report unlawful conduct by the NSA to the appropriate arm of government, probably a Congressional committee. But he knew that a previous whistleblower, Bill Binney, had been arrested and harassed after trying to do that. In hindsight, that aggressive approach was unwise, as President Obama's NSA review group eventually conceded. At the less exalted level of a commercial firm, if one of your staff is stealing your money, and another wants to tell you about it, you'd better make that work.

2.4 Geeks

Our third category of attacker are the people like me – researchers who investigate vulnerabilities and report them so they can be fixed. Academics look for new attacks out of curiosity, and get rewarded with professional acclaim – which can lead to promotion for professors and jobs for the students who help us. Researchers working for security companies also look for newsworthy exploits; publicity at conferences such as Black Hat can win new customers. Hobby hackers break into stuff as a challenge, just as people climb mountains or play chess; hacktivists do it to annoy companies they consider to be wicked. Whether on the right side of the law or not, we tend to be curious introverts who need to feel in control, but accept challenges and look for the 'rush'. Our reward is often fame – whether via academic publications, by winning customers for a security consulting business, by winning medals from academic societies or government agencies, or even on social media. Sometimes we break stuff out of irritation, so we can circumvent something that stops us fixing something we own; and sometimes there's an element of altruism. For example, people have come to us in the past complaining that their bank cards had been stolen and used to buy stuff, and the banks wouldn't give them a refund, saying their PIN must have been used, when it hadn't. We looked into some of these cases and discovered the No-PIN and preplay attacks on chip and PIN systems, which I'll describe in the chapter on banking (the bad guys had actually discovered these attacks, but we replicated them and got justice for some of the victims).

Security researchers who discovered and reported vulnerabilities to a software vendor or system operator used to risk legal threats, as companies sometimes thought this would be cheaper than fixing things. So some researchers took to disclosing bugs anonymously on mailing lists; but this meant that the bad guys could use them at once. By the early 2000s, the IT industry had evolved practices of responsible disclosure whereby researchers disclose the bug to the maintainer some months in advance of disclosure. Many firms operate bug-bounty programs that offer rewards for vulnerabilities; as a result, independent researchers can now make serious money selling vulnerabilities, and more than one assiduous researcher has now earned over $1m doing this. Since the Stuxnet worm, governments have raced to stockpile vulnerabilities, and we now see some firms that buy vulnerabilities from researchers in order to weaponise them, and sell them to cyber-arms suppliers. Once they're used, they spread, are eventually reverse-engineered and patched. I'll discuss this ecosystem in more detail in the chapters on economics and assurance.

Some more traditional sectors still haven't adopted responsible disclosure. Volkswagen sued researchers in the universities of Birmingham and Nijmegen who reverse-engineered some online car theft tools and documented how poor their remote key entry system was. The company lost, making fools of themselves and publicising the insecurity of their vehicles (I'll discuss the technical details in section 4.3.1 and the policy in section 27.5.7.2). Eventually, as software permeates everything, software industry ways of working will become more widespread too. In the meantime, we can expect turbulence. Firms that cover up problems that harm their customers will have to reckon with the possibility that either an internal whistleblower, or an external security researcher, will figure out what's going on, and when that happens there will often be an established responsible disclosure process to invoke. This will impose costs on firms that fail to align their business models with it.

2.5 The swamp

Our fourth category is abuse, by which we usually mean offences against the person rather than against property. These range from cyber-bullying at schools all the way to state-sponsored Facebook advertising campaigns that get people to swamp legislators with death threats. I'll deal first with offences that scale, including political harassment and child sex abuse material, and then with offences that don't, ranging from school bullying to intimate partner abuse.

2.5.1 Hacktivism and hate campaigns

Propaganda and protest evolved as technology did. Ancient societies had to make do with epic poetry; cities enabled people to communicate with hundreds of others directly, by making speeches in the forum; and the invention of writing enabled a further scale-up. The spread of printing in the sixteenth century led to wars of religion in the seventeenth, daily newspapers in the eighteenth and mass-market newspapers in the nineteenth. Activists learned to compete for attention in the mass media, and honed their skills as radio and then TV came along.

Activism in the Internet age started off with using online media to mobilise people to do conventional lobbying, such as writing to legislators; organisations such as Indymedia and Avaaz developed expertise at this during the 2000s. In 2011, activists such as Wael Ghonim used social media to trigger the Arab Spring, which we discuss in more detail in section 26.4.1. Since then, governments have started to crack down, and activism has spread into online hate campaigns and radicalisation. Many hate campaigns are covertly funded by governments or opposition parties, but by no means all: single-issue campaign groups are also players. If you can motivate hundreds of people to send angry emails or tweets, then a company or individual on the receiving end can have a real problem. Denial-of-service attacks can interrupt operations while doxxing can do real brand damage as well as causing distress to executives and staff.

Activists vary in their goals, in their organisational coherence and in the extent to which they'll break the law. There's a whole spectrum, from the completely law-abiding NGOs who get their supporters to email legislators to the slightly edgy, who may manipulate news by getting bots to click on news stories, to game the media analytics and make editors pay more attention to their issue. Then there are whistleblowers who go to respectable newspapers, political partisans who harass people behind the mild anonymity of Twitter accounts, hackers who break into target firms and vandalise their websites or even doxx them. The Climategate scandal, described in 2.2.5 above, may be an example of doxxing by a hacktivist. At the top end, there are the hard-core types who end up in jail for terrorist offences.

During the 1990s, I happily used email and usenet to mobilise people against surveillance bills going through the UK parliament, as I'll describe later in section 26.2.7. I found myself on the receiving end of hacktivism in 2003 when the Animal Liberation Front targeted my university because of plans to build a monkey house, for primates to be used in research. The online component consisted of thousands of emails sent to staff members with distressing images of monkeys with wires in their brains; this was an early example of 'brigading', where hundreds of people gang up on one target online. We dealt with that online attack easily enough by getting their email accounts closed down. But they persisted with physical demonstrations and media harassment; our

Vice-Chancellor decided to cut her losses, and the monkey house went to Oxford instead. Some of the leaders were later jailed for terrorism offences after they assaulted staff at a local pharmaceutical testing company and placed bombs under the cars of medical researchers [21].

Online shaming has become popular as a means of protest. It can be quite spontaneous, with a flash mob of vigilantes forming when an incident goes viral. An early example happened in 2005 when a young lady in Seoul failed to clean up after her dog defecated in a subway carriage. Another passenger photographed the incident and put it online; within days the 'dog poo girl' had been hounded into hiding, abandoning her university course [420]. There have been many other cases since.

The power of platforms such as Twitter became evident in Gamergate, a storm sparked by abusive comments about a female game developer made publicly by a former boyfriend in August 2014, and cascading into a torrent of misogynistic criticism of women in the gaming industry and of feminists who had criticised the industry's male-dominated culture. A number of people were doxxed, SWATted, or hounded from their homes [1936]. The harassment was coordinated on anonymous message boards such as 4chan and the attackers would gang up on a particular target – who then also got criticised by mainstream conservative journalists [1132]. The movement appeared leaderless and evolved constantly, with one continuing theme being a rant against 'social justice warriors'. It appears to have contributed to the development of the alt-right movement which influenced the 2016 election two years later.

A growing appreciation of the power of angry online mobs is leading politicians to stir them up, at all levels from local politicians trying to undermine their rivals to nation states trying to swing rival states' elections. Angry mobs are an unpleasant enough feature of modern politics in developed countries; in less developed countries things get even worse, with real lynchings in countries such as India (where the ruling BJP party has been building a troll army since at least 2011 to harrass political opponents and civil-society critics [1640]). Companies are targeted less frequently, but it does happen. Meanwhile the social-media companies are under pressure to censor online content, and as it's hard for an AI program to tell the difference between a joke, abuse, a conspiracy theory and information warfare by a foreign government, they end up having to hire more and more moderators. I will return to the law and policy aspects of this in 26.4 below.

2.5.2 Child sex abuse material

When the Internet came to governments' attention in the 1990s and they wondered how to get a handle on it, the first thing to be regulated was images of child sex abuse (CSA), in the Budapest Convention in 2001. We have little data on the real prevalence of CSA material as the legal restrictions make it hard for anyone outside law enforcement to do any research. In many countries, the approach to CSA material has less focus on actual harm reduction than it deserves. Indeed, many laws around online sexual offences are badly designed, and seem to be driven more by exploiting outrage than by minimising the number of victims and the harm they suffer. CSA may be a case study on how not to do online regulation because of forensic failures, takedown failures, weaponisation and the law-norm gap.

The most notorious forensic failure was Britain's Operation Ore, which I describe in more detail in 26.5.3. Briefly, several thousand men were arrested on suspicion of CSA offences after their credit card numbers were found on an abuse website, and perhaps half of them turned out to be victims of credit card fraud. Hundreds of innocent men had their lives ruined. Yet nothing was done for the child victims in Brazil and Indonesia, and the authorities are still nowhere near efficient at taking down websites that host CSA material. In most countries, CSA takedown is a monopoly of either the police, or a regulated body that operates under public-sector rules (NCMEC in the USA and the IWF in the UK), and takes from days to weeks; things would go much more quickly if governments were to use the private-sector contractors that banks use to deal with phishing sites [940]. The public-sector monopoly stems from laws in many countries that make the possession of CSA material a strict-liability offence. This not only makes it hard to deal with such material using the usual abuse channels, but also allows it to be weaponised: protesters can send it to targets and then report them to the police. It also makes it difficult for parents and teachers to deal sensibly with incidents that arise with teens using dating apps or having remote relationships. The whole thing is a mess, caused by legislators wanting to talk tough without understanding the technology. (CSA material is now a significant annoyance for some legislators' staff, and also makes journalists at some newspapers reluctant to make their email addresses public.)

There is an emerging law-norm gap with the growth in popularity of sexting among teenagers. Like it or not, sending intimate photographs to partners (real and intended) became normal behaviour for teens in many countries when smartphones arrived in 2008. This was a mere seven years after the Budapest convention, whose signatories may have failed to imagine that sexual images of under-18s could be anything other than abuse. Thanks to the convention, possessing an intimate photo of anyone under 18 can now result in a prison sentence in any of the 63 countries that have ratified it. Teens laugh at lectures from schoolteachers to not take or share such photos, but the end result is real harm. Kids may be tricked or pressured into sharing photos of themselves, and even if the initial sharing is consensual, the recipient can later use it for blackmail or just pass it round for a laugh. Recipients – even if innocent – are also committing criminal offences by simply having the photos on their phones, so kids can set up other kids and denounce them. This leads to general issues of bullying and more specific issues of intimate partner abuse.

2.5.3 School and workplace bullying

Online harassment and bullying are a fact of life in modern societies, not just in schools but in workplaces too, as people jostle for rank, mates and resources. From the media stories of teens who kill themselves following online abuse, you might think that cyber-bullying now accounts for most of the problem – at least at school – but the figures show that it's less than half. An annual UK survey discloses that about a quarter of children and young people are constantly bullied (13% verbal, 5% cyber and 3% physical) while about half are bullied sometimes (24%, 8% and 9% respectively) [565]. The only national survey of all ages of which I'm aware is the French national victimisation survey, which since 2007 has collected data not just on physical crimes such as burglary and online crimes such as fraud, but on harassment too [1460]. This is based on face-to-face interviews with 16,000 households and the 2017 survey reported two million cases of threatening behaviour, 7% were made on social networks and a further 9% by phone. But have social media made this worse? Research suggests that the effects of social media use on adolescent well-being are nuanced, small at best, and contingent on analytic methods [1475].

Yet there is talk in the media of a rise in teen suicide which some commentators link to social media use. Thankfully, the OECD mortality statistics show that this is also untrue: suicides among 15–19 year olds have declined slightly from about 8 to about 7 cases per 100,000 over the period 1990–2015 [1479].

2.5.4 Intimate relationship abuse

Just as I ended the last section by discussing whistleblowers – the insider threat to companies – I'll end this section with intimate relationship abuse, the insider threat to families and individuals. Gamergate may have been a flashbulb example, but protection from former intimate partners and other family members is a real problem that exists at scale – with about half of all marriages ending in divorce, and not all breakups being amicable. Intimate partner abuse has been suffered by 27% of women and 11% of men. Stalking is not of course limited to former partners. Celebrities in particular can be stalked by people they've never met – with occasional tragic outcomes, as in the case of John Lennon. But former partners account for most of it, and law enforcement in most countries have historically been reluctant to do anything effective about them. Technology has made the victims' plight worse.

One subproblem is the publication of non-consensual intimate imagery (NCII), once called 'revenge porn' – until California Attorney General Kamala

Harris objected that this is cyber-exploitation and a crime. Her message got through to the big service firms who since 2015 have been taking down such material on demand from the victims [1693]. This followed an earlier report in 2012 where Harris documented the increasing use of smartphones, online marketplaces and social media in forcing vulnerable people into unregulated work including prostitution – raising broader questions about how technology can be used to connect with, and assist, crime victims [867].

The problems faced by a woman leaving an abusive and controlling husband are among the hardest in the universe of information security. All the usual advice is the wrong way round: your opponent knows not just your passwords but has such deep contextual knowledge that he can answer all your password recovery questions. There are typically three phases: a physical control phase where the abuser has access to your device and may install malware, or even destroy devices; a high-risk escape phase as you try to find a new home, a job and so on; and a life-apart phase when you might want to shield location, email address and phone numbers to escape harassment, and may have lifelong concerns. It takes seven escape attempts on average to get to life apart, and disconnecting from online services can cause other abuse to escalate. After escape, you may have to restrict childrens' online activities and sever mutual relationships; letting your child post anything can leak the school location and lead to the abuser turning up. You may have to change career as it can be impossible to work as a self-employed professional if you can no longer advertise.

To support such users, responsible designers should think hard about usability during times of high stress and high risk; they should allow users to have multiple accounts; they should design things so that someone reviewing your history should not be able to tell you deleted anything; they should push two-factor authentication, unusual activity notifications, and incognito mode. They should also think about how a survivor can capture evidence for use in divorce and custody cases and possibly in criminal prosecution, while minimising the trauma [1250]. But that's not what we find in real life. Many banks don't really want to know about disputes or financial exploitation within families. A big problem in some countries is stalkerware – apps designed to monitor partners, ex-partners, children or employees. A report from Citizen Lab spells out the poor information security practices of these apps, how they are marketed explicitly to abusive men, and how they break the law in Europe and Canada; as for the USA and Australia, over half of abusers tracked women using stalkerware [1497]. And then there's the Absher app, which enables men in Saudi Arabia to control their women in ways unacceptable in developed countries; its availability in app stores has led to protests against Apple and Google elsewhere in the world, but as of 2020 it's still there.

Intimate abuse is hard for designers and others to deal with as it's entangled with normal human caregiving between partners, between friends and colleagues, between parents and young children, and later between children and elderly parents. Many relationships are largely beneficent but with some abusive aspects, and participants often don't agree on which aspects. The best analysis I know, by Karen Levy and Bruce Schneier, discusses the combination of multiple motivations, copresence which leads to technical vulnerabilities, and power dynamics leading to relational vulnerabilities [1156]. Technology facilitates multiple privacy invasions in relationships, ranging from casual annoyance to serious crime; designers need to be aware that households are not units, devices are not personal, and the purchaser of a device is not the only user. I expect that concerns about intimate abuse will expand in the next few years to concerns about victims of abuse by friends, teachers and parents, and will be made ever more complex by new forms of home and school automation.

2.6 Summary

The systems you build or operate can be attacked by a wide range of opponents. It's important to work out who might attack you and how, and it's also important to be able to figure out how you were attacked and by whom. Your systems can also be used to attack others, and if you don't think about this in advance you may find yourself in serious legal or political trouble.

In this chapter I've grouped adversaries under four general themes: spies, crooks, hackers and bullies. Not all threat actors are bad: many hackers report bugs responsibly and many whistleblowers are public-spirited. ('Our' spies are of course considered good while 'theirs' are bad; moral valence depends on the public and private interests in play.) Intelligence and law enforcement agencies may use a mix of traffic data analysis and content sampling when hunting, and targeted collection for gathering; collection methods range from legal coercion via malware to deception. Both spies and crooks use malware to establish botnets as infrastructure. Crooks typically use opportunistic collection for mass attacks, while for targeted work, spear-phishing is the weapon of choice; the agencies may have fancier tools but use the same basic methods. There are also cybercrime ecosystems attached to specific business sectors; crime will evolve where it can scale. As for the swamp, the weapon of choice is the angry mob, wielded nowadays by states, activist groups and even individual orators. There are many ways in which abuse can scale, and when designing a system you need to work out how crimes against it, or abuse using it, might scale. It's not enough to think about usability; you need to think about abusability too.

Personal abuse matters too. Every police officer knows that the person who assaults you or murders you isn't usually a stranger, but someone you know – maybe another boy in your school class, or your stepfather. This has been ignored by the security research community, perhaps because we're mostly clever white or Asian boys from stable families in good neighbourhoods.

If you're defending a company of any size, you'll see enough machines on your network getting infected, and you need to know whether they're just zombies on a botnet or part of a targeted attack. So it's not enough to rely on patching and antivirus. You need to watch your network and keep good enough logs that when an infected machine is spotted you can tell whether it's a kid building a botnet or a targeted attacker who responds to loss of a viewpoint with a scramble to develop another one. You need to make plans to respond to incidents, so you know who to call for forensics – and so your CEO isn't left gasping like a landed fish in front of the TV cameras. You need to think systematically about your essential controls: backup to recover from ransomware, payment procedures to block business email compromise, and so on. If you're advising a large company they should have much of this already, and if it's a small company you need to help them figure out how to do enough of it.

The rest of this book will fill in the details.

Research problems

Until recently, research on cybercrime wasn't really scientific. Someone would get some data – often under NDA from an anti-virus company – work out some statistics, write up their thesis, and then go get a job. The data were never available to anyone else who wanted to check their results or try a new type of analysis. Since 2015 we've been trying to fix that by setting up the Cambridge Cybercrime Centre, where we collect masses of data on spam, phish, botnets and malware as a shared resource for researchers. We're delighted for other academics to use it. If you want to do research on cybercrime, call us.

We also need something similar for espionage and cyber warfare. People trying to implant malware into control systems and other operational technology are quite likely to be either state actors, or cyber-arms vendors who sell to states. The criticisms made by President Eisenhower of the 'military-industrial complex' apply here in spades. Yet not one of the legacy think-tanks seems interested in tracking what's going on. As a result, nations are more likely to make strategic miscalculations, which could lead not just to cyber-conflict but the real kinetic variety, too.

As for research into cyber abuse, there is now some research, but the technologists, the psychologists, the criminologists and the political scientists aren't talking to each other enough. There are many issues, from the welfare and rights of children and young people, through the issues facing families separated by prison, to our ability to hold fair and free elections. We need to engage more technologists with public-policy issues and educate more policy people about the realities of technology. We also need to get more women involved, and people from poor and marginalised communities in both developed and less developed countries, so we have a less narrow perspective on what the real problems are.

Further reading

There's an enormous literature on the topics discussed in this chapter but it's rather fragmented. A starting point for the Snowden revelations might be Glenn Greenwald's book *'No Place to Hide'* [817]; for an account of Russian strategy and tactics, see the 2018 report to the US Senate's Committee on Foreign Relations [387]; and for a great introduction to the history of propaganda see Tim Wu's *'The Attention Merchants'* [2052]. For surveys of cybercrime, see our 2012 paper "Measuring the Cost of Cybercrime" [91] and our 2019 follow-up "Measuring the Changing Cost of Cybercrime" [92]. Criminologists such as Bill Chambliss have studied state-organised crime, from piracy and slavery in previous centuries through the more recent smuggling of drugs and weapons by intelligence agencies to torture and assassination; this gives the broader context within which to assess unlawful surveillance. The story of Gamergate is told in Zoë Quinn's *'Crash Override'* [1570]. Finally, the tale of Marcus Hutchins, the malware expert who stopped Wannacry, is at [812].

CHAPTER

3

Psychology and Usability

Humans are incapable of securely storing high-quality cryptographic keys, and they have unacceptable speed and accuracy when performing cryptographic operations. (They are also large, expensive to maintain, difficult to manage, and they pollute the environment. It is astonishing that these devices continue to be manufactured and deployed. But they are sufficiently pervasive that we must design our protocols around their limitations.)
– KAUFMANN, PERLMAN AND SPECINER [1028]

Only amateurs attack machines; professionals target people.
– BRUCE SCHNEIER

Metternich told lies all the time, and never deceived any one; Talleyrand never told a lie and deceived the whole world.
– THOMAS MACAULAY

3.1 Introduction

Many real attacks exploit psychology at least as much as technology. We saw in the last chapter how some online crimes involve the manipulation of angry mobs, while both property crimes and espionage make heavy use of *phishing*, in which victims are lured by an email to log on to a website that appears genuine but that's actually designed to steal their passwords or get them to install malware.

Online frauds like phishing are often easier to do, and harder to stop, than similar real-world frauds because many online protection mechanisms are neither as easy to use nor as difficult to forge as their real-world equivalents. It's much easier for crooks to create a bogus bank website that passes casual inspection than to build an actual bogus bank branch in a shopping street.

We've evolved social and psychological tools over millions of years to help us deal with deception in face-to-face contexts, but these are less effective when we get an email that asks us to do something. For an ideal technology, good use would be easier than bad use. We have many examples in the physical world: a potato peeler is easier to use for peeling potatoes than a knife is, but a lot harder to use for murder. But we've not always got this right for computer systems yet. Much of the asymmetry between good and bad on which we rely in our daily business doesn't just depend on formal exchanges – which can be automated easily – but on some combination of physical objects, judgment of people, and the supporting social protocols. So, as our relationships with employers, banks and government become more formalised via online communication, and we lose both physical and human context, the forgery of these communications becomes more of a risk.

Deception, of various kinds, is now the principal mechanism used to defeat online security. It can be used to get passwords, to compromise confidential information or to manipulate financial transactions directly. Hoaxes and frauds have always happened, but the Internet makes some of them easier, and lets others be repackaged in ways that may bypass our existing controls (be they personal intuitions, company procedures or even laws).

Another driver for the surge in attacks based on social engineering is that people are getting better at technology. As designers learn how to forestall the easier technical attacks, psychological manipulation of system users or operators becomes ever more attractive. So the security engineer absolutely must understand basic psychology, as a prerequisite for dealing competently with everything from passwords to CAPTCHAs and from phishing to social engineering in general; a working appreciation of risk misperception and scaremongering is also necessary to understand the mechanisms underlying angry online mobs and the societal response to emergencies from terrorism to pandemic disease. So just as research in security economics led to a real shift in perspective between the first and second editions of this book, research in security psychology has made much of the difference to how we view the world between the second edition and this one.

In the rest of this chapter, I'll first survey relevant research in psychology, then work through how we apply the principles to make password authentication mechanisms more robust against attack, to security usability more generally, and beyond that to good design.

3.2 Insights from psychology research

Psychology is a huge subject, ranging from neuroscience through to clinical topics, and spilling over into cognate disciplines from philosophy through artificial intelligence to sociology. Although it has been studied for much longer than computer science, our understanding of the mind is much less complete: the brain is so much more complex. There's one central problem – the nature of consciousness – that we just don't understand at all. We know that 'the mind is what the brain does', yet the mechanisms that underlie our sense of self and of personal history remain obscure.

Nonetheless a huge amount is known about the functioning of the mind and the brain, and we're learning interesting new things all the time. In what follows I can only offer a helicopter tour of three of the themes in psychology research that are very relevant to our trade: cognitive psychology, which studies topics such as how we remember and what sort of mistakes we make; social psychology, which deals with how we relate to others in groups and to authority; and behavioral economics, which studies the heuristics and biases that lead us to make decisions that are consistently irrational in measurable and exploitable ways.

3.2.1 Cognitive psychology

Cognitive psychology is the classical approach to the subject – building on early empirical work in the nineteenth century. It deals with how we think, remember, make decisions and even daydream. Twentieth-century pioneers such as Ulric Neisser discovered that human memory doesn't work like a video recorder: our memories are stored in networks across the brain, from which they are reconstructed, so they change over time and can be manipulated [1429]. There are many well-known results. For example, it's easier to memorise things that are repeated frequently, and it's easier to store things in context. Many of these insights are used by marketers and scammers, but misunderstood or just ignored by most system developers.

For example, most of us have heard of George Miller's result that human short-term memory can cope with about seven (plus or minus two) simultaneous choices [1319] and, as a result, many designers limit menu choices to about five. But this is not the right conclusion. People search for information first by recalling where to look, and then by scanning; once you've found the relevant menu, scanning ten items is only twice as hard as scanning five. The real limits on menu size are screen size, which might give you ten choices, and with spoken menus, where the average user has difficulty dealing with more than three or four [1547]. Here, too, Miller's insight is misused because spatio-structural memory is a different faculty from echoic memory. This illustrates why a broad idea like 7+/-2 can be hazardous; you need to look at the detail.

In recent years, the centre of gravity in this field has been shifting from applied cognitive psychology to the human-computer interaction (HCI) research community, because of the huge amount of empirical know-how gained not just from lab experiments, but from the iterative improvement of fielded systems. As a result, HCI researchers not only model and measure human performance, including perception, motor control, memory and problem-solving; they have also developed an understanding of how users' mental models of systems work, how they differ from developers' mental models, and of the techniques (such as task analysis and cognitive walkthrough) that we can use to explore how people learn to use and understand systems.

Security researchers need to find ways of turning these ploughshares into swords (the bad guys are already working on it). There are some low-hanging fruit; for example, the safety research community has put a lot of effort into studying the errors people make when operating equipment [1592]. It's said that 'to err is human' and error research confirms this: the predictable varieties of human error are rooted in the very nature of cognition. The schemata, or mental models, that enable us to recognise people, sounds and concepts so much better than computers, also make us vulnerable when the wrong model gets activated.

Human errors made while operating equipment fall into broadly three categories, depending on where they occur in the 'stack': slips and lapses at the level of skill, mistakes at the level of rules, and misconceptions at the cognitive level.

- Actions performed often become a matter of skill, but we can slip when a manual skill fails – for example, pressing the wrong button – and we can also have a lapse where we use the wrong skill. For example, when you intend to go to the supermarket on the way home from work you may take the road home by mistake, if that's what you do most days (this is also known as a *capture error*). Slips are exploited by typosquatters, who register domains similar to popular ones, and harvest people who make typing errors; other attacks exploit the fact that people are trained to click 'OK' to pop-up boxes to get their work done. So when designing a system you need to ensure that dangerous actions, such as installing software, require action sequences that are quite different from routine ones. Errors also commonly follow interruptions and perceptual confusion. One example is the *post-completion error*: once they've accomplished their immediate goal, people are easily distracted from tidying-up actions. More people leave cards behind in ATMs that give them the money first and the card back second.
- Actions that people take by following rules are open to errors when they follow the wrong rule. Various circumstances – such as information overload – can cause people to follow the strongest rule they know, or the most general rule, rather than the best one. Phishermen use many tricks to get people to follow the wrong rule, ranging from using `https` (because 'it's secure') to starting URLs with the impersonated bank's name, as `www.citibank.secureauthentication.com` – for most people, looking for a name is a stronger rule than parsing its position.
- The third category of mistakes are those made by people for cognitive reasons – either they simply don't understand the problem, or pretend

> that they do, and ignore advice in order to get their work done. The seminal paper on security usability, Alma Whitten and Doug Tygar's "Why Johnny Can't Encrypt", demonstrated that the encryption program PGP was simply too hard for most college students to use as they didn't understand the subtleties of private versus public keys, encryption and signatures [2022]. And there's growing realisation that many security bugs occur because most programmers can't use security mechanisms either. Both access control mechanisms and security APIs are hard to understand and fiddly to use; security testing tools are often not much better. Programs often appear to work even when protection mechanisms are used in quite mistaken ways. Engineers then copy code from each other, and from online code-sharing sites, so misconceptions and errors are propagated widely [11]. They often know this is bad, but there's just not the time to do better.

There is some important science behind all this, and here are just two examples. James Gibson developed the concept of action possibilities or *affordances*: the physical environment may be climbable or fall-off-able or get-under-able for an animal, and similarly a seat is sit-on-able. People have developed great skill at creating environments that induce others to behave in certain ways: we build stairways and doorways, we make objects portable or graspable; we make pens and swords [763]. Often perceptions are made up of affordances, which can be more fundamental than value or meaning. In exactly the same way, we design software artefacts to train and condition our users' choices, so the affordances of the systems we use can affect how we think in all sorts of ways. We can also design traps for the unwary: an animal that mistakes a pitfall for solid ground is in trouble.

Gibson also came up with the idea of optical flows, further developed by Christopher Longuet-Higgins [1187]. As our eyes move relative to the environment, the resulting *optical flow field* lets us interpret the image, understanding the size, distance and motion of objects in it. There is an elegant mathematical theory of optical parallax, but our eyes deal with it differently: they contain receptors for specific aspects of this flow field which assume that objects in it are rigid, which then enables us to resolve rotational and translational components. Optical flows enable us to understand the shapes of objects around us, independently of binocular vision. We use them for some critical tasks such as landing an aeroplane and driving a car.

In short, cognitive science gives useful insights into how to design system interfaces so as to make certain courses of action easy, hard or impossible. It is increasingly tied up with research into computer human interaction. You can make mistakes more or less likely by making them easy or difficult; in section 28.2.2 I give real examples of usability failures causing serious accidents involving both medical devices and aircraft. Yet security can be even harder than safety if we have a sentient attacker who can provoke exploitable errors.

What can the defender expect attackers to do? They will use errors whose effect is predictable, such as capture errors; they will exploit perverse affordances; they will disrupt the flows on which safe operation relies; and they will look for, or create, exploitable dissonances between users' mental models of a system and its actual logic. To look for these, you should try a cognitive walkthrough aimed at identifying attack points, just as a code walkthough can be used to search for software vulnerabilities. Attackers also learn by experiment and share techniques with each other, and develop tools to look efficiently for known attacks. So it's important to be aware of the attacks that have already worked. (That's one of the functions of this book.)

3.2.2 Gender, diversity and interpersonal variation

Many women die because medical tests and technology assume that patients are men, or because engineers use male crash-test dummies when designing cars; protective equipment, from sportswear through stab-vests to spacesuits, gets tailored for men by default [498]. So do we have problems with information systems too? They are designed by men, and young geeky men at that, yet over half their users may be women. This realisation has led to research on *gender HCI* – on how software should be designed so that women can also use it effectively. Early experiments started from the study of behaviour: experiments showed that women use peripheral vision more, and it duly turned out that larger displays reduce gender bias. Work on American female programmers suggested that they tinker less than males, but more effectively [203]. But how much is nature, and how much nurture? Societal factors matter, and US women who program appear to be more thoughtful, but lower self-esteem and higher risk-aversion leads them to use fewer features.

Gender has become a controversial topic in psychology research. In the early 2000s, discussion of male aptitude for computer science was sometimes in terms of an analysis by Simon Baron-Cohen which gives people separate scores as systemisers (good at geometry and some kinds of symbolic reasoning) and as empathisers (good at intuiting the emotions of others and social intelligence generally) [177]. Most men score higher at systematising, while most women do better at empathising. The correspondence isn't exact; a minority of men are better at empathising while a minority of women are better at systematising. Baron-Cohen's research is in Asperger's and autism spectrum disorder, which he sees as an extreme form of male brain. This theory gained some traction among geeks who saw an explanation of why we're often introverted with more aptitude for understanding things than for understanding people. If we're born that way, it's not out fault. It also suggests an explanation for why geek couples often have kids on the spectrum.

Might this explain why men are more interested in computer science than women, with women consistently taking about a sixth of CS places in the USA and the UK? But here, we run into trouble. Women make up a third of CS students in the former communist countries of Poland, Romania and the Baltic states, while numbers in India are close to equal. Male dominance of software is also a fairly recent phenomenon. When I started out in the 1970s, there were almost as many women programmers as men, and many of the pioneers were women, whether in industry, academia or government. This suggests that the relevant differences are more cultural than genetic or developmental. The argument for a 'male brain / female brain' explanation has been progressively undermined by work such as that of Daphna Joel and colleagues who've shown by extensive neuroimaging studies that while there are recognisable male and female features in brains, the brains of individuals are a mosaic of both [987]. And although these features are visible in imaging, that does not mean they're all laid down at birth: our brains have a lot of plasticity. As with our muscles the tissues we exercise grow bigger. Perhaps nothing else might have been expected given the variance in gender identity, sexual preference, aggression, empathy and so on that we see all around us.

Other work has shown that gender performance differences are absent in newborns, and appear round about age 6–7, by which time children have long learned to distinguish gender and adapt to the social cues all around them, which are reinforced in developed countries by a tsunami of blue/pink gendered toys and marketing. (Some believe that women are happier to work in computing in India because India escaped the home computer boom in the 1980s and its evolution into gaming.) This is reinforced in later childhood and adolescence by gender stereotypes that they internalise as part of their identity; in cultures where girls aren't supposed to be good at maths or interested in computers, praise for being 'good at maths' can evoke a *stereotype threat* (the fear of confirming a negative stereotype about a group to which one belongs). Perhaps as a result, men react better to personal praise ('That was really clever of you!') while women are motivated better by performance praise ('You must have put in a hell of a lot of effort'). So it may not be surprising that we see a deficit of women in disciplines that praise genius, such as mathematics. What's more, similar mechanisms appear to underlie the poorer academic performance of ethnic groups who have been stigmatised as non-academic. In short, people are not just born different; we learn to be different, shaped by power, by cultural attitudes, by expectations and by opportunities. There are several layers between gene and culture with emergent behaviour, including the cell and the circuit. So if we want more effective interventions in the pipeline from school through university to professional development, we need a better understanding of the underlying neurological and cultural mechanisms. For a survey of this, see Gina Rippon [1608].

Gender matters at many levels of the stack, from what a product should do through how it does it. For example, should a car be faster or safer? This is entangled with social values. Are men better drivers because they win car races, or are women better drivers because they have fewer insurance claims? Digging down, we find gendered and cultural attitudes to risk. In US surveys, risks are judged lower by white people and by men, and on closer study this is because about 30% of white males judge risks to be extremely low. This bias is consistent across a wide range of hazards but is particularly strong for handguns, second-hand cigarette smoke, multiple sexual partners and street drugs. Asian males show similarly low sensitivity to some hazards, such as motor vehicles. White males are more trusting of technology, and less of government [693].

We engineers must of course work with the world as it is, not as it might be if our education system and indeed our culture had less bias; but we must be alert to the possibility that computer systems discriminate because they are built by men for men, just like cars and spacesuits. For example, Tyler Moore and I did an experiment to see whether anti-phishing advice given by banks to their customers was easier for men to follow than women, and we found that indeed it was [1339]. No-one seems to have done much work on gender and security usability, so there's an opportunity.

But the problem is much wider. Many systems will continue to be designed by young fit straight clever men who are white or Asian and may not think hard or at all about the various forms of prejudice and disability that they do not encounter directly. You need to think hard about how you mitigate the effects. It's not enough to just have your new product tested by a token geek girl on your development team; you have to think also of the less educated and the vulnerable – including older people, children and women fleeing abusive relationships (about which I'll have more to say later). You really have to think of the whole stack. Diversity matters in corporate governance, market research, product design, software development and testing. If you can't fix the imbalance in dev, you'd better make it up elsewhere. You need to understand your users; it's also good to understand how power and culture feed the imbalance.

As many of the factors relevant to group behaviour are of social origin, we next turn to social psychology.

3.2.3 Social psychology

This attempts to explain how the thoughts, feelings, and behaviour of individuals are influenced by the actual, imagined, or implied presence of others. It has many aspects, from the identity that people derive from belonging to groups – whether of gender, tribe, team, profession or even religion – through the self-esteem we get by comparing ourselves with others. The results that put it on the map were three early papers that laid the groundwork for understanding the abuse of authority and its relevance to propaganda, interrogation and aggression. They were closely followed by work on the bystander effect which is also highly relevant to crime and security.

3.2.3.1 Authority and its abuse

In 1951, Solomon Asch showed that people could be induced to deny the evidence of their own eyes in order to conform to a group. Subjects judged the lengths of lines after hearing wrong opinions from other group members, who were actually the experimenter's stooges. Most subjects gave in and conformed, with only 29% resisting the bogus majority [136].

Stanley Milgram was inspired by the 1961 trial of Nazi war criminal Adolf Eichmann to investigate how many experimental subjects were prepared to administer severe electric shocks to an actor playing the role of a 'learner' at the behest of an experimenter while the subject played the role of the 'teacher' – even when the 'learner' appeared to be in severe pain and begged the subject to stop. This experiment was designed to measure what proportion of people will obey an authority rather than their conscience. Most did – Milgram found that consistently over 60% of subjects would do downright immoral things if they were told to [1314]. This experiment is now controversial but had real influence on the development of the subject.

The third was the Stanford Prisoner Experiment which showed that normal people can behave wickedly even in the absence of orders. In 1971, experimenter Philip Zimbardo set up a 'prison' at Stanford where 24 students were assigned at random to the roles of 12 warders and 12 inmates. The aim of the experiment was to discover whether prison abuses occurred because warders (and possibly prisoners) were self-selecting. However, the students playing the role of warders rapidly became sadistic authoritarians, and the experiment was halted after six days on ethical grounds [2076]. This experiment is also controversial now and it's unlikely that a repeat would get ethical approval today. But abuse of authority, whether real or ostensible, is a real issue if you are designing operational security measures for a business.

During the period 1995–2005, a telephone hoaxer calling himself 'Officer Scott' ordered the managers of over 68 US stores and restaurants in 32 US states (including at least 17 McDonald's stores) to detain some young employee on suspicion of theft and strip-search them. Various other degradations were ordered, including beatings and sexual assaults [2036]. A former prison guard was tried for impersonating a police officer but acquitted. At least 13 people who obeyed the caller and did searches were charged with crimes, and seven were convicted. McDonald's got sued for not training its store managers properly, even years after the pattern of hoax calls was established; and in October 2007, a jury ordered them to pay $6.1 million dollars to one of the victims, who had been strip-searched when she was an 18-year-old employee. It was a nasty case, as she was left by the store manager in the custody of her boyfriend, who then committed a further indecent assault on her. The boyfriend got five years, and the manager pleaded guilty to unlawfully detaining her. McDonald's argued that she was responsible for whatever damages she suffered for not realizing it was a hoax, and that the store manager had failed to apply common sense. A Kentucky jury didn't buy this and ordered McDonald's to pay up. The store manager also sued, claiming to be another victim of the firm's negligence to warn her of the hoax, and got $1.1 million [1090]. So US employers now risk heavy damages if they fail to train their staff to resist the abuse of authority.

3.2.3.2 *The bystander effect*

On March 13, 1964, a young lady called Kitty Genovese was stabbed to death in the street outside her apartment in Queens, New York. The press reported that thirty-eight separate witnesses had failed to help or even to call the police, although the assault lasted almost half an hour. Although these reports were later found to be exaggerated, the crime led to the nationwide 911 emergency number, and also to research on why bystanders often don't get involved.

John Darley and Bibb Latané reported experiments in 1968 on what factors modulated the probability of a bystander helping someone who appeared to be having an epileptic fit. They found that a lone bystander would help 85% of the time, while someone who thought that four other people could see the victim would help only 31% of the time; group size dominated all other effects. Whether another bystander was male, female or even medically qualified made essentially no difference [513]. The diffusion of responsibility has visible effects in many other contexts. If you want something done, you'll email one person to ask, not three people. Of course, security is usually seen as something that other people deal with.

However, if you ever find yourself in danger, the real question is whether at least one of the bystanders will help, and here the recent research is much more positive. Lasse Liebst, Mark Levine and others have surveyed CCTV footage of a number of public conflicts in several countries over the last ten years, finding that in 9 out of 10 cases, one or more bystanders intervened to de-escalate a fight, and that the more bystanders intervene, the more successful they are [1166]. So it would be wrong to assume that bystanders generally pass by on the other side; so the bystander effect's name is rather misleading.

3.2.4 The social-brain theory of deception

Our second big theme, which also fits into social psychology, is the growing body of research into deception. How does deception work, how can we detect and measure it, and how can we deter it?

The modern approach started in 1976 with the social intelligence hypothesis. Until then, anthropologists had assumed that we evolved larger brains in order to make better tools. But the archaeological evidence doesn't support this. All through the paleolithic period, while our brains evolved from chimp size to human size, we used the same simple stone axes. They only became more sophisticated in the neolithic period, by which time our ancestors were anatomically modern homo sapiens. So why, asked Nick Humphrey, did we evolve large brains if we didn't need them yet? Inspired by observing the behaviour of both caged and wild primates, his hypothesis was that the primary function of the intellect was social. Our ancestors didn't evolve bigger brains to make better tools, but to use other primates better as tools [936]. This is now supported by a growing body of evidence, and has transformed psychology as a discipline. Social psychology had been a poor country cousin until then and was not seen as rigorous; since then, people have realised it was probably the driving force of cognitive evolution. Almost all intelligent species developed in a social context. (One exception is the octopus, but even it has to understand how predators and prey react.)

The primatologist Andy Whiten then collected much of the early evidence on tactical deception, and recast social intelligence as the Machiavellian brain hypothesis: we became smart in order to deceive others, and to detect deception too [362]. Not everyone agrees completely with this characterisation, as the positive aspects of socialisation, such as empathy, also matter. But Hugo Mercier and Dan Sperber have recently collected masses of evidence that the modern human brain is more a machine for arguing than anything else [1296]. Our goal is persuasion rather than truth; rhetoric comes first, and logic second.

The second thread coming from the social intellect hypothesis is theory of mind, an idea due to David Premack and Guy Woodruff in 1978 but developed by Heinz Wimmer and Josef Perner in a classic 1983 experiment to determine when children are first able to tell that someone has been deceived [2032]. In this experiment, the Sally-Anne test, a child sees a sweet hidden under a cup by Sally while Anne and the child watch. Anne then leaves the room and Sally switches the sweet to be under a different cup. Anne then comes back and the child is asked where Anne thinks the sweet is. Normal children get the right answer from about age five; this is when they acquire the ability to discern others' beliefs and intentions. Simon Baron-Cohen, Alan Leslie and Uta Frith then showed that children on the Aspergers / autism spectrum acquire this ability significantly later [178].

Many computer scientists and engineers appear to be on the spectrum to some extent, and we're generally not as good at deception as neurotypical people are. This has all sorts of implications! We're under-represented in politics, among senior executives and in marketing. Oh, and there was a lot less cybercrime before underground markets brought together geeks who could write wicked code with criminals who could use it for wicked purposes. Geeks are also more likely to be whistleblowers; we're less likely to keep quiet about an uncomfortable truth just to please others, as we place less value on their opinions. But this is a complex field. Some well-known online miscreants who are on the spectrum were hapless more than anything else; Gary McKinnon claimed to have hacked the Pentagon to discover the truth about flying saucers and didn't anticipate the ferocity of the FBI's response. And other kinds of empathic deficit are involved in many crimes. Other people with dispositional empathy deficits include psychopaths who disregard the feelings of others but understand them well enough to manipulate them, while there are many people whose deficits are situational, ranging from Nigerian scammers who think that any white person who falls for their lure must think Africans are stupid, so they deserve it, right through to soldiers and terrorists who consider their opponents to be less than human or to be morally deserving of death. I'll discuss radicalisation in more detail later in section 26.4.2.

The third thread is self-deception. Robert Trivers argues that we've evolved the ability to deceive ourselves in order to better deceive others: "If deceit is fundamental in animal communication, then there must be strong selection to spot deception and this ought, in turn, to select for a degree of self-deception, rendering some facts and motives unconscious so as to not betray – by the subtle signs of self-knowledge – the deception being practiced" [906]. We forget inconvenient truths and rationalise things we want to believe. There may well be a range of self-deception abilities from honest geeks through to the great salesmen who have a magic ability to believe completely in their product. But it's controversial, and at a number of levels. For example, if Tony Blair really believed that Iraq had weapons of mass destruction when he persuaded Britain to go to war in 2003, was it actually a lie? How do you define sincerity? How can you measure it? And would you even elect a national leader if you expected that they'd be unable to lie to you? There is a lengthy discussion in [906], and the debate is linked to other work on motivated reasoning. Russell Golman, David Hagman and George Loewenstein survey research on how people avoid information, even when it is free and could lead to better decision-making: people at risk of illness avoid medical tests, managers avoid information that might show they made bad decisions, and investors look at their portfolios less when markets are down [782]. This strand of research goes all the way back to Sigmund Freud, who described various aspects of the *denial* of unpleasant information, including the ways in which we try to minimise our feelings of guilt for the bad things we do, and to blame others for them.

It also links up with filter-bubble effects on social media. People prefer to listen to others who confirm their beliefs and biases, and this can be analysed in terms of the hedonic value of information. People think of themselves as honest and try to avoid the *ethical dissonance* that results from deviations [173]; criminologists use the term *neutralisation* to describe the strategies that rule-breakers use to minimise the guilt that they feel about their actions (there's an overlap with both filter effects and self-deception). A further link is to Hugo Mercier and Dan Sperber's work on the brain as a machine for argument, which I mentioned above.

The fourth thread is intent. The detection of hostile intent was a big deal in our ancestral evolutionary environment; in pre-state societies, perhaps a quarter of men and boys die of homicide, and further back many of our ancestors were killed by animal predators. So we appear to have evolved a sensitivity to sounds and movements that might signal the intent of a person, an animal or even a god. As a result, we now spend too much on defending against threats that involve hostile intent, such as terrorism, and not enough on defending against epidemic disease, which kills many more people – or climate change, which could kill even more.

There are other reasons why we might want to think about intent more carefully. In cryptography, we use logics of belief to analyse the security of authentication protocols, and to deal with statements such as 'Alice believes that Bob believes that Charlie controls the key *K*'; we'll come to this in the next chapter. And now we realise that people use theories of mind to understand each other, philosophers have got engaged too. Dan Dennett derived the intentional stance in philosophy, arguing that the propositional attitudes we use when reasoning – beliefs, desires and perceptions – come down to the intentions of people and animals.

A related matter is socially-motivated reasoning: people do logic much better if the problem is set in a social role. In the Wason test, subjects are told they have to inspect some cards with a letter grade on one side, and a numerical code on the other, and given a rule such as "If a student has a grade D on the front of their card, then the back must be marked with code 3". They are shown four cards displaying (say) D, F, 3 and 7 and then asked "Which cards do you have to turn over to check that all cards are marked correctly?" Most subjects get this wrong; in the original experiment, only 48% of 96 subjects got the right answer of D and 7. However the evolutionary psychologists Leda Cosmides and John Tooby found the same problem becomes easier if the rule is changed to 'If a person is drinking beer, he must be 20 years old' and the individuals are a beer drinker, a coke drinker, a 25-year-old and a 16-year old. Now three-quarters of subjects deduce that the bouncer should check the age of the beer drinker and the drink of the 16-year-old [483]. Cosmides and Tooby argue that our ability to do logic and perhaps arithmetic evolved as a means of policing social exchanges.

The next factor is minimsation – the process by which people justify bad actions or make their harm appear to be less. I mentioned Nigerian scammers who think that white people who fall for their scams must be racist, so they deserve it; there are many more examples of scammers working up reasons why their targets are fair game. The criminologist Donald Cressey developed a *Fraud Triangle* theory to explain the factors that lead to fraud: as well as motive and opportunity, there must be a rationalisation. People may feel that their employer has underpaid them so it's justifiable to fiddle expenses, or that the state is wasting money on welfare when they cheat on their taxes. Minimisation is very common in cybercrime. Kids operating DDoS-for-hire services reassured each other that offering a 'web stresser' service was legal, and said on their websites that the service could only be used for legal purposes. So undermining minimisation can work as a crime-fighting tool. The UK National Crime Agency bought Google ads to ensure that anyone searching for a web stresser service would see an official warning that DDoS was a crime. A mere £3,000 spent between January and June 2018 suppressed demand growth; DDoS revenues remained constant in the UK while they grew in the USA [457].

Finally, the loss of social context is a factor in online disinhibition. People speak more frankly online, and this has both positive and negative effects. Shy people can find partners, but we also see vicious flame wars. John Suler analyses the factors as anonymity, invisibility, asynchronicity and the loss of symbols of authority and status; in addition there are effects relating to psychic boundaries and self-imagination which lead us to drop our guard and express feelings from affection to aggression that we normally rein in for social reasons [1849].

Where all this leads is that the nature and scale of online deception can be modulated by suitable interaction design. Nobody is as happy as they appear on Facebook, as attractive as they appear on Instagram or as angry as they appear on Twitter. They let their guard down on closed groups such as those supported by WhatsApp, which offer neither celebrity to inspire performance, nor anonymity to promote trolling. However, people are less critical in closed groups, which makes them more suitable for spreading conspiracy theories, and for radicalisation [523].

3.2.5 Heuristics, biases and behavioural economics

One field of psychology that has been applied by security researchers since the mid-2000s has been *decision science*, which sits at the boundary of psychology and economics and studies the heuristics that people use, and the biases that influence them, when making decisions. It is also known as *behavioural economics*, as it examines the ways in which people's decision processes depart from the rational behaviour modeled by economists. An early pioneer was

Herb Simon – both an early computer scientist and a Nobel-prizewinning economist – who noted that classical rationality meant doing whatever maximizes your expected utility regardless of how hard that choice is to compute. So how would people behave in a realistic world of bounded rationality? The real limits to human rationality have been explored extensively in the years since, and Daniel Kahneman won the Nobel prize in economics in 2002 for his major contributions to this field (along with the late Amos Tversky) [1006].

3.2.5.1 Prospect theory and risk misperception

Kahneman and Tversky did extensive experimental work on how people made decisions faced with uncertainty. They first developed *prospect theory* which models risk appetite: in many circumstances, people dislike losing $100 they already have more than they value winning $100. Framing an action as avoiding a loss can make people more likely to take it; phishermen hook people by sending messages like 'Your PayPal account has been frozen, and you need to click here to unlock it.' We're also bad at calculating probabilities, and use all sorts of heuristics to help us make decisions:

- we often base a judgment on an initial guess or comparison and then adjust it if need be – the *anchoring effect*;
- we base inferences on the ease of bringing examples to mind – the *availability heuristic*, which was OK for lion attacks 50,000 years ago but gives the wrong answers when mass media bombard us with images of terrorism;
- we're more likely to be sceptical about things we've heard than about things we've seen, perhaps as we have more neurons processing vision;
- we worry too much about events that are very unlikely but have very bad consequences;
- we're more likely to believe things we've worked out for ourselves rather than things we've been told.

Behavioral economics is not just relevant to working out how likely people are to click on links in phishing emails, but to the much deeper problem of the perception of risk. Many people perceive terrorism to be a much worse threat than epidemic disease, road traffic accidents or even food poisoning: this is wrong, but hardly surprising to a behavioural economist. We overestimate the small risk of dying in a terrorist attack not just because it's small but because of the visual effect of the 9/11 TV coverage, the ease of remembering the event, the outrage of an enemy attack, and the effort we put into thinking and worrying about it. (There are further factors, which we'll explore in Part 3 when we discuss terrorism.)

The misperception of risk underlies many other public-policy problems. The psychologist Daniel Gilbert, in an article provocatively entitled 'If only gay sex caused global warming', compares our fear of terrorism with our fear of climate change. First, we evolved to be much more wary of hostile intent than of nature; 100,000 years ago, a man with a club (or a hungry lion) was a much worse threat than a thunderstorm. Second, global warming doesn't violate anyone's moral sensibilities; third, it's a long-term threat rather than a clear and present danger; and fourth, we're sensitive to rapid changes in the environment rather than slow ones [765]. There are many more risk biases: we are less afraid when we're in control, such as when driving a car, as opposed to being a passenger in a car or airplane; and we are more afraid of uncertainty, that is, when the magnitude of the risk is unknown (even when it's small) [1674, 1678]. We also indulge in *satisficing* which means we go for an alternative that's 'good enough' rather than going to the trouble of trying to work out the odds perfectly, especially for small transactions. (The misperception here is not that of the risk taker, but of the economists who ignored the fact that real people include transaction costs in their calculations.)

So, starting out from the folk saying that a bird in the hand is worth two in the bush, we can develop quite a lot of machinery to help us understand and model people's attitudes towards risk.

3.2.5.2 Present bias and hyperbolic discounting

Saint Augustine famously prayed 'Lord, make me chaste, but not yet.' We find a similar sentiment with applying security updates, where people may pay more attention to the costs as they're immediate and determinate in time, storage and bandwidth, than the unpredictable future benefits. This *present bias* causes many people to decline updates, which was the major source of technical vulnerability online for many years. One way software companies pushed back was by allowing people to delay updates: Windows has 'restart / pick a time / snooze'. Reminders cut the ignore rate from about 90% to about 34%, and may ultimately double overall compliance [726]. A better design is to make updates so painless that they can be made mandatory, or nearly so; this is the approach now followed by some web browsers, and by cloud-based services generally.

Hyperbolic discounting is a model used by decision scientists to quantify present bias. Intuitive reasoning may lead people to use utility functions that discount the future so deeply that immediate gratification seems to be the best course of action, even when it isn't. Such models have been applied to try to explain the *privacy paradox* – why people say in surveys that they care about privacy but act otherwise online. I discuss this in more detail in section 8.67: other factors, such as uncertainty about the risks and about the efficacy of privacy measures, play a part too. Taken together, the immediate and determinate positive utility of getting free stuff outweighs the random future costs of disclosing too much personal information, or disclosing it to dubious websites.

3.2.5.3 Defaults and nudges

This leads to the importance of defaults. Many people usually take the easiest path and use the standard configuration of a system, as they assume it will be good enough. In 2009, Richard Thaler and Cass Sunstein wrote a bestseller *'Nudge'* exploring this, pointing out that governments can achieve many policy goals without infringing personal liberty simply by setting the right defaults [1879]. For example, if a firm's staff are enrolled in a pension plan by default, most will not bother to opt out, while if it's optional most will not bother to opt in. A second example is that many more organs are made available for transplant in Spain, where the law lets a dead person's organs be used unless they objected, than in Britain where donors have to consent actively. A third example is that tax evasion can be cut by having the taxpayer declare that the information in the form is true when they start to fill it out, rather than at the end. The set of choices people have to make, the order in which they make them, and the defaults if they do nothing, are called the *choice architecture*. Sunnstein got a job in the Obama administration implementing some of these ideas while Thaler won the 2017 economics Nobel prize.

Defaults matter in security too, but often they are set by an adversary so as to trip you up. For example, Facebook defaults to fairly open information sharing, and whenever enough people have figured out how to increase their privacy settings, the architecture is changed so you have to opt out all over again. This exploits not just hazardous defaults but also the *control paradox* – providing the illusion of control causes people to share more information. We like to feel in control; we feel more comfortable driving in our cars than letting someone else fly us in an airplane – even if the latter is an order of magnitude safer. "Privacy control settings give people more rope to hang themselves," as behavioral economist George Loewenstein puts it. "Facebook has figured this out, so they give you incredibly granular controls." [1536]

3.2.5.4 The default to intentionality

Behavioral economists follow a long tradition in psychology of seeing the mind as composed of interacting rational and emotional components – 'heart' and 'head', or 'affective' and 'cognitive' systems. Studies of developmental biology have shown that, from an early age, we have different mental processing systems for social phenomena (such as recognising parents and siblings) and physical phenomena. Paul Bloom argues that the tension between them explains why many people believe that mind and body are basically different [269]. Children try to explain what they see using physics, but when their understanding falls short, they explain phenomena in terms of intentional action. This has survival value to the young, as it disposes them to get advice from parents or other adults about novel natural phenomena. Bloom suggests that it has an interesting side effect: it predisposes humans to believe that body and soul are different, and thus lays the ground for religious belief. This argument may not overwhelm the faithful (who will retort that Bloom simply stumbled across a mechanism created by the Intelligent Designer to cause us to have faith in Him). But it may have relevance for the security engineer.

First, it goes some way to explaining the *fundamental attribution error* – people often err by trying to explain things from intentionality rather than from context. Second, attempts to curb phishing by teaching users about the gory design details of the Internet – for example, by telling them to parse URLs in emails that seem to come from a bank – will be of limited value once they get bewildered. If the emotional is programmed to take over whenever the rational runs out, then engaging in a war of technical instruction and counter-instruction with the phishermen is unsound, as they'll be better at it. Safe defaults would be better.

3.2.5.5 The affect heuristic

Nudging people to think in terms of intent rather than of mechanism can exploit the *affect heuristic*, explored by Paul Slovic and colleagues [1791]. The idea is that while the human brain can handle multiple threads of cognitive processing, our emotions remain resolutely single-threaded, and they are even less good at probability theory than the rational part of our brains. So by making emotion salient, a marketer or a fraudster can try to get you to answer questions using emotion rather than reason, and using heuristics rather than calculation. A common trick is to ask an emotional question (whether 'How many dates did you have last month?' or even 'What do you think of President Trump?') to make people insensitive to probability.

So it should not surprise anyone that porn websites have been used to install a lot of malware – as have church websites, which are often poorly maintained and easy to hack. Similarly, events that evoke a feeling of dread – from cancer to terrorism – not only scare people more than the naked probabilities justify, but also make those probabilities harder to calculate, and deter people from even making the effort.

Other factors that can reinforce our tendency to explain things by intent include cognitive overload, where the rational part of the brain simply gets tired. Our capacity for self-control is also liable to fatigue, both physical and mental; some mental arithmetic will increase the probability that we'll pick up a chocolate rather than an apple. So a bank that builds a busy website may be able to sell more life insurance, but it's also likely to make its customers more vulnerable to phishing.

3.2.5.6 Cognitive dissonance

Another interesting offshoot of social psychology is cognitive dissonance theory. People are uncomfortable when they hold conflicting views; they seek out information that confirms their existing views of the world and of themselves, and try to reject information that conflicts with their views or might undermine their self-esteem. One practical consequence is that people are remarkably able to persist in wrong courses of action in the face of mounting evidence that things have gone wrong [1866]. Admitting to yourself or to others that you were duped can be painful; hustlers know this and exploit it. A security professional should 'feel the hustle' – that is, be alert for a situation in which recently established social cues and expectations place you under pressure to 'just do' something about which you'd normally have reservations. That's the time to step back and ask yourself whether you're being had. But training people to perceive this is hard enough, and getting the average person to break the social flow and say 'stop!' is hard. There have been some experiments, for example with training health-service staff to not give out health information on the phone, and training people in women's self-defence classes to resist demands for extra personal information. The problem with mainstreaming such training is that the money available for it is orders of magnitude less than the marketing budgets of the firms whose business model is to hustle their customers.

3.2.5.7 The risk thermostat

Some interesting empirical work has been done on how people manage their exposure to risk. John Adams studied mandatory seat belt laws, and established that they don't actually save lives: they just transfer casualties from vehicle occupants to pedestrians and cyclists [20]. Seat belts make drivers feel safer, so they drive faster in order to bring their perceived risk back up to its previous level. He calls this a *risk thermostat* and the model is borne out in other applications too [19]. The lesson is that testing needs to have ecological validity: you need to evaluate the effect of a proposed intervention in as realistic a setting as possible.

3.3 Deception in practice

This takes us from the theory to the practice. Deception often involves an abuse of the techniques developed by *compliance professionals* – those people whose job it is to get other people to do things. While a sales executive might dazzle you with an offer of a finance plan for a holiday apartment, a police officer might nudge you by their presence to drive more carefully, a park ranger might tell you to extinguish campfires carefully and not feed the bears, and a corporate lawyer might threaten you into taking down something from your website.

The behavioural economics pioneer and apostle of 'nudge', Dick Thaler, refers to the selfish use of behavioural economics as 'sludge' [1878]. But it's odd that economists ever thought that the altruistic use of such techniques would ever be more common than the selfish ones. Not only do marketers push the most profitable option rather than the best value, but they use every other available trick too. Stanford's Persuasive Technology Lab has been at the forefront of developing techniques to keep people addicted to their screens, and one of their alumni, ex-Googler Tristan Harris, has become a vocal critic. Sometimes dubbed 'Silicon valley's conscience', he explains how tech earns its money by manipulating not just defaults but choices, and asks how this can be done ethically [868]. Phones and other screens present menus and thus control choices, but there's more to it than that. Two techniques that screens have made mainstream are the casino's technique of using intermittent variable rewards to create addiction (we check our phones 150 times a day to see if someone has rewarded us with attention) and bottomless message feeds (to keep us consuming even when we aren't hungry any more). But there are many older techniques that predate computers.

3.3.1 The salesman and the scamster

Deception is the twin brother of marketing, so one starting point is the huge literature about sales techniques. One eminent writer is Robert Cialdini, a psychology professor who took summer jobs selling everything from used cars to home improvements and life insurance in order to document the tricks of the trade. His book *'Influence: Science and Practice'* is widely read by sales professionals and describes six main classes of technique used to influence people and close a sale [426].

These are:

1. Reciprocity: most people feel the need to return favours;
2. Commitment and consistency: people suffer cognitive dissonance if they feel they're being inconsistent;
3. Social proof: most people want the approval of others. This means following others in a group of which they're a member, and the smaller the group the stronger the pressure;
4. Liking: most people want to do what a good-looking or otherwise likeable person asks;

5. Authority: most people are deferential to authority figures (recall the Milgram study mentioned above);
6. Scarcity: we're afraid of missing out, if something we might want could suddenly be unavailable.

All of these are psychological phenomena that are the subject of continuing research. They are also traceable to pressures in our ancestral evolutionary environment, where food scarcity was a real threat, strangers could be dangerous and group solidarity against them (and in the provision of food and shelter) was vital. All are used repeatedly in the advertising and other messages we encounter constantly.

Frank Stajano and Paul Wilson built on this foundation to analyse the principles behind scams. Wilson researched and appeared in nine seasons of TV programs on the most common scams – 'The Real Hustle' – where the scams would be perpetrated on unsuspecting members of the public, who would then be given their money back, debriefed and asked permission for video footage to be used on TV. The know-how from experimenting with several hundred frauds on thousands of marks over several years was distilled into the following seven principles [1823].

1. Distraction – the fraudster gets the mark to concentrate on the wrong thing. This is at the heart of most magic performances.
2. Social compliance – society trains us not to question people who seem to have authority, leaving people vulnerable to conmen who pretend to be from their bank or from the police.
3. The herd principle – people let their guard down when everyone around them appears to share the same risks. This is a mainstay of the three-card trick, and a growing number of scams on social networks.
4. Dishonesty – if the mark is doing something dodgy, they're less likely to complain. Many are attracted by the idea that 'you're getting a good deal because it's illegal', and whole scam families – such as the resale of fraudulently obtained plane tickets – turn on this.
5. Kindness – this is the flip side of dishonesty, and an adaptation of Cialdini's principle of reciprocity. Many social engineering scams rely on the victims' helpfulness, from tailgating into a building to phoning up with a sob story to ask for a password reset.
6. Need and greed – sales trainers tell us we should find what someone really wants and then show them how to get it. A good fraudster can help the mark dream a dream and use this to milk them.
7. Time pressure – this causes people to act viscerally rather than stopping to think. Normal marketers use this all the time ('only 2 seats left at this price'); so do crooks.

The relationship with Cialdini's principles should be obvious. A cynic might say that fraud is just a subdivision of marketing; or perhaps that, as marketing becomes ever more aggressive, it comes to look ever more like fraud. When we investigated online accommodation scams we found it hard to code detectors, since many real estate agents use the same techniques. In fact, the fraudsters' behaviour was already well described by Cialdini's model, except the scamsters added appeals to sympathy, arguments to establish their own credibility, and ways of dealing with objections [2065]. (These are also found elsewhere in the regular marketing literature.)

Oh, and we find the same in software, where there's a blurry dividing line between illegal malware and just-about-legal 'Potentially Unwanted Programs' (PUPs) such as browser plugins that replace your ads with different ones. One good distinguisher seems to be technical: malware is distributed by many small botnets because of the risk of arrest, while PUPs are mostly distributed by one large network [956]. But crooks use regular marketing channels too: Ben Edelman found in 2006 that while 2.73% of companies ranked top in a web search were bad, 4.44% of companies that appeared alongside in the search ads were bad [612]. Bad companies were also more likely to exhibit cheap trust signals, such as TRUSTe privacy certificates on their websites. Similarly, bogus landlords often send reference letters or even copies of their ID to prospective tenants, something that genuine landlords never do.

And then there are the deceptive marketing practices of 'legal' businesses. To take just one of many studies, a 2019 crawl of 11K shopping websites by Arunesh Mathur and colleagues found 1,818 instances of 'dark patterns' – manipulative marketing practices such as hidden subscriptions, hidden costs, pressure selling, sneak-into-basket tactics and forced account opening. Of these at least 183 were clearly deceptive [1244]. What's more, the bad websites were among the most popular; perhaps a quarter to a third of websites you visit, weighted by traffic, try to hustle you. This constant pressure from scams that lie just short of the threshold for a fraud prosecution has a chilling effect on trust generally. People are less likely to believe security warnings if they are mixed with marketing, or smack of marketing in any way. And we even see some loss of trust in software updates; people say in surveys that they're less likely to apply a security-plus-features upgrade than a security patch, though the field data on upgrades don't (yet) show any difference [1594].

3.3.2 Social engineering

Hacking systems through the people who operate them is not new. Military and intelligence organisations have always targeted each other's staff; most of the intelligence successes of the old Soviet Union were of this kind [119]. Private investigation agencies have not been far behind.

Investigative journalists, private detectives and fraudsters developed the false-pretext phone call into something between an industrial process and an art form in the latter half of the 20th century. An example of the industrial process was how private detectives tracked people in Britain. Given that the country has a National Health Service with which everyone's registered, the trick was to phone up someone with access to the administrative systems in the area you thought the target was, pretend to be someone else in the health service, and ask. Colleagues of mine did an experiment in England in 1996 where they trained the staff at a local health authority to identify and report such calls[1]. They detected about 30 false-pretext calls a week, which would scale to 6000 a week or 300,000 a year for the whole of Britain. That eventually got sort-of fixed but it took over a decade. The real fix wasn't the enforcement of privacy law, but that administrators simply stopped answering the phone.

Another old scam from the 20th century is to steal someone's ATM card and then phone them up pretending to be from the bank asking whether their card's been stolen. On hearing that it has, the conman says 'We thought so. Please just tell me your PIN now so I can go into the system and cancel your card.' The most rapidly growing recent variety is the 'authorised push payment', where the conman again pretends to be from the bank, and persuades the customer to make a transfer to another account, typically by confusing the customer about the bank's authentication procedures, which most customers find rather mysterious anyway[2].

As for art form, one of the most disturbing security books ever published is Kevin Mitnick's *'Art of Deception'*. Mitnick, who was arrested and convicted for breaking into US phone systems, related after his release from prison how almost all of his exploits had involved social engineering. His typical hack was to pretend to a phone company employee that he was a colleague, and solicit 'help' such as a password. Ways of getting past a company's switchboard and winning its people's trust are a staple of sales-training courses, and hackers apply these directly. A harassed system administrator is called once or twice on trivial matters by someone claiming to be the CEO's personal assistant; once this idea has been accepted, the caller demands a new password for the boss. Mitnick became an expert at using such tricks to defeat company security procedures, and his book recounts a fascinating range of exploits [1327].

Social engineering became world headline news in September 2006 when it emerged that Hewlett-Packard chairwoman Patricia Dunn had hired private investigators who used pretexting to obtain the phone records of other board members of whom she was suspicious, and of journalists she considered hostile. She was forced to resign. The detectives were convicted of fraudulent wire communications and sentenced to do community service [139]. In the same

[1]The story is told in detail in chapter 9 of the second edition of this book, available free online.

[2]Very occasionally, a customer can confuse the bank; a 2019 innovation was the 'callhammer' attack, where someone phones up repeatedly to 'correct' the spelling of 'his name' and changes it one character at a time into another one.

year, the UK privacy authorities prosecuted a private detective agency that did pretexting jobs for top law firms [1140].

Amid growing publicity about social engineering, there was an audit of the IRS in 2007 by the Treasury Inspector General for Tax Administration, whose staff called 102 IRS employees at all levels, asked for their user IDs, and told them to change their passwords to a known value; 62 did so. What's worse, this happened despite similar audit tests in 2001 and 2004 [1676]. Since then, a number of audit firms have offered social engineering as a service; they phish their audit clients to show how easy it is. Since the mid-2010s, opinion has shifted against this practice, as it causes a lot of distress to staff without changing behaviour very much.

Social engineering isn't limited to stealing private information. It can also be about getting people to believe bogus public information. The quote from Bruce Schneier at the head of this chapter appeared in a report of a stock scam, where a bogus press release said that a company's CEO had resigned and its earnings would be restated. Several wire services passed this on, and the stock dropped 61% until the hoax was exposed [1673]. Fake news of this kind has been around forever, but the Internet has made it easier to promote and social media seem to be making it ubiquitous. We'll revisit this issue when I discuss censorship in section 26.4.

3.3.3 Phishing

While phone-based social engineering was the favoured tactic of the 20th century, online phishing seems to have replaced it as the main tactic of the 21st. The operators include both criminals and intelligence agencies, while the targets are both your staff and your customers. It is difficult enough to train your staff; training the average customer is even harder. They'll assume you're trying to hustle them, ignore your warnings and just figure out the easiest way to get what they want from your system. And you can't design simply for the average. If your systems are not safe to use by people who don't speak English well, or who are dyslexic, or who have learning difficulties, you are asking for serious legal trouble. So the easiest way to use your system had better be the safest.

The word 'phishing' appeared in 1996 in the context of the theft of AOL passwords. By then, attempts to crack email accounts to send spam had become common enough for AOL to have a 'report password solicitation' button on its web page; and the first reference to 'password fishing' is in 1990, in the context of people altering terminal firmware to collect Unix logon passwords [445]. Also in 1996, Tony Greening reported a systematic experimental study: 336 computer science students at the University of Sydney were sent an email message asking them to supply their password on the pretext that it was required to 'validate' the password database after a suspected break-in. 138 of them returned a valid password. Some were suspicious: 30 returned a plausible looking but invalid password, while over 200 changed their passwords without official prompting. But very few of them reported the email to authority [813].

Phishing attacks against banks started seven years later in 2003, with half-a-dozen attempts reported [443]. The early attacks imitated bank websites, but were both crude and greedy; the attackers asked for all sorts of information such as ATM PINs, and their emails were also written in poor English. Most customers smelt a rat. By about 2008, the attackers learned to use better psychology; they often reused genuine bank emails, with just the URLs changed, or sent an email saying something like 'Thank you for adding a new email address to your PayPal account' to provoke the customer to log on to complain that they hadn't. Of course, customers who used the provided link rather than typing in `www.paypal.com` or using an existing bookmark would get their accounts emptied. By then phishing was being used by state actors too; I described in section 2.2.2 how Chinese intelligence compromised the Dalai Lama's private office during the 2008 Olympic games. They used crimeware tools that were originally used by Russian fraud gangs, which they seemed to think gave them some deniability afterwards.

Fraud losses grew rapidly but stabilised by about 2015. A number of countermeasures helped bring things under control, including more complex logon schemes (using two-factor authentication, or its low-cost cousin, the request for some random letters of your password); a move to webmail systems that filter spam better; and back-end fraud engines that look for cashout patterns. The competitive landscape was rough, in that the phishermen would hit the easiest targets at any time in each country, both in terms of stealing their customer credentials and using their accounts to launder stolen funds. Concentrated losses caused the targets to wake up and take action. Since then, we've seen large-scale attacks on non-financial firms like Amazon; in the late 2000s, the crook would change your email and street address, then use your credit card to order a wide-screen TV. Since about 2016, the action has been in gift vouchers.

As we noted in the last chapter, phishing is also used at scale by botmasters to recruit new machines to their botnets, and in targeted ways both by crooks aiming at specific people or firms, and by intelligence agencies. There's a big difference between attacks conducted at scale, where the economics dictate that the cost of recruiting a new machine to a botnet can be at most a few cents, and targeted attacks, where spies can spend years trying to hack the phone of a rival head of government, or a fraudster can spend weeks or months of effort stalking a chief financial officer in the hope of a large payout. The lures and techniques used are different, even if the crimeware installed on the target's laptop or phone comes from the same stable. Cormac Herley argues that this gulf between the economics of targeted crime and volume crime is one of the reasons why cybercrime isn't much worse than it is [889]. After all, given that we depend on computers, and that all computers are insecure, and that there are attacks all the time, how come civilisation hasn't collapsed? Cybercrime can't always be as easy as it looks.

Another factor is that it takes time for innovations to be developed and disseminated. We noted that it took seven years for the bad guys to catch up with Tony Greening's 1995 phishing work. As another example, a 2007 paper by Tom Jagatic and colleagues showed how to make phishing much more effective by automatically personalising each phish using context mined from the target's social network [973]. I cited that in the second edition of this book, and in 2016 we saw it in the wild: a gang sent hundreds of thousands of phish with US and Australian banking Trojans to individuals working in finance departments of companies, with their names and job titles apparently scraped from LinkedIn [1299]. This seems to have been crude and hasn't really caught on, but once the bad guys figure it out we may see spear-phishing at scale in the future, and it's interesting to think of how we might respond. The other personalised bulk scams we see are blackmail attempts where the victims get email claiming that their personal information has been compromised and including a password or the last four digits of a credit card number as evidence, but the yield from such scams seems to be low.

As I write, crime gangs have been making ever more use of spear-phishing in targeted attacks on companies where they install ransomware, steal gift coupons and launch other scams. In 2020, a group of young men hacked Twitter, where over a thousand employees had access to internal tools that enabled them to take control of user accounts; the gang sent bitcoin scam tweets from the accounts of such well-known users as Bill Gates, Barack Obama and Elon Musk [1294]. They appear to have honed their spear-phishing skills on SIM swap fraud, which I'll discuss later in sections 3.4.1 and 12.7.4. The spread of such 'transferable skills' among crooks is similar in many ways to the adoption of mainstream technology.

3.3.4 Opsec

Getting your staff to resist attempts by outsiders to inveigle them into revealing secrets, whether over the phone or online, is known in military circles as *operational security* or opsec. Protecting really valuable secrets, such as unpublished financial data, not-yet-patented industrial research and military plans, depends on limiting the number of people with access, and also on doctrines about what may be discussed with whom and how. It's not enough for rules to exist; you have to train the staff who have access, explain the reasons behind the rules, and embed them socially in the organisation. In our medical privacy case, we educated health service staff about pretext calls and set up a strict callback policy: they would not discuss medical records on the phone unless they had called a number they had got from the health service internal phone book rather than from a caller. Once the staff have detected and defeated a few false-pretext calls, they talk about it and the message gets embedded in the way everybody works.

Another example comes from a large Silicon Valley service firm, which suffered intrusion attempts when outsiders tailgated staff into buildings on campus. Stopping this with airport-style ID checks, or even card-activated turnstiles, would have changed the ambience and clashed with the culture. The solution was to create and embed a social rule that when someone holds open a building door for you, you show them your badge. The critical factor, as with the bogus phone calls, is social embedding rather than just training. Often the hardest people to educate are the most senior; in my own experience in banking, the people you couldn't train were those who were paid more than you, such as traders in the dealing rooms. The service firm in question did better, as its CEO repeatedly stressed the need to stop tailgating at all-hands meetings.

Some opsec measures are common sense, such as not throwing sensitive papers in the trash, or leaving them on desks overnight. (One bank at which I worked had the cleaners move all such papers to the departmental manager's desk.) Less obvious is the need to train the people you trust. A leak of embarrassing emails that appeared to come from the office of UK Prime Minister Tony Blair and was initially blamed on 'hackers' turned out to have been fished out of the trash at his personal pollster's home by a private detective [1210].

People operate systems however they have to, and this usually means breaking some of the rules in order to get their work done. Research shows that company staff have only so much *compliance budget*, that is, they're only prepared to put so many hours a year into tasks that are not obviously helping them achieve their goals [197]. You need to figure out what this budget is, and use it wisely. If there's some information you don't want your staff to be tricked into disclosing, it's safer to design systems so that they just can't disclose it, or at least so that disclosures involve talking to other staff members or jumping through other hoops.

But what about a firm's customers? There is a lot of scope for phishermen to simply order bank customers to reveal their security data, and this happens at scale, against both retail and business customers. There are also the many small scams that customers try on when they find vulnerabilities in your business processes. I'll discuss both types of fraud further in the chapter on banking and bookkeeping.

3.3.5 Deception research

Finally, a word on deception research. Since 9/11, huge amounts of money have been spent by governments trying to find better lie detectors, and deception researchers are funded across about five different subdisciplines of psychology. The polygraph measures stress via heart rate and skin conductance; it has been around since the 1920s and is used by some US states in criminal investigations, as well as by the Federal government in screening people for Top Secret clearances. The evidence on its effectiveness is patchy at best, and surveyed extensively by Aldert Vrij [1974]. While it can be an effective prop in the hands of a skilled interrogator, the key factor is the skill rather than the prop. When used by unskilled people in a lab environment, against experimental subjects telling low-stakes lies, its output is little better than random. As well as measuring stress via skin conductance, you can measure distraction using eye movements and guilt by upper body movements. In a research project with Sophie van der Zee, we used body motion-capture suits and also the gesture-recognition cameras in an Xbox and got slightly better results than a polygraph [2066]. However such technologies can at best augment the interrogator's skill, and claims that they work well should be treated as junk science. Thankfully, the government dream of an effective interrogation robot is some way off.

A second approach to dealing with deception is to train a machine-learning classifier on real customer behaviour. This is what credit-card fraud engines have been doing since the late 1990s, and recent research has pushed into other fields too. For example, Noam Brown and Tuomas Sandholm have created a poker-playing bot called Pluribus that beat a dozen expert players over a 12-day marathon of 10,000 hands of Texas Hold 'em. It doesn't use psychology but game theory, playing against itself millions of times and tracking regret at bids that could have given better outcomes. That it can consistently beat experts without access to 'tells' such as its opponents' facial gestures or body language is itself telling. Dealing with deception using statistical machine learning rather than physiological monitoring may also be felt to intrude less into privacy.

3.4 Passwords

The management of passwords gives an instructive context in which usability, applied psychology and security meet. Passwords have been one of the biggest practical problems facing security engineers since perhaps the 1970s. In fact, as the usability researcher Angela Sasse puts it, it's hard to think of a worse authentication mechanism than passwords, given what we know about human memory: people can't remember infrequently-used or frequently-changed items; we can't forget on demand; recall is harder than recognition; and non-meaningful words are more difficult.

To place the problem in context, most passwords you're asked to set are not for your benefit but for somebody else's. The modern media ecosystem is driven by websites seeking to maximise both their page views and their registered user bases so as to maximise their value when they are sold. That's why, when you're pointed to a news article that's so annoying you feel you have to leave a comment, you find you have to register. Click, and there's a page of ads. Fill out the form with an email address and submit. Got the CAPTCHA wrong, so do it again and see another page of ads. Click on the email link, and see a page with another ad. Now you can add a comment that nobody will ever read. In such circumstances you're better to type random garbage and let the browser remember it; or better still, don't bother. Even major news sites use passwords against the reader's interest, for example by limiting the number of free page views you get per month unless you register again with a different browser. This ecosystem is described in detail by Ryan Holiday [915].

Turning now to the more honest uses, the password system used by a big modern service firm has a number of components.

1. The visible part is the logon page, which asks you to choose a password when you register and probably checks its strength in some way. It later asks for this password whenever you log on.
2. There will be recovery mechanisms that enable you to deal with a forgotten password or even a compromised account, typically by asking further security questions, or via your primary email account, or by sending an SMS to your phone.
3. Behind this lie technical protocol mechanisms for password checking, typically routines that encrypt your password when you enter it at your laptop or phone, and then either compare it with a local encrypted value, or take it to a remote server for checking.
4. There are often protocol mechanisms to synchronise passwords across multiple platforms, so that if you change your password on your laptop, your phone won't let you use that service until you enter the new one there too. And these mechanisms may enable you to blacklist a stolen phone without having to reset the passwords for all the services it was able to access.
5. There will be intrusion-detection mechanisms to propagate an alarm if one of your passwords is used somewhere it probably shouldn't be.
6. There are single-signon mechanisms to use one logon for many websites, as when you use your Google or Facebook account to log on to a newspaper.

Let's work up from the bottom. Developing a full-feature password management system can be a lot of work, and providing support for password recovery also costs money (a few years ago, the UK phone company BT had two hundred people in its password-reset centre). So outsourcing 'identity management' can make business sense. In addition, intrusion detection works best at scale: if someone uses my gmail password in an Internet cafe in Peru while

Google knows I'm in Scotland, they send an SMS to my phone to check, and a small website can't do that. The main cause of attempted password abuse is when one firm gets hacked, disclosing millions of email addresses and passwords, which the bad guys try out elsewhere; big firms spot this quickly while small ones don't. The big firms also help their customers maintain situational awareness, by alerting you to logons from new devices or from strange places. Again, it's hard to do that if you're a small website or one that people visit infrequently.

As for syncing passwords between devices, only the device vendors can really do that well; and the protocol mechanisms for encrypting passwords in transit to a server that verifies them will be discussed in the next chapter. That brings us to password recovery.

3.4.1 Password recovery

The experience of the 2010s, as the large service firms scaled up and people moved en masse to smartphones, is that password recovery is often the hardest aspect of authentication. If people you know, such as your staff, forget their passwords, you can get them to interact with an administrator or manager who knows them. But for people you don't know such as your online customers it's harder. And as a large service firm will be recovering tens of thousands of accounts every day, you need some way of doing it without human intervention in the vast majority of cases.

During the 1990s and 2000s, many websites did password recovery using 'security questions' such as asking for your favourite team, the name of your pet or even that old chestnut, your mother's maiden name. Such near-public information is often easy to guess so it gave an easier way to break into accounts than guessing the password itself. This was made even worse by everyone asking the same questions. In the case of celebrities – or abuse by a former intimate partner – there may be no usable secrets. This was brought home to the public in 2008, when a student hacked the Yahoo email account of US Vice-Presidential candidate Sarah Palin via the password recovery questions – her date of birth and the name of her first school. Both of these were public information. Since then, crooks have learned to use security questions to loot accounts when they can; at the US Social Security Administration, a common fraud was to open an online account for a pensioner who's dealt with their pension by snail mail in the past, and redirect the payments to a different bank account. This peaked in 2013; the countermeasure that fixed it was to always notify beneficiaries of account changes by snail mail.

In 2015, five Google engineers published a thorough analysis of security questions, and many turned out to be extremely weak. For example, an attacker could get a 19.7% success rate against 'Favourite food?' in English.

Some 37% of people provided wrong answers, in some cases to make them stronger, but sometimes not. Fully 16% of people's answers were public. In addition to being insecure, the 'security questions' turned out to be hard to use: 40% of English-speaking US users were unable to recall the answers when needed, while twice as many could recover accounts using an SMS reset code [292].

Given these problems with security and memorability, most websites now let you recover your password by an email to the address with which you first registered. But if someone compromises that email account, they can get all your dependent accounts too. Email recovery may be adequate for websites where a compromise is of little consequence, but for important accounts – such as banking and email itself – standard practice is now to use a second factor. This is typically a code sent to your phone by SMS, or better still using an app that can encrypt the code and tie it to a specific handset. Many service providers that allow email recovery are nudging people towards using such a code instead where possible. Google research shows that SMSs stop all bulk password guessing by bots, 96% of bulk phishing and 76% of targeted attacks [574].

But this depends on phone companies taking care over who can get a replacement SIM card, and many don't. The problem in 2020 is rapid growth in attacks based on intercepting SMS authentication codes, which mostly seem to involve SIM swap, where the attacker pretends to be you to your mobile phone company and gets a replacement SIM card for your account. SIM-swap attacks started in South Africa in 2007, became the main form of bank fraud in Nigeria, then caught on in America – initially as a means of taking over valuable Instagram accounts, then to loot people's accounts at bitcoin exchanges, then for bank fraud more generally [1094]. I will discuss SIM-swap attacks in more detail in section 12.7.4.

Attackers have also exploited the SS7 signalling protocol to wiretap targets' mobile phones remotely and steal codes [485]. I'll discuss such attacks in more detail in the chapters on phones and on banking. The next step in the arms race will be moving customers from SMS messages for authentication and account recovery to an app; the same Google research shows that this improves these last two figures to 99% for bulk phishing and 90% for targeted attacks [574]. As for the targeted attacks, other research by Ariana Mirian along with colleagues from UCSD and Google approached gangs who advertised 'hack-for-hire' services online and asked them to phish Gmail passwords. Three of the gangs succeeded, defeating SMS-based 2fa with a middleperson attack; forensics then revealed 372 other attacks on Gmail users from the same IP addresses during March to October 2018 [1324]. This is still an immature criminal market, but to stop such attacks an app or authentication token is the way to go. It also raises further questions about account recovery. If I use a hardware security key on my Gmail, do I need a second one in a safe as a recovery mechanism? (Probably.) If I use one app on my phone to do banking and another as an authenticator, do I comply with rules on two-factor authentication? (See section 12.7.4 in the chapter on banking.)

Email notification is the default for telling people not just of suspicious login attempts, but of logins to new devices that succeeded with the help of a code. That way, if someone plants malware on your phone, you have some chance of detecting it. How a victim recovers then is the next question. If all else fails, a service provider may eventually let them speak to a real person. But when designing such a system, never forget that it's only as strong as the weakest fall-back mechanism – be it a recovery email loop with an email provider you don't control, a phone code that's vulnerable to SIM swapping or mobile malware, or a human who's open to social engineering.

3.4.2 Password choice

Many accounts are compromised by guessing PINs or passwords. There are botnets constantly breaking into online accounts by guessing passwords and password-recovery questions, as I described in 2.3.1.4, in order to use email accounts to send spam and to recruit machines to botnets. And as people invent new services and put passwords on them, the password guessers find new targets. A recent example is cryptocurrency wallets: an anonymous 'bitcoin bandit' managed to steal $50m by trying lots of weak passwords for ethereum wallets [810]. Meanwhile, billions of dollars' worth of cryptocurrency has been lost because passwords were forgotten. So passwords matter, and there are basically three broad concerns, in ascending order of importance and difficulty:

1. Will the user enter the password correctly with a high enough probability?
2. Will the user remember the password, or will they have to either write it down or choose one that's easy for the attacker to guess?
3. Will the user break the system security by disclosing the password to a third party, whether accidentally, on purpose, or as a result of deception?

3.4.3 Difficulties with reliable password entry

The first human-factors issue is that if a password is too long or complex, users might have difficulty entering it correctly. If the operation they're trying to perform is urgent, this might have safety implications. If customers have difficulty entering software product activation codes, this can generate expensive calls to your support desk. And the move from laptops to smartphones during the 2010s has made password rules such as 'at least one lower-case letter, upper-case letter, number and special character' really fiddly and annoying.

This is one of the factors pushing people toward longer but simpler secrets, such as passphrases of three or four words. But will people be able to enter them without making too many errors?

An interesting study was done for the STS prepayment meters used to sell electricity in many less-developed countries. The customer hands some money to a sales agent, and gets a 20-digit number printed out on a receipt. They take this receipt home, enter the numbers at a keypad in the meter, and the lights come on. The STS designers worried that since a lot of the population was illiterate, and since people might get lost halfway through entering the number, the system might be unusable. But illiteracy was not a problem: even people who could not read had no difficulty with numbers ('everybody can use a phone', as one of the engineers said). The biggest problem was entry errors, and these were dealt with by printing the twenty digits in two rows, with three groups of four digits in the first row followed by two in the second [94]. I'll describe this in detail in section 14.2.

A quite different application is the firing codes for US nuclear weapons. These consist of only 12 decimal digits. If they are ever used, the operators will be under extreme stress, and possibly using improvised or obsolete communications channels. Experiments suggested that 12 digits was the maximum that could be conveyed reliably in such circumstances. I'll discuss how this evolved in section 15.2.

3.4.4 Difficulties with remembering the password

Our second psychological issue is that people often find passwords hard to remember [2079]. Twelve to twenty digits may be easy to copy from a telegram or a meter ticket, but when customers are expected to memorize passwords, they either choose values that are easy for attackers to guess, or write them down, or both. In fact, standard password advice has been summed up as: "Choose a password you can't remember, and don't write it down".

The problems are not limited to computer access. For example, one chain of cheap hotels in France introduced self service. You'd turn up at the hotel, swipe your credit card in the reception machine, and get a receipt with a numerical access code to unlock your room door. To keep costs down, the rooms did not have en-suite bathrooms. A common failure mode was that you'd get up in the middle of the night to go to the bathroom, forget your access code, and realise you hadn't taken the receipt with you. So you'd have to sleep on the bathroom floor until the staff arrived the following morning.

Password memorability can be discussed under five main headings: naïve choice, user abilities and training, design errors, operational failures and vulnerability to social-engineering attacks.

3.4.4.1 *Naïve choice*

Since the mid-1980s, people have studied what sort of passwords people choose, and found they use spouses' names, single letters, or even just hit carriage return giving an empty string as their password. Cryptanalysis of tapes from a 1980 Unix system showed that of the pioneers, Dennis Ritchie used 'dmac' (his middle name was MacAlistair); the later Google chairman Eric Schmidt used 'wendy!!!' (his wife's name) and Brian Kernighan used '/.,/.,' [796]. Fred Grampp and Robert Morris's classic 1984 paper on Unix security [806] reports that after software became available which forced passwords to be at least six characters long and have at least one nonletter, they made a file of the 20 most common female names, each followed by a single digit. Of these 200 passwords, at least one was in use on each of several dozen machines they examined. At the time, Unix systems kept encrypted passwords in a file `/etc/passwd` that all system users could read, so any user could verify a guess of any other user's password. Other studies showed that requiring a non-letter simply changed the most popular password from 'password' to 'password1' [1675].

In 1990, Daniel Klein gathered 25,000 Unix passwords and found that 21–25% of passwords could be guessed depending on the amount of effort put in [1058]. Dictionary words accounted for 7.4%, common names for 4%, combinations of user and account name 2.7%, and so on down a list of less probable choices such as words from science fiction (0.4%) and sports terms (0.2%). Other password guesses used patterns, such as by taking an account *'klone'* belonging to the user 'Daniel V. Klein' and trying passwords such as klone, klone1, klone123, dvk, dvkdvk, leinad, neilk, DvkkvD, and so on. The following year, Alec Muffett released 'crack', software that would try to brute-force Unix passwords using dictionaries and patterns derived from them by a set of mangling rules.

The largest academic study of password choice of which I am aware is by Joe Bonneau, who in 2012 analysed tens of millions of passwords in leaked password files, and also interned at Yahoo where he instrumented the login system to collect live statistics on the choices of 70 million users. He also worked out the best metrics to use for password guessability, both in standalone systems and where attackers use passwords harvested from one system to crack accounts on another [290]. This work informed the design of password strength checkers and other current practices at the big service firms.

3.4.4.2 *User abilities and training*

Sometimes you can train the users. Password checkers have trained them to use longer passwords with numbers as well as letters, and the effect spills over to websites that don't use them [446]. But you do not want to drive customers away, so the marketing folks will limit what you can do. In fact, research shows that password rule enforcement is not a function of the value at risk, but of whether the website is a monopoly. Such websites typically have very annoying rules, while websites with competitors, such as Amazon, are more usable, placing more reliance on back-end intrusion-detection systems.

In a corporate or military environment you can enforce password choice rules, or password change rules, or issue random passwords. But then people will have to write them down. So you can insist that passwords are treated the same way as the data they protect: bank master passwords go in the vault overnight, while military 'Top Secret' passwords must be sealed in an envelope, in a safe, in a room that's locked when not occupied, in a building patrolled by guards. You can send guards round at night to clean all desks and bin everything that hasn't been locked up. But if you want to hire and retain good people, you'd better think things through a bit more carefully. For example, one Silicon Valley firm had a policy that the root password for each machine would be written down on a card and put in an envelope taped to the side of the machine – a more human version of the rule that passwords be treated the same way as the data they protect. The domestic equivalent is the card in the back of your wifi router with the password.

While writing the first edition of this book, I could not find any account of experiments on training people in password choice that would hold water by the standards of applied psychology (i.e., randomized controlled trials with adequate statistical power). The closest I found was a study of the recall rates, forgetting rates, and guessing rates of various types of password [347]; this didn't tell us the actual effects of giving users various kinds of advice. We therefore decided to see what could be achieved by training, and selected three groups of about a hundred volunteers from our first-year science students [2058]:

- the red (control) group was given the usual advice (password at least six characters long, including one nonletter);
- the green group was told to think of a passphrase and select letters from it to build a password. So 'It's 12 noon and I am hungry' would give `'I'S12&IAH'`;
- the yellow group was told to select eight characters (alpha or numeric) at random from a table we gave them, write them down, and destroy this note after a week or two once they'd memorized the password.

What we expected to find was that the red group's passwords would be easier to guess than the green group's which would in turn be easier than the yellow group's; and that the yellow group would have the most difficulty remembering their passwords (or would be forced to reset them more often), followed by green and then red. But that's not what we found.

About 30% of the control group chose passwords that could be guessed using Alec Muffett's 'crack' software, versus about 10 percent for the other two groups. So passphrases and random passwords seemed to be about equally effective. When we looked at password reset rates, there was no significant difference between the three groups. When we asked the students whether they'd found their passwords hard to remember (or had written them down), the yellow group had significantly more problems than the other two; but there was no significant difference between red and green.

The conclusions we drew were as follows.

- For users who follow instructions, passwords based on mnemonic phrases offer the best of both worlds. They are as easy to remember as naively selected passwords, and as hard to guess as random passwords.
- The problem then becomes one of *user compliance*. A significant number of users (perhaps a third of them) just don't do what they're told.

So when the army gives soldiers randomly-selected passwords, its value comes from the fact that the password assignment compels user compliance, rather than from the fact that they're random (as mnemonic phrases would do just as well).

But centrally-assigned passwords are often inappropriate. When you are offering a service to the public, your customers expect you to present broadly the same interfaces as your competitors. So you must let users choose their own website passwords, subject to some lightweight algorithm to reject passwords that are 'clearly bad'. (GCHQ suggests using a 'bad password list' of the 100,000 passwords most commonly found in online password dumps.) In the case of bank cards, users expect a bank-issued initial PIN plus the ability to change the PIN afterwards to one of their choosing (though again you may block a 'clearly bad' PIN such as 0000 or 1234). Over half of cardholders keep a random PIN, but about a quarter choose PINs such as children's birth dates which have less entropy than random PINs would, and have the same PIN on different cards. The upshot is that a thief who steals a purse or wallet may have a chance of about one in eleven to get lucky, if he tries the most common PINs on all the cards first in offline mode and then in online mode, so he gets six goes at each. Banks that forbid popular choices such as 1234 can increase the odds to about one in eighteen [296].

3.4.4.3 Design errors

Attempts to make passwords memorable are a frequent source of severe design errors. The classic example of how not to do it is to ask for 'your mother's maiden name'. A surprising number of banks, government departments and other organisations still authenticate their customers in this way, though nowadays it tends to be not a password but a password recovery question. You could always try to tell 'Yngstrom' to your bank, 'Jones' to the phone company, 'Geraghty' to the travel agent, and so on; but data are shared extensively between companies, so you could easily end up confusing their systems – not to mention yourself. And if you try to phone up your bank and tell them that you've decided to change your mother's maiden name from Yngstrom to `yGt5r4ad` – or even Smith – then good luck. In fact, given the large number of data breaches, you might as well assume that anyone who wants to can get all your common password recovery information – including your address, your date of birth, your first school and your social security number, as well as your mother's maiden name.

Some organisations use contextual security information. A bank I once used asks its business customers the value of the last check from their account that was cleared. In theory, this could be helpful: if someone overhears me doing a transaction on the telephone, then it's not a long-term compromise. The details bear some attention though. When this system was first introduced, I wondered whether a supplier, to whom I'd just written a check, might impersonate me, and concluded that asking for the last three checks' values would be safer. But the problem we actually had was unexpected. Having given the checkbook to our accountant for the annual audit, we couldn't talk to the bank. I also don't like the idea that someone who steals my physical post can also steal my money.

The sheer number of applications demanding a password nowadays exceeds the powers of human memory. A 2007 study by Dinei Florêncio and Cormac Herley of half a million web users over three months showed that the average user has 6.5 passwords, each shared across 3.9 different sites; has about 25 accounts that require passwords; and types an average of 8 passwords per day. Bonneau published more extensive statistics in 2012 [290] but since then the frequency of user password entry has fallen, thanks to smartphones. Modern web browsers also cache passwords; see the discussion of password managers at section 3.4.11 below. But many people use the same password for many different purposes and don't work out special processes to deal with their high-value logons such as to their bank, their social media accounts and their email. So you have to expect that the password chosen by the customer of the electronic banking system you've just designed, may be known to a Mafia-operated porn site as well. (There's even a website, `http://haveibeenpwned.com`, that will tell you which security breaches have leaked your email address and password.)

One of the most pervasive and persistent errors has been forcing users to change passwords regularly. When I first came across enforced monthly password changes in the 1980s, I observed that it led people to choose passwords such as 'julia03' for March, 'julia04' for April, and so on, and said as much in the first (2001) edition of this book (chapter 3, page 48). However, in 2003, Bill Burr of NIST wrote password guidelines recommending regular update [1098].

This was adopted by the Big Four auditors, who pushed it out to all their audit clients[3]. Meanwhile, security usability researchers conducted survey after survey showing that monthly change was suboptimal. The first systematic study by Yinqian Zhang, Fabian Monrose and Mike Reiter of the password transformation techniques users invented showed that in a system with forced expiration, over 40% of passwords could be guessed from previous ones, that forced change didn't do much to help people who chose weak passwords, and that the effort of regular password choice may also have diminished password quality [2073]. Finally a survey was written by usability guru Lorrie Cranor while she was Chief Technologist at the FTC [492], and backed up by an academic study [1507]. In 2017, NIST recanted; they now recommend long passphrases that are only changed on compromise[4]. Other governments' agencies such as Britain's GCHQ followed, and Microsoft finally announced the end of password-expiration policies in Windows 10 from April 2019. However, many firms are caught by the PCI standards set by the credit-card issuers, which haven't caught up and still dictate three-monthly changes; another problem is that the auditors dictate compliance to many companies, and will no doubt take time to catch up.

The current fashion, in 2020, is to invite users to select passphrases of three or more random dictionary words. This was promoted by a famous xkcd cartoon which suggested 'correct horse battery staple' as a password. Empirical research, however, shows that real users select multi-word passphrases with much less entropy than they'd get if they really did select at random from a dictionary; they tend to go for common noun bigrams, and moving to three or four words brings rapidly diminishing returns [297]. The Electronic Frontier Foundation now promotes using dice to pick words; they have a list of 7,776 words (6^5, so five dice rolls to pick a word) and note that a six-word phrase has 77 bits of entropy and is memorable [291].

3.4.4.4 *Operational failures*

The most pervasive operational error is failing to reset default passwords. This has been a chronic problem since the early dial access systems in the 1980s attracted attention from mischievous schoolkids. A particularly bad example is where systems have default passwords that can't be changed, checked by software that can't be patched. We see ever more such devices in the Internet of Things; they remain vulnerable for their operational lives. The Mirai botnets have emerged to recruit and exploit them, as I described in Chapter 2.

[3]Our university's auditors wrote in their annual report for three years in a row that we should have monthly enforced password change, but couldn't provide any evidence to support this and weren't even aware that their policy came ultimately from NIST. Unimpressed, we asked the chair of our Audit Committee to appoint a new lot of auditors, and eventually that happened.
[4]NIST SP 800-63-3

Passwords in plain sight are another long-running problem, whether on sticky notes or some electronic equivalent. A famous early case was R v Gold and Schifreen, where two young hackers saw a phone number for the development version of Prestel, an early public email service run by British Telecom, in a note stuck on a terminal at an exhibition. They dialed in later, and found the welcome screen had a maintenance password displayed on it. They tried this on the live system too, and it worked! They proceeded to hack into the Duke of Edinburgh's electronic mail account, and sent mail 'from' him to someone they didn't like, announcing the award of a knighthood. This heinous crime so shocked the establishment that when prosecutors failed to persuade the courts to convict the young men, Britain's parliament passed its first Computer Misuse Act.

A third operational issue is asking for passwords when they're not really needed, or wanted for dishonest reasons, as I discussed at the start of this section. Most of the passwords you're forced to set up on websites are there for marketing reasons – to get your email address or give you the feeling of belonging to a 'club' [295]. So it's perfectly rational for users who never plan to visit that site again to express their exasperation by entering '123456' or even ruder words in the password field.

A fourth is atrocious password management systems: some don't encrypt passwords at all, and there are reports from time to time of enterprising hackers smuggling back doors into password management libraries [429].

But perhaps the biggest operational issue is vulnerability to social-engineering attacks.

3.4.4.5 *Social-engineering attacks*

Careful organisations communicate security context in various ways to help staff avoid making mistakes. The NSA, for example, had different colored internal and external telephones, and when an external phone in a room is off-hook, classified material can't even be discussed in the room – let alone on the phone.

Yet while many banks and other businesses maintain some internal security context, they often train their customers to act in unsafe ways. Because of pervasive phishing, it's not prudent to try to log on to your bank by clicking on a link in an email, so you should always use a browser bookmark or type in the URL by hand. Yet bank marketing departments send out lots of emails containing clickable links. Indeed much of the marketing industry is devoted to getting people to click on links. Many email clients – including Apple's, Microsoft's, and Google's – make plaintext URLs clickable, so their users may never see a URL that isn't. Bank customers are well trained to do the wrong thing.

A prudent customer should also be cautious if a web service directs them somewhere else – yet bank systems use all sorts of strange URLs for their services. A spam from the Bank of America directed UK customers to mynewcard.com and got the certificate wrong (it was for mynewcard.bankofamerica.com). There are many more examples of major banks training their customers to practice unsafe computing – by disregarding domain names, ignoring certificate warnings, and merrily clicking links [582]. As a result, even security experts have difficulty telling bank spam from phish [445].

It's not prudent to give out security information over the phone to unidentified callers – yet we all get phoned by bank staff who demand security information. Banks also call us on our mobiles now and expect us to give out security information to a whole train carriage of strangers, rather than letting us text a response. (I've had a card blocked because a bank security team phoned me while I was driving; it would have been against the law to deal with the call other than in hands-free mode, and there was nowhere safe to stop.) It's also not prudent to put a bank card PIN into any device other than an ATM or a PIN entry device (PED) in a store; and Citibank even asks customers to disregard and report emails that ask for personal information, including PIN and account details. So what happened? You guessed it – it sent its Australian customers an email asking customers 'as part of a security upgrade' to log on to its website and authenticate themselves using a card number and an ATM PIN [1089]. And in one 2005 case, the Halifax sent a spam to the mother of a student of ours who contacted the bank's security department, which told her it was a phish. The student then contacted the ISP to report abuse, and found that the URL and the service were genuine [1243]. The Halifax disappeared during the crash of 2008, and given that their own security department couldn't tell spam from phish, perhaps that was justice (though it cost us taxpayers a shedload of money).

3.4.4.6 Customer education

After phishing became a real threat to online banking in the mid-2000s, banks tried to train their customers to look for certain features in websites. This has been partly risk reduction, but partly risk dumping – seeing to it that customers who don't understand or can't follow instructions can be held responsible for the resulting loss. The general pattern has been that as soon as customers are trained to follow some particular rule, the phishermen exploit this, as the reasons for the rule are not adequately explained.

At the beginning, the advice was 'Check the English', so the bad guys either got someone who could write English, or simply started using the banks' own emails but with the URLs changed. Then it was 'Look for the lock symbol', so the phishing sites started to use SSL (or just forging it by putting graphics of lock symbols on their web pages). Some banks started putting the last four digits of the customer account number into emails; the phishermen responded by putting in the first four (which are constant for a given bank and card product). Next the advice was that it was OK to click on images, but not on URLs; the phishermen promptly put in links that appeared to be images but actually pointed at executables. The advice then was to check where a link would really go by hovering your mouse over it; the bad guys then either inserted a non-printing character into the URL to stop Internet Explorer from displaying the rest, or used an unmanageably long URL (as many banks also did).

This sort of arms race is most likely to benefit the attackers. The countermeasures become so complex and counterintuitive that they confuse more and more users – exactly what the phishermen need. The safety and usability communities have known for years that 'blame and train' is not the way to deal with unusable systems – the only real fix is to design for safe usability in the first place [1453].

3.4.4.7 Phishing warnings

Part of the solution is to give users better tools. Modern browsers alert you to wicked URLs, with a range of mechanisms under the hood. First, there are lists of bad URLs collated by the anti-virus and threat intelligence community. Second, there's logic to look for expired certificates and other compliance failures (as the majority of those alerts are false alarms).

There has been a lot of research, in both industry and academia, about how you get people to pay attention to warnings. We see so many of them, most are irrelevant, and many are designed to shift risk to us from someone else. So when do people pay attention? In our own work, we tried a number of things and found that people paid most attention when the warnings were not vague and general (*'Warning - visiting this web site may harm your computer!'*) but specific and concrete (*'The site you are about to visit has been confirmed to contain software that poses a significant risk to you, with no tangible benefit. It would try to infect your computer with malware designed to steal your bank account and credit card details in order to defraud you*) [1329]. Subsequent research by Adrienne Porter Felt and Google's usability team has tried many ideas including making warnings psychologically salient using faces (which doesn't work), simplifying the text (which helps) and making the safe defaults both attractive and prominent (which also helps). Optimising these factors improves compliance from about 35% to about 50% [675]. However, if you want to stop the great majority of people from clicking on known-bad URLs, then voluntary compliance isn't enough. You either have to block them at your firewall, or block them at the browser (as both Chrome and Firefox do for different types of certificate error – a matter to which we'll return in 21.6).

3.4.5 System issues

Not all phishing attacks involve psychology. Some involve technical mechanisms to do with password entry and storage together with some broader system issues.

As we already noted, a key question is whether we can restrict the number of password guesses. Security engineers sometimes refer to password systems as 'online' if guessing is limited (as with ATM PINs) and 'offline' if it is not (this originally meant systems where a user could fetch the password file and take it away to try to guess the passwords of other users, including more privileged users). But the terms are no longer really accurate. Some offline systems can restrict guesses, such as payment cards which use physical tamper-resistance to limit you to three PIN guesses, while some online systems cannot. For example, if you log on using Kerberos, an opponent who taps the line can observe your key encrypted with your password flowing from the server to your client, and then data encrypted with that key flowing on the line; so they can take their time to try out all possible passwords. The most common trap here is the system that normally restricts password guesses but then suddenly fails to do so, when it gets hacked and a one-way encrypted password file is leaked, together with the encryption keys. Then the bad guys can try out their entire password dictionary against each account at their leisure.

Password guessability ultimately depends on the entropy of the chosen passwords and the number of allowed guesses, but this plays out in the context of a specific threat model, so you need to consider the type of attacks you are trying to defend against. Broadly speaking, these are as follows.

Targeted attack on one account: an intruder tries to guess a specific user's password. They might try to guess a rival's logon password at the office, in order to do mischief directly.

Attempt to penetrate any account belonging to a specific target: an enemy tries to hack any account you own, anywhere, to get information that might might help take over other accounts, or do harm directly.

Attempt to penetrate any account on a target system: the intruder tries to get a logon as any user of the system. This is the classic case of the phisherman trying to hack any account at a target bank so he can launder stolen money through it.

Attempt to penetrate any account on any system: the intruder merely wants an account at any system in a given domain but doesn't care which one. Examples are bad guys trying to guess passwords on any online email service so they can send spam from the compromised account, and a targeted attacker who wants a logon to any random machine in the domain of a target company as a beachhead.

Attempt to use a breach of one system to penetrate a related one: the intruder has got a beachhead and now wants to move inland to capture higher-value targets.

Service-denial attack: the attacker may wish to block one or more legitimate users from using the system. This might be targeted on a particular account or system-wide.

This taxonomy helps us ask relevant questions when evaluating a password system.

3.4.6 Can you deny service?

There are basically three ways to deal with password guessing when you detect it: lockout, throttling, and protective monitoring. Banks may freeze your card after three wrong PINs; but if they freeze your online account after three bad password attempts they open themselves up to a denial-of-service attack. Service can also fail by accident; poorly-configured systems can generate repeat fails with stale credentials. So many commercial websites nowadays use throttling rather than lockout. In a military system, you might not want even that, in case an enemy who gets access to the network could jam it with a flood of false logon attempts. In this case, protective monitoring might be the preferred option, with a plan to abandon rate-limiting if need be in a crisis. Joe Bonneau and Soren Preibusch collected statistics of how many major websites use account locking versus various types of rate control [295]. They found that popular, growing, competent sites tend to be more secure, as do payment sites, while content sites do worst. Microsoft Research's Yuan Tian, Cormac Herley and Stuart Schechter investigated how to do locking or throttling properly; among other things, it's best to penalise guesses of weak passwords (as otherwise an attacker gets advantage by guessing them first), to be more aggressive when protecting users who have selected weak passwords, and to not punish IPs or clients that repeatedly submit the same wrong password [1892].

3.4.7 Protecting oneself or others?

Next, to what extent does the system need to protect users and subsystems from each other? In global systems on which anyone can get an account – such as mobile phone systems and cash machine systems – you must assume that the attackers are already legitimate users, and see to it that no-one can use the service at someone else's expense. So knowledge of one user's password will not allow another user's account to be compromised. This has both personal aspects, and system aspects.

On the personal side, don't forget what we said about intimate partner abuse in 2.5.4: the passwords people choose are often easy for their spouses or partners to guess, and the same goes for password recovery questions: so some thought needs to be given to how abuse victims can recover their security.

On the system side, there are all sorts of passwords used for mutual authentication between subsystems, few mechanisms to enforce password quality in server-server environments, and many well-known issues (for example, the default password for the Java trusted keystore file is 'changeit'). Development teams often share passwords that end up in live systems, even 30 years after this practice led to the well-publicised hack of the Duke of Edinburgh's email described in section 3.4.4.4. Within a single big service firm you can lock stuff down by having named crypto keys and seeing to it that each name generates a call to an underlying hardware security module; or you can even use mechanisms like SGX to tie keys to known software. But that costs real money, and money isn't the only problem. Enterprise system components are often hosted at different service companies, which makes adoption of better practices a hard coordination problem too. As a result, server passwords often appear in scripts or other plaintext files, which can end up in Dropbox or Splunk. So it is vital to think of password practices beyond end users. In later chapters we'll look at protocols such as Kerberos and ssh; for now, recall Ed Snowden's remark that it was trivial to hack the typical large company: just spear-phish a sysadmin and then chain your way in. Much of this chapter is about the 'spear-phish a sysadmin' part; but don't neglect the 'chain your way in' part.

3.4.8 Attacks on password entry

Password entry is often poorly protected.

3.4.8.1 *Interface design*

Thoughtless interface design is all too common. Some common makes of cash machine have a vertical keyboard at head height, making it simple for a pickpocket to watch a woman enter her PIN before lifting her purse from her handbag. The keyboards may have been at a reasonable height for the men who designed them, but women who are a few inches shorter are exposed.

When entering a card number or PIN in a public place, I usually cover my typing hand with my body or my other hand – but you can't assume that all your customers will. Many people are uncomfortable shielding a PIN as it's a signal of distrust, especially if they're in a supermarket queue and a friend is standing nearby. UK banks found that 20% of users never shield their PIN [128] – and then used this to blame customers whose PINs were compromised by an overhead CCTV camera, rather than designing better PIN entry devices.

3.4.8.2 *Trusted path, and bogus terminals*

A *trusted path* is some means of being sure that you're logging into a genuine machine through a channel that isn't open to eavesdropping. False terminal attacks go back to the dawn of time-shared computing. A public terminal would be left running an attack program that looks just like the usual logon screen – asking for a user name and password. When an unsuspecting user did this, it would save the password, reply 'sorry, wrong password' and then vanish, invoking the genuine password program. The user assumed they'd made a typing error and just entered the password again. This is why Windows had a *secure attention sequence*; hitting `ctrl-alt-del` was guaranteed to take you to a genuine password prompt. But eventually, in Windows 10, this got removed to prepare the way for Windows tablets, and because almost nobody understood it.

ATM skimmers are devices that sit on an ATM's throat, copy card details, and have a camera to record the customer PIN. There are many variants on the theme. Fraudsters deploy bad PIN entry devices too, and have even been jailed for attaching password-stealing hardware to terminals in bank branches. I'll describe this world in much more detail in the chapter on banking and bookkeeping; the long-term solution has been to move from magnetic-strip cards that are easy to copy to chip cards that are much harder. In any case, if a terminal might contain malicious hardware or software, then passwords alone will not be enough.

3.4.8.3 *Technical defeats of password retry counters*

Many kids find out that a bicycle combination lock can usually be broken in a few minutes by solving each ring in order of looseness. The same idea worked against a number of computer systems. The PDP-10 TENEX operating system checked passwords one character at a time, and stopped as soon as one of them was wrong. This opened up a *timing attack*: the attacker would repeatedly place a guessed password in memory at a suitable location, have it verified as part of a file access request, and wait to see how long it took to be rejected [1131]. An error in the first character would be reported almost at once, an error in the second character would take a little longer to report, and in the third character a little longer still, and so on. So you could guess the characters one after another, and instead of a password of N characters drawn from an alphabet of A characters taking $A^N/2$ guesses on average, it took $AN/2$. (Bear in mind that in thirty years' time, all that might remain of the system you're building today is the memory of its more newsworthy security failures.)

These same mistakes are being made all over again in the world of embedded systems. With one remote car locking device, as soon as a wrong byte was transmitted from the key fob, the red telltale light on the receiver came on. With some smartcards, it has been possible to determine the customer PIN by trying each possible input value and looking at the card's power consumption, then issuing a reset if the input was wrong. The reason was that a wrong PIN caused a PIN retry counter to be decremented, and writing to the EEPROM memory which held this counter caused a current surge of several milliamps – which could be detected in time to reset the card before the write was complete [1107]. These implementation details matter. Timing channels are a serious problem for people implementing cryptography, as we'll discuss at greater length in the next chapter.

A recent high-profile issue was the PIN retry counter in the iPhone. My colleague Sergei Skorobogatov noted that the iPhone keeps sensitive data encrypted in flash memory, and built an adapter that enabled him to save the encrypted memory contents and restore them to their original condition after several PIN attempts. This enabled him to try all 10,000 possible PINs rather than the ten PINs limit that Apple tried to impose [1781][5].

3.4.9 Attacks on password storage

Passwords have often been vulnerable where they are stored. In MIT's 'Compatible Time Sharing System' `ctss` – a 1960s predecessor of Multics – it once happened that one person was editing the message of the day, while another was editing the password file. Because of a software bug, the two editor temporary files got swapped, and everyone who logged on was greeted with a copy of the password file! [476].

Another horrible programming error struck a UK bank in the late 1980s, which issued all its customers with the same PIN by mistake [55]. As the procedures for handling PINs meant that no one in the bank got access to anyone's PIN other than their own, the bug wasn't spotted until after thousands of customer cards had been shipped. Big blunders continue: in 2019 the security company that does the Biostar and AEOS biometric lock system for building entry control and whose customers include banks and police forces in 83 countries left a database unprotected online with over a million people's IDs, plaintext passwords, fingerprints and facial recognition data; security researchers who discovered this from an Internet scan were able to add themselves as users [1867].

Auditing provides another hazard. When systems log failed password attempts, the log usually contains a large number of passwords, as users get the 'username, password' sequence out of phase. If the logs are not well protected then someone who sees an audit record of a failed login with a

[5]This was done to undermine an argument by then FBI Director James Comey that the iPhone was unhackable and so Apple should be ordered to produce an operating system upgrade that created a backdoor; see section 26.2.7.4.

non-existent user name of `e5gv*8yp` just has to try this as a password for all the valid user names.

3.4.9.1 One-way encryption

Such incidents taught people to protect passwords by encrypting them using a one-way algorithm, an innovation due to Roger Needham and Mike Guy. The password, when entered, is passed through a one-way function and the user is logged on only if it matches a previously stored value. However, it's often implemented wrong. The right way to do it is to generate a random key, historically known in this context as a *salt*; combine the password with the salt using a slow, cryptographically strong one-way function; and store both the salt and the hash.

3.4.9.2 Password cracking

Some systems that use an encrypted password file make it widely readable. Unix used to be the prime example – the password file `/etc/passwd` was readable by all users. So any user could fetch it and try to break passwords by encrypting all the passwords in a dictionary and comparing them with the encrypted values in the file. We already mentioned in 3.4.4.1 the 'Crack' software that people have used for years for this purpose.

Most modern operating systems have sort-of fixed this problem; in modern Linux distributions, for example, passwords are salted, hashed using 5000 rounds of SHA-512, and stored in a file that only the root user can read. But there are still password-recovery tools to help you if, for example, you've encrypted an Office document with a password you've forgotten [1677]. Such tools can also be used by a crook who has got root access, and there are still lots of badly designed systems out there where the password file is vulnerable in other ways.

There is also *credential stuffing*: when a system is hacked and passwords are cracked (or were even found unencrypted), they are then tried out on other systems to catch the many people who reused them. This remains a live problem. So password cracking is still worth some attention. One countermeasure worth considering is deception, which can work at all levels in the stack. You can have honeypot systems that alarm if anyone ever logs on to them, honeypot accounts on a system, or password canaries – bogus encrypted passwords for genuine accounts [998].

3.4.9.3 Remote password checking

Many systems check passwords remotely, using cryptographic protocols to protect the password in transit, and the interaction between password security and network security can be complex. Local networks often use a protocol called Kerberos, where a server sends you a key encrypted under your password; if you know the password you can decrypt the key and use it to get tickets that give you access to resources. I'll discuss this in the next chapter, in section 4.7.4; it doesn't always protect weak passwords against an opponent who can wiretap encrypted traffic. Web servers mostly use a protocol called TLS to encrypt your traffic from the browser on your phone or laptop; I discuss TLS in the following chapter, in section 5.7.5. TLS does not protect you if the server gets hacked. However there is a new protocol called Simultaneous Authentication of Equals (SAE) which is designed to set up secure sessions even where the password is guessable, and which has been adopted from 2018 in the WPA3 standard for WiFi authentication. I'll discuss this later too.

And then there's OAuth, a protocol which allows access delegation, so you can grant one website the right to authenticate you using the mechanisms provided by another. Developed by Twitter from 2006, it's now used by the main service providers such as Google, Microsoft and Facebook to let you log on to media and other sites; an authorisation server issues access tokens for the purpose. We'll discuss the mechanisms later too. The concomitant risk is cross-site attacks; we are now (2019) seeing OAuth being used by state actors in authoritarian countries to phish local human-rights defenders. The technique is to create a malicious app with a plausible name (say 'Outlook Security Defender') and send an email, purportedly from Microsoft, asking for access. If the target responds they end up at a Microsoft web page where they're asked to authorise the app to have access to their data [47].

3.4.10 Absolute limits

If you have confidence in the cryptographic algorithms and operating-system security mechanisms that protect passwords, then the probability of a successful password guessing attack is a function of the entropy of passwords, if they are centrally assigned, and the psychology of users if they're allowed to choose them. Military sysadmins often prefer to issue random passwords, so the probability of password guessing attacks can be managed. For example, if L is the maximum password lifetime, R is login attempt rate, S is the size of the password space, then the probability that a password can be guessed in its lifetime is $P = LR/S$, according to the US Department of Defense password management guideline [546].

There are issues with such a 'provable security' doctrine, starting with the attackers' goal. Do they want to crack a target account, or just any account? If an army has a million possible passwords and a million users, and the alarm goes off after three bad password attempts on any account, then the attacker can just try one password for every different account. If you want to stop this, you have to do rate control not just for every account, but for all accounts.

To take a concrete example, Unix systems used to be limited to eight character passwords, so there were 96^8 or about 2^{52} possible passwords. Some UK government systems used to issue passwords randomly selected with a fixed template of consonants, vowels and numbers designed to make them easier to remember, such as CVCNCVCN (e.g. `fuR5xEb8`). If passwords are not case sensitive, the guess probability is cut drastically, to only one in $21^4.5^2.10^2$ or about 2^{-29}. So if an attacker could guess 100 passwords a second – perhaps distributed across 10,000 accounts on hundreds of machines on a network, so as not to raise the alarm – then they would need about 5 million seconds, or two months, to get in. If you're defending such a system, you might find it prudent to do rate control: set a limit of say one password guess per ten seconds per user account, and perhaps by source IP address. You might also count the failed logon attempts and analyse them: is there a constant series of guesses that suggests an attacker using a botnet, or some other attempted intrusion? And what will you do once you notice one? Will you close the system down? Welcome back to the world of service denial.

With a commercial website, 100 passwords per second may translate to one compromised user account per second, because of poor user password choices. That may not be a big deal for a web service with 100 million accounts – but it may still be worth trying to identify the source of any industrial-scale password-guessing attacks. If they're from a small number of IP addresses, you can block them, but doing this properly is harder than it looks, as we noted in section 3.4.6 above. And if an automated guessing attack does persist, then another way of dealing with it is the CAPTCHA, which I'll describe in section 3.5.

3.4.11 Using a password manager

Since the 1980s, companies have been selling single sign-on systems that remember your passwords for multiple applications, and when browsers came along in the mid-1990s and people started logging into dozens of websites, password managers became a mass-market product. Browser vendors noticed, and started providing much the same functionality for free.

Choosing random passwords and letting your browser remember them can be a pragmatic way of operating. The browser will only enter the password into a web page with the right URL (IE) or the same hostname and field name (Firefox). Browsers let you set a master password, which encrypts all the individual site passwords and which you only have to enter when your browser is updated. The main drawbacks of password managers in general are that you might forget the master password; and that all your passwords may be compromised at once, since malware writers can work out how to hack common products. This is a particular issue when using a browser, and another is that a master password is not always the default so many users don't set one. (The same holds for other security services you get as options with platforms, such as encrypting your phone or laptop.) An advantage of using the browser is that you may be able to sync passwords between the browser in your phone and that in your laptop.

Third-party password managers can offer more, such as choosing long random passwords for you, identifying passwords shared across more than one website, and providing more controllable ways for you to manage the backup and recovery of your password collection. (With a browser, this comes down to backing up your whole laptop or phone.) They can also help you track your accounts, so you can see whether you had a password on a system that's announced a breach. The downside is that many products are truly dreadful, with even some hardware password managers storing all your secrets in the clear [131], while the top five software products suffer from serious and systemic vulnerabilities, from autocomplete to ignoring subdomains [391]. How do you know that any given product is actually sound?

Many banks try to disable storage, whether by setting `autocomplete="off"` in their web pages or using other tricks that block password managers too. Banks think this improves security, but I'm not at all convinced. Stopping people using password managers or the browser's own storage will probably make most of them use weaker passwords. The banks may argue that killing autocomplete makes compromise following device theft harder, and may stop malware stealing the password from the database of your browser or password manager, but the phishing defence provided by that product is disabled – which may expose the average customer to greater risk [1357]. It's also inconvenient; one bank that suddenly disabled password storage had to back down the following day, because of the reaction from customers [1280]. People manage risk in all sorts of ways. I personally use different browsers for different purposes, and let them store low-value passwords; for important accounts, such as email and banking, I always enter passwords manually, and always navigate to them via bookmarks rather than by clicking on links. But most people are less careful. And be sure to think through backup and recovery, and exercise it to make sure it works. What happens when your laptop dies? When your phone dies? When someone persuades your phone company to link your phone number to their SIM? When you die – or when you fall ill and your partner needs to manage your stuff? Do they know where to find the master passwords? Writing them down in a book can make sense, if all you (and your executor) have to remember is 'page 169, Great Expectations.' Writing them down in a diary you tote with you, on a page saying 'passwords', is not so great. Very few people get all this right.

3.4.12 Will we ever get rid of passwords?

Passwords are annoying, so many people have discussed getting rid of them, and the move from laptops to phones gives us a chance. The proliferation of IoT devices that don't have keyboards will force us to do without them for some purposes. A handful of firms have tried to get rid of them completely. One example is the online bank Monzo, which operates exclusively via an app. They leave it up to the customer whether they protect their phone using a fingerprint, a pattern lock, a PIN or a password. However they still use email to prompt people to upgrade, and to authenticate people who buy a new phone, so account takeover involves either phone takeover, or guessing a password or a password recovery question. The most popular app that uses SMS to authenticate rather than a password may be WhatsApp. I expect that this will become more widespread; so we'll see more attacks based on phone takeover, from SIM swaps through Android malware, SS7 and RCS hacking, to simple physical theft. In such cases, recovery often means an email loop, making your email password more critical than ever – or phoning a call centre and telling them your mother's maiden name. So things may change less than they seem.

Joe Bonneau and colleagues analysed the options in 2012 [293]. There are many criteria against which an authentication system can be evaluated, and we've worked through them here: resilience to theft, to physical observation, to guessing, to malware and other internal compromise, to leaks from other verifiers, to phishing and to targeted impersonation. Other factors include ease of use, ease of learning, whether you need to carry something extra, error rate, ease of recovery, cost per user, and whether it's an open design that anyone can use. They concluded that most of the schemes involving net benefits were variants on single sign-on – and OpenID has indeed become widespread, with many people logging in to their newspaper using Google or Facebook, despite the obvious privacy cost[6]. Beyond that, any security improvements involve giving up one or more of the benefits of passwords, namely that they're easy, efficient and cheap.

Bonneau's survey gave high security ratings to physical authentication tokens such as the CAP reader, which enables people to use their bank cards to log on to online banking; bank regulators have already mandated two-factor

[6]Government attempts to set up single sign-on for public services have been less successful, with the UK 'Verify' program due to be shuttered in 2020 [1394]. There have been many problems around attempts to entrench government's role in identity assurance, which I'll discuss further in the chapter on biometrics, and which spill over into issues from online services to the security of elections. It was also hard for other private-sector firms to compete because of the network effects enjoyed by incumbents. However in 2019 Apple announced that it would provide a new, more privacy-friendly single sign-on mechanism, and use the market power of its app store to force websites to support it. Thus the quality and nature of privacy on offer is becoming a side-effect of battles fought for other motives. We'll analyse this in more depth in the chapter on economics.

authentication in a number of countries. Using something tied to a bank card gives a more traditional root of trust, at least with traditional high-street banks; a customer can walk into a branch and order a new card[7]. Firms that are targets of state-level attackers, such as Google and Microsoft, now give authentication tokens of some kind or another to all their staff.

Did the survey miss anything? Well, the old saying is 'something you have, something you know, or something you are' – or, as Simson Garfinkel engagingly puts it, 'something you had once, something you've forgotten, or something you once were'. The third option, biometrics, has started coming into wide use since high-end mobile phones started offering fingerprint readers. Some countries, like Germany, issue their citizens with ID cards containing a fingerprint, which may provide an alternate root of trust for when everything else goes wrong. We'll discuss biometrics in its own chapter later in the book.

Both tokens and biometrics are still mostly used with passwords, first as a backstop in case a device gets stolen, and second as part of the process of security recovery. So passwords remain the (shaky) foundation on which much of information security is built. What may change this is the growing number of devices that have no user interface at all, and so have to be authenticated using other mechanisms. One approach that's getting ever more common is trust on first use, also known as the 'resurrecting duckling' after the fact that a duckling bonds on the first moving animal it sees after it hatches. We'll discuss this in the next chapter, and also when we dive into specific applications such as security in vehicles.

Finally, you should think hard about how to authenticate customers or other people who exercise their right to demand copies of their personal information under data-protection law. In 2019, James Pavur sent out 150 such requests to companies, impersonating his fiancée [1890]. 86 firms admitted they had information about her, and many had the sense to demand her logon and password to authenticate her. But about a quarter were prepared to accept an email address or phone number as authentication; and a further 16 percent asked for easily forgeable ID. He collected full personal information about her, including her credit card number, her social security number and her mother's maiden name. A threat intelligence firm with which she'd never interacted sent a list of her accounts and passwords that had been compromised. Given that firms face big fines in the EU if they don't comply with such requests within 30 days, you'd better work out in advance how to cope with them, rather than leaving it to an assistant in your law office to improvise a procedure. If you abolish passwords, and a former customer claims their phone was stolen, what do you do then? And if you hold personal data on people who have never been your customers, how do you identify them?

[7]This doesn't work for branchless banks like Monzo; but they do take a video of you when you register so that their call centre can recognise you later.

3.5 CAPTCHAs

Can we have protection mechanisms that use the brain's strengths rather than its weaknesses? The most successful innovation in this field is probably the CAPTCHA – the 'Completely Automated Public Turing Test to Tell Computers and Humans Apart'. These are the little visual puzzles that you often have to solve to post to a blog, to register for a free online account, or to recover a password. The idea is that people can solve such problems easily, while computers find them hard.

CAPTCHAs first came into use in a big way in 2003 to stop spammers using scripts to open thousands of accounts on free email services, and to make it harder for attackers to try a few simple passwords with each of a large number of existing accounts. They were invented by Luis von Ahn and colleagues [1973], who were inspired by the test famously posed by Alan Turing as to whether a computer was intelligent: you put a computer in one room and a human in another, and invite a human to try to tell them apart. The test is turned round so that a computer can tell the difference between human and machine.

Early versions set out to use a known 'hard problem' in AI such as the recognition of distorted text against a noisy background. The idea is that breaking the CAPTCHA was equivalent to solving the AI problem, so an attacker would actually have to do the work by hand, or come up with a real innovation in computer science. Humans were good at reading distorted text, while programs were less good. It turned out to be harder than it seemed. A lot of the attacks on CAPTCHAs, even to this day, exploit the implementation details.

Many of the image recognition problems posed by early systems also turned out not to be too hard at all once smart people tried hard to solve them. There are also protocol-level attacks; von Ahn mentioned that in theory a spammer could get people to solve them as the price of access to free porn [1972]. This soon started to happen: spammers created a game in which you undress a woman by solving one CAPTCHA after another [192]. Within a few years, we saw commercial CAPTCHA-breaking tools arriving on the market [844]. Within a few more, generic attacks using signal-processing techniques inspired by the human visual system had become fairly efficient at solving at least a subset of most types of text CAPTCHA [746]. And security-economics research in underground markets has shown that by 2011 the action had moved to using humans; people in countries with incomes of a few dollars a day will solve CAPTCHAs for about 50c per 1000.

From 2014, the CAPTCHA has been superseded by the ReCAPTCHA, another of Luis von Ahn's inventions. Here the idea is to get a number of users to do some useful piece of work, and check their answers against each other. The service initially asked people to transcribe fragments of text from Google books that confused OCR software; more recently you get a puzzle with eight pictures asking 'click on all images containing a shop front', which helps Google train its vision-recognition AI systems[8]. It pushes back on the cheap-labour attack by putting up two or three multiple-choice puzzles and taking tens of seconds over it, rather than allowing rapid responses.

The implementation of CAPTCHAs is often thoughtless, with accessibility issues for users who are visually impaired. And try paying a road toll in Portugal where the website throws up a CAPTCHA asking you to identify pictures with an object, if you can't understand Portuguese well enough to figure out what you're supposed to look for!

3.6 Summary

Psychology matters to the security engineer, because of deception and because of usability. Most real attacks nowadays target the user. Various kinds of phishing are the main national-security threat, the principal means of developing and maintaining the cybercrime infrastructure, and one of the principal threats to online banking systems. Other forms of deception account for much of the rest of the cybercrime ecosystem, which is roughly equal to legacy crime in both volume and value.

Part of the remedy is security usability, yet research in this field was long neglected, being seen as less glamorous than cryptography or operating systems. That was a serious error on our part, and from the mid-2000s we have started to realise the importance of making it easier for ordinary people to use systems in safe ways. Since the mid-2010s we've also started to realise that we also have to make things easier for ordinary programmers; many of the security bugs that have broken real systems have been the result of tools that were just too hard to use, from cryptographic APIs that used unsafe defaults to the C programming language. Getting usability right also helps business directly: PayPal has built a $100bn business through being a safer and more convenient way to shop online[9].

In this chapter, we took a whistle-stop tour through psychology research relevant to deception and to the kinds of errors people make, and then tackled authentication as a case study. Much of the early work on security usability focused on password systems, which raise dozens of interesting questions. We now have more and more data not just on things we can measure in the lab such as guessability, memorability, and user trainability, but also on factors that can

[8]There's been pushback from users who see a ReCAPTCHA saying 'click on all images containing a helicopter' and don't want to help in military AI research. Google's own staff protested at this research too and the military program was discontinued. But other users still object to working for Google for free.

[9]Full disclosure: I consult for them.

only be observed in the field such as how real systems break, how real attacks scale and how the incentives facing different players lead to unsafe equilibria.

At the end of the first workshop on security and human behavior in 2008, the psychologist Nick Humphrey summed up a long discussion on risk. "We're all agreed," he said, "that people pay too much attention to terrorism and not enough to cybercrime. But to a psychologist this is obvious. If you want people to be more relaxed in airports, take away the tanks and guns, put in some nice sofas and Mozart in the loudspeakers, and people will relax soon enough. And if you want people to be more wary online, make everyone use Jaws as their screen saver. But that's not going to happen as the computer industry goes out of its way to make computers seem a lot less scary than they used to be." And of course governments want people to be anxious about terrorism, as it bids up the police budgets and helps politicians get re-elected. So we give people the wrong signals as well as spending our money on the wrong things. Understanding the many tensions between the demands of psychology, economics and engineering is essential to building robust systems at global scale.

Research problems

Security psychology is one of the hot topics in 2020. In the second edition of this book, I noted that the whole field of security economics had sprung into life since the first edition in 2001, and wrote 'We also need more fundamental thinking about the relationship between psychology and security'. Security usability has become a discipline too, with the annual Symposium on Usable Privacy and Security, and we've been running workshops to bring security engineers together with anthropologists, psychologists, philosophers and others who work on risk and how people cope with it.

My meta-algorithm for finding research topics is to look first at applications and then at neighbouring disciplines. An example of the first is safe usability: as safety-critical products from cars to medical devices acquire not just software and Internet connections, but complex interfaces and even their own apps, how can we design them so that they won't harm people by accident, or as a result of malice?

An example of the second, and the theme of the Workshop on Security and Human Behaviour, is what we can learn from disciplines that study how people deal with risk, ranging from anthropology and psychology to sociology, history and philosophy. Our 2020 event is hosting leading criminologists. The pandemic now suggests that maybe we should work with architects too. They're now working out how people can be physically distant but socially engaged, and their skill is understanding how form facilitates human experience and human interaction. There's more to design than just hacking code.

Further reading

The Real Hustle videos are probably the best tutorial on deception; a number of episodes are on YouTube. Meanwhile, the best book on social engineering is still Kevin Mitnick's *'The Art of Deception'* [1327]. Amit Katwala wrote a short survey of deception detection technologies [1027] while Tony Docan-Morgan has edited a 2019 handbook on the state of deception research with 51 chapters by specialists on its many aspects [569].

For how social psychology gets used and abused in marketing, the must-read book is Tim Wu's *'The Attention Merchants'* which tells the history of advertising [2052].

In the computer science literature, perhaps a good starting point is James Reason's *'Human Error'*, which tells us what the safety-critical systems community has learned from many years studying the cognate problems in their field [1592]. Then there are standard HCI texts such as [1547], while early papers on security usability appeared as [493] and on phishing appeared as [978]. As we move to a world of autonomous devices, there is a growing body of research on how we can get people to trust robots more by Disneyfication – for example, giving library robots eyes that follow the direction of travel, and making them chirp with happiness when they help a customer [1690]. Similar research on autonomous vehicles shows that people trust such vehicles more if they're given some personality, and the passengers are given some strategic control such as the ability to select routes or even just to order the car to stop.

As for behavioral economics, I get my students to read Danny Kahneman's Nobel prize lecture. For more technical detail, there's a volume of papers Danny edited just before that with Tom Gilovich and Dale Griffin [770], or the pop science book *'Thinking, Fast and Slow'* that he wrote afterwards [1007]. An alternative view, which gives the whole history of behavioral economics, is Dick Thaler's *'Misbehaving: The Making of Behavioural Economics'* [1877]. For the applications of this theory in government and elsewhere, the standard reference is Dick Thaler and Cass Sunnstein's *'Nudge'* [1879]. Dick's later second thoughts about 'Sludge' are at [1878].

For a detailed history of passwords and related mechanisms, as well as many empirical results and an analysis of statistical techniques for measuring both guessability and recall, I strongly recommend Joe Bonneau's thesis [290], a number of whose chapters ended up as papers I cited above.

Finally, if you're interested in the dark side, *'The Manipulation of Human Behavior'* by Albert Biderman and Herb Zimmer reports experiments on interrogation carried out after the Korean War with US Government funding [240]. Known as the Torturer's Bible, it describes the relative effectiveness of sensory deprivation, drugs, hypnosis, social pressure and so on when interrogating and brainwashing prisoners. As for the polygraph and other deception-detection techniques used nowadays, the standard reference is by Aldert Vrij [1974].

CHAPTER

4

Protocols

It is impossible to foresee the consequences of being clever.

– CHRISTOPHER STRACHEY

If it's provably secure, it probably isn't.

– LARS KNUDSEN

4.1 Introduction

Passwords are just one example of a more general concept, the security protocol. If security engineering has a core theme, it may be the study of security protocols. They specify the steps that principals use to establish trust relationships. They are where the cryptography and the access controls meet; they are the tools we use to link up human users with remote machines, to synchronise security contexts, and to regulate key applications such as payment. We've come across a few protocols already, including challenge-response authentication and Kerberos. In this chapter, I'll dig down into the details, and give many examples of how protocols fail.

A typical security system consists of a number of principals such as people, companies, phones, computers and card readers, which communicate using a variety of channels including fibre, wifi, the cellular network, bluetooth, infrared, and by carrying data on physical devices such as bank cards and transport tickets. The security protocols are the rules that govern these communications. They are designed so that the system will survive malicious acts such as people telling lies on the phone, hostile governments jamming radio, or forgers altering the data on train tickets. Protection against all possible attacks is often too expensive, so protocol designs make assumptions about threats. For example, when we get a user to log on by entering a password into a machine, we implicitly assume that she can enter it into the right machine. In the old days of hard-wired terminals in the workplace, this was reasonable;

now that people log on to websites over the Internet, it is much less obvious. Evaluating a protocol thus involves two questions: first, is the threat model realistic? Second, does the protocol deal with it?

Protocols may be very simple, such as swiping a badge through a reader to enter a building. They often involve interaction, and are not necessarily technical. For example, when we order a bottle of fine wine in a restaurant, the standard protocol is that the wine waiter offers us the menu (so that we see the prices but our guests don't); they bring the bottle, so we can check the label, the seal and the temperature; they open it so we can taste it; and then serve it. This has evolved to provide some privacy (our guests don't learn the price), some integrity (we can be sure we got the right bottle and that it wasn't refilled with cheap plonk) and non-repudiation (we can't complain afterwards that the wine was off). Matt Blaze gives other non-technical protocol examples from ticket inspection, aviation security and voting in [261]. Traditional protocols like these often evolved over decades or centuries to meet social expectations as well as technical threats.

At the technical end of things, protocols get a lot more complex, and they don't always get better. As the car industry moved from metal keys to electronic keys with buttons you press, theft fell, since the new keys were harder to copy. But the move to keyless entry has seen car crime rise again, as the bad guys figured out how to build relay devices that would make a key seem closer to the car than it actually was. Another security upgrade that's turned out to be tricky is the move from magnetic-strip cards to smartcards. Europe made this move in the late 2000s while the USA is only catching up in the late 2010s. Fraud against cards issued in Europe actually went up for several years; clones of European cards were used in magnetic-strip cash machines in the USA, as the two systems' protection mechanisms didn't quite mesh. And there was a protocol failure that let a thief use a stolen chipcard in a store even if he didn't know the PIN, which took the banks several years to fix.

So we need to look systematically at security protocols and how they fail.

4.2 Password eavesdropping risks

Passwords and PINs are still the foundation for much of computer security, as the main mechanism used to authenticate humans to machines. We discussed their usability in the last chapter; now let's consider the kinds of technical attack we have to block when designing protocols that operate between one machine and another.

Remote key entry is a good place to start. The early systems, such as the remote control used to open your garage or to unlock cars manufactured up to the mid-1990's, just broadcast a serial number. The attack that killed them was the 'grabber', a device that would record a code and replay it later. The first grabbers, seemingly from Taiwan, arrived on the market in about 1995; thieves would lurk in parking lots or outside a target's house, record the signal used to lock the car and then replay it once the owner had gone[1].

The first countermeasure was to use separate codes for lock and unlock. But the thief can lurk outside your house and record the unlock code before you drive away in the morning, and then come back at night and help himself. Second, sixteen-bit passwords are too short. Occasionally people found they could unlock the wrong car by mistake, or even set the alarm on a car whose owner didn't know he had one [309]. And by the mid-1990's, devices appeared that could try all possible codes one after the other. A code will be found on average after about 2^{15} tries, and at ten per second that takes under an hour. A thief operating in a parking lot with a hundred vehicles within range would be rewarded in less than a minute with a car helpfully flashing its lights.

The next countermeasure was to double the length of the password from 16 to 32 bits. The manufacturers proudly advertised 'over 4 billion codes'. But this only showed they hadn't really understood the problem. There were still only one or two codes for each car, and grabbers still worked fine.

Using a serial number as a password has a further vulnerability: lots of people have access to it. In the case of a car, this might mean all the dealer staff, and perhaps the state motor vehicle registration agency. Some burglar alarms have also used serial numbers as master passwords, and here it's even worse: when a bank buys a burglar alarm, the serial number may appear on the order, the delivery note and the invoice. And banks don't like sending someone out to buy something for cash.

Simple passwords are sometimes the appropriate technology. For example, a monthly season ticket for our local swimming pool simply has a barcode. I'm sure I could make a passable forgery, but as the turnstile attendants get to know the 'regulars', there's no need for anything more expensive. For things that are online, however, static passwords are hazardous; the Mirai botnet got going by recruiting wifi-connected CCTV cameras which had a password that couldn't be changed. And for things people want to steal, like cars, we also need something better. This brings us to cryptographic authentication protocols.

[1]With garage doors it's even worse. A common chip is the Princeton PT2262, which uses 12 tri-state pins to encode 3^{12} or 531,441 address codes. However implementers often don't read the data sheet carefully enough to understand tri-state inputs and treat them as binary instead, getting 2^{12}. Many of them only use eight inputs, as the other four are on the other side of the chip. And as the chip has no retry-lockout logic, an attacker can cycle through the combinations quickly and open your garage door after 2^7 attempts on average. Twelve years after I noted these problems in the second edition of this book, the chip has not been withdrawn. It's now also sold for home security systems and for the remote control of toys.

4.3 Who goes there? – simple authentication

A simple modern authentication device is the token that some multistorey parking garages give subscribers to raise the barrier. The token has a single button; when you press it, it first transmits its serial number and then sends an authentication block consisting of the same serial number, followed by a random number, all encrypted using a key unique to the device, and sent to the garage barrier (typically by radio at 434MHz, though infrared is also used). We will postpone discussion of how to encrypt data to the next chapter, and simply write $\{X\}_K$ for the message X encrypted under the key K.

Then the protocol between the access token and the parking garage can be written as:

$$T \rightarrow G : T, \{T, N\}_{KT}$$

This is standard protocol notation, so we'll take it slowly.

The token T sends a message to the garage G consisting of its name T followed by the encrypted value of T concatenated with N, where N stands for 'number used once', or *nonce*. Everything within the braces is encrypted, and the encryption binds T and N together as well as obscuring their values. The purpose of the nonce is to assure the recipient that the message is *fresh*, that is, it is not a replay of an old message. Verification is simple: the garage reads T, gets the corresponding key KT, deciphers the rest of the message, checks that the nonce N has not been seen before, and finally that the plaintext contains T.

One reason many people get confused is that to the left of the colon, T identifies one of the principals (the token that represents the subscriber) whereas to the right it means the name (that is, the unique device number) of the token. Another is that once we start discussing attacks on protocols, we may find that a message intended for one principal was intercepted and played back by another. So you might think of the $T \rightarrow G$ to the left of the colon as a hint as to what the protocol designer had in mind.

A *nonce* can be anything that guarantees the freshness of a message. It can be a random number, a counter, a random challenge received from a third party, or even a timestamp. There are subtle differences between them, such as in the level of resistance they offer to various kinds of replay attack, and the ways in which they increase system cost and complexity. In very low-cost systems, random numbers and counters predominate as it's cheaper to communicate in one direction only, and cheap devices usually don't have clocks.

Key management in such devices can be very simple. In a typical garage token product, each token's key is just its unique device number encrypted under a global master key KM known to the garage:

$$KT = \{T\}_{KM}$$

This is known as *key diversification* or *key derivation*. It's a common way of implementing access tokens, and is widely used in smartcards too. The goal is that someone who compromises a token by drilling into it and extracting the key cannot masquerade as any other token; all he can do is make a copy of one particular subscriber's token. In order to do a complete break of the system, and extract the master key that would enable him to pretend to be any of the system's users, an attacker has to compromise the central server at the garage (which might protect this key in a tamper-resistant smartcard or hardware security module).

But there is still room for error. A common failure mode is for the serial numbers – whether unique device numbers or protocol counters – not to be long enough, so that someone occasionally finds that their remote control works for another car in the car park as well. This can be masked by cryptography. Having 128-bit keys doesn't help if the key is derived by encrypting a 16-bit device number, or by taking a 16-bit key and repeating it eight times. In either case, there are only 2^{16} possible keys, and that's unlikely to be enough even if they appear to be random[2].

Protocol vulnerabilities usually give rise to more, and simpler, attacks than cryptographic weaknesses do. An example comes from the world of prepayment utility meters. Over a million households in the UK, plus over 400 million in developing countries, have an electricity or gas meter that accepts encrypted tokens: the householder buys a magic number and types it into the meter, which then dispenses the purchased quantity of energy. One early meter that was widely used in South Africa checked only that the nonce was different from last time. So the customer could charge their meter indefinitely by buying two low-value power tickets and then feeding them in one after the other; given two valid codes *A* and *B*, the series *ABABAB*... was seen as valid [94].

So the question of whether to use a random number or a counter is not as easy as it looks. If you use random numbers, the lock has to remember a lot of past codes. There's the *valet attack*, where someone with temporary access, such as a valet parking attendant, records some access codes and replays them later to steal your car. In addition, someone might rent a car, record enough unlock codes, and then go back later to the rental lot to steal it. Providing enough non-volatile memory to remember thousands of old codes might add a few cents to the cost of your lock.

If you opt for counters, the problem is synchronization. The key might be used for more than one lock; it may also be activated repeatedly by accident (I once took an experimental token home where it was gnawed by my dogs). So you need a way to recover after the counter has been incremented hundreds or possibly even thousands of times. One common product uses a sixteen bit

[2] We'll go into this in more detail in section 5.3.1.2 where we discuss the birthday theorem in probability theory.

counter, and allows access when the deciphered counter value is the last valid code incremented by no more than sixteen. To cope with cases where the token has been used more than sixteen times elsewhere (or gnawed by a family pet), the lock will open on a second press provided that the counter value has been incremented between 17 and 32,767 times since a valid code was entered (the counter rolls over so that 0 is the successor of 65,535). This is fine in many applications, but a thief who can get six well-chosen access codes – say for values 0, 1, 20,000, 20,001, 40,000 and 40,001 – can break the system completely. In your application, would you be worried about that?

So designing even a simple token authentication mechanism is not as easy as it looks, and if you assume that your product will only attract low-grade adversaries, this assumption might fail over time. An example is *accessory control*. Many printer companies embed authentication mechanisms in printers to ensure that genuine toner cartridges are used. If a competitor's product is loaded instead, the printer may quietly downgrade from 1200 dpi to 300 dpi, or simply refuse to work at all. All sorts of other industries are getting in on the act, from scientific instruments to games consoles. The cryptographic mechanisms used to support this started off in the 1990s being fairly rudimentary, as vendors thought that any competitor who circumvented them on an industrial scale could be sued or even jailed under copyright law. But then a judge found that while a vendor had the right to hire the best cryptographer they could find to lock their customers in, a competitor also had the right to hire the best cryptanalyst they could find to set them free to buy accessories from elsewhere. This set off a serious arms race, which we'll discuss in section 24.6. Here I'll just remark that security isn't always a good thing. Security mechanisms are used to support many business models, where they're typically stopping the device's owner doing things she wants to rather than protecting her from the bad guys. The effect may be contrary to public policy; one example is cellphone locking, which results in hundreds of millions of handsets ending up in landfills each year, with toxic heavy metals as well as the embedded carbon cost.

4.3.1 Challenge and response

Since 1995, all cars sold in Europe were required to have a 'cryptographically enabled immobiliser' and by 2010, most cars had remote-controlled door unlocking too, though most also have a fallback metal key so you can still get into your car even if the key fob battery is flat. The engine immobiliser is harder to bypass using physical means and uses a two-pass *challenge-response protocol* to authorise engine start. As the car key is inserted into the steering lock, the engine controller sends a challenge consisting of a random n-bit number to the key using short-range radio. The car key computes a response by encrypting the challenge; this is often done by a separate RFID chip that's powered by the incoming radio signal and so keeps on working even if the battery is flat. The frequency is low (125kHz) so the car can power the transponder directly, and the exchange is also relatively immune to a noisy RF environment.

Writing E for the engine controller, T for the transponder in the car key, K for the cryptographic key shared between the transponder and the engine controller, and N for the random challenge, the protocol may look something like:

$$\begin{aligned} E \rightarrow T: &\quad N \\ T \rightarrow E: &\quad T, \{T, N\}_K \end{aligned}$$

This is sound in theory, but implementations of security mechanisms often fail the first two or three times people try it.

Between 2005 and 2015, all the main remote key entry and immobiliser systems were broken, whether by security researchers, car thieves or both. The attacks involved a combination of protocol errors, poor key management, weak ciphers, and short keys mandated by export control laws.

The first to fall was TI's DST transponder chip, which was used by at least two large car makers and was also the basis of the SpeedPass toll payment system. Stephen Bono and colleagues found in 2005 that it used a block cipher with a 40-bit key, which could be calculated by brute force from just two responses [298]. This was one side-effect of US cryptography export controls, which I discuss in 26.2.7.1. From 2010, Ford, Toyota and Hyundai adopted a successor product, the DST80. The DST80 was broken in turn in 2020 by Lennert Wouters and colleagues, who found that as well as side-channel attacks on the chip, there are serious implementation problems with key management: Hyundai keys have only 24 bits of entropy, while Toyota keys are derived from the device serial number that an attacker can read (Tesla was also vulnerable but unlike the older firms it could fix the problem with a software upgrade) [2050]. Next was Keeloq, which was used for garage door openers as well as by some car makers; in 2007, Eli Biham and others found that given an hour's access to a token they could collect enough data to recover the key [244]. Worse, in some types of car, there is also a protocol bug, in that the key diversification used exclusive-or: $KT = T \oplus KM$. So you can rent a car of the type you want to steal and work out the key for any other car of that type.

Also in 2007, someone published the Philips Hitag 2 cipher, which also had a 48-bit secret key. But this cipher is also weak, and as it was attacked by various cryptanalysts, the time needed to extract a key fell from days to hours to minutes. By 2016, attacks took 8 authentication attempts and a minute of computation on a laptop; they worked against cars from all the French and Italian makers, along with Nissan, Mitsubishi and Chevrolet [748].

The last to fall was the Megamos Crypto transponder, used by Volkswagen and others. Car locksmithing tools appeared on the market from 2008, which included the Megamos cipher and were reverse engineered by researchers from Birmingham and Nijmegen – Roel Verdult, Flavio Garcia and Barış Ege – who cracked it [1956]. Although it has a 96-bit secret key, the effective key length is only 49 bits, about the same as Hitag 2. Volkswagen got an injunction in the High Court in London to stop them presenting their work at Usenix 2013, claiming that their trade secrets had been violated. The researchers resisted, arguing that the locksmithing tool supplier had extracted the secrets. After two years of argument, the case settled without admission of liability on either side. Closer study then threw up a number of further problems. There's also a protocol attack as an adversary can rewrite each 16-bit word of the 96-bit key, one after another, and search for the key 16 bits at a time; this reduces the time needed for an attack from days to minutes [1957].

Key management was pervasively bad. A number of Volkswagen implementations did not diversify keys across cars and transponders, but used a fixed global master key for millions of cars at a time. Up till 2009, this used a cipher called AUT64 to generate device keys; thereafter they moved to a stronger cipher called XTEA but kept on using global master keys, which were found in 23 models from the Volkswagen-Audi group up till 2016 [748][3].

It's easy to find out if a car is vulnerable: just try to buy a spare key. If the locksmith companies have figured out how to duplicate the key, your local garage will sell you a spare for a few bucks. We have a spare key for my wife's 2005 Lexus, bought by the previous owner. But when we lost one of the keys for my 2012 Mercedes, we had to go to a main dealer, pay over £200, show my passport and the car log book, have the mechanic photograph the vehicle identification number on the chassis, send it all off to Mercedes and wait for a week. We saw in Chapter 3 that the hard part of designing a password system was recovering from compromise without the recovery mechanism itself becoming either a vulnerability or a nuisance. Exactly the same applies here!

But the worst was still to come: passive keyless entry systems (PKES). Challenge-response seemed so good that car vendors started using it with just a push button on the dashboard to start the car, rather than with a metal key. Then they increased the radio frequency to extend the range, so that it worked not just for short-range authentication once the driver was sitting in the car, but as a keyless entry mechanism. The marketing pitch was that so long as

[3]There are some applications where universal master keys are inevitable, such as in communicating with a heart pacemaker – where a cardiologist may need to tweak the pacemaker of any patient who walks in, regardless of where it was first fitted, and regardless of whether the network's up – so the vendor puts the same key in all its equipment. Another example is the subscriber smartcard in a satellite-TV set-top box, which we'll discuss later. But they often result in a break-once-run-anywhere (BORA) attack. To install universal master keys in valuable assets like cars in a way that facilitated theft and without even using proper tamper-resistant chips to protect them was an egregious error.

you keep the key in your pocket or handbag you don't have to worry about it; the car will unlock when you walk up to it, lock as you walk away, and start automatically when you touch the controls. What's not to like?

Well, now you don't have to press a button to unlock your car, it's easy for thieves to use devices that amplify or relay the signals. The thief sneaks up to your front door with one relay while leaving the other next to your car. If you left your keys on the table in the hall, the car door opens and away he goes. Even if the car is immobilised he can still steal your stuff. And after many years of falling car thefts, the statistics surged in 2017 with 56% more vehicles stolen in the UK, followed by a further 9% in 2018 [824][4].

The takeaway message is that the attempt since about 1990 to use cryptography to make cars harder to steal had some initial success, as immobilisers made cars harder to steal and insurance premiums fell. It has since backfired, as the politicians and then the marketing people got in the way. The politicians said it would be disastrous for law enforcement if people were allowed to use cryptography they couldn't crack, even for stopping car theft. Then the immobiliser vendors' marketing people wanted proprietary algorithms to lock in the car companies, whose own marketing people wanted passive keyless entry as it seemed cool.

What can we do? Well, at least two car makers have put an accelerometer in the key fob, so it won't work unless the key is moving. One of our friends left her key on the car seat while carrying her child indoors, and got locked out. The local police advise us to use old-fashioned metal steering-wheel locks; our residents' association recommends keeping keys in a biscuit tin. As for me, we bought such a car but found that the keyless entry was simply too flaky; my wife got stranded in a supermarket car park when it just wouldn't work at all. So we took that car back, and got a second-hand one with a proper push-button remote lock. There are now chips using AES from NXP, Atmel and TI – of which the Atmel is open source with an open protocol stack.

However crypto by itself can't fix relay attacks; the proper fix is a new radio protocol based on ultrawideband (UWB) with intrinsic ranging, which measures the distance from the key fob to the car with a precision of 10cm up to a range of 150m. This is fairly complex to do properly, and the design of the new 802.15.4z Enhanced Impulse Radio is described by Srdjan Capkun and colleagues [1768]; the first chip became available in 2019, and it will ship in cars from 2020. Such chips have the potential to replace both the Bluetooth and NFC protocols, but they might not all be compatible; there's a low-rate pulse (LRP) mode that has an open design, and a high-rate pulse (HRP) variant that's partly proprietary. Were I advising a car startup, LRP would be my starting point.

[4]To be fair this was not due solely to relay attacks, as about half of the high-value thefts seem to involve connecting a car theft kit to the onboard diagnostic port under the glove box. As it happens, the authentication protocols used on the CAN bus inside the vehicle are also vulnerable in a number of ways [893]. Updating these protocols will take many years because of the huge industry investment.

Locks are not the only application of challenge-response protocols. In HTTP Digest Authentication, a web server challenges a client or proxy, with whom it shares a password, by sending it a nonce. The response consists of the hash of the nonce, the password, and the requested URI [715]. This provides a mechanism that's not vulnerable to password snooping. It's used, for example, to authenticate clients and servers in SIP, the protocol for Voice-Over-IP (VOIP) telephony. It's much better than sending a password in the clear, but like keyless entry it suffers from middleperson attacks (the beneficiaries seem to be mostly intelligence agencies).

4.3.2 Two-factor authentication

The most visible use of challenge-response is probably in *two-factor authentication*. Many organizations issue their staff with password generators to let them log on to corporate computer systems, and many banks give similar devices to customers. They may look like little calculators (and some even work as such) but their main function is as follows. When you want to log in, you are presented with a random nonce of maybe seven digits. You key this into your password generator, together with a PIN of maybe four digits. The device encrypts these eleven digits using a secret key shared with the corporate security server, and displays the first seven digits of the result. You enter these seven digits as your password. This protocol is illustrated in Figure 4.1. If you had a password generator with the right secret key, and you entered the PIN right, and you typed in the result correctly, then you get in.

Formally, with S for the server, P for the password generator, PIN for the user's Personal Identification Number, U for the user and N for the nonce:

$$\begin{aligned} S \rightarrow U &: \quad N \\ U \rightarrow P &: \quad N, PIN \\ P \rightarrow U &: \quad \{N, PIN\}_K \\ U \rightarrow S &: \quad \{N, PIN\}_K \end{aligned}$$

These devices appeared from the early 1980s and caught on first with phone companies, then in the 1990s with banks for use by staff. There are simplified versions that don't have a keyboard, but just generate new access codes by encrypting a counter or a clock. And they work; the US Defense Department announced in 2007 that an authentication system based on the DoD Common Access Card had cut network intrusions by 46% in the previous year [321].

This was just when crooks started phishing bank customers at scale, so many banks adopted the technology. One of my banks gives me a small calculator that generates a new code for each logon, and also allows me to authenticate new payees by using the last four digits of their account number in place of the challenge. My other bank uses the Chip Authentication Program (CAP), a calculator in which I can insert my bank card to do the crypto.

Figure 4.1: Password generator use

But this still isn't foolproof. In the second edition of this book, I noted 'someone who takes your bank card from you at knifepoint can now verify that you've told them the right PIN', and this now happens. I also noted that 'once lots of banks use one-time passwords, the phishermen will just rewrite their scripts to do real-time man-in-the-middle attacks' and this has also become widespread. To see how such attacks work, let's look at a military example.

4.3.3 The MIG-in-the-middle attack

The first use of challenge-response authentication protocols was probably in the military, with 'identify-friend-or-foe' (IFF) systems. The ever-increasing speeds of warplanes in the 1930s and 1940s, together with the invention of the jet engine, radar and rocketry, made it ever more difficult for air defence forces to tell their own craft apart from the enemy's. This led to a risk of pilots shooting down their colleagues by mistake and drove the development of automatic systems to prevent this. These were first fielded in World War II, and enabled an airplane illuminated by radar to broadcast an identifying number to signal friendly intent. In 1952, this system was adopted to identify civil aircraft to air traffic controllers and, worried about the loss of security once it became widely used, the US Air Force started a research program to incorporate cryptographic protection in the system. Nowadays, the typical air defense system sends random challenges with its radar signals, and friendly aircraft can identify themselves with correct responses.

It's tricky to design a good IFF system. One of the problems is illustrated by the following story, which I heard from an officer in the South African Air Force (SAAF). After it was published in the first edition of this book, the story was disputed – as I'll discuss below. Be that as it may, similar games have been played with other electronic warfare systems since World War 2. The 'MIG-in-the-middle' story has since become part of the folklore, and it nicely illustrates how attacks can be carried out in real time on challenge-response protocols.

In the late 1980's, South African troops were fighting a war in northern Namibia and southern Angola. Their goals were to keep Namibia under white rule, and impose a client government (UNITA) on Angola. Because the South African Defence Force consisted largely of conscripts from a small white population, it was important to limit casualties, so most South African soldiers remained in Namibia on policing duties while the fighting to the north was done by UNITA troops. The role of the SAAF was twofold: to provide tactical support to UNITA by bombing targets in Angola, and to ensure that the Angolans and their Cuban allies did not return the compliment in Namibia.

Suddenly, the Cubans broke through the South African air defenses and carried out a bombing raid on a South African camp in northern Namibia, killing a number of white conscripts. This proof that their air supremacy had been lost helped the Pretoria government decide to hand over Namibia to the insurgents –itself a huge step on the road to majority rule in South Africa several years later. The raid may also have been the last successful military operation ever carried out by Soviet bloc forces.

Some years afterwards, a SAAF officer told me how the Cubans had pulled it off. Several MIGs had loitered in southern Angola, just north of the South African air defense belt, until a flight of SAAF Impala bombers raided a target in Angola. Then the MIGs turned sharply and flew openly through the SAAF's air defenses, which sent IFF challenges. The MIGs relayed them to the Angolan air defense batteries, which transmitted them at a SAAF bomber; the responses were relayed back to the MIGs, who retransmitted them and were allowed through – as in Figure 4.2. According to my informant, this shocked the general staff in Pretoria. Being not only outfought by black opponents, but actually outsmarted, was not consistent with the world view they had held up till then.

After this tale was published in the first edition of my book, I was contacted by a former officer in SA Communications Security Agency who disputed the story's details. He said that their IFF equipment did not use cryptography yet at the time of the Angolan war, and was always switched off over enemy territory. Thus, he said, any electronic trickery must have been of a more primitive kind. However, others tell me that 'Mig-in-the-middle' tricks were significant in Korea, Vietnam and various Middle Eastern conflicts.

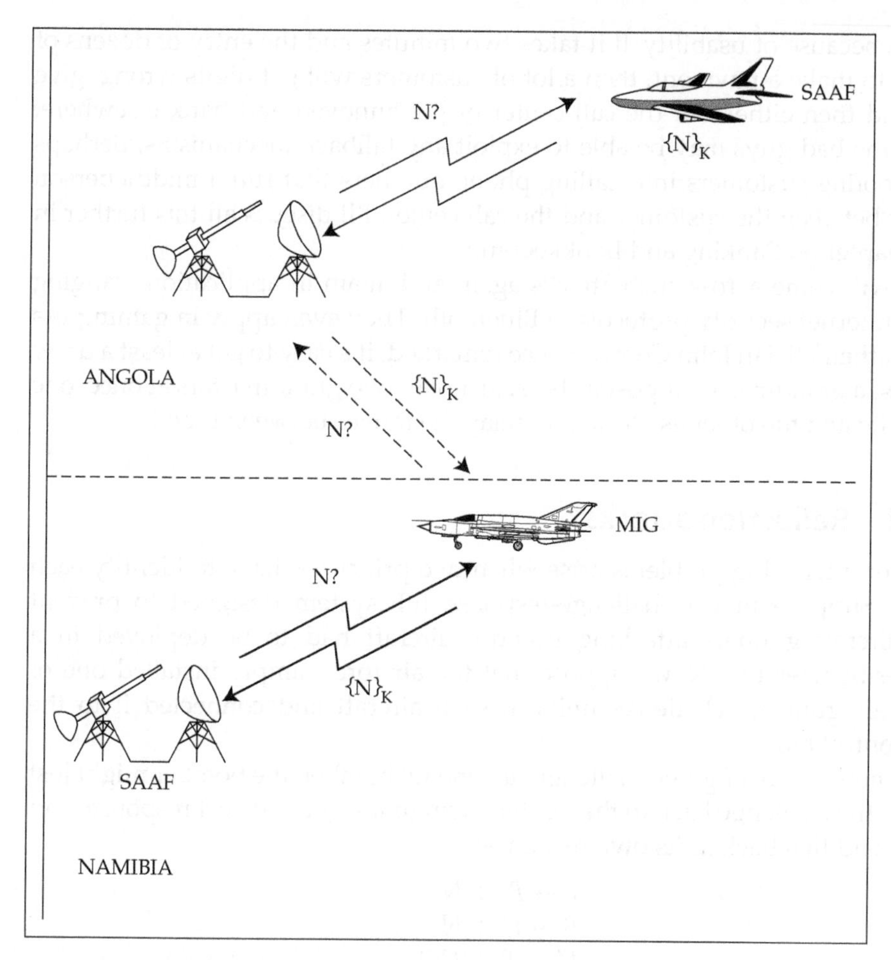

Figure 4.2: The MIG-in-the middle attack

In any case, the tale gives us another illustration of the man-in-the-middle attack. The relay attack against cars is another example. It also works against password calculators: the phishing site invites the mark to log on and simultaneously opens a logon session with his bank. The bank sends a challenge; the phisherman relays this to the mark, who uses his device to respond to it; the phisherman relays the response to the bank, and the bank now accepts the phisherman as the mark.

Stopping a middleperson attack is harder than it looks, and may involve multiple layers of defence. Banks typically look for a known machine, a password, a second factor such as an authentication code from a CAP reader, and a risk assessment of the transaction. For high-risk transactions, such as adding a new payee to an account, both my banks demand that I compute an authentication code on the payee account number. But they only authenticate the last four digits, because of usability. If it takes two minutes and the entry of dozens of digits to make a payment, then a lot of customers will get digits wrong, give up, and then either call the call center or get annoyed and bank elsewhere. Also, the bad guys may be able to exploit any fallback mechanisms, perhaps by spoofing customers into calling phone numbers that run a middleperson attack between the customer and the call center. I'll discuss all this further in the chapter on Banking and Bookkeeping.

We will come across such attacks again and again in applications ranging from Internet security protocols to Bluetooth. They even apply in gaming. As the mathematician John Conway once remarked, it's easy to get at least a draw against a grandmaster at postal chess: just play two grandmasters at once, one as white and the other as black, and relay the moves between them!

4.3.4 Reflection attacks

Further interesting problems arise when two principals have to identify each other. Suppose that a challenge-response IFF system designed to prevent anti-aircraft gunners attacking friendly aircraft had to be deployed in a fighter-bomber too. Now suppose that the air force simply installed one of their air gunners' challenge units in each aircraft and connected it to the fire-control radar.

But now when a fighter challenges an enemy bomber, the bomber might just reflect the challenge back to the fighter's wingman, get a correct response, and then send that back as its own response:

$$\begin{aligned} F \rightarrow B &: N \\ B \rightarrow F' &: N \\ F' \rightarrow B &: \{N\}_K \\ B \rightarrow F &: \{N\}_K \end{aligned}$$

There are a number of ways of stopping this, such as including the names of the two parties in the exchange. In the above example, we might require a friendly bomber to reply to the challenge:

$$F \rightarrow B : N$$

with a response such as:

$$B \rightarrow F : \{B, N\}_K$$

Thus a reflected response $\{F', N\}$ from the wingman F' could be detected[5].

This serves to illustrate the subtlety of the trust assumptions that underlie authentication. If you send out a challenge N and receive, within 20 milliseconds, a response $\{N\}_K$, then – since light can travel a bit under 3,730 miles in 20 ms – you know that there is someone with the key K within 2000 miles.

[5]And don't forget: you also have to check that the intruder didn't just reflect your own challenge back at you. You must be able to remember or recognise your own messages!

But that's all you know. If you can be sure that the response was not computed using your own equipment, you now know that there is someone *else* with the key K within two thousand miles. If you make the further assumption that all copies of the key K are securely held in equipment which may be trusted to operate properly, and you see $\{B, N\}_K$, you might be justified in deducing that the aircraft with callsign B is within 2000 miles. A careful analysis of trust assumptions and their consequences is at the heart of security protocol design.

By now you might think that we understand all the protocol design aspects of IFF. But we've omitted one of the most important problems – and one which the designers of early IFF systems didn't anticipate. As radar is passive the returns are weak, while IFF is active and so the signal from an IFF transmitter will usually be audible at a much greater range than the same aircraft's radar return. The Allies learned this the hard way; in January 1944, decrypts of Enigma messages revealed that the Germans were plotting British and American bombers at twice the normal radar range by interrogating their IFF. So more modern systems authenticate the challenge as well as the response. The NATO mode XII, for example, has a 32 bit encrypted challenge, and a different valid challenge is generated for every interrogation signal, of which there are typically 250 per second. Theoretically there is no need to switch off over enemy territory, but in practice an enemy who can record valid challenges can replay them as part of an attack. Relays are made difficult in mode XII using directionality and time-of-flight.

Other IFF design problems include the difficulties posed by neutrals, error rates in dense operational environments, how to deal with equipment failure, how to manage keys, and how to cope with multinational coalitions. I'll return to IFF in Chapter 23. For now, the spurious-challenge problem serves to reinforce an important point: that the correctness of a security protocol depends on the assumptions made about the requirements. A protocol that can protect against one kind of attack (being shot down by your own side) but which increases the exposure to an even more likely attack (being shot down by the other side) might not help. In fact, the spurious-challenge problem became so serious in World War II that some experts advocated abandoning IFF altogether, rather than taking the risk that one bomber pilot in a formation of hundreds would ignore orders and leave his IFF switched on while over enemy territory.

4.4 Manipulating the message

We've now seen a number of middleperson attacks that reflect or spoof the information used to authenticate a participant. However, there are more complex attacks where the attacker doesn't just impersonate someone, but manipulates the message content.

One example we saw already is the prepayment meter that remembers only the last ticket it saw, so it can be recharged without limit by copying in the codes from two tickets *A* and *B* one after another: *ABABAB*.... Another is when dishonest cabbies insert pulse generators in the cable that connects their taximeter to a sensor in their taxi's gearbox. The sensor sends pulses as the prop shaft turns, which lets the meter work out how far the taxi has gone. A pirate device can insert extra pulses, making the taxi appear to have gone further. A truck driver who wants to drive faster or further than regulations allow can use a similar device to discard some pulses, so he seems to have been driving more slowly or not at all. We'll discuss such attacks in the chapter on 'Monitoring Systems', in section 14.3.

As well as monitoring systems, control systems often need to be hardened against message-manipulation attacks. The Intelsat satellites used for international telephone and data traffic have mechanisms to prevent a command being accepted twice – otherwise an attacker could replay control traffic and repeatedly order the same maneuver to be carried out until the satellite ran out of fuel [1529]. We will see lots of examples of protocol attacks involving message manipulation in later chapters on specific applications.

4.5 Changing the environment

A common cause of protocol failure is that the environment changes, so that the design assumptions no longer hold and the security protocols cannot cope with the new threats.

A nice example comes from the world of cash machine fraud. In 1993, Holland suffered an epidemic of 'phantom withdrawals'; there was much controversy in the press, with the banks claiming that their systems were secure while many people wrote in to the papers claiming to have been cheated. Eventually the banks noticed that many of the victims had used their bank cards at a certain filling station near Utrecht. This was staked out and one of the staff was arrested. It turned out that he had tapped the line from the card reader to the PC that controlled it; his tap recorded the magnetic stripe details from their cards while he used his eyeballs to capture their PINs [55]. Exactly the same fraud happened in the UK after the move to 'chip and PIN' smartcards in the mid-2000s; a gang wiretapped perhaps 200 filling stations, collected card data from the wire, observed the PINs using CCTV cameras, then made up thousands of magnetic-strip clone cards that were used in countries whose ATMs still used magnetic strip technology. At our local filling station, over 200 customers suddenly found that their cards had been used in ATMs in Thailand.

Why had the system been designed so badly, and why did the design error persist for over a decade through a major technology change? Well, when the standards for managing magnetic stripe cards and PINs were developed in the early 1980's by organizations such as IBM and VISA, the engineers had made two assumptions. The first was that the contents of the magnetic strip – the card number, version number and expiration date – were not secret, while the PIN was [1303]. (The analogy used was that the magnetic strip was your name and the PIN your password.) The second assumption was that bank card equipment would only be operated in trustworthy environments, such as in a physically robust automatic teller machine, or by a bank clerk at a teller station. So it was 'clearly' only necessary to encrypt the PIN, on its way from the PIN pad to the server; the magnetic strip data could be sent in clear from the card reader.

Both of these assumptions had changed by 1993. An epidemic of card forgery, mostly in the Far East in the late 1980's, drove banks to introduce authentication codes on the magnetic strips. Also, the commercial success of the bank card industry led banks in many countries to extend the use of debit cards from ATMs to terminals in all manner of shops. The combination of these two environmental changes destroyed the assumptions behind the original system architecture. Instead of putting a card whose magnetic strip contained no security data into a trusted machine, people were putting a card with clear security data into an untrusted machine. These changes had come about so gradually, and over such a long period, that the industry didn't see the problem coming.

4.6 Chosen protocol attacks

Governments keen to push ID cards have tried to get them used for many other transactions; some want a single card to be used for ID, banking and even transport ticketing. Singapore went so far as to experiment with a bank card that doubled as military ID. This introduced some interesting new risks: if a Navy captain tries to withdraw some cash from an ATM after a good dinner and forgets his PIN, will he be unable to take his ship to sea until Monday morning when they open the bank and give him his card back?

Some firms are pushing multifunction authentication devices that could be used in a wide range of transactions to save you having to carry around dozens of different cards and keys. A more realistic view of the future may be that people's phones will be used for most private-sector authentication functions.

But this too may not be as simple as it looks. The idea behind the 'Chosen Protocol Attack' is that given a target protocol, you design a new protocol that will attack it if the users can be inveigled into reusing the same token or crypto key. So how might the Mafia design a protocol to attack the authentication of bank transactions?

Here's one approach. It used to be common for people visiting a porn website to be asked for 'proof of age,' which usually involves giving a credit card number, whether to the site itself or to an age checking service. If smartphones are used to authenticate everything, it would be natural for the porn site to ask the customer to authenticate a random challenge as proof of age. A porn site might then mount a 'Mafia-in-the-middle' attack as shown in Figure 4.3. They wait until an unsuspecting customer visits their site, then order something resellable (such as gold coins) from a dealer, playing the role of the coin dealer's customer. When the coin dealer sends them the transaction data for authentication, they relay it through their porn site to the waiting customer. The poor man OKs it, the Mafia gets the gold coins, and when thousands of people suddenly complain about the huge charges to their cards at the end of the month, the porn site has vanished – along with the gold [1034].

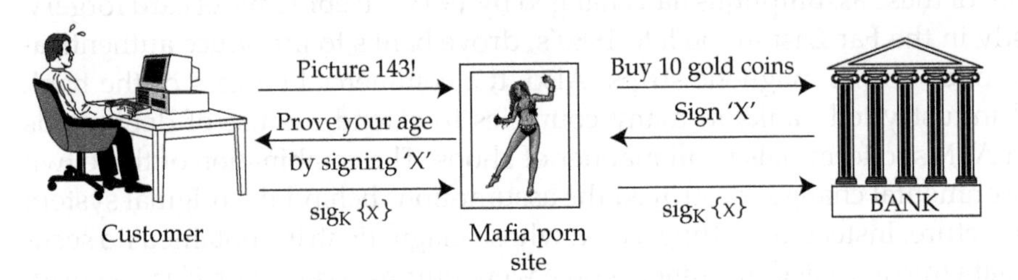

Figure 4.3: The Mafia-in-the-middle attack

In the 1990s a vulnerability of this kind found its way into international standards: the standards for digital signature and authentication could be run back-to-back in this way. It has since been shown that many protocols, though secure in themselves, can be broken if their users can be inveigled into reusing the same keys in other applications [1034]. This is why, if we're going to use our phones to authenticate everything, it will be really important to keep the banking apps and the porn apps separate. That will be the subject in Chapter 6 on Access Control.

In general, using crypto keys (or other authentication mechanisms) in more than one application is dangerous, while letting other people bootstrap their own application security off yours can be downright foolish. The classic case is where a bank relies for two-factor authentication on sending SMSes to customers as authentication codes. As I discussed in section 3.4.1, the bad guys have learned to attack that system by SIM-swap fraud – pretending to the phone company that they're the target, claiming to have lost their phone, and getting a replacement SIM card.

4.7 Managing encryption keys

The examples of security protocols that we've discussed so far are mostly about authenticating a principal's name, or application data such as the impulses driving a taximeter. There is one further class of authentication protocols that is very important – the protocols used to manage cryptographic keys.

4.7.1 The resurrecting duckling

In the Internet of Things, keys can sometimes be managed directly and physically, by local setup and a policy of *trust-on-first-use* or TOFU.

Vehicles provided an early example. I mentioned above that crooked taxi drivers used to put interruptors in the cable from their car's gearbox sensor to the taximeter, to add additional mileage. The same problem happened in reverse with tachographs, the devices used by trucks to monitor drivers' hours and speed. When tachographs went digital in the late 1990s, we decided to encrypt the pulse train from the sensor. But how could keys be managed? The solution was that whenever a new tachograph is powered up after a factory reset, it trusts the first crypto key it receives over the sensor cable. I'll discuss this further in section 14.3.

A second example is Homeplug AV, the standard used to encrypt data communications over domestic power lines, and widely used in LAN extenders. In the default, 'just-works' mode, a new Homeplug device trusts the first key it sees; and if your new wifi extender mates with the neighbour's wifi instead, you just press the reset button and try again. There is also a 'secure mode' where you open a browser to the network management node and manually enter a crypto key printed on the device packaging, but when we designed the Homeplug protocol we realised that most people have no reason to bother with that [1439].

The TOFU approach is also known as the 'resurrecting duckling' after an analysis that Frank Stajano and I did in the context of pairing medical devices [1822]. The idea is that when a baby duckling hatches, it imprints on the first thing it sees that moves and quacks, even if this is the farmer – who can end up being followed everywhere by a duck that thinks he's mummy. If such false imprinting happens with an electronic device, you need a way to kill it and resurrect it into a newborn state – which the reset button does in a device such as a LAN extender.

4.7.2 Remote key management

The more common, and interesting, case is the management of keys in remote devices. The basic technology was developed from the late 1970s to manage keys in distributed computer systems, with cash machines being an early application. In this section we'll discuss shared-key protocols such as Kerberos, leaving public-key protocols such as TLS and SSH until after we've discussed public-key cryptology in Chapter 5.

The basic idea behind key-distribution protocols is that where two principals want to communicate, they may use a trusted third party to introduce them. It's customary to give them human names in order to avoid getting lost in too much algebra. So we will call the two communicating principals 'Alice' and 'Bob', and the trusted third party 'Sam'. Alice, Bob and Sam are likely to be programs running on different devices. (For example, in a protocol to let a car dealer mate a replacement key with a car, Alice might be the car, Bob the key and Sam the car maker.)

A simple authentication protocol could run as follows.

1. Alice first calls Sam and asks for a key for communicating with Bob.
2. Sam responds by sending Alice a pair of certificates. Each contains a copy of a key, the first encrypted so only Alice can read it, and the second encrypted so only Bob can read it.
3. Alice then calls Bob and presents the second certificate as her introduction. Each of them decrypts the appropriate certificate under the key they share with Sam and thereby gets access to the new key. Alice can now use the key to send encrypted messages to Bob, and to receive messages from him in return.

We've seen that replay attacks are a known problem, so in order that both Bob and Alice can check that the certificates are fresh, Sam may include a timestamp in each of them. If certificates never expire, there might be serious problems dealing with users whose privileges have been revoked.

Using our protocol notation, we could describe this as

$$\begin{aligned} A \rightarrow S: &\quad A, B \\ S \rightarrow A: &\quad \{A, B, K_{AB}, T\}_{K_{AS}}, \{A, B, K_{AB}, T\}_{K_{BS}} \\ A \rightarrow B: &\quad \{A, B, K_{AB}, T\}_{K_{BS}}, \{M\}_{K_{AB}} \end{aligned}$$

Expanding the notation, Alice calls Sam and says she'd like to talk to Bob. Sam makes up a message consisting of Alice's name, Bob's name, a session key for them to use, and a timestamp. He encrypts all this under the key he shares with Alice, and he encrypts another copy of it under the key he shares with Bob. He gives both ciphertexts to Alice. Alice retrieves the session key from the ciphertext that was encrypted to her, and passes on to Bob the ciphertext encrypted for him. She now sends him whatever message she wanted to send, encrypted using this session key.

4.7.3 The Needham-Schroeder protocol

Many things can go wrong, and here is a famous historical example. Many existing key distribution protocols are derived from the Needham-Schroeder protocol, which appeared in 1978 [1428]. It is somewhat similar to the above, but uses nonces rather than timestamps. It runs as follows:

$$\begin{aligned} &\text{Message 1} \quad A \rightarrow S: \quad A, B, N_A \\ &\text{Message 2} \quad S \rightarrow A: \quad \{N_A, B, K_{AB}, \{K_{AB}, A\}_{K_{BS}}\}_{K_{AS}} \\ &\text{Message 3} \quad A \rightarrow B: \quad \{K_{AB}, A\}_{K_{BS}} \\ &\text{Message 4} \quad B \rightarrow A: \quad \{N_B\}_{K_{AB}} \\ &\text{Message 5} \quad A \rightarrow B: \quad \{N_B - 1\}_{K_{AB}} \end{aligned}$$

Here Alice takes the initiative, and tells Sam: 'I'm Alice, I want to talk to Bob, and my random nonce is N_A.' Sam provides her with a session key, encrypted using the key she shares with him. This ciphertext also contains her nonce so she can confirm it's not a replay. He also gives her a certificate to convey this key to Bob. She passes it to Bob, who then does a challenge-response to check that she is present and alert.

There is a subtle problem with this protocol – Bob has to assume that the key K_{AB} he receives from Sam (via Alice) is fresh. This is not necessarily so: Alice could have waited a year between steps 2 and 3. In many applications this may not be important; it might even help Alice to cache keys against possible server failures. But if an opponent – say Charlie – ever got hold of Alice's key, he could use it to set up session keys with many other principals. And if Alice ever got fired, then Sam had better have a list of everyone in the firm to whom he issued a key for communicating with her, to tell them not to believe it any more. In other words, revocation is a problem: Sam may have to keep complete logs of everything he's ever done, and these logs would grow in size forever unless the principals' names expired at some fixed time in the future.

Almost 40 years later, this example is still controversial. The simplistic view is that Needham and Schroeder just got it wrong; the view argued by Susan Pancho and Dieter Gollmann (for which I have some sympathy) is that this is a protocol failure brought on by shifting assumptions [781, 1493]. 1978 was a kinder, gentler world; computer security then concerned itself with keeping 'bad guys' out, while nowadays we expect the 'enemy' to be among the users of our system. The Needham-Schroeder paper assumed that all principals behave themselves, and that all attacks came from outsiders [1428]. Under those assumptions, the protocol remains sound.

4.7.4 Kerberos

The most important practical derivative of the Needham-Schroeder protocol is Kerberos, a distributed access control system that originated at MIT and is now one of the standard network authentication tools [1829]. It has become part of the basic mechanics of authentication for both Windows and Linux, particularly when machines share resources over a local area network. Instead of a single trusted third party, Kerberos has two kinds: authentication servers to which users log on, and ticket granting servers which give them tickets allowing access to various resources such as files. This enables scalable access management. In a university, for example, one might manage students through their colleges or halls of residence but manage file servers by departments; in a company, the personnel people might register users to the payroll system while departmental administrators manage resources such as servers and printers.

First, Alice logs on to the authentication server using a password. The client software in her PC fetches a ticket from this server that is encrypted under her password and that contains a session key K_{AS}. Assuming she gets the password right, she now controls K_{AS} and to get access to a resource B controlled by the ticket granting server S, the following protocol takes place. Its outcome is a key K_{AB} with timestamp T_S and lifetime L, which will be used to authenticate Alice's subsequent traffic with that resource:

$$\begin{aligned} A \rightarrow S: &\quad A, B \\ S \rightarrow A: &\quad \{T_S, L, K_{AB}, B, \{T_S, L, K_{AB}, A\}_{K_{BS}}\}_{K_{AS}} \\ A \rightarrow B: &\quad \{T_S, L, K_{AB}, A\}_{K_{BS}}, \{A, T_A\}_{K_{AB}} \\ B \rightarrow A: &\quad \{T_A + 1\}_{K_{AB}} \end{aligned}$$

Translating this into English: Alice asks the ticket granting server for access to B. If this is permissible, the ticket $\{T_S, L, K_{AB}, A\}_{K_{BS}}$ is created containing a suitable key K_{AB} and given to Alice to use. She also gets a copy of the key in a form readable by her, namely encrypted under K_{AS}. She now verifies the ticket by sending a timestamp T_A to the resource, which confirms it's alive by sending back the timestamp incremented by one (this shows it was able to decrypt the ticket correctly and extract the key K_{AB}).

The revocation issue with the Needham-Schroeder protocol has been fixed by introducing timestamps rather than random nonces. But, as in most of life, we get little in security for free. There is now a new vulnerability, namely that the clocks on our various clients and servers might get out of sync; they might even be desynchronized deliberately as part of a more complex attack.

What's more, Kerberos is a *trusted third-party* (TTP) protocol in that S is trusted: if the police turn up with a warrant, they can get Sam to turn over the keys and read the traffic. Protocols with this feature were favoured during the 'crypto wars' of the 1990s, as I will discuss in section 26.2.7. Protocols that involve no or less trust in a third party generally use public-key cryptography, which I describe in the next chapter.

A rather similar protocol to Kerberos is OAuth, a mechanism to allow secure delegation. For example, if you log into Doodle using Google and allow Doodle to update your Google calendar, Doodle's website redirects you to Google, which gets you to log in (or relies on a master cookie from a previous login) and asks you for consent for Doodle to write to your calendar. Doodle then gives you an access token for the calendar service [864]. I mentioned in section 3.4.9.3 that this poses a cross-site phishing risk. OAuth was not designed for user authentication, and access tokens are not strongly bound to clients. It's a complex framework within which delegation mechanisms can be built, with both short-term and long-term access tokens; the details are tied up with how cookies and web redirects operate and optimised to enable servers to be stateless, so they scale well for modern web services. In the example above, you want to be able to revoke Doodle's access at Google, so behind the scenes Doodle only gets short-lived access tokens. Because of this complexity, the OpenID Connect protocol is a 'profile' of OAuth which ties down the details for the case where the only service required is authentication. OpenID Connect is what you use when you log into your newspaper using your Google or Facebook account.

4.7.5 Practical key management

So we can use a protocol like Kerberos to set up and manage working keys between users given that each user shares one or more long-term keys with a server that acts as a key distribution centre. But there may be encrypted passwords for tens of thousands of staff and keys for large numbers of devices too. That's a lot of key material. How is it to be managed?

Key management is a complex and difficult business and is often got wrong because it's left as an afterthought. You need to sit down and think about how many keys are needed, how they're to be generated, how long they need to remain in service and how they'll eventually be destroyed. There is a much longer list of concerns – many of them articulated in the Federal Information Processing Standard for key management [1410]. And things go wrong as applications evolve; it's important to provide headroom to support next year's functionality. It's also important to support recovery from security failure. Yet there are no standard ways of doing either.

Public-key cryptography, which I'll discuss in Chapter 5, can simplify the key-management task slightly. In banking the usual answer is to use dedicated cryptographic processors called hardware security modules, which I'll describe in detail later. Both of these introduce further complexities though, and even more subtle ways of getting things wrong.

4.8 Design assurance

Subtle difficulties of the kind we have seen above, and the many ways in which protection properties depend on subtle assumptions that may be misunderstood, have led researchers to apply formal methods to protocols. The goal of this exercise was originally to decide whether a protocol was right or wrong: it should either be proved correct, or an attack should be exhibited. We often find that the process helps clarify the assumptions that underlie a given protocol.

There are several different approaches to verifying the correctness of protocols. One of the best known is the *logic of belief*, or *BAN logic*, named after its inventors Burrows, Abadi and Needham [352]. It reasons about what a principal might reasonably believe having seen certain messages, timestamps and so on. Other researchers have applied mainstream formal methods such as CSP and verification tools such as Isabelle.

Some history exists of flaws being found in protocols that had been proved correct using formal methods; I described an example in Chapter 3 of the second edition, of how the BAN logic was used to verify a bank card used for stored-value payments. That's still used in Germany as the 'Geldkarte' but elsewhere its use has died out (it was Net1 in South Africa, Proton in Belgium, Moneo in France and a VISA product called COPAC). I've therefore decided to drop the gory details from this edition; the second edition is free online, so you can download and read the details.

Formal methods can be an excellent way of finding bugs in security protocol designs as they force the designer to make everything explicit and thus confront difficult design choices that might otherwise be fudged. But they have their limitations, too.

We often find bugs in verified protocols; they're just not in the part that we verified. For example, Larry Paulson verified the SSL/TLS protocol using his Isabelle theorem prover in 1998, and about one security bug has been found every year since then. These have not been flaws in the basic design but exploited additional features that had been added later, and implementation issues such as timing attacks, which we'll discuss later. In this case there was no failure of the formal method; that simply told the attackers where they needn't bother looking.

For these reasons, people have explored alternative ways of assuring the design of authentication protocols, including the idea of *protocol robustness*. Just as structured programming techniques aim to ensure that software is designed methodically and nothing of importance is left out, so robust protocol design is largely about explicitness. Robustness principles include that the interpretation of a protocol should depend only on its content, not its context; so everything of importance (such as principals' names) should be stated explicitly in the messages. It should not be possible to interpret data in more than one way; so the message formats need to make clear what's a name, what's an address, what's a timestamp, and so on; string formats have to be unambiguous and it should be impossible to use the protocol itself to mount attacks on the software that handles it, such as by buffer overflows. There are other issues concerning the freshness provided by counters, timestamps and random challenges, and on the way encryption is used. If the protocol uses public key cryptography or digital signature mechanisms, there are more subtle attacks and further robustness issues, which we'll start to tackle in the next chapter. To whet your appetite, randomness in protocol often helps robustness at other layers, since it makes it harder to do a whole range of attacks – from those based on mathematical cryptanalysis through those that exploit side-channels such as power consumption and timing to physical attacks that involve microprobes or lasers.

4.9 Summary

Passwords are just one example of a more general concept, the security protocol. Protocols specify the steps that principals use to establish trust relationships in a system, such as authenticating a claim to identity, demonstrating ownership of a credential, or establishing a claim on a resource. Cryptographic authentication protocols are used for a wide range of purposes, from basic entity authentication to providing infrastructure for distributed systems that allows trust to be taken from where it exists to where it is needed. Security protocols are fielded in all sorts of systems from remote car door locks through military IFF systems to authentication in distributed computer systems.

Protocols are surprisingly difficult to get right. They can suffer from a number of problems, including middleperson attacks, modification attacks, reflection attacks, and replay attacks. These threats can interact with implementation vulnerabilities and poor cryptography. Using mathematical techniques to verify the correctness of protocols can help, but it won't catch all the bugs. Some of the most pernicious failures are caused by creeping changes in the environment for which a protocol was designed, so that the protection it gives is no longer relevant. The upshot is that attacks are still found frequently on protocols that we've been using for years, and sometimes even on protocols for which we thought we had a security proof. Failures have real consequences, including the rise in car crime worldwide since car makers started adopting passive keyless entry systems without stopping to think about relay attacks. Please don't design your own protocols; get a specialist to help, and ensure that your design is published for thorough peer review by the research community. Even specialists get the first versions of a protocol wrong (I have, more than once). It's a lot cheaper to fix the bugs before the protocol is actually deployed, both in terms of cash and in terms of reputation.

Research problems

At several times during the past 30 years, some people have thought that protocols had been 'done' and that we should turn to new research topics. They have been repeatedly proved wrong by the emergence of new applications with a new crop of errors and attacks to be explored. Formal methods blossomed in the early 1990s, then key management protocols; during the mid-1990's the flood of proposals for electronic commerce mechanisms kept us busy. Since 2000, one strand of protocol research has acquired an economic flavour as security mechanisms are used more and more to support business models; the designer's 'enemy' is often a commercial competitor, or even the customer. Another has applied protocol analysis tools to look at the security of application programming interfaces (APIs), a topic to which I'll return later.

Much protocol research is problem-driven, but there are still deep questions. How much can we get out of formal methods, for example? And how do we manage the tension between the principle that robust protocols are generally those in which everything is completely specified and checked and the system engineering principle that a good specification should not overconstrain the implementer?

Further reading

Research papers on security protocols are scattered fairly widely throughout the literature. For the historical background you might read the original Needham-Schroeder paper [1428], the Burrows-Abadi-Needham authentication logic [352], papers on protocol robustness [2, 113] and a survey paper by Anderson and Needham [114]. Beyond that, there are many papers scattered around a wide range of conferences; you might also start by studying the protocols used in a specific application area, such as payments, which we cover in more detail in Part 2. As for remote key entry and other security issues around cars, a good starting point is a tech report by Charlie Miller and Chris Valasek on how to hack a Jeep Cherokee [1318].

CHAPTER

5

Cryptography

ZHQM ZMGM ZMFM

– G JULIUS CAESAR

KXJEY UREBE ZWEHE WRYTU HEYFS KREHE GOYFI WTTTU OLKSY CAJPO BOTEI ZONTX BYBWT GONEY CUZWR GDSON SXBOU YWRHE BAAHY USEDQ

– JOHN F KENNEDY

5.1 Introduction

Cryptography is where security engineering meets mathematics. It gives us the tools that underlie most modern security protocols. It is the key technology for protecting distributed systems, yet it is surprisingly hard to do right. As we've already seen in Chapter 4, "Protocols," cryptography has often been used to protect the wrong things, or to protect them in the wrong way. Unfortunately, the available crypto tools aren't always very usable.

But no security engineer can ignore cryptology. A medical friend once told me that while she was young, she worked overseas in a country where, for economic reasons, they'd shortened their medical degrees and concentrated on producing specialists as quickly as possible. One day, a patient who'd had both kidneys removed and was awaiting a transplant needed her dialysis shunt redone. The surgeon sent the patient back from the theater on the grounds that there was no urinalysis on file. It just didn't occur to him that a patient with no kidneys couldn't produce any urine.

Just as a doctor needs to understand physiology as well as surgery, so a security engineer needs to be familiar with at least the basics of crypto (and much else). There are, broadly speaking, three levels at which one can approach crypto. The first consists of the underlying intuitions; the second of the mathematics that we use to clarify these intuitions, provide security proofs where possible and tidy up the constructions that cause the most confusion;

and the third is the cryptographic engineering – the tools we commonly use, and the experience of what can go wrong with them. In this chapter, I assume you have no training in crypto and set out to explain the basic intuitions. I illustrate them with engineering, and sketch enough of the mathematics to help give you access to the literature when you need it. One reason you need some crypto know-how is that many common constructions are confusing, and many tools offer unsafe defaults. For example, Microsoft's Crypto API (CAPI) nudges engineers to use electronic codebook mode; by the end of this chapter you should understand what that is, why it's bad, and what you should do instead.

Many crypto textbooks assume that their readers are pure maths graduates, so let me start off with non-mathematical definitions. *Cryptography* refers to the science and art of designing ciphers; *cryptanalysis* to the science and art of breaking them; while *cryptology*, often shortened to just crypto, is the study of both. The input to an encryption process is commonly called the *plaintext* or *cleartext*, and the output the *ciphertext*. Thereafter, things get somewhat more complicated. There are a number of basic building blocks, such as *block ciphers*, *stream ciphers*, and *hash functions*. Block ciphers may either have one key for both encryption and decryption, in which case they're called *shared-key* (also *secret-key* or *symmetric*), or have separate keys for encryption and decryption, in which case they're called *public-key* or *asymmetric*. A *digital signature scheme* is a special type of asymmetric crypto primitive.

I will first give some historical examples to illustrate the basic concepts. I'll then fine-tune definitions by introducing the security models that cryptologists use, including perfect secrecy, concrete security, indistinguishability and the random oracle model. Finally, I'll show how the more important cryptographic algorithms actually work, and how they can be used to protect data. En route, I'll give examples of how people broke weak ciphers, and weak constructions using strong ciphers.

5.2 Historical background

Suetonius tells us that Julius Caesar enciphered his dispatches by writing 'D' for 'A', 'E' for 'B' and so on [1847]. When Augustus Caesar ascended the throne, he changed the imperial cipher system so that 'C' was now written for 'A', 'D' for 'B' etcetera. In modern terminology, we would say that he changed the key from *'D'* to 'C'. Remarkably, a similar code was used by Bernardo Provenzano, allegedly the *capo di tutti capi* of the Sicilian mafia, who wrote '4' for 'a', '5' for 'b' and so on. This led directly to his capture by the Italian police in 2006 after they intercepted and deciphered some of his messages [1538].

The Arabs generalised this idea to the *monoalphabetic substitution*, in which a keyword is used to permute the cipher alphabet. We will write the plaintext in lower case letters, and the ciphertext in upper case, as shown in Figure 5.1:

```
abcdefghijklmnopqrstuvwxyz
SECURITYABDFGHJKLMNOPQVWXZ
```

Figure 5.1: Monoalphabetic substitution cipher

`OYAN RWSGKFR AN AH RHTFANY MSOYRM OYSH SMSEAC NCMAKO;` but it's a pencil and paper puzzle to break ciphers of this kind. The trick is that some letters, and combinations of letters, are much more common than others; in English the most common letters are e,t,a,i,o,n,s,h,r,d,l,u in that order. Artificial intelligence researchers have experimented with programs to solve monoalphabetic substitutions. Using letter and digram (letter pair) frequencies alone, they typically need about 600 letters of ciphertext; smarter strategies such as guessing probable words can cut this to about 150 letters; and state-of-the-art systems that use neural networks and approach the competence of human analysts are also tested on deciphering ancient scripts such as Ugaritic and Linear B [1196].

There are basically two ways to make a stronger cipher – the *stream cipher* and the *block cipher*. In the former, you make the encryption rule depend on a plaintext symbol's position in the stream of plaintext symbols, while in the latter you encrypt several plaintext symbols at once in a block.

5.2.1 An early stream cipher – the Vigenère

This early stream cipher is commonly ascribed to the Frenchman Blaise de Vigenère, a diplomat who served King Charles IX. It works by adding a key repeatedly into the plaintext using the convention that 'A' = 0, 'B' = 1, …, 'Z' = 25, and addition is carried out modulo 26 – that is, if the result is greater than 25, we subtract as many multiples of 26 as are needed to bring it into the range [0, …, 25], that is, [A, …, Z]. Mathematicians write this as

$$C = P + K \bmod 26$$

So, for example, when we add P (15) to U (20) we get 35, which we reduce to 9 by subtracting 26. 9 corresponds to J, so the encryption of P under the key U (and of U under the key P) is J, or more simply U + P = J. In this notation, Julius Caesar's system used a fixed key K = D, while Augustus Caesar's used K = C and Vigenère used a repeating key, also known as a *running key*. Techniques were developed to do this quickly, ranging from printed tables to brass cipher wheels. Whatever the technology, the encryption using a repeated keyword for the key would look as shown in Figure 5.2:

Plain	tobeornottobethatisthequestion
Key	runrunrunrunrunrunrunrunrunrun
Cipher	KIOVIEEIGKIOVNURNVJNUVKHVMGZIA

Figure 5.2: Vigenère (polyalphabetic substitution cipher)

A number of people appear to have worked out how to solve polyalphabetic ciphers, from the womaniser Giacomo Casanova to the computing pioneer Charles Babbage. But the first published solution was in 1863 by Friedrich Kasiski, a Prussian infantry officer [1023]. He noticed that given a long enough piece of ciphertext, repeated patterns will appear at multiples of the keyword length.

In Figure 5.2, for example, we see 'KIOV' repeated after nine letters, and 'NU' after six. Since three divides both six and nine, we might guess a keyword of three letters. Then ciphertext letters one, four, seven and so on were all enciphered under the same keyletter; so we can use frequency analysis techniques to guess the most likely values of this letter, and then repeat the process for the remaining letters of the key.

5.2.2 The one-time pad

One way to make a stream cipher of this type proof against attacks is for the key sequence to be as long as the plaintext, and to never repeat. This is known as the *one-time pad* and was proposed by Gilbert Vernam during World War I [1003]; given any ciphertext, and any plaintext of the same length, there's a key that decrypts the ciphertext to the plaintext. So regardless of the amount of computation opponents can do, they're none the wiser, as given any ciphertext, all possible plaintexts of that length are equally likely. This system therefore has *perfect secrecy*.

Here's an example. Suppose you had intercepted a message from a wartime German agent which you knew started with 'Heil Hitler', and the first ten letters of ciphertext were `DGTYI BWPJA`. So the first ten letters of the one-time pad were `wclnb tdefj`, as shown in Figure 5.3:

Plain	heilhitler
Key	wclnbtdefj
Cipher	DGTYIBWPJA

Figure 5.3: A spy's message

But once he's burnt the piece of silk with his key material, the spy can claim that he's actually a member of the underground resistance, and the message actually said 'Hang Hitler'. This is also possible, as the key material could just as easily have been `wggsb tdefj`, as shown in Figure 5.4:

Cipher	DGTYIBWPJA
Key	wggsbtdefj
Plain	hanghitler

Figure 5.4: What the spy can claim he said

Now we rarely get anything for nothing in cryptology, and the price of the perfect secrecy of the one-time pad is that it fails completely to protect message integrity. So if you wanted to get this spy into trouble, you could change the ciphertext to `DCYTI BWPJA` (Figure 5.5):

Cipher	DCYTIBWPJA
Key	wclnbtdefj
Plain	hanghitler

Figure 5.5: Manipulating the message to entrap the spy

Leo Marks' engaging book on cryptography in the Special Operations Executive in World War II [1226] relates how one-time key material was printed on silk, which agents could conceal inside their clothing; whenever a key had been used it was torn off and burnt. In fact, during the war, Claude Shannon proved that a cipher has perfect secrecy if and only if there are as many possible keys as possible plaintexts, and every key is equally likely; so the one-time pad is the only kind of system that offers perfect secrecy. He was finally allowed to publish this in 1948 [1717, 1718].

The one-time tape was used for top-level communications by both sides from late in World War II, then for strategic communications between NATO allies, and for the US-USSR hotline from 1963. Thousands of machines were produced in total, using paper tapes for key material, until they were eventually replaced by computers from the mid-1980s[1]. But such cryptography is too expensive for most applications as it consumes as much key material as there is traffic. It's more common for stream ciphers to use a pseudorandom number generator to expand a short key into a long keystream. The data is then encrypted by combining the keystream, one symbol at a time, with the data. It's not enough for the keystream to appear "random" in the sense of passing the standard statistical randomness tests: it must also have the property that an opponent who gets his hands on even quite a lot of keystream symbols should not be able to predict any more of them.

[1]Information about the machines can be seen at the Crypto Museum, `https://www.cryptomuseum.com`.

An early example was *rotor machines*, mechanical stream-cipher devices that produce a very long sequence of pseudorandom states[2] and combine them with plaintext to get ciphertext. These machines were independently invented by a number of people from the 1920s, many of whom tried to sell them to the banking industry. Banks weren't in general interested, for reasons we'll discuss below, but rotor machines were very widely used by the combatants in World War II to encipher radio traffic, and the efforts made by the Allies to decipher German traffic included the work by Alan Turing and others on Colossus, which helped kickstart the computer industry after the war.

Stream ciphers have been widely used in hardware applications where the number of gates had to be minimised to save power. However, block ciphers are more flexible and are more common in systems being designed now, so let's look at them next.

5.2.3 An early block cipher – Playfair

The Playfair cipher was invented in 1854 by Sir Charles Wheatstone, a telegraph pioneer who also invented the concertina and the Wheatstone bridge. The reason it's not called the Wheatstone cipher is that he demonstrated it to Baron Playfair, a politician; Playfair in turn demonstrated it to Prince Albert and to Viscount Palmerston (later Prime Minister), on a napkin after dinner.

This cipher uses a 5 by 5 grid, in which we place the alphabet, permuted by the key word, and omitting the letter 'J' (see Figure 5.6):

P	A	L	M	E
R	S	T	O	N
B	C	D	F	G
H	I	K	Q	U
V	W	X	Y	Z

Figure 5.6: The Playfair enciphering table

The plaintext is first conditioned by replacing 'J' with 'I' wherever it occurs, then dividing it into letter pairs, preventing double letters occurring in a pair by separating them with an 'x', and finally adding a 'z' if necessary to complete the last letter pair. The example Playfair wrote on his napkin was 'Lord Granville's letter' which becomes '`lo rd gr an vi lx le sl et te rz`'.

[2]letters in the case of the Hagelin machine used by the USA, permutations in the case of the German Enigma and the British Typex

Plain	`lo rd gr an vi lx le sl et te rz`
Cipher	`MT TB BN ES WH TL MP TA LN NL NV`

Figure 5.7: Example of Playfair enciphering

It is then enciphered two letters at a time using the following rules:

- if the two letters are in the same row or column, they are replaced by the succeeding letters. For example, '`am`' enciphers to '`LE`';
- otherwise the two letters stand at two of the corners of a rectangle in the table, and we replace them with the letters at the other two corners of this rectangle. For example, '`lo`' enciphers to '`MT`'.

We can now encipher our specimen text as follows:

Variants of this cipher were used by the British army as a field cipher in World War I, and by the Americans and Germans in World War II. It's a substantial improvement on Vigenère as the statistics that an analyst can collect are of *digraphs* (letter pairs) rather than single letters, so the distribution is much flatter and more ciphertext is needed for an attack.

Again, it's not enough for the output of a block cipher to just look intuitively "random". Playfair ciphertexts look random; but they have the property that if you change a single letter of a plaintext pair, then often only a single letter of the ciphertext will change. Thus using the key in Figure 5.7, `rd` enciphers to `TB` while `rf` enciphers to `OB` and `rg` enciphers to `NB`. One consequence is that given enough ciphertext, or a few probable words, the table (or an equivalent one) can be reconstructed [740]. In fact, the quote at the head of this chapter is a Playfair-encrypted message sent by the future President Jack Kennedy when he was a young lieutenant holed up on a small island with ten other survivors after his motor torpedo boat had been sunk in a collision with a Japanese destroyer. Had the Japanese intercepted it, they might possibly have decrypted it, and history could be different. For a stronger cipher, we will want the effects of small changes in the cipher's input to diffuse completely through its output. Changing one input bit should, on average, cause half of the output bits to change. We'll tighten these ideas up in the next section.

The security of a block cipher can also be greatly improved by choosing a longer block length than two characters. For example, the *Data Encryption Standard* (DES), which is widely used in payment systems, has a block length of 64 bits and the *Advanced Encryption Standard* (AES), which has replaced it in most other applications, has a block length of twice this. I discuss the internal details of DES and AES below; for the time being, I'll just remark that we need more than just an adequate block size.

For example, if a bank account number always appears at the same place in a transaction, then it's likely to produce the same ciphertext every time a transaction involving it is encrypted with the same key. This might allow an opponent to cut and paste parts of two different ciphertexts in order to produce a valid but unauthorised transaction. Suppose a crook worked for a bank's phone company, and monitored an enciphered transaction that he knew said "Pay IBM $10,000,000". He might wire $1,000 to his brother causing the bank computer to insert another transaction saying "Pay John Smith $1,000", intercept this instruction, and make up a false instruction from the two ciphertexts that decrypted as "Pay John Smith $10,000,000". So unless the cipher block is as large as the message, the ciphertext will contain more than one block and we'll need some way of binding the blocks together.

5.2.4 Hash functions

The third classical type of cipher is the *hash function*. This evolved to protect the integrity and authenticity of messages, where we don't want someone to be able to manipulate the ciphertext in such a way as to cause a predictable change in the plaintext.

After the invention of the telegraph in the mid-19th century, banks rapidly became its main users and developed systems for transferring money electronically. What's 'wired' is a payment instruction, such as:

> *'To Lombard Bank, London. Please pay from our account with you no. 1234567890 the sum of £1000 to John Smith of 456 Chesterton Road, who has an account with HSBC Bank Cambridge no. 301234 4567890123, and notify him that this was for "wedding present from Doreen Smith". From First Cowboy Bank of Santa Barbara, CA, USA. Charges to be paid by us.'*

Since telegraph messages were relayed from one office to another by human operators, it was possible for an operator to manipulate a payment message.

In the nineteenth century, banks, telegraph companies and shipping companies developed *code books* that could not only protect transactions but also shorten them – which was important given the costs of international telegrams at the time. A code book was essentially a block cipher that mapped words or phrases to fixed-length groups of letters or numbers. So "Please pay from our account with you no." might become 'AFVCT'. Sometimes the codes were also enciphered.

The banks realised that neither stream ciphers nor code books protect message authenticity. If, for example, the codeword for '1000' is 'mauve' and for '1,000,000' is 'magenta', then the crooked telegraph clerk who can compare the coded traffic with known transactions should be able to figure this out and substitute one for the other.

The critical innovation, for the banks' purposes, was to use a code book but to make the coding one-way by adding the code groups together into a number called a *test key*. (Modern cryptographers would describe it as a *hash value* or *message authentication code*, terms I'll define more carefully later.)

Here is a simple example. Suppose the bank has a code book with a table of numbers corresponding to payment amounts as in Figure 5.8.

	0	1	2	3	4	5	6	7	8	9
x 1000	14	22	40	87	69	93	71	35	06	58
x 10,000	73	38	15	46	91	82	00	29	64	57
x 100,000	95	70	09	54	82	63	21	47	36	18
x 1,000,000	53	77	66	29	40	12	31	05	87	94

Figure 5.8: A simple test key system

Now in order to authenticate a transaction for £376,514 we might add together 53 (no millions), 54 (300,000), 29 (70,000) and 71 (6,000) ignoring the less significant digits. This gives us a test key of 207.

Most real systems were more complex than this; they usually had tables for currency codes, dates and even recipient account numbers. In the better systems, the code groups were four digits long rather than two, and in order to make it harder for an attacker to reconstruct the tables, the test keys were compressed: a key of '7549' might become '23' by adding the first and second digits, and the third and fourth digits, ignoring the carry.

This made such test key systems into *one-way functions* in that although it was possible to compute a test from a message, given knowledge of the key, it was not possible to reverse the process and recover either a message or a key from a single test – the test just did not contain enough information. Indeed, one-way functions had been around since at least the seventeenth century. The scientist Robert Hooke published in 1678 the sorted anagram 'ceiiinosssttuu' and revealed two years later that it was derived from 'Ut tensio sic uis' – 'the force varies as the tension', or what we now call Hooke's law for a spring. (The goal was to establish priority for the idea while giving him time to do more work on it.)

Banking test keys are not strong by the standards of modern cryptography. Given between a few dozen and a few hundred tested messages, depending on the design details, a patient analyst could reconstruct enough of the tables to forge a transaction. With a few carefully chosen messages inserted into the banking system by an accomplice, it's even easier. But the banks got away with it: test keys worked fine from the late nineteenth century through the 1980s. In several years working as a bank security consultant, and listening to elderly auditors' tales over lunch, I only ever heard of two cases of fraud that exploited it: one external attempt involving cryptanalysis, which failed because the attacker didn't understand bank procedures, and one successful but small fraud involving a crooked staff member. I'll discuss the systems that replaced test keys in the chapter on Banking and Bookkeeping.

However, test keys are our historical example of an algebraic function used for authentication. They have important modern descendants in the authentication codes used in the command and control of nuclear weapons, and also with modern block ciphers. The idea in each case is the same: if you can use a unique key to authenticate each message, simple algebra can give you ideal security. Suppose you have a message M of arbitrary length and want to compute an authentication code or tag A of 128 bits length, and the property you want is that nobody should be able to find a different message M' whose authentication code under the same key will also be A, unless they know the key, except by a lucky guess for which the probability is 2^{-128}. You can simply choose a 128-bit prime number p and compute $A = k_1M + k_2 \pmod{p}$ where the key consists of two 128-bit numbers k_1 and k_2.

This is secure for the same reason the one-time pad is: given any other message M' you can find another key (k'_1, k'_2) that authenticates M' to A. So without knowledge of the key, the adversary who sees M and A simply has no information of any use in creating a valid forgery. As there are 256 bits of key and only 128 bits of tag, this holds even for an adversary with unlimited computing power: such an adversary can find the 2^{128} possible keys for each pair of message and tag but has no way to choose between them. I'll discuss how this *universal hash function* is used with block ciphers below, and how it's used in nuclear command and control in Part 2.

5.2.5 Asymmetric primitives

Finally, some modern cryptosystems are asymmetric, in that different keys are used for encryption and decryption. So, for example, most web sites nowadays have a certificate containing a *public key* with which people can encrypt their session using a protocol called TLS; the owner of the web page can decrypt the traffic using the corresponding *private key*. We'll go into the details later.

There are some pre-computer examples of this too; perhaps the best is the postal service. You can send me a private message by addressing it to me and dropping it into a post box. Once that's done, I'm the only person who'll be able to read it. Of course, many things can go wrong: you might get the wrong address for me (whether by error or as a result of deception); the police might get a warrant to open my mail; the letter might be stolen by a dishonest postman; a fraudster might redirect my mail without my knowledge; or a thief might steal the letter from my doormat. Similar things can go wrong with public key cryptography: false public keys can be inserted into the system, computers can be hacked, people can be coerced and so on. We'll look at these problems in more detail in later chapters.

Another asymmetric application of cryptography is the *digital signature*. The idea here is that I can sign a message using a private *signature key* and then anybody can check this using my public *signature verification key*. Again, there are pre-computer analogues in the form of manuscript signatures and seals; and again, there is a remarkably similar litany of things that can go wrong, both with the old way of doing things and with the new.

5.3 Security models

Before delving into the detailed design of modern ciphers, I want to look more carefully at the various types of cipher and the ways in which we can reason about their security.

Security models seek to formalise the idea that a cipher is "good". We've already seen the model of *perfect secrecy*: given any ciphertext, all possible plaintexts of that length are equally likely. Similarly, an authentication scheme that uses a key only once can be designed so that the best forgery attack on it is a random guess, whose probability of success can be made as low as we want by choosing a long enough tag.

The second model is *concrete security*, where we want to know how much actual work an adversary has to do. At the time of writing, it takes the most powerful adversary in existence – the community of bitcoin miners, burning about as much electricity as the state of Denmark – about ten minutes to solve a 68-bit cryptographic puzzle and mine a new block. So an 80-bit key would take them 2^{12} times as long, or about a month; a 128-bit key, the default in modern systems, is 2^{48} times harder again. So even in 1000 years the probability of finding the right key by chance is 2^{-35} or one in many billion. In general, a system is (t, ϵ)-secure if an adversary working for time t succeeds in breaking the cipher with probability at most ϵ.

The third model, which many theoreticians now call the standard model, is about *indistinguishability*. This enables us to reason about the specific properties of a cipher we care about. For example, most cipher systems don't hide the length of a message, so we can't define a cipher to be secure by just requiring that an adversary not be able to distinguish ciphertexts corresponding to two messages; we have to be more explicit and require that the adversary not be able to distinguish between two messages $M1$ and $M2$ of the same length. This is formalised by having the cryptographer and the cryptanalyst play a game in which the analyst wins by finding an efficient discriminator of something she shouldn't be able to discriminate with more than negligible probability. If the cipher doesn't have perfect security this can be *asymptotic*, where we typically want the effort to grow faster than any polynomial function of a security parameter n – say the length of the key in bits. A security proof typically consists of a *reduction* where we show that if there exists a randomised (i.e., probabilistic) algorithm running in time polynomial in n that learns information it shouldn't with non-negligible probability, then this would give an efficient discriminator for an underlying cryptographic primitive that we already trust. Finally, a construction is said to have *semantic security* if there's no efficient distinguisher for the plaintext regardless of any side information the analyst may have about it; even if she knows all but one bit of it, and even if she can get a decryption of any other ciphertext, she can't learn anything more from the target ciphertext. This skips over quite a few mathematical details, which you can find in a standard text such as Katz and Lindell [1025].

The fourth model is the random oracle model, which is not as general as the standard model but which often leads to more efficient constructions. We call a cryptographic primitive *pseudorandom* if there's no efficient way of distinguishing it from a random function of that type, and in particular it passes all the statistical and other randomness tests we apply. Of course, the cryptographic primitive will actually be an algorithm, implemented as an array of gates in hardware or a program in software; but the outputs should "look random" in that they're indistinguishable from a suitable random oracle given the type and the number of tests that our model of computation permits.

To visualise a random oracle, we might imagine an elf sitting in a black box with a source of physical randomness and some means of storage (see Figure 5.9) – represented in our picture by the dice and the scroll. The elf will accept inputs of a certain type, then look in the scroll to see whether this query has ever been answered before. If so, it will give the answer it finds there; if not, it will generate an answer at random by throwing the dice, and keep a record for future reference. We'll further assume finite bandwidth – the elf

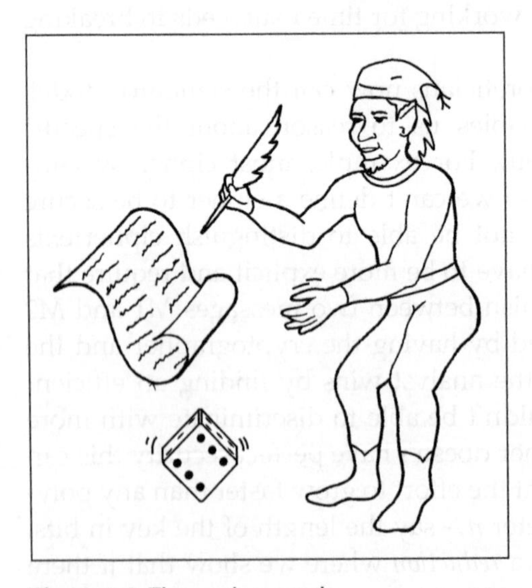

Figure 5.9: The random oracle

will only answer so many queries every second. What's more, our oracle can operate according to several different rules.

5.3.1 Random functions – hash functions

The first type of random oracle is the random function. A random function accepts an input string of any length and outputs a string of fixed length, say n bits long. The same input gives the same output, but the set of outputs appears random. So the elf just has a simple list of inputs and outputs, which grows steadily as it works.

Random functions are our model for *cryptographic hash functions*. These were first used in computer systems for one-way encryption of passwords in the 1960s and have many more uses today. For example, if the police seize your laptop, the standard forensic tools will compute checksums on all the files, to identify which files are already known (such as system files) and which are novel (such as user data). These hash values will change if a file is corrupted and so can assure the court that the police haven't tampered with evidence. And if we want evidence that we possessed a given electronic document by a certain date, we might submit it to an online time-stamping service or have it mined into the Bitcoin blockchain. However, if the document is still secret – for example an invention for which we want to establish a priority date – then we would not upload the whole document, but just the message hash. This is the modern equivalent of Hooke's anagram that we discussed in section 5.2.4 above.

5.3.1.1 Properties

The first main property of a random function is one-wayness. Given knowledge of an input x we can easily compute the hash value $h(x)$, but it is very difficult given $h(x)$ to find x if such an input is not already known. (The elf will only pick outputs for given inputs, not the other way round.) As the output is random, the best an attacker can do to invert a random function is to keep on feeding in more inputs until he gets lucky; with an n-bit output this will take about 2^{n-1} guesses on average. A pseudorandom function will have the same properties, or they could be used to distinguish it from a random function, contrary to our definition. So a pseudorandom function will also be a *one-way function*, provided there are too many possible outputs for the opponent to guess an input that has a desired target output by chance. This means choosing n so that the opponent can't do anything near 2^n computations. If we claim, for example, that SHA256 is a pseudorandom function, then we're saying that there's no practical way to find an input that hashes to a given 256-bit value, unless you knew it already and used it to compute that value.

A second property of pseudorandom functions is that the output will not give any information at all about even part of the input. So we can get a one-way encryption of the value x by concatenating it with a secret key k and computing $h(x, k)$. If the hash function isn't random enough, though, using it for one-way encryption in this manner is asking for trouble. (I'll discuss an example later in section 22.3.1: the hash function used by many phone companies in the 1990s and early 2000s to authenticate mobile phone users wasn't random enough, which led to attacks.)

A third property of pseudorandom functions with sufficiently long outputs is that it is hard to find *collisions*, that is, different messages $M_1 \neq M_2$ with $h(M_1) = h(M_2)$. Unless the opponent can find a shortcut attack (which would mean the function wasn't pseudorandom) then the best way of finding a collision is to collect a large set of messages M_i and their corresponding hashes $h(M_i)$, sort the hashes, and look for a match. If the hash function output is an n-bit number, so that there are 2^n possible hash values, then the number of hashes the enemy will need to compute before he can expect to find a match will be about the square root of this, namely $2^{n/2}$ hashes. This fact is of huge importance in security engineering, so let's look at it more closely.

5.3.1.2 The birthday theorem

The birthday theorem gets its name from the following problem. A maths teacher asks a class of 30 pupils what they think is the probability that two of them have the same birthday. Most pupils intuitively think it's unlikely, and the maths teacher then asks the pupils to state their birthdays one after another. The odds of a match exceed 50% once 23 pupils have been called. As this surprises most people, it's also known as the 'birthday paradox'.

The birthday theorem was first used in the 1930's to count fish, so it's also known as *capture-recapture statistics* [1668]. Suppose there are N fish in a lake and you catch m of them, ring them and throw them back, then when you first catch a fish you've ringed already, m should be 'about' the square root of N. The intuitive reason why this holds is that once you have $\sqrt{N}$ samples, each could potentially match any of the others, so the number of possible matches is about $\sqrt{N}$ x $\sqrt{N}$ or N, which is what you need[3].

This theorem has many applications for the security engineer. For example, if we have a biometric system that can authenticate a person's claim to identity with a probability of only one in a million that two randomly selected subjects will be falsely identified as the same person, this doesn't mean that we can use it as a reliable means of identification in a university with a user population of

[3]More precisely, the probability that m fish chosen randomly from N fish are different is $\beta = N(N-1)\ldots(N-m+1)/N^m$ which is asymptotically solved by $N \simeq m^2/2log(1/\beta)$ [1039].

twenty thousand staff and students. This is because there will be almost two hundred million possible pairs. In fact, you expect to find the first *collision* – the first pair of people who can be mistaken for each other by the system – once you have somewhat over a thousand people enrolled. It may well, however, be OK to use it to verify a claimed identity (though many other things can go wrong; see the chapter on Biometrics in Part 2 for a discussion).

There are some applications where collision-search attacks aren't a problem, such as in challenge-response protocols where an attacker has to find the answer to the challenge just issued, and where you can prevent challenges repeating. In identify-friend-or-foe (IFF) systems, for example, common equipment has a response length of 48 to 80 bits. You can't afford much more than that, as it costs radar accuracy.

But there are other applications in which collisions are unacceptable. When we design digital signature systems, we typically pass the message M through a cryptographic hash function first, and then sign the hash $h(M)$, for a number of reasons we'll discuss later. In such an application, if it were possible to find collisions with $h(M_1) = h(M_2)$ but $M_1 \neq M_2$, then a Mafia owned bookstore's web site might precalculate suitable pairs M_1, M_2, get you to sign an M_1 saying something like "I hereby order a copy of Rubber Fetish volume 7 for \$32.95" and then present the signature together with an M_2 saying something like "I hereby mortgage my house for \$75,000 and please send the funds to Mafia Holdings Inc., Bermuda."

For this reason, hash functions used with digital signature schemes have n large enough to make them collision-free. Historically, the two most common hash functions have been MD5, which has a 128-bit output and will thus require at most 2^{64} computations to break, and SHA1 with a 160-bit output and a work factor for the cryptanalyst of at most 2^{80}. However, collision search gives at best an upper bound on the strength of a hash function, and both these particular functions have turned out to be disappointing, with cryptanalytic attacks that I'll describe later in section 5.6.2.

To sum up: if you need a cryptographic hash function to be collision resistant, then you'd better choose a function with an output of at least 256 bits, such as SHA-2 or SHA-3. However if you only need to be sure that nobody will find a second preimage for an existing, externally given hash, then you can perhaps make do with less.

5.3.2 Random generators – stream ciphers

The second basic cryptographic primitive is the *random generator*, also known as a *keystream generator* or *stream cipher*. This is also a random function, but it's the reverse of the hash function in that it has a short input and a long output. If we had a good pseudorandom function whose input and output were long enough, we could turn it into a hash function by throwing away all but a few hundred bits of the output, and turn it into a stream cipher by padding all but a few hundred bits of the input with a constant and using the output as a keystream.

It can be used to protect the confidentiality of our backup data as follows: we go to the keystream generator, enter a key, get a long file of random bits, and exclusive-or it with our plaintext data to get ciphertext, which we then send to our backup service in the cloud. (This is also called an *additive stream cipher* as exclusive-or is addition modulo 2.) We can think of the elf generating a random tape of the required length each time he is presented with a new key, giving it to us and keeping a copy on his scroll for reference in case he's given the same input key again. If we need to recover the data, we go back to the generator, enter the same key, get the same keystream, and exclusive-or it with our ciphertext to get our plaintext back again. Other people with access to the keystream generator won't be able to generate the same keystream unless they know the key. Note that this would not give us any guarantee of file integrity; as we saw in the discussion of the one-time pad, adding a keystream to plaintext can protect confidentiality, but it can't detect modification of the file. For that, we might make a hash of the file and keep that somewhere safe. It may be easier to protect the hash from modification than the whole file.

One-time pad systems are a close fit for our theoretical model, except in that they are used to secure communications across space rather than time: the two communicating parties have shared a copy of a keystream in advance. Vernam's original telegraph cipher machine used punched paper tape; Marks describes how SOE agents' silken keys were manufactured in Oxford by retired ladies shuffling counters; we'll discuss modern hardware random number generators in the chapter on Physical Security.

A real problem with keystream generators is to prevent the same keystream being used more than once, whether to encrypt more than one backup tape or to encrypt more than one message sent on a communications channel. During World War II, the amount of Russian diplomatic traffic exceeded the quantity of one-time tape they had distributed in advance to their embassies, so it was reused. But if $M_1 + K = C_1$ and $M_2 + K = C_2$, then the opponent can combine the two ciphertexts to get a combination of two messages: $C_1 - C_2 = M_1 - M_2$, and if the messages M_i have enough redundancy then they can be recovered. Text messages do in fact contain enough redundancy for much to be recovered; in the case of the Russian traffic this led to the Venona project in which the US and UK decrypted large amounts of wartime Russian traffic from 1943 onwards and broke up a number of Russian spy rings. In the words of one former NSA chief scientist, it became a "two-time tape".

To avoid this, the normal engineering practice is to have not just a key but also a *seed* (also known as an *initialisation vector* or IV) so we start the keystream at a different place each time. The seed N may be a sequence number, or generated from a protocol in a more complex way. Here, you need to ensure that both parties synchronise on the right working key even in the presence of an adversary who may try to get you to reuse old keystream.

5.3.3 Random permutations – block ciphers

The third type of primitive, and the most important in modern cryptography, is the block cipher, which we model as a *random permutation*. Here, the function is invertible, and the input plaintext and the output ciphertext are of a fixed size. With Playfair, both input and output are two characters; with DES, they're both bit strings of 64 bits. Whatever the number of symbols and the underlying alphabet, encryption acts on a block of fixed length. (So if you want to encrypt a shorter input, you have to pad it as with the final 'z' in our Playfair example.)

We can visualise block encryption as follows. As before, we have an elf in a box with dice and a scroll. This has on the left a column of plaintexts and on the right a column of ciphertexts. When we ask the elf to encrypt a message, it checks in the left-hand column to see if it has a record of it. If not, it rolls the dice to generate a random ciphertext of the appropriate size (and which doesn't appear yet in the right-hand column of the scroll), and then writes down the plaintext/ciphertext pair in the scroll. If it does find a record, it gives us the corresponding ciphertext from the right-hand column.

When asked to decrypt, the elf does the same, but with the function of the columns reversed: he takes the input ciphertext, looks for it on the right-hand scroll, and if he finds it he gives the message with which it was previously associated. If not, he generates a new message at random, notes it down and gives it to us.

A *block cipher* is a keyed family of pseudorandom permutations. For each key, we have a single permutation that's independent of all the others. We can think of each key as corresponding to a different scroll. The intuitive idea is that a cipher machine should output the ciphertext given the plaintext and the key, and output the plaintext given the ciphertext and the key, but given only the plaintext and the ciphertext it should output nothing. Furthermore, nobody should be able to infer any information about plaintexts or ciphertexts that it has not yet produced.

We will write a block cipher using the notation established for encryption in the chapter on protocols:

$$C = \{M\}_K$$

The random permutation model also allows us to define different types of attack on block ciphers. In a *known plaintext attack*, the opponent is just given a number of randomly chosen inputs and outputs from the oracle corresponding to a target key. In a *chosen plaintext attack*, the opponent is allowed to put a certain number of plaintext queries and get the corresponding ciphertexts. In a *chosen ciphertext attack* he gets to make a number of ciphertext queries. In a *chosen plaintext/ciphertext attack* he is allowed to make queries of either type. Finally, in a *related key attack* he can make queries that will be answered using keys related to the target key K, such as $K + 1$ and $K + 2$.

In each case, the objective of the attacker may be either to deduce the answer to a query he hasn't already made (a *forgery attack*), or to recover the key (unsurprisingly known as a *key recovery attack*).

This precision about attacks is important. When someone discovers a vulnerability in a cryptographic primitive, it may or may not be relevant to your application. Often it won't be, but will have been hyped by the media – so you will need to be able to explain clearly to your boss and your customers why it's not a problem. So you have to look carefully to find out exactly what kind of attack has been found, and what the parameters are. For example, the first major attack announced on the Data Encryption Standard algorithm (differential cryptanalysis) required 2^{47} chosen plaintexts to recover the key, while the next major attack (linear cryptanalysis) improved this to 2^{43} known plaintexts. While these attacks were of huge scientific importance, their practical engineering effect was zero, as no practical systems make that much known text (let alone chosen text) available to an attacker. Such impractical attacks are often referred to as *certificational* as they affect the cipher's security certification rather than providing a practical exploit. They can have a commercial effect, though: the attacks on DES undermined confidence and started moving people to other ciphers. In some other cases, an attack that started off as certificational has been developed by later ideas into an exploit.

Which sort of attacks you should be worried about depends on your application. With a broadcast entertainment system, for example, a hacker can buy a decoder, watch a lot of movies and compare them with the enciphered broadcast signal; so a *known-plaintext attack* might be the main threat. But there are surprisingly many applications where *chosen-plaintext attacks* are possible. A historic example is from World War II, where US analysts learned of Japanese intentions for an island 'AF' which they suspected meant Midway. So they arranged for Midway's commander to send an unencrypted message reporting problems with its fresh water condenser, and then intercepted a Japanese report that 'AF is short of water'. Knowing that Midway was the Japanese objective, Admiral Chester Nimitz was waiting for them and sank four Japanese carriers, turning the tide of the war [1003].

The other attacks are more specialised. *Chosen plaintext/ciphertext* attacks may be a worry where the threat is a *lunchtime attack*: someone who gets temporary access to a cryptographic device while its authorised user is out, and tries out the full range of permitted operations for a while with data of their choice. *Related-key attacks* are a concern where the block cipher is used as a building block in the construction of a hash function (which we'll discuss below).

To exclude all such attacks, the goal is semantic security, as discussed above; the cipher should not allow the inference of unauthorised information (whether of plaintexts, ciphertexts or keys) other than with negligible probability.

5.3.4 Public key encryption and trapdoor one-way permutations

A *public-key encryption* algorithm is a special kind of block cipher in which the elf will perform the encryption corresponding to a particular key for anyone who requests it, but will do the decryption operation only for the key's owner. To continue with our analogy, the user might give a secret name to the scroll that only she and the elf know, use the elf's public one-way function to compute a hash of this secret name, publish the hash, and instruct the elf to perform the encryption operation for anybody who quotes this hash. This means that a principal, say Alice, can publish a key and if Bob wants to, he can now encrypt a message and send it to her, even if they have never met. All that is necessary is that they have access to the oracle.

The simplest variation is the *trapdoor one-way permutation*. This is a computation that anyone can perform, but which can be reversed only by someone who knows a *trapdoor* such as a secret key. This model is like the 'one-way function' model of a cryptographic hash function. Let us state it formally nonetheless: a public key encryption primitive consists of a function which given a random input R will return two keys, KR (the public encryption key) and KR^{-1} (the private decryption key) with the properties that

1. Given KR, it is infeasible to compute KR^{-1} (so it's not possible to compute R either);
2. There is an encryption function $\{\ldots\}$ which, applied to a message M using the encryption key KR, will produce a ciphertext $C = \{M\}_{KR}$; and
3. There is a decryption function which, applied to a ciphertext C using the decryption key KR^{-1}, will produce the original message $M = \{C\}_{KR^{-1}}$.

For practical purposes, we will want the oracle to be replicated at both ends of the communications channel, and this means either using tamper-resistant hardware or (more commonly) implementing its functions using mathematics rather than metal.

In most real systems, the encryption is randomised, so that every time someone uses the same public key to encrypt the same message, the answer is different; this is necessary for semantic security, so that an opponent cannot check whether a guess of the plaintext of a given ciphertext is correct. There are even more demanding models than this, for example to analyse security in the case where the opponent can get ciphertexts of their choice decrypted, with the exception of the target ciphertext. But this will do for now.

5.3.5 Digital signatures

The final cryptographic primitive we'll define here is the *digital signature*. The basic idea is that a signature on a message can be created by only one principal, but checked by anyone. It can thus perform the same function in the electronic world that ordinary signatures do in the world of paper. Applications include signing software updates, so that a PC can tell that an update to Windows was really produced by Microsoft rather than by a foreign intelligence agency.

Signature schemes, too, can be deterministic or randomised: in the first, computing a signature on a message will always give the same result and in the second, it will give a different result. (The latter is more like handwritten signatures; no two are ever alike but the bank has a means of deciding whether a given specimen is genuine or forged.) Also, signature schemes may or may not support *message recovery*. If they do, then given the signature, anyone can recover the message on which it was generated; if they don't, then the verifier needs to know or guess the message before they can perform the verification.

Formally, a signature scheme, like a public key encryption scheme, has a keypair generation function which given a random input R will return two keys, σR (the private signing key) and VR (the public signature verification key) with the properties that

1. Given the public signature verification key VR, it is infeasible to compute the private signing key σR;
2. There is a digital signature function which given a message M and a private signature key σR, will produce a signature $Sig_{\sigma R}\{M\}$; and
3. There is a verification function which, given a signature $Sig_{\sigma R}\{M\}$ and the public signature verification key VR, will output TRUE if the signature was computed correctly with σR and otherwise output FALSE.

Where we don't need message recovery, we can model a simple digital signature algorithm as a random function that reduces any input message to a one-way hash value of fixed length, followed by a special kind of block cipher in which the elf will perform the operation in one direction, known as *signature*, for only one principal. In the other direction, it will perform verification for anybody.

For this simple scheme, signature verification means that the elf (or the signature verification algorithm) only outputs TRUE or FALSE depending on whether the signature is good. But in a scheme with *message recovery*, anyone can input a signature and get back the message corresponding to it. In our elf model, this means that if the elf has seen the signature before, it will give the message corresponding to it on the scroll, otherwise it will give a random value (and record the input and the random output as a signature and message pair). This is sometimes desirable: when sending short messages over a low bandwidth channel, it can save space if only the signature has to be sent rather than the signature plus the message. An application that uses message recovery is machine-printed postage stamps, or *indicia*: the stamp consists of a 2-d barcode with a digital signature made by the postal meter and which contains information such as the value, the date and the sender's and recipient's post codes. We discuss this at the end of section 16.3.2.

In the general case we do not need message recovery; the message to be signed may be of arbitrary length, so we first pass it through a hash function and then sign the hash value. We need the hash function to be not just one-way, but also collision resistant.

5.4 Symmetric crypto algorithms

Now that we've tidied up the definitions, we'll look under the hood to see how they can be implemented in practice. While most explanations are geared towards graduate mathematics students, the presentation I'll give here is based on one I developed over the years with computer science undergraduates, to help the non-specialist grasp the essentials. In fact, even at the research level, most of cryptography is as much computer science as mathematics: modern attacks on ciphers are put together from guessing bits, searching for patterns, sorting possible results and so on, and require ingenuity and persistence rather than anything particularly highbrow.

5.4.1 SP-networks

Claude Shannon suggested in the 1940s that strong ciphers could be built by combining substitution with transposition repeatedly. For example, one might add some key material to a block of input text, and then shuffle subsets of the input, and continue in this way a number of times. He described the properties of a cipher as being *confusion* and *diffusion* – adding unknown key values will confuse an attacker about the value of a plaintext symbol, while diffusion means spreading the plaintext information through the ciphertext. Block ciphers need diffusion as well as confusion.

The earliest block ciphers were simple networks which combined substitution and permutation circuits, and so were called SP-networks [1011]. Figure 5.10 shows an SP-network with sixteen inputs, which we can imagine as the bits of a sixteen-bit number, and two layers of four-bit invertible substitution boxes (or *S-boxes*), each of which can be visualised as a lookup table containing some permutation of the numbers 0 to 15.

The point of this arrangement is that if we were to implement an arbitrary 16 bit to 16 bit function in digital logic, we would need 2^{20} bits of memory – one lookup table of 2^{16} bits for each single output bit. That's hundreds of thousands

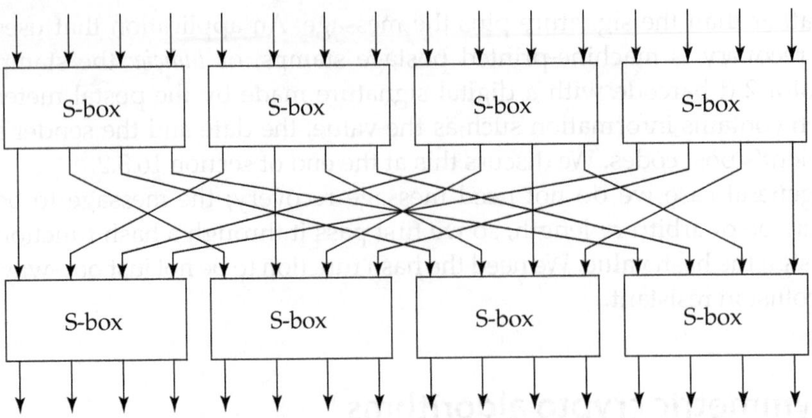

Figure 5.10: A simple 16-bit SP-network block cipher

of gates, while a four bit to four bit function takes only 4 x 2^4 or 64 bits of memory. One might hope that with suitable choices of parameters, the function produced by iterating this simple structure would be indistinguishable from a random 16 bit to 16 bit function to an opponent who didn't know the value of the key. The key might consist of some choice of a number of four-bit S-boxes, or it might be added at each round to provide confusion and the resulting text fed through the S-boxes to provide diffusion.

Three things need to be done to make such a design secure:

1. the cipher needs to be "wide" enough
2. it needs to have enough rounds, and
3. the S-boxes need to be suitably chosen.

5.4.1.1 Block size

First, a block cipher which operated on sixteen bit blocks would be rather limited, as an opponent could just build a dictionary of plaintext and ciphertext blocks as they were observed. The birthday theorem tells us that even if the input plaintexts were random, he'd expect to find a match as soon as he had seen a few hundred blocks. So a practical block cipher will usually deal with plaintexts and ciphertexts of 64 bits, 128 bits or even more. So if we are using four-bit to four-bit S-boxes, we may have 16 of them (for a 64 bit block size) or 32 of them (for a 128 bit block size).

5.4.1.2 Number of rounds

Second, we have to have enough rounds. The two rounds in Figure 5.10 are completely inadequate, as an opponent can deduce the values of the S-boxes by tweaking input bits in suitable patterns. For example, he could hold the rightmost 12 bits constant and try tweaking the leftmost four bits, to deduce the values in the top left S-box. (The attack is slightly more complicated than this, as sometimes a tweak in an input bit to an S-box won't produce a change in any output bit, so we have to change one of its other inputs and tweak again. But it is still a basic student exercise.)

The number of rounds we need depends on the speed with which data diffuse through the cipher. In our simple example, diffusion is very slow because each output bit from one round of S-boxes is connected to only one input bit in the next round. Instead of having a simple permutation of the wires, it is more efficient to have a linear transformation in which each input bit in one round is the exclusive-or of several output bits in the previous round. If the block cipher is to be used for decryption as well as encryption, this linear transformation will have to be invertible. We'll see some concrete examples below in the sections on AES and DES.

5.4.1.3 *Choice of S-boxes*

The design of the S-boxes also affects the number of rounds required for security, and studying bad choices gives us our entry into the deeper theory of block ciphers. Suppose that the S-box were the permutation that maps the inputs (0,1,2, … ,15) to the outputs (5,7,0,2,4,3,1,6,8,10,15,12,9,11,14,13). Then the most significant bit of the input would come through unchanged as the most significant bit of the output. If the same S-box were used in both rounds in the above cipher, then the most significant bit of the input would pass through to become the most significant bit of the output. We certainly couldn't claim that our cipher was pseudorandom.

5.4.1.4 *Linear cryptanalysis*

Attacks on real block ciphers are usually harder to spot than in this example, but they use the same ideas. It might turn out that the S-box had the property that bit one of the input was equal to bit two plus bit four of the output; more commonly, there will be linear approximations to an S-box which hold with a certain probability. *Linear cryptanalysis* [897, 1246] proceeds by collecting a number of relations such as "bit 2 plus bit 5 of the input to the first S-box is equal to bit 1 plus bit 8 of the output, with probability 13/16", then searching for ways to glue them together into an algebraic relation between input bits, output bits and key bits that holds with a probability different from one half. If we can find a linear relationship that holds over the whole cipher with probability $p = 0.5 + 1/M$, then according to the sampling theorem in probability theory we can expect to start recovering keybits once we have about M^2 known texts.

If the value of M^2 for the best linear relationship is greater than the total possible number of known texts (namely 2^n where the inputs and outputs are n bits wide), then we consider the cipher to be secure against linear cryptanalysis.

5.4.1.5 Differential cryptanalysis

Differential Cryptanalysis [246, 897] is similar but is based on the probability that a given change in the input to an S-box will give rise to a certain change in the output. A typical observation on an 8-bit S-box might be that "if we flip input bits 2, 3, and 7 at once, then with probability 11/16 the only output bits that will flip are 0 and 1". In fact, with any nonlinear Boolean function, tweaking some combination of input bits will cause some combination of output bits to change with a probability different from one half. The analysis procedure is to look at all possible input difference patterns and look for those values δ_i, δ_o such that an input change of δ_i will produce an output change of δ_o with particularly high (or low) probability.

As in linear cryptanalysis, we then search for ways to join things up so that an input difference which we can feed into the cipher will produce a known output difference with a useful probability over a number of rounds. Given enough chosen inputs, we will see the expected output and be able to make deductions about the key. As in linear cryptanalysis, it's common to consider the cipher to be secure if the number of texts required for an attack is greater than the total possible number of different texts for that key. (We have to be careful of pathological cases, such as if you had a cipher with a 32-bit block and a 128-bit key with a differential attack whose success probability given a single pair was 2^{-40}. Given a lot of text under a number of keys, we'd eventually solve for the current key.)

There are many variations on these two themes. For example, instead of looking for high probability differences, we can look for differences that can't happen (or that happen only rarely). This has the charming name of *impossible cryptanalysis*, but it is quite definitely possible against many systems [243][4].

Block cipher design involves a number of trade-offs. For example, we can reduce the per-round information leakage, and thus the required number of rounds, by designing the rounds carefully. But a complex design might be slow in software, or need a lot of gates in hardware, so using simple rounds but more of them might have been better. Simple rounds may also be easier to analyse. A prudent designer will also use more rounds than are strictly necessary to block the attacks known today, in order to give some safety margin, as attacks only ever get better. But while we may be able to show that a cipher resists all the attacks we know of, and with some safety margin, this says little about

[4]This may have been used first at Bletchley in World War II where a key insight into breaking the German Enigma machine was that no letter ever enciphered to itself.

whether it will resist novel types of attack. (A general security proof for a block cipher would appear to imply a result such as $P \neq NP$ that would revolutionise computer science.)

5.4.2 The Advanced Encryption Standard (AES)

The Advanced Encryption Standard (AES) is an algorithm originally known as Rijndael after its inventors Vincent Rijmen and Joan Daemen [507]. It acts on 128-bit blocks and can use a key of 128, 192 or 256 bits in length. It is an SP-network; in order to specify it, we need to fix the S-boxes, the linear transformation between the rounds, and the way in which the key is added into the computation.

AES uses a single S-box that acts on a byte input to give a byte output. For implementation purposes it can be regarded simply as a lookup table of 256 bytes; it is actually defined by the equation $S(x) = M(1/x) + b$ over the field $GF(2^8)$ where M is a suitably chosen matrix and b is a constant. This construction gives tight differential and linear bounds.

The linear transformation is based on arranging the 16 bytes of the value being enciphered in a square and then doing bytewise shuffling and mixing operations. The first step is the *shuffle*, in which the top row of four bytes is left unchanged while the second row is shifted one place to the left, the third row by two places and the fourth row by three places. The second step is a column-mixing step in which the four bytes in a column are mixed using matrix multiplication. This is illustrated in Figure 5.11, which shows, as an example, how a change in the value of the third byte in the first column is propagated. The effect of this combination is that a change in the input to the cipher can potentially affect all of the output after just two rounds – an *avalanche* effect that makes both linear and differential attacks harder.

The key material is added byte by byte after the linear transformation. This means that 16 bytes of key material are needed per round; they are derived from the user supplied key material by means of a recurrence relation.

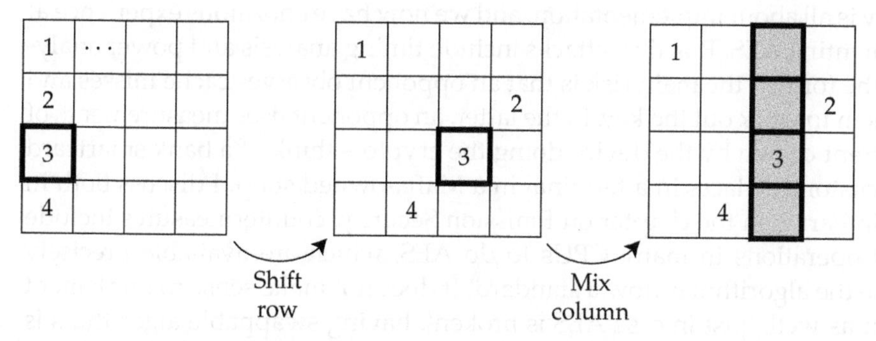

Figure 5.11: The AES linear transformation, illustrated by its effect on byte 3 of the input

The algorithm uses 10 rounds with 128-bit keys, 12 rounds with 192-bit keys and 14 rounds with 256-bit keys. These are enough to give practical, but not certificational, security – as indeed we expected at the time of the AES competition, and as I described in earlier editions of this chapter. The first key-recovery attacks use a technique called biclique cryptanalysis and were discovered in 2009 by Andrey Bogdanov, Dmitry Khovratovich, and Christian Rechberger [274]; they give only a very small advantage, with complexity now estimated at 2^{126} for 128-bit AES and $2^{254.3}$ for 256-bit AES, as opposed to 2^{127} and 2^{255} for brute-force search. Faster shortcut attacks are known for the case where we have related keys. But none of these attacks make any difference in practice, as they require infeasibly large numbers of texts or very special combinations of related keys.

Should we trust AES? The governments of Russia, China and Japan try to get firms to use local ciphers instead, and the Japanese offering, Camellia, is found in a number of crypto libraries alongside AES and another AES competition finalist, Bruce Schneier's Twofish. (Camellia was designed by a team whose own AES candidate was knocked out at the first round.) Conspiracy theorists note that the US government picked the weakest of the five algorithms that were finalists in the AES competition. Well, I was one of the designers of the AES finalist Serpent [95], which came second in the competition: the winner Rijndael got 86 votes, Serpent 59 votes, Twofish 31 votes, RC6 23 votes and MARS 13 votes. Serpent has a simple structure that makes it easy to analyse – the structure of Figure 5.10, but modified to be wide enough and to have enough rounds – and was designed to have a much larger security margin than Rijndael in anticipation of the attacks that have now appeared. Yet the simple fact is that while Serpent is more secure, Rijndael is faster; industry and crypto researchers voted for it at the last AES conference, and NIST approved it as the standard.

Having been involved in the whole process, and having worked on the analysis and design of shared-key ciphers for much of the 1990s, I have a high level of confidence that AES is secure against practical attacks based on mathematical cryptanalysis. And even though AES is less secure than Serpent, practical security is all about implementation, and we now have enormous experience at implementing AES. Practical attacks include timing analysis and power analysis. In the former, the main risk is that an opponent observes cache misses and uses them to work out the key. In the latter, an opponent uses measurements of the current drawn by the device doing the crypto – think of a bank smartcard that a customer places in a terminal in a Mafia-owned shop. I discuss both in detail in Part 2, in the chapter on Emission Security; countermeasures include special operations in many CPUs to do AES, which are available precisely because the algorithm is now a standard. It does not make sense to implement Serpent as well, 'just in case AES is broken': having swappable algorithms is known as *pluggable cryptography*, yet the risk of a fatal error in the algorithm negotiation protocol is orders of magnitude greater than the risk that anyone will come up with a production attack on AES. (We'll see a number of examples later where using multiple algorithms caused something to break horribly.)

The back story is that, back in the 1970s, the NSA manipulated the choice and parameters of the previous standard block cipher, the *Data Encryption Standard* (DES) in such a way as to deliver a cipher that was good enough for US industry at the time, while causing foreign governments to believe it was insecure, so they used their own weak designs instead. I'll discuss this in more detail below, once I've described the design of DES. AES seems to have followed this playbook; by selecting an algorithm that was only just strong enough mathematically and whose safe implementation requires skill and care, the US government saw to it that firms in Russia, China, Japan and elsewhere will end up using systems that are less secure because less skill and effort has been invested in the implementation. However, this was probably luck rather than Machiavellian cunning: the relevant committee at NIST would have had to have a lot of courage to disregard the vote and choose another algorithm instead. Oh, and the NSA has since 2005 approved AES with 128-bit keys for protecting information up to SECRET and with 192-bit or 256-bit keys for TOP SECRET. So I recommend that you use AES instead of GOST, or Camellia, or even Serpent. The definitive specification of AES is Federal Information Processing Standard 197, and its inventors have written a book describing its design in detail [507].

5.4.3 Feistel ciphers

Many block ciphers use a more complex structure, which was invented by Feistel and his team while they were developing the Mark XII IFF in the late 1950s and early 1960s. Feistel then moved to IBM and founded a research group that produced the Data Encryption Standard (DES) algorithm, which is still a mainstay of payment system security.

A Feistel cipher has the ladder structure shown in Figure 5.12. The input is split up into two blocks, the left half and the right half. A *round function* f_1 of the left half is computed and combined with the right half using exclusive-or (binary addition without carry), though in some Feistel ciphers addition with carry is also used. (We use the notation $\oplus$ for exclusive-or.) Then, a function f_2 of the right half is computed and combined with the left half, and so on. Finally (if the number of rounds is even) the left half and right half are swapped.

A notation which you may see for the Feistel cipher is $\psi(f, g, h, ...)$ where f, g, h, ... are the successive round functions. Under this notation, the above

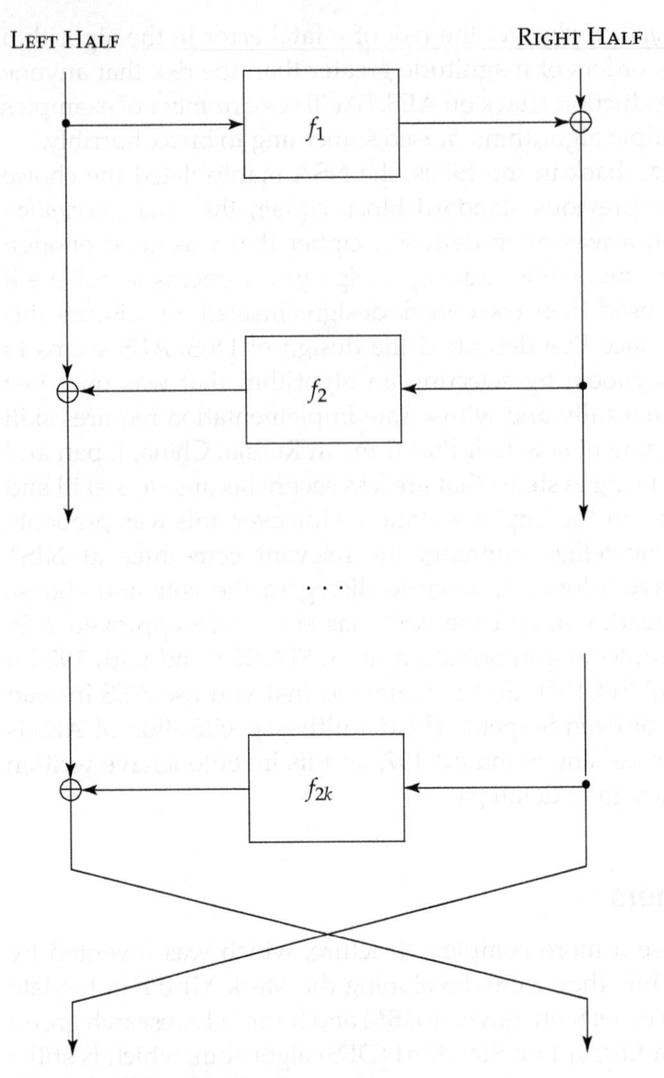

Figure 5.12: The Feistel cipher structure

cipher is $\psi(f_1, f_2, \dots f_{2k-1}, f_{2k})$. The basic result that enables us to decrypt a Feistel cipher – and indeed the whole point of his design – is that:

$$\psi^{-1}(f_1, f_2, \dots, f_{2k-1}, f_{2k}) = \psi(f_{2k}, f_{2k-1}, \dots, f_2, f_1)$$

In other words, to decrypt, we just use the round functions in the reverse order. Thus the round functions f_i do not have to be invertible, and the Feistel structure lets us turn any one-way function into a block cipher. This means that we are less constrained in trying to choose a round function with good diffusion and confusion properties, and which also satisfies any other design constraints such as code size, software speed or hardware gate count.

5.4.3.1 The Luby-Rackoff result

The key theoretical result on Feistel ciphers was proved by Mike Luby and Charlie Rackoff in 1988. They showed that if f_i were random functions, then $\psi(f_1,f_2,f_3)$ was indistinguishable from a random permutation under chosen-plaintext attack, and this result was soon extended to show that $\psi(f_1,f_2,f_3,f_4)$ was indistinguishable under chosen plaintext/ciphertext attack – in other words, it was a pseudorandom permutation. (I omit a number of technicalities.)

In engineering terms, the effect is that given a really good round function, four rounds of Feistel are enough. So if we have a hash function in which we have confidence, it is straightforward to construct a block cipher from it: use four rounds of keyed hash in a Feistel network.

5.4.3.2 DES

The DES algorithm is widely used in banking and other payment applications. The 'killer app' that got it widely deployed was ATM networks; from there it spread to prepayment meters, transport tickets and much else. In its classic form, it is a Feistel cipher, with a 64-bit block and 56-bit key. Its round function operates on 32-bit half blocks and consists of three operations:

- first, the block is expanded from 32 bits to 48;
- next, 48 bits of round key are mixed in using exclusive-or;
- the result is passed through a row of eight S-boxes, each of which takes a six-bit input and provides a four-bit output;
- finally, the bits of the output are permuted according to a fixed pattern.

The effect of the expansion, key mixing and S-boxes is shown in Figure 5.13:

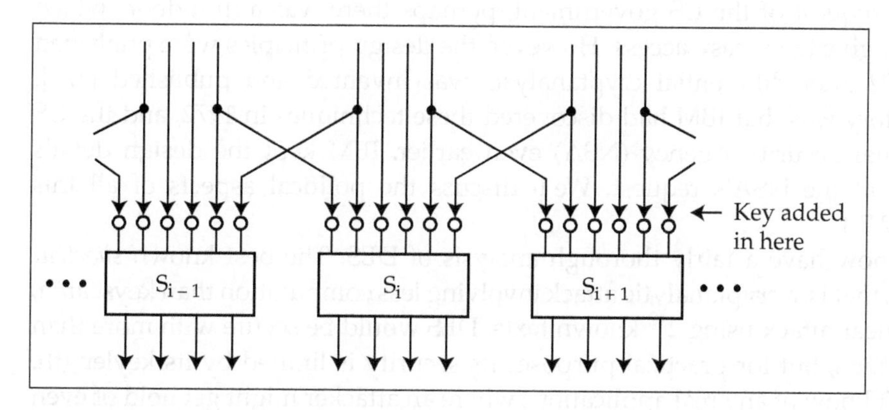

Figure 5.13: The DES round function

The round keys are derived from the user-supplied key by using each user key bit in twelve different rounds according to a slightly irregular pattern. A full specification of DES is given in [1399].

DES was introduced in 1974 and immediately caused controversy. The most telling criticism was that the key is too short. Someone who wants to find a 56 bit key using brute force, that is by trying all possible keys, will have a *total exhaust time* of 2^{56} encryptions and an *average solution time* of half that, namely 2^{55} encryptions. Whit Diffie and Martin Hellman argued in 1977 that a DES keysearch machine could be built with a million chips, each testing a million keys a second; as a million is about 2^{20}, this would take on average 2^{15} seconds, or a bit over 9 hours, to find the key. They argued that such a machine could be built for $20 million in 1977 [557]. IBM, whose scientists invented DES, retorted that they would charge the US government $200 million to build such a machine. (In hindsight, both were right.)

During the 1980's, there were persistent rumors of DES keysearch machines being built by various intelligence agencies, but the first successful public keysearch attack took place in 1997. In a distributed effort organised over the net, 14,000 PCs took more than four months to find the key to a challenge. In 1998, the Electronic Frontier Foundation (EFF) built a DES keysearch machine called Deep Crack for under $250,000, which broke a DES challenge in 3 days. It contained 1,536 chips run at 40MHz, each chip containing 24 search units which each took 16 cycles to do a test decrypt. The search rate was thus 2.5 million test decryptions per second per search unit, or 60 million keys per second per chip. The design of the cracker is public and can be found at [619]. By 2006, Sandeep Kumar and colleagues at the universities of Bochum and Kiel built a machine using 120 FPGAs and costing $10,000, which could break DES in 7 days on average [1110]. A modern botnet with 100,000 machines would take a few hours. So the key length of single DES is now inadequate.

Another criticism of DES was that, since IBM kept its design principles secret at the request of the US government, perhaps there was a 'trapdoor' which would give them easy access. However, the design principles were published in 1992 after differential cryptanalysis was invented and published [473]. The story was that IBM had discovered these techniques in 1972, and the US National Security Agency (NSA) even earlier. IBM kept the design details secret at the NSA's request. We'll discuss the political aspects of all this in 26.2.7.1.

We now have a fairly thorough analysis of DES. The best known *shortcut attack*, that is, a cryptanalytic attack involving less computation than keysearch, is a linear attack using 2^{42} known texts. DES would be secure with more than 20 rounds, but for practical purposes its security is limited by its keylength. I don't know of any real applications where an attacker might get hold of even 2^{40} known texts. So the known shortcut attacks are not an issue. However, its vulnerability to keysearch makes single DES unusable in most applications. As with AES, there are also attacks based on timing analysis and power analysis.

The usual way of dealing with the DES key length problem is to use the algorithm multiple times with different keys. Banking networks have largely moved to *triple-DES*, a standard since 1999 [1399]. Triple-DES does an encryption, then a decryption, and then a further encryption, all with independent keys. Formally:

$$3DES(k_0, k_1, k_2; M) = DES(k_2; DES^{-1}(k_1; DES(k_0; M)))$$

By setting the three keys equal, you get the same result as a single DES encryption, thus giving a backwards compatibility mode with legacy equipment. (Some banking systems use *two-key triple-DES* which sets $k_2 = k_0$; this gives an intermediate step between single and triple DES.) Most new systems use AES as the default choice, but many banking systems are committed to using block ciphers with an eight-byte block, because of the message formats used in the many protocols by which ATMs, point-of-sale terminals and bank networks talk to each other, and because of the use of block ciphers to generate and protect customer PINs (which I discuss in the chapter on Banking and Bookkeeping). Triple DES is a perfectly serviceable block cipher for such purposes for the foreseeable future.

Another way of preventing keysearch (and making power analysis harder) is *whitening*. In addition to the 56-bit key, say k_0, we choose two 64-bit whitening keys k_1 and k_2, xor'ing the first with the plaintext before encryption and the second with the output of the encryption to get the ciphertext afterwards. This composite cipher is known as DESX. Formally,

$$DESX(k_0, k_1, k_2; M) = DES(k_0; M \oplus k_1) \oplus k_2$$

It can be shown that, on reasonable assumptions, DESX has the properties you'd expect; it inherits the differential strength of DES but its resistance to keysearch is increased by the amount of the whitening [1049]. Whitened block ciphers are used in some applications, most specifically in the XTS mode of operation which I discuss below. Nowadays, it's usually used with AES, and AESX is defined similarly, with the whitening keys used to make each block encryption operation unique – as we shall see below in section 5.5.7.

5.5 Modes of operation

A common failure is that cryptographic libraries enable or even encourage developers to use an inappropriate *mode of operation*. This specifies how a block cipher with a fixed block size (8 bytes for DES, 16 for AES) can be extended to process messages of arbitrary length.

There are several standard modes of operation for using a block cipher on multiple blocks [1406]. It is vital to understand them, so you can choose the right one for the job, especially as some common tools provide a weak one by default. This weak mode is electronic code book (ECB) mode, which we discuss next.

5.5.1 How not to use a block cipher

In electronic code book mode, we just encrypt each succeeding block of plaintext with our block cipher to get ciphertext, as with the Playfair example above. This is adequate for protocols using single blocks such as challenge-response and some key management tasks; it's also used to encrypt PINs in cash machine systems. But if we use it to encrypt redundant data the patterns will show through, giving an opponent information about the plaintext. For example, figure 5.14 shows what happens to a cartoon image when encrypted using DES in ECB mode. Repeated blocks of plaintext all encrypt to the same ciphertext, leaving the image quite recognisable.

In one popular corporate email system from the last century, the encryption used was DES ECB with the key derived from an eight-character password. If you looked at a ciphertext generated by this system, you saw that a certain block was far more common than the others – the one corresponding to a plaintext of nulls. This gave one of the simplest attacks ever on a fielded DES encryption system: just encrypt a null block with each password in a dictionary and sort the answers. You can now break at sight any ciphertext whose password was one of those in your dictionary.

In addition, using ECB mode to encrypt messages of more than one block length which require authenticity – such as bank payment messages – is

(a) plaintext (b) ECB ciphertext

Figure 5.14: The Linux penguin, in clear and ECB encrypted (from Wikipedia, derived from images created by Larry Ewing).

particularly foolish, as it opens you to a *cut and splice* attack along the block boundaries. For example, if a bank message said "Please pay account number X the sum Y, and their reference number is Z" then an attacker might initiate a payment designed so that some of the digits of X are replaced with some of the digits of Z.

5.5.2 Cipher block chaining

Most commercial applications which encrypt more than one block used to use cipher block chaining, or CBC, mode. Like ECB, this was one of the original modes of operation standardised with DES. In it, we exclusive-or the previous block of ciphertext to the current block of plaintext before encryption (see Figure 5.15).

This mode disguises patterns in the plaintext: the encryption of each block depends on all the previous blocks. The input initialisation vector (IV) ensures that stereotyped plaintext message headers won't leak information by encrypting to identical ciphertexts, just as with a stream cipher.

However, an opponent who knows some of the plaintext may be able to cut and splice a message (or parts of several messages encrypted under the same key). In fact, if an error is inserted into the ciphertext, it will affect only two blocks of plaintext on decryption, so if there isn't any integrity protection on the plaintext, an enemy can insert two-block garbles of random data at locations of their choice. For that reason, CBC encryption usually has to be used with a separate authentication code.

More subtle things can go wrong, too; systems have to pad the plaintext to a multiple of the block size, and if a server that decrypts a message and finds incorrect padding signals this fact, whether by returning an 'invalid padding' message or just taking longer to respond, then this opens a *padding oracle attack*

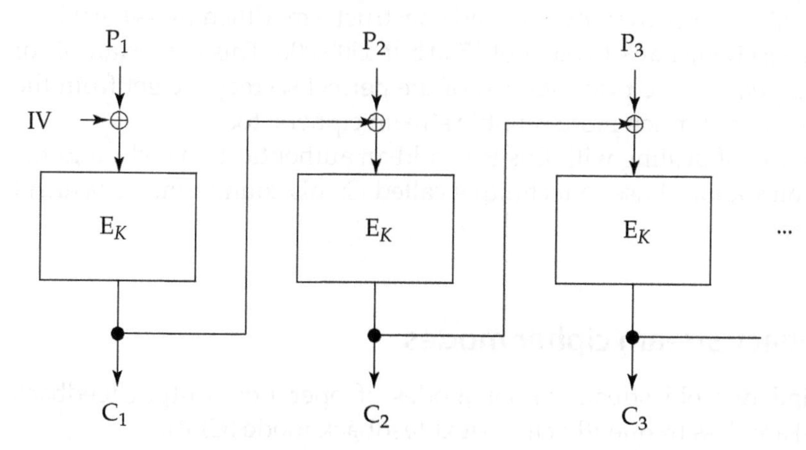

Figure 5.15: Cipher Block Chaining (CBC) mode

in which the attacker tweaks input ciphertexts, one byte at a time, watches the error messages, and ends up being able to decrypt whole messages. This was discovered by Serge Vaudenay in 2002; variants of it were used against SSL, IPSEC and TLS as late as 2016 [1953].

5.5.3 Counter encryption

Feedback modes of block cipher encryption are falling from fashion, and not just because of cryptographic issues. They are hard to parallelise. With CBC, a whole block of the cipher must be computed between each block input and each block output. This can be inconvenient in high-speed applications, such as protecting traffic on backbone links. As silicon is cheap, we would rather pipeline our encryption chip, so that it encrypts a new block (or generates a new block of keystream) in as few clock ticks as possible.

The simplest solution is to use AES as a stream cipher. We generate a keystream by encrypting a counter starting at an initialisation vector: $K_i = \{IV + i\}_K$, thus expanding the key K into a long stream of blocks K_i of keystream, which is typically combined with the blocks of a message M_i using exclusive-or to give ciphertext $C_i = M_i \oplus K_i$.

Additive stream ciphers have two systemic vulnerabilities, as we noted in section 5.2.2 above. The first is an attack in depth: if the same keystream is used twice, then the xor of the two ciphertexts is the xor of the two plaintexts, from which plaintext can often be deduced, as with Venona. The second is that they fail to protect message integrity. Suppose that a stream cipher were used to encipher fund transfer messages. These messages are highly structured; you might know, for example, that bytes 37–42 contain the sum being transferred. You could then cause the data traffic from a local bank to go via your computer, for example by an SS7 exploit. You go into the bank and send $500 to an accomplice. The ciphertext $C_i = M_i \oplus K_i$, duly arrives in your machine. You know M_i for bytes 37–42, so you can recover K_i and construct a modified message which instructs the receiving bank to pay not $500 but $500,000! This is an example of an *attack in depth*; it is the price not just of the perfect secrecy we get from the one-time pad, but of much more humble stream ciphers, too.

The usual way of dealing with this is to add an authentication code, and the most common standard uses a technique called Galois counter mode, which I describe later.

5.5.4 Legacy stream cipher modes

You may find two old stream-cipher modes of operation, output feedback mode (OFB) and less frequently ciphertext feedback mode (CFB).

Output feedback mode consists of repeatedly encrypting an initial value and using this as a keystream in a stream cipher. Writing IV for the initialization vector, we will have $K1 = \{IV\}_K$ and $Ki = \{IV\}_{K(i-1)}$. However an n-bit block cipher in OFB mode will typically have a cycle length of $2^{n/2}$ blocks, after which the birthday theorem will see to it that we loop back to the IV. So we may have a cycle-length problem if we use a 64-bit block cipher such as triple-DES on a high-speed link: once we've called a little over 2^{32} pseudorandom 64-bit values, the odds favour a match. (In CBC mode, too, the birthday theorem ensures that after about $2^{n/2}$ blocks, we will start to see repeats.) Counter mode encryption, however, has a guaranteed cycle length of 2^n rather than $2^{n/2}$, and as we noted above is easy to parallelise. Despite this OFB is still used, as counter mode only became a NIST standard in 2002.

Cipher feedback mode is another kind of stream cipher, designed for use in radio systems that have to resist jamming. It was designed to be self-synchronizing, in that even if we get a burst error and drop a few bits, the system will recover synchronization after one block length. This is achieved by using our block cipher to encrypt the last n bits of ciphertext, adding the last output bit to the next plaintext bit, and shifting the ciphertext along one bit. But this costs one block cipher operation per bit and has very bad error amplification properties; nowadays people tend to use dedicated link layer protocols for synchronization and error correction rather than trying to combine them with the cryptography at the traffic layer.

5.5.5 Message authentication code

Another official mode of operation of a block cipher is not used to encipher data, but to protect its integrity and authenticity. This is the *message authentication code*, or MAC. To compute a MAC on a message using a block cipher, we encrypt it using CBC mode and throw away all the output ciphertext blocks except the last one; this last block is the MAC. (The intermediate results are kept secret in order to prevent splicing attacks.)

This construction makes the MAC depend on all the plaintext blocks as well as on the key. It is secure provided the message length is fixed; Mihir Bellare, Joe Kilian and Philip Rogaway proved that any attack on a MAC under these circumstances would give an attack on the underlying block cipher [212].

If the message length is variable, you have to ensure that a MAC computed on one string can't be used as the IV for computing a MAC on a different string, so that an opponent can't cheat by getting a MAC on the composition of the two strings. In order to fix this problem, NIST has standardised CMAC, in which a variant of the key is xor-ed in before the last encryption [1407]. (CMAC is based on a proposal by Tetsu Iwata and Kaoru Kurosawa [967].) You may see legacy systems in which the MAC consists of only half of the last output block, with the other half thrown away, or used in other mechanisms.

There are other possible constructions of MACs: the most common one is HMAC, which uses a hash function with a key; we'll describe it in section 5.6.2.

5.5.6 Galois counter mode

The above modes were all developed for DES in the 1970s and 1980s (although counter mode only became an official US government standard in 2002). They are not efficient for bulk encryption where you need to protect integrity as well as confidentiality; if you use either CBC mode or counter mode to encrypt your data and a CBC-MAC or CMAC to protect its integrity, then you invoke the block cipher twice for each block of data you process, and the operation cannot be parallelised.

The modern approach is to use a mode of operation designed for authenticated encryption. Galois Counter Mode (GCM) has taken over as the default since being approved by NIST in 2007 [1409]. It uses only one invocation of the block cipher per block of text, and it's parallelisable so you can get high throughput on fast data links with low cost and low latency. Encryption is performed in a variant of counter mode; the resulting ciphertexts are also used as coefficients of a polynomial which is evaluated at a key-dependent point over a Galois field of 2^{128} elements to give an authenticator tag. The tag computation is a universal hash function of the kind I described in section 5.2.4 and is provably secure so long as keys are never reused. The supplied key is used along with a random IV to generate both a unique message key and a unique authenticator key. The output is thus a ciphertext of the same length as the plaintext, plus an IV and a tag of typically 128 bits each.

GCM also has an interesting incremental property: a new authenticator and ciphertext can be calculated with an amount of effort proportional to the number of bits that were changed. GCM was invented by David McGrew and John Viega of Cisco; their goal was to create an efficient authenticated encryption mode suitable for use in high-performance network hardware [1270]. It is the sensible default for authenticated encryption of bulk content. (There's an earlier composite mode, CCM, which you'll find used in Bluetooth 4.0 and later; this combines counter mode with CBC-MAC, so it costs about twice as much effort to compute, and cannot be parallelised or recomputed incrementally [1408].)

5.5.7 XTS

GCM and other authenticated encryption modes expand the plaintext by adding a message key and an authenticator tag. This is very inconvenient in applications such as hard disk encryption, where we prefer a mode of operation that preserves plaintext length. Disk encryption systems used to use CBC with the sector number providing an IV, but since Windows 10, Microsoft has been using a new mode of operation, XTS-AES, inspired by GCM and standardised in 2007. This is a codebook mode but with the plaintext whitened by a *tweak key* derived from the disk sector. Formally, the message M_i encrypted with the key K at block j is

$$AESX(KT_j, K, KT_j; M)$$

where the tweak key KT_j is derived by encrypting the IV using a different key and then multiplying it repeatedly with a suitable constant so as to give a different whitener for each block. This means that if an attacker swaps two encrypted blocks, all 256 bits will decrypt to randomly wrong values. You still need higher-layer mechanisms to detect ciphertext manipulation, but simple checksums will be sufficient.

5.6 Hash functions

In section 5.4.3.1 I showed how the Luby-Rackoff theorem enables us to construct a block cipher from a hash function. It's also possible to construct a hash function from a block cipher[5]. The trick is to feed the message blocks one at a time to the key input of our block cipher, and use it to update a hash value (which starts off at say $H_0 = 0$). In order to make this operation non-invertible, we add feedforward: the $(i-1)$st hash value is exclusive or'ed with the output of round i. This *Davies-Meyer construction* gives our final mode of operation of a block cipher (Figure 5.16).

The birthday theorem makes another appearance here, in that if a hash function h is built using an n bit block cipher, it is possible to find two messages $M_1 \neq M_2$ with $h(M_1) = h(M_2)$ with about $2^{n/2}$ effort (hash slightly more than that many messages M_i and look for a match). So a 64 bit block cipher is not adequate, as forging a message would cost of the order of 2^{32} messages, which is just too easy. A 128-bit cipher such as AES used to be just about adequate, and in fact the AACS content protection mechanism in Blu-ray DVDs used 'AES-H', the hash function derived from AES in this way.

5.6.1 Common hash functions

The hash functions most commonly used through the 1990s and 2000s evolved as variants of a block cipher with a 512 bit key and a block size increasing from

[5]In fact, we can also construct hash functions and block ciphers from stream ciphers – so, subject to some caveats I'll discuss in the next section, given any one of these three primitives we can construct the other two.

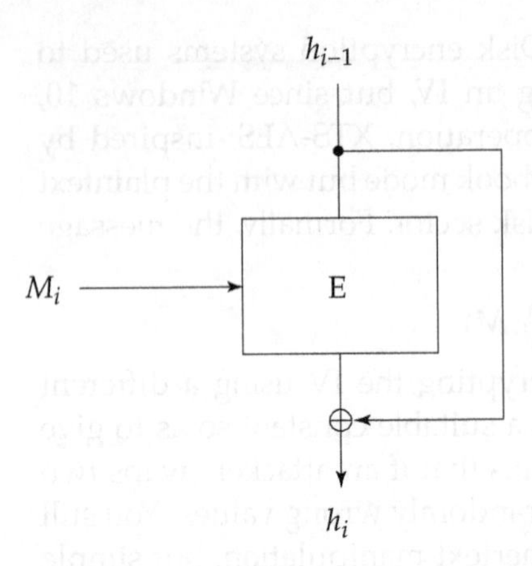

Figure 5.16: Feedforward mode (hash function)

128 to 512 bits. The first two were designed by Ron Rivest and the others by the NSA:

- MD4 has three rounds and a 128 bit hash value, and a collision was found for it in 1998 [568];
- MD5 has four rounds and a 128 bit hash value, and a collision was found for it in 2004 [1983, 1985];
- SHA-1, released in 1995, has five rounds and a 160 bit hash value. A collision was found in 2017 [1831], and a more powerful version of the attack in 2020 [1148];
- SHA-2, which replaced it in 2002, comes in 256-bit and 512-bit versions (called SHA256 and SHA512) plus a number of variants.

The block ciphers underlying these hash functions are similar: their round function is a complicated mixture of the register operations available on 32 bit processors [1670]. Cryptanalysis has advanced steadily. MD4 was broken by Hans Dobbertin in 1998 [568]; MD5 was broken by Xiaoyun Wang and her colleagues in 2004 [1983, 1985]; collisions can now be found easily, even between strings containing meaningful text and adhering to message formats such as those used for digital certificates. Wang seriously dented SHA-1 the following year in work with Yiqun Lisa Yin and Hongbo Yu, providing an algorithm to find collisions in only 2^{69} steps [1984]; it now takes about 2^{60} computations. In February 2017, scientists from Amsterdam and Google published just such a collision, to prove the point and help persuade people to move to stronger hash functions such as SHA-2 [1831] (and from earlier versions of TLS to TLS 1.3). In 2020, Gaëtan Leurent and Thomas Peyrin developed an improved attack that computes chosen-prefix collisions, enabling certificate forgery at a cost of several tens of thousands of dollars [1148].

In 2007, the US National Institute of Standards and Technology (NIST) organised a competition to find a replacement hash function family [1411]. The winner, Keccak, has a quite different internal structure, and was standardised as SHA-3 in 2015. So we now have a choice of SHA-2 and SHA-3 as standard hash functions.

A lot of deployed systems still use hash functions such as MD5 for which there's an easy collision-search algorithm. Whether a collision will break any given application can be a complex question. I already mentioned forensic systems, which keep hashes of files on seized computers, to reassure the court that the police didn't tamper with the evidence; a hash collision would merely signal that someone had been trying to tamper, whether the police or the defendant, and trigger a more careful investigation. If bank systems actually took a message composed by a customer saying 'Pay X the sum Y', hashed it and signed it, then a crook could find two messages 'Pay X the sum Y' and 'Pay X the sum Z' that hashed to the same value, get one signed, and swap it for the other. But bank systems don't work like that. They typically use MACs rather than digital signatures on actual transactions, and logs are kept by all the parties to a transaction, so it's not easy to sneak in one of a colliding pair. And in both cases you'd probably have to find a preimage of an existing hash value, which is a much harder cryptanalytic task than finding a collision.

5.6.2 Hash function applications – HMAC, commitments and updating

But even though there may be few applications where a collision-finding algorithm could let a bad guy steal real money today, the existence of a vulnerability can still undermine a system's value. Some people doing forensic work continue to use MD5, as they've used it for years, and its collisions don't give useful attacks. This is probably a mistake. In 2005, a motorist accused of speeding in Sydney, Australia was acquitted after the New South Wales Roads and Traffic Authority failed to find an expert to testify that MD5 was secure in this application. The judge was "not satisfied beyond reasonable doubt that the photograph [had] not been altered since it was taken" and acquitted the motorist; his strange ruling was upheld on appeal the following year [1434]. So even if a vulnerability doesn't present an engineering threat, it can still present a *certificational* threat.

Hash functions have many other uses. One of them is to compute MACs. A naïve method would be to hash the message with a key: $MAC_k(M) = h(k, M)$. However the accepted way of doing this, called HMAC, uses an extra step in which the result of this computation is hashed again. The two hashing operations are done using variants of the key, derived by exclusive-or'ing them with two different constants. Thus $HMAC_k(M) = h(k \oplus B, h(k \oplus A, M))$.

A is constructed by repeating the byte `0x36` as often as necessary, and B similarly from the byte `0x5C`. If a hash function is on the weak side, this construction can make exploitable collisions harder to find [1091]. HMAC is now FIPS 198-1.

Another use of hash functions is to make commitments that are to be revealed later. For example, I might wish to timestamp a digital document in order to establish intellectual priority, but not reveal the contents yet. In that case, I can publish a hash of the document, or send it to a commercial timestamping service, or have it mined into the Bitcoin blockchain. Later, when I reveal the document, the timestamp on its hash establishes that I had written it by then. Again, an algorithm that generates colliding pairs doesn't break this, as you have to have the pair to hand when you do the timestamp.

Merkle trees hash a large number of inputs to a single hash output. The inputs are hashed to values that form the leaves of a tree; each non-leaf node contains the hash of all the hashes at its child nodes, so the hash at the root is a hash of all the values at the leaves. This is a fast way to hash a large data structure; it's used in code signing, where you may not want to wait for all of an application's files to have their signatures checked before you open it. It's also widely used in blockchain applications; in fact, a blockchain is just a Merkle tree. It was invented by Ralph Merkle, who first proposed it to calculate a short hash of a large file of public keys [1298], particularly for systems where public keys are used only once. For example, a Lamport digital signature can be constructed from a hash function: you create a private key of 512 random 256-bit values k_i and publish the verification key V as their Merkle tree hash. Then to sign $h = \text{SHA256}(M)$ you would reveal k_{2i} if the i-th bit of h is zero, and otherwise reveal k_{2i+1}. This is secure if the hash function is, but has the drawback that each key can be used only once. Merkle saw that you could generate a series of private keys by encrypting a counter with a master secret key, and then use a tree to hash the resulting public keys. However, for most purposes, people use signature algorithms based on number theory, which I'll describe in the next section.

One security-protocol use of hash functions is worth a mention: key updating and autokeying. *Key updating* means that two or more principals who share a key pass it through a one-way hash function at agreed times: $K_i = h(K_{i-1})$. The point is that if an attacker compromises one of their systems and steals the key, he only gets the current key and is unable to decrypt back traffic. The chain of compromise is broken by the hash function's one-wayness. This property is also known as *backward security*. A variant is *autokeying* where the principals update a key by hashing it with the messages they have exchanged since the last key change: $K_{i+1} = h(K_i, M_{i1}, M_{i2}, \ldots)$. If an attacker now compromises one of their systems and steals the key, then as soon as they exchange a message which he can't observe or guess, security will be recovered; again, the chain of compromise is broken. This property is known as *forward security*. It was first used in banking in EFT payment terminals in Australia [208, 210]. The use of asymmetric cryptography allows a slightly stronger form of forward security, namely that as soon as a compromised terminal exchanges a message with an uncompromised one which the opponent doesn't control, security can be recovered even if the message is in plain sight. I'll describe how this works next.

5.7 Asymmetric crypto primitives

The commonly used building blocks in *asymmetric cryptography*, public-key encryption and digital signature are based on number theory. I'll give a brief overview here, and look in more detail at some of the mechanisms in Part 2 when I discuss applications.

The basic idea is to make the security of the cipher depend on the difficulty of solving a mathematical problem that's known to be hard, in the sense that a lot of people have tried to solve it and failed. The two problems used in almost all real systems are factorization and discrete logarithm.

5.7.1 Cryptography based on factoring

The *prime numbers* are the positive whole numbers with no proper divisors: the only numbers that divide a prime number are 1 and the number itself. By definition, 1 is not prime; so the primes are {2, 3, 5, 7, 11, … }. The *fundamental theorem of arithmetic* states that each natural number greater than 1 factors into prime numbers in a way that is unique up to the order of the factors. It is easy to find prime numbers and multiply them together to give a composite number, but much harder to resolve a composite number into its factors. And lots of smart people have tried really hard since we started using cryptography based on factoring. The largest composite product of two large random primes to have been factorized in 2020 was RSA-250, an 829-bit number (250 decimal digits). This took the equivalent of 2700 years' work on a single 2.2GHz core; the previous record, RSA-240 in 2019, had taken the equivalent of 900 years [302]. It is possible for factoring to be done surreptitiously, perhaps using a botnet; in 2001, when the state of the art was factoring 512-bit numbers, such a challenge was set in Simon Singh's 'Code Book' and solved by five Swedish students using several hundred computers to which they had access [44]. As for 1024-bit numbers, I expect the NSA can factor them already, and I noted in the second edition that 'an extrapolation of the history of factoring records suggests the first factorization will be published in 2018.' Moore's law is slowing down, and we're two years late. Anyway, organisations that want keys to remain secure for many years are already using 2048-bit numbers at least.

The algorithm commonly used to do public-key encryption and digital signatures based on factoring is RSA, named after its inventors Ron Rivest, Adi Shamir and Len Adleman. It uses *Fermat's little theorem*, which states that for all primes p not dividing a, $a^{p-1} \equiv 1 \pmod p$ (proof: take the set $\{1, 2, \ldots, p-1\}$ and multiply each of them modulo p by a, then cancel out $(p-1)!$ each side). For a general integer n, $a^{\phi(n)} \equiv 1 \pmod p$ where Euler's function $\phi(n)$ is the number of positive integers less than n with which it has no divisor in common (the proof is similar). So if n is the product of two primes pq then $\phi(n) = (p-1)(q-1)$.

In RSA, the encryption key is a modulus N which is hard to factor (take $N = pq$ for two large randomly chosen primes p and q, say of 1024 bits each) plus a public exponent e that has no common factors with either $p-1$ or $q-1$. The private key is the factors p and q, which are kept secret. Where M is the message and C is the ciphertext, encryption is defined by

$$C \equiv M^e \pmod N$$

Decryption is the reverse operation:

$$M \equiv \sqrt[e]{C} \pmod N$$

Whoever knows the private key – the factors p and q of N – can easily calculate $\sqrt[e]{C} \pmod N$. As $\phi(N) = (p-1)(q-1)$ and e has no common factors with $\phi(N)$, the key's owner can find a number d such that $de \equiv 1 \pmod{\phi(N)}$ – she finds the value of d separately modulo $p-1$ and $q-1$, and combines the answers. $\sqrt[e]{C} \pmod N$ is now computed as $C^d \pmod N$, and decryption works because of Fermat's theorem:

$$C^d \equiv \{M^e\}^d \equiv M^{ed} \equiv M^{1+k\phi(N)} \equiv M.M^{k\phi(N)} \equiv M.1 \equiv M \pmod N$$

Similarly, the owner of a private key can operate on a message with it to produce a signature

$$Sig_d(M) \equiv M^d \pmod N$$

and this signature can be verified by raising it to the power e mod N (thus, using e and N as the public signature verification key) and checking that the message M is recovered:

$$M \equiv (Sig_d(M))^e \pmod N$$

Neither RSA encryption nor signature is safe to use on its own. The reason is that, as encryption is an algebraic process, it preserves certain algebraic properties. For example, if we have a relation such as $M_1 M_2 = M_3$ that holds among plaintexts, then the same relationship will hold among ciphertexts $C_1 C_2 = C_3$ and signatures $Sig_1 Sig_2 = Sig_3$. This property is known as a *multiplicative homomorphism*; a homomorphism is a function that preserves some mathematical structure. The homomorphic nature of raw RSA means that it doesn't meet the random oracle model definitions of public key encryption or signature.

Another general problem with public-key encryption is that if the plaintexts are drawn from a small set, such as 'attack' or 'retreat', and the encryption process is deterministic (as RSA is), then an attacker might just precompute the possible ciphertexts and recognise them when they appear. With RSA, it's also dangerous to use a small exponent e to encrypt the same message to multiple recipients, as this can lead to an algebraic attack. To stop the guessing attack, the low-exponent attack and attacks based on homomorphism, it's sensible to add in some randomness, and some redundancy, into a plaintext block before encrypting it. Every time we encrypt the same short message, say 'attack', we want to get a completely different ciphertext, and for these to be indistinguishable from each other as well as from the ciphertexts for 'retreat'. And there are good ways and bad ways of doing this.

Crypto theoreticians have wrestled for decades to analyse all the things that can go wrong with asymmetric cryptography, and to find ways to tidy it up. Shafi Goldwasser and Silvio Micali came up with formal models of *probabilistic encryption* in which we add randomness to the encryption process, and *semantic security*, which we mentioned already; in this context it means that an attacker cannot get any information at all about a plaintext M that was encrypted to a ciphertext C, even if he is allowed to request the decryption of any other ciphertext C' not equal to C [778]. In other words, we want the encryption to resist chosen-ciphertext attack as well as chosen-plaintext attack. There are a number of constructions that give semantic security, but they tend to be too ungainly for practical use.

The usual real-world solution is *optimal asymmetric encryption padding* (OAEP), where we concatenate the message M with a random nonce N, and use a hash function h to combine them:

$$C_1 = M \oplus h(N)$$

$$C_2 = N \oplus h(C_1)$$

In effect, this is a two-round Feistel cipher that uses h as its round function. The result, the combination C_1, C_2, is then encrypted with RSA and sent. The recipient then computes N as $C_2 \oplus h(C_1)$ and recovers M as $C_1 \oplus h(N)$ [213]. This was eventually proven to be secure. There are a number of public-key cryptography standards; PKCS #1 describes OAEP [995]. These block a whole lot of attacks that were discovered in the 20th century and about which people have mostly forgotten, such as the fact that an opponent can detect if you encrypt the same message with two different RSA keys. In fact, one of the things we learned in the 1990s was that randomisation helps make crypto protocols more robust against all sorts of attacks, and not just the mathematical ones. Side-channel attacks and even physical probing of devices take a lot more work.

With signatures, things are slightly simpler. In general, it's often enough to just hash the message before applying the private key: $Sig_d = [h(M)]^d \pmod N$;

PKCS #7 describes simple mechanisms for signing a message digest [1010]. However, in some applications one might wish to include further data in the signature block, such as a timestamp, or some randomness to make side-channel attacks harder.

Many of the things that have gone wrong with real implementations have to do with side channels and error handling. One spectacular example was when Daniel Bleichenbacher found a way to break the RSA implementation in SSL v 3.0 by sending suitably chosen ciphertexts to the victim and observing any resulting error messages. If he could learn from the target whether a given c, when decrypted as $c^d \pmod{n}$, corresponds to a PKCS #1 message, then he could use this to decrypt or sign messages [265]. There have been many more side-channel attacks on common public-key implementations, typically via measuring the precise time taken to decrypt. RSA is also mathematically fragile; you can break it using homomorphisms, or if you have the same ciphertext encrypted under too many different small keys, or if the message is too short, or if two messages are related by a known polynomial, or in several other edge cases. Errors in computation can also give a result that's correct modulo one factor of the modulus and wrong modulo the other, enabling the modulus to be factored; errors can be inserted tactically, by interfering with the crypto device, or strategically, for example by the chipmaker arranging for one particular value of a 64-bit multiply to be computed incorrectly. Yet other attacks have involved stack overflows, whether by sending the attack code in as keys, or as padding in poorly-implemented standards.

5.7.2 Cryptography based on discrete logarithms

While RSA was the first public-key encryption algorithm deployed in the SSL and SSH protocols, the most popular public-key algorithms now are based on discrete logarithms. There are a number of flavors, some using normal modular arithmetic while others use *elliptic curves*. I'll explain the normal case first.

A *primitive root* modulo p is a number whose powers generate all the nonzero numbers mod p; for example, when working modulo 7 we find that $5^2 = 25$ which reduces to 4 (modulo 7), then we can compute 5^3 as $5^2 \times 5$ or 4×5 which is 20, which reduces to 6 (modulo 7), and so on, as in Figure 5.17.

Thus 5 is a primitive root modulo 7. This means that given any y, we can always solve the equation $y = 5^x \pmod{7}$; x is then called the discrete logarithm of y modulo 7. Small examples like this can be solved by inspection, but for a large random prime number p, we do not know how to do this efficiently. So the mapping $f : x \rightarrow g^x \pmod{p}$ is a one-way function, with the additional properties that $f(x+y) = f(x)f(y)$ and $f(nx) = f(x)^n$. In other words, it is a *one-way homomorphism*. As such, it can be used to construct digital signature and public key encryption algorithms.

5^1		$= 5$	(mod 7)
$5^2 =$	25	$\equiv 4$	(mod 7)
$5^3 \equiv$	4 x 5	$\equiv 6$	(mod 7)
$5^4 \equiv$	6 x 5	$\equiv 2$	(mod 7)
$5^5 \equiv$	2 x 5	$\equiv 3$	(mod 7)
$5^6 \equiv$	3 x 5	$\equiv 1$	(mod 7)

Figure 5.17: Example of discrete logarithm calculations

5.7.2.1 One-way commutative encryption

Imagine we're back in ancient Rome, that Anthony wants to send a secret to Brutus, and the only communications channel available is an untrustworthy courier (say, a slave belonging to Caesar). Anthony can take the message, put it in a box, padlock it, and get the courier to take it to Brutus. Brutus could then put his own padlock on it too, and have it taken back to Anthony. He in turn would remove his padlock, and have it taken back to Brutus, who would now at last open it.

Exactly the same can be done using a suitable encryption function that commutes, that is, has the property that $\{\{M\}_{KA}\}_{KB} = \{\{M\}_{KB}\}_{KA}$. Alice can take the message M and encrypt it with her key KA to get $\{M\}_{KA}$ which she sends to Bob. Bob encrypts it again with his key KB getting $\{\{M\}_{KA}\}_{KB}$. But the commutativity property means that this is just $\{\{M\}_{KB}\}_{KA}$, so Alice can decrypt it using her key KA getting $\{M\}_{KB}$. She sends this to Bob and he can decrypt it with KB, finally recovering the message M.

How can a suitable commutative encryption be implemented? The one-time pad does indeed commute, but is not suitable here. Suppose Alice chooses a random key xA and sends Bob $M \oplus xA$ while Bob returns $M \oplus xB$ and Alice finally sends him $M \oplus xA \oplus xB$, then an attacker can simply exclusive-or these three messages together; as $X \oplus X = 0$ for all X, the two values of xA and xB both cancel out, leaving the plaintext M.

The discrete logarithm problem comes to the rescue. If the discrete log problem based on a primitive root modulo p is hard, then we can use discrete exponentiation as our encryption function. For example, Alice encodes her message as the primitive root g, chooses a random number xA, calculates g^{xA} modulo p and sends it, together with p, to Bob. Bob likewise chooses a random number xB and forms g^{xAxB} modulo p, which he passes back to Alice. Alice can now remove her exponentiation: using Fermat's theorem, she calculates $g^{xB} = (g^{xAxB})^{(p-xA)}$ (mod p) and sends it to Bob. Bob can now remove his exponentiation, too, and so finally gets hold of g. The security of this scheme depends on the difficulty of the discrete logarithm problem. In practice, it can be tricky to encode a message as a primitive root; but there's a simpler way to achieve the same effect.

5.7.2.2 Diffie-Hellman key establishment

The first public-key encryption scheme to be published, by Whitfield Diffie and Martin Hellman in 1976, has a fixed primitive root g and uses g^{xAxB} modulo p as the key to a shared-key encryption system. The values xA and xB can be the private keys of the two parties.

Let's walk through this. The prime p and generator g are common to all users. Alice chooses a secret random number xA, calculates $yA = g^{xA}$ and publishes it opposite her name in the company phone book. Bob does the same, choosing a random number xB and publishing $yB = g^{xB}$. In order to communicate with Bob, Alice fetches yB from the phone book, forms yB^{xA} which is just g^{xAxB}, and uses this to encrypt the message to Bob. On receiving it, Bob looks up Alice's public key y_A and forms yA^{xB} which is also equal to g^{xAxB}, so he can decrypt her message.

Alternatively, Alice and Bob can use transient keys, and get a mechanism for providing forward security. As before, let the prime p and generator g be common to all users. Alice chooses a random number R_A, calculates g^{R_A} and sends it to Bob; Bob does the same, choosing a random number R_B and sending g^{R_B} to Alice; they then both form $g^{R_A R_B}$, which they use as a session key (see Figure 5.18).

Alice and Bob can now use the session key $g^{R_A R_B}$ to encrypt a conversation. If they used transient keys, rather than long-lived ones, they have managed to create a shared secret 'out of nothing'. Even if an opponent had inspected both their machines before this protocol was started, and knew all their stored private keys, then provided some basic conditions were met (e.g., that their random number generators were not predictable and no malware was left behind) the opponent could still not eavesdrop on their traffic. This is the strong version of the forward security property to which I referred in section 5.6.2. The opponent can't work forward from knowledge of previous keys, however it was obtained. Provided that Alice and Bob both destroy the shared secret after use, they will also have backward security: an opponent who gets access to their equipment later cannot work backward to break their old traffic. In what follows, we may write the Diffie-Hellman key derived from R_A and R_B as $DH(R_A, R_B)$ when we don't have to be explicit about which group we're working in, and don't need to write out explicitly which is the private key R_A and which is the public key g^{R_A}.

$$
\begin{aligned}
A \rightarrow B &: \quad g^{R_A} \pmod{p} \\
B \rightarrow A &: \quad g^{R_B} \pmod{p} \\
A \rightarrow B &: \quad \{M\}_{g^{R_A R_B}}
\end{aligned}
$$

Figure 5.18: The Diffie-Hellman key exchange protocol

Slightly more work is needed to provide a full solution. Some care is needed when choosing the parameters p and g; we can infer from the Snowden disclosures, for example, that the NSA can solve the discrete logarithm problem for commonly-used 1024-bit prime numbers[6]. And there are several other details which depend on whether we want properties such as forward security.

But this protocol has a small problem: although Alice and Bob end up with a session key, neither of them has any real idea who they share it with.

Suppose that in our padlock protocol Caesar had just ordered his slave to bring the box to him instead, and placed his own padlock on it next to Anthony's. The slave takes the box back to Anthony, who removes his padlock, and brings the box back to Caesar who opens it. Caesar can even run two instances of the protocol, pretending to Anthony that he's Brutus and to Brutus that he's Anthony. One fix is for Anthony and Brutus to apply their seals to their locks.

With the Diffie-Hellman protocol, the same idea leads to a middleperson attack. Charlie intercepts Alice's message to Bob and replies to it; at the same time, he initiates a key exchange with Bob, pretending to be Alice. He ends up with a key $DH(R_A, R_C)$ which he shares with Alice, and another key $DH(R_B, R_C)$ which he shares with Bob. So long as he continues to sit in the middle of the network and translate the messages between them, they may have a hard time detecting that their communications are compromised. The usual solution is to authenticate transient keys, and there are various possibilities.

In the STU-2 telephone, which is now obsolete but which you can see in the NSA museum at Fort Meade, the two principals would read out an eight-digit hash of the key they had generated and check that they had the same value before starting to discuss classified matters. Something similar is implemented in Bluetooth versions 4 and later, but is complicated by the many versions that the protocol has evolved to support devices with different user interfaces. The protocol has suffered from multiple attacks, most recently the Key Negotiation of Bluetooth (KNOB) attack, which allows a middleperson to force one-byte keys that are easily brute forced; all devices produced before 2018 are vulnerable [125]. The standard allows for key lengths between one and sixteen bytes; as the keylength negotiation is performed in the clear, an attacker can force the length to the lower limit. All standards-compliant chips are vulnerable; this may be yet more of the toxic waste from the Crypto Wars, which I discuss in section 26.2.7. Earlier versions of Bluetooth are more like the 'just-works' mode of the HomePlug protocol described in section 4.7.1 in that they were principally designed to help you set up a pairing key with the right device in a benign

[6]The likely discrete log algorithm, NFS, involves a large computation for each prime number followed by a smaller computation for each discrete log modulo that prime number. The open record is 795 bits, which took 3,100 core-years in 2019 [302], using a version of NFS that's three times more efficient than ten years ago. There have been persistent rumours of a further NSA improvement and in any case the agency can throw a lot more horsepower at an important calculation.

environment, rather than defending against a sophisticated attack in a hostile one. The more modern ones appear to be better, but it's really just theatre.

So many things go wrong: protocols that will generate or accept very weak keys and thus give only the appearance of protection; programs that leak keys via side channels such as the length of time they take to decrypt; and software vulnerabilities leading to stack overflows and other hacks. If you're implementing public-key cryptography you need to consult up-to-date standards, use properly accredited toolkits, and get someone knowledgeable to evaluate what you've done. And please don't write the actual crypto code on your own – doing it properly requires a lot of different skills, from computational number theory to side-channel analysis and formal methods. Even using good crypto libraries gives you plenty of opportunities to shoot your foot off.

5.7.2.3 ElGamal digital signature and DSA

Suppose that the base p and the generator g are public values chosen in some suitable way, and that each user who wishes to sign messages has a private signing key X with a public signature verification key $Y = g^X$. An ElGamal signature scheme works as follows. Choose a message key k at random, and form $r = g^k \pmod{p}$. Now form the signature s using a linear equation in k, r, the message M and the private key X. There are a number of equations that will do; the one that happens to be used in ElGamal signatures is

$$rX + sk = M$$

So s is computed as $s = (M - rX)/k$; this is done modulo $\phi(p)$. When both sides are passed through our one-way homomorphism $f(x) = g^x \bmod p$ we get:

$$g^{rX} g^{sk} \equiv g^M$$

or

$$Y^r r^s \equiv g^M$$

An ElGamal signature on the message M consists of the values r and s, and the recipient can verify it using the above equation.

A few more details need to be fixed up to get a functional digital signature scheme. As before, bad choices of p and g can weaken the algorithm. We will also want to hash the message M using a hash function so that we can sign messages of arbitrary length, and so that an opponent can't use the algorithm's algebraic structure to forge signatures on messages that were never signed. Having attended to these details and applied one or two optimisations, we get the *Digital Signature Algorithm* (DSA) which is a US standard and widely used in government applications.

DSA assumes a prime p of typically 2048 bits[7], a prime q of 256 bits dividing $(p-1)$, an element g of order q in the integers modulo p, a secret signing key x and a public verification key $y = g^x$. The signature on a message M, $Sig_x(M)$, is (r, s) where

$$r \equiv (g^k \pmod p) \pmod q$$

$$s \equiv (h(M) - xr)/k \pmod q$$

The hash function used by default is SHA256[8].

DSA is the classic example of a randomised digital signature scheme without message recovery. The most commonly-used version nowadays is ECDSA, a variant based on elliptic curves, which we'll discuss now – this is for example the standard for cryptocurrency and increasingly also for certificates in bank smartcards.

5.7.3 Elliptic curve cryptography

Discrete logarithms and their analogues exist in many other mathematical structures. *Elliptic curve cryptography* uses discrete logarithms on an elliptic curve – a curve given by an equation like $y^2 = x^3 + ax + b$. These curves have the property that you can define an addition operation on them and the resulting *Mordell group* can be used for cryptography. The algebra gets a bit complex and this book isn't the place to set it out[9]. However, elliptic curve cryptosystems are interesting for at least two reasons.

First is performance; they give versions of the familiar primitives such as Diffie-Hellmann key exchange and the Digital Signature Algorithm that use less computation, and also have shorter variables; both are welcome in constrained environments. Elliptic curve cryptography is used in applications from the latest versions of EMV payment cards to Bitcoin.

Second, some elliptic curves have a *bilinear pairing* which Dan Boneh and Matt Franklin used to construct cryptosystems where your public key is your name [287]. Recall that in RSA and Diffie-Hellmann, the user chose his private key and then computed a corresponding public key. In a so-called *identity-based cryptosystem*, you choose your identity then go to a central authority that issues you with a private key corresponding to that identity. There is a global public key, with which anyone can encrypt a message

[7] In the 1990s p could be in the range 512–1024 bits and q 160 bits; this was changed to 1023–1024 bits in 2001 [1404] and 1024–3072 bits in 2009, with q in the range 160–256 bits [1405].

[8] The default sizes of p are chosen to be 2048 bits and q 256 bits in order to equalise the work factors of the two best known cryptanalytic attacks, namely the number field sieve whose running speed depends on the size of p and Pollard's rho which depends on the size of q. Larger sizes can be chosen if you're anxious about Moore's law or about progress in algorithms.

[9] See Katz and Lindell [1025] for an introduction.

to your identity; you can decrypt this using your private key. Earlier, Adi Shamir had discovered *identity-based signature schemes* that allow you to sign messages using a private key so that anyone can verify the signature against your name [1707]. In both cases, your private key is computed by the central authority using a system-wide private key known only to itself. Identity-based primitives have been used in a few specialist systems: in Zcash for the payment privacy mechanisms, and in a UK government key-management protocol called Mikey-Sakke. Computing people's private keys from their email addresses or other identifiers may seem a neat hack, but it can be expensive when government departments are reorganised or renamed [116]. Most organisations and applications use ordinary public-key systems with certification of public keys, which I'll discuss next.

5.7.4 Certification authorities

Now that we can do public-key encryption and digital signature, we need some mechanism to bind users to keys. The approach proposed by Diffie and Hellman when they invented digital signatures was to have a directory of the public keys of a system's authorised users, like a phone book. A more common solution, due to Loren Kohnfelder, is for a *certification authority* (CA) to sign the users' public encryption keys or their signature verification keys giving certificates that contain a user's name, one or more of their public keys, and attributes such as authorisations. The CA might be run by the local system administrator; but it is most commonly a third party service such as Verisign whose business is to sign public keys after doing some due diligence about whether they are controlled by the principals named in them.

A certificate might be described symbolically as

$$C_A = Sig_{K_S}(T_S, L, A, K_A, V_A) \tag{5.1}$$

where T_S is the certificate's starting date and time, L is the length of time for which it is valid, A is the user's name, K_A is her public encryption key, and V_A is her public signature verification key. In this way, only the administrator's public signature verification key needs to be communicated to all principals in a trustworthy manner.

Certification is hard, for a whole lot of reasons. Naming is hard, for starters; we discuss this in Chapter 7 on Distributed Systems. But often names aren't really what the protocol has to establish, as in the real world it's often about authorisation rather than authentication. Government systems are often about establishing not just a user's name or role but their security clearance level. In banking systems, it's about your balance, your available credit and your authority to spend it. In commercial systems, it's often about linking remote users to role-based access control. In user-facing systems, there is a tendency to dump on the customer as many of the compliance costs as possible [524]. There are many other things that can go wrong with certification at the level of systems engineering. At the level of politics, there are hundreds of certification authorities in a typical browser, they are all more or less equally trusted, and many nation states can coerce at least one of them[10]. The revocation of bad certificates is usually flaky, if it works at all. There will be much more on these topics later. With these warnings, it's time to look at the most commonly used public key protocol, TLS.

5.7.5 TLS

I remarked above that a server could publish a public key KS and any web browser could then send a message M containing a credit card number to it encrypted using KS: $\{M\}_{KS}$. This is in essence what the TLS protocol (then known as SSL) was designed to do, at the start of e-commerce. It was developed by Paul Kocher and Taher ElGamal in 1995 to support encryption and authentication in both directions, so that both `http` requests and responses can be protected against both eavesdropping and manipulation. It's the protocol that's activated when you see the padlock on your browser toolbar.

Here is a simplified description of the basic version of the protocol in TLS v1:

1. the client sends the server a *client hello* message that contains its name C, a transaction serial number C#, and a random nonce N_C;
2. the server replies with a *server hello* message that contains its name S, a transaction serial number $S\#$, a random nonce N_S, and a certificate CS containing its public key KS. The client now checks the certificate CS, and if need be checks the key that signed it in another certificate, and so on back to a root certificate issued by a company such as Verisign and stored in the browser;
3. the client sends a *key exchange* message containing a *pre-master-secret* key, K_0, encrypted under the server public key KS. It also sends a *finished* message with a message authentication code (MAC) computed on all the messages to date. The key for this MAC is the *master-secret*, K_1. This key is computed by hashing the pre-master-secret key with the nonces sent by the client and server: $K_1 = h(K_0, N_C, N_S)$. From this point onward, all the traffic is encrypted; we'll write this as $\{...\}_{KCS}$ in the client-server direction and $\{...\}_{KSC}$ from the server to the client. These keys are generated in turn by hashing the nonces with K_1.

[10]The few that can't, try to cheat. In 2011 Iran hacked the CA Diginotar, and in 2019 Kazakhstan forced its citizens to add a local police certificate to their browser. In both cases the browser vendors pushed back fast and hard: Diginotar failed after it was blacklisted, while the Kazakh cert was blocked even if its citizens installed it manually. This of course raises issues of sovereignty.

4. The server also sends a *finished* message with a MAC computed on all the messages to date. It then finally starts sending the data.

$$\begin{array}{ll} C \rightarrow S: & C, C\#, N_C \\ S \rightarrow C: & S, S\#, N_S, CS \\ C \rightarrow S: & \{K_0\}_{KS} \\ C \rightarrow S: & \{finished, MAC(K_1, everythingtodate)\}_{KCS} \\ S \rightarrow C: & \{finished, MAC(K_1, everythingtodate)\}_{KSC}, \{data\}_{KSC} \end{array}$$

Once a client and server have established a pre-master-secret, no more public-key operations are needed as further master secrets can be obtained by hashing it with new nonces.

5.7.5.1 TLS uses

The full protocol is more complex than this, and has gone through a number of versions. It has supported a number of different ciphersuites, initially so that export versions of software could be limited to 40 bit keys – a condition of export licensing that was imposed for many years by the US government. This led to downgrade attacks where a middleperson could force the use of weak keys. Other ciphersuites support signed Diffie-Hellman key exchanges for transient keys, to provide forward and backward secrecy. TLS also has options for bidirectional authentication so that if the client also has a certificate, this can be checked by the server. In addition, the working keys *KCS* and *KSC* can contain separate subkeys for encryption and authentication, as is needed for legacy modes of operation such as CBC plus CBC MAC.

As well as being used to encrypt web traffic, TLS has also been available as an authentication option in Windows from Windows 2000 onwards; you can use it instead of Kerberos for authentication on corporate networks. I will describe its use in more detail in the chapter on network attack and defence.

5.7.5.2 TLS security

Although early versions of SSL had a number of bugs [1977], SSL 3.0 and later appear to be sound; the version after SSL 3.0 was renamed TLS 1.0. It was formally verified by Larry Paulson in 1998, so we know that the idealised version of the protocol doesn't have any bugs [1504].

However, in the more than twenty years since then, there have been over a dozen serious attacks. Even in 1998, Daniel Bleichenbacher came up with the first of a number of attacks based on measuring the time it takes a server to decrypt, or the error messages it returns in response to carefully-crafted protocol responses [265]. TLS 1.1 appeared in 2006 with protection against exploits of CBC encryption and of padding errors; TLS 1.2 followed two years later, upgrading the hash function to SHA256 and supporting authenticated encryption; and meanwhile there were a number of patches dealing with various attacks that had emerged. Many of these patches were rather inelegant because of the difficulty of changing a widely-used protocol; it's difficult to change both the server and client ends at once, as any client still has to interact with millions of servers, many running outdated software, and most websites want to be able to deal with browsers of all ages and on all sorts of devices. This has been dealt with by the big service firms changing their browsers to reject obsolete ciphersuites, and to add features like *strict transport security* (STS) whereby a website can instruct browsers to only interact with it using https in future (to prevent downgrade attacks). The browser firms have also mandated a number of other supporting measures, from shorter certificate lifetimes to certificate transparency, which we'll discuss in the chapter on network attack and defence.

5.7.5.3 TLS 1.3

The most recent major upgrade to the core protocol, TLS 1.3, was approved by the IETF in January 2019 after two years of discussion. It has dropped backwards compatibility in order to end support for many old ciphers, and made it mandatory to establish end-to-end forward secrecy by means of a Diffie-Hellman key exchange at the start of each session. This has caused controversy with the banking industry, which routinely intercepts encrypted sessions in order to do monitoring for compliance purposes. This will no longer be possible, so banks will have to bear the legal discomfort of using obsolete encryption or the financial cost of redeveloping systems to monitor compliance at endpoints instead[11].

5.7.6 Other public-key protocols

Dozens of other public-key protocols have found wide use, including the following, most of which we'll discuss in detail later. Here I'll briefly mention code signing, PGP and QUIC.

5.7.6.1 Code signing

Code signing was introduced in the 1990s when people started downloading software rather than getting it on diskettes. It is now used very widely to

[11]The COVID-19 pandemic has given some respite: Microsoft had been due to remove support for legacy versions of TLS in spring 2020 but has delayed this.

assure the provenance of software. You might think that having a public signature-verification key in your software so that version N can verify an update to version $N + 1$ would be a simple application of public-key cryptography but this is far from the case. Many platforms sign their operating-system code, including updates, to prevent persistent malware; the mechanisms often involve trusted hardware such as TPMs and I'll discuss them in the next chapter in section 6.2.5. Some platforms, such as the iPhone, will only run signed code; this not only assures the provenance of software but enables platform owners to monetise apps, as I will discuss in section 22.4.2; games consoles are similar. As some users go to great lengths to jailbreak their devices, such platforms typically have trustworthy hardware to store the verification keys. Where that isn't available, verification may be done using code that is obfuscated to make it harder for malware (or customers) to tamper with it; this is a constant arms race, which I discuss in section 24.3.3. As for the signing key, the developer may keep it in a hardware security module, which is expensive and breaks in subtle ways discussed in section 20.5; there may be a chain of trust going back to a commercial CA, but then have to worry about legal coercion by government agencies, which I discuss in section 26.2.7; you might even implement your own CA for peace of mind. In short, code signing isn't quite as easy as it looks, particularly when the user is the enemy.

5.7.6.2 PGP/GPG

During the 'Crypto Wars' in the 1990s, cyber-activists fought governments for the right to encrypt email, while governments pushed for laws restricting encryption; I'll discuss the history and politics in section 26.2.7. The crypto activist Phil Zimmermann wrote an open-source encryption product *Pretty Good Privacy* (PGP) and circumvented U.S. export controls by publishing the source code in a paper book, which could be posted, scanned and compiled. Along with later compatible products such as GPG, it has become fairly widely used among geeks. For example, sysadmins, Computer Emergency Response Teams (CERTs) and malware researchers use it to share information about attacks and vulnerabilities. It has also been built into customised phones sold to criminal gangs to support messaging; I'll discuss this later in section 25.4.1.

PGP has a number of features but, in its most basic form, each user generates private/public keypairs manually and shares public keys with contacts. There are command-line options to sign a message with your signature key and/or encrypt it using the public key of each of the intended recipients. Manual key management avoids the need for a CA that can be cracked or coerced. Many things were learned from the deployment and use of PGP during the 1990s. As I described in section 3.2.1, Alma Whitten and Doug Tygar wrote the seminal paper on security usability by assessing whether motivated but cryptologically unsophisticated users could understand it well enough to drive the program safely. Only four of twelve subjects were able to correctly send encrypted email to the other subjects, and every subject made at least one significant error.

5.7.6.3 QUIC

QUIC is a new UDP-based protocol designed by Google and promoted as an alternative to TLS that allows quicker session establishment and cutting latency in the ad auctions that happen as pages load; sessions can persist as people move between access points. This is achieved by a cookie that holds the client's last IP address, encrypted by the server. It appeared in Chrome in 2013 and now has about 7% of Internet traffic; it's acquired a vigorous standardisation community. Google claims it reduces search latency 8% and YouTube buffer time 18%. Independent evaluation suggests that the benefit is mostly on the desktop rather than mobile [1009], and there's a privacy concern as the server can use an individual public key for each client, and use this for tracking. As a general principle, one should be wary of corporate attempts to replace open standards with proprietary ones, whether IBM's EBCDIC coding standard of the 1950s and SNA in the 1970s, or Microsoft's attempts to 'embrace and extend' both mail standards and security protocols since the 1990s, or Facebook's promotion of Internet access in Africa that kept users largely within its walled garden. I'll discuss the monopolistic tendencies of our industry at greater length in Chapter 8.

5.7.7 Special-purpose primitives

Researchers have invented a large number of public-key and signature primitives with special properties. Two that have so far appeared in real products are threshold cryptography and blind signatures.

Threshold crypto is a mechanism whereby a signing key, or a decryption key, can be split up among n principals so that any k out of n can sign a message (or decrypt). For $k = n$ the construction is easy. With RSA, for example, you can split up the private key d as $d = d_1 + d_2 + \ldots + d_n$. For $k < n$ it's slightly more complex (but not much – you use the Lagrange interpolation formula) [554]. Threshold signatures were first used in systems where a number of servers process transactions independently and vote independently on the outcome; they have more recently been used to implement business rules on cryptocurrency wallets such as 'a payment must be authorised by any two of the seven company directors'.

Blind signatures are a way of making a signature on a message without knowing what the message is. For example, if we are using RSA, I can take a random number R, form $R^eM \pmod n$, and give it to the signer who computes

$(R^e M)^d = R.M^d \pmod{n}$. When he gives this back to me, I can divide out R to get the signature M^d. Now you might ask why on earth someone would want to sign a document without knowing its contents, but there are some applications.

The first was in *digital cash*; you might want to be able to issue anonymous payment tokens to customers, and the earliest idea, due to David Chaum, was a way to sign 'digital coins' without knowing their serial numbers [413]. A bank might agree to honour for $10 any string M with a unique serial number and a specified form of redundancy, bearing a signature that verified as correct using the public key (e, n). The blind signature protocol ensures a customer can get a bank to sign a coin without the banker knowing its serial number, and it was used in prototype road toll systems. The effect is that the digital cash can be anonymous for the spender. The main problem with digital cash was to detect people who spend the same coin twice, and this was eventually fixed using blockchains or other ledger mechanisms, as I discuss in section 20.7. Digital cash failed to take off because neither banks nor governments really want payments to be anonymous: anti-money-laundering regulations since 9/11 restrict anonymous payment services to small amounts, while both banks and bitcoin miners like to collect transaction fees.

Anonymous digital credentials are now used in attestation: the TPM chip on your PC motherboard might prove something about the software running on your machine without identifying you. Unfortunately, this led to designs for attestation in SGX (and its AMD equivalent) which mean that a single compromised device breaks the whole ecosystem. Anonymous signatures are also found in prototype systems for conducting electronic elections, to which I will return in section 25.5.

5.7.8 How strong are asymmetric cryptographic primitives?

In order to provide the same level of protection as a symmetric block cipher, asymmetric cryptographic primitives generally require at least twice the block length. Elliptic curve systems appear to achieve this bound; a 256-bit elliptic scheme could be about as hard to break as a 128-bit block cipher with a 128-bit key; and the only public-key encryption schemes used in the NSA's Suite B of military algorithms are 384-bit elliptic curve systems. The traditional schemes, based on factoring and discrete log, now require 3072-bit keys to protect material at Top Secret, as there are shortcut attack algorithms such as the number field sieve. As a result, elliptic curve cryptosystems are faster.

When I wrote the first edition of this book in 2000, the number field sieve had been used to attack keys up to 512 bits, a task comparable in difficulty to keysearch on 56-bit DES keys; by the time I rewrote this chapter for the second edition in 2007, 64-bit symmetric keys had been brute-forced, and the 663-bit challenge number RSA-200 had been factored. By the third edition in 2019, bitcoin miners are finding 68-bit hash collisions every ten minutes, RSA-768 has been factored and Ed Snowden has as good as told us that the NSA can do discrete logs for a 1024-bit prime modulus.

There has been much research into *quantum computers* – devices that perform a large number of computations simultaneously using superposed quantum states. Peter Shor has shown that if a sufficiently large quantum computer could be built, then both factoring and discrete logarithm computations will become easy [1728]. So far only very small quantum devices have been built; although there are occasional claims of 'quantum supremacy' – of a quantum computer performing a task sufficiently faster than a conventional one to convince us that quantum superposition or entanglement is doing any real work – they seem to lead nowhere. I am sceptical (as are many physicists) about whether the technology will ever threaten real systems. I am even more sceptical about the value of quantum cryptography; it may be able to re-key a line encryption device that uses AES for bulk encryption on a single uninterrupted fibre run, but we already know how to do that.

What's more, I find the security proofs offered for entanglement-based quantum cryptography to be unconvincing. Theoretical physics has been stalled since the early 1970s when Gerard 't Hooft completed the Standard Model by proving the renormalisability of Yang-Mills. Since then, a whole series of ideas have come and gone, such as string theory [2035]. Quantum information theory is the latest enthusiasm. Its proponents talk up the mystery of the Bell tests, which are supposed to demonstrate that physics cannot be simultaneously local and causal. But alternative interpretations such as 't Hooft's cellular automaton model [918] and Grisha Volovik's superfluid model [1971] suggest that the Bell tests merely demonstrate the existence of long-range order in the quantum vacuum, like the order parameter of a superfluid. Since 2005, we've had lab experiments involving bouncing droplets on a vibrating fluid bath that demonstrate interesting analogues of quantum-mechanical properties relevant to the Bell tests [1560]. This book is not the place to discuss the implications in more detail; for that, see [312]. There is a whole community of physicists working on emergent quantum mechanics – the idea that to make progress beyond the Standard Model, and to reconcile the apparent conflict between quantum mechanics and general relativity, we may need to look at things differently. Meantime, if anyone claims their system is secure 'because quantum mechanics' then scepticism may be in order.

I think it more likely that a major challenge to public-key cryptography could come in the form of a better algorithm for computing discrete logarithms on elliptic curves. These curves have a lot of structure; they are studied intensively by some of the world's smartest pure mathematicians; better discrete-log algorithms for curves of small characteristic were discovered in 2013 [169]; and the NSA is apparently moving away from using elliptic-curve crypto.

If quantum computers ever work, we have other 'post-quantum' algorithms ready to go, for which quantum computers give no obvious advantage. In 2020, NIST began the third round of public review of submissions for the Post-Quantum Cryptography Standardization Process. The 65 initial submissions have been cut to 15 through two rounds of review[12]. One or more algorithms will now be chosen and standardised, so ciphersuites using them could be dropped into protocols such as TLS as upgrades. Many protocols in use could even be redesigned to use variants on Kerberos. If elliptic logarithms become easy, we have these resources and can also fall back to discrete logs in prime fields, or to RSA. But if elliptic logs become easy, bitcoins will become trivial to forge, and the cryptocurrency ecosystem would probably collapse, putting an end to the immensely wasteful mining operations I describe in section 20.7. So mathematicians who care about the future of the planet might do worse than to study the elliptic logarithm problem.

5.7.9 What else goes wrong

Very few attacks on systems nowadays involve cryptanalysis in the sense of a mathematical attack on the encryption algorithm or key. There have indeed been attacks on systems designed in the 20th century, mostly involving keys that were kept too short by export-control rules, clueless designs or both. I already discussed in section 4.3.1 how weak crypto has facilitated a wave of car theft, as all the devices used for remote key entry were defeated one after another in 2005–15. In later chapters, I give examples of how the crypto wars and their export control rules resulted in attacks on door locks (section 13.2.5), mobile phones (section 22.3.1) and copyright enforcement (section 24.2.5).

Most attacks nowadays exploit the implementation. In chapter 2, I mentioned the scandal of NIST standardising a complicated random number generator based on elliptic curves that turned out to contain an NSA backdoor; see section 2.2.1.5. Poor random number generators have led to many other failures: RSA keys with common factors [1142], predictable seeds for discrete logs [1679], etc. These vulnerabilities have continued; thanks to the Internet of Things, the proportion of RSA certs one can find out there on the Internet that share a common factor with other RSA keys has actually risen between 2012 and 2020; 1 in 172 IoT certs are trivially vulnerable [1048].

Many of the practical attacks on cryptographic implementations that have forced significant changes over the past 20 years have exploited side channels such as timing and power analysis; I devote Chapter 19 to these.

[12]One of them, the McEliece cryptosystem, has been around since 1978; we've had digital signatures based on hash functions for about as long, and some of us used them in the 1990s to avoid paying patent royalties on RSA.

In Chapter 20, I'll discuss a number of systems that use public-key mechanisms in intricate ways to get interesting emergent properties, including the Signal messaging protocol, the TOR anonymity system, and cryptocurrencies. I'll also look at the crypto aspects of SGX enclaves. These also have interesting failure modes, some but not all of them relating to side channels.

In Chapter 21, I'll discuss protocols used in network infrastructure such as DKIM, DNSSec versus DNS over HTTP, and SSH.

5.8 Summary

Many ciphers fail because they're used badly, so the security engineer needs a clear idea of what different types of cipher do. This can be tackled at different levels; one is at the level of crypto theory, where we can talk about the random oracle model, the concrete model and the semantic security model, and hopefully avoid using weak modes of operation and other constructions. The next level is that of the design of individual ciphers, such as AES, or the number-theoretic mechanisms that underlie public-key cryptosystems and digital signature mechanisms. These also have their own specialised fields of mathematics, namely block cipher cryptanalysis and computational number theory. The next level involves implementation badness, which is much more intractable and messy. This involves dealing with timing, error handling, power consumption and all sorts of other grubby details, and is where modern cryptosystems tend to break in practice.

Peering under the hood of real systems, we've discussed how block ciphers for symmetric key applications can be constructed by the careful combination of substitutions and permutations; for asymmetric applications such as public key encryption and digital signature one uses number theory. In both cases, there is quite a large body of mathematics. Other kinds of ciphers – stream ciphers and hash functions – can be constructed from block ciphers by using them in suitable modes of operation. These have different error propagation, pattern concealment and integrity protection properties. A lot of systems fail because popular crypto libraries encourage programmers to use inappropriate modes of operation by exposing unsafe defaults. Never use ECB mode unless you really understand what you're doing.

There are many other things that can go wrong, from side channel attacks to poor random number generators. In particular, it is surprisingly hard to build systems that are robust even when components fail (or are encouraged to) and where the cryptographic mechanisms are well integrated with other measures such as access control and physical security. I'll return to this repeatedly in later chapters.

The moral is: Don't roll your own! Don't design your own protocols, or your own ciphers; and don't write your own crypto code unless you absolutely have to. If you do, then you not only need to read this book (and then read it again, carefully); you need to read up the relevant specialist material, speak to experts, and have capable motivated people try to break it. At the very least, you need to get your work peer-reviewed. Designing crypto is a bit like juggling chainsaws; it's just too easy to make fatal errors.

Research problems

There are many active threads in cryptography research. Many of them are where crypto meets a particular branch of mathematics (number theory, algebraic geometry, complexity theory, combinatorics, graph theory, and information theory). The empirical end of the business is concerned with designing primitives for encryption, signature and composite operations, and which perform reasonably well on available platforms. The two meet in the study of subjects ranging from cryptanalysis, to the search for primitives that combine provable security properties with decent performance.

The best way to get a flavor of what's going on at the theoretical end of things is to read the last few years' proceedings of research conferences such as Crypto, Eurocrypt and Asiacrypt; work on cipher design appears at Fast Software Encryption; attacks on implementations often appear at CHES; while attacks on how crypto gets used in systems can be found in the systems security conferences such as IEEE Security and Privacy, CCS and Usenix.

Further reading

The classic papers by Whit Diffie and Martin Hellman [556] and by Ron Rivest, Adi Shamir and Len Adleman [1610] are the closest to required reading in this subject. Bruce Schneier's *Applied Cryptography* [1670] covers a lot of ground at a level a non-mathematician can understand, and got crypto code out there in the 1990s despite US export control laws, but is now slightly dated. Alfred Menezes, Paul van Oorshot and Scott Vanstone's *Handbook of Applied Cryptography* [1291] is one reference book on the mathematical detail. Katz and Lindell is the book we get our students to read for the math. It gives an introduction to the standard crypto theory plus the number theory you need for public-key crypto (including elliptic curves and index calculus) but is also dated: they don't mention GCM, for example [1025].

There are many more specialist books. The bible on differential cryptanalysis is by its inventors Eli Biham and Adi Shamir [246], while a good short tutorial on linear and differential cryptanalysis was written by Howard Heys [897]. Doug Stinson's textbook has another detailed explanation of linear cryptanalysis [1832]; and the modern theory of block ciphers can be traced through the papers in the *Fast Software Encryption* conference series. The original book on modes of operation is by Carl Meyer and Steve Matyas [1303]. Neal Koblitz has a good basic introduction to the mathematics behind public key cryptography [1062]; and the number field sieve is described by Arjen and Henrik Lenstra [1143]. For the practical attacks on TLS over the past twenty years, see the survey paper by Christopher Meyer and Joerg Schwenk [1304] as well as the chapter on Side Channels later in this book.

If you want to work through the mathematical detail of theoretical cryptology, there's an recent graduate textbook by Dan Boneh and Victor Shoup [288]. A less thorough but more readable introduction to randomness and algorithms is in [836]. Research at the theoretical end of cryptology is found at the FOCS, STOC, Crypto, Eurocrypt and Asiacrypt conferences.

The history of cryptology is fascinating, and so many old problems keep on recurring that anyone thinking of working with crypto should study it. The standard work is Kahn [1003]; there are also compilations of historical articles from *Cryptologia* [529–531] as well as several books on the history of cryptology in World War II by Kahn, Marks, Welchman and others [440, 1004, 1226, 2011]. The NSA Museum at Fort George Meade, Md., is also worth a visit, but perhaps the best is the museum at Bletchley Park in England.

Finally, no chapter that introduces public key encryption would be complete without a mention that, under the name of 'non-secret encryption,' it was first discovered by James Ellis in about 1969. However, as Ellis worked for GCHQ, his work remained classified. The RSA algorithm was then invented by Clifford Cocks, and also kept secret. This story is told in [626]. One effect of the secrecy was that their work was not used: although it was motivated by the expense of Army key distribution, Britain's Ministry of Defence did not start building electronic key distribution systems for its main networks until 1992. And the classified community did not pre-invent digital signatures; they remain the achievement of Whit Diffie and Martin Hellman.

CHAPTER

6

Access Control

Anything your computer can do for you it can potentially do for someone else.

– ALAN COX

Microsoft could have incorporated effective security measures as standard, but good sense prevailed. Security systems have a nasty habit of backfiring and there is no doubt they would cause enormous problems.

– RICK MAYBURY

6.1 Introduction

I first learned to program on an IBM mainframe whose input was punched cards and whose output was a printer. You queued up with a deck of cards, ran the job, and went away with printout. All security was physical. Then along came machines that would run more than one program at once, and the *protection problem* of preventing one program from interfering with another. You don't want a virus to steal the passwords from your browser, or patch a banking application so as to steal your money. And many reliability problems stem from applications misunderstanding each other, or fighting with each other. But it's tricky to separate applications when the customer wants them to share data. It would make phishing much harder if your email client and browser ran on separate machines, so you were unable to just click on URLs in emails, but that would make life too hard.

From the 1970s, access control became the centre of gravity of computer security. It's where security engineering meets computer science. Its function is to control which principals (persons, processes, machines, . . .) have access to which resources in the system – which files they can read, which programs they can execute, how they share data with other principals, and so on. It's become horrendously complex. If you start out by leafing through the 7000-plus pages of Arm's architecture reference manual or the equally complex arrangements for Windows, your first reaction might be 'I wish I'd studied music instead!' In this chapter I try to help you make sense of it all.

Access control works at a number of different levels, including at least:

1. Access controls at the application level may express a very rich, domain-specific security policy. The call centre staff in a bank are typically not allowed to see your account details until you have answered a couple of security questions; this not only stops outsiders impersonating you, but also stops the bank staff looking up the accounts of celebrities, or their neighbours. Some transactions might also require approval from a supervisor. And that's nothing compared with the complexity of the access controls on a modern social networking site, which will have a thicket of rules about who can see, copy, and search what data from whom, and privacy options that users can set to modify these rules.
2. The applications may be written on top of middleware, such as a web browser, a bank's bookkeeping system or a social network's database management system. These enforce a number of protection properties. For example, bookkeeping systems ensure that a transaction that debits one account must credit another, with the debits and credits balancing so that money cannot be created or destroyed; they must also allow the system's state to be reconstructed later.
3. As the operating system constructs resources such as files and communications ports from lower level components, it has to provide ways to control access to them. Your Android phone treats apps written by different companies as different users and protects their data from each other. The same happens when a shared server separates the VMs, containers or other resources belonging to different users.
4. Finally, the operating system relies on the processor and its associated memory-management hardware, which control which memory addresses a given process or thread can access.

As we work up from the hardware through the operating system and middleware to the application layer, the controls become progressively more complex and less reliable. And we find the same access-control functions being implemented at multiple layers. For example, the separation between different phone apps that is provided by Android is mirrored in your browser which separates web page material according to the domain name it came from (though this separation is often less thorough). And the access controls built at the application layer or the middleware layer may largely duplicate access controls in the underlying operating system or hardware. It can get very messy, and to make sense of it we need to understand the underlying principles, the common architectures, and how they have evolved.

I will start off by discussing operating-system protection mechanisms that support the isolation of multiple processes. These came first historically – being invented along with the first time-sharing systems in the 1960s – and they remain the foundation on which many higher-layer mechanisms are built, as well as inspiring similar mechanisms at higher layers. They are often described as *discretionary access control* (DAC) mechanisms, which leave protection to the machine operator, or *mandatory access control* (MAC) mechanisms which are typically under the control of the vendor and protect the operating system itself from being modified by malware. I'll give an introduction to software attacks and techniques for defending against them – MAC, ASLR, sandboxing, virtualisation and what can be done with hardware. Modern hardware not only provides CPU support for virtualisation and capabilities, but also hardware support such as TPM chips for trusted boot to stop malware being persistent. These help us tackle the toxic legacy of the old single-user PC operating systems such as DOS and Win95/98 which let any process modify any data, and constrain the many applications that won't run unless you trick them into thinking that they are running with administrator privileges.

6.2 Operating system access controls

The access controls provided with an operating system typically authenticate principals using a mechanism such as passwords or fingerprints in the case of phones, or passwords or security protocols in the case of servers, then authorise access to files, communications ports and other system resources.

Access controls can often be modeled as a matrix of access permissions, with columns for files and rows for users. We'll write r for permission to read, w for permission to write, x for permission to execute a program, and - for no access at all, as shown in Figure 6.1.

In this simplified example, Sam is the system administrator and has universal access (except to the audit trail, which even he should only be able to read). Alice, the manager, needs to execute the operating system and application, but only through the approved interfaces – she mustn't have the ability to tamper

	Operating System	Accounts Program	Accounting Data	Audit Trail
Sam	rwx	rwx	rw	r
Alice	x	x	rw	–
Bob	rx	r	r	r

Figure 6.1: Naive access control matrix

with them. She also needs to read and write the data. Bob, the auditor, can read everything.

This is often enough, but in the specific case of a bookkeeping system it's not quite what we need. We want to ensure that transactions are well-formed – that each debit is balanced by credits somewhere else – so we don't want Alice to have uninhibited write access to the account file. We would also rather that Sam didn't have this access. So we would prefer that write access to the accounting data file be possible only via the accounting program. The access permissions might now look like in Figure 6.2:

User	Operating System	Accounts Program	Accounting Data	Audit Trail
Sam	rwx	rwx	r	r
Alice	rx	x	–	–
Accounts program	rx	rx	rw	w
Bob	rx	r	r	r

Figure 6.2: Access control matrix for bookkeeping

Another way of expressing a policy of this type would be with *access triples* of *(user, program, file)*. In the general case, our concern isn't with a program so much as a *protection domain* which is a set of processes or threads that share access to the same resources.

Access control matrices (whether in two or three dimensions) can be used to implement protection mechanisms as well as just model them. But they don't scale well: a bank with 50,000 staff and 300 applications would have a matrix of 15,000,000 entries, which might not only impose a performance overhead but also be vulnerable to administrators' mistakes. We will need a better way of storing and managing this information, and the two main options are to compress the users and to compress the rights. With the first, we can use groups or roles to manage large sets of users simultaneously, while with the second we may store the access control matrix either by columns (access control lists) or rows (capabilities, also known as 'tickets' to protocol engineers and 'permissions' on mobile phones) [1642, 2024].

6.2.1 Groups and roles

When we look at large organisations, we usually find that most staff fit into one of a small number of categories. A bank might have 40 or 50: teller, call centre operator, loan officer and so on. Only a few dozen people (security manager, chief foreign exchange dealer, ...) will need personally customised access rights.

So we need to design a set of groups, or functional roles, to which staff can be assigned. Some vendors (such as Microsoft) use the words *group* and *role* almost interchangeably, but a more careful definition is that a group is a list of principals, while a role is a fixed set of access permissions that one or more principals may assume for a period of time. The classic example of a role is the officer of the watch on a ship. There is exactly one watchkeeper at any one time, and there is a formal procedure whereby one officer relieves another when the watch changes. In most government and business applications, it's the role that matters rather than the individual.

Groups and roles can be combined. *The officers of the watch of all ships currently at sea* is a group of roles. In banking, the manager of the Cambridge branch might have their privileges expressed by membership of the group *manager* and assumption of the role *acting manager of Cambridge branch*. The group *manager* might express a rank in the organisation (and perhaps even a salary band) while the role *acting manager* might include an assistant accountant standing in while the manager, deputy manager, and branch accountant are all off sick.

Whether we need to be careful about this distinction is a matter for the application. In a warship, even an ordinary seaman may stand watch if everyone more senior has been killed. In a bank, we might have a policy that "transfers over $10m must be approved by two staff, one with rank at least manager and one with rank at least assistant accountant". If the branch manager is sick, then the assistant accountant acting as manager might have to get the regional head office to provide the second signature on a large transfer.

6.2.2 Access control lists

The traditional way to simplify the management of access rights is to store the access control matrix a column at a time, along with the resource to which the column refers. This is called an *access control list* or ACL (pronounced 'ackle'). In the first of our above examples, the ACL for file 3 (the account file) might look as shown here in Figure 6.3.

User	Accounting Data
Sam	rw
Alice	rw
Bob	r

Figure 6.3: Access control list (ACL)

ACLs have a number of advantages and disadvantages as a means of managing security state. They are a natural choice in environments where users manage their own file security, and became widespread in Unix systems from the 1970s. They are the basic access control mechanism in Unix-based systems such as Linux and Apple's macOS, as well as in derivatives such as Android and iOS. The access controls in Windows were also based on ACLs, but have become more complex over time. Where access control policy is set centrally, ACLs are suited to environments where protection is data-oriented; they are less suited where the user population is large and constantly changing, or where users want to be able to delegate their authority to run a particular program to another user for some set period of time. ACLs are simple to implement, but are not efficient for security checking at runtime, as the typical operating system knows which user is running a particular program, rather than what files it has been authorized to access since it was invoked. The operating system must either check the ACL at each file access, or keep track of the active access rights in some other way.

Finally, distributing the access rules into ACLs makes it tedious to find all the files to which a user has access. Verifying that no files have been left world-readable or even world-writable could involve checking ACLs on millions of user files; this is a real issue for large complex firms. Although you can write a script to check whether any file on a server has ACLs that breach a security policy, you can be tripped up by technology changes; the move to containers has led to many corporate data exposures as admins forgot to check the containers' ACLs too. (The containers themselves are often dreadful as it's a new technology being sold by dozens of clueless startups.) And revoking the access of an employee who has just been fired will usually have to be done by cancelling their password or authentication token.

Let's look at an important example of ACLs – their implementation in Unix (plus its derivatives Android, MacOS and iOS).

6.2.3 Unix operating system security

In traditional Unix systems, files are not allowed to have arbitrary access control lists, but simply `rwx` attributes that allow the file to be read, written and executed. The access control list as normally displayed has a flag to show whether the file is a directory, then flags r, w and x for owner, group and world respectively; it then has the owner's name and the group name. A directory with all flags set would have the ACL:

```
drwxrwxrwx Alice Accounts
```

In our first example in Figure 6.1, the ACL of file 3 would be:

```
-rw-r----- Alice Accounts
```

This records that the file is simply a file rather than a directory; that the file owner can read and write it; that group members (including Bob) can read it but not write it; that non-group members have no access at all; that the file owner is Alice; and that the group is Accounts.

The program that gets control when the machine is booted (the operating system kernel) runs as the supervisor, and has unrestricted access to the whole machine. All other programs run as users and have their access mediated by the supervisor. Access decisions are made on the basis of the userid associated with the program. However if this is zero (`root`), then the access control decision is 'yes'. So root can do what it likes – access any file, become any user, or whatever. What's more, there are certain things that only root can do, such as starting certain communication processes. The root userid is typically made available to the system administrator in systems with discretionary access control.

This means that the system administrator can do anything, so we have difficulty implementing an audit trail as a file that they cannot modify. In our example, Sam could tinker with the accounts, and have difficulty defending himself if he were falsely accused of tinkering; what's more, a hacker who managed to become the administrator could remove all evidence of his intrusion. The traditional, and still the most common, way to protect logs against root compromise is to keep them separate. In the old days that meant sending the system log to a printer in a locked room; nowadays, it means sending it to another machine, or even to a third-party service. Increasingly, it may also involve mandatory access control, as we discuss later.

Second, ACLs only contain the names of users, not of programs; so there is no straightforward way to implement access triples of (user, program, file). Instead, Unix provides an indirect method: the *set-user-id* (`suid`) file attribute. The owner of a program can mark the file representing that program as `suid`, which enables it to run with the privilege of its owner rather than the privilege of the user who has invoked it. So in order to achieve the functionality needed by our second example above, we could create a user '`account-package`' to own file 2 (the accounts package), make the file `suid` and place it in a directory to which Alice has access. This special user can then be given the access that the accounts program needs.

But when you take an access control problem that has three dimensions – (user, program, data) – and implement it using two-dimensional mechanisms, the outcome is much less intuitive than triples and people are liable to make mistakes. Programmers are often lazy or facing tight deadlines; so they just make the application `suid root`, so it can do anything. This practice leads to some shocking security holes. The responsibility for making access control decisions is moved from the operating system environment to the application program, and most programmers are insufficiently experienced to check everything they should. (It's hard to know what to check, as the person invoking a `suid root` program controls its environment and could manipulate this in unexpected ways.)

Third, ACLs are not very good at expressing mutable state. Suppose we want a transaction to be authorised by a manager and an accountant before it's acted on; we can either do this at the application level (say, by having queues of transactions awaiting a second signature) or by doing something fancy with `suid`. Managing stateful access rules is difficult; they can complicate the revocation of users who have just been fired, as it can be hard to track down the files they've opened, and stuff can get stuck.

Fourth, the Unix ACL only names one user. If a resource will be used by more than one of them, and you want to do access control at the OS level, you have a couple of options. With older systems you had to use groups; newer systems implement the Posix system of extended ACLs, which may contain any number of named user and named group entities. In theory, the ACL and `suid` mechanisms can often be used to achieve the desired effect. In practice, programmers are often in too much of a hurry to figure out how to do this, and security interfaces are usually way too fiddly to use. So people design their code to require much more privilege than it strictly ought to have, as that seems to be the only way to get the job done.

6.2.4 Capabilities

The next way to manage the access control matrix is to store it by rows. These are called *capabilities*, and in our example in Figure 6.1 above, Bob's capabilities would be as in Figure 6.4 here:

User	Operating System	Accounts Program	Accounting Data	Audit Trail
Bob	rx	r	r	r

Figure 6.4: A capability

The strengths and weaknesses of capabilities are roughly the opposite of ACLs. Runtime security checking is more efficient, and we can delegate a right without much difficulty: Bob could create a certificate saying 'Here is my capability and I hereby delegate to David the right to read file 4 from 9am to 1pm, signed Bob'. On the other hand, changing a file's status becomes tricky as it can be hard to find out which users have access. This can be tiresome when we have to investigate an incident or prepare evidence. In fact, scalable systems end up using de-facto capabilities internally, as instant system-wide revocation is just too expensive; in Unix, file descriptors are really capabilities, and continue to grant access for some time even after ACL permissions or even file owners change. In a distributed Unix, access may persist for the lifetime of Kerberos tickets.

Could we do away with ACLs entirely then? People built experimental machines in the 1970s that used capabilities throughout [2024]; the first commercial product was the Plessey System 250, a telephone-switch controller [1578]. The IBM AS/400 series systems brought capability-based protection to the mainstream computing market in 1988, and enjoyed some commercial success. The public key certificates used in cryptography are in effect capabilities, and became mainstream from the mid-1990s. Capabilities have started to supplement ACLs in operating systems, including more recent versions of Windows, FreeBSD and iOS, as I will describe later.

In some applications, they can be the natural way to express security policy. For example, a hospital may have access rules like 'a nurse shall have access to all the patients who are on his or her ward, or who have been there in the last 90 days'. In early systems based on traditional ACLs, each access control decision required a reference to administrative systems to find out which nurses and which patients were on which ward, when – but this made both the HR system and the patient administration system safety-critical, which hammered reliability. Matters were fixed by giving nurses ID cards with certificates that entitle them to access the files associated with a number of wards or hospital departments [535, 536]. If you can make the trust relationships in systems mirror the trust relationships in that part of the world you're trying to automate, you should. Working with the grain can bring advantages at all levels in the stack, making things more usable, supporting safer defaults, cutting errors, reducing engineering effort and saving money too.

6.2.5 DAC and MAC

In the old days, anyone with physical access to a computer controlled all of it: you could load whatever software you liked, inspect everything in memory or on disk and change anything you wanted to. This is the model behind *discretionary access control* (DAC): you start your computer in supervisor mode and then, as the administrator, you can make less-privileged accounts available for less-trusted tasks – such as running apps written by companies you don't entirely trust, or giving remote logon access to others. But this can make things hard to manage at scale, and in the 1970s the US military started a huge computer-security research program whose goal was to protect classified information: to ensure that a file marked 'Top Secret' would never be made available to a user with only a 'Secret' clearance, regardless of the actions of any ordinary user or even of the supervisor. In such a *multilevel secure* (MLS) system, the sysadmin is no longer the boss: ultimate control rests with a remote government authority that sets security policy. The mechanisms started to be described as *mandatory access control* (MAC). The supervisor, or root access if you will, is under remote control. This drove development of technology for mandatory access control – a fascinating story, which I tell in Part 2 of the book.

From the 1980s, safety engineers also worked on the idea of *safety integrity levels*; roughly, that a more dependable system must not rely on a less dependable one. They started to realise they needed something similar to multilevel security, but for safety. Military system people also came to realise that the tamper-resistance of the protection mechanisms themselves was of central importance. In the 1990s, as computers and networks became fast enough to handle audio and video, the creative industries lobbied for *digital rights management* (DRM) in the hope of preventing people undermining their business models by sharing music and video. This is also a form of mandatory access control – stopping a subscriber sharing a song with a non-subscriber is in many ways like stopping a Top Secret user sharing an intelligence report with a Secret user.

In the early 2000s, these ideas came together as a number of operating-system vendors started to incorporate ideas and mechanisms from the MAC research programme into their products. The catalyst was an initiative by Microsoft and Intel to introduce cryptography into the PC platform to support DRM. Intel believed the business market for PCs was saturated, so growth would come from home sales where, they believed, DRM would be a requirement. Microsoft started with DRM and then realised that offering rights management for documents too might be a way of locking customers tightly into Windows and Office. They set up an industry alliance, now called the Trusted Computing Group, to introduce cryptography and MAC mechanisms into the PC platform. To do this, the operating system had to be made tamper-resistant, and this is achieved by means of a separate processor, the Trusted Platform Module (TPM), basically a smartcard chip mounted on the PC motherboard to support trusted boot and hard disk encryption. The TPM monitors the boot process, and at each stage a hash of everything loaded so far is needed to retrieve the key needed to decrypt the next stage. The real supervisor on the system is now no longer you, the machine owner – it's the operating-system vendor.

MAC, based on TPMs and trusted boot, was used in Windows 6 (Vista) from 2006 as a defence against persistent malware[1]. The TPM standards and architecture were adapted by other operating-system vendors and device OEMs,

[1]Microsoft had had more ambitious plans; its project Palladium would have provided a new, more trusted world for rights-management apps, alongside the normal one for legacy software. They launched Information Rights Management – DRM for documents – in 2003 but corporates didn't buy it, seeing it as a lock-in play. A two-world implementation turned out to be too complex for Vista and after two separate development efforts it was abandoned; but the vision persisted from 2004 in Arm's TrustZone, which I discuss below.

and there is now even a project for an open-source TPM chip, OpenTitan, based on Google's product. However the main purpose of such a design, whether the design itself is open or closed, is to lock a hardware device to using specific software.

6.2.6 Apple's macOS

Apple's macOS operating system (formerly called OS/X or Mac OS X) is based on the FreeBSD version of Unix running on top of the Mach kernel. The BSD layer provides memory protection; applications cannot access system memory (or each others') unless running with advanced permissions. This means, for example, that you can kill a wedged application using the 'Force Quit' command without having to reboot the system. On top of this Unix core are a number of graphics components, including OpenGL, Quartz, QuickTime and Carbon, while at the surface the Aqua user interface provides an elegant and coherent view to the user.

At the file system level, macOS is almost a standard Unix. The default installation has the root account disabled, but users who may administer the system are in a group 'wheel' that allows them to su to root. If you are such a user, you can install programs (you are asked for the root password when you do so). Since version 10.5 (Leopard), it has been based on TrustedBSD, a variant of BSD that incorporates mandatory access control mechanisms, which are used to protect core system components against tampering by malware.

6.2.7 iOS

Since 2008, Apple has led the smartphone revolution with the iPhone, which (along with other devices like the iPad) uses the iOS operating system – which is now (in 2020) the second-most popular. iOS is based on Unix; Apple took the Mach kernel from CMU and fused it with the FreeBSD version of Unix, making a number of changes for performance and robustness. For example, in vanilla Unix a filename can have multiple pathnames that lead to an inode representing a file object, which is what the operating system sees; in iOS, this has been simplified so that files have unique pathnames, which in turn are the subject of the file-level access controls. Again, there is a MAC component, where mechanisms from Domain and Type Enforcement (DTE) are used to tamper-proof core system components (we'll discuss DTE in more detail in chapter 9). Apple introduced this because they were worried that apps would brick the iPhone, leading to warranty claims.

Apps also have *permissions*, which are capabilities; they request a capability to access device services such as the mobile network, the phone, SMSes, the camera, and the first time the app attempts to use such a service. This is granted if the user consents[2]. The many device services open up possible side-channel attacks; for example, an app that's denied access to the keyboard could deduce keypresses using the accelerometer and gyro. We'll discuss side channels in Part 2, in the chapter on that subject.

The Apple ecosystem is closed in the sense that an iPhone will only run apps that Apple has signed[3]. This enables the company to extract a share of app revenue, and also to screen apps for malware or other undesirable behaviour, such as the exploitation of side channels to defeat access controls.

The iPhone 5S introduced a fingerprint biometric and payments, adding a *secure enclave* (SE) to the A7 processor to give them separate protection. Apple decided to trust neither iOS nor TrustZone with such sensitive data, since vulnerabilities give transient access until they're patched. Its engineers also worried that an unpatchable exploit might be found in the ROM (this eventually happened, with Checkm8). While iOS has access to the system partition, the user's personal data are encrypted, with the keys managed by the SE. Key management is bootstrapped by a unique 256-bit AES key burned into fusible links on the system-on-chip. When the device is powered up, the user has ten tries to enter a passcode; only then are file keys derived from the master key and made available[4]. When the device is locked, some keys are still usable so that iOS can work out who sent an incoming message and notify you; the price of this convenience is that forensic equipment can get some access to user data. The SE also manages upgrades and prevents rollbacks. Such public information as there is can be found in the iOS Security white paper [129].

The security of mobile devices is a rather complex issue, involving not just access controls and tamper resistance, but the whole ecosystem – from the provision of SIM cards through the operation of app stores to the culture of how people use devices, how businesses try to manipulate them and how government agencies spy on them. I will discuss this in detail in the chapter on phones in Part 2.

6.2.8 Android

Android is the world's most widely used operating system, with 2.5 billion active Android devices in May 2019, according to Google's figures. Android

[2]The trust-on-first-use model goes back to the 1990s with the Java standard J2ME, popularised by Symbian, and the Resurrecting Duckling model from about the same time. J2ME also supported trust-on-install and more besides. When Apple and Android came along, they initially made different choices. In each case, having an app store was a key innovation; Nokia failed to realise that this was important to get a two-sided market going. The app store does some of the access control by deciding what apps can run. This is hard power in Apple's case, and soft power in Android's; we'll discuss this in the chapter on phones.

[3]There are a few exceptions: corporates can get signing keys for internal apps, but these can be blacklisted if abused.

[4]I'll discuss fusible links in the chapter on tamper resistance, and iPhone PIN retry defeats in the chapter on surveillance and privacy.

is based on Linux; apps from different vendors run under different userids. The Linux mechanisms control access at the file level, preventing one app from reading another's data and exhausting shared resources such as memory and CPU. As in iOS, apps have *permissions*, which are in effect capabilities: they grant access to device services such as SMSes, the camera and the address book.

Apps come in signed packages, as .apk files, and while iOS apps are signed by Apple, the verification keys for Android come in self-signed certificates and function as the developer's name. This supports integrity of updates while maintaining an open ecosystem. Each package contains a manifest that demands a set of permissions, and users have to approve the 'dangerous' ones – roughly, those that can spend money or compromise personal data. In early versions of Android, the user would have to approve the lot on installation or not run the app. But experience showed that most users would just click on anything to get through the installation process, and you found even flashlight apps demanding access to your address book, as they could sell it for money. So Android 6 moved to the Apple model of trust on first use; apps compiled for earlier versions still demand capabilities on installation.

Since Android 5, SELinux has been used to harden the operating system with mandatory access controls, so as not only to protect core system functions from attack but also to separate processes strongly and log violations. SELinux was developed by the NSA to support MAC in government systems; we'll discuss it further in chapter 9. The philosophy is actions require the consent of three parties: the user, the developer and the platform.

As with iOS (and indeed Windows), the security of Android is a matter of the whole ecosystem, not just of the access control mechanisms. The new phone ecosystem is sufficiently different from the old PC ecosystem, but inherits enough of the characteristics of the old wireline phone system, that it merits a separate discussion in the chapter on Phones in Part Two. We'll consider other aspects in the chapters on Side Channels and Surveillance.

6.2.9 Windows

The current version of Windows (Windows 10) appears to be the third-most popular operating system, having achieved a billion monthly active devices in March 2020 (until 2016, Windows was the leader). Windows has a scarily complex access control system, and a quick canter through its evolution may make it easier to understand what's going on.

Early versions of Windows had no access control. A break came with Windows 4 (NT), which was very much like Unix, and was inspired by it, but with some extensions. First, rather than just *read*, *write* and *execute* there were separate attributes for *take ownership*, *change permissions* and *delete*, to support more flexible delegation. These attributes apply to groups as well as users, and group permissions allow you to achieve much the same effect as `suid` programs in Unix. Attributes are not simply on or off, as in Unix, but have multiple values: you can set *AccessDenied*, *AccessAllowed* or *SystemAudit*. These are parsed in that order: if an `AccessDenied` is encountered in an ACL for the relevant user or group, then no access is permitted regardless of any conflicting `AccessAllowed` flags. The richer syntax lets you arrange matters so that everyday configuration tasks, such as installing printers, don't have to require full administrator privileges.

Second, users and resources can be partitioned into domains with distinct administrators, and trust can be inherited between domains in one direction or both. In a typical large company, you might put all the users into a personnel domain administered by HR, while assets such as servers and printers may be in resource domains under departmental control; individual workstations may even be administered by their users. Things can be arranged so that the departmental resource domains trust the user domain, but not vice versa – so a hacked or careless departmental administrator can't do too much external damage. The individual workstations would in turn trust the department (but not vice versa) so that users can perform tasks that require local privilege (such as installing software packages). Limiting the damage a hacked administrator can do still needs careful organisation. The data structure used to manage all this, and hide the ACL details from the user interface, is called the *Registry*. Its core used to be the *Active Directory*, which managed remote authentication – using either a Kerberos variant or TLS, encapsulated behind the *Security Support Provider Interface* (SSPI), which enables administrators to plug in other authentication services. Active Directory is essentially a database that organises users, groups, machines, and organisational units within a domain in a hierarchical namespace. It lurked behind Exchange, but is now being phased out as Microsoft becomes a cloud-based company and moves its users to Office365.

Windows has added capabilities in two ways which can override or complement ACLs. First, users or groups can be either allowed or denied access by means of profiles. Security policy is set by groups rather than for the system as a whole; group policy overrides individual profiles, and can be associated with sites, domains or organisational units, so it can start to tackle complex problems. Policies can be created using standard tools or custom coded.

The second way in which capabilities insinuate their way into Windows is that in many applications, people use TLS for authentication, and TLS certificates provide another, capability-oriented, layer of access control outside the purview of the Active Directory.

I already mentioned that Windows Vista introduced trusted boot to make the operating system itself tamper-resistant, in the sense that it always boots into a known state, limiting the persistence of malware. It added three further protection mechanisms to get away from the previous default of all software running as root. First, the kernel was closed off to developers; second, the graphics subsystem and most drivers were removed from the kernel; and third, *User Account Control* (UAC) replaced the default administrator privilege with user defaults instead. Previously, so many routine tasks needed administrative privilege that many enterprises made all their users administrators, which made it difficult to contain malware; and many developers wrote their software on the assumption that it would have access to everything. According to Microsoft engineers, this was a major reason for Windows' lack of robustness: applications monkey with system resources in incompatible ways. So they added an Application Information Service that launches applications which require elevated privilege and uses virtualisation to contain them: if they modify the registry, for example, they don't modify the 'real' registry but simply the version of it that they can see.

Since Vista, the desktop acts as the parent process for later user processes, so even administrators browse the web as normal users, and malware they download can't overwrite system files unless given later authorisation. When a task requires admin privilege, the user gets an *elevation prompt* asking them for an admin password. (Apple's macOS is similar although the details under the hood differ somewhat.) As admin users are often tricked into installing malicious software, Vista added mandatory access controls in the form of file integrity levels. The basic idea is that low-integrity processes (such as code you download from the Internet) should not be able to modify high-integrity data (such as system files) in the absence of some trusted process (such as verification of a signature by Microsoft on the code in question).

In 2012, Windows 8 added *dynamic access control* which lets you control user access by context, such as their work PC versus their home PC and their phone; this is done via account attributes in Active Directory, which appear as claims about a user, or in Kerberos tickets as claims about a domain. In 2016, Windows 8.1 added a cleaner abstraction with *principals*, which can be a user, computer, process or thread running in a security context or a group to which such a principal belongs, and *security identifiers* (SIDs), which represent such principals. When a user signs in, they get tickets with the SIDs to which they belong. Windows 8.1 also prepared for the move to cloud computing by adding *Microsoft accounts* (formerly LiveID), whereby a user signs in to a Microsoft cloud service rather than to a local server. Where credentials are stored locally, it protects them using virtualisation. Finally, Windows 10 added a number of features to support the move to cloud computing with a diversity of client devices, ranging from certificate pinning (which we'll discuss in the chapter on Network Security) to the abolition of the old secure attention sequence ctrl-alt-del (which is hard to do on touch-screen devices and which users didn't understand anyway).

To sum up, Windows evolved to provide a richer and more flexible set of access control tools than any system previously sold in mass markets. It was driven by corporate customers who need to manage tens of thousands of staff performing hundreds of different job roles across hundreds of different sites, providing internal controls to limit the damage that can be done by small numbers of dishonest staff or infected machines. (How such controls are actually designed will be our topic in the chapter on Banking and Bookkeeping.) The driver for this development was the fact that Microsoft made over half of its revenue from firms that licensed more than 25,000 seats; but the cost of the flexibility that corporate customers demanded is complexity. Setting up access control for a big Windows shop is a highly skilled job.

6.2.10 Middleware

Doing access control at the level of files and programs was fine in the early days of computing, when these were the resources that mattered. Since the 1980s, growing scale and complexity has led to access control being done at other levels instead of (or as well as) at the operating system level. For example, bookkeeping systems often run on top of a database product such as Oracle, which looks to the operating system as one large file. So most of the access control has to be done in the database; all the operating system supplies may be an authenticated ID for each user who logs on. And since the 1990s, a lot of the work at the client end has been done by the web browser.

6.2.10.1 Database access controls

Before people started using websites for shopping, database security was largely a back-room concern. But enterprises now have critical databases to handle inventory, dispatch and e-commerce, fronted by web servers that pass transactions to the databases directly. These databases now contain much of the data that matter to our lives – bank accounts, vehicle registrations and employment records – and failures sometimes expose them to random online users.

Database products, such as Oracle, DB2 and MySQL, have their own access control mechanisms, which are modelled on operating-system mechanisms, with privileges typically available for both users and objects (so the mechanisms are a mixture of access control lists and capabilities). However, the typical database access control architecture is comparable in complexity with Windows; modern databases are intrinsically complex, as are the things they support – typically business processes involving higher levels of abstraction than files or domains. There may be access controls aimed at preventing any user learning too much about too many customers; these tend to be stateful, and may deal with possible statistical inference rather than simple yes-no access rules. I devote a whole chapter in Part 2 to exploring the topic of Inference Control.

Ease of administration is often a bottleneck. In companies I've advised, the operating-system and database access controls have been managed by different departments, which don't talk to each other; and often IT departments have to put in crude hacks to make the various access control systems seem to work as one, but which open up serious holes.

Some products let developers bypass operating-system controls. For example, Oracle has both operating system accounts (whose users must be authenticated externally by the platform) and database accounts (whose users are authenticated directly by the Oracle software). It is often convenient to use the latter, to save the effort of synchronising with what other departments are doing. In many installations, the database is accessible directly from the outside; and even where it's shielded by a web service front-end, this often contains loopholes that let SQL code be inserted into the database.

Database security failures can thus cause problems directly. The Slammer worm in 2003 propagated itself using a stack-overflow exploit against Microsoft SQL Server 2000 and created large amounts of traffic as compromised machines sent floods of attack packets to random IP addresses.

Just as Windows is tricky to configure securely, because it's so complicated, the same goes for the typical database system. If you ever have to lock one down – or even just understand what's going on – you had better read a specialist textbook, such as [1175], or get in an expert.

6.2.10.2 Browsers

The web browser is another middleware platform on which we rely for access control and whose complexity often lets us down. The main access control rule is the *same-origin policy* whereby JavaScript or other active content on a web page is only allowed to communicate with the IP address that it originally came from; such code is run in a *sandbox* to prevent it altering the host system, as I'll describe in the next section. But many things can go wrong.

In previous editions of this book, we considered web security to be a matter of how the servers were configured, and whether this led to cross-site vulnerabilities. For example a malicious website can include links or form buttons aimed at creating a particular side-effect:

```
https://mybank.com/transfer.cgi?amount=10000USD&recipient=thief
```

The idea is that if a user clicks on this who is logged into `mybank.com`, there may be a risk that the transaction will be executed, as there's a valid session cookie. So payment websites deploy countermeasures such as using short-lived sessions and an anti-CSRF token (an invisible MAC of the session cookie), and checking the `Referer:` header. There are also issues around web authentication mechanisms; I described OAuth briefly in section 4.7.4. If you design web pages for a living you had better understand the mechanics of all this in rather more detail (see for example [120]); but many developers don't take enough care. For example, as I write in 2020, Amazon Alexa has just turned out to have a misconfigured policy on cross-origin resource sharing, which meant that anyone who compromised another Amazon subdomain could replace the skills on a target Alexa with malicious ones [1483].

By now there's a realisation that we should probably have treated browsers as access control devices all along. After all, the browser is the place on your laptop were you run code written by people you don't want to trust and who will occasionally be malicious; as we discussed earlier, mobile-phone operating systems run different apps as different users to give even more robust protection. Even in the absence of malice, you don't want to have to reboot your browser if it hangs because of a script in one of the tabs. (Chrome tries to ensure this by running each tab in a separate operating-system process.)

Bugs in browsers are exploited in *drive-by download* attacks, where visiting an attack web page can infect your machine, and even without this the modern web environment is extremely difficult to control. Many web pages are full of trackers and other bad things, supplied by multiple ad networks and data brokers, which make a mockery of the intent behind the same-origin policy. Malicious actors can even use web services to launder origin: for example, the attacker makes a mash-up of the target site plus some evil scripts of his own, and then gets the victim to view it through a proxy such as Google Translate. A prudent person will go to their bank website by typing in the URL directly, or using a bookmark; unfortunately, the marketing industry trains everyone to click on links in emails.

6.2.11 Sandboxing

The late 1990s saw the emergence of yet another type of access control: the software *sandbox*, introduced by Sun with its Java programming language. The model is that a user wants to run some code that she has downloaded as an applet, but is concerned that the applet might do something nasty, such as stealing her address book and mailing it off to a marketing company, or just hogging the CPU and running down the battery.

The designers of Java tackled this problem by providing a 'sandbox' – a restricted environment in which the code has no access to the local hard disk (or at most only temporary access to a restricted directory), and is only allowed to communicate with the host it came from (the *same-origin policy*). This is enforced by having the code executed by an interpreter – the Java Virtual Machine (JVM) – with only limited access rights [784]. This idea was adapted to JavaScript, the main scripting language used in web pages, though it's actually a different language; and other active content too. A version of Java is also used on smartcards so they can support applets written by different firms.

6.2.12 Virtualisation

Virtualisation is what powers cloud computing; it enables a single machine to emulate a number of machines independently, so that you can rent a *virtual machine* (VM) in a data centre for a few tens of dollars a month rather than having to pay maybe a hundred for a whole server. Virtualisation was invented in the 1960s by IBM [496]; a single machine could be partitioned using VM/370 into multiple virtual machines. Initially this was about enabling a new mainframe to run legacy apps from several old machine architectures; it soon became normal for a company that bought two computers to use one for its production environment and the other as a series of logically separate machines for development, testing, and minor applications. It's not enough to run a virtual machine monitor (VMM) on top of a host operating system, and then run other operating systems on top; you have to deal with sensitive instructions that reveal processor state such as absolute addresses and the processor clock. Working VMMs appeared for Intel platforms with VMware ESX Server in 2003 and (especially) Xen in 2003, which accounted for resource usage well enough to enable AWS and the cloud computing revolution. Things can be done more cleanly with processor support, which Intel has provided since 2006 with VT-x, and whose details I'll discuss below. VM security claims rest to some extent on the argument that a VMM hypervisor's code can be much smaller than an operating system and thus easier to code-review and secure; whether there are actually fewer vulnerabilities is of course an empirical question [1578].

At the client end, virtualisation allows people to run a guest operating system on top of a host (for example, Windows on top of macOS), which offers not just flexibility but the prospect of better containment. For example, an employee might have two copies of Windows running on their laptop – a locked-down version with the office environment, and another for use at home. Samsung offers Knox, which creates a virtual machine on a mobile phone that an employer can lock down and manage remotely, while the user enjoys a normal Android as well on the same device.

But using virtualisation to separate security domains on clients is harder than it looks. People need to share data between multiple VMs and if they use ad-hoc mechanisms, such as USB sticks and webmail accounts, this undermines the separation. Safe data sharing is far from trivial. For example, Bromium[5] offers VMs tailored to specific apps on corporate PCs, so you have one VM for Office, one for Acrobat reader, one for your browser and so on. This enables firms to work reasonably securely with old, unsupported software. So how do you download an Office document? Well, the browser exports the file from its VM to the host hard disc, marking it 'untrusted', so when the user tries to open it they're given a new VM with that document plus Office and nothing else.

[5]Now owned by HP

When they then email this untrusted document, there's an Outlook plugin that stops it being rendered in the 'sent mail' pane. Things get even more horrible with network services integrated into apps; the rules on what sites can access which cookies are complicated, and it's hard to deal with single signon and workflows that cross multiple domains. The clipboard also needs a lot more rules to control it. Many of the rules change from time to time, and are heuristics rather than hard, verifiable access logic. In short, using VMs for separation at the client requires deep integration with the OS and apps if it's to appear transparent to the user, and there are plenty of tradeoffs made between security and usability. In effect, you're retrofitting virtualisation on to an existing OS and apps that were not built for it.

Containers have been the hot new topic in the late 2010s. They evolved as a lightweight alternative to virtualisation in cloud computing and are often confused with it, especially by the marketing people. My definition is that while a VM has a complete operating system, insulated from the hardware by a hypervisor, a container is an isolated guest process that shares a kernel with other containers. Container implementations separate groups of processes by virtualising a subset of operating-system mechanisms, including process identifiers, interprocess communication, and namespaces; they also use techniques such as sandboxing and system call filtering. The business incentive is to minimise the guests' size, their interaction complexity and the costs of managing them, so they are deployed along with orchestration tools. Like any other new technology, there are many startups with more enthusiasm than experience. A 2019 survey by Jerry Gamblin disclosed that of the top 1000 containers available to developers on Docker Hub, 194 were setting up blank root passwords [743]. If you're going to use cloud systems, you need to pay serious attention to your choice of tools, and also learn yet another set of access control mechanisms – those offered by the service provider, such as the Amazon AWS Identity and Access Management (IAM). This adds another layer of complexity, which people can get wrong. For example, in 2019 a security firm providing biometric identification services to banks and the police left its entire database unprotected; two researchers found it using Elasticsearch and discovered millions of people's photos, fingerprints, passwords and security clearance levels on a database that they could not only read but write [1867].

But even if you tie down a cloud system properly, there are hardware limits on what the separation mechanisms can achieve. In 2018, two classes of powerful side-channel attacks were published: Meltdown and Spectre, which I discuss in the following section and at greater length in the chapter on side channels. Those banks that use containers to deploy payment processing rely, at least implicitly, on their containers being difficult to target in a cloud the size of Amazon's or Google's. For a comprehensive survey of the evolution of virtualisation and containers, see Randal [1578].

6.3 Hardware protection

Most access control systems set out not just to control what users can do, but to limit what programs can do as well. In many systems, users can either write programs, or download and install them, and these programs may be buggy or even malicious.

Preventing one process from interfering with another is the *protection problem*. The *confinement problem* is that of preventing programs communicating outward other than through authorized channels. There are several flavours of each. The goal may be to prevent active interference, such as memory overwriting, or to stop one process reading another's memory directly. This is what commercial operating systems set out to do. Military systems may also try to protect *metadata* – data about other data, or subjects, or processes – so that, for example, a user can't find out what other users are logged on to the system or what processes they're running.

Unless one uses sandboxing techniques (which are too restrictive for general programming environments), solving the protection problem on a single processor means, at the very least, having a mechanism that will stop one program from overwriting another's code or data. There may be areas of memory that are shared to allow interprocess communication; but programs must be protected from accidental or deliberate modification, and must have access to memory that is similarly protected.

This usually means that hardware access control must be integrated with the processor's memory management functions. A classic mechanism is *segment addressing*. Memory is addressed by two registers, a segment register that points to a segment of memory, and an address register that points to a location within that segment. The segment registers are controlled by the operating system, often by a component of it called the *reference monitor* which links the access control mechanisms with the hardware.

The implementation has become more complex as processors themselves have. Early IBM mainframes had a two-state CPU: the machine was either in authorized state or it was not. In the latter case, the program was restricted to a memory segment allocated by the operating system; in the former, it could write to segment registers at will. An authorized program was one that was loaded from an authorized library.

Any desired access control policy can be implemented on top of this, given suitable authorized libraries, but this is not always efficient; and system security depended on keeping bad code (whether malicious or buggy) out of the authorized libraries. So later processors offered more complex hardware mechanisms. Multics, an operating system developed at MIT in the 1960s and which inspired Unix, introduced *rings of protection* which express differing levels of privilege: ring 0 programs had complete access to disk, supervisor states ran in ring 2, and user code at various less privileged levels [1687]. Many of its features have been adopted in more recent processors.

There are a number of general problems with interfacing hardware and software security mechanisms. For example, it often happens that a less privileged process such as application code needs to invoke a more privileged process (e.g., a device driver). The mechanisms for doing this need to be designed with care, or security bugs can be expected. Also, performance may depend quite drastically on whether routines at different privilege levels are called by reference or by value [1687].

6.3.1 Intel processors

The Intel 8088/8086 processors used in early PCs had no distinction between system and user mode, and thus any running program controlled the whole machine[6]. The 80286 added protected segment addressing and rings, so for the first time a PC could run proper operating systems. The 80386 had built-in virtual memory, and large enough memory segments (4 Gb) that they could be ignored and the machine treated as a 32-bit flat address machine. The 486 and Pentium series chips added more performance (caches, out of order execution and additional instructions such as MMX).

The rings of protection are supported by a number of mechanisms. The current privilege level can only be changed by a process in ring 0 (the kernel). Procedures cannot access objects in lower-level rings directly but there are *gates* that allow execution of code at a different privilege level and manage the supporting infrastructure, such as multiple stack segments.

From 2006, Intel added hardware support for x86 virtualisation, known as Intel VT, which helped drive the adoption of cloud computing. Some processor architectures such as S/370 and PowerPC are easy to virtualise, and the theoretical requirements for this had been established in 1974 by Gerald Popek and Robert Goldberg [1535]; they include that all sensitive instructions that expose raw processor state must be privileged instructions. The native Intel instruction set, however, has sensitive user-mode instructions, requiring messy workarounds such as application code rewriting and patches to hosted operating systems. Adding VMM support in hardware means that you can run an operating system in ring 0 as it was designed; the VMM has its own copy of the memory architecture underneath. You still have to trap sensitive opcodes, but system calls don't automatically require VMM intervention, you can run unmodified operating systems, things go faster and systems are generally more robust. Modern Intel CPUs now have nine rings: ring 0–3 for normal code,

[6]They had been developed on a crash programme to save market share following the advent of RISC processors and the market failure of the iAPX432.

under which is a further set of ring 0–3 VMM root mode for the hypervisor, and at the bottom is *system management mode* (SMM) for the BIOS. In practice, the four levels that are used are SMM, ring 0 of VMX root mode, the normal ring 0 for the operating system, and ring 3 above that for applications.

In 2015, Intel released Software Guard eXtensions (SGX), which lets trusted code run in an *enclave* – an encrypted section of the memory – while the rest of the code is executed as usual. The company had worked on such architectures in the early years of the Trusted Computing initiative, but let things slide until it needed an enclave architecture to compete with TrustZone, which I discuss in the next section. The encryption is performed by a Memory Encryption Engine (MEE), while SGX also introduces new instructions and memory-access checks to ensure non-enclave processes cannot access enclave memory (not even root processes). SGX has been promoted for DRM and securing cloud VMs, particularly those containing crypto keys, credentials or sensitive personal information; this is under threat from Spectre and similar attacks, which I discuss in detail in the chapter on side channels. Since SGX's security perimeter is the CPU, its software is encrypted in main memory, which imposes real penalties in both time and space. Another drawback used to be that SGX code had to be signed by Intel. The company has now delegated signing (so bad people can get code signed) and from SGXv2 will open up the root of trust to others. So people are experimenting with SGX malware, which can remain undetectable by anti-virus software. As SGX apps cannot issue syscalls, it had been hoped that enclave malware couldn't do much harm, yet Michael Schwarz, Samuel Weiser and Daniel Gruss have now worked out how to mount stealthy return-oriented programming (ROP) attacks from an enclave on a host app; they argue that the problem is a lack of clarity about what enclaves are supposed to do, and that any reasonable threat model must include untrusted enclaves [1691]. This simple point may force a rethink of enclave architectures; Intel says 'In the future, Intel's control-flow enforcement technology (CET) should help address this threat inside SGX'[7]. As for what comes next, AMD released full system memory encryption in 2016, and Intel announced a competitor. This aimed to deal with cold-boot and DMA attacks, and protect code against an untrusted hypervisor; it might also lift space and performance limits on next-generation enclaves. However, Jan Werner and colleagues found multiple inference and data-injection attacks on AMD's offering when it's used in a virtual environment. [2014]. There's clearly some way to go.

As well as the access-control vulnerabilities, there are crypto issues, which I'll discuss in the chapter on Advanced Cryptographic Engineering.

[7]The best defence against ROP attacks in 2019 appears to be Apple's mechanism, in the iPhone X3 and later, for signing pointers with a key that's kept in a register; this stops ROP attacks as the attacker can't guess the signatures.

6.3.2 Arm processors

The Arm is the processor core most commonly used in phones, tablets and IoT devices; billions have been used in mobile phones alone, with a high-end device having several dozen Arm cores of various sizes in its chipset. The original Arm (which stood for *Acorn Risc Machine*) was the first commercial RISC design; it was released in 1985, just before MIPS. In 1991, Arm became a separate firm which, unlike Intel, does not own or operate any fabs: it licenses a range of processor cores, which chip designers include in their products. Early cores had a 32-bit datapath and contained fifteen registers, of which seven were shadowed by banked registers for system processes to cut the cost of switching context on interrupt. There are multiple supervisor modes, dealing with fast and normal interrupts, the system mode entered on reset, and various kinds of exception handling. The core initially contained no memory management, so Arm-based designs could have their hardware protection extensively customized; there are now variants with *memory protection units* (MPUs), and others with *memory management units* (MMUs) that handle virtual memory as well.

In 2011, Arm launched version 8, which supports 64-bit processing and enables multiple 32-bit operating systems to be virtualised. Hypervisor support added yet another supervisor mode. The cores come in all sizes, from large 64-bit superscalar processors with pipelines over a dozen stages deep, to tiny ones for cheap embedded devices.

TrustZone is a security extension that supports the 'two worlds' model mentioned above and was made available to mobile phone makers in 2004 [45]. Phones were the 'killer app' for enclaves as operators wanted to lock subsidised phones and regulators wanted to make the baseband software that controls the RF functions tamper-resistant [1241]. TrustZone supports an open world for a normal operating system and general-purpose applications, plus a closed enclave to handle sensitive operations such as cryptography and critical I/O (in a mobile phone, this can include the SIM card and the fingerprint reader). Whether the processor is in a secure or non-secure state is orthogonal to whether it's in user mode or a supervisor mode (though the interaction between secure mode and hypervisor mode can be nontrivial). The closed world hosts a single *trusted execution environment* (TEE) with separate stacks, a simplified operating system, and typically runs only trusted code signed by the OEM – although Samsung's Knox, which sets out to provide 'home' and 'work' environments on your mobile phone, allows regular rich apps to execute in the secure environment.

Although TrustZone was released in 2004, it was kept closed until 2015; OEMs used it to protect their own interests and didn't open it up to app developers, except occasionally under NDA. As with Intel SGX, there appears to be no way yet to deal with malicious enclave apps, which might come bundled as DRM with gaming apps or be mandated by authoritarian states; and, as with Intel SGX, enclave apps created with TrustZone can raise issues of transparency and control, which can spill over into auditability, privacy and much else. Again, company insiders mutter 'wait and see'; no doubt we shall.

Arm's latest offering is CHERI[8] which adds fine-grained capability support to Arm CPUs. At present, browsers such as Chrome put tabs in different processes, so that one webpage can't slow down the other tabs if its scripts run slowly. It would be great if each object in each web page could be sandboxed separately, but this isn't possible because of the large cost, in terms of CPU cycles, of each inter-process context switch. CHERI enables a process spawning a subthread to allocate it read and write accesses to specific ranges of memory, so that multiple sandboxes can run in the same process. This was announced as a product in 2018 and we expect to see first silicon in 2021. The long-term promise of this technology is that, if it were used thoroughly in operating systems such as Windows, Android or iOS, it would have prevented most of the zero-day exploits of recent years. Incorporating a new protection technology at scale costs real money, just like the switch from 32-bit to 64-bit CPUs, but it could save the cost of lots of patches.

6.4 What goes wrong

Popular operating systems such as Android, Linux and Windows are very large and complex, with their features tested daily by billions of users under very diverse circumstances. Many bugs are found, some of which give rise to vulnerabilities, which have a typical lifecycle. After discovery, a bug is reported to a CERT or to the vendor; a patch is shipped; the patch is reverse-engineered, and an exploit may be produced; and people who did not apply the patch in time may find that their machines have been compromised. In a minority of cases, the vulnerability is exploited at once rather than reported – called a *zero-day* exploit as attacks happen from day zero of the vulnerability's known existence. The economics, and the ecology, of the vulnerability lifecycle are the subject of study by security economists; I'll discuss them in Part 3.

The traditional goal of an attacker was to get a normal account on the system and then become the system administrator, so they could take over the system completely. The first step might have involved guessing, or social-engineering, a password, and then using an operating-system bug to escalate from user to root [1131].

The user/root distinction became less important in the twenty-first century for two reasons. First, Windows PCs were the most common online devices

[8]Full disclosure: this was developed by a team of my colleagues at Cambridge and elsewhere, led by Robert Watson.

(until 2017 when Android overtook them) so they were the most common attack targets; and as they ran many applications as administrator, an application that could be compromised typically gave administrator access. Second, attackers come in two basic types: targeted attackers, who want to spy on a specific individual and whose goal is typically to acquire access to that person's accounts; and scale attackers, whose goal is typically to compromise large numbers of PCs, which they can organise into a botnet. This, too, doesn't require administrator access. Even if your mail client does not run as administrator, it can still be used by a spammer who takes control.

However, botnet herders do prefer to install *rootkits* which, as their name suggests, run as root; they are also known as *remote access trojans* or RATs. The user/root distinction does still matter in business environments, where you do not want such a kit installed as an *advanced persistent threat* by a hostile intelligence agency, or by a corporate espionage firm, or by a crime gang doing reconnaissance to set you up for a large fraud.

A separate distinction is whether an exploit is *wormable* – whether it can be used to spread malware quickly online from one machine to another without human intervention. The Morris worm was the first large-scale case of this, and there have been many since. I mentioned Wannacry and NotPetya in chapter 2; these used a vulnerability developed by the NSA and then leaked to other state actors. Operating system vendors react quickly to wormable exploits, typically releasing out-of-sequence patches, because of the scale of the damage they can do. The most troublesome wormable exploits at the time of writing are variants of Mirai, a worm used to take over IoT devices that use known root passwords. This appeared in October 2016 to exploit CCTV cameras, and hundreds of versions have been produced since, adapted to take over different vulnerable devices and recruit them into botnets. Wormable exploits often use root access but don't have to; it is sufficient that the exploit be capable of automatic onward transmission[9]. I will discuss the different types of malware in more detail in section 21.3.

However, the basic types of technical attack have not changed hugely in a generation and I'll now consider them briefly.

6.4.1 Smashing the stack

The classic software exploit is the memory overwriting attack, colloquially known as 'smashing the stack', as used by the Morris worm in 1988; this infected so many Unix machines that it disrupted the Internet and brought

[9]In rare cases even human transmission can make malware spread quickly: an example was the ILoveYou worm which spread itself in 2000 via an email with that subject line, which caused enough people to open it, running a script that caused it to be sent to everyone in the new victim's address book.

malware forcefully to the attention of the mass media [1810]. Attacks involving violations of memory safety accounted for well over half the exploits against operating systems in the late 1990s and early 2000s [484] but the proportion has been dropping slowly since then.

Programmers are often careless about checking the size of arguments, so an attacker who passes a long argument to a program may find that some of it gets treated as code rather than data. The classic example, used in the Morris worm, was a vulnerability in the Unix `finger` command. A common implementation of this would accept an argument of any length, although only 256 bytes had been allocated for this argument by the program. When an attacker used the command with a longer argument, the trailing bytes of the argument ended up overwriting the stack and being executed by the system.

The usual exploit technique was to arrange for the trailing bytes of the argument to have a *landing pad* – a long space of *no-operation* (NOP) commands, or other register commands that didn't change the control flow, and whose task was to catch the processor if it executed any of them. The landing pad delivered the processor to the attack code which will do something like creating a shell with administrative privilege directly (see Figure 6.5).

Stack-overwriting attacks were around long before 1988. Most of the early 1960s time-sharing systems suffered from this vulnerability, and fixed it [805]. Penetration testing in the early '70s showed that one of the most frequently-used attack strategies was still "unexpected parameters" [1168]. Intel's 80286 processor introduced explicit parameter checking instructions – verify read, verify write, and verify length – in 1982, but they were avoided by most software designers to prevent architecture dependencies. Stack overwriting attacks have been found against all sorts of programmable devices – even against things like smartcards and hardware security modules, whose designers really should have known better.

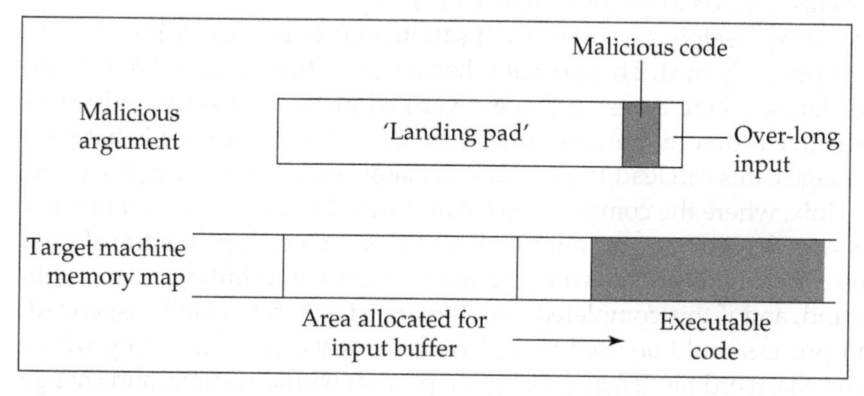

Figure 6.5: Stack smashing attack

6.4.2 Other technical attacks

Many vulnerabilities are variations on the same general theme, in that they occur when data in grammar A is interpreted as being code in grammar B. A stack overflow is when data are accepted as input (e.g. a URL) and end up being executed as machine code. These are failures of *type safety*. In fact, a stack overflow can be seen either as a memory safety failure or as a failure to sanitise user input, but there are purer examples of each type.

The *use after free* type of safety failure is now the most common cause of remote execution vulnerabilities and has provided a lot of attacks on browsers in recent years. It can happen when a chunk of memory is freed and then still used, perhaps because of confusion over which part of a program is responsible for freeing it. If a malicious chunk is now allocated, it may end up taking its place on the heap, and when an old innocuous function is called a new, malicious function may be invoked instead. There are many other variants on the memory safety theme; buffer overflows can be induced by improper string termination, passing an inadequately sized buffer to a path manipulation function, and many other subtle errors. See Gary McGraw's book *'Software Security* [1268] for a taxonomy.

SQL injection attacks are the most common attack based on failure to sanitise input, and arise when a careless web developer passes user input to a back-end database without checking to see whether it contains SQL code. The game is often given away by error messages, from which a capable and motivated user may infer enough to mount an attack. There are similar command-injection problems afflicting other languages used by web developers, such as PHP. The usual remedy is to treat all user input as suspicious and validate it. But this can be harder than it looks, as it's difficult to anticipate all possible attacks and the filters written for one shell may fail to be aware of extensions present in another. Where possible, one should only act on user input in a safe context, by designing such attacks out; where it's necessary to blacklist specific exploits, the mechanism needs to be competently maintained.

Once such type-safety and input-sanitisation attacks are dealt with, *race conditions* are probably next. These occur when a transaction is carried out in two or more stages, where access rights are verified at the first stage and something sensitive is done at the second. If someone can alter the state in between the two stages, this can lead to an attack. A classic example arose in early versions of Unix, where the command to create a directory, '`mkdir`', used to work in two steps: the storage was allocated, and then ownership was transferred to the user. Since these steps were separate, a user could initiate a '`mkdir`' in background, and if this completed only the first step before being suspended, a second process could be used to replace the newly created directory with a link to the password file. Then the original process would resume, and change ownership of the password file to the user.

A more modern example arises with the wrappers used in containers to intercept system calls made by applications to the operating system, parse them, and modify them if need be. These wrappers execute in the kernel's address space, inspect the enter and exit state on all system calls, and encapsulate only security logic. They generally assume that system calls are atomic, but modern operating system kernels are highly concurrent. System calls are not atomic with respect to each other; there are many possibilities for two system calls to race each other for access to shared memory, which gives rise to *time-of-check-to-time-of-use* (TOCTTOU) attacks. An early (2007) example calls a path whose name spills over a page boundary by one byte, causing the kernel to sleep while the page is fetched; it then replaces the path in memory [1996]. There have been others since, and as more processors ship in each CPU chip as time passes, and containers become an ever more common way of deploying applications, this sort of attack may become more and more of a problem. Some operating systems have features specifically to deal with concurrency attacks, but this field is still in flux.

A different type of timing attack can come from backup and recovery systems. It's convenient if you can let users recover their own files, rather than having to call a sysadmin – but how do you protect information assets from a time traveller? People can reacquire access rights that were revoked, and play even more subtle tricks.

One attack that has attracted a lot of research effort recently is *return-oriented programming* (ROP) [1711]. Many modern systems try to prevent type safety attacks by *data execution prevention* – marking memory as either code or data, a measure that goes back to the Burroughs 5000; and if all the code is signed, surely you'd think that unauthorised code cannot be executed? Wrong! An attacker can look for *gadgets* – sequences of instructions with some useful effect, ending in a return. By collecting enough gadgets, it's possible to assemble a machine that's Turing powerful, and implement our attack code as a chain of ROP gadgets. Then all one has to do is seize control of the call stack. This evolved from the *return-to-libc attack* which uses the common shared library `libc` to provide well-understood gadgets; many variants have been developed since, including an attack that enables malware in an SGX enclave to mount stealthy attacks on host apps [1691]. The latest attack variant, *block-oriented programming* (BOP), can often generate attacks automatically from crashes discovered by program fuzzing, defeating current control-flow integrity controls [966]. This coevolution of attack and defence will no doubt continue.

Finally there are *side channels*. The most recent major innovation in attack technology targets CPU pipeline behaviour. In early 2018, two game-changing attacks pioneered the genre: *Meltdown*, which exploits side-channels created by out-of-order execution on Intel processors [1173], and *Spectre*, which exploits speculative execution on Intel, AMD and Arm processors [1070]. The basic idea is that large modern CPUs' pipelines are so long and complex that they look ahead and anticipate the next dozen instructions, even if these are instructions that the current process wouldn't be allowed to execute (imagine the access check is two instructions in the future and the read operation it will forbid is two instructions after that). The path not taken can still load information into a cache and thus leak information in the form of delays. With some cunning, one process can arrange things to read the memory of another. I will discuss Spectre and Meltdown in more detail later in the chapter on side channels. Although mitigations have been published, further attacks of the same general kind keep on being discovered, and it may take several years and a new generation of processors before they are brought entirely under control. It all reminds me of a saying by Roger Needham, that optimisation consists of replacing something that works with something that almost works, but is cheaper. Modern CPUs are so heavily optimised that we're bound to see more variants on the Spectre theme. Such attacks limit the protection that can be offered not just by containers and VMs, but also by enclave mechanisms such as TrustZone and SGX. In particular, they may stop careful firms from entrusting high-value cryptographic keys to enclaves and prolong the service life of old-fashioned hardware cryptography.

6.4.3 User interface failures

A common way to attack a fortress is to trick the guards into helping you, and operating systems are no exception. One of the earliest attacks was the *Trojan Horse*, a program the administrator is invited to run but which contains a nasty surprise. People would write games that checked whether the player was the system administrator, and if so would create another administrator account with a known password. A variant was to write a program with the same name as a common system utility, such as the `ls` command which lists all the files in a Unix directory, and design it to abuse the administrator privilege (if any) before invoking the genuine utility. You then complain to the administrator that something's wrong with the directory. When they enter the directory and type `ls` to see what's there, the damage is done. This is an example of the *confused deputy* problem: if A does some task on behalf of B, and its authority comes from both A and B, and A's authority exceeds B, things can go wrong. The fix in this particular case was simple: an administrator's 'PATH' variable (the list of directories to be searched for a suitably-named program when a command is invoked) should not contain '.' (the symbol for the current directory). Modern Unix versions ship with this as a default. But it's still an example of how you have to get lots of little details right for access control to be robust, and these details aren't always obvious in advance.

Perhaps the most serious example of user interface failure, in terms of the number of systems historically attacked, consists of two facts: first, Windows is forever popping up confirmation dialogues, which trained people to click boxes away to get their work done; and second, that until 2006 a user needed to be the administrator to install anything. The idea was that restricting software installation to admins enabled Microsoft's big corporate customers, such as banks and government departments, to lock down their systems so that staff couldn't run games or other unauthorised software. But in most environments, ordinary people need to install software to get their work done. So hundreds of millions of people had administrator privileges who shouldn't have needed them, and installed malicious code when a website simply popped up a box telling them to do something. This was compounded by the many application developers who insisted that their code run as root, either out of laziness or because they wanted to collect data that they really shouldn't have had. Windows Vista started to move away from this, but a malware ecosystem is now well established in the PC world, and one is starting to take root in the Android ecosystem as businesses pressure people to install apps rather than using websites, and the apps demand access to all sorts of data and services that they really shouldn't have. We'll discuss this later in the chapter on phones.

6.4.4 Remedies

Software security is not all doom and gloom; things got substantially better during the 2000s. At the turn of the century, 90% of vulnerabilties were buffer overflows; by the time the second edition of this book came out in 2008, it was just under half, and now it's even less. Several things made a difference.

1. The first consists of specific defences. *Stack canaries* are a random number inserted by the compiler next to the return address on the stack. If the stack is overwritten, then with high probability the canary will change [484]. *Data execution prevention* (DEP) marks all memory as either data or code, and prevents the former being executed; it appeared in 2003 with Windows XP. *Address space layout randomisation* (ASLR) arrived at the same time; by making the memory layout different in each instance of a system, it makes it harder for an attacker to predict target addresses. This is particularly important now that there are toolkits to do ROP attacks, which bypass DEP. *Control flow integrity* mechanisms involve analysing the possible control-flow graph at compile time and enforcing this at runtime by validating indirect control-flow transfers; this appeared in 2005 and was incorporated in various products over the following decade [351]. However the analysis is not precise, and block-oriented programming attacks are among the tricks that have evolved to exploit the gaps [966].
2. The second consists of better general-purpose tools. Static-analysis programs such as Coverity can find large numbers of potential software

bugs and highlight ways in which code deviates from best practice; if used from the start of a project, they can make a big difference. (If added later, they can throw up thousands of alerts that are a pain to deal with.) The radical solution is to use a better language; my colleagues increasingly write systems code in Rust rather than in C or C++[10].

3. The third is better training. In 2002, Microsoft announced a security initiative that involved every programmer being trained in how to write secure code. (The book they produced for this, *'Writing Secure Code'* [929], is still worth a read.) Other companies followed suit.
4. The latest approach is DevSecOps, which I discuss in section 27.5.6. Agile development methodology is extended to allow very rapid deployment of patches and response to incidents; it may enable the effort put into design, coding and testing to be aimed at the most urgent problems.

Architecture matters; having clean interfaces that evolve in a controlled way, under the eagle eye of someone experienced who has a long-term stake in the security of the product, can make a huge difference. Programs should only have as much privilege as they need: the *principle of least privilege* [1642]. Software should also be designed so that the default configuration, and in general, the easiest way of doing something, should be safe. Sound architecture is critical in achieving safe defaults and using least privilege. However, many systems are shipped with dangerous defaults and messy code, exposing all sorts of interfaces to attacks like SQL injection that just shouldn't happen. These involve failures of incentives, personal and corporate, as well as inadequate education and the poor usability of security tools.

6.4.5 Environmental creep

Many security failures result when environmental change undermines a security model. Mechanisms that worked adequately in an initial environment often fail in a wider one.

Access control mechanisms are no exception. Unix, for example, was originally designed as a 'single user Multics' (hence the name). It then became an operating system to be used by a number of skilled and trustworthy people in a laboratory who were sharing a single machine. In this environment the function of the security mechanisms is mostly to contain mistakes; to prevent one user's typing errors or program crashes from deleting or overwriting another user's files. The original security mechanisms were quite adequate for this purpose.

[10]Rust emerged from Mozilla research in 2010 and has been used to redevelop Firefox; it's been voted the favourite language in the Stack Overflow annual survey from 2016–2019.

But Unix security became a classic 'success disaster'. Over the 50 years since Ken Thomson started work on it at Bell Labs in 1969, Unix was repeatedly extended without proper consideration being given to how the protection mechanisms also needed to be extended. The Berkeley versions assumed an extension from a single machine to a network of machines that were all on one LAN and all under one management. The Internet mechanisms (telnet, ftp, DNS, SMTP) were originally written for mainframes on a secure network. Mainframes were autonomous, the network was outside the security protocols, and there was no transfer of authorisation. So remote authentication, which the Berkeley model really needed, was simply not supported. The Sun extensions such as NFS added to the party, assuming a single firm with multiple trusted LANs. We've had to retrofit protocols like Kerberos, TLS and SSH as duct tape to hold the world together. The arrival of billions of phones, which communicate sometimes by wifi and sometimes by a mobile network, and which run apps from millions of authors (most of them selfish, some of them actively malicious), has left security engineers running ever faster to catch up.

Mixing many different models of computation together has been a factor in the present chaos. Some of their initial assumptions still apply partially, but none of them apply globally any more. The Internet now has billions of phones, billions of IoT devices, maybe a billion PCs, and millions of organisations whose managers not only fail to cooperate but may be in conflict. There are companies that compete; political groups that despise each other, and nation states that are at war with each other. Users, instead of being trustworthy but occasionally incompetent, are now largely unskilled – but some are both capable and hostile. Code used to be simply buggy – but now there is a lot of malicious code out there. Attacks on communications used to be the purview of intelligence agencies – now they can be done by youngsters who've downloaded attack tools from the net and launched them without any real idea of how they work.

6.5 Summary

Access control mechanisms operate at a number of levels in a system, from the hardware up through the operating system and middleware like browsers to the applications. Higher-level mechanisms can be more expressive, but also tend to be more vulnerable to attack for a variety of reasons ranging from intrinsic complexity to implementer skill.

The main function of access control is to limit the damage that can be done by particular groups, users, and programs whether through error or malice. The most widely fielded examples are Android and Windows at the client end and Linux at the server end; they have a common lineage and many architectural similarities. The basic mechanisms (and their problems) are pervasive. Most attacks involve the opportunistic exploitation of bugs; products that are complex, widely used, or both are particularly likely to have vulnerabilities found and turned into exploits. Many techniques have been developed to push back on the number of implementation errors, to make it less likely that the resulting bugs give rise to vulnerabilties, and harder to turn the vulnerabilities into exploits; but the overall dependability of large software systems improves only slowly.

Research problems

Most of the issues in access control were identified by the 1960s or early 1970s and were worked out on experimental systems such as Multics [1687] and the CAP [2024]. Much of the research in access control systems since then has involved reworking the basic themes in new contexts, such as mobile phones.

Recent threads of research include enclaves, and the CHERI mechanisms for adding finer-grained access control. Another question is: how will developers use such tools effectively?

In the second edition I predicted that 'a useful research topic for the next few years will be how to engineer access control mechanisms that are not just robust but also usable – by both programmers and end users.' Recent work by Yasemin Acar and others has picked that up and developed it into one of the most rapidly-growing fields of security research [11]. Many if not most technical security failures are due at least in part to the poor usability of the protection mechanisms that developers are expected to use. I already mention in the chapter on cryptography how crypto APIs often induce people to use really unsafe defaults, such as encrypting long messages with ECB mode; access control is just as bad, as anyone coming cold to the access control mechanisms in a Windows system or either an Intel or Arm CPU will find.

As a teaser, here's a new problem. Can we extend what we know about access control at the technical level – whether hardware, OS or app – to the organisational level? In the 20th century, there were a number of security policies proposed, from Bell-LaPadula to Clark-Wilson, which we discuss at greater length in Part 2. Is it time to revisit this for a world of deep outsourcing and virtual organisations, now that we have interesting technical analogues?

Further reading

There's a history of virtualisation and containers by Allison Randal at [1578]; a discussion of how mandatory access controls were adapted to operating systems such as OS X and iOS by Robert Watson in [1997]; and a reference book for Java security written by its architect Li Gong [784]. The Cloud Native Security Foundation is trying to move people towards better open-source practices around containers and other technologies for deploying and managing cloud-native software. Going back a bit, the classic descriptions of Unix security are by Fred Grampp and Robert Morris in 1984 [806] and by Simson Garfinkel and Eugene Spafford in 1996 [753], while the classic on Internet security by Bill Cheswick and Steve Bellovin [222] gives many examples of network attacks on Unix systems.

Carl Landwehr gives a useful reference to many of the flaws found in operating systems in the 1960s through the 1980s [1131]. One of the earliest reports on the subject (and indeed on computer security in general) is by Willis Ware in 1970 [1990]; Butler Lampson's seminal paper on the confinement problem appeared in 1970s [1127] and three years later, another influential early paper was written by Jerry Saltzer and Mike Schroeder [1642]. The textbook we get our students to read on access control issues is Dieter Gollmann's *'Computer Security'* [780]. The standard reference on Intel's SGX and indeed its CPU security architecture is by Victor Costan and Srini Devadas [479].

The field of software security is fast-moving; the attacks change significantly (at least in their details) from one year to the next. The classic starting point is Gary McGraw's 2006 book [1268]. Since then we've had ROP attacks, Spectre and much else; a short but useful update is Matthias Payer's *Software Security* [1506]. But to really keep up, it's not enough to just read textbooks; you need to follow security conferences such as Usenix and CCS as well as the security blogs such as Bruce Schneier, Brian Krebs and – dare I say it – our own `lightbluetouchpaper.org`. The most detail on the current attacks is probably in Google's Project Zero blog; see for example their analysis of attacks on iPhones found in the wild for an insight into what's involved in hacking modern operating systems with mandatory access control components [205].

CHAPTER

7

Distributed Systems

A distributed system is one in which the failure of a computer you didn't even know existed can render your own computer unusable.

– LESLIE LAMPORT [1125]

What's in a name? That which we call a rose by any other name would smell as sweet.

– WILLIAM SHAKESPEARE

7.1 Introduction

We need a lot more than authentication, access control and cryptography to build a robust distributed system of any size. Some things need to happen quickly, or in the right order, and matters that are trivial to deal with for a few machines become a big deal once we have hyperscale data centres with complex arrangements for resilience. Everyone must have noticed that when you update your address book with an online service provider, the update might appear a second later on another device, or perhaps only hours later.

Over the last 50 years, we've learned a lot about issues such as concurrency, failure recovery and naming as we've built things ranging from phone systems and payment networks to the Internet itself. We have solid theory, and a lot of hard-won experience. These issues are central to the design of robust secure systems but are often handled rather badly. I've already described attacks on protocols that arise as concurrency failures. If we replicate data to make a system fault-tolerant, then we may increase the risk of data theft. Finally, naming can be a thorny problem. There are complex interactions of people and objects with accounts, sessions, documents, files, pointers, keys and other ways of naming stuff. Many organisations are trying to build larger, flatter namespaces – whether using identity cards to track citizens or using device ID to track objects – but there are limits to what we can practically do. Big data means dealing with lots of identifiers, many of which are ambiguous or even changing, and a lot of things can go wrong.

7.2 Concurrency

Processes are called *concurrent* if they can run at the same time, and this is essential for performance; modern computers have many cores and run many programs at a time, typically for many users. However, concurrency is hard to do robustly, especially when processes can act on the same data. Processes may use old data; they can make inconsistent updates; the order of updates may or may not matter; the system might deadlock; the data in different systems might never converge to consistent values; and when it's important to make things happen in the right order, or even to know the exact time, this can be trickier than you might think. These issues go up and down the entire stack.

Systems are becoming ever more concurrent for a number of reasons. First is scale: Google may have started off with four machines but their fleet passed a million in 2011. Second is device complexity; a luxury car can now contain dozens to hundreds of different processors. The same holds for your laptop and your mobile phone. Deep within each CPU, instructions are executed in parallel, and this complexity leads to the Spectre attacks we discussed in the chapter on access control. On top of this, virtualization technologies such as Xen are the platforms on which modern cloud services are built, and they may turn a handful of real CPUs in a server into hundreds or even thousands of virtual CPUs. Then there's interaction complexity: going up to the application layer, an everyday transaction such as booking a rental car may call other systems to check your credit card, your credit reference agency score, your insurance claim history and much else, while these systems in turn may depend on others.

Programming concurrent systems is hard, and the standard textbook examples come from the worlds of operating system internals and of performance measurement. Computer scientists are taught Amdahl's law: if the proportion that can be parallelised is p and s is the speedup from the extra resources, the overall speedup is $(1 - p + p/s)^{-1}$. Thus if three-quarters of your program can be parallelised but the remaining quarter cannot be, then the maximum speedup you can get is four times; and if you throw eight cores at it, the practical speedup is not quite three times[1]. But concurrency control in the real world is also a security issue. Like access control, it is needed to prevent users interfering with each other, whether accidentally or on purpose. And concurrency problems can occur at many levels in a system, from the hardware right up to the business logic. In what follows, I provide a number of concrete examples; they are by no means exhaustive.

[1] $\left(1 - \frac{3}{4} + \frac{3}{4}\cdot\frac{1}{8}\right)^{-1} = (0.25 + 0.09375)^{-1} = (0.34375)^{-1} = 2.909$

7.2.1 Using old data versus paying to propagate state

I've already described two kinds of concurrency problem: replay attacks on protocols, where an attacker manages to pass off out-of-date credentials; and race conditions, where two programs can race to update some security state. As an example, I mentioned the 'mkdir' vulnerability from Unix, in which a privileged instruction that is executed in two phases could be attacked halfway through by renaming the object on which it acts. Another example goes back to the 1960s, where in one of the first multiuser operating systems, IBM's OS/360, an attempt to open a file caused it to be read and its permissions checked; if the user was authorised to access it, it was read again. The user could arrange things so that the file was altered in between [1131].

These are examples of a *time-of-check-to-time-of-use* (TOCTTOU) attack. We have systematic ways of finding such attacks in file systems [252], but attacks still crop up both at lower levels, such as system calls in virtualised environments, and at higher levels such as business logic. Preventing them isn't always economical, as propagating changes in security state can be expensive.

A good case study is card fraud. Since credit and debit cards became popular in the 1970s, the banking industry has had to manage lists of *hot* cards (whether stolen or abused), and the problem got steadily worse in the 1980s as card networks went international. It isn't possible to keep a complete hot card list in every merchant terminal, as we'd have to broadcast all loss reports instantly to tens of millions of devices, and even if we tried to verify all transactions with the bank that issued the card, we'd be unable to use cards in places with no network (such as in remote villages and on airplanes) and we'd impose unacceptable costs and delays elsewhere. Instead, there are multiple levels of stand-in processing, exploiting the fact that most payments are local, or low-value, or both.

Merchant terminals are allowed to process transactions up to a certain limit (the *floor limit*) offline; larger transactions need online verification with the merchant's bank, which will know about all the local hot cards plus foreign cards that are being actively abused; above another limit it might refer the transaction to a network such as VISA with a reasonably up-to-date international list; while the largest transactions need a reference to the card-issuing bank. In effect, the only transactions that are checked immediately before use are those that are local or large.

Experience then taught that a more centralised approach can work better for bad terminals. About half the world's ATM transactions use a service that gets alerts from subscribing banks when someone tries to use a stolen card at an ATM, or guesses the PIN wrong. FICO observed that criminals take a handful of stolen cards to a cash machine and try them out one by one; they maintain a list of the 40 ATMs worldwide that have been used most recently for attempted fraud, and banks that subscribe to their service decline all transactions at those machines – which become unusable by those banks' cards for maybe half an hour. Most thieves don't understand this and just throw them away.

Until about 2010, payment card networks had the largest systems that manage the global propagation of security state, and their experience taught us that revoking compromised credentials quickly and on a global scale is expensive. The lesson was learned elsewhere too; the US Department of Defense, for example, issued 16 million certificates to military personnel during 1999–2005, by which time it had to download 10 million revoked certificates to all security servers every day, and some systems took half an hour to do this when they were fired up [1301].

The costs of propagating security state can lead to centralisation. Big service firms such as Google, Facebook and Microsoft have to maintain credentials for billions of users anyway, so they offer logon as a service to other websites. Other firms, such as certification authorities, also provide online credentials. But although centralisation can cut costs, a compromise of the central service can be disruptive. In 2011, for example, hackers operating from Iranian IP addresses compromised the Dutch certification authority Diginotar. On July 9th, they generated fake certificates and did middleperson attacks on the gmail of Iranian activists. Diginotar noticed on the 19th that certificates had been wrongly issued but merely called in its auditors. The hack became public on the 29th, and Google reacted by removing all Diginotar certificates from Chrome on September 3rd, and getting Mozilla to do likewise. This led immediately to the failure of the company, and Dutch public services were unavailable online for many days as ministries scrambled to get certificates for their web services from other suppliers [471].

7.2.2 Locking to prevent inconsistent updates

When people work concurrently on a document, they may use a version control system to ensure that only one person has write access at any one time to any given part of it, or at least to warn of contention and flag up any inconsistent edits. *Locking* is one general way to manage contention for resources such as filesystems and to make conflicting updates less likely. Another approach is *callback*; a server may keep a list of all those clients which rely on it for security state and notify them when the state changes.

Credit cards again provide an example of how this applies to security. If I own a hotel and a customer presents a credit card on check-in, I ask the card company for a *pre-authorisation*, which records that I will want to make a debit in the near future; I might register a claim on 'up to $500'. This is implemented by separating the authorisation and settlement systems. Handling the failure modes can be tricky. If the card is cancelled the following day, my bank can call me and ask me to contact the police, or to get her to pay cash[2]. This is an example of the *publish-register-notify* model of how to do robust authorisation in distributed systems (of which there's a more general description in [153]).

Callback mechanisms don't provide a universal solution, though. The credential issuer might not want to run a callback service, and the customer might object on privacy grounds to the issuer being told all her comings and goings. Consider passports as another example. In many countries, government ID is required for many transactions, but governments won't provide any guarantee, and most citizens would object if the government kept a record of every time an ID document was presented. Indeed, one of the frequent objections to the Indian government's requirement that the Aadhar biometric ID system be used in more and more transactions is that checking citizens' fingerprints or iris codes at all significant transactions creates an audit trail of all the places where they have done business, which is available to officials and to anyone who cares to bribe them.

There is a general distinction between those credentials whose use gives rise to some obligation on the issuer, such as credit cards, and the others, such as passports. Among the differences is whether the credential's use changes important state, beyond possibly adding to a log file or other surveillance system. This is linked with whether the order in which updates are made is important.

7.2.3 The order of updates

If two transactions arrive at the government's bank account – say a credit of $500,000 and a debit of $400,000 – then the order in which they are applied may not matter much. But if they're arriving at my bank account, the order will have a huge effect on the outcome! In fact, the problem of deciding the order in which transactions are applied has no clean solution. It's closely related to the problem of how to parallelise a computation, and much of the art of building efficient distributed systems lies in arranging matters so that processes are either simply sequential or completely parallel.

The traditional bank algorithm was to batch the transactions overnight and apply all the credits for each account before applying all the debits. Inputs from devices such as ATMs and check sorters were first batched up into journals before the overnight reconciliation. Payments which bounce then

[2]My bank might or might not have guaranteed me the money; it all depends on what sort of contract I've got with it. There were also attacks for a while when crooks figured out how to impersonate a store and cancel an authorisation so that a card could be used to make multiple big purchases. And it might take a day or three for the card-issuing bank to propagate an alarm to the merchant's bank. A deep dive into all this would be a book chapter in itself!

have to be reversed out – and in the case of ATM and debit transactions where the cash has already gone, you can end up with customers borrowing money without authorisation. In practice, chains of failed payments terminate. In recent years, one country after another has introduced *real-time gross settlement* (RTGS) systems in which transactions are booked in order of arrival. There are several subtle downsides. First, at many institutions, the real-time system for retail customers is an overlay on a platform that still works by overnight updates. Second, the outcome can depend on the order of transactions, which can depend on human, system and network vagaries, which can be an issue when many very large payments are made between financial institutions. Credit cards operate a hybrid strategy, with credit limits run in real time while settlement is run just as in an old-fashioned checking account.

In the late 2010s, the wave of interest in cryptocurrency led some entrepreneurs to believe that a blockchain might solve the problems of inconsistent update, simplifying applications such as supply-chain management. The energy costs rule out a blockchain based on proof-of-work for most applications; but might some other kind of append-only public ledger find a killer app? We will have to wait and see. Meanwhile, the cryptocurrency community makes extensive use of off-chain mechanisms that are often very reminiscent of the checking-account approach: disconnected applications propose tentative updates that are later reconciled and applied to the main chain. Experience suggests that there is no magic solution that works in the general case, short perhaps of having a small number of very large banks that are very competent at technology. We'll discuss this further in the chapter on banking.

In other systems, the order in which transactions arrive is much less important. Passports are a good example. Passport issuers only worry about their creation and expiration dates, not the order in which visas are stamped on them[3].

7.2.4 Deadlock

Another problem is deadlock, where two systems are each waiting for the other to move first. Edsger Dijkstra famously explained this problem, and its possible solutions, via the *dining philosophers' problem*. A number of philosophers are seated round a table, with a chopstick between each of them; and a philosopher can only eat when they can pick up the two chopsticks on either side. So if all of them try to eat at once and each picks up the chopstick on their right, they get stuck [560].

[3]Many Arab countries won't let you in with an Israeli stamp on your passport, but most pure identification systems are essentially stateless.

This can get really complex when you have multiple hierarchies of locks distributed across systems, some of which fail (and where failures can mean that the locks aren't reliable) [152]. And deadlock is not just about technology; the phrase 'Catch-22' has become popular to describe deadlocks in bureaucratic processes [4]. Where a process is manual, some fudge may be found to get round the catch, but when everything becomes software, this option may no longer be available.

In a well known business problem – the *battle of the forms* – one company issues an order with its own contract terms attached, another company accepts it subject to its own terms, and trading proceeds without any further agreement. In the old days, the matter might only be resolved if something went wrong and the companies ended up in court; even so, one company's terms might specify an American court while the other's specify one in England. As trading has become more electronic, the winner is often the company that can compel the loser to trade using its website and thus accept its terms and conditions. Firms increasingly try to make sure that things fail in their favour. The resulting liability games can have rather negative outcomes for both security and safety; we'll discuss them further in the chapter on economics.

7.2.5 Non-convergent state

When designing protocols that update the state of a distributed system, the 'motherhood and apple pie' is ACID – that transactions should be *atomic, consistent, isolated and durable*. A transaction is atomic if you 'do it all or not at all' – which makes it easier to recover after a failure. It is consistent if some invariant is preserved, such as that the books must still balance. This is common in banking systems, and is achieved by insisting that the sum total of credits and debits made by each transaction is zero (I'll discuss this more in the chapter on banking and bookkeeping). Transactions are isolated if they are serialisable, and they are durable if once done they can't be undone.

These properties can be too much, or not enough, or both. On the one hand, each of them can fail or be attacked in numerous obscure ways; on the other, it's often sufficient to design the system to be *convergent*. This means that, if the transaction volume were to tail off, then eventually there would be consistent state throughout [1355]. Convergence is usually achieved using semantic tricks such as timestamps and version numbers; this can often be enough where transactions get appended to files rather than overwritten.

In real life, you also need ways to survive things that go wrong and are not completely recoverable. The life of a security or audit manager can be a constant battle against entropy: apparent deficits (and surpluses) are always

[4]Joseph Heller's 1961 novel of that name described multiple instances of inconsistent and crazy rules in the World War 2 military bureaucracy.

turning up, and sometimes simply can't be explained. For example, different national systems have different ideas of which fields in bank transaction records are mandatory or optional, so payment gateways often have to guess data in order to make things work. Sometimes they guess wrong; and sometimes people see and exploit vulnerabilities which aren't understood until much later (if ever). In the end, things may get fudged by adding a correction factor and setting a target for keeping it below a certain annual threshold.

Durability is a subject of debate in transaction processing. The advent of phishing and keylogging attacks has meant that some small proportion of bank accounts will at any time be under the control of criminals; money gets moved both from them and through them. When an account compromise is detected, the bank moves to freeze it and perhaps to reverse payments that have recently been made from it. The phishermen naturally try to move funds through institutions, or jurisdictions, that don't do transaction reversal, or do it at best slowly and grudgingly [76]. This sets up a tension between the recoverability and thus the resilience of the payment system on the one hand and transaction durability and finality on the other[5].

7.2.6 Secure time

The final concurrency problem of special interest to the security engineer is the provision of accurate time. As authentication protocols such as Kerberos can be attacked by inducing clock error, it's not enough to simply trust a random external time source. One possibility is a *Cinderella attack*: if a security critical program such as a firewall has a licence with a timelock, an attacker might wind your clock forward "and cause your firewall to turn into a pumpkin". Given the spread of IoT devices that may be safety-critical and use time in ways that are poorly understood, there is now some concern about possible large-scale service denial attacks. Time is a lot harder than it looks: even if you have an atomic clock, leap seconds cannot be predicted but need to be broadcast somehow; some minutes have 61 and even 62 seconds; odd time effects can be a security issue[6]; and much of the world is not using the Gregorian calendar.

Anyway, there are several possible approaches to the provision of secure time. You can give every computer a radio clock, and indeed your smartphone

[5]This problem goes back centuries, with a thicket of laws around whether someone acting in good faith can acquire good title to stolen goods or stolen funds. The Bills of Exchange Act 1882 gave good title to people who bought bills of exchange in good faith, even if they were stolen. Something similar used to hold for stolen goods bought in an open market, but that was eventually repealed. In the case of electronic payments, the banks acted as a cartel to make payments final more quickly, both via card network rules and by lobbying European institutions over the Payment Services Directives. As for the case of bitcoin, it's still in flux; see section 20.7.5.

[6]Some ATMs didn't check customer balances for a few days after Y2K, leading to unauthorised overdrafts once the word got round.

has GPS – but that can be jammed by a passing truck driver. You can abandon absolute time and instead use *Lamport time*, in which all you care about is whether event A happened before event B rather than what date it is [1124]. For robustness reasons, Google doesn't use time in its internal certificates, but uses ranges of serial numbers coupled to a revocation mechanism [23].

In many applications, you may end up using the *network time protocol* (NTP). This has a moderate amount of protection, with clock voting and authentication of time servers, and is dependable enough for many purposes. However, you still need to take care. For example, Netgear hardwired their home routers to use an NTP server at the University of Wisconsin-Madison, which was swamped with hundreds of thousands of packets a second; Netgear ended up having to pay them $375,000 to maintain the time service for three years. Shortly afterwards, D-Link repeated the same mistake [447]. Second, from 2016 there have been denial-of-service attacks using NTP servers as force multipliers; millions of servers turned out to be abusable, so many ISPs and even IXPs started blocking them. So if you're planning to deploy lots of devices outside your corporate network that will rely on NTP, you'd better think hard about which servers you want to trust and pay attention to the latest guidance from CERT [1801].

7.3 Fault tolerance and failure recovery

Failure recovery is often the most important aspect of security engineering, yet it is one of the most neglected. For many years, most of the research papers on computer security have dealt with confidentiality, and most of the rest with authenticity and integrity; availability has almost been ignored. Yet the actual expenditures of a modern information business – whether a bank or a search engine – are the other way round. Far more is spent on availability and recovery mechanisms, such as multiple processing sites and redundant networks, than on integrity mechanisms such as code review and internal audit, and this in turn is way more than is spent on encryption. As you read through this book, you'll see that many other applications, from burglar alarms through electronic warfare to protecting a company from DDoS attacks, are fundamentally about availability. Fault tolerance and failure recovery are often the core of the security engineer's job.

Classical fault tolerance is usually based on redundancy, fortified using mechanisms such as logs and locking, and is greatly complicated when it must withstand malicious attacks on these mechanisms. Fault tolerance interacts with security in a number of ways: the failure model, the nature of resilience, the location of redundancy used to provide it, and defence against service denial attacks. I'll use the following definitions: a *fault* may cause an *error*, which is an incorrect state; this may lead to a *failure*, which is a deviation from the system's specified behavior. The resilience which we build into a system to tolerate faults and recover from failures will have a number of components, such as fault detection, error recovery and if necessary failure recovery. The meaning of *mean-time-before-failure* (MTBF) and *mean-time-to-repair* (MTTR) should be obvious.

7.3.1 Failure models

In order to decide what sort of resilience we need, we must know what sort of attacks to expect. Much of this will come from an analysis of threats specific to our system's operating environment, but some general issues bear mentioning.

7.3.1.1 Byzantine failure

First, the failures with which we are concerned may be normal or malicious, and we often model the latter as *Byzantine*. Byzantine failures are inspired by the idea that there are n generals defending Byzantium, t of whom have been bribed by the attacking Turks to cause as much confusion as possible. The generals can pass oral messages by courier, and the couriers are trustworthy, so each general can exchange confidential and authentic communications with each other general (we could imagine them encrypting and computing a MAC on each message). What is the maximum number t of traitors that can be tolerated?

The key observation is that if we have only three generals, say Anthony, Basil and Charalampos, and Anthony is the traitor, then he can tell Basil "let's attack" and Charalampos "let's retreat". Basil can now say to Charalampos "Anthony says let's attack", but this doesn't let Charalampos conclude that Anthony's the traitor. It could just as easily have been Basil; Anthony could have said "let's retreat" to both of them, but Basil lied when he said "Anthony says let's attack".

This beautiful insight is due to Leslie Lamport, Robert Shostak and Marshall Pease, who proved that the problem has a solution if and only if $n \geq 3t + 1$ [1126]. Of course, if the generals are able to sign their messages, then no general dare say different things to two different colleagues. This illustrates the power of digital signatures in particular and of end-to-end security mechanisms in general. There is now a substantial literature on Byzantine fault tolerance – the detailed design of systems able to withstand this kind of failure; see for example the algorithm by Miguel Castro and Barbara Liskov [396].

Another lesson is that if a component which fails (or can be induced to fail by an opponent) gives the wrong answer rather than just no answer, then it's much harder to use it to build a resilient system. It can be useful if components that fail just stop, or if they can at least be quickly identified and blacklisted.

7.3.1.2 Interaction with fault tolerance

So we can constrain the failure rate in a number of ways. The two most obvious are by using *redundancy* and *fail-stop processes.* The latter process error-correction information along with data, and stop when an inconsistency is detected; for example, bank transaction processing will typically stop if an out-of-balance condition is detected after a processing task. The two may be combined; the processors used in some safety-critical functions in cars and aircraft typically have two or more cores. There was pioneering work on a *fault-tolerant multiprocessor* (FTMP) in the 1970s, driven by the Space Shuttle project; this explored which components should be redundant and the associated design trade-offs around where the error detection takes place and how closely everything is synchronised [922]. Such research ended up driving the design of fault-tolerant processors used in various submarines and spacecraft, as well as architectures used by Boeing and Airbus. The FTMP idea was also commercialised by Tandem and then by Stratus, which sold machines for payment processing. The Stratus had two disks, two buses and even two CPUs, each of which would stop if it detected errors; the fail-stop CPUs were built by having two CPU chips on the same card and comparing their outputs. If they disagreed the output went open-circuit. A replacement card would arrive in the post; you'd take it down to the machine room, notice that card 5 had a flashing red light, pull it out and replace it with the new one – all while the machine was processing dozens of transactions per second. Nowadays, the data centres of large service firms have much more elaborate protocols to ensure that if a machine fails, another machine takes over; if a rack fails, another rack takes over; and even if a data centre fails, its workload is quickly recovered on others. Google was a leader in developing the relevant software stack, having discovered in the early 2000s that it was much cheaper to build large-scale systems with commodity PCs and smart software than to buy ever-larger servers from specialist vendors.

While redundancy can make a system more *resilient,* it has costs. First, we have to deal with a more complex software stack and toolchain. Banks eventually moved away from Stratus because they found it was less reliable overall than traditional mainframes: although there was less downtime due to hardware failure, this didn't compensate for the extra software failure caused by an unfamiliar development environment. Second, if I have multiple sites with backup data, then confidentiality could fail if any of them gets compromised[7]; and if I have some data that I have a duty to destroy, then purging it from multiple backup tapes can be a headache. The modern-day issue with developing software in containers on top of redundant cloud services is not so much the

[7]Or the communications between your data centres get tapped; we discussed in section 2.2.1.3 how GCHQ did that to Google.

programming languages, or compromise via data centres; it's that developers are unfamiliar with the cloud service providers' access control tools and all too often leave sensitive data world-readable.

There are other traps for the unwary. In one case in which I was called as an expert, my client was arrested while using a credit card in a store, accused of having a forged card, and beaten up by the police. He was adamant that the card was genuine. Much later, we got the card examined by VISA, who confirmed that it was indeed genuine. What happened, as well as we can reconstruct it, was this. Credit cards have two types of redundancy on the magnetic strip – a simple checksum obtained by combining together all the bytes on the track using exclusive-or, and a cryptographic checksum which we'll describe in detail later in section 12.5.1. The former is there to detect errors, and the latter to detect forgery. It appears that in this particular case, the merchant's card reader was out of alignment in such a way as to cause an even number of bit errors which cancelled each other out by chance in the simple checksum, while causing the crypto checksum to fail. The result was a false alarm, and a major disruption in my client's life.

Redundancy is hard enough to deal with in mechanical systems. For example, training pilots to handle multi-engine aircraft involves drilling them on engine failure procedures, first in the simulator and then in real aircraft with an instructor. Novice pilots are in fact more likely to be killed by an engine failure in a multi-engine plane than in a single; landing in the nearest field is less hazardous for them than coping with sudden asymmetric thrust. The same goes for instrument failures; it doesn't help to have three artificial horizons in the cockpit if, under stress, you rely on the one that's broken. Aircraft are much simpler than many modern information systems – yet there are still air crashes when pilots fail to manage the redundancy that's supposed to keep them safe. There are also complex failures, as when two Boeing 737 Max aircraft crashed because of failures in a single sensor, when the plane had two but the software failed to read them both, and the pilots hadn't been trained how to diagnose the problem and manage the consequences. All too often, system designers put in multiple protection mechanisms and don't think through the consequences carefully enough. Many other safety failures are failures of usability, and the same applies to security, as we discussed in Chapter 3; redundancy isn't an antidote to poor design.

7.3.2 What is resilience for?

When introducing redundancy or other resilience mechanisms into a system, we need to understand what they're for and the incentives facing the various actors. It therefore matters whether the resilience is local or crosses geographical or organisational boundaries.

In the first case, replication can be an internal feature of the server to make it more trustworthy. I already mentioned 1980s systems such as Stratus and Tandem; then we had replication of standard hardware at the component level, such as *redundant arrays of inexpensive disks* (RAID). Since the late 1990s there has been massive investment in developing rack-scale systems that let multiple cheap PCs do the work of expensive servers, with mechanisms to ensure a single server that fails will have its workload taken over rapidly by another, and indeed a rack that fails can also be recovered on a hot spare. These are now a standard component of cloud service architecture: any firm operating hundreds of thousands of servers will have so many failures that recovery must be largely automated.

But often things are much more complicated. A service may have to assume that some of its clients are trying to cheat it and may also have to rely on a number of services, none of which is completely accurate. When opening a bank account, or issuing a passport, we might want to check against services from voter rolls through credit reference agencies to a database of driver's licences, and the results may often be inconsistent. Trust decisions may involve complex logic, not entirely unlike the systems used in electronic warfare to try to work out which of your inputs are being jammed. (I'll discuss these further in the chapter on electronic and information warfare.)

The direction of mistrust has an effect on protocol design. A server faced with multiple untrustworthy clients and a client relying on multiple servers that may be incompetent, unavailable or malicious will both wish to control the flow of messages in a protocol in order to contain the effects of service denial. It's hard to design systems for the real world in which everyone is unreliable and all are mutually suspicious.

Sometimes the emphasis is on *security renewability*. The obvious example here is bank cards: a bank can upgrade security from time to time by mailing out newer versions of its cards, whether upgrading from mag strip to chip or from cheap chips to more sophisticated ones; and it can recover from a compromise by mailing out cards out of cycle to affected customers. Pay TV and mobile phones are somewhat similar.

7.3.3 At what level is the redundancy?

Systems may be made resilient against errors, attacks and equipment failures at a number of levels. As with access control, these become progressively more complex and less reliable as we go up to higher layers in the system.

Some computers have been built with redundancy at the hardware level, such as Stratus systems and RAID discs I mentioned earlier. But simple replication cannot provide a defense against malicious software, or against an intruder who exploits faulty software.

At the next level up, there is *process group redundancy*. Here, we may run multiple copies of a system on multiple servers in different locations and compare their outputs. This can stop the kind of attack in which the opponent gets physical access to a machine and subverts it, whether by mechanical destruction or by inserting unauthorised software. It can't defend against attacks by authorised users or damage by bad authorised software, which could simply order the deletion of a critical file.

The next level is *backup*, where we typically take a copy of the system (a *checkpoint*) at regular intervals. The copies are usually kept on media that can't be overwritten such as write-protected tapes or discs with special software. We may also keep *journals* of all the transactions applied between checkpoints. Whatever the detail, backup and recovery mechanisms not only enable us to recover from physical asset destruction, they also ensure that if we do get an attack at the logical level, we have some hope of recovering. The classic example in the 1980s would have been a time bomb that deletes the customer database on a specific date; since the arrival of cryptocurrency, the fashion has been for ransomware.

Businesses with critical service requirements, such as banks and retailers, have had backup data centres for many years. The idea is that if the main centre goes down, the service will *failover* to a second facility. Maintaining such facilities absorbed most of a typical bank's information security budget.

Backup is not the same as *fallback*. A fallback system is typically a less capable system to which processing reverts when the main system is unavailable. One example was the use of manual imprinting machines to capture credit card transactions from the card embossing when electronic terminals failed. Fallback systems are an example of redundancy in the application layer – the highest layer we can put it.

It is important to realise that these are different mechanisms, which do different things. Redundant disks won't protect against a malicious programmer who deletes all your account files, and backups won't stop him if rather than just deleting files he writes code that slowly inserts more and more errors[8]. Neither will give much protection against attacks on data confidentiality. On the other hand, the best encryption in the world won't help you if your data processing center burns down. Real-world recovery plans and mechanisms involve a mixture of all of the above.

The remarks that I made earlier about the difficulty of redundancy, and the absolute need to plan and train for it properly, apply in spades to system backup. When I was working in banking in the 1980s, we reckoned that we could probably get our backup system working within an hour or so of our

[8]Nowadays the really serious ransomware operators will hack your system, add file encryption surreptitiously and wait before they pounce – so they hold hostage not just your current data but several weeks' backups too

main processing centre being destroyed, but the tests were limited by the fact that we didn't want to risk processing during business hours: we would recover the main production systems on our backup data centre one Saturday a year. By the early 1990s, Tesco, a UK supermarket, had gotten as far as live drills: they'd pull the plug on the main processing centre once a year without warning the operators, to make sure the backup came up within 40 seconds. By 2011, Netflix had developed 'chaos monkeys' – systems that would randomly knock out a machine, or a rack, or even a whole data centre, to test resilience constantly. By 2019, large service firms have gotten to such a scale that they don't need this. If you have three million machines across thirty data centres, then you'll lose machines constantly, racks frequently, and whole data centres often enough that you have to engineer things to keep going. So nowadays, you can simply pay money and a cloud service provider will worry about a lot of the detail for you. But you need to really understand what sort of failures Amazon or Google or Microsoft can handle for you and what you have to deal with yourself. The standard service level agreements of the major providers allow them to interrupt your service for quite a few hours per month, and if you use a smaller cloud service (even a government cloud), it will have capacity limits about which you have to think carefully.

It's worth trying to work out which services you depend on that are outside your direct supply chain. For example, Britain suffered a fuel tanker drivers' strike in 2001, and some hospitals had to close because of staff shortages, which was supposed to not happen. The government had allocated petrol rations to doctors and nurses, but not to schoolteachers. So the schools closed, and the nurses had to stay home to look after their kids, and this closed hospitals too. This helped the strikers defeat Prime Minister Tony Blair: he abandoned his signature environmental policy of steadily increasing fuel duty. As we become increasingly dependent on each other, contingency planning gets ever harder.

7.3.4 Service-denial attacks

One of the reasons we want security services to be fault-tolerant is to make service-denial attacks less attractive, less effective, or both. Such attacks are often used as part of a larger plan. For example, one might take down a security server to force other servers to use cached copies of credentials, or swamp a web server to take it temporarily offline and then get another machine to serve the pages that victims try to download.

A powerful defense against service denial is to prevent the opponent from mounting a selective attack. If principals are anonymous – say there are several equivalent services behind a load balancer, and the opponent has no idea which one to attack – then he may be ineffective. I'll discuss this further in the context of burglar alarms and electronic warfare.

Where this isn't possible, and the opponent knows where to attack, then there are some types of service-denial attacks that can be stopped by redundancy and resilience mechanisms and others that can't. For example, the TCP/IP protocol has few effective mechanisms for hosts to protect themselves against network flooding, which comes in a wide variety of flavours. Defense against this kind of attack tends to involve moving your site to a beefier hosting service with specialist packet-washing hardware – or tracing and arresting the perpetrator.

Distributed denial-of-service (DDoS) attacks came to public notice when they were used to bring down Panix, a New York ISP, for several days in 1996. During the late 1990s they were occasionally used by script kiddies to take down chat servers. In 2001 I mentioned them in passing in the first edition of this book. Over the following three years, extortionists started using them; they'd assemble a *botnet*, a network of compromised PCs, which would flood a target webserver with packet traffic until its owner paid them to desist. Typical targets were online bookmakers, and amounts of $10,000 – $50,000 were typically demanded to leave them alone, and the typical bookie paid up the first time this happened. When the attacks persisted, the first solution was replication: operators moved their websites to hosting services such as Akamai whose servers are so numerous (and so close to customers) that they can shrug off anything the average botnet could throw at them. In the end, the blackmail problem was solved when the bookmakers met and agreed not to pay any more blackmail money, and the Ukrainian police were prodded into arresting the gang responsible.

By 2018, we had come full circle, and about fifty bad people were operating DDoS-as-a-service, mostly for gamers who wanted to take down their opponents' teamspeak servers. The services were sold online as 'booters' that would boot your opponents out of the game; a few dollars would get a flood of perhaps 100Gbit/sec. Service operators also called them, more euphemistically, 'stressors' – with the line that you could use them to test the robustness of your own website. This didn't fool anyone, and just before Christmas 2018 the FBI took down fifteen of these sites, arresting a number of their operators and causing the volumes of DDoS traffic to drop noticeably for several months [1447].

Finally, where a more vulnerable fallback system exists, a common technique is to use a service-denial attack to force victims into fallback mode. The classic example is in payment cards. Smartcards are generally harder to forge than magnetic strip cards, but perhaps 1% of them fail every year, thanks to static electricity and worn contacts. Also, some tourists still use magnetic strip cards. So most card payment systems still have a fallback mode that uses the magnetic strip. A simple attack is to use a false terminal, or a bug inserted into the cable to a genuine terminal, to capture card details and then write them to the magnetic strip of a card with a dead chip.

7.4 Naming

Naming is a minor if troublesome aspect of ordinary distributed systems, but it becomes surprisingly hard in security engineering. During the dotcom boom in the 1990s, when SSL was invented and we started building public-key certification authorities, we hit the problem of what names to put on certificates. A certificate that says simply "the person named Ross Anderson is allowed to administer machine X" is little use. I used to be the only Ross Anderson I knew of; but as soon as the first search engines came along, I found dozens of us. I am also known by different names to dozens of different systems. Names exist in contexts, and naming the principals in secure systems is becoming ever more important and difficult.

Conceptually, namespaces can be hierarchical or flat. You can identify me as 'The Ross Anderson who teaches computer science at Cambridge, England' or as 'The Ross Anderson who's `rossjanderson@gmail.com`' or even as 'the Ross Anderson with such-and-such a passport number'. But these are not the same kind of thing, and linking them causes all sorts of problems.

In general, using more names increases complexity. A public-key certificate that simply says "this is the key to administer machine X" is a bearer token, just like a metal door key; whoever controls the private key for that certificate is the admin, just as if the root password were in an envelope in a bank vault. But once my name is involved, and I have to present some kind of passport or ID card to prove who I am, the system acquires a further dependency. If my passport is compromised the consequences could be far-reaching, and I really don't want to give the government an incentive to issue a false passport in my name to one of its agents.

After 9/11, governments started to force businesses to demand government-issue photo ID in places where this was not previously thought necessary. In the UK, for example, you can no longer board a domestic flight using just the credit card with which you bought the ticket; you have to produce a passport or driving license – which you also need to order a bank transfer in a branch for more than £1000, to rent an apartment, to hire a lawyer or even to get a job. Such measures are not only inconvenient but introduce new failure modes into all sorts of systems.

There is a second reason that the world is moving towards larger, flatter name spaces: the growing dominance of the large service firms in online authentication. Your name is increasingly a global one; it's your Gmail or Hotmail address, your Twitter handle, or your Facebook account. These firms have not merely benefited from the technical externalities, which we discussed in the chapter on authentication, and business externalities, which we'll discuss in the chapter on economics, they have sort-of solved some of the problems of naming. But we can't be complacent as many other problems remain. So it's useful to canter through what a generation of computer science researchers have learned about naming in distributed systems.

7.4.1 The Needham naming principles

During the last quarter of the twentieth century, engineers building distributed systems ran up against many naming problems. The basic algorithm used to bind names to addresses is known as *rendezvous*: the principal exporting a name advertises it somewhere, and the principal seeking to import and use it searches for it. Obvious examples include phone books and file system directories.

People building distributed systems soon realised that naming gets complex quickly, and the lessons are set out in a classic article by Needham [1426]. Here are his ten principles.

1. *The function of names is to facilitate sharing.* This continues to hold: my bank account number exists in order to share the information that I deposited money last week with the teller from whom I am trying to withdraw money this week. In general, names are needed when the data to be shared is changeable. If I only ever wished to withdraw exactly the same sum as I'd deposited, a bearer deposit certificate would be fine. Conversely, names need not be shared – or linked – where data will not be; there is no need to link my bank account number to my telephone number unless I am going to pay my phone bill from the account.

2. *The naming information may not all be in one place, and so resolving names brings all the general problems of a distributed system.* This holds with a vengeance. A link between a bank account and a phone number assumes both of them will remain stable. So each system relies on the other, and an attack on one can affect the other. Many banks use two-channel authorisation to combat phishing – if you order a payment online, you get a text message on your mobile phone saying 'if you want to pay $X to account Y, please enter the following four-digit code into your browser'. The standard attack is for the crook to claim to be you to the phone company and report the loss of your phone. So they give him a new SIM that works for your phone number, and he makes off with your money. The phone company could stop that, but it doesn't care too much about authentication, as all it stands to lose is some airtime, whose marginal cost is zero. And the latest attack is to use Android malware to steal authentication codes. Google could stop that by locking down the Android platform as tightly as Apple – but it lacks the incentive to do so.

3. *It is bad to assume that only so many names will be needed*. The shortage of IP addresses, which motivated the development of IP version 6 (IPv6), is well enough discussed. What is less well known is that the most expensive upgrade the credit card industry ever had to make was the move from thirteen-digit credit card numbers to sixteen. Issuers originally assumed that thirteen digits would be enough, but the system ended up with tens of thousands of banks – many with dozens of products – so a six-digit bank identification number was needed. Some issuers have millions of customers, so a nine-digit account number is the norm. And there's also a *check digit* to detect errors.
4. *Global names buy you less than you think*. For example, the 128-bit address in IPv6 can in theory enable every object in the universe to have a unique name. However, for us to do business, a local name at my end must be resolved into this unique name and back into a local name at your end. Invoking a unique name in the middle may not buy us anything; it may even get in the way if the unique naming service takes time, costs money, or occasionally fails (as it surely will). In fact, the name service itself will usually have to be a distributed system, of the same scale (and security level) as the system we're trying to protect. So we can expect no silver bullets from this quarter. Adding an extra name, or adopting a more complicated one, has the potential to add extra costs and failure modes.
5. *Names imply commitments, so keep the scheme flexible enough to cope with organisational changes*. This sound principle was ignored in the design of the UK government's key management system for secure email [116]. There, principals' private keys are generated from their email addresses. So the frequent reorganisations meant that the security infrastructure had to be rebuilt each time – and that more money had to be spent solving secondary problems such as how people access old material.
6. *Names may double as access tickets, or capabilities*. We have already seen a number of examples of this in Chapters 2 and 3. In general, it's a bad idea to assume that today's name won't be tomorrow's password or capability – remember the Utrecht fraud we discussed in section 4.5. Norway, for example, used to consider the citizen's ID number to be public, but it ended up being used as a sort of password in so many applications that they had to relent and make it private. There are similar issues around the US Social Security Number (SSN). So the Department of Defense created a surrogate number called the EDIPI, which was supposed to be not sensitive; but, sure enough, people started using it as an authenticator instead of as an identifier.

I've given a number of examples of how things go wrong when a name starts being used as a password. But sometimes the roles of name and password are ambiguous. In order to get entry to a car park I used to use at the university, I had to speak my surname and parking badge number into a microphone at the barrier. So if I say, "Anderson, 123", which of these is the password? In fact it was "Anderson", as anyone can walk through the car park and note down valid badge numbers from the parking permits on the car windscreens.

7. *Things are made much simpler if an incorrect name is obvious.* In standard distributed systems, this enables us to take a liberal attitude to caching. In payment systems, credit card numbers used to be accepted while the terminal was offline so long as the credit card number appears valid (i.e., the last digit is a proper check digit of the first fifteen) and it is not on the hot card list. The certificates on modern chip cards provide a higher-quality implementation of the same basic concept; authentication mechanisms such as crypto and security printing can give the added benefit of making names resilient to spoofing. As an example of what can still go wrong, the Irish police created over 50 dockets for Mr 'Prawo Jazdy', wanted for failing to pay over fifty traffic tickets – until they realised that this is Polish for 'Driving licence' [193].
8. *Consistency is hard, and is often fudged. If directories are replicated, then you may find yourself unable to read, or to write, depending on whether too many or too few directories are available.* Naming consistency causes problems for business in a number of ways, of which perhaps the most notorious is the bar code system. Although this is simple enough in theory – with a unique numerical code for each product – in practice different manufacturers, distributors and retailers attach quite different descriptions to the bar codes in their databases. Thus a search for products by 'Kellogg's' will throw up quite different results depending on whether or not an apostrophe is inserted, and this can cause confusion in the supply chain. Proposals to fix this problem can be surprisingly complicated [916]. There are also the issues of convergence discussed above; data might not be consistent across a system, even in theory. There are also the problems of timeliness, such as whether a product has been recalled.
9. *Don't get too smart. Phone numbers are much more robust than computer addresses.* Early secure messaging systems – from PGP to government systems – tried to link keys to email addresses, but these change when people's jobs do. More modern systems such as Signal and WhatsApp use mobile phone numbers instead. In the same way, early attempts to replace bank account numbers and credit card

numbers with public-key certificates in protocols like SET failed, though in some mobile payment systems, such as Kenya's M-Pesa, they've been replaced by phone numbers. (I'll discuss further specific problems of public key infrastructures in section 21.6.)

10. *Some names are bound early, others not; and in general it is a bad thing to bind early if you can avoid it.* A prudent programmer will normally avoid coding absolute addresses or filenames as that would make it hard to upgrade or replace a machine. It's usually better to leave this to a configuration file or an external service such as DNS. Yet secure systems often want stable and accountable names as any third-party service used for last-minute resolution could be a point of attack. Designers therefore need to pay attention to where the naming information goes, how devices get personalised with it, and how they get upgraded – including the names of services on which the security may depend, such as the NTP service discussed in section 7.2.6 above.

7.4.2 What else goes wrong

The Needham principles were crafted for the world of the early 1990s in which naming systems could be imposed at the system owner's convenience. Once we moved to the reality of modern web-based (and interlinked) service industries, operating at global scale, we found that there is more to add.

By the early 2000s, we had learned that no naming system can be globally unique, decentralised and human-meaningful. In fact, it's a classic trilemma: you can only have two of those attributes (Zooko's triangle) [38]. In the past, engineers went for naming systems that were unique and meaningful, like URLs, or unique and decentralised, as with public keys in PGP or the self-signed certificates that function as app names in Android. Human names are meaningful and local but don't scale to the Internet. I mentioned above that as soon as the first search engines came along, I could instantly find dozens of other people called Ross Anderson, but it's even worse than that; half a dozen worked in fields I've also worked in, such as software engineering and electricity distribution.

The innovation from sites like Facebook is to show on a really large scale that names don't have to be unique. We can use social context to build systems that are both decentralised and meaningful – which is just what our brains evolved to cope with. Every Ross Anderson has a different set of friends and you can tell us apart that way.

How can we make sense of all this, and stop it being used to trip people up? It is sometimes helpful to analyse the properties of names in detail.

7.4.2.1 Naming and identity

First, the principals in security protocols are usually known by many different kinds of name – a bank account number, a company registration number, a personal name plus a date of birth or a postal address, a telephone number, a passport number, a health service patient number, or a userid on a computer system.

A common mistake is to confuse naming with identity. *Identity* is when two different names (or instances of the same name) correspond to the same principal (this is known to computer scientists as an *indirect name* or *symbolic link*). One classic example comes from the registration of title to real estate. Someone who wishes to sell a house often uses a different name than they did at the time it was purchased: they might have changed their name on marriage, or on gender transition, or started using their middle name instead. A land-registration system must cope with a lot of identity issues like this.

There are two types of identity failure leading to compromise: where I'm happy to impersonate anybody, and where I want to impersonate a specific individual. The former case includes setting up accounts to launder cybercrime proceeds, while an example of the latter is SIM replacement (I want to clone a CEO's phone so I can loot a company bank account). If banks (or phone companies) just ask people for two proofs of address, such as utility bills, that's easy. Demanding government-issue photo ID may require us to analyse statements such as "The Aaron Bell who owns bank account number 12345678 is the Aaron James Bell with passport number 98765432 and date of birth 3/4/56". This may be seen as a symbolic link between two separate systems – the bank's and the passport office's. Note that the latter part of this 'identity' encapsulates a further statement, which might be something like "The US passport office's file number 98765432 corresponds to the entry in the New York birth register for 3/4/56 of one Aaron James Bell." If Aaron is commonly known as Jim, it gets messier still.

In general, names may involve several steps of recursion, which gives attackers a choice of targets. For example, a lot of passport fraud is *pre-issue fraud*: the bad guys apply for passports in the names of genuine citizens who haven't applied for a passport already and for whom copies of birth certificates are easy to obtain. Postmortem applications are also common. Linden Labs, the operators of Second Life, introduced a scheme whereby you prove you're over 18 by providing the driver's license number or social security number of someone who is. Now a web search quickly pulls up such data for many people, such as the rapper Tupac Amaru Shakur; and yes, Linden Labs did accept Mr Shakur's license number – even through the license had expired and he's dead.

There can also be institutional failure. For example, the United Arab Emirates started taking iris scans of all visitors after women who had been deported to Pakistan for prostitution offences would turn up a few weeks later with a genuine Pakistani passport in a different name and accompanied by a different 'husband'. Similar problems led many countries to issue biometric visas so they don't have to depend on passport issuers in countries they don't want to have to trust.

In addition to corruption, a pervasive failure is the loss of original records. In countries where registers of births, marriages and deaths are kept locally and on paper, some are lost, and smart impersonators exploit these. You might think that digitisation is fixing this problem, but the long-term preservation of digital records is a hard problem even for rich countries; document formats change, software and hardware become obsolete, and you either have to emulate old machines or translate old data, neither of which is ideal. Various states have run pilot projects on electronic documents that must be kept forever, such as civil registration, but we still lack credible standards. Sensible developed countries still keep paper originals as the long-term document of record. In less developed countries, you may have to steer between the Scylla of flaky government IT and the Charybdis of natural disasters – while listening to the siren song of development consultants saying 'put it on the blockchain!

7.4.2.2 Cultural assumptions

The assumptions that underlie names change from one country to another. In the English-speaking world, people may generally use as many names as they please; a name is simply what you are known by. But some countries forbid the use of aliases, and others require them to be registered. The civil registration of births, marriages, civil partnerships, gender transitions and deaths is an extremely complex one, often politicised, tied up with religion in many countries and with the issue of ID documents as well. And incompatible rules between countries cause real problems for migrants, for tourists and indeed for companies with overseas customers.

In earlier editions of this book, I gave as an example that writers who change their legal name on marriage often keep publishing using their former name. So my lab colleague, the late Professor Karen Spärck Jones, got a letter from the university every year asking why she hadn't published anything (she was down on the payroll as Karen Needham). The publication-tracking system just could not cope with everything the personnel system knew. And as software gets in everything and systems get linked up, conflicts can have unexpected remote effects. For example, Karen was also a trustee of the British Library and was not impressed when it started to issue its own admission tickets using the name on the holder's home university library card. Such issues caused even more friction when the university introduced an ID card system keyed to payroll names to give unified access to buildings, libraries and canteens. These issues with multiple names are now mainstream; it's not just professors, musicians and novelists who use more than one name. Trans people who want to stop firms using names from a previous gender; women who want to stop using a married name when they separate or divorce, and who perhaps need to if they're fleeing an abusive partner; people who've assumed new names following religious conversion – there's no end of sources of conflict. If you're building a system that you hope will scale up globally, you'll eventually have to deal with them all.

Human naming conventions also vary by culture. Chinese may have both English and Chinese given names if they're from Hong Kong, with the English one coming before and the Chinese one coming after the family name. Many people in South India, Indonesia and Mongolia have only a single name – a mononym. The Indian convention is to add two initials – for your place of birth and your father's name. So 'BK Rajan' may mean Rajan, son of Kumar, from Bangalore. A common tactic among South Indian migrants to the USA is to use the patronymic (here, Kumar) as a surname; but when western computer systems misinterpret Rajan as a surname, confusion can arise. Russians are known by a forename, a patronymic and a surname. Icelanders have no surname; their given name is followed by a patronymic if they are male and a matronymic if they are female. In the old days, when 'Maria Trosttadóttir' arrived at US immigration and the officer learned that 'Trosttadóttir' isn't a surname or even a patronymic, their standard practice was to compel her to adopt as a surname a patronymic (say, 'Carlsson' if her father was called Carl). Many Indians in the USA have had similar problems, all of which cause unnecessary offence. And then there are cultures where your name changes after you have children.

Another cultural divide is often thought to be that between the English-speaking countries, where identity cards were unacceptable on privacy grounds[9], and the countries conquered by Napoleon or by the Soviets, where identity cards are the norm. What's less well known is that the British Empire happily imposed ID on many of its subject populations, so the real divide is perhaps whether a country was ever conquered.

The local history of ID conditions all sorts of assumptions. I know Germans who have refused to believe that a country could function at all without a proper system of population registration and ID cards yet admit they are asked for their ID card only rarely (for example, to open a bank account or get married). Their card number can't be used as a name because it is a document number and changes every time a new card is issued. The Icelandic ID card number, however, is static; it's just the citizen's date of birth plus two further digits. What's more, the law requires that bank account numbers contain the account holder's ID number. These are perhaps the extremes of private and public ID numbering.

[9] unless they're called drivers' licences or health service cards!

Finally, in many less developed countries, the act of registering citizens and issuing them with ID is not just inefficient but political [89]. The ruling tribe may seek to disenfranchise the others by making it hard to register births in their territory or by making it inconvenient to get an ID card. Sometimes cards are reissued in the run-up to an election in order to refresh or reinforce the discrimination. Cards can be tied to business permits and welfare payments; delays can be used to extract bribes. Some countries (such as Brazil) have separate registration systems at the state and federal level, while others (such as Malawi) have left most of their population unregistered. There are many excluded groups, such as refugee children born outside the country of their parents' nationality, and groups made stateless for religious or ideological reasons. Target 16.9 of the United Nations' Sustainable Development Goals is to 'provide legal identity for all, including birth registration'; and a number of companies sell ID systems and voting systems financed by development aid. These interact with governments in all sorts of complex ways, and there's a whole research community that studies this [89]. Oh, and if you think this is a third-world problem, there are several US states using onerous registration procedures to make it harder for Black people to vote; and in the Windrush scandal, it emerged that the UK government had deported a number of foreign-born UK residents who were automatically entitled to citizenship as they had not maintained a good enough paper trail of their citizenship to satisfy increasingly xenophobic ministers.

In short, the hidden assumptions about the relationship between governments and people's names vary in ways that constrain system design and cause unexpected failures when assumptions are carried across borders. The engineer must always be alert to the fact that a service-oriented ID is one thing and a legal identity or certificate of citizenship is another. Governments are forever trying to entangle the two, but this leads to all sorts of pain.

7.4.2.3 Semantic content of names

Changing from one type of name to another can be hazardous. A bank got sued after they moved from storing customer data by account number to storing it by name and address. They wrote a program to link up all the accounts operated by each of their customers, in the hope that it would help them target junk mail more accurately. The effect on one customer was serious: the bank statement for the account he kept for his mistress got sent to his wife, who divorced him.

The semantics of names can change over time. In many transport systems, tickets and toll tags can be bought for cash, which defuses privacy concerns, but it's more convenient to link them to bank accounts, and these links accumulate over time. The card that UK pensioners use to get free bus travel also started out anonymous, but in practice the bus companies try to link up the card numbers to other passenger identifiers. In fact, I once got a hardware store loyalty card with a random account number (and no credit checks). I was offered the chance to change this into a bank card after the store was taken over by a supermarket and the supermarket started a bank.

7.4.2.4 Uniqueness of names

Human names evolved when we lived in small communities. We started off with just forenames, but by the late Middle Ages the growth of travel led governments to bully people into adopting surnames. That process took a century or so and was linked with the introduction of paper into Europe as a lower-cost and more tamper-resistant replacement for parchment; paper enabled the badges, seals and other bearer tokens, which people had previously used for road tolls and the like, to be replaced with letters that mentioned their names.

The mass movement of people, business and administration to the Internet has been too fast for social adaptation. There are now way more people (and systems) online than we're used to dealing with. So how can we make human-memorable names unique? As we discussed above, Facebook tells one John Smith from another the way humans do, by clustering each one with his set of friends and adding a photo.

Perhaps the other extreme is cryptographic names. Names are hashes either of public keys or of other stable attributes of the object being named. All sorts of mechanisms have been proposed to map real-world names, addresses and even document content indelibly and eternally on to the bitstring outputs of hash functions (see, for example, [846]). You can even use hashes of biometrics or the surface microstructure of objects, coupled with a suitable error-correction code. The world of cryptocurrency and blockchains makes much use of hash-based identifiers. Such mechanisms can make it impossible to reuse names; as expired domain names are often bought by bad people and exploited, this is sometimes important.

This isn't entirely new, as it has long been common in transaction processing to just give everything and everyone a number. This can lead to failures, though, if you don't put enough uniqueness in the right place. For example, a UK bank assigned unique sequence numbers to transactions by printing them on the stationery used to capture the deal. Once, when they wanted to send £20m overseas, the operator typed in £10m by mistake. A second payment of £10m was ordered – but this acquired the same transaction sequence number from the paperwork. So two payments were sent to SWIFT with the same date, payee, amount and sequence number – and the second was discarded as a duplicate [310].

7.4.2.5 Stability of names and addresses

Many names include some kind of address, yet addresses change. While we still had a phone book in Cambridge, about a quarter of the addresses changed every year; with work email, the turnover is probably higher. When we tried in the late 1990s to develop a directory of people who use encrypted email, together with their keys, we found that the main cause of changed entries was changes of email address [104]. (Some people had assumed it would be the loss or theft of keys; the contribution from this source was precisely zero.) Things are perhaps more stable now. Most people try to keep their personal mobile phone numbers, so they tend to be long-lived, and the same goes increasingly for personal email addresses. The big service providers like Google and Microsoft generally don't issue the same email address twice, but other firms still do.

Distributed systems pioneers considered it a bad thing to put addresses in names [1355]. But hierarchical naming systems can involve multiple layers of abstraction with some of the address information at each layer forming part of the name at the layer above. Also, whether a namespace is better flat depends on the application. Often people end up with different names at the departmental and organisational level (such as `rja14@cam.ac.uk` and `ross.anderson@cl.cam.ac.uk` in my own case). So a clean demarcation between names and addresses is not always possible.

Authorisations have many (but not all) of the properties of addresses. Kent's Law tells designers that if a credential contains a list of what it may be used for, then the more things there are on this list the shorter its period of usefulness. A similar problem besets systems where names are composite. For example, some online businesses recognize me by the combination of email address and credit card number. This is clearly bad practice. Quite apart from the fact that I have several email addresses, I have several credit cards.

There are good reasons to use pseudonyms. Until Facebook came along, people considered it sensible for children and young people to use online names that weren't easily linkable to their real names and addresses. When you go for your first job on leaving college aged 22, or for a CEO's job at 45, you don't want a search to turn up all your teenage rants. Many people also change email addresses from time to time to escape spam; I used to give a different email address to every website where I shop. On the other hand, some police and other agencies would prefer people not to use pseudonyms, which takes us into the whole question of traceability online – which I'll discuss in Part 2.

7.4.2.6 Restrictions on the use of names

The interaction between naming and society brings us to a further problem: some names may be used only in restricted circumstances. This may be laid down by law, as with the US social security number and its equivalents in some other countries. Sometimes it is a matter of marketing: a significant minority of customers avoid websites that demand too much information.

Restricted naming systems interact in unexpected ways. For example, it's fairly common for hospitals to use a patient number as an index to medical record databases, as this may allow researchers to use pseudonymous records for some purposes. This causes problems when a merger of health maintenance organisations, or a policy change, forces the hospital to introduce uniform names. There have long been tussles in Britain's health service, for example, about which pseudonyms can be used for which purposes.

Finally, when we come to law and policy, the definition of a name throws up new and unexpected gotchas. For example, regulations that allow police to collect communications data – that is, a record of who called whom and when – are usually much more lax than the regulations governing phone tapping; in many countries, police can get communications data just by asking the phone company. This led to tussles over the status of URLs, which contain data such as the parameters passed to search engines. Clearly some policemen would like a list of everyone who hit a URL like `http://www.google.com/search?q=cannabis+cultivation`; just as clearly, many people would consider such large-scale trawling to be an unacceptable invasion of privacy. The resolution in UK law was to define traffic data as that which was sufficient to identify the machine being communicated with, or in lay language 'Everything up to the first slash.' I discuss this in much more detail later, in the chapter 'Surveillance or Privacy?'

7.4.3 Types of name

Not only is naming complex at all levels – from the technical up through the organisational to the political – but some of the really wicked issues go across levels. I noted in the introduction that names can refer not just to persons (and machines acting on their behalf), but also to organisations, roles ('the officer of the watch'), groups, and compound constructions: *principal in role* – Alice as manager; *delegation* – Alice for Bob; *conjunction* – Alice and Bob. Conjunction often expresses implicit access rules: 'Alice acting as branch manager plus Bob as a member of the group of branch accountants'.

That's only the beginning. Names also apply to services (such as NFS, or a public-key infrastructure) and channels (which might mean wires, ports or crypto keys). The same name might refer to different roles: 'Alice as a computer game player' ought to have less privilege than 'Alice the system administrator'. The usual abstraction used in the security literature is to treat them as different principals. So there's no easy mapping between names and principals, especially when people bring their own devices to work or take work devices home, and therefore may have multiple conflicting names or roles on the same platform. Many organisations are starting to distinguish carefully between 'Alice in person', 'Alice as a program running on Alice's home laptop' and 'a program running on Alice's behalf on the corporate cloud', and we discussed some of the possible mechanisms in the chapter on access control.

Functional tensions are often easier to analyse if you work out how they're driven by the underlying business processes. Businesses mainly want to get paid, while governments want to identify people uniquely. In effect, business wants your credit card number while government wants your passport number. An analysis based on incentives can sometimes indicate whether a naming system might be better open or closed, local or global, stateful or stateless – and whether the people who maintain it are the same people who will pay the costs of failure (economics is one of the key issues for dependability,and is the subject of the next chapter).

Finally, although I've illustrated many of the problems of naming with respect to people – as that makes the problems more immediate and compelling – many of the same problems pop up in various ways for cryptographic keys, unique product codes, document IDs, file names, URLs and much more. When we dive into the internals of a modern corporate network we may find DNS Round Robin to multiple machines, each on its own IP addresses, behind a single name; or Anycast to multiple machines, each on the same IP address, behind a single name; or Cisco's HSRP protocol, where the IP address and the Ethernet MAC address move from one router to another router. (I'll discuss more technical aspects of network security in Part 2.) Anyway, as systems scale, it becomes less realistic to rely on names that are simple, interchangeable and immutable. You need to scope naming carefully, understand who controls the names on which you rely, work out how slippery they are, and design your system to be dependable despite their limitations.

7.5 Summary

Many secure distributed systems have incurred large costs, or developed serious vulnerabilities, because their designers ignored the basics of how to build (and how not to build) distributed systems. Most of these basics have been in computer science textbooks for a generation.

Many security breaches are concurrency failures of one kind or another; systems use old data, make updates inconsistently or in the wrong order, or assume that data are consistent when they aren't or even can't be. Using time to order transactions may help, but knowing the right time is harder than it seems.

Fault tolerance and failure recovery are critical. Providing the ability to recover from security failures, as well as from random physical and software failures, is the main purpose of the protection budget for many organisations. At a more technical level, there are significant interactions between protection and resilience mechanisms. Byzantine failure – where defective processes conspire rather than failing randomly – is an issue, and it interacts with our choice of cryptographic tools.

There are many different flavors of redundancy, and we have to use the right combination. We need to protect not just against failures and attempted manipulation, but also against deliberate attempts to deny service that may be part of larger attack plans.

Many problems also arise from trying to make a name do too much, or making assumptions about it which don't hold outside of one particular system, culture or jurisdiction. For example, it should be possible to revoke a user's access to a system by cancelling their user name without getting sued on account of other functions being revoked. The simplest solution is often to assign each principal a unique identifier used for no other purpose, such as a bank account number or a system logon name. But many problems arise when merging two systems that use naming schemes that are incompatible. Sometimes this can even happen by accident.

Research problems

I've touched on many technical issues in this chapter, from secure time protocols to the complexities of naming. But perhaps the most important research problem is to work out how to design systems that are resilient in the face of malice, that degrade gracefully, and whose security can be recovered simply once the attack is past. All sorts of remedies have been pushed in the past, from getting governments to issue everyone with ID to putting it all on the blockchain. However these magic bullets don't seem to kill any of the goblins.

It's always a good idea for engineers to study failures; we learn more from the one bridge that falls down than from the thousand that don't. We now have a growing number of failed ID systems, such as the UK government's Verify scheme – an attempt to create a federated logon system for public service that was abandoned in 2019 [1394]. There is a research community that studies failures of ID systems in less developed countries [89]. And then there's the failure of blockchains to live up to their initial promise, which I'll discuss in Part 2 of this book.

Perhaps we need to study more carefully the conditions under which we can recover neatly from corrupt security state. Malware and phishing attacks mean that at any given time a small (but nonzero) proportion of customer bank accounts are under criminal control. Yet the banking system carries on. The proportion of infected laptops, and phones, varies quite widely by country, and the effects might be worth more careful study.

Classical computer science theory saw convergence in distributed systems as an essentially technical problem, whose solution depended on technical properties (at one level, atomicity, consistency, isolation and durability; at another, digital signatures, dual control and audit). Perhaps we need a higher-level view in which we ask how we obtain sufficient agreement about the state of the world and incorporate not just technical resilience mechanisms and protection technologies, but also the mechanisms whereby people who have been victims of fraud obtain redress. Purely technical mechanisms that try to obviate the need for robust redress may actually make things worse.

Further reading

If the material in this chapter is unfamiliar to you, you may be coming to the subject from a maths/crypto background or chips/engineering or even law/policy. Computer science students get many lectures on distributed systems; to catch up, I'd suggest Saltzer and Kaashoek [1643]. Other books we've recommended to our students over the years include Tanenbaum and van Steen [1863] and Mullender [1355]. A 2003 report from the US National Research Council, *'Who Goes There? Authentication Through the Lens of Privacy'*, discusses the tradeoffs between authentication and privacy and how they tend to scale poorly [1041]. Finally, there's a recent discussion of naming by Pat Helland [882].

CHAPTER

8

Economics

The great fortunes of the information age lie in the hands of companies that have established proprietary architectures that are used by a large installed base of locked-in customers.

– CARL SHAPIRO AND HAL VARIAN

There are two things I am sure of after all these years: there is a growing societal need for high assurance software, and market forces are never going to provide it.

– EARL BOEBERT

The law locks up the man or woman
Who steals the goose from off the common
But leaves the greater villain loose
Who steals the common from the goose.

– TRADITIONAL, 17th CENTURY

8.1 Introduction

Round about 2000, we started to realise that many security failures weren't due to technical errors so much as to wrong incentives: if the people who guard a system are not the people who suffer when it fails, then you can expect trouble. In fact, security mechanisms are often designed deliberately to shift liability, which can lead to even worse trouble.

Economics has always been important to engineering, at the raw level of cost accounting; a good engineer was one who could build a bridge safely with a thousand tons of concrete when everyone else used two thousand tons. But the perverse incentives that arise in complex systems with multiple owners make economic questions both more important and more subtle for the security engineer. Truly global-scale systems like the Internet arise from the actions of millions of independent principals with divergent interests; we hope that reasonable global outcomes will result from selfish local actions. The outcome we get is typically a market equilibrium, and often a surprisingly stable one. Attempts to make large complex systems more secure, or safer, will usually fail if this isn't understood. At the macro level, cybercrime patterns have been remarkably stable through the 2010s even though technology changed completely, with phones replacing laptops, with society moving to social networks and servers moving to the cloud. Network insecurity is somewhat like air pollution or congestion, in that people who connect insecure machines to the Internet do not bear the full consequences of their actions while people who try to do things right suffer the side-effects of others' carelessness.

In general, people won't change their behaviour unless they have an incentive to. If their actions take place in some kind of market, then the equilibrium will be where the forces pushing and pulling in different directions balance each other out. But markets can fail; the computer industry has been dogged by monopolies since its earliest days. The reasons for this are now understood, and their interaction with security is starting to be.

Security economics has developed rapidly as a discipline since the early 2000s. It provides valuable insights not just into 'security' topics such as privacy, bugs, spam, and phishing, but into more general areas of system dependability. For example, what's the optimal balance of effort by programmers and testers? (For the answer, see section 8.6.3.) It also enables us to analyse many important policy problems – such as the costs of cybercrime and the most effective responses to it. And when protection mechanisms are used to limit what someone can do with their possessions or their data, questions of competition policy and consumer rights follow – which we need economics to analyse. There are also questions of the balance between public and private action: how much of the protection effort should be left to individuals, and how much should be borne by vendors, regulators or the police? Everybody tries to pass the buck.

In this chapter I first describe how we analyse monopolies in the classical economic model, how information goods and services markets are different, and how network effects and technical lock-in make monopoly more likely. I then look at asymmetric information, another source of market power. Next is game theory, which enables us to analyse whether people will cooperate or compete; and auction theory, which lets us understand the working of the ad markets that drive much of the Internet – and how they fail. These basics then let us analyse key components of the information security ecosystem, such as the software patching cycle. We also get to understand why systems are less reliable than they should be: why there are too many vulnerabilities and why too few cyber-crooks get caught.

8.2 Classical economics

Modern economics is an enormous field covering many different aspects of human behaviour. The parts of it that have found application in security so far are largely drawn from microeconomics, game theory and behavioral economics. In this section, I'll start with a helicopter tour of the most relevant ideas from microeconomics. My objective is not to provide a tutorial on economics, but to get across the basic language and ideas, so we can move on to discuss security economics.

The modern subject started in the 18th century when growing trade changed the world, leading to the industrial revolution, and people wanted to understand what was going on. In 1776, Adam Smith's classic *'The Wealth of Nations'* [1792] provided a first draft: he explained how rational self-interest in a free market leads to progress. Specialisation leads to productivity gains, as people try to produce something others value to survive in a competitive market. In his famous phrase, "It is not from the benevolence of the butcher, the brewer, or the baker, that we can expect our dinner, but from their regard to their own interest." The same mechanisms scale up from a farmers' market or small factory to international trade.

These ideas were refined by nineteenth-century economists; David Ricardo clarified and strengthened Smith's arguments in favour of free trade, while Stanley Jevons, Léon Walras and Carl Menger built detailed models of supply and demand. One of the insights from Jevons and Menger is that the price of a good, at equilibrium in a competitive market, is the marginal cost of production. When coal cost nine shillings a ton in 1870, that didn't mean that every mine dug coal at this price, merely that the marginal producers – those who were only just managing to stay in business – could sell at that price. If the price went down, these mines would close; if it went up, even more marginal mines would open. That's how supply responded to changes in demand. (It also gives us an insight into why so many online services nowadays are free; as the marginal cost of duplicating information is about zero, lots of online businesses can't sell it and have to make their money in other ways, such as from advertising. But we're getting ahead of ourselves.)

By the end of the century Alfred Marshall had combined models of supply and demand in markets for goods, labour and capital into an overarching 'classical' model in which, at equilibrium, all the excess profits would be competed away and the economy would be functioning efficiently. By 1948, Kenneth Arrow and Gérard Debreu had put this on a rigorous mathematical foundation by proving that markets give efficient outcomes, subject to certain conditions, including that the buyers and sellers have full property rights, that they have complete information, that they are rational and that the costs of doing transactions can be neglected.

Much of the interest in economics comes from the circumstances in which one or more of these conditions aren't met. For example, suppose that transactions have side-effects that are not captured by the available property rights. Economists call these *externalities*, and they can be either positive or negative. An example of a positive externality is scientific research, from which everyone can benefit once it's published. As a result, the researcher doesn't capture the full benefit of their work, and we get less research than would be ideal (economists reckon we do only a quarter of the ideal amount of research). An example of a negative externality is environmental pollution; if I burn a coal fire, I get the positive effect of heating my house but my neighbour gets the negative effect of smell and ash, while everyone shares the negative effect of increased CO_2 emissions.

Externalities, and other causes of market failure, are of real importance to the computer industry, and to security folks in particular, as they shape many of the problems we wrestle with, from industry monopolies to insecure software. Where one player has enough power to charge more than the market clearing price, or nobody has the power to fix a common problem, then markets alone may not be able to sort things out. Strategy is about acquiring power, or preventing other people having power over you; so the most basic business strategy is to acquire market power in order to extract extra profits, while distributing the costs of your activity on others to the greatest extent possible. Let's explore that now in more detail.

8.2.1 Monopoly

As an introduction, let's consider a textbook case of monopoly. Suppose we have a market for apartments in a university town, and the students have different incomes. We might have one rich student able to pay \$4000 a month, maybe 300 people willing to pay at least \$2000 a month, and (to give us round numbers) at least 1000 prepared to pay at least \$1000 a month. That gives us the *demand curve* shown in Figure 8.1.

So if there are 1000 apartments being let by many competing landlords, the market-clearing price will be at the intersection of the demand curve with the vertical supply curve, namely \$1000. But suppose the market is rigged – say the landlords have set up a cartel, or the university makes its students rent through a tied agency. A monopolist landlord examines the demand curve, and notices that if he rents out only 800 apartments, he can get \$1400 per month for each of them. Now 800 times \$1400 is \$1,120,000 per month, which is more than the million dollars a month he'll make from the market price at \$1000. (Economists would say that his 'revenue box' is the box CBFO rather than EDGO in Figure 8.1.) So he sets an artificially high price, and 200 apartments remain empty.

This is clearly inefficient, and the Italian economist Vilfredo Pareto invented a neat way to formalise this. A *Pareto improvement* is any change that would make some people better off without making anyone else worse off, and an allocation is *Pareto efficient* if there isn't any Pareto improvement available.

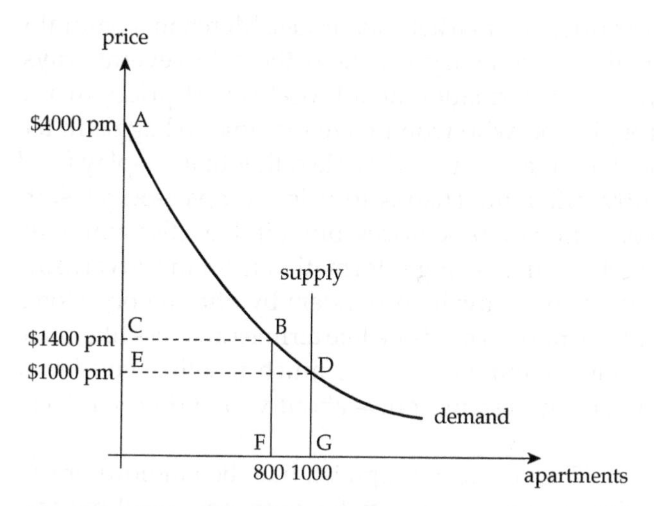

Figure 8.1: The market for apartments

Here, the allocation is not efficient, as the monopolist could rent out one empty apartment to anyone at a lower price, making both him and them better off. Now Pareto efficiency is a rather weak criterion; both perfect communism (everyone gets the same income) and perfect dictatorship (the king gets the lot) are Pareto-efficient. In neither case can you make anyone better off without making someone else worse off! Yet the simple monopoly described here is not efficient even in this very weak sense.

So what can the monopolist do? There is one possibility – if he can charge everyone a different price, then he can set each student's rent at exactly what they are prepared to pay. We call such a landlord a *price-discriminating monopolist*; he charges the rich student exactly $4000, and so on down to the 1000th student whom he charges exactly $1000. The same students get apartments as before, yet almost all of them are worse off. The rich student loses $3000, money that he was prepared to pay but previously didn't have to; economists refer to this money he saved as *surplus*. The discriminating monopolist manages to extract all the consumer surplus.

Merchants have tried to price-discriminate since antiquity. The carpet seller in Istanbul who expects you to haggle down his price is playing this game, as is an airline selling first, business and cattle class seats. The extent to which firms can charge people different prices depends on a number of factors, principally their *market power* and their *information asymmetry*. Market power is a measure of how close a merchant is to being a monopolist; under monopoly the merchant is a *price setter*, while under perfect competition he is a *price taker* who has to accept whatever price the market establishes. Merchants naturally try to avoid this. Information asymmetry can help them in several ways. A carpet seller has much more information about local carpet prices than a tourist who's passing through, and who won't have the time to haggle in ten different shops. So the merchant may prefer to haggle rather than display fixed prices. An airline is slightly different. Thanks to price-comparison sites, its passengers have good information on base prices, but if it does discount to fill seats, it may be able to target its offers using information from the advertising ecosystem. It can also create its own loyalty ecosystem by offering occasional upgrades. Technology tends to make firms more like airlines and less like small carpet shops; the information asymmetry isn't so much whether you know about average prices, as what the system knows about you and how it locks you in.

Monopoly can be complex. The classic monopolist, like the landlord or cartel in our example, may simply push up prices for everyone, resulting in a clear loss of consumer surplus. Competition law in the USA looks for welfare loss of this kind, which often happens where a cartel operates price discrimination. During the late 19th century, railroad operators charged different freight rates to different customers, depending on how profitable they were, how perishable their goods were and other factors – basically, shaking them all down according to their ability to pay. This led to massive resentment and to railway regulation. In the same way, telcos used to price-discriminate like crazy; SMSes used to cost a lot more than voice, and voice a lot more than data, especially over distance. This led to services like Skype and WhatsApp which use data services to provide cheaper calls and messaging, and also to net neutrality regulation in a number of countries. This is still a tussle space, with President Trump's appointee at the FCC reversing many previous net neutrality rulings.

However, many firms with real market power like Google and Facebook give their products away free to most of their users, while others, like Amazon (and Walmart), cut prices for their customers. This challenges the traditional basis that economists and lawyers used to think about monopoly, in the USA at least. Yet there's no doubt about monopoly power in tech. We may have gone from one dominant player in the 1970s (IBM) to two in the 1990s (Microsoft and Intel) and a handful now (Google, Facebook, Amazon, Microsoft, maybe Netflix) but each dominates its field; although Arm managed to compete with Intel, there has been no new search startup since Bing in 2009 (whose market share is slipping), and no big social network since Instagram in 2011 (now owned by Facebook). So there's been a negative effect on innovation, and the question what we do about it is becoming a hot political topic. The EU has fined tech majors multiple times for competition offences.

To understand what's going on, we need to dive more deeply into how information monopolies work.

8.3 Information economics

The information and communications industries are different from traditional manufacturing in a number of ways, and among the most striking is that these markets have been very concentrated for generations. Even before computers came along, newspapers tended to be monopolies, except in the biggest cities. Much the same happened with railways, and before that with canals. When electrical tabulating equipment came along in the late 19th century, it was dominated by NCR, until a spin-off from NCR's Manhattan sales office called IBM took over. IBM dominated the computer industry in the 1960s and 70s, then Microsoft came along and took pole position in the 90s. Since then, Google and Facebook have come to dominate advertising, Apple and Google sell phone operating systems, ARM and Intel do CPUs, while many other firms dominate their own particular speciality. Why should this be so?

8.3.1 Why information markets are different

Recall that in a competitive equilibrium, the price of a good should be its marginal cost of production. But for information that's almost zero! That's why there is so much free stuff online; zero is its fair price. If two or more suppliers compete to offer an operating system, or a map, or an encyclopedia, that they can duplicate for no cost, then they will keep on cutting their prices without limit. Take for example encyclopedias; the Britannica used to cost $1,600 for 32 volumes; then Microsoft brought out Encarta for $49.95, forcing Britannica to produce a cheap CD edition; and now we have Wikipedia for free [1721]. One firm after another has had to move to a business model in which the goods are given away free, and the money comes from advertising or in some parallel market. And it can be hard to compete with services that are free, or are so cheap it's hard to recoup the capital investment you need to get started. So other industries with high fixed costs and low marginal costs tend to be concentrated – such as newspapers, airlines and hotels.

Second, there are often *network externalities*, whereby the value of a network grows more than linearly in the number of users. Networks such as the telephone and email took some time to get going because at the start there were only a few other enthusiasts to talk to, but once they passed a certain threshold in each social group, everyone needed to join and the network rapidly became mainstream. The same thing happened again with social media from the mid-2000s; initially there were 40–50 startups doing social networks, but once Facebook started to pull ahead, suddenly all young people had to be there, as that was where all your friends were, and if you weren't there then you missed out on the party invitations. This *positive feedback* is one of the mechanisms by which network effects can get established. It can also operate in a *two-sided market* which brings together two types of user. For example, when local newspapers got going in the nineteenth century, businesses wanted to advertise in the papers with lots of readers, and readers wanted papers with lots of small ads so they could find stuff. So once a paper got going, it often grew to be a local monopoly; it was hard for a competitor to break in. The same thing happened when the railways allowed the industrialisation of agriculture; powerful firms like Cargill and Armour owned the grain elevators and meat packers, dealing with small farmers on one side and the retail industry on the other. We saw the same pattern in the 1960s when IBM mainframes dominated computing: firms used to develop software for IBM as they'd have access to more users, while many users bought IBM because there was more software for it. When PCs came along, Microsoft beat Apple for the same reason; and now that phones are replacing laptops, we see a similar pattern with Android and iPhone. Another winner was eBay in the late 1990s: most people wanting to auction stuff will want to use the largest auction, as it will attract more bidders. Network effects can also be negative; once a website such as Myspace starts losing custom, negative feedback can turn the loss into a rout.

Third, there are various supply-side scale economies enjoyed by leading information services firms, ranging from access to unmatchable quantities of user data to the ability to run large numbers of A/B tests to understand user preferences and optimise system performance. These enable early movers to create, and incumbents to defend, competitive advantage in service provision.

Fourth, there's often lock-in stemming from *interoperability*, or a lack thereof. Once a software firm commits to using a platform such as Windows or Oracle for its product, it can be expensive to change. This has both technical and human components, and the latter are often dominant; it's cheaper to replace tools than to retrain programmers. The same holds for customers, too: it can be hard to close a sale if they not only have to buy new software and convert files, but retrain their staff too. These *switching costs* deter migration. Earlier platforms where interoperability mattered included the telephone system, the telegraph, mains electricity and even the railways.

These four features separately – low marginal costs, network externalities, supply-side scale economies and technical lock-in – can lead to industries with dominant firms; in combination, they are even more likely to. If users want to be compatible with other users (and with vendors of complementary products such as software) then they will logically buy from the vendor they expect to win the biggest market share.

8.3.2 The value of lock-in

There is an interesting result, due to Carl Shapiro and Hal Varian: that the value of a software company is the total lock-in (due to both technical and network effects) of all its customers [1721]. To see how this might work, consider a firm with 100 staff each using Office, for which it has paid $150 per copy. It could save this $15,000 by moving to a free program such as LibreOffice, so if the costs of installing this product, retraining its staff, converting files and so on – in other words the total switching costs – were less than $15,000, it would switch. But if the costs of switching were more than $15,000, then Microsoft would put up its prices.

As an example of the link between lock-in, pricing and value, consider how prices changed over a decade. In the second edition of this book, this example had the cost of Office as $500; since then, cloud-based services that worked just like Office, such as Google Docs, cut the costs of switching – so Microsoft had to slash its prices. As I started writing this edition in 2019, I saw standalone Office for sale at prices ranging between $59.99 and £164. Microsoft's response since 2013 has been trying to move its customers to an online subscription service (Office365) which costs universities a few tens of pounds per seat depending on what options they choose and how good they are at negotiating, while Google is also trying to move organisations away from their free services to paid G Suite versions that cost about the same. Charging $30 a year for an online service is better business than charging $60 for a program that the customer might use for five years or even seven. When I revised this chapter in 2020, I saw I can now get a 'lifetime key' for about double the cost of a standalone product last year. There's a new form of lock-in, namely that the cloud provider now looks after all your data.

Lock-in explains why so much effort gets expended in standards wars and antitrust suits. It also helps explain the move to the cloud (though cost cutting is a bigger driver). It's also why so many security mechanisms aim at controlling compatibility. In such cases, the likely attackers are not malicious outsiders, but the owners of the equipment, or new firms trying to challenge the incumbent by making compatible products. This doesn't just damage competition, but innovation too. Locking things down too hard can also be bad for business, as innovation is often incremental, and products succeed when new firms find killer applications for them [905]. The PC, for example, was designed by IBM as a machine to run spreadsheets; if they had locked it down to this application alone, then a massive opportunity would have been lost. Indeed, the fact that the IBM PC was more open than the Apple Mac was a factor in its becoming the dominant desktop platform. (That Microsoft and Intel later stole IBM's lunch is a separate issue.)

So the law in many countries gives companies a right to reverse-engineer their competitors' products for compatibility [1650]. Incumbents try to build ecosystems in which their offerings work better together than with their competitors'. They lock down their products using digital components such as cloud services and cryptography so that even if competitors have the legal right to try to reverse engineer these products, they are not always going to succeed in practice. Incumbents also use their ecosystems to learn a lot about their customers, the better to lock them in; and a variety of digital mechanisms are used to control aftermarkets and enforce planned obsolescence. I will discuss these more complex ecosystem strategies in more detail below in section 8.6.4.

8.3.3 Asymmetric information

Another way markets can fail, beyond monopoly and public goods, is when some principals know more than others, or know it slightly earlier, or can find it out more cheaply. We discussed how an old-fashioned carpet trader has an information advantage over tourists buying in his store; but the formal study of *asymmetric information* was kicked off by a famous paper in 1970 on the 'market for lemons' [35], for which George Akerlof won a Nobel prize. It presents the following simple yet profound insight: suppose that there are 100 used cars for sale in a town: 50 well-maintained cars worth $2000 each, and 50 'lemons' worth $1000. The sellers know which is which, but the buyers don't. What is the market price of a used car?

You might think $1500; but at that price, no good cars will be offered for sale. So the market price will be close to $1000. This is why, if you buy a new car, maybe 20% falls off the price the second you drive it out of the dealer's lot. Asymmetric information is also why poor security products dominate some markets. When users can't tell good from bad, they might as well buy the cheapest. When the market for antivirus software took off in the 1990s, people would buy the $10 product rather than the $20 one. (Nowadays there's much less reason to buy AV, as the malware writers test their code against all available products before releasing it – you should focus on patching systems instead. That people still buy lots of AV is another example of asymmetric information.)

A further distinction can be drawn between hidden information and hidden action. For example, Volvo has a reputation for building safe cars that help their occupants survive accidents, yet Volvo drivers have more accidents. Is this because people who know they're bad drivers buy Volvos so they're less likely to get killed, or because people in Volvos believe they're safer and drive faster? The first is the hidden-information case, also known as *adverse selection*, while the second is the hidden-action case, also known as *moral hazard*. Both effects are important in security, and both may combine in specific cases. (In the case of drivers, people adjust their driving behaviour to keep their risk exposure at the level with which they're comfortable. This also explains why mandatory seat-belt laws tend not to save lives overall, merely to move fatalities from vehicle occupants to pedestrians and cyclists [19].)

Asymmetric information explains many market failures in the real world, from low prices in used-car markets to the high price of cyber-risks insurance (firms who know they cut corners may buy more of it, making it expensive for the careful). In the world of information security, it's made worse by the fact that most stakeholders are not motivated to tell the truth; police and intelligence agencies, as well as security vendors, try to talk up the threats while software vendors, e-commerce sites and banks downplay them [112].

8.3.4 Public goods

An interesting case of positive externalities is when everyone gets the same quantity of some good, whether they want it or not. Classic examples are air quality, national defense and scientific research. Economists call these *public goods*, and the formal definition is that such goods are non-rivalrous (my using them doesn't mean there's less for you) and non-excludable (there's no practical way to stop people consuming them). Uncoordinated markets are generally unable to provide public goods in socially optimal quantities.

Public goods may be supplied by governments directly, as with national defense, or by using indirect mechanisms such as laws on patents and copyrights to encourage people to produce inventions, books and music by giving them a temporary monopoly. Very often, public goods are provided by some mix of public and private action; scientific research is done in universities that get some public subsidy, earn some income from student fees, and get some research contracts from industry (which may get patents on the useful inventions).

Many aspects of security are public goods. I do not have an anti-aircraft gun on the roof of my house; air-defense threats come from a small number of actors, and are most efficiently dealt with by government action. So what about Internet security? Certainly there are strong externalities; people who connect insecure machines to the Internet end up dumping costs on others, as they enable bad actors to build botnets. Self-protection has some aspects of a public good, while insurance is more of a private good. So what should we do about it?

The answer may depend on whether the bad actors we're concerned with are concentrated or dispersed. In our quick survey of cybercrime in section 2.3 we noted that many threats have consolidated as malware writers, spammers and others have become commercial. By 2007, the number of serious spammers had dropped to a handful, and by 2020, the same had become true of denial-of-service (DoS) attacks: there seems to be one dominant DoS-for-hire provider. This suggests a more centralised defence strategy, namely, finding the bad guys and throwing them in jail.

Some have imagined a gentler government response, with rewards paid to researchers who discover vulnerabilities, paid for by fines imposed on the firms whose software contained them. To some extent this happens already via bug bounty programs and vulnerability markets, without government intervention. But a cynic will point out that in real life what happens is that vulnerabilities are sold to cyber-arms manufacturers who sell them to governments who then stockpile them – and industry pays for the collateral damage, as with NotPetya. So is air pollution the right analogy – or air defense? This brings us to game theory.

8.4 Game theory

Game theory has some of the most fundamental insights of modern economics. It's about when we cooperate, and when we fight.

There are really just two ways to get something you want if you can't find or make it yourself. You either make something useful and trade it; or you take what you need, by force, by the ballot box or whatever. Choices between cooperation and conflict are made every day at all sorts of levels, by both humans and animals.

The main tool we can use to study and analyse them is *game theory* – the study of problems of cooperation and conflict among independent decision makers. Game theory provides a common language used by economists, biologists and political scientists as well as computer scientists, and is a useful tool for building collaboration across disciplines. We're interested in games of strategy, and we try to get to the core of a decision by abstracting away much of the detail. For example, consider the school playground game of 'matching pennies': Alice and Bob toss coins and reveal them simultaneously, upon which Alice gets Bob's penny if they're different and Bob gets Alice's penny if they're the same. I'll write this as in Figure 8.2:

		BOB	
		H	T
Alice	H	−1,1	1,−1
	T	1,−1	−1,1

Figure 8.2: Matching pennies

Each entry in the table shows first Alice's outcome and then Bob's. Thus if the coins fall (H,H) Alice loses a penny and Bob gains a penny. This is an example of a *zero-sum game*: Alice's gain is Bob's loss.

Often we can solve a game quickly by writing out a *payoff matrix* like this. Here's an example (Figure 8.3):

		BOB	
		Left	Right
Alice	Top	1,2	0,1
	Bottom	2,1	1,0

Figure 8.3: Dominant strategy equilibrium

In game theory, a *strategy* is just an algorithm that takes a game state and outputs a move[1]. In this game, no matter what Bob plays, Alice is better off playing 'Bottom'; and no matter what Alice plays, Bob is better off playing 'Left'. Each player has a *dominant strategy* – an optimal choice regardless of what the other does. So Alice's strategy should be a constant 'Bottom' and Bob's a constant 'Left'. We call this a *dominant strategy equilibrium.*

Another example is shown in Figure 8.4:

		BOB	
		Left	Right
Alice	Top	2,1	0,0
	Bottom	0,0	1,2

Figure 8.4: Nash equilibrium

Here each player's optimal strategy depends on what they think the other player will do. We say that two strategies are in Nash equilibrium when Alice's choice is optimal given Bob's, and vice versa. Here there are two symmetric Nash equilibria, at top left and bottom right. You can think of them as being like local optima while a dominant strategy equilibrium is a global optimum.

8.4.1 The prisoners' dilemma

We're now ready to look at a famous problem that applies to many situations from international trade negotiations through cooperation between hunting animals to whether the autonomous systems that make up the Internet cooperate effectively to protect its infrastructure. It was first studied by scientists at the Rand corporation in 1950 in the context of US and USSR defense spending; Rand was paid to think about possible strategies in nuclear war. But they presented it using the following simple example.

Two prisoners are arrested on suspicion of planning a bank robbery. The police interview them separately and tell each of them: "If neither of you confesses you'll each get a year for carrying a concealed firearm without a permit. If only one of you confesses, he'll go free and the other will get 6 years for conspiracy to rob. If both of you confess, you will each get three years."

[1]In business and politics, a strategy is a means of acquiring power, such as monopoly power or military advantage, by a sequence of moves; the game-theoretic meaning is a somewhat simplified version, to make problems more tractable.

What should the prisoners do? Figure 8.5 shows their payoff matrix:

		Benjy	
		Confess	Deny
Alfie	Confess	−3,−3	0,−6
	Deny	−6,0	−1,−1

Figure 8.5: The prisoners' dilemma

When Alfie looks at this table, he will reason as follows: "If Benjy's going to confess then I should too as then I get 3 years rather than 6; and if he's going to deny then I should still confess as I'll walk rather than doing a year". Benjy will reason similarly. The two of them confess, and get three years each. This is not just a Nash equilibrium; it's a dominant strategy equilibrium. Each prisoner should confess regardless of what the other does.

But hang on, you say, if they had agreed to keep quiet then they'll get a year each, which is a better outcome for them! In fact the strategy (deny,deny) is Pareto efficient, while the dominant strategy equilibrium is not. (That's one reason it's useful to have concepts like 'Pareto efficient' and 'dominant strategy equilibrium' rather than just arguing over 'best'.)

So what's the solution? Well, so long as the game is going to be played once only, and this is the only game in town, there isn't a solution. Both prisoners will confess and get three years.

You may think this is fair enough, as it serves them right. However, the Prisoners' Dilemma can be used to model all sorts of interactions where we decide whether or not to cooperate: international trade, nuclear arms control, fisheries protection, the reduction of CO_2 emissions, and the civility of political discourse. Even matters of self-control such as obesity and addiction can be seen as failures of cooperation with our future selves. In these applications, we really want cooperation so we can get good outcomes, but the way a single-shot game is structured can make them really hard to achieve. We can only change this if somehow we can change the game itself.

There are many possibilities: there can be laws of various kinds from international treaties on trade to the gangster's *omertà*. In practice, a prisoner's dilemma game is changed by altering the rules or the context so as to turn it into another game where the equilibrium is more efficient.

8.4.2 Repeated and evolutionary games

Suppose the game is played repeatedly – say Alfie and Benjy are career criminals who expect to be dealing with each other again and again. Then of course there can be an incentive for them to cooperate. There are at least two ways of modelling this.

In the 1970s, Bob Axelrod started thinking about how people might play many rounds of prisoners' dilemma. He set up a series of competitions to which people could submit programs, and these programs played each other repeatedly in tournaments. He found that one of the best strategies overall was *tit-for-tat*, which is simply that you cooperate in round one, and at each subsequent round you do to your opponent what he or she did in the previous round [148]. It began to be realised that strategy evolution could explain a lot. For example, in the presence of noise, players tend to get locked into (defect, defect) whenever one player's cooperative behaviour is misread by the other as defection. So in this case it helps to 'forgive' the other player from time to time.

A parallel approach was opened up by John Maynard Smith and George Price [1253]. They considered what would happen if you had a mixed population of aggressive and docile individuals, 'hawks' and 'doves', with the behaviour that doves cooperate; hawks take food from doves; and hawks fight, with a risk of death. Suppose the value of the food at each interaction is v and the risk of death in a hawk fight is c per encounter. Then the payoff matrix looks like Figure 8.6:

	Hawk	Dove
Hawk	$\frac{v-c}{2}, \frac{v-c}{2}$	$v, 0$
Dove	$0, v$	$\frac{v}{2}, \frac{v}{2}$

Figure 8.6: The hawk-dove game

Here, if $v > c$, the whole population will become hawk, as that's the dominant strategy, but if $c > v$ (fighting is too expensive) then there is an equilibrium where the probability p that a bird is a hawk sets the hawk payoff and the dove payoff equal, that is

$$p\frac{v-c}{2} + (1-p)v = (1-p)\frac{v}{2}$$

which is solved by $p = v/c$. In other words, you can have aggressive and docile individuals coexisting in a population, and the proportion of aggressive individuals will be a function of the costs of aggression; the more dangerous a fight is, the fewer combative individuals there will be. Of course, the costs can change over time, and diversity can be a good thing in evolutionary terms, as a society with some hard men may be at an advantage when war breaks out. But it takes generations for a society to move to equilibrium. Perhaps our current high incidence of aggression reflects conditions in pre-state societies. Indeed, anthropologists believe that tribal warfare used to be endemic in such societies; the archaeological record shows that until states came along, about a quarter to a third of men and boys died of homicide [1134]. Maybe we just haven't been civilised long enough for evolution to catch up.

Such insights, along with Bob Axelrod's simulation methodology, got many people from moral philosophers to students of animal behaviour interested in evolutionary game theory. They offer further insights into how cooperation evolved. It turns out that many primates have an inbuilt sense of fairness and punish individuals who are seen to be cheating – the instinct for vengeance is one mechanism to enforce sociality. Fairness can operate in a number of different ways at different levels. For example, doves can get a better result against hawks if they can recognise each other and interact preferentially, giving a model for how some social movements and maybe even some religions establish themselves [1788]. Online reputation systems, as pioneered by eBay and now used by firms like Uber and AirBnB, perform a similar function: they help doves avoid hawks by making interactions into iterated games.

Of course, the basic idea behind tit-for-tat goes back a long way. The Old Testament has 'An eye for an eye' and the New Testament 'Do unto others as you'd have them do unto you' – the latter formulation being the more fault-tolerant – and versions of it can be found in Aristotle, in Confucius and elsewhere. More recently, Thomas Hobbes used similar arguments in the seventeenth century to argue that a state did not need the Divine Right of Kings to exist, paving the way for revolutions, republics and constitutions in the eighteenth.

Since 9/11, people have used hawk-dove games to model the ability of fundamentalists to take over discourse in religions at a time of stress. Colleagues and I have used evolutionary games to model how insurgents organise themselves into cells [1375]. Evolutionary games also explain why cartel-like behaviour can appear in industries even where there are no secret deals.

For example, Internet service in the UK involves a regulated monopoly that provides the local loop, and competing retail companies that sell Internet service to households. If the local loop costs the ISPs £6 a month, how come the ISPs all charge about £30? Well, if one were to undercut the others, they'd all retaliate by cutting their own prices, punishing the defector. It's exactly the same behavior you see where three airlines operate a profitable route, and one lowers its prices to compete for volume; the others will often respond by cutting prices even more sharply to punish it and make the route unprofitable. And just as airlines offer all sorts of deals, air miles and so on to confuse the customer, so also the telecomms providers offer their own confusion pricing. Similar structures lead to similar behaviour. Tacit collusion can happen in both industries without the company executives actually sitting down and agreeing to fix prices (which would be illegal). As pricing becomes more algorithmic, both lawyers and economists may need to understand more computer science; and computer scientists need to understand economic analysis tools such as game theory and auction theory.

8.5 Auction theory

Auction theory is vital for understanding how Internet services work, and what can go wrong. Much online activity is funded by the ad auctions run by firms like Google and Facebook, and many e-commerce sites run as auctions.

Auctions have been around for millennia, and are the standard way of selling livestock, fine art, mineral rights, bonds and much else; many other transactions from corporate takeovers to house sales are also really auctions. They are the fundamental way of discovering prices for unique goods. There are many issues of game play, asymmetric information, cheating – and some solid theory to guide us.

Consider the following five traditional types of auction.

1. In the English, or ascending-bid, auction, the auctioneer starts at a reserve price and then raises the price until only one bidder is left. This is used to sell art and antiques.
2. In the Dutch, or descending-bid, auction, the auctioneer starts out at a high price and cuts it gradually until someone bids. This is used to sell flowers.
3. In the first-price sealed-bid auction, each bidder is allowed to make one bid. After bidding closes, all the bids are opened and the highest bid wins. This has been used to auction TV rights; it's also used for government contracts, where it's the lowest bid that wins.
4. In the second-price sealed-bid auction, or Vickrey auction, we also get sealed bids and the highest bid wins, but that bidder pays the price in the second-highest bid. This is familiar from eBay, and is also how online ad auctions work; it evolved to sell rare postage stamps, though the earliest known use was by the poet Goethe to sell a manuscript to a publisher in the 18th century.
5. In the all-pay auction, every bidder pays at every round, until all but one drop out. This is a model of war, litigation, or a winner-take-all market race between several tech startups. It's also used for charity fundraising.

The first key concept is *strategic equivalence*. The Dutch auction and the first-price sealed-bid auction give the same result, in that the highest bidder gets the goods at his *reservation price* – the maximum he's prepared to bid. Similarly, the English auction and the Vickrey auction give the same result (modulo the bid increment). However the two pairs are not strategically equivalent. In a Dutch auction, you should bid low if you believe your valuation is a lot higher than anybody else's, while in a second-price auction it's best to bid truthfully.

The second key concept is *revenue equivalence*. This is a weaker concept; it's not about who will win, but how much money the auction is expected to raise.

The interesting result here is the *revenue equivalence theorem*, which says that you get the same revenue from any well-behaved auction under ideal conditions. These conditions include risk-neutral bidders, no collusion, Pareto efficiency (the highest bidder gets the goods) and independent valuations (no externalities between bidders). In such circumstances, the bidders adjust their strategies and the English, Dutch and all-pay auctions all yield the same. So when you design an auction, you have to focus on the ways in which the conditions aren't ideal. For details and examples, see Paul Klemperer's book [1059].

And there are many things that can go wrong. There may be bidding rings, where all the buyers collude to lowball the auction; here, a first-price auction is best as it takes only one defector to break ranks, rather than two. Second, there's entry detection: in one UK auction of TV rights, bidders had to submit extensive programming schedules, which involved talking to production companies, so everyone in the industry knew who was bidding and the franchises with only one bidder went for peanuts. Third, there's entry deterrence: bidders in corporate takeovers often declare that they will top any other bid. Fourth, there's risk aversion: if you prefer a certain profit of $1 to a 50% chance of $2, you'll bid higher at a first-price auction. Fifth, there are signaling games; in US spectrum auctions, some bidders broke anonymity by putting zip codes in the least significant digits of their bids, to signal what combinations of areas they were prepared to fight for, and to deter competitors from starting a bidding war there. And then there are budget constraints: if bidders are cash-limited, all-pay auctions are more profitable.

Advertisement auctions are big business, with Google, Facebook and Amazon making about $50bn, $30bn and $10bn respectively in 2019, while the rest of the industry gets about $40bn. The ad auction mechanism pioneered by Google is a second-price auction tweaked to optimise revenue. Bidders offer to pay prices b_i, the platform estimates their ad quality as e_i, based on the ad's relevance and clickthrough rate. It then calculates 'ad rank' as $a_i = b_i e_i$. The idea is that if my ad is five times as likely to be clicked on as yours, then my bid of 10c is just as good as your bid of 50c. This is therefore a second-price auction, but based on ranking a_i rather than b_i. Thus if I have five times your ad quality, I bid 10c and you bid 40c, then I get the ad and pay 8c. It can be shown that under reasonable assumptions, this maximises platform revenue.

There's one catch, though. Once media become social, then ad quality can easily segue into virality. If your ads are good clickbait and people click on them, you pay less. One outcome was that in the 2016 US Presidential Election, Hilary Clinton paid a lot more per ad than Donald Trump did [1236]. Both auction theory and empirical data show how the drive to optimise platform revenue may lead to ever more extreme content: in addition to virality effects at the auction step, Facebook's delivery algorithms put ads in front of the people most likely to click on them, strengthening the effect of filter bubbles, and that this is not all due to user actions [41]. Some people feel this 'delivery optimisation' should be prohibited by electoral law; certainly it's one more example of mechanisms with structural tension between efficiency and fairness. In fact, in the UK, election ads aren't permitted on TV, along with some other categories such as tobacco. In my opinion, the cleanest solution in such jurisdictions is to ban them online too, just like tobacco.

Ad pricing isn't the only way market mechanisms drive social media to promote extreme content. As former Googler Tristan Harris has explained, the platforms' recommender algorithms are optimised to maximise the time people spend on-site, which means not just providing bottomless scrolling feeds and letting users accumulate followers, but also a bias towards anxiety and outrage. At YouTube, such algorithms gave recommendations that heavily favoured Trump in 2016 [1886]. What's more, ad delivery can be skewed by factors such as gender and race, as advertisers compete for more 'valuable' demographics, and by content effects because of the appeal of ad headlines or images. This can be deliberate or accidental, and can affect a broad range of ads including employment and housing [40]. This all raises thorny political issues at the boundary between economics and psychology, which are at the centre of policy debates around regulating tech. Economic tools such as auction theory can often be used to unpick them.

8.6 The economics of security and dependability

Economists used to see a simple interaction between economics and security: richer nations could afford bigger armies. But after 1945, nuclear weapons were thought to decouple national survival from economic power, and the fields of economics and strategic studies drifted apart [1240]. It has been left to the information security world to re-establish the connection.

Round about 2000, a number of us noticed persistent security failures that appeared at first sight to be irrational, but which we started to understand once we looked more carefully at the incentives facing the various actors. I observed odd patterns of investment by banks in information security measures [55, 56]. Hal Varian looked into why people were not spending as much money on anti-virus software as the vendors hoped [1947]. When the two of us got to discussing these cases in 2001, we suddenly realised that there was an interesting and important research topic here, so we contacted other people with similar interests and organised a workshop for the following year. I was writing the first edition of this book at the time, and found that describing many of the problems as incentive problems made the explanations much more compelling; so I distilled what I learned from the book's final edit into a paper 'Why Information Security is Hard – An Economic Perspective". This paper, plus the first edition of this book, got people talking [73]. By the time they came out, the 9/11 attacks had taken place and people were searching for new perspectives on security.

We rapidly found many other examples of security failure associated with institutional incentives, such as hospital systems bought by medical directors and administrators that support their interests but don't protect patient privacy. (Later, we found that patient safety failures often had similar roots.) Jean Camp had been writing about markets for vulnerabilities, and two startups had set up early vulnerability markets. Networking researchers were starting to use auction theory to design strategy-proof routing protocols. The Department of Defense had been mulling over its failure to get vendors to sell them secure systems, as you can see in the second quote at the head of this chapter. Microsoft was thinking about the economics of standards. All these ideas came together at the Workshop on the Economics of Information Security at Berkeley in June 2002, which launched security economics as a new field of study. The picture that started to emerge was of system security failing because the people guarding a system were not the people who suffered the costs of failure. Sometimes, security mechanisms are used to dump risks on others, and if you are one of those others you'd be better off with an insecure system. Put differently, security is often a power relationship; the principals who control what it means in a given system often use it to advance their own interests.

This was the initial insight, and the story of the birth of security economics is told in [79]. But once we started studying the subject seriously, we found that there's a lot more to it than that.

8.6.1 Why is Windows so insecure?

The hot topic in 2002, when security economics got going, was this. Why is Windows so insecure, despite Microsoft's dominant market position? It's possible to write much better software, and there are fields such as defense and healthcare where a serious effort is made to produce dependable systems. Why do we not see a comparable effort made with commodity platforms, especially since Microsoft has no real competitors?

By then, we understood the basics of information economics: the combination of high fixed and low marginal costs, network effects and technical lock-in makes platform markets particularly likely to be dominated by single vendors, who stand to gain vast fortunes if they can win the race to dominate the market. In such a race, the Microsoft philosophy of the 1990s – 'ship it Tuesday and get it right by version 3' – is perfectly rational behaviour. In such a race, the platform vendor must appeal not just to users but also to complementers – to the software companies who decide whether to write applications for its platform or for someone else's. Security gets in the way of applications, and it tends to be a lemons market anyway. So the rational vendor engaged in a race for platform dominance will enable all applications to run as root on his platform[2], until his position is secure. Then he may add more security – but will be tempted to engineer it in such a way as to maximise customer lock-in, or to appeal to complementers in new markets such as digital media.

The same pattern was also seen in other platform products, from the old IBM mainframe operating systems through telephone exchange switches to the early Symbian operating system for mobile phones. Products are insecure at first, and although they improve over time, many of the new security features are for the vendor's benefit as much as the user's. And this is exactly what we saw with Microsoft's product lines. DOS had no protection at all and kick-started the malware market; Windows 3 and Windows 95 were dreadful; Windows 98 was only slightly better; and security problems eventually so annoyed Microsoft's customers that finally in 2003 Bill Gates decided to halt development until all its engineers had been on a secure coding course. This was followed by investment in better testing, static analysis tools, and regular patching. The number and lifetime of exploitable vulnerabilities continued to fall through later releases of Windows. But the attackers got better too, and the protection in Windows isn't all for the user's benefit. As Peter Gutmann points out, much more effort went into protecting premium video content than into protecting users' credit card numbers [843].

From the viewpoint of the consumer, markets with lock-in are often 'bargains then rip-offs'. You buy a nice new printer for $39.95, then find to your disgust after just a few months that you need two new printer cartridges for $19.95 each. You wonder whether you'd not be better off just buying a new printer. From the viewpoint of the application developer, markets with standards races based on lock-in look a bit like this. At first it's really easy to write code for them; later on, once you're committed, there are many more hoops to jump through. From the viewpoint of the poor consumer, they could be described as 'poor security, then security for someone else'.

The same pattern can be seen with externalities from security management costs to infrastructure decisions that the industry takes collectively. When racing to establish a dominant position, vendors are tempted to engineer products so that most of the security management cost is dumped on the user. A classic example is SSL/TLS encryption. This was adopted in the mid-1990s as Microsoft and Netscape battled for dominance of the browser market. As we discussed in Chapter 5, SSL leaves it up to the user to assess the certificate offered by a web site and decide whether to trust it; and this led to all kinds of phishing and other attacks. Yet dumping the compliance costs on the user made perfect sense at the time; competing protocols such as SET would have saddled banks with the cost of issuing certificates to every customer who wanted to buy

[2]To make coding easier, and enable app developers to steal the user's other data for sale in secondary markets.

stuff online, and that would just have cost too much [524]. The world ended up with an insecure system of credit card payments on the Internet, and with most of the stakeholders trying to dump liability on others in ways that block progress towards something better.

There are also network effects for bads, as well as for goods. Most malware writers targeted Windows rather than Mac or Linux through the 2000s and 2010s as there are simply more Windows machines to infect – leading to an odd equilibrium in which people who were prepared to pay more for their laptop could have a more secure one, albeit one that didn't run as much software. This model replicated itself when smartphones took over the world in the 2010s; since Android took over from Windows as the world's most popular operating system, we're starting to see a lot of bad apps for Android, while people who pay more for an iPhone get better security but less choice. We will discuss this in detail in the chapter on phones.

8.6.2 Managing the patching cycle

The second big debate in security economics was about how to manage the patching cycle. If you discover a vulnerability, should you just publish it, which may force the vendor to patch it but may leave people exposed for months until they do so? Or should you report it privately to the vendor – and risk getting a lawyer's letter threatening an expensive lawsuit if you tell anyone else, after which the vendor just doesn't bother to patch it?

This debate goes back a long way; as we noted in the preface, the Victorians agonised over whether it was socially responsible to publish books about lockpicking, and eventually concluded that it was [1899]. People have worried more recently about whether the online availability of the US Army Improvised Munitions Handbook [1928] helps terrorists; in some countries it's a crime to possess a copy.

Security economics provides both a theoretical and a quantitative framework for discussing some issues of this kind. We started in 2002 with simple models in which bugs were independent, identically distributed and discovered at random; these have nice statistical properties, as attackers and defenders are on an equal footing, and the dependability of a system is a function only of the initial code quality and the total amount of time spent testing it [75]. But is the real world actually like that? Or is it skewed by correlated bugs, or by the vendor's inside knowledge? This led to a big policy debate. Eric Rescorla argued that software is close enough to the ideal that removing one bug makes little difference to the likelihood of an attacker finding another one later, so frequent disclosure and patching were an unnecessary expense unless the same vulnerabilities were likely to be rediscovered [1599]. Ashish Arora and others responded with data showing that public disclosure made vendors fix bugs more quickly; attacks increased to begin with, but reported vulnerabilities declined over time [134]. In 2006, Andy Ozment and Stuart Schechter found that the rate at which unique vulnerabilities were disclosed for the core OpenBSD operating system decreased over a six-year period [1490]. In short, in the right circumstances, software can be more like wine than like milk – it improves with age. (Sustainability is a holy grail, and I discuss it in more detail in Part 3.)

Several further institutional factors helped settle the debate in favour of *responsible disclosure*, also known as *coordinated disclosure*, whereby people report bugs to vendors or to third parties that keep them confidential for a period until patches are available, then let the reporters get credit for their discoveries. One was the political settlement at the end of Crypto War I whereby bugs would be reported to CERT which would share them with the NSA during the bug-fixing process, as I will discuss later in section 26.2.7.3. This got governments on board. The second was the emergence of commercial vulnerability markets such as those set up by iDefense and TippingPoint, where security researchers could sell bugs; these firms would then disclose each bug responsibly to the vendor, and also work out indicators of compromise that could be sold to firms operating firewall or intrusion-detection services. Third, smart software firms started their own bug-bounty programs, so that security researchers could sell their bugs directly, cutting out middlemen such as CERT and iDefense.

This marketplace sharpened considerably after Stuxnet drove governments to stockpile vulnerabilities. We've seen the emergence of firms like Zerodium that buy bugs and sell them to state actors, and to cyberweapons suppliers that also sell to states; zero-day exploits for platforms such as the iPhone can now sell for a million dollars or more. This had knock-on effects on the supply chain. For example, in 2012 we came across the first case of a volunteer deliberately contributing vulnerable code to an open-source project[3], no doubt in the hope of a six-figure payoff if it had found its way into widely-used platforms. Already in 2010, Sam Ransbotham had shown that although open-source and proprietary software are equally secure in an ideal model, bugs get turned into exploits faster in the open source world, so attackers target it more [1582]. In 2014, Abdullah Algarni and Yashwant Malaiya surveyed vulnerability markets and interviewed some of the more prolific researchers: a combination of curiosity and economic incentives draw in many able young men, many from less developed countries. Some disclose responsibly, some use vulnerability markets to get both money and recognition, while others sell for more money to the black hats. Some will offer bugs to the vendor, but if not treated properly will offer them to the bad guys instead. Vendors have responded with comparable offers: at Black Hat 2019, Apple announced a bug bounty schedule that

[3]Webkit, which is used in mobile phone browsers

goes up to $1m for exploits that allow zero-click remote command execution on iOS. Oh, and many of the bug hunters retire after a few years [39]. Like it or not, volunteers running open-source projects now find themselves some capable motivated opponents if their projects get anywhere, and even if they can't match Apple's pocket, it's a good idea to keep as many of the researchers onside as possible.

The lifecycle of a vulnerability now involves not just its discovery, but perhaps some covert use by an intelligence agency or other black-hat actor; then its rediscovery, perhaps by other black hats but eventually by a white hat; the shipment of a patch; and then further exploitation against users who didn't apply the patch. There are tensions between vendors and their customers over the frequency and timing of patch release, as well as with complementers and secondary users over trust. A vulnerability in Linux doesn't just affect the server in your lab and your kid's Raspberry Pi. Linux is embedded everywhere: in your air-conditioner, your smart TV and even your car. This is why responsible disclosure is being rebranded as coordinated disclosure. There may be simply too many firms using a platform for the core developers to trust them all about a forthcoming patch release. There are also thousands of vulnerabilities, of which dozens appear each year in the exploit kits used by criminals (and some no doubt used only once against high-value targets, so they never become known to defense systems). We have to study multiple overlapping ecosystems – of the vulnerabilities indexed by their CVE numbers; of the Indicators of Compromise (IoCs) that get fed to intrusion detection systems; of disclosure to vendors directly, via markets, via CERTs and via ISACs; of the various botnets, crime gangs and state actors; and of the various recorded crime patterns. We have partial correlations between these ecosystems, but the data are generally noisy. I'll come back to all this and discuss the technical details in section 27.5.7.

8.6.3 Structural models of attack and defence

The late Jack Hirshleifer, the founder of conflict theory, told the story of Anarchia, an island whose flood defences were constructed by individual families each of whom maintained a section of the flood wall. The island's flood defence thus depended on the weakest link, that is, the laziest family. He compared this with a city whose defences against missile attack depend on the single best defensive shot [908]. Another example of best-shot is medieval warfare, where there could be a single combat between the two armies' champions. This can lead to different political systems. Medieval Venice, the best example of weakest-link defence because of the risk of flooding, had strong central government, with the merchant families electing a Doge with near-dictatorial powers over flood defence. In much of the rest of late medieval Europe, kings or chieftains led their own armies to kill enemies and seize land; the strongest king built the biggest empire, and this led to a feudal system that optimised the number of men at arms.

Hal Varian extended this model to the dependability of information systems – where performance can depend on the weakest link, the best effort, or the sum-of-efforts [1949]. This last case, the sum-of-efforts, is the modern model for warfare: we pay our taxes and the government hires soldiers. It's more efficient than best-shot (where most people will free-ride behind the heroes), which in turn is more efficient than weakest-link (where everyone will be vulnerable via the laziest). Information security is an interesting mix of all three modes. Program correctness can depend on the weakest link (the most careless programmer introducing a vulnerability) while software vulnerability testing may depend on the sum of everyone's efforts. Security may also depend on the best effort – the actions taken by an individual champion such as a security architect. As more agents are added, systems become more reliable in the sum-of-efforts case but less reliable in the weakest-link case. So as software companies get bigger, they end up hiring more testers and fewer (but more competent) programmers; Microsoft found by the early 2000s that they had more test engineers than software engineers.

Other models of attack and defence include epidemic models of malware spread, which were important back when computer viruses spread from machine to machine via floppy disks, but are of less interest now that we see relatively few wormable exploits; and models of security games that hinge on timing, notably the game of FlipIt by Ron Rivest and colleagues [559]; indeed, there's a whole conference (Gamesec) devoted to game theory and information security. There are also models of social networks. For example, most social networks owe their connectivity to a relatively small number of nodes that have a relatively high number of links to other nodes [1998]. Knocking out these nodes can rapidly disconnect things; William the Conqueror consolidated England after 1066 by killing the Anglo-Saxon nobility and replacing them with Normans, while Stalin killed the richer peasants. US and British forces similarly targeted highly-connected people in counterinsurgency operations during the Iraq war (and the resulting social breakdown in Sunni areas helped the emergence of Islamic State). Such models also suggest that for insurgents to form into cells is the natural and most effective response to repeated decapitation attacks [1375].

George Danezis and I also showed that where solidarity is needed for defence, smaller and more homogeneous groups will be more effective [511]. Rainer Böhme and Tyler Moore studied what happens where it isn't – if people use defense mechanisms that bring only private benefit, then the weakest-link model becomes one of low-hanging fruit. Examples include spammers who simply guess enough weak passwords to replenish their stock of compromised email accounts, and some types of card-not-present fraud [277].

In short, the technology of conflict in any age can have deep and subtle effects on politics, as it conditions the kind of institutions that can survive and thrive. These institutions in turn shape the security landscape. Tyler Moore, Allan Friedman and Ariel Procaccia studied whether a national agency such as the NSA with both defensive and offensive missions would disclose vulnerabilities so they could be fixed, or stockpile them; they concluded that if it could ignore the social costs that fall on others, it would stockpile [1340]. However the biggest institutions in the security ecosystem are probably not the government agencies but the dominant firms.

8.6.4 The economics of lock-in, tying and DRM

Technical lock-in is one of the factors that lead to dominant-firm markets, and software firms have spent billions over more than thirty years on mechanisms that make it hard for their customers to leave but easy for their competitors to defect. The 1980s saw file format wars where companies tried to stop anyone else accessing the word-processing files or spreadsheets their software generated. By the 1990s, the fight had shifted to network compatibility as Microsoft tried to exclude other operating systems from LANs, until SAMBA created interoperability with Apple; in the wake of a 1993 anti-trust suit, Microsoft held back from using the Windows contract to block it. Adversarial interoperability emerged as a kind of judo to fight network effects [570]. Similar mechanisms are used to control markets in neighbouring or complementary goods and services, examples being tying ink cartridges to printers, and digital rights management (DRM) systems that lock music and videos to a specific machine or family of machines, by preventing users from simply copying them as files. In an early security-economics paper, Hal Varian pointed out in 2002 that their unfettered use could damage competition [1948].

In 2003, Microsoft, Intel and others launched a 'Trusted Computing' initiative that extended rights management to other types of file, and Windows Server 2003 offered 'Information Rights Management' (IRM) whereby I could email you a Word document that you could only read on screen, not print, and only till the end of the month. There was obvious potential for competitive abuse; by transferring control of user data from the owner of the machine on which it is stored to the creator of the file in which it is stored, the potential for lock-in is hugely increased [74]. Think of the example in section 8.3.2 above, in which a firm has 100 staff, each with a PC on which they install Office for $150. The $15,000 they pay Microsoft is roughly equal to the total costs of switching to (say) LibreOffice, including training, converting files and so on. However, if control of the files moves to its thousands of customers, and the firm now has to contact each customer and request a digital certificate in order to migrate the file, then clearly the switching costs have increased – so you could expect the cost of Office to increase too. IRM failed to take off at the time: corporate America quickly understood that it was a lock-in play, European governments objected to the fact that the Trusted Computing initiative excluded small firms, and Microsoft couldn't get the mechanisms to work properly with Vista. (But now that email has moved to the cloud, both Microsoft and Google are offering restricted email services of just the type that was proposed, and objected to, back in 2003.)

Another aspect concerns DRM and music. In the late 1990s and early 2000s, Hollywood and the music industry lobbied hard for mandatory DRM in consumer electronics equipment, and we still pay the costs of that in various ways; for example, when you switch your presentation from a VGA adapter to HDMI and you lose the audio. Hollywood's claim that unlicensed peer-to-peer filesharing would destroy the creative industries was always shaky; a 2004 study showed that downloads didn't harm music industry revenues overall [1459] while a later one suggested that downloaders actually bought more CDs [51]. However the real issue was explained in 2005 by Google's chief economist [1950]: that a stronger link between the tech industry and music would help tech firms more than the music industry, because tech was more concentrated (with only three serious music platforms then – Microsoft, Sony and Apple). The content industry scoffed, but by the end of that year music publishers were protesting that Apple was getting too large a share of the cash from online music sales. Power in the supply chain moved from the music majors to the platforms, so the platforms (now Apple, Google, Amazon and Spotify) got most of the money and the residual power in the music industry shifted from the majors to the independents – just as airline deregulation favoured aircraft makers and low-cost airlines. This is a striking demonstration of the predictive power of economic analysis. By fighting a non-existent threat, the record industry let the computer industry eat its lunch. I discuss this in more detail in section 24.5.

DRM had become much less of an issue by 2020; the move from removable media to streaming services means that few people copy music or movies any more; the question is whether you pay a subscription to avoid the ads. Similarly, the move to cloud-based services means that few people steal software. As a result, crimes involving copyright infringement have dropped sharply [92].

However, the move to the cloud is making lock-in a more complex matter, operating at the level of ecosystems as well as of individual products. We discussed above how competition from Google Docs cut the price of Office, and so Microsoft responded with a move to Office365; and how the total cost of ownership of either that service or G-suite is greater than a standalone productivity product. So where is the lock-in? Well, if you opt for the Google ecosystem, you'll probably be using not just Gmail and Google Docs but a Google calendar, maps and much else. Although you can always download all your data, reinstalling it on a different platform (such as Microsoft's or Apple's) will be a lot of bother, so you'll probably just grit your teeth and pay for more storage when the free quota runs out. Similarly, if you start using tools like Slack or Splunk in an IT company, you'll end up customising them in all sorts of ways that make it difficult to migrate. Again, this is nothing new; my own university's dreadful accounting system has been a heavily customised version of Oracle Financials for about 20 years. Now everyone's playing the lock-in game by inducing customers to buy or build complementary assets, or even to outsource whole functions. Salesforce has taken over many companies' sales admin, Palantir has locked in many US police forces, and the big academic publishers are usurping the functions of university libraries. Where there's no viable competition, there's a real policy issue. The depth of Microsoft lock-in on public-sector IT is illustrated by the brave attempts made by the city of Munich to break away and use Linux in public administration: this was eventually reverted after 15 years, several visits of Bill Gates, and a new mayor [760]. The IT industry now has such global scale and influence that we need to see its competition problems in a larger context.

8.6.5 Antitrust law and competition policy

The control of whole ecosystems by cartels is nothing new. Tim Wu reminds us that both the English civil war and the American revolution started as revolts against royal monopolies, while US antitrust law was inspired by Louis Brandeis' campaign against J.P. Morgan's railway empire, and its European equivalent by the help that German monopolists gave Hitler in his rise to power [2053]. Joshua Specht tells the history of how big food companies like Cargill and Armour grabbed control of the two-sided markets opened up by the railroads, consolidated their power by buying infrastructure such as grain elevators, dumped climate risk on small farmers, ran union organisers out of town and even got the politicians to pass 'ag-gag' laws that define animal-rights activism as terrorism [1812]. There are echoes of this in the way the big IT service firms have built out their market power, controlling everything from the ad ecosystem through operating systems to datacentres, and seeking to marginalise their critics.

US antitrust activity has been on the wane since the 2000 election, after which the new President Bush ended a big case against Microsoft. This was coupled with US competition law turning its focus to consumer surplus, at the expense of the other effects of monopoly [2053]. In fact, the whole global economy has become more monopolistic over the first two decades of the twenty-first century, and IT appears to account for much of the growth in industry concentration [235]. But it isn't the only factor. The USA has also seen a wave of corporate mergers, and there is a growing literature on *moats* – structural barriers to competition, of which network effects and technical lock-in are merely two examples. Others range from patents and regulatory capture to customer insight derived from control of data [1433]. (The word 'moat' appears due to Warren Buffett, who became one of the world's richest men by buying shares in several dozen companies with captive markets [1834].) The dynamics of the information industries compound many of these existing problems and can make both effective competition, and effective regulation, even harder. However a clear pattern is now emerging: that US markets are becoming steadily less competitive, while markets in Europe are becoming slightly more so [1524].

A new generation of competition-law scholars, such as Lina Khan of Harvard, argues that American law needs to take a much broader view of competition abuse than consumer surplus, just as Europe has always done [1046]. So should Amazon and Facebook be broken up, just like AT&T? President Obama's antitrust economist Carl Shapiro argue that antitrust law is ill-suited to tackle the political power that large corporations wield, and so remedies should be targeted at specific harms [1719]. Carl does however concede that US antitrust law has been excessively narrowed by the Supreme Court in the last 40 years, that the consumer-welfare test is inadequate, that dominant firms' exclusionary conduct and labour-market practices both need to be tackled, and that the USA needs to control horizontal mergers better [1720].

European competition law has for many years forbidden firms from using a dominant position in one market to establish a dominant position in another, and we've seen a whole series of judgements against the big tech firms in the European courts. Regulators are designed to be more independent, since no one member state wants to risk them being captured by any other [1524]. As for the likely future direction, a 2019 report for the European Commission's Directorate-General of Competition by Jacques Crémer, Yves-Alexandre de Montjoye and Heike Schweizter highlights not just the tech majors' network externalities and extreme returns to scale, but also the fact that they control more and more of the data thanks to the move to online services and cloud computing [497]. As a result they have economies of scope: succeeding in one business makes it easier to succeed in another. It concludes that the EU's competition-law framework is basically sound but needs some tuning: regulators need to protect both competition for the market and competition in the market, such as on dominant platforms, which have a responsibility not to distort competition there. In this environment, regulators must pay attention to multihoming, switching, interoperability, data portability and the effect on aftermarkets.

Tying spare parts is already regulated in Europe, with specific laws in some sectors requiring vendors to let other firms make compatible spare parts, and in others requiring that they make spares available for a certain period of time. Some very specific policy issues can arise if you use security mechanisms to tie products to each other. This links in with laws on planned obsolescence, which is reinforced for goods with digital components when the vendors limit the time period for which software updates are made available. The rules have recently been upgraded in the European Union by a new Sales of Goods Directive (2019/771) that from January 2022 requires firms selling goods with digital components – whether embedded software, cloud services or associated phone apps – to maintain this software for at least two years after the goods are sold, and for longer if this is the reasonable expectation of the customer (for cars and white goods it's likely to mean ten years). Such regulations will become more of an issue now we have software in durable goods such as cars and medical devices; I'll discuss sustainability in the last chapter of this book.

8.6.6 Perversely motivated guards

"There's nane sae blind as them that will na see", goes an old Scots proverb, and security engineering throws up lots of examples.

- There's very little police action against cybercrime, as they found it simpler to deter people from reporting it. As we noted in section 2.3, this enabled them to claim that crime was falling for many years even though it was just moving online like everything else.
- Governments have imposed a duty on banks to spot money laundering, especially since 9/11. However no banker really wants to know that one of his customers is a Mafioso. So banks lobby for risk reduction to be formalised as due diligence; they press for detailed regulations that specify the forms of ID they need for new account opening, and the processing to be done to identify suspicious transactions.
- When it comes to fraud, spotting a rare bank fraud pattern means a payment service provider should now carry the loss rather than just telling the customer she must be mistaken or lying. So they're tempted to wait and learn about new fraud types from industry or from academics, rather than doing serious research of their own.
- Click fraud is similar. Spotting a pattern of 'inorganic clicks' from a botnet means you can't charge the advertisers for those clicks any more. You have to do some work to mitigate the worst of it, but if you have a dominant market position then the harder you work at fighting click fraud, the less revenue you earn.
- Finding bugs in your own code is another example. Of course you have to tweak the obvious bugs that stop it working, but what about the more subtle bugs that can be exploited by attackers? The more time you spend looking for them, the more time you have to spend fixing them. You can always go and buy static analysis tools, but then you'll find thousands more bugs and your ship date will slip by months. So firms tend to do that only if their customers demand it, and it's only cheap if you do it from the start of a project (but in that case you could just as well write the code in Rust rather than in C).

There are more subtle examples, such as when it's not politically acceptable to tell the truth about threats. In the old days, it was hard to talk to a board of directors about the insider threat, as directors mostly preferred to believe the best about their company; so a typical security manager would make chilling presentations about 'evil hackers' in order to get the budget to build internal controls. Nowadays, the security-policy space in many companies has been captured by the big four accountancy firms, whose consensus on internal controls is tied to their thought leadership on governance, which a cynic might say is optimised for the welfare not of their ostensible client, the shareholders, but for their real client, the CEO. Executive frauds are rarely spotted unless they bring the company down; the effort goes instead into the annoying and irrelevant, such as changing passwords every month and insisting on original paper receipts. I discuss all this in detail in section 12.2.2.

Or consider the 2009 parliamentary expenses scandal in the UK described in section 2.3.6. Perhaps the officers of the Houses of Parliament didn't defend the expenses system more vigorously because they have to think of MPs and peers as 'honourable members' in the context of a government that was pushing harsh surveillance legislation with a slogan of 'If you've nothing to hide you have nothing to fear'. The author of that slogan, then Home Secretary Jacqui Smith, may have had nothing to hide, but her husband did: he was watching porn and charging it to her parliamentary expenses. Jacqui lost her job, and her seat in Parliament too. Had officers known that the information on the expenses server could cost a cabinet minister her job, they probably ought to have classified it Top Secret and kept it in a vault. But how could the extra costs have been justified to the Treasury? On that cheerful note, let's go on to privacy.

8.6.7 Economics of privacy

The privacy paradox is that people say that they value privacy, yet act otherwise. If you stop people in the street and ask them their views, about a third say they are privacy fundamentalists and will never hand over their personal information to marketers or anyone else; about a third say they don't care; and about a third are in the middle, saying they'd take a pragmatic view of the risks and benefits of any disclosure. However, their shopping behavior – both online and offline – is quite different; the great majority of people pay little heed to privacy, and will give away the most sensitive information for little benefit. Privacy-enhancing technologies have been offered for sale by various firms, yet most have failed in the marketplace. Why should this be?

Privacy is one aspect of information security that interested economists before 2000. In 1978, Richard Posner defined privacy in terms of secrecy [1539], and the following year extended it to seclusion [1540]. In 1980, Jack Hirshleifer published a seminal paper in which he argued that rather than being about withdrawing from society, privacy was a means of organising society, arising from evolved territorial behavior; internalised respect for property supports autonomy. In 1996, Hal Varian analysed privacy in terms of information markets [1944]. Consumers want to not be annoyed by irrelevant marketing calls while marketers do not want to waste effort; yet both are frustrated, because of search costs, externalities and other factors. Varian suggested giving consumers rights in information about themselves, and letting contracts sort it out.

However, as we've seen, the information industries are prone to market failures leading to monopoly, and the proliferation of dominant, information-intensive business models demands a different approach. Andrew Odlyzko argued in 2003 that these monopolies simultaneously increase both the incentives and the opportunities for price discrimination [1464]. Companies mine online interactions for data revealing individuals' willingness to pay, and while the differential pricing we see in many markets from airline yield-management systems to telecommunications prices may be economically efficient, it is increasingly resented. Peter Swire argued that we should measure the externalities of privacy intrusion [1856]. If a telesales operator calls 100 prospects, sells three of them insurance, and annoys 80, then the conventional economic analysis considers only the benefit to the three and to the insurer. But persistent annoyance causes millions of people to go ex-directory, screen calls through an answering machine, or just not have a landline at all. The long-run societal costs of robocalls can be considerable. Empirical studies of people's privacy valuations have supported this.

The privacy paradox has generated a significant literature, and is compounded by at least three factors. First, there are many different types of privacy harm, from discrimination in employment, credit and insurance, through the kind of cybercrime that presents as payment fraud, to personal crimes such as stalking and non-consensual intimate imagery.

Second, the behavioral factors we discussed in section 3.2.5 play a large role. Leslie John and colleagues demonstrated the power of context with a neat experiment. She devised a 'privacy meter' in the form of a list of embarrassing questions; the score was how many questions a subject would answer before they balked. She tried this on three groups of students: a control group in a neutral university setting, a privacy treatment group who were given strong assurances that their data would be encrypted, their IP addresses not stored, and so on; and a gamer treatment group that was taken to an external website (`howbadareyou.com` with a logo of a smiling devil). You might think that the privacy treatment group would disclose more, but in fact they disclosed less – as privacy had been made salient to them. As for the gamer group, they happily disclosed twice as much as the control group [989].

Third, the industry understands this, and goes out of its way to make privacy risks less salient. Privacy policies are usually not on the front page, but are easily findable by concerned users; policies typically start with anodyne text and leave the unpleasant stuff to the end, so they don't alarm the casual viewer, but the vigilant minority can quickly find a reason not to use the site, so they also don't stop the other users clicking on the ads. The cookie warnings mandated in Europe are mostly anodyne, though some firms give users fine-grained control; as noted in section 3.2.5, the illusion of control is enough to reassure many.

So what's the overall effect? In the 2000s and early 2010s there was evidence that the public were gradually learning what we engineers already understood about the risks; we could see this for example in the steadily rising proportion of Facebook users who opt to use privacy controls to narrow that system's very open defaults.

In 2015, almost two years after the Snowden revelations, two surveys conducted by Pew Research disclosed a growing sense of learned helplessness among the US public. 93% of adults said that being in control of who can get information about them is important, and 90% that controlling what information is collected about them is important; 88% said it's important that no-one watch or listen to them without their permission. Yet just 6% of adults said they were 'very confident' that government agencies could keep their records private and secure, while another 25% said they were 'somewhat confident.' The figures for phone companies and credit card companies were similar while those for advertisers, social media and search engines were significantly worse. Yet few respondents had done anything significant, beyond occasionally clearing their browser history or refusing particularly inappropriate demands for personal information [1206].

These tensions have been growing since the 1960s, and have led to complex privacy regulation that differs significantly between the US and Europe. I'll discuss this in much more detail in section 26.6.

8.6.8 Organisations and human behaviour

Organisations often act in apparently irrational ways. We frequently see firms and even governments becoming so complacent that they're unable to react to a threat until it's a crisis, when they panic. The erosion of health service resilience and pandemic preparedness in Europe and North America in the century since the 1918–19 Spanish flu is merely the most salient of many examples. As another example, it seems that there's always one phone company, and one bank, that the bad guys are picking on. A low rate of fraud makes people complacent, until the bad guys notice. The rising tide of abuse is ignored, or blamed on customers, for as long as possible. Then it gets in the news and executives panic. Loads of money get spent for a year or two, stuff gets fixed, and the bad guys move on to the next victim.

So the security engineer needs to anticipate the ways in which human frailties express themselves through organizational behaviour.

There's a substantial literature on institutional economics going back to Thorstein Veblen. One distinguished practitioner, Herb Simon, was also a computing pioneer and founded computer science at CMU. In a classic book on administrative behaviour, he explained that the decisions taken by managers are not just about efficiency but also organisational loyalty and authority, and the interaction between the organisation's goals and the incentives facing individual employees; there are messy hierarchies of purpose, while values and facts are mixed up [1758]. A more modern analysis of these problems typically sees them as principal-agency issues in the framework of microeconomics; this is a typical approach of professors of accountancy. We will discuss the failures of the actual practice of accountancy later, in section 12.2. Another approach is public-choice economics, which applies microeconomic methods to study the behaviour of politicians, civil servants and people in public-sector organsations generally. I summarise public choice in section 26.3.3; the principles are illustrated well in the TV sitcom "Yes Minister' which explores the behaviour of British civil servants. Cynics note that bureaucracies seem to evolve in such a way as to minimise the likelihood of blame.

My own observation, having worked in banks, tech companies big and small and in the university sector too, is that competition is more important than whether an enterprise is publicly or privately owned. University professors compete hard with each other; our customer isn't our Vice-Chancellor but the Nobel Prize committee or equivalent. But as university administrators work in a hierarchy with the VC at the top, they face the same incentives as civil servants and display many of the same strengths and weaknesses. Meanwhile, some private firms have such market power that internally they behave just like government (though with much better pay at the top).

8.6.9 Economics of cybercrime

If you're going to protect systems from attack, it's a good idea to know who the attackers are, how many they are, where they come from, how they learn their jobs and how they're motivated. This brings us to the economics of cybercrime. In section 2.3 we gave an overview of the cybercrime ecosystem, and there are many tools we can use to study it in more detail. At the Cambridge Cybercrime Centre we collect and curate the data needed to do this, and make it available to over a hundred researchers worldwide. As in other economic disciplines, there's an iterative process of working out what the interesting questions are and collecting the data to answer them. The people with the questions are not just economists but engineers, psychologists, lawyers, law enforcement and, increasingly, criminologists.

One approach to crime is that of Chicago-school economists such as Gary Becker, who in 1968 analysed crime in terms of rewards and punishments [201]. This approach gives many valuable insights but isn't the whole story. Why is crime clustered in bad neighbourhoods? Why do some kids from these neighbourhoods become prolific and persistent offenders? Traditional criminologists study questions like these, and find explanations of value in crime prevention: the worst offenders often suffer multiple deprivation, with poor parenting, with substance and alcohol abuse, and get drawn into cycles of offending. The earlier they start in their teens, the longer they'll persist before they give up. Critical criminologists point out that laws are made by the powerful, who maintain their power by oppressing the poor, and that bad neighbourhoods are more likely to be over-policed and stigmatised than the nice suburbs where the rich white people live.

Drilling down further, we can look at the bad neighbourhoods, the psychology of offenders, and the pathways they take into crime. Since the 1960s there has been a substantial amount of research into using environmental design to suppress crime, initially in low-cost housing and then everywhere. For example, courtyards are better than parks, as residents are more likely to identify and challenge intruders; many of these ideas for *situational crime prevention* go across from criminology into systems design. In section 13.2.2 we'll discuss this in more detail.

Second, psychologically normal people don't like harming others; people who do so tend to have low empathy, perhaps because of childhood abuse, or (more often) to have minimisation strategies to justify their actions. Bank robbers see bankers as the real exploiters; soldiers dehumanise the enemy as 'gooks' or 'terrs'; and most common murderers see their crimes as a matter of honour. "She cheated on me" and "He disrespected me" are typical triggers; we discussed the mechanisms in section 3.2.4. These mechanisms go across to the world of online and electronic fraud. Hackers on the wrong side of the law tend to feel their actions are justified anyway: hacktivists are political activists after all, while cyber-crooks use a variety of minimisation strategies to avoid feeling guilty. Some Russian cybercrooks take the view that the USA screwed Russia over after 1989, so they're just getting their own back (and they're supported in this by their own government's attitudes and policies). As for bankers who dump fraud risks on customers, they talk internally about 'the avalanche of fraudulent risks of fraud' they'd face if they owned up to security holes.

Third, it's important to understand the pathways to crime, the organisation of criminal gangs, and the diffusion of skills. Steve Levitt studied the organisation and finances of Chicago crime gangs, finding that the street-level dealers were earning less than minimum wage [1153]. They were prepared to stand in the rain and be shot at for a chance to make it to the next level up, where the neighbourhood boss drove around in a BMW with three girls. Arresting the boss won't make any difference as there are dozens of youngsters who'll fight to replace him. To get a result, the police should target the choke point, such as the importer's system administrator. These ideas also go across. Many cyber-criminals start off as gamers, then cheat on games, then deal in game cheats, then learn how to code game cheats, and within a few years the more talented have become malware devs. So one policy intervention is to try to stop kids crossing the line between legal and illegal game cheating. As I mentioned in section 3.2.4, the UK National Crime Agency bought Google ads which warned people in Britain searching for DDoS-for-hire services that the use of such services was illegal. Ben Collier and colleagues used our Cybercrime Centre data to show that this halted the growth of DDoS attacks in the UK, compared with the USA where they continued to grow [457].

We discussed the overall costs of cybercrime in section 2.3, noting that the ecosystem has been remarkably stable over the past decade, despite the fact that the technology has changed; we now go online from phones more than laptops, use social networks, and keep everything in the cloud. Most acquisitive crime is now online; in 2019 we expect that about a million UK households suffered a burglary or car theft, while over two million suffered a fraud or scam, almost always online. (In 2020 the difference will be even more pronounced; burglary has fallen still further with people staying at home through the lockdown.) Yet policy responses lag almost everywhere. Studies of specific crimes are reported at various places in this book.

The effects of cybercrime are also studied via the effects of breach disclosures. Alessandro Acquisti and colleagues have studied the effects on the stock price of companies of reporting a security or privacy breach [15]; a single breach tends to cause a small dip that dissipates after a week or so, but a double breach can impair investor confidence over the longer term. Breach disclosure laws have made breaches into insurable events; if TJX loses 47m records and has to pay $5 to mail each customer, that's a claim; we'll discuss cyber-insurance later in section 28.2.9.

Overall, though, measurement is tricky. Most of the relevant publications come from organisations with an incentive to talk up the losses, from police agencies to anti-virus vendors; our preferred methodology is to count the losses by modus operandi and by sector, as presented in section 2.3.

8.7 Summary

Many systems fail because the incentives are wrong, rather than because of some technical design mistake. As a result, the security engineer needs to understand basic economics as well as the basics of crypto, protocols, access controls and psychology. Security economics has grown rapidly to explain many of the things that we used to consider just 'bad weather'. It constantly throws up fascinating new insights into all sorts of questions from how to optimise the patching cycle through whether people really care about privacy.

Research problems

So far, three areas of economics have been explored for their relevance to security, namely microeconomics, game theory and behavioural economics. But economics is a vast subject. What other ideas might it give us?

In the history paper I wrote on the origins of security economics, I suggested a new research student might follow the following heuristics to select a research topic. First, think of security and *X* for other subfields *X* of economics. Second, think about the security economics of *Y* for different applications *Y*; there have already been some papers on topics like payments, pornography, gaming, and censorship, but these aren't the only things computers are used for. Third, where you find gold, keep digging (e.g. behavioral privacy) [79]. Since then I would add the following.

Fourth, there is a lot of scope for data-driven research now that we're starting to make large datasets available to academics (via the Cambridge Cybercrime Centre) and many students are keen to develop skills in data science. A related problem is how to gather more data that might be useful in exploring other fields, from the productivity of individual security staff to how security works within institutions, particularly large complex institutions such as governments and healthcare systems. Is there any good way of measuring the quality of a security culture?

Fifth, now we're starting to put software and online connectivity in durable safety-critical things like cars and medical devices, we need to know a lot more about the interaction between security and safety, and about how we can keep such systems patched and running for decades. This opens up all sorts of new topics in dependability and sustainability.

The current research in security economics is published mostly at the Workshop on the Economics of Information Security (WEIS), which has been held annually since 2002 [77]. There are liveblogs of all but one of the workshops, which you can find on our blog `https://www.lightbluetouchpaper.org`.

Further reading

The classic introduction to information economics is Shapiro and Varian's *'Information Rules'* which remains remarkably fresh for a book written twenty years ago [1721]. This is still on our student reading list. The most up-to-date summary is probably Jacques Crémer, Yves-Alexandre de Montjoye and Heike

Schweizter's 2019 report for the European Commission's Directorate-General of Competition, which analyses what goes wrong with markets in which information plays a significant role [497]; I would read also Carl Shapiro's 2019 review of the state of competition policy in the USA[1720]. Tim Wu's "The Master Switch" discusses monopoly in telecomms and the information industries generally, including the breakup of AT&T, which was essential to the development of the Internet as we know it today – one of antitrust law's greatest achievements [2051]. His later book, "The Curse of Bigness", tells the broader antitrust story, including the antitrust case against IBM that spawned the modern software industry [2053]. If you're seriously interested in antitrust and competition policy you need to dive into the detail, for which I'd suggest Thomas Philippon's "The Great Reversal – How America Gave up on Free Markets" [1524]. This analyses multiple aspects of market power across several industries in America and Europe, and explains the machinery economists use for the purpose.

The early story of security economics is told in [79]; there's an early (2007) survey of the field that I wrote with Tyler Moore at [111], and a more comprehensive 2011 survey, also with Tyler, at [112]. For privacy economics, see Alessandro Acquisti's online bibliography, and the survey paper he wrote with George Loewenstein and Laura Brandimarte [16]; there's also a survey of the literature on the privacy paradox by Spiros Kokolakis [1078]. Then, to dive into the research literature, I'd suggest the WEIS conference papers and liveblogs.

A number of economists study related areas. I mentioned Jack Hirshleifer's conflict theory [909]; another important strand is the economics of crime, which was kick-started by Gary Becker [201], and has been popularised by Steve Levitt and Stephen Dubner's "Freakonomics" [1153]. Diego Gambetta is probably the leading scholar of organised crime; his *'Codes of the Underworld: How Criminals Communicate'* is a classic [742]. Finally, there is a growing research community and literature on cyber-criminology, for which the website of our Cambridge Cybercrime Centre might be a reasonable starting point.

If you plan to do research in security economics and your degree wasn't in economics, you might work through a standard textbook such as Varian [1945] or the Core Economics website. Adam Smith's classic *'An inquiry into the nature and causes of the wealth of nations'* is still worth a look, while Dick Thaler's *'Misbehaving'* tells the story of behavioural economics.

PART II

In this second part of the book, I describe a large number of applications of secure systems, many of which introduce particular protection concepts or technologies.

There are three broad themes. Chapters 9–12 look at conventional computer security issues, and by discussing what we're trying to do and how it's done in different environments – the military, healthcare, the census and banking – we introduce security policy models which set out the protection concepts that real systems try to implement. These range from multilevel security through compartments to anonymisation and internal control. We introduce our first detailed case studies, from government networks through medical records to payment systems.

Chapters 13–20 look at the hardware and system engineering aspects of information security. This ranges from biometrics, through the design of hardware security mechanisms from physical locks, security printing and seals, to chip-level tamper-resistance and emission security. We study applications that illustrate these technologies, ranging from burglar alarms through curfew tags, utility meters and payment cards to the control of nuclear weapons. We end up with a chapter on advanced cryptographic engineering, where hardware and software security meet: there we discuss topics from secure messaging and anonymous communications through hardware security modules and enclaves to blockchains.

Our third theme is attacks on networks and on highly-networked systems. We start off in Chapter 21 with attacks on computer networks and defensive technologies ranging from firewalls to PKI. We then study the phone ecosystems in Chapter 22, from bad apps down through switching exploits and out to the policy tussles over 5G. Chapter 23 tackles electronic and information warfare, showing how far techniques of denial, deception and exploitation can be taken by a serious combatants, and helping us hone our appreciation of anonymity and traffic analysis. Chapter 24 shows how some of these techniques are adapted in systems for digital rights management.

Finally, in Chapter 25 I present four areas of bleeding-edge security research in 2020. First are autonomous vehicles, including the 'autopilot' systems starting to appear in family cars. Second, we look at the machine-learning systems on which such vehicles increasingly rely, and which are starting to be used in many other applications. Third, we work through the realistic options for people to protect ourselves using privacy technology and operational security measures in a world where surveillance is being turbocharged by machine-learning techniques. Finally, we look at elections, which are becoming ever more fraught with claims (whether true or false) of interference and cheating.

This ordering tries to give the chapters a logical progression. Thus, for example, I discuss frauds against magnetic stripe bank cards before going on to describe the smartcards which replaced them and the phone payment systems which rely on smartcards for the SIMs that authenticate devices to the network, but which have so many more vulnerabilities thanks to the rich environment that has evolved since the launch of the iPhone.

Often a technology has evolved through a number of iterations over several applications. In such cases I try to distill what I know into a history. It can be confusing and even scary when you first dive into a 5,000-page manual for something that's been evolving for thirty years like the card payment system, or an Intel or Arm CPU; the story of how it evolved and why is often what you need to make sense of it.

CHAPTER

9

Multilevel Security

Most high assurance work has been done in the area of kinetic devices and infernal machines that are controlled by stupid robots. As information processing technology becomes more important to society, these concerns spread to areas previously thought inherently harmless, like operating systems.

– EARL BOEBERT

The password on the government phone always seemed to drop, and I couldn't get into it.

– US diplomat and former CIA officer KURT VOLKER, explaining why he texted from his personal phone

I brief; you leak; he/she commits a criminal offence by divulging classified information.

– BRITISH CIVIL SERVICE VERB

9.1 Introduction

In the next few chapters I'm going to explore the concept of a security policy using case studies. A security policy is a succinct description of what we're trying to achieve; it's driven by an understanding of the bad outcomes we wish to avoid and in turn drives the engineering. After I've fleshed out these ideas a little, I'll spend the rest of this chapter exploring the *multilevel security* (MLS) policy model used in many military and intelligence systems, which hold information at different levels of classification (Confidential, Secret, Top Secret, ...), and have to ensure that data can be read only by a principal whose clearance level is at least as high. Such policies are increasingly also known as *information flow control* (IFC).

They are important for a number of reasons, even if you're never planning to work for a government contractor:

1. from about 1980 to about 2005, the US Department of Defense spent several billion dollars funding research into multilevel security. So the

model was worked out in great detail, and we got to understand the second-order effects of pursuing a single policy goal with great zeal;

2. the *mandatory access control* (MAC) systems used to implement it have now appeared in all major operating systems such as Android, iOS and Windows to protect core components against tampering by malware, as I described in Chapter 6;
3. although multilevel security concepts were originally developed to support confidentiality in military systems, many commercial systems now use multilevel integrity policies. For example, safety-critical systems use a number of safety integrity levels[1].

The poet Archilochus famously noted that a fox knows many little things, while a hedgehog knows one big thing. Security engineering is usually in fox territory, but multilevel security is an example of the hedgehog approach.

9.2 What is a security policy model?

Where a top-down approach to security engineering is possible, it will typically take the form of *threat model – security policy – security mechanisms*. The critical, and often neglected, part of this process is the security policy.

By a security policy, we mean a document that expresses clearly and concisely what the protection mechanisms are to achieve. It is driven by our understanding of threats, and in turn drives our system design. It will often take the form of statements about which users may access which data. It plays the same role in specifying the system's protection requirements, and evaluating whether they have been met, that the system specification does for functionality and the safety case for safety. Like the specification, its primary function is to communicate.

Many organizations use the phrase 'security policy' to mean a collection of vapid statements, as in Figure 9.1:

Megacorp, Inc. security policy

1. This policy is approved by Management.
2. All staff shall obey this security policy.
3. Data shall be available only to those with a "need-to-know".
4. All breaches of this policy shall be reported at once to Security.

Figure 9.1: typical corporate policy language

[1]Beware though that terminology varies between different safety-engineering disciplines. The safety integrity levels in electricity generation are similar to Biba, while automotive safety integrity levels are set in ISO 26262 as a hazard/risk metric that depends on the likelihood that a fault will cause an accident, together with the expected severity and controllability.

This sort of language is common, but useless – at least to the security engineer. It dodges the central issue, namely 'Who determines "need-to-know" and how?' Second, it mixes statements at different levels (organizational approval of a policy should logically not be part of the policy itself). Third, there is a mechanism but it's implied rather than explicit: 'staff shall obey' – but what does this mean they actually have to do? Must the obedience be enforced by the system, or are users 'on their honour'? Fourth, how are breaches to be detected and who has a specific duty to report them?

When you think about it, this is political language. A politician's job is to resolve the tensions in society, and this often requires vague language on which different factions can project their own wishes; corporate executives are often operating politically, to balance different factions within a company[2].

Because the term 'security policy' is often abused to mean using security for politics, more precise terms have come into use by security engineers.

A *security policy model* is a succinct statement of the protection properties that a system must have. Its key points can typically be written down in a page or less. It is the document in which the protection goals of the system are agreed with an entire community, or with the top management of a customer. It may also be the basis of formal mathematical analysis.

A *security target* is a more detailed description of the protection mechanisms that a specific implementation provides, and how they relate to a list of control objectives (some but not all of which are typically derived from the policy model). The security target forms the basis for testing and evaluation of a product.

A *protection profile* is like a security target but expressed in a manner that is independent of the implementation, so as to enable comparable evaluations across products and versions. This can involve the use of a semi-formal language, or at least of suitable security jargon. A protection profile is a requirement for products that are to be evaluated under the *Common Criteria* [1398]. (I discuss the Common Criteria in section 28.2.7; they are used by many governments for mutual recognition of security evaluations of defense information systems.)

When I don't have to be so precise, I may use the phrase 'security policy' to refer to either a security policy model or a security target. I will never use it to refer to a collection of platitudes.

Sometimes, we're confronted with a completely new application and have to design a security policy model from scratch. More commonly, there already exists a model; we just have to choose the right one, and develop it into

[2]Big projects often fail in companies when the specification becomes political, and they fail even more often when run by governments – issues I'll discuss further in Part 3.

a security target. Neither of these steps is easy. In this section of the book, I provide a number of security policy models, describe them in the context of real systems, and examine the engineering mechanisms (and associated constraints) which a security target can use to meet them.

9.3 Multilevel security policy

On March 22, 1940, President Roosevelt signed Executive Order 8381, enabling certain types of information to be classified Restricted, Confidential or Secret [980]. President Truman later added a higher level of Top Secret. This developed into a common protective marking scheme for the sensitivity of documents, and was adopted by NATO governments too in the Cold War. *Classifications* are labels, which run upwards from *Unclassified* through *Confidential, Secret* and *Top Secret* (see Figure 9.2). The original idea was that information whose compromise could cost lives was marked 'Secret' while information whose compromise could cost many lives was 'Top Secret'. Government employees and contractors have *clearances* depending on the care with which they've been vetted; in the USA, for example, a 'Secret' clearance involves checking FBI fingerprint files, while 'Top Secret' also involves background checks for the previous five to fifteen years' employment plus an interview and often a polygraph test [548]. Candidates have to disclose all their sexual partners in recent years and all material that might be used to blackmail them, such as teenage drug use or gay affairs[3].

The access control policy was simple: you can read a document only if your clearance is at least as high as the document's classification. So an official cleared to 'Top Secret' could read a 'Secret' document, but not vice versa. So information may only flow upwards, from confidential to secret to top secret, but never downwards – unless an authorized person takes a deliberate decision to declassify it.

The system rapidly became more complicated. The damage criteria for classifying documents were expanded from possible military consequences to economic harm and even political embarrassment. Information that is neither classified nor public is known as 'Controlled Unclassified Information' (CUI) in the USA while Britain uses 'Official'[4].

[3]In June 2015, the clearance review data of about 20m Americans was stolen from the Office of Personnel Management by the Chinese intelligence services. By then, about a million Americans had a Top Secret clearance; the OPM data also covered former employees and job applicants, as well as their relatives and sexual partners. With hindsight, collecting all the dirt on all the citizens with a sensitive job may not have been a great idea.

[4]Prior to adopting the CUI system, the United States had more than 50 different markings for data that was controlled but not classified, including For Official Use Only (FOUO), Law Enforcement Sensitive (LES), Proprietary (PROPIN), Federal Tax Information (FTI), Sensitive but Unclassified (SBU), and many, many others. Some agencies made up their own labels, without any

TOP SECRET
SECRET
CONFIDENTIAL
UNCLASSIFIED

Figure 9.2: multilevel security

There is also a system of codewords whereby information, especially at Secret and above, can be restricted further. For example, information that might reveal intelligence sources or methods – such as the identities of agents or decryption capabilities – is typically classified 'Top Secret Special Compartmented Intelligence' or TS/SCI, which means that so-called *need to know* restrictions are imposed as well, with one or more codewords attached to a file. Some codewords relate to a particular military operation or intelligence source and are available only to a group of named users. To read a document, a user must have all the codewords that are attached to it. A classification label, plus a set of codewords, makes up a *security category* or (if there's at least one codeword) a *compartment*, which is a set of records with the same access control policy. Compartmentation is typically implemented nowadays using discretionary access control mechanisms; I'll discuss it in the next chapter.

There are also *descriptors, caveats* and *IDO markings*. Descriptors are words such as 'Management', 'Budget', and 'Appointments': they do not invoke any special handling requirements, so we can deal with a file marked 'Confidential – Management' as if it were simply marked 'Confidential'. Caveats are warnings such as "UK Eyes Only", or the US equivalent, "NOFORN"; they do create restrictions. There are also *International Defence Organisation* markings such as *NATO*[5]. The lack of obvious differences between codewords, descriptors, caveats and IDO marking helps make the system confusing. A more detailed explanation can be found in [1565].

9.3.1 The Anderson report

In the 1960s, when computers started being widely used, the classification system caused serious friction. Paul Karger, who worked for the USAF then, described having to log off from a Confidential system, walk across the yard

coordination. Further problems arose when civilian documents marked Confidential ended up at the National Archives and Records Administration, where CONFIDENTIAL was a national security classification. Moving from this menagerie of markings to a single centrally-managed government-wide system has taken more than a decade and is still ongoing. The UK has its own post-Cold-War simplification story.

[5]Curiously, in the UK 'NATO Secret' is less secret than 'Secret', so it's a kind of anti-codeword that moves the content down the lattice rather than up.

to a different hut, show a pass to an armed guard, then go in and log on to a Secret system – over a dozen times a day. People soon realised they needed a way to deal with information at different levels at the same desk, but how could this be done without secrets leaking? As soon as one operating system bug was fixed, some other vulnerability would be discovered. The NSA hired an eminent computer scientist, Willis Ware, to its scientific advisory board, and in 1967 he brought the extent of the computer security problem to official and public attention [1989]. There was the constant worry that even unskilled users would discover loopholes and use them opportunistically; there was also a keen and growing awareness of the threat from malicious code. (Viruses were not invented until the 1980s; the 70's concern was Trojans.) There was then a serious scare when it was discovered that the Pentagon's World Wide Military Command and Control System (WWMCCS) was vulnerable to Trojan Horse attacks; this had the effect of restricting its use to people with a 'Top Secret' clearance, which was inconvenient.

The next step was a 1972 study by James Anderson for the US government which concluded that a secure system should do one or two things well; and that these protection properties should be enforced by mechanisms that were simple enough to verify and that would change only rarely [52]. It introduced the concept of a *reference monitor* – a component of the operating system that would mediate access control decisions and be small enough to be subject to analysis and tests, the completeness of which could be assured. In modern parlance, such components – together with their associated operating procedures – make up the *Trusted Computing Base* (TCB). More formally, the TCB is defined as the set of components (hardware, software, human, …) whose correct functioning is sufficient to ensure that the security policy is enforced, or, more vividly, whose failure could cause a breach of the security policy. The Anderson report's goal was to make the security policy simple enough for the TCB to be amenable to careful verification.

9.3.2 The Bell-LaPadula model

The multilevel security policy model that gained wide acceptance was proposed by Dave Bell and Len LaPadula in 1973 [211]. Its basic property is that information cannot flow downwards. More formally, the *Bell-LaPadula* (BLP) model enforces two properties:

- The *simple security property*: no process may read data at a higher level. This is also known as *no read up (NRU)*;
- The **-property*: no process may write data to a lower level. This is also known as *no write down (NWD)*.

The *-property was Bell and LaPadula's critical innovation. It was driven by the WWMCCS debacle and the more general fear of Trojan-horse attacks. An uncleared user might write a Trojan and leave it around where a system administrator cleared to 'Secret' might execute it; it could then copy itself into the 'Secret' part of the system, read the data there and try to signal it down somehow. It's also quite possible that an enemy agent could get a job at a commercial software house and embed some code in a product that would look for secret documents to copy. If it could then write them down to where its creator could read them, the security policy would have been violated. Information might also be leaked as a result of a bug, if applications could write down.

Vulnerabilities such as malicious and buggy code are assumed to be given. It is also assumed that most staff are careless, and some are dishonest; extensive operational security measures have long been used, especially in defence environments, to prevent people leaking paper documents. So the pre-existing culture assumed that security policy was enforced independently of user actions; Bell-LaPadula sets out to enforce it not just independently of users' direct actions, but of their indirect actions (such as the actions taken by programs they run).

So we must prevent programs running at 'Secret' from writing to files at 'Unclassified'. More generally we must prevent any process at High from signalling to any object at Low. Systems that enforce a security policy independently of user actions are described as having *mandatory access control*, as opposed to the *discretionary access control* in systems like Unix where users can take their own access decisions about their files.

The Bell-LaPadula model enabled designers to prove theorems. Given both the simple security property (no read up), and the star property (no write down), various results can be proved: in particular, if your starting state is secure, then your system will remain so. To keep things simple, we will generally assume from now on that the system has only two levels, High and Low.

9.3.3 The standard criticisms of Bell-LaPadula

The introduction of BLP caused a lot of excitement: here was a security policy that did what the defence establishment thought it wanted, was intuitively clear, yet still allowed people to prove theorems. Researchers started to beat up on it and refine it.

The first big controversy was about John McLean's *System Z*, which he defined as a BLP system with the added feature that a user can ask the system administrator to temporarily declassify any file from High to Low. In this way, Low users can read any High file without breaking the BLP assumptions. Dave Bell countered that System Z cheats by doing something his model doesn't allow (changing labels isn't a valid operation on the state), and John McLean's retort was that it didn't explicitly tell him so: so the BLP rules were not in themselves enough. The issue is dealt with by introducing a *tranquility property*. Strong tranquility says that security labels never change during system operation, while weak tranquility says that labels never change in such a way as to violate a defined security policy.

Why weak tranquility? In a real system we often want to observe the principle of least privilege and start off a process at the uncleared level, even if the owner of the process were cleared to 'Top Secret'. If they then access a confidential email, their session is automatically upgraded to 'Confidential'; in general, a process is upgraded each time it accesses data at a higher level (the *high water mark* principle). As subjects are usually an abstraction of the memory management sub-system and file handles, rather than processes, this means that state changes when access rights change, rather than when data actually moves.

The practical implication is that a process acquires the security labels of all the files it reads, and these become the default label set of every file that it writes. So a process which has read files at 'Secret' and 'Crypto' will thereafter create files marked 'Secret Crypto'. This will include temporary copies made of other files. If it then reads a file at 'Secret Nuclear' then all files it creates after that will be labelled 'Secret Crypto Nuclear', and it will not be able to write to any temporary files at 'Secret Crypto'.

The effect this has on applications is one of the serious complexities of multilevel security; most application software needs to be rewritten (or at least modified) to run on MLS platforms. Real-time changes in security level mean that access to resources can be revoked at any time, including in the middle of a transaction. And as the revocation problem is generally unsolvable in modern operating systems, at least in any complete form, the applications have to cope somehow. Unless you invest some care and effort, you can easily find that everything ends up in the highest compartment – or that the system fragments into thousands of tiny compartments that don't communicate at all with each other. In order to prevent this, labels are now generally taken outside the MLS machinery and dealt with using discretionary access control mechanisms (I'll discuss this in the next chapter).

Another problem with BLP, and indeed with all mandatory access control systems, is that separating users and processes is the easy part; the hard part is when some controlled interaction is needed. Most real applications need some kind of *trusted subject* that can break the security policy; the classic example was a trusted word processor that helps an intelligence analyst scrub a Top Secret document when she's editing it down to Secret [1272]. BLP is silent on how the system should protect such an application. So it becomes part of the Trusted Computing Base, but a part that can't be verified using models based solely on BLP.

Finally it's worth noting that even with the high-water-mark refinement, BLP still doesn't deal with the creation or destruction of subjects or objects (which is one of the hard problems of building a real MLS system).

9.3.4 The evolution of MLS policies

Multilevel security policies have evolved in parallel in both the practical and research worlds.

The first multilevel security policy was a version of high water mark written in 1967–8 for the ADEPT-50, a mandatory access control system developed for the IBM S/360 mainframe [2010]. This used triples of level, compartment and group, with the groups being files, users, terminals and jobs. As programs (rather than processes) were subjects, it was vulnerable to Trojan horse compromises. Nonetheless, it laid the foundation for BLP, and also led to the current IBM S/390 mainframe hardware security architecture [942].

The next big step was Multics. This had started as an MIT project in 1965 and developed into a Honeywell product; it became the template and inspirational example for 'trusted systems'. The evaluation that was carried out on it by Paul Karger and Roger Schell was hugely influential and was the first appearance of the idea that malware could be hidden in the compiler [1022] – and led to Ken Thompson's famous paper 'Reflections on Trusting Trust' ten years later [1887]. Multics had a derivative system called SCOMP that I'll discuss in section 9.4.1.

The torrent of research money that poured into multilevel security from the 1980s led to a number of alternative formulations. *Noninterference* was introduced by Joseph Goguen and Jose Meseguer in 1982 [774]. In a system with this property, High's actions have no effect on what Low can see. *Nondeducibility* is less restrictive and was introduced by David Sutherland in 1986 [1851] to model applications such as a LAN on which there are machines at both Low and High, with the High machines encrypting their LAN traffic[6]. Nondeducibility turned out to be too weak, as there's nothing to stop Low making deductions about High input with 99% certainty. Other theoretical models include *Generalized Noninterference* and *restrictiveness* [1278]; the *Harrison-Ruzzo-Ullman* model tackles the problem of how to deal with the creation and deletion of files, on which BLP is silent [869]; and the *Compartmented Mode Workstation* (CMW) policy attempted to model the classification of information using floating labels, as in the high water mark policy [808,2042].

Out of this wave of innovation, the model with the greatest impact on modern systems is probably the *type enforcement* (TE) model, due to Earl Boebert and Dick Kain [272], later extended by Lee Badger and others to *Domain and Type*

[6]Quite a lot else is needed to do this right, such as padding the High traffic with nulls so that Low users can't do traffic analysis – see [1635] for an early example of such a system. You may also need to think about Low traffic over a High network, such as facilities for soldiers to phone home.

Enforcement (DTE) [154]. This assigns subjects to *domains* and objects to *types*, with matrices defining permitted domain-domain and domain-type interactions. This is used in SELinux, now a component of Android, which simplifies it by putting both subjects and objects in types and having a matrix of allowed type pairs [1189]. In effect this is a second access-control matrix; in addition to having a user ID and group ID, each process has a security ID (SID). The Linux Security Modules framework provides pluggable security where you can set rules that operate on SIDs.

DTE introduced a language for configuration (DTEL), and implicit typing of files based on pathname; so all objects in a given subdirectory may be declared to be in a given domain. DTE is more general than BLP, as it starts to deal with integrity as well as confidentiality concerns. One of the early uses was to enforce trusted pipelines: the idea is to confine a set of processes in a pipeline so that each can only talk to the previous stage and the next stage. This can be used to assemble guards and firewalls that cannot be bypassed unless at least two stages are compromised [1432]. Type-enforcement mechanisms can be aware of code versus data, and privileges can be bound to code; in consequence the tranquility problem can be dealt with at execute time rather than as data are read. This can make things much more tractable. They are used, for example, in the Sidewinder firewall.

The downside of the greater flexibility and expressiveness of TE/DTE is that it is not always straightforward to implement policies like BLP, because of state explosion; when writing a security policy you have to consider all the possible interactions between different types. Other mechanisms may be used to manage policy complexity, such as running a prototype for a while to observe what counts as normal behaviour; you can then turn on DTE and block all the information flows not seen to date. But this doesn't give much assurance that the policy you've derived is the right one.

In 1992, *role-based access control* (RBAC) was introduced by David Ferraiolo and Richard Kuhn to manage policy complexity. It formalises rules that attach primarily to roles rather than to individual users or machines [678, 679]. Transactions that may be performed by holders of a given role are specified, then mechanisms for granting membership of a role (including delegation). Roles, or groups, had for years been the mechanism used in practice in organizations such as banks to manage access control; the RBAC model started to formalize this. It can be used to give finer-grained control, for example by granting different access rights to 'Ross as Professor', 'Ross as member of the Admissions Committee' and 'Ross reading private email'. A variant of it, aspect-based access control (ABAC), adds context, so you can distinguish 'Ross at his workstation in the lab' from 'Ross on his phone somewhere on Earth'. Both have been supported by Windows since Windows 8.

SELinux builds it on top of TE, so that users are mapped to roles at login time, roles are authorized for domains and domains are given permissions to types.

On such a platform, RBAC can usefully deal with integrity issues as well as confidentiality, by allowing role membership to be revised when certain programs are invoked. Thus, for example, a process calling untrusted software that had been downloaded from the net might lose the role membership required to write to sensitive system files. I discuss SELinux in more detail at 9.5.2.

9.3.5 The Biba model

The incorporation into Windows 7 of a multilevel integrity model revived interest in a security model devised in 1975 by Ken Biba [238], which deals with integrity alone and ignores confidentiality. Biba's observation was that confidentiality and integrity are in some sense dual concepts – confidentiality is a constraint on who can read a message, while integrity is a constraint on who can write or alter it. So you can recycle BLP into an integrity policy by turning it upside down.

As a concrete application, an electronic medical device such as an ECG may have two separate modes: calibration and use. Calibration data must be protected from corruption, so normal users should be able to read it but not write to it; when a normal user resets the device, it will lose its current user state (i.e., any patient data in memory) but the calibration must remain unchanged. Only an authorised technician should be able to redo the calibration.

To model such a system, we can use a multilevel integrity policy with the rules that we can read data at higher levels (i.e., a user process can read the calibration data) and write to lower levels (i.e., a calibration process can write to a buffer in a user process); but we must never read down or write up, as either could allow High integrity objects to become contaminated with Low – i.e., potentially unreliable – data. The Biba model is often formulated in terms of the *low water mark* principle, which is the dual of the high water mark principle discussed above: the integrity of an object is the lowest level of all the objects that contributed to its creation.

This was the first formal model of integrity. A surprisingly large number of real systems work along Biba lines. For example, the passenger information system in a railroad may get information from the signalling system, but shouldn't be able to affect it; and an electricity utility's power dispatching system will be able to see the safety systems' state but not interfere with them. The safety-critical systems community talks in terms of *safety integrity levels*, which relate to the probability that a safety mechanism will fail and to the level of risk reduction it is designed to give.

Windows, since version 6 (Vista), marks file objects with an integrity level, which can be Low, Medium, High or System, and implements a default policy of NoWriteUp. Critical files are at System and other objects are at Medium by default – except for the browser which is at Low. So things downloaded using

IE can read most files in a Windows system, but cannot write to them. The goal is to limit the damage that can be done by malware.

As you might expect, Biba has the same fundamental problems as Bell-LaPadula. It cannot accommodate real-world operation very well without numerous exceptions. For example, a real system will usually require trusted subjects that can override the security model, but Biba on its own cannot protect and confine them, any more than BLP can. For example, a car's airbag is on a less critical bus than the engine, but when it deploys you assume there's a risk of a fuel fire and switch the engine off. There are other real integrity goals that Biba also cannot express, such as assured pipelines. In the case of Windows, Microsoft even dropped the NoReadDown restriction and did not end up using its integrity model to protect the base system from users, as this would have required even more frequent user confirmation. In fact, the Type Enforcement model was introduced by Boebert and Kain as an alternative to Biba. It is unfortunate that Windows didn't incorporate TE.

9.4 Historical examples of MLS systems

The second edition of this book had a much fuller history of MLS systems; since these have largely gone out of fashion, and the MLS research programme has been wound down, I give a shorter version here.

9.4.1 SCOMP

A key product was the *secure communications processor* (SCOMP), a derivative of Multics launched in 1983 [710]. This was a no-expense-spared implementation of what the US Department of Defense believed it wanted for handling messaging at multiple levels of classification. It had formally verified hardware and software, with a minimal kernel to keep things simple. Its operating system, STOP, used Multics' system of rings to maintain up to 32 separate compartments, and to allow appropriate one-way information flows between them.

SCOMP was used in applications such as military *mail guards*. These are firewalls that allow mail to pass from Low to High but not vice versa [538]. (In general, a device which supports one-way flow is known as a *data diode*.) SCOMP's successor, XTS-300, supported C2G, the Command and Control Guard. This was used in the time phased force deployment data (TPFDD) system whose function was to plan US troop movements and associated logistics. SCOMP's most significant contribution was to serve as a model for the *Orange Book* [544] – the US Trusted Computer Systems Evaluation Criteria. This was the first systematic set of standards for secure computer systems, being introduced in 1985 and finally retired in December 2000. The Orange

Book was enormously influential not just in the USA but among allied powers; countries such as the UK, Germany, and Canada based their own national standards on it, until these national standards were finally subsumed into the Common Criteria [1398].

The Orange Book allowed systems to be evaluated at a number of levels with A1 being the highest, and moving downwards through B3, B2, B1 and C2 to C1. SCOMP was the first system to be rated A1. It was also extensively documented in the open literature. Being first, and being fairly public, it set a target for the next generation of military systems.

MLS versions of Unix started to appear in the late 1980s, such as AT&T's System V/MLS [48]. This added security levels and labels, showing that MLS properties could be introduced to a commercial operating system with minimal changes to the system kernel. By this book's second edition (2007), Sun's Solaris had emerged as the platform of choice for high-assurance server systems and for many clients as well. *Comparted Mode Workstations* (CMWs) were an example of the latter, allowing data at different levels to be viewed and modified at the same time, so an intelligence analyst could read 'Top Secret' data in one window and write reports at 'Secret' in another, without being able to accidentally copy and paste text downwards [934]. For the engineering, see [635, 636].

9.4.2 Data diodes

It was soon realised that simple mail guards and crypto boxes were too restrictive, as more complex networked services were developed besides mail. First-generation MLS mechanisms were inefficient for real-time services.

The US Naval Research Laboratory (NRL) therefore developed the *Pump* – a one-way data transfer device (a data diode) to allow secure one-way information flow (Figure 9.3. The main problem is that while sending data from Low to

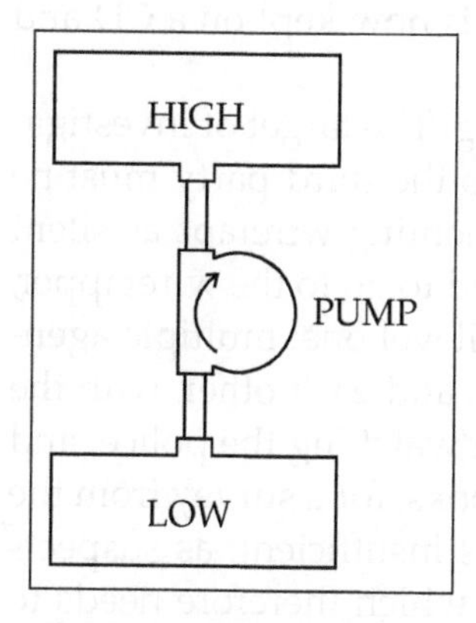

Figure 9.3: The NRL pump

High is easy, the need for assured transmission reliability means that acknowledgement messages must be sent back from High to Low. The Pump limits the bandwidth of possible backward leakage using a number of mechanisms such as buffering and random timing of acknowledgements [1014,1016, 1017]. The attraction of this approach is that one can build MLS systems by using data diodes to connect separate systems at different security levels. As these systems don't process data at more than one level – an architecture called *system high* – they can be built from cheap *commercial-off-the-shelf* (COTS) components. You don't need to worry about applying MLS internally, merely protecting them from external attack, whether physical or network-based. As the cost of hardware has fallen, this has become the preferred option, and the world's military bases are now full of KVM switches (which let people switch their keyboard, video display and mouse between Low and High systems) and data diodes (to link Low and High networks). The pump's story is told in [1018].

An early application was logistics. Some signals intelligence equipment is 'Top Secret', while things like jet fuel and bootlaces are not; but even such simple commodities may become 'Secret' when their quantities or movements might leak information about tactical intentions. The systems needed to manage all this can be hard to build; MLS logistics projects in both the USA and UK have ended up as expensive disasters. In the UK, the Royal Air Force's Logistics Information Technology System (LITS) was a 10 year (1989–99), £500m project to provide a single stores management system for the RAF's 80 bases [1388]. It was designed to operate on two levels: 'Restricted' for the jet fuel and boot polish, and 'Secret' for special stores such as nuclear bombs. It was initially implemented as two separate database systems connected by a pump to enforce the MLS property. The project became a classic tale of escalating costs driven by creeping changes in requirements. One of these changes was the easing of classification rules with the end of the Cold War. As a result, it was found that almost all the 'Secret' information was now static (e.g., operating manuals for air-drop nuclear bombs that are now kept in strategic stockpiles rather than at airbases). To save money, the 'Secret' information is now kept on a CD and locked up in a safe.

Another major application of MLS is in wiretapping. The target of investigation should not know they are being wiretapped, so the third party must be silent – and when phone companies started implementing wiretaps as silent conference calls, the charge for the conference call had to go to the wiretapper, not to the target. The modern requirement is a multilevel one: multiple agencies at different levels may want to monitor a target, and each other, with the police tapping a drug dealer, an anti-corruption unit watching the police, and so on. Eliminating covert channels is harder than it looks; for a survey from the mid-2000s, see [1710]; a pure MLS security policy is insufficient, as suspects can try to hack or confuse wiretapping equipment, which therefore needs to resist online tampering. In one notorious case, a wiretap was discovered on the mobile phones of the Greek Prime Minister and his senior colleagues during the Athens olympics; the lawful intercept facility in the mobile phone company's switchgear was abused by unauthorised software, and was detected when the buggers' modifications caused some text messages not to be delivered [1553]. The phone company was fined 76 million Euros (almost $100m). The clean way to manage wiretaps nowadays with modern VOIP systems may just be to write everything to disk and extract what you need later.

There are many military embedded systems too. In submarines, speed, reactor output and RPM are all Top Secret, as a history of these three measurements would reveal the vessel's performance – and that's among the few pieces of information that even the USA and the UK don't share. The engineering is made more complex by the need for the instruments not to be Top Secret when the vessel is in port, as that would complicate maintenance. And as for air combat, some US radars won't display the velocity of a US aircraft whose performance is classified, unless the operator has the appropriate clearance. When you read stories about F-16 pilots seeing an insanely fast UFO whose speed on their radar didn't make any sense, you can put two and two together. It will be interesting to see what sort of other side-effects follow when powerful actors try to bake MAC policies into IoT infrastructure, and what sort of superstitious beliefs they give rise to.

9.5 MAC: from MLS to IFC and integrity

In the first edition of this book, I noted a trend to use mandatory access controls to prevent tampering and provide real-time performance guarantees [1021, 1315], and ventured that "perhaps the real future of multilevel systems is not in confidentiality, but integrity." Government agencies had learned that MAC was what it took to stop malware. By the second edition, multilevel integrity had hit the mass market in Windows, which essentially uses the Biba model.

9.5.1 Windows

In Windows, all processes do, and all securable objects (including directories, files and registry keys) may, have an integrity-level label. File objects are labelled 'Medium' by default, while Internet Explorer (and everything downloaded using it) is labelled 'Low'. User action is therefore needed to upgrade downloaded content before it can modify existing files. It's also possible to implement a crude BLP policy using Windows, as you can also set 'NoReadUp' and 'NoExecuteUp' policies. These are not installed as default; Microsoft was concerned about malware installing itself in the system and then hiding. Keeping the browser 'Low' makes installation harder, and allowing all processes (even Low ones) to inspect the rest of the system makes hiding harder. But this integrity-only approach to MAC does mean that malware running at Low can steal all your data; so some users might care to set 'NoReadUp' for sensitive directories. This is all discussed by Joanna Rutkowska in [1637]; she also describes some interesting potential attacks based on virtualization.

9.5.2 SELinux

The case of SELinux is somewhat similar to Windows in that the immediate goal of mandatory access control mechanisms was also to limit the effects of a compromise. SELinux [1189] was implemented by the NSA, based on the Flask security architecture [1815], which separates the policy from the enforcement mechanism; a security context contains all of the security attributes associated with a subject or object in Flask, where one of those attributes includes the Type Enforcement type attribute. A security identifier is a handle to a security context, mapped by the security server. This is where policy decisions are made and resides in the kernel for performance [820]. It has been mainstream since Linux 2.6. The server provides a security API to the rest of the kernel, behind which the security model is hidden. The server internally implements a general constraints engine that can express RBAC, TE, and MLS. In typical Linux distributions from the mid-2000s, it was used to separate various services, so an attacker who takes over your web server does not thereby acquire your DNS server as well. Its adoption by Android has made it part of the world's most popular operating system, as described in Chapter 6.

9.5.3 Embedded systems

There are many fielded systems that implement some variant of the Biba model. As well as the medical-device and railroad signalling applications I already mentioned, there are utilities. In an electricity utility, for example, there is typically a hierarchy of safety systems, which operate completely independently at the highest safety integrity level; these are visible to, but cannot be influenced by, operational systems such as power dispatching; retail-level metering systems can be observed by, but not influenced by, the billing system. Both retail meters and the substation-level meters in the power-dispatching system feed information into fraud detection, and finally there are the executive information systems, which can observe everything while having no direct effect on operations. In cars, most makes have separate CAN buses for the powertrain and for the cabin, as you don't want a malicious app on your radio to be able to operate your brakes (though in 2010, security researchers found that the separation was completely inadequate [1087]).

It's also worth bearing in mind that simple integrity controls merely stop malware taking over the machine – they don't stop it infecting a Low compartment and using that as a springboard from which to spread elsewhere, or to issue instructions to other machines.

To sum up, many of the lessons learned in the early multilevel systems go across to a number of applications of wider interest. So do a number of the failure modes, which I'll now discuss.

9.6 What goes wrong

Engineers learn more from the systems that fail than from those that succeed, and here MLS systems have been an effective teacher. The billions of dollars spent on building systems to follow a simple policy with a high level of assurance have clarified many second-order and third-order consequences of information flow controls. I'll start with the more theoretical and work through to the business and engineering end.

9.6.1 Composability

Consider a simple device that accepts two 'High' inputs H_1 and H_2; multiplexes them; encrypts them by xor'ing them with a one-time pad (i.e., a random generator); outputs the other copy of the pad on H_3; and outputs the ciphertext, which being encrypted with a cipher system giving perfect secrecy, is considered to be low (output L), as in Figure 9.4.

In isolation, this device is provably secure. However, if feedback is permitted, then the output from H_3 can be fed back into H_2, with the result that the high input H_1 now appears at the low output L. Timing inconsistencies can also break the composition of two secure systems (noted by Daryl McCullough [1262]).

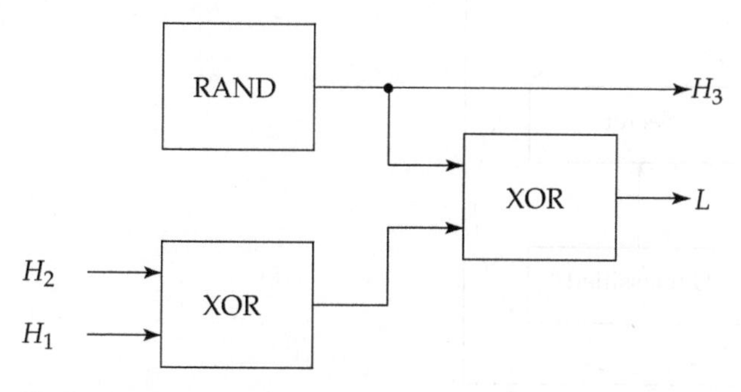

Figure 9.4: Insecure composition of secure systems with feedback

In general, the *composition problem* – how to compose two or more secure components into a secure system – is hard, even at the relatively uncluttered level of proving results about ideal components [1432]. (Simple information flow doesn't compose; neither does noninterference or nondeducibility.) Most of the low-level problems arise when some sort of feedback is introduced; without it, composition can be achieved under a number of formal models [1279]. However, in real life, feedback is pervasive, and composition of security properties can be made even harder by interface issues, feature interactions and so on. For example, one system might produce data at such a rate as to perform a service-denial attack on another. And the composition of secure components is often frustrated by higher-level incompatibilities. Components might have been designed in accordance with two different security policies, or designed according to inconsistent requirements.

9.6.2 The cascade problem

An example of the composition problem is given by the *cascade problem* (Figure 9.5). After the Orange book introduced a series of evaluation levels, this led to span-limit rules about the number of levels at which a system can operate [548]. For example, a system evaluated to B3 was in general allowed to process information at Unclassified, Confidential and Secret, or at Confidential, Secret and Top Secret; there was no system permitted to process Unclassified and Top Secret data simultaneously [548].

As the diagram shows, it is straightforward to connect together two B3 systems in such a way that this policy is broken. The first system connects together Unclassified and Secret, and its Secret level communicates with the second system – which also processes Top Secret information [925]. This defeats the span limit.

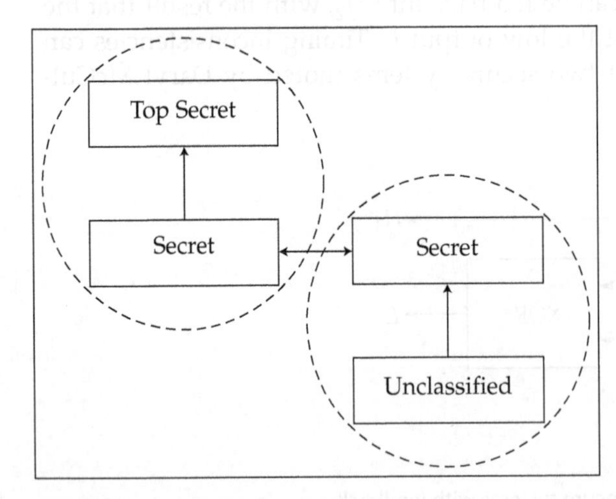

Figure 9.5: The cascade problem

9.6.3 Covert channels

One of the reasons why span limits are imposed on multilevel systems emerges from a famous – and extensively studied – problem: the *covert channel*. First pointed out by Lampson in 1973 [1127], a covert channel is a mechanism that was not designed for communication but that can nonetheless be abused to allow information to be communicated down from High to Low.

A typical covert channel arises when a high process can signal to a low one by affecting some shared resource. In a modern multicore CPU, it could increase the clock frequency of the CPU core it's using at time t_i to signal that the *i*-th bit in a Top Secret file was a 1, and let it scale back to signal that the bit was a 0. This gives a covert channel capacity of several tens of bits per second [36]. Since 2018, CPU designers have been struggling with a series of covert channels that exploit the CPU microarchitecture; with names like Meltdown, Spectre, and Foreshadow, they have provided not just ways for High to signal to Low but for Low to circumvent access control and read memory at High. I will discuss these in detail in the chapter on side channels.

The best that developers have been able to do consistently with confidentiality protection in regular operating systems is to limit it to 1 bit per second or so. (That is a DoD target [545], and techniques for doing a systematic analysis may be found in Kemmerer [1038].) One bit per second may be tolerable in an environment where we wish to prevent large TS/SCI files – such as satellite photographs – leaking down from TS/SCI users to 'Secret' users. However, it's potentially a lethal threat to high-value cryptographic keys. This is one of the reasons for the military and banking doctrine of doing crypto in special purpose hardware.

The highest-bandwidth covert channel of which I'm aware occurs in large early-warning radar systems, where High – the radar processor – controls hundreds of antenna elements that illuminate Low – the target – with high speed pulse trains, which are modulated with pseudorandom noise to make jamming harder. In this case, the radar code must be trusted as the covert channel bandwidth is many megabits per second.

9.6.4 The threat from malware

The defense computer community was shocked when Fred Cohen wrote the first thesis on computer viruses, and used a virus to penetrate multilevel secure systems easily in 1983. In his first experiment, a file virus that took only eight hours to write managed to penetrate a system previously believed to be multilevel secure [452]. People had been thinking about malware since the 1960s and had done various things to mitigate it, but their focus had been on Trojans.

There are many ways in which malicious code can be used to break access controls. If the reference monitor (or other TCB components) can be corrupted, then malware can deliver the entire system to the attacker, for example by issuing an unauthorised clearance. For this reason, slightly looser rules apply to so-called *closed security environments* which are defined to be those where 'system applications are adequately protected against the insertion of malicious logic' [548], and this in turn created an incentive for vendors to tamper-proof the TCB, using techniques such as TPMs. But even if the TCB remains intact, malware could still copy itself up from Low to High (which BLP doesn't prevent) and use a covert channel to signal information down.

9.6.5 Polyinstantiation

Another problem that exercised the research community is *polyinstantiation*. Suppose our High user has created a file named `agents`, and our Low user now tries to do the same. If the MLS operating system prohibits him, it will have leaked information – namely that there is a file called `agents` at High. But if it lets him, it will now have two files with the same name.

Often we can solve the problem by a naming convention, such as giving Low and High users different directories. But the problem remains a hard one for databases [1652]. Suppose that a High user allocates a classified cargo to a ship. The system will not divulge this information to a Low user, who might think the ship is empty, and try to allocate it another cargo or even to change its destination.

Here the US and UK practices diverge. The solution favoured in the USA is that the High user allocates a Low cover story at the same time as the real High cargo. Thus the underlying data will look something like Figure 9.6.

In the UK, the theory is simpler – the system will automatically reply 'classified' to a Low user who tries to see or alter a High record. The two available views would be as in Figure 9.7.

This makes the system engineering simpler. It also prevents the mistakes and covert channels that can still arise with cover stories (e.g., a Low user tries to add a container of ammunition for Cyprus). The drawback is that everyone tends to need the highest available clearance in order to get their work done. (In practice, cover stories still get used in order not to advertise the existence of a covert mission any more than need be.)

Level	Cargo	Destination
Secret	Missiles	Iran
Restricted	–	–
Unclassified	Engine spares	Cyprus

Figure 9.6: how the USA deals with classified data

Level	Cargo	Destination
Secret	Missiles	Iran
Restricted	Classified	Classified
Unclassified	–	–

Figure 9.7: how the UK deals with classified data

9.6.6 Practical problems with MLS

Multilevel secure systems are surprisingly expensive and difficult to build and deploy. There are many sources of cost and confusion.

1. They are built in small volumes, and often to high standards of physical robustness, using elaborate documentation, testing and other quality control measures driven by military purchasing bureaucracies.
2. MLS systems have idiosyncratic administration tools and procedures. A trained Unix administrator can't just take on an MLS installation without significant further training; so many MLS systems are installed without their features being used.
3. Many applications need to be rewritten or at least greatly modified to run under MLS operating systems [1632].
4. Because processes are automatically upgraded as they see new labels, the files they use have to be too. New files default to the highest label belonging to any possible input. The result of all this is a chronic tendency for things to be overclassified. There's a particular problem when system components accumulate all the labels they've seen, leading to *label explosion* where they acquire such a collection that no single principal can access them any more. So they get put in the trusted computing base, which ends up containing a quite uncomfortably large part of the operating system (plus utilities, plus windowing system software, plus middleware such as database software). This 'TCB bloat' constantly pushes up the cost of evaluation and reduces assurance.
5. The classification of data can get complex:
   - in the run-up to a conflict, the location of 'innocuous' stores such as food could reveal tactical intentions, and so may be suddenly upgraded;
   - classifications are not always monotone. Equipment classified at 'confidential' may easily contain components classified 'secret', and on the flip side it's hard to grant access at 'secret' to secret information in a 'top secret' database;

- information may need to be downgraded. An intelligence analyst might need to take a satellite photo classified at TS/SCI, and paste it into an assessment for field commanders at 'secret'. In case information was covertly hidden in the image by a virus, this may involve special filters, lossy compression of images and so on. One option is a 'print-and-fax' mechanism that turns a document into a bitmap, and logs it for traceability.
- we may need to worry about the volume of information available to an attacker. For example, we might be happy to declassify any single satellite photo, but declassifying the whole collection would reveal our surveillance capability and the history of our intelligence priorities. (I will look at this *aggregation problem* in more detail in section 11.2.)
- Similarly, the output of an unclassified program acting on unclassified data may be classified, for example if standard data mining techniques applied to an online forum throw up a list of terror suspects.

6. Although MLS systems can prevent undesired things (such as information leakage), they also prevent desired things too (such as building a search engine to operate across all an agency's Top Secret compartmented data). So even in military environments, the benefits can be questionable. After 9/11, many of the rules were relaxed, and access controls above Top Secret are typically discretionary, to allow information sharing. The cost of that, of course, was the Snowden disclosures.

7. Finally, obsessive government secrecy is a chronic burden. The late Senator Daniel Moynihan wrote a critical study of its real purposes, and its huge costs in US foreign and military affairs [1348]. For example, President Truman was never told of the Venona decrypts because the material was considered 'Army Property'. As he put it: "Departments and agencies hoard information, and the government becomes a kind of market. Secrets become organizational assets, never to be shared save in exchange for another organization's assets."

   More recent examples of MLS doctrine impairing operational effectiveness include the use of unencrypted communications to drones in the Afghan war (as the armed forces feared that if they got the NSA bureaucracy involved, the drones would be unusable), and the use of the notoriously insecure Zoom videoconferencing system for British government cabinet meetings during the coronavirus crisis (the government's encrypted videoconferencing terminals are classified, so ministers aren't allowed to take them home). This brings to mind a quip from an exasperated British general: "What's the difference between Jurassic Park and the Ministry of Defence? One's a theme park full of dinosaurs, and the other's a movie!"

There has been no shortage of internal strategic critique. A 2004 report by Mitre's JASON programme of the US system of classification concluded that it was no longer fit for purpose [980]. There are many interesting reasons, including the widely different risk/benefit calculations of the producer and consumer communities; classification comes to be dominated by distribution channels rather than by actual risk. The relative ease of attack has led government systems to be too conservative and risk-averse. It noted many perverse outcomes; for example, Predator imagery in Iraq is Unclassified, and was for some time transmitted in clear, as the Army feared that crypto would involve the NSA bureaucracy in key management and inhibit warfighting.

Mitre proposed instead that flexible compartments be set up for specific purposes, particularly when getting perishable information to tactical compartments; that intelligent use be made of technologies such as rights management and virtualisation; and that lifetime trust in cleared individuals be replaced with a system focused on transaction risk.

Anyway, one of the big changes since the second edition of this book is that the huge DoD research programme on MLS has disappeared, MLS equipment is no longer very actively promoted on the government-systems market, and systems have remained fairly static for a decade. Most government systems now operate system high – that is, entirely at Official, or at Secret, or at Top Secret. The difficulties discussed in the above section, plus the falling cost of hardware and the arrival of virtualisation, have undermined the incentive to have different levels on the same machine. The deployed MLS systems thus tend to be firewalls or mail guards between the different levels, and are often referred to by a new acronym, MILS (for multiple independent levels of security). The real separation is at the network level, between unclassified networks, the Secret Internet Protocol Router Network (SIPRNet) which handles secret data using essentially standard equipment behind crypto, and the Joint Worldwide Intelligence Communications System (JWICS) which handles Top Secret material and whose systems are kept in Secure Compartmentalized Information Facilities (SCIFs) – rooms shielded to prevent electronic eavesdropping, which I'll discuss later in the chapter on side channels.

There are occasional horrible workarounds such as 'browse-down' systems that will let someone at High view a website at Low; they're allowed to click on buttons and links to navigate, just not to enter any text. Such ugly hacks have clear potential for abuse; at best they can help keep honest people from careless mistakes.

9.7 Summary

Mandatory access control was initially developed for military applications, where it is still used in specialized firewalls (guards and data diodes). The main use of MAC mechanisms nowadays, however, is in platforms such as Android, iOS and Windows, where they protect the operating systems themselves from malware. MAC mechanisms have been a major subject of computer security research since the mid-1970's, and the lessons learned in trying to use them for military multilevel security underlie many of the schemes used for security evaluation. It is important for the practitioner to understand both their strengths and limitations, so that you can draw on the research literature when it's appropriate, and avoid being dragged into overdesign when it's not.

There are many problems which we need to be a 'fox' rather than a 'hedgehog' to solve. By trying to cast all security problems as hedgehog problems, MLS often leads to inappropriate security goals, policies and mechanisms.

Research problems

A standing challenge, sketched out by Earl Boebert in 2001 after the NSA launched SELinux, is to adapt mandatory access control mechanisms to safety-critical systems (see the quote at the head of this chapter, and [271]). As a tool for building high-assurance, special-purpose devices where the consequences of errors and failures can be limited, mechanisms such as type enforcement and role-based access control should be useful outside the world of security. Will we see them widely used in the Internet of Things? We've mentioned Biba-type mechanisms in applications such as cars and electricity distribution; will the MAC mechanisms in products such as SELinux, Windows and Android enable designers to lock down information flows and reduce the likelihood of unanticipated interactions?

The NSA continues to fund research on MLS, now under the label of IFC, albeit at a lower level than in the past. Doing it properly in a modern smartphone is hard; for an example of such work, see the Weir system by Adwait Nadkarni and colleagues [1374]. In addition to the greater intrinsic complexity of modern operating systems, phones have a plethora of side-channels and their apps are often useful only in communication with cloud services, where the real heavy lifting has to be done. The commercial offering for separate 'low' and 'high' phones consists of products such as Samsung's Knox.

A separate set of research issues surround actual military opsec, where reality falls far short of policy. All armed forces involved in recent conflicts, including US and UK forces in Iraq and Afghanistan, have had security issues around their personal mobile phones, with insurgents in some cases tracing their families back home and harassing them with threats. The Royal Navy tried to ban phones in 2009, but too many sailors left. Tracking ships via Instagram is easy; a warship consists of a few hundred young men and women, aged 18-24, with nothing much else to do but put snaps on social media. Discipline tends to focus on immediate operational threats, such as when a sailor is seen snapchatting on mine disposal: there the issue is the risk of using a radio near a mine! Different navies have tried different things: the Norwegians have their own special network for sailors and the USA is trying phones with MLS features. But NATO exercises have shown that for one navy to hack another's navigation is shockingly easy. And even the Israelis have had issues with their soldiers using mobiles on the West Bank and the Golan Heights.

Further reading

The unclassified manuals for the UK government's system of information classification, and the physical, logical and other protection mechanisms required at the different levels, have been available publicly since 2013, with the latest documents (at the time of writing) having been released in November 2018 on the Government Security web page [803]. The report on the Walker spy ring is a detailed account of a spectacular failure, and brings home the sheer complexity of running a system in which maybe three million people have a clearance at any one time, with a million applications being processed each year [878]. And the classic on the abuse of the classification process to cover up waste, fraud and mismanagement in the public sector is by Chapman [409].

On the technical side, textbooks such as Dieter Gollmann's *Computer Security* [780] give an introduction to MLS systems, while many of the published papers on actual MLS systems can be found in the proceedings of two conferences: academics' conference is the *IEEE Symposium on Security & Privacy* (known in the trade as 'Oakland' as that's where it used to be held), while the NSA supplier community's unclassified bash is the *Computer Security Applications Conference* (ACSAC) whose proceedings are (like Oakland's) published by the IEEE. Fred Cohen's experiments on breaking MLS systems using viruses are described in his book [452]. Many of the classic early papers in the field can be found at the NIST archive [1397]; NIST ran a conference series on multilevel security up till 1999. Finally, a history of the Orange Book was written by Steve Lipner [1172]; this also tells the story of the USAF's early involvement and what was learned from systems like WWMCCS.

CHAPTER

10

Boundaries

They constantly try to escape
From the darkness outside and within
By dreaming of systems so perfect that no one will need to be good.
– TS ELIOT

You have zero privacy anyway. Get over it.
– SCOTT MCNEALY

10.1 Introduction

When we restrict information flows to protect privacy or confidentiality, a policy goal is usually not to prevent information flowing 'down' a hierarchy but to prevent it flowing 'across' between smaller groups.

1. If you give the million US Federal employees and contractors with a Top Secret clearance access to too much Top Secret data, then you get a whistleblower like Ed Snowden if you're lucky, or a traitor like Aldrich Ames if you're not.
2. As mobile phones spread round the world, they've made wildlife crime easier. Game rangers and others who fight poaching face organised crime, violence and insider threats at all levels, but unlike in national intelligence there's no central authority to manage clearances and counterintelligence.
3. If you let too many people in a health service see patient records, you get scandals where staff look up data on celebrities. And the existence of big central systems can lead to big scandals, such as where a billion English medical records going back a decade were sold to multiple drug companies.

4. Similar issues arise in social care and in education. There are frequent calls for data sharing, yet attempts to do it in practice cause all sorts of problems.
5. If you let everyone in a bank or an accountancy firm see all the customer records, then an unscrupulous manager could give really good advice to a client by looking at the confidential financial information of that client's competitors.

The basic problem is that if you centralise systems containing sensitive information, you create a more valuable asset and simultaneously give more people access to it. Just as the benefits of networks can scale more than linearly, so can the harms.

A common mitigation is to restrict how much information any individual sees. In our five example cases above:

1. Intelligence services put sensitive information into compartments, so that an analyst working on Argentina might see only the Top Secret reports relating to Argentina and its neighbouring countries;
2. Systems that support game conservation have to do something similar, but access control has to be a federated effort involving multiple conservancies, researchers, rangers and other actors;
3. Many hospital systems limit staff access to the wards or departments where they work, to the extent that this is reasonably practical, and patients have a right to forbid the use of their data outside their direct care. Both are becoming more difficult to implement as systems get more complex and their operators lack the incentive to make the effort;
4. In 2010, the UK parliament closed down a system that was supposed to give doctors, teachers and social workers shared access to all childrens' data, as they realised it was both unsafe and illegal. Yet there's constant pressure for information sharing, and all sorts of issues with schools and other institutions using dubious cloud services;
5. Financial firms have 'Chinese walls' between different parts of the business, and bank staff are now often limited to accessing records for which they have a recent customer authorisation, such as by the customer answering security questions over the phone.

We will discuss these kinds of access control in this chapter. There are several aspects: what sort of technical designs are feasible, the operational costs they impose on the organisation, and – often the critical factor – whether the organisation is motivated to implement and police them properly.

In the last chapter, we discussed multilevel security and saw that it can be hard to get the mechanisms right. In this chapter, we'll see that when we go for fine-grained access controls, it's also hard to get the policy right. Are the groups or roles static or dynamic? Are they set by national policy, by commercial law, by professional ethics, or – as with your group of Facebook friends – by the system's users? What happens when people fight over the rules, or deceive each other? Even where everyone is working for the same boss, different parts of an organisation can have quite different incentives. Some problems can be technically complex but simple in policy terms (wildlife) while others use standard mechanisms but have wicked policy problems (healthcare).

To start with a simpler case, suppose you're trying to set security policy at the tax collection office. Staff have been caught in the past making improper access to the records of celebrities, selling data to outsiders, and leaking income details in alimony cases [189]. How might you go about stopping that?

Your requirement might be to stop staff looking at tax records belonging to a different geographical region, or a different industry – except under strict controls. Thus instead of the information flow control boundaries being horizontal as we saw in the classic civil service model in Figure 10.1, we actually need the boundaries to be mostly vertical, as shown in Figure 10.2.

Lateral information flow controls may be organizational, as when an intelligence agency keeps the names of agents working in one foreign country secret from the department responsible for spying on another. They may be relationship-based, as in a law firm where different clients' affairs, and the clients of different partners, must be kept separate. They may be a mixture of the two, as in medicine where patient confidentiality is based in law on the rights of the patient but may be enforced by limiting access to a particular hospital department or medical practice. They may be volumetric, as when a game conservancy doesn't mind declassifying a handful of leopard photos but doesn't want the poachers to get the whole collection, as that would let them work out the best places to set traps.

Doctors, bankers and spies have all learned that as well as preventing overt information flows, they also have to prevent information leakage through side-channels such as billing data. The mere fact that patient X paid doctor Y suggests that X suffered from something in Y's speciality.

TOP SECRET
SECRET
CONFIDENTIAL
OPEN

Figure 10.1: Multilevel security

A	B	C	D	E
shared data				

Figure 10.2: Multilateral security

10.2 Compartmentation and the lattice model

The United States and its allies restrict access to secret information by *codewords* as well as classifications. These are pre-computer mechanisms for expressing an access control group, such as the codeword *Ultra* in World War 2, which referred to British and American decrypts of messages that had been enciphered using the German Enigma machine. The fact that the Enigma had been broken was worth protecting at almost any cost. So Ultra clearances were given to only a small group of people – in addition to the cryptologists, translators and analysts, the list included the Allied leaders and their senior generals. No-one who had ever held an Ultra clearance could be placed at risk of capture; and the intelligence could never be used in such a way as to let Hitler suspect that his principal cipher had been broken. So when Ultra told of a target, such as an Italian convoy to North Africa, the Allies would send over a plane to 'spot' it an hour or so before the attack. This policy was enforced by special handling rules; for example, Churchill got his Ultra summaries in a special dispatch box to which he had a key but his staff did not. (Ultra security is described by David Kahn [1004] and Gordon Welchman [2011].)

Much the same precautions are in place today. Information whose compromise could expose intelligence sources or methods is marked TS/SCI for 'Top Secret – Special Compartmented Intelligence' and may have one or more codewords. A classification plus a set of codewords gives a *compartment* or security context. So if you have N codewords, you can have 2^N compartments; some intelligence agencies have had over a million of them active. This caution was a reaction to a series of disastrous insider threats. Aldrich Ames, a CIA officer who had accumulated access to a large number of compartments by virtue of long service and seniority, and because he worked in counterintelligence, was able to betray almost the entire US agent network in Russia. The KGB's overseas operations were similarly compromised by Vassily Mitrokhin – an officer who'd become disillusioned with communism and who was sent to work in the archives while waiting for his pension [119]. There was an even earlier precedent in the Walker spy case. There, an attempt to keep naval vessels in compartments just didn't work, as a ship could be sent anywhere without notice, and for a ship to have no local key material was operationally unacceptable. So the US Navy's 800 ships all ended up with the same set of cipher keys, which the Walker family sold to the Russians [878]. You clearly don't want anybody to have access to too much, but how can you do that?

Attempts were made to implement compartments using mandatory access controls, leading to the *lattice model*. Classifications together with codewords form a lattice – a mathematical structure in which any two objects A and B can be in a dominance relation $A > B$ or $B > A$. They don't have to be: A and B could simply be incomparable (but in this case, for the structure to be a lattice, they will have a least upper bound and a greatest lower bound). As an illustration, suppose we have a codeword, say 'Crypto'. Then someone cleared to 'Top Secret' would be entitled to read files classified 'Top Secret' and 'Secret', but would have no access to files classified 'Secret Crypto' unless he also had a crypto clearance. This can be expressed as shown in Figure 10.3.

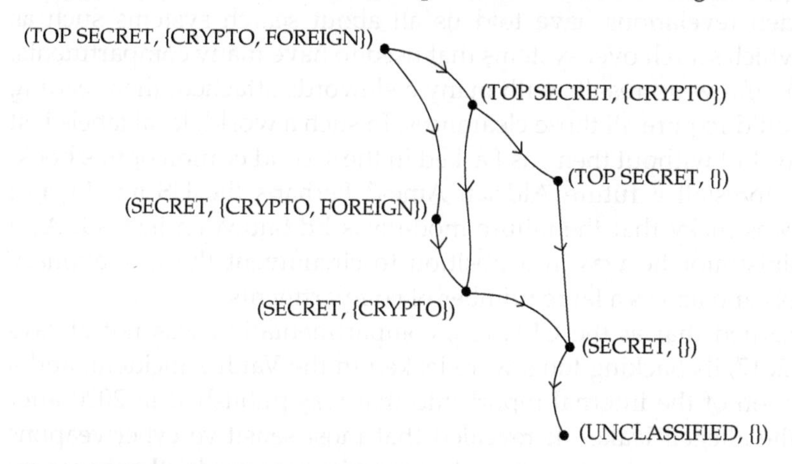

Figure 10.3: A lattice of security labels

As it happens, the Bell-LaPadula model can work more or less unchanged. We still have information flows between High and Low as before, where High is a compartment that dominates Low. If two nodes in a lattice are incompatible — as with 'Top Secret' and 'Secret Crypto' in Figure 10.3 – then there should be no information flow between them at all. In fact, the lattice and Bell-LaPadula models are essentially equivalent, and were developed in parallel. Most products built in the 20th century for the multilevel secure market could be used in compartmented mode. For a fuller history, see the second edition of this book.

In practice, mandatory access control products turned out to be not that effective for compartmentation. It is easy to use such a system to keep data in different compartments separate – just give them incompatible labels ('Secret Tulip', 'Secret Daffodil', 'Secret Crocus', ...). But the operating system has now become an isolation mechanism, rather than a sharing mechanism; and the real problems facing users of intelligence systems have to do with combining data in different compartments, and downgrading it after sanitization. Lattice security models offer little help here.

There was a sea change in the US intelligence community after 9/11. Leaders claimed that the millions of compartments had got in the way of the war on terror, and that better information sharing might have enabled the community to forestall the attack, so President Bush ordered more information sharing within the intelligence community. There was a drive by NSA Director Keith Alexander to 'collect it all', and rather than minimising data collection to maximise it instead and make everything searchable. So nowadays, government systems use mandatory access control to keep the Secret systems apart from the unclassified stuff, and the Top Secret systems from both, using data diodes and other mechanisms that we discussed in the previous chapter. The stuff above Top Secret now appears to be mostly managed using discretionary access controls.

The Snowden revelations have told us all about search systems such as XKeyscore, which search over systems that used to have many compartments. If a search can throw up results with many codewords attached, then reading that result would require all those clearances. In such a world, local labels just get in the way; but without them, as I asked in the second edition of this book, how do you forestall a future Aldrich Ames? Perhaps the US intelligence community was lucky that the failure mode was Ed Snowden instead. As a system administrator he was in a position to circumvent the discretionary access controls and access a large number of compartments.

We later learned that at the CIA, too, compartmentation was not always effective. In 2017, its hacking tools were leaked in the Vault 7 incident, and a redacted version of the internal report into that was published in 2020 after the trial of the alleged leaker. It revealed that most sensitive cyberweapons were not compartmented, users shared sysadmin passwords, there was no user activity monitoring and historical data were available indefinitely. They did not notice the loss until the tools ended up on Wikileaks a year later. In fact, the Joint worldwide Intel Communications System (JWICS), which the intel community uses for Top Secret data, did not yet use two-factor authentication [2054].

There are a few compartments Ed Snowden didn't get to, such as the details of which cryptographic systems the NSA can exploit and how – this was marked 'extremely compartmented information' (ECI). Commercial firms may also have special mechanisms for protecting material such as unpublished financial results; at my university we compile exam papers on machines that are not even attached to the network. In such cases, what's happening may be not so much a compartment as a whole new level above Top Secret.

10.3 Privacy for tigers

People involved in fighting wildlife crime face a fascinating range of problems. The threats range from habitat encroachment through small-scale poaching for bushmeat to organised crime gangs harvesting ivory, rhino horn and tiger body parts on an industrial scale. The gangs may be protected by disaffected communities; even heads of government can be a threat, whether by undermining environmental laws or even by protecting poaching gangs. And often the best poacher is a former ranger.

Even where sovereign threats are absent, public-sector defenders often work for mutually suspicious governments; protecting the snow leopard from poachers involves rangers in India, Pakistan, China, Nepal and Tajikistan, while the illegal ivory trade in East Africa spills over borders from Kenya down to South Africa. And technology is making matters worse; as mobile phone masts have gone up in less developed countries, so has poaching. Its military, insider-threat and political aspects are thus similar in many ways to traditional security and intelligence work. The critical difference is that the defenders are a loose coalition of NGOs, park rangers and law-enforcement agencies. There isn't a central bureaucracy to manage classifications, clearances and counterintelligence.

We had a project with Tanya Berger-Wolf, the leader of Wildbook, an ecological information management system that uses image recognition to match and analyse data collected on animals via tourist photos, camera traps, drones and other data sources [93]. Her idea was that if we could link up the many photographs taken of individual wild animals, we could dramatically improve the science of ecology and population biology, together with the resource management, biodiversity, and conservation decisions that depend on them. Modern image-recognition software makes this feasible, particularly for large animals with distinctive markings, such as elephants, giraffes and zebras. Wildbook is now deployed for over a dozen species at over a dozen locations.

In 2015, two Spanish citizens were arrested in Namibia's Knersvlagte nature reserve with 49 small succulent plants; a search of their hotel room revealed 2000 more, of which hundreds were threatened species. It turned out that they sold these plants through a website, had made numerous collecting trips, and found rare specimens via botanical listservs and social networks. They pleaded guilty, paid a $160,000 fine and were banned from the country for life. It turned out that they had also used another citizen-science website, iSpot [2013]. Incidents like this showed that wildlife aggregators need access control, and are also leading to a rethink among botanists, zoologists and others about open data [1169]. So what should the policy be?

What one needs to protect varies by species and location. With rare plants, we don't want thieves to learn the GPS location of even a single specimen. With endangered Coahuilan box tortoises, we don't want thieves stealing them from the wild and selling them as pets with false documents claiming they were bred in captivity. There, the goal is a public database of all known tortoises, and conservators are busy photographing all the wild specimens in their range, a 360 km^2 region of Mexico. This will enable the US Fish and Wildlife Service to check shipments. With the snow leopard, Wildbook had three years of camera-trap data from one Nepal conservancy, and wanted a security policy to help this scale to five locations in Nepal, India and Pakistan. This is a Red List species with only a few hundred individuals in each of these three countries. In Africa the picture is similar; Wildbook started out by tracking zebras, of which the Grévy's zebra is endangered. Animals cross borders between mutually suspicious countries, and tourists post tagged photos despite leaflets and warnings that they should not geotag [2077]. Some tourists simply don't know how to turn off tagging; some are so dumb they get out of their cars and get eaten. The protection requirements also vary by country; in Namibia the authorities are keen to stop tourists posting tagged photos of rhino, while in Kenya the rhinos all have their own armed guards and the authorities are less bothered.

The new wildlife aggregation sites can use image recognition to identify individual animals and link up sightings into location histories; other machine-learning techniques then aggregate these histories into movement models. We rapidly find sensitive outputs, such as which waterhole has lots of leopards, or which island has lots of breeding whales. This is one of the ways animal privacy differs from the human variety: highly abstracted data are often more sensitive rather than less. In effect, our machine-learning models acquire the 'lore' that an individual ranger might learn after a decade working at a conservancy. As such individuals make the best poachers if they go over to the dark side, we need to keep models that learn their skills out of the poachers' hands. And we need to be smart about sensitivity: it's not enough to protect only the data and movement models of snow leopards, if a poacher can also track them by tracking the mountain goats that they eat.

Our primary protection goal is to not give wildlife criminals actionable intelligence, such as "an animal of species A is more likely to be at location X at time T". In particular, we don't want the citizen-science data platforms we build to make the situation worse. Our starting point is to use an operations-research model as a guide to derive access rules for (a) recent geotagged photos, (b) predictive models and (c) photo collections. And we need to be able to tweak the rules by species and location.

There are four levels of access. The core Wildbook team maintains the software and has operational access to almost everything; we might call this level zero. At level one are the admins of whom there might be maybe 20 per species; as access control is delegated there will be further admins per conservancy or per reserve. At level two are hundreds of people who work for conservancies collecting and contributing data, and who at present are sort-of known to Wildbook; as the system scales up, we need to cope with delegated administration. At level three there are thousands of random citizens who contribute photos and are rewarded with access to non-sensitive outputs. Our threat model is that the set of citizen scientists at level 3 will always include poachers; the set of conservancy staff at level 2 will include a minority who are careless or disloyal; and we hope that the level 1 admins usually won't be in cahoots with poachers.

The focus of our insider threat mitigation is conservancy staff who may be tempted to defect. Given that conservancies often operate in weak states, the threat of eventual detection and imprisonment can seem remote. The most powerful deterrent available is the social pressure from conservancy peers: loyalty to colleagues, a sense of teamwork and a sense of mission. The task is to find a technical means of supporting group cohesion and loyalty. The civil-service approach of having a departmental security officer who looks over everyone's shoulder all the time is not feasible anyway in a financially-stretched conservancy employing ten or twenty people on low wages in less-developed country (LDC) conditions.

The problem is not just one of providing analytics so that we can alarm if a member of staff starts looking at lots of records of rhino, or lots of records at a Serengeti waterhole. We already have admins per species and per location. The problem is motivating people to pay attention and take action. Our core strategy is local public auditability for situational awareness and deterrence, based on two-dimensional transparency. All conservancy staff are in at least one group, relating to the species of interest to them or the park where they work. Staff in the rhino group therefore see who's been looking at rhino records – including individual sighting records and models – while staff working in the Serengeti see who's interested in data and models there. In effect it's a matrix system for level 2 staff; you get to see Serengeti rhinos if you're there or if you're a rhino expert, and in either case you share first-line responsibility for vigilance. Level 1 staff can enrol level 2 staff and make peering arrangements with other conservancies, but their relevant actions are visible to level 2 colleagues. We will have to see how this works in the field.

10.4 Health record privacy

Perhaps the most complex and instructive example of security policies where access control supports privacy is found in clinical information systems. The healthcare sector spends a much larger share of national income than the military in all developed countries, and although hospitals are still less automated, they are catching up fast. The protection of medical information is thus an important case study for us all, with many rich and complex tradeoffs.

Many countries have laws regulating healthcare safety and privacy, which help shape the health IT sector. In the USA, the Health Insurance Portability and Accountability Act (HIPAA) was passed by Congress in 1996 following a number of privacy failures. In one notorious case, a convicted child rapist working as an orthopedic technician at Newton-Wellesley Hospital in Newton, Massachusetts, was caught using a former employee's password to go through the records of 954 patients (mostly young females) to get the phone numbers of girls to whom he then made obscene phone calls [318]. He ended up doing jail time, and the Massachusetts senator Edward Kennedy was one of HIPAA's sponsors.

The HIPAA regulations have changed over time. The first set, issued by the Clinton administration in December 2000, were moderately robust, and based on assessment of the harm done to people who were too afraid to seek treatment in time because of privacy concerns. In the run-up to the rulemaking, HHS estimated that privacy concerns led 586,000 Americans to delay seeking cancer treatment, and over 2 million to delay seeking mental health treatment. Meanwhile, over 1 million simply did not seek treatment for sexually transmitted infections [875]. In 2002, President Bush rewrote and relaxed them to the 'Privacy Rule'; this requires *covered entities* such as hospitals and insurers to maintain certain security standards and procedures for *protected health information* (PHI), with both civil and criminal penalties for violations (although very few penalties were imposed in the first few years). The rule also gave patients the right to demand copies of their records. Covered entities can disclose information to support treatment or payment, but other disclosures require patient consent; this led to complaints by researchers. The privacy rule was followed by further 'administrative simplification' rules in 2006 to promote healthcare systems interoperability. This got a further boost when President Obama's stimulus bill allocated billions of dollars to health IT, and slightly increased the penalties for privacy violations; in 2013 his administration extended the rules to the business associates of covered entities. But grumbling continues. Health privacy advocates note that the regime empowered health data holders to freely and secretly aggregate and broker protected health information, while hospitals complain that it adds to their costs and patient advocates have been complaining for over a decade that it's often used by hospital staff as an excuse to be unhelpful – such as by preventing people tracing injured relatives [828]. Although HIPAA regulation gives much less privacy than in Europe, it is still the main driver for information security in healthcare, which accounts for over 10% of the U.S. economy. Another driver is local market effects: in the USA, for example, systems are driven to some extent by the need to generate billing records, and the market is also concentrated with Epic having a 29% market share for electronic medical record systems in 2019 while Cerner had 26% [1353].

In Europe, data-protection law sets real boundaries. In 1995, the UK government attempted to centralise all medical records, which led to a confrontation with the doctors' professional body, the British Medical Association (BMA). The BMA hired me to devise a policy for safety and privacy of clinical information, which I'll discuss later in this chapter. The evolution of medical privacy over the 25 years since is a valuable case study; it's remarkable how little the issues have changed despite the huge changes in technology.

Debates about the safety and privacy tradeoffs involved with medical information started around this time in other European countries too. The Germans put summary data such as current prescriptions and allergies on the medical insurance card that residents carry; other countries held back, reasoning that if emergency data are moved from a human-readable MedAlert bracelet to a smartcard, this could endanger patients who fall ill on an airplane or a foreign holiday. There was a series of scandals in which early centralised systems were used to get information on celebrities. There were also sharp debates about whether people could stop their records being used in research, whether out of privacy concerns or for religious reasons – for example, a Catholic woman might want to forbid her gynaecological records being sold to a drug company doing research on abortion pills.

European law around consent and access to records was clarified in 2010 by the European Court of Human Rights in the case I v Finland. The complainant was a nurse at a Finnish hospital, and also HIV-positive. Word of her condition spread among colleagues, and her contract was not renewed. The hospital's access controls were not sufficient to prevent colleagues accessing her record, and its audit trail was not sufficient to determine who had compromised her privacy. The court's view was that health care staff who are not involved in the care of a patient must be unable to access that patient's electronic medical record: "What is required in this connection is practical and effective protection to exclude any possibility of unauthorised access occurring in the first place." This judgment became final in 2010, and since then health providers have been supposed to design their systems so that patients can opt out effectively from secondary uses of their data.

10.4.1 The threat model

The appropriate context to study health IT threats is not privacy alone, but safety and privacy together. The main objective is safety, and privacy is often subordinate. The two are also intertwined, though in many ways.

There are various hazards with medical systems, most notably safety usability failures, which are reckoned to kill about as many people as road traffic accidents. I will discuss these issues in the chapter on Assurance and Sustainability. They interact directly with security; vulnerabilities are particularly likely to result in the FDA mandating recalls of products such as infusion pumps. The public are much more sensitive to safety issues if they have a security angle; we have much less tolerance of hostile action than of impersonal risk.

A second hazard is that loss of confidence in medical privacy causes people to avoid treatment, or to seek it too late.

1. The most comprehensive data were collected by the US Department of Health and Human Services prior to the HIPAA rulemaking under President Clinton. HHS estimated that privacy concerns led 586,000 Americans to delay seeking cancer treatment, and over 2 million to

delay seeking mental health treatment. Meanwhile, over 1 million simply did not seek treatment for sexually transmitted infections [875];

2. The Rand corporation found that over 150,000 soldiers who served in Iraq and Afghanistan failed to seek treatment for post-traumatic stress disorder (PTSD), which is believed to contribute to the suicide rate among veterans being about double that of comparable civilians – a significant barrier being access to confidential treatment [1864];
3. The most authoritative literature review concluded that many patients, particularly teenagers, gay men and prostitutes, withheld information or simply failed to seek treatment because of confidentiality concerns. Anonymised HIV testing more than doubled the testing rate among gay men [1654].

So poor privacy is a safety issue, as well as a critical factor in providing equal healthcare access to a range of citizens, from veterans to at-risk and marginalised groups. The main privacy threat comes from insiders, with a mix of negligence and malice, in roughly three categories:

1. There are targeted attacks on specific individuals, ranging from creepy doctors looking up the records of a date on a hospital computer, to journalists stalking a politician or celebrity. These cause harm to individuals directly;
2. There are bulk attacks, as where governments or hospitals sell millions of records to a drug company, sometimes covertly and sometimes with the claim that the records have been 'anonymised' and are thus no longer personal health information;
3. Most of the reported breaches are accidents, for example where a doctor leaves a laptop on a train, or when a misconfigured cloud server leaves millions of people's records online [768]. These are reported at five times the rate of breaches at private firms, as healthcare providers have a reporting duty. Sometimes accidental leaks lead to opportunistic attacks.

The resulting press coverage, which is mostly of bulk attacks and accidents, causes many to fear for the privacy of their health data, although they may not be directly at risk. The bulk attacks also offend many people's sense of justice, violate their autonomy and agency, and undermine trust in the system.

So how big is the direct risk? And how much of the risk is due to technology? As things get centralised, we hit a fundamental scaling problem. The likelihood that a resource will be abused depends on its value and on the number of people with access to it. Aggregating personal information into large databases increases both these risk factors at the same time. Over the past 25 years, we've moved from a world in which each doctor's receptionist had access to maybe 5,000 patients' records in a paper library or on the practice PC, to one in which the records of thousands of medical practices are hosted on common platforms. Some shared systems give access to data on many patients and have been abused. This was already a concern 25 years ago as people started building centralised systems to support emergency care, billing and research, and it has become a reality since. Even local systems can expose data at scale: a large district hospital is likely to have records on over a million former patients. And privacy issues aren't limited to organizations that treat patients directly: some of the largest collections of personal health information are in the hands of health insurers and research organizations.

To prevent abuses scaling, lateral information flow controls are needed. Early hospital systems that gave all staff access to all records led to a number of privacy incidents, of which the most notable was the one that led to the I v Finland judgment of the European court; but there were similar incidents in the UK going back to the mid-1990s. All sorts of ad hoc privacy mechanisms had been tried, but by the mid-1990s we felt the need for a proper access control policy, thought through from first principles and driven by a realistic model of the threats.

10.4.2 The BMA security policy

By 1995, most medical practices had computer systems to keep records; the suppliers were small firms that had often been started by doctors whose hobby was computing rather than golf or yachting, and they were attuned to doctors' practical needs. Hospitals had central administrative systems to take care of billing, and some were moving records from paper to computers. There was pressure from the government, which pays for about 90% of medical care in Britain through the National Health Service; officials believed that if they had access to all the information, they could manage things better, and this caused tension with doctors who cared about professional autonomy. One of the last things done by Margaret Thatcher's government, in 1991, had been to create an 'internal market' in the health service where regional commissioners act like insurers and hospitals bill them for treatments; implementing this was a work in progress, both messy and contentious. So the Department of Health announced that it wanted to centralise all medical records. The Internet boom had just started, and medics were starting to send information around by private email; enthusiasts were starting to build systems to get test results electronically from hospitals to medical practices. The BMA asked whether personal health information should be encrypted on networks, but the government refused to even consider this (the crypto wars were getting underway; see 26.2.7.3 for that story). This was the last straw; the BMA realised they'd better get an expert and asked me what their security policy should be. I worked with their staff and members to develop one.

We rapidly hit a problem. The government strategy assumed a single electronic patient record (EPR) that would follow the patient around from conception to autopsy, rather than the traditional system of having different records on the same patient at different hospitals and doctors' offices, with information flowing between them in the form of referral and discharge letters. An attempt to devise a security policy for the EPR that would observe existing ethical norms became unmanageably complex [822], with over 60 rules. Different people have access to your record at different stages of your life; your birth record is also part of your mother's record, your record while you're in the army or in jail might belong to the government, and when you get treatment for a sexually transmitted disease you may have the right to keep that completely private.

The Department of Health next proposed a multilevel security policy: sexually transmitted diseases would be at a level corresponding to Secret, normal patient records at Confidential and administrative data such as drug prescriptions and invoices at Restricted. But this was obviously a non-starter. For example, how should a prescription for anti-retroviral drugs be classified? As it's a prescription, it should be Restricted; but as it identifies a person as HIV positive, it should be Secret. It was wrong in all sorts of other ways too; some people with HIV are open about their condition while others with minor conditions are very sensitive about them. Sensitivity is a matter for the patient to decide, not the Prime Minister. Patient consent is central: records can only be shared with third parties if the patient agrees, or in a limited range of legal exceptions, such as contact tracing for infectious diseases like TB.

Medical colleagues and I realised that we needed a security context with finer granularity than a lifetime record, so we decided to let existing law and practice set the granularity, then build the policy on that. We defined a record as the maximum set of facts to which the same people have access: patient + doctor, patient + doctor plus surgery staff, patient + patient's mother + doctor + staff, and so on. So a patient will usually have more than one record, and this offended the EPR advocates.

A really hard problem was the secondary use of records. In the old days, this meant a researcher or clinical auditor sitting in the library of a hospital or medical practice, patiently collecting statistics; consent consisted of a notice in the waiting room saying something like 'We use our records in medical research to improve care for all; if you don't want your records used in this way, please speak to your doctor.' By 1995, we'd already seen one company offering subsidised computers to General Practitioners (GPs)[1] in return for allowing remote queries by drug companies to return supposedly anonymous data.

[1]Britain's GPs are the equivalent of family doctors in the USA; they have historically acted as gatekeepers to the system and as custodians of each patient's lifetime medical record. They also act as the patient's advocate and join up care between medical practice, hospital and community. This helps keeps healthcare costs down in the UK, compared with the USA.

The goals of the BMA security policy were therefore to enforce the principle of consent, and to prevent too many people getting access to too many records. It did not try to do anything new, but merely to codify existing best practice, and to boil it down into a page of text that everyone – doctor, engineer or administrator – could understand.

Starting from these principles and insights, we proposed a policy of nine principles.

1. Access control: each identifiable clinical record shall be marked with an access control list naming the people who may read it and append data to it.
2. Record opening: a clinician may open a record with herself and the patient on the access control list. Where a patient has been referred, she may open a record with herself, the patient and the referring clinician(s) on the access control list.
3. Control: One of the clinicians on the access control list must be marked as being responsible. Only she may alter the access control list, and she may only add other health care professionals to it.
4. Consent and notification: the responsible clinician must notify the patient of the names on his record's access control list when it is opened, of all subsequent additions, and whenever responsibility is transferred. His consent must also be obtained, except in emergency or in the case of statutory exemptions.
5. Persistence: no-one shall have the ability to delete clinical information until the appropriate time period has expired.
6. Attribution: all accesses to clinical records shall be marked on the record with the subject's name, as well as the date and time. An audit trail must also be kept of all deletions.
7. Information flow: Information derived from record A may be appended to record B if and only if B's access control list is contained in A's.
8. Aggregation control: there shall be effective measures to prevent the aggregation of personal health information. In particular, patients must receive special notification if any person whom it is proposed to add to their access control list already has access to personal health information on a large number of people.
9. Trusted computing base: computer systems that handle personal health information shall have a subsystem that enforces the above principles in an effective way. Its effectiveness shall be subject to evaluation by independent experts.

From the technical viewpoint, this policy is strictly more expressive than the Bell-LaPadula model of the last chapter, as it contains an information flow control mechanism in principle 7, but also contains state. In fact, it takes compartmentation to the logical limit, as there are more compartments than patients. A discussion for a technical audience can be found at [60]. The full policy dealt with a lot more issues, such as access to records by vulnerable patients who might be coerced [59].

Similar policies were developed by other medical bodies including the Swedish and German medical associations; the Health Informatics Association of Canada, and an EU project (these are surveyed in [1079]). The BMA model was adopted by the Union of European Medical Organisations (UEMO) in 1996, and feedback from public consultation on the policy can be found in [61].

10.4.3 First practical steps

Feedback from the field came from a pilot implementation in a medical practice [871], which was positive, and from a hospital system developed in Hastings, which controlled access using a mixture of roles and capabilities, rather than the ACLs in which the BMA model was expressed. It turned out that the practical way to do access control at hospital scale was by rules such as 'a ward nurse can see the records of all patients who have within the previous 90 days been on her ward', 'a junior doctor can see the records of all patients who have been treated in her department', and 'a senior doctor can see the records of all patients, but if she accesses the record of a patient who has never been treated in her department, then the senior doctor responsible for that patient's care will be notified'[2].

The technical lessons learned are discussed in [535, 536, 871]. With hindsight, the BMA model was a lossless compression of what doctors said they did while the role-based model was a slightly lossy version but which implemented what hospitals do in practice and worked well in that context. One of the BMA rules, though, created difficulty in both contexts: the desire for a small trusted computing base. GPs ended up having to trust all the application code that they got from their suppliers, and while they could influence its evolution, there was no useful trusted subset. The hospital records system was much worse: it had to rely on the patient administrative system (PAS) to tell it which patients, and which nurses, are on which ward. The PAS was flaky and often down, so it wasn't acceptable to make a safety-critical system depend on it. The next iteration was to give each hospital staff member a smartcard containing credentials for their departments or wards.

[2]The Hastings system was initially designed independently of the BMA project. When we learned of each other we were surprised at how much our approaches coincided, and reassured that we had captured the profession's expectations in a reasonably consistent way.

The policy response from the Department of Health was to set up a committee of inquiry under Dame Fiona Caldicott. She acknowledged that some 60 established flows of information within the NHS were unlawful, and recommended the appointment of a responsible privacy officer in each healthcare organisation [369]. This was at least a start, but it created a moral hazard: while the privacy officer, typically a senior nurse, was blamed when things went wrong, the actual policy was set by ministers – leading to the classic security-economics gotcha we discussed in Chapter 8, of Bob guarding the system while Alice pays the cost of failure. Anyway, the government changed, and the new administration of Tony Blair went for a legal rather than a technical fix – with a data-protection law that allowed data controllers to pretend that data were anonymous so long as they themselves could not re-identify them, even if others could re-identify them by matching them with other data[3]. We will discuss the limits of anonymisation in the following chapter.

10.4.4 What actually goes wrong

In his second term as Prime Minister, Tony Blair announced a £6bn plan to modernise health service computing in England. The National Programme for IT (NPfIT), as it came to be known, turned out to be the world's most expensive civilian IT disaster. After David Cameron came to power in 2010, an inquiry from the National Audit Office noted of a total expenditure of about £10bn, some £2bn spent on broadband networking and digital X-ray imaging resulted in largely working systems, while the rest didn't give value for money, and the core aim that every patient should have an electronic care record would not be achieved [1392]. Cameron formally killed the project, but its effects continued for years because of entrenched supplier contracts, and health IT was held up for a decade [1562].

NPfIT had called for all hospital systems to be replaced during 2004–2010 with standard ones, to give each NHS patient a single electronic care record. The security policy had three main mechanisms.

1. There are role-based access controls like those pioneered at Hastings.
2. In order to access patient data, a staff member also needs a *legitimate relationship*. This abstracts the Hastings idea of 'her department'.
3. There was a plan that patients would be able to seal certain parts of their records, making them visible only to a particular care team. However, the providers never got round to implementing this. It wasn't

[3]The UK law was supposed to transpose the EU Data Protection Directive (95/46/EC) into UK law to provide a level playing field on privacy; this loophole was one of several that allowed UK firms a lot of wriggle room, annoying the French and Germans [597]. The EU eventually pushed through the stricter General Data Protection Regulation (2016/679).

> consistent with the doctrine of a single electronic health record, which had been repeated so often by ministers that it had become an article of religious faith. As late as 2007, Parliament's Health Committee noted that suppliers hadn't even got a specification yet [927].

As a result, patients receiving outpatient psychiatric care at a hospital found that the receptionist could see their case notes. Formerly, the notes were kept in paper in the psychiatrist's filing cabinet; all the receptionist got to know was that Mrs Smith was seen once a month by Dr Jones. But now the receptionist role had to be given access to patient records so that they could see and amend administrative data such as appointment times; and everyone working reception in the hospital wing where Dr Jones had his office had a legitimate relationship. So they all got access to everything. This illustrates why the doctrine of a single record with a single security context per patient was a bad idea. Thanks to project mismanagement, less than ten percent of England's hospitals actually installed these systems, though the doctrine of 'RBAC + relationship' has affected others since. It now looks like the failure to support multiple security contexts per patient is about to become an issue in the USA as firms start pushing health apps supported by the FHIR standard, to which I'll return in section 10.4.5.

10.4.4.1 Emergency care

The next thing to go wrong was emergency medical records. One of the stories used by politicians to sell NPfIT had been 'Suppose you fall ill in Aberdeen and the hospital wants access to your records in London …'. This was, and remains, bogus. Paramedics and emergency-room physicians are trained to treat what they see, and assume nothing; the idea that they'd rely on a computer to tell the blood group of an unconscious patient is simply daft. But policy was policy, and in Scotland the government created an 'emergency care record' of prescriptions and allergies that is kept on a central database for use by emergency room clinicians, paramedics and the operators of out-of-hours medical helpline services. Sensitive information about 2.5 million people was made available to tens of thousands of people, and the inevitable happened; one doctor of Queen Margaret Hospital in Dunfermline was arrested and charged for browsing the health records of then Prime Minister Gordon Brown, First Minister Alex Salmond and various sports and TV personalities. The case was eventually dropped as 'not in the public interest' to prosecute [1745]. Patients had been offered the right to opt out of this system, but it was a very odd opt-out: if you did nothing, your data were collected from your GP and made available to the Department of Health in Edinburgh and also to the ambulance service. If you opted out, your data were still collected from your GP and made available to the Department of Health; they just weren't shared with the ambulance crew.

This was also policy in England where it was called 'consent-to-view': the state would collect everything and show users only what they were allowed to see. Everybody's records would be online, and doctors would only be allowed to look at them if they claimed the patient had consented. Officials assured Parliament that this was the only practical way to build NPfIT; they described this as 'an electronic version of the status quo' [927]. The English emergency system, the Summary Care Record (SCR), also has sensitive data on most citizens, is widely accessible, but is little used; if you end up in an ambulance, they'll take a medical history from you en route to hospital, just as they always have[4]. Something similar also happened in the Netherlands, where a database of citizens' medical insurance details ended up being accessible not just by doctors and pharmacists but alternative healers and even taxi firms, with entirely predictable results [187].

10.4.4.2 Resilience

The move to centralised systems typically makes failures rarer but larger, and health systems are no exception. The NPfIT's only real achievement was to standardise all X-ray imaging in England using digital machines and cloud storage. An early warning of fragility came on 11th December 2005, when a leak of 250,000 litres of petrol at the Buncefield oil storage depot formed a vapour cloud and detonated – the largest peacetime explosion in Europe. Oil companies were later fined millions of pounds for safety breaches. Our local hospital lost X-ray service as both the primary and backup network connections to the cloud service passed nearby. A further warning came when the Wannacry worm infected machines at another nearby hospital in 2017; managers foolishly closed down the network, in the hope of preventing further infection, and then found that they had to close the emergency room and send patients elsewhere. With no network they could do no X-rays (and get no pathology test results either, even from the hospital's own lab). There have been further incidents of hospitals closed by ransomware since, particularly in the USA.

10.4.4.3 Secondary uses

Databases relating to payment usually don't allow a real opt-out, and the UK example is the Hospital Episode Statistics (HES) database, which collects bills sent by hospitals to the commissioning bodies that pay them, and has

[4]In the coronavirus crisis, the SCR was 'enriched' by adding a lot of data from the GP record, making it available to planners, and making it opt-out by default. It's still not clear that any worthwhile use has been made of it.

extensive information on every state-funded hospital visit and test in England and Wales since 1998 – about a billion records in total[5]. These records have proved impossible to protect, not just because anonymisation of complete records is impractical but because of the intense political pressure for access by researchers. More and more people had got access under the 1997–2010 Labour government; and after David Cameron became Prime Minister in 2010, the floodgates opened. Cameron hired a 'transparency tsar' who'd previously run a health IT business, and announced 'Open Data measures' in 2011 which had the goal that every NHS patient would be a research patient, in order to make Britain a world leader in pharmaceutical research. Officials claimed that 'All necessary safeguards would be in place to ensure protection of patients' details – the data will be anonymised and the process will be carefully and robustly regulated' [1811]. Anonymisation meant that your personal details were redacted down to your postcode and date of birth; this is quite inadequate, as we'll discuss in the next chapter.

In 2013 the government announced that records would also be harvested from GP systems; GPs were given eight weeks to inform their patients of the impending upload. This caused enough disquiet that privacy campaigners, GPs and others got together to set up a medical privacy campaign group, `medConfidential.org`. The initial impetus was consent, and in particular that patients who tried to exercise their European-law rights to opt out of such systems have ended up being ignored or even de-registered from the health service. Campaigners pushed for the government to obey the newly clarified European law on consent; the government wriggled and evaded. How could doctors' bonuses be calculated if some of their records could not be uploaded?

In January 2014, some digging revealed that the HES data had been sold to over 1000 drug companies, universities and others round the world – often in the form of a set of DVDs containing a billion episodes going back to 1998. A medic revealed that the data had appeared online; it was quickly taken down [1803]. This 'care.data' scandal, as it became known after the proposal to collect all the GP data, went mainstream. Surveys show that most people are prepared to let their data be used in academic research, so long as they're asked; but most are not prepared to share it with for-profit researchers, and most object to having it simply taken. On inspection, it turned out to be easy to re-identify patients, even if their postcode and date of birth had not been included in the dataset; we'll discuss the technical details in the following

[5]HES is advertised as 'a data warehouse containing details of all admissions, outpatient appointments and A and E attendances at NHS hospitals in England' including private and foreign patients treated at NHS hospitals, and treatments at private hospitals for which the NHS pays. It is now claimed that 'We apply a strict statistical disclosure control in accordance with the NHS Digital protocol, to all published HES data. This suppresses small numbers to stop people identifying themselves and others, to ensure that patient confidentiality is maintained.'. See `https://digital.nhs.uk/data-and-information/data-tools-and-services/data-services/hospital-episode-statistics`.

chapter. There was a financial scandal: despite ministers talking of the huge value of research data to the health service, the data had been sold on a cost-recovery basis, for a few thousand dollars a set. There was also an issue of jurisdiction: it turned out that PA Consulting had loaded the HES data to a Google cloud system for resale to its clients, as at 20Gb it was too big for Excel.

But hang on, said members of parliament, how can that be legal? Google didn't have any data centres in the UK, and there are all sorts of regulations against taking NHS data overseas [1576]. Also, officials had promised that UK data wouldn't be sold overseas, yet they were advertised in the USA; and it turned out that even the regulator, the Medicines and Healthcare Products Regulatory Agency (MHRA)[6], had been selling personal data [1648]. Ministers went into damage-containment mode; the privacy regulator was persuaded to believe that the exported data were anonymous enough, and the UK website of a firm claiming to be able to identify patients from these records was taken offline [1577]. Ministers talked of lessons being learned, and a review of all data releases was commissioned; but when this appeared, it only investigated whether internal guidelines had been followed, not whether they were legal [1498].

UK health privacy scandals have continued at the rate of about once a year since then:

- In 2015, Google Deepmind obtained a copy of all the 1.6m patient records from the Royal Free Hospital in London, claiming that it wanted to develop an app to detect acute kidney injury (it took all the records, not just those of kidney patients). Patient consent was not sought, the deal was later found to be unlawful, and when the app was developed using US data obtained from the VA instead, it was unimpressive [1544]. The Information Commissioner reprimanded the hospital but failed to order Google Deepmind to delete the data. Eventually Deepmind transferred the records to Google, contrary to previous assurances [1283].
- Also in 2015, a tabloid newspaper discovered the online pharmacy Pharmacy2U selling thousands of patients' details to predatory marketers, including lottery fraudsters who targeted unwell elderly men and a healthcare supplement vendor that had already been sanctioned for misleading advertising and unauthorised health claims [662]. The firm was fined £130,000 and its commercial director suspended by the General Pharmaceutical Council. A major backer, the UK's largest GP software supplier EMIS, sold its shareholding.

[6]The MHRA had also been a lot less keen about making data about adverse clinical trial results available to medics who wanted it. The essence of the complaint against it was that it acted more in the interests of the drug companies and medical device makers rather than in the interest of patients, becoming in effect a captured regulator.

- SCR data were also sold to Boots, a high-street pharmacy chain that pressures its staff to market aggressively, leading to regulatory hearings [407].
- In 2017, leading GP software supplier TPP which has 6,000 customers including 2,700 GP practices – a third of all practices in England, with records on 26 million patients – switched on 'enhanced data sharing' so that records could be seen by doctors at local hospitals. It was soon noticed that records could be seen at all other practices that were TPP customers; GPs had not been aware of this [577]. The records were also visible to TPP customers in care homes, prisons and immigration detention centres. TPP failed to answer questions about whether any of its customers in India, China and the UAE had access.
- In 2018, the records of all 180,000 lung cancer patients diagnosed in England from 2008-2013 were given to a tobacco company by Public Health England, which had claimed that cancer registry data would only be sold for a 'medical purpose'.

Standard central systems do have real advantages. In the USA, the Veterans' Administration runs such systems for its hospital network; after Hurricane Katrina, veterans from Louisiana who'd ended up as refugees in Texas or Florida, or even Minnesota, could go straight to local VA hospitals and find their notes there at the doctor's fingertips, when patients of many other hospitals in New Orleans lost their notes altogether.

But there have also been controversies in the USA. In November 2019, it emerged that Google had done an outsourcing deal to process the medical records of 50 million Americans on behalf of Ascension, and a whistleblower revealed that the data were not even being lightly de-identified; staff at both Google and Ascension had full access to patient data. A federal inquiry was started into whether the arrangement was HIPAA compliant [122].

Google also got VA data from the USA, which it used in place of the London data once the ICO ruled against it there. With a few such exceptions in egregious cases, policymakers find it hard to resist lobbying from marketers and researchers for access. The EU General Data Protection Regulation has a convenient exemption for 'research', put there by the pharma lobby, which doesn't exclude market research. And, of course, law enforcement and intelligence agencies demand access. This started off in the 1990s with the collection of opiate prescribing records and has greatly expanded.

10.4.5 Confidentiality – the future

What can we say about healthcare privacy now, almost a quarter of a century after the BMA policy? Well, some things change, but a surprising number of things stay the same. We noted in Chapter 2 that the cybercrime ecosystem had not been changed much by the huge technological changes of the past decade; much the same holds for the health privacy ecosystem. The move to cloud-based medical records is hard to resist as it saves individual care providers the trouble and expense of maintaining servers and backups. The move to ever more complex outsourcing also seems inexorable; we can expect that specialist firms will handle X-ray images, pathology tests and the like, while subject specialists will support care for specific diseases such as diabetes.

Since 2014, there has emerged a draft standard for Fast Healthcare Interoperability Resources (FHIR, pronounced 'fire'), which describes how two systems talk to each other once you've allowed them to. The security engineering is outside this standard; Deepmind's smartphone apps, for example, use OAuth 2. FHIR has been mandated in the NHS from 2021. In America, new federal information-sharing rules may require providers to send your record to third-party apps, like Apple's Health Records, after you have authorized the data exchange. The details alarm doctors who note that once you do that you'll be open to serious abuse, as the data will fall outside HIPAA and the apps can sell it off as they please. Data such as substance abuse could not only limit access to insurance but even be demanded by employers and others. The government responds that opening up health data will enable people to manage their care better and understand costs, while opening the sector up to competitive innovation [1818]. Quite apart from whether people would trust Microsoft, Amazon and Google with their health data, you have to share it all or not at all; there is no provision for finer-grained access control than your whole lifetime record. The last 25 years' experience suggests that this will not be satisfactory.

In the UK, the medical professors and drug companies are having another push to collect all the GP data, talking about three big new health industries, based on medical records, AI and genomics. Research policy is that while R&D should be 2% of GDP, only a third of that should be from the state and the rest from industry. It was announced in 2019 that five hospitals had done deals with a pharmaceutical company run by a former minister: they supply 'anonymised' data for research in return for an equity stake [500]. On the other hand, the UK's biggest medical-research charity, the Wellcome Trust, is predicting that as many as 40% of patients might opt out of having their data being used in research if there's another scandal on the scale of care.data. Certainly the data show that while about 80% of people trust doctors with their health data, this falls to just over 50% for health insurers and pharmacies, around 40% for researchers, 20% for drug companies and 10% for tech [1102]. How can we navigate this thicket?

The view of the UK campaign group medConfidential is that three things are needed.

1. First, to enable us to enforce our rights under European law, there must be real patient consent. This means a single opt-out from secondary uses, rather than the current Facebook-like approach of changing the opt-out

mechanisms every year or two and forcing people to opt out all over again.

2. Second, it should not be the patient's job to defend their data, so both the privacy architecture and the security engineering must be safe by default. People must not be quietly opted in to secondary data uses that are misdescribed or not mentioned at all; and there must be appropriate security mechanisms about which patients are told the truth, particularly when they fail.
3. Third, there must still be real transparency. At present my GP can see who has had access to my record, but I want to see too. If tens of millions of patients can audit access, then even if only a few hundred thousand actually do so, this should deter most of the abuse.

History should have taught us that it's best to be honest with patients. In the UK we've wasted 20 years: a decade with NPfIT and a further decade trying to sell data while pretending not to. Yet hospitals that set out to get positive consent for the use of data in research get it 70–80% of the time, and we have had large collaborative research projects such as UK Biobank where 500,000 people not only consented in 2006–10 to lifetime monitoring but also provided blood samples, so that researchers could sequence their DNA and correlate that with health outcomes. There's a further research database of 100,000 genomes collected from other patients who consented.

Another development is the OpenSAFELY collaboration, which has been pioneering rapid analysis of the Covid-19 epidemic by working in situ with the live medical records held by TPP, a large provider of cloud electronic health record services that supports about 40% of GPs in England. They imported a list of death notifications and were able to analyse mortality not just by age and sex, as in official statistics, but by social deprivation, race, smoking history, body mass index and specific comorbidities, establishing risk factors over more than 17 million patients and over 6,000 deaths over February to April 2020 [2029]. They were first to establish, for example, that the excess mortality observed in black and Asian patients was significantly greater than could be explained by social deprivation alone. The speed and scale of this study were unprecedented and make the case for taking ethically-approved queries directly to the live data and taking away only statistics, rather than abstracting anonymised subsets for offsite use that still carry privacy hazards (as we'll discuss at length in the next chapter). The privacy risks may be more controllable as there are fewer copies of the data and as patient opt-outs can be enforced. And although this might be seen as a 'new' research technique, enabled by the emergence of cloud-based medical records, it's actually a very old technique. In the days before computers, observational epidemiology meant sitting in the library of a hospital or surgery, sifting through thousands of paper records, looking for diagnoses of interest, and departing after weeks or months of work with statistical tables rather than with identifiable personal information.

10.4.6 Ethics

So researchers working with health data had better pay attention to ethics. In 2014–5, the Nuffield Bioethics Council commissioned a dozen of us from a variety of backgrounds in tech, genetics, medicine, insurance and ethics to write a detailed report on what happens to medical ethics in a world of cloud-based medical records and pervasive genomics [1603]. Historically, it was a series of ethical abuses in medical research that drove the development of research ethics more generally.

- In the Tuskegee syphilis experiment, US doctors studied the progression of untreated syphilis in rural African-American men who were led to believe they were getting free healthcare. The experiment ran from 1932 to 1972, but even after effective antibiotic treatments became available in 1947, infected men were not treated.
- Dr Karl Brandt was Hitler's personal physician, and ran a euthanasia program from 1939. He also did human experiments on prisoners of war and the civilians of occupied countries without their consent, as did his colleague Dr Josef Mengele who experimented on twins at Birkenau from 1943–5; subjects were often killed and dissected afterwards. Brandt was convicted at the Nuremberg trials and hanged in 1948.
- In the UK Alder Hey scandal, the press discovered that pathologists were routinely saving 'interesting' body samples from patients living and dead, without any kind of consent. Parents discovered that body parts of their dead children had been kept without their knowledge. This did serious damage to public trust and the consequences impaired research in pathology in the UK. There was a similar scandal in Ireland.

The Nazi doctors' trial led to the Nuremberg code in 1948, under which the voluntary and informed consent of subjects is essential. The subject must have the freedom to choose, without deceit or duress, and must be able to exit from the experiment at any time. This led later to the Declaration of Helsinki on ethics in medical research in 1964, which was revised in 1975 after Tuskegee to incorporate the need for an independent institutional review board or ethics committee, and subsequently in 1983, 1989, 1996, 2000 and 2008. The Declaration is managed by the World Medical Association and is ethically binding on physicians. The Declaration upholds the right of patients to make informed decisions about participation in research, both initially and afterwards.

Until about the mid-1990s, the main ethical debates were related to drug trials: was it wrong to give placebos to HIV sufferers once effective anti-retroviral drugs existed? And was it ethical to test drugs in less developed countries if their citizens or health services could not afford them? Since then, the growing issues have been informational: is it ethical to use whole populations as subjects in observational epidemiology and research, without giving them a right to opt out? And what are the ethical issues arising from low-cost sequencing of the human genome?

After spending a year considering in detail the history and issues I've summarised in this section, we concluded that, when working in such a complex and fast-moving ethical field, that holds a lot of promise but is also riven with vested interests and political chicanery, it's not enough for researchers to hide behind the law or just act in accordance with this year's government guidelines. A morally reasonable set of expectations should embody four principles. To quote the report:

1. The set of expectations about how data will be used in a data initiative should be grounded in the principle of respect for persons. This includes recognition of a person's profound moral interest in controlling others' access to and disclosure of information relating to them held in circumstances they regard as confidential.
2. The set of expectations about how data will be used in a data initiative should be determined with regard to established human rights. This will include limitations on the power of states and others to interfere with the privacy of individual citizens in the public interest (including to protect the interests of others).
3. The set of expectations about how data will be used (or re-used) in a data initiative, and the appropriate measures and procedures for ensuring that those expectations are met, should be determined with the participation of people with morally relevant interests. This participation should involve giving and receiving a public account of the reasons for establishing, conducting and participating in the initiative in a form that is accepted as reasonable by all. Where it is not feasible to engage all those with relevant interests – which will often be the case in practice – the full range of values and interests should be fairly represented.
4. A data initiative should be subject to effective systems of governance and accountability that are themselves morally justified. This should include both structures of accountability that invoke legitimate judicial and political authority, and social accountability arising from engagement of people in a society. Maintaining effective accountability must include effective measures for communicating expectations and failures of governance, execution and control to people affected and to the society more widely.

In short, you have to treat people as ends rather than means, and not just treat their data as an industrial raw material; you have to tell people in advance what you're doing, and if you can't tell everyone you must tell a good sample, not just some friends on your ethics committee; you have to obey the law, including the difficult bits of human-rights law; and you have to tell people what you've done afterwards – which includes public breach disclosure [1603]. Beware, though, that there is a lot of moral hazard around ethics processes; big firms who abuse data routinely set up ethics bodies to excuse what they do. I'll return to this ethics washing in section 11.4.4.

Since then we have used this model to guide our own research in cybercrime, which is similar in a number of ways. For example, we may sometimes use data that may be of questionable origin and from which it may be possible to draw inferences about living people who did not give consent. However, in many cases, an ethical case for an investigation can be made but the processes for taking and recording such decisions need careful thought. Transparency is vital; we put all the papers we write on our website, so everyone can see what's been done with the data.

The same principles may be a good starting point for thinking about the ethics of machine learning. Many if not most of the AI ethics controversies in the real world so far have been around health data.

10.4.7 Social care and education

The same issues have spilled over into education and social care. While building the NHS national programme for IT, the UK government also started to build a national database of all children, for child-protection and welfare purposes, containing a list of all professionals with which each child has contact. In 2006, the UK Information Commissioner asked a group of us to study the safety and privacy aspects of this. Now the fact that child X is registered with family doctor Y may be innocuous, but a child's registration with a social work department is different; teachers have lower expectations of children whom they know to have been in contact with social workers. And a record of contact with drug-addiction services or prostitution services is highly stigmatizing. We concluded that the failure to keep such metadata private is both unsafe and unlawful [102].

This became an even hotter political issue in November 2007, when the tax authorities lost two DVDs containing the UK's entire child benefit database – personal information on every family in Britain with children. A charity associated with the Liberal Democrat party commissioned a further report entitled 'Database State' on the safety, privacy and legality of a range of public-sector systems [103]; the coalition government of which the Liberal Democrats were part after the 2010 election killed the children's database as well as discontinuing NPfIT, repealing the previous Labour government's legislation to make ID cards compulsory, and destroying the data and hardware associated with that project. After a further review, it also abandoned a plan for a new 'eCaf' system to organise social workers involved in child protection. There the issue was not just privacy but also poor design, as eCaf demanded so much information that social workers were starting to spend more time 'feeding the beast' than they did actually talking to children and their families [1356].

Attempts to share data between medicine and social care by direct electronic access threw up issues of integrity as well as privacy. As an example, when social workers in Oxford were given access to GP records, a social worker could enter 'diabetic?' directly into a GP system – which would interpret this as a diagnosis and start trying to schedule all the rest of the diabetes care machinery. The GP would have their work cut out stopping this, as medical records are append-only; and they might start failing to meet their targets for scheduling eye tests for diabetics, which would cut their income. There are also problems with automating exchanges between care services and schools; in fact, any automated interaction between different types of professional practice needs to be designed with extensive consultation and exploration of a lot of edge cases.

The 'Database State' report also highlighted privacy in education. In England, the Department for Education had set up a National Pupil Database that initially held census data but gradually accreted test results, behaviour and attendance data, whether the child was poor enough to get free school meals and whether they were in care. In addition, schools started adding further surveillance ranging from fingerprint scanners to record attendance and library book loans, to CCTV recording the classroom continuously (with the sales pitch that teachers could defend themselves against false accusations by children).

In Scotland, the government proposed a 'named person' scheme in 2014, whereby each child would be allocated one public-sector worker (typically a teacher or health visitor) to promote and safeguard their wellbeing. Rather than stigmatising the poor children who have a social worker, why not give everybody one? This aroused widespread opposition, was defeated in the Supreme Court in 2016, and finally abandoned in 2019 after ministers couldn't figure out a way to do it that was both legal and politically acceptable. A body set up to devise a statutory code of practice decided it 'would not be desirable as the complexity of this would mean it would not be easy to understand or apply in practice' [520].

Following sporadic protests by parents, there is now at least one NGO working for children's rights[7]. Concerns range from biometrics to the widespread

[7] https://www.defenddigitalme.org

adoption of cloud services in education, with numerous small providers selling a huge range of teaching support and other services, and children's data getting everywhere. Even the privacy regulator, the Information Commissioner, has been criticised for being blind to children's issues, for example using Vimeo to make instructional videos available on her website, when its terms of service prohibit use by under-13s. If even the regulator can't manage her own website, what chance does the average school have? More fundamentally, should a school treat each pupil as a citizen/customer – responsible and in control – or as a suspect/recidivist to be tracked, scanned and fingerprinted? The temptation with young people is the latter.

Looking back at almost a quarter century of tussles around the safety and privacy of health IT, and the related subjects of IT in education and social care, one can see the failures conforming to political stereotypes. Britain's Labour governments from 1997–2010 failed in a typical left-wing way. They were well-meaning but naïve; they could only think in terms of bureaucratic centralism and billion-pound contracts (some with firms that hired ministers before or after their term of office); they had no idea how to write the specifications; they lied like mad when things went wrong; and they were suckers for special interests such as medical researchers demanding access to everything. The Conservative governments since 2010 have failed in a typical right-wing way[8] : talking about rights and freedoms but cynically selling off data to their friends in the drug companies, and for a pittance; lying like mad when things went wrong; while undermining regulators and appointing leaders disposed to turn a blind eye to both safety and privacy failures.

10.4.8 The Chinese Wall

Our final flavour of multilateral security is the Chinese Wall model, formalised by David Brewer and Michael Nash [320]. Financial services firms from investment banks to accountants are required by their regulators to have internal rules designed to prevent conflicts of interest wherever two of their clients are competitors, and these controls are called Chinese Walls.

The model's scope is wider than finance. There are many service firms whose clients may be in competition with each other: advertising agencies are another example. A typical rule is that 'a partner who has worked recently for one company may not see the papers of any other company in the same sector'. So once a copywriter has worked on the Shell account, they will not be allowed to work on another oil company's account for some fixed period of time.

The Chinese Wall model thus mixes free choice and mandatory access control: a partner can choose which oil company to work for, but once that decision is

[8]This was despite the fact that the 2010–15 government had Liberal Democrat coalition partners.

taken their actions in that sector are constrained. It also introduces the concept of *separation of duty* into access control; a given user may perform transaction A or transaction B, but not both. Access controls thus become stateful.

Part of the attraction of the Chinese Wall model to the security research community comes from the fact that it's easy to formalise; in fact, it can be expressed in terms similar to Bell-LaPadula. If we write, for each object c, $y(c)$ for c's company and $x(c)$ for c's conflict-of-interest class, then like BLP it can be expressed in two properties:

- The *simple security property*: a subject s has access to c if and only if, for all c' which s can read, either $y(c) \notin x(c')$ or $y(c) = y(c')$;
- The **-property*: a subject s can write to c only if s cannot read any c' with $x(c') \neq \emptyset$ and $y(c) \neq y(c')$.

The Chinese Wall model sparked a debate about the extent to which it is consistent with the BLP tranquility properties, and some work on the formal semantics of such systems[9]. There are also some interesting new questions about covert channels. For example, could an oil company find out whether a competitor which used the same investment bank was planning a bid for a third oil company, by asking which specialists were available for consultation and noticing that their number had dropped suddenly?

In practice Chinese Walls still get implemented using manual methods. One large software consultancy has each of its staff maintain an 'unclassified' CV containing entries that have been sanitized and agreed with the customer. A typical entry might be:

> ***Sep 17 – Apr 18:*** consulted on security requirements for a new branch accounting system for a major US retail bank

This is not the only control. A consultant's manager should be aware of possible conflicts and not forward the CV to the client if in doubt; if this fails, the client can spot potential conflicts himself from the CV; and if this also fails then the consultant is duty bound to report any potential conflicts as soon as they appear.

There remains the issue of micro-level access. What if a bank manager simply looks at the bank statements of his best customer's competitors? Here, modern systems tend to limit access except where the staff member has established a security context for that customer, for example by getting the customer to answer some authentication questions. I'll discuss this further in the chapter on Banking and Bookkeeping.

[9]See, for example, Foley [700] on the relationship with non-interference. The practical resolution of tranquility is usually a cooling-off period: having worked for one oil company, you might be forbidden to work for another for two years.

One conspicuous failure mode of Chinese walls is where the conflict period is too short. Governments typically have conflict rules that prevent a minister working in any sector that they have regulated for six months after leaving office. This is way too little. Someone who was an energy minister six months ago still knows all the top people in the industry, and anyone who's benefited from their policy may express their gratitude by hiring them. Five years might be more sensible, but if you think you can get your local legislature to pass such a law, good luck.

10.5 Summary

In this chapter, we looked at the problem of setting boundaries when systems scale up to collect large amounts of sensitive information, to which many people need access in order to do their jobs. This is an issue in many information security problems, ranging from the protection of national intelligence data and data about wildlife at risk from poaching, through the privacy and confidentiality of medical and social-care information, to professional practice in general.

We looked at medical records in the greatest detail, and found that the easy problem is setting up access controls in a direct care setting so that access to each record is limited to a sensible number of staff. Such systems can be designed by automating existing working practices, and role-based access controls are a natural way to implement them. However, the incentives in health-care systems are such that the implementation is often poor, and needs regulation to enforce compliance. The traditional approach to privacy, which might be summarised as 'consent or anonymise', is being undermined by growing complexity with many outsourced systems that are often opaque even to doctors (let alone patients). The harder problems are the growing number of central systems, particularly those related to payments, from which opt-outs aren't available; the growing use of genetic data, and the effects of social media from which sensitive personal health information can often be inferred. Here, too, the governance problems are even less tractable than the technical ones. The only realistic solution lies in regulation, and here the USA and the EU are moving ever further apart. Europe gives its citizens the right to restrict their personal health information to the clinicians involved directly in their case; America does not. However it can be hard for Europeans to enforce our rights. Both America and Europe have huge lobbying and financial pressures from drug firms and others who want all our data; politicians tend to side with the industry and undermine the regulators.

Since the 1990s, health providers and services have tried to have their cake and eat it by building 'anonymised' databases of medical records (or school records, or census returns) so as to allow researchers to make statistical enquiries without compromising individuals' privacy. There are some applications where this is a complete non-starter, such as in fighting wildlife crime; there, the aggregate data are even more valuable to poachers than individual sightings. In the case of medical records, computer scientists have known since the 1980s that anonymising rich data is a lot harder than it looks, and in recent years we've acquired a robust theory of this that lets us work out when it can work and when it won't. I'll discuss this in the next chapter.

Another takeaway message is this. Just as multilevel security was the 'hedgehog' approach to information security, where you hope to get a good result by just getting one big thing right, multilateral security requires the 'fox' approach; you need to understand your application in detail, learn what's gone wrong in the past – and also be good at adversarial thinking if you want to anticipate what's likely to go wrong in future.

Research problems

The coronavirus pandemic is likely to make health surveillance much more pervasive so personal health information will become more widespread and the conflicts discussed here will spread way beyond the healthcare sector. What will that entail, and how should technical and policy mechanisms evolve to cope?

Also, in the near future, more and more medical treatment will involve genetic information. Is there any sensible way in which privacy models can be extended to deal with multiple individuals? For example, in many countries you have the right not to know the outcome of a DNA test that a relative has for an inheritable disease such as Huntington's Chorea, as it may affect the odds that you have it too. Your relative does have a right to know, and may tell others – so unwelcome news might reach you indirectly. As I write, there are cases going through the courts in the UK and Germany that push in different directions on the rights of the children of people diagnosed with Huntington's [606]. Such tensions over information rights long predate the Internet and cannot be managed purely by technological mechanisms. But social media change the scaling factors in such a way as to make them more widespread and acute. The long-term solutions may well involve some mix of laws, social norms and technology support; but they are likely to take years to work out, and we may well end up with different solutions in different cultures. For example, East Asian countries have tolerated much more intrusive surveillance, and have suffered far fewer deaths in the pandemic, at least so far. Might that change attitudes elsewhere?

Further reading

The literature on compartmented-mode security is scattered: most of the public-domain papers are in the proceedings of the NCSC/NISSC and ACSAC conferences, while Amoroso [48] and Gollmann [780] cover the basics of the lattice and Chinese-wall models. For a survey of privacy failures in health, social care and education in the UK in 2009, see *'Database State'* [103]. For a case study of the NHS National Programme for IT, see [381], and for a later report on total costs by the UK Parliament's Public Accounts Committee, see [1562]. For the BMA model see the policy itself [59], the Oakland version [60], the proceedings of a conference on the policy [64], and the papers on the pilot system at Hastings [535, 536]. For a National Research Council study of medical privacy in the USA, see [1414]; there is also an HHS report on the use of de-identified data in research at [1193]. But the best sources for up-to-date news on medical privacy issues are the websites of the relevant lobby groups: medConfidential for the UK, and Patient Privacy Rights for the USA.

CHAPTER

11

Inference Control

Privacy is a transient notion. It started when people stopped believing that God could see everything and stopped when governments realised there was a vacancy to be filled.

– ROGER NEEDHAM

"Anonymized data" is one of those holy grails, like "healthy ice-cream" or "selectively breakable crypto".

– CORY DOCTOROW

11.1 Introduction

Just as Big Tobacco spent decades denying that smoking causes lung cancer, and Big Oil spent decades denying climate change, so also Big Data has spent decades pretending that sensitive personal data can easily be 'anonymised' so it can be used as an industrial raw material without infringing on the privacy rights of the data subjects.

Anonymisation is an aspirational term that means stripping identifying information from data in such a way that useful statistical research can be done without leaking information about identifiable data subjects. Its limitations have been explored in four waves of research, each responding to the technology of the day. The first wave came in the late 1970s and early 1980s in the context of the US census, which contained statistics that were sensitive of themselves but where aggregate totals were required for legitimate reasons such as allocating money to states; and in the context of other structured databases from college marks through staff salaries to bank transactions. Statisticians started to study how information could leak, and to develop measures for inference control.

The second wave came in the 1990s as medical records were computerised. Both health service administrators and medical researchers saw this as a treasure trove, and hoped that removing patients' names and addresses would be enough to make the data non-personal. This turned out to be insufficient because of the richness of the data, which led to tussles in several countries including the USA, the UK, Germany and Iceland. There have since been multiple scandals when inadequately anonymised data were leaked or even sold.

The third wave, in the mid-2000s, came when people realised they could use search engines to identify people in large datasets of consumer preferences such as movie ratings and search engine logs. An advance in theory came in 2006, when Cynthia Dwork and colleagues developed the theory of *differential privacy*, which quantifies the extent to which inferences can be prevented by limiting queries and adding noise, enabling us to add noise where it's needed. This is now being used in the US census, whose experience teaches a lot about its practical limits.

The fourth wave came upon us in the late 2010s with social media, pervasive genomics and large databases of personal location histories collected by phone apps and widely sold to marketers. Ever more companies who sell personal information at scale pretend that it isn't personal because names are somehow tokenised. Ever more press articles show how bogus such claims usually are. For example, in December 2019 the New York Times reported analysing the mobile-phone location history of 12 million Americans over a few months, locating celebrities, rioters, police, Secret Service officers and even sex-industry customers without difficulty [1889].

We face a yawning gap between what can be done using anonymisation and related privacy technologies, and what stakeholders from medical researchers through marketers to politicians would like to believe is possible. This gap has been the subject of much discussion and, as with tobacco and carbon emissions, political argument. As our knowledge of the re-identification risks becomes ever more detailed and certain, so the hopes of both governments and industry become ever more unrealistic. Governments repeatedly call for proposals, and data users call for contractors, to create services that cannot be created; all too often, contracts for privacy services are won by the more ignorant or unscrupulous operators.

It must be said that not all governments have simply been ignorant. Both the UK and Ireland, for example, annoyed other EU member states for years by allowing firms to pretend that data were anonymous when they clearly weren't, and this was one of the factors that led the EU to pass the General Data Protection Regulation (GDPR), as I will discuss later in section 26.6.1. Since it came into force, the wriggle room for wishful thinking has become less – though even the European institutions have sometimes had a rosy view of what can be achieved by de-identification.

11.2 The early history of inference control

Inference control goes back to the 1920s when economic data were compiled in ways that masked the contribution of individual firms, but it was first studied systematically in the context of census data. A census collects a lot of sensitive information about individuals, including names, addresses, family relationships, race, employment, educational attainment and income, and then makes statistical summaries available by geographical and governmental units such as states, counties, districts and wards. This information is used to determine electoral districts, to set levels of government funding for public services, and as inputs to all sorts of other policy decisions. Census data are a good simple case with which to start as the data are in a standard format, and the allowable queries are generally known in advance.

There are two broad approaches, depending on whether the data are sanitised once and for all before publication, or whether the privacy mechanisms operate one query at a time and work out whether it's allowable. Mathematically, the two types of processing are the same. For data of a particular type subject to given privacy constraints, only a certain number of queries will be allowable; the question is whether you determine these in advance, or dynamically in response to user demand.

An example of the first type comes from the US census data up till the 1960s. One record in a thousand was made available on tape – minus names, exact addresses and other sensitive data. There was also noise added to the data in order to prevent people with some extra knowledge (such as of the salaries paid by the employer in a company town) from tracing individuals. In addition to the sample records, local averages were also given for various attributes. But records with extreme values – such as very high incomes – were suppressed. Without such suppression, a wealthy family living in a small village might increase the average village income by enough for their own family income to be deduced.

In the second type of processing, identifiable data are stored in a database, and privacy protection comes from restricting the queries that may be made. For example, a simple rule might be that you answer no question unless the result is computed using the data of three or more data subjects – the so-called *rule of three*. Early attempts at this were not very successful, as people kept on coming up with new attacks based on inference. A typical attack would construct a number of queries about samples containing a target individual, and work back to infer some confidential fact. You might for example ask 'tell me the number of two-person households earning between $50,000 and $55,000', 'tell me the proportion of households headed by a man aged

40–45 years earning between $50,000 and $55,000', 'tell me the proportion of households headed by a man earning between $50,000 and $55,000 whose children have grown up and left home', and so on, until you home in on the target individual. Queries to which we successively add context to defeat query controls are known as *trackers*.

Related problems arise in many contexts. For example, a New Zealand journalist deduced the identities of many officers in that country's signals intelligence service, GCSB, by scrutinising lists of military and diplomatic personnel for patterns of postings over time [850]. Combining low-level sources to draw a high-level conclusion is known as an *aggregation attack* in the national security context.

11.2.1 The basic theory of inference control

The basic theory of inference control was developed by Dorothy Denning and others in the late 1970s and early 1980s, largely in response to problems of the US census [538]. This wave of research is summarised in a 1989 survey paper by Adam and Wortman [17]. The developers of many modern privacy systems are often unaware of this work, and repeat many of the mistakes of the 1960s. The following is an overview of the basic ideas.

A *characteristic formula* is the expression (in some database query language) that selects a *query set* of records. An example might be 'all female employees of the Computer Laboratory at the grade of professor'. The smallest query sets, obtained by the logical AND of all the attributes (or their negations) are known as *elementary sets* or *cells*. The statistics corresponding to query sets may be *sensitive statistics* if the set size is too small. The objective of inference control is to prevent the disclosure of sensitive statistics.

If we let D be the set of statistics that are disclosed and P the set that are sensitive and must be protected, then we need $D \subseteq P'$ for privacy, where P' is the complement of P. If $D = P'$, then the protection is said to be *precise*. Protection that is not precise will usually carry some cost in terms of the range of queries that the database can answer and may therefore degrade its usefulness.

11.2.1.1 Query set size control

The simplest protection mechanism is to specify a minimum query set size, so that no question is answered if the number of records from which the answer is calculated is less than some threshold t. But this is not enough. Say $t = 6$; then an obvious tracker attack is to make an enquiry on six patients' records, and then on those records plus the target's. And you must also prevent the attacker from querying all but one of the records: if there are N records and a query set size threshold of t, then between t and $N - t$ records must be the subject of a query for it to be allowed. This also applies to subsets. For example, when I wrote the first edition of this book, only one of the full professors in our lab was female. So we could have found out her salary with just two queries: 'Average salary professors?' and 'Average salary male professors?'. So you have to avoid successive queries of record sets K and L if $K \subset L$ and $|L| - |K| < t$.

11.2.1.2 Trackers

That is an example of an *individual tracker*, a custom formula that allows us to calculate the answer to a forbidden query indirectly. There are also *general trackers* – sets of formulae that will enable any sensitive statistic to be revealed. A somewhat depressing discovery made in the late 1970s, due to Dorothy Denning, Peter Denning and Mayer Schwartz, was that general trackers are usually easy to find. Provided the minimum query set size n is less than a quarter of the total number of statistics N, and there are no further restrictions on the type of queries that are allowed, then we can find formulae that provide general trackers [541]. So tracker attacks are easy, unless we restrict the query set size or control the allowed queries in some other way. Such *query auditing* turns out to be an NP-complete problem.

11.2.1.3 Cell suppression

The next question is how to deal with the side-effects of suppressing sensitive statistics. The UK rules for the 2010 census, for example, required that it be 'unlikely that any statistical unit, having identified themselves, could use that knowledge, by deduction, to identify other statistical units in National Statistics outputs' [1418]. To take a simple concrete example, suppose that a university wants to release average marks for various combinations of courses, so that people can check that the marking is fair across courses. Suppose now that the table in Figure 11.1 contains the number of students studying two science subjects, one as their major subject and one as their minor subject.

Major:	Biology	Physics	Chemistry	Geology
Minor:				
Biology	-	16	17	11
Physics	7	-	32	18
Chemistry	33	41	-	2
Geology	9	13	6	-

Figure 11.1: Table containing data before cell suppression

The UK census rules imply a minimum query set size of 3, which makes sense here too: if we set it at 2, then either of the two students who studied 'geology-with-chemistry' could work out the other's mark. So we cannot release the average for 'geology-with-chemistry'. But if the average mark for chemistry is known, then it could be reconstructed from the averages for 'biology-with-chemistry' and 'physics-with-chemistry'. So we have to suppress at least one other mark in the chemistry row, and for similar reasons we need to suppress one in the geology column. But if we suppress 'geology-with-biology' and 'physics-with-chemistry', then we'd also better suppress 'physics-with-biology' to prevent these values being worked out in turn. Our table will now look like Figure 11.2, where 'D' means 'value suppressed for disclosure purposes'.

Major:	Biology	Physics	Chemistry	Geology
Minor:				
Biology	-	D	17	D
Physics	7	-	32	18
Chemistry	33	D	-	D
Geology	9	13	6	-

Figure 11.2: Table after cell suppression

This process, due to Tore Dalenius, is called *complementary cell suppression*. If there are further attributes in the database schema – for example, if figures are also broken down by race and sex, to show compliance with anti-discrimination laws – then even more information may be lost. Where a database scheme contains *m*-tuples, blanking a single cell generally means suppressing $2^m - 1$ other cells, arranged in a hypercube with the sensitive statistic at one vertex. So even precise protection can rapidly make the database unusable. Sometimes complementary cell suppression can be avoided, as when large incomes (or rare diseases) are tabulated nationally and excluded from local figures. But it is often necessary when we are publishing micro-statistics, as in the above tables of exam marks. It may still not be sufficient, unless we can add noise to the totals – as the possible values of the confidential data are limited still further by the information we disclose, and there may also be side information such as the fact that no totals are negative.

11.2.1.4 Other statistical disclosure control mechanisms

Another approach is *k-anonymity*, due to Pierangela Samarati and Latanya Sweeney, which means that each individual whose data is used in calculating a release of data cannot be distinguished from $k - 1$ others [1646]. Its limitation is that it's an operational definition of a privacy mechanism rather than a mathematical definition of a privacy property; it's not much help if k individuals all possess the same sensitive attribute. Where the database is open for online queries, we can use *implied queries control*: we allow a query on m attribute values only if every one of the 2^m implied query sets given by setting the m attributes to true or false, has at least k records. An alternative is to limit the type of inquiries. *Maximum order control* limits the number of attributes any query can have. However, to be effective, the limit may have to be severe. It takes only 33 bits of information to identify a human, and most datasets are of much smaller populations. A more thorough approach (where it is feasible) is to reject queries that would partition the sample population into too many sets.

We saw in the previous chapter how lattices can be used in compartmented security to define a partial order of permitted information flows between compartments with combinations of codewords. They can also be used in a slightly different way to systematize query controls in some databases. If we have, for example, three attributes A, B and C (say area of residence, birth year and medical condition), we may find that while enquiries on any one of these attributes are non-sensitive, as are enquiries on A and B and on B and C, the combination of A and C might be sensitive. It follows that an enquiry on all three would not be permissible either. So the lattice divides naturally into a 'top half' of prohibited queries and a 'bottom half' of allowable queries, as shown in Figure 11.3.

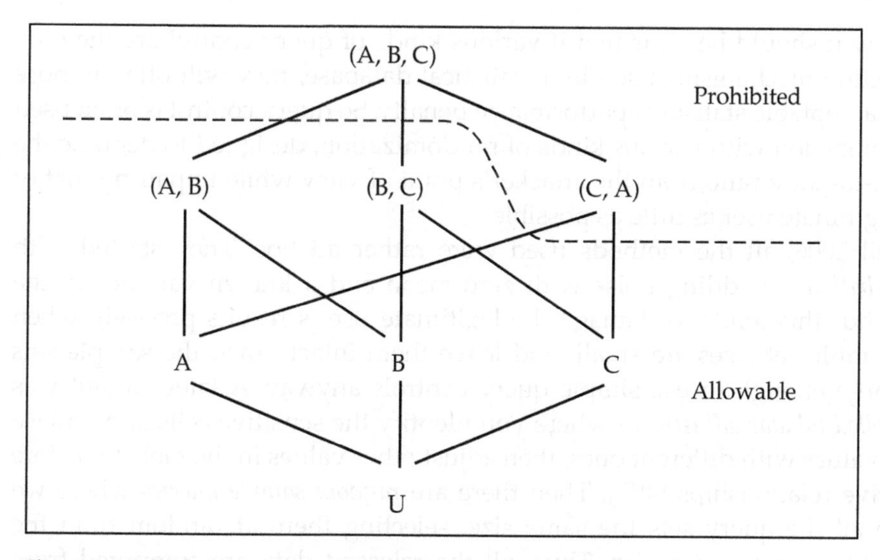

Figure 11.3: Table lattice for a database with three attributes

11.2.1.5 More sophisticated query controls

There are a number of alternatives to simple query control. During the late 20th century, the US census used the 'n-respondent, k%-dominance rule': it would not release a statistic of which k% or more was contributed by n values or less. Other techniques included suppressing data with extreme values. A census may include high-net-worth individuals in national statistics but not in the local figures, while some medical databases do the same for less common diseases. For example, a UK prescribing statistics system from that period suppressed sales of AIDS drugs from local statistics [1251]; even during the AIDS crisis in the early 1990s, there were counties with only one single patient receiving such treatment.

Some systems try to get round the limits imposed by static query control by keeping track of who accessed what. Known as *query overlap control*, this involves rejecting any query from a user that, combined with what the user knows already, would disclose a sensitive statistic. This may sound like a good idea, but in practice it suffers from two usually insurmountable drawbacks. First, the complexity of the processing involved increases over time, and often exponentially. Second, it's extremely hard to be sure that your users don't collude, or that one user has registered under two different names. Even if your users are all honest and distinct persons today, it's always possible that one of them will get taken over tomorrow.

11.2.1.6 Randomization

By now it should be clear that if various kinds of query control are the only protection mechanisms used in a statistical database, they will often impose an unacceptable statistical performance penalty. So query control is often used in conjunction with various kinds of randomization, designed to degrade the signal-to-noise ratio from the attacker's point of view while impairing that of the legitimate user as little as possible.

Until 2006, all the methods used were rather ad hoc. They started with *perturbation*, or adding noise with zero mean and a known variance to the data; but this tends to damage the legitimate user's results precisely when the sample set sizes are small, and leave them intact when the sample sets are large enough to use simple query controls anyway. A later variant was *controlled tabular adjustment* where you identify the sensitive cells and replace their values with different ones, then adjust other values in the table to restore additive relationships [490]. Then there are *random sample queries* where we make all the query sets the same size, selecting them at random from the available relevant statistics. Thus, all the released data are computed from small samples rather than from the whole database, and we can use a pseudorandom number generator keyed to the input query to make the results repeatable. Random sample queries are a natural protection mechanism where the correlations being investigated are strong enough that a small sample is sufficient. Finally, there's *swapping*, another of Tore Dalenius' innovations;

Week:	1	2	3	4
Doctor A	17	26	19	22
Doctor B	25	31	9	29
Doctor C	32	30	39	27
Doctor D	16	19	18	13

Figure 11.4: Sample of de-identified drug prescribing data

many census bureaux swap a proportion of records so that a family with two young teenage kids and an income in the second quartile might be swapped for a similar family in a town in the next county.

Since 2006, we have a solid theory of exactly how much protection we can get from adding randomness: *differential privacy*. This is now being used for the 2020 US census, and we'll discuss it in more detail later in this chapter.

11.2.2 Limits of classical statistical security

As with any protection technology, statistical security can only be evaluated in a particular environment and against a particular threat model. Whether it is adequate or not depends on the details of the application.

One example is a system developed in the mid-1990s by a company then called Source Informatics for analysing trends in drug prescribing, which figured in the key UK lawsuit about the privacy of anonymised data[1]. The system's goal is to tell drug companies how effective their sales staff are, by tracking sales of different medicines by district. The privacy goal was to not leak any information about identifiable patients or about the prescribing habits of individual physicians[2]. So prescriptions were collected (minus patient names) from pharmacies, and then a further stage of de-identification removed the doctors' identities too.

The first version of this system merely replaced the names of doctors in a cell of four or five practices with 'doctor A', 'doctor B' and so on, as in Figure 11.4. When evaluating it, we realised that an alert drug rep could identify doctors from prescribing patterns: "Well, doctor B must be Susan Jones because she went skiing in the third week in January and look at the fall-off in prescriptions here. And doctor C is probably Mervyn Smith who was covering for her". The fix was to replace absolute numbers of prescriptions with the percentage of each doctor's prescribing which went on each particular drug, to drop some

[1]Full disclosure: I was the evaluator, acting on behalf of the British Medical Association.
[2]Doctors are hounded all the time by drug sales reps and often say they'll use some product or other just to get them out of the surgery. It's curious that such an important privacy case had as its privacy objective a doctor's ability to continue telling white lies.

doctors at random, and to randomly perturb the timing by shifting the figures backwards or forwards a few weeks [1251].

This is a good example of the sort of system where classical statistical security techniques can give a robust solution. The application is well-defined, the database is not too rich, the allowable queries are fairly simple, and they remain stable over time. Even so, the UK Department of Health sued the database operator, alleging that the database might compromise privacy. The Department's motive was to maintain a monopoly on the supply of such data to industry. They lost, and this established the precedent that (in Britain at least) inference security controls may, if they are robust, exempt statistical data from being considered as 'personal information' for the purpose of privacy laws [1808].

In general, though, it's not so easy. For a start, privacy mechanisms don't compose: it's easy to have two separate applications, each of which provides the same results via perturbed versions of the same data, but where an attacker with access to both of them can easily identify individuals. This actually happened in the Source Informatics case; by 2015, another competing system was available that used different mechanisms, and people realised that a drug company with access to both systems could occasionally deduce some doctors' prescribing behaviour. If we were re-implementing such a system today, we'd prevent this by using differential privacy, which I'll describe later in this chapter.

11.2.3 Active attacks

The Source Informatics system added a new tranche of records every week, but it can sometimes happen that users have the ability to insert single identifiable records into the database. In that case, *active attacks* can be particularly powerful. A prominent case in the late 1990s was a medical research database in Iceland. A Swiss drug company funded a local startup to offer the Reykjavik government a deal: we'll build you a modern health cards system if you'll let us mine it for research. The government signed up, but Iceland's doctors mostly opposed the deal, seeing it as a threat both to patient privacy and professional autonomy.

Under their proposed design, every time a medical record was generated, it would be sent to the Iceland privacy commissioner whose system would strip out the patient's name and address, replacing it with an encrypted version of their Social Security number, and pass it to a research database. The privacy commissioner controlled the encryption key. However, anyone in the system who wanted to find (say) the Prime Minister's medical records would merely have to enter some record or other – say a prescription for aspirin – and then watch it pop up on the research system a second or two later. The Icelandic government pressed ahead anyway, with a patient opt-out. Many doctors advised patients to opt out, and 11% of the population did so. Eventually, the Icelandic Supreme Court found that European privacy law required the database to be opt-in rather than opt-out, which put paid to the national project and forced the company to switch to encouraging large-scale volunteering.

Iceland remains particularly attractive to researchers as the population is very homogeneous, being descended from a small number of settlers a thousand years ago, and there are good genealogical records. This also made privacy problems in the Icelandic database more acute. By linking medical records to genealogies, which are public, patients can be identified by such factors as the number of their uncles, aunts, great-uncles, great-aunts and so on – in effect by the shape of their family trees. There was much debate about whether the design could even theoretically meet legal privacy requirements [67], and European privacy officials expressed grave concern about the possible consequences for Europe's system of privacy laws [515]. This brings us to the broader question of rich contextual data, which drove the second wave of work on inference control.

11.2.4 Inference control in rich medical data

The second half of the 1990s saw the 'dotcom boom'. The worldwide web was new, and a torrent of money flowed into tech as businesses (and governments) tried to figure out how to move their operations online. Healthcare IT people struggled with many questions around safety and privacy; records had already been moving from paper to computers, but now all the computers started talking to each other [64]. Could you use email to send test results from a hospital to a doctor's surgery, or would it be a web form? How would you encrypt it, and who'd manage the keys? And could you make complete medical records safe enough for use in research by removing names and addresses, as opposed to just episode data such as individual prescriptions? Researchers had previously done epidemiology by sitting in hospital libraries reading paper records, and it would 'obviously' be better if you could do this at your desk. However, an epidemiologist will usually want to be able to link up episodes over a patient's lifetime, so they can see long-term effects of treatments and lifestyle choices. That is much harder to anonymise.

Health IT people faced this problem in many countries at once. New Zealand set up a database with encrypted patient names plus a rule that no query may answered with respect to fewer than six records, but realised that that was not enough and restricted access to a small number of specially cleared medical statisticians [1424]. The fall of the Berlin Wall caused an acute problem for Germany, as the former East Germany had cancer registries with first-class data that were really useful for research but had patient names and rich contextual data, and these now fell under West Germany's strict privacy laws.

The registry had to install protection mechanisms rapidly, which involve both de-identification and strict usage controls [267]. In Switzerland too, some research systems were replaced at the insistence of privacy regulators [1684]. The British Medical Association objected to a proposal for a centralised research database in 1995–6 and a committee was set up under an eminent psychiatrist, Dame Fiona Caldicott, to suggest a way forward.

The fact that the rich context of medical records had changed the statistical security game was then brought into focus in 1997 by Latanya Sweeney who tried, in her PhD thesis, to build a system that would anonymise medical records properly, and discovered how hard it is. She showed that even the Health Care Finance Administration's 'public-use' files could often be re-identified by cross-correlating them with commercial databases [1853]. She showed that 69% of US residents can be identified by date of birth and zip code, and discussed the extreme difficulty of scrubbing medical records that contain all sorts of contextual data, including free-form text [1853]. At the time, the Medicare system considered *beneficiary-encrypted* records – with patients' names and Social Security numbers encrypted – to be personal data and thus only usable by trusted researchers. There were also *public-access* records, stripped of identifiers down to the level where patients are only identified in general terms such as 'a white female aged 70–74 living in Vermont'. Nonetheless, researchers have found that many patients can still be identified by cross-correlating the public access records with commercial databases. Sweeney brought this to public attention by identifying the records of Massachusetts governor William Weld. This got the anonymity of medical research data on to the US political agenda.

As I describe in section 10.4, the Clinton administration issued a privacy rule in 2000 under HIPAA that defined a 'Safe Harbor' standard for the public sharing of data, and then in 2002 the Bush administration adopted a more relaxed rule. In 2017 Sweeney and colleagues examined a 2006 public-health study of 50 homes in California, which had been cited hundreds of times in the research literature, and showed they could identify 25% of the participants by name and 28% by address [1854]. Even after redacting participants' birth years to 10-year ranges, they could still pinpoint 3% by name and 18% by address – because of side information such as the type of housing.

The UK followed a similar trajectory. Dame Fiona Caldicott's report identified over sixty illegal information flows within the health service [369]. Some research datasets were de-identified very carelessly; others (including data on people with HIV/AIDS) were re-identified deliberately afterwards, so that people and HIV charities whose data had been collected under a promise of anonymity were deceived. Parliament then passed a law giving ministers the power to regulate secondary uses of medical data, but the broad direction was trusted researchers; a committee vetted applications for data access. Patient consent was obtained in some cases, but not for research involving the

Hospital Episode Statistics database, which contains records of over a billion hospital treatments in England and Wales from 1998 to the present day. HES data are made available to researchers with the patient's name and address removed and replaced with an encrypted identifier. (The encryption key is different for each research organisation that licenses the data.)

But encrypting patient names isn't enough. Suppose I want to look up the record of former Prime Minister Tony Blair. A quick web search reveals that he was treated in Hammersmith Hospital in London for an irregular heartbeat on 19th October 2003 and 1st October 2004. That's more than enough to pick out his encrypted ID and look up everything else he's had done. Such a leak can be intrusive for anybody; for a celebrity, it can be newsworthy. What's more, in many systems there's a cleartext postcode and date of birth; again, this combination is enough to identify about 98% of UK residents[3]. Even if the date of birth is replaced by a year of birth, I am still likely to be able to compromise patient privacy if the records are detailed, or if records of different individuals can be linked. For example, a query such as 'show me the records of all women aged 36 with daughters aged 14 and 16 such that the mother and exactly one daughter have psoriasis' can find one individual out of millions. Query set size control might stop this kind of tracker, but researchers do want to make complex queries with lots of conditions to find disease clusters with a few hundreds or even a few dozens of patients. Such queries could be composed, whether deliberately or by accident, in such a way as to identify individuals.

In 2006, UK privacy groups organised a campaign to alert people to the risks and invite them to exercise their right to opt out of secondary data use. In 2007, Parliament's Health Select Committee conducted an inquiry into the Electronic Patient Record, heard evidence from a wide range of viewpoints[4] and made many recommendations, including that patients should be permitted to prevent the use of their data in research [927]. Privacy concerns are not the only reason that a patient might reasonably request that their data not be used; for example, a devout Catholic woman might demand that her data not be used to develop pills for abortion or birth control. The Government rejected this.

David Cameron's government, elected in 2010, weakened privacy protection, just as George Bush had done ten years earlier. Amidst talk of abolishing red tape and making the UK the best place in the world for medical research, as I discussed at greater length in section 10.4.4.3, he launched 'care.data', a central research database that would add test results, prescriptions and GP data to the existing HES database. In November 2013 it emerged that HES data were available via BT for sale online [950], and in February 2014, it emerged that copies of the HES database had been sold to 1,200 organisations worldwide, including

[3]UK postcodes have more resolution than US zip codes, with typically 30 buildings in each postcode. The 1% or so of people for whom postcode plus date of birth is not unique are mostly identical twins, or young people living in college halls of residence or military barracks.
[4]Declaration of interest: I was a Special Adviser to the Committee.

not just academic researchers but commercial firms, from drug companies to consultancies [775]. One of the big US consultancies had uploaded all 23GB of data to the Google cloud 'as it was too big for Excel' and was making it available to clients, despite laws that required the data to remain in the UK. The data had been used for non-health purposes, specifically by actuaries to refine insurance premiums. A law was quickly passed stating that health and social data could be shared and analyzed only when there was a 'benefit to healthcare', and never for other purposes. Another consultancy was hired to produce another report, and people who'd opted out were told to opt out all over again. An academic case study tells the story, analyses the tensions between healthcare law and data-protection law, and remarks that 'this debate centers on the ability to protect and maintain the anonymity of patient data, and there are no easy answers' [1551].

11.2.5 The third wave: preferences and search

The next wave broke in 2006, by which time a significant number of transactions had moved online, recommender systems had emerged thanks to eBay and Amazon, and search engines made it easy to find needles in haystacks. Two incidents that year brought this home to the public.

First, AOL released the supposedly anonymous records of 20 million search queries made over three months by 657,000 people. Searchers' names and IP addresses were replaced with numbers, but that didn't help. Investigative journalists looked through the searches and rapidly identified some of the searchers, who were shocked at the privacy breach [168]. The data were released 'for research purposes': the leak led to complaints being filed with the FTC, following which the company's CTO resigned, and the firm fired both the employee who released the data and their supervisor. Search history, or equivalently your clickstream, is highly sensitive as it reflects your thoughts and intentions.

Second, Netflix offered a $1m prize for a better recommender algorithm and published the viewer ratings of 500,000 subscribers with their names removed. At the time, it had only 6 million US customers and shipped them physical DVDs, so this was a significant minority of its customers. Arvind Narayanan and Vitaly Shmatikov showed that many subscribers could be reidentified by comparing the anonymous records with preferences publicly expressed in the Internet Movie Database [1386]. This is partly due to the 'long tail' effect: once you disregard the 100 or so movies everyone watches, people's viewing preferences are pretty unique. As US law protects movie rental privacy, the attack was a serious embarrassment for Netflix.

The response of privacy regulators in Europe and Canada was to promote *Privacy Enhancing Technologies* (PETs) – they hoped that if security researchers were to work harder, we could come up with more effective ways of anonymising rich data [649]. Researchers at Microsoft took them at their word, and developed the theory of differential privacy, which I explain in 11.3. This does not get the privacy regulators off the hook, as it clarifies the limitations of anonymisation. Yet for years policy people talked about it as a solution without understanding that it explains in more detail why we cannot resolve the tension between researchers' demand for detailed data, and the right of data subjects to privacy.

11.2.6 The fourth wave: location and social

During the 2010s, the world was changed by smartphones and social networks. Chapter 23 in the second edition of this book in 2008 describes the early social network scene, as Facebook was just taking over from Myspace. I noted that Robert Putman's book *'Bowling Alone'* had documented the decline of social engagement through voluntary associations such as churches, clubs and societies with the arrival of TV in the 1960s [1566], and the fact that the Internet's early Usenet newsgroups and mailing lists had managed to put some of that back. The sweet spot the social networks hit was rolling this out to everybody. However recondite your interests, you can connect with people who share them, wherever in the world they are. We predicted that social networks would bring all sorts of privacy problems directly, as social context makes it hard to hide. (Is there anyone other than me who hangs out with cryptographers, with digital-rights activists, and with people interested in the dance music of 200 years ago?) Persistence adds further hazards, as when teens' boasts about sex and drugs come back to haunt them later in job interviews. Two things we missed were the fact that masses of data have migrated to the cloud, and the sheer amount of sensitive personal information that can be deduced from contextual data about people. By 2011 Google was describing its core competence as 'the statistical data mining of crowdsourced data'; as the datasets got larger, and basic statistical techniques were augmented with machine learning, the amount we can learn has grown.

An example of 'more data' is location history. By 2012, Yves-Alexandre de Montjoye and his colleagues had shown that four mobile-phone locations are in general enough to identify someone, even when you only get their cell-tower location [1335]. Nowadays much more high-resolution data are widely available, as many smartphone apps ask for access to your location – which can involve not just GPS (with an average accuracy of perhaps 8m outdoors) but also which wifi hotspots are in range (which can tell where you are in a building). Most people click to agree without a second thought, and there's now a whole ecoystem of companies buying and selling location trace data – which is now accurate to a few metres rather than a few hundred. The data were sold not just to marketing firms, but to private detectives, including bounty hunters who use it to track down people who've jumped bail [487].

In December 2019 the New York Times got hold of the location traces of 12 million Americans over a few months and demonstrated graphically how closely people can now be tracked. Your daily trace shows your home, when you left, how you traveled to work, where you stopped for a coffee en route, where your office is, where you went for lunch – everything. The journalists found in their database a celebrity who had sung at a church service for President Trump; hundreds of people working at the Pentagon and the CIA, as well as the President's Secret Service bodyguards, all of whom they could follow home; and people visiting the sex industry. They found one man who'd worked at Microsoft, then visited Amazon, then started working at Amazon the following month. They looked at a riot, and found they could follow both rioters and police officers home [1889]. There's a stark contrast between the ease of buying this data on the open market, and the hoops that law enforcement have to jump through to get it by means of warrants. The location data companies all claim that their data are anonymous; yet even though they might not actually use the phone book or the voters' roll to look up your name from your street address, several sell your location data tied to an advertising identifier based on one or more cookies in your browser. With low-resolution location data, when you go to Black Hat in Las Vegas, online gambling companies can put ads in front of you. With high-resolution data, a foreign intelligence agency could locate people who work at the Pentagon and also visit gay clubs or brothels. It can also follow them home.

An example of 'better inference' comes from the behavioural analysis of social-network data. The headline case here started when Michal Kosinski and colleagues wrote a Facebook app that offered free psychometric testing and persuaded tens of thousands of people to use it. They figured out that they could tell whether someone was straight or gay from four Facebook likes; given sixty likes, they could assess the user's 'Big Five' personality traits: whether you are open to experience or cautious, conscientious or easygoing, extravert or introvert, agreeable or detached, and neurotic or confident [1088]. They can also tell whether you're white or black, conservative or liberal, Christian or Muslim, whether you smoke, whether you drink, whether you're in a relationship, and whether you use drugs – with varying degrees of accuracy. This led some of his colleagues to collect Facebook data on an industrial scale for marketing and political campaigning, leading to the Cambridge Analytica scandal, which I'll discuss in Part 3. Later research showed that having behavioural data gives publishers only an extra 4% of ad income compared with what they get over contextual ads, so conceivably this practice might simply be banned [1230]. However, industry observers note that the platforms earn more than this, as they get the lion's share of ad income – so they can be expected to resist any such privacy law [1182].

In many cases, you can get both location data and social data, and get them at scale. For example, the government of Victoria, Australia, made public a database of transport ticket use covering a billion journeys by 15m tickets from 2015–8. Although the card IDs had been anonymised, it usually took only one or two journeys for a resident to identify their own card from the touch on and touch off times; researchers found they could then identify their co-travelers [502]. Next they identified people using Australian federal parliamentary passes, who routinely get the train to their constituencies; hypotheses could be confirmed from the parliamentarians' tweets. This dataset enabled the researchers to analyse the sensitivity of travel time. They found that even if travel times were truncated to the day, with hours and minutes thrown away, four locations would identify over a third of travelers.

We now have many social side channels as well as location data. Location history leaks so much data as it reveals who we live with, work with and party with. Social networks are even richer with our contacts, preferences and selfies, and can make these measurements more accurate. And social analysis can reach right down into the lowest layers of the stack. For example, it turns out to be fairly easy to match up two social graphs, even if they are not exact copies of each other; so given a country's anonymised mobile phone call data records, you can re-identify them by comparing them with (say) the friend graph of a social network [1722]. Mobile phone data already leak lots of information about our personalities: extraverts make more calls, agreeable people get more calls, and the variance of time between phone calls predicts conscientiousness [1336].

The combination of more data and better inference led to fresh controversy in medical research too. Google's AI subsidiary DeepMind announced a collaboration in 2016 with a London hospital to develop an app to diagnose kidney injury. The following year, it turned out that the hospital had given DeepMind not just the records of kidney injury sufferers, but all 1.6m fully-identifiable records of all its patients, without getting their consent [1545]. The privacy regulator reprimanded the hospital, as such access should be given only to firms involved in direct patient care rather than for product research; however it did not attempt to force DeepMind to delete the data. The company used VA data from the USA instead to develop diagnostic apps. It did set up an Ethics Board that it claimed would control the technology, and did undertake not to give the hospital data to its parent Google, but in 2017 an eminent member of the ethics board resigned claiming it was window-dressing, and in 2018 it was announced that Google was absorbing DeepMind's health operation [911]. This slow train wreck was followed by the news that Google was already under fire for acquiring the records of 50 million US patients [122].

So is it possible to do anonymisation properly? The answer is yes; in certain circumstances, it is. Although it is not possible to create anonymous datasets that can be used to answer any question, we can sometimes provide a dependable measure of privacy when we set out to answer a specific set of research questions. This brings us to the theory of differential privacy.

11.3 Differential privacy

In 2006, Cynthia Dwork, Frank McSherry, Kobbi Nissim and Adam Smith published a seminal paper showing how you could systematically analyse privacy systems that added noise to prevent disclosure of sensitive statistics in a database [595]. Their theory, *differential privacy*, enables the security engineer to limit the probability of disclosure, even in the presence of an adversary with unbounded computational power and copious side information, and can thus be seen as the equivalent of the one-time pad and unconditionally secure authentication codes in cryptography. Although it started as a paper on theoretical cryptography, it has come to be seen as the gold standard for both statistical database security and for anonymisation in general. The starting point was an earlier paper by Kobbi Nissim and Irit Dinur, who had shown in 2003 that if queries on a database each returned an approximation to a linear function of private bits of information, then so long as the error was small enough the number of queries required to reconstruct the database would not grow too quickly; such reconstruction attacks are, after all, based on linear algebra, so rather than making carefully targeted tracker attacks, an attacker can just make a whole lot of random queries, then do the algebra and get everything out [562]. So the defender has to add noise if there will be more than a limited number of queries, and the question is how much.

The key insight of differential privacy is that, to avoid inadvertent disclosure, no individual's contribution to the results of queries should make too much of a difference, so you calibrate the standard deviation of the noise according to the sensitivity of the data. A privacy mechanism is called ϵ-indistinguishable if for all databases X and X' differing in a single row, the probability of getting any answer from X is within a multiplicative factor of $(1 + \epsilon)$ of getting it from X'; in other words, you bound the logarithm of the ratios. It follows that you can use noise with a Laplace distribution to get indistinguishability with noisy sums, and things compose, so it all becomes mathematically tractable. The value of ϵ, which sets the trade-off between accuracy and privacy, has to be set by policy. Small values give strong privacy; but setting $\epsilon = 1000$ is basically publishing your raw data.

There is now a growing research literature exploring how such mechanisms can be extended for static to dynamic databases, to data streams, to mechanism design and to machine learning. But can the promise of learning nothing useful about individuals while learning useful information about a population, be realised in practical applications?

Differential privacy is now getting a full-scale test in the 2020 US census. The census is not allowed to publish anything that identifies the data of any individual or establishment; collected data must by law be kept confidential for 72 years and used only for statistical purposes until then. First, the Census Bureau reviewed the security of the 2010 census in the light of modern analysis tools [752]. In 2010, the aggregated *census edited file* (CEF) of data collected from US residents and then edited to get rid of duplicates and fill in missing entries from data such as tax returns, had 44 bits of confidential data on each resident (a total of 1.7Gb). The problem is that the microdata summaries simply contained a lot more data than this; writing everything out, you get several billion simultaneous equations and can in theory solve for the confidential data.

What about in practice? Census staff implemented ideas based on Kobbi Nissim and Irit Dinur's work, and found that they got all the variables right about 38% of the time, covering a bit under 20% of the population. It took one month on four servers, so it's not entirely trivial. However, the lesson is that the traditional approaches to statistical database security don't really work. They did provide some privacy, because the 2010 census swapped very identifiable households with other blocks, so not everyone was compromised. If they'd swapped all the households, it would have been OK, but the users wouldn't have put up with that; the fact that they gave exact population counts for a block was a real vulnerability. Dealing with database reconstruction piecemeal is hard; that's the value of differential privacy.

The big policy question is where you set ϵ. This is also an empirical question. In 2018, census staff did an end-to-end test reporting four tables. In 2020 the full system will process the CEF into a *microdata details file* (MDF) from which the tabulations will be derived. Foreseeable issues include that numbers won't add up; so the number of members of the separate Native American tribes won't add up to the total of Native Americans, and that will have to be explained to the public. The differential-privacy approach will protect everyone, while the old system only protected people who were swapped, and it has to be done all at once. Every record may be modified subject to an overall privacy budget, so there's no exact mapping between the CEF and the MDF.

The new top-down algorithm generates a national histogram without geographic identifiers, then sets out to build a geographic histogram top-down, such that the state figures add up to the national figures (which is needed for Congressional redistricting). The construction is then done recursively down through state, county, tract, block group and block, after which they generate the microdata. This can be done in parallel and enables sparsity discovery (e.g., there are very few people over 100 belonging to 5 or more races). The top-down approach turns out to be much more accurate than applying noise block-by-block, in that county data have less error than blocks, and national data have essentially no error. There are several edge cases needing special handling: a prison won't be turned into a college dorm, but if there are five dorms, you might report four or six. Person-household joins are also hard; you can do the number of men on a block, or the number of households, but the number of children in households headed by a single man is more sensitive. But many things that used to be suppressed no longer have to be; you no longer have to enumerate all the sources of side information that might be used; and there will at last be published error statistics.

Now that the outline design has been done, there's a simulator you can use to explore possible values of ϵ. You can plug this into an economic analysis of the tradeoff between the marginal social benefit of better stats with the marginal social costs of identity theft [930]; the outcome suggests a value of ϵ between 4 and 6.

11.4 Mind the gap?

On the political side, the use of lightly-deidentified data in research, whether medical research or market research, has involved sporadic guerilla warfare between privacy advocates and data users for years, with regulators usually siding with the data users except in the aftermath of a scandal. The regulators are both overwhelmed and conflicted, as I'll describe in section 26.6.1, and mostly do not have the political support to take on big Internet service firms or government departments. These 'Big Data' interests are generally adept at capturing regulators anyway. For example, in 2008 Prime Minister Gordon Brown asked the UK Information Commissioner and the head of Britain's largest medical-research charity to come up with guidelines on using data in research; they ignored privacy rights, took an instrumental view of costs and benefits, and spun the secondary use of data as 'data sharing'. As you might expect, neither privacy lawyers nor security academics were pleased with the result [97].

In 2009 a highly influential paper, 'Broken promises of privacy', was written by Paul Ohm, a distinguished US law professor [1467]. He noted that "scientists have demonstrated they can often 'reidentify' or 'deanonymize' individuals hidden in anonymized data with astonishing ease" and confessed "we have made a mistake, labored beneath a fundamental misunderstanding, which has assured us much less privacy than we have assumed. This mistake pervades nearly every information privacy law, regulation, and debate, yet regulators and legal scholars have paid it scant attention." For the previous thirty years, computer scientists had known that anonymisation doesn't really work, but law and policy people had stopped their ears. Here at last was an eminent lawyer spelling out the facts, telling the story of AOL and Netflix, in a law journal and using lawyer-accessible language. Among other things he ridiculed Google's claim that IP addresses were not personal information (it argued that its search logs should therefore fall outside the scope of data protection), denounced the binary mindset of data as either personal or not, and called for a more realistic debate on privacy and data protection. Might this change things?

In 2012, a report from the Royal Society called for scientists to publish their data openly where possible but acknowledged the reality of re-identification risks: 'However, a substantial body of work in computer science has now demonstrated that the security of personal records in databases cannot be guaranteed through anonymisation procedures where identities are actively sought' [1630]. In that year, the UK Information Commissioner also developed a code of practice on anonymisation [81]; as the ICO is the privacy regulator, such a code can shield firms from liability, and it was the target of vigorous lobbying. The eventual code required data users to only describe their mechanisms in general terms, and shifted the burden of proof on to anyone who objected [82]. This was a less stringent burden than the ICO applies in freedom-of-information cases, where a request for public data can be refused on the presumption that the data subjects' 'friends, former colleagues, or acquaintances' may know relevant context. This tiptoes round a concept of some relevance to tactical anonymity – the *privacy set*, or the set of people whom I might want to not know some fact about me. For most people, this is your family, friends and work colleagues – perhaps 100–200 people. For celebrities, it can be everybody; and problems can arise when someone suddenly becomes famous. Most of us can be anonymous in a big city, but a celebrity can't.

Another useful but quite different concept is the *anonymity set*, which is the set of people with whom you might be confused. We're all familiar with detective films or novels, where Poirot steadily reduces the number of people who might have committed the murder from a dozen to one. Strategic mechanisms like differential privacy focus on keeping the anonymity set large enough, while many tactical mechanisms assess the risk that people with access to some application will overlap your privacy set.

But you always have to think carefully about the threat model. While it may be enough to worry about your privacy set when the concern is embarrassment, when it's scam artists you need to worry about the anonymity set. As we noted in Chapter 3, phishing attacks often involve information leaks about the victim that enable an attacker to impersonate the victim to some service, or impersonate the service to the victim. In short, when it comes to phishing, anyone who can tie your identity to some relevant context may be able to attack you.

11.4.1 Tactical anonymity and its problems

The ICO also set up the UK Anonymisation Network (UKAN), which is coordinated by academics and by the Office of National Statistics. In 2016 UKAN produced a book of guidance on how firms should make decisions on anonymisation, duly signed off by the ICO [627]. Its authors see confidentiality as being about risk rather than duty; decisions have to be taken not just according to the technical possibility of identifying data subjects but the institutional and social context that determines whether this might be attempted. The threat model should be based on plausible intruder scenarios. They talk of governance processes rather than side channels; they dismiss differential privacy as 'extreme'; they see anonymisation as a process and advise against using 'success terms' like 'anonymised'; and they define 'de-identified' as 'can't be re-identified from the data directly'. Measures to manage re-identification risk should be proportional to risk and its likely impact; and anonymisation measures may have a limited lifetime because of eventual triangulation from other datasets. Such mechanisms therefore have to be seen as tactical anonymity, as opposed to the strategic anonymity that is being carefully engineered into the US census. The UKAN authors do not seem to have considered differential privacy seriously.

Despite its flaws, the UKAN framework requires attention if you're going to rely on anonymisation, whether tactical or strategic, in the UK, as it's the yardstick by which the regulator will decide whether or not to take enforcement action against you. It is likely to provide a shock absorber and liability shield for both data users and regulators as anonymisation becomes steadily less effective. It would have provided some protection for firms that based their EU operations in the UK, but with Britain having left the EU this will no longer hold. It does however contain a reasonable amount of practical advice on assessing the risks of tactical anonymisation in applications where both the data and the environment are reasonably well understood. As a result, there are now several firms whose products and services aim at helping data users comply with it.

An example of a firm operating openly under this framework is the mobile network operator Vodafone, which sells 'location insight' products. The company aggregates the mobile phone locations of its customers into journeys with implied origin, destination and mode of transport. The origin-destination matrices are sold to local government and transport firms along with flows along main roads and railways. The privacy mechanisms consist of first, allowing all subscribers an opt-out and second, encrypting phone IMSIs to give a different pseudonym per device, with a slowly changing key; the cell towers are easily re-identifiable. One can indeed make an argument that the risk here is low; maybe the analysts at the local council or bus company can identify you, especially if you live in a small hamlet (as I do; four houses 200m from the nearest village). So the anonymity set can be too small. Then you have to look at the privacy set size. But suppose you work at a firm that becomes a target for activists. If they recruit someone at the council, they could target company staff who live in isolated houses in order to intimidate them or their families[5].

The practical problems that have become evident have to do first with scale and second with the inherent conflicts of self-regulation. The scale is evident not just in the number of data sources that might be matched externally to identify people, but in the growing size and complexity of organisations' internal data warehouses too. A decisive factor has been Hadoop[6]: a firm can now store everything, so it's hard to keep track of what's stored. As there are no database schemas but the data are just piled up, you have no idea of linkage risks, especially if your firm has a multitenant cluster with all sorts of stuff from different subsidiaries. Such data warehouses are now used for fraud prevention, customer analytics and targeted marketing. Firms want to be responsible, but how do you give live data to your development and test teams? How can you collaborate with academics and startups? How can you sell data products? Anonymisation technology is all pretty rudimentary at this scale, and as you just don't know what's going on, it's beyond the scope of differential privacy or anything else you can analyse cleanly. You can tokenise the data on ingest to get rid of the obvious names, then control access and use special tricks for time series and location streams, but noise addition doesn't work on trajectories and there are lots of creative ways to re-identify location data (e.g., photos of celebs getting in and out of taxis). Things get even harder where people are partially authorised and have partial access.

Future problems may come from AI and machine learning; that's the fashion now, following the 'Big Data' fashion of the mid-2010s that led firms to set up large data warehouses. You're now training up systems that generally can't explain what they do, on data you don't really understand. We already know of lots of things that can go wrong. Insurance systems jack up premiums in minority neighbourhoods, breaking anti-discrimination laws. And machine learning systems inhale existing social prejudices along with their training data; as machine-translation systems read gigabytes of online text, they become much better at translation but they also become racist, sexist and homophobic (we'll discuss this in more detail in section 25.3). Another problem is that if a neural network is trained on personal data, then it will often be able to identify some of those persons if it comes across them again – so you can't just train it and then release it in the hope that its knowledge is somehow anonymous, as

[5]In 2003 I was an elected member of our university's governing body, and we were targeted by animal rights activists after the university proposed a new building for animals to be used in medical research. Some colleagues had activists turning up at their homes to shout at them, and a couple of activists were later convicted of terrorism offences after a similar campaign at Oxford. Just about anyone can suddenly become a target.

[6]Open-source software originally developed by Yahoo to store data at petabyte scale on clusters of servers and access it using NoSQL.

we might hope for averages derived from large aggregates of data. Again, you just don't understand what the ML system is doing, so any claim you make to anonymity should be treated with scepticism. And it's not enough to say 'We don't sell your data, we just target ads': if you let the Iranian secret police target ads at gay people who speak Farsi, they can simply pop up ads offering free pizza.

As the Information Commissioner's Office doesn't appear to have the capability or motivation to police anonymity services and applications, the industry self-regulates; in effect, firms mark their own homework. This means adverse selection, as the least conscientious provider will promise the most functionality. As I already noted, there are many firms selling fine-grained location data, social data and the like who claim it's anonymous even when it clearly isn't. Even where organisations are well-meaning, it's rare for them to really understand the issues until they hit trouble, and on more than one occasion we've had providers approaching us for advice after they'd bitten off more than they could chew. The data users often don't want to talk to real experts once they hit a problem as they realise that the more they know, the more expensive things will be to fix. As for beefing up the regulator, the more a government did that, the less competitive its information industries would become. One of the reasons anonymisation is such a wicked problem is that its security economics are truly dreadful.

11.4.2 Incentives

Even imperfect de-identification may protect data against casual browsing and against some uses that are unsafe or even predatory. However, it may make rascals feel empowered to do rascally things (especially since UKAN). So in statistical security, the question of whether one should let the best be the enemy of the good can require a finer judgment call than elsewhere. As I discussed in the chapter on economics, the most common cause of security failure in large systems with many stakeholders is when the incentives are wrong – when Alice guards a system and Bob pays the cost of failure. So what are the incentives here?

The overall picture is not good. For example, medical privacy is conditioned by how people pay for healthcare. If you see a psychoanalyst privately and pay cash, then the incentives are aligned; the analyst will lock up your notes. But in the US, healthcare is generally paid for by your employer; and in Britain, the government pays for most of it. In both cases, attempts to centralise control for management purposes have driven conflict with doctors and patients. While such conflicts can be masked for a while by claims about anonymity, it is unlikely that they can be resolved by any feasible privacy technology. Once people accept this, a more realistic political conversation can begin.

11.4.3 Alternatives

One approach is to combine weak anonymity with access control, whether requiring the researcher to visit a secure site (as in New Zealand, and also for research on tax data in the UK) or requiring licensing incorporating a non-disclosure agreement plus access and use controls that forbid any attempt at identifying subjects (as in Germany). This can be robust provided it is done:

1. competently, with decent security engineering;
2. honestly, without false claims that the data are no longer personal; and
3. within the law, which in the EU will involve giving data subjects a right to opt out that is respected.

In medicine, the gold standard is doing research with explicit patient consent. This not only allows full access to data, but provides motivated subjects and much higher-quality clinical information than can be harvested simply as a byproduct of normal clinical activities. For example, a network of researchers into ALS (the motor-neurone disease from which Cambridge astronomer Stephen Hawking suffered) shares fully-identifiable information between doctors and other researchers in over a dozen countries with the full consent of the patients and their families. This network allows data sharing between Germany, with very strong privacy laws, and Japan, with almost none; and data continued to be shared between researchers in the USA and Serbia even when the USAF was bombing Serbia. The consent model is spreading. A second example is Biobank, a UK research project in which several hundred thousand volunteers gave researchers not just full access to their records for the rest of their lives, but answered an extensive questionnaire and gave blood samples so that those who develop interesting diseases in later life can have their genetic and proteomic makeup analysed. Needless to say, access with full consent also requires robust security engineering as consent will be contingent on access being restricted to researchers.

Whether you go the trusted-researcher route or the full-consent route, access for research will also depend on ethical approval. In section 10.4.6 we discussed the origins of medical ethics, in the Tuskegee experiments in the US and the experiments performed by Nazi doctors in Germany, and the safeguards that have now arisen: Institutional Review Boards (IRBs) in America and ethics committees in Europe. If you're a medical researcher with no realistic alternative to using records collected from medical practice on a shaky legal basis and protected using leaky de-identification mechanisms, then you have no real choice but to rely on your IRB or ethics committee. Although the exact processes differ between (and within) institutions the key principle is that such research has to be approved by someone independent of the researcher – typically one or more anonymous colleagues, who assess both the aims of the investigation and the proposed methods. There are, however, some serious moral hazards.

11.4.4 The dark side

Ethics review processes provide researchers with a liability shield at two levels. First, if something goes wrong and the researcher is sued for negligence, this is assessed using 'the standards of the industry' as a yardstick. If you follow the same processes as everybody else, and have each project approved by an ethics committee that contains 'independent' members (which in practice means professors from other universities, rather than representatives of the real data subjects) then you can make a strong case that you followed those standards. Second, if the worst happens and you face the possibility of criminal prosecution, in common-law countries that involves a dual test: of 'mens rea' or wrongful intent, as well as 'actus reus' or a prohibited act. Ethical approval processes are designed to provide evidence that there was no mens rea. If you did what you said you'd do, and for reasons that independent people approved, how can that be wrongful intent? In short, ethics review processes are optimised to protect the researcher and the institution, not the data subject.

This has not escaped the attention of Big Data. In section 11.2.6 I mentioned Google DeepMind's ethics board and its failure to prevent the scandal; Google managed to escape censure from the Information Commissioner (unlike the hospital that handed over all its medical records). Unsurprisingly, ethics boards are proliferating, especially as firms start throwing artificial intelligence and machine learning techniques at large data warehouses with little clear idea of what the outcome might be. AI ethics is a hot topic in academia and a rapidly-growing source of jobs. The cynical operator will go through the motions of complying with some of the UKAN recommendations and then hire some unemployed philosophers to talk about moral philosophy and the nature of intelligence, while getting on with the business of selling your most intimate personal information to the spammers. Ethics washing and data abuse now go hand in hand.

What's more, the existence of publicly-advertised privacy mechanisms may deflect attention from abuse of the underlying personal data. In March 2007, historians Margo Anderson and William Seltzer found that census confidentiality was suspended in 1942, and microdata on Japanese Americans living in Washington DC was given to the Secret Service in 1943 [1702]. Block-level data were given to officials in California, where they rounded up Japanese-Americans for internment. The single point of failure there appears to have been Census Bureau director JC Capt, who released the data to the Secret Service following a request from Treasury Secretary Henry Morgenthau. The Bureau has since publicly apologised [1321]. But this was nothing new. The British government used the 1911 census to target aliens for expulsion when WWI broke out in 1914; the 1941 census was brought forward to 1939 to serve as a basis for conscription, rationing and internment; and the security services continued to have a back door into the census until the 1980s. Elsewhere, the Germans used census data to round up Jews not only in Germany but in the Netherlands and other occupied territories. More recently, Cambridge Analytica and its parent company SCL were granted covert access to full national census data by a number of countries where they helped the incumbent government win re-election [2055].

There are many examples of publicly-advertised privacy mechanisms that are less effective than they seem. The UK is building a system of 'smart meters' that report everyone's gas and electricity consumption via a central clearing-house, from which it gets sent to your utility so they can bill you; other firms need an approved privacy plan to get access to the data. However, when we look at a typical privacy plan, we see a distribution network operator getting access to half-hourly meter data for its distribution area, the Midlands, the South West and Wales [2015]. The purpose is to predict when substation transformers will have to be replaced. The distributor promises to aggregate this feed into half-hourly totals for each feeder – these are the cables that leave the transformers and supply a number of houses. But looking at the data, we see that 0.96% of feeders serve only one house and 2.67% serve 3 or fewer. A more robust privacy regulator would have told them to just install their own meters at their own transformers. In fact, more sensible public policy would have been to not do the smart meter project at all; I discuss this in Chapter 14.

As for medicine, the US HIPAA system empowers the DHHS to regulate health plans, healthcare clearinghouses, and healthcare providers, but leaves many other organisations that process medical data such as lawyers, employers and universities, outside its scope. Big tech companies may escape the regulations depending on who they say they're processing data for. In the UK, as we already noted, neither the patient opt-outs nor the advertised de-identification mechanisms are effective. In many countries, more organisations than you might think have access to fully-identifiable data.

11.5 Summary

Lots of people want to believe that you can turn sensitive personal data into an industrial raw material by stripping off overt identifiers such as names. This only works in some well-defined special cases, such as a national census – where we have a solid theory in the form of differential privacy. In most cases, the data are just too rich and re-identification of data subjects is easy.

However policymakers, marketers, medical researchers and others want so hard to believe that anonymity provides a magic solution to using personal data that it's difficult to disabuse them. The constant hype around big data and machine learning makes the education task harder, just as these technologies are making anonymity much harder still. We may expect serious trouble as the scale and the scope of the privacy lawbreaking become ever more clear to the public. It will probably take a scandal to bring real change, and when this eventually happens, the disruption is likely to be non-trivial.

Research problems

At present there are several lively threads of research around anonymity and privacy. First, there are practical researchers who look for new ways of deriving sensitive data from existing public data, or try to understand exploits being carried out by marketers and cybercriminals. Second, there are mathematicians looking at ways of doing differentially-private machine learning in various contexts, such as learning from data held by mutually mistrustful firms. Third, there are privacy law scholars trying to work out how the gap between law and practice could be closed. Fourth, there are practical campaigners (such as EPIC, Privacy International and Max Schrems) who bring lawsuits to try to stop practices that are becoming common yet which appear to violate the laws we already have. This ecosystem of theory, practice, scholarship and campaigning will no doubt continue to evolve as yet more of the stuff around us becomes 'smart'. Will 'smart cities' simply mean even more pervasive surveillance? In the limit, will there be so much contextual information available that nothing short of differential privacy will do? Or will society eventually say that enough is enough, and impose radical limits on the collection, analysis and use of data – and what limits might have some chance of working? Finally, the latest magic potion is privacy-preserving federated machine learning. I've no doubt one can find edge cases in which something like that can be made to work, as with differential privacy. But I suspect it will turn out to be just a variant of the snake oil we've been fed about anonymisation over the past forty years. (Hey, if you boil snake oil with sodium hydroxide, you should get snake soap.) What's the best way to debunk that?

Further reading

If you want to dive into the details of differential privacy, a good starting point might be a long survey paper by Cynthia Dwork and Aaron Roth [594]. The classic reference on inference control is Dorothy Denning's 1982 book [538]; the 1989 survey paper by Adam and Wortman is a good summary of the state of the art then [17]. An important reference for statisticians involved in US government work is the Federal Committee on Statistical Methodology's *'Report on Statistical Disclosure Limitation Methodology'* which introduces the tools and methods used in various US departments and agencies [667]; this dates back to 2005, so it's somewhat out of date and is currently being rewritten. The UKAN book is a must-read if you're doing anonymisation for a client operating within the UK's jurisdiction [627]. As an example of a quite different application, Mark Allman and Vern Paxson discuss the problems of anonymizing IP packet traces for network systems research in [43]. Finally, Margo Anderson and William Seltzer's papers on the abuses of census data in the US, particularly during World War 2, can be found at [53].

CHAPTER

12

Banking and Bookkeeping

Against stupidity, the Gods themselves contend in vain.
– JC FRIEDRICH VON SCHILLER

As a dog returneth to his vomit, so a fool returneth to his folly.
– PROVERBS 26:11

12.1 Introduction

The cashless payment industry is one of the winners from the coronavirus pandemic, as people worldwide abandon cash in favour of card and phone payments. The underlying banking systems range from payment card processing and home banking through high-value interbank money transfers to the back-end bookkeeping systems that keep track of it all and settle up afterwards. There are specialised networks for everything from stock trading to trade payments, many of which are open to other companies too. Larger companies have internal bookkeeping and cash management systems that mirror many of the functions of a bank.

Such systems matter to the security engineer for a number of reasons. First, they're a core professional competence. You need to understand transaction processing to tackle the wider problems of fraud, and this chapter will give you a road map. You also need to understand internal controls based on bookkeeping, as these not only give early warnings when things go wrong, but also drive corporate risk management. You have to be able to carry a conversation about Gramm-Leach-Bliley, Sarbanes-Oxley and PCI DSS to have credibility with your CFO. When you propose protection mechanisms, one of the first things you're likely to be asked is how they'll help executives discharge their fiduciary responsibilities to shareholders.

Second, bookkeeping drove the computer industry. The first computer outside the military and academia was the Leo, which did bookkeeping for the Lyons chain of coffee houses from 1951. Banking rapidly became the most intensive application area for computing, which spread into other firms via the automation of bookkeeping from the 1960s. So the protection of bookkeeping systems is of both historical and practical importance. It also gives us a well-understood model of protection in which confidentiality plays little role, but where the integrity of records (and their immutability once made) is paramount. A banking system should prevent customers from cheating each other, or the bank; it should prevent bank staff from cheating the bank, or its customers; and the evidence it provides should be good enough that none of them can get away with falsely accusing others of cheating. Banking and bookkeeping pioneered the use of dual control, also known nowadays as multi-party authorisation.

Third, transaction processing systems – whether for $50 ATM withdrawals, or $100m wire transfers – were the application that launched commercial cryptology as a separate discipline outside the military. They drove the development of encryption algorithms and protocols, as well as the supporting technology such as smartcards. Many instructive mistakes were first made (or at least publicly documented) in the area of financial cryptography.

Finally, many of the global-scale systems we've built this century were designed to circumvent the checks and balances that had evolved over centuries in the local and manual systems they replaced. Google's mission was to make all the world's information available by disrupting the previous implicit and explicit controls of locality, scale, confidence and copyright. Uber planned to become the global taxi company by circumventing taxi regulations in thousands of towns and cities worldwide. It's hardly surprising that a successful startup often has to reinvent controls, whether under pressure from fraud and abuse, or under pressure from lawmakers.

In this chapter, I'll first describe the bookkeeping systems used to track assets and manage the risk of corrupt staff; such accounting systems are also used by other companies of any size. I'll then describe the international funds-transfer systems used for interbank payments. Next, I'll describe ATM systems, the public face of banking, whose technology has also been adopted in applications such as utility meters. I'll follow with the story of credit cards, which have become the main payment mechanism online. I'll then move on to more recent technical advances, including contactless payments, phone payments and open banking.

12.2 Bookkeeping systems

Bookkeeping appears to have been invented in the Middle East in about 8500 BC, just after agriculture [1666]. When people started to produce surplus food, they started to store and trade it. Suddenly they needed a way to keep track of which villager put what in the communal warehouse. To start with, each unit of food (sheep, wheat, oil, …) was represented by a clay token, or *bulla*, which was placed inside a clay envelope, sealed by rolling it with the pattern of the warehouse keeper and then baked in a kiln, as we can see in Figure 12.1. When the farmer wanted to get his food back, the seal was broken by the keeper in the presence of a witness. (This may be the oldest known security protocol.) By about 3000BC, this had led to the invention of writing [1517]; after another thousand years, we find equivalents of promissory notes, bills of lading, and so on. At about the same time, metal ingots started to be used as an intermediate commodity, often sealed inside a bulla by an assayer. In 700BC, Lydia's King Croesus started stamping the metal directly and thus invented coins [1554]. By the Athens of Pericles, a number of wealthy individuals were in business as bankers [773].

Figure 12.1: Clay envelope and its content of tokens representing 7 jars of oil, from Uruk, present day Iraq, ca. 3300 BC (courtesy Denise Schmandt-Besserat and the Louvre Museum)

The next significant innovation dates to medieval times. As the dark ages came to a close and trade started to grow, some businesses became too large for a single family to manage. The earliest recognisably modern banks date to this period; by having branches in a number of cities, they could finance trade. But for firms to grow beyond the ability of the owner's family to supervise them directly, they had to hire managers from outside. The mechanism that evolved to control the risk of fraud was *double-entry bookkeeping*. Historians have found double-entry records created by Jewish merchants in twelfth-century Cairo [1694], though the first book on the subject did not appear until 1494 [522].

12.2.1 Double-entry bookkeeping

The idea behind double-entry bookkeeping is simple: each transaction is posted to two separate books, as a credit in one and a debit in the other. For example, when a firm sells a customer $100 worth of goods on credit, it posts a $100 credit on the Sales account, and a $100 debit to the Receivables account. When the customer pays the money, it will credit the Receivables account (thereby reducing the asset of 'money receivable'), and debit the Cash account. (The principle taught in accountancy school is 'debit the receiver, credit the giver'.) At the end of the day, the books should *balance*, that is, add up to zero; the assets and the liabilities should be equal. In all but the smallest firms, the books were kept by different clerks.

We arrange things so that each branch can be balanced separately. Each cashier will balance their cash tray before locking it in the vault overnight; the debits in the cash ledger should exactly balance the physical banknotes they've collected. So most frauds need the collusion of two or more people, and this principle of *split responsibility*, also known as *dual control* or *multi-party authorisation* (MPA), is complemented by audit. Not only are the books audited at year end, but there are random audits too; inspectors may descend on a branch at no notice and insist that all the books are balanced before the staff go home.

Technology arrived in 1879, when the 'Incorruptible Cashier' patent of James Ritty of Dayton, Ohio, introduced the cash register with a bell and a paper tape. Ritty was a saloon owner whose employees stole money from him. He sold his patent to John H. Patterson, who founded the National Cash Register Company, which not only became a leading supplier of banking and bookkeeping equipment, but spun off IBM, which dominated the computer industry until Microsoft displaced it in the 1990s.

12.2.2 Bookkeeping in banks

Banks were early adopters of computers for bookkeeping. Starting in the late 1950s and early 1960s with applications such as cheque processing, they found that even the slow and expensive computers of the time were much cheaper than armies of clerks. The 1960s saw banks offering automated payroll services to their corporate customers. ATMs arrived en masse in the 1970s, with the first online banking systems in the 1980s; web-based banking followed in the 1990s. Yet today's slick online systems still rely on legacy back-office automation.

The law in the US, Europe and most developed countries requires not just banks but all public companies to have effective internal controls, and makes executives responsible for them. Such laws are the main drivers of investment in information security mechanisms. Computer systems used for bookkeeping typically claim to implement variations on the double-entry theme, but the quality is variable. The separation-of-duty features may be just a skin in the user interface, while the underlying data are open to manipulation by technical staff. For example, if the ledgers are all just views of one single database, then someone with physical access and a database editing tool might bypass the controls. Staff may also notice loopholes and exploit them. For example, one bank didn't audit address changes, until a cashier found he could change a customer's address, issue an extra bank card, and change it back again [55]. So we need to look at the mechanics, and banking is the natural place to start.

A traditional core banking system has a number of data structures: an *account master file*, which contains each customer's current balance together with previous transactions for a period of perhaps ninety days; a number of *ledgers* which track cash and other assets on their way through the system; various *journals* of transactions that have been received from cash machines, teller stations, merchant terminals and so on, but not yet posted to the ledgers; and an *audit trail* that records who did what and when. The systems used by the large UK banks are relatively unchanged since the last century, though a number of peripherals have been added, notably phone banking[1].

The core banking software will apply the transactions from the journals to the various ledgers and the account master file. So when a customer walks into a branch and pays $100 into their savings account, the teller will make a transaction that records a credit to the customer's savings account of $100 while debiting the same amount to the cash ledger recording the amount of money in the drawer.

This was traditionally done overnight in a batch process but increasingly involves real-time online processing, so things can go wrong more quickly. The fact that all the ledgers should always add up to zero provides an important check. If the bank (or one of its branches) is ever out of balance, an alarm will go off, some processing will stop, and inspectors will start looking for the cause. So a programmer who wants to add to their own account balance has to take the money from some other account, rather than just creating it out of thin air by tweaking the account master file. Just as a traditional business had different ledgers managed by different clerks, so a banking data processing shop will have different development teams in charge of different subsystems. In addition, all code is subjected to scrutiny by an internal auditor, and to testing by a separate test department. Once it has been approved, it will be run on a production machine that does not have a development environment, but only approved object code and data. (The principle that a different team runs production systems than the developers who wrote it is now coming under strain in the new world of DevOps.)

[1]Most retail banking transactions nowadays are balance enquiries from phones, which are typically dealt with by a front end that gets regular updates from the core system. This minimises load on the core system, and also minimises the complaints when it goes down.

12.2.3 The Clark-Wilson security policy model

Although such systems had evolved since the 1960s, a formal model of their security policy was only introduced in 1987 by Dave Clark and Dave Wilson (the former a computer scientist, and the latter an accountant) [438]. In this model, some data items are constrained so that they can only be acted on by a certain set of transformation procedures.

More formally, there are special procedures whereby data can be input – turned from an *unconstrained data item*, or UDI, into a *constrained data item*, or CDI; *integrity verification procedures* (IVPs) to check the validity of any CDI (e.g., that the books balance); and *transformation procedures* (TPs), which may be thought of in the banking case as transactions that preserve balance. In the general case, they maintain the integrity of CDIs. They also write enough information to an append-only CDI (the audit trail) for transactions to be reconstructed. Access control is by means of triples *(subject, TP, CDI)*, which are so structured that a multi-party authorisation policy is enforced. In the formulation in [48]:

1. the system will have an IVP for validating the integrity of any CDI;
2. the application of a TP to any CDI must maintain its integrity;
3. a CDI can only be changed by a TP;
4. subjects can only initiate certain TPs on certain CDIs;
5. triples must enforce an appropriate separation-of-duty policy on subjects;
6. certain special TPs on UDIs can produce CDIs as output;
7. each application of a TP must cause enough information to reconstruct it to be written to a special append-only CDI;
8. the system must authenticate subjects attempting to initiate a TP;
9. the system must let only special subjects (i.e., security officers) make changes to authorization-related lists.

A number of things bear saying. First, unlike Bell-LaPadula, the Clark-Wilson model involves maintaining state. In addition to the audit trail, this is usually necessary for dual control as you have to keep track of which transactions have been partially approved – such as those approved by only one manager and waiting for sign-off by a second.

Second, the model doesn't do everything. It captures the idea that state transitions should preserve an invariant such as balance, but not that state transitions should be correct. This model doesn't stop you paying cash into the wrong bank account.

Third, the hard question remains, namely: how do we control the risks from dishonest staff? Rule 5 says that 'an appropriate separation-of-duty policy' must be supported, but nothing about what this means. Indeed, it's difficult to find any systematic discussion in the accounting literature of how you design internal controls.

What happens in practice is that the big four accountancy firms have a list of controls that they push to their audit clients – a typical company may have a checklist of about 300 internal controls that it has to maintain, depending on what sector it's in. These lists get steadily longer in response to incidents, fears, and regulatory requirements. Many controls are formal compliance rather than real risk reduction, and some are actually harmful. I discussed in section 3.4.4.3 how the big four auditors seized on NIST advice in the 1990s to get people to change their passwords every month; at the time of writing (2020) they are still pushing their audit clients to do this. Yet NIST retracted its advice years ago in the face of the evidence, and Britain's GCHQ also advises companies against password aging.

A principled approach to internal control is possible, and indeed desirable. In the following section, I try to distill the experience gained from working at the coalface in banking and consultancy, and more recently in university governance.

12.2.4 Designing internal controls

Over the years, various standards for bookkeeping and internal control have been promoted by the accountancy profession, by lawgivers and by banking regulators. In the US, there's the *Committee of Sponsoring Organizations* (COSO), a group of accounting and auditing bodies [462]. However, self-regulation failed to stop the excesses of the dotcom era, and following the collapse of Enron there was intervention from US lawmakers in the form of the *Sarbanes-Oxley Act* (SOX) of 2002. SOX regulates all US public companies, making senior executives responsible for the accuracy and completeness of financial reports, whose truthfulness CEOs have to certify; protecting whistle-blowers, who are the main source of information on insider fraud; and making managers responsible for maintaining "adequate internal control structure and procedures for financial reporting". It also demands that auditors disclose any "material weaknesses". Most of the compliance costs of SOX are reckoned to come from internal controls. Earlier, the *Gramm-Leach-Bliley Act* (GLBA) of 1999 had liberalised bank regulation in many respects but obliged banks to have security mechanisms to protect information from foreseeable threats in security and integrity. Along with HIPAA in the medical sector, and PCI DSS that I'll discuss later in section 12.5.2, GLBA and SOX have driven much of the investment in information security and internal control. These regulations have helped consolidate the Big Four accountancy firms' influence over corporate policy on internal control.

In this section, our focus is on the technical aspects. Modern risk-management systems typically require a company to identify and assess its risks, and then build controls to mitigate them. The company will typically have a risk register containing many pages of major risk items such as 'loss of working capital due to large unauthorised bank transaction by insider' (I'll discuss this in more detail in section 27.2). Some of them will be mitigated using non-technical measures such as insurance, but all should have a risk owner among the senior executives, and a number of these risks will end up in the CIO's lap[2].

The auditors' work will be driven by the International Auditing and Assurance Standard Board's "International Standard on Auditing 315" [952]. ISA 315 focuses on the risk of a material misstatement in an organisation's accounts, whether due to error or to fraud. The auditors are supposed to understand the business and its system of internal control; they will identify significant accounts (such as Cash), significant assertions for each account (such as Existence) and the significant business processes (such as Sales) that impact them, along with the controls those processes contain. They then work through the risk that each assertion might be false and whether the risk is material. So how do you engineer proper controls? The latest version of ISA 315 has quite a few pages on this, but they are mostly somewhat general[3], so their interpretation is often down to the accountancy firms.

As we'll discuss in Part 3, there are two basic approaches to assuring safety against errors and security against attacks. You can work top-down, starting off from the list of bad things you want to not happen, such as 'large unauthorised wire transfer', then enumerating the possible causes and identifying controls to mitigate the risks; or you can work bottom-up, starting off from things that might fail, such as 'a member of staff being blackmailed', work out what harm might result, and again identify appropriate controls. You may often have to use both approaches. When supporting audit, you need to pay attention to the risks to assertions on which the financial statements rely. However, you cannot ignore other risks that might affect the firm's ability to operate, such as the loss of a data centre. The internal controls will not be all of your security posture.

Having identified those risks that need to be mitigated by separation of duty, you can do this in two ways: *dual control*, also known as *multi-party authorisation*, and *functional separation*.

In dual control, two or more principals act together to authorize a transaction. The classic military example is in nuclear command systems, which may require two officers to turn their keys simultaneously in consoles that are too far apart for either to reach both locks (I'll discuss this in detail in section 15.4). The classic civilian example is when a bank issues a letter of guarantee, which may

[2]For a description of risk governance in a UK bank, see the Financial Conduct Authority's report into the 2016 fraud against Tesco Bank [687], which I discuss in section 12.6.3.

[3]See paragraphs A6, A123–181, A198, A224–229 and Appendix 3 paragraphs 15–24.

undertake to carry the loss should a loan made by another bank go sour. Guarantees are particularly prone to fraud. If you can get bank A to guarantee a loan to your business from bank B, then bank B is supervising your account while bank A's money is at risk. A crook with a forged or corruptly-obtained guarantee can take their time to plunder the loan account at bank B, with the alarm only being raised when they default and bank B asks bank A for the money. You don't want a single manager to be able to issue such an instrument[4].

With functional separation of duty, two or more staff members act on a transaction in complementary ways. The classic example is corporate purchasing. A line manager takes a purchase decision and tells the purchasing department; a clerk there raises a purchase order; the store clerk records the goods' arrival; an invoice arrives at accounts; the accounts clerk correlates it with the purchase order and the stores receipt and raises a cheque; and the accounts manager signs the cheque.

However, it doesn't stop there. The line manager now gets a debit on their monthly statement for that internal account, their boss reviews the accounts to make sure the division's profit targets are likely to be met, the internal audit department can descend at any time to audit the division's books, and when the external auditors come in once a year they will check the books of a randomly selected sample of departments. Finally, when frauds are discovered, the company's lawyers may make vigorous efforts to get the money back.

The model can be summarised as *prevent – detect – recover*. The reliance placed on each of these three legs will depend on the application. Where detection may be delayed, and recovery may therefore be difficult – as with corrupt bank guarantees – you put extra effort into prevention, perhaps using dual control. Where it's prevention that's hard, you can make detection fast enough, and recovery vigorous enough, to provide a deterrent. The classic example here is that bank cashiers can easily take cash, so you count the money every day before they go home.

Management control based on bookkeeping is not only one of the earliest security systems; it has given rise to a lot of management science and civil law. Controls work best where the roles are complementary parts of the existing business process, and some processes have evolved over centuries to support them. Controls are not only entwined with these processes, but exist in the firm's cultural context. In Swiss banks, there are two managers' signatures on almost everything, while Americans are much more relaxed. In most countries' banks, staff can be moved randomly from one task to another, and are forced to take a one-week or even two-week holiday, with no computer or building access, at least once a year. This would not be acceptable in a university – but in academia there's a lot less to steal.

[4]Nowadays the issue is not just whether two managers might collude, or one of them impersonate the other, but whether malware might take over both their accounts. I'll discuss this further in section 12.3.3.

Designing an internal control system is highly interdisciplinary. The financial controllers, the personnel department, the lawyers, the auditors and the systems people all come at the problem from different directions, offer partial solutions, fail to understand each other's control objectives, and things fall down the hole in the middle. Human factors are often neglected, and systems end up vulnerable when helpful subordinates or authoritarian managers circumvent the control to get their work done. It's important to match the controls to the culture, and motivate people to use them; the better run banks sell management controls to staff as a means of protecting them against blackmail and kidnapping. As we noted in Chapter 3, staff in an organisation only have so much compliance budget – they're only prepared to spend so much time and effort performing security rituals that get in the way. Controls that become rituals may also be practised for many years after their purpose has been forgotten or become irrelevant. You have to understand all this and spend the compliance budget wisely on achieving culturally feasible effects. A culture of limited trust of close colleagues is particularly difficult to sustain (another reason why functional controls split across business units may be more effective).

And just as you will try to require more than one banker to approve a large transaction, you may want to require more than one engineer to approve code to run on a live system. But this is hard to do thoroughly for a number of reasons. First, many interfaces provide single points of failure. Second, split-responsibility systems administration is just too tedious. With care you can make it auditable[5]. Third, dual controls often require persistent state, which is in tension with programmers' wish to keep things simple by making transactions atomic. And as that state needs to be managed, there are always some trusted sysadmins who need full access in order to do their jobs. Fourth, as firms move to integrating development and operations as DevOps, and then add security to make it DevSecOps, they may end up with more trusted staff. At the very least, the location of trust may change, as more of it shifts to the source code review phase. Fifth, there are emergencies. The ATM system goes down at the weekend, and the ATM team's on-call engineer gets access to the live system from home to fix the bug. You log such accesses and get your auditors to stare at the logs, as with the sysadmins. Finally, it's inevitable that your top engineers will be so much more knowledgeable than your auditors that they could do bad things if they really wanted to.

So there are always engineers who could commit fraud. A sysadmin might create two shadow users who between them authorise a large payment, or a payment system maintainer might pop an extra payment into the queue. Where they get caught is when the balancing controls set off the alarm after a

[5]Old-time banking systems were built on the IBM operating system MVS, which would let the sysadmin do anything, except finding out which of their activities the auditor was monitoring [225].

day or two, and the money-laundering controls at the bank to which they wire the money stop them getting away with very much. I'll discuss this further in section 12.3.3. The take-home is that functional controls along the *prevent – detect – recover* model are often more important than shared control, as they separate know-how as well as access. But for functional separation to work, the mechanisms need to be engineered into the application, so they may be proprietary, obscure and less well tested than the mechanisms that come with operating systems. And there are limits to how much you can separate know-how. Some people have to understand it all, such as the security architect and the chief auditor.

The same analysis holds for the business processes themselves. Some people end up having to take high-value decisions quickly and have to understand all the aspects of a deal. At a real bank, you might find thirty or forty people you just have to trust – the CEO, the chief dealer, the top sysadmins and a number of others. It's important to know who they are, to minimise their numbers, to pay them well, and to watch them discreetly.

A final remark on dual control is that it gets fragile at organizational interfaces. One example is that banks in California suddenly started ignoring requests that cheques have two signatures after they installed new processing equipment [1624]. Some organisations are unwilling to show competitors who's trusted to sign and for how much. And then there's dispute resolution: 'My two managers say the money was sent!' 'But my two say it wasn't!'

12.2.5 Insider frauds

Theft and fraud can take many forms. Most thefts from the average company are due to insiders, and automation seems to be making the incidents both rarer and larger.

Back when most bankers worked in branches, banks in the English-speaking world sacked some 1% of staff each year. The typical offence was minor embezzlement with a loss of a few thousand dollars. No-one found an effective way of predicting which staff would go bad; previously loyal staff can be thrown off the rails by shocks such as divorce, or by getting a new manager they just can't stand. Losing a few hundred tellers a year was just a cost of doing business. These numbers are falling now that most staff work in call centres; the customers they deal with are allocated randomly to them, so it's hard to collude with a friend. It's also harder nowadays for staff to sell customers' personal information, since staff have to walk a customer through security questions to get access to their record. Staff at well-run banks are typically forbidden from taking phones or even pens and paper into call centres so they can't leak data to outsiders at any scale[6].

[6]Such opsec rules are making it harder for call centres to get staff to work from home during the Covid pandemic.

Notable insider cases include:

- The biggest recent UK bank fraud was pulled off by a gangster from the East End of Glasgow, Feezan Hameed. 'Fizzy' got sent down for 11 years in 2016 for stealing at least £113m from business customers of Lloyds' Bank in the UK during 2013–15, of which only £47m was recovered[7]. He subverted two members of staff who spotted target companies – typically medium-sized firms with over £1m in their accounts. Fizzy would then phone up the business owner or financial controller, claim to be from the bank, 'authenticate' himself by reading them a couple of recent transactions, and ask them to 'authenticate' themselves in return by computing an authorisation code on their second-factor device. Before he did this, he'd log on as them and set up a batch of payments for large five-figure sums. The code he got from the victim would release the batch [821].
- A password reset clerk at HSBC conspired with persons unknown to change the password used by AT&T to access their bank account with HSBC. The new password was used to transfer over $20 million to offshore companies, from which it was not recovered. The clerk was a vulnerable young man who had been employed on password reset after failing internal exams; the court took mercy, and he got away with five years [1572]. It was alleged that an AT&T employee had conspired to cover up the transactions, but that gentleman was acquitted.
- One rapidly-growing bank fraud in the 2010s has involved spear-phishing accounts staff at medium-sized firms and taking over a couple of staff accounts. Owning two clerks' PCs is simpler than suborning two clerks, and if a firm's PCs all have the same configuration and update status, it may not be too hard. As a bank may pay extra attention to large transactions, the game is often to make a lot of four-figure payments before the company notices. In the US, companies that don't notice a fraudulent payment the following day usually have no redress. A typical attack might net half a million.

12.2.6 Executive frauds

All the famous large financial frauds – nine figures and up – have involved senior insiders. The collapse of Barings Bank is a good example: managers failed to control rogue trader Nick Leeson, blinded by greed for the bonuses his apparent trading profits earned them. Other examples include the Equity

[7]Full disclosure: I acted as expert witness for one of the victim companies, and we had to threaten to sue Lloyds to get our money back.

Funding scandal, in which an insurance company's management created thousands of fake people on their computer system, insured them, and sold the policies on to reinsurers; and Robert Maxwell's looting of the Daily Mirror newspaper pension funds in Britain. Either the victim's executives were grossly negligent, as in the case of Barings, or were the perpetrators, as with Equity Funding and Maxwell. And these patterns repeat; for example, Wells Fargo was fined $3bn in 2020 for opening millions of accounts without the customers' knowledge, just as in the Equity Funding case [699].

Economists and accountancy professors analyse such issues as problems of *agency*: a principal A hires an agent B to manage an asset and wants to know how can B's performance be monitored and assessed. The same principles apply whether the principal is the bank's CEO and the agent is a manager contemplating a fraud; or whether the principal consists of the shareholders and the agent is the CEO. In theory, the internal controls and the internal audit department are the tool used by the CEO to keep track of more junior staff, while the external auditors are the tool used by the shareholders to keep track of the CEO and the senior executives.

That's the theory. The practice was analysed by Alexander Dyck, Adair Morse and Luigi Zingales in a survey of 230 cases of corporate fraud against quoted US companies between 1996 and 2004 [596]. Before Sarbanes-Oxley, only a minority of frauds were revealed by the people mandated to spot them: 14% by the auditors and 6% by the SEC. Most were detected by actors with other incentives: 19% by employees, 16% by industry regulators, 14% by financial analysts and 14% by the media. Stock-exchange regulators, commercial banks and insurance underwriters are notable for their complete absence. After Sarbanes-Oxley the performance of mandated actors improved slightly but still to just over half the total. Their analysis of incentives shows that actors with the strongest incentive to blow the whistle, such as short sellers, were least active, while the most active, employees, often had negative incentives in that they got fired. This suggests that the dominating factor is who actually knows what's going on. Second, rewards promote disclosure: in addition to the effects of Sarbanes-Oxley, many government actors (such as the taxman) reward whistleblowers, with positive effects.

In theory, external auditors are appointed by the board's audit committee, which is chaired by an external director; but who appoints the external directors? In my experience, the external directors tend to be friendly with the CEO and the auditors go out of their way to schmooze the CFO[8]. They offer cheap audits to get their foot in the door, and make their real money from consultancy; this was a structural problem for decades, and eventually in February

[8]The legal infighting following the collapse of Enron destroyed its auditors Arthur Andersen, reducing the 'big five' audit firms to the 'big four'; now auditors go out of their way to avoid liability for fraud.

2020, the UK Financial Reporting Council ordered audit and consultancy to be separated [1051]. The big audit firms have a pernicious effect on the information security world by pushing their own list of favourite controls, regardless of the client's real risks. They maximise their income by nit-picking and compliance; the Sarbanes-Oxley regulations cost the average US public company over $1m a year in audit fees.

Quite apart from the pure economic incentives, bosses find it hard to cope with evidence that senior colleagues are incompetent or dishonest. There's a whole literature on information avoidance, which I mentioned in section 3.2.4: people are reluctant to learn things that will cause them pain, stress or extra work. And risks that managers are unwilling to confront, they are often unable to control. No-one at Barings wanted to think that their star dealer Nick Leeson might be a crook; and pop went the bank. Such risks are not being mitigated by technology; if anything they may be growing.

12.2.6.1 The post office case

Executives can also be unwilling to believe that anything might be going systematically wrong with their accounting systems. Even if they suspect, there's a social reflex to close ranks under criticism, and lawyers may advise clients to just deny everything.

The case worth studying here is the failure of the Post Office accounting system in the UK. The Post Office doesn't just ship letters but is a significant financial institution too, most of whose branches are run by sub-postmasters – typically shopkeepers with a franchised Post Office counter on their premises. To control them, the Post Office built an accounting system called Horizon, which had multiple bugs that caused many franchisees to be charged money they didn't owe. Thousands of people had their lives ruined; some lost their businesses and were bankrupted, some staff were wrongly fired, and several people were jailed for frauds they did not commit. Eventually 587 sub-postmasters sued the Post Office, and in December 2019 they won an apology and £58m. The judge found that Horizon 'was not remotely robust' [186].

This is the first and only case, so far as I know, where an accounting system has been subjected to a proper test in aggressive litigation. Many legal systems presume that accounting systems are working properly unless someone can produce evidence to the contrary, and this can be hard: a lot of the legal effort went into forcing the Post Office to give the claimants access to the software and its documentation so it could be examined by their experts. Incidentally, the total losses to franchisees appear to be in the mid-hundreds of millions; they'll get maybe £11m of the £58m settlement, with the rest going to the lawyers and to the hedge fund that bankrolled the litigation. Most staff at the

Post Office took a pay cut while the CEO Paula Vennels, an ordained minister, got a substantial raise [359]. She eventually left. It may be that the software supplier, Fujitsu, will end up paying for the settlement, but that may require further litigation.

12.2.6.2 Other failures

Most accounting system failures are less spectacular, but there are many failures that have significant effects on the ability of financial and other firms to operate. We'll see more examples as we work through payments in this chapter and other applications in later chapters, but here's a start sample.

1. As computer systems get more complex over time, they accumulate cruft that makes them more fragile and harder to maintain. Software engineers refer to this as *technical debt*: it means that changes become slower and more expensive, and recovery from failures can be complex [42]. Bookkeeping systems are no exception. For example, in June 2012, 6.5 million customers of the Natwest Bank had service disrupted for several weeks following a software upgrade that went wrong and had to be reversed. People were stranded overseas with no money and some companies couldn't make payroll. The bank was fined £42m [686]; it was then largely owned by the UK government as it had gone bust in the crash of 2008. Had the service failure gone on another week, it might well have gone bust again, costing taxpayers tens of billions and causing widespread disruption. So the fear of a catastrophic failure closing a money-centre bank is a real one. But replacing a crufty old core banking system with a new one is a major project taking years and costing nine figures, with its own strategic risks. As a young man I worked on a couple of such projects: they have their nail-biting moments.
2. We find similar project risks further down the food chain. Our university's accounting system was replaced in the early 2000s, and a project that should have cost £3m cost £11m instead. We ended up suing the accountancy firm that installed it, and published a detailed report of what went wrong [691].
3. The system is still, years later, a pain to use, and the reason why may be of interest. At our university, 35 finance-office staff have more say in the design of the finance system than 1,500 professors. The clerks care more, as they use it all the time, while we professors might use it for an hour or two a week. The time saved by clerks is less than the time wasted by professors, but the concentrated interest usually wins.

So even if your bookkeeping system uses a standard core that enforces the basic Clark-Wilson properties of balance and integrity, there's still a lot to go wrong.

12.2.6.3 *Ecological validity*

And it's not enough to just check that the books are internally consistent. You also need to check that they correspond to external reality. The series of scandals that shaped modern audit requirements and practice began with the collapse in 1938 of McKesson and Robbins, a well-known drug and chemical company with reported assets of $100m[9]. It turned out that 20% of the recorded assets and inventory did not exist. The president, Philip Musica, turned out to be a bootlegger with a previous fraud conviction; with his three brothers, he inflated the firm's figures using a fake foreign drug business involving a bogus shipping agent and a fake Montreal bank. The auditors had accepted the McKesson account without making enquiries about the company's bosses; they failed to check inventories, verify accounts receivable with customers, or think about separation of duties within the company [1619].

The famous case for the next generation was the salad oil scandal of 1963, involving the bankruptcy of the Allied Crude Oil Refining Corporation and the prosecution by Robert F. Kennedy of its CEO, Tino de Angelis. Allied had borrowed millions from American Express and others against tanks of soybean oil that were actually mostly water, and used this to trade heavily in futures [1444]. American Express stock dropped by 50% after a whistleblower told it of the fraud; it lost $58m. (Warren Buffett then bought 5% of the company and made a fortune.)

The requirement that all big firms be audited has entangled audit firms in pretty well every major financial scandal. I already mentioned Enron, whose failure in 2001 led to the Sarbanes-Oxley Act, and then there was the financial crisis in 2008 caused in part by trading complicated financial derivatives that turned out to be based on near-worthless mortgages. And one issue with the blockchain systems currently being promoted for some payment and bookkeeping applications is that while the mathematical structure may give guarantees of consistency and consensus, there is no information whatsoever about whether the assets referred to are sound, or even exist. So you might be somewhat sceptical when you see a bank talking about a blockchain to register mortgages, on which smart contracts will allow financial innovation. I'll return to this in section 20.7.

The most recent scandal as this book went to press in September 2020 was Wirecard. A payment service firm, it had started out processing card payments to porn sites, online casinos and other merchants that normal banks wouldn't touch. It grew rapidly to displace Commerzbank in the Dax 30 – the index of Germany's 30 biggest quoted companies, and was celebrated in Germany as a rare local firm able to challenge Silicon Valley. But in June 2020, as it was attempting to buy Deutsche Bank (Germany's largest bank, with a market cap

[9] About $1.8bn in 2020 dollars

of about $20bn), Wirecard's auditors EY disclosed that a quarter of its claimed assets, some €2.1bn supposedly held in the Philippines, could not be found. (EY had failed to verify its bank statements with its bankers for three years, relying instead on 'screenshots' provided by the company itself [1838].) The firm filed for bankruptcy and its CEO, Markus Braun, was arrested. A string of fintech startups that used it to process payments stopped trading, leaving millions of cardholders inside and outside Germany unable to access their money. Yet investors and regulators had ignored numerous red flags, going back as far as 2008 [1258]. Worse, when the Financial Times published an analysis in 2019 of Wirecard's dubious accounting practices – pointing out that its Dubai subsidiary seemed to have no customers, that the address of one alleged Philippines subsidiary was a small bus company, that another was the home of a retired seaman, and that whistle blowers in its Singapore subsidiary had reported they were being ordered to cook the books [1285] – the German regulator BaFin had responded not by investigating the company but by starting a criminal investigation of the journalists and banning short selling of the company's shares [610]. BaFin had for some years defended the company against critics rather than investigating their criticisms. This was one of the largest frauds in European history, destroying over €20bn in apparent shareholder value, as well as public confidence in German financial regulation. En route Wirecard had taken in firms such as Moodys, Credit Suisse and Softbank. It was quite astonishing to see how little the lessons of McKesson and Robbins had been heeded; checking overseas cash balances really should have been audit 101. Yet the audit industry has persistent structural problems, ranging from the fact that auditors sell to CFOs to the fact that almost all the work is done by juniors [703].

12.2.6.4 Control tuning and corporate governance

The main reason internal control structures tend to be conservative, expensive and ineffective is that while in theory organizations develop them in the light of experience, in practice this experience is relayed through the auditor cartel. In theory there is some governance behind this. The most influential internal audit standard is the Risk Management Framework from the *Committee of Sponsoring Organizations* (COSO), a group of US accounting and auditing bodies [462]. This is one yardstick by which your system will be judged if it's used in the US public sector or by companies quoted on US equity markets. The COSO model is targeted not just on internal control but on the reliability of financial reporting and compliance with laws and regulations. Its basic process is an evolutionary cycle: in a given environment, you assess the risks, design controls, monitor their performance, and then go round the loop again. COSO emphasizes soft aspects of corporate culture more than hard system design issues, so it may be seen as a guide to managing and documenting the process by which your system evolves. In theory, its core consists of senior management checking that their control policies are being implemented and achieving their objectives, and modifying them if not. In practice, the auditors have captured it.

The Information Systems Audit and Control Association (ISACA), which administers the Certified Information Systems Auditor (CISA) exam, has a refinement of COSO known as the *Control Objectives for Information and related Technology* (CoBIT), which is more international [948]. It extends from the technical aspects of internal audit to personnel management, change control and project management. More concrete standards emerge from auditors' interpretation of specific sectoral regulations, such as Sarbanes-Oxley for US publicly-listed companies, Gramm-Leach-Bliley for US financial-sector firms, HIPAA for US healthcare providers and GDPR for the personal information of residents of EU member states. And, as we noted in the chapter on banking and bookkeeping, the standards set by the PCI trade association govern data relating to payment cards. There's also ISO 27001 on security management. Whatever sectors you or your customers operate in, it's worthwhile paying attention to evolving cybersecurity standards. Many of these are standards because everyone can agree on them, so they're by no means sufficient. Pretty well every big breach involves a firm with ISO 27001 certification; the auditors said something was OK when it wasn't. We'll return to this in section 28.2.9.

12.2.7 Finding the weak spots

If you are ever responsible for security in an organisation, you should not just think about which components might, by their failure, cause a bad enough loss to make a material difference to the bottom line. You need to think about the people too, and their external relationships. Which of your managers could defraud your company by colluding with customers or suppliers? Could a branch manager be lending money to a dodgy business run by his cousin against forged collateral? Could he have sold life-insurance policies to nonexistent people and forged their death certificates? Could an operations manager be taking bribes from a supplier? Could your call-centre staff be selling data from the accounts they've dealt with to a phishing gang who use this data to impersonate your company to your customers? Lots of things can go wrong. You have to figure out which of them matter, and how you get to find out. Remember the old experience of 1% of staff falling into temptation every year. Remember that a trusted person is one who can damage you. Who can damage you, and how? This is what a control maintainer must constantly think about.

The lessons to be learned include the following:

- Maintaining effective controls is hard in a changing environment and needs someone senior to own it.
- If you rely on complaints from customers or staff to alert you to fraud and system failures, you'd better have a good way for them to contact you and for you to listen to them. Many companies cut costs by being hard to contact, but this has consequences.
- The main exposure is to the company's own staff and contractors, so you'd better talk to enough of them and ask questions like 'If you wanted to defraud the company, how would you do it?'
- Don't just think in terms of transactions and processes, but about people, incentives, social norms and the power to manipulate or intimidate others. Do you expect people to keep each other honest without any motivating structure, and nothing but risk for whistle blowers?
- No security policy can achieve full compliance, as workarounds will be needed for people to cope with real life.
- These workarounds naturally create vulnerabilities, so you'd better design controls that people can comply with.
- You'd better have a working relationship with the firm's executive leadership, so you understand which of them might be incurring risks relevant to your responsibilities, and so they understand what you're doing too.

There will always be residual risks. Managing these residual risks remains one of the hardest and most neglected of jobs. It's an extremely bad idea to adopt a doctrine that some particular system is foolproof – because if you assign its failure an a priori probability of zero, then evidence won't shift it and things could go badly wrong when it eventually fails. More generally, you need to help the firm learn from experience. And experience means not just loss history: controls that get in the way need to be identified and improved. If you're seen as contributing to profits rather than just as another compliance burden, you'll be listened to a lot more. For example, if you can fix the password reset function so it needs fewer staff, or improve the fraud engine so that the company's website rejects fewer shopping baskets, the board will listen to you a lot more readily.

Finally, your risk management systems will have to pay some homage to one or more compliance regimes, depending on the industry. The international standard ISO 27001 on security management is used in some industries: it demands that you analyse the risks systematically and subject the unacceptable ones to some form of risk treatment (control, avoidance, transfer); and have a management process to ensure that the controls are updated. In many companies, this will be driven by your auditors anyway. And there are many sector-specific regulatory regimes to deal with. In healthcare you have to worry about HIPAA (see section 10.4); and as for banking and payments, we turn to that next.

12.3 Interbank payment systems

When people think of electronic fraud, they often envisage a Hollywood scene in which crafty Russian hackers break a bank's codes and send zillion-dollar wire transfers to tax havens. Systems for transferring money are indeed a crime target, and have been for a century and a half. We'll look first at the systems used to transfer money between banks, and then at those used by bank customers, whether individuals or merchants.

12.3.1 A telegraphic history of E-commerce

Many people assume that e-commerce is something invented in the mid-1990s. But it goes back much further.

Governments used visual signalling from classical times, including heliographs (which used mirrors to flash sunlight at the receiver), semaphores (which used the positions of moving arms to signal letters and numbers) and flags. Land-based systems sent messages along chains of beacon towers, and naval systems relayed them between ships. After the Napoleonic War, the French government opened its heliograph network to commercial use, and soon the first frauds took place. For two years up till they were discovered in 1836, two bankers bribed an operator to signal the movements of the stock market to them covertly by making errors in transmissions that they could observe from a safe distance. Other techniques were devised to signal the results of horse races. Bookies learned to 'call time' by a clock, rather than waiting for a result and hoping that they were the first to hear it.

From the 1760s to the 1840s, the electric telegraph was developed by a number of pioneers, of whom the most influential was Samuel Morse. He persuaded Congress in 1842 to fund an experimental line from Washington to Baltimore. This so impressed people that serious commercial investment started, and by the end of that decade there were 12,000 miles of line operated by 20 companies. This was in many ways like the Internet boom of the late 1990s.

Banks were the first big users, and found that they needed mechanisms to prevent transactions being altered by crooked operators en route: I discussed the *test key* systems they developed for the purpose in section 5.2.4. Telegrams were also used to create national markets. For the first time, commodity traders in New York could find out within minutes what prices had been set in auctions in Chicago, and fishing skippers arriving in Boston could find out the price of cod in Gloucester. The history of the period shows that most of the concepts and problems of e-commerce were familiar to the Victorians [1821]. How do you know who you're speaking to? How do you know if they're trustworthy? How do you know whether the goods will be delivered, and whether payments will arrive? The nineteenth-century answer was trusted intermediaries – principally banks who helped business manage risk using references, guarantees and letters of credit.

By the 1970s, bankers started to realise that this worthy old Victorian system was due for an overhaul.

First, as I noted earlier in section 5.2.4, most test-key systems were vulnerable to cryptanalysis; someone who observed a number of transactions could gradually work out the key material.

Second, the test key system didn't support dual control. The secret tables were kept in a safe, and two clerks would sit together to work out a test and check it; but there was nothing really to stop staff members working out tests for unauthorised messages at the same time.

Third, the real concern was cost and errors. The use of manual cryptography meant that each transaction was typed on a keyboard at least three times: once into the paying bank's computer, which would print out a transaction in the telex room, where a test was computed manually; then a second time to send a telex to the receiving bank, who would check the test manually; then the third time as that bank fed it into their own computer. Errors were much more of a problem than frauds. Surely the payments could flow directly from one bank's computer to another?

12.3.2 SWIFT

A consortium of banks set up the Society for Worldwide Interbank Financial Telecommunications (SWIFT) in the 1970s to provide a more secure, efficient and controllable mechanism for sending payment instructions between member banks. It can be thought of as an email system with built-in authentication and non-repudiation services, plus optional encryption. It's used to ship trillions of dollars round the world daily, and its design has been copied in systems processing the title to many other kinds of asset, such as the bills of lading that prove ownership of ships' cargoes.

The design constraints are interesting. The banks did not wish to trust SWIFT to the point that its employees could forge bank transactions. The authenticity mechanisms had to be independent of the confidentiality mechanisms, since at the time a number of countries (such as France) forbade the civilian use of cryptography for confidentiality. The non-repudiation functions could not use digital signatures, as they hadn't been invented yet. Finally, the banks had to be able to enforce auditable dual controls over interbank transactions.

The design of SWIFT I is summarized in Figure 12.2. Authenticity of messages was assured by computing a message authentication code (MAC) at the sending bank and checking it at the receiving bank. The keys used to be managed using *bilateral key exchange*: whenever a bank set up a relationship overseas, the senior manager who negotiated it would exchange keys with his opposite number, whether in a face-to-face meeting or afterwards by post to each others' home addresses. There were two key components to minimize the risk of compromise, with one sent in each direction (even if a bank manager's mail is read in his mailbox by a criminal at one end, it's not likely to happen at both). Authentication was not enabled until both banks confirmed that the other's key had been safely received and installed.

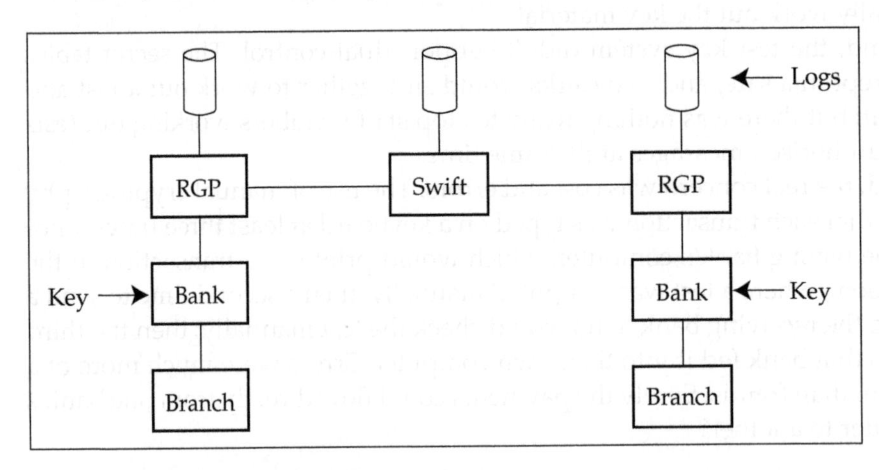

Figure 12.2: Architecture of SWIFT

This way, SWIFT had no part in the message authentication; so long as the authentication algorithm in use was sound, none of their staff could forge a transaction. The authentication algorithm was supposed to be a trade secret, but as banks like their security mechanisms to be international standards, people figured out to look at ISO 8731 [1634]. Pretty quickly, an attack was found and published in [1548]. Fortunately, this attack takes over 100,000 messages to recover a key – which was too large for a practical attack on a closed system and gave the banks time to migrate to more modern mechanisms.

Although SWIFT itself was not trusted for authentication, it did provide a non-repudiation service. Banks in each country sent their messages to a *Regional General Processor* (RGP), which logged them and forwarded them to SWIFT, which also logged them and sent them on to the recipient via the RGP in its country, which also logged them. The RGPs were generally run by different service firms. Thus, any banker wishing to dishonestly repudiate a transaction would have to subvert not just the local SWIFT application and its surrounding controls, but two independent contractors in different countries. And logs are easier for judges to understand than cryptography.

Confidentiality was an optional add-on. It was provided by line encryption devices between the banks and the RGP node, and between these nodes and the main SWIFT processing sites. Keys were hand-carried between the devices at either end of a leased line. In countries where confidentiality was illegal, these devices could be omitted without impairing the authenticity and non-repudiation mechanisms[10].

Dual control was provided either by specialized terminals or by software packages that could be integrated with other bank systems. The usual method of operation is to have three separate staff to do a SWIFT transaction: one to enter it, one to check it, and one to authorize it[11]. There's a further functional control in that you reconcile accounts by checking transactions against statements every day. So a bogus payment instruction that gets past the entry controls should result in an alarm the following business day.

12.3.3 What goes wrong

SWIFT I ran for twenty years without a single report of external fraud against the system itself. In the mid 1990s, after the attack on the MAC algorithm was published, it was enhanced by adding public key mechanisms: SWIFT II still used bilateral key exchange, but with MAC keys shared between correspondent banks using public-key cryptography and the MACs themselves further protected by a digital signature. The key-management mechanisms were ensconced as ISO 11166, and there was some debate over the security of this architecture [113, 1634]. Quite apart from the centralization of trust brought about by the adoption of public key cryptography – in that a central certification authority could falsely certify a key as belonging to a bank when it doesn't – at least one early deployment adopted 512-bit public keys because of US export controls, and by 2000 at least one RSA public key of this length had been factored surreptitiously by a group of students [44]. Bilateral key exchange was replaced in 2009 with a new system whose cryptographic mechanisms are proprietary. The messaging standard is being replaced by ISO 20022.

A political row arose once the crypto started to be toughened up and to offer confidentiality by default. The New York Times disclosed in June 2006

[10] In one country, a bank that attempted to install line encryptors found noise appearing on the line after a few hours. This only appeared on the live line, not the backup one, only after a delay, and swapping the equipment between the two lines didn't help. The bank realised that the local secret police wouldn't tolerate encryption and gave up.

[11] As the checker can modify the payee and the amount, this is really only dual control, not triple control – and the programmers who maintain the interface can always attack the system there, unless you can maintain separation of duty on the systems side too.

that the NSA was accessing the entire transaction stream, whereupon the NSA simply demanded access to everything. This caused a confrontation with privacy-conscious Europeans, but eventually after President Obama succeeded President Bush, the EU agreed a treaty under which the US Treasury Department can serve subpoenas on SWIFT [343]. Payments within Europe were supposedly excluded, but since Ed Snowden revealed the scale of collection of such payments, the issue has been raised repeatedly by the European Parliament and by privacy authorities[12].

Criminal (as opposed to governmental) attacks on interbank systems have not involved the payment mechanisms themselves but the surrounding business processes. It does happen from time to time that a bank programmer inserts a bogus message into the processing queue, but it usually fails because he doesn't understand the business process. How an international wire transfer actually works is that banks maintain accounts with each other, so when bank A sends money to a customer of bank B, it actually sends an instruction 'please pay this customer the following sum out of our account with you'. As these accounts have both balances and credit limits, and as payments may have to go through one or more correspondent banks, large payments need human interventions to make the money available. There are also filters that look for large transactions so that the bank can report them to the money-laundering authorities [76]. So a naive programmer who sneaks in a bogus transaction to an account he's set up at a Swiss bank usually gets arrested when he turns up to collect the cash.

The most famous attack carried out via SWIFT was in 4–5 February 2016 when North Korean agents stole $63m from the Bank of Bangladesh. They appear to have used Dridex malware to steal the credentials of bank staff and then ordered four transactions that transferred $81m from the bank's account at the Federal Reserve in New York to the Philippines, of which only $18m was recovered; the rest got laundered through a local casino. A further 30 transactions for a total of $851m were flagged for manual review by the Fed and not sent; another for $20m was sent to Sri Lanka, but recovered after the paying bank noticed a spelling error and stopped payment. This was not actually an attack on SWIFT, but an attack on the Bank of Bangladesh's own gateway to the SWIFT system [859].

But if your life's goal is to get rich from bank fraud, you're probably better off getting a law degree and working as a bank manager rather than messing about with computers. In fact, most significant frauds have exploited procedural vulnerabilities rather than technical attacks.

[12]One might ask why banks don't just build new systems with end-to-end crypto, but bank regulators demand access to all message traffic between banks, and some traffic within banks, to enforce rules against insider trading.

- Perhaps the first famous wire fraud was in 1979 when Stanley Rifkin, a computer consultant, embezzled over ten million dollars from Security Pacific National Bank. He got round the controls by agreeing to buy a large shipment of diamonds from a Russian government agency in Switzerland. He observed an authorization code used internally when dictating transfers to the wire transfer department, and used it over the telephone – a classic example of dual control breakdown at a system interface. He gave himself extra time to escape by doing the deal just before a US bank holiday. Where he went wrong was in not planning what to do after he collected the stones. If he'd hidden them in Europe, gone back to the US and helped investigate the fraud, he might well have got away with it; as it was, he went on the run and got caught.
- A fraud of a slightly different type took place in 1986 between London and Johannesburg. At that time, the South African government operated two exchange rates, and in one bank the manager responsible for deciding which rate applied to each transaction conspired with a rich man in London. They sent money out to Johannesburg at an exchange rate of seven Rand to the Pound, and back again the following day at four. After two weeks of this, the central bank sent the police round. When he saw them in the dealing room, the manager fled without stopping to collect his jacket, drove over the border to Swaziland, and flew via Nairobi to London. There, he boasted to the press about how he had defrauded the wicked apartheid system. As the UK had no exchange controls, exchange control fraud wasn't an offence, so he couldn't be extradited. This is perhaps the only case I know where the perp not only got away with several million but also got to brag about it.
- I've seen bad guys getting away with fraud using a letter of guarantee. It's common enough for a company in one country to ask their bank to guarantee a loan to a company in another. This can be set up as a SWIFT message, or even a paper letter, between the two banks. But as no cash changes hands at the time, the balancing controls are inoperative. If a forged guarantee is accepted as genuine, the 'beneficiary' can take his time borrowing money from the accepting bank, laundering it, and disappearing. Only when the lending bank realises that the loan has gone sour and tries to call in the guarantee is the forgery discovered. Then you can end up with a computer forensics case as two banks argue over whose fault it was.

The lesson is to be alert to anything that can defeat dual control. But you need to see this in a broader context. It's not just the technical problems of systems administration, interfaces or even shared-control crypto: the core is the business process design. And quite often, critical transactions don't appear as such at a casual inspection. Proper split control usually needs functional separation, and for that you need to really understand the application in its social and economic context.

12.4 Automatic teller machines

Our second set of lessons emerges from studying payment cards. This story has at least four components: first, *automatic teller machines* (ATMs); second, credit cards; third, the chip cards that have taken over as both debit and credit cards since the mid-2000s; and fourth, contactless payments including phone banking.

ATMs were one of the most influential technological innovations of the 20th century. They were devised in 1938 by the inventor Luther Simjian, who also thought up the teleprompter and the self-focusing camera. He persuaded Citicorp to install his 'Bankamat' machine in New York in 1939, but they withdrew it after six months, saying 'the only people using the machines were a small number of prostitutes and gamblers who didn't want to deal with tellers face to face' [1747]. Its comeback was in 1967, when a machine made by De La Rue was installed by Barclays Bank in Enfield, London. According to the World Bank, there are now over 2.4m machines, or 41 per 100,000 adults [2043]. Card payments with PINs are now used in many terminals in shops, and the technology, including block ciphers, tamper-resistant hardware and the supporting protocols, ended up being adapted for many other applications from postal franking machines to lottery ticket terminals. In short, ATMs were the 'killer app' that got modern commercial cryptology and retail payment technology off the ground.

12.4.1 ATM basics

Most ATMs operate using some variant of a system developed by IBM for its 3624 series cash machines in the late 1970s. The card's magnetic strip contains the customer's *primary account number* (PAN) and an expiry date. A secret key, called the 'PIN key', is used to encrypt the PAN, then decimalize it and truncate it. The result of this operation is called the 'natural PIN'; an offset can be added to give the PIN that the customer must enter. The offset has no cryptographic function; it just enables customers to choose their own PIN. An example of the process is shown in Figure 12.3.

In the first ATMs to use PINs, each ATM contained a copy of the PIN key, and each card contained the offset as well as the primary account number. So each ATM could verify all customer PINs. Early ATMs also operated offline; if your cash withdrawal limit was $500 per week, a counter was kept on the card. From the mid-1990s, networks became more dependable, and ATMs have tended to

PAN:	8807012345691715
PIN key KP:	FEFEFEFEFEFEFEFE
Result of DES $\{PAN\}_{KP}$:	A2CE126C69AEC82D
$\{N\}_{KP}$ decimalized:	0224126269042823
Natural PIN:	0224
Offset:	6565
Customer PIN:	6789

Figure 12.3: IBM method for generating bank card PINs

operate online only, which simplified the design. Starting in 2003, magnetic strips were supplemented with smartcard chips, followed by contactless payment from 2012; I'll describe these enhancements in later sections. But the basic principle remains: PINs are generated and protected using cryptography.

A cryptographic processor, known as a *hardware security module* (HSM), is kept in the bank's server room and manages customer PINs so as to enforce a dual-control policy.

1. Operations on the clear values of customer PINs, and on the keys used to protect them, are always done in a *secure cryptographic device* (SCD), so that no member of the bank's staff ever gets to see a PIN other than their own. SCDs include the HSMs in the bank server room[13] along with crypto modules in ATMs and other PIN-entry devices.
2. Thus, for example, the cards are personalized in a facility with machines to emboss the card, encode the mag strip and initialise the chip, while the PIN mailers are printed in a separate facility containing a printer attached to an HSM. They're mailed out a few days apart.
3. A *terminal master key* is supplied to each ATM in the form of two printed components, which are carried to the branch by separate people, input at the ATM's rear keyboard, and combined to form the key. Similar ceremonies (but with three people) are used to set up master keys between banks and network switches such as VISA.
4. If ATMs perform PIN verification locally, then the PIN key is encrypted under the terminal master key and sent to the ATM. Keys are stored in a local SCD – a tamper-resistant chip next to the keyboard – which either verifies PINs as they're entered or encrypts them so they can be sent from the ATM to a central HSM for checking.
5. If the bank's ATMs are to accept other banks' cards, then the PIN will be encrypted in the ATM's SCD and sent to the bank, which will

[13] Or nowadays, also in a cloud service provider or other service contractor

decrypt it and re-encrypt it using a key shared with the switch operator, such as VISA. This *PIN translation* function is done entirely within an HSM. VISA similarly uses an HSM to translate the PIN to a key shared with the card-issuing bank, so it can be verified by an HSM there.

The ATM network rapidly became orders of magnitude bigger than SWIFT. Rather than being used by a few thousand banks, it was soon connecting tens of thousands of banks and hundreds of millions of cardholders. It was not feasible to do either key exchange or financial settlement bilaterally between 20,000 banks, so each bank connects to a switch provided by a switching organization such as VISA, and these switches' HSMs translate the traffic. The switches also do accounting, so banks can settle their accounts for each day's transactions with a single debit or credit, rather than each having to maintain accounts with thousands of other institutions.

The switches are trusted, so if something goes wrong, there the consequences can be severe. This seems to happen about once a decade. In one case a switch manager ended up a fugitive from justice, and in another, a Y2K-related software upgrade at a switch was bungled, with the result that cardholders in one country found that for a day or two they could withdraw money even if their accounts were empty. The bill in each case was in seven figures.

The engineers who designed ATM networks and security systems in the 1980s (of whom I was one) assumed that criminals would be relatively sophisticated, fairly well-informed about the system design, and rational in their choice of attack methods. We worried about the many banks that were slow to buy security modules. We worried about banks cutting corners such as omitting authentication codes on authorization responses. We agonized over whether the encryption algorithms were strong enough, whether the tamper-resistant HSMs were tamper-resistant enough, and whether the random number generators used to generate keys were random enough. We knew we just couldn't enforce dual control properly: bank managers considered it beneath their dignity to touch a keyboard, so rather than entering the ATM master key components themselves after a maintenance visit, most of them would just give both key components to the ATM engineer. Above all, we worried that a repairman would get his hands on a bank's PIN key, force the reissue of millions of cards and wreck public confidence in electronic banking. This was our doomsday scenario.

Doomsday eventually happened. In December 2017, a key at Postbank in South Africa was compromised while kept on a laptop during a data centre move. Somehow, it was copied to a memory stick; the CEO also had a copy. The copies were supposed to be destroyed in front of witnesses but somehow a stick got lost. From March 2018 to December 2019, R56m (US $3.4m) was stolen in 56,000 transactions, mostly from cards issued to poor pensioners to pay state benefits. In February 2019, the central bank ordered Postbank to reissue all its 12m cards, which cost R1bn (US $60m) [1239].

However, the millions of frauds against PIN-based payment cards over the past 50 years turned out to be very much more diverse.

12.4.2 What goes wrong

Card payment systems have huge transaction volumes, a wide diversity of operators, and plenty of capable motivated opponents. There have been successive waves of card fraud, where vulnerabilities were discovered, exploited and then eventually fixed. The overall pattern is that card fraud has increased in value over time but decreased as a proportion of the transactions; the system is slowly getting more secure as it grows in both size and experience [92].

The first wave, in the early 1990s, exploited the poor implementation and management of early magnetic-strip card systems. In the UK, one prolific fraudster, Andrew Stone, was convicted three times of ATM fraud, the last time getting five-and-a-half years in prison. He started when he discovered by chance an 'encryption replacement' trick: he changed the account number on his bank card to his wife's and found that he could take money out of her account using his PIN. In fact, he could take money out of any account at that bank using his PIN. This happened because his bank wrote the encrypted PIN to the card's magnetic strip without linking it to the account number. His second method was 'shoulder surfing': he'd stand in line behind a victim, observe the entered PIN, and pick up the discarded ATM slip. Most banks at the time printed the full account number on the slip, and a card would work with no other correct information on it.

Stone's methods spread via people he trained as his accomplices, and via a 'Howto' manual he wrote in prison. Some two thousand victims of his (and other) frauds banded together to bring a class action against thirteen banks to get their money back. The banks beat this by arguing that the facts in each case were different, and split it into thousands of small-claims cases that the victims did not have the expertise to pursue. I was an expert in this case, and used it to write a couple of papers on what went wrong [55, 56]. The fraud eventually spread worldwide, as criminals in Romania and elsewhere started designing ATM skimming equipment and sold it online. Here I'll summarize the more important and interesting lessons we learned.

Most of the actual 'phantom withdrawals' in the early 1990s appeared to have one of the following three causes:

- Simple processing errors give rise to a steady background noise of disputes. Developed countries get about four transactions per head per month; that's 240m a month in the UK alone. If the error rate is only 1 in 100,000, that's a lot of disputes. Even if your core banking system has good balancing controls, the peripheral systems that feed it can be flaky. One source of errors we tracked down was that a large bank's ATMs would send a transaction again if the network went down before a confirmation message was received from the bank's server; periodically, the server itself crashed and forgot about open transactions, causing debits to be duplicated. We also found customers whose accounts were debited with other customers' transactions, and other customers who were never debited at all for their card transactions. (We used to call these cards 'directors' cards' and joked that they were issued to bank directors.)

- Thefts from the mail were reckoned in the 1990s to account for 30% of all UK payment card losses, and postal control procedures remained dismal for years. For example, when I moved to Cambridge in February 1992 my bank sent not one, but two, cards and PINs through the post, and they arrived only a few days after intruders had got hold of our apartment block's mail and torn it up looking for valuables. In 2003–5, when magnetic-strip cards were replaced with chip cards, there was another surge in thefts from the mail – see Figure 12.4. The main fix was to make you phone a call centre or visit a website to activate a card before you can use it.
- Frauds involving dishonest or negligent bank staff appeared to be the third big cause of phantoms. We've had occasional cases of ATM service staff installing wiretaps inside an ATM to record customer card and PIN data, and one case back in the 1990s of crooked insiders working out PINs for stolen cards for £50 a time. More recently we've had bigger cases of crooks working out how to social-engineer bank call centres to issue new cards to addresses they control [2017]. Insider frauds were particularly common in countries like Britain where the law generally made the customer pay for fraud, and rarer in countries like the US where the bank paid; British bank staff knew that customer complaints wouldn't be investigated carefully.

However, there were plenty of frauds due to careless design or that taught technical security lessons.

- The shoulder-surfing trick of standing in an ATM queue, observing a customer's PIN, picking up the discarded ticket and copying the data to a blank card, was first reported in New York in the mid-1980s; and it was still working in the Bay Area in the mid-1990s. By then it had been automated; Bay Area criminals used video cameras with motion sensors to snoop on PINs, whether by renting an apartment overlooking an ATM or even parking a rented van there. Visual copying is easy to stop: the standard nowadays is to print only the last four digits of the account number on the ticket, and since the early 1990s, cards have a three-digit *card verification value* (CVV) on the magnetic strip that must never be printed. Yet the CVV is not always checked.

- There were many losses due to bugs and blunders. One ATM sold in the 1980s had a 'test dispense' code that would output ten banknotes of the lowest available denomination whenever a certain fourteen-digit sequence was entered at the keyboard. One bank printed this sequence in its branch manual, and three years later there was a sudden spate of losses. All the banks using the machine had to rush out a patch to disable the test dispense transaction. And despite the fact that I documented this in 1993, and again in the first edition of this book in 2001, similar incidents were still reported as late as 2007.
- Some makes of ATM used in convenience stores could be reprogrammed into thinking that they were dispensing $1 bills when in fact they were dispensing twenties; it just took a default master password that was printed in the online manuals. Any passer-by who knew this could stroll up to the machine, reset the bill value, withdraw $400, and have their account debited only $20. The store owners who leased the machines were not told of the vulnerability, and were left to pick up the tab [1542].
- Many banks' operational security procedures were dire. As an experiment, my wife went into a branch of our bank in 1993 with a witness and told them she'd forgotten her PIN. The teller helpfully printed her a new PIN mailer from a printer attached to a PC behind the counter – just like that! It was not the branch where our account is kept. Nobody knew her, and all the identification she offered was our bank card and her checkbook. When anyone who's snatched a handbag can walk in off the street and get a PIN for the card in it at any branch, no amount of encryption technology will do much good. (That bank later went bust in 2008.)
- One technique that's worked consistently for 40 years – and still works nowadays with many ATMs – is the *Lebanese loop*. The crook fits a loop of tape, perhaps from an old videocassette, into the ATM throat and waits for a victim. The card gets snagged in the loop, and the victim abandons it. The crook retrieves it, and if he managed to see the victim's PIN, goes shopping. Some ATMs have mechanisms to frustrate this, and some don't. Some banks just don't care: one victim of such a fraud, in a bank lobby, went straight inside the bank to complain but was fobbed off by staff who didn't want to get involved. After her card was looted, her card-issuing bank blamed her, and this ended up as a dispute.
- The high-tech modus operandi was using false terminals or skimmers to collect card and PIN data. The first report was from the USA in 1988; there, crooks built a vending machine that would accept any card and PIN, and dispense a pack of cigarettes. In

1993, two villains bought a real ATM and a software development kit for it, programmed it to steal card data and PINs, and installed it in the Buckland Hills Mall in Connecticut [990].

- False terminal attacks spread to Europe and to point-of-sale systems in the 90s. I mentioned in section 4.5, a tap on a garage point-of-sale terminal was used to harvest card and PIN data in Utrecht, in the Netherlands; and in 1994, crooks in London set up to a whole bogus bank branch [945]. Eventually, by the mid-2000s, card skimmers became widely available on the black market. By 2015 a Romanian gang was caught operating 100 ATMs in tourist spots in Mexico, stealing $20m a month [1096]. Magnetic strip cards were just too easy to copy, and the card technology had to change.
- Since the mid-2010s, we have seen occasional 'jackpotting' attacks where crooks hack ATMs so that they keep on dispensing bills until they're empty. This can involve infecting ATMs with malware, whether online or by getting physical access to a USB port, or physically inserting rogue electronics [485].
- There are occasional frauds when an insider gets at one of the servers in the back-end system, or when one of them fails insecure. This can result in customers being able to use cards with any PIN (if the online PIN checking process fails) or in customers with the right PIN being able to run up unlimited overdrafts (if the balance inquiry process fails). One such failure was deliberate: after 9/11 damaged its ATM network, the Municipal Credit Union decided to let customers in New York withdraw money without checking their balances until things could be fixed. That cost $15m, and 118 customers ended up being charged with theft [1660].

I reckon the first thing we did wrong when designing ATM security systems in the 1980s was to worry about criminals being clever, when we should rather have worried about our customers – the banks' system designers, implementers and testers – being unable to use the security systems we designed. In recent years, research by Yasemin Acar, Sascha Fahl and others has shown that many if not most security failures can be seen as programmer usability failures; normal programmers can't cope with the complicated crypto APIs and access control mechanisms that security geeks love to build [11]. Security geeks pay attention to crypto because the maths are interesting, but less so to the 'boring' bits such as creating tools that non-specialists can actually use. So it's rare that the bad guys have to break the crypto. And modern payment networks have so many users that we must expect the chance discovery of vulnerabilities that were too obscure to be caught in testing.

The second thing we did wrong was to not figure out what attacks could be industrialised, and focus on those. In the case of ATMs, the false-terminal attack is the one that eventually made the big time. The first hint of organised crime involvement was in 1999 in Canada, where dozens of alleged Eastern European organized-crime figures were arrested in the Toronto area for deploying doctored point-of-sale terminals [130, 217]. Since about 2005, skimmers made in Eastern Europe are sold on underground markets, designed to be attached to the throats of cash machines to read the magnetic strip and also capture the PIN using a tiny camera or a keyboard overlay. I'll discuss these in more detail in the next section. The remedy has been moving from magnetic-strip cards to chip cards, but this has taken over fifteen years, and magnetic-strip fraud has cost a lot of money in the meantime. The curious thing may be that it took 40 years from the launch of magnetic-strip ATM cards until skimmers made them too easy to attack. The key factor was that criminals started to specialise and organise, as I discussed in section 2.3.

12.4.3 Incentives and injustices

In the US, the banks carry a lot of the risks associated with new technology. In a historic case, Judd v Citibank, bank customer Dorothy Judd claimed that she had not made some disputed withdrawals, and Citibank said that as its systems were secure, she must have done. The judge ruled that he "was not prepared to go so far as to rule that when a credible witness is faced with the adverse 'testimony' of a machine, he is as a matter of law also faced with an unmeetable burden of proof" – and gave her her money back [997]. The US Federal Reserve incorporated this view into 'Regulation E', which requires banks to refund all disputed transactions unless they can prove fraud by the customer [639]. This has led to some minor abuse, but typically less than the losses from vandalism [2048].

In other countries – such as the UK, the Netherlands and Norway – the banks got away for years with claiming that their ATM systems were infallible. Phantom withdrawals, they maintained, could not happen, and a customer who complained of one must be mistaken or lying. This position was somewhat undermined in the UK when Stone and his followers started being jailed for ATM fraud, and there were some rather unpleasant incidents. One example was the Munden case [56].

John Munden was one of our local police constables, based in Bottisham, Cambridgeshire; his beat included the village of Lode where I lived at the time. He came home from holiday in September 1992 to find his account at the Halifax Building Society empty. He asked for a statement, found six withdrawals for a total of £460 that he did not recall making, and complained. The Halifax had him prosecuted for attempting to obtain money by deception. It came out during the trial that their IT was somewhat ramshackle; the disputed transactions had not been properly investigated; and they made all sorts of wild claims, such as that their ATM system couldn't suffer from bugs as its software was written in assembler. Nonetheless, it was his word against theirs. He was convicted in February 1994 and suspended from the police force. Just before the appeal was due to be heard, the prosecution served up a report from the Halifax's auditors claiming that their system was secure. The defense demanded equal access to the bank's systems for its own expert. The Halifax refused, so the court disallowed all its computer evidence. The case collapsed, John Munden was acquitted, and he got his job back.

Once the fuss died down, the banks went back to claiming that their systems were secure, and the same drama played itself out again when Jane Badger, of Burton-on-Trent, England, was prosecuted for complaining about phantom withdrawals. The case against her collapsed in January 2008. If a system is to provide evidence, then dual control is not enough. It must be able to withstand examination by hostile experts. The security property the bank really needed wasn't dual control but *non-repudiation*: the ability for the principals in a transaction to prove afterwards what happened. This might have been provided by installing ATM cameras; although these were mandatory in the state of New York as an anti-mugging measure, they were not used in Britain. Indeed, during the 1992–4 wave of ATM frauds, the few banks who had installed ATM cameras were pressured by the other banks into withdrawing them; camera evidence was a threat to the banks' collective stance that their systems were infallible. It would be a further 25 years before the Post Office case I mentioned in section 12.2.6.1 would finally expose a bank's systems to thorough scrutiny, and have them condemned as unreliable in the High Court.

12.5 Credit cards

The second component that led to modern card payment systems was the credit card. For years after their invention by Diners Club in the 1950s, credit cards were treated by most banks as a loss leader with which to attract high-value customers. Eventually, the number of merchants and cardholders reached critical mass and the transaction volume took off. In Britain, from the mid-80s, the credit card business was suddenly extremely profitable[14].

When you use a credit card to pay for a purchase in a store, the transaction flows from the merchant to their bank (the *acquiring bank*), which pays them after deducting a *merchant discount* of typically just under 2% for a small merchant[15]. If the card was issued by a different bank, the transaction now flows

[14]Payment systems have strong network externalities, just like communications technologies or computer platforms: the service provider must recruit enough merchants to appeal to cardholders, and vice versa, so new payment mechanisms can take years to get established, then suddenly take off like a rocket.

[15]Debit cards are cheaper, and big merchants can pay under 1% even for credit card transactions.

to a switch such as VISA, which passes it to the *issuing bank* for payment. Each transaction involves two components: *authorisation*, when you present your card at a merchant and they want to know right now whether to give you the goods, and *settlement*, which flows through a separate system and gets money to the merchant, often two or three days later. The issuer also gets a slice of the merchant discount, but makes most of its money from extending credit to cardholders.

12.5.1 Credit card fraud

From the 1950s to the 1990s, credit card transactions were processed by making a paper sales draft on a multipart form using the embossing on the card, writing in the amount, getting the customer to sign it, and processing it like a check. The risk of fraud using stolen credit cards was traditionally managed by *hot card lists* and merchant *floor limits*. Each merchant got a local 'hot card list' plus a limit set by their acquiring bank above which they have to call for online authorization. In the 1980s, electronic terminals were introduced so a sales clerk could swipe a card and get an authorization automatically. The crooks' response was a flood of forged cards: between 1989 and 1992, magnetic strip counterfeiting grew from an occasional nuisance into half the total fraud losses [12].

The introduction of mail-order and telephone sales led to *card not present* (CNP) transactions where the merchant was not able to inspect the card. Banks managed the risk by using the expiry date as a password, lowering the floor limits, increasing the merchant discount and insisting on delivery to a cardholder address, of which the numerical part is supposed to be checked during authorization. But the main change was to shift liability so that the merchant bore the risk of disputes. If you challenge an online credit card transaction (or in fact any transaction made under CNP rules), the full amount is immediately debited back to the merchant, together with a significant handling fee. This applies whether the debit is a fraud, a dispute or a return.

VISA's response to growing card forgery and online fraud was *card verification values* (CVVs) – three-digit MACs computed on the card strip contents (account number, version number, expiry date) and written at the end of the strip. They worked: in the first quarter of 1994, VISA's fraud losses dropped by 15.5%, while Mastercard's rose 67% [388]. So Mastercard adopted CVVs too. They also appeared on debit cards, which converged with credit cards technically: this was an extended process as banks first allowed credit cards to be used in ATMs too and then let debit cards be used at the point of sale, at different times in different countries.

The crooks moved to *skimming* – operating businesses where genuine customer cards were swiped through an extra, unauthorized, terminal to grab a copy of the magnetic strip, which would then be re-encoded on a genuine card. (In countries where PINs were already used in point-of-sale terminals, this allowed forged cards to be used in ATMs directly.) The banks' response was intrusion detection systems that tried to identify criminal businesses by correlating the purchase histories of customers who complained. By the late 1990s, the smarter crooked businesses learned to absorb the cost of the customer's transaction. You have a drink at a Mafia-owned bistro, offer a card, sign the voucher, and fail to notice when the charge doesn't appear on your bill. A month or two later, there's a huge bill for jewelry, electrical goods or even casino chips. By then you've forgotten about the bistro, and the bank never had a record of it [720].

In the early 2000s, high-tech criminals became better organised as electronic crime became specialised. The emergence of online criminal forums, starting in Russia and Ukraine in 2003, enabled malware writers, botnet herders, phishing site operators and cash-out specialists to trade with each other and get good at their jobs. This spilled over from targeting online transactions to attacks on retail terminals. Forums offered fake terminals and skimmers that record mag-strip card and PIN data, so as to make card clones. In the Far East, wiretaps were used to harvest card data from the mid-2000s [1160].

Europe introduced smartcards in 2003–5, and the crooks came up with devices that copy data from chip cards to mag-strip cards for use in terminals that still accepted mag-strip transactions. Some of them used vulnerabilities in the EMV protocol, and so I'll come back to them after I've described EMV and chip cards in the next section.

Regardless of whether the card has a chip or not, there are many scams involving cards that are never received by genuine customers. There's *pre-issue fraud* including thefts from the mail of the 'pre-approved' cards that arrive in junk mail. There are applications made in the names of people who exist but are not aware of the application (often misrepresented as 'identity theft' by banks that would like to pretend that it was your identity that was stolen rather than their money [1326]). And there are scams where crooks get careless bank staff to send a replacement card for your account to an address they control [2017]. The remaining line of defence against such scams – until the customer gets a bill and complains – is automatic fraud detection, which I'll discuss in section 12.5.4.

12.5.2 Online card fraud

Turning now from traditional credit card fraud to the online variety, I first helped the police investigate an online credit card fraud in 1987. In that case, the suspect got a list of hot credit card numbers from his partner who worked in a supermarket, and used them to buy software from companies overseas, which he downloaded to order for his customers. Hot card lists at the time carried only those cards that were being abused in that country; using a local hot card overseas meant that the bank would carry the can, not an innocent customer. As it happens, the suspect quit before there was enough evidence to arrest him. A rainstorm washed away the riverbank opposite his house and exposed a hide the police had built to stake him out.

From about 1995, the dotcom boom got underway, and businesses rushed to build websites. There was anxiety that the use of credit cards on the Internet would lead to an avalanche of fraud, as 'evil hackers' intercepted emails and web forms and harvested credit card numbers by the million. These fears drove Microsoft and Netscape to introduce SSL/TLS to encrypt credit card transactions en route from browsers to web servers.

The reality is a bit more complex. Intercepting email and web traffic is indeed possible, especially at endpoints, but can be difficult to do at scale. Lots of websites ran for many years with no encryption, or weak encryption, and the real issue turned out to be not wiretapping but phishing. Even this only got going at scale after 2004; and there (as I remarked in Chapter 3) the issue is more psychology than cryptography. TLS per se doesn't help, as bad guys who can set up man-in-the-middle attacks can just get certificates and encrypt the traffic. The site will have a different domain name, but it's unreasonable to expect most members of the public to notice that, especially as banks and merchants use all sorts of variant domains themselves[16].

Second, most of the credit card numbers that are traded online got into bad hands because someone hacked a merchant's computer. VISA had rules for years that prohibited merchants from storing credit card data once the transaction had been processed, but many merchants ignored them. There followed the *Payment Card Industry Data Security Standard* (PCI-DSS), a joint effort by the Payment Card Industry Security Standards Council[17]. PCI DSS rules require basic hygiene for systems holding cardholder data such as account numbers and expiry dates[18] while sensitive data such as CVVs and PINs can't be stored at all. Finally, enforcement started to bite, and by in October 2007, the US National Retail Federation asked credit card companies to stop forcing retailers to store credit card data at all (they were supposed to store card numbers temporarily in case of chargebacks) [1961]. PCI DSS has now become a significant piece of compliance for firms that accept credit card

[16]There are now some technical fixes, such as certificate transparency, which I'll discuss in section 21.5.1.

[17]This was set up by VISA, Mastercard, Amex, JCB and Discover; it now has other stakeholders too.

[18]Cardholder data must be encrypted when they go over networks, and when stored, they must be protected by a firewall and AV; default passwords can't be used; and you must have a security policy, need-to-know access controls, testing, and since 2017 a secure software development lifecycle. It adds up to quite a bundle of documentation and a lot of jobs for accountants to check it.

transactions; it provides little liability cover, since if fraud happens the banks can usually blame the merchant anyway even if it was certified compliant.

Other real incentives facing merchants are, first, the cost of disputes, and second, security-breach disclosure laws. While the details differ between countries, disclosure laws have made a difference as notifying customers costs real money and the stock prices of companies suffering a breach can fall several percent. As for disputes, consumer protection laws in many countries make it easy to repudiate a transaction. Basically all the customer has to do is call the credit card company and say "I didn't authorize that" and the merchant is saddled with the bill. This was workable in the days when almost all credit card transactions took place locally and most were for significant amounts. If a customer fraudulently repudiated a transaction, the merchant would pursue them through the courts. Nowadays many transactions are international, amounts are small, and verifying overseas addresses via the credit card system is flaky. So the opportunity for repudiating transactions – and getting away with it – is increased.

On the other hand, some market sectors have many websites that exploit their customers, and porn sites have been a running sore. A common scam was to offer a 'free tour' of the site and demand a credit card number, supposedly to verify that the user was over 18, and then bill him anyway. Some sites billed other consumers who have never visited them at all [923]. Even apparently large and 'respectable' web sites like `playboy.com` were criticised for such practices, and at the bottom end of the porn industry, things are atrocious. The worst case so far was probably Operation Ore, in which some three thousand victims of credit card fraud were wrongly arrested on suspicion of buying child sex abuse material, and at least one killed himself. I discuss the Operation Ore case in section 26.5.3.

The main brake on wicked websites is the credit-card chargeback. A bank will typically charge the merchant $100–200 in fees for each of them, as well as debiting the transaction amount from his account. So if more than a small percentage of the transactions on your site are challenged by customers, your margins will be eroded. If chargebacks go over perhaps 10%, your bank may terminate your service. This has motivated merchants to take care – to beware of odd orders (e.g., for four watches), orders from dodgy countries, customers using free email services, requests for expedited delivery, and so on. But leaving the bulk of the liability for mail-order transactions with them is suboptimal: the banks know much more about fraud patterns. Shared liability might well be better, but legal systems are not good at that. One lobbyist beats another when the law gets written, or one legal team beats the other when the key precedent is set, and we get stuck with it.

One systematic attack involves progressive guessing. All websites must ask for the primary account number and expiry date, but a merchant may also ask for the CVV printed on the back of the card, and digits from the cardholder address. Starting from a valid account number, you guess the expiry date by testing it on merchant websites that check only that; then you guess the CVV on websites that check that too, then the postcode digits, and finally guess the house number from the websites that check that too. There are enough websites out there for this to work for VISA cards; Mastercard has central monitoring, and they hot-list a number after about ten failed guesses (though this can lead to denial-of-service attacks) [1].

Another attack is *credential stuffing*, where the bad guys get millions of email/password combinations from compromised websites and try them out in other sites from which value can be extracted. Such attacks, plus the increasing availability of stolen credit card data on underground markets, have driven the development of better cardholder authentication, at least for larger transactions.

12.5.3 3DS

3D Secure is a single sign-on system designed by the payment card industry[19]. When the merchant captures a payment transaction past some threshold, they redirect to a bank server that invites the customer to authenticate the transaction using a password or a second-factor such as a code sent to their mobile by SMS. It is increasingly used for large payment card transactions.

3DS acquired users rapidly because customers who used it were held liable for fraud where possible, so merchants paid less. Customer onboarding was a soft spot for years. Many banks initially let the 3DS servers enrol their customers directly and solicit a password the first time their card was used at a participating merchant, a process called *activation during shopping* (ADS). Some even let customers re-enrol if they forgot the password, so initially the system was easy to hack. It also got customers used to entering bank passwords at a site whose URL has nothing to do with the bank, and one bank even got customers to enter their ATM PINs there [1364]. Now, a decade after its initial roll-out, 3DS is moving to an (incompatible) second version endorsed as an EMV standard. A factor has been government mandates to use two-factor authentication, which results in most banks knowing their customers' mobile phone numbers. However, SMS-based two-factor authentication is now reaching the end of its useful life, as discussed previously in section 3.4.1 and later in section 12.7.4. Some 3DS implementations still use bank passwords.

[19]It is variously branded as 'Mastercard SecureCode', 'Verified by VISA', 'Amex SafeKey' and 'Discover ProtectBuy'.

12.5.4 Fraud engines

People started working from the mid-1990s on better financial intrusion detection, and by now all websites of any size that accept card-not-present transactions have a fraud engine that decides whether to accept or decline each transaction. There are two approaches: anomaly detection, which uses various thresholding and other techniques to look for unusual patterns, and abuse detection, which looks for known fraud patterns. The big problem in both cases is false positives. We all have experience of cards being blocked, and in many cases the triggers are obvious. Small transactions used to cause alarms as they suggested a thief testing stolen cards to see which are still live. Another issue was multiple transactions overseas; in the 1990s, whenever I went to the US, my debit card would do three transactions and then stop working. Modern machine-learning techniques have made such mechanisms slightly less annoying, but the sheer scale of modern payment systems with tens of thousands of transactions per second means that even a 0.1% false positive rate will create a firehose of customer complaints.

More convincing are projects that look for known patterns of misuse. For example, FICO maintains a list of the most suspicious ATMs. Banks that subscribe to its service tell it whenever a transaction is declined, whether because of a stolen card, a wrong PIN or an empty account. The ATM is then bumped up the 'hot ATM' list. When a crook takes a fistful of stolen cards to an ATM, it will get to the top of the list within three or four cards and then decline any card issued by a bank that subscribes to FICO's service. The crook will assume they're no good and throw them away. Over 40% of the world's banks, by card issuing volume, now subscribe.

An important success factor in running an intrusion detection system is the incentives. Websites in the UK can turn away as much as 4% of offered shopping baskets because of their fraud engines. If security is the responsibility of the CFO, he'll see it as a cost centre and try to minimise it; but for the chief marketing officer, a 25% improvement in the false positive rate translates to '1% more sales', for which they'll happily pay real money.

The core of a good fraud engine tends to be several dozen signals extracted from the transaction stream on the basis of a set of well-understood threat vectors (such as bad IP addresses, or too many logons from the same IP address) and a set of quality signals (such as 'card old but good'). These signals are then fed to a machine-learning system that scores the transactions. The signals appear to be the most important part of the design, not whether you use an SVM or a Bayesian network. The signals need to be continuously curated and updated as the bad guys learn new tricks, and the fraud engine needs to be well integrated with the human processes. As for how fraud engines fail, the regulator's report into a 2016 fraud against Tesco Bank found that the staff failed to 'exercise due skill, care and diligence' over the fraud detection rules, and to 'respond to the attack with sufficient rigor, skill and urgency' [687]. In that case, the bank failed to update its fraud engine following a warning from Mastercard the previous day of a new type of card scam. We'll discuss this case further in section 12.6.3 once we've explained chip cards.

12.6 EMV payment cards

The biggest investment since 2003 has been in new card technologies, with banks replacing both credit cards and debit cards with EMV smartcards, followed by contactless payments with both cards and phones. Card payments have become both complex and diverse; the best way to understand them may be to follow their evolution.

When integrated circuits came along in the 1960s and microprocessors in the 1970s, various people proposed putting them in bank cards. The Germans consider the smartcard to have been invented by Helmut Gröttrup and Jürgen Dethloff in 1968, when they proposed and patented a custom IC for a card; the Japanese point to a patent by Kunitaka Arimura in 1970; while the French credit Roland Moreno, who proposed memory chips in cards in 1973, and Michel Ugon who proposed adding a microprocessor in 1977. The French company Honeywell-Bull patented a chip containing memory, a microcontroller and everything else needed to do transactions in 1982; they started being used in French pay phones in 1983, and in banking from the mid-1980s.

Norway was second with some banks issuing chip cards from 1986. Britain's NatWest Bank developed the Mondex electronic purse system in the early 90s, piloted it in Swindon, then sold it to Mastercard; the software evolved into Multos, a card operating system that's still in use. There was a patent fight between VISA and Mastercard. There is more detail on these early pilot projects in Chapter 3 of the second edition of this book. That was all good learning experience. But for a payment card to be really useful, it has to work internationally – and especially in Europe with many small countries jammed up close together, where millions of people cross borders for their weekly shop or even on their commute to work. So the banks finally got together in the late 1990s and hammered out a standard.

12.6.1 Chip cards

The EMV standards specify chip cards and the supporting protocols for use in ATMs and retail payment terminals. They were initially developed by Europay, Mastercard and VISA, who then set up EMVCo to maintain and extend the standards. Chip cards were rolled out in the UK from 2003–6 and then in other

European countries, most of which use PINs for authentication in stores as well as ATMs, leading to the system being called 'chip and PIN'. In the US and Singapore, chip cards are now used with signatures, and the system's called 'chip and signature'. The standards run to many thousands of pages; they now extend to contactless payments, online payments and much else; and there are further documents specific to particular countries, and to individual banks. To make sense of it all, let's start with the basic protocol for using an EMV card with a PIN to buy goods from a shop.

First, the card sends its credentials to the *PIN entry device* (PED) or terminal, consisting of the primary account number (PAN) and a certificate signed by the card issuing bank. Then the terminal sends an *unpredictable number* or nonce N, the date t and the requested payment amount X, along with the PIN entered by the cardholder. The card checks the PIN, and if it's correct, it computes an *authentication request cryptogram* (ARQC), which is a message authentication code (MAC) on N, d_3 and X. Each message has some extra data d_i which we'll discuss later.

$$
\begin{aligned}
C \rightarrow T: &\quad PAN, d_1, Cert_{KB}(PAN, d_1) \\
T \rightarrow C: &\quad N, t, X, d_2, PIN \\
C \rightarrow T: &\quad d_3, MAC_{KCB}(d_3, T, N, t, X)
\end{aligned}
$$

The ARQC is computed using a key *KCB* shared between the card and the bank[20]. The merchant can't check this, so must either accept the risk of an offline payment or send the transaction to the card-issuing bank through the payment network. The bank checks the ARQC and the available funds, and if all's well sends a response that also includes an *authorisation response cryptogram* (ARPC) for the card. The card responds with a further MAC called the *transaction certificate.*

EMV allows many options, some of which are dangerous, either individually or in combination, and can be thought of as a construction kit for building payment systems, with which you can build systems that are quite secure, or very insecure. It's the switch specifications from VISA and Mastercard that really constrain the crypto as most banks want to be able to rely on their stand-in processing. Things got tightened up steadily over 2005–17 as a succession of frauds exploited the less secure versions. The simplest way to understand the protocol suite may be to follow this history.

12.6.1.1 Static data authentication

The default EMV variant up till 2011 in many countries was *static data authentication* (SDA). As this used cheap cards that could not do public-key

[20]The long-term key *KCB* is actually used to generate a *derived unique key per transaction* (DUKPT, pronounced duck-put) as a countermeasure to power analysis. I'm omitting such details here and will discuss power analysis later in the chapter on side channels.

cryptography, there's no card public key *KC*, and the PIN is sent to the card in the clear. So it's still vulnerable to sniffing by a man-in-the-middle device, just as with the magnetic strip cards that EMV was replacing. The terminal verifies the certificate and digital signature, but has no way to verify the MAC[21]. As before, merchants have a floor limit below which offline transactions are permitted, so they don't have to stop trading when the network or the acquiring bank are down[22].

To begin with, the commonly-exploited vulnerability was backwards compatibility with magnetic strip cards. The certificate initially contained all the information needed to forge a mag-strip card, and as the introduction of chip and PIN meant that people started to enter PINs everywhere rather than just at cash machines[23], gangs either set up false terminals or used various wiretap devices to collect card data from genuine terminals and then cashed out via mag-strip forgeries. Initially these were used in local ATMs that would fall back to mag-strip processing for reliability and compatibility during the changeover. From the late 2000s, the crooks targeted countries such as the USA and Thailand that hadn't adopted EMV yet. This wave of mag-strip fallback fraud is visible in the counterfeit line in Figure 12.4, which surges between 2006 and 2010.

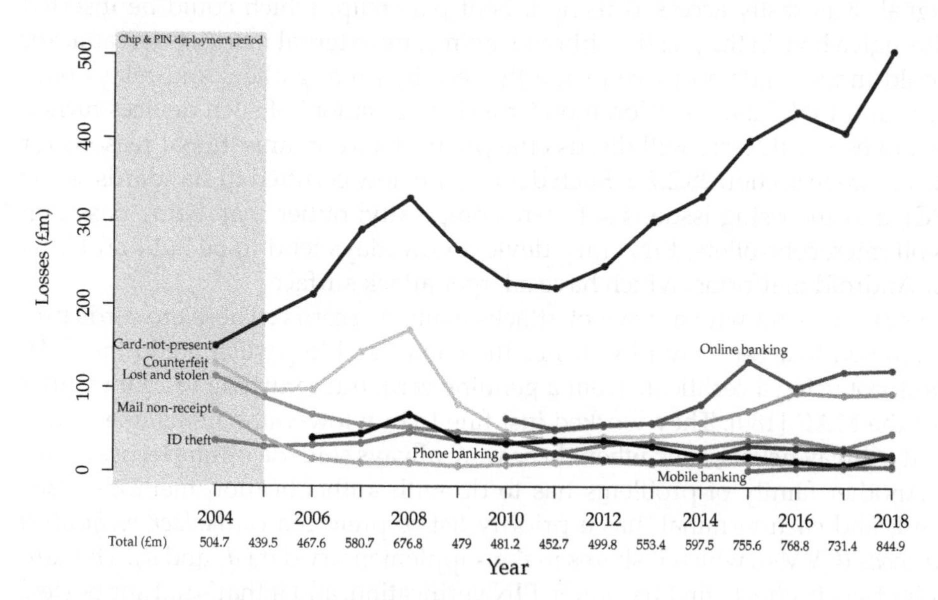

Figure 12.4: Card fraud in the UK from 2004 to 2018

[21]The bank could thus use any algorithm it liked, but the default was DES-CBC-MAC with triple-DES for the last block.

[22]Floor limits were first cut to zero in Spain, and this seems to be happening in the UK too, which seems daft; stations should not stop selling tickets when the phone line goes down, except possibly for season tickets.

[23]In the UK, at 900,000 shop terminals as well as 50,000 ATMs.

Part of the crime wave of 2006–9 targeted petrol stations. An attack on our local BP garage in Cambridge involved a CCTV camera fitted in the ceiling to capture the PINs plus a wiretap to get the card data; over 200 local people found that copies of their cards were used in ATMs in Thailand. BP's competitor Shell was hit even harder, and fell back to mag-strip operation for a while after some of their PIN pads were replaced with tampered ones by crooks pretending to be maintenance engineers. The most spectacular fraud was discovered in 2008, when a gang apparently intercepted PIN entry devices in a warehouse in Dubai, en route from the factory in China to the UK and the Netherlands, and installed in them miniature mobile phones that sent the gang the card and PIN data. Shops in the UK and banks in the Netherlands installed new devices straight out of the box – which promptly started SMSing their customers' data to a server in Karachi [1732]. The gang was arrested and brought to trial in the UK, but the case failed when the banks declined to provide evidence.

Colleagues and I therefore investigated a sample of PIN pads and found that such attacks were easy. For example, the Ingenico i3300, the most widely-deployed terminal in the UK in 2007, had a user-accessible compartment, shown in Figure 12.5, which gives access to the bottom layer of the circuit board. We found that a 1 mm diameter via, carrying the serial data signal, was easily accessed using a bent paperclip, which could be inserted through a hole in the plastic without leaving any external marks. So an attacker could indeed hide a device inside the terminal that gathers and relays both card and PIN data. The 'Common Criteria Evaluation' of such devices turned out to be worthless; I will discuss the political and organisational reasons for its failure in section 28.2.7.2. Such devices are now certified to standards set by PCI, and the rising issue is software complexity; rather than being based on 8-bit microcontrollers, PIN entry devices nowadays tend to be built on Linux or Android platforms, which have a larger attack surface.

France was hit with a wave of attacks using 'yescards'. These are cards programmed to accept any PIN (hence the name) and to participate in the EMV protocol using a certificate from a genuine card, but returning random values for the MAC [180]. They worked just fine to buy low-value items like snacks and subway tickets, back when these were always sold via offline transactions.

Another family of problems has to do with authentication methods. Each card, and each terminal, has a priority list of preferred *cardholder verification methods* (CVMs), which it shares in the supplementary data d_1 and d_2. The card might say in effect: 'first try online PIN verification, and if that's not supported, use local PIN verification, and if that's not possible then a signature will do, and if you can't even get that, then you don't need to authenticate the customer at all'. It might seem surprising that 'no authentication' is an option, but it's needed to support devices such as parking meters that don't have PIN pads. As well as PIN, signature or nothing, the terminal CVM list can specify authentication on a device, such as the biometric scanner on a phone. Both card and terminal can have risk-management logic to set monetary limits for different methods. But EMV version 1 has a flaw: the list of authentication methods isn't itself authenticated, so a crook can manipulate it in a false-terminal attack [170].

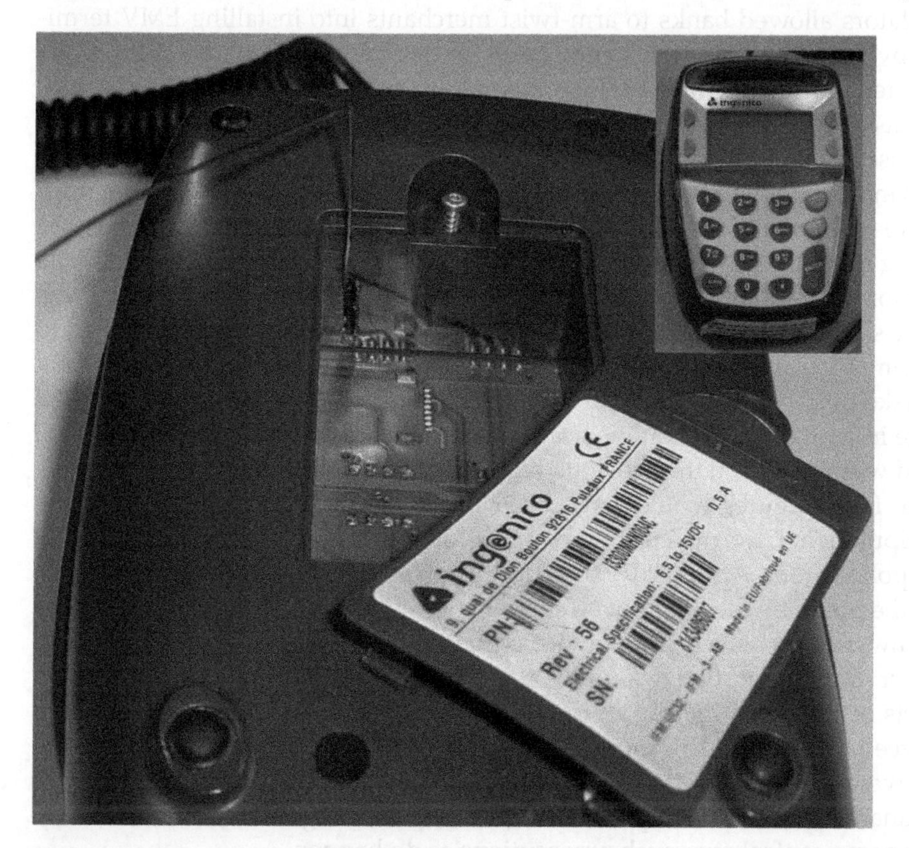

Figure 12.5: A rigid wire is inserted through a hole in the Ingenico's concealed compartment wall to intercept the smartcard data. The front of the device is shown on the top right.

Many attacks become possible once you have a man-in-the-middle device. Two students of ours implemented a *relay attack* for a TV programme; a bogus terminal in a café was hooked up via radio to a bogus card. When a journalist in the café went to pay £5 for some cake to a till operated by one student, the transaction was relayed to the false card carried by the other, who was lingering in a bookstore waiting to buy a book for £50. The £50 transaction went through successfully [584]. There are many entertaining variants on the theme. We don't find them in the wild, though, as they're hard to scale.

The scale of fraud varies quite a lot between countries, and this teaches that the practical security of EMV depends on contextual factors and implementation details – such as the extent to which local ATMs will do fallback magnetic-strip processing, the proportion of local shops open to various kinds of skimmer attack, and – as always – incentives. Do the banks carry the can for fraud as in the US, which makes them take care, or are they able to dump the costs on merchants and cardholders?

A landmark during EMV roll-out was the 'liability shift'. In many countries, regulators allowed banks to arm-twist merchants into installing EMV terminals by changing their terms and conditions so that merchants were liable for disputed transactions if EMV wasn't used, but the banks became liable if it was. In that case, banks in much of Europe simply blamed the customer: 'Your card was used, and so was your PIN, so you're liable.' So in theory fraud wasn't the bank's problem anymore. In practice, fraud went up, as you can see from Figure 12.4. Fraud rose initially, thanks to the many cards stolen from the mail during the changeover period; the banks rushed the roll-out as the merchants paid for the fraud until they had EMV terminals, which took time[24]. There was then a surge in counterfeit, as shops started to get terminals, people got used to entering PINs in them, and the bad guys used bad terminals to steal card data to make mag-strip copies for use in ATMs. The biggest change though was a surge in mail order and online fraud. The net effect was that by October 2007 fraud was up 26% on the previous year [127].

The fraud figures would have been higher were it not for some blatant manipulation. UK bank customers were stopped from reporting card fraud to the police from April 2007; this deal was negotiated between the banks and the police by the Blair government in order to massage the crime statistics downwards, for which it was twice criticised by a parliamentary committee. Proper fraud reporting was only reintroduced in 2015[25]. You can see the effects of this from the dip in the top, 'card-not-present', line in Figure 12.4 between 2008 and 2016; those missing millions include a lot of fraud costs that were simply dumped on cardholders. The banks also took over much of the financing of the small police unit that does investigate card fraud, so they have some control over such prosecutions as do happen.

12.6.1.2 ICVVs, DDA and CDA

In order to stop mag-strip fallback fraud, banks started from the mid-2000s to implement the *integrated circuit card verification value* (iCVV), a CVV that is different in the card data in the chip from the versions on the magnetic

[24]This led to years of bad blood between merchants and banks.

[25]By then it had served its political purpose. From 2007–2015 crime fell steadily, as it was moving online like everything else, and the online part wasn't being counted properly. When Theresa May stood for election as leader of the Conservative Party in 2016, one of her claims to party members was that she'd cut crime despite cutting police numbers from 140,000 to 120,000. This claim was technically true, of reported crime at least. When Boris Johnson stood to replace her in 2019, he claimed that crime had fallen while he was Mayor of London from 2008–16. This claim was not even technically true, as once the Office of National Statistics insisted on counting properly from 2015, reported crime in Britain doubled.

strip (which is read in mag-strip ATM transactions) and on the signature strip (which is used online). Once all three are different, a chip-only skimmer can't in theory be used to make working mag-strip forgeries, and even if a merchant breaks the PCI DSS rules by keeping the signature-strip CVV on a database that then gets hacked, this CVV should not be enough to allow either a mag-strip forgery or a yes-card forgery (this is known as *channel separation*). The three CVVs are all calculated the same way – as a three-digit MAC on the PAN, version number and expiry date, computed using triple-DES, but with different values of a service code in the computation.

Dynamic data authentication (DDA) is the current default variant of EMV. It was used initially in Germany and from 2011 throughout Europe. DDA cards can do public-key cryptography: each has a private key *KC*, whose public key is embedded in the card certificate. The cryptography is used for two functions. First, when the card is first inserted into the terminal, it's sent a nonce, which it signs, assuring the terminal that the card is present (somewhere). The terminal then sends a block containing the 'unpredictable number' and the PIN encrypted using the card's public key, followed by the transaction data, and the card returns the application data cryptogram as before. This blocks skimmers from collecting the PIN[26]. Back in the 2000s, DDA cards cost twice as much as SDA cards; cards are now very much cheaper, and the main extra cost of DDA is that card personalisation is slower.

Combined data authentication (CDA) is the Rolls-Royce variant. It's like DDA except that the card also computes a signature on the MAC. This enables safer offline operation, as the terminal can now verify the transaction. It ties the transaction data to the public key and to the fact that a PIN verification was performed – assuming, that is, the bank selected the option of including a PIN-verification flag in the transaction data. As for why this matters, consider the No-PIN attack.

12.6.1.3 The No-PIN attack

In 2009, we got credible complaints from several fraud victims that their cards had been stolen and then used in shops in transactions that their bank refused to refund, claiming that their PIN had been used – while they insisted that it could not have been compromised. Steven Murdoch, Saar Drimer and I investigated and found that a man-in-the-middle device could tell the terminal that the card had accepted the PIN, while telling the card that the terminal had initiated a chip-and-signature transaction [1366]. Banks in some countries don't use PINs, typically because regulators didn't allow the liability shift;

[26] As the card data are still in clear, a bad guy can still collect the PINs by visual observation and try mag-strip fallback, in the hope that the card issuer doesn't check CVVs; some banks apparently still don't.

and some banks in the UK allow customers to refuse a PIN and get a US-style chip-and-signature card instead.

In the protocol, the card data d_3 contains a flag indicating whether the PIN was verified or not, and the terminal separately returns a flag to its acquiring bank with the same information. However, the card flag is proprietary to the issuer, rather than an EMV standard, so it wasn't checked by default.

Four criminals were arrested in France in May 2011, and a forensic report was published by Houda Ferradi et al. in 2015 after their last appeals ran out. The No-PIN attack was accomplished by cutting out the chip from a stolen card and bonding it underneath the chip of a hobbyist smartcard, which was then programmed to perform the man-in-the-middle attack [680]. The gang stole some €600,000 over 7,000 transactions using 40 modified cards, of which 25 were seized by the police.

One UK bank blocked the attack in late 2010, but the block was removed in early 2011, perhaps because strict error handling was causing too many false positives (the terminal flag may be missing or wrong). The response to our disclosure of the vulnerability was somewhat negative; the banks' trade association wrote to the university asking it to take down the master's thesis of a student whose project had been to build a more robust man-in-the-middle device to investigate such issues (the university refused) [78]. It wasn't until 2017 that the attack definitively stopped working in the UK. However, if either the card or the merchant terminal was issued by a non-UK bank, the attack may still work.

Overlay smartcards may have been used in China and possibly Italy for such an attack in late 2018. These are very thin smartcards – about 180 microns thick – with contacts top and bottom. They were developed in China to support mobile phone roaming; the idea is that you stick one on top of your normal phone SIM to provide an alternative. The overlay acts as a classic man-in-the-middle. These devices are ideal for attacks; they're widely available, they save you having to build fiddly custom hardware, and they are easy to use (you program them in Java Card).

12.6.2 The preplay attack

On the 29th of June 2011, a Maltese customer of HSBC on holiday in Majorca found four ATM transactions debited to his account despite the fact that he had the card in his possession at the time. He'd eaten a meal the previous evening at a restaurant where he thought the staff suspicious, and wondered if his card had been copied. HSBC refused him a refund. So he contacted us, and we advised him to demand the transaction logs. It turned out that the 'unpredictable number' generated by the ATM was just a 16-bit counter that cycled every 3 minutes.

For a DDA/CDA card, the authentication step of EMV is:

$$T \rightarrow C: \quad T, N, t, X, d_2, \{PIN\}_{KC}$$
$$C \rightarrow T: \quad d_3, MAC_{KCB}(d_3, T, N, t, X)$$

If I know which 'unpredictable number' N a given terminal will generate when the date t is tomorrow, and I have your card in my hand today, then I can work out an ARQC $MAC_{KCB}(d_3, T, N, t, X)$ that will work tomorrow in that machine. Mike Bond, Marios Choudary, Steven Murdoch, Sergei Skorobogatov and I therefore instrumented a payment card, by attaching tiny microcontroller, memory and clock chips, and investigated ATMs around Cambridge, England. We found that almost half of them used counters as 'unpredictable numbers'. Others had random number generators with stuck bits. We then went back to the EMV specs and found that the test routine for a terminal only required the tester to draw three 'unpredictable numbers' and check that they were different. So could this be exploited at scale in Britain?

The next data point came in September 2012, when a Scottish sailor ordered a drink in a bar in Las Ramblas, a tourist street in Barcelona. He paid €33 with his EMV card, or so he thought. He passed out, woke up the following morning, and found later that day that his account at Lloyds Bank had been hit with ten debits of €3,300 each – a total of £24,000 at the time. The bank claimed that as the chip and PIN had been used, he was liable. He instructed lawyers who engaged us, and got the transaction logs from the bank. It turned out that the ten transactions had been spaced evenly, filed through three different acquiring banks, and that although they had been made in the same terminal, the terminal was registered with different characteristics at each of these banks. This was clear evidence of technical manipulation, and the sailor got his money back. We dubbed this the 'pre-play attack', as the essence is that rather than replaying old transactions, you record transactions that you will book in the future. If the same terminal will be used, then the fact that it's the terminal that generates the 'unpredictable number' makes the attack easy [283].

Since then, we've seen cases of pre-play attacks in a number of countries in Europe, typically against customers of strip clubs and other sex industry firms. In the UK, a customer of a lap-dancing club in Bournemouth complained in 2014 that the staff got him drunk and charged him £7,500 in 13 transactions [335]. Following press publicity, over a dozen other victims came forward, including people who'd suffered debits after they were back home in bed [1952]. This suggested a pre-play attack rather than a simple case of whores rolling drunken customers; the local authority took an interest, and the club was put 'on probation' for six months. However, we could not persuade the police to raid the club and look for evidence, and eventually it got its full license back. In 2020, a club in London actually lost its license after making multiple charges to customers, with some victims being taken for tens of thousands [1343]. Elsewhere in Europe too, it's turned out to be hard; one such club in Cracow, Poland, got raided but the police didn't look for technical evidence. Terminals can be compromised in various ways: apart from poor random number generators, their vendors can fail to patch their software, and some nowadays even let operators run apps on them[27]. So the preplay problem persists, and I fear that eventually we'll have a homicide case on our hands. Pimps who do pre-play attacks often spike the victim's drink, and if you anaesthetise drunks and leave them to sleep it off on a whorehouse sofa while you loot their bank accounts, then sooner or later one of them will inhale some vomit.

An interesting point about security usability is that if you have four or five cards in your wallet or purse, then if you add up all their balances and credit limits, plus the extra 'unauthorised overdrafts' the card firms might give you, you're probably walking around with the price of a car. If you had that much cash in your pockets you'd probably not go into a bad part of town. You might not even be comfortable walking along the high street unless you had a couple of big friends with you. Payment cards obscure this prudential reflex, and enable us to spend much more than we would when calm and sober. Quite apart from fraud there are issues of vulnerability. The UK government, for example, has just banned the use of credit cards in casinos. If you're designing a system that takes payments online for regulated products, or if your products might be regulated in future because they can be addictive, then there's a bunch of issues you need to work through from ethics to geolocation to arbitration.

12.6.3 Contactless

Contactless payment was pioneered in the US by Mobil in 1997 and adopted in the 2000s in a number of transport systems from London to Tokyo. By 2007, you could just touch your phone on Japanese subway turnstiles in order to get through. Barclays issued the first contactless bank cards in the same year; VISA and Mastercard developed contactless variants of EMV for payment; and Google launched Android Pay in 2011 using the Mastercard PayPass standard[28]. These early adopters struggled to get merchants to change their payment terminals, while the press and public remained sceptical. The market tipped in 2014 when Apple launched Apple Pay. By 2017 card payments had overtaken cash payments in the UK, because of the convenience of tap-and-pay; in 2018, debit cards overtook cash in the USA, and the share of US consumers using mobile online apps rose from 40% to 60% [707]. The

[27]Dixons Carphone was fined £500,000 in 2020 after malware infected 5,390 tills, compromising the personal data of 14 million people and the data from 5.6 million cards. The previous year they'd been fined £400,000 for similar failures [2041].

[28]Full disclosure: I did some work for Google on the design.

coronavirus pandemic in 2020 caused a further large-scale switch from cash to contactless, with UK ATM transactions falling from 232m in January to 91m in April and cash transactions falling from one in three to one in ten, while the contactless limit was raised from £30 to £45.

The basic idea is simple. In the USA, the terminal generates an 'unpredictable number' *N*, the card uses *KC* to generate a dynamic CVV as a 3-digit MAC on selected transaction data, and this is sent to the card-issuing bank along with *N*. In order to scale processing, the CVV keys may be made available to the HSMs of acquiring banks and to service firms that stand in for them. Risk is mitigated by transaction limits – in 2020, $100 in the USA and £30 in the UK. Some issuers have a policy that after a certain number of contactless transactions, the cardholder must do a full EMV transaction with a PIN; this causes complications in some applications. There's a variant in the UK and Europe where the card is made to generate an ARQC, which may be sent to the bank network for checking on a random basis.

As with regular EMV, *N* is generated by the terminal rather than by the bank, so pre-play attacks are possible, but in most countries are not an issue because of the transaction limits[29]. However, the extension of contactless payments from cards to phones led to additional complexity, and the systems we have now are a mash-up of competing proposals from the two card schemes. In some Android phones, the credit card becomes a virtual credit card, implemented in Java Card in a secure element in the NFC chip that does the contactless RF protocol; Apple is something similar but with the key material in the iPhone's secure enclave. Other Android phones use *host card emulation* where the NFC function is provided in software. NFC chips, or functionality, are starting to appear in watches, bracelets and other devices too. Many use *tokenization*, where the phone or other device is provisioned with a token[30] and key material by an online *tokenization service provider* (TSP) that acts on behalf of the banks. The merchant sends the transaction to the TSP, which performs the appropriate cryptographic operations in its HSM and forwards the transaction to the customer's bank.

When contactless cards were rolled out, there were the usual implementation failures. In some stores, you could be charged for a transaction twice if you paid using a contact transaction yet left your wallet or purse near the terminal with a different, contactless, card in it. Researchers also wondered whether a crook could harvest credit card numbers, security codes and expiry dates by doing RFID transactions with victims' cards as he brushes past them in the street – or by reading cards that have been sent in the mail, without opening the envelopes [896]. Martin Emms and colleagues from Newcastle showed this

[29]In Germany, you do high-value card payments by doing a contactless payment, combined with online PIN verification as in an ATM transaction, but I'm not aware of any pre-play incidents.
[30]There's a *payment account reference* (PAR), a permanent pseudonym for the card number.

was possible, and found some even more interesting flaws: one UK bank even let you make one guess at a PIN; with others, the cash limit failed with foreign currency transactions [629]. On November 5th 2016 this led to a major fraud against Tesco Bank in the UK, when crooks in Brazil posted high-value transactions by using mag-strip data on a contactless interface on a mobile device. The bogus transactions amounted to £2.2m from 8,261 customer accounts and, although the eventual losses were only £700,000, the attack created a flood of fraud alerts with which the bank's weekend working procedures could not cope. It took until November 7th to block the fraudulent transaction stream, many legitimate transactions were also blocked, and normal customer service only restarted on the 9th. For this failure, and the distress caused to customers, the regulator fined the bank £16.4m [687].

In 2019, Leigh-Anne Galloway and Tim Yunusov found you could increase the contactless limit from £30 to £5500 by pretending to be a phone, and there's also an exploitable preplay attack. These attacks exploit the phone/card/terminal complexity. Android phones can have multiple limits depending on whether the screen is off or on, and whether the user has recently authenticated; and the phone and terminal send unauthenticated flags to each other [736]. In 2020, David Basin, Ralf Sasse, and Jorge Toro found an improved middleperson attack where a transaction is routed from a stolen card through two phones to a contactless terminal, which accepts a claim that the cardholder was verified using the phone's own authentication mechanism, such as a biometric [183]. Possibly such attacks could be prevented from scaling by the banks' fraud engines, and they haven't appeared in the statistics (yet). However, we still get complaints from cardholders who have been victims of fraud after their cards were stolen, and who claim their PIN wasn't compromised while their bank claims it must have been.

We're starting to see innovative variants that don't rely on specific hardware but allow other channels to be used to run the protocol, such as QR codes. We'll have to wait and see whether these lead to man-in-the-middle attacks at scale. The designers of second-generation EMV are talking of closing all the plaintext gaps and even adding distance bounding as an option. Such techniques could thwart many of the attacks described here. But the principal problems with contactless now that it has been running for several years are more prosaic, and include card collisions: if you have three cards in your wallet and you wave the wallet over a subway turnstile, which of them gets debited? The card-choice mechanisms aren't robust enough to give repeatable answers [1289]. This is an issue in London, where if you tap into the local transport system and fail to tap out again, you get billed the maximum fare. If the entry and exit turnstiles see different cards in your wallet, you end up paying double the maximum.

A recent development is *Software PIN on COTS* (SPoC) where the old assumption of a sort-of cleartext magnetic strip plus a strongly encrypted PIN is turned on its head: the SPoC rule is that devices where the PIN can't be strongly protected must never learn the associated card data. If a PIN is entered in a merchant's iPhone, as we now see at Apple stores, there's another component called a *Secure Card Reader – PIN* (SCRP) that plugs into the phone and accepts the customer card. Even if the phone app is compromised, the bad guy doesn't know which card the PIN will work for. The phone also passes the customer PIN to the SCRP where it's encrypted and sent off for online verification. There's also work on ways to accept contactless payments on ordinary phones; and presumably the next step will be to pay people by tapping phones together, with one emulating the card and another the terminal. Direct phone-to-phone payments are already routine for tens of millions of people in countries such as Kenya and Bangladesh, as I'll describe below in section 12.8.1. It will be an interesting challenge to join up such systems with the world of EMV and make the whole thing safe to use.

12.7 Online banking

After credit and debit cards, the third thread in the world of payments is banking from your PC or phone.

In 1985, the first home banking service in the world was offered by the Bank of Scotland, whose customers could use Prestel, a proprietary email system operated by British Telecom, to make payments. When Steve Gold and Robert Schifreen hacked Prestel – as described previously in section 3.4.4.4 – it scared the press and the bankers. But there was little real risk. The system allowed only *nominated account payments* – you could only send money between your own accounts and to accounts you'd notified to the bank, such as your gas and electricity suppliers. In the early days this meant visiting a branch, filling a paper consent form, and waiting until the cashier checked the payee account number.

The early 1990s saw the rapid growth of phone banking, followed by bank websites from the late 1990s, and then the phishermen arrived.

12.7.1 Phishing

In section 3.3.3 I summarised the history of phishing from its beginnings in the 1990s to its use against online bank accounts from 2003. The bad guys started with crude lures from typosquatted domains like `http://www.barqlays.com` to deceptive ones like `http://www.barclays.othersite.com`; the banks' initial response was to blame their customers. The gangs rapidly got more sophisticated, as underground crime forums got going from around 2005 that supported increasing specialisation, just as in the normal economy. One gang would write the malware, another would herd the botnet, and we started to see specialists who would accept hot money and launder it. The usual technique was to loot whatever customer accounts you could and send the money to compromised accounts at whatever bank was slowest at recovery. Of the £35m lost by UK banks in 2006, over £33m was lost by a single bank. One of its competitors told us that the secret was to spot account takeovers quickly and follow them up aggressively; if money's sent to a mule's account, he should find his account frozen before he can walk to Western Union. So the laundrymen learned to avoid them.

The industry learned to take down phishing websites as quickly as possible, and specialist takedown companies got good at this. The bad guys responded with tricks such as fast flux, where phishing sites were hosted on botnets and each mark who answered a lure was sent to a different IP address.

The second battlefield was asset recovery: the fraudsters would try to get the money overseas quickly and launder it, while the industry and law enforcement would try to stop them. Until May 2007, the preferred route was eGold, a company operated from Florida but with a legal domicile in the Caribbean, which offered unregulated electronic payment. After eGold got raided and closed down by the FBI, the villains started to send money through banks in Finland to their subsidiaries in the Baltic states and on to Russia. The third choice was wire-transfer firms like Western Union: the phishermen recruit *mules* by offering jobs in which they work from home and earn a commission as an agent for a foreign company. They are told their work is to receive several payments a week, deduct their own commission, and then send the balance onwards via Western Union [790]. There have also been various electronic money services in Russia and the Middle East [76]. Regulators played whack-a-mole: after one channel got closed down, another would open up. Banks through which money laundering was easy – known in the industry as 'mule banks' – even suffered less fraud, as the big gangs avoided targeting their customers in the hope that they'd stay useful for longer as the second link in the chain. This battle continues, with funds laundered through everything from cryptocurrencies to Amazon gift cards.

This emphasises the importance of the *prevent – detect – recover* model we introduced in section 12.2.4 above. Where authentication alone can't do the job, and you can't find other vulnerable points in the kill chain, you need to beef up the intrusion-detection mechanisms that complement them.

12.7.2 CAP

In 2006, the banks announced a two-factor authentication standard based on EMV, and this was launched the following year. The *Chip Authentication Program* (CAP)[31] consists of a handheld password calculator in which you can

[31] This is its brand name for Mastercard, which invented it; VISA calls it *Dynamic Passcode Authentication* (DPA).

put your EMV bank card. You enter a PIN; the device gets the card to check this; you can then do one of three functions. You can get a one-time password to log on, you can answer a logon challenge, or you can authenticate a series of digits, typically from a payee account number and amount.

Current versions use a custom app on the EMV card, which uses a key shared with the issuing bank to compute a MAC on the supplied data and on an *application transaction counter* (ATC) (which is different from the one used for point-of-sale transactions). The response code is a truncated MAC and a truncated ATC. The security is discussed in [585]; briefly, if you put your card in a bad terminal, this can generate a CAP code to log on to your online banking service, though that's hard to scale as you typically also need a password. The availability of CAP readers means that a mugger who holds you up for your card can demand your PIN and check it, without having to march you to an ATM and risk being seen on CCTV. This has led to homicides, and was negligent design: other password calculators just return the wrong result if you supply the wrong PIN, including the early designs from the 1980s that I described in section 4.3.2.

12.7.3 Banking malware

As banks made simple phishing attacks harder by using ever more elaborate authentication mechanisms from partial password questions to the early two-factor authentication schemes, some bad guys just worked harder at persuasion. Even in Germany, whose banks gave their customers printed lists of one-time passwords, the crooks persuaded some customers to type them all in at once. Other bad guys turned to automation, in the form of banking malware. From 2007, a series of malware strains such as Zeus, Torpig, SpyEye, EMotet, Trickbot and Dridex stole hundreds of millions from banks and their customers worldwide, spreading by various techniques including Word macros and drive-by downloads. By 2011, man-in-the-middle attacks developed into *man-in-the-browser* attacks: when the user of an infected PC sets out to use their bank account, browser malware can actively modify transaction data so that what they see isn't what they authorise. This is why prudent banks now use a second factor such as CAP to authenticate at least the last four digits of the account number of any new payee. Banks who don't use CAP may use a dedicated authentication device instead, or a phone-based second factor.

12.7.4 Phones as second factors

Another response to the wave of phishing in the mid-2000s was to use the customer's phone as a second factor. It seems natural to send a confirmation, such as: 'If you really want to send $7500 to Russian Real Estate LLC, please enter 4716 now in your browser.' This appears to give the same benefits as CAP, but with a nicer user interface.

However, after South African banks started implementing this in 2007, they quickly saw the first *SIM swap* fraud. Some Johannesburg crooks got a new SIM for the phone number of the CFO of a charity that looks after orphaned and vulnerable children, and stole R90,460 from its bank account [1516]. The bank complained to the phone company, which was unsympathetic: phone companies sell minutes, not banking authentication services. As I discussed in section 3.4.1, such frauds spread from South Africa to Nigeria, then to the US from about 2014–5 where they were initially used to steal Instagram accounts, and from 2018 to loot people's accounts at bitcoin exchanges [1094].

Such attacks now involve phone company insiders. In a 2019 case, an AT&T contractor in Tucson, Arizona, helped a SIM-swap gang steal $2m from 29 victims [711]. In 2020, Kevin Lee and colleagues tried to swap ten SIMs on each of five US phone companies and found it to be easy: with the big companies, it worked every time. Vulnerabilities included authenticating people by asking about recent calls and recent top-ups, both of which can be manipulated by an attacker [1138]. It was also reported that SIM swappers were hacking phone company staff, by social-engineering them into installing remote access tools on their PCs, and then using the subverted machines to reassign target phone numbers to SIMs they controlled [486]. Tens of thousands of customer service reps are in a position to be careless, to get hacked or to take bribes from SIM swap gangs. Some already take bribes to unlock stolen phones, and once these underground communities link up we can expect things to get worse. There have also been a couple of cases, in Germany and the UK, where attackers exploited the SS7 signalling protocol to wiretap targets' mobile phones remotely and steal codes that way [485] (I'll discuss this further in section 22.2.3). In China, the law requires you to visit a phone shop and show ID to buy a SIM; in India, you need a biometric check and the phone company is also made partly liable for SIM-swap fraud. However, the direction of travel in the US and Europe is away from SMS as a second factor and towards a custom phone app[32].

But as I wrote in the second edition of this book in 2007, "Two-channel authentication relies for its security on the independence of the channels ... if everyone starts using an iPhone, or doing VoIP telephony over wireless access points, then the assumption of independence breaks down."

In the EU, the second payment services directive now requires banks to use two-factor authentication. So it's becoming universal, and the bad guys are getting a lot of practice at breaking it. But what happens if you do your banking

[32]Data on which banks use hardware tokens as second factors, or software tokens, or SMS, or no second factor at all, can be found at `https://twofactorauth.org/#banking`.

not on your laptop but on a phone app, and use another phone app as your second factor? If malware roots your phone, might it take over both apps, and loot your account?

At the time of writing (2020), the European Central Bank takes the view that two apps are OK so long as you use *runtime application self-protection* (RASP), which means that you obfuscate the app code using the kind of techniques developed during the 1980s for software copy protection and the 1990s for digital rights management. This makes experienced security engineers wince, as the history of such mechanisms is not a good one; it's told in the chapter on Copyright and DRM, and I discuss RASP further there in section 24.3.3. It is very hard to get any assurance of how long an obfuscation scheme will take to break; a break must be expected at any time, and the user of such a scheme had better be ready to patch it immediately that happens. And maybe all an attacker might need to do is shim one of the methods in the network stack to get at the strings containing the authentication exchange. So they might not need to extract the key or otherwise break the RASP mechanism itself.

12.7.5 Liability

One long-running argument has been over liability. The rush to online banking led many banks to adopt contract terms that put the risk of fraud on customers, in conflict with consumer law and traditional banking practice [278]. Unfortunately, the EU's Payment Services Directives of 2007 and 2015 went along with this by leaving a loophole in dispute resolution procedures[33].

A study of the bank fraud reimbursement terms and conditions of 30 banks operating in 25 countries showed a great variety of security advice, with much of it being vague, impractical or even conflicting [202]. For example, HSBC required unique PINs and passwords per account, contrary to advice given earlier by the UK banks' trade association which recommended customers to change all their PINs to the PIN issued for one of their cards. It also had the most onerous demands for Internet banking, including that the bank's URL must always be typed into the browser manually. It, and many other banks, required customers to use antivirus software; fewer required that software be patched up-to-date.

Banks meanwhile trained their customers to be vulnerable by business practices such as telling their customers to reveal their security data, even when making unsolicited calls. I've personally received an unsolicited call from my

[33]British banks got the UK government to insert 'necessarily' into article 72(2): 'Where a payment service user denies having authorised an executed payment transaction, the use of a payment instrument recorded by the payment service provider, including the payment initiation service provider as appropriate, shall in itself not necessarily be sufficient to prove either that the payment transaction was authorised by the payer or that the payer acted fraudulently or failed with intent or gross negligence to fulfil one or more of the obligations under Article 69.'

bank saying 'Hello, this is Lloyds TSB, can you tell me your mother's maiden name?' You're sorely tempted to tell them to get lost, but if you do it will be a bother to reactivate or replace your payment cards. And even if the security ritual is made more complicated, the phishermen can still talk the marks through it, if need be as a man-in-the-middle (or browser) attack.

However, round about 2015, the bad guys started to evolve a better way.

12.7.6 Authorised push payment fraud

Authorised push payment (APP) fraud refers to bank transfers that customers are tricked into making. Figures only started to get collected in 2017 and the 2018 figures are not calculated in the same way to 2017, so we don't have those on the graph in Figure 12.4. However the total, at £354.3 million, is second only to remote purchase fraud and more than the remainder put together.

A typical modus operandi is to look for someone who's buying a house and send an email that seems to be from their lawyer informing them that the firm's bank account number has changed. Another is to target vulnerable elderly people. In one case, a 92-year old war veteran was called by crooks pretending to be from his bank, bank A, who told him that the bank had been hacked, so he had to transfer his life savings of £120,000 to bank B for safekeeping. Two days later, his son visited and learned what had happened. In this particular case, their lawyers demanded that bank B produce the know-your-customer documents with which the mule account was opened. A few days later, bank B (which had a reputation as a 'mule bank') sheepishly refunded the money.

That victim was lucky, but many were less so. Large frauds had become easy because the banks had made large payments easy; in the old days, taking out £120,000 would have involved arranging a meeting with a bank manager at the very least. Yet online banking had been combined with a system of instantaneous payments which meant that fraudsters could get away with five-figure and even six-figure sums. In the UK this became such a sore point that Parliament's Treasury committee noted that rapid irrevocable payments were simply the wrong default [1363], and the Payment Services Regulator changed the rules so that the banks now carry some of the liability. As a result, it has become significantly more complicated to make large bank transfers. Even medium-sized transactions get held up; if you try to pay your plumber a few thousand for renovating your bathroom, you're likely to get anxious calls from the bank and be put through some security ceremonies.

Similar frauds have also been growing steadily against companies. Known as *business email compromise* (BEC), they now account for several billion dollars a year in losses [92]. In one recent case, a museum in the Netherlands agreed to buy an 1855 painting by John Constable for £2.4m from a London art dealer, but sent the money to the wrong account after crooks hacked the museum's email account and sent emails appearing to come from the dealer. The museum sued the dealer but lost [506]. Victim firms have much less protection than consumers do, but there are some mitigations that help both. For example, the UK regulator ordered banks to implement *confirmation of payee*: when you first make a payment to a new account, you'll be asked for the account holder's name and you'll be alerted if it's wrong [1363]. Still, prudent practice is now to hard-code company bank account numbers in business contracts, so that if firm A pays crook C instead of firm B, there's no room for argument over whose fault it was. In Germany – where firms have been using direct bank payments since the 20th century – it has been a legal requirement for years that companies print their bank account numbers on their letterheads.

12.8 Nonbank payments

There are many ways of making payments other than through banks. PayPal is the survivor of a number of email-based payment service providers that sprung up at the time of the dotcom boom, and has now in effect grown into a bank, with a portfolio of payment services both traditional and novel. A more traditional service is *hawala*, a term that refers to money-changers that serve communities of immigrants from South Asia and the Middle East, helping them to send money home. They compete with Western Union, which grew up with the Victorian telegraph network, and more modern payment service providers who provide low-cost foreign exchange transactions. Some of these services are used by cybercriminals, most notably PayPal and Western Union. Western Union is a particular problem for law enforcement as criminals can send money to any one of its many branches and withdraw it in cash. All such providers are regulated in the European Union by the E-money directive of 2009, which sets rules for capital and liquidity. There are also cryptocurrencies such as bitcoin, which some regulators currently exempt from e-money regulation, and which I'll discuss in the chapter on Advanced Cryptographic Engineering.

Two particular types of payment service merit separate discussion: phone payments and overlay payments, of which the leading examples are M-Pesa, AliPay/WeChat Pay, and Sofort.

12.8.1 M-Pesa

M-Pesa is a mobile phone banking service in Kenya, launched in 2007 by Vodafone. It took off rapidly and the firm that operates it, Safaricom, is now Kenya's largest financial institution. Over 200 similar services have been launched in less developed countries, and have been transformative in about 20 of them;

the largest such service now may be B-Kash in Bangladesh. Many such services have been growing rapidly during the 2020 coronavirus lockdown.

M-Pesa got going as a means for migrant workers in Nairobi and Mombasa to send money home to rural relatives. Before mobile phones came along, this meant posting cash, or sending it with friends or bus drivers. This was both inconvenient and risky, especially during a period of civil unrest in 2008 after a disputed election the year before. Once mobile phones became widespread, people started buying airtime as a means of transferring value, and from there it was a small step to transfer actual value. The security mechanisms of such systems tend to be simple, with an encrypted PIN, payee and value sent over SMS or USSD. The key success factor is that phone companies have built networks of tens of thousands of sales agents who can turn cash into digital credit and back again – networks that reach the smallest villages, unlike the legacy banks. The operational problems have to do with people sending money to the wrong phone number by mistake, and integrating incoming M-Pesa payments with business systems.

12.8.2 Other phone payment systems

Many other countries have phone payment systems, or have widely-used proprietary payment systems that work reasonably well on phones. An example of these is PayPal, which redirects you from a merchant website to PayPal's, where you log in to authorise payment. Up until 2013, this was the world's leading phone payment system. Since then the leading phone payment mechanism has been AliPay, a proprietary payment app run by the Alibaba group in China. It is closely followed by Tencent's WeChat Pay; in 2020 they had 54% and 39% of the Chinese mobile-payment market respectively. Smartphone payments took off rapidly in China, as M-Pesa did in Kenya, because banking used to be unsatisfactory outside the main cities [608]. They have become the default payment mechanism in China, and use a visual payment channel: a merchant displays a QR code that the customer scans to send the right amount to the right account. AliPay and WeChat Pay operate not just as business platforms but as national infrastructure, and since 2018 are closely regulated: the People's Bank of China gets copies of all transaction data [1532]. This fits with the Chinese approach to information sovereignty we discussed in section 2.2.2. And both apps now support payment using your face, aligning with the growing use in China of face recognition, a technology I discuss in section 17.3. India also has a low-cost phone payment system in UPI, linked to the national Aadhaar biometric card; on these national payment and identity layers sit a number of competing payment apps.

12.8.3 Sofort, and open banking

Credit cards were not traditionally used in Germany, which was inconvenient when people started shopping online. One approach was to order goods from a website, get the merchant's bank account details and a transaction reference number, go to your bank and pay, and then go back to the merchant's website the next day and put in the payment details.

Sofortüberweisung is German for 'immediate payment' and set out to solve this problem by means of an industrialised man-in-the-middle attack. In order to buy a plane ticket, for example, you click the 'sofort' ('immediate') button on the airline's checkout page, and the service opens up a frame in which you enter your bank name and account number. Sofort then logs on to your bank as you, and presents you with the bank's authentication challenge. Once you pass this, it goes into your account, checks that there's enough money, and sends itself the payment. It then redirects back to the airline and you get your ticket [80]. The effect is to make online shopping easier, but also to deprive the banks of card transaction fees (the merchant pays about a third as much as they'd have paid for a card transaction).

The banks sued Sofort for unfair competition and for inciting customers to breach bank terms of service by entering their credentials at Sofort's website. They lost after the German Federal Antitrust Office argued that the banks' terms of service hindered competition and were designed to exclude new business models like Sofort's. Sofort got a banking licence and the other banks just had to compete.

The upshot was the EU's second payment services directive (PSD2), also known as 'open banking'. Since January 2018, banks must open up their systems, not just by releasing transaction data in a standard format to other regulated financial institutions if their customer requests it, but allowing the other institution to act as the customer does. The upside will include banks and fintech companies offering dashboards that will let you see all your holdings across all the banks with which you have an account, and move money between them to get the best deals. The downside is that fraud and money laundering are migrating rapidly to open banking channels. If a crook sets up an account at bank A, fills it with stolen money, authorises an account at fintech B to operate it, then uses B to get A to send money to C, A is not allowed to refuse the transaction. The upshot is that traditional controls on fraud and money laundering become much less effective. So there will be more jobs for security engineers[34]. We will have to wait and see how all this develops.

[34]Open Banking means migrating from the old ISO 8583 standard to the newer ISO 20022. This enables a move from 8-byte PIN blocks to 16-byte and thus from 3DES to AES; from later batch settlement of transactions to real-time gross settlement; and much much more.

The introduction of QR code based payment into the EMV standards opens up the possibility of scaling something like Sofort's payment mechanism worldwide. As well as the customer presenting a payment instrument as a QR code, the merchant can present a payment demand in this way, so that the customer's phone can initiate an online bank payment. Existing phone payment systems like M-Pesa also require the customer to scan a QR code or enter data manually if their phone can't do this. There may be some scope for innovation and convergence here, so we'll have to wait and see how it develops.

12.9 Summary

Banking systems are critical to the security engineer because that's how stolen money gets moved – and fascinating in other ways too. Bookkeeping gives us a mature example of systems oriented towards authenticity and accountability rather than confidentiality. The Clark-Wilson security policy provides a model of this approach, which evolved over centuries. Making it work well in practice means sophisticated functional separation, whose design involves input from many disciplines. The threat model has a particular emphasis on insiders.

Payment systems played a significant role in the development of cryptology through their use in the first generation of ATM systems; the adoption of smartcard-based payments has changed the fraud landscape once more.

Finally, we have seen several waves of attacks on electronic banking systems since the mid-2000s – by phishing account credentials, by man-in-the-browser attacks by specialised malware, by SIM swap attacks on the mobile phones used as a second authentication factor, and by social engineering customers to send their money to the bad guys directly. These have progressively explored the possible combinations of high tech and low cunning, and they teach the importance of a holistic approach to fraud mitigation. The turbulence caused by the pandemic is likely to emphasise this, but at least the mechanisms whose use is surging, such as contactless payments in developed countries and phone payments elsewhere, have had a few years to bed down.

Research problems

I've always distrusted the cartel of big accountancy firms – down from the Big Eight in the 1980s to the Big Four now, following three mergers and the failure of Arthur Anderson in the Enron scandal. A student and I once wondered whether being a client of a big accountancy firm was a signal of wrongdoing, but a brief analysis threw up no evidence either way. Thereafter when I served on a governing body or audit committee, I always proposed using a local firm, as it was cheaper, but only once managed to get a change (and that was from one big firm to another). When I served on our university's governing body I had to put up with this cartel shaking us down for a million a year and providing nothing useful in return; most of the work was done by juniors. I thought the Germans might be better off as their rules prevent auditors selling consultancy services, but the Wirecard scandal punctured that illusion. The UK government still decided after that scandal (and many others) that from 2024, the audit firms must separate their audit and consulting practices in such a way that audit partners' remuneration comes only from the audit business and is not cross-subsidised from consultancy [1052]. It would be great if that works, but I fail to see how it can have any real effect on most of the concrete problems described in this book, whether the internal control issues analysed in this chapter or the assurance issues which I tackle in section 28.1. The audit cartel imposes huge social costs and is not quite what we expect from standard economic analysis[35]. It needs to be understood better.

Designing internal controls is still pre-scientific; we could do with tools to help us do it in a more systematic, less error-prone way. Just as many security failures come from poor usability at the level of both users (who are offered dangerous choices as defaults) and programmers (who're given access-control and other tools that are insanely tricky to use), so many internal control failures come from administrative mechanisms that are designed for the comfort of the auditor rather than to be actually usable in real organisations. How can we do this better?

Payment systems are at the one time deeply conservative, being in many ways little changed since the 1970s, and also constantly evolving, as the mechanisms moved from ATMs and HSMs to chip cards and to crypto chips in mobile phones. The ground's also shifting as attacks evolve (as with SIM swap) and the environment changes (as with open banking). Maintaining resilience in the face of such change takes work. As EMV implementations get tightened up, and as the second version of EMV starts to tackle the residual vulnerabilities described here, we can expect fraud to move to the periphery: to the customer, via account takeover; to the merchant, via hacking attacks, refund scams, coupon scams and the like; and to the bank, via pre-issue frauds and technical attacks on the systems for authorisation and settlement.

If account takeover is going to become ever-more pervasive, what are the implications? I suspect that our regulatory approach needs an overhaul: blaming ordinary customers for harm they suffer from systems designed by others is wrong. But what should we do? Should we go for radical transparency, impose

[35]See the Lerner-Tirole model discussed in section 28.2.8 for a model of how firms faced with a compliance requirement usually choose the cheapest supplier. Why do most large firms and even large universities go for famous but expensive firms when they're all but useless at detecting whether executives are crooks or firms are trading while insolvent?

payment delays, or put more weight on rapid asset recovery? Is there some smart combination, such as making the speed and finality of payment a function of the known standing of both payer and payee? Or should regulators just keep pushing liability back to the banks and let them work it out?

The context in early 2020 was that retail banks are making less money than they used to, because of low interest rates and growing competition, so bank security engineers are being asked to do more with less. Social media are making downtime more painful; if a bank's mobile app is down for 15 minutes because of a DDoS attack on a gateway, there can be a twitter storm that causes directors to phone the Chief Operating Officer. Such incentives push in the direction of moving stuff to the cloud, but this raises further problems; we'll discuss cloud HSMs later in the chapter on Advanced Cryptographic Engineering. The coronavirus pandemic has been great for payment service providers, with PayPal's share price up by about a half; as to where it may drive fintech innovation, perhaps it will be around video. Videoconferencing is having to replace in-branch meetings for complex and high-value transactions such as loans. The latest wave of fintechs such as Monzo were already getting customers to record a selfie video as part of the onboarding process, so that call centre staff helping a customer recover an account from a lost or stolen phone could check they're the same person who opened the account. What else?

Further reading

Andrew Jamieson wrote a 100-page ebook on EMV for Underwriters' Laboratories – ten times what I had space for here [979] – and that may be a useful stepping stone from my short summary to the thousands of pages of specifications from PCI SSC and EMVco [630]. I don't know of any comprehensive book on core banking systems, although there are many papers on payment systems available from the Bank for International Settlements: the most recent, as we go to press in 2020, analyses quality of service and notes that while payments within Europe mostly take under 30 minutes, a combination of multiple intermediaries, business hours, time zones, capital controls, liquidity and ancient technology mean that payments to Asia and Africa can take hours to days [163]. If you're going to do any real work on internal control, you'd better read ISA 315 [952]; its interpretation by the big four accountancy firms now makes the weather on internal controls. I'll revisit this topic in Part 3. To understand what can actually go wrong, read the judgment in the Horizon case [186] and the survey of corporate fraud by Alexander Dyck, Adair Morse and Luigi Zingales [596].

The IBM system of generating and protecting ATM PINs was described in a number of articles, such as [521] and [953], while early ATM networks are described in [764]. For the basics of ATM fraud, see [56]; while the transcript of the trial of an HSBC insider gives a snapshot of typical internal controls in electronic banking systems [1572]. The first survey of underground markets was 2007 by Jason Franklin, Vern Paxson, Adrian Perrig and Stefan Savage [714]; even then, the focus was on bank fraud rather than on drugs or malware. There's a rich literature since then on topics from the social dynamics of underground communities [1347] to the Russians behind the Dridex malware campaign [1625]. Colleagues and I have contributed to big surveys of cybercrime in 2012 [91] and 2019 [92]. There's a collection of our group's writings on bank fraud at our Bank Fraud Resource Page, at `https://www.cl.cam.ac.uk/~rja14/banksec.html`. For an authoritative case study of a large card fraud, see the FCA's 2018 ruling against Tesco Bank [687]. This not only sets out how the fraud was done, but how the controls failed at multiple points and how the regulators calculated the fine.

Finally, for the political and legislative history of the US intelligence initiative against terrorist finance and its efforts to get SWIFT data by covert or legislative means, see David Bulloch's thesis [343].

CHAPTER

13

Locks and Alarms

For if a man watch too long, it is odds he will fall asleepe.
– FRANCIS BACON

The greatest of faults, I should say, is to be conscious of none.
– THOMAS CARLYLE

13.1 Introduction

Most security engineers nowadays focus on electronic systems, but physical protection cannot be neglected. First, if you're advising on a company's overall risk management, then walls and locks are a factor. Second, as it's easier to teach someone with an electrical engineering or computer science background the basics of physical security than the other way round, interactions between physical and logical protection are usually up to the systems person to manage. Third, you will often be asked for your opinion on your client's installations – which may have been built by contractors with little understanding of system issues. You'll need to be able to give informed, but diplomatic, advice. Fourth, many information security mechanisms can be defeated if a bad man gets physical access, whether at the factory, or during shipment, or before installation. Fifth, many mechanical locks have recently been completely compromised by 'bumping', an easy covert-entry technique; their manufacturers often seem unaware of vulnerabilities that enable their products to be quickly bypassed. Finally, many of the electronic locks that are replacing them are easy to compromise, either because they use cryptography that's been broken (such as Mifare classic) or because of poor integration of the mechanical and digital components.

Much of physical security is just common sense, but there are some non-obvious twists, and there have been significant recent advances in technology. There are useful ideas from criminology and architecture on how you can reduce the incidence of crime around your facilities; some of these may go across into system design too. And there's a very interesting case study in burglar alarms.

For example, in order to defeat a burglar alarm it's enough to make it stop working, or even just to persuade the guards that it has become unreliable. This gives a new perspective on *denial-of-service attacks*. Just as we've seen military messaging systems designed to enforce confidentiality and bookkeeping systems whose goal is preserving record authenticity, monitoring gives us the classic example of systems that need to be dependably available. If there is a burglar in my bank vault, then I don't care very much who else gets to know (so I'm not worried about confidentiality), or who it was who told me (so authenticity isn't a major concern); but I do care very much that an attempt to tell me is not thwarted. Historically, about 90% of computer security research was about confidentiality, about 9% about authenticity and 1% about availability. But actual attacks – and companies' infosec expenditures – are often the other way round, with more spent on availability than on authenticity and confidentiality combined. And it's alarm systems, above all else, that can teach us about availability.

13.2 Threats and barriers

Physical security engineering is no different at heart from the digital variety: you perform a threat analysis, then design a system that involves equipment and procedures, then test it. You evaluate it according to criteria agreed with the customer, which in 2020 may mean that a bank headquarters building has a specification setting out five years' maintenance cost, building software penetration testing and a security policy [355]. The design and testing of entry controls and alarms are driven by a policy based on:

Deter – detect – alarm – delay – respond

A facility can deter intruders using hard methods such as concrete walls, or softer methods such as being inconspicuous. It will then have one or more layers of barriers and sensors whose job is to keep out casual intruders, detect deliberate intruders, and make it difficult for them to get in too quickly. This will be complemented by an alarm system designed to get a response to the scene in time. As the barriers will have doors for authorized staff to go in and out, there will be entry control that could be anything from metal keys to biometric scanners. Finally, these measures will be supported by operational controls. How do you cope, for example, with your facility manager having his family taken hostage?

As I noted earlier, one of the ways in which you get your staff to accept dual controls and integrate them into their work culture is that these controls protect them, as well as protecting the assets. You need to embed the operational aspects of security in the firm's culture or they won't work well, and this applies to physical security just as much as to the computer variety. It's also vital to get unified operational security across the physical, business and information domains: there's little point in spending $10m to protect a vault containing $100m of diamonds if a bad man can sneak a false delivery order into your system, and send a courier to pick up the diamonds from reception. That is another reason why, as the information security expert, you have to pay attention to the physical side too.

13.2.1 Threat model

An important design consideration is the attacker's level of skill, equipment and motivation. And as we've seen in one context after another, security isn't a scalar. It doesn't make sense to ask 'Is device X secure?' without a context: 'secure against whom and in what environment?'

In the absence of an 'international standard burglar', the nearest I know to a working classification is one developed by a US Army expert [174].

- *Derek* is a 19-year old addict. He's looking for a low-risk opportunity to steal something he can sell for his next fix.
- *Charlie* is a 40-year old inadequate with seven convictions for burglary. He's spent seventeen of the last twenty-five years in prison. Although not very intelligent, he is cunning and experienced; he has picked up a lot of 'lore' during his spells inside. He steals from small shops and suburban houses, taking whatever he thinks he can sell to local fences.
- *Bruno* is a 'gentleman criminal'. His business is mostly stealing art. As a cover, he runs a small art gallery. He has a (forged) university degree in art history on the wall, and one conviction for robbery eighteen years ago. After two years in jail, he changed his name and moved to a different part of the country. He has done occasional 'black bag' jobs for intelligence agencies who know his past. He'd like to get into computer crime, but the most he's done so far is lock hacking and alarm tampering.
- *Abdurrahman* heads a cell of a dozen agents, most with military training. They have access to weapons and explosives, with PhD-grade technical support provided by his home country. Abdurrahman himself came third out of a class of 280 at its military academy. His mission is to deal with the country's opponents overseas, typically by covert entry into their homes or offices to plant listening devices or to install malware into their computers and phones. One of the possible missions that his agency and government are considering is to steal plutonium. He thinks of himself as a good man rather than a bad man.

So Derek is unskilled, Charlie is skilled, Bruno is highly skilled and may have the help of an unskilled insider such as a cleaner, while Abdurrahman is not only highly skilled but has substantial resources. He may even have the help of one or more skilled insiders who have been suborned. (It's true that many terrorists these days are barely at Charlie's level, but it would not be prudent to design a nuclear power station on the assumption that Charlie would be the highest grade of attacker you have to worry about. And now that your power station's dozens of contractors are moving their systems to the cloud, you can bet that one of them will be vulnerable to a capable motivated hacker.)

While the sociologists focus on Derek, the criminologists on Charlie and the military on Abdurrahman, our concern is mainly with Bruno. He isn't the highest available grade of 'civilian' criminal: that distinction probably goes to the bent bankers and lawyers who launder money for drug gangs, or the guys who write malware for online crime gangs. But the physical defenses of banks and computer rooms tend to be designed with Bruno in mind.

13.2.2 Deterrence

The first consideration is whether you can prevent bad people from ever trying to break in. It's a good idea to make your asset anonymous and inconspicuous if you can. It might be a nondescript building in the suburbs; in somewhere like Hong Kong, with its sky-high property prices, it might be half a floor of a nondescript office block.

Location matters; some neighbourhoods have much less crime than others. Part of this has to do with whether other property nearby is protected, and how easy it is for a crook to tell which properties are protected. If owners just install visible alarms, they may redistribute crime to their neighbours; but invisible alarms that get criminals caught rather than just sent next door can deter crime in a whole neighbourhood. For example, Ian Ayres and Steven Levitt studied the effect on auto thefts of Lojack, a radio tag that's embedded invisibly in cars and lets the police find them if they're stolen. In towns where a lot of cars have Lojack, car thieves are caught quickly, and 'chop-shops' that break up stolen cars for parts are closed down. Ayres and Levitt found that although a motorist who installs Lojack pays about $100 a year, the social benefit from their doing this – the reduced car crime suffered by others – is $1500 [149]. The same applies to real estate; a neighbourhood in which lots of houses have high-grade alarms that quietly call the police is a dangerous place for a burglar to work. In fact, physical property crimes have fallen substantially in the USA, the UK and many other countries since the early 1990s.

But that's not all. Since the 1960s, there has arisen a substantial literature on using environmental design to deflect and deter threats. Much of this evolved in the context of low-income housing, as criminologists and architects learned which designs made crime more or less likely. In 1961, Elizabeth Wood urged architects to improve the visibility of apartment units by residents, and create communal spaces where people would gather and keep apartment entrances in view, thus fostering social surveillance; areas that are out of sight are more vulnerable [2039]. In 1972, Oscar Newman developed this into the concept of 'Defensible Space': buildings should 'release the latent sense of territoriality and community' of residents [1437]. Small courtyards are better than large parks, as intruders are more likely to be identified, and residents are more likely to challenge them. At the same time, Ray Jeffery developed a model that is based on psychology rather than sociology and thus takes account of the wide differences between individual offenders; it is reflected in our four 'model' villains. Intruders are not all the same, and not all rational [1612].

Jeffery's 'Crime Prevention Through Environmental Design' has been influential and challenges a number of old-fashioned ideas about deterrence. Old-timers liked bright security lights; but they create glare, and pools of shadow in which villains can lurk. It's better to have a civilised front, with windows overlooking sidewalks and car parks. In the old days, cyclone fences with barbed wire were thought to be a good thing; but they communicate an absence of personal control. A communal area with picnic seating, in which activities happen frequently, has a greater deterrent effect. Trees also help, as they make shared areas feel safer (perhaps a throwback to an ancestral environment where grassland with some trees helped us see predators coming and take refuge from them). Access matters too; defensible spaces should have single egress points, so that potential intruders are afraid of being trapped. It's been found, for example, that CCTV cameras only deter crime in facilities such as car parks where there's a single exit [767]. There are also many tricks developed over the years, from using passing vehicles to enhance site visibility to planting low thorn bushes under windows. Railings can make better barriers than walls, as you can see through them. Advice on these can be found in modern standards such as [325].

Another influential idea is the broken-windows theory of George Kelling and Catherine Coles [1032]. They noted that if a building has a broken window that's not repaired, then soon vandals will break more, and perhaps squatters or drug dealers will move in; if litter is left on a sidewalk, then eventually people will start dumping their trash there. So problems should be fixed when they're still small. Kelling was hired as a consultant to help New York clean up its vandalised subways, and inspired the zero-tolerance movement of police chief William Bratton, who cracked down on public drinkers, squeegee men and other nuisances. Both petty crime and serious crime in New York fell sharply. Criminologists still argue about whether the fall was due to zero tolerance, or to other simultaneous changes such as demographics [1153] and right-to-carry laws [1190].

A related set of ideas can be found in the situational crime prevention theory of Ronald Clarke. This builds on the work of Jeffery and Newman, and is broader than just property crime; it proposes a number of principles for reducing crime generally by increasing the risks and effort, reducing the rewards and provocations, and removing excuses. Its focus is largely on designing crime out of products and out of the routines of everyday life; it's pragmatic and driven by applications [442]. It involves detailed study of specific threats; for example, car theft is considered to be a number of different problems, such as joyriding by juveniles, theft to get home at night and theft by professional gangs of cars for dismantling or sale abroad – these threats are best countered by quite different measures. Such empirical studies may be criticised by criminologists with a sociology background as lacking 'theory', but are gaining influence and are not far from what security engineers do. Many of the mechanisms discussed in this book fit easily within a framework of application-level opportunity reduction.

This framework naturally accommodates the extension of environmental controls to other topics when needed. So if you're planning on anonymity of your hosting centres as a defence against targeted attack, you have to think about how you limit the number of people who know where those premises are. At least, that was the traditional approach; but it may not be the last word. Many firms have moved entirely to third-party cloud services and have no hosting centres any more. This can save physical security costs, as well as sysadmin salaries and electricity.

13.2.3 Walls and barriers

Once you've decided what environmental features you'll use to deter Derek or Charlie from trying to break into your site, and how you make it harder for Bruno to find out which of your sites he should break into, you then have the problem of designing the physical barriers.

Your first task is to figure out what you're really trying to protect. In the old days, banks used to go to great lengths to make life really tough for robbers, but this has its limits: a robber can always threaten to shoot a customer. So by the 1980s, the philosophy had shifted to 'give him all the cash he can see'. This philosophy has spread to the rest of retail. In 1997, Starbucks reviewed physical security following an incident in which three employees were shot dead in a bungled robbery. They decided to move the safes from the manager's office to the front of the store, and made these safes highly visible not just to staff, customers and passers-by, but also to the control room via CCTV. A side benefit was improved customer service. The new design was tested at a number of US locations, where increased sales and loss reductions gave a good return on investment [505]. I notice that people increasingly leave their car keys just inside the front door at home, rather than keeping them on their bedside table. If someone breaks into your house at night to steal your car, do you really want to engage them in hand-to-hand combat?

Second, having settled your protection goals, you have to decide what perimeters or boundaries you'll have for what purposes, and where. A growth industry recently has been vehicle traps to prevent cars or trucks being brought close to iconic targets, whether to carry bombs or to run down sightseers. But it's a mistake to focus on rare but 'exciting' threats at the expense of mundane ones. Many buildings have stout walls but roofs that are easy to penetrate; perhaps a terrorist would blow himself up at your main gate to no effect, but an environmental protester could cripple your fab and cost you hundreds of millions in lost production by climbing on the roof, cutting a hole and dropping some burning newspaper.

For this reason, organisations such as NIST, the Builders' Hardware Manufacturers' Association, Underwriters' Laboratories, and their equivalents in other countries have a plethora of test results and standards for walls, roofs, safes and so on. The basic idea is to assess how long a barrier will resist an attacker who has certain resources – typically hand tools or power tools. Normal building materials don't offer much delay at all; you get through a cavity brick wall in less than a minute with a sledgehammer, and regardless of how expensive a lock you put on your front door, a SWAT team will just break the door off its hinges with a battering-ram. So could a robber. So the designers of data centres, bank vaults and the like favour reinforced concrete walls, floors and roofs, with steel doorframes. But if the bad guys can work undisturbed all weekend, even concrete won't keep them out. In England's biggest burglary, a gang of elderly criminals drilled through the 20-inch concrete wall of a safe deposit company in Hatton Garden in 2015 and made off with £14m in diamonds. Four years later, the ringleader was caught, and it emerged at trial how he'd posed as a phone company engineer to tamper with the security system, then used a mobile phone jammer to block the alarm signal [1550].

Beware that the organisations that certify locks, safes and vaults often make outdated assumptions about attack tools. The lock on your car steering wheel is certified to resist a man putting his weight on it; but car thieves have learned to use a scaffolding pole, which gives the leverage to break it. The typical bank vault is certified to resist attack for ten minutes, yet your local fire department can get through in two minutes using a modern angle grinder. And if the bad guys have access to proper explosives, they can get through almost anything in seconds. Another issue is the thermic lance, or burning bar, which will cut through most barrier materials quickly: safe engineers use such things to get into a vault whose combination has been lost. Robbers can get them too. So barriers can't be seen in isolation. You have to be aware of assumptions about the threats, and about the intrusion detection and response on which you can rely.

13.2.4 Mechanical locks

The locksmithing industry has been seriously upset in recent years by developments that have exposed the vulnerability of many low-cost mechanical and electronic locks.

The first of these is *bumping*. This technique enables many mechanical locks to be opened quickly and without damage by unskilled people using tools that are now readily available. Its main target is the pin-tumbler lock originally patented by Linus Yale in 1860 (see Figure 13.1). This was actually used in ancient Egypt, but Yale rediscovered it, and it's often known as a 'Yale lock', although many other firms make them too nowadays.

These locks have a cylindrical plug set inside a shell, and prevented from rotating by a number of *pin stacks*. Each stack usually consists of two or three pins, one on top of the other. The *bottom pin* or *key pin* makes direct contact with the key; behind it is a spring-loaded *top pin* or *driver pin* that forces the bottom pin as far down as possible in the keyway. When the correct key is inserted, the gaps between the top pin and the bottom pin in each stack align with the edge of the plug, creating a *shear line*; the plug can now be turned. A typical house or office lock might have five or six pins each of which could have the gap in ten different positions, giving a theoretical key diversity of 10^5 or 10^6 possible *key differs*. The actual number will be less because of mechanical tolerances and key-cutting restrictions.

It had been known for years that such locks can be picked, given special tools. You can find details in the MIT Lock Picking Manual [1900] or in treatises such as that by Marc Weber Tobias [1895]: the basic idea is that you twist the plug slightly using a tension wrench, and then manipulate the pins with a lockpick until they all line up along the shear line. Such techniques have been used by specialists such as locksmiths for years; but they take a lot of practice, and it's unlawful to possess the tools in many jurisdictions (for the laws in the USA, see [1897]). Until recently, lockpicking was generally thought to be a threat only to high-value targets such as investment banks and embassies.

Figure 13.1: A cutaway pin-tumbler lock (courtesy of Marc Weber Tobias)

The new discovery was that an attacker can insert a specially made *bump key* each of whose teeth is set at the lowest pin position and whose shoulder is slightly rounded. (Such keys are also known as '999' keys as all the teeth are at the lowest position, or *bitting*, namely number 9.) The intruder can then place the key under slight torsion with their fingertips and tap the key head with a rubber mallet. The shock causes the pins to bounce upwards; the applied torsion causes them to stick as the spring pushes them back down, but with the gap at the cylinder edge. The net effect is that with a few taps of the mallet, the lock can be opened.

This trick had been known for years, but became more effective because of better tools and techniques. It was publicised by a 2005 white paper written by Barry Wels and Rop Gonggrijp of The Open Organization Of Lockpickers (TOOOL), a Dutch 'lock sports' group (as amateur locksmithing is now known [2012]). TV coverage spread the message to a wide audience. The view of experts is that bumping deskills lockpicking, with potentially serious consequences [1896]. It's been found, for example, that the locks in US mailboxes can be opened easily, as can the pin-tumbler locks with 70% of the US domestic market. The Dutch paper, and the subsequent publicity, kicked off an arms race, with vendors producing more complex designs and amateur locksmiths reporting bumping attacks on many of them. We now have lockpicking kits at my lab so schoolkids can play with them during open days. They love it!

Just about all metal locks have been broken. When I worked in banking, locks from Medeco were thought to be unpickable (and even certified as such), and were used to protect the hardware security modules in which the bank's most important cryptographic keys were kept. The company had a dominant position in the high-security lock market. Medeco uses secondary keying in the angle at which cuts are made in the key. In this 'biaxial' system, angled cuts rotate the pins to engage sliders. In 2005, Medeco introduced the m3, which also has a simple sidebar in the form of a slider cut into the side of the key. Yet in 2007, Tobias reported an attack on the m3 and biaxial locks, using a bent paperclip to set the slider and then a combination of bumping and picking to rotate the plug [1898].

What can a householder do? As an experiment, I replaced my own front door lock. The only high-security product I could find in a store within an hour's drive turned out to be a rebranded Mul-T-Lock device from Israel. It took two attempts to install, jamming the first time; it then took about a week for family members to learn to use the more complex deadbolt, which can easily fail open if operated carelessly. And the next time we were visited by someone with an intelligence background, he remarked that in the UK only drug dealers fitted such locks; so if the police ever pass by, I might end up on their database as a suspect. The lock did not wear well; after a few years it started sticking open, and when I removed it I noted that some ball bearings had come out. This dubious improvement to my home security cost me £200 as opposed to £20 for a standard product; and as in practice a burglar could always break a window, our actual protection still depends more on our location and our dogs than on ironmongery. Indeed, Yochanan Shachmurove and colleagues surveyed the residents of Greenwich, Connecticut, and built a model of how domestic burglaries varied as a function of the precautions taken; locks and deadbolts had essentially no effect, as there were always alternative means of entry such as windows. The most effective deterrents were alarms and visible signs of occupancy such as cars in the drive [1712].

The situation for commercial firms is slightly better (but not much). The usual standards for high-security locks in the USA, UL 437 and ANSI 156.30, specify resistance to picking and drilling, but not to bumping; and although pick-resistant locks are generally more difficult to bump, this is no guarantee. Knowledge does exist about which lock designs resist bumping, but you have to look for it. (Tobias' paper and `www.toool.org` are good starting points.)

Purchasers therefore face a lemons market – as one might suspect anyway from the glossiness, fluffiness and lack of technical content of most lock vendors' marketing literature. And even expensive pick-resistant locks are often poorly installed by builders or OEMs; when I once had to break into a cryptographic processor with a Medeco lock, I found that it turned a cam made of white metal, which bent easily when we tried to lever it open. Indeed, a recent security alert by Tobias disclosed that one of the most popular high security deadbolts could be mechanically bypassed by sliding a narrow screwdriver down the keyway, catching the bolt at the end and turning it, even without defeating the extensive security protections within the lock. This design had existed for more than twenty years, and the vulnerability was unknown to the manufacturer before the disclosure. Many high-security installations employ similar hardware.

The second recent class of problems are *master-key attacks*. These were also known to locksmiths for some time but were improved and published by Matt Blaze[1]. Master-key systems are designed so that in addition to the individual key for each door in a building, there can be a top-level master key that opens them all – say, for use by the cleaners. More complex schemes are common; in our building, for example, I can open my students' doors while the system administrators and cleaners can open mine. In pin-tumbler locks, such schemes are implemented by having extra cuts in some of the pin stacks. Thus instead of having a top pin and a bottom pin with a single cut between them, some of the pin stacks will have a middle pin as well.

The master-key attack is to search for the extra cuts one at a time. Suppose my key bitting is 557346, and the master key for my corridor is 232346. I make

[1]There was an interesting response: "For a few days, my e-mail inbox was full of angry letters from locksmiths, the majority of which made both the point that I'm a moron, because everyone knew about this already, as well as the point that I'm irresponsible, because this method is much too dangerous to publish". The paper is [260].

a key with the bitting 157346, and try it in the lock. It doesn't work. I then file the first position down to 257346. As 2 is a valid bitting for the first pin, this opens the lock, and as it's different from my user bitting of 5, I know it's the master key bitting for that pin. I will have to try on average four bittings for each pin, and if three pins are master-keyed, then I'll have a master key after about twelve tests. So master keying allows much greater convenience not just to the building occupants but also to the serious burglar. This matters, as most large commercial premises that still have metal keys use master keying. There are master-keying systems that resist this attack – for example, the Austrian lockmaker Evva has a system involving magnets embedded in metal keys that are much harder to duplicate. But most fielded systems appear vulnerable, and the invention of 3-d printing has made them even more so.

A big headache with mechanical master-keying systems is revocation. Keyholders leave, and may be dishonest or careless. They may have cut a copy of their key, and sold it to an attacker. Or someone may have taken a photo of their key, and used it to print a copy. Master-key attacks are important here, and many expensive, pick-resistant locks actually make the problem worse. They often depend on a secondary keying mechanism such as a sidebar: the keys look like two normal pin-tumbler keys welded together, as in Figure 13.2. The sidebar is often the same for all the locks in the building (master-keyed systems generally require common sidebars in locks that share master keys). So if a bad man can take a picture of a genuine key belonging to one of my students, he may be able to turn it into a bump key that will open my door, and indeed every door in the building, as in Figure 13.3. This may not be a problem in university premises, where there's nothing much to steal but books. But it definitely is for banks, bullion dealers and jewelers where attackers might spend two years planning a raid. If such a facility had a master-keying system using sidebar locks, and a staff member were even suspected of having leaked a key, the prudent thing would be to replace every single lock. So while mechanical locks are easy to change singly, systems that integrate hundreds of locks in one building may end up locking the building owner in to the lock vendor more than they lock the burglar out of the premises.

The combined effect of bumping, bad deadbolts, master-key attacks and 3-d printing might be summarised as follows. As the tools and knowledge spread,

Figure 13.2: Key for a sidebar lock

Figure 13.3: Sidebar bump key

a career criminal like Charlie will be able to open almost any house lock quickly and without leaving any forensic trace, while more professional attackers like Bruno and Abdurrahman will be able to open the locks in most commercial premises too. House locks may not matter all that much, as Charlie will just go through the window anyway; but the vulnerability of most mechanical locks in commercial premises could have much more complex and serious implications. If your responsibilities include the physical protection of server rooms or other assets, it's time to start thinking about them.

13.2.5 Electronic locks

The difficulty of revocation is just one reason why electronic locks are getting ever more market share. They've been around for a long time – hotels have been using card locks since the 1970s. There's a host of products, using all sorts of mechanisms from contactless smartcards through PIN pads to biometrics. Many of them can be bypassed in various ways, and most of the chapters of this book can be applied in one way or another to their design, evaluation and assurance. There are also some electromechanical locks that combine mechanical and electronic (or magnetic) components; but it's hard to get the locksmithing, the cryptography and the electromagnetic mechanisms to work together seamlessly; and you can never tell until you test them. Such locks not only cost more money than simple metal locks or card locks, but often fail in interesting ways; there's a whole literature of attacks on them [1293, 1843].

But, from the viewpoint of a big company using locks to protect large and complex premises, the problem is not so much the locks themselves but how you manage dozens or hundreds of locks in a building, especially when you have dozens or hundreds of buildings worldwide.

Newer buildings are starting to become aware of who is where, using multiple sensors, and integrating physical with logical access control. In an ideal world, you'd know who went through which door in real time and be able to line this up with security policies on information; for example, if classified material is being handled, you can sound an alarm if there's anyone in the room without the right clearance. Buildings can monitor objects as well as people; in an experiment at our lab, both people and devices carried active badges for location tracking [1986]. Electronic systems can be fully, or almost always, online, making revocation much easier. As well as enforcing security policy, smart buildings could provide other benefits, such as saving energy by turning lights off and by tailoring air conditioning to the presence of occupants. But it will be a long haul.

One practical problem, as we found with one organisation I worked with, is that only a few firms sell large-scale entry control systems, and they're hard to customise. In one building project, we found the vendors' protocols didn't support the kit we ideally wanted to use, and we didn't have the time or the people to build our own entry control system from scratch. The legacy entry-control vendors operate just as other systems houses do: they make their money from lock-in (in the economic, rather than locksmithing sense). You end up paying $200 for a door lock that cost maybe $10 to manufacture, because of proprietary cabling systems and card designs. The main limit to the lock-in is the cost of ripping and replacing the whole system – hence the proprietary cabling.

We settled for a card system to control access to sections of the building, and used Mifare contactless smartcards as they were available from multiple entry-control vendors. Other buildings operated by the same organisation used this system, and it allowed more complex access control policies that were a function of the time of day. On the office doors themselves we had metal door keys, which just have a matrix specifying which key opens which lock (this means a master keying system as described above). The organisation hoped to migrate to a more fully electronic system in time, once they could get the sort of components that would make decent systems integration possible – such as reasonably-priced door locks that run off the building's standard Ethernet.

Then an attack was found on the underlying card system, the Mifare Classic, sold by NXP Semiconductors. This used a proprietary cipher called Crypto-1 whose key had been limited to 48 bits as a result of export controls imposed during the crypto wars of the 1990s, which I discuss in 26.2.7. Mifare Classic had other flaws including a weak random number generator and a protocol that leaked keystream material via error messages. Although mostly used for transport ticketing, it also had an installed base of tens of thousands of buildings and was supported by several major building entry control vendors.

The Mifare Classic was partially reverse engineered by Karsten Nohl and colleagues in 2007 [1452]; Flavio Garcia and colleagues at Nijmegen finished the job the following year, publishing a complete analysis of the chip and showing how a version used in tickets for all Dutch public transport could be subverted [747]. NXP tried to get a court to suppress this research, but failed. The effect of these attacks on Mifare was to force transport systems to deploy intrusion-detection systems to detect fare dodgers; the effect on entry control systems was that card keys became easy to clone. Anyone with appropriate equipment who got temporary possession of a key could make a working copy, just as with a traditional metal key. What's more, an ingenious attacker could deploy a fake lock and copy the key of anyone who went through it. That would include cleaners, whose keys open all the locks in a building, and security patrol staff whose keys open all the locks in all the company's buildings. You can even put a contactless reader into a coffee cup and hold it at chest height to clone the keys of people who keep them on lanyards.

Some lock vendors were badly hit. One vendor sold locks to hotels at near cost price, reckoning on making its profits by selling replacement card stock for $1 a key. The Mifare break meant that competitors from Taiwan could sell compatible stock for a few cents, destroying their business model. NXP responded with a product that added a digital signature to the card, so that the lock could tell that although it was a weak key, it was a genuine weak key.

The consequence for organisations with dozens of buildings using Mifare locks operated by a common staff card was that to move to a more secure lock they had to either replace all the locks and cards at once, or else stick with NXP, who produced two series of successor cards. The first were 'hardened' classic cards that still used the weak Crypto 1 cipher but fixed the implementation mistakes that made the initial attacks easier; but as the underlying cipher is weak, these were broken too [1286]. The second product line used better algorithms, with the DESfire card, for example, using two-key triple-DES. However, David Oswald and Christof Paar promptly discovered a timing attack on the DESfire [1486]. The problem was partly mitigated by entrepreneurial lock vendors who started to produce card readers that could cope with multiple product lines; one will cope not only with Mifare but also with NFC (for Android phones) and Bluetooth (for phones made by Apple, which locks down the NFC chip to Apple Pay). Others are embracing new technologies such as the new 802.15.4z standard for UWB radio, which I mentioned in section 4.3.1.

In short, NXP managed to maintain much of its lock-in by migrating its customers to new products but at some cost in security. Some of the externalities this created were captured by more alert card reader vendors. However, the whole field has become way too complex for the traditional lock buyer, who was an architect or building services manager. That's yet another reason why the CISO's security engineering team needs to take an interest in physical security too.

13.3 Alarms

Alarms are used to deal with much more than burglary. Their applications range from monitoring freezer temperatures in supermarkets (so staff don't 'accidentally' switch off freezer cabinets in the hope of being given food to take home), right through to improvised explosive devices in conflict zones that are often booby-trapped. However, it's convenient to discuss them in the context of burglary and of protecting server rooms, bank vaults or art galleries. Alarms also give us a good grounding in the wider problem of service denial attacks, which are an issue everywhere from gaming to electronic warfare.

Standards for building alarms vary between countries and between different types of risk. As with locks, you'll normally use a specialist firm for this kind of work; but you must be aware of the technical issues. My own professional experience has ranged from the alarms built into automatic teller machines, through the security of the communications used by an alarm system for large risks such as wholesale jewelers, to the systems used to protect bank computer rooms.

An alarm in a server room is well protected from tampering (at least by outsiders). So I'll take as my case study an art gallery. This has the interesting design problem of safeguarding precious objects and also displaying them. Attackers can come in during the day as members of the public, and we'll assume that the attacker is Bruno – the educated professional art thief. The movie scriptwriter's view of Bruno is that he organizes cunning attacks on alarms, having spent days poring over the building plans in the town hall:

How to steal a painting (1)

A Picasso is stolen from a gallery with 'state-of-the-art' alarm systems by a thief who removes a dozen roofing tiles and lowers himself down a rope so as not to activate the pressure mats under the carpet. He grabs the painting, climbs back out without touching the floor, and is paid by a wealthy gangster who commissioned the theft.

The press loves this kind of stuff, and it does happen from time to time. Reality is both simpler and stranger. Let's work through the threat scenarios systematically.

13.3.1 How not to protect a painting

A common mistake when designing alarm systems is to be captivated by the latest sensor technology. There's a lot of impressive stuff on the market, such as a fiber-optic cable which you loop round protected objects and which will alarm if the cable is stretched or relaxed by less than 100nm – a ten-thousandth of a millimeter. Isn't modern science marvellous? So the naïve art gallery owner will buy a few feet of this magic cable, glue it to the back of his prize Picasso and connect it to an alarm company. That would detect the chap in the bosun's chair. So how would you defeat it? Well, that's easy.

How to steal a painting (2)

Bruno comes in as a tourist and hides in a broom cupboard. At one in the morning, he emerges, snatches the painting and heads for the fire exit. Off goes the alarm, but so what! In less than a minute, he'll be on his motorbike. By the time the cops arrive twelve minutes later he's gone.

Alarms are rarely integrated well with building entry controls. Many designers don't realise that unless you can positively account for all the people who've entered the premises during the day, you'd better take precautions against the 'stay-behind' villain – even if this is only an inspection tour after the gallery has closed. Serious physical security means serious controls on people. In fact, the first recorded use of the RSA cryptosystem – in 1978 – was not to encrypt communications but to provide digital signatures on credentials used by staff to get past the entry barrier to a plutonium reactor at Idaho Falls. The credentials contained data such as body weight and hand geometry [1751, 1755]. But I'm still amazed by the ease with which building entry controls are defeated at most secure sites I visit – whether by mildly technical means, such as sitting on somebody else's shoulders to go through an entry booth, or (most often) by helpful people holding the door open.

What's more, the alarm response process often hasn't been thought through. (The *Titanic Effect* of over-reliance on the latest technology often blinds people to common sense.)

So we mustn't think of the alarm mechanism in isolation. As I mentioned above, a physical protection system has the steps *deter – detect – alarm – delay – respond*, and the emphasis will vary from one application to another. If our opponent is Derek or Charlie, we'll mostly be concerned with deterrence. At the sort of targets where Abdurrahman might try to steal fissile materials, an attack will almost certainly be detected; the main problem is to delay him long enough for the Marines to arrive. Bruno is the most interesting case as we won't have the military budget to spend on keeping him out, and there are many more premises whose defenders worry about Bruno than about Abdurrahman. So you have to look carefully and decide whether the bigger problem is with detection, with delay or with response.

13.3.2 Sensor defeats

Burglar alarms use a wide range of *sensors*, including:

- vibration detectors, to sense fence disturbance, footsteps, breaking glass or other attacks on buildings or perimeters;
- switches on doors and windows;
- passive infrared devices to detect body heat;
- motion detectors using ultrasonics or microwave;
- invisible barriers of microwave or infrared beams;
- pressure pads under the carpet, which in extreme cases may extend to instrumenting the entire floor with pressure transducers under each tile;

- video cameras, nowadays often with movement detectors and even face detectors, to alarm automatically or provide a live video feed to a monitoring center;
- movement sensors on equipment, ranging from simple tie-down cables through seismometers to loops of optical fiber.

Most sensors can be circumvented. Fence disturbance sensors can be defeated by vaulting the fence; motion sensors by moving very slowly; door and window switches by breaking through a wall. Designing a good combination of sensors comes down to skill and experience (with the latter not always guaranteeing the former). A standard, if slightly dated, reference on sensor installation is [410].

The main problem is limiting the number of false alarms. Ultrasonics don't perform well near moving air such as central heating inlets, while vibration detectors can be rendered useless by traffic. Severe weather, such as lightning, will trigger most systems, and a hurricane can swamp a town's police force not just with rain but with thousands of false alarms. In some places, even normal weather can make protection difficult: how do you defend a site where the intruder might be able to ski over your sensors (and even over your fence)[2]?

But regardless of whether you're in Alaska or Arizona, the principal dilemma is that the closer you get to the object being protected, the more tightly you can control the environment and so the lower the achievable false alarm rate. Conversely, at the perimeter it's hard to keep the false alarm rate down. But to delay an intruder long enough for the guards to get there, the outer perimeter is exactly where you need reliable sensors.

How to steal a painting (3)

So Bruno's next attack is to wait for a dark and stormy night. He sets off the alarm somehow, taking care not to get caught on CCTV or leave any other hard evidence that the alarm was a real one. He retires a few hundred yards and hides in the bushes. The guards come out and find nothing. He waits half an hour and sets off the alarm again. This time the guards don't bother, so in he goes.

False alarms – whether induced deliberately or not – are the bane of the industry. They are a denial-of-service attack on the alarm response force. Experience from electronic warfare is that a false alarm rate of greater than about 15% degrades the performance of radar operators; and most intruder alarm responders are operating well above this threshold. Deliberately induced false alarms are especially effective against sites that don't have round-the-clock guards. Many police forces have a policy that after a certain number of false alarms from a given site (typically three to five per year), they will no longer send a

[2]For an instructive worked example of intruder detection for a nuclear power station in a snow zone see [174].

squad car there until the alarm company, or another keyholder, has been there to check.

False alarms degrade systems in other ways. The rate at which they are caused by environmental stimuli such as weather conditions and traffic noise limits the sensitivity of the sensors that can usefully be deployed. Also, the very success of the alarm industry has greatly increased the total number of alarms and thus decreased police tolerance of false ones. A common strategy is to have remote video surveillance as a second line of defense, so the customer's premises can be inspected by the alarm company's dispatcher; many police forces prioritize alarms confirmed in this way [981]. But even video links are not a panacea. The attacker can disable the lighting, start a fire, or set off alarms in other buildings in the same street. The failure of a telephone exchange, as a result of a flood or hurricane, may lead to opportunistic looting.

After traffic and weather, Bruno's next ally is time. Vegetation grows into the path of sensor beams, fences get slack so the vibration sensors don't work so well, the criminal community learns new tricks, and meanwhile the sentries become complacent.

So sites needing serious physical protection often have several perimeters: an outer fence to keep out the drunks and the wildlife; then level grass with buried sensors, an inner fence with an infrared barrier, and finally a massive enough building to delay the bad guys until the cavalry gets there. The regulations laid down by the International Atomic Energy Agency for sites that hold more than 15g of plutonium are an instructive read [951].

At most sites this kind of protection will be too expensive. And even if you have loads of money, you may be somewhere like Manhattan or Hong Kong where real estate is expensive: if you have to be near the exchange to trade quickly enough, your bank computer room may just be a floor of an office building and you'll have to protect it as best you can. A good example comes from a gang of jewel thieves in Florida who targeted retail stores that shared a wall with a store such as a nail salon that had no reason to install an alarm. They broke in there, then cut through the wall into the jewelry store [1217].

Anyway, the combination of sensors and physical barriers still makes up less than half the story.

13.3.3 Feature interactions

Intruder alarms and barriers interact in a number of ways with other services. The most obvious of these is electricity. A power cut will leave many sites dark and unprotected, so a serious alarm installation needs backup power. A less obvious interaction is with fire alarms and firefighting.

How to steal a painting (4)

Bruno visits the gallery as a tourist and leaves a smoke grenade on a timer. It goes off at one in the morning and sets off the fire alarm, which in turn causes the burglar alarm to ignore signals from its passive infrared sensors. (If it doesn't, the alarm dispatcher will ignore them anyway as he concentrates on getting the fire trucks to the scene.) Bruno smashes his way in through a fire exit and grabs the Picasso. He'll probably manage to escape in the general chaos, but if he doesn't, he can always claim he was a public-spirited bystander who saw the fire and risked his life to save the town's priceless cultural heritage. The police might not believe him, but they'll have a hard time convicting him.

The largest ever burglary – the theft in 2019 of about a billion Euros' worth of treasures from the Grüne Gewölbe in Dresden, the home of Augustus the Strong's treasure chamber and a dozen other rooms of priceless antiquities – used arson [470]. A fire at a nearby building site disabled the local electricity substation, turning off local streetlights as well as the power to the museum [1047]. Its security guards eventually saw intruders on CCTV and called the police, but they didn't get there in time.

The interaction between fire and intrusion is always difficult. At nuclear reactors, there's typically a rule that if a bomb is discovered, the site is locked down, with no-one allowed in or out; and a fire safety rule that in the event of a blaze, much of the staff have to be evacuated (plus perhaps some of the local population too). This raises the interesting question of which rule prevails should a bomb ever go off. And some fire precautions may only be used if you can keep out innocent intruders. Many server rooms have automatic fire extinguishers, and this often means flooding with carbon dioxide. A CO_2 dump can be lethal to untrained people: you have to get out of the room on the air you have in your lungs as visibility drops to a few inches and you're disoriented by the terrible shrieking noise of the dump. A nitrogen dump is less spectacular but also lethal; a falling oxygen level doesn't provoke a panic response the way a rising CO_2 level does.

But the most severe feature interactions are between alarms and communications.

13.3.4 Attacks on communications

A sophisticated attacker is at least as likely to attack the communications as the sensors. Sometimes this will mean the cabling between the sensors and the alarm controller.

How to steal a painting (5)

Bruno goes into an art gallery and, while the staff are distracted, he cuts the wire from a window switch. He goes back that evening and helps himself.

It's also possible that one of your staff, or a cleaner, will be bribed, seduced or coerced into creating a vulnerability. In Britain's biggest robbery, in February 2006 from the Securitas Cash Management depot in Tonbridge, Kent, robbers took the manager and his family hostage, pretending to be police officers. They then compelled him to let them in, taking £53,116,760; although five of the robbers were caught and jailed, others escaped, and most of the money was never recovered. When I worked in banking back in the 1980s, we took care to brief our cash centre managers that the controls were there to stop their families being taken hostage. It's great to have knowledgeable and motivated defenders, but the dual-control defence must be carried through in depth. High-value sites with capable defenders insist that alarm maintenance and testing be done by two people rather than one. Even then, dual control isn't always enough, especially if your opponent is Abdurrahman rather than Bruno. In Britain's fourth-largest ever robbery, the Provisional IRA kidnapped two keyholders at the Northern Bank in December 2004 and held their families at gunpoint, to force them to let them into the bank's Belfast headquarters the next day. The terrorists escaped with £26.4m, and in order to make most of the money useless, the £50 notes they stole were withdrawn from circulation. Another edge case is the prison system, where attacks on sensors, cabling and indeed the very fabric of the building are so frequent that a continuing program of test and inspection is essential. It can be useful to ask yourself, "How would I do this differently if half my staff were convicts on day release?" and "How would I cope if a handful of my staff were working for an organisation that decided to rob me?" I will discuss the implications of dual control in more detail in the chapter on banking and bookkeeping.

The old-fashioned way of protecting the communications between the alarm sensors and the controller was physical: lay multiple wires to each sensor and bury them in concrete, or use armored gas-pressurized cables. The more modern way is to encrypt the communications [706]. So how do you attack those?

How to steal a painting (6)

Bruno phones up a rival gallery claiming to be from the security company that handles their alarms. He says that they're updating their computers so could they please tell him the serial number on their alarm controller unit? An office junior helpfully does so – not realising that the serial number on the box is also the crypto key that secures the communications. Bruno buys an identical controller for $200 and now has a functionally identical unit that he splices into his rival's phone line. This continues to report 'all's well' even when it isn't.

Substituting bogus alarm equipment, or a computer that mimics it, is known as 'spoofing'. There have been reports for many years of black boxes that spoof various alarm controllers. As early as 1981, thieves made off with $1.5 million in jade statues and gold jewelry imported from China, driving the importer into bankruptcy. The alarm system protecting its warehouse in Hackensack, New Jersey, was cut off. Normally that would trigger an alarm at a security company, but the burglars attached a homemade electronic device to an external cable to ensure continuous voltage [862]. And I mentioned in section 13.2.3 how Britain's biggest burglary involved jamming the alarm signal.

With the better modern systems, either the alarm controller in the vault sends a cryptographic pseudorandom sequence to the alarm company, which will assume the worst if it's interrupted, or the alarm company sends periodic random challenges to the controller that are encrypted and returned, just as with IFF. However, the design is often faulty, having been done by engineers with no training in security protocols. The crypto algorithm may be weak, or its key may be too short (whether because of incompetence or export regulations). Even if not, Bruno might be able to record the pseudorandom sequence and replay it slightly more slowly, so that by early Monday morning he might have accumulated five minutes of 'slack' to cover a lightning raid.

An even more frequent cause of failure is the gross design blunder. One is making the crypto key equal to the device serial number. This often appears in the purchase order, invoice, and other paperwork that lots of people get to see. (It's a good idea to buy your alarm controller for cash. This also makes it less likely that you'll get one that's been 'spiked'. But big firms often have difficulty doing this.)

By now you've probably decided not to go into the art gallery business. But I've saved the best for last. Here is the most powerful attack on burglar alarm systems. It's a variant on (3) but rather than targeting the sensors, it goes for the communications.

How to steal a painting (7)

Bruno cuts the phone line to his rival's gallery and hides a few hundred yards away in the bushes. He counts the number of men in blue uniforms who arrive, and the number who depart. If the two numbers are equal, then it's a fair guess the custodian has said, 'Oh bother, we'll fix it in the morning', or words to that effect. He now knows he has several hours to work.

This is more or less the standard way to attack a bank vault, and it's also been used on computer installations. The modus operandi can vary from simply reversing a truck into the phone company's kerbside junction box, to more sophisticated attempts to cause multiple simultaneous alarms in different premises and swamp the local police force. (This is why it's so much more powerful than just rattling the fence.)

In one case, thieves in New Jersey cut three main telephone cables, knocking out phones and alarm apparatus in three police stations and thousands of homes and businesses in the Hackensack Meadowlands. They used this opportunity to steal Lucien Piccard wristwatches from the American distributor, with a value of $2.1 million wholesale and perhaps $8 million retail [862]. In another, an Oklahoma deputy sheriff cut the phone lines to 50,000 homes in Tulsa before burgling a narcotics warehouse [1927]. In a third, a villain blew up a telephone exchange, interrupting service to dozens of shops in London's jewelry quarter. Blanket service denial attacks of this kind, which saturate the response force's capacity, are the burglarious equivalent of a nuclear strike. The move from phones to broadband has changed nothing; instead of cutting the BT phone line, a British burglar now cuts the BT Openreach DSL line, which is the same piece of copper, but now carrying digital signals. In places where the cable company carries broadband, you cut that; so an American burglar will learn how to recognise Comcast cables, if they're the local supplier. Alarm services often partner with the broadband providers, leaving the firms that supply the sensors competing in low-cost volume markets where they don't have the incentive to do anything sophisticated.

Future attacks might not involve snips or explosives, but a distributed denial-of-service attack on network facilities. Rather than causing all the alarms to go off in the neighborhood of a local telephone exchange (which could be protected to some extent by swamping it with police), it might be possible to set off several thousand alarms all monitored by the same alarm company, or by attacking some other component in the response chain. This might include attacks on police communications, or on 4G networks now that these are used for more alarm communications than wireline. One way of minimising the number of vulnerable components is by making the alarm communications anonymous, so that service-denial attacks can't be targeted [1425].

For years, the rule in the London insurance market (which does most of the world's major reinsurance business) was that alarm controllers in premises insured for over £20 million must have two independent means of communication. The traditional approach was one alarm using wireline communications and one using cellular radio; by 2019 we're seeing offerings that use two different 4G radio services. This opens the prospect of jamming, as used in the 2015 Hatton Garden burglary mentioned in section 13.2.3. In the nuclear world, IAEA regulations stipulate that sites containing more than 500g of plutonium or 2kg of U-235 must have both their alarm control center and an armed response force on the premises [951].

Where the asset you're protecting isn't a vault but a hosting center, the network is also critical to your operations. There's little point in having eight-inch concrete walls and roofs if the single fibre connecting you to the world runs through a kerbside junction box. You'll want at least two buried fibres going to at least two different telcos – and you will want them to be using switches and routers from two different vendors. Even so, the simplest way for a knowledgeable opponent to take out a hosting centre is usually to cut its communications. That's one reason why small firms have two centres and the big service firms have dozens. If you're not operating at cloud scale, you may want to ask yourself: who wants to dig, who knows where to, and would you detect them in time?

Finally, it's worth bearing in mind that many physical security incidents arise from angry people coming into the workplace – whether spouses, former employees or customers. In countries where private ownership of firearms is widespread, you have to plan for shooters.

13.3.5 Lessons learned

The reader might still ask why a book that's essentially about security in computer systems should spend several pages describing walls, locks and alarm systems. There are more reasons than the obvious ones.

- Most locks can be defeated. Metal keys can be photographed and forgeries made with a 3-d printer, or even an old-fashioned file; the locks they open can often be bumped. Card keys can often be cloned if you can get close. So alarms matter.
- Dealing with service denial attacks is the hardest part of many secure system designs, and also often the most important. Intruder alarms give us applicable knowledge and experience.
- One very general lesson is that one must look at the overall system – from deterrence through detection, alarm, delay and response.
- Another is the observation that the outermost perimeter defenses are the ones that you'd most like to rely on, but also the ones on which the least reliance can be placed.
- The trade-off between the missed alarm rate and the false alarm rate – the receiver operating characteristic – is also a pervasive problem in security engineering.
- It's hard work to keep guards alert, especially in jobs where almost all alarms are false alarms. The classic example is airport screening, where the US Transportation Security Administration puts test guns into suitcases, whether physically or using software in the X-ray machines. They have found that only about 20% of threats get through if you test screeners several times per checkpoint per shift, but this rises to 60–75% if you only test once [713].

- Failure to understand the threat model – designing for Charlie and hoping to keep out Bruno – causes many real-life failures. You need to know what actually goes wrong, not just what crime writers think goes wrong.
- And finally, you can't just leave the technical aspects of a security engineering project to specialist subcontractors, as critical stuff will always fall down between the cracks.

There are other applications where the experience of the alarm industry is relevant. In a later chapter, I'll discuss tamper-resistant processors that are designed to detect attempts to penetrate them and respond by destroying all their cryptographic key material.

13.4 Summary

Security engineers have to deal with physical protection as well as with computers and cipher systems. Just as the confluence of computers and telecoms saw computer-industry equipment and methods displace the old phone-company ways of doing things, so the automation of physical protection systems is steadily bringing the world of barriers, locks and alarms within our orbit. The move to 'smart buildings' means entry controls, alarms and system security integrated with energy management and much else. The design, implementation and management of such complex artefacts will increasingly be the job of systems security people.

In this chapter, I highlighted a few things worth noting. First, environmental deterrence matters; things like architecture, landscaping and lighting can make a real difference to the likelihood of intrusion.

Second, locks are not as secure as you might think. Recent developments in covert entry technology have led to wide publication of attacks that compromise most mechanical locks, and even the expensive 'high-security' offerings. Many card key systems are also vulnerable, as the most common products were compromised by US export controls in the 1990s and the process of replacing them with better ones has been held up by industry structures and incentives. Knowing what's good and what's not is not possible unless you understand at least the basics of cryptography, protocols and tamper-resistance; it's a job for security engineers, not for retired cops.

Third, there's quite a lot to learn from the one aspect of physical security that's already fairly well automated, namely alarms. Alarms provide us with a good example of a system whose security policy hinges on availability rather than on confidentiality or integrity. They can give us some useful insights when dealing with service-denial attacks in other contexts.

Research problems

At the strategic level, the confluence of physical security and systems security is bound to throw up all sorts of new problems. I expect that novel research challenges will be found by those who explore the information / physical security boundary; an example that came up as we were going to press in 2020 is the use of acoustic side-channels. Given a decent microphone, you can record the clicks as a Yale key is pushed into a keyway, and use it to deduce the key bitting [1227]. No doubt there will be more results of this kind. From the viewpoint of security economics, the problems of the locksmithing industry would make an excellent thesis topic: how the vulnerabilities found in Mifare and other products have been dealt with all along the supply chain is a complex story that nobody, as far as I'm aware, has really analysed systematically. It might be fascinating to compare this with how other complex ecosystems have responded to the security failure of critical components.

At the technical level, we will probably need better mechanisms for specifying and implementing policy engines that can manage both physical and other forms of protection. As for low-level mechanisms, we could do with better tools to manage keys in embedded systems. As one engineer from Philips put it to me, will the smart building mean that I have to perform a security protocol every time I change a light bulb? And will smart buildings end up being open, in the sense that so many different service firms will have access to the plans that all capable opponents must be assumed to have a copy? But if you really want the bad guys to not know the precise location of the alarm response centre in your nuclear power station, how do you keep that information confidential? All your contractors will happily claim to be ISO 27001 certified, but then so is almost every firm that owns up to a big data breach.

Further reading

The classic reference on alarm systems is [174] while some system issues are discussed in [1425]. Resources for specific countries are often available through trade societies such as the American Society for Industrial Security [46], and through the local insurance industry; many countries have a not-for-profit body such as Underwriters' Laboratories [1920] in the USA, and schemes to certify products, installations or both. For progress on lock bumping and related topics, I'd monitor the TOOOL group, Marc Weber Tobias, and Matt Blaze; Matt has also written on safecracking [262]. Research papers on the latest sensor technologies appear at the IEEE Carnahan conferences [954]. Finally, the systems used to monitor compliance with nuclear arms control treaties are written up in [1752].

CHAPTER

14

Monitoring and Metering

Management is that for which there is no algorithm. Where there is an algorithm, it's administration.

– ROGER NEEDHAM

The market is not an invention of capitalism. It has existed for centuries. It is an invention of civilization.

– MIKHAIL GORBACHEV

14.1 Introduction

In addition to the burglar alarms we discussed in the last chapter, your home will likely have a number of other monitoring devices: utility meters, baby monitors, smoke detectors, exercise equipment, health trackers and connected appliances. You may also buy value online for some metering systems, from a prepayment utility meter in your home through prepaid postage labels. An increasing number of systems are concerned with monitoring and metering human activities and indeed the natural environment too. They go back a long way. James Watt, the steam engine pioneer, didn't just sell engines; he licensed his patents using a sealed counter that measured the number of revolutions an engine had made. His inspectors read these from time to time and billed the customer for royalties.

Electronic systems that use cryptography and tamper-resistance have displaced most of the older mechanical systems and opened up all sorts of new applications. Ticketing is huge, from transport tickets through sports events to coupons; my case study for ticketing is the prepayment meters used for gas and electricity. Then I'll turn to vehicle systems. The most familiar of these may be taxi meters, but as these are being replaced by phone apps, I'll mainly discuss tachographs – devices used in Europe and Australia to record the speed and working hours of truck and coach drivers, and in the USA to record the comings and goings of bank trucks. My third case study is the curfew tags used in the USA to monitor criminal suspects before trial and in the UK for parolees after release. My fourth is the electronic postage meters used to frank letters and packages.

Many of these new applications follow the traditional IT industry mantra of 'ship it Tuesday and get it right by version 3'. We do have the beginnings of general standards for IoT security, such as the draft ETSI standard EN 303 645, which lays out the usual motherhood-and-apple-pie stuff like no default passwords, protecting crypto keys, updateable software, minimising the attack surface and allowing users to delete personal information [640]. But turning basic principles into good engineering takes effort, and we can learn a lot from applications that have already gone through at least one iteration of attack and defence. I hope the case studies in this chapter will give some of the needed contextual insight.

You'll recall that in order to defeat a burglar alarm it is sufficient to make it appear unreliable. Meters add further subtleties.

When we discussed an alarm in a bank vault, we were largely concerned with attacks on communications (though sensor defeats also matter). But many metering systems are much more exposed physically. A taxi driver may want the meter to read more miles or more minutes than were actually worked, so may manipulate it into over-measuring. With tachographs, it's the reverse: the truck driver usually wants to drive above the speed limit, or work dangerously long hours, so wants the tachograph to ignore some driving. Utility consumers may want their meters to ignore some of the passing electricity or gas. Criminal defendants and parolees may want to evade a curfew order. In such cases, the subject of surveillance may cause the device to make false readings, or simply to fail. There are also underground markets for exploits of various kinds.

Many metering and monitoring systems are also concerned with evidence. An opponent could get an advantage either by manipulating communications (such as by replaying old messages) or by falsely claiming that someone else had done so. With postal franking systems, it's not sufficient for the attacker to cause a failure (as then he can't post his letters). And we need to understand the real threats. The post office is mostly concerned with stopping wholesale fraud, such as crooked direct marketers who bribe postal employees to slip a truckload of mail into the system. The system may look like it's designed to stop external fraud, but its real focus is internal.

14.2 Prepayment tokens

There are many systems where the user pays in one place for a token – whether a magic number, or a cardboard ticket with a magnetic strip, or an app that displays a QR code, or even a rechargeable chip card – and uses the stored value somewhere else. Examples include transport tickets, photocopier cards in libraries, lift passes at ski resorts, and washing-machine tokens in university halls of residence.

The main protection goal is usually to prevent the tokens being forged at scale. Duplicating a single ticket is not too hard, and repeating a magic number is easy. Such scams can be prevented if we make all the tokens unique and all the devices online. But that makes things fragile; if people can't get on the bus in a mobile network black spot, or can't use a ski lift or a washing machine if a data centre is down, that can damage the business and cost real money. So the replay and forgery detection must sometimes be done offline. But if we simply encipher all our tokens using a universal master key, a villain could extract it from a stolen terminal and set up in business selling tokens. What are our options?

In most ticketing systems, procedural fraud is easy. A free rider can jump the barrier at a subway station; an electricity meter can have a bypass switch wired across it. But most people won't cheat unless someone makes it seem easy and safe by industrialising it. To maximise revenue, petty fraud should be at least slightly inconvenient and – more importantly – there should be mechanisms to prevent anyone forging tickets at scale.

The first example I'll discuss is the prepayment electricity meter. I chose this because I was lucky enough to consult on a project to electrify three million households in South Africa (a central election pledge made by Nelson Mandela when he took power). This work is described in some detail in [94]. By December 2019, the STS specification we developed was used in 68 million meters in 98 countries. Most of the lessons learned apply directly to other ticketing systems.

14.2.1 Utility metering

Householders who can't get credit buy gas and electricity services using prepayment meters (Figure 14.1). In the old days they were coin-operated, but the costs of coin collection led vendors to develop token-based meters instead. This technology was driven by less developed countries, and most notably by South Africa, where it became a national priority to electrify the townships; as many of the houses were informally constructed, and the owners did not even have addresses (let alone credit ratings), prepayment was the only way to go. Over 2 million meters were installed during Nelson Mandela's term of office as President, and there are now an estimated 10 million in use there. The largest installation is 35 million in Indonesia, and they are common in Africa, Asia and Latin America, as well as in some developed countries; most meters in Northern Ireland are prepayment. The typical developed country might have about 10% of households using prepayment meters, because they're on welfare or have court judgments against them.

Figure 14.1: A prepayment electricity meter (courtesy of Schlumberger)

The customer goes to a shop and buys a token, which can be a card, a cardboard ticket with a magnetic strip, or a 20-digit magic number. Most of South Africa's meters use a magic number. This is convenient for the customer, as a ticket can be bought at a supermarket checkout, at an ATM, over the phone or online.

The token is really just one or more instructions, encrypted using a key unique to the meter, and saying something like 'meter 12345 – dispense 50KWh of electricity!' The meter interrupts the supply when the credit runs out. Some tokens have engineering functions too. Special tokens may be used to change prices: if the power company charges different rates for the daytime and evening, the meter may need updates on the relative prices and the times at which the tariffs change.

Of the UK's electricity meters, about twice as many use smartcards as magnetic tickets. The former do not use the STS standard but are able to report consumption patterns, tampering attempts and so on back to the power company. The magnetic-ticket and magic-number meters do not have such a back channel. There is currently a project to replace all the meters in most EU countries with *smart meters*, which report readings and other data over a radio link, and which can be set remotely into prepayment mode. Smart meters have already been installed in other countries with mixed results. I'll return to them later.

Prepayment was the only way that less developed countries could electrify millions of homes quickly. In the developed world, the main incentive was reducing bad debts and other administrative costs. An added benefit is energy saving. In areas where most meters are prepaid, electricity consumption is up to 10% lower, as its cost becomes more salient to the householder.

14.2.2 How the STS system works

The security requirements for prepayment meters seem straightforward. Tokens should not be easy to forge, while genuine tokens should not work in the wrong meter, or in the right meter twice. The usual strategy is to tie each token to a unique meter, so that someone can't use the same magic number in two different meters, and also make each token unique using serial numbers or random numbers, so that the same token can't be used twice in the same meter. But it took a surprising amount of experience to develop this simple idea into a robust system.

Each meter has a crypto key to authenticate its instructions from the vending machine. Early systems had one for each neighbourhood, usually in a local store. It had a vend key K_V, which is the master key for a neighborhood, and each meter has a device key K_{ID} derived by encrypting its meter ID under the vend key:

$$K_{ID} = \{ID\}_{K_V}$$

This is the same key diversification technique described for parking lot access devices in Chapter 4, and it works fine where all the tokens are bought locally. But real life is usually more complicated. In Britain, deregulation of the electricity industry led to dozens of electricity companies who buy power from generators and sell it onward to households through a common infrastructure, so meters change ownership between multiple power companies with different tariff structures. In South Africa, many people commute long distances, so they want to buy tickets where they work. So we started with protocols to send a customer meter key from the vending station that 'owns' the meter to another station, and to pass sales data in the opposite direction for balancing and settlement, somewhat like in ATM networks. In 2007 we introduced online vending; a central server has a hardware security module with all the vend keys, so a customer can buy a magic number over the Internet or via their mobile phone. This server sells directly to seven million customers and also via about 10,000 online vend points such as ATMs and shops.

Statistical balancing is used to detect *non-technical losses*, that is, theft of power through meter tampering or unauthorized connections to mains cables. We compare the readings on a feeder meter, which might supply 30 houses, with token sales to those houses. But customers hoard tickets and meter readers lie about when they read the meter, so the discrepancy is a noisy signal. You can use it as a source of leads for your investigation team, and as a statistical check on your bookkeeping systems, but that's about it.

There were cases where vending machines were stolen and used to sell tokens in competition with the utility. Eliminating such a 'ghost vendor' generally means changing the keys in all the local meters; there are a few stolen machines still out there, operated by crime syndicates. The countermeasure was to maintain a credit balance in the vending machine's security chip that also protects vend keys and foreign meter keys. The balance is decremented with each sale and only credited again when cash is banked; the operating company then sends a magic number that reloads the chip with credit. So we have an accounting system enforced by a value counter at the point of sale, rather than by ledger data kept on servers at the utility. However, the strategic direction was centralisation, to save the effort and expense of managing resellers, and operators have replaced offline vending machines by online vending points that get their tokens in real time from a central service.

14.2.3 What goes wrong

As with burglar alarms, environmental robustness is critical. Apart from the huge range of temperatures (as variable in South Africa as in the continental USA) many areas have severe thunderstorms: the meter can be thought of as a microprocessor with a 3-kilometer lightning conductor attached.

When meters were destroyed by lightning, the customers complained and got credit for the value they said was still unused. So their next step was to poke live mains wires into the meter to try to emulate the effects of the lightning. One make of meter would give unlimited credit if the circuitry under the token slot was destroyed, so service-denial attacks worked well enough to become popular.

It was to get worse. Kids in Soweto observed that when there was a brown-out – a fall in voltage from 220 to 180 volts – a particular make of meter went to maximum credit. Soon they were throwing steel chains over the 11KV feeders and crediting all the meters in the neighborhood. This bug wasn't picked up because brown-out testing hadn't been specified. Developed-country environmental standards were inadequate for use in Africa. The responsible company almost went bust after 100,000 meters had to be pulled out and re-ROMmed.

There were numerous other bugs. One make of meter didn't vend a specified quantity of electricity, but so much worth of electricity at such-and-such a rate. Vending staff discovered that the tariff could be set to a minute amount, and the meter would operate almost forever. Another allowed refunds, but a copy of the refunded token could still be used. Another meter remembered only the last token serial number entered, so by alternately entering duplicates of two tokens it could be charged up indefinitely.

As elsewhere, the real security breaches resulted from bugs and blunders that were discovered by accident and exploited in quite opportunistic ways. Some of the exploits scaled up and cost millions to fix.

Other lessons learned, which we wrote up in [94], were:

- prepayment may be cheap and simple so long as you control the marketing channel, but when you try to sell tokens through third parties such as convenience stores, banks and supermarkets, it can become expensive, complicated and risky;
- if you don't get the security infrastructure right first time, then changing it can be expensive – as was the case with the need to sell meter tokens at distant shops, to support commuters;
- recycle technology if you can, as it's likely to have fewer bugs. Much of what we needed was borrowed from the world of cash machines;
- use multiple experts. One expert alone cannot usually span all the issues, and even the best will miss things;
- you absolutely need prolonged field testing. This is where many errors and impracticalities will first make themselves known.

The main lesson learned in the years after the initial deployment was to design out scalable fraud, which meant centralisation. There are still procedural exploits; for example, as any company can become a reseller, buying meters and a vending station on the market, crooked firms can set up rogue meters in community housing estates and direct the tenants to buy tokens from them instead. So prepayment does not entirely abolish the need for good old-fashioned audit, energy balancing and inspection – and neither does it entirely solve the problems of local corruption or broader state capture in less developed countries.

What we learned ended up in the STS specifications that are now used by dozens of manufacturers worldwide. One compromise did come back to bite us, though. The date in the STS meters rolls over in 2024, which was the distant future back in the early 1990s when we were doing the work[1]. Now that there are 60 million meters in almost 100 countries, it's going to cost utilities hundreds of millions to give each customer a special key-change ticket to manage the rollover. (The positive side of the key change is that the remaining ghost vending machines will be finally put out of business.) So, when designing a

[1]We had to fit everything into the 66 bits of a 20-digit token, and although we thought of having an extra bit in the counter to get an extra 31 years, that would have meant a time unit of 2 minutes rather than one, which would have made selling multiple tokens for a meter at the same time tricky. But we did have the foresight to provide for resetting the counter on key change.

new system, please think of sustainability not just as 'Will this system be OK for the next 30 years?' but 'Will this be OK for the next 100 years?' You may just live long enough to be embarrassed!

14.2.4 Smart meters and smart grids

In the early 2000s, the metering industry started selling the idea of a *smart meter* – a meter with real-time communications to a central server so that it could be read remotely. This had been patented as long ago as the 1970s but was developed into a broader concept involving not just billing, and prepayment if need be, but fine-grained pricing, power outage reporting and power quality monitoring. *Automatic meter reading* (AMR) was superseded by *advanced metering infrastructure* (AMI); the latter has two-way communications, so commands can be sent to the meter remotely. Pricing can be complex, including both time-of-day and demand-response tariffs. The benefits sold to utilities included reduced billing costs and easier debt collection. The case made to governments included reducing peak demand and thus the number of power stations required. Marketers talked about 'smart grids', talked excitedly of your meter being able to control domestic appliances and to negotiate real-time tariffs with the market. A more sober claim was that smart meters would pay for themselves by making users more conscious of how much electricity they used, thus saving money. The benefit to the meter vendor was replacing a product that cost $15 and lasted for 50 years with one that cost at least $50 and lasted for maybe 15.

There are many issues with smart metering. Researchers first raised general privacy concerns about fine-grained consumption data going to utilities; if the meter is set to monitor consumption by the minute or even by the second, the utility can work out how many people are in the home, when they eat, when they shower and when they sleep. This leads to direct concerns around predatory marketing, and indirect concerns around third-party access – whether via law-enforcement warrants, abuse of authorised access, or the perhaps inevitable intrusion of the advertising ecosystem. This led to debates about the time granularity of measurement, and how much data should be held in the meter versus centrally. Then we noticed that putting a remotely commandable off switch in all of a country's homes creates a major cyber-war threat; if an enemy can switch off your electricity supply, they can quickly close down your economy, or hold you to ransom [106]. This led to a scramble by the national-security agencies. But perhaps the biggest bundle of issues was around the diverging incentives of the various stakeholders. Utilities want to sell lots of energy, while governments want to save it and to reduce peak demand. So who would win?

The pioneer was Italy, where the utility ENEL started installing smart meters in 2001. Their main concern was power theft, particularly in southern Italy where enforcement staff sent to disconnect non-paying customers were threatened by gangsters. Smart meters enabled defaulters to be switched remotely to a prepayment regime. This was seen as a success, and the lobbyists got to work. The concept of a smart grid became US policy with the Energy Independence and Security Act of 2007 and came forcefully to public attention when President Obama allocated $4.5bn to its development as the headline measure of the American Recovery and Reinvestment Act; the European Parliament followed with a 2009 law requiring member states to conduct an economic assessment of smart metering by 2012, and if they found it beneficial, mandate its use by 2022 (with 80% adoption by 2020) [645]. Many countries have now launched national or regional smart meter programmes as have a number of US utilities, and we have some experience of the successes (such as Spain) and failures (including the UK and Ontario).

While US utilities tend to be regulated local monopolies, the European model has competitive generation, regulated transmission and distribution monopolies, and competitive retailers. Whether the meters belong to the distribution network operator or the retailer is a matter of historical accident. It turned out that where the distributor owned the meter, replacing all the meters with smart meters was straightforward, as a contractor could do a whole street at a time, and the meters could be connected to the utility via power-line communications with the substation. In Spain, the utilities set up a buyers' cartel and insisted that every supplier's meter would work with every other supplier's headend, so they got commodity hardware costing under €50 a meter.

However, in countries where the retailer owns the meter, things were not so simple. There is a serious problem with incentives: if smart meters are to pay for themselves by saving energy, then it makes no sense to put them under the control of the retailer, which maximises its profit by maximising energy sales. Germany did an honest assessment, decided that smart meters would be uneconomic, and abandoned the project. Britain unfortunately plowed ahead. Its Department of Energy and Climate Change had already had economic assessments in 2004, 2007 and 2008, which showed a negative return on the investment. Undeterred, they stretched the assumptions about costs, benefits, electricity prices and interest rates, came up with a positive assessment in 2009, and committed Britain to introducing smart meters not just for electricity but for gas too [885].

Outside Europe, the same problems arose where meters were owned by multiple retailers. New Zealand made smart meters optional, calculating they would be worthwhile only for large houses. In Ontario, as in Britain, the government pressed on, leading to an expensive failure, documented in the 2014 Annual Report of the Auditor General [1199]. The province dealt with 73 local distribution companies by building a central system to collect all the meter readings and making them available to retailers, as well as regulators. The goal of the system, to cut peak demand, was not realised at all; the peak-to-trough price variation that politicians were prepared to tolerate was not enough to change behaviour. The Ontario cost-benefit analysis that had been prepared in 2005 (a year after ministers announced the project) turned out to have overestimated benefits as $600m when they were at most $88m, while costs ballooned to $2bn; the largest retailer spent over $500 per meter on the devices and the systems to support them. Overall, energy planning was so poor that the province ended up selling surplus power to the USA, subsidising utilities in Michigan and in New York State to the tune of billions of dollars.

In Britain, smart metering has evolved into what may be the largest ever civilian project disaster. Successive governments (Labour, coalition and Conservative) committed to rolling out smart meters by 2020 as nobody wanted to be accused of not being 'green'. To my way of thinking, wasting £20 billion without saving any energy, and displacing better projects that could have yielded real savings, was about as un-green as you can get. The project was gold-plated at every level, with each home having up to four devices: smart meters for gas and electricity, a home hub to connect them to a wireless network, and an in-home display so the bill payer could track consumption. (The project started in 2009 just as people started to use smartphones but was too rigid to switch to using apps instead.) Ministers followed the Ontario route of a central meter-reading server, but nonetheless a UK householder who accepts a smart meter from one vendor and then moves to a different supplier to save money usually has to submit manual readings thereafter. It took years to agree a national standard for a second-generation meter and most of the deployed meter fleet consists of older incompatible models; the vendors fought for years to get their own patents in there and the officials didn't have the technical knowledge or political support to bang heads together. Security mechanisms were retrofitted in a panic in the mid-2010s once we pointed out that a hostile state could simply turn off British households' power at a time of tension [106]. Whistleblowers who threatened to expose the project's failure, and a likely cost increase from £11bn to £23bn, were threatened with prison [921]. The National Audit Office then reported at the end of 2018 that the project was falling materially short of expectations: the plan had been to replace 80% of UK meters by the end of 2020, but only 12.5m had been done, with 39m yet to do [1393]. What's more, 70% of the meters lost functionality when customers switched supplier (as you have to do annually to get decent prices). If government follows its declared strategy of moving everyone to second-generation meters, all these old ones will have to be replaced; according to a report from November 2019, only 2.3m of the meters were the new ones. Cost savings are unlikely as the industry will have to support good old-fashioned meters, several types of obsolete smart meter and the new smart meters through the 2020s. As for energy savings, there's no sign. (The government could save a lot of energy if it used the meters to move everyone to prepayment, but that's not on the agenda, and could have been done with much cheaper kit.) Nobody's using the data for anything but billing. And now officials just don't want to know: in the words of the NAO report, "The Department currently has no plans to continue engagement with consumers after the rollout is complete."

Two final remarks on smart grids. While the meter makers were doing their big marketing push in the late 2000s, there was breathless talk of meters helping to stabilise the grid by creating demand response and improving measurement. The scepticism expressed at the time by experienced power engineers has turned out to be justified. Grids have indeed become more fragile as generation capacity has moved from large spinning machines attached to the core transmission network to hundreds of thousands of windmills and solar panels embedded in the wider distribution systems. Recent large outages, such as in South Australia on 28 September 2016 and the UK on 9 August 2019, were cascade failures, caused when a local issue (a storm in Australia, and a lightning strike in England) caused a rate of change of frequency in excess of the safety limit, causing further loads to be shed, resulting in undervoltage and further load shedding. A complicating factor in each case is that now we have a lot of generation capacity embedded on people's rooftops, shedding load doesn't work as well as it used to. The takeaway is not that we need smart meters, even at the substation level, but that we need more inertia in the system – which means buying batteries or synchronous condensers. We also need to make the rest of the infrastructure more tolerant of outages. Much of the political fury in Britain over the 2019 power cut came from London commuters being stuck in trains for hours. This happened because 60 Siemens Desiro class trains tripped at 49Hz when they should have tripped at 48.5Hz, and half of them would not restart because of a software bug. Getting them going again required a visit from a technician with a laptop[2].

Demand response was also supposed to help with peak demand reduction. Nowhere have smart meters helped. Many countries now have capacity markets where grid operators can buy extra megawatts, on timescales of seconds to minutes, but these operate using dedicated systems. For example, data centre operators who have standby diesel generators and have to run them for half an hour a month to make sure they still work, are paid to start them when they're needed. In warmer countries, some people get discounts on their electricity bills for allowing their air conditioners to be switched off for

[2]UK trains and railway signals are not allowed to do over-the-air software upgrade because of national security rules, as the railways are considered to be critical national infrastructure. This also means that security patches take days to ship. Well done, MI5!

half an hour during demand peaks. Eventually, the chargers for electric cars will contribute to this too, once there are enough of them. But the equipment to do this is always separate from the main utility meter; no entrepreneur starting a capacity company would want to get entangled with the regulated mess that is metering. As for the smart meter marketing vision of your home hub negotiating energy prices and turning off your cooker or water heater in response to a price surge, that is remote from commercial reality. Firms that sell things like cookers and heaters are indeed putting CPUs and communications in them, but they talk to the firm's own servers, not to other devices; and the idea that politicians would allow retail prices to surge to match those on capacity markets is naïve. All that smart meters have achieved in Britain is to put a few tens of thousands of meter readers out of work, at a cost to the bill payer of £20 billion. Ontario was the same, but with one less trailing zero.

14.2.5 Ticketing fraud

Transport ticketing is a larger application than utility metering, but I don't know of any serious and publicly available study of the failure modes of train, bus and subway tickets. In the case of London, deregulation of the railways led to problems with train companies manipulating ticket sales by booking them at stations where they got a larger percentage of the takings; if you're designing a system that shares revenue between vendors, you should try to design out the incentive for stakeholders to cheat. There was also a scare after the break of Mifare Classic described in section 13.2.5; Transport for London scrambled to add intrusion-detection systems to detect fraud.

One type of ticketing on which we do have some real fraud data is the airline variety. During the 2010s, there emerged an ecosystem of fraudulently obtained air tickets and of channels for reselling them. The tickets are obtained by a variety of methods, ranging from compromised credit cards through dishonest staff at airlines and travel agencies through stolen air miles and hacked booking systems; the marketing channels include spam, affiliate marketing, sales to migrant communities and sales to human traffickers. This is all documented by Alice Hutchings [938, 939]. The key factors are that plane tickets, unlike subway tickets, are sufficiently valuable for such an ecosystem to develop; and that while some of the customers know they're getting bogus tickets, enough of them are simply suckers, so you can't just arrest everyone who turns up for a flight with an invalid ticket.

I'll now look at a class of applications where the attacks are more severe and prolonged than on electricity meters. The threat model includes sensor manipulation, service denial, accounting fiddles, procedural defeats and the corruption of operating staff. This exemplary field of study is vehicle monitoring systems.

14.3 Taxi meters, tachographs and truck speed limiters

A number of systems are designed to monitor and control vehicles. The most familiar is probably the odometer in your car. When buying a used car, you'll worry whether the car has been *clocked*, that is, had its indicated mileage reduced. As odometers became digital, clocking became a kind of computer fraud [393]. A related problem is *chipping*, that is, replacing or reprogramming the engine controller. This can be done for two basic reasons. First, the engine controller acts as the server for the remote key-entry systems that protect most modern cars from theft, as described in Chapter 4; so if you want to steal a car without stealing the key, you might replace the controller in the street, or else tow the car and replace or reprogram the controller later. Second, people reprogram their cars' engine controllers to make them go faster, and the manufacturers dislike this because of the increased warranty claims from burned-out engines. So they try to make the controllers more tamper-resistant, or at least tamper-evident. This arms race is described in [625].

Many vehicles now keep logs that are uploaded to the manufacturer during servicing. General Motors started equipping some vehicles with black boxes to record crash data in 1990. By the time the logging became public in 1999, some six million vehicles had been instrumented, and the disclosure caused protests from privacy activists [1942]. Indeed, there's a whole conference, ESCAR, devoted to electronic security in cars. Vehicle security is becoming a hot topic again in 2019 because of the growing interest in autonomous operation[3].

Other vehicle monitoring systems are fitted after manufacture, and the most familiar may be the taxi meter. A taxi driver has an incentive to manipulate the meter to show more miles travelled (or minutes waited) if he can get away with it. There are various other kinds of 'black box' used to record the movement of vehicles from aircraft through fishing vessels to armored bank trucks, and their operators have differing levels of motive for tampering with them. Insurers who sell 'pay-as-you-drive' insurance to young and high-risk drivers demand that they fit black boxes with satellite navigation devices that let the insurer charge a couple of pennies a mile for driving along a country road in the afternoon but a couple of dollars a mile for evening driving in an inner city [1913]. Any young man who wants to impress a lady by driving around town on a Saturday night will have an incentive to beat the black box.

14.3.1 The tachograph

The case study I'm going to use here is the tachograph. These devices are used to monitor truck drivers' speed and working hours; in Europe, the traditional

[3]Full disclosure: one of my research students is funded by Bosch.

analogue devices were replaced by digital ones from 2006, and as a truck lasts about ten years, most of the fleet is now digital. This gives us some interesting data on how such equipment works, and can fail; and it's an example of how a move to digital technology didn't make things better. What was actually needed wasn't whizzy technology but more enforcement.

Vehicle accidents resulting from a driver falling asleep at the wheel cause several times more accidents than drunkenness (20 percent versus 3 percent of accidents in the UK, for example). Accidents involving trucks are more likely to lead to fatal injuries because of the truck's mass. So most countries regulate truck drivers' working hours. While these laws are enforced in the USA using weigh stations and drivers' logbooks, countries in Europe use tachographs that record a 24-hour history of the vehicle's speed. Until 2005–6, this was recorded on a circular waxed paper chart (Figure 14.2); since then, digital tachographs have been introduced and the old system has been largely phased out[4].

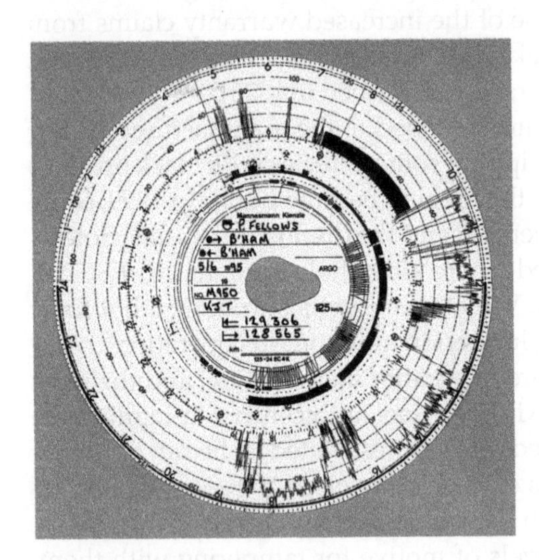

Figure 14.2: A tachograph chart

First let's look at the old analogue system as our baseline; it's still in use by old trucks and buses on Europe's roads.

The analogue system uses a waxed paper chart that is loaded into the tachograph, which is part of the vehicle's speedometer/odometer unit. It turns slowly on a turntable inside the instrument that turns once every 24 hours, and a speed history is inscribed by a fine stylus connected to the speedometer. With some exceptions that needn't concern us, it is an offence to drive a truck in Europe unless you have a tachograph; if it's analogue you

[4]Vehicles registered since August 2004 in the UK had to have digital systems fitted, driver cards have been issued since June 2005 and the use of digital systems in new vehicles became mandatory in August 2006; the dates vary slightly for other EU countries.

must have a chart installed, and have written on it your starting time and location. You must also keep several days' charts with you to establish that you've complied with the relevant driving hours regulations (typically 8.5 hours per day with rules for rest breaks per day and rest days per week). If it's digital, you have to have a driver card plugged into it; the card and the vehicle unit both keep records.

European law also restricts trucks to 100 km/h (62 mph) on freeways and less on other roads. This is enforced not just by police speed traps and the tachograph record, but directly by a speed limiter that is also driven by the tachograph. Tachograph charts are also used to investigate other offences, such as unlicensed waste dumping, and by fleet operators to detect fuel theft. So there are lots of reasons why a truck driver might want to fiddle his tachograph. Indeed, it's a general principle in security engineering that one shouldn't aggregate targets. Forcing a truck driver to defeat his tachograph in order to circumvent his speed limiter, and vice versa, was a design error – but one that's now too entrenched to change easily.

Most of what we have to say applies just as well to taxi meters and other monitoring devices. While the truck driver wants his vehicle to appear to have gone less distance, the taxi driver wants the opposite. This has little effect on the actual tampering techniques.

14.3.2 What goes wrong

According to a survey of 1060 convictions of drivers and operators done before the introduction of the new digital system [65], the offences were distributed as follows.

14.3.2.1 How most tachograph manipulation is done

About 70% of offences that result in conviction did not involve tampering but exploited procedural weaknesses. For example, a company with premises in Dundee and Southampton should have four drivers in order to operate one vehicle per day in each direction, as the distance is about 500 miles and the journey takes about 10 hours – which is illegal for a single driver to do every day. The standard fiddle is to have two drivers who meet at an intermediate point such as Penrith, change trucks, and insert new paper charts into the tachographs. So the driver who had come from Southampton now returns home with the vehicle from Dundee. When stopped and asked for his charts, he shows the current chart from Penrith to Southampton, the previous day's for Southampton to Penrith, the day before's for Penrith to Southampton, and so on. In this way he can give the false impression that he spent every other night in Penrith and was thus legal. This practice of swapping vehicles halfway through the working day is called *ghosting*. It's even harder to detect in mainland Europe, where a driver might be operating out of a depot in France on Monday, in Belgium on Tuesday and in Holland on Wednesday.

Simpler frauds included setting the clock wrongly, pretending that a hitch-hiker is a relief driver, and recording the start point as a village with a very common name – such as 'Milton' in England or 'La Hoya' in Spain. If stopped, the driver can claim he started from a nearby Milton or La Hoya.

Such tricks often involve collusion between the driver and the operator. When the operator is ordered to produce charts and supporting documents such as pay records, weigh station slips and ferry tickets, his office may well conveniently burn down. (It's remarkable how many truck companies operate out of cheap wooden sheds at a safe distance from the trucks in their yard.)

14.3.2.2 Tampering with the supply

The next largest category of fraud, amounting to about 20% of the total, involved tampering with the supply to the tachograph instrument, including interference with the power and impulse supply, cables and seals.

The earliest tachographs used a rotating wire cable – as did the speedometers in cars up until the early 1980s – that was hard to fiddle with. If you jammed the truck's odometer, it was quite likely that you'd shear off the cable. More recent analogue tachographs are 'electronic', in that they use electric cables rather than rotating wire. The input comes from a sensor in the gearbox, which sends electrical impulses as the prop shaft rotates. This has made fiddling much easier! A common attack is to unscrew the sensor about a tenth of an inch, which causes the impulses to cease, as if the vehicle were stationary. To prevent this, sensors are fixed in place with a wire and lead seal. Fitters are bribed to wrap the wire anticlockwise rather than clockwise, which causes it to loosen rather than break when the sensor is unscrewed. The fact that seals are issued to workshops rather than to individual fitters complicates prosecution.

But most of the fiddles are much simpler still. Drivers short out the cable or replace the tachograph fuse with a blown one. (One manufacturer tried to stop this trick by putting the truck's anti-lock braking system on the same fuse. Many drivers preferred to get home sooner than to drive a safe vehicle.) There's evidence of power-supply interruption on the chart in Figure 14.2: around 11am, there are several places where the speed indicated in the outside trace goes suddenly from zero to over 100 km/h. These indicate power interruptions, except where there's also a discontinuity in the distance trace. There, the unit was open.

14.3.2.3 Tampering with the instrument

The third category of fraud was tampering with the tachograph unit itself. The typical offence in this category is miscalibration, usually done in cahoots with the fitter but sometimes by the driver defeating the seal on the device. This amounted for some 6% of offences, but declined through the 1990s as the introduction of digital communications made it easier to tamper with the cable instead.

14.3.2.4 High-tech attacks

The state of the tampering art at the time of the survey was the equipment in Figure 14.3. The plastic cylinder on the left of the photo is marked 'Voltage Regulator — Made in Japan' but is certainly not a voltage regulator. (It appears to be made in Italy.) It is spliced into the tachograph cable and controlled by the driver using the remote control key fob. A first press causes the indicated speed to drop by 10%, a second press causes a drop of 20%, a third press causes it to fall to zero, and a fourth causes the device to return to proper operation.

This kind of device accounted for under 1% of convictions, but its use was believed to be much more widespread. It's extremely hard to find as it can be hidden at many different places in the truck's cable harness. Police officers who stop a speeding truck equipped with such a device, and can't find it, have difficulty getting a conviction: the sealed and apparently correctly calibrated tachograph contradicts the evidence from their radar or camera.

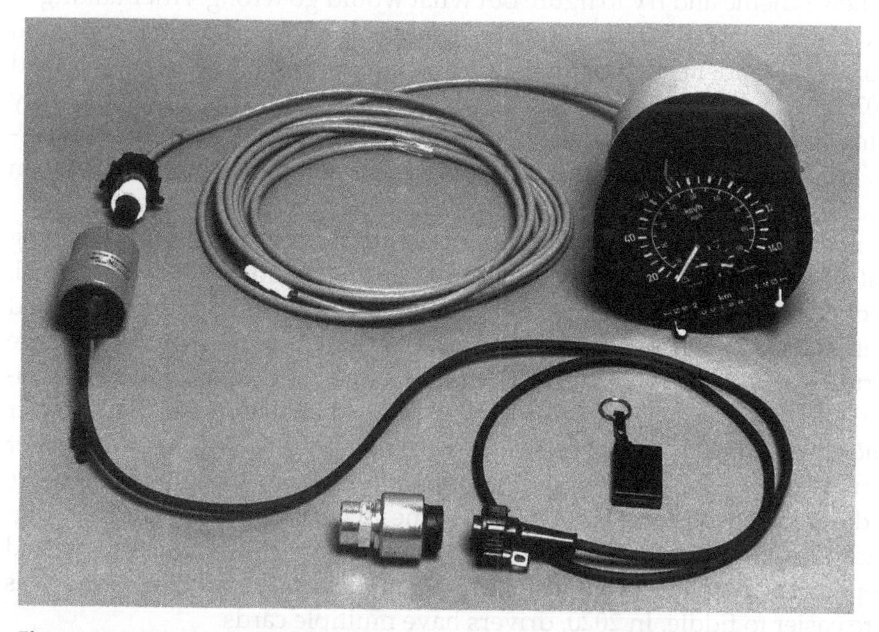

Figure 14.3: A tachograph with an interruptor controlled by the driver using a radio key fob (courtesy of Hampshire Constabulary, England)

14.3.3 Digital tachographs

The countermeasures taken against tachograph manipulation vary by country. In Britain, trucks are stopped at the roadside for random checks by vehicle inspectors, and suspect trucks may be shadowed across the country. In the Netherlands, inspectors prefer to descend on a trucking company and audit their delivery documents, drivers' timesheets, fuel records etc. In Italy, data from the toll booths on the freeways are used to prosecute drivers who've averaged more than the speed limit (you can often see trucks parked just in front of Italian toll booths). But drivers can arbitrage between the differing control regimes. For example, a truck driver operating between France and Holland can keep his documents at a depot in France where the Dutch vehicle inspectors can't get at them. The weakness in the UK system was that when a vehicle inspector stopped a truck and found evidence of a violation, this would result in a prosecution some months later in the local magistrate's court. Foreign drivers often just didn't appear.

So the European Union took the initiative to design a unified electronic tachograph system to replace the existing paper-based charts with smartcards. Each driver now has a driver card that contains a record of his driving hours over the last 28 days. Every vehicle registered since 2006 has a vehicle unit that can hold a year's history. There are also workshop cards used by mechanics to calibrate devices, and control cards used by law enforcement officers to read them out at the roadside. In 1998, I was hired by the UK Department of Transport to look at the new scheme and try to figure out what would go wrong. After talking to a wide range of people from policemen and vehicle inspectors to tachograph vendors and accident investigators, I wrote a report [65]. I revisited the field in 2007 when writing the second edition of this book; it was simultaneously pleasing and depressing to find that I'd mostly predicted the problems correctly. However a few interesting new twists also emerged. Finally, in 2020, in the third edition, we can take a more mature view.

The main objection raised to the project was that it was not clear how going digital would help combat the procedural frauds that made up 70% of the total. Indeed, our pair of drivers 'ghosting' between Dundee and Southampton had their lives made even easier. It took fourteen years – more than the lifetime of a truck – to change over to the new system and meantime a crooked company could run one new digital truck and one old analogue one. Each driver will now have one chart and one card, with five hours a day on each, rather than two charts which they might accidentally mix up when stopped. This turned out to be well-founded. By 2008, some 20% of the vehicle fleet had digital tachographs – somewhat more than would be expected – which suggested that operators may have been installing digital devices before they need to as they're easier to fiddle. In 2020, drivers have multiple cards.

Another objection was that enforcement would be made harder by the loss of detailed speed and driving hours information. Back in 1998, the Germans had wanted the driver card to be a memory device so it could contain detailed records; the French insisted on a smartcard, thanks to lobbying from their smartcard industry. So the driver card has limited memory, and can only contain a limited number of alarm events.

14.3.3.1 System-level problems

The response to the loss of fine-grained data varies by country. Germany went for an infrastructure of fleet management systems that accept digital tachograph data, digitized versions of the analog data from the existing paper charts, fuel data, delivery data and even payroll, and reconcile them all to provide not just management information for the trucking company but surveillance data for the police. Britain has something similar, although it's up to the police to decide which companies to inspect; unless they do so, data on driving infringements is only available to the employer. There are third-party service firms who will analyse this for companies who are keen on saving time, or just demonstrating compliance. Germany has also introduced a system of road pricing for heavy goods vehicles that gives further inputs into fleet management.

Britain has a network of automatic number plate reader (ANPR) cameras, initially installed around London to make IRA bombing attacks harder; after the Good Friday agreement in 1997 ended that threat, ANPR was not decommissioned but extended nationwide. That was justified on the basis of detecting car tax evaders, but we then saw ANPR data adduced in more and more prosecutions, for everything from terrorism down to burglary. In the case of drivers' hours enforcement, the strategy is to verify a sample of logged journeys against the ANPR database; where discrepancies are found, the company's operations are then scrutinised more closely.

However, disagreements about privacy and about national economic interests hindered EU-wide standardization. It's up to individual countries whether they require truck companies to download and analyze the data from their trucks. And even among countries that require this, there's still arbitrage. For example, the German police are much more vigorous at enforcing drivers' hours regulations than their Italian counterparts. So, under the old analogue system, an Italian driver who normally didn't bother to put a chart in his machine did so while driving over the Alps. Meanwhile, the driver of the German truck going the other way took his chart out. The net effect was that all drivers in a given country were subject to the same level of enforcement. But if the driving data got uploaded from the Italian driver's card and kept on a PC at a truck company in Rome then they were subject to Italian levels of enforcement (or even less if the police in Rome didn't care about accidents in Germany). The fix was extraterritoriality; an Italian truck driver stopped in Germany can now be prosecuted there if he can't show satisfactory records of his driving in Italy for the week before he crossed the border.

In the UK, foreign drivers who were stopped and ordered to appear at a magistrates' court often didn't turn up. The real fix turned out to be not technological, but legal. In March 2018, Britain changed the law to allow spot fines at the roadside. Previously, officers could only issue spot fines for ongoing offences, rather than for offences visible in the truck or driver records. This change led to a near-tenfold increase in fines [926].

14.3.3.2 Other problems

Overall, the move from analogue to digital wasn't an improvement. While comparative fraud statistics of digital and analogue devices have not been collected, the view of officials is that while the initial detection of an unrealistic journey remains much the same, the sophistication of digital defeat devices makes them harder to find [1729]. And there are other interesting problems with tachographs becoming digital.

First, digital tachographs were the first system that caused digital signatures to turn up in court in large numbers. For years, security researchers have been writing academic papers with punchlines like "the judge then raises X to the power Y, finds it's equal to Z, and sends Bob to jail." The reality is different. Judges found digital signatures difficult as they were presented as hexadecimal strings on little tickets printed out from vehicle units, with no approved apparatus for verification. The police solved the problem by applying standard procedures for "securing" evidence. When they raid a dodgy trucking company, they image the PC's disk drive and take copies on DVDs that are sealed in evidence bags. One gets given to the defence and one kept for appeal. The paper logs documenting the copying are available for Their Worships to inspect, along with the printouts from the vehicle units.

Second, many drivers have more than one driver card. This is an offence everywhere but that doesn't stop it! Drivers borrow them from friends who use them only occasionally – for example because they usually drive trucks under 3.5 tonnes. And thanks to EU freedom of movement, drivers can easily have more than one address: the Jean Moulin of Toulouse may also be Jean Moulin of Antwerp. A database, Tachonet, was set up to try to catch duplicate applications across European countries but it doesn't seem to work very well. For example, drivers may forget their middle name in one of their countries of residence. From 2018 it was made mandatory for Member States to share data with it.

Third, there are new kinds of service-denial attacks (as well as the traditional ones on gearbox sensors, fuses and so on). A truck driver can destroy his smartcard by feeding it with mains electricity (even a truck's 24 volts will do fine). Under the regulations he is allowed to drive for 15 days while waiting for a replacement. As static electricity destroys maybe 1% of cards a year anyway, it's hard to prosecute drivers for doing this occasionally.

Fourth, I mentioned that the loss of detailed, redundant data on the tachograph chart makes enforcement harder. In the old analogue days, experienced vehicle inspectors had a 'feel' for when a chart isn't right, but the analogue trace was replaced by a binary signal saying either that the driver infringed the regulations or that he didn't. This spills over into other enforcement tasks; analogue charts were often used to collect evidence of illegal toxic waste dumping, for example, as the recorded speed history often gave an inspector a good idea of the truck's route.

Next, some of the cards in the system (notably the workshop cards used to set up the instruments, and the control cards used by police and vehicle inspectors) are very powerful. They can be used to erase evidence of wrongdoing. For example, if you use a workshop card to wind back the clock in a vehicle unit from 10th July to 8th July, then the entries for July 9th and 10th become unreadable. Some countries have therefore gone to great lengths to minimise the number of workshop cards that fall into bad hands. In the UK, for example, truck mechanics have to pass a criminal records check to get one; yet this isn't foolproof as it's often companies that get convicted, and the wealthy owners of crooked truck-maintenance firms just set up new firms. There's no company licensing scheme, and although wrongdoers can be blacklisted from acting as directors of licensed firms, crooks just hide behind nominee directors.

There is one interesting spin-off from the world of tachographs. In the late 1990s, a European Union regulation decreed that, in order to frustrate the use of interruptors of the kind shown in Figure 14.3, all digital tachographs had to encrypt the pulse train from the gearbox sensor to the vehicle unit. As both of these devices contain a microcontroller, and the data rate is fairly low, this shouldn't in theory have been a problem. But how on earth could we distribute the keys? If we just set up a hotline that garages could call, it is likely to be abused. There's a long history of fitters conspiring with truck drivers to defeat the system, and of garage staff abusing helplines to get unlocking data for stolen cars and even PIN codes for stolen car radios. The solution was given by the *resurrecting duckling* security policy model, more prosaically known as *trust on first use*, which we discussed in 4.7.1. This is named after the fact that a duckling emerging from its egg will recognize as its mother the first moving object it sees that makes a sound: this is called imprinting. Similarly, a 'newborn' vehicle unit, just removed from the shrink wrap, can recognize as its owner the first gearbox sensor that sends it a secret key. The sensor does this on power-up. As soon as this key is received, the vehicle unit is no longer a newborn and will stay faithful to the gearbox sensor for the rest of its 'life'. If the sensor fails and has to be replaced, a workshop card can be used to 'kill' the vehicle unit's key store and resurrect it as a newborn, whereupon it can imprint on the new sensor. Each act of resurrection is indelibly logged in the vehicle unit to make abuse harder. (This at least was the theory – the implementation fell somewhat short in that in one unit the error code for sensor rekeying is the same as the error code for a power outage.)

14.3.4 Sensor defeats and third-generation devices

However, even if the protocols can be secured, the sensors can still be attacked directly. Since digital tachographs started shipping, the folks who brought you the interruptor now have a new product: a black box containing electromagnets and electronics to simulate a gearbox. The errant truck driver unscrews his gearbox sensor and places it in this simulator, which comes with its own cable and a sensor that he plugs into his actual gearbox. The system now operates as before; on command it will either relay impulses faithfully, or discard them, or filter some of them out. The dodgy pulse-train arrives at the tachograph as before, but this time beautifully encrypted using triple-DES. Secure sensing is harder than it looks!

This became such a nuisance that the EU passed a law in 2009 specifically prohibiting, and requiring Member States to check for, "any device, or devices, intended to destroy, suppress, manipulate or alter any data, or which is intended to interfere with any part of the electronic data exchange between the component parts of recording equipment, or which inhibits or alters the data in such ways prior to encryption" [651]. It also upgraded the regulations to require that vehicles registered from 2012 have the 'third version tachograph', which requires an extra motion sensor as a countermeasure to sensor defeats.

14.3.5 The fourth generation – smart tachographs

In 2014 the regulations were updated to introduce the smart tachograph, which is required in vehicles registered for the first time as from 15 June 2019, and adds:

- better security mechanisms to make fraud more difficult;
- a satellite navigation system, which will record the truck's location at the start and end of each trip, and every three hours if the trip's longer than that;
- a radio link for a cop at the roadside to read tachograph data when the vehicle is moving.

By now, the reader might feel a certain cynicism about anything called 'smart'. The regulations are a further move in the direction of pervasive enforcement, but stop short of demanding that vehicle units keep detailed GPS history. Privacy law in some countries would make that difficult; in egregious cases, such as toxic waste dumping, the authorities can always subpoena the driver's mobile phone history[5]. Meanwhile, vendors offer fleet management systems with automatic infringement checking, assuring firms that this will minimise liability. We will have to wait and see how this all works out.

But what might be the practicalities of requiring constant GPS monitoring? We can get some insight from our next application.

14.4 Curfew tags: GPS as policeman

My third case study of monitoring and metering is the curfew tags that criminal suspects and paroled offenders wear on their ankles in order to constrain and monitor their movements. Introduced in Britain in 1999, they are used to cut the prison population. Most offenders are released after serving half their sentence and spend some of their parole period under curfew, which typically means that they must stay at home from 7pm to 7am. They wear a curfew tag on an ankle bracelet which communicates with a home monitoring station. Others receive community sentences instead of prison, with a curfew. Some 20,000 offenders may be 'on tag' at any one time.

Curfew tags have spread to many other countries too. The more expensive tags contain GPS chips and report the tag wearer's location constantly to the police. In Britain, these devices are worn by sex offenders whose curfews prohibit them from going near schools, by persistent offenders in some police areas, and by terrorism suspects. In France, they're being introduced in domestic violence cases [478]. In the USA, they're offered to many suspects pre-trial as a condition of bail (of whom the most famous may have been Harvey Weinstein). There, the issue is that while the Federal government pays for its prisoners' tags, 90% of cases are raised by states and cities, which mostly force the tag wearer to pay. Monitoring is dominated by two companies that typically charge $10 a day, with $350 up front. (When government pays, they only get $2–3 a day.) So poor defendants get into debt, or get jailed for nonpayment. This is short-sighted, as jail costs about $100 a day. Given that the USA has about a million people awaiting trial in jail at any time, this is a policy issue with real consequences; the number of tag wearers is over 125,000 and has been rising since the First Step Act of 2018. Judges see monitoring orders as cost-free; they issue them defensively, steadily widening

[5] All vehicles under 3.5 tons in Europe are required to have embedded phones for eCall emergency service; this is unfortunately not mandatory for larger vehicles, no doubt because of industry lobbying.

the scope; two-thirds of tag wearers are African American; and unlike with bail, defendants don't get their money back if acquitted [1076].

In 2013–6, I was involved as an expert witness in a number of curfew-tag cases. The first, in 2013, involved a woman convicted of shoplifting who was accused of tampering with her curfew tag as it indicated on several occasions that she'd left home in the evening. Analysis of the logs relating to my defendant's case showed large numbers of false alarms; some of these had good explanations (such as power cuts), but many didn't. The overall picture was of an unreliable technology surrounded by chaotic procedures and conflicts of interest. The tagging contractor, Serco, not only supplied the tags and the back-end systems, but the call centre and the interface to the court system. What's more, if you break your curfew, it isn't the public prosecutor that takes you before the magistrates, but the contractor – relying on expert evidence from one of its subcontractors, who helped design the system. We asked the court for access to the tag in the case, plus a set of tagging equipment for testing, the system specifications, false alarm statistics and audit reports. The contractor promptly replied that "although we continue to feel that the defendant is in breach of the order, our attention has been drawn to a number of factors that would allow me to properly discontinue proceedings in the public interest" [84].

Several months later, there was a case involving several men subject to 'terrorism prevention and investigation measures' (TPIM) orders. These were a measure introduced in 2011 that allows the UK government to impose curfews on individuals believed to be a terrorist threat but against whom there is insufficient evidence to mount a prosecution; they have been controversial on human-rights grounds. A number of individuals were served with orders restricting their movements and fitted with GPS tags to monitor compliance. These tags tended to break off after about six months, whereupon the men were prosecuted for tag tampering and imprisoned. As this was covered by a secrecy order, the pattern only came to light when it was noticed by a London law firm that represented three of them. Again, the government refused to expose any evidence to expert examination, and the three men were acquitted, causing embarrassment to the then Home Secretary, Theresa May [1907]. A few days later, one of them evaded surveillance by donning a niqab in a London mosque and leaving as a woman. This caused outrage in the press [1908]. The following month, it turned out that the two main UK curfew tag contractors – Serco and G4S – had been defrauding the government at scale, by charging tag fees for offenders who had been acquitted or who were in prison, abroad or dead, and that this had been going on since the contracts started in 2005. They were stripped of their contracts, and the matter was referred to the Serious Fraud Office [1288]. Serco was eventually fined £19.2m in 2019 and ordered to pay £3.7m costs; its accountants, Deloitte, were fined £4.2m for audits they conducted of the tagging operation; and finally, in 2020, G4S was fined £44.4m by the UK Serious Fraud Office.

The dependability of curfew tags came to trial in 2014 in the case of yet another terrorism suspect who was being held in immigration detention, accused of tag tampering, which he denied. This time the government decided to risk a trial. The suspect's lawyers instructed me and a colleague at our Materials Science department as experts. We formed the hypothesis that the stress of wearing a heavy tag would lead to a fracture of the strap's fixing, particularly for a devout Muslim who prayed five times a day. The court duly ordered that the two of us, and a Saudi research student at our lab, be fitted with GPS tags, and we rigged up accelerometers and strain gauges to monitor the test. While the student's tag survived several days of prayer, my tag broke off when I caught it on a radiator at home, and my colleague's after he wore it while playing football. The specification called for the tag to withstand a 50kg pull, and the operating company (which had taken over the business from G4S but still used the same specialist subcontractors) claimed that the material from which it was made was not liable to fatigue fractures. The government refused however 'for reasons of commercial confidentiality' to reveal what this material was. No matter; a test of a sliver from the broken fixing lug revealed that it was a polycarbonate that does indeed suffer fatigue fractures. The court ordered us to hand back all our samples 'to protect the contractor's intellectual property' but did not impose a secrecy order on our expert report, which can be found at [86]. This suspect was also eventually freed by the court.

By 2015–6 GPS tags, from a new supplier, were being used by the Kent police to monitor petty offenders. The supplier initially made inaccurate claims about GPS accuracy (salesmen don't like to admit anything is less than perfect), and there were a couple of trials. This forced us to study the security and reliability of GPS, or more generally GNSS (a term that includes not just the original US service but the European Galileo system plus the Russian and Chinese offerings). In such services, a constellation of satellites each broadcasts a very accurate time signal, and a receiver seeing four or more of these can solve for its position and time. In practice it takes more than that. First, the signal's propagation depends on conditions in the ionosphere, which are variable, leading to error unless this can be calibrated against reference stations – a technique called augmentation, which is used in aircraft navigation and can result in a precision of 2m. The accuracy of consumer equipment is more like 10m on average, but it can be significantly worse, for several reasons.

First, if the visible satellites are clustered close together this dilutes the precision, which may happen if only a few satellites are visible. In this case, you can look up the resulting *dilution of precision* and use it to estimate the error. (For the key fixes in our first case, only five satellites were visible and the expected error was 45m; there are websites where you can look this up as a function of location and time.) Second, many consumer devices (such as phones) have *snap-to-fit* software that automatically places the device on the nearest road or path. Third, even larger errors can come from multipath – typically when a signal reflected from a building competes with the direct signal. The combination of multipath and snap-to-fit is what causes your phone or your navigator to jump from one street to another when driving or walking through a town with tall buildings. Finally, there are various kinds of jamming, ranging from barrage jamming that simply denies service to more sophisticated strategies such as *meaconing* in which a decoy retransmits the radio spectrum observed at another location, causing GPS equipment to believe it is at that location instead. Until recently, GPS jamming was something governments did, but the advent of low-cost software radios is starting to spread the fun. If I were a gangster on tag, I could use meaconing to provide an alibi: it would tell the police I'd been at home while I'd actually gone out and shot someone.

If you're going to base a business on GPS, whether directly or by relying on an underlying mapping service, it's a good idea to understand not just the average error but the worst case, and the circumstances in which such outliers can arise[6]. It's possible to do better than commodity equipment, whether by using professional equipment or by using clever signal processing. One of my postdocs, Ramsey Faragher, did a startup (Focal Point Positioning) which applies interferometry to successive GPS fixes in order to increase accuracy and detect both multipath and many kinds of jamming, supporting precision of about one metre[7].

At the organisational level, the court cases gave insight into how the technology was working its way into police practice. A significant proportion of burglaries are committed by 'prolific persistent offenders' – typically men with drug and alcohol problems with dozens of convictions for minor offences. (Our first case was of a man alleged to have snuck into someone's kitchen and stolen a bottle of wine from the fridge.) If police fit their 'frequent fliers' with curfew tags, then when a burglary was reported, they can simply look up to see if any of them had been within 100 yards, and if so send a car to pick them up. This may help the police drive down the crime statistics by locking up the frequent fliers for ever longer sentences; it might be less optimal socially if it fills up the jails with men who should be on rehab or receiving psychiatric care – or if it diverts attention from the more capable offenders.

14.5 Postage meters

My fourth case history of metering is the postage meter. Postage stamps were introduced in Britain 1840 by Sir Rowland Hill to simplify charging for post,

[6]You should employ at least one engineer who's read up on the subject (such as via [1020]) and follows the relevant blogs (such as https://www.insidegnss.com).
[7]Full disclosure: I invested in the company.

and developed into a special currency that could be used for certain purposes, from paying for postage to paying certain taxes and topping up the value of postal money orders. Bulk users of the postal system started to find stamps unsatisfactory by the late 19th century, and the postage meter was invented in 1889 by Josef Baumann. Its first commercial use was in Norway in 1903; in the USA Arthur Pitney and Walter Bowes had a meter approved for use in 1920 and built a large business on it. Early postal meters were analogue, and would print a stamp (known as an indicium) on a letter, or on a tape to stick on a parcel. The indicium had a date so that old indicia couldn't be peeled off and reused. Each meter had a mechanical value counter, protected by a physical seal; every so often you'd take your meter into the post office to be read and reset. Fraud prevention relied on users taking their mail to the local post office, which knew them; the clerk could check the date and the meter serial number.

In 1979, Pitney Bowes introduced a 'reset-by-phone' service, which enabled firms to buy an extra $500 worth of credit over the phone; the implementation involved a mechanical one-time pad, with the meter containing a tape with successive recharge codes [477]. In 1981, this was upgraded to a DES-based system that enabled a meter to be recharged with any sum of money. The recharge codes were calculated in part from the value counter – so if the firm lied about how much postage they'd used, they couldn't recharge the device. However, these meters still produced inked indicia.

In 1990, José Pastor of Pitney Bowes suggested replacing stamps and indicia with printed digital signatures [1499]. This caught the attention of the US Postal Service, which started a program to investigate whether cryptography could help produce better postage meters. One concern was whether the availability of color scanners and copiers would make stamps and indicia too easy to forge. A threat analysis done for them by Doug Tygar, Bennett Yee and Nevin Heintze revealed that the big problem was not so much the forging or copying of stamps, or even tampering with meters to get extra postage. It was bulk mailers corrupting Postal Service employees so as to insert truckloads of junk mail into the system without paying for them [1916]. As a bulk mailer on the fiddle would risk arousing the suspicion of postal staff, there was a temptation to cut them in on the deal; and then it was natural to forge a meter plate whose inducting post office was elsewhere. By 1990 US Postal service losses were in nine figures, and through the 1990s there were a number of high-profile convictions of bulk mailers who had manipulated their meters, getting away with millions of dollars of free postage [266].

This led to a development programme for a meter using digital signatures, generated by tamper-resistant processors in the postage meters. This was developed into an open standard available to multiple competing manufacturers. The basic idea is that the indicium, which is machine-readable, contains both the sender and recipient postal codes, the meter number, the date, the postage rate, the amount of postage ever sold by the meter and the amount of credit remaining in it, all protected with a digital signature. The private signature key is kept in the meter's processor while its corresponding public signature verification key is kept in a Postal Service directory, indexed by the meter serial number. In this way, postal inspectors can sample mail in bulk at sorting offices, checking that each item is not only franked but on a logical route from its ostensible source to its destination.

The USA introduced the technology in 2000, with traditional suppliers such as Pitney Bowes selling traditional meters while startups such as `stamps.com` obtained licenses to generate indicia online so that customers could download them and print them on their computers at home. Germany and the UK were next in 2004 and Canada in 2006; other countries followed suit. By 2006, all US postal facilities had the scanners needed to read the new indicia, of which an example is illustrated in Figure 14.4 below.

Such indicia can be produced by postage meters that are drop-in replacements for the old-fashioned devices; you weigh a letter, frank it, and get billed at the end of the month. You don't have to take the meter in to be read though, as that can be done over the Internet for a credit meter, while if you buy a pre-payment meter, you replenish it by phoning a call centre and buying a magic number with your credit card. This works in much the same way as the pre-payment electricity meters discussed earlier in this chapter.

Indicia can also be bought over the Internet by simply specifying the sender and destination postal codes. This 'online postage' is aimed at small firms and people working from home who don't send enough mail for it to be worth their while buying a meter. Both metered and online postage are cheaper than stamps to distribute. It has also become possible to manage the system much better, by tracking volumes and profitability of mail down to local level. So, all

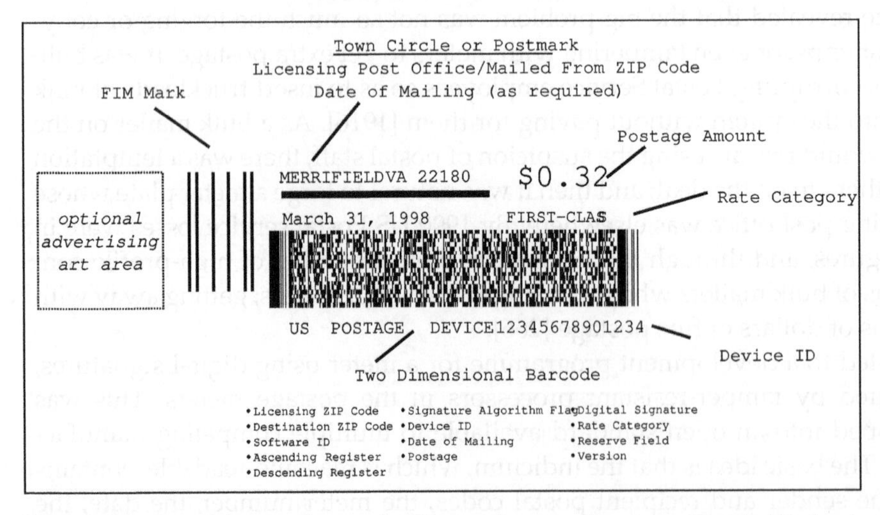

Figure 14.4: One of the new formats for US postal meters (courtesy of Symbol Technologies)

told, digital post offers more flexibility to both users and postal services. But what about security?

Postage meters are a slight extension of the utility metering model. There's a tamper-resistant processor, either in the meter itself, or attached to a web server in the case of online postage; this has a value counter and a crypto key. It dispenses value by creating indicia until the value counter is exhausted, then requires replenishment from a control unit higher up in the chain. There are some additional features in each case. Many postage meters include a 'Clark-Wilson' feature whereby the value counter actually consists of two counters, an Ascending Register (AR) containing the total value ever dispensed by the meter, and a Descending Register (DR) indicating the remaining credit. The balancing control is AR + DR = TS, the 'total setting', that is, the total of all the sales made by or authorised for that device. If the balance fails, the meter locks up and can only be accessed by inspectors.

The full threat model includes stolen postage meters, meters that have been tampered with to provide free postage, genuine meters used by unauthorised people, mail pieces with indicia of insufficient value to cover the weight and service class, and straightforward copies of valid indicia. Various sampling and other tests are used to control these risks. Subtleties include how you deal with features like certified mail and reply mail. There are also national differences on matters ranging from which authentication algorithms are used to what sort of usage data the meters have to upload back to the postal service.

Once operators got real experience, the industry started to move away from digital signatures to message authentication codes. Signatures appealed because they were elegant; but in real life, signature verification is expensive, and has also turned out to be unnecessary. Equipment at major sorting offices must process thousands of mail pieces a minute, and postal services usually verify indicia as an offline batch operation. Forged mail pieces go through initially and are only intercepted once a pattern of abuse emerges. Once verification is centralised, MACs make more sense than signatures; the central servers have hardware security modules with master keys that are diversified to a MAC key in each meter, just as with utility meters. It turns out that two-digit MACs are enough to detect systematic abuse before it becomes significant [477].

In many countries, the postal service contracts all the cryptography out to the meter vendors. So indicia are verified only in the home postal system, as overseas systems will often use different vendors. We also see a diversity of architectures. Canada, for example, uses both signatures and MACs on its indicia. (And if you want to bribe a postal employee to let a few tons of junk mail into the system, the place to do it is now at a border crossing.)

How stuff actually breaks in real life is – as always – instructive. In the German post office's 'Stampit' scheme, a user buys 'smart pdf' files that contact the post office to say they're being printed, without any interaction with the user or her software. If the paper jams, or the printer is out of toner, then tough. So users arrange to photocopy the stamp, or to copy it to a file from which it can be printed again if need be. The UK system has learnt from this: although a stamp is grey-listed when a user PC reports that it's been printed, the grey doesn't turn to black until the stamp appears at the sorting office. The difference in syntax is subtle: the German system tried to stop you printing the stamp more than once, while the British system more realistically tries to stop you using it more than once [886].

All told, moving to digital postal meters enabled much better control than was possible in the old days, when postal inspectors had to refer to paper records of mechanical meter readings. It also facilitates business models that extend the service to many more customers and that also improve the post office's cash flow and credit control. Unlike digital tachographs, digital postal meters have brought real benefits.

14.6 Summary

Many security systems are concerned one way or another with monitoring or metering some aspect of the environment. They range from utility meters to taxi meters, tachographs, and postal meters. We'll come across further metering and payment systems in later chapters, such as the mechanisms used to stop printer cartridges working once they have printed a certain number of pages.

Many monitoring, metering and payment systems have been redesigned as the world moved from analogue to digital technology. Some of the redesigns have been a success, and others less so. Digital prepayment electricity meters have been a success, as they enable utility companies in the developing world to sell power to hundreds of millions of people who don't even have addresses, let alone credit ratings. Digital tachographs have been less impressive; they just do what the old analogue systems did, but less well. Their slow evolution was perhaps inevitable given the many entrenched stakeholders and the lack of opportunity for a disruptive process change, as the goal was securing compliance by a mature industry with existing safety law. Our third example, the curfew tag, extends location monitoring from vehicles to human beings. It has supported some innovation, since technical offender monitoring is a new industry; it also teaches us some of the limits of using GPS in large complex systems. Our fourth example, the postage meter, did allow some competitive innovation and has been a success.

As with burglar alarms, the protection of monitoring systems is tied up with dependability. You have to think long and hard about what sort of service-denial attacks are possible. Key management can be an issue, especially in low-cost widely-distributed systems where you can't provide a central key management facility or hire enough trustworthy people. Systems may have to deal with numerous mutually suspicious parties, and must often be implemented on the cheapest possible hardware. Many of the monitoring devices are in the hands of opponents. And there are all sorts of application-level subtleties that have to be understood if you want your design to succeed.

Research problems

There's a lot of talk about the 'Internet of Things' but few concrete examples for researchers to think about. Case studies such as those described here may help. Although the mechanisms (and products) developed for payment networks can be adapted (and are), much of the design work has to be redone and the end result often has vulnerabilities. Metering applications are particularly useful because of the pervasive mutual mistrust caused not just by competing commercial entities but by the presence of dishonest staff at every level, as well as dishonest customers; and the fact that most of the equipment is in the custody of the attackers.

Again, there are questions for security economists and scholars of innovation. Why did some digital transformations of existing metering systems work well (utilities, postage) while others were less impressive (tachographs)? Why were some disruptive, in that new entrants successfully challenged the previous incumbent suppliers, while in other cases (such as postage) the existing suppliers managed the transition to better digital systems and survived despite innovative competition from dotcom startups?

Further reading

Prepayment electricity meters are described in [94]. Tachographs are written up in [65]; other papers relevant to transport appear in the annual ESCAR conference on electronic security in cars. The early work on postal meters is in [1916] and the US regulations can be found in [1322]. However the most detailed exposition of postage meter security is a book by Gerrit Bleumer of Francotyp-Postalia, which played a leading role in the program [266].

CHAPTER

15

Nuclear Command and Control

In Germany and Turkey they viewed scenes that were particularly distressing. On the runway stood a German (or Turkish) quick-reaction alert airplane loaded with nuclear weapons and with a foreign pilot in the cockpit. The airplane was ready to take off at the earliest warning, and the nuclear weapons were fully operational. The only evidence of U.S. control was a lonely 18-year-old sentry armed with a carbine and standing on the tarmac. When the sentry at the German airfield was asked how he intended to maintain control of the nuclear weapons should the pilot suddenly decide to scramble (either through personal caprice or through an order from the German command circumventing U.S. command), the sentry replied that he would shoot the pilot; Agnew directed him to shoot the bomb.

– Jerome Wiesner, reporting to President Kennedy on nuclear arms command and control after the Cuban crisis

15.1 Introduction

The catastrophic harm that could result from the unauthorized use of a nuclear weapon, or from the proliferation of nuclear technology, has led the US and other nuclear powers to spend colossal amounts of money protecting not just nuclear warheads but also the supporting infrastructure, industry and materials. Nuclear arms control is at the heart of international diplomacy: while North Korea now has the bomb, South Africa and Libya were persuaded to give it up, Iran's program has been stopped (by both diplomatic and cyber means) while Iraq and Syria have had their WMD programs terminated by force.

A surprising amount of nuclear security know-how has been published. In fact, there are limits on how much could be kept secret even if this was thought desirable. Many countries are capable of producing nuclear weapons but have decided not to (Japan, Australia, Switzerland, ...) so maintain controls on nuclear materials in a civilian context. Much of the real force of nonproliferation is cultural, built over the years through diplomacy and through the restraint of nuclear powers who since 1945 forbore use of these weapons even when facing defeat at the hands of non-nuclear states. This is backed by international agreements, such as the Nonproliferation Treaty and the Convention on the Physical Protection of Nuclear Material [951], enforced by the International Atomic Energy Agency (IAEA).

About ten tons of plutonium are produced by civil reactors each year, and if the human race is to rely on nuclear power long-term, then we'll be burning it in reactors as well as just making it as a side-effect of burning uranium. So we have to guard the stuff, in ways that inspire international confidence – not just between governments but from an increasingly sceptical public[1].

A vast range of security technology has spun off from the nuclear program. The US Department of Energy weapons laboratories – Sandia, Lawrence Livermore and Los Alamos – have worked for two generations to make nuclear weapons and materials as safe as can be achieved. I've already mentioned some of their more pedestrian spin-offs, from the discovery that passwords of more than twelve digits were not usable under battlefield conditions to high-end burglar alarm systems. The trick of wrapping an optical fiber round the devices to be protected and using interference effects to detect a change in length of less than a micron, is also one of theirs – it was designed to loop round the warheads in an armoury and alarm without fail if any of them are moved.

In later chapters, we'll see still more technology of nuclear origin. For example, iris recognition – the most accurate system known for biometric identification of individuals, and now used in India's Aadhaar identity system – was developed using US Department of Energy funds to control entry to the plutonium store, and much of the expertise in tamper-resistance and tamper-sensing technology originally evolved to prevent the abuse of stolen weapons or control devices. After 9/11, the USA and its allies took many aggressive steps to control nuclear proliferation including:

1. the invasion of Iraq in March 2003, for which the casus belli was a claim that Iraq possessed weapons of mass destruction;
2. an agreement by Libya in December 2003 to abandon an undeclared weapons program;
3. the disclosure in 2004 that Abdul Qadeer Khan, a senior scientist with Pakistan's nuclear program, had helped a number of other countries including Syria, Libya, Iran and North Korea get hold of weapons technology, and the dismantling of his network;
4. the Israeli operation 'Outside the Box' where a suspected Syrian reactor near Deir-ez-Zor was bombed on September 6th, 2007;

[1]For example, the British government was seriously embarrassed in 2007 when the safety of its plutonium stockpile was criticised by eminent scientists [1629], and again in 2018 when parliament's public accounts committee criticised the weapons program's crumbling facilities, aging workforce, specialist staff shortages and endemic funding and practical problems [1563].

5. the 2015 Joint Comprehensive Plan of Action whereby Iran agreed with the USA, the UK, Russia, China, France, Germany and the EU to halt its weapons program.

Not all of the efforts were successful, the obvious case in point being North Korea, which had signed a treaty with the USA in 1994 to halt weapons development in return for oil shipments and help developing civil nuclear energy. This collapsed in 2003, after which Pyongyang withdrew from the Non-Proliferation Treaty and developed weapons. This history makes many people apprehensive of the possible long-term effects of the Trump administration's 2018 abandonment of the agreement with Iran (even though Iran was abiding by it). And then there's also its 2019 abandonment of the Intermediate-Range Nuclear Forces Treaty with Russia (even though that was the result of Russian cheating); and the fact that the New START treaty, signed in 2010 by Barack Obama, will run out in February 2021, unless America elects a president in November 2020 who agrees to renew it.

Nuclear controls apply to more than just warheads and the fissile materials required for their construction. Following 9/11, we learned that Al-Qaida had talked about a 'dirty bomb' – a device that would disperse radioactive material over a city block – which might not kill anyone but could lead to panic, and in a financial center could cause great economic damage. So in 2007, GAO investigators set up a bogus company and got a license from the Nuclear Regulatory Commission authorizing them to buy isotopes. The license was printed on ordinary paper; the investigators altered it to change the quantity of material they were allowed to buy, then used it to order dozens of moisture density gauges containing americium-241 and cesium-137, which could have been used in a dirty bomb [1114]. Thanks to the fear of terrorism, the control of nuclear materials has tightened and spread more widely in the economy.

Nuclear safety continually teaches us lessons about the limits of assurance. For example, it's tempting to assume that if a certain action that you don't want to happen has a probability of 1 in 10 of happening through human error, then by getting five different people to check, you can reduce the probability to 1 in 100,000. The US Air Force thought so too. Yet in October 2007, six US hydrogen bombs went missing for 36 hours after a plane taking cruise missiles from Minot Air Force Base in North Dakota to Barksdale in Louisiana was mistakenly loaded with six missiles armed with live warheads. All the missiles were supposed to be inspected by handlers in the storage area and checked against a schedule (which was out of date), by ground crew waiting for the inspection to finish before moving any missiles (they didn't), by ground crew inspecting the missiles (they didn't look in the glass portholes to see whether the warheads were real or dummy), by the driver calling in the identification numbers to a control centre (nobody there bothered to check), and finally by the navigator during his preflight check (he didn't look at the wing with the live missiles).

The plane took off, flew to Louisiana, landed, and sat unguarded on the runway for nine hours before the ground crew arrived to unload the missiles and discovered they were live [188, 549]. This illustrates one of the limits to shared control. People will rely on others and slack off – a lesson also known in the world of medical safety. Indeed, in the USAF case it turned out that the airmen had replaced the official procedures with an 'informal' checklist of their own. So how can you design systems that don't fail in this way?

In this chapter I describe the nuclear safety environment and some of the tricks that might find applications (or pose threats) elsewhere. It has been assembled from public sources – but even so there are useful lessons to be drawn.

15.2 The evolution of command and control

The first atomic bomb to be used in combat was the 'Little Boy' dropped on Hiroshima. Its safety was somewhat improvised. It came with three detonators, and the weapon officer was supposed to replace green dummy ones with red live ones once the plane was airborne. However, a number of heavily loaded B-29s had crashed on takeoff from Tinian, the base they used. The Enola Gay weapon officer, Navy Captain Deak Parsons, reckoned that if the plane crashed, the primer might explode, detonating the bomb and wiping out the island. So he spent the day before the raid practising removing and reinstalling the primer – a gunpowder charge about the size of a loaf of bread – so he could install it after takeoff instead.

Doctrine has rather moved away from improvisation, and if anything we're at the other extreme now, with mechanisms and procedures tested and drilled and exercised and analysed by multiple experts from different agencies. It has been an evolutionary process. When weapons started being carried in single-seat tactical aircraft in the 1950s, and being slung under the wings rather than in a bomb bay, it was no longer possible to insert a bag of gunpowder manually. There was a move to combination locks: the pilot would arm the bomb after takeoff by entering a six-digit code into a special keypad with a wired-seal lid. This enabled some central control; the pilot might only get the code once airborne. But both the technical and procedural controls in the 1950s were primitive.

15.2.1 The Kennedy memorandum

The Cuban missile crisis changed all that. The Soviet B-59 was a Foxtrot-class diesel-electric submarine that came under attack on 27th October 1962 when a US battle group consisting of the aircraft carrier USS Randolph and 11 destroyers started dropping depth charges nearby. These were practice rounds, dropped in an attempt to force the submarine to the surface for identification; but the ship's captain, Valentin Savitsky, thought he was under attack, that war had started, and so he should fire a nuclear torpedo to destroy the carrier. But this could only be done if the three senior officers on board agreed, and luckily one of them, Vasily Arkhipov, refused. Eventually the submarine surfaced and returned to Russia.

This made the risk that a world war might start by accident salient to US policymakers, and President Kennedy ordered his science adviser Jerome Wiesner to investigate. He reported that hundreds of US nuclear weapons were kept in allied countries such as Greece and Turkey, which were not particularly stable and occasionally fought with each other. These weapons were protected by token US custodial forces, so there was no physical reason why the weapons couldn't be seized in time of crisis. There was also some worry about unauthorized use of nuclear weapons by US officers – for example, if a local commander under pressure felt that 'if only they knew in Washington how bad things were here, they would let us use the bomb.' In [1828] we find the passage quoted at the head of this chapter.

Kennedy's response was National Security Action Memo no. 160 [218]. This ordered that America's 7,000 nuclear weapons then dispersed to NATO commands should be got under positive US control using technical means, whether they were in the custody of US or allied forces. Although this policy was sold to Congress as protecting US nuclear weapons from foreigners, the worries about a crazy 'Dr Strangelove' (or a real-life Captain Savitsky) were actually at the top of Wiesner's list.

The Department of Energy was already working on weapon safety devices. The basic principle was that a unique aspect of the environment had to be sensed before the weapon would arm. For example, missile warheads and some free-fall bombs had to experience zero gravity, while artillery shells had to experience an acceleration of thousands of G. There was one exception: atomic demolition munitions. These are designed to be taken to their targets by ground troops and detonated using time fuses. There appears to be no scope for a unique environmental sensor to prevent accidental or malicious detonation.

The solution then under development was a secret arming code that activated a solenoid safe lock buried deep in the plutonium pit at the heart of the weapon. The main engineering problem was maintenance. When the lock was exposed, for example to replace the power supply, the code might become known. So it was not acceptable to have the same code in every weapon. Group codes were one possibility – firing codes shared by only a small batch of warheads.

Following the Kennedy memo, it was proposed that all nuclear bombs should be protected using code locks, and that there should be a 'universal unlock' action message that only the president or his legal successors could give. The problem was to find a way to translate this code securely to a large number of individual firing codes, each of which enabled a small batch of weapons. The problem became worse in the 1960s and 1970s when the doctrine changed from massive retaliation to 'measured response'. Instead of arming all nuclear weapons or none, the President now needed to be able to arm selected batches (such as 'all nuclear artillery in Germany'). This starts to lead us to a system of some complexity, especially when we realise we need disarming codes too, for maintenance purposes, and some means of navigating the trade-offs between weapons safety and effective command.

15.2.2 Authorization, environment, intent

The deep question was the security policy that nuclear safety systems, and command systems, should enforce. What emerged in the USA was the rule of 'authorization, environment, intent'. For a warhead to detonate, three conditions must be met.

Authorization: the use of the weapon in question must have been authorized by the *national command authority* (i.e., the President and his lawful successors in office).

Environment: the weapon must have sensed the appropriate aspect of the environment. (With atomic demolition munitions, this requirement is replaced by the use of a special container.)

Intent: the officer commanding the aircraft, ship or other unit must unambiguously command the weapon's use.

In early systems, 'authorization' meant the entry into the device of a four-digit authorization code.

The means of signalling 'intent' depended on the platform. Aircraft typically use a six-digit arming or 'use control' code. The command consoles for intercontinental ballistic missiles are operated by two officers, each of whom must enter and turn a key to launch the rocket. Whatever the implementation, there must be a unique signal; 22 bits derived from a six-digit code are believed to be a good tradeoff between a number of factors from usability to minimising the risk of accidental arming [1351].

15.3 Unconditionally secure authentication

Nuclear command and control drove the development of a theory of one-time authentication codes. As I described in Chapter 5, "Cryptography", these are similar in concept to the test keys invented to protect telegraphic money transfers, in that a keyed transformation is applied to the message in order to yield a short authentication code, also known as an *authenticator* or *tag*. As the keys are only used once, authentication codes can be made unconditionally secure, in that the protection they give is independent of the computational resources available to the attacker. So they do for authentication what the one-time pad does for confidentiality.

Recall that we still have to choose the code length to bound the probability of a successful guess; this might be different depending on whether the opponent was trying to guess a valid message from scratch (*impersonation*) or modify an existing valid message so as to get another one (*substitution*). In the GCM mode of operation discussed in Chapter 5, these are set equal at 2^{128} but this need not be the case.

An example should make this clear. Suppose a commander has agreed an authentication scheme with a subordinate under which an instruction is to be encoded as a three-digit number from 000 to 999. The instruction may have two values: 'Attack Russia' and 'Attack China'. One of these will be encoded as an even number, and the other by an odd number: which is which will be part of the secret key. The authenticity of the message will be vouched for by making its remainder, when divided by 337, equal to a secret number that is the second part of the key.

Suppose the key is that:

- 'Attack Russia' codes to even numbers, and 'Attack China' to odd
- an authentic message has the remainder 12 when divided by 337.

So 'Attack Russia' is '686' (or '12') and 'Attack China' is '349'.

An enemy who has taken over the communications channel between the commander and the subordinate, and who knows the scheme but not the key, has a probability of only 1 in 337 of successfully impersonating the commander. However, once he sees a valid message (say '12' for 'Attack Russia'), then he can easily change it to the other by adding 337, and so (provided he understood the commander's intent) he can send the missiles to the other country. So the probability of a successful substitution attack in this case is 1.

As with computationally secure authentication, the unconditional variety can provide message secrecy or not: it might work like a block cipher, or like a MAC on a plaintext message. Similarly, it can use an arbitrator or not. One might even want multiple arbitrators, so that they don't have to be trusted individually. Schemes may also combine unconditional and computational security. For example, an unconditional code without secrecy could have computationally secure secrecy added by simply enciphering the message and the authenticator using a conventional cipher system.

Authentication is in some sense the dual of coding in that in the latter, given an incorrect message, we want to find the nearest correct one efficiently; in the former, we want finding a correct message to be impossible unless you've seen it already or are authorized to construct it. And just as the designer of an error-correcting code wants the shortest length of code for a given error recovery capability, so the designer of an authentication code wants to minimize the key length required to achieve a given bound on the deception probabilities.

Quite a few details have to be fixed before you have a fully-functioning command and control system. You have to work out ways to build the key control mechanisms into warheads in ways that will resist disarming or dismantling by people without disarming keys. You need mechanisms for generating keys and embedding them in weapons and control devices. You have to think of all the ways an attacker might social-engineer maintenance staff, and what you'll do to forestall this. And there is one element of cryptographic complexity. How do you introduce an element of one-wayness, so that a maintenance man who disarms a bomb to change the battery doesn't end up knowing the universal unlock code? You may need to be able to derive the code to unlock this one specific device from the universal unlock, but not vice versa. What's more, you need serviceable mechanisms for recovery and re-keying in the event that a crisis causes you to authorize some weapons, that thankfully are stood down rather than used. US systems now use public-key cryptography to implement this one-wayness, but you could also use one-way functions. In either case, you will end up with an interesting mix of unconditional and computational security.

One interesting spin-off from authentication research was the GCM mode of operation for block ciphers, described in the chapter on cryptography, which has become the most common mode of operation in modern ciphersuites.

15.4 Shared control schemes

The nuclear command and control business became even more complex with the concern, from the late 1970s, that a Soviet decapitation strike against the US national command authority might leave the arsenal intact but useless. There was also concern that past a certain threshold of readiness, it wasn't sensible to assume that communications between the authority and field commanders could be maintained, because of the likely damage from electromagnetic pulses (and other possible attacks on communications).

The solution was found in another branch of cryptomathematics known as *secret sharing*, whose development it helped to inspire. The idea is that in time of tension a backup control system will be activated in which combinations of office holders or field commanders can jointly allow a weapon to be armed. Otherwise, the problems of maintaining detailed central control of a large number of weapons would likely become insoluble. A particular case of this is in submarine-launched ballistic missiles. These exist to provide a second-strike capability – to take vengeance on a country that has destroyed your country with a first strike. The UK government was concerned that, under the US doctrine, it is possible for the submarine commander to be left unable to arm his weapons if the USA is destroyed, and the President and his lawful successors in office are killed. So the British approach is for arming material to be kept in safes under the control of the boat's officers, along with a letter from the Prime Minister on the circumstances in which weapons are to be used. If the officers agree, then the missiles can be fired.

How can this be generalised? Well, you might just give half of the authentication key to each of two people, but then you need twice the length of key, assuming that the original security parameter must apply even if one of them is suborned. An alternative approach is to give each of them a number and have the two of them add up to the key. This is how keys for automatic teller machines are managed[2]. But this may not be enough in command applications, as one cannot be sure that the people operating the equipment will consent, without discussion or query, to unleash Armageddon. So a more general approach was invented independently by Blakley and Shamir in 1979 [257, 1706]. Their basic idea is illustrated in Figure 15.1.

Suppose the rule Britain wants to enforce is that if the Prime Minister is assassinated, then a weapon can be armed either by any two cabinet ministers, or by any three generals, or by a cabinet minister and two generals. To implement this, let the point C on the z axis be the unlock code that has to be supplied to the weapon. We now draw a line at random through C and give each cabinet minister a random point on the line. Now any two of them together can work out the coordinates of the line and find the point C where it meets the z axis. Similarly, we embed the line in a random plane and give each general a random point on the plane. Now any three generals, or two generals plus a minister, can reconstruct the plane and thence the firing code C.

By generalizing this simple construction to geometries of n dimensions, or to general algebraic structures rather than lines and planes, this technique enables weapons, commanders and options to be linked together with a complexity limited only by the available bandwidth. An introduction to secret sharing can be found in [1832] and a more detailed exposition in [1754]. This inspired the development of threshold signature schemes, as described in Chapter 5, 'Cryptography', and can be used in products that enforce a rule such as 'Any two vice-presidents of the exchange may activate a cold bitcoin wallet'.

In the typical military application, two-out-of-n control is used; n must be large enough that at least two of the keyholders will be ready and able to do the job, despite combat losses. Many details need attention. For example, the death of a commander shouldn't give his deputy both halves of the key, and

[2] Combining keys using addition or exclusive-or turns out to be a bad idea for ATMs as it opens up the system to attacks that I'll discuss later under the rubric of 'API security'. However, in the context of unconditionally-secure authentication codes, addition may be OK.

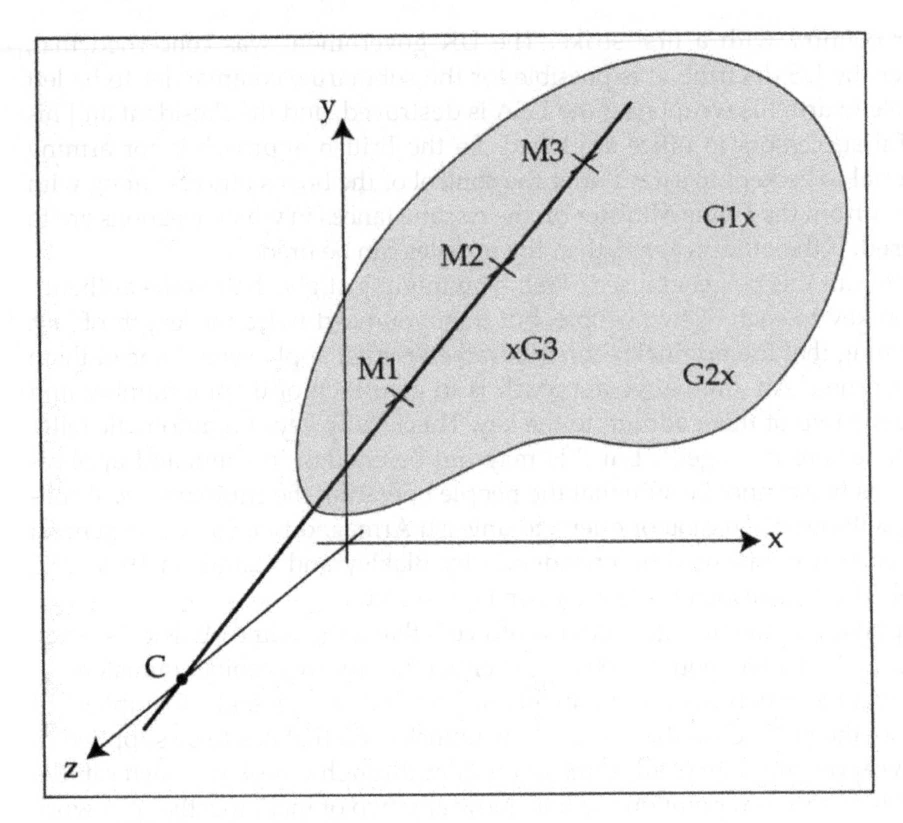

Figure 15.1: Shared control using geometry

there are all sorts of nitty-gritty issues such as who shoots whom when (on the same side). Banking is much the same; it may take two officers to release a large payment, and you need to take care that delegation rules don't allow both keys to fall into the one pair of hands.

In some civilian applications, a number of insiders may conspire to break your system. The classic example is pay-TV where a pirate may buy several dozen subscriber cards and reverse engineer them for their secrets. So the pay-TV operator wants a system that's robust against multiple compromised subscribers. I'll talk about this *traitor tracing* problem more in the chapter on copyright.

15.5 Tamper resistance and PALs

In modern weapons the solenoid safe locks have been superseded by *permissive action links* (PALs), which are used to protect most US nuclear devices. A summary of the published information about PALs can be found in [218]. PAL development started in about 1961, but deployment was slow. Even twenty years later, about half the US nuclear warheads in Europe still used four-digit code locks [3]. As more complex arming options were introduced, the codes increased in length from 4 to 6 and finally to 12 digits. Devices started to have multiple codes, with separate 'enable' and 'authorize' commands and also the ability to change codes in the field (to recover from false alarms).

The PAL system is supplemented by various coded switch systems and operational procedures, and in the case of weapons such as atomic demolition munitions, which are not big and complex enough for the PAL to be made inaccessible, the weapon is also stored in tamper-sensing containers called *prescribed action protective system* (PAPS). Other mechanisms used to prevent accidental detonation include the deliberate weakening of critical parts of the detonator system, so that they will fail if exposed to certain abnormal environments.

Whatever combination of systems is used, there are penalty mechanisms to deny a thief the ability to obtain a nuclear yield from a stolen weapon. These mechanisms vary from one weapon type to another but include gas bottles to deform the pit and hydride the plutonium in it, shaped charges to destroy components such as neutron generators and the tritium boost, and asymmetric detonation that results in plutonium dispersal rather than yield. This self-destruct procedure will render them permanently inoperative, without yield, if enemy capture is threatened. It is always a priority to destroy the code. It is assumed that a renegade government prepared to deploy "terrorists" to steal a shipment of bombs would be prepared to sacrifice some of the bombs (and some technical personnel) to obtain a single serviceable weapon.

To perform authorized maintenance, the tamper protection must be disabled, and this requires a separate unlock code. The devices that hold the various unlock codes – for servicing and firing – are themselves protected in similar ways to the weapons.

The assurance target is summarized in [1828]:

> *It is currently believed that even someone who gained possession of such a weapon, had a set of drawings, and enjoyed the technical capability of one of the national laboratories would be unable to successfully cause a detonation without knowing the code.*

Meeting such an ambitious goal requires a very substantial effort. There are several examples of the level of care needed:

- after tests showed that 1 mm chip fragments survived the protective detonation of a control device carried aboard airborne command posts, the software was rewritten so that all key

[3]Bruce Blair says that Strategic Air Command resisted the new doctrine and kept Minuteman authorization codes at '00000000' until 1977, lying to a succession of Presidents and Defense Secretaries [256]. Others say that this was just the use control code.

material was stored as two separate components, which were kept at addresses more than 1 mm apart on the chip surface;

- the 'football', the command device carried around behind the President, is as thick as it is because of fear that shaped charges might be used to disable its protective mechanisms. Shaped charges can generate a plasma jet with a velocity of 8000m/s, which could in theory be used to disable tamper sensing circuitry. So some distance may be needed to give the alarm circuit enough time to zeroize the code memory.

This care must extend to many details of implementation and operation. The weapons testing process includes not just independent verification and validation, but hostile 'black hat' penetration attempts by competing agencies. Even then, all practical measures are taken to prevent access by possible opponents. The devices (both munition and control) are defended in depth by armed forces; there are frequent zero-notice challenge inspections; and staff may be made to re-sit the relevant examinations at any time of the day or night. Finally, at all levels below the President, there is dual control as in banking; no unaccompanied person may approach a nuclear weapon.

I discuss tamper resistance in much more detail in its own chapter, as it's widely used in applications such as bank cards and phones. However, tamper resistance, secret sharing and one-time authenticators aren't the only technologies to have benefited from the nuclear industry's interest. There are more subtle system lessons too.

15.6 Treaty verification

A variety of verification systems are used to monitor compliance with nuclear nonproliferation treaties. For example, the IAEA and the US Nuclear Regulatory Commission (NRC) monitor fissile materials in licensed civilian power reactors and other facilities.

An interesting example comes from the tamper-resistant seismic sensor devices designed to monitor the Comprehensive Test Ban Treaty [1751]. The goal in this application was to have sufficiently sensitive sensors in each signatory's test sites that any violation of the treaty (such as by testing too large a device) can be detected with high probability. The tamper sensing here is fairly straightforward: the seismic sensors are fitted in a steel tube and inserted into a drill hole that is backfilled with concrete. The whole assembly is so solid that the seismometers themselves can be relied upon to detect tampering events with a fairly high probability. This physical protection is reinforced by random challenge inspections.

The authentication process becomes somewhat more complex because of the assumption of pervasive deceit. Because there is no third party trusted by both sides, and because the quantity of seismic data being transmitted is of the order of 10^8 bits per day, a digital signature scheme (RSA) was used instead of one-time authentication tags. But this is only part of the answer. One party might always disavow a signed message by saying that the official responsible for generating it had defected, and so the signature was forged. So the keys had to be generated within the seismic package itself once it had been sealed by both sides. Also, if one side builds the equipment, the other will suspect it of having hidden functionality. Several protocols were proposed of the *cut and choose* variety, in which one party would produce several devices of which the other party would dismantle a sample for inspection. A number of these issues have since resurfaced in electronic commerce. (Many system designers since could have saved themselves a lot of grief if they'd read the account of these treaty monitoring systems by Sandia's former crypto chief Gus Simmons in [1751].)

15.7 What goes wrong

Despite the huge amounts of money invested in developing high-tech protection mechanisms, nuclear control and safety systems appear to suffer from just the same kind of design bugs, implementation blunders and careless operations as any others.

15.7.1 Nuclear accidents

The main risk may be just an accident. We've already had two nuclear accidents rated at 7[4] on the International Nuclear and Radiological Event Scale, namely those at Chernobyl and Fukushima, and quite a few less serious ones. Britain's main waste reprocessing plant at Sellafield, which stores 160 tonnes of plutonium – the world's largest stockpile – has been plagued with scandals for decades. Waste documentation has been forged; radiation leaks have been covered up; workers altered entry passes so they could bring their cars into restricted areas; there have been reports of sabotage; and the nuclear police force only manage to clear up 10–20% of cases of theft or criminal damage [1133]. The task of cleaning it all up could take a century and cost over $100bn; meanwhile it has to be guarded [1870]. There are significant and pervasive problems elsewhere in the defence nuclear enterprise, including at the nuclear weapons factories and the submarine bases, ranging from dilapidated facilities, incompetent contractors, poor morale, project delays, spiralling costs, and 20 old submarines awaiting disposal – nine of which still contain fuel [1563]. The situation in Russia appears to be even worse. A survey

[4]The definition is 'Major release of radioactive material with widespread health and environmental effects requiring implementation of planned and extended countermeasures'

of nuclear safekeeping described how dilapidated their security mechanisms became following the collapse of the USSR, with fissile materials occasionally appearing on the black market and whistleblowers being prosecuted [955].

15.7.2 Interaction with cyberwar

A second, and growing, concern is that nuclear safety might be undermined by the possibility of cyber-attack. Even if the command and control channel itself has been made invulnerable to manipulation using the cryptographic and tamper-resistance mechanisms described here, it might be subject to service-denial attack; and in 2018, the Trump administration changed doctrine to allow the first use of nuclear weapons in response to such an attack. Another vital question is whether commanders can believe what they see on their screens. In 1983, a new Soviet early-warning system malfunctioned at a time of international tension, reporting that the USA had launched five Minuteman missiles at Russia. The commander in the Moscow bunker, lieutenant-colonel Stanislav Petrov, decided it was probably a false alarm, as launching only five missiles would have been illogical, and held fire until satellites confirmed it was indeed a false alarm. That was probably the closest that the world got to accidental nuclear war (there had also been a US false alarm three years previously). How would such a system failure play out today, now that we have much more complex systems, with AI creeping into the command chain in all sorts of places without our even realising it? And never mind failures – what about attacks on our intelligence, surveillance and reconnaissance (ISR) capability, including the satellites that watch for missile launches, detect nuclear detonations and pass on orders?

A 2018 report from the Nuclear Threat Initiative describes the concerns in some detail [1837]. It's not enough to protect the weapons themselves, as a cyber-attack on the planning, early-warning or communications systems could also have catastrophic consequences. The main risk is of use because of false warnings or miscalculation; there are also external dependencies, from networks to the electricity grid. Attacks on conventional command-and-control networks could be seen as strategic threats if these networks are also used for nuclear forces. Such issues have been acknowledged in the Trump administration's 2018 Nuclear Posture Review. Technical cybersecurity measures alone are unlikely to be enough, as there are significant soft issues, such as whether key people can be undermined by making them look incompetent.

There may also be fears that an opponent's capability at cyber operations may render one's own deterrent less effective or overconfidence that one's own capability might make attacking a rival less risky. I was personally told by a senior official in the signals intelligence agency of a non-NATO nuclear power that in a confrontation they 'had the drop on' a regional rival. Regardless of whether this was actually true or not, such sentiments, when expressed in the corridors of power, can undermine deterrence and make nuclear conflict more likely. More recently, the US National Security Commission on Artificial Intelligence warned in 2019 that nuclear deterrence could be undermined if AI-equipped systems succeed in tracking and targeting previously invulnerable military assets [1417].

And it's not just the declared nuclear states. There are currently 22 countries with fissile materials in sufficient quantity and quality to be useful in weapons, and 44 with civil nuclear programs (45 once the UAE goes critical). Of these countries, 15 don't even have cybersecurity laws; energy companies generally won't invest in cybersecurity unless their regulators tell them to, while some companies (and countries) have no real capability.

This has all been made highly salient to governments by the US/Israeli attack on Iran's uranium enrichment capability at Natanz using the Stuxnet virus. In 2009 their output of enriched uranium fell by 30%, and in 2010 the virus came to light. It had infected the centrifuge controllers, causing them to spin up and then slow down in such a way as to destroy about 1000 of Iran's fleet of 4,700. US government involvement was finally admitted in 2012 [1031].

15.7.3 Technical failures

There have also been a number of interesting high-tech security failures. One example is a possible attack discovered on a nuclear arms reduction treaty, which led to the development of a new branch of cryptomathematics – the study of subliminal channels – and is relevant to later work on copyright marking and steganography.

The story is told in [1757]. During the Carter administration, the USA proposed a deal with the USSR under which each side would cooperate with the other to verify the number of intercontinental ballistic missiles. In order to protect US Minuteman missiles against a Soviet first strike, it was proposed that 100 missiles be moved randomly around a field of 1000 silos by giant trucks, which were designed so that observers couldn't determine whether they were moving a missile or not. So the Soviets would have had to destroy all 1,000 silos to make a successful first strike, which was thought impractical.

But how could the USA assure the Soviets that there were at most 100 missiles in the silo field, but without letting them find out where? The proposed solution was that the silos would have a Russian sensor package that would detect the presence or absence of a missile, sign this single bit of information, and send it via a US monitoring facility to Moscow. The catch was that only this single bit of information could be sent; if the Russians could smuggle any more information into the message, they could locate the full silos – as it would take only ten bits of address information to specify a single silo in the field. (There were many other security requirements to prevent either side cheating, or falsely accusing the other of cheating: for more details, see [1756].)

To see how subliminal channels work, consider the Digital Signature Algorithm described in the chapter on cryptography. The system-wide values are a prime number p, a prime number q dividing $p - 1$, and a generator g of a subgroup of F_p^* of order q. The signature on the message M is r, s where $r = (g^k \pmod p) \pmod q$, and k is a random session key. The mapping from k to r is fairly random, so a signer who wishes to hide ten bits of information in this signature for covert transmission to an accomplice can first agree a convention about how the bits will be hidden (such as 'bits 72–81') and second, try out one value of k after another until the resulting value r has the desired substring.

This could have caused a disastrous failure of the security protocol. But in the end, the "missile shell game", as it had become known in the press, wasn't used. Eventually the medium range ballistic missile treaty (MRBM) used statistical methods. The Russians could say 'we'd like to look at the following 20 silos' and they would be uncapped for their satellites to take a look. With the end of the Cold War, inspections have become much more intimate with inspection flights in manned aircraft, with observers from both sides, rather than satellites.

Still, the discovery of subliminal channels was significant. Ways in which they might be abused include putting HIV status, or the fact of a felony conviction, into a digital passport or identity card. Where this is unacceptable, the remedy is to use a completely deterministic signature scheme such as RSA instead of one that uses a random session key like DSA.

15.8 Secrecy or openness?

Finally, the nuclear industry provides a nice case history of secrecy. In the 1930s, physicists from many countries had freely shared the scientific ideas that led to the bomb, but after the 'atomic spies' (Fuchs, the Rosenbergs and others) had leaked the designs of the Hiroshima and Nagasaki devices to the Soviet Union, things swung to the other extreme. The USA adopted a policy that atomic knowledge was born classified. That meant that if you were within US jurisdiction and had an idea relevant to nuclear weapons, you had to keep it secret regardless of whether you held a security clearance or even worked in the nuclear industry. This was in tension with the Constitution. Things have greatly relaxed since then, as the protection issues were thought through in detail.

"We've a database in New Mexico that records the physical and chemical properties of plutonium at very high temperatures and pressures", a former head of US nuclear security once told me. "At what level should I classify that? Who's going to steal it, and will it do them any good? The Russians, they've got that data for themselves. The Israelis can figure it out. Gaddafi? What the hell will he do with it?"

As issues like this got worked through, a lot of the technology has been declassified and published, at least in outline. Starting from early publication at scientific conferences of results on authentication codes and subliminal channels in the early 1980s, the benefits of public design review have been found to outweigh the advantage to an opponent of knowing broadly the system in use.

Many implementation details are kept secret, including information that could facilitate sabotage, such as which of a facility's fifty buildings contains the alarm response force. Yet the big picture is fairly open, with command and control technologies on offer at times to other states, including potentially hostile ones. The benefits of reducing the likelihood of an accidental war were considered to outweigh the possible benefits of secrecy. Post-9/11, we'd rather have decent command and control systems in Pakistan than risk having one of their weapons used against us by some mid-level officer suffering from an attack of religious zealotry. This is a modern reincarnation of Kerckhoffs' doctrine, the nineteenth-century maxim that the security of a system must depend on its key, not on its design remaining obscure [1044].

The nuclear lessons could be learned more widely. Post-9/11, a number of governments talked up the possibility of terrorists using biological weapons, and imposed controls on research and teaching in bacteriology, virology, toxicology and indeed medicine. My faculty colleagues in these disciplines were deeply unimpressed. "You just shouldn't worry about anthrax," one of the UK's top virologists told me. "The real nasties are the things Mother Nature dreams up like HIV and SARS and bird flu. If these policies mean that there aren't any capable public health people in Khartoum next time a virus comes down the Nile, we'll be sorry." Sadly, the events of 2020 confirm this wisdom.

15.9 Summary

The control of nuclear weapons, and subsidiary activities from protecting the integrity of the national command system through physical security of nuclear facilities to monitoring international arms control treaties, has made a huge contribution to the development of security technology.

The rational decision that weapons and fissile material had to be protected almost regardless of the cost drove the development of a lot of mathematics and science that has found application elsewhere. The particular examples we've looked at in this chapter are authentication codes, shared control schemes and subliminal channels. There are other examples scattered through the rest of this book, from alarms to iris biometrics and from tamper-resistant electronic devices to seals.

Yet even though we can protect the command and control channel that authorises the use of nuclear weapons, that is by no means the whole story. If cyber-attacks can undermine confidence in deterrence by targeting a country's intelligence, surveillance and reconnaissance capabilities, they can still be seriously destabilising. At a time of nuclear brinkmanship, each side could think they have an advantage because of an undeclared cyber capability. And given that US presidents have used nuclear threats about a dozen times since 1945 (Cuba, Vietnam and Iraq being merely the more obvious examples), we might expect several such crises each generation.

Research problems

The research problem I set at the end of this chapter in the first edition in 2001 was 'Find interesting applications for technologies developed in this area, such as authentication codes.' By the second edition the Galois Counter mode of operation of block ciphers had been standardised, and by now it's pervasive. What else might there be?

The most serious research problem now might be the interaction between silicon and plutonium. The US/Israeli attack on Iran's uranium enrichment program in 2009–10 gave the world an example of cyber-attacks being used in the nuclear world. In what ways might the threat of such attacks increase the risk of nuclear conflict, and what can we do about it? Given that we can't harden everything the way we harden the command and control channel, what can we do to maintain trust in the supporting systems such as surveillance, or at least ensure that they degrade in ways that don't lead to lethal false alarms?

Further reading

As my own direct experience of nuclear weapons is rather dated – consisting of working in the 1970s on the avionics of nuclear-capable aircraft – this chapter has been assembled from published sources and conversations with insiders. One of the best sources of public information on nuclear weapons is the Federation of American Scientists, who discuss everything from bomb design to the rationale for the declassification of many nuclear arms technologies [672]. Declassification issues are also discussed in [2047], and the publicly available material on PALs has been assembled by Steve Bellovin [218].

Gus Simmons was the guy at Sandia who designed the football; he was a pioneer of authentication codes, shared control schemes and subliminal channels.

His book [1753] remains the best reference for most of the technical material discussed in this chapter. A more concise introduction to both authentication and secret sharing can be found in Doug Stinson's textbook [1832].

Control failures in nuclear installations are documented in many places. The problems with Russian installations are discussed in [955]; US nuclear safety is overseen by the Nuclear Regulatory Commission [1457]; and shortcomings with UK installations are documented in the quarterly reports posted by the Health and Safety Executive [876]. The best and most up-to-date survey of problems can be found in the Public Accounts Committee's 2018 report *'Ministry of Defence nuclear programme'* [1563]. As for the interaction 'between silicon and plutonium', there's a recent report on the subject from Chatham House [27].

CHAPTER

16

Security Printing and Seals

A seal is only as good as the man in whose briefcase it's carried.

– KAREN SPÄRCK JONES

You can't make something secure if you don't know how to break it.

– MARC WEBER TOBIAS

16.1 Introduction

Many computer systems rely to some extent on secure printing, packaging and seals to guarantee important aspects of their protection.

- Most security products can be defeated if the opponent can get at them before you install them. Seals, and tamper-evident packaging generally, can help with *trusted distribution*, that is, assuring the user that the product hasn't been tampered with since leaving the factory.
- We saw how monitoring systems, such as utility meters and tachographs, often use seals to make it harder for users to tamper with input. No matter how sophisticated the cryptography, a defeat for the seals can be a defeat for the system.
- I also discussed how the contactless cards used in most building entry control systems can be cloned, thanks to the attacks on Mifare and some of its successors. If you're scrutinising the ID of an engineer before you let him into your hosting centre, it can be a good idea to eyeball the ID as well as reading it electronically. Even with electronic ID cards, the security printing can still matter.
- In general, it may be a more realistic goal to make credentials *tamper evident* rather than tamper proof: if someone dismantles their smartcard and gets the keys out, they should not be able to reassemble it into something that will pass close examination. Security printing can help here.

Quite apart from these direct applications of printing and sealing technology, the ease with which modern color scanners and printers can be used to make passable forgeries has opened up another front. Since the late 1990s, banknote printers have been promoting digital protection techniques [254]. These include watermarks that stop compliant scanners and printers being used for forgery, and invisible copyright marks that can enable forgeries to be detected in vending machines [831]. Meanwhile, vendors of color copiers and printers embed forensic tracking codes in their printed output that contain the machine serial number, date and time [621]. So the digital world and the world of 'funny inks' have been growing closer.

16.2 History

Seals have a long and interesting history. In the chapter on banking systems, I discussed how bookkeeping systems had their origin in the clay tablets, or bullae, used by neolithic warehouse keepers in Mesopotamia as receipts for produce. Over 5000 years ago, the bulla system was adapted to resolve disputes by having the warehouse keeper bake the bulla in a clay envelope with his mark on it.

Seals were used to authenticate documents in the ancient Mediterranean and China. They were used in medieval Europe as a means of social control before paper came along; a carter would be given a lead seal at one tollbooth and hand it in at the next, while pilgrims would get lead tokens from shrines to prove that they had gone on pilgrimage (indeed, the young Gutenberg got his first break in business by inventing a way of embedding slivers of mirror in lead seals to prevent forgery and protect church revenues) [826]. Even after handwritten signatures had taken over as the principal authentication mechanism for letters, seals lingered as a secondary mechanism. Until the nineteenth century, letters were not placed in envelopes, but folded over several times and sealed using hot wax and a signet ring.

Seals are still the preferred authentication mechanism for important documents in China, Japan and Korea. Elsewhere, traces of their former importance survive in the company seals and notaries' seals affixed to important documents, and the national seals that some countries' heads of state apply to archival copies of legislation, and in the demand in some European countries for electronic signatures that comply with the EU's eIDAS standards.

However, by the middle of the 20th century, their use with documents had become less important in the West than their use to authenticate packaging. The move from loose goods to packaged goods, and the growing importance of brands, created not just the potential for greater quality control but also the vulnerability that bad people might tamper with products. The USA suffered an epidemic of tampering incidents, particularly of soft drinks and medical products, leading to a peak of 235 reported cases in 1993 [1030]. This helped push many manufacturers towards making products tamper-evident.

The ease with which software can be copied, and consumer resistance to technical copy-protection mechanisms from the mid-1980s, led software companies to rely increasingly on packaging to deter counterfeiters. That was just part of a much larger market in preventing the forgery of high value branded goods ranging from perfume and cigarettes through aircraft spares to pharmaceuticals. In short, huge amounts of money have poured into seals and other kinds of secure packaging.

Unfortunately, most seals are still fairly easy to defeat. The typical seal consists of a substrate with security printing, which is then glued or tied round the object being sealed. So we must first look at security printing. If the whole seal can be forged easily, then no amount of glue or string is going to help.

16.3 Security printing

The introduction of paper money into Europe by Napoleon in the early 1800s, and of other valuable documents such as bearer securities and passports, kicked off a battle between security printers and counterfeiters that exhibits many of the characteristics of a coevolution of predators and prey. Photography (1839) helped the attackers, then color printing and steel etching (1850s) the defenders. In recent years, the color copier and the cheap scanner have been countered by holograms and other optically variable devices. Sometimes the same people were involved on both sides, as when a government's intelligence services try to forge another government's passports – or even its currency, as both sides did in World War Two.

On occasion, the banknote designers succumb to the Titanic Effect, of believing too much in the latest technology, and place too much faith in some particular trick. An example comes from the forgery of British banknotes in the 1990s. These notes have a *window thread* – a metal strip through the paper that is about 1 mm wide and comes to the paper surface every 8 mm. So when you look at the note in reflected light, it appears to have a dotted metallic line running across it, but when you hold it up and view it through transmitted light, the metal strip is dark and solid. Duplicating this was thought to be hard. Yet a criminal gang came up with a beautiful hack. They used a cheap hot stamping process to lay down a metal strip on the surface of the paper, and then printed a pattern of solid bars over it using white ink to leave the expected metal pattern visible. They were found at their trial to have forged tens of millions of pounds' worth of notes over a period of several years [697]. British banknotes are now being migrated to plastic, a process pioneered in Australia.

16.3.1 Threat model

As always we have to evaluate a protection technology in the context of a model of the threats. Broadly speaking, the threat can be from a major organization (such as one country trying to forge another's banknotes), from a medium-sized organization (whether a criminal gang forging several million dollars a month or a distributor forging labels on vintage wines), to amateurs using equipment they have at home or in the office.

In the banknote business, the big growth area in the last years of the twentieth century was amateur forgery. Knowledge had spread in the printing trade of how to manufacture high-quality forgeries of many banknotes, which one might have thought would increase the level of professional forgery. But the spread of high-quality color scanners and printers has put temptation in the way of many people who would never have dreamed of getting into forgery in the days when it required messy wet inks. Amateurs used to be thought a minor nuisance, but since the late 1990s they have accounted for most of the forgeries detected in the USA. Amateur forgers are hard to combat as there are many of them; they mostly work on such a small scale that their product takes a long time to come to the attention of authority; and they are less likely to have criminal records. The notes they produce are often not good enough to pass a bank teller, but are uttered in places such as dark and noisy nightclubs.

The industry distinguishes three different levels of inspection of a forged banknote or document [1939]:

1. a *primary* inspection is one performed by an untrained inexperienced person, such as a member of the public or a new cashier at a store. Often the primary inspector has no motivation, or even a negative motivation. If he gets a banknote that feels slightly dodgy, he may try to pass it on without looking at it closely enough to have to decide between becoming an accomplice or going to the hassle of reporting it;
2. a *secondary* inspection is one performed in the field by a competent and motivated person, such as an experienced bank teller in the case of banknotes or a trained manufacturer's inspector in the case of product labels. This person may have some special equipment such as an ultraviolet lamp, a pen with a chemical reagent, or even a scanner and a PC. However the equipment will be limited in both cost and bulk, and will be completely understood by serious counterfeiters;
3. a *tertiary* inspection is one performed at the laboratory of the manufacturer or the note issuing bank. The experts who designed the security printing (and perhaps even the underlying industrial processes) will be on hand, with substantial equipment and support.

The state of the security printing art can be summarised as follows. Getting a counterfeit past a primary inspection is usually easy, while getting it past tertiary inspection is usually impossible if the product and the inspection process have been competently designed. So secondary inspection is the battleground – except in a few applications such as banknote printing where attention is now being paid to the primary level, where the limitations are skill and, above all, motivation. The main limits on what sort of counterfeits can be detected by the secondary inspector in the field have to do with the bulk and the cost of the equipment needed.

16.3.2 Security printing techniques

Traditional security documents utilize a number of printing processes, including:

- *intaglio*, a process where an engraved pattern is used to press the ink on to the paper with great force, leaving a raised ink impression with high definition. This is often used for scroll work on paper banknotes and passports;
- *letterpress* in which the ink is rolled on raised type that is then pressed on to the page, leaving a depression. The numbers on paper banknotes are usually printed this way, often with numbers of different sizes and using different inks to prevent off-the-shelf numbering equipment being used;
- special printing presses, called *Simultan presses*, which transfer all the inks, for both front and back, to the paper simultaneously. The printing on front and back can therefore be accurately aligned; patterns can be printed partly on the front and partly on the back so that they match up perfectly when the note is held up to the light (*see-through register*). Reproducing this is believed to be hard on cheap color printing equipment. Simultan presses also have special ducting to make ink colors vary along the line (*rainbowing*);
- rubber stamps that are used to endorse documents, or to seal photographs to them;
- embossing and laminates that are also used to seal photographs, and on bank cards to push up the cost of forgery. Embossing can be physical, or use laser engraving techniques to burn a photo into an ID card;
- *watermarks* are an example of putting protection features in the paper. They are more translucent areas inserted into the paper by varying its thickness when it is manufactured. Many other special materials, such as fluorescent threads, are used for similar purposes.

More modern techniques include:

- Modern plastic notes, first introduced in Australia, allow a variety of features to be embedded in a see-through window;
- optically variable inks that change color from green to gold depending on the viewing angle;
- inks with magnetic, photochromic or thermochromic properties;
- printing features visible only with special equipment, such as the microprinting on US bills, which requires a magnifying glass to see, and printing in ultraviolet, infrared or magnetic inks (the last of these being used in the black printing on US bills);
- metal threads and foils, from simple iridescent features to foil color copying through to foils with optically variable effects such as *holograms* and *kinegrams*. Holograms are typically produced optically, and look like a solid object behind the film, while kinegrams are produced by computer and may show a number of startlingly different views from slightly different angles;
- *screen traps* such as details too faint to scan properly, and *alias band structures*, which contain detail at the correct size to form interference effects with the dot separation of common scanners and copiers;
- *digital copyright marks*, which may vary from images hidden by microprinting their Fourier transforms directly, to proprietary spread spectrum signals that will be recognized by a color copier, scanner or printer and cause it to stop. The best-known is the yellow pattern of stars, in the shape of the Southern Cross, that is embedded in the design of many banknotes and that stops compliant scanners and printers from processing it;
- unique stock, such as the Sandia proposal of paper with optical fibers randomly spread through it during manufacture so that each sheet has a characteristic pattern that can be digitally signed and printed on the document using a barcode [1750].

For the design of the US $100 bill, see [1369]; and for a study of counterfeit banknotes, with an analysis of which features provide what evidence, see [1940]. In general, banknotes' genuineness cannot readily be confirmed by the inspection of a single security feature. Many of the older techniques, and some of the newer, can be mimicked in ways that will pass primary inspection. The tactile effects of intaglio and letterpress printing wear off, so crumpling and dirtying a forged note is standard practice, and skilled banknote forgers mimic watermarks with faint grey printing (though watermarks remain surprisingly effective against amateurs). Holograms and kinegrams can be vulnerable to people using electrochemical techniques to make mechanical copies; if not, then villains may originate their own master copies from scratch.

When a hologram of Shakespeare was introduced on UK bank cards in 1988, I visited the factory as the representative of a bank and was told proudly that, as the industry had demanded a second source of supply, they had given a spare set of plates to a large security printing firm – and this competitor of theirs had been quite unable to manufacture acceptable foils. (The Shakespeare foil was the first commercially used diffraction hologram to be in full color and to move as the viewing angle changed.) Surely a device that couldn't be forged, even by a major security printing company with access to genuine printing plates, must give total protection? But when I visited Singapore seven years later, I bought a similar (but larger) hologram of Shakespeare in the flea market. This was clearly a boast by the maker that he could forge UK bank cards if he wished to. By then, a police expert estimated that there were over 100 forgers in China with the skill to produce passable forgeries [1442].

When polymer notes were introduced into the UK, in 2016 for the £5 note and 2017 for the £10, we were told they were unforgeable. But by 2018 we were being told how to spot forgeries. One victim reported 'I looked closer and saw the Big Ben was missing and part of the serial number and the Queen's face were coming off. When I compared it to a genuine note I already had, I also saw the silver strips were green' [1614]. Later that year, enterprising villains were passing off plastic £20 notes, even though the official £20 note wasn't due to launch till 2020.

So the technology constantly moves on, and it is imprudent to rely on a single protection technology. Even if one defense is completely defeated (such as if it becomes easy to make mechanical copies of metal foils), you have at least one completely different trick to fall back on (such as optically variable ink).

But designing a security document is much harder than this. There are complex trade-offs between protection, aesthetics and robustness, and the business focus can also change. For many years, banknote designers aimed at preventing forgeries passing secondary or tertiary inspection rather than on the more common primary inspection. Much time was spent hand-wringing about the difficulty of training people to examine documents properly, and not enough attention was paid to studying how the typical user of a product such as a banknote actually decides subconsciously whether it's acceptable. In other words, the technological focus had usurped the business focus.

The lessons drawn so far are [1939]:

- security features should convey a message relevant to the product. So it's better to use iridescent ink to print the denomination of a banknote than some obscure feature nobody looks at;
- security features should obviously belong where they are, so they become embedded in the user's cognitive model of the object;

- their effects should be obvious, distinct and intelligible;
- they should not have existing competitors that can provide a basis for imitations;
- they should be standardized.

This work deserves much wider attention, as the banknote community is one of the few subdisciplines of our trade to have devoted a lot of thought to security usability. (We've seen over and over again that one of the main failings of security products is that usability gets ignored.) When it comes to documents other than banknotes, such as passports, there are also issues relating to the political environment of the country and the mores of the society in which they will be used [1295].

Usability also matters during second-line inspection, but here the issues are more subtle and focus on the process that the inspector has to follow to distinguish genuine from fake.

With banknotes, the theory is that you design a note with perhaps twenty features that are not advertised to the public. A number of features are made known to secondary inspectors such as bank staff. In due course these become known to the forgers. As time goes on, more and more features are revealed. Eventually, when they are all exposed, the note is retired from circulation and replaced. This process may become harder if the emphasis switches from manual to automatic verification. A thief who steals a vending machine, dismantles it, and reads out the software, gains a complete and accurate description of the checks currently in use. Having once spent several weeks or months doing this, he will find it much easier the second time round. So when the central bank tells manufacturers the secret polynomial for the second-level digital watermark (or whatever), and this gets fielded, he can steal another machine and get the new data within days. So failures can be more sudden and complete than with manual systems, and the cycle of feature life, death and rebirth could turn more quickly than in the past. Another possibility, of course, is that developed countries move entirely to card payments, the path of rich early adopters such as Sweden and Finland.

With product packaging, the typical business model is that samples of forgeries are found and taken to the laboratory, where the scientists find some way in which they are different – perhaps the hologram is not quite right. Kits are then produced for field inspectors to go out and track down the source. If these kits are bulky and expensive, fewer of them can be fielded. If there are many different forgery detection devices from different companies, then it is hard to persuade customs officers to use any of them. Ideas such as printing individual microscopic ultraviolet bar codes on plastic product shrink-wrap often fail because of the cost of the microscope, laptop and online connection needed to do the verification. As with banknotes, you can get a much more robust system with multiple features, but this pushes the cost and bulk of the reading device up still further.

With financial instruments, and especially checks, alteration is a much bigger problem than copying or forgery from scratch. In numerous scams, villains got genuine checks from businesses by tricks such as by prepaying deposits or making reservations in cash and then cancelling the order. The victim duly sends out a check, which is altered to a much larger amount, often using readily available domestic solvents. The standard countermeasure is background printing using inks that discolor and run in the presence of solvents. But the protection isn't complete because of tricks for removing laser printer toner (and even simple things like typewriter correction ribbon). One enterprising villain even presented his victims with pens that had been specially selected to have easily removable ink [8].

Check fraud used to be many times greater in value than card fraud, and also difficult to deal with because of the huge volume of checks processed daily. This makes scrutiny impossible except for very large amounts. In the Far East, where people use a personal *chop* or signature stamp to sign checks, low-cost automatic verification is possible [931]. However, with handwritten signatures, automated verification with acceptable error rates is still beyond the state of the art (I'll discuss it in section 17.2). The future for businesses is to move payments to bank transfer; the early adopter here, Germany, largely suppressed check frauds by the early 2000s. SEPA payments are now making electronic payments much quicker and cheaper than check payments in the Euro zone.

Of course, document alterations aren't just a banking problem. Most fake travel documents are altered rather than counterfeited from scratch. Names are changed, photographs are replaced, or pages are added and removed. For this reason, developed countries have largely moved to chip-based passports; visitors from countries that don't have electronic passports yet may have to get visas that contain chips or that point to an online database storing the traveler's biometric.

16.4 Packaging and seals

Supply-chain security involves problems of packaging and seals. A seal, in the definition of the Los Alamos vulnerability assessment team, is 'a tamper-indicating device designed to leave non-erasable, unambiguous evidence of unauthorized entry or tampering.'

Most seals work by applying some kind of security printing to a substrate to get a tag and then fixing this tag to the material to be protected. Applications range from pharmaceutical products through cargo containers to ballot boxes. Other products follow the same general philosophy but using different materials; at the bottom end we find plastic straps that are easy to tighten but hard to loosen without cutting, while at the top there are optical fibres that loop around the protected object and are actively monitored for stretching by an attached laser tag.

16.4.1 Substrate properties

Some systems add random variability to the substrate material. We mentioned the trick of loading paper with optical fibers; there are also *watermark magnetics* in which a random high-coercivity signal is embedded in a card strip that can subsequently be read and written using standard low-coercivity equipment without the unique random pattern being disturbed. These were used in bank cards in Sweden, telephone cards in Korea, and entry control cards in some of the buildings in my university.

A similar idea was used in arms control during the Cold War. Many weapons and materials have surfaces that are unique; see for example Figure 16.1 for the surface of paper. Other material surfaces can be made unique; for example, a patch can be eroded on a tank gun barrel using a small explosive charge. The pattern is measured using laser speckle techniques, and either recorded in a log or attached to the device as a machine-readable digital signature [1753]. This makes it easy to identify capital equipment such as heavy artillery where identifying each gun barrel is enough to prevent either side from cheating. You can even authenticate a piece of paper using laser speckle to encode its surface roughness into a code that is robust to creasing, drying, scribbling and even scorching [333]. The problem there is finding an application where you can justify using expensive scanners at each end of the process.

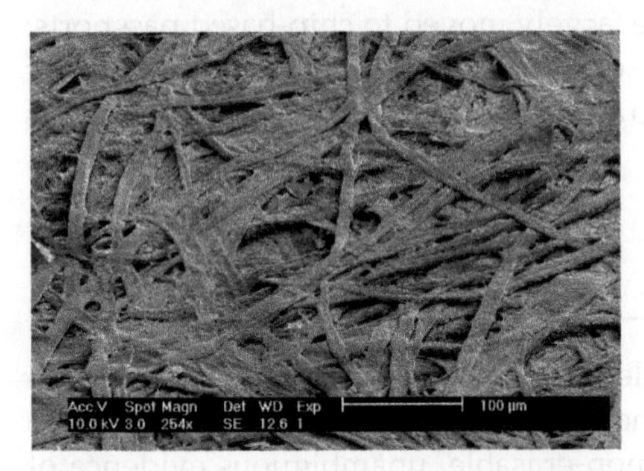

Figure 16.1: Scanning electron micrograph of paper (courtesy Ingenia Technology Ltd)

16.4.2 The problems of glue

Although a tag's uniqueness can be a side effect of its manufacture, most seals still work by fixing a security-printed tag on to the target object. This raises the question of how the beautiful piece of iridescent printed art can be attached to a crude physical object in a way that is very hard to remove.

In the particular case of tamper-evident packaging, the attachment is part of an industrial process; it could be a pressurized container with a pop-up button or a break-off lid. The usual answer is to use a glue that is stronger than the seal substrate itself, so that the seal will tear or at least deform noticeably if pulled away. This is the case with foil seals under drink caps and blister packs of pills.

However, in most products, the implementation is rather poor. Many seals are vulnerable to direct removal using only hand tools and a little patience. Take a sharp knife and experiment with the next few letters that arrive in self-seal envelopes. Many of these envelopes are supposed to tear, rather than peel open; the flap may have a few vertical slots cut into it for this purpose. But this hoped-for tamper evidence usually assumes that people will open them by pulling the envelope flap back from the body. By raising the flap slightly and working the knife back and forth, it is often possible to cut the glue without damaging the flap and so open the envelope without leaving suspicious marks. (Some glues should be softened first using a hairdryer, or made more fragile by freezing.) Or open the envelope at the other end, where the glue is not designed to be mildly tamper-evident. Either way you'll probably get an envelope that looks slightly crumpled on careful examination. If it's noticeable, iron out the crumples. This attack usually works against a primary inspection, probably fails a tertiary inspection, and may well pass secondary inspection: crumples happen in the post anyway.

Many of the seals on the market can be defeated using similarly simple tricks. A notorious example is the *vignette*, or motorway toll sticker, used in Switzerland and Austria. There, you have to pay a road toll for which you get a sticker that goes on your windscreen to certify that you have paid your dues for a year, or a shorter period if you rent a car. If you tear a sticker off your windscreen to use it on another car, some of the ink comes with it while some sticks to the windscreen. So people get dust on the glue before sticking it on, by brushing the sticker back and forth on the dashboard. This has now been made an offence, and you're fined if you get caught [1470].

16.4.3 PIN mailers

Many banks now print customer PINs on special print stocks. In the old days, PIN mailers used multipart stationery and impact printers; you got the PIN by ripping the envelope open and pulling out a slip on which the PIN had been impressed. The move from impact to laser technology led to a number of companies inventing letter stationery from which you pull a tab to read the PIN. The idea is that just as a seal can't be moved without leaving visible evidence, with this stationery the secret can't be extracted without leaving visible evidence. A typical mechanism is to have a patch on the paper that's printed with an obscuring pattern and that also has an adhesive film over it, on which the PIN is printed. Behind the film is a die-cut tab in the paper that can be pulled away with the obscuring background, making the PIN visible.

My students Mike Bond, Steven Murdoch and Jolyon Clulow had some fun finding vulnerabilities with successive versions of these products. The early products could be read by holding them up to the light, so that the light glanced off the surface at about 10 degrees; the opaque toner showed up clearly against the shiny adhesive film. The next attack was to scan the printing into Photoshop and filter out the dense black of the toner from the grey of the underlying printing. Another was thermal transfer; put a blank sheet of paper on top of the mailer and run an iron over it. Yet another was chemical transfer using blotting paper and organic solvents. This work was reported to the banking industry in 2004, and finally published in 2005 [285]. The banks have now issued test standards for mailers. Yet to this day we keep getting mailers on which the PIN is easy to read.

This is an example of a system that doesn't work, and yet persists. If a crook knows I'm getting a new bank card, and can steal from my mail, he'll just take both the card and the PIN. It's hard to think of any real attacks that the 'tamper-evident' PIN mailer prevents. It might occasionally prevent a family member learning a PIN by accident; equally, there might be an occasional customer who reads the PIN without tearing the tab, withdraws a lot of money, then claims he didn't do it, in which case the bank will probably just say "so sue us" and disown its own mailer. But the threats are vestigial compared with the amount that's being spent on all this fancy stationery. The driver for such behaviour is probably compliance; it's too much bother to rethink card scheme rules, audit procedures and insurance inspections that evolved in an age of impact printers.

16.5 Systemic vulnerabilities

We turn now from the specific threats against particular printing tricks and glues to the system level threats, of which there are many.

At our local swimming pool, congestion is managed by issuing swimmers with wristbands during busy periods. A different color is issued every twenty minutes or so, and from time to time all people with bands of a certain color are asked to leave. The band is made of waxed paper. At one end it has a printed pattern and serial number on one side, and glue on the other; the paper is cross-cut with the result that it is completely destroyed if you tear it off carelessly; see Figure 16.2. (It's similar to the luggage seals used at some airports.)

Figure 16.2: A wristband seal from our local swimming pool

The simplest attack is via the supplier's website, where boxes of 100 wristbands cost about $8. If you don't want to spend money, you can use each band once, then ease it off gently by pulling it alternately from different directions, giving the result shown in the photo. The printing is crumpled, though intact; the damage isn't such as to be visible by a poolside attendant, and could in fact have been caused by careless application. The point is that the damage done to the seal by fixing it twice, carefully, is not easily distinguishable from the effects of a naive user fixing it once. An even more powerful attack is to not remove the backing tape from the seal at all, but use a safety pin, or your own glue, to fix it.

Despite this, the wristband seal is perfectly fit for purpose. There is little incentive to cheat: the Olympic hopefuls who swim lengths for two hours at a stretch use the pool when it's not congested. They also buy a season ticket, so they can go out at any time to get a fresh wristband. But it illustrates many of the things that can go wrong. The customer is the enemy; it's the customer who applies the seal; the effects of seal re-use are indistinguishable from those of random failure; unused seals can be bought in the marketplace; counterfeit seals could also be manufactured at little cost; and effective inspection is infeasible. (And yet this swimming-pool seal is still harder to defeat than many sealing products sold for high-value industrial applications.)

16.5.1 Peculiarities of the threat model

In military systems the opponent is the disloyal soldier, or the other side's special forces trying to sabotage your equipment. In nuclear monitoring systems it can be the host government trying to divert fissile materials from a licensed civilian reactor. With voting machines, most attacks come from election officials.

Some of the most difficult sealing tasks arise where it's the enemy who will apply the seal. A typical business application is where a company subcontracts the manufacture of some of its products and is afraid that the contractor will produce more of the goods than agreed. Overproduction is the main source by value of counterfeit goods worldwide; the perpetrators have access to the authorized manufacturing process and raw materials, and grey markets provide natural distribution channels. Even detecting such frauds – let alone proving them to a court – can be hard.

A typical solution for high-value goods such as cosmetics may involve sourcing packaging materials from a number of different companies, whose identities are kept secret from the firm operating the final assembly plant. Some of these materials may have serial numbers embedded in various ways (such as by laser engraving in bottle glass, or printing on cellophane using inks visible only under UV light). There may be an online service whereby the manufacturer's field agents can verify the serial numbers of samples purchased randomly in shops, or there might be a digital signature on the packaging that links all the various serial numbers together for offline checking.

There are limits on what seals can achieve in isolation. Sometimes the brand owner himself is the villain, as when a vineyard falsely labels as vintage an extra thousand cases of wine that were actually made from bought-in blended grapes. So bottles of South African wine all carry a government regulated seal with a unique serial number; here, the seal doesn't prove the fraud but makes it harder for a dishonest vintner to evade the other controls such as inspection and audit. Sealing mechanisms usually must be designed with the complementary control processes in mind.

Inspection can be harder than one would think. The distributor who has bought counterfeit goods on the grey market, believing them to be genuine, may set out to deceive the inspectors without any criminal intent. Where grey markets are an issue, the products bought from 'Fred' will be pushed out rapidly to the customers, ensuring that the inspectors see only authorized products in his stockroom. Also, the distributor may be completely in the dark; it could be his staff who are peddling the counterfeits. A well-known scam is for airline staff to buy counterfeit perfumes, watches and the like when they visit countries with unregulated markets, and sell them in-flight to customers [1144]. The stocks in the airline's warehouses (and in the duty-free carts after the planes land) will all be completely genuine. So it is usually essential to have agents go out and make sample purchases, and the sealing mechanisms must support this.

16.5.2 Anti-gundecking measures

Whether the seal adheres properly to the object being sealed may also depend on the honesty and diligence of low-level staff. I mentioned in section 14.3.2.2 how in truck speed limiter systems, the gearbox sensor is secured using a piece of wire that the calibrating garage seals with a lead disc that is crimped in place with special tongs. The defeat is to bribe the garage mechanic to wrap the wire the wrong way, so that when the sensor is unscrewed from the gearbox the wire will loosen, instead of tightening and breaking the seal. This is simpler than going to amateur sculptor classes so that you can take a cast of the seal and forge a pair of sealing tongs out of bronze.

The people who apply seals can be careless as well as corrupt. Some airports apply tape seals to checked bags after X-raying them using a machine near the check-in queue. On about half of the occasions this has been done to my baggage, the tape has been poorly fixed; either it didn't cross the fastener between the suitcase and the lid, or it came off at one end, or the case had several compartments big enough to hold a bomb but only one of their fasteners was sealed. But airport security is mostly theatre anyway.

Much of the interesting research in seals has focused on usability. One huge problem is checking whether staff who're supposed to inspect seals have actually done so. *Gundecking* is a naval term used to refer to people who pretend to have done their duty, but were actually down on the gun deck having a smoke. So if your task is to inspect the seals on thousands of shipping containers arriving at a port, how do you ensure that your staff actually look at each one?

One approach is to include in each container seal a small processor with a cryptographic keystream generator that produces a new number every minute or so. Then the inspector's task is to visit all the inbound containers and record the numbers they display. If a tampering event is detected, the device erases its key, and can generate no more numbers. If your inspector doesn't bring back a valid seal code from one of the containers, you know something's wrong, whether with it or with him. Such seals are also known as 'anti-evidence' seals: the idea is that you store information that a device hasn't been tampered with, and destroy it when tampering occurs, leaving nothing for an adversary to counterfeit.

Carelessness and corruption interact. If enough of the staff applying or verifying a seal are careless, then if I bribe one of them the resulting defect doesn't of itself prove dishonesty.

16.5.3 The effect of random failure

There are similar effects when seals can break for completely innocent reasons. For example, speed-limiter seals often break when a truck engine is steam-cleaned, so a driver will not be prosecuted for tampering if a broken seal is all the evidence the traffic policeman can find. (Truck drivers know this.)

After opening a too-well-sealed envelope, a spy can close it again with a sticker saying 'Opened by customs' or 'Burst in transit – sealed by the Post Office'. He could even just tape it shut and scrawl 'delivered to wrong address try again' on the front.

The consequences of such failures and attacks have to be thought through carefully. If the protection goal is to prevent large-scale forgery of a product, occasional breakages may not matter; but if it is to support prosecutions, spontaneous seal failure can be a serious problem. In extreme cases, placing too much trust in the robustness of a seal might lead to a miscarriage of justice and undermine the sealing product's evidential (and thus commercial) value.

My example of this comes from the curfew tags which I described in detail in section 14.4. There, the tag vendors made grandiose marketing claims about the tamper-resistance of their products, but refused to make samples available for testing by the defence when challenged in court. Terrorism suspects were released when their control orders could no longer be justified, and eventually the tag firms lost their contracts for criminal misconduct: they had billed the Ministry of Justice for tagging people who were dead or in jail, and ended up paying multimillion-pound fines, as did their auditors [194].

16.5.4 Materials control

Another common vulnerability is that supplies of sealing materials are uncontrolled. Corporate seals are a nice example. In the UK, these typically consist of two metal embossing plates that are inserted into special pliers and were used to crimp important documents. Several suppliers manufacture the plates, and a lawyer who has ordered hundreds of them tells me that no check was ever made. Although it might be slightly risky to order a seal for 'Microsoft Corporation', it should be easy to have a seal made for almost any less well known target: all you have to do is write a letter that looks like it came from a law firm. The real purpose of sealing is not to prevent forgery but to enable law firms to charge extra for documents that have to have seals attached.

A more serious example is the reliance of the pharmaceutical industry on blister packs, sometimes supplemented with holograms and color-shifting inks. All these technologies are freely available to anyone who cares to buy them, and they are not particularly expensive either. Or consider the plastic envelopes used by some courier companies, which are designed to stretch and tear when opened. So long as you can walk in off the street and pick up virgin envelopes at the depot, they are unlikely to deter anyone who invests some time and thought in planning an attack; he can substitute the packaging either before, or after, a parcel's trip through the courier's network.

It is also an 'urban myth' that the police and security services cannot open envelopes tracelessly if the flaps have been reinforced with sticky tape that has been burnished down by rubbing it with a thumbnail (I recently received some paperwork from a bank that had been sealed in just this way). This is not entirely believable – even if no police lab has invented a magic solvent for sellotape glue, the nineteenth century Tsarist police already used forked sticks to wind up letters inside a sealed envelope so that they could be pulled out, read, and then put back [1003]; letter writers there and indeed all over Europe used *letterlocking* – complex systems of folds, slits and seals that they hoped would make tampering evident [368].

Even if sellotape were guaranteed to leave a visible mark on an envelope, one would have to assume that the police's envelope-steaming department have no stock of comparable envelopes, and that the recipient would be observant enough to spot a forged envelope. Given the ease with which an envelope with a company logo can be scanned and then duplicated using a cheap color printer, these assumptions are fairly ambitious. In any case, the arrival of desktop color printers has caused a lot of organizations to stop using preprinted stationery. This makes the forger's job much easier.

16.5.5 Not protecting the right things

Where a value token encodes value in two different ways, you may expect criminals to exploit any difference, or indeed to create one. Credit cards became vulnerable to forgery in the late 1980s as banks introduced authorization terminals that read the magnetic strip, while the imprinting machines used by most merchants to print out vouchers for the customer to sign used the embossing, and most merchants banked the signed vouchers as if they were checks. Crooks who changed the mag strip but not the embossing defeated the system. There are also attacks involving partial alterations. For example, credit cards used to have holograms, but as they covered only the last four digits, the attacker could always change the other twelve. When the algorithm the bank used to generate credit card numbers was known, this involved only flattening, reprinting and re-embossing the rest of the card, which could be done with cheap equipment. Such attacks are now obsolete, as the old Addressograph draft capture machines are no longer used. In any case, all the hologram said was 'This was once a valid card' and most banks have now discontinued it.

Finally, food and drug producers often use shrink-wrap or blister packaging, which if well designed can be moderately difficult for amateurs to forge well enough to withstand close inspection. However when selecting protective measures you have to be very clear about the threat model – is it counterfeiting, alteration, duplication, simulation, diversion, dilution, substitution or something else [1527]? If the threat model is a psychotic with a syringe full of poison, then simple blister or shrink-wrap packaging is not quite enough. What's really needed is a tamper sensing membrane, which will react visibly and irreversibly to even a tiny penetration. (Such membranes exist but are still too expensive for consumer products. I'll discuss them in the chapter on tamper resistance.)

16.5.6 The cost and nature of inspection

There are many stories in the industry of villains replacing the hologram on a bank card with something else – say a rabbit instead of a dove – whereupon the response of shopkeepers is just to say: 'Oh, look, they changed the hologram!' This isn't a criticism of holograms but is a much deeper issue of applied psychology and public education. It's a worry for bankers when new notes are being introduced – the few weeks during which everyone is getting familiar with the new notes can be a bonanza for forgers.

A related problem is the huge variety of passports, driver's licenses, letterheads, corporate seals, and variations in packaging. Without samples of genuine articles for comparison, inspection is more or less limited to the primary level and so forgery is easy. Even though bank clerks have books with pictures of foreign banknotes, and immigration officers similarly have pictures of foreign passports, there is often only sketchy information on security features. Crooks frequently get genuine passports and ID cards by corrupt means (and not just from less developed countries). Oh, and the absence of real physical samples means that the tactile aspects cannot be properly examined.

A somewhat shocking experiment was performed by Sonia Trujillo at the 7th Security Seals Symposium in Santa Barbara in March 2006. She tampered with nine out of thirty different food and drug products, using only low-tech attacks, and invited 71 tamper-detection experts to tell them apart. Each subject was asked to pick exactly three out of ten products that they thought had been tampered. The experts did no better than random, even though most of them took significantly longer than the four seconds per product that they were directed to. If even the experts can't detect tampering, even when they're told it has been happening, what chance does the average consumer have?

So the seal that can be checked by the public or by staff with minimal training, and without access to an online database, remains an ideal rather than a reality. The main purpose of tamper-evident packaging is to reassure the customer; secondary purposes include minimising product returns, due diligence and reducing the size of jury awards. Deterring incompetent tamperers might just about be in there somewhere.

Firms that take forgery seriously, like luxury goods makers, have adopted many of the techniques pioneered by banknote printers. But high-value product packages are harder to protect than banknotes. Familiarity is important: people get a 'feel' for things they handle frequently such as local money, but are much less likely to notice something wrong with a package they see only rarely – such as a fancy cosmetic or an expensive bottle of wine. For this reason, much of the work in protecting products that contain electronics has shifted to online registration mechanisms. Some products have acquired electronics for this purpose, while others that already have electronics are acquiring wifi chips.

One of the possibilities is to enlist the public as inspectors, not so much of the packaging, but of unique serial numbers. Instead of having these numbers hidden from view in RFID chips, vendors can print them on product labels, and people who're concerned about whether they got a genuine product could call in to verify. This may often get the incentives aligned better, but can be harder than it looks. For example, when Microsoft first shipped its antispyware beta, I installed it on a family PC – whose copy of Windows was immediately denounced as evil. Now that PC was bought at a regular store, and I simply did not need the hassle of explaining this. I particularly did not like their initial negotiating position, namely that I should send them more money. Eventually they gave us another copy of Windows. But we didn't buy another Windows machine after that.

16.6 Evaluation methodology

This discussion suggests a systematic way to evaluate a seal product for a given application. Rather than just asking, "Can you remove the seal in ways other than the obvious one?" we need to follow it from design and field test through manufacture, application, use, checking, destruction and finally retirement from service. Here are some of the questions that should be asked:

- If a seal is forged, who's supposed to spot it? If it's the public, then how often will they see genuine seals? Has the vendor done proper experiments to establish the likely false accept and false reject rates? If it's your inspectors in the field, how much will their equipment and training cost? And how well are these inspectors – public or professional – motivated to find and report defects?

- Has anybody who really knows what they're doing tried hard to defeat the system? And what's a defeat anyway – tampering, forgery, alteration, erosion of evidential value or a 'PR' attack on your commercial credibility?
- What is the reputation of the team that designed it – did they have a history of successfully defeating opponents' products?
- How long has it been in the field, and how likely is it that progress will make a defeat significantly easier?
- Who else can buy, forge or steal the sealing materials?
- Will the person who applies the seal ever be careless or corrupt, and if so, how will you cope?
- Will the seal protect the right part (or enough) of the product?
- What are the quality issues? What about the effects of dirt, oil, noise, vibration, cleaning, and manufacturing defects? Will the product have to survive outdoor weather, petrol splashes, being carried next to the skin or being dropped in a glass of beer? Or is it supposed to respond visibly if such a thing happens? How often will there be random seal failures and what effect will they have?
- If you're going to end up in court, are there experts other than your own (or the vendor's) on whom the other side can rely? If the answer is no, then is this a good thing or a bad thing? Why should the jury believe you, the system's inventor, rather than the sweet little old lady in the dock? Will the judge let her off on fair trial grounds – because rebutting your technical claims would be an impossible burden of proof for her to discharge? And what happens if you sell your company to someone who sells it to a crook?
- Once the product is used, how will the seals be disposed of – are you bothered if someone recovers a few old seals from the trash?

Remember that defeating seals is about fooling people, not beating hardware. So think hard whether the people who apply and check the seals will perform their tasks faithfully and effectively; analyze motive, opportunity, skills, audit and accountability. Be particularly cautious where the seal is applied by the enemy (as in the case of contract manufacture) or by someone open to corruption (such as the garage eager to win the truck company's business). Finally, think through the likely consequences of seal failure and inspection error rates not just from the point of view of the client company and its opponents, but also from the points of view of innocent system users and of legal evidence.

This whole-life-cycle assurance process is just a microcosm of the assurance process you need to apply to systems in general. I'll discuss that in more detail in Part 3.

16.7 Summary

Most commercially available sealing products are relatively easy to defeat, and this is particularly true when seal inspection is performed casually by people who are untrained, unmotivated or both (as is often the case). Sealing has to be evaluated over the whole lifetime of the seal from manufacture through materials control, application, verification and eventual destruction; hostile testing is highly advisable in critical applications. Seals often depend on security printing, about which broadly similar comments may be made.

Research problems

This is an area in which a lot of ideas have come and gone without making much impact. No doubt lots of fancy new technologies will be touted for product safety and counterfeit detection, from nanoparticles through ferrofluids to DNA; but so long as the markets are broken, and people ignore the system-level issues, what good will they do? Do any of them have novel properties that enable us to tackle the hard problems of primary inspectability?

Automatic inspection systems may be one way forward. One example is in cold chain assurance. Some products such as vaccines need to be kept at less than 4^0C, and already ship with loggers in the container or pallet that monitor the temperature and allow failures to be identified. There are also telltale paper strips that display a different bar code, on the basis of a chemical reaction, if the threshold is exceeded. Regulated industries with safety-critical products, such as pharma, might be a good place to try out new ideas.

A much harder problem is how to help the consumer in less regulated industries. Most of the counterfeits and poisoned products are introduced at the retail level, which used to be highly dispersed. But tech is fixing that, and perhaps the solution doesn't lie in packaging but in regulatory action against large retailers like Amazon. Its marketplace and fulfilment services are reportedly becoming the most concerning distribution channel for many counterfeit products, as well as products that have been declared unsafe by government agencies, are deceptively labeled or are banned by regulators, including children's toys containing dangerous levels of lead [591]. This is looking like becoming one of the big regulatory battles between governments and Big Tech. Perhaps it's an inevitable effect of scale; if everybody's on Facebook then that includes all the world's creeps, bullies and extremists, and if all the world's merchants use Amazon to ship their products then something similar can be expected. Eventually, I suspect, Amazon will be compelled to hire tens of thousands of product safety and compliance inspectors, just as Facebook has been compelled to hire tens of thousands of content moderators. But laws usually lag technology by fifteen years or so, and in the meantime secure printing and sealing will continue – albeit with a continuing move to online product registration.

Further reading

The definitive textbook on security printing is van Renesse [1939], which goes into not just the technical tricks such as holograms and kinegrams, but how they work in a variety of applications from banknote printing through passports to packaging. This is very important background reading.

The essential writing on seals can be found in the many publications by Roger Johnston's seal vulnerability assessment team (e.g., [991]).

The history of counterfeiting is fascinating. From Independence to the Civil War, Americans used banknotes issued by private banks rather than by the government, and counterfeiting was pervasive. Banks could act against local forgers, but by about 1800 there had arisen a network of engravers, papermakers, printers, wholesalers, retailers and passers, with safe havens in the badlands on the border between Vermont and Canada; neither the US nor the Canadian government wanted to take ownership of the problem [1313].

More recently there's been the Supernote controversy. In the late 2000s, a few million dollars a year worth of counterfeit US currency turned up that was perfect in almost every respect: it was printed with the right presses, on the right paper, and tracked the small changes accurately – except in that it did not use the right magnetic and infrared security features. The US government accused North Korea of forgery and used this to impose sanctions; others suggested that the notes were more likely produced by the CIA in order to trace cash money flows. These notes turned up in only tiny quantities, and only in the hands of people of interest to the CIA such as North Korean diplomats and central Asian warlords. They had been carefully designed to pass all inspections other than the counting machines used by money-centre banks, which would prevent them getting into circulation at scale; and the volumes that turned up were at least one order of magnitude less than a forger would have produced, and would have needed to produce in order to pay for the equipment [622].

CHAPTER

17

Biometrics

And the Gileadites took the passages of Jordan before the Ephraimites: and it was so, that when those Ephraimites which were escaped said, Let me go over; that the men of Gilead said unto him, Art thou an Ephraimite? If he said, Nay; Then said they unto him, Say now Shibboleth: and he said Sibboleth: for he could not frame to pronounce it right. Then they took him, and slew him at the passages of the Jordan: and there fell at that time of the Ephraimites forty and two thousand.

– JUDGES 12:5–6

17.1 Introduction

The above quotation may be the first recorded military use of a security protocol in which the authentication relies on a property of the human being – in this case his accent. (There had been less formal uses before this, as when Isaac tried to identify Esau by his bodily hair but got deceived by Jacob, or indeed when people recognized each other by their faces – which I'll discuss later.)

Biometrics identify people by measuring some aspect of individual anatomy or physiology (such as your hand geometry or fingerprint), some deeply ingrained skill or behavior (such as your handwritten signature), or some combination of the two (such as your voice).

In the 21st century the market has really taken off, with three major changes since the second edition of this book in 2008.

1. There are many large-scale programs by states to identify citizens using biometrics, of which the biggest single programme may be India's Aadhaar project, which has recorded the iris codes and fingerprints of over a billion people. International travel has been speeded up by international standard biometric travel documents, the US-VISIT program that fingerprints visitors to the USA, and face-recognition passport booths at the borders of the European Union.
2. There has been a massive improvement in face recognition technology, brought about by the revolution in deep neural networks since 2012.

This has made passport booths steadily faster and more reliable, made mass surveillance easier, and led to concerns about privacy and human rights – particularly given its deployment in China.

3. Automatic fingerprint readers are no longer a niche product for bank vaults and welfare offices, but are deployed on hundreds of millions of mobile phones. Now that people keep their entire lives in their phones, or on web services for which their phones have the credentials, they are relied on to stop a lost or stolen phone turning from annoyance into disaster.

The biometric systems market has taken off like a rocket, growing from $50m in 1998 to over $1.5bn in 2005 [999] and $33bn in 2019 [2040].

I'll start off by describing the biometric techniques that predate the computer age – handwritten signatures, facial features and fingerprints – then describe how they have been automated, and then go on to explore some more modern techniques.

17.2 Handwritten signatures

Handwritten signatures had been used in classical China, but carved personal seals came to be considered higher status; they are still used for serious transactions in China, Japan and Korea. Europe was the other way round: seals had been used in medieval times, but as writing spread after the Renaissance, people increasingly just wrote their names to assent to documents. Over time, the signature became the standard. Every day, billions of dollars' worth of contracts are still concluded by handwritten signatures; how these will be replaced by electronic mechanisms remains a live policy and technology issue.

Handwritten signatures are a weak authentication mechanism in that they're easy to forge, but they worked well enough for centuries because of the context of their use. An important factor is the liability for forgery. Britain's Bills of Exchange Act 1882 provides that a forged handwritten signature is null and void, and this has survived in the laws of many countries that were part of the British Empire at the time, such as Canada and Australia. In these countries, manuscript signatures are better for the customer, as the bank carries most of the risk, but PINs and electronic tokens can be better for the bank – and so have largely replaced them. Europe also went for electronic signatures following lobbying by the French and German smartcard industries. In the USA, the law makes banks liable for the electronic systems they deploy, so US banks generally stuck with chip and signature cards rather than going for chip and PIN. Courier companies also collect handwritten signatures as proof of receipt as they're the only thing that works for all recipients. So the verification of handwritten signatures continues to matter.

Now the probability that a forged signature will be accepted as genuine mainly depends on the amount of care taken when examining it. Many bank card transactions in stores are accepted without even a glance at the specimen signature on the card – so much so that many Americans don't even bother to sign their credit cards[1]. But even diligent signature checking doesn't reduce the risk to zero. An experiment showed that 105 professional document examiners, who each did 144 pairwise comparisons, misattributed 6.5% of documents. Meanwhile, a control group of 34 untrained people of the same educational level got it wrong 38.3% of the time [1012], and the nonprofessionals' performance couldn't be improved by giving them monetary incentives [1013]. Errors made by professionals are a subject of continuing discussion in the industry but are thought to reflect the examiner's preconceptions [199] and context [587]. As the participants in these tests were given reasonable handwriting samples rather than just a signature, it seems fair to assume that the results for verifying signatures on checks or delivery receipts would be even worse.

In most of the English-speaking world, most documents do not need to be authenticated by special measures. The essence of a signature is the intent of the signer, so an illiterate's 'X' on a document is perfectly valid. A plaintext name at the bottom of an email message therefore has full legal force [2044], except where there are specific regulations to the contrary.

The exceptions come from conventions and special rules that vary from one country to another. For example, to buy a house in England using money borrowed from a bank of which you're not an established customer, the procedure is to go to a lawyer's office with a document such as a passport, sign the property transfer and loan contracts, and get them countersigned by the lawyer. The requirement for government-issued photo ID was originally imposed by the lender's insurers, and became a 'know-your-customer' (KYC) provision of anti-money-laundering regulations; the requirement that a real-estate purchase be in writing was imposed centuries ago in order to collect tax on property transactions.

Other types of document (such as expert testimony) may have to be notarized in particular ways. Many of the anomalies go back to the nineteenth century, and the invention of the typewriter. Some countries require that machine written contracts be initialled on each page, while some don't; clashes in conventions still cause serious problems.

It's rare for signatures to be disputed in court cases, as the context mostly makes it clear who did what. So this weak biometric mechanism actually works fairly well in practice – the real problems come from a thicket of procedural

[1]Indeed, it's not in the cardholder's interest to give a specimen signature to a thief – if the thief has to make a random signature on a voucher or signature tablet, it's easier for the real cardholder to disown it. Signing the card is in the bank's interest but not the customer's.

rules that vary by country and by application. Lawmakers have made various attempts to sort out the mess, and impose uniform rules for electronic documents.

In section 26.5.2 I discuss the Electronic Signatures in Global and National Commerce ('ESIGN') Act of 2000, which legitimised contracts made by clicking on buttons in web pages, and the much more heavyweight European eIDAS Regulation (910/2014), which requires all Member States to accept electronic signatures made using approved products. This was originally designed to help the smartcard industry, but as many people and firms need to sign things occasionally and don't want to buy special hardware, the latest regulation now allows online signature service firms to generate signatures in their cloud service that are considered legally binding, even though the security of the customer's phone or laptop may leave a lot to be desired. Signature services typically generate an electronic document with a machine-written signature that we're supposed to pretend was handwritten; there's also an electronic signature whose verification by the service provider we're supposed to trust.

A separate topic is the automatic recognition of handwritten signatures, such as on checks. This became one of the earliest topics of serious biometric research in the 1980s by firms selling check-processing equipment to banks. In early systems, an operator was presented with the check image and the customer's reference signature on a screen, and took the decision. To save money, this was only done for amounts over a few thousand dollars; smaller checks just went straight through, and it was up to the account holder to dispute them. From the early 1990s there were signature tablets that record not just the shape of the curve but also its dynamics (the velocity of the hand, where the pen was lifted off the paper, and so on). These are used by delivery drivers to collect receipts for goods and also for credit card transactions. Since the early 1990s some products have been able to compare captured signatures against specimens enrolled previously.

Like alarms, most biometric systems have a tradeoff between false-accept and false-reject rates, often referred to in the banking industry as the *fraud* and *insult* rates and in the biometric literature as *type 1* and *type 2* errors. Many systems can be tuned to favor one over the other. The tradeoff is known as the *receiver operating characteristic*, a term first used by radar operators; if you turn up the gain on your radar set too high, you can't see the target for clutter, while if it's too low, you can't see it at all. So the radar operator has to select a suitable point on the curve. The *equal error rate* is when the system is tuned so that the probabilities of false-accept and false-reject are equal. For tablet-based signature recognition systems, the equal error rate is at best 1%; for purely optical comparison, it's several percent. This isn't fatal in an operation such as a check processing centre, as the automated comparison is used as a filter to select checks for human scrutiny. However, it's a show-stopper in a retail store. If one transaction in a hundred fails, the aggravation to customers would be unacceptable.

So back in the 1990s, UK banks set a target for biometrics of a fraud rate of 1% and an insult rate of 0.01%, which was beyond the state of the art in signature verification and fingerprint scanning – as indeed it still is [719]. In fact, even the 1% equal error rate for tablets was achieved by excluding *goats* – a term used by the biometric community for people whose templates don't classify well. Vendors typically exclude people without eyes from statistics on iris scanners and manual workers with worn fingertips from fingerprint statistics. This can lead to deceptive performance claims and hide issues of social exclusion.

In general, biometric mechanisms tend to be more robust in attended operation where they assist a guard rather than replacing them.

17.3 Face recognition

Recognizing people by their facial features is the oldest identification mechanism of all, going back at least to our early primate ancestors. Biologists believe that a significant part of our cognitive function evolved to provide efficient ways of recognizing other people's facial features and expressions [1607]. For example, we are very good at detecting whether another person is looking at us or not.

The human ability to recognize faces is an important baseline for many reasons, of which one is the reliance placed on photo ID. Drivers' licenses, passports and other kinds of identity card are not only used to control entry to computer rooms directly, but also to bootstrap most other systems. The issue of a password, or a smartcard, for access to a system is often the end point of a process that was started by that person presenting photo ID when applying for a job or opening a bank account.

So how good are we at identifying strangers by photo ID, as opposed to identifying friends in the flesh?

The simple answer is that we're not. Psychologists at the University of Westminster conducted a fascinating experiment with the help of a supermarket chain and a bank [1037]. They recruited 44 students and issued each of them four credit cards each with a different photograph on it:

- one of the photos was a 'good, good' one. It was genuine and recent;
- the second was a 'bad, good one'. It was genuine but a bit old, and the student now had different clothing, hairstyle or whatever. In other words, it was typical of the photo that most people have on their photo ID;
- the third was a 'good, bad one'. From a pile of a hundred or so random photographs of different people, investigators chose the one that most looked like the subject. In other words, it was typical of the match that criminals could get with a stack of stolen cards;

- the fourth was a 'bad, bad' one. It was chosen at random except that it had the same sex and race as the subject. In other words, it was typical of the match that really lazy, careless criminals would get.

The experiment was conducted in a supermarket after normal business hours, but with experienced cashiers on duty, and aware of the purpose of the experiment. Each student made several trips past the checkout using different cards. It transpired that none of the checkout staff could tell the difference between 'good, bad' photos and 'bad, good' photos. In fact, some of them could not even tell the difference between 'good, good' and 'bad, bad'. Now this experiment was done under optimum conditions, with experienced staff, plenty of time, and no threat of embarrassment or violence if a card was declined. Real-life performance can be expected to be worse. In fact, many stores do not pass on to their checkout staff the reward offered by credit card companies for capturing stolen cards. So even the most basic incentive is absent. Yet at least two banks that had experimented with photos on credit cards had experienced a substantial drop in fraud [155]. The conclusion was that the benefit to be had from photo ID at the time was basically its deterrent effect [689].

So maybe people won't use their facial-recognition skills effectively in identification contexts, or maybe the information we use to identify people in social contexts is stored differently in our brains from information we get by looking at a single photo. Recognising passing strangers is in any case much harder than recognising people you know. It's reckoned that misidentifications are the main cause of false imprisonment, with 20% of witnesses making mistakes in identity parades [2046] – not as bad as the near-random outcomes when comparing faces with photos, but still not good.

Since photo-ID doesn't work well with human guards, many people have tried to automate the process. Attempts go back to the nineteenth century, when Francis Galton devised a series of spring-loaded "mechanical selectors" for facial measurements [738]. But automated face recognition actually subsumes a number of separate problems, in most of which we don't have the luxury of taking careful 3-d measurements of the subject. Automated passport control booths may be the easiest: the subject looks straight at the camera under controlled lighting conditions, and their face is compared with the one on file. In forensics, we may be trying to establish whether a suspect's face fits a low-quality recording on a security video. The hardest of all is surveillance, where we may want to scan a moving crowd of people at an airport and try to pick out anyone who is on a list of thousands of known suspects.

Early applications of face recognition were often just security theater. In 1998, the London borough of Newham placed video cameras prominently in the high street and ran a PR campaign about how their new computer system constantly scanned the faces in the crowd for several hundred known local criminals. They got a significant reduction in reported burglary, shoplifting and street crime, but later admitted that they only had 20 or 25 villains' faces on the system, and it never recognised any of them [1284]. After 9/11, a number of places tried this. In Tampa, Florida, a similar system was abandoned in 2003 after an ACLU freedom-of-information request discovered that it had recognised no villains [1600]. Face recognition was also tried at Boston's Logan airport; passengers passing through security screening were observed and matched. The system was found to be impractical, with no useful balance between non-matches and false alarms [317]. The Illinois Department of Motor Vehicles adopted face recognition in 2003 to detect people applying for extra drivers' licenses in false names [663]. In such an application, it may be worthwhile to try to detect wrongdoers even if you only catch a quarter of them.

As a baseline, tests done in 2001 by the UK National Physical Laboratory (NPL) of a number of biometric technologies found that face recognition was almost the worst; its single-attempt equal-error rate was almost 10% [1219]. A UK Passport Office trial in 2005, which was a better approximation to field conditions, found it recognised only 69% of users (and only 48% of disabled participants) [1924]. Face recognition was still adopted by the ICAO as a standard for passports and ID cards with embedded chips; iris codes and fingerprints were optional extras. The typical installation has a row of booths relaying both live and file photos to a human operator who is alerted to suspected mismatches.

However, since the neural network revolution began in 2012, the performance of facial recognition has improved remarkably, with error rates falling by an order of magnitude. Getting through a passport booth is often a lot quicker now than in 2010, and you don't always have to take off your glasses. But what about data? The best are probably from NIST's Face Recognition Vendor Test (FRVT) that tests products against millions of law-enforcement mugshots, prison webcam images and wild photos for 1:1 verification, one-to-many identification, face morph detection and face image quality assessment. According to the 2018 report, massive gains in accuracy were achieved in 2013–2018, and largely due to the adoption of convolutional neural networks (CNNs). The most accurate algorithms will find matching entries when present, in galleries containing 12 million individuals, with a miss rate approaching 0.1%; but in about 5% of images the identification succeeds with low confidence and human adjudication is necessary. A few algorithms correctly match side-view photos to galleries of frontal photos; such *pose invariance* has been a long-sought milestone in face recognition research.

There is measurable racial bias. US-developed algorithms had significantly higher rates of false positives in one-to-one matching of Asians, African Americans and American Indians, while for one-to-many matching the highest false positive rates were for African American females. Algorithms developed in Asia did equally well for Asians and whites. The remaining errors are in large part due to long-run ageing, facial injury, poor image quality or a second face in shot, such as a face printed on a T-shirt [829].

A 2018 study pitted face recognition algorithms against professional forensic face examiners, untrained superrecognisers (highly talented individuals), and a control group of random people. It found that both types of human expert were significantly better than the control group, and that four deep CNNs, developed between 2015 and 2017, identified faces within the range of human experts, with the most recent scoring above the median of the forensic experts. However, the best results could be achieved if algorithms and human experts worked together [1525].

As for what's under the hood, a 2019 survey paper by Guodong Guo and Na Zhang explores the use of deep learning in face image analysis and recognition, and discusses how systems handle variations in pose, age, illumination and expression [835]. Most systems are CNNs but with a range of adaptations, e.g., with multiple CNNs looking for different types of feature in different regions of two candidate faces simultaneously and an autoencoder looking for common latent features to give pose robustness; there are then various kinds of fusion, aggregation and filtering. There may also be mechanisms to correct for makeup and for facial expressions. There are complex tradeoffs in algorithm choice, with the best algorithm in ROC terms taking time linear in the gallery size, meaning half a second to match against 10m other faces; accuracy can double if three or more mugshots are available, as this enables the CNN to allow for ageing. But blur in video images is still a significant problem, as is matching still images to video and visible-light images to near-infrared.

The face-recognition revolution is continuing apace, with NIST reporting that some algorithms doubled in accuracy during 2018 alone. It is also becoming controversial. Do we face a dystopian future where every other lamp post has a 5G base station with an embedded CCTV that recognises all passers-by? All of a sudden, CCTV changes from a tool for crime-scene forensics to one that does real-time person recognition and tracking. This appears to be the Chinese vision; firms there are training cameras not just to recognise individuals but also groups, with classifiers that alert if the subject appears to be an ethnic Uighur or Tibetan. This has been interrupted by mandatory face masks during the coronavirus pandemic, but it will no doubt resume afterwards. Russia has been using its cameras to spot people breaking coronavirus quarantine orders, and claims to have deployed 178,000 of them [1911]. Even in the West, do we face a future in which the police get a feed not just from the automatic number-plate recognition systems that already track road vehicles, but a system that tracks pedestrians too? Cynics would say that mobile phone location history already works fine even if you're wearing shades or a mask, so what's the fuss about? But there are now companies with much larger collections of faces than law enforcement, as they don't face the legal restrictions, and whose services help law enforcement solve crimes committed by people with no mugshots on file. These firms appear set to offer services more widely; they could potentially enable users of augmented-reality glasses to identify most of the people they see – whether an attractive stranger on a subway, or a protester at a demonstration. You could find out their names, where they live and what they do online. The company's backer has a rather casual approach to privacy law: "Laws have to determine what's legal, but you can't ban technology. Sure, that might lead to a dystopian future or something, but you can't ban it" [899].

The political and legal pushback has started. A family in Evanston, Illinois found that photos of their kids that they'd uploaded into Flickr in 2005 had ended up in a database called MegaFace, used to train many of the new recognition systems. This is against Illinois law, and there are now several class actions in progress. As a result, some face-tagging features on social media don't work in Illinois (or Texas for that matter) [900]. In 2018, Google decided not to make face-recognition APIs available in its cloud platforms until their use was regulated. If you train a system on criminal mugshots, it can look at any passer-by and say 'This robber is the closest match'. Where the police are trigger-happy, that can kill. In May 2019, San Francisco banned the use of face recognition by its agencies including the transport authority and law enforcement. In June 2020, following worldwide protests over racism and biased policing, Amazon announced a one-year pause in making its Rekognition face-recognition software available to law enforcement; their technology had been criticised for misidentifying people of colour. The ACLU had shown that Amazon's system generated false matches of 28 members of Congress against mugshots of people who had been arrested. IBM and Microsoft also announced that they would stop selling face-recognition products [2008]. As the technology is now a commodity, the self-restraint of the big four doesn't stop second-tier firms selling it. So the big four are now pushing for face-recognition products to be regulated. Courts are already engaged: in August 2020, the Court of Appeal in London found that the use of facial recognition by South Wales police breached privacy rights, data protection laws and equality laws [1595].

Finally, facial recognition can be enhanced with special hardware. In 2017, Apple introduced it on the iPhone X, in which a dot projector paints your face with tens of thousands of dots and a camera reads them. This deals with makeup, some sunglasses and facial hair, and was claimed to have a false acceptance rate of one in a million – as opposed to one in 50,000 for the fingerprint reader that previous iPhones used. However my eldest granddaughter's iPhone can be unlocked by both of her younger siblings, and this is a general problem for families [526].

17.4 Fingerprints

Automatic fingerprint identification systems (AFIS) have been around for years. In 1998, they accounted for 78% of the $50m sales of biometric technology; this had fallen to 43.5% of $1,539m by 2005[2]. AFIS products look at the friction ridges that cover the fingertips and classify patterns of *minutiae* such as branches and endpoints of the ridges. Some also look at the pores in the skin of the ridges [1215].

The use of fingerprints to identify people was discovered independently a number of times. Mark Twain mentions thumbprints in 1883 in *Life on the Mississippi* where he claims to have learned about them from an old Frenchman who had been a prison-keeper; his 1894 novel *Pudd'nhead Wilson* made the idea popular in the USA. Long before that, fingerprints were accepted in a seventh-century Chinese legal code as an alternative to a seal or a signature, and required by an eighth-century Japanese code when an illiterate man wished to divorce his wife. They were also used in India centuries ago. Following the invention of the microscope, they were mentioned by the English botanist Nathaniel Grew in 1684, and by Marcello Malpighi in Italy in 1686; in 1691, 225 citizens of Londonderry in Ireland used their fingerprints to sign a petition asking King William for reparations following the siege of the city.

The first modern systematic use was in India from 1858, by William Herschel, grandson of the astronomer and a colonial magistrate. He introduced handprints and then fingerprints to sign contracts, stop impersonation of pensioners who had died, and prevent rich criminals paying poor people to serve their jail sentences for them. Henry Faulds, a medical missionary in Japan, discovered them independently in the 1870s, and came up with the idea of using latent prints from crime scenes to identify criminals. Faulds brought fingerprints to the attention of Charles Darwin, who in turn motivated Francis Galton to study them. Galton wrote an article in *Nature* [738]; this got him in touch with the retired Herschel, whose data convinced Galton that fingerprints persisted throughout a person's life. Galton went on to collect many more prints and devise a scheme for classifying their patterns [739]. The Indian history is told by Chandak Sengoopta, whose book also makes the point that fingerprinting saved two somewhat questionable Imperial institutions, namely, the indentured labor system and the opium trade [1704].

The practical introduction of the technique owes a lot to Sir Edward Henry, who had been a policeman in Bengal. He wrote a book in 1900 describing a simpler and more robust classification, of *loops*, *whorls*, *arches* and *tents*, that he had developed with his assistants Azizul Haque and Hem Chandra Bose, and that is still in use today. In the same year he became Commissioner of the Metropolitan Police in London from where the technique spread round the world[3]. Henry's real scientific contribution was to develop Galton's classification into an indexing system. By assigning one bit to whether or not each of

[2]I don't have comparable figures for 2019 as fingerprint tech is now bundled with phones or with other biometrics in systems such as Aadhaar.

[3]In the Spanish version of history, they were first used in Argentina where they secured a murder conviction in 1892; while Cuba, which set up its fingerprint bureau in 1907, beat the USA whose

a suspect's ten fingers had a whorl – a type of circular pattern – he divided the fingerprint files into 1024 bins. In this way, it was possible to reduce the number of records that had to be searched by orders of magnitude. Meanwhile, as Britain had stopped sending convicted felons to Australia, there was a perceived need to identify previous offenders, so that they could be given longer jail sentences.

Fingerprints are used by the world's police forces for essentially two different purposes: identifying people (their main use in the USA), and crime scene forensics (their main use in Europe).

17.4.1 Verifying positive or negative identity claims

In America nowadays – as in nineteenth-century England – quite a few criminals change their names and move somewhere new on release from prison. This is fine when offenders go straight, but what about fugitives and recidivists? American police forces have historically used fingerprints to identify arrested suspects to determine whether they're currently wanted by other agencies, whether they have criminal records and whether they've previously come to attention under other names. The FBI maintains the *Next Generation Identification* (NGI) service system for this purpose; it identifies about eight thousand fugitives a month [1813]. Anyone wanting a US government clearance at Secret or above must have an FBI fingerprint check, and checks are also run on some people applying to work with children or the elderly. Up to 100,000 checks are made a day, and about a million federal, local and state officers have access. There's a 'rap-back' service to alert the employer of anyone with a clearance who gets into trouble with the law [1380]; it's also used to track reoffending by probationers, parolees and sex offenders. The Department of Homeland Security's IDENT system holds fingerprints on 200 million aliens who have arrived at US ports; it matches them against a watch list of bad guys, compiled with the help of police forces and intelligence services worldwide.

These are examples of one type of identity verification – checking against a blacklist. The other type is where the system checks a claim to identity, with the main US applications being building entry control and welfare payment [588]. Banks have used them for years to identify customers in countries such as India and Saudi Arabia, where the use of ink fingerprints was already common thanks to high levels of illiteracy. India now has a national system, Aadhaar, with fingerprints and iris codes of most residents, designed initially to support

first conviction was in Illinois in 1911. The Croatian version notes that the Argentinian system was developed by one Juan Vucetich, who had emigrated from Dalmatia. The German version refers to Professor Purkinje of Breslau, who wrote about fingerprints in 1828. Success truly has many fathers!

welfare payments and ensure that nobody can claim twice. Its use has become mandatory for many other transactions too.

Fingerprints have never taken off for authenticating bank customers in North America or Europe, though a few US banks do ask for fingerprints if you cash a check there and are not a customer. They find this cuts check fraud by about a half. Some have gone as far as fingerprinting new customers, and found that customer resistance is less than expected, especially if they use scanners rather than ink and paper [716]. These applications are not authentication, but rather an attempt to identify and even deter customers who later turn out to be bad – another example being the large British van-hire company that demands a thumbprint when you rent a van. If the vehicle isn't returned, or if it's used in a crime, the thumbprint is given to the police. They're thus really a crime-scene forensics application, which I'll discuss in the following section.

So how good are automatic fingerprint identification systems? A good rule of thumb (if one might call it that) is that to verify a claim to identity, it may be enough to scan a single finger, while to check someone against a blacklist of millions of felons, you had better scan all ten. After the US DHS program set out to scan the two index fingers of each arriving visitor, it was overwhelmed by false matches. With 6,000,000 bad guys on the database, the false match rate in 2004 was 0.31% and the missed match rate 4% [2031]. The program moved to '10-prints', where each visitor must present the four fingers of each hand, and then both thumbs, in three successive scans. The European Union will be adopting a combination of 4-prints plus facial recognition from 2020; nonresidents will need both to get in, and either to get out.

This is all about the trade-off between false negatives and false positives – the receiver operating characteristic, described in the previous section. The better systems have an equal error rate of slightly below 1% per finger. False accepts happen because of features incorporated to reduce the false-reject rate – such as allowance for distortion and flexibility in feature selection [1613]. Spotting returning fugitives with high enough probability to deter them and high enough certainty to detain them (which means keeping false alarms at manageable levels) requires several fingers to be matched – perhaps eight out of ten. This does cause delays; a UK Passport Office study found that about 20% of participants failed to register properly when taking a 10-print, and that 10-print verification took over a minute [1924]. This is approximately my experience while flying in and out of the USA during the 2010s. The cost of fingerprinting everybody is that a US airport getting a planeload of 300 international arrivals every 15 minutes needs an extra 10 working immigration lanes. The extra building and staffing costs swamp anything spent on hardware and software. (For more on algorithms and systems, see [975,1213,1215].)

Errors are not uniformly distributed. A number of people such as manual workers and pipe smokers damage their fingerprints frequently, and both the young and the old have faint prints [394]. Automated systems also have problems with amputees, people with birth defects such as extra fingers, and the (rare) people born without conventional fingerprint patterns at all [1122]. When I was a kid, I slashed my left middle finger while cutting an apple, and this left a scar about half an inch long. When I presented this finger to the system used in 1989 by the FBI for building entry control, my scar crashed the scanner. (It worked OK when I tried again ten years later.)

Fingerprint identification systems can be attacked in many ways. An old trick was for a crook to distract (or bribe) the officer fingerprinting him, so that the officer takes the fingers in the wrong order and instead of the hand being indexed under the Henry system as '01101' it becomes perhaps '01011', so his record isn't found and he gets the lighter sentence due a first offender [1122].

The first high-profile technical attack was in 2002, when Tsutomu Matsumoto and colleagues showed that fingerprints could be molded and cloned quickly and cheaply using cooking gelatin [1248]. He tested eleven commercially available fingerprint readers and easily fooled all of them. This prompted the German computer magazine C'T to test a number of biometric devices that were offered for sale at the CeBIT electronic fair in Hanover – nine fingerprint readers, one face-recognition system and one iris scanner. They were all easy to fool – the low-cost capacitive sensors fell to such simple tricks as breathing on a finger scanner to reactivate a latent print left by a previous user [1880]. Latent fingerprints can also be reactivated – or transferred – using adhesive tape. The more expensive thermal scanners could still be defeated by rubber molded fingers.

In 2013, Apple introduced a fingerprint scanner on the iPhone 5S and other phone makers raced to follow suit. Hackers duly demonstrated attacks, with a 2014 CCC presentation of a model of the German defence minister's finger, created from a photograph [314]. Scanners on phones typically store 8–12 partial prints on registration and will unlock against any of them, which makes the scanner more usable but also more vulnerable. In 2016, Aditi Roy and colleagues invented the 'masterprint': a fake fingerprint that can be worn on your fingertip and that's designed to match at least one of the partial prints derived from a typical finger; it works against 6% of users' prints [1628]. In 2017, Apple moved from fingerprints to face recognition, as I discussed above, but most Android OEMs still use fingerprints. In 2019, it turned out that a new ultrasonic scanner on the Samsung S10 enrolled the screen protector instead of the customer's finger, leading to the phone being blocked from running a number of banks' apps [467].

There are other angles too. For example, the San Bernardino shooter used an iPhone 5C, the last made without a scanner; if he'd used a later version, the FBI could have unlocked it by taking it to the morgue and pressing it against his finger, or by making a fingertip mould from his file print. And as government agencies collect more and more prints, they will be less and less private.

(The Chinese already got all US federal employees' prints via the OPM hack I discussed in section 2.2.2.) Fingerprint systems have also expanded rapidly into low-assurance applications, from entry into golf club car parks to automatic book borrowing in school libraries. (Most European countries' privacy authorities have banned fingerprint scanners in schools; Britain allows them, which causes pushback from privacy-conscious parents [191].) And the latest twist comes from a Mitre project that developed software to harvest people's fingerprints from photos they post on social media; these often show fingers in enough detail to get matches against FBI databases [322].

One final reason for the success of fingerprint identification systems is their deterrent effect, which is particularly pronounced in welfare payments. Even though the cheap fingerprint readers used to authenticate welfare claimants have an error rate as much as 5% [385], they turned out to be such an effective way of reducing the welfare rolls that they were adopted in one place after another during the nineties [1317].

17.4.2 Crime scene forensics

The second use of fingerprint recognition is in crime scene forensics – the main application in Europe. Prints found at a crime scene are matched against database records, and any that match to more than a certain level are taken as evidence that a suspect visited the crime scene. They are often enough to secure a conviction on their own. In many countries, fingerprints are required from all citizens and all resident foreigners.

The forensic error rate has become extremely controversial in recent years, the critical limitation being the size and quality of the image taken from the crime scene. The quality and procedure rules vary from one country to another. The UK used to require that fingerprints match in sixteen *points* (corresponding minutiae), and a UK police expert claimed that this will only happen by chance somewhere between one in four billion and one in ten billion matches [1122]. Greece accepts 10, Turkey 8, while the USA has no set limit (it certifies examiners instead). This means that in the USA, matches can be found with poorer quality prints but they can be open to challenge in court.

In the UK, fingerprint evidence went for almost a century without a successful challenge; a 16-point fingerprint match was considered hanging evidence. The courts' confidence was shattered by the McKie case [1275]. Shirley McKie, a Scottish policewoman, was prosecuted on the basis of a fingerprint match on the required sixteen points, verified by four examiners of the Scottish Criminal Records Office. She denied that it was her fingerprint, and found that she could not get an independent expert in Britain to support her; the profession closed ranks. She called two American examiners who presented testimony that it is not an identification. The crime scene and file prints are side-by-side at Figure 17.1.

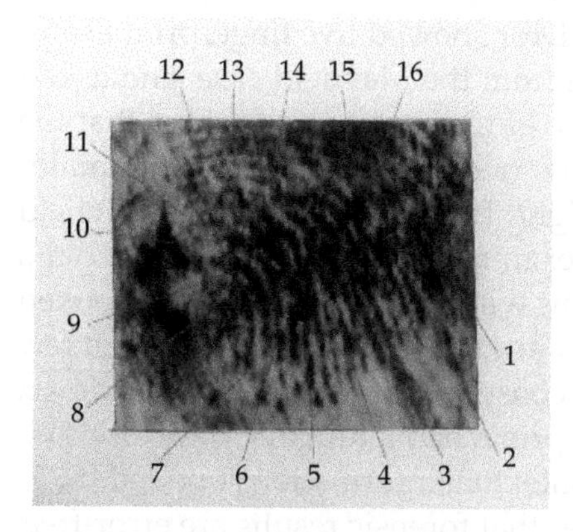

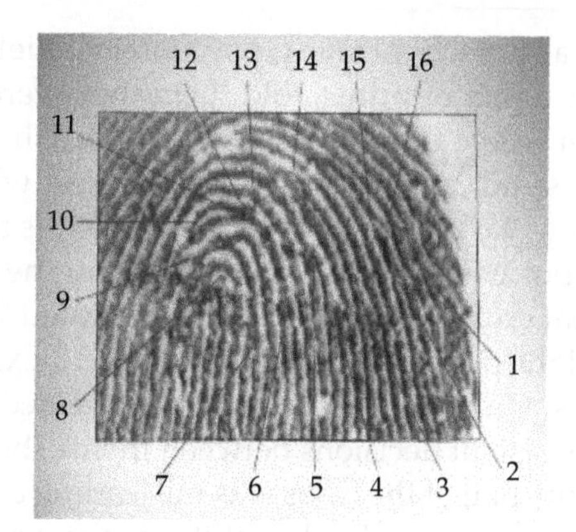

Figure 17.1: The prints in the McKie case

She was acquitted, which led to a political drama that ran on for years [1274]. The first problem was the nature of the case against her [1275]. A number of senior police officers had tried to persuade her to make a false statement in order to explain the presence, at the scene of a gruesome murder, of the misidentified print. Her refusal to do so led to her being prosecuted for perjury, as a means of discrediting her. Her acquittal cast doubt on the reliability of police testimony, not just in her specific case but more generally. The man convicted of the murder was acquitted on appeal and sued the police for compensation. The government panicked at the prospect of dozens more appeals in other cases, and prosecuted its four fingerprint experts for perjury. That didn't get anywhere either. The issue went back to the Scottish parliament again and again. The police refused to reinstate Shirley McKie, the officers involved got promoted, and the row got ever more acrimonious. Eventually she won £750,000 compensation from the government [190].

The case led to wide discussion among experts of the value of fingerprint identification, and to fingerprint evidence being successfully challenged in a number of other countries [761]. Two high-profile cases in the USA were Stephan Cowans and Brandon Mayfield. Stephan Cowans had been convicted of shooting a police officer in 1997 following a robbery, but was acquitted on appeal six years later after he argued that his print was a misidentification and saved up enough money to have the evidence tested for DNA. The DNA didn't match, which got the Boston and State police to reanalyze the fingerprint, whereupon they realised it was not a match after all. Brandon Mayfield was an Oregon lawyer who was mistakenly identified by the FBI as one of the perpetrators of the Madrid bombing, and held for two weeks until the Madrid police arrested another man whose fingerprint was a better match. The FBI, which had called their match 'absolutely incontrovertible', agreed to pay Mayfield $2m in 2006.

In a subsequent study, psychologist Itiel Dror showed five fingerprint examiners a pair of prints, told them they were from the Mayfield case, and asked them where the FBI had gone wrong. Three of the examiners decided that the prints did not match and pointed out why; one was unsure; and one maintained that they did match. He alone was right. The prints weren't the Mayfield set, but were in each case a pair that the examiner himself had matched in a recent criminal case [586]. Dror repeated this with six experts who each looked at eight prints, all of which they had examined for real in the previous few years. Only two of the experts remained consistent; the other four made six inconsistent decisions between them. The prints had a range of difficulty, and in only half of the cases was misleading contextual information supplied [587].

Prosecutors and police still insist to juries that forensic results are error-free, when FBI proficiency exams have long had an error rate of about one percent [206], and misleading contextual information can push this up to ten percent or in some cases over fifty percent.

Four comments are in order.

- As Figure 17.1 should make clear, fingerprint impressions are often very noisy, being obscured by dirt. So mistakes are quite possible, and the skill (and prejudices) of the examiner enter into the equation in a much bigger way than was accepted until uproar caused by the McKie and Mayfield cases. Dror's work confirmed that the cases in which misidentifications occur tend to be the difficult ones [587]. Yet the forensic culture was such that only certainty was acceptable; the International Association for Identification, the largest forensic group, held that testifying about "possible, probable or likely identification shall be deemed ... conduct unbecoming" [206].
- Even if the probability of a false match on sixteen points were one in ten billion (10^{-10}) as claimed by police optimists, once many prints are compared against each other, probability theory starts to bite. A system that worked fine in the old days as a crime scene print would be compared manually with the records of a hundred and fifty-seven known local burglars, breaks down once thousands of prints are compared every year with an online database of millions. It was inevitable that sooner or later, enough matches would have been done to find a 16-point mismatch. Indeed, as most people on the fingerprint database are petty criminals who will not be able to muster the resolute defence that Shirley McKie did, I would be surprised if there hadn't been other wrongful convictions already. And things may get worse, because European police forces now link up their biometric databases (both fingerprints and DNA) so that police forces can search for matches across all EU member states [1909]. They may eventually need more robust ways of handling false positives.

- The belief that any security mechanism is infallible creates the complacency and carelessness needed to undermine its proper use. No consideration appears to have been given to increasing the number of points required from sixteen to (say) twenty with the introduction of computer matching. Sixteen was tradition, and nobody wanted either to challenge the system or make public funds available for defendants' experts. In the UK, all the experts were policemen or former policemen, so there were no independents available for hire anyway. Even so, it would have been possible to use randomised matching with multiple experts; but if the fingerprint bureau had had to tell the defence in the perhaps 5–10% of cases when (say) one of four experts disagreed, then more defendants would have been acquitted.
- A belief of infallibility ensures that the consequences of the eventual failure will be severe. As with the Munden case described in section 12.4.3, which helped torpedo claims about cash machine security, an assumption that a security mechanism is infallible causes procedures, cultural assumptions and even laws to spring up to ensure that its eventual failure will be denied for as long as possible, and will thus have real impact when it can no longer be postponed. In the Scottish case, there appears to have arisen a hierarchical risk-averse culture in which examiners were predisposed to confirm identifications made by colleagues (especially senior colleagues). This risk aversion backfired when four of them were tried for perjury.

However, even when we do have a correct match, its implications are not always entirely obvious. Fingerprints can be transferred using adhesive tape, and moulds can be made, using techniques originally devised for police use. So it's possible that the suspect whose print is found at the crime scene was framed by another criminal (or by the police – most fabrication cases involve law-enforcement personnel rather than other suspects [255]). And even if the villain wasn't framed, he can always claim that he was (and the jury might believe him).

In the USA, the Supreme Court in its Daubert judgment held that trial judges should screen the principles and methodology behind forensic evidence to ensure it is relevant and reliable [516]. The judge ought to consider the refereed scientific literature – and in the case of fingerprints this has been lacking, as law enforcement agencies have been generally unwilling to submit their examination procedures to rigorous double-blind testing. A number of Daubert hearings relating to forensic fingerprint evidence have been held in US trials, and the FBI has generally prevailed [762]. However, the bureau's traditional line that fingerprint examination has a zero error rate is now widely ridiculed [1813].

17.5 Iris codes

We turn now from the traditional ways of identifying people to the modern and innovative. Recognizing people by the patterns in the irises of their eyes has far and away the best error rates of any automated biometric system when measured under lab conditions. The initial research was funded by the Department of Energy, which wanted the best possible way of securing entry to premises such as plutonium stores, and the technology is now used in applications from immigration to welfare. The international standards for machine-readable travel documents mandate the use of photographs, and permit both fingerprints and irises.

So far as is known, every human iris is measurably unique. It is fairly easy to detect in a video picture, it does not wear out, and it is isolated from the external environment by the cornea (which in turn has its own cleaning mechanism). The iris pattern contains a large amount of randomness, and appears to have many times the number of degrees of freedom of a fingerprint. It is formed between the third and eighth months of gestation, and (like the fingerprint pattern) appears to be under limited genetic influence; the mechanisms that form it appear to be chaotic. The patterns are different even for identical twins (and for the two eyes of a single individual), and they appear to be stable throughout life.

Leonard Flom and Aran Safir patented the idea of an iris identification system in 1987, observing that every iris is different. In 1993, John Daugman figured out how to make the idea work, developing signal-processing techniques that extract the information from an image of the iris into a 256 byte *iris code*. This involves a circular wavelet transform taken at a number of concentric rings between the pupil and the outside of the iris (Figure 17.2). The resulting iris codes have the neat property that two codes computed from the same iris will typically match in 90% of their bits [517]. This is much simpler than in fingerprint scanners where orienting and classifying the minutiae is a fiddly computational task. The speed and accuracy of iris coding, and the expiry of the Daugman patents, have led to a number of commercial iris recognition products [2000]. Iris codes provide the lowest false-accept rates of any known verification system – zero, in tests conducted by both the US Department of Energy and the NPL [1219]. The equal error rate has been shown to be better than one in a million, and if one is prepared to tolerate a false-reject rate of one in ten thousand, then the theoretical false-accept rate would be less than one in a trillion. In practice, the false-reject rate is significantly higher than this; many things, from eyelashes to hangovers, can cause the camera to not see enough of the iris. The US Department of Defense found a 6% false-reject rate in its 2002 field trials [1260]; a UK Passport Office trial found 4% for normal users and 9% for disabled users [1924]. A further problem is failure to enrol; the Passport

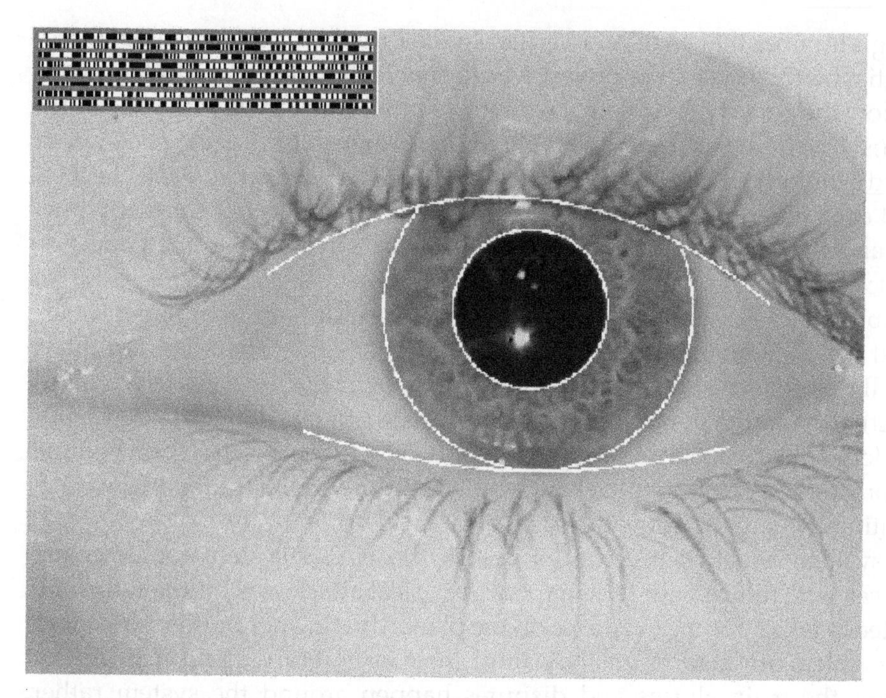

Figure 17.2: an iris with iris code (courtesy John Daugman)

Office trial failed to enrol 10% of participants, and the rate was higher among black users, the over-60s and the disabled.

One practical problem with iris scanning used to be getting the picture cheaply without being too intrusive. The iris is small (less than half an inch) and an image with several hundred pixels of iris is needed. A cooperative subject can place his eye within a few inches of a video camera, and the best standard equipment will work up to a distance of two or three feet. All current iris scanning systems use infrared light, and some people feel uncomfortable when this is shone in their eyes. Given more sophisticated cameras, with automatic facial feature recognition, pan and zoom, it is now possible to capture iris codes from airline passengers covertly as they walk along a corridor [1242], and the cost came down after the key patent ran out in 2011.

The first large-scale deployment was in the United Arab Emirates, which wanted to track people expelled from the country, particularly for prostitution offences. Expellees would turn up again some weeks later with new and completely valid passports from certain Asian countries, obtained by corruption. Since its deployment in 2003, this has led to the detention of over 330,000 people attempting to enter the country despite a ban or with false papers.

The largest deployment is the Aadhaar system in India, under which all residents had their fingerprints and irises scanned. They get an Aadhaar card with a 10-digit number that enables a verifier to look up their profile in a database. The initial motivation for the project was to enable the 300 million Indians who live below the poverty line and get welfare, to move into the cities to seek work. Previously welfare was only available in their towns or villages. The system enrolled a billion people between 2011 and 2016, and all iris codes were checked against each other for uniqueness. Aadhaar is now mandatory for many purposes, and the collected fingerprints are also made available to the police for crime scene forensics.

Possible attacks on iris recognition systems include – in unattended operation at least – a simple photograph of the target's iris. There are terminals that will detect such simple fakes, for example by measuring *hippus* – a natural fluctuation in the diameter of the pupil that happens at about 0.5 Hz. But the widely-sold cheap terminals don't do this, and if liveness detection became widespread then no doubt attackers would try more sophisticated tricks, such as printing the target's iris patterns on a contact lens.

The system in active use the longest is the UAE's system for detecting deportees who return with false papers. A typical attack was for the returning deportee to take atropine eyedrops on the plane, dilating her pupils; nowadays such travelers are held in custody until their eyes return to normal. As for Aadhaar, the main abuses and disputes happen around the system rather than through it. In 2019, a hot issue is the authorities' reluctance to register Muslims in Assam and other border regions, part of a larger policy of trying to portray them as illegal immigrants. The Supreme Court of India has ruled that services should not be withheld from people who are not registered, but this has not stopped registration being a requirement in practice for opening a bank account, buying a phone or SIM card, and school enrolment.

Despite the difficulties, iris codes are in some sense the most powerful biometric as they can, in the correct circumstances, assure you that the individual in front of you is the same human as the one whose iris was initially registered. They alone can meet the goal of automatic recognition with zero false acceptances.

17.6 Voice recognition and morphing

Voice recognition – also known as *speaker recognition* – is the problem of identifying a speaker from a short utterance. While *speech recognition* systems are concerned with transcribing speech and need to ignore speech idiosyncrasies, voice recognition systems need to amplify and classify them. There are many subproblems, such as whether the recognition is text-dependent or not, whether the environment is noisy, whether operation must be real time and whether one needs only to verify speakers or to recognize them from a large set.

As with fingerprints, the technology is used for both identification and forensics. In *forensic phonology*, the task is usually to match a recorded telephone conversation, such as a bomb threat, to speech samples from a number of suspects. Typical techniques involve filtering and extracting features from the spectrum; for more details see [1060]. A more straightforward biometric authentication objective is to verify a claim to identity in some telephone systems. These range from telephone banking to the identification of military personnel, with the NSA maintaining a standard corpus of test data for evaluating speaker recognition systems. In the UK, asylum seekers are required to ring in several times every week [1906]. Such systems tend to use caller-ID to establish where people are, and are also used for people like football hooligans who're under court orders not to go to certain places at certain times. The only system I've used personally is run by one of the banks I use, and authenticates you to their phone app when you change your phone. But a major UK bank was embarrassed when it fielded a voice biometric system in a phone app in 2016, only to have it broken the following year by a BBC reporter who got his non-identical twin to mimic his voice [1748].

Quite apart from the possibility that a relative or a villain might somehow manage to imitate you, there are some powerful attacks. In [730] there is a description of a 1990s system fielded in US EP-3 aircraft that breaks up intercepted messages from enemy aircraft and ground controllers into quarter second segments that are then cut and pasted to provide new, deceptive messages. That was primitive compared with what can now be done two decades later. There are now many videos online of public figures appearing to say inappropriate things, and 'Deepfake' editing software now enables such voice and image morphing to be done in near real time. Most recently, criminals used AI to impersonate a chief executive's voice and order a payment of €220,000: the victim of that deception wasn't even a machine, but another executive [1845]. This may be the first case of voice morphing software being used in a real fraud; we can be sure it won't be the last.

17.7 Other systems

Many other biometric technologies have been proposed [1317]. Typing patterns were used in products in the 1980s but don't appear to have been successful (typing patterns, also known as keystroke dynamics, had a famous precursor in the wartime technique of identifying wireless telegraphy operators by their *fist*, the way in which they used a Morse key). Vein patterns have been used in one or two systems but don't seem to have been widely sold (in the NPL trials, the vein was the worst of the lot [1219]). Hand geometry was used for a while in some airports, and has a historic predecessor in the system of Bertillonage, whereby the French police in the 19th century identified criminals by a system of physical measurements.

There has been growing interest recently in *stylometry*, the science of identifying authors, whether of text or of code, from their writing styles. This goes back at least a century; as a young man, the famous cryptologist William Friedman was hired along with his wife Elizebeth by an eccentric millionaire to study whether Bacon wrote Shakespeare. (They eventually debunked the idea but got interested in cryptography in the process.) Computers make it possible to run ever more subtle statistical tests, and modern applications range from trying to identify people who post to cybercrime markets and extremist web forums to the detection of plagiarism by college students [3]. Researchers have shown that people can change their writing styles enough to defeat simple stylometry if they try [319]. But most people don't, and with a bit more work, the fact of an attempted obfuscation can usually be detected [28]. Stylometry also extends to code; programmers can be recognised from their coding style [372].

Other proposals include *facial thermograms* (maps of the surface temperature of the face, derived from infrared images), the shape of the ear, gait, lip prints and electrocardiograms. Bertillon used the shape of the ear in nineteenth-century Paris. And perhaps the huge investment in developing digital noses for quality control in the food and drink industries may lead to personal devices that recognize their master by scent.

One final biometric deserves mention – DNA. This has become a valuable tool for crime scene forensics and for determining parenthood in child support cases, but it is way too slow and expensive for real-time applications. Being genotypic rather than phenotypic, its accuracy is limited by the incidence of monozygotic twins: about one white person in 120 has an identical twin. There's also a privacy problem in that it is possible to reconstruct a growing amount of information about an individual from their DNA sample. There have been major procedural problems, with false matches resulting from sloppy lab procedure. And there are also major data quality problems; the UK police have the biggest DNA database in the world, with records on almost six million people, but got the names misspelled or even wrong for about half a million of them [880]. They also had court judgments against them for retaining the DNA of innocent people, from acquitted suspects to bystanders [103]. The processes that work for local policing don't always scale nationally – small errors from mistyped records, to suspects giving false names that were never discovered because they weren't prosecuted, accumulate along with lab errors until the false-positive rate becomes a serious operational and political issue. In this context, many were concerned when in 2019, a Florida detective managed to get a warrant to search all million records held by a private DNA testing company GEDmatch [901]. It will be interesting to see whether this undermines the business of the larger consumer

DNA firms, such as 23andMe and `ancestry.com`, enough for them to lobby for stronger privacy laws.

17.8 What goes wrong

As with other aspects of security, we find the usual crop of failures due to bugs, blunders and complacency. In section 3.4.9 I noted a report that the firm which supplies biometric building entry control systems to 5,700 organisations in 83 countries left its database unprotected online. And the second time Uber lost its London operating licence, it was because they failed to stop banned drivers re-registering, thanks to a photo checking bug [311]. And the main problem faced by DNA typing was an initially high rate of false positives, due to careless laboratory procedure. This led to disputed court cases and miscarriages of justice. As with fingerprints, any system that's believed to be infallible will make its operators careless enough to break it.

Biometrics are also like many other physical protection mechanisms (alarms, seals, tamper sensing enclosures, ...) in that environmental conditions can cause havoc. Noise, dirt, vibration and unreliable lighting conditions all take their toll. Some systems, like speaker recognition, are vulnerable to alcohol intake and stress. Changes in environmental assumptions, such as from closed to open systems, from small systems to large ones, from attended to stand-alone, from cooperative to recalcitrant subjects, and from verification to identification, can all break things.

Many interesting attacks are more specific to biometric systems and apply to more than one type of biometric.

- Forensic biometrics often don't tell as much as one might assume. Apart from the possibility that a fingerprint or DNA sample might have been planted by the police, it may just be old. The age of a fingerprint can't be determined directly, and prints on areas with public access say little. A print on a bank door says much less than a print in a robbed vault. So in premises vulnerable to robbery, cleaning procedures may be critical for evidence. If a suspect's prints are found on a bank counter, and he claims that he had gone there three days previously, he may be convicted by evidence that the branch counter is polished every evening. Putting this in system terms, freshness is often a critical issue, and some quite unexpected things can find themselves inside the 'trusted computing base'.
- Another aspect of freshness is that most biometric systems can, at least in theory, be attacked using suitable recordings. We mentioned direct attacks on voice recognition, attacks on iris scanners by photos on a contact lens, and moulds of fingerprints. Even simpler still, in countries like South Africa where fingerprints are used to pay pensions, there

are persistent tales of 'Granny's finger in the pickle jar' being the most valuable property she bequeathed to her family. The lesson to be learned here is that unattended operation of biometric authentication devices is tricky. Attacks aren't always straightforward; although it's easy to make a mould from a good fingerprint [408], the casual prints that people leave lying around on doorknobs, beer glasses and so on are often too smudged and fragmentary to pass an identification system. But attacks are definitely possible, and definitely happen. Defences are also possible; voice recognition systems can demand that you read out an unpredictable challenge to thwart recordings, while one version of the app that EU citizens use to apply for residence in the UK post-Brexit took a video of your face as colours change on the phone screen in front of you.

- Most biometrics are not as accurate for all people, and some of the population can't be identified as reliably as the rest (or even at all). The elderly, and manual workers, often have damaged or abraded fingerprints; there's a tradition of hardcore criminals doing this deliberately. People with dark eyes, and large pupils, give poorer iris codes. Disabled people with no fingers, or no eyes, risk exclusion. (That's one reason Aadhaar uses both irises and fingerprints.) Illiterates who make an 'X' are more at risk from signature forgery.

  Biometric engineers sometimes refer to such subjects dismissively as 'goats', but this is foolish and discriminatory. A biometric system that is (or is seen to be) socially regressive – that puts the disabled, the poor, the old and ethnic minorities at greater risk of impersonation – should meet with principled resistance. It might be defeated by legal challenges [1555]. It may also be defeated by villains who pretend to be disabled. And sometimes the lack of heed for minority population groups is so offensive as to be unlawful. For example, in 2019 the UK Home Office deployed a passport app despite knowing that it didn't work properly for black people [1954].

- A point that follows from this is that systems may be vulnerable to collusion. Alice opens a bank account and her accomplice Betty withdraws money from it; Alice then complains of theft and produces a watertight alibi. Quite apart from simply letting Betty take a rubber impression of her fingertip, Alice might voluntarily decrease handwriting ability; by giving several slightly different childish sample signatures, she can force the machine to accept a lower threshold than usual. She can spend a couple of weeks building a wall in her garden, and wear her fingerprints flat, so as to degrade registration in a fingerprint system. She might register for a voice recognition system when drunk.

- The next issue is compulsion. If you get arrested in China, and since August 2020 in Hong Kong, the police will hold your finger to your phone to unlock it. If it uses face recognition, they'll pin your head and point your phone at you; if you want to resist, you have to close your eyes and scrunch up your face [1350].
- The statistics are often not understood by system designers, and the birthday theorem is a big soft spot. With 10,000 biometrics in a database, for example, there are about 50,000,000 pairs. So even with a false-accept rate of only one in a million, the likelihood of there being at least one false match will rise above one-half as soon as there are somewhat over a thousand people enrolled[4]. So identification is a lot tougher than verification. The practical consequence is that a system designed for authentication may fail when you try to rely on it for evidence.
- Another aspect of statistics comes into play when designers assume that by combining biometrics they can get a lower error rate. But a combination will often improve either the false-accept rate or the false-reject rate, while making the other worse. If you install two different burglar alarms at your home, then the probability that they will be simultaneously defeated goes down while the number of false alarms goes up.
- The statistics are often somewhat uneven, so that as well as so-called 'goats', whose biometrics typically fall outside the normal parameter range, there may be 'lambs' who are particularly easy to impersonate, and 'wolves' who are particularly good at impersonating others. So it is vital to test systems thoroughly on substantial and diverse populations before deployment.
- Many vendors have claimed that their products protect privacy, as what's stored is not the image of your face or fingerprint or iris, but rather a template that's derived from it, somewhat like a one-way hash, and from which you can't be identified. It's been argued from this that biometric data are not personal data, in terms of privacy law, and can thus be passed around without restriction. These claims were exploded by Andy Adler who came up with an interesting *hill-climbing attack* on face recognition systems. Given a recogniser that outputs how close an input image is to a target template, the input face is successively altered to increase the match. With the tested systems, this led rapidly to a recognizable image of the target – a printout of which would be accepted as the target's face [24].

[4]More precisely, 1177: a false match pairing in a database of N people becomes likelier than not as soon as $N > \sqrt{1.386/f}$ where f is the single false-match rate, here 10^{-6} [519]. Check: 1177 people make 1177 x 1176 / 2 = 692,076 pairings, and the probability that none of these makes a false match is: $0.999999^{692,076} = 0.500$.

He then showed how this hill-climbing technique could be used to attack other biometrics, including some based on fingerprints [25].

- It's worth thinking what happens when humans and computers disagree. Iris data can't be matched by unaided humans at all; most of the iris code is derived from phase information to which the human eye is not sensitive. But what happens when a guard and a program disagree on whether a subject's face matches a file photo? Psychologists advise that biometric systems should be used in ways that support and empower human cognition and that work within our social norms [586]. Yet we engineers often find it easier to treat the users as a nuisance that must adapt to our technology. This may degrade the performance of the humans. For example, when an automated fingerprint database pulls out what it thinks is the most likely print and presents it to the examiner: is he not likely to be biased in its favour? Would it not perhaps be better for the computer to test the examiner's alertness constantly by giving him the three best matches plus two poor matches, or would that be too annoying?
- Finally, Christian fundamentalists are uneasy about biometrics. They find Revelation 13:16-18 talking about the Antichrist: 'And he causes all, both small and great, rich and poor, free and slave, to receive a mark on their right hand or on their foreheads, and that no one may buy or sell except one who has the mark or the name of the beast, or the number of his name.'

So there are some non-trivial problems. But biometrics have now gone mainstream, and a good security engineer needs to know how to use them appropriately.

17.9 Summary

Biometric measures of one kind or another have been used to identify people since ancient times, with handwritten signatures, facial features and fingerprints being the traditional methods. Three systems are now deployed at scale: fingerprint recognition on our phones, iris recognition in India and the Middle East, and facial recognition – which has become rapidly more accurate thanks to the neural network revolution. These systems have different strengths and weaknesses, and the statistics of error rates can be deceptively difficult.

When a biometric becomes very widely used, there may be an increased risk of forgery in unattended operation: photographs of irises, fingerprint moulds and even good old-fashioned forged signatures must all be thought of in system design. Context matters; even a weak biometric like handwritten signature verification can be effective if it is well embedded in the social and legal matrix.

Biometrics are usually more powerful in attended operation, where with good system design the relative strengths and weaknesses of the human and the machine may complement one another. Forensic uses are problematic, and courts are much less blindly trusting of even fingerprint evidence than they were ten years ago. Historically, many biometric systems achieved most of their effect by deterring criminals rather than actually identifying them. And although there's now the prospect of identifying people at scale from face recognition, and authoritarian countries like Russia and China are doing it, there's now serious debate about whether we should allow the large-scale routine use of this technology in democracies.

Research problems

Many practical research problems relate to the design, or improvement, of biometric systems. The hot topic in 2019 is the scalability of mass surveillance CCTV systems, and the policy questions this raises about privacy, autonomy and sovereignty. Given that facial recognition technology is still improving rapidly and finding new applications, the debate is likely to run for some time and to drive technical research on related topics.

One idea I thought up while writing this chapter for the first edition in 2000 was instrumenting a car so as to identify a driver by the way in which he operated the gears and the clutch. If your car thinks it's been stolen, it phones a control center that calls you to check. There is now research showing that users of haptic systems can be recognised by the way in which they use tools [1480]. So here's another idea. Can we identify humans, and AI/ML systems, by other learned skills? For example, the quote at the head of this chapter – where the Ephraimites were spotted and killed for their inability to say the Hebrew letter 'shin' – is actually about a skill that people learn when young or, with more difficulty, as an adult. The ability to speak a language fluently in the local dialect is one of the most universal and visceral ways of identifying the in-group from the out-group. The cool crowd speak the latest slang and dance the latest dance. Now that robots, as well as humans, have skills that are acquired only with effort, does this lead anywhere interesting?

Further reading

The standard British history of fingerprints is by Commander G.T.C. Lambourne [1122], while the history in India is told by Chandak Sengoopta [1704]. The McKie case is described in a book by Ian McKie and Michael Russella [1275]. A good technical reference on automated fingerprint identification systems is the book by Davide Maltoni, Dario Maio, Anil Jain and Salil Prabhakar [1215]. As for facial recognition, see Guodong Guo and Na Zhang [835]. The standard work on iris codes is by John Daugman [517]. For speaker recognition forensics, see Richard Klevans and Robert Rodman [1060].

As for the future, the US Department of Homeland Security is building a new Homeland Advanced Recognition Technology (HART) database that will include multiple forms of biometrics, from face recognition to DNA, and consolidate records on both US residents and foreigners; there's a description and a discussion of the policy implications by the EFF [1198]. And the errors in biometric forensics are mirrored in other forensic techniques; a 2009 report from the US National Research Council showed that apart from DNA analysis, most forensic methods were unreliable in various ways, relating not only to the underlying science and technology but also to the fragmented nature of forensic practice, the lack of standards and poor governance [1415]. As a recent example, Sophie Nightingale and Hany Farid found that a common method of identifying denim clothes by seam patterns was nowhere near as reliable or reproducible as forensic examiners had claimed for many years [1449].

CHAPTER

18

Tamper Resistance

It is relatively easy to build an encryption system that is secure if it is working as intended and is used correctly but it is still very hard to build a system that does not compromise its security in situations in which it is either misused or one or more of its sub-components fails (or is 'encouraged' to misbehave) ... this is now the only area where the closed world is still a long way ahead of the open world and the many failures we see in commercial cryptographic systems provide some evidence for this.

– BRIAN GLADMAN

The amount of careful, critical security thinking that has gone into a given security device, system or program is inversely proportional to the amount of high-technology it uses.

– ROGER JOHNSTON

18.1 Introduction

Tamper-resistant devices are everywhere now. Examples we've discussed so far include:

- the EMV chips used in bank cards and the SIMs used in mobile phones for *authentication*;
- the contactless cards used as transport tickets and the smartcards used in pay-TV decoders for *service control*;
- chips used for *accessory control* in printer toner cartridges and game-console accessories;
- the TPM chips in phones, laptops and servers to provide a *root of trust* to support secure boot and hard-disk encryption;
- hardware security modules used to encrypt bank PINs, not just in bank server farms but in ATMs and some point-of-sale terminals;
- the NFC chips used in Android phones to store contactless payment credentials, and the enclave chips in iPhones that store your fingerprint and crypto keys;

- cryptographic modules buried in vending machines that sell everything from railway tickets through postage stamps to the magic numbers that activate your electricity meter;
- various chips used for *manufacturing control* by firms who want to have their products made by low-cost overseas manufacturers but don't want to see extra products made without their consent on a 'third shift' and sold on the grey market.

Many of the devices on the market are insecure. In section 4.3.1 I described how reverse engineering remote key entry devices for cars led to class breaks that notably increased car theft; in section 13.2.5 I described how reverse engineering the Mifare card compromised many building locks and transport ticketing systems; and in section 12.6.1.1, I described card payment terminals that could be compromised trivially, leading to card counterfeiting and transaction manipulation attacks.

Yet some are pretty good. The best cryptographic modules used in banking and government withstand all known types of physical attack, and can only be defeated when people either run insecure software on them or rely on insecure devices to interface with users. Smartcard tamper resistance has evolved in a long war between pay-TV pirates cloning subscriber cards and the pay-TV industry trying to stop them, and was honed in an arms race between firms that wanted to lock down their products, and others who wanted to unlock them. The tussles over printer cartridges were important here, as both the printer makers who were trying to control aftermarkets, and the independent cartridge makers who were trying to break into these markets, are acting lawfully. Other hackers work for lawyers, reverse engineering products to prove patent infringements. There are academics who hack systems for glory, and to push forward the state of the art. And finally there are lots of grey areas. If you find a way to unlock a mobile phone, so that it can be used on any network, is that a crime? It depends on how you do it, and on what country you're in.

Given the wide range of products and the huge variation in quality, the security engineer needs to understand what tamper resistance is, and what it can and can't do. In this chapter I'm going to take you through the past thirty years of evolution of attack and defence.

If a computer cannot resist physical tampering, an attacker can simply change the software. Computers in data centres are protected by physical barriers, sensors and alarms. And an ATM is basically a PC in a safe with banknote dispensers and alarm sensors, often bolted to a wall or a plinth.

Where tamper resistance is needed purely for integrity and availability, it can sometimes be implemented using replication on different servers that perform transactions simultaneously and vote on the result; this is being reinvented nowadays with blockchains and other consensus protocols. The threshold schemes discussed in section 15.4 can also provide confidentiality for key material. But tamper-resistant devices can provide confidentiality for the data too, and the arrival of CPUs that support enclaves such as SGX and TrustZone hold out the prospect of computing with encrypted data in cloud services.

18.2 History

The use of tamper resistance in cryptography goes back centuries [1003]. Naval codebooks were weighted so they could be thrown overboard if capture was imminent; the dispatch boxes used by British government ministers' aides to carry state papers were lead-lined to make sure they'd sink. Codes have been printed in water-soluble ink; Russian one-time pads were printed on cellulose nitrate, so they'd burn furiously if lit; and one US wartime cipher machine came with self-destruct thermite charges. But key material was often captured in surprise attacks, so attempts were made to automate the tamper response process. Some mechanical cipher machines were built so that opening the case erased the key settings, and early electronic devices followed suit.

After the notorious Walker family sold US Navy key material to the Russians for over 20 years [878], engineers paid more attention to the question of how to protect keys in transit too. The goal was 'to reduce the street value of key material to zero', and this can be achieved either by *tamper resistant* devices from which the key cannot be readily extracted, or *tamper evident* ones from which key extraction would be obvious.

Paper keys were once carried in 'tattle-tale containers', designed to show evidence of tampering. When electronic key distribution came along, a typical solution was the 'fill gun': a portable device that dispenses crypto keys in a controlled way. Nowadays the physical transport of crypto key material usually involves a smartcard, or a similar chip packaged as a key. Your SIM card and bank card are just the most visible examples. The control of key material also acquired broader purposes, with both the US and the UK governments using it to restrict their networks to approved devices. Live key material would only be supplied once the system had been properly accredited.

Once initial keys have been loaded, further keys may be distributed using authentication protocols. Our subject here is the physical defenses against tampering.

18.3 Hardware security modules

The IBM 4758 (Figures 18.1 and 18.2) was the leading commercial cryptographic processor in the early 2000s, and is important for four reasons. First,

Figure 18.1: The IBM 4758 cryptoprocessor (courtesy of Steve Weingart)

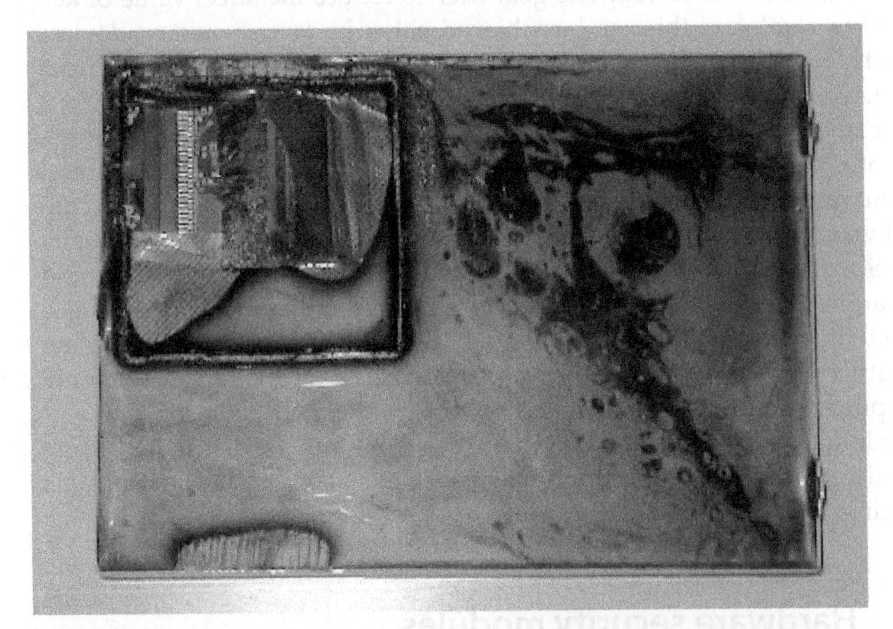

Figure 18.2: The 4758 partially opened showing (from top left downward) the circuitry, aluminium electromagnetic shielding, tamper-sensing mesh and potting material (courtesy of Frank Stajano)

it was the first commercial product to be evaluated to the highest level of tamper resistance (FIPS 140-1 level 4) [1401] then set by the US government. Second, there is an extensive literature about it, including its history, hardware and software [1646, 2002, 2005]. Third, it was therefore a high-profile target, and from 2000–2005 my students and I put a lot of effort into attacking it and understanding the residual vulnerabilities. Fourth, the current IBM flagship product, the 4765, isn't hugely changed except for fixing some of the bugs we found.

The back story starts in the 1970s, when Mikhail Atalla had the idea of a black-box cryptographic module to manage bank PINs. As early cryptographic schemes for ATMs were rather weak, IBM developed a better block cipher that became the Data Encryption Standard, as described in Chapter 5. There followed a period of intense research about precisely how block ciphers could be used to manage PINs in a single bank, and then in a network of many banks [1303]. The banking community realised that commercial operating systems were likely to remain insufficient to protect PINs, particularly from bank insiders, and decided to use separate hardware to manage them.

This led to the development of standalone cryptographic modules or *hardware security modules* (HSMs), as fintech people call them. These are microcomputers encased in robust metal enclosures, with encryption hardware and special *key memory*, static RAM that is zeroized when the enclosure is opened. Initially, this just involved wiring the power supply to the key memory through a number of lid switches. So whenever the maintenance crew came to replace batteries, they'd open the lid and destroy the keys. Once they'd finished, the HSM custodians would reload the key material. In this way, the HSM's owner could hope that its keys were under the unique control of its own trustworthy staff.

How to hack a cryptoprocessor (1)

The obvious attack is just to steal the keys. In early HSMs, the master keys were kept in PROMs that were loaded into a special socket in the device to be read during initialization, or as strings of numbers that were typed in at a console. The PROMs could be pocketed, taken home and read out. Cleartext paper keys were even easier: just scribble down a copy.

The fix was shared control – to have two or three master key components, and make the actual master key by combining them. The PROMs (or paper keys) would be kept in different safes under the control of different departments. This taught us that shared control is a serious security usability hazard. The manual may tell the custodians to erase the live keys, let the engineer fix the device, and then re-load the keys afterwards. But many senior men used to think that touching keyboards was women's work, and even today they think that technical work is beneath them. And who reads the manual anyway? So managers often give both keys to the engineer to save the bother. In one case, a dishonest engineer got them to enter the keys using a laptop that acted as a terminal but had logging switched on [55]. I've even come across cases of paper master keys for an automatic teller machine being kept in the correspondence file in a bank branch, where any of the staff could look them up.

How to hack a cryptoprocessor (2)

Early devices were vulnerable to attackers cutting through the casing. Second-generation devices made physical attacks harder by adding photocells and tilt switches. But the difficult opponent is the maintenance engineer – who could disable the sensors on one visit and extract the keys on the next.

By about 2000, the better products separated all the components that can be serviced (such as batteries) from the core of the device (such as the tamper sensors, cryptoprocessor, key memory and alarm circuits). The core was then potted into a solid block of a hard, opaque substance such as epoxy. The idea was that any physical attack would involve cutting or drilling, which could be detected by the guard who accompanies the engineer into the bank computer room[1]. At least it should leave evidence of tampering after the fact. This is the level of protection needed for medium-level evaluations under the FIPS standard.

How to hack a cryptoprocessor (3)

However, if a competent attacker can get unsupervised access to the device for even a short period of time – and, to be realistic, that's what the maintenance engineer probably has, as the guard doesn't understand what's going on – then potting the device core is inadequate. For example, you might scrape away the potting with a knife and drop the probe from a logic analyzer on to one of the chips. In theory, scraping the sticky epoxy should damage the components inside; in practice, it's just a matter of patience. Cryptographic algorithms such as RSA, DES and AES have the property that an attacker who can monitor any bitplane during the computation can recover the key [861].

So the high-end products acquired a tamper-sensing barrier. An early example appeared in IBM's μABYSS system in the mid-1980s, which used loops of 40-gauge nichrome wire wound loosely around the device as it was embedded in epoxy, and then connected to a sensing circuit [2002]. The theory was that techniques such as milling, etching and laser ablation would break the wire, erasing the keys. But the wire-in-epoxy technique can be vulnerable to slow erosion using sand blasting; when the sensing wires become visible at the surface of the potting, shunts can be connected round them. In 2018 Sergei Skorobogatov managed to use a combination of acid etching and masking to expose a battery-powered chip, on the Vasco Digipass 270, showing that given

[1]That at least was the theory; experience suggests it's a bit much to ask a minimum-wage guard to ensure that a specialist in some exotic piece of equipment repairs it using some tools but not others.

decent lab technique you can indeed attack live circuits protected by wires in epoxy [1785].

The next major product from IBM, the 4753, used a metal shield combined with a membrane printed with a pattern of conductive ink and surrounded by a more durable material of similar chemistry. The idea was that any attack would break the membrane with high probability. The 4758 had an improved tamper-sensing membrane in which four overlapping zig-zag conducting patterns were doped into a urethane sheet, which was potted in a chemically similar substance so that an attacker cutting into the device had difficulty even detecting the conductive path, let alone connecting to it. This potting surrounds the metal shielding, which in turn contains the cryptographic core. The design is described in more detail in [1799].

How to hack a cryptoprocessor (4)

The next class of attack exploited *memory remanence*, the fact that many kinds of computer memory retain some trace of data that have been stored there. Once a certain security module had run for some years using the same master keys, their values *burned in* to the device's static RAM. On power-up, about 90% of the relevant memory bits would assume the values of the previously stored secret keybits, which was quite enough to recover the keys [108]. Memory remanence affects not just static and dynamic RAM, but other storage media too. The relevant engineering and physics issues are discussed in [838] and [841], and in 2005 Sergei Skorobogatov discovered how to extract data from Flash memory in microcontrollers, even after it had been 'erased' several times [1774]; like it or not, the wear-levelling processors in Flash chips become part of your trusted computing base. RAM contents can also be *burned in* by ionising radiation, so radiation sensing or hardening might make sense too.

How to hack a cryptoprocessor (5)

Computer memory can also be frozen by low temperatures. By the 1980s it was realized that below about −20° C, static RAM contents can persist for several seconds after power is removed. This extends to minutes at the temperatures of liquid nitrogen. So an attacker might freeze a device, remove the power, cut through the tamper sensing barrier, extract the RAM chips containing the keys, and power them up again in a test rig.

In 2008, Alex Halderman and colleagues developed this into the *cold boot attack* on encryption keys in PCs and phones [855]. Modern DRAM retains memory contents for several seconds after power is removed, and even longer at low temperatures; by chilling memory with a freezing spray, then rebooting the device with a lightweight operating system, keys can often be read out. Software encryption of disk contents can be defeated unless there are mechanisms to zeroise the keys on power-down. Even keeping keys in special hardware such as a TPM isn't enough if all it's doing is limiting the number of times you can guess the hard disk encryption password, but then copying the master key to main memory once you get the password right so that the CPU can do the rest of the work. You need to really understand what guarantees the crypto chip is giving you – a matter we'll discuss at greater length in the chapter on advanced cryptographic engineering.

Anyway, the better cryptographic devices have temperature and radiation alarms. But modern RAM chips exhibit a wide variety of memory remanence behaviors; remanence seems to have got longer as feature sizes have shrunk, and in unpredictable ways even within standard product lines. So although your product might pass a remanence test using a given make of SRAM chip, it might fail the same test with the same make of chip purchased a year later [1772]. This shows the dangers of relying on a property of some component to whose manufacturer this property is unimportant.

The main constraints on the HSM alarms are similar to those we encountered with more general alarms. There's a tradeoff between the false alarm rate and the missed alarm rate, and thus between security and robustness. Vibration, power transients and electromagnetic interference can be a problem, but temperature is the worst. A device that self-destructs if frozen can't be sent reliably through normal distribution channels, as aircraft holds can get as low as −40°C. (We've bought crypto modules on eBay and found them dead on arrival.) Military equipment makers have the converse problem: their kit must be rated from −55° to +155° C. Some military devices use protective detonation; memory chips are potted in steel cans with a thermite charge precisely calculated to destroy the chip without causing gas release from the can. Meeting simultaneous targets for tamper resistance, temperature tolerance, radiation hardening, shipping safety, weight and cost can be nontrivial.

How to hack a cryptoprocessor (6)

The next set of attacks on cryptographic hardware involves monitoring the RF and other electromagnetic signals emitted by the device, or even injecting signals into it and measuring their externally visible effects. This technique, which is variously known as 'Tempest', 'power analysis,' 'side-channel attacks' or 'emission security', is such a large subject that I devote the next chapter to it.

As far as the 4758 was concerned, the strategy was to have solid aluminium shielding and to low-pass filter the power supply to block the egress of any signals at the frequencies used internally for computation. This shielding is inside the tamper-sensing membrane, to prevent an opponent cutting a slot that could function as an antenna.

How to hack a cryptoprocessor (7)

We never figured out how to attack the hardware of the 4758. The attacks we have seen on high-end systems have involved the exploitation of logical rather than physical flaws. One hardware security module, the Chrysalis-ITS

Luna CA3, had its key token's software reverse engineered by Mike Bond, Daniel Cvrček and Steven Murdoch who found code that enabled an unauthenticated "Customer Verification Key" to be introduced and used to certify the export of live keys [284]. Most recently, in 2019, Gabriel Campana and Jean-Baptiste Bédrune found a buffer overflow attack on the Gemalto Safenet Protect Server PSI-E2/PSE2 by fuzzing the HSM emulator that came with its software development kit, then checked this on a real HSM, and wrote code to upload arbitrary firmware, which is persistent and can download all the secrets [204].

This did not happen to IBM's 4758, which had a formally verified operating system. But most of its users ran a banking crypto application called CCA that is described in [917]. Mike Bond and I discovered that the application programming interface (API) that CCA exposed to the host contained a number of exploitable flaws. The effect was that a programmer with access to the host could send the security module a series of commands that would cause it to leak PINs or keys. These vulnerabilities were largely the legacy of previous encryption devices with which 4758 users needed to be backward compatible, and in fact most other security modules were worse. Such attacks were hard to stop, as from time to time Visa would mandate new cryptographic operations to support new payment network features and these would introduce new systemic vulnerabilities across the whole fleet of security modules [22]. Some HSMs now have two APIs: an internal one which the vendor tries to keep clean (but which needs to have the ability to import and export keys) and an external one that implements the standards of whatever industry the HSM is being used to support. The software between the two APIs may be trusted, but can be hard to make trustworthy if the external API is insecure. In effect, it has to anticipate and block API attacks. The end result is that many banks pay top dollar for secure HSMs which they use for formal compliance, while relying on other access control mechanisms to shield these precious devices from attack. There are even specialist firms selling firewalls to shield HSMs from software-based harm. I'll discuss API attacks in detail in the chapter on advanced cryptographic engineering.

18.4 Evaluation

A few comments about the evaluation of HSMs are in order before we go on to discuss cheaper devices. When IBM launched the 4753 in 1991, they proposed the following classification of attackers in the associated white paper [9]:

1. Class 1 attackers – 'clever outsiders' – are often very intelligent but may have insufficient knowledge of the system. They may have access to only moderately sophisticated equipment. They often try to take advantage of an existing weakness in the system, rather than try to create one.

2. Class 2 attackers – 'knowledgeable insiders' – have substantial specialized technical education and experience. They have varying degrees of understanding of parts of the system but potential access to most of it. They often have highly sophisticated tools and instruments for analysis.
3. Class 3 attackers – 'funded organizations' – are able to assemble teams of specialists with related and complementary skills backed by great funding resources. They are capable of in-depth analysis of the system, designing sophisticated attacks, and using the most advanced analysis tools. They may use Class 2 adversaries as part of the attack team.

Within this scheme, the typical microcontroller is aimed at blocking clever outsiders; the early 4753 aimed at stopping knowledgeable insiders, and the 4758 was aimed at (and certified for) blocking funded organizations. This classification is now a bit dated; we see class 1 attackers renting access to class 3 equipment, while class 3 attackers nowadays are not just national labs, but commercial competitors and even university security teams. In our case, we have people with backgrounds in maths, physics, software and banking, and we've had friendly manufacturers giving us samples of their competitors' products for us to break.

The FIPS certification scheme is operated by laboratories licensed by the US government. The original 1994 standard, FIPS 140-1, set out four levels of protection, with level 4 being the highest, and this remained in the next version, FIPS 140-2, which was introduced in 2001. There was a huge gap between level 4 and level 3; devices at that level were often easy for experts to attack. In fact, the original paper on evaluation by IBM engineers proposed six levels [2005]; the FIPS standard adopted the first three of these as its levels 1–3, and the proposed level 6 as its level 4 (the 4758 designer Steve Weingart tells the story in [2004]). The gap, commonly referred to as level 3.5 or 3+, is where many of the better commercial systems were aimed from the 1990s through 2019. Such equipment attempts to keep out the class 1 attack community, while making life hard for class 2 and expensive for class 3.

There was about a decade of consultation about whether to abandon FIPS 140 in favour of ISO 19790 – a move supported by vendors, particularly those outside the USA. Critics of the FIPS approach noted that it didn't cover non-invasive security such as buffer overflows and API attacks; that its concept of roles was tied to human actors in companies, rather than other system components; that it failed to cover some methods of side-channel analysis; that it was generally aimed at outdated technology; that the FIPS standard includes the dual elliptic curve deterministic random bit generator, known to contain an NSA backdoor; and that it was changed too often by NIST issuing implementation guidelines, rather than by updating the standard regularly [1412]. Eventually, the US Department of Commerce gave up and approved an updated version, FIPS 140-3, which simply refers to the ISO standards 19790:2012 and 24759:2017, and specifies some refinements. This came into force in September 2019 and in 2021 testing under FIPS 140-2 will cease.

18.5 Smartcards and other security chips

While there are tens of thousands of HSMs in use, there are billions of self-contained one-chip crypto modules containing nonvolatile memory, I/O, usually a CPU, often some specialised logic, and mechanisms to protect memory from being read out. Most are packaged as cards, while some look like physical keys. They range from transport tickets at the low end, through smartcards and the TPMs that now ship with most computers and phones, up to pay-TV cards and accessory control chips designed to withstand attack by capable motivated opponents for as long as possible.

Many attacks have been developed; we discussed the consequences of the breaks of the Mifare cards in section 13.2.5 and of car keys in section 4.3.1. Pay-TV subscriber cards in particular have been subjected to intensive attacks as they often have a universal shared secret key, so a compromise enables an attacker to make lots of counterfeit cards, while a break of a bank smartcard only lets the attacker loot that specific bank account. The accessory control chips in printer cartridges also protect a lot of 'value', and have driven real innovation in both attack and defence. I'll describe both pay-TV and accessory control in the chapter on copyright; in this section, I'll tell the story of how chip-level security evolved.

18.5.1 History

Smartcards were developed in France from the mid-70s to mid-80s; for the early history, see [833]. From the late 1980s, they started to be used at scale, initially as the *subscriber identity modules* (SIMs) in GSM mobile phones and as subscriber cards for satellite-TV stations. They started being used as bank cards in France and South Africa in 1994, followed by trials in the UK and Norway; this led to the EMV standard I mentioned in the chapter on banking and bookkeeping, with deployment in the rest of Europe from 2003 and the USA from about 2015.

A smartcard is a self-contained microcontroller, with a microprocessor, memory and a serial interface integrated in a single chip and packaged in a plastic card. Smartcards used in banking use a standard-size bank card, while in modern mobile phones a much smaller size is used. Smartcard chips are also packaged in other ways. In the STU-III secure telephones used in the US government from 1987–2009, each user had a 'crypto ignition key', packaged to look and feel like a physical key; some prepayment electricity meters and pay-TV set-top boxes used the same approach. The TPM chips built into computer motherboards to support trusted boot are basically smartcard chips with an added parallel port, so the TPM can verify that the right software is being used to start up the computer. Contactless smartcards contain a smartcard chip plus a wire-loop antenna; most car keys are a slightly more complex version of the same idea, with an added battery to give greater range. In what follows I'll mostly disregard the packaging form factor and just refer to single-chip cryptographic modules as 'smartcards' or 'chipcards'.

Apart from bank cards, the single most widespread application is the mobile phone SIM. The handsets are personalized for each user by the SIM, which contains the key with which you authenticate yourself to the network. The strategy of using a cheap card to personalise a more expensive electronic device is found in other applications from pay-TV set-top boxes to smart meters. The device can be manufactured in bulk for global markets, while each subscriber gets a card to pay for service. The cards can also be replaced relatively quickly and cheaply in the event of a successful attack.

18.5.2 Architecture

The typical smartcard consists of a single die of up to 25 square millimeters of silicon containing a microprocessor (larger dies are more likely to break as the card is flexed). Cheap products have an 8-bit processor such as an 8051 or 6805, and the more expensive products have either a modular multiplication circuit to do public-key cryptography, or a 32-bit processor such as an Arm, or indeed both (hardware crypto is easier to protect against side-channel attacks). The high-end ones also tend to have a hardware random number generator. There's also serial I/O and a hierarchy of memory – ROM or Flash to hold the program and immutable data, Flash or EEPROM to hold customer data such as the user's account number, crypto keys, PIN retry counters and value counters; and RAM to hold transient data during computation.

The memory is limited by the standards of normal computers; outside the device, the only connections are for power, reset, a clock and a serial port. The physical, electrical and low-level logical connections, together with a file-system-like access protocol, are specified in ISO 7816. There are several main software architectures on offer, including at the bottom end the *Application Programming Data Units* (APDUs) defined by ISO 7816 which allow a reader to invoke specific applications directly, through the Multos operating system, to JavaCard which lets the card run apps written in a subset of the Java language, and which you (and your opponents in the underground) can use to code up custom apps[2]. You can even buy overlay SIMs – smartcards 160 microns thick with contacts top and bottom, which you can program in JavaCard to carry out middleperson attacks on other smartcards (you stick the overlay on top of the target device).

18.5.3 Security evolution

When I first heard a sales pitch from a smartcard vendor – in 1986 when I was working as a banker – I asked how come the device was secure. I was assured that since the machinery needed to make the card cost $20m, just as for making banknotes, the system must be secure. I didn't believe this but didn't have the time or the tools to prove the salesman wrong. I later learned from industry executives that none of their customers were prepared to pay for serious security until about 1995; until then they relied on the small size of the devices, the obscurity of their design, and the inaccessibility of chip testing tools to make attacks more difficult. In any case, so long as they were only used for SIM cards, there were no capable motivated opponents. All I can achieve by hacking my SIM card is the ability to charge calls to my own account.

The application that changed this was satellite TV. TV operators broadcast their signals over a large footprint – such as all of Europe – and give each subscriber a card to compute the keys needed to decipher the channels they've paid for. Since the operators had usually only bought the rights to the movies for one or two countries, they couldn't sell subscriber cards elsewhere. This created a black market, into which forged cards could be sold. A critical factor was that 'Star Trek', which people in Europe had picked up from UK satellite broadcasts for years, was suddenly encrypted in 1993. In some countries, such as Germany, it wasn't available legally at any price. This motivated a lot of keen young computer science and engineering students to look for vulnerabilities. A further factor was that some countries, notably Ireland and Canada, didn't have laws yet against selling forged pay-TV cards; Canada didn't do this until 2002. So hackers could sell their wares openly.

This rapidly had knock-on effects. The first large financial fraud reported to involve a cloned smartcard was about a year later, in February/March 1995. The perpetrator targeted a card used to give Portuguese farmers rebates on fuel, conspiring with petrol stations who registered other fuel sales to the bogus cards in return for a share of the proceeds. The proceeds were reported to have been about $30m [1332].

How to hack a smartcard (1)

The earliest hacks targeted the protocols rather than the cards themselves. For example, some early pay-TV systems gave each customer a card with access

[2]JavaCard has quietly become one of the most widely deployed operating systems in the world with over 6 billion cards sold [1252].

to all channels, and then sent messages over the air to cancel those channels to which the customer hadn't subscribed after an introductory period. This opened an attack in which a device was inserted between the smartcard and the decoder to intercept and discard any messages addressed to the card. So you could cancel your subscription without the vendor being able to cancel your service. The same kind of attack was launched on the German phone card system, with handmade chip cards sold in brothels and in hostels for asylum seekers [185,1817].

How to hack a smartcard (2)

As smartcards use an external power supply, and store security state such as crypto keys and value counters in EEPROM, an attacker could freeze the EEPROM contents by removing the programming voltage, V_{PP}. Early smartcards received V_{PP} from the card reader on a dedicated contact. So by covering this contact with sticky tape, cardholders could prevent a value counter from being decremented. With some payphone chipcards, this gave infinite units.

The fix was to generate V_{PP} internally from the supply voltage V_{CC} using a voltage multiplier. However, this isn't foolproof as the circuit can be destroyed by an attacker, for example with a laser shot. As well as bypassing value controls, they can also bypass a PIN retry counter and try every possible PIN, one after another. So a prudent programmer won't just ask for a customer PIN and decrement the counter if it fails. You decrement the counter, check it, get the PIN, verify it, and if it's correct then increment the counter again[3].

How to hack a smartcard (3)

Another early attack was to read the voltages on the chip surface using a scanning electron microscope (SEM). The low-cost SEMs found in universities back then couldn't do voltage contrast microscopy at more than a few tens of kilohertz, so attackers would slow down the clock. In one card, attackers found they read out RAM contents with a suitable transaction after reset, as working memory wasn't zeroized.

Modern smartcard processors have a watchdog timer or other circuit to detect low clock frequency and reset the card, or else use dynamic logic. And the attacker could sometimes single-step the program by repeatedly resetting the card and clocking it n times, then $n+1$ times, and so on. But as with burglar alarms, there's a tradeoff between false alarms and missed alarms. Cheap card readers can have wild fluctuations in clock frequency when a card is powered up, causing many false alarms. Eventually, cards acquired an internal clock.

[3]Such *defensive programming* was common in the early days of computing, when computers used valves rather than transistors and used to break down every few hours. Back then, if you masked off three bits, you'd check the result was no more than seven, just to make sure.

How to hack a smartcard (4)

Once pay-TV operators had blocked the easy attacks, pirates turned to physical probing. Early smartcards had no protection against physical tampering except the microscopic scale of the circuit, a thin glass *passivation layer* on the surface of the chip, and potting that is typically some kind of epoxy. Techniques for depackaging chips are well known, and discussed in detail in standard works on semiconductor testing, such as [198]. In most cases, a milliliter of fuming nitric acid is more than enough to dissolve the epoxy.

Probing stations consist of microscopes with micromanipulators attached for landing fine probes on the surface of the chip. They are used in the semiconductor industry for testing production-line samples, and can be bought second-hand (see Figure 18.3). They may have specialized accessories, such as a laser to shoot holes in the chip's passivation layer.

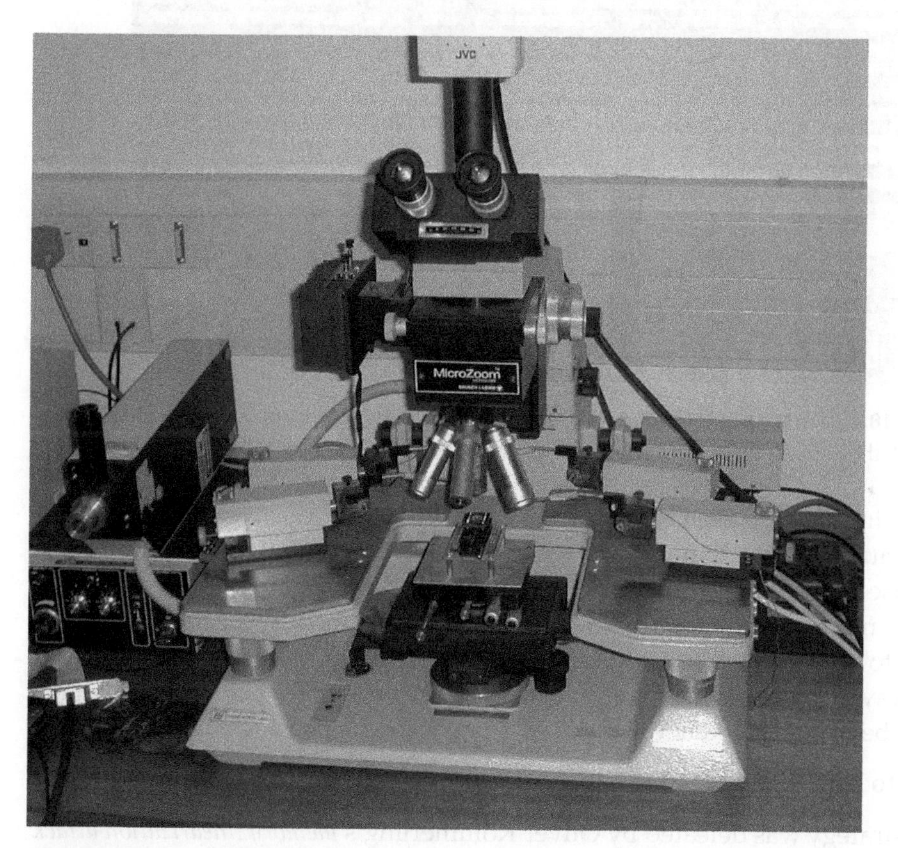

Figure 18.3: Our probing station

The usual target of a probing attack is the processor's bus. If the bus traffic can be recorded, this gives a trace of the program's operation. (It was once a recommended industry practice for the card to compute a checksum on memory immediately after reset – giving a complete listing of all code and data.) So the attacker will find the bus and expose it for probing (see Figure 18.4). If the chip is using algorithms like AES and RSA, then unless there's some defense mechanism that masks the computation, a trace from even a single bus line will be enough to reconstruct the key [861].

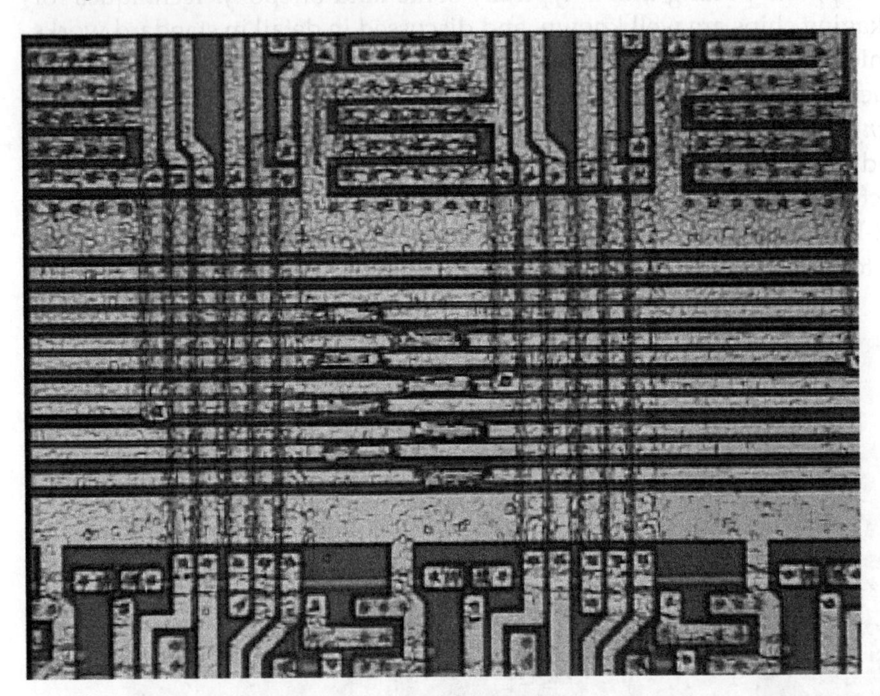

Figure 18.4: The data bus of an ST16 smartcard prepared for probing by excavating eight trenches through the passivation layer with laser shots (courtesy Oliver Kömmerling)

The first defense used by the pay-TV card industry was to endow each card with multiple keys or algorithms, and arrange things so that only those in current use would appear on the processor bus. Whenever pirate cards appeared on the market, a command would be issued over the air to cause legitimate cards to activate new keys or algorithms from previously unused memory. In this way, the pirates' customers would suffer a loss of service until the attack could be repeated and new pirate cards or updates could be distributed [2067].

How to hack a smartcard (5)

This strategy was defeated by Oliver Kömmerling's *memory linearization attack* in which the analyst damages the chip's instruction decoder in such a way that instructions such as jumps and calls – which change the program address other than by incrementing it – are broken [1080]. One way to do this is to drop a grounded microprobe needle on the control line to the instruction latch, so that whatever instruction happens to be there on power-up is executed repeatedly. The memory contents can now be read off the bus. In fact, once some of the device's ROM and EEPROM is understood, the attacker can skip over unwanted instructions and cause the device to execute only instructions of their choice. So with a single probing needle, they can get the card to execute arbitrary code, and in theory could get it to output its secret key material on the serial port. This can be thought of as an early version of the return-oriented programming attack. But probing the memory contents off the bus is usually more convenient.

There are often several places in the instruction decoder where a grounded needle will prevent programmed changes in the control flow. So even if it isn't fully understood, memory linearization can often be achieved by trial and error. One particularly vulnerable smartcard family was the Hitachi H8/300 architecture, which had a 16-bit bus with the property that if the most significant bit equals 1 then the CPU will always execute single-cycle instructions without any branches. So by shooting the MSB bus line with a laser, the memory could be easily read out [1785]. Other CPUs based on RISC cores also tend to suffer from this. Some of the more modern processors have traps which prevent memory linearization, such as watchdog timers that reset the card unless they themselves are reset every few thousand instructions.

Memory linearization is an example of a *fault induction attack*. There are many other examples. Faults can be injected into processors in many ways, from hardware probing through power transients and laser illumination. One common target is the test circuitry. A typical chip has a self-test routine in ROM that is executed in the factory and allows all the memory contents to be read and verified. In some cases, a fuse is blown in the chip to stop an attacker using the facility. But the attacker can cause a fault in this mechanism – whether by flipping a bit in Flash memory [1780], or just finding the fuse and bridging it with two probing needles [303]. In other cases, the test routine is protected with a password, which can be found [1779].

We noted in section 5.7.1 that the RSA algorithm is fragile in the presence of failure; one laser shot is all it takes to cause a signature to be right modulo p and wrong modulo q, enabling the attacker to factor the key pq. Adi Shamir pointed out that if a CPU has an error in its multiply unit – even just a single computation $ab = c$ whose result is returned consistently wrong in a single bit – then you can design an RSA ciphertext for decryption (or an RSA plaintext for signature) so that the computation will be done correctly mod p but incorrectly mod q, again enabling you to factor the key [1708]. So a careful programmer will always check the results of critical computations, and think hard about what error messages might disclose.

How to hack a smartcard (6)

The next thing the pay-TV card industry tried was to incorporate hardware cryptographic processors, in order to force attackers to reconstruct hardware circuits rather than simply clone software, and to force them to use more expensive processors in their pirate cards. In the first such implementation, the crypto processor was a separate chip packaged into the card, and it had an interesting protocol failure: it would always work out the key needed to decrypt the current video stream, and then pass it to the CPU which would decide whether or not to pass it on to the outside world. Hackers just tapped the wire between the two chips.

The next version had the crypto hardware built into the CPU itself. Where this consists of just a few thousand gates, an attacker can trace the circuit manually from micrographs. But with larger gate counts and deep submicron processes, a successful attack needs serious tools: you need to etch or grind away the layers of the chip, take electron micrographs, and use image processing software to reconstruct the circuit [270]. Equipment can now be rented and circuit-reconstruction software can be bought; the short resource now is skilled reverse engineers.

By the late 1990s, some pirates had started to get commercial reverse-engineering labs to reconstruct chips for them. Such labs get much of their business from analyzing integrated circuits on behalf of chip makers' competitors, looking for patent infringements. They also reverse chips used for accessory control, as doing this for compatibility rather than piracy is lawful. Many labs were located in Canada, where copying pay-TV cards wasn't a crime until 2002 (though there were at least two cases where these labs were sued by pay-TV operators). Some labs are now in China, whose legal system is harder for outsiders to navigate.

How to hack a smartcard (7)

In 1995 STM pioneered a new defence, a protective shield on the chip surface. This was a serpentine sensor line, zig-zagging round ground lines in a top metal layer. Any break or short would be sensed as soon as the chip was powered up, whereupon the chip would overwrite the keys.

Sensor mesh shields can really push up the cost of an attack. One bypass is to hold the sensor line to V_{DD} with a needle, but this can be fragile; and other vendors have multiple sensor lines with real signals on them. So if you cut them, you have to repair them, and the tool for the job is the *Focused Ion Beam Workstation* (FIB). This is a device similar to a scanning electron microscope but which uses a beam of ions instead of electrons. By varying the beam current, it can be used either as a microscope or as a milling machine, with a useful resolution under 10 nanometers. By introducing a gas that's broken down by the ion beam, you can lay down either conductors or insulators with a precision of a few tens of nanometers. For a detailed description of FIBs and other semiconductor test equipment that can be used in reverse engineering, see [1235].

FIBs are so useful in all sorts of applications, from semiconductor testing through metallurgy and forensics to nanotechnology, that they are widely available in physics and material-science labs, and can be rented for about a hundred dollars an hour.

Given such a tool, it is straightforward to attack a shield that is not powered up. The direct approach is to drill a hole through the mesh to the metal line that carries the desired signal, fill it up with insulator, drill another hole through the center of the insulator, fill it with metal, and plate a contact on top – typically a platinum 'X' a few microns wide, which you then contact with a needle from your probing station (see Figure 18.5). There are many more tricks, such as using the voltage contrast and backscatter modes of your electron microscope to work out exactly where to cut, so you can disable a whole section of the mesh. John Walker has a video tutorial on how to use these tricks to defeat a shield at [1979].

Many other defenses can force the attacker to do more work. Some chips have protective coatings of silicon carbide or boron nitride, which can force the FIB operator to go slowly rather than damage the chip through a build-up of electrical charge. Chips with protective coatings are on display at the NSA Museum at Fort Meade, Maryland.

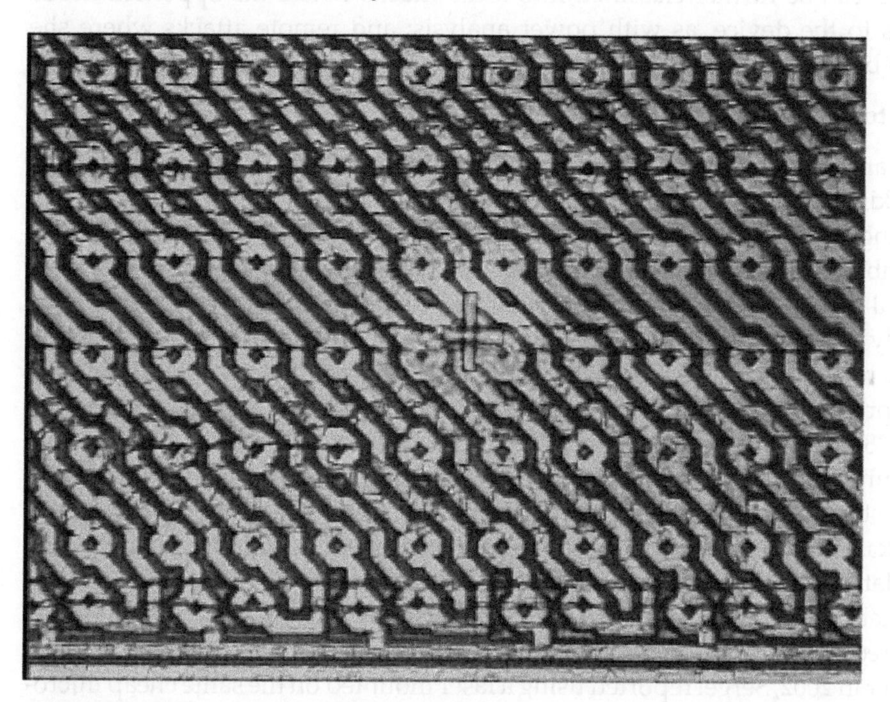

Figure 18.5: The protective mesh of an ST16 smartcard with a FIB cross for probing the bus line visible underneath (courtesy Oliver Kömmerling)

How to hack a smartcard (8)

In 1998, the smartcard industry was shaken when Paul Kocher announced a new attack known as *differential power analysis* (DPA). This relies on the fact that different instructions consume different amounts of power, so by measuring the current drawn by a chip it was possible to extract the key. Smartcard makers had known since the 1980s that this was theoretically possible, and had even patented some crude countermeasures. But Paul came up with efficient signal processing techniques that made it easy, and which I'll describe in the following chapter. He came up with even simpler attacks based on timing; if cryptographic operations don't take the same number of clock cycles, this can leak key material too[4]. Power and timing attacks are examples of *side-channel attacks*, where the opponent can observe some extra information about the processor's state during a cryptographic computation. All the smartcards on the market in 1998 turned out to be highly vulnerable to DPA, and this held up the industry's development for a couple of years while countermeasures were developed.

Attacks were traditionally classed as either *invasive attacks* such as mechanical probing, which involves penetrating the passivation layer, and *noninvasive attacks* such as power analysis, which leaves the card untouched. Noninvasive attacks can be further classified into local attacks where the opponent needs access to the device, as with power analysis; and remote attacks where she could be anywhere, such as timing attacks. But that was not the whole story.

How to hack a smartcard (9)

Mechanical probing techniques have been getting steadily harder because of shrinking feature sizes. The next attack technology to develop was optical probing. The first report was from Sandia National Laboratories who in 1995 described a way to read out a voltage directly using a laser [33]. Since 2001 optical probing has been developed into an effective and low-cost technology, largely by my Cambridge colleague Sergei Skorobogatov. In 2002 Sergei and I reported using a photographic flashgun, mounted on the microscope of a probing station, to induce transient faults in selected transistors of an IC [1786]. The light ionises the silicon, causing transistors to conduct. Once you understand photoconductivity and learn to focus the light on single transistors, by upgrading from a flashgun to a laser, this enables many direct attacks. For example, microcontrollers can be opened by toggling the flip-flop that latches their protection state. This gave a new way of causing not just transient fault attacks, as on fragile cryptosystems such as RSA, but faults that are precisely directed and controlled in both space and time.

Later in 2002, Sergei reported using a laser mounted on the same cheap microscope to read out a microcontroller's memory directly. The basic idea is simple: if you shine a laser on a transistor, that will induce a photocurrent and increase

[4]On larger processors, it can be even worse; a number of researchers developed attacks on crypto algorithms such as AES based on cache misses during the 2000s, and in 2018 we had the Spectre and Meltdown attacks that exploit transient execution. See the chapter on side channels.

the device's power consumption – unless it was conducting already. So by scanning the laser across the device, you map which transistors are off and which are on. We developed this into a reasonably dependable way of reading out flip-flops and RAM memory [1651]. We named our attack *semi-invasive analysis* as it lies between the existing categories of invasive and non-invasive. It's not invasive, as we don't break the passivation; but we do remove the epoxy, so it doesn't count as non-invasive either.

Optical probing from the front side of the chip remained the state of the art for about five years. By the time of this book's second edition (2007), smartcard vendors were using 0.18 and 0.13 micron processes, typically with seven metal layers. Direct optical probe attacks from the chip surface had become difficult, not so much because of the feature size but because the metal layers get in the way. In addition, the sheer size and complexity of the chips was making it difficult to know where to aim. The difficulty was increased by *glue logic* – essentially randomised place-and-route.

Older chips have clearly distinguishable blocks, and quite a lot can be learned about their structure and organisation just by looking. Bus lines could be picked out and targeted for attack. However, the SX28 in Figure 18.6 just

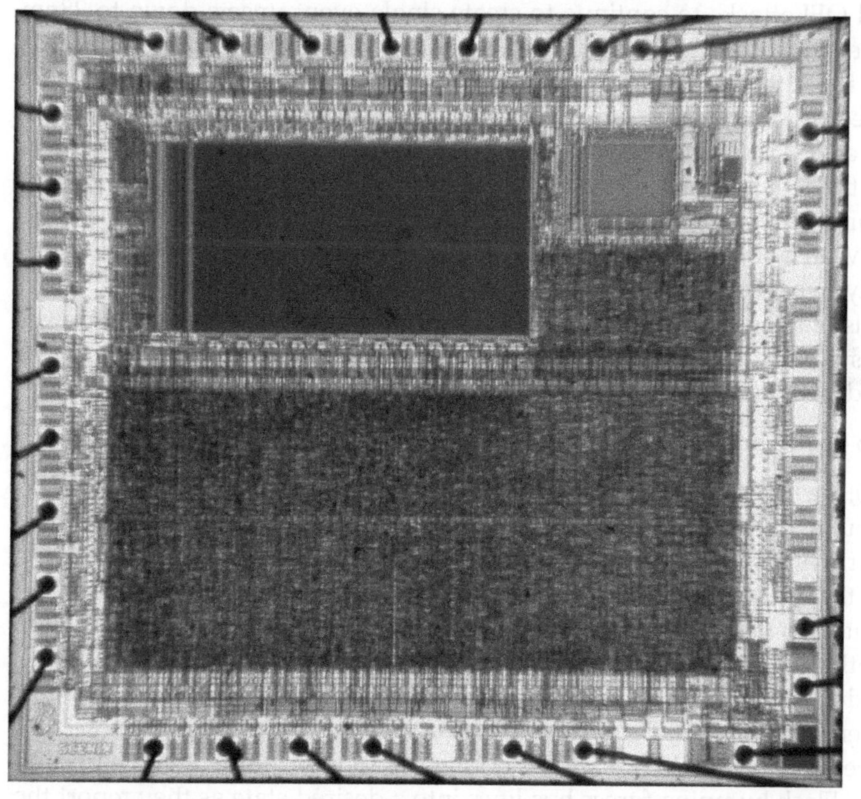

Figure 18.6: SX28 microcontroller with 'glue logic' (courtesy of Sergei Skorobogatov)

looks like a random sea of gates. The only easily distinguishable features are the EEPROM (at top left) and the RAM (at top right). It takes some work to find the CPU, the instruction decoder and the bus.

I wrote in the second edition, "The two current windows of vulnerability are the memory and the rear side." These have provided our Tamper Lab's main research targets during the decade since.

How to hack a smartcard (10)

Rear-side attacks are the practical semi-invasive option once you get below 0.35μ. You go through the back of the chip using an infrared laser at a wavelength around 1.1μ where silicon is transparent. For feature sizes below 65nm, you need to thin down the chip to 2–5μ using some combination of mechanical polishing and chemical etching; and there are now special methods to improve the resolution, such as silicon immersion lenses. One physical limit is you can't get a bandwidth of much over a few MHz because of the time taken for the charge carriers to recombine.

Rear-side attacks can sometimes be used to extract ROM contents by direct observation, but the main technique is optical fault induction (OFI), which has now become a standard security test procedure. Silicon immersion lenses have enabled OFI attacks to continue to create single-event upsets down to 28nm silicon, even though the laser spot size is about a micron [593]. Most smartcards current in 2019 tend to use about 90nm with the smallest about 65nm [1865]. The three big vendors have all announced 40nm products. So OFI will continue to be practical for some time.

With the smaller feature sizes, you have to accept that your aim in both space and time will often be fuzzy, and you may use the laser in combination with another more precise technique. One starting point here was optically-enhanced position-locked power analysis. By illuminating the *n* channels of a memory cell, the signal observed from a state change by power analysis is increased; with higher light levels, even read accesses can be detected. This enables much more selective analysis [1775].

How to hack a smartcard (11)

By 2010, the logic in most security chips was glue logic with few discernible features, but since Flash memory needs high voltages and large charge pumps, Flash arrays are large and easily identifiable. Chipmakers worried that the attacks that targeted chips with a separate V_{PP} programming voltage might be reinvented by using a laser to interfere with the charge pumps. So they tried to stop both memory corruption and the exploitation of memory readback access by making secure Flash with a per-block verify-only operation when memory is written. Sergei's *bumping attack* was inspired by the bumping attacks on locks described in Chapter 13. Just as lock bumping forces cylinders into a desired state, so Flash bumping forces bus lines into a desired state as they report the results of memory verification [1778].

But perhaps the most significant recent breakthrough was in 2016, when Franck Courbon, Sergei Skorobogatov and Chris Woods discovered how to use the latest generation of scanning electron microscopes to automate the direct read-out of Flash and EEPROM. As the memory cells store a bit by the presence or absence of a few hundred electrons in a floating gate, it's tricky to read them out without using the circuits designed for the purpose – especially when using a beam consisting of billions of electrons, aimed through the rear side of the chip. (We used to compare this with reading a palimpsest with a blowlamp.) Making it work requires very careful sample preparation, a SEM that supports passive voltage contrast (PVC), fine-tuned scan acquisition and efficient image processing [480]. Using such tools and techniques, it's now possible to read out the 256K of Flash or EEPROM from a typical smartcard or other security chip with perhaps half a dozen single-bit errors. This had been predicted as long ago as 2000 by Steve Weingart, the 4758 designer [2003]; PVC made it a reality. The effect on the smartcard industry is that the entire memory of the chip can now be read out. Reverse engineering is a matter of figuring out the CPU's instruction set, how the memory is encrypted, and so on.

How to hack a smartcard (12)

Reverse engineering services in China now charge 30c per gate, so the brute-force approach is to just reverse the whole chip and drop it in a simulator without trying to understand it in detail. Given that a typical smartcard has 100,000 gates, this means you can get a simulator for $30,000. Then you have all sorts of options. Once you have sufficiently understood one card of a particular type, the per-card cloning cost is now the cost of memory extraction. You can also use the simulation to look for side-channel attacks, to plan FIB edits, or to fuzz the device and look for other vulnerabilities.

As smartcards are computers, they can sometimes fall to the usual computer attacks, such as stack overwriting, by sending too long a string of parameters. As early as 1996, the Mondex card, used in a payment trial by the UK's NatWest Bank, boasted a formally verified operating system. Yet as late as 2019, software attacks worked against at least one SIM card. Malicious SMSes were used by nation-state attackers to download malware into the SIMs of target users so that their location could be tracked [575].

18.5.4 Random number generators and PUFs

Many crypto chips are offered with a random number generator, a physical unclonable function, or both.

Hardware random number generators (RNGs) are used to produce protocol nonces and session keys. Weak generators have led to many catastrophic security failures, of which a number pop up in this book. Poor nonces lead to replay attacks, while weak session keys can compromise long-term signing keys in cryptographic algorithms such as ECDSA. During the 1990s, the fashion was for algorithmic random number generation; this is properly known as a *pseudorandom number generator* (PRNG). A crypto chip might have had a special key-generation key that was used in counter encryption mode; operating systems often had something similar. However, if the counter is reset, then the output is repeated; there have been several variants on this theme. I also mentioned the NIST Dual-EC-DRBG, which was built into Windows and seemed to have contained an NSA trapdoor [1737]; Ed Snowden later confirmed that the NSA paid RSA $10m to use this standard in tools that many tech companies licensed [1292].

Hardware random number generators typically quantise jitter or use some source of metastability such as a cross-coupled inverter pair. Such generators are notoriously difficult to test; faults can be induced by external noise such as temperature, supply voltage and radiation. Standards such as NIST SP800-A/B/C call for RNG output to be run through test circuits. Crypto products often mix together the randomness from a number of sources both environmental and internal [839], and this is a requirement for the highest levels of certification. The way these sources are combined is often the critical thing and one should beware of designs that try to be too clever [1035]. One must also beware that hardware RNGs are usually proprietary, obscure designs, sometimes specific to a single fab, so it's hard to check that the design is sound, let alone that it doesn't contain a subtle backdoor. An example of conservative design may be that used in Intel chips since 2012, which combines both a hardware RNG and a software PRNG that follows it [857].

The manufacture of crypto chips typically involves a personalisation stage where serial numbers and crypto keys are loaded into Flash or EEPROM. This is another attack point: Ed Snowden reported that GCHQ had hacked the mechanisms used by Gemalto to personalise cards, and got copies of the keys in millions of SIMs. So one might ask whether chips could be manufactured with an intrinsic key that would never leave the device. Each chip would create a private key and export the public key, which the vendor would certify during personalisation. But this takes time, and also seems to need an RNG on the chip. Is there another way?

A physical unclonable function (PUF) is a means of identifying a device from variations that occur naturally during manufacture. In the 1980s, Sandia National Laboratories were asked by the US Federal Reserve whether it was possible to make unforgeable banknote paper, and they came up with the idea of chopping up optical fibre into the mash, so you could recognise each note by a unique speckle pattern [1750]. Such a mechanism should be unclonable, and its behaviour should change detectably if it's tampered with. Could something similar be devised for integrated circuits? In 2000, Oliver and Fritz Kömmerling proposed loading chip packaging with metal fibres and measuring its properties to generate a key with which the chip contents would be encrypted, so that drilling through the packaging would destroy the key [1081]. In 2002 Blaise Gassend, Dwaine Clarke, Marten Van Dijk and Srini Devadas proposed using process variability in the silicon itself, suggesting that a collection of ring oscillators might be chaotic enough to be unique [754]. There followed the usual coevolution of attack and defence as people proposed designs and others broke them.

Through the 2010s we've started to see PUFs appearing in significant numbers of low-cost chips as well as in higher-value products such as FPGAs. The typical 'weak PUF' generates a consistent random number on power-up from process variability; an SRAM PUF reads the initial state of some SRAM cells and is used, with error correction, as a stable random ID or as an AES key to encrypt memory or to drive a PRNG. If your opponent is capable of reversing your circuit and scanning your Flash memory, a PUF may at least force them to go to the trouble of probing the key off the bus, or inducing faults one bus line at a time to read it out using differential fault analysis.

PUF marketing often claims much more, and one claim (as well as a research goal) is a 'strong PUF' which would act as a hardware challenge-response mechanism. Given an input, it would return an output that would be sufficiently different for each chip (and each input) to be usable as a cryptographic primitive in itself. For example, one might send a thousand challenges to the chip at personalisation and store the responses for later key updating. Note that this would not of itself have stopped the NSA attack on Gemalto, as they hacked the personalisation files and if PUFs had been used they'd have got the challenge-response pair files too.

The state of the art in 2020 appears to be *XOR arbiter PUFs*, which consist of a chain of multiplexers followed by an arbiter. The challenge to the PUF is input to the address lines of the multiplexers that select a route for signals to race through them to get to the arbiter. To make it harder for an attacker to work out the relative delay on each circuit path, the outputs of a number of arbiters are XORed together. However, Fatemeh Ganji, Shahin Tajik and Jean-Pierre Seifert have shown that suitable machine-learning techniques can be used to model the underlying circuits [745]. The same authors worked with Heiko Lohrke and Christian Boit to develop laser fault induction attacks, guided by the chip's optical emissions, that disable some arbiters so that others can be learned more quickly, and thus significantly reduce the PUFs' entropy [1862]. There are always probing attacks, as some routine on the chip has to be able to read the PUF for it to do any work, and this means the bootloader or the monitor. As these are often left open to parts of the supply chain for personalisation, warranty and upgrade purposes, it's hard to see what extra protection such devices would give, even if we could invent one that works properly. Also, using such devices at scale would tend to make personalisation slower and protocols more complex. Finally, the strength of a PUF depends on variation that the fab tries its best to eliminate, so a change in silicon process can suddenly make a PUF design insecure.

18.5.5 Larger chips

There's a growing number of larger chips with embedded security functions, typically aimed at manufacturing control or accessory control. The granddaddy of these products may be the *Clipper chip*, which the Clinton administration proposed in 1993 as a replacement for DES. Also known as the *Escrowed Encryption Standard* (EES), this was a tamper-resistant chip containing the Skipjack block cipher and a protocol designed to allow the FBI to decrypt any traffic encrypted using it. When you gave Clipper some plaintext and a key to encrypt it, the chip returned not just the ciphertext but also a *Law Enforcement Access Field* (LEAF), which contained the user-supplied key encrypted under an FBI key embedded in the device. To prevent people cheating by sending the wrong LEAF with a message, the LEAF had a MAC computed with a 'family key' shared by all Clipper chips – which had to be tamper-resistant to keep both the Skipjack block cipher and the LEAF family key secret.

As often happens, it wasn't the tamper-resistance that failed, but the protocol. Almost as soon as Clipper hit the market, Matt Blaze found a vulnerability: as the MAC used to bind the LEAF to the message was only 16 bits long, it was possible to feed message keys into the device until you got one with a given LEAF, so a message could be sent with a LEAF that would reveal nothing to the government [259]. Clipper was replaced with the Capstone chip, the crypto wars continued by other means, and the Skipjack block cipher was placed in the public domain [1402].

Of interest in this chapter are the tamper protection mechanisms used, which were claimed at the time to be sufficient to withstand a 'very sophisticated, well funded adversary' [1400]. Although it was claimed that the Clipper chip would be unclassified and exportable, I was never able to get hold of a sample despite repeated attempts. It used *Vialink read only memory* (VROM) in which bits are set by blowing antifuses between the metal 1 and metal 2 layers on the chip. A high-voltage programming pulse is used to melt a conducting path through the polysilicon between two metal layers. This technology was also used in the QuickLogic FPGA, which was advertised as a way for firms to conceal proprietary algorithms, and claimed to be 'virtually impossible to reverse engineer'; further details and micrographs appeared in its data book [802]. A recent variant is the *spot breakdown PUF* where a high enough voltage is applied to a bank of transistors for just long enough that about half of them suffer breakdown of the gate oxide, creating random failures that can be read as ones and zeros [424].

Fusible links are used on other devices too; recent iPhones, for example, have an AES key burned into the system-on-chip. There are basically three approaches to reverse engineering an antifuse device.

- The first thing to look at is the programming circuitry. All such chips have a test circuit used to read back and verify the bitstream during programming, and many disabled this by melting a single fuse afterwards. If you can get sample devices and a programmer, you can maybe find this fuse using differential optical probing [1776]. You then use a FIB to repair it, or bridge it with two probe needles, and read out the bitstream. This attack technique works not just for antifuse FPGAs but also for the Flash and EEPROM varieties.
- Where you need to read out many fuses, as where they're used to store an AES key, the brute-force approach is to strip the chip down one layer at a time and read the fuses directly; they turn out to be visible under a suitable chemical stain. As this attack is destructive it is typically of limited interest against keys that are different in each device (as in the iPhone, or a spot breakdown PUF).
- Where the device implements a cryptographic algorithm, a side-channel attack may be the fastest way in. Most devices manufactured before about 2000 are rather vulnerable to power analysis, and while smartcard chipmakers have incorporated defences, the makers of larger chips may have preferred to avoid paying royalties to Cryptography Research, which patented many of the best ones. You can always try optical fault induction to read the key one bit at a time, and since the late 2000s we also know how to work with optical emissions, which I'll discuss later.

Secure FPGAs became big business in the 21st century as firms outsource the manufacture of electronic goods to the Far East but want to control at least one critical component to prevent overbuild and counterfeiting. Most FPGAs sold now have conventional memory rather than antifuse, so they can be made reprogrammable. If you use a volatile FPGA that stores the bitstream in SRAM, you will want one or more embedded keys kept in nonvolatile memory, so the bitstream is uploaded and then decrypted on power-up. For faster power-up you might choose a non-volatile device that stores the whole bitstream in Flash. In both cases, there may be fuses to protect the key material and the security state [583]. But do watch out for service-denial attacks via the upgrade mechanism. For example, a Flash FPGA may only have enough memory for one copy of the bitstream, not two; so the naïve approach is to read in the bitstream once to decrypt it and verify the MAC, and then a second time to reprogram the part. But if the bitstream supplied the second time is corrupt, will you have a dead product? And if you allow rollback, your customers can perhaps escape upgrades by replaying old bitstreams. And if an attacker gets your products to load a random encrypted bitstream, this could cause short circuits and brick the part. So stop and think whether anyone might try to destroy your product base via a corrupt upgrade; if so, you might consider a secure bitstream loader. You might also consider a more expensive FPGA with enough on-chip memory to support old and new bitstreams at the same time.

The second type of large-chip security product is the *system-on-chip* (SoC) with inbuilt authentication logic. The pioneer may have been Sony's Playstation 2 in 2000, which fielded MagicGate, a cryptographic challenge-response protocol run between the device's graphics chip and small authentication chips embedded in legitimate accessories. The business model of games console manufacturers included charging premium prices for software and additional memory cards, whose sellers had to use copy-control technology and pay the console vendor a royalty; this was used to subsidise the initial cost of the console. Of course, aftermarket operators would then hack their copy-control mechanisms, so Sony set out to dominate its aftermarket with a better copy-control technology. This used some interesting protection tricks; the MagicGate protocol was both simple (so protocol attacks couldn't be found) and randomised (so attackers couldn't learn anything from repeating transactions). It took several years and millions of dollars for the aftermarket firms to catch up. While the authentication logic in a small chip may need a top metal shield, copy traps and layout obfuscation to hide it, the same logic in a large chip can hide among the billions of other transistors.

By the mid-to-late 2000s, similar logic was appearing in system-on-chip products in other industries – sometimes for accessory control, and sometimes to enable one product to be sold with several different levels of performance as a means of price discrimination. This practice has led to some interesting edge cases. For example, in 2017 Tesla temporarily 'upgraded' the batteries of its model S and X cars so that owners could get out of the path of Hurricane Irma [1934].

So how can you hack the magic devices that we find everywhere nowadays? Memory readout can be the most dependable attack path. As an example, Sergei Skorobogatov used the new PVC Flash / EEPROM readout technique to reverse the OmniPod insulin pump. Diabetics who know how to program prefer to control their own insulin pumps but vendors try to stop them, for both market control and liability reasons. The OmniPod's system-on-chip therefore runs an authentication protocol with the device's authorised controller, and the Nightscout Foundation, an NGO that supports diabetics, wanted to extract the keys so patients could optimise the control for their own health needs rather than following the treatment protocols devised by Omnipod. The analysis is described in [1782].

A second attack path is to look to see whether the device computes with encrypted data, and if so look for a protocol failure or side channel that gives a way in. An early example was the *cipher instruction search attack* invented by Markus Kuhn on the DS5002 processor [1104]. This device pioneered *bus encryption* with hardware that encrypts memory addresses and contents on the fly as data are loaded and stored, so it was not limited to the small amount of RAM that could be fitted into a low-cost tamper-sensing package at the time (1995). Markus noticed that some of the processor's instructions have a visible external effect; one instruction in particular caused the next byte in memory to be output to the device's parallel port. So if you intercept the bus between the processor and memory using a test clip, you can feed in all possible 8-bit instruction bytes at some point in the instruction stream until you see a one-byte output. After using this technique to tabulate the encryption function for a few bytes, you can encipher and execute a short program to dump the entire memory contents. Similar tricks are still used today, and variants on the attack still work. In 2017 Sergei Skorobogatov demonstrated an active attack on a system-on-chip used in the car industry, which used memory encryption to make bus probing harder. By selectively injecting wrong opcodes into the bus, he was able to reverse the encryption function [1783].

A tougher problem was presented by the iPhone. In March 2016 FBI director James Comey demanded that Apple produce a law-enforcement 'upgrade' to its iOS operating system to enable access to locked iPhones, claiming that the FBI would otherwise be unable to unlock the phone of the San Bernardino shooter. Sergei set out to prove him wrong and by August had a working attack. The phone in question, the Apple 5c, has an SoC with an embedded AES key, set up by burning fusible links; as these can be seen under an electron microscope, read-out may be possible but would destroy the SoC. AES isn't vulnerable to cryptanalysis, and the encryption appears to work one cache line at a time, so cipher instruction search won't work. But no matter, as there's a *NAND mirroring attack*. The phone's non-volatile memory is a NAND Flash chip whose contents are encrypted, one cache line at a time, by the embedded device key, so that the chip from one phone can't be read in another. The attack is to desolder the memory chip, mount it in a socket, and copy its contents. You then make half a dozen PIN guesses, and the phone starts to slow down (it locks after ten). Next, you remove the memory chip and restore its original contents. You can now make half a dozen more attempts. With a bit more work, you can clone the chip or build a circuit board to emulate it, so you can guess faster. The details can be found in [1781]. In the end, the FBI used a service from Cellebrite, a forensics company, which later turned out to be exploiting the Checkm8 bug in the iPhone ROM [794].

The third type of attack I'll mention is *optical emission analysis*, which is strictly speaking a side channel but which I'll introduce here as it's becoming one of the main ways of attacking high-grade crypto chips. Photons are emitted when semiconductor junctions switch, and photon emission microscopy is an established failure analysis technique, with silicon emitting mostly in the near infrared near the drain area of n-MOS transistors. This was first used to attack a crypto implementation in 2008 by Julie Ferrigno and Martin Hlavac, who used an expensive single-photon counting photomultiplier to read out AES keys from an outdated 0.8μ microcontroller, but worried that their technique would not work for technologies smaller than 0.12μ [681]. By the following year, Sergei Skorobogatov found that a photomultiplier sold to hobby astronomers was near ideal and discovered a voltage boost trick: increasing the chip supply voltage from 1.5V to 2V increases the photon output sixfold. He found he was almost able to read out the AES keys from the internal crypto engine of a modern chip, the Actel ProASIC3 FGPA. Then, once the AES algorithm timing had been established, and he knew each round key took $1.6\mu s$, he further increased the voltage to 2.5V for the $0.2\mu s$ of an individual bus write, giving a further fourfold increase in the photon output plus temporal resolution, which enabled him to read each word of round key clearly off the bus. This was all rather embarrassing as I'd consulted on the design to Actel back in 2001. The ProASIC3 was fabricated in a 0.13μ technology with 7 metal layers and flash memory, and we had built in all sorts of countermeasures to block the attacks we knew about at the time; reading it out invasively would have been tedious. That was a sharp reminder that it's hard to block the attacks that haven't been invented yet, and that attacks can improve very quickly once experts start to hone them. Optical emission analysis is now used in combination attacks: if you want to attack a chip that's too big to reverse engineer, you observe the emissions as it does the cryptography and this tells you where to aim your laser as you try a fault attack or optically-enhanced power analysis. It can also suggest where you might lay down a few probe points with your FIB.

18.5.6 The state of the art

How well can you protect a single-chip product against a capable motivated opponent? In the late 1990s, everything got broken, and in the 2001 edition of this book, I wrote, "there isn't any technology, or combination of technologies, known to me which can make a smartcard resistant to penetration by a skilled and determined attacker." During the 2000s, the defence improved because of the efforts of the pay-TV firms and the banking industry, so in the second edition I wrote "This is still almost true, but … you can be looking at a year's delay, a budget of over a million dollars, and no certainty of success."

Now, in 2019, Moore's law has run out of steam; crypto chips are mostly stuck at about 100nm, while the semiconductor test equipment industry is aiming to support 9nm processing and still turning out innovations such as passive voltage contrast microscopy; and researchers are finding innovative ways to use their products. So the attackers are starting to catch up. The scope of the industry is also increasing. In 2007, we had a handful of smartcard OEMs, a handful of reversing labs and a handful of interested academics; now many chipmakers are being asked by their customers for some tamper-resistance, as products from routers to the Raspberry Pi acquire some kind of secure boot capability to defeat persistent malware. So there are ever more medium-grade products that are suitable for grad students to learn the art and craft of hardware reverse engineering[5]. And the growing demand, particularly in China, to reverse devices for compatibility drives the growth of commercial reversing labs. The market is now big enough for people to make a living selling specialist tools such as layout-reconstruction software and optical fault induction workstations. As a result, attackers are getting more numerous and more efficient. I suspect that the cost of cloning a smartcard will steadily come down through the tens of thousands and perhaps into the single thousands.

Security economics remains a big soft spot, with security chips being in many ways a market for lemons. A banker buying HSMs probably won't be aware of the huge gap between FIPS level 3 and level 4, and understand that level 3 can sometimes be defeated with a Swiss army knife. The buying incentive there is compliance, and where real security clashes with operations it's not surprising to see weaker standards designed to make compliance easier. API security is too hard, and the difference between HSMs' internal and external APIs makes it too confusing. The near-abdication of FIPS in favour of ISO 19790 and various protection profiles touted under the Common Criteria will confuse things further, as will the UK's move away from the Criteria. Confusion marketing and liability games appear set to continue. But does this matter?

First, most of the HSM business is moving to the cloud, with Azure and AWS each having of the order of 2,000 HSMs, and Google playing catchup. Instead of having a few thousand banks each running a few, or a few dozen, HSMs we'll have three companies running a few thousand. As the prices are driven down, the HSM vendor engineers' expertise will be lost; and as the cloud service providers guard their datacentres, HSMs are likely to be replaced by crypto chips.

Second, most of the volume smartcard markets – SIM cards and EMV cards – have only moderate physical protection requirements as a full compromise enables the attacker to exploit one account only. You don't want a bad terminal to be able to do production power-analysis attacks on every EMV card it sees, but even if that were to happen it's not the end of the world, as that's how mag-stripe cards got cloned, and we know how to limit the damage. The pay-TV markets used to lead innovation and customise the chips they used, as a single break can enable a pirate to sell hundreds of thousands of clone cards. But pay-TV is now moving to wireline broadband, and the companies learned that more secure chips aren't the only way to cut losses: more complex smartcards played a role, but much of the improvement came from legal action against pirates, and from making technical and legal measures

[5]My colleagues Franck Courbon, Markus Kuhn and Sergei Skorobogatov now run just such a course for our graduate students.

work together efficiently. Gadget makers nowadays lock their products into ecosystems with cloud services and apps, which makes manufacturing control less dependent on tamper-proof FPGAs.

I therefore expect that although the number and variety of crypto chips will continue to increase, the quality of physical protection will remain indifferent. Vendors will spend only as much money as they need to in order to meet certification requirements, which will remain slippery and will be gamed. Security engineers will have to get used to building systems out of grey-box components – chips from which keys and algorithms can be extracted, given some effort.

I suspect that accessory control will remain the toughest hardware battlefield. Aftermarket control isn't just about printer cartridges nowadays but extends to vehicles, medical devices and other high-value products. But where at least one of the two devices that authenticate each other goes online at least occasionally, the protection requirements are much less severe than for satellite TV. The real question will be how to stop attacks scaling.

18.6 The residual risk

The security engineer will therefore have to pay attention to the many failure modes of systems involving tamper-resistant processors that are more or less independent of the price or technical tamper-resistance of the device.

18.6.1 The trusted interface problem

None of the devices described in the above sections has a really trustworthy user interface[6]. Some of the bank security modules have a physical lock (or two) on the front to ensure that only the person with a given metal key (or smartcard) can perform privileged transactions. But whether you use a $2000 4765 or a $2 smartcard to do digital signatures, you still trust the PC that drives them. If it shows you a text saying "Please pay amazon.com $67.99 for a copy of Anderson's *Security Engineering*" while the message it actually sends for signature is "Please remortgage my house at 13 Acacia Avenue and pay the proceeds to Mafia Real Estate Inc", then the tamper resistance hasn't bought you much.

Indeed, it probably makes your situation worse. Nick Bohm, Ian Brown and Brian Gladman pointed out that when you use a qualifying electronic signature device, you're saying 'I agree to be unreservedly liable for all signatures that are verified by the key that I now present to you and I will underwrite all

[6]The iPhone secure enclave processor (SEP) has a direct link to the fingerprint reader but relies on the main application processor for everything else including FaceID.

the risks taken by anyone as a result of relying on it' [278]. I will discuss the history and politics of this later in section 26.5.2. The EU eIDAS regulation requires all EU governments to accept qualifying electronic signatures for transactions where they previously required ink on paper, and set standards for technical certification of signature devices. The industry has duly produced dozens of certified products. Given the liability shift compared with ink-on-paper signatures, no sensible person would use a qualifying electronic signature device unless they had to. So the lobbyists have been at work, and some countries now insist you use them to file your taxes. This has led researchers in Germany to look closely at how signatures, signature verification services and PDF files interact; as you might expect, the results are somewhat shocking. Vladislav Mladenov, Christian Mainka, Karsten Meyer zu Selhausen, Martin Grothe and Jörg Schwenk created a document signed by Amazon in Germany and backed by all the official machinery, certifying that you are due a refund of one trillion dollars. They found three new attacks on pdf signatures, worked out how to bypass signature validation in 21 out of 22 viewers, and cheated 6 of 8 online validation services [1328]. It's a fair bet that this is just the tip of an iceberg.

Another example comes from the hardware wallets that some people use to store cryptocurrency. Early products had no trusted display and were thus vulnerable to malware. Some later ones combined a smartcard chip acting as a secure element, with a less secure microcontroller driving a display. This opens a number of possibilities – including an *evil maid attack* described by Saleem Rashid where someone with temporary access to the device, such as a hotel maid, reflashes the microcontroller software [1583]. In this case the secure element had no idea whether the main processor was running compromised code.

Trustworthy interfaces aren't always needed, as tamper-resistant processors are often able to do useful work without having to authenticate users. Recall the example of prepayment electricity metering in section 14.2: there, tamper-resistant processors can maintain a value counter, enforcing a credit limit on each operator and limiting the loss when a vending machine is stolen. Postal meters work the same way. In many other applications from printer ink cartridges through games consoles to prepaid phone cards, the vendor mainly cares about use control.

18.6.2 Conflicts

A further set of issues is that where an application is implemented on devices under the control of different parties, you have to consider what happens when each party attacks the others. In banking, the card issuer, the terminal owner and the customer are different; all the interactions of cloned cards, bogus terminals, gangland merchants and cheating banks need to be thought through.

A particular source of conflict and vulnerability is that many of the users of tamper resistance have business models that make their customers the enemy – such as rights management and accessory control. Their customers may own the product, but have the incentive to tamper with it if they can. In the case of accessory control, they may also have a legal right to try to break it; and where the mechanisms are used to limit device lifetime and thus contribute to environmental pollution, they may even feel they have a moral duty.

18.6.3 The lemons market, risk dumping and evaluation games

Each of the product categories discussed here, from HSMs down through FPGAs to smartcards, has a wide range of offerings with wide variability in the quality of protection. Many products have evaluations, but interpreting them is hard.

First, there are relatively few offerings at high levels of assurance – whether FIPS-140 level 4 or Common Criteria levels above 4. There are many at lower levels, where the tests are fairly easy to pass, and where vendors can shop around for a lab that will give them an easy ride. This leads to a lemons market in which all but the best informed buyers will be tempted to go for the cheapest FIPS level 3 or CC EAL4 product.

Second, evaluation certificates don't mean what they seem. Someone buying a 4758 in 2001 might have interpreted its level 4 evaluation to mean that it was unbreakable – and then been startled when we broke it. In fact, the FIPS certificate referred only to the hardware, and we found vulnerabilities in the software. It's happened the other way too: there's been a smartcard with a Common Criteria level 6 evaluation, but that referred only to the operating system – which ran on a chip with no real defences against microprobing. I'll discuss the failings of evaluation systems at greater length in Part 3.

Third, while HSMs tend to be evaluated under FIPS, smartcard vendors tend to use the Common Criteria. There the tussles are about which protection profile to use; vendors naturally want the labs to evaluate the aspects of security they think they're good at.

Finally, many firms use secure processors to dump risk rather than minimise it. Banks love to be able to say 'your chip and PIN card was used, so it's your fault' and in many countries the regulators let them get away with it. There are many environments, from medicine to defense, where buyers want a certificate of security rather than real protection, and this interacts in many ways with the flaws in the evaluation system. Indeed, the main users of evaluated products are precisely those system operators whose focus is on due diligence rather than risk reduction.

18.6.4 Security-by-obscurity

Many designers have tried hard to keep their cryptoprocessor secret. You have almost always had to sign an NDA to get smartcard development tools. The protection profiles still used for evaluating many smartcards under the Common Criteria emphasise design obscurity. Chip masks have to be secret, instruction set architectures are proprietary, staff have to be vetted, developers have to sign NDAs – these all pushed up industry's costs [656]. Obscurity was also a common requirement for export approval, leading to a suspicion that it covers up deliberate vulnerabilities. For example, a card we tested would always produce the same value when instructed to generate a private/public keypair and output the public part. Many products that incorporate encryption have been broken because their random number generators weren't random enough [576,776] and as we discussed, the NSA got NIST to standardise a weak one.

Some HSM vendors have been an honourable exception; IBM's Common Cryptographic Architecture has been well documented from the beginning, as has Intel's SGX and the core mechanisms of Arm's TrustZone. This openness has facilitated the discovery of API attacks on IBM's product, as well as side-channel and ROP attacks on Intel's and more recently Arm's. But most such attacks have been disclosed responsibly and the learning process has improved their products.

One tussle in 2020 is over whether the development environment needs to be air-gapped. This has been common practice for years in smartcard OEMs; one lab we visited had only a single PC connected to the Internet (painted red, on a pedestal) so staff could book flights and hotels. These firms are now pushing evaluators to emphasise the risk that an attacker ends up owning the entire company infrastructure using an advanced persistent threat. That would make life inconvenient for firms that have always operated online, as they would have to rebuild toolchains and change their workflows.

A smart evaluator would not be taken in by such gamesmanship. Almost none of the actual attacks on smartcards used inside information; most of them started out with a probing attack or side-channel attack on a card bought at retail. As the industry did not do hostile attacks on its own products in the early years, its products were weak and were eventually broken by others. Since the late 1990s some organisations, such as VISA, have specified penetration testing [1967]. But the incentives are still wrong; a sensible vendor will go to whatever evaluation lab offers the easiest ride. We'll discuss the underlying economics and politics of evaluation in Section 28.2.7.2.

18.6.5 Changing environments

We've already seen examples of how function creep and changes in the environment have broken systems by undermining their design assumptions. A general problem is 'leverage' – where firms try to exploit infrastructure maintained by others, without negotiating proper contracts. We've seen how the SIM card that was previously just a means of identifying people to the phone company became a token that controls access to their bank accounts. In the second edition of this book, I wrote "Does this matter? ... I'd say it probably doesn't; using text messages to confirm bank transactions gives a valuable second authentication channel at almost zero marginal cost to both the bank and the customer." At that time, we had one reported case of a SIM swap attack, in South Africa.

In the following paragraph, I wrote: "But what will happen in five or ten years' time, once everyone is doing it? What if the iPhone takes off as Apple hopes, so that everyone uses an iPhone not just as their phone, but as their web browser? All of a sudden the two authentication channels have shrunk to one." And so it is; SIM swap is now going mainstream in the USA.

This is actually tied up with local law and regulation. In most countries, phone companies are not liable to banks for failing to authenticate their customers properly. After all, phone companies just sell minutes, and the marginal cost of stolen minutes is near zero. But one country with little SIM swap fraud is India, where regulators decided that phone companies must share liability for SIM swap fraud, and where the phone company is required to check a customer's fingerprint against the national Aadhar database before selling them a SIM.

18.7 So what should one protect?

In such a complex world, what value can tamper-resistant chips add?

First, they can tie information processing to a single physical token. A pay-TV subscriber card can be bought and sold in a grey market, but so long as it isn't copied the station operator isn't losing much revenue. This also applies to accessory control, where a printer vendor wants their product to work with any genuine ink cartridge, just not with a cheap competitor.

Second, they can maintain value counters, as with the postal metering discussed in Chapter 13. Even if the device is stolen, the total value of the service it can vend is limited. In printers, ink cartridges can be programmed to dispense only so much ink and then declare themselves dry.

Third, they can reduce the need to trust human operators. Their main purpose in some government systems was 'reducing the street value of key material to zero'. A crypto ignition key for a secure phone should allow a thief only to masquerade as the rightful owner, and only if they have access to an actual device, and only so long as neither the key nor the phone has been reported stolen. The same general considerations applied in ATM networks, which not only implement a separation-of-duty policy, but transfer a lot of the trust from people to things.

Fourth, they can protect a physical root of trust that monitors secure boot, and thus make it hard for malware to be persistent. This mission of its own does not require high-grade physical protection; security against capable motivated software attackers is the key. One question is whether activists who want to run their own favoured version of Linux on their devices actually have to break the TPM, or whether they can just ignore it and manage the malware risk themselves.

Fifth, they can control the risk of overproduction by untrusted hardware contractors: sometimes called the 'third shift' problem, where the factory you hire runs two shifts to make devices for you and a third shift to make some more for grey-market sale. This can involve embedding part of the design in an FPGA that's hard to reverse engineer, or by having a TPM to control the credentials necessary for the device to work in your ecosystem. As things acquire cloud services and apps, firms are moving from the former strategy to the latter, which has lower hardware costs and is easier to manage. You just release as many credentials as the factory ships you products.

Sixth, such techniques can control some of the more general risk from counterfeit electronic parts. This covers a multitude of sins, from cheap knock-offs that cause early product failure through to sophisticated supply-chain attacks by state adversaries. For a survey, see Guin et al [834]. The techniques described in this chapter also find use in the fight against counterfeiting, as do many of the tools. As for supply-chain attacks, the most pernicious may be hardware trojans. One national-security concern is that as defence systems increasingly depend on chips fabricated overseas, the fabs might introduce extra circuitry to facilitate later attack. For example, some extra logic might cause a 64-bit multiply with two specific inputs to function as a kill switch. This has been the subject of significant research since about 2010, and mechanisms have been developed for Trojan detection both pre-silicon and post-silicon; for example, you can do a differential side-channel analysis of a 'golden' reference chip and a target of evaluation [1779]. This of course assumes that you can produce a reference chip in a trustworthy fab. For a survey of this field, see Xiao et al [2056].

This is an incomplete list. But what these applications have in common is that a security property can be provided independently of the trustworthiness of the surrounding environment. But beware: the actual protection properties that are required and provided can be quite subtle, and tamper-resistant devices are more often a useful component than a full solution. Generic mechanisms fail again and again; security is not some kind of magic pixie dust that you sprinkle on a system to cause bad things to not happen. You need to work out what bad things you want to stop. If you're not careful you can find yourself paying for smartcards and crypto modules in applications where they add rather little; and if you're really unlucky you may find that the industry lobbied for legal mandates or industry standards to force you to use their products.

18.8 Summary

Tamper-resistant devices and systems have a long history. Computers can be protected against physical tampering in a number of ways, from keeping them locked up in a guarded room, through putting them in tamper-sensing boxes, to making them into single chips with shields against probing and defences against side-channel attacks.

I've told the story of how hardware tamper-resistance developed through a series of cycles of attack and defence, and given examples of applications. Security processors are typically vulnerable to attacks on interfaces (human, sensor or system) but can often deliver value in applications where we need to link processing to physical objects and to protect security state against scalable threats, particularly in environments where any online service may be intermittent.

Research problems

There are basically two strands of research in tamper-resistant processor design. The first concerns itself with making 'faster, better, cheaper, more secure' processors: how can the protection offered by a high-end device be brought to chips that cost under a dollar? The second concerns itself with pushing forward the state of the attack art. How can the latest chip testing technologies be used to make 'faster, better, cheaper, novel' attacks? The best guide for the second may be Sergei Skorobogatov's 2018 talk, "Hardware Security: Present challenges and Future directions" [1784].

A broader area of research is how to build more secure systems out of less secure components. How can moderately protected chips be used effectively to stop various kinds of attack scaling?

Further reading

I'm not aware of any up-to-date systematisation of knowledge paper on hardware tamper resistance. Colleagues and I wrote a survey of security processors in 2005 [101], which might serve as a more detailed starting point, if slightly dated; of the same vintage are a summer school on attack techniques [1776] as well as reviews of FPGA security [583] and microcontroller security [1771,1773]. Bunnie Huang's book on hacking the Xbox is still a good read [932]. A slightly later summary, from an industry perspective, is by Randy Torrance and Dick James of Chipworks in 2009 [1901].

As for the last decade of research, the best current papers often appear at conferences such as CHES (for the crypto), HOST (Trojans and backdoors), FDTC (fault attacks) and Cardis (smartcards). Failure analysis research tends to appear at ISTFA and IPFA.

For the early history – the weighted codebooks and water-soluble inks – read David Kahn's book *'The Code Breakers'* [1003]. For a handbook on the chip card technology of the mid-to-late 1990s, see [1581], while the gory details of how we started tampering with those generations of cards can be found in [107,108,1080]. The IBM products mentioned have extensive documentation online [953], where you can also find the US FIPS documents [1399].

For modern chip testing techniques, I recommend the video of a keynote talk by John Walker at Hardwear.IO 2019 on how to use FIBs in reverse engineering [1979] as well as the talks at the same event by Chris Tarnovsky on the evolution of chip defense technology [1865]. Finally, for a detailed description of a non-trivial attack, see Chris Gerlinsky's 2016 talk on how he broke VideoCipher [759].

CHAPTER

19

Side Channels

The hum of either army stilly sounds,
That the fixed sentinels almost receive
The secret whispers of each others' watch;
Fire answers fire, and through their paly flames
Each battle sees the other's umber'd face.
– WILLIAM SHAKESPEARE, KING HENRY V, ACT IV

Optimisation consists of taking something that works and replacing it with something that almost works but is cheaper.
– ROGER NEEDHAM

19.1 Introduction

Electronic devices such as computers and phones leak information in all sorts of ways. A *side channel* is where information leaks accidentally via some medium that was not designed or intended for communication; a *covert channel* is where the leak is deliberate. Side channel attacks are everywhere, and 3–4 of them have caused multi-billion dollar losses.

1. First, there are conducted or radiated electromagnetic signals, which can compromise information locally and occasionally at longer ranges. These 'Tempest' attacks led NATO governments to spend billions of dollars a year on shielding equipment, starting in the 1960s. After the end of the Cold War, people started to realise that there had usually been nobody listening.
2. Second, side channels leak data between tasks on a single device, or between devices that are closely coupled; these can exploit both power and timing information, and also contention for shared system resources. The discovery of Differential Power Analysis in the late 1990s held up the deployment of smartcards in banking and elsewhere by 2–3 years once it was realised that all the cards then on sale were vulnerable.

3. The third multibillion-dollar incident started in January 2018 with the announcement of the 'Spectre' and 'Meltdown' attacks, which exploit speculative execution to enable one process on a CPU to snoop on another, for example to steal its cryptographic keys. This will probably force the redesign of all superscalar CPUs over 2020–5.
4. There are attacks that exploit shared local physical resources, such as when a phone listens to keystrokes entered on a nearby keyboard, or indeed on a keyboard on its own touch screen – whether that sensing is done with microphones, the accelerometer and gyro, or even the camera. Another example is that a laser pulse can create a click on a microphone, so a voice command can be given to a home assistant through a window. So far, none of the side-channel attacks on phones and other IoT devices has scaled up to have major impact – but there are ever more of them.
5. Finally, there are attacks that exploit shared social resources. An example is identifying someone in a supposedly anonymous dataset from patterns of communications, location history or even just knowing when they went on holiday. This has led to many poor policy decisions and much wishful thinking around whether personal data can be anonymised sufficiently to escape privacy law. There have been both scandalous data leaks, and complaints that data should be made more available for research and other uses. It's hard to put a dollar value on this, but it is significant in fields such as medical research, as we discussed in Chapter 11.

We have known about side channels for years but have consistently underestimated the importance of some, while spending unreasonable sums on defending against others. A security engineer who wants to protect systems long-term without either overlooking real and scalable threats, or wasting money chasing shadows, needs to understand the basics.

19.2 Emission security

Emission security, or Emsec, is about preventing attacks using *compromising emanations*, namely conducted or radiated electromagnetic signals. It's mostly military organizations that worry about *Tempest*, where the stray RF emitted by computers and other electronic equipment is picked up by an opponent and used to reconstruct the data being processed. It has become an issue for voting machines too, after a Dutch group found they could tell at a distance which party a voter had selected on a voting machine, and attacks have also been demonstrated on automatic teller machines (though these don't really scale).

Both active and passive emission security measures are closely related to *electromagnetic compatibility* (EMC) and *radio frequency interference* (RFI), which can disrupt systems accidentally, as well as *electromagnetic pulse* (EMP) weapons, which disrupt them deliberately. (I discuss these in more detail in the chapter on electronic warfare.) As more and more everyday devices get hooked up to wireless networks, and as devices acquire more sensors, all these problems – RFI/EMC, side channels and electronic warfare threats – may get worse.

19.2.1 History

Crosstalk between telephone wires was well known to the 19th century telephony pioneers, whose two-wire circuits were stacked on tiers of crosstrees on supporting poles. They learned to cross the wires over at intervals to make each circuit a twisted pair. Crosstalk first came to the attention of the military in 1884–85, and the first known combat exploit was in 1914. Field telephone wires were laid to connect units bogged down in the mud of Flanders, and often ran for miles, parallel to enemy trenches a few hundred yards away. An early WWI phone circuit was a single-core insulated cable which used earth return in order to halve the cable's weight and bulk. It was soon discovered that earth leakage caused crosstalk, including messages from the enemy side. Listening posts were quickly established and protective measures were introduced, including the use of twisted-pair cable. By 1915, valve amplifiers had extended the earth leakage listening range to 100 yards for telephony and 300 yards for Morse code. People found that the tangle of abandoned telegraph wire in no-man's land provided such a good communications channel, and leaked so much traffic, that clearing it away become a task for which lives were spent. By 1916, earth return circuits had been abolished within 3000 yards of the front [1382].

The intelligence community discovered side-channel attacks on cryptographic equipment around World War 2, when Bell sold the US government a mixer to add one-time tapes to telegraph traffic and discovered plaintext leaking out in ciphertext. Through the 1950s, both the USA and the UK struggled to suppress electromagnetic and acoustic emanations from their own cipher machines; from 1957 there was a machine, the KW-27, which was 'reasonably well protected' against Tempest emissions. In 1960, after the UK Prime Minister ordered surveillance on the French embassy during negotiations about joining the European Economic Community, his security service's scientists noticed that the enciphered traffic from the embassy carried a faint plaintext signal, and constructed equipment to recover it. By the 1960s, NATO started work on Tempest standards; America and Britain gave their European allies selective and incomplete security advice, so they could continue to spy on them. Meanwhile the Russians developed serious proficiency at exploiting spurious emissions and spied on all of them. When the Americans and British realised this, they used manual one-time pads as a stopgap for traffic at Secret and above, then started putting crypto equipment in shielded rooms in vulnerable embassies [600]. There was a brief public reference to the possibility that computer data might leak in Rand Corporation reports by Willis Ware in 1967 and 1970 [1989, 1990]. After that, emission security became a classified topic, with secret NATO standards set by 1980 that were only declassified in 2000.

Meanwhile the stray RF leaking from the local oscillator signals in domestic television sets was being targeted by direction-finding equipment in 'TV detector vans' in Britain, where TV owners must pay an annual license fee to support public broadcast services. The fact that computer data might also leak came to public attention in 1985 when Wim van Eck, a Dutch researcher, published an article describing how to reconstruct the picture on a VDU at a distance using a modified TV set [601]. The story of the leaky French cipher machine was leaked by the security service whistleblower Peter Wright in 1987 [2049]. Published research in emission security and related topics took off in the 1990s, as I'll discuss shortly.

19.2.2 Technical surveillance and countermeasures

Before we dive into the details of Tempest attacks, it is worth noting that the simplest and most widespread attacks that use the electromagnetic spectrum are not those exploiting unintended RF emissions of innocuous equipment, but where a listening device is introduced by the attacker, or (more recently) when a target's device is compromised by malware. No matter how well it is protected by encryption and access controls while in transit or storage, most highly confidential information comes into being either as speech or as keystrokes on a laptop or phone. If it can be captured by the opponent at this stage, then no subsequent protective measures are likely to help very much.

An extraordinary range of bugs is available on the market:

- At the low end, a few tens of dollars will buy a simple radio microphone that you can stick under a table when visiting the target. Battery life is the main constraint on these devices. They typically have a range of only a few hundred yards, and a lifetime of days to weeks.
- At the next step up are devices that draw their power from the mains, a telephone cable or some other external electricity supply, and so can last indefinitely. As a historical example, the UK Security Service got entry to the Egyptian embassy in London during the Suez crisis and modified the telephone to listen in when the clerk was entering the day's key settings into the cipher machine [600]. Some modern equivalents clip into a keyboard cable and look like a connector; others look like

electrical adaptors but send audio and video back to their owner. Police covert-entry teams install such bugs in the homes and cars of serious crime suspects. Most now use mobile-phone technology: they can be seen as custom handsets that listen and watch when called.

- One exotic device, on show at the NSA Museum in Fort Meade, was presented to the US ambassador in Moscow in 1946 by a class of schoolchildren. It was a wooden replica of the Great Seal of the United States, and the ambassador hung it on the wall of the office in his residence. In 1952, it was discovered to contain a resonant cavity that acted as a microphone when illuminated by microwaves from outside the building, and retransmitted the conversations that took place in his office. Right up to the end of the Cold War, embassies in Moscow were regularly irradiated with microwaves, so variants of the technique presumably remained in use.
- Bugs are also implanted in equipment. In 1984, sixteen bugs were discovered in IBM Selectric typewriters in the US embassy in Moscow; each stored eight key presses and then transmitted them in a single burst. There have been many *keyloggers* designed and fielded since then in keyboards and keyboard cables, using a wide variety of sensors and side channels [1333].
- Laser microphones work by shining a laser beam at a reflective or partially reflective surface, such as a window pane, in the room where the target conversation is taking place. The sound waves induce vibration in the surface which modulates the reflected light, and this can be picked up and decoded at a distance.
- However, it's now possible that the bulk of surveillance worldwide is done by creepware – by software installed on the target's phone either remotely by a skilled attacker, or by a coercive or manipulative family member, or sometimes even as a condition of employment.

An expert in *technical surveillance countermeasures* (TSCM) will have a whole bag of tools to provide protection against such attacks.

- The better *surveillance receivers* sweep the radio spectrum from about 10 KHz to 3 GHz every few tens of seconds, and look for signals that can't be explained as broadcast, police, air traffic control and so on. Direct-sequence spread spectrum can be spotted from its power spectrum, and frequency hoppers will typically be observed at different frequencies on successive sweeps. Burst transmission does better. But the effectiveness of surveillance receivers is limited by the bugs that use the same frequencies and protocols as legitimate mobile phones. Many organizations tried to forbid the use of mobiles, but most have given up; even the Royal Navy eventually had to allow sailors to keep their phones on board ship as too many of them left.

- The *nonlinear junction detector* can find hidden devices at close range. It broadcasts a weak radio signal and listens for odd harmonics, generated when the transistors, diodes and other nonlinear junctions in the equipment rectify the signal. However, if the bug has been planted in or near legitimate equipment, then the nonlinear junction detector is not much help. There are also expensive bugs designed not to re-radiate at all.
- Breaking the line of sight, such as by planting trees around your laboratory, can be effective against laser microphones but is often impractical.
- It's possible to detect hidden wireless cameras that just use the normal building wifi by their traffic patterns, and researchers have developed apps for this purpose [417].
- Some facilities have shielded rooms, so that even if bugs are introduced their signals can't be heard outside [133]. In NATO countries, Top Secret material is supposed to be kept in a *secure compartmented information facility* (SCIF) that has both physical security and acoustic shielding, and is swept regularly for bugs; a SCIF may have electromagnetic shielding too if a threat assessment suggests that capable motivated opponents might get close enough. Shielded rooms are required in the UK for researchers to access sensitive personal data held by government, such as tax records. There are vendors who sell prefabricated rooms with acoustic and electromagnetic shielding. But this is harder than it looks. A new US embassy building in Moscow had to be abandoned after large numbers of microphones were found in the structure, and Britain's counterintelligence service decided to tear down and rebuild a large part of a new headquarters building, at a cost of about $50m, after an employee of one of the building contractors was found to have past associations with the Provisional IRA.
- After the Obama administration kicked out three dozen Russian diplomats for eavesdropping on US officials' mobile phones, it was reported that the Russians had even picked up conversations in unshielded SCIFs by hacking officials' phones [579].

Technological developments are steadily making life easier for the bugger and harder for the defender. As more and more devices acquire intelligence and short-range radio or infrared communications – as the 'Internet of Things' becomes the 'Internet of Targets' – there is ever more scope for attacks via equipment that's already there rather than stuff that needs to emplaced for the purpose. It's not just that your laptop, tablet or mobile phone might be running creepware that records audio and uploads it later. The NSA banned Furby toys in its buildings, as the Furby remembers (and randomly repeats) things said in its presence. The Cayla talking doll was banned in Germany as strangers could use it to listen to a child remotely, and speak to them too.

But there are many more subtle ways in which existing electronic equipment can be exploited.

19.3 Passive attacks

We'll first consider passive attacks, that is, attacks in which the opponent exploits electromagnetic signals that are presented to him without any effort on his part to create them. I'll exclude optical signals for now, and discuss them along with acoustic attacks later.

Broadly speaking, there are two categories of electromagnetic attack. The signal can either be conducted over some kind of circuit (such as a power line or phone line), or it may be radiated as radio frequency energy. These are referred to by the military as 'Hijack' and 'Tempest' respectively. They are not mutually exclusive; RF threats often have a conducted component. For example, radio signals emitted by a computer can be picked up by the power main and conducted into nearby buildings.

19.3.1 Leakage through power and signal cables

Every hardware engineer knows that high-frequency signals leak everywhere and you need to work hard to stop them causing problems. Conducted information leakage can be suppressed by careful design, with power supplies and signal cables suitably filtered. But civilian equipment only needs to be well-enough shielded that it doesn't interfere with radio and TV; it's a much harder task to prevent any exploitable leak of information.

In military parlance, *red* equipment (carrying confidential data) has to be isolated by filters and shields from *black* equipment (that can send signals directly to the outside world). Equipment with both red and black connections, such as cipher machines, is tricky to get right, and shielded equipment tends to be available only in small quantities, made for government markets. But the costs don't stop there. The operations room at an air base can have hundreds of cables leading from it; filtering them all, and imposing strict configuration management to preserve red/black separation, can cost millions. The contractors are expensive, as the staff all need clearances – the NATO standard SDIP-20 for emission security (formerly AMSG 720B) is classified.

19.3.2 Leakage through RF signals

When I first learned to program in 1972 at the Glasgow Schools' Computer Centre, we had an IBM 1401 with a 1.5 MHz clock. A radio tuned to this frequency in the machine room would emit a loud whistle, which varied depending on the data being processed. Some people used this as a debugging aid. A school colleague had a better idea: he wrote a set of subroutines of different lengths so that by calling them in sequence, the computer could play a tune. It never occurred to us that this could be used for mischief as well as fun.

Moving now to more modern equipment, the VDUs used as monitors until the early 2000s naturally emit a TV signal – a VHF or UHF radio signal modulated with the image currently being displayed. The beam current is modulated with the video signal, which contains many harmonics of the dot rate, some of which resonate with metal components and radiate better than others. Given a broadband receiver, these emissions can be picked up and reconstituted as video. Wim van Eck discovered this and made it public in 1985 [601]; equipment design is discussed in his paper and in much more detail in [1107]. Contrary to popular belief, the more modern flat displays are also generally easy to snoop on; a typical laptop has a serial line going through the hinge from the system unit to the display and this carries the video signal (Figure 19.1).

Other researchers started to experiment with snooping on everything from fax machines through shielded RS-232 cables to ethernet [534, 1800]. Hans-Georg Wolf demonstrated a Tempest attack that could recover card and PIN data from a cash machine at a distance of eight meters [1097]. Most business sectors just ignored the problem, as countermeasures such as shielding and jamming are difficult and expensive to do properly [144]. The military's expertise and equipment remained classified and unavailable outside the defence world. Finally, in October 2006, a Dutch group opposed to electronic voting machines demonstrated that the machine used to collect 90% of the election ballots in the Netherlands could be eavesdropped from a distance of several tens of meters [786]. This led to a Dutch government requirement that voting equipment be Tempest-tested to a level of 'Zone 1 - 12dB'.

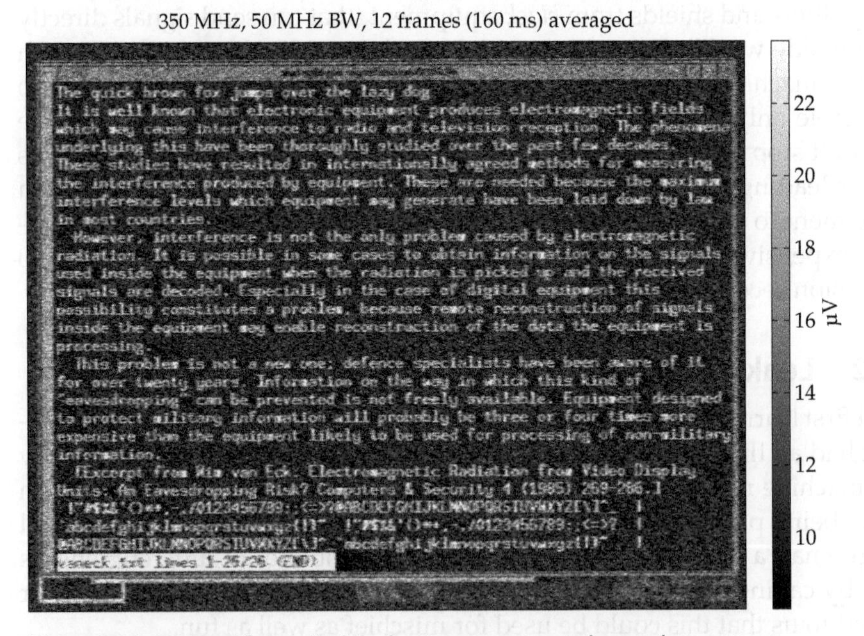

Figure 19.1: RF signal from a Toshiba laptop reconstructed several rooms away, through three plasterboard walls (courtesy of Markus Kuhn [1106])

The *zone* system works as follows. Equipment certified as Zone 0 should not emit any signals that are exploitable at a distance of one meter; it should protect data from electronic eavesdropping even if the opponent is in the next room, and the wall is something flimsy like plasterboard. Zone 1 equipment should be safe from opponents at a distance of 20 meters, so the Dutch 'Zone 1 - 12dB' criterion means that a voting machine should not leak any data on what vote was cast to an eavesdropper 5 meters away. Zone 2 and Zone 3 mean 120 and 1200 meters respectively. Technical details of zoning were briefly published by the Germans in 2007, as [345]. This document was then withdrawn, perhaps because the Americans objected. But everything in it was already in the public domain except the zone limit curves, which are worst-case relative attenuations between distances of 20m, 120m and 1200m from a small dipole or loop antenna, taking into account the difference between nearfield and farfield dropoff. Any competent RF engineer can reverse engineer the rest of it.

The zone system has come into wide governmental use since the end of the Cold War slashed military budgets. Governments faced up to the fact that there are almost no attacks, except on high-value targets to which an opponent can get really close, such as diplomatic missions. The Snowden papers revealed that the US's principal Tempest target was the UN diplomatic missions in New York, and even there, such techniques were only used against the handful of nations whose computers couldn't be compromised using malware.

Governments realised they had been wasting billions on shielding everything, and cost cuts forced them to use commercial off-the-shelf (COTS) equipment for almost everything. COTS equipment tends to be zone 2 when tested, with some particularly noisy pieces of kit in zone 3. By knowing which equipment radiates what, you can keep your most sensitive data on equipment furthest from the facility perimeter, and shield stuff only when you really have to. Zoning has greatly cut the costs of emission security.

Markus Kuhn and I developed a lower-cost protection technology, called 'Soft Tempest', which was deployed for a while in some products, from email encryption programs to Dutch voting machines [1107]. It uses software techniques to filter or mask the information-bearing electromagnetic emanations from a computer system. We discovered that most of the information-bearing RF energy from a VDU was concentrated in the top of the spectrum, so we removed the top 30% of the Fourier transform of a standard font by convolving it with a suitable low-pass filter (see Figures 19.2 and 19.3).

TrustNo1

Figure 19.2: Normal text

TrustNo1

Figure 19.3: Text low-pass filtered

This has an almost imperceptible effect on the screen contents as seen by the user. Figures 19.4 and 19.5 display photographs of the screen with the two video signals from Figures 19.2 and 19.3.

Figure 19.4: Screen, normal text

Figure 19.5: Screen, filtered text

However, the difference in the emitted RF is dramatic, as illustrated in the photographs in Figures 19.6 and 19.7. These show the potentially compromising emanations, as seen by a Tempest monitoring receiver.

Using Soft Tempest techniques on VDUs translated to a difference of a zone [109]. Less can be done for modern flat screens, but for some devices, there may still be useful gains to be had.

However, the attacker can use active as well as passive techniques. The phenomenon we observed with the IBM 1401 – that a suitable program would turn a computer into a radio broadcast transmitter – is easy to reimplement on a modern computer. Figures 19.8 and 19.9 show what the screen on a PC looks like when the video signal is an RF carrier at 2 MHz, modulated with pure tones of 300 and 1200 Hz.

Using such tricks, malware can infect a machine that's air-gapped from the Internet and exfiltrate data to a radio receiver hidden nearby [1107]. And the intelligence community knew this: there had been a report of the CIA using software-based RF exploits in economic espionage in a TV documentary in 1995 [1064]. Material declassified by the NSA in response to a FOIA request [988] revealed that the codeword *Teapot* refers to "the investigation, study, and control of intentional compromising emanations (i.e., those that are hostilely induced or provoked) from telecommunications and automated

Figure 19.6: Page of normal text

Figure 19.7: Page of filtered text

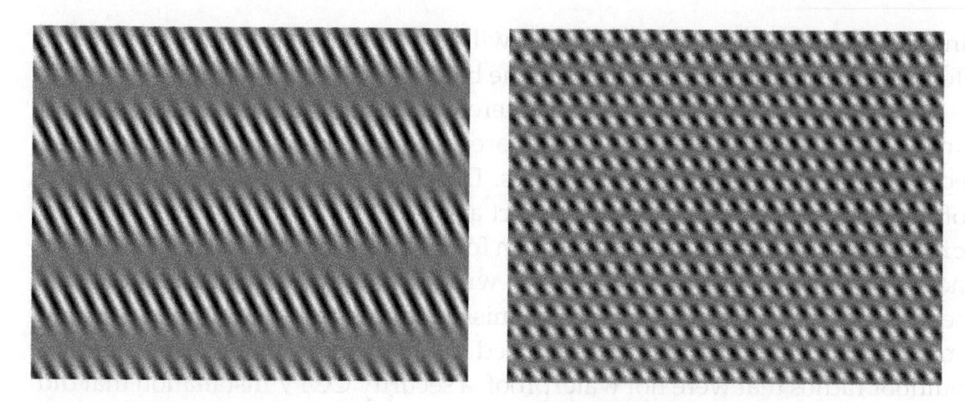

Figure 19.8: Hz AM signal **Figure 19.9:** 1200 Hz AM signal

information systems equipment." The possibility of malware is one reason why Tempest testing involves not just listening passively to the device under test, but injecting into it signals that simulate the worst-case attack in which the opponent has used a software exploit to take over the device and tries to set up a covert channel [253].

The final class of classical Emsec attacks is the exploitation of RF emanations that are accidentally induced by nearby RF sources, called *Nonstop* by the US military [133]. If equipment processing sensitive data is used near a mobile phone, then the phone's transmitter may induce currents in the equipment that get modulated with sensitive data by the nonlinear junction effect and re-radiated. For this reason, it used to be forbidden to use a mobile phone within 5 meters of classified equipment. Nonstop attacks are also the main Emsec concern for ships and aircraft; here, an attacker who can get close enough to do a passive Tempest attack can probably do much more serious harm than eavesdropping, but as military ships and aircraft often carry very powerful radios and radars, one must be careful that their signals don't get modulated accidentally with something useful to the enemy. In one case, Soviet spy ships were found to be listening to US military data in Guam from outside the 3-mile limit.

19.3.3 What goes wrong

As Ed Snowden confirmed, the Emsec threats to embassies in hostile countries are real. The UK embassy in one hostile Arab country used to be on the second floor of an office block whose first and third floors were occupied by the Mukhabarat, the local secret police; if that's what you get given as diplomatic premises, then shielding all electronic equipment (except that used for deception) will be part of the solution. It won't be all of it; your cleaning staff will be in the pay of the Mukhabarat so they will helpfully loosen your equipment's Tempest gaskets, just as they change the batteries in the room bugs.

As for the defensive side of things, there was a scandal in April 2007 when it emerged that Lockheed Martin had ignored Tempest standards when installing equipment in US Coast Guard vessels. Documents were left on the website of the Coast Guard's Deepwater project and ended up on an activist website, `cryptome.org`, which was closed down for a while. The documents tell a story not just of emission security defects – wrong cable types, violations of cable separation rules, incorrect grounding, missing filters, red/black violations, and so on – but of a more generally botched job. The ships also had hull cracks, outdoor radios that were not waterproof, a security CCTV installation that did not provide the specified 360 degree coverage, and much more [501]. This led to a Congressional inquiry. The documents provide some insight into Tempest and Nonstop accreditation procedures.

The most recent development has been Tempest attacks on smartphones. Such devices do not have a design requirement to withstand a capable motivated opponent sitting in the next room with decent radio equipment; so it should have been no surprise when, in 2015, Gabriel Goller and Georg Sigl described how to go about extracting private keys from smartphones at a distance using passive RF monitoring [779]. The main difficulty with such attacks is that a phone's clock frequency typically varies with workload; if this frequency can somehow be fixed (e.g., by malware) then attacks become much easier – in fact, they reduce to a standard timing attack, of a kind I will now describe.

19.4 Attacks between and within computers

In the chapter on multilevel security, I remarked that Butler Lampson pointed out in 1973 covert channels may allow a process at high to signal down to low [1127]. As a simple example, the high process can keep some shared resource busy at time t_i to signal that the i-th bit of a secret key is 1. If a machine is shared between high and low, and resources are not allocated in fixed slices, then the high process can signal by filling up the disk drive, or by using a lot of CPU cycles (some people call the former case a *storage channel* and the latter a *timing channel*, though in practice they can often be converted into each other). There are many others such as sequential process IDs, shared file locks and last access times on files – reimplementing all of these in a multilevel secure way is an enormous task. It's also possible to limit the covert channel capacity by introducing noise. Some machines have had randomised system clocks for this purpose. But some covert channel capacity almost always remains [809].

In classical multilevel-secure systems, it was considered a good result to get covert channel bandwidth down to one bit per second. This would make it hard to leak many Top Secret satellite images, but of course it would be trivial to leak a 256-bit crypto key. This is one of the reasons the NSA was traditionally suspicious of crypto in software. And covert channels are even harder to analyse and block in distributed systems where the software can initiate communications on the network. DNS supports covert channels, for example, which are hard to block because of the service's legitimate use, but which have been used by malware to exfiltrate credit card numbers [1373]. Such channels have easily enough bandwidth to smuggle out crypto keys.

In the mid-1990s, side-channel research was invigorated by the discovery of novel attacks on smartcards and other crypto implementations.

19.4.1 Timing analysis

In 1996, Paul Kocher showed that many implementations of public-key algorithms such as RSA and DSA leaked key information through the amount of time they took [1066]. When doing exponentiation, software typically steps through the secret exponent one bit at a time, and if the next bit is a one it does a multiply. Paul's idea was to guess the exponent one bit at a time, work through the consequences of this guess for the timing measurements, and see if it reduced their variance. This clever signal-processing technique was steadily refined. By 2003, David Brumley and Dan Boneh implemented a timing attack against Apache using OpenSSL, and showed how to extract the private key from a remote server by timing about a million decryptions [331]. Some implementations of public-key algorithms use blinding to prevent such attacks (OpenSSL did offer it as an option, but Apache didn't use it). In fact, there was a whole series of timing attacks on SSL/TLS; despite this protocol's having been proven secure in the late 1990s, there has been about one attack a year since on its implementation, mostly using side channels.

Symmetric-key block ciphers are vulnerable too. John Kelsey, Bruce Schneier, David Wagner and Chris Hall had pointed out in 1998 that Rijndael, the algorithm that later became AES, is vulnerable to timing attacks based on cache misses [1036]. The attacker can verify guesses about the output of the first round of the cipher by predicting whether the guessed value would cause a cache miss on S-box lookup, and verifying this against observation. A number of researchers improved this attack steadily since then, and a naïve implementation of AES can be broken by observing a few hundred encryptions [233, 1485, 1491]. Many crypto libraries and toolkits are vulnerable; you need to work out whether they are an issue for your application and if so what you're going to do. And it's not just the algorithms that leak; protocol and implementation features such as padding and error handling leak secrets too.

19.4.2 Power analysis

Timing attacks can work from a distance, but if you can get up close to the target equipment, there's a lot more you can do. Smartcard makers were aware from the 1980s that information could leak through the power line and patented various defences; by the early 1990s, it appears to have been known to pay-TV hackers and to some government agencies that information could be gathered by simply measuring the current a card drew. Known as *power analysis* or *rail noise analysis*, this may involve as little as inserting a resistor in the ground line and connecting a digital storage scope across it to observe the device's current draw. An example of such a power trace can be seen in Figure 19.10. This shows how a password can be extracted from a microcontroller by guessing it a byte at a time and looking for a change in the power trace when you guess right.

Different instructions have quite different power profiles, and, as you can see, the power consumption also depends on the data being processed. The main data-dependent contribution in many circumstances is from the bus driver transistors, which are quite large. Depending on the design, the current may vary by several hundred microamps over a period of several hundred nanoseconds for each bit of the bus whose state is changed [1300]. Thus the Hamming

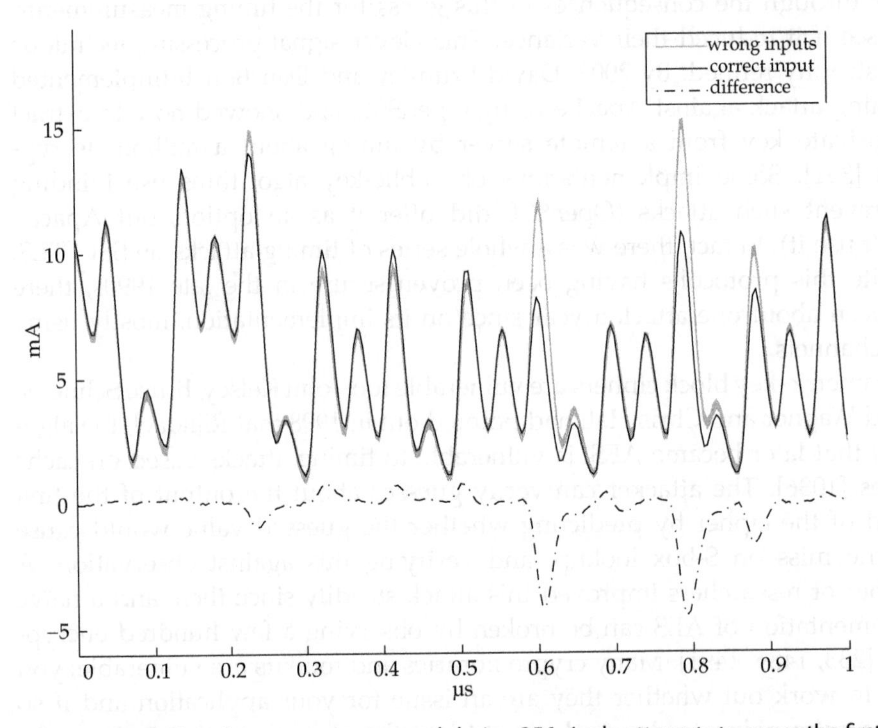

Figure 19.10: Plot of the current measured during 256 single attempts to guess the first byte of a service password stored in the microcontroller at the heart of a car immobilizer (courtesy of Markus Kuhn and Sergei Skorobogatov)

weight of the difference between each data byte and the preceding byte on the bus (the *transition count*) is visible to an attacker. In some devices, the Hamming weight of each data byte is available too [1305]. EEPROM reads and writes can give even stronger signals. If a wrong PIN guess leads to a PIN-retry counter being decremented, this may cause a sharp increase in current draw as a charge pump prepares to write memory (at this point, an attacker might even reset the card and try another PIN).

The effect of this leakage is not limited to password extraction. An attacker who understands (or guesses) how a cipher is implemented can obtain significant information about the card's secrets and in many cases deduce the value of the key in use. This was brought forcefully to the industry's attention in 1998 by Paul Kocher, when he adapted the signal-processing ideas developed for timing attacks into an efficient technique to extract the key bits used in a block cipher such as DES from a collection of power traces, without knowing any implementation details of the card software [1067]. This technique, known as *differential power analysis*, involves partitioning a set of power traces into subsets, then computing the difference of the averages of these subsets. If the subsets are correlated with information of interest, the difference should be nonzero [1069].

As a concrete example, the attacker might collect several hundred traces of transactions with a target card, for which either the plaintext or the ciphertext is known. They then guess some of the cipher's internal state. In the case of DES, each round of the cipher has eight table look-ups in which six bits of the current input are xor'ed with six bits of key, and then used to look up a four-bit output from an S-box. So if it's the ciphertext to which the attacker has access, they will guess the six input bits to an S-box in the last round. The power traces are then sorted into two sets based on this guess and synchronized. Average traces are then computed and compared. The difference between the two average traces is called a *differential trace*.

The process is repeated for each of the 64 possible six-bit inputs to the target S-box. The correct input value – which separates the power traces into two sets each with a different S-box output value – will typically give a differential trace with a noticeable peak. Wrong guesses, however, give randomly-sorted traces, so the differential trace looks like random noise. In this way, the six keybits that go to the S-box in question can be found, followed by the others used in the last round of the cipher. In the case of DES, this gives 48 of the 56 keybits, so the remainder can be found trivially.

The industry had not anticipated this attack, and all smartcards then on the market appeared vulnerable [1067]. As it is a noninvasive attack, it can be carried out by modified terminal equipment against a bank card carried by an unsuspecting customer. So once the attacker has taken the trouble to understand a card and design a Trojan terminal, a large number of cards may be compromised at little marginal cost.

Paul's discovery held up the deployment of smartcards in banking for two or three years while people worked on defences. In fact, his company had patented many of the best ones, and ended up licensing them to most crypto vendors. Some work at the protocol level; for example, the EMV protocol for bank cards mandates (from version 4.1) that the key used to compute the MAC on a transaction be a session key derived from an on-card master key by encrypting a counter. In this way, no two ciphertexts visible outside the card are ever generated using the same key. Other defences include randomised clocking, to make trace alignment harder, and masking, where you introduce some offsets in each round and recalculate the S-boxes to compensate for them. This way, the implementation of the cipher changes every time it's invoked. With public-key algorithms, there are even stronger arguments for masking, because they also help mitigate fault attacks, which I'll discuss below. The more expensive cards have dedicated crypto engines for modular multiplication and for DES/AES. Testing a device for DPA resistance is not straightforward; there is a discussion by Paul Kocher at [1068] and a 2011 survey article that discusses the practicalities of attack and defence at [1069].

There are many variants on the theme. Attacks based on cache misses can measure power as well as the time taken to encrypt, as a miss activates a lot of circuitry to read nonvolatile memory; you can't stop cache attacks on AES just by using a timer to ensure that each encryption takes the same number of clock cycles. Another variant is to use different sensors: David Samyde and Jean-Jacques Quisquater created *electromagnetic analysis*, in which they move a tiny pickup coil over the surface of the chip to pick up local signals rather than relying simply on the whole device's current draw [1571]. And, as I noted in the last chapter, DPA can be combined with optical probing; Sergei Skorobogatov's optically-enhanced position-locked power analysis uses a laser to illuminate a single target transistor for half of the test runs, giving access not just to a Hamming weight of a computation, but a single targeted bit [1775].

A spectacular demonstration of power analysis arrived in 2016 when Eyal Ronen, Colin O'Flynn, Adi Shamir and Achi-Or Weingarten demonstrated a worm that could take over Philips Hue lamps, after they developed an improved power-analysis attack to retrieve the AES key that these lamps used to authenticate firmware updates [1617]. Philips had made several other mistakes: relying on a single AES key, present in millions of low-cost devices, to protect updates, using the same key for CBC and MAC, and having two bugs in the light link protocol they used. As updates could propagate by ZigBee, malware could spread in a chain reaction from one lamp to the next; the authors showed that in a city such as Paris, there were enough lamps for such a chain reaction to be self-sustaining, like nuclear fission.

The state of the art in 2019 is probably the *template attack* where the attacker studies a device's current draw closely for the instructions of interest and builds a multivariate Gaussian distribution giving the probability distribution for an observed trace given the instruction, the operands, the results and the state. For details, see for example Marios Choudary and Markus Kuhn [421]. It is also possible to use special hardware tools to capture a power trace with less noise, a significant factor in power analysis [1787].

19.4.3 Glitching and differential fault analysis

In 1996 Markus Kuhn and I reported that many smartcards could be broken by inserting transients, or *glitches*, in their power or clock lines [107]. For example, one smartcard used in early banking applications had the feature that an unacceptably high clock frequency only triggered a reset after a number of cycles, so that transients would be less likely to cause false alarms. You could replace a single clock pulse with two much narrower pulses without causing a reset, but forcing the processor to execute a NOP instead of the instruction it was supposed to execute. This gives rise to a *selective code execution* attack where the attacker can step over jump instructions to bypass access controls, or construct his own program out of gadgets found in the card's own code.

The following year, Dan Boneh, Richard DeMillo and Richard Lipton noticed that a number of public key cryptographic algorithms break horribly if a random error can be induced [286]. For example, when doing an RSA signature the secret computation $S = h(m)^d \pmod{pq}$ is carried out mod p, then mod q, and the results are then combined, as this is much faster. But if the card returns a defective signature S_p which is correct modulo p but incorrect modulo q, then we will have

$$p = \gcd(pq, S_p^e - h(m))$$

which breaks the system at once.

Also in 1997, Eli Biham and Adi Shamir pointed out that if we can set a given bit of memory to zero (or one), and we know where in memory a key is kept, we can find out the key by just doing an encryption, zeroising the leading bit, doing another encryption and seeing if the result's different, then zeroising the next bit and so on [247]. Optical probing turned out to be just the tool for this [1651], and using a laser to set key bits to zero one at a time has now become a routine reverse-engineering technique.

Glitches induced by lasers are not limited to attacks on chips. It turns out that if you fire a laser at a MEMS microphone, as used in phones and in voice-controlled digital assistants such as Google Home and Amazon Alexa, it records a click. Kevin Fu and colleagues found that by modulating a laser pointer with spoken commands, they could activate such devices from tens of meters away – so they could order Alexa to unlock a house's front door by shining a laser pointer through the window from the garden [1848].

Many real-world attacks now use a combination of active and passive methods. In section 19.3 above, I discussed optically enhanced position-locked power analysis, which uses a laser to partially ionise a target transistor during power analysis. And you can use a power glitch to greatly increase the optical emissions from a chip for a short period of time, in order to distinguish specific memory writes, as I discussed in section 18.5.5.

19.4.4 Rowhammer, CLKscrew and Plundervolt

One very serious chip-level side channel is when DRAM memory contents can leak into adjacent rows. In 2014, Yoongu Kim and colleagues at CMU found that DRAM manufactured in 2012 and 2013 was vulnerable to disturbance errors; repeatedly accessing a row in a modern DRAM chip causes bit flips in physically-adjacent rows at consistently predictable bit locations, an attack now known as Rowhammer [1050]. The following year, Mark Seaborn and Thomas Dullien found how this hardware fault could be exploited by application code to gain kernel privileges [1697]. By the year after that, Kaveh Razavi and colleagues had shown how to use the technique to replace a strong public key with a weak one – with the effect that one virtual machine could attack a co-hosted target machine by subverting its OpenSSH public-key authentication, and also compromise the software update mechanism by forging GPG signatures from trusted keys [1590]. The vulnerable type of DRAM is still in such wide use and the attacks can target so many different software mechanisms, that they may be around for some time. The first generation of hardware mitigation from vendors includes *target row refresh* (TRR) where the DRAM chip controller refreshes rows to block the most common hammering patterns; Pietro Frigo and colleagues built a fuzzer to analyse 42 chips with TRR defences, and found other patterns that gave attacks on 13 of them [725]. And in 2020, Andrew Kwong and colleagues found that the mechanism could be used to read as well as write; an attacker can exploit the dependence between Rowhammer-induced bit flips and the bits in adjacent rows to deduce those bits – and what's more, this works even when ECC memory detects and corrects each bit flip [1116].

CPUs are also vulnerable to hardware fault injection, using dynamic scaling of frequency and voltage. To save power, many modern CPUs change frequency in response to load, and scale the voltage appropriately. In 2017 Adrian Tang, Simha Sethumadhavan, and Sal Stolfo discovered the CLKscrew attack, where they overclocked the Arm processor on a Nexus 6 to defeat TrustZone, extracting crypto keys and escalating privilege [1861]. In 2019, Kit Murdock and colleagues discovered Plundervolt: here an undocumented voltage scaling interface in Intel Core processors is exploited to cause an undervoltage that induces faults in multiply and AES-NI operations that allow RSA and AES keys to be extracted using fault analysis, as well as mistakes in pointer arithmetic that leak arbitrary memory contents from SGX exclaves [1368].

Although Arm and Intel released microcode patches for CLKscrew and Plundervolt, we may expect other CPU attacks of the same genre. Rowhammer / RAMBleed attacks remain an issue. In the long term, hardware security will require more defensive design. This will not be trivial: just increasing the DRAM refresh rate increases device power consumption, as would less aggressive frequency scaling. Two of the scientists who discovered Rowhammer, Onur Mutlu and Jeremie Kim, suggest that when the memory controller closes a row, then it refreshes the adjacent rows with a probability tuned to the dependability of the chip [1371]. This may in turn add more complexity at the system level. Given that ever more side channels will lurk in new chip technologies as firms push devices ever closer to the boundaries set by physics, a more principled approach is needed to semiconductor security. Chip vendors are learning the hard way that they need to involve good security engineers at design time, rather than just hoping to patch stuff later. When failures emerge at the level of a popular semiconductor process, or a widely-used CPU, remediation is expensive.

19.4.5 Meltdown, Spectre and other enclave side channels

The latest tsunami to hit the chipmakers (and indeed the whole information security world) is a family of attacks based on CPU microarchitecture. The story starts in 2005, when Colin Percival found that AES cache misses could be used by an attacker to observe an encryption operation in another hyperthread on the same Intel CPU; by pulling data into the L1 cache, then measuring a moment later how long it takes to access the same data, you can see whether your data were evicted by the other hyperthread [1510]. Two years later, Onur Acıiçmez, Çetin Kaya Koç and Jean-Pierre Seifert invented branch prediction analysis (BPA). Modern high-performance CPUs have a superscalar architecture in which the CPU no longer fetches and executes one instruction at a time, but has a pipeline that fetches as many as a dozen instructions ahead, and tries to predict which branch the code will take. BPA enabled a spy thread to extract a secret key from a parallel crypto thread by observing the CPU's branch-prediction state; a misprediction imposed a penalty of 20 cycles at the time; in the best circumstances, an RSA private key could be extracted from observing a single signature [13]. Others explored other cache behaviour; in 2015, Fangfei Liu, Yuval Yarom and colleagues showed that the L3 cache gave practical *prime and probe* cross-core attacks that enabled the recovery of GPG private keys [1177]. By 2017, the Cachezoom attack allowed an attacker to extract keys from SGX enclaves [1330]. The most recent such attack is the Membuster attack by Dayeol Lee and colleagues, which uses OS privilege to induce cache misses that leak data [1136]. (Intel's response has been simply to declare such attacks to be out of scope.) This was a field in which, over more than a decade of work, many ideas came together; the CPU vendors should have been paying more attention.

The most impactful attacks were Meltdown and Spectre, disclosed in early 2018. They both exploit speculative memory reads, and build on the previous work on prime-and-probe, branch prediction and cache side-channels. They are so serious that both Intel and Arm announced that they will redesign their CPUs to block them; but that will take years, and in the meantime software mitigations (where available) may cause a 15% performance hit with some workloads, and occasional reboots. Given that the world's data centres consume perhaps 3% of all electric power, this is potentially a big deal.

Meltdown creates a race condition between memory access and privilege checking, and reads out forbidden memory via a cache side channel. It was discovered independently by multiple researchers who disclosed their findings responsibly to the chip makers and then consolidated their results [1173]. The chip makers spent much of 2017 working secretly on bug fixes.

Spectre was disclosed at the same time, having also been discovered by many of the same teams. It's actually a (growing) family of vulnerabilities exploiting the branch prediction logic that is a special case of speculative execution. This logic tries to guess which code path will be taken after a conditional jump, and rogue software can train it to mispredict. The CPU will then fetch instructions that will never be executed, and if some of these perform forbidden operations – such as when a user program reads protected kernel memory – then the protected pages may be fetched from cache. Even if they are never read – so the access-control check is never done – this gives a reliable timing side-channel that enables an attacker to observe crypto key material [1071]. In short, even if a CPU's execution is formally correct, all sorts of lower-level optimisations can make the timing depend on secret data, and a whole series of Spectre variants have come along to exploit this. While Meltdown reads a target process's data directly, Spectre tricks the target process into revealing its data via side-channels.

The Spectre family of attacks keeps on growing; shortly after Spectre was announced, researchers discovered a variant called Foreshadow that cracks many of the features on Intel processors that Spectre didn't, including SGX and system management mode [340]. The 2019 security conferences brought a whole series of other attacks that exploit subtle microarchitectural features: Zombieload, Fallout, Smotherspectre and RAMBleed to name but four, while 2020 brought Load Value Injection, which combines ideas from Meltdown and Spectre [341], and CrossTalk, which enables one core in a CPU to attack another [1573]. Pretty well all CPUs now use branch prediction – except the tiniest – and have become so complex that there are lots of side channels. Finding them at design time isn't easy, as the tools the chipmakers developed for verifying their designs merely check that the logic gives the right answer – not how long it takes. The reason they're now being found is that the formerly sleepy backwater of microarchitectural covert channels suddenly became the hottest topic in security research, and hundreds of bright research students are suddenly looking hard. Fixing everything they find will take years, and given the nature of the technology I doubt that everything will ever be fixed. Arm, for example, has introduced new barrier instructions CSDB, SSBB and PSSBB. After CSDB appears in code, for example, no instruction may be speculatively executed using predicted data or state [132]. There's also a new data field CVS2 from v8.5A onwards to indicate the presence of mitigations against adversarial prediction training. It will take perhaps four years to get this all into silicon, and several more for the necessary support to appear in software toolchains – and longer still for programmers to learn to use it all. Many programmers won't bother, and many managers' reaction to such wicked and complex problems will be denial.

So, during the 2020s, any crypto that you do on CPUs that also run untrustworthy processes is potentially at risk. Quite possibly all CPUs of any size will acquire cryptoprocessors, with hardware engines that do AES, ECDH, ECDSA and so on in constant time. (But that then opens up several new cans of worms, as we'll discuss in the chapter on advanced cryptographic engineering.)

19.5 Environmental side channels

The past twenty years have seen a host of side-channel attacks that exploit human behaviour and the environment of the device. Such attacks exploit acoustics, optics, device motion and combinations too; once attackers figure out how to recover text from the sound of someone typing, they can apply the same techniques to keystroke timings observed by other means, such as on the network or by measuring device motion.

19.5.1 Acoustic side channels

Acoustic security has a long history in terms of preventing people or devices eavesdropping on sensitive conversations, as I mentioned in section 19.2.2. As for listening to machines, the first case may have been during the Suez crisis in 1956, when the British figured out the settings of the Egyptian embassy's Hagelin cipher machine using a phone bug. There was later a 'folk rumour' that the agencies were able to tell what someone was typing on the old IBM Selectric typewriter by just recording the sound they made, and that data could be recovered from the noise made by dot matrix printers [324]. It later turned out that the KGB had indeed bugged IBM typewriters in the US embassy in Moscow from 1976 to 1984, though they used magnetic bugs rather than microphones [791].

In 2001, Dawn Song, David Wagner and Xuqing Tian showed that the timing of keystrokes contained enough information for an opponent to recover a lot of information merely by observing traffic encrypted under SSH. As each keystroke is sent in a separate packet when SSH is used in interactive mode, encrypted packet timing gives precise inter-keystroke timing and even a simple hidden Markov model gives about one bit of information per keystroke pair about the content; they noted that this would enable an attacker about a factor of 50 advantage in guessing a password whose encrypted value he'd observed [1807].

In 2004, Dmitri Asonov and Rakesh Agrawal showed that the different keys on a computer keyboard made sufficiently different sounds. They trained a neural network to recognise the clicks made by key presses on a target keyboard and concluded that someone's typing could be picked up from acoustic emanations with an error rate of only a few percent [137]. In 2005, Li Zhuang, Feng Zhou, and Doug Tygar combined these threads to come up with an even more powerful attack. Given a recording of someone typing text in English for about ten minutes on an unknown keyboard, they recognised the individual keys, then used the inter-keypress times and the known statistics of English to figure out which key was which. Thus they could decode text from a recording of a keyboard to which they had never had access [2075]. Other researchers quickly joined in; by the following year, Yigael Berger, Avishai Wool, and Arie Yeredor had shown that with improved signal-processing algorithms, acoustic reconstruction could be made much more efficient [229].

Others took acoustic analysis down to a much lower level: Eran Tromer and Adi Shamir showed that keys leak via the acoustic emanations from a PC, generated mostly at frequencies above 10KHz by capacitors on the motherboard [1912].

The deep neural network revolution that began in 2012 enabled much more information to be wrung out of such signals, and by 2016 Alberto Compagno and colleagues had shown that if you type while talking to someone over Skype, they can reconstruct a lot of what you're typing [465]. Also in 2016, Mengyuan Li and colleagues had shown that when you type on a smartphone, your finger motions interfere with the RF signal in ways that change the multipath behaviour on wifi enough to modulate the channel state information; this enables a rogue wifi hotspot to infer keystroke information [1164]. By 2017, Ilia Shumailov had figured out how one app on a mobile phone could recover passwords and PINs typed into another app by listening to the taps on the screen, using the two microphones in the device [1734]. Such *time-difference-of-arrival* (TDOA) processing had previously been the domain of sophisticated electronic-warfare kit; here was an application in your pocket, and that would enable a rogue app to steal your online banking password, even despite the protection available if the password entry mechanism is implemented in the Trusted Execution Environment, so malware cannot tap it directly.

19.5.2 Optical side channels

Turning now to optics, there are obvious optical side-channels such as *shoulder surfing*, where someone watches your PIN over your shoulder at an ATM and then picks your pocket; ATM crime gangs have also used CCTV cameras in shop ceilings above a PIN entry device, and even in furniture vans parked next to a cash machine. And now that everyone has a camera in their pocket and a 3-d printer in their den, physical keys are easy to duplicate – even by someone watching at a distance. But there is much, much more.

Have you ever looked across a city at night, and seen someone working late in their office, their face and shirt lit up by the diffuse reflected glow from their computer monitor? Did you ever stop to wonder whether any information might be recovered from the glow? In 2002 Markus Kuhn showed that the answer was 'pretty well everything': he hooked up a high-performance photomultiplier tube to an oscilloscope, and found that the light from the blue and green phosphors used in common VDU tubes decays after a few microseconds. As a result, the diffuse reflected glow contains much of the screen information, encoded in the time domain. Thus, given a telescope, a photomultiplier tube and suitable image-processing software, it was possible to read the computer screen at which a banker was looking by decoding the light scattered from his face or his shirt [1105]. (According to Ed Snowden, this was one of the techniques the NSA used to spy on foreign embassies, and went under the code-name 'Ocean'.)

The next headline was from Joe Loughry and David Umphress, who looked at the LED status indicators found on the data serial lines of PCs, modems, routers and other communications equipment. They found that a significant number of them were transmitting the serial data optically: 11 out of 12 modems tested, 2 out of 7 routers, and one data storage device. The designers were just driving the tell-tale light off the serial data line, without stopping to realise that the LED had sufficient bandwidth to transmit the data to a waiting telescope [1191].

The latest discovery, by Ben Nassi and colleagues in 2020, is the lamphone channel. Speech or music in a room induces vibration in a hanging lightbulb, which can be read from across the street using a telescope and a suitable photodiode [1389]. Unlike a laser microphone that picks up sound from a window, this is entirely passive, and the direction is less sensitive.

19.5.3 Other side-channels

Thermal covert channels arrived in 2006, when Steven Murdoch discovered that a typical computer's clock skew, which can be measured remotely, showed diurnal variation, and realised this was a function of ambient temperature. His experiments showed that unless a machine's owner takes countermeasures, anyone who can extract accurate timestamps from it can measure its CPU load; and this raises the question of whether an attacker can find where in the world a hidden machine is located. The longitude comes from the time zone, and the latitude (more slowly) from the seasons. So hiding behind an anonymity service such as Tor might not be as easy as it looks [1358, 1360].

It had long been known that oily fingerprint residues can compromise fingerprint scanners, as we discuss in the chapter on biometrics. However, they also leave traces on touchscreens. After these screens started being used on phones, Adam Aviv documented the *smudge attack*: these residues are a very effective way of breaking the pattern lock commonly used on Android devices [146]. (Smudges also help guess the PINs used on all sorts of touchscreen devices – even your Tesla.)

Adam also developed the use of the smartphone's accelerometer as a side-channel, finding that the phone's rocking motion as the user typed would reveal significant information. Even in uncontrolled settings, while users were walking, his model could classify 20% of PINs and 40% of unlock patterns within 5 attempts [147]. The accelerometer had already been used by Philip Marquardt and others to decode the vibrations from a nearby conventional computer keyboard [1231]. Liang Cai and Hao Chen then studied using both the accelerometer and gyro, finding that the latter was more effective, and allowed a 4-digit PIN to be guessed about 80 times better than by chance [367]. Laurent Simon and I then played with turning the camera into a virtual gyroscope, as the phone tilts when you tap in a PIN; we found that camera plus microphone was just as good as the gyro for keystroke inference [1760]. Gesture typing also leaks; text entered into one app can be read by others, although this is a technical side channel that exploits shared interrupt state [1763].

The arrival of the Apple watch in 2015 inspired more people to study smartwatch side channels; by the end of the year, Xiangyu Liu and colleagues had shown that a smartwatch not only allows you to do the accelerometer inference attacks on smartphone PIN entry, but also to reconstruct text typed at a normal keyboard – though if you wear it on your left wrist you get more accuracy with the left-hand letters [1178].

Are these side channels a big deal? The answer appears to be 'not yet'. Joel Reardon and colleagues studied 88,000 apps from the Google Play Store and reported in 2019 that while over 12,000 had the means to exploit side channels to observe other apps or system data, or to communicate in ways that they shouldn't, only 61 actually did so [1591]. However, the security engineer must remain aware that as we move to devices such as smartphones with a rich set of sensors, we get a rich set of side channels that make it ever more difficult to confine information to specific apps and contexts. As we move to a world with gazillions of smart objects, the number and type of side channels will multiply. We might expect this to give us a nasty surprise one day.

19.6 Social side channels

Many side channels occur at the application layer, and are often overlooked. One classic example is an increase in pizza deliveries to the Pentagon leaking the fact of a forthcoming military operation. A more subtle example is that personal health information derived from visits to genitourinary medicine clinics is considered specially sensitive in the UK, and can't be shared with the GP unless the patient consents. In one case, a woman's visit to a GUM clinic leaked when the insurer failed to recall her for a smear test that her GP knew was due [1312]. The insurer knew that a smear test had been done already by the clinic, and didn't want to pay twice.

I've already discussed such issues at length in the chapter on inference control and don't propose to duplicate that discussion here. I'll merely note that this is also a high-impact family of side channels. Policymakers and the tech industry have both pretended for years to believe that de-identification of sensitive data such as medical records makes it non-sensitive and thus suitable to be treated as an industrial raw material. This is emphatically not the case, as one scandal after another has brought home – leading among other things to the EU General Data Protection Regulation.

Social side channels also play a role on the philosophical side of technology policy debates; for example, Helen Nissenbaum has gone so far as to define privacy as 'contextual integrity'. Most privacy failures that do real harm result from information from one context (such as the clinic) ending up in another (such as a newspaper). Ubiquitous devices with complex side channels are not the only issue; the mass collection of data that's used for advertising without effective opt-outs leads to much more leakage. I'll discuss this later in the chapter on 'Surveillance or Privacy?'

19.7 Summary

Side-channel attacks include a whole range of threats in which the security of systems can be subverted by compromising emanations, whether from unintentional radio frequency or conducted electromagnetic signals, to leakage through shared computational state, to the wide range of sensors found in modern mobile phones and other consumer devices and to leakage via social context too. Side channel leakage is a huge topic and it will get more complex still as we get software and sensors in just about everything. Which side channels pose a real threat will of course depend on the application, and most of them will remain of academic interest most of the time. But occasionally, they'll bite. So the security engineer needs to be aware of the risks.

Research problems

Many of the research papers in the top security conferences in 2019 are about side channels, particularly side-channel attacks on processors that undermine access controls and enclaves, and side-channel attacks on security chips that enable TPMs or payment cards to be defeated. Back in 2015, the emphasis was on side-channel attacks on phones, smart watches and other physical devices. Social side-channels continue to be of interest and drive research into privacy.

Side-channel vulnerabilities are becoming ubiquitous as systems get more complex. More complex supply chains made bug fixes harder, and sometimes vulnerabilities just won't be fixed as it would cost too much in terms of performance, effort or cash. Attacks become easier as techniques are honed and software gets passed around. This applies to classical Tempest attacks too, as *software radios* – radios that digitize a signal at the intermediate frequency stage and do all the subsequent processing in software – are no longer an expensive military curiosity [1119] but are now ubiquitous in cellular radio base stations, GPS receivers, IoT devices, and even hobbyists' bedrooms. The explosion of interest in machine learning is bound to have an effect, improving attacks everywhere from Tempest through power analysis to the exploitation of social channels. It's hard to predict which side channels will scale up to become another billion-dollar issue, but it's a good bet that some of them will.

Further reading

A recent history of Tempest by David Easter tells of the Cold War struggles between Russia, the USA, the UK and their European allies [600]. The classic van Eck article [601] is still worth a read, and our work on Soft Tempest, Teapot and related topics can be found in [1107]. For power analysis, see the papers by Paul Kocher [1067] and Thomas Messergues [1300]. For timing and power analysis, the original papers by Paul Kocher and his colleagues are the classic references [1066, 1067]; there's a textbook by Stefan Mangard, Elisabeth Oswald and Thomas Popp that covers all the major aspects [1216], while Paul Kocher's 2011 survey paper, "Introduction to differential power analysis" explains the engineering detail of both attack and defence [1069]. A 2020 survey by Mark Randolph and William Diehl covers more recent work [1579].

To keep up with progress in timing and power attacks on security chips, you really need to follow the current research literature, as attack techniques improve all the time. For example, in November 2019, Daniel Moghimi, Berk Sunar, Thomas Eisenbarth and Nadia Henninger found timing attacks on a TPM made by STM that had been certified secure to Common Criteria EAL4+ and on a virtual TPM in Intel CPUs, enabling them to extract ECDSA keys; the latter case led to a real attack on a VPN product [1331]. More than twenty years after timing attacks came along, you still can't rely on either certified products or big brand names to withstand them.

Attacks on mainstream computer hardware are still developing quickly. For attacks on memory, see the 2019 survey paper on Rowhammer by Onur Mutlu and Jeremie Kim [1371]. As for attacks on CPUs exploiting speculative execution, the Meltdown and Spectre attacks attracted so much publicity that microarchitectural security turned overnight from a backwater into one of the hottest research areas in the field. For years the CPU designers (and almost everyone else) had assumed that if hardware had been verified, then it did what it said in the manual, so there was no point looking for bugs. Now we know that the verification tools had nothing to say about side channels, there are hundreds of smart people beating up on CPUs. The bug reports just keep on coming, and CPUs have meanwhile got so complex that it may take years before we get some stability. The best starting point in 2020 is probably the survey paper by Claudio Canella and colleagues at the Usenix Security Symposium [382]. Claudio and colleagues have also broken the first-generation Meltdown mitigations with an attack called EchoLoad [383].

CHAPTER

20

Advanced Cryptographic Engineering

Give me a rock on which to stand, and I will move the world.

– ARCHIMEDES

Whoever thinks his problem can be solved using cryptography, doesn't understand his problem and doesn't understand cryptography.

– Attributed by Roger Needham and Butler Lampson to each other

20.1 Introduction

Cryptography is often used to build a trustworthy component on which more complex designs can rely. Such designs come from three rather different backgrounds. The first is the government systems world we described in Chapter 9, where the philosophy is to minimise the trusted computing base using mechanisms like data diodes and multilevel secure encryption devices. The second is the world of banking described in Chapter 12 where smartcards are used as authentication tokens while HSMs are used to protect PINs and keys. The third is the world of cryptography research in the 1980s and 1990s where people dreamed of solving social problems using mathematics: of creating anonymous communications so that oppressed groups could evade state surveillance, leading to censorship-resistant publishing, untraceable digital cash and electronic elections that would be impossible to rig. In all these cases, real life turned out to be somewhat messier than we anticipated.

There are even more complex cryptographic components that we use as platforms. But the engineering isn't just about reducing the attack surface, or simplifying our fault tree analysis. In most cases there's a significant interaction with policy, liability and other complicating factors.

In this chapter I'm going to discuss six examples of cryptographic engineering – full disk encryption, the Signal protocol, Tor, hardware security modules, enclaves and blockchains. The first is a simple example to set the scene;

the other five use crypto in more complex ways to support a wide range of applications, including payments in the case of the last three. All but HSMs are used by cybercriminals.

Hard disk encryption has been around since the 1980s and is one of the simplest security products, at least conceptually. By encrypting the data on your hard disk when the machine's in use, you ensure that a thief can only steal the hardware, not the data.

Signal is a protocol for secure messaging between phones. It is perhaps the next level up in complexity and is about enabling people to manage a social network as securely as possible in the face of equipment compromise. Signal does private contact discovery by means of enclaves.

Tor takes this to the next level by providing anonymity, when you don't want someone observing your traffic to know who you're talking to or which websites you're visiting.

HSMs have provided a trust platform for payment services since the 1980s. But the crypto apps that run on them can suffer from attacks on their *application programming interfaces* that are so deeply entangled with payment applications that they are very hard to fix.

Enclaves are an attempt by CPU vendors to provide a general-purpose crypto platform: we've had Arm's TrustZone since 2004 and Intel's SGX since 2015. They are starting to replace HSMs in payment applications, and also support private contact discovery in Signal. But they have been plagued with problems from side-channel attacks to class breaks. For example, if you can extract the master secret key from an SGX chip, you can break the whole ecosystem.

Finally, for a quite different kind of trusted computer, we look at Bitcoin. This is a project, since 2009, to create a digital currency based on a shared ledger that emerges using cryptographic mechanisms from the cooperation of mutually mistrustful parties. Many of the stakeholders are far from trustworthy, and there are dominant players at several levels in the technology stack. Yet a trusted computer has somehow emerged, thanks to a combination of cryptography and economic incentives, and has kept going despite the huge amounts of money that could be taken in a successful attack.

It may be useful to bring together in one chapter the trusted platforms of both bankers and gangsters, so we can contrast them. Some striking facts emerge. For example, the best attempts of the top technology companies to produce trusted computers have produced flawed products, while the gangsters seem to have created something that works – at least for now.

20.2 Full-disk encryption

The idea behind *full-disk encryption* (FDE) is simple. You encrypt data as it's written to disk, and do decryption as it's read again. The key depends on an initial authentication step such as a password, which is forgotten when the machine sleeps or is switched off. So if a doctor leaves their laptop on a train, only the hardware is lost; the medical records are not. FDE has become a regulatory requirement in many industries. In Europe, privacy regulators generally see the loss of machines with FDE as not serious enough to attract a fine or to need mandatory notification of data subjects. Many phones and laptops come with FDE; with some it's enabled by default (Android) while with others it just takes a click (Mac).

Scratch a little under the surface, though, and there's a wide variance in quality. From the early days of hard disks in 1980s, software FDE products were available but imposed a performance penalty, while hardware products cost more and were export-controlled. The engineering isn't trivial, as you need a platform on which to run the initial authentication step. Early products offered an extra encrypted volume but did not protect the host operating system and could be defeated by malware. The initial authentication is tricky in other ways. If you derive the disk key from a user password, then a thief can try zillions of them offline, as we discussed in section 3.4.4.1, and guess anything a normal user sets up. A hardware TPM chip can limit password guessing, and from 2007 this became available for Windows with BitLocker. Integrating FDE into a platform enables the vendor to design coherent mechanisms for trusted boot of an authentic copy of the operating system, setting up and managing recovery keys, and coping with quite complex interactions with software upgrade, swap space, device repairs, the backup and recovery of user data, and factory reset when the device is sold.

Third-party offerings started to offer some extra features: TrueCrypt, for example, offered a steganographic file system where the very existence of a disk volume would remain hidden unless the user knew the right password [115][1]. A crypto phone sold to criminals, EncroChat, had a whole hidden partition containing encrypted chat and VOIP apps; I'll discuss such products in more detail in section 25.4.1. However most people now use the FDE facility provided by the vendor of their phone or laptop, as proper integration involves quite a lot of the platform. Since 2010 we've had a special mode of operation, XTS-AES, designed for FDE; it encrypts each block salted with the sector number, and has a mechanism to fit disc blocks to block ciphers. Offerings such as Microsoft's BitLocker and Apple's FileVault have an overhead of only a few percent, when run on CPUs with AES support.

Yet attacks continue. In 2008, Alex Halderman and colleagues at Princeton came up with *cold boot attacks*, which defeated the principal FDE products then

[1]That product was suddenly discontinued and its anonymous developers recommended that users migrate to other products because of an unspecified vulnerability; some suspect that this was a 'warrant canary', a pre-planned warning message whose transmission the developers suppress by certifying regularly that they are not subject to coercion, but which fires off a warning once they're served with a subpoena or warrant [62].

on the market and can still present a problem for many machines [855]. As I described in section 18.3, you freeze a computer's DRAM in which the transient encryption key is stored, then reboot the device with a lightweight operating system and acquire a memory image, from which the key can be read. In 2015, we found that most Androids were insecure: the factory reset function was so badly engineered by most OEMs that credentials, including FDE keys, could be recovered from second-hand devices [1761]. And most Android phones don't get patched once they're no longer on sale. And in 2019, Carlo Meijer and Bernard van Gastel found that the three third-party FDE products that held 60% of the market were insecure, that open-source software encryption would have been better, and that BitLocker turned itself off if one of these hardware products appeared to be present; thanks to their work, it no longer does so [1287]. And then there's the collateral damage. Now that lots of sensitive data are kept not on hard disks but in Amazon S3 buckets, auditors routinely demand that these buckets are encrypted; but as the failure mode of an S3 bucket isn't a burglar in Amazon's data centre but negligence over access controls, it's unclear that S3 bucket encryption achieves anything other than tick-box compliance.

And finally one has to consider abusability, of which there are at least two significant kinds. First, the wide availability of FDE code is one of the two components that led to the recent wave of ransomware attacks, where a gang penetrates your systems, installs FDE, lets it run until you've encrypted enough backups to make recovery painful, then demands a ransom for the key. (The other component is cryptocurrency, which I'll discuss later in this chapter.) Second, many people consider FDE to be magic insurance against compromise, and won't report a laptop left on a train if it had FDE enabled (or was supposed to), even if the finder might have seen the password or be able to guess it.

So even the simplest of encryption products has a significant entanglement with compliance, is much more complex under the hood than you might think at first glance, usually imposes some performance penalty, and can be vulnerable to a capable opponent – even years after the relevant attacks have been published.

20.3 Signal

As smartphones spread round the world, people switched from SMS to messaging apps such as WhatsApp, Telegram and Signal; they're cheaper and more flexible, allowing you to create groups of families and friends. Pretty soon they started supporting voice and video calls too, and offering end-to-end encryption. It had previously been possible to encrypt email using programs like PGP, but it was rather fiddly (as we discussed in section 3.2.1) and remained a niche activity. The arrival of new platforms meant that message encryption could be made universal, shipped as a default with the app; and the Snowden disclosures helped stoke the public demand.

Signal is a free messaging app, initially developed by a man who uses the name of Moxie Marlinspike. It set the standard for end-to-end encryption of messaging, and its mechanisms have been adopted by competing products including WhatsApp. Mobile messages can be highly sensitive, with everything from lovers' assignations through business deals to political intrigues at diplomatic summits; yet mobile phones are often lost or stolen, or sent in for repair when the screens break. So key material in phones is frequently exposed to compromise, and it's not enough to just have a single long-lived private key in an app. The Signal protocol therefore provides the properties of *forward secrecy*, that a key compromise today won't expose any future traffic, and *backward secrecy*, which means that it won't expose previous traffic either. These are now formalised as *post-compromise security* [453].

The protocol has three main components: the *Extended Triple Diffie-Hellman* (X3DH) protocol to set up keys between Alice, Bob and the server; a ratchet protocol to derive message keys once a secret key is established; and mechanisms for finding the Signal keys of other people in your address book.

We can't use vanilla Diffie-Hellman to establish a fresh key between Alice and Bob, as they might not be online at the same time. So in the X3DH protocol [1229], each user U publishes an identity key IK_U and a prekey SK_U to a server, together with a signature on the latter that can be verified using the former. The algorithms are elliptic-curve Diffie-Hellman and elliptic-curve DSA. When Alice wants to send a message to Bob, she fetches Bob's keys IK_B and SK_B from the server, generates an ephemeral Diffie-Hellman key EK_A, and combines them with Bob's keys in all the feasible ways: $DH(IK_A, SPK_B)$, $DH(EK_A, IK_B)$, and $DH(EK_A, SPK_B)$. These are hashed together to give a fresh key K_{AB}. Alice then sends Bob an initial message containing her keys IK_A and EK_A, a note of which of Bob's prekeys she used, and a ciphertext encrypted using K_{AB} so that he can check he's got it too. Optionally, Bob can upload a one-time ephemeral key that Alice will combine with EK_A and hash into the mix.

Given an initial Diffie-Hellman key K_{AB}, Alice and Bob then use the *double ratchet algorithm* to derive message keys for individual texts and calls. Its purpose is to recover security if one of their phones is compromised. It uses two mechanisms: a *key derivation function* (KDF) or one-way hash function to update stored secret keys, and further Diffie-Hellman key exchanges. Alice and Bob each maintain separate *KDF chains* for sending and for receiving, each with a shared-secret key and a Diffie-Hellman key. Each message carries a new Diffie Hellman key part which is combined with the key for the relevant chain, while the shared-secret key is passed through the KDF. The actual details are slightly more fiddly, because of the need to deal with out-of-order messages [1514]. The goal is that an opponent must compromise either Alice's phone or Bob's continuously in order to get access to the traffic between them.

The really tricky part is the initial authentication step. If Charlie could take over the server and send Alice his own *IK* instead of Bob's, all bets are off. This is the attack being mounted on messaging apps by some intelligence agencies. Systems such as Apple's iMessage don't just send a single identity key *IK* to your counterparty but a whole keyring of device keys – one for each of your MacBooks, iPhones and other Apple devices. Ian Levy and Crispin Robinson of GCHQ propose that laws such as the UK's Investigatory Powers Bill be used to compel providers to add an extra law-enforcement key to the keyring of any user against whom they get a warrant [1155]. This has led to policy tussles in the USA, the UK and elsewhere, to which I return in section 26.2.7.4. Signal attempts to forestall such attacks by being open source, so that Alice and Bob can more easily work out whether their private conversation has been joined by Charlie as a silent conference call partner, or 'ghost user'. Keeping such surveillance covert may be easier if the phone app software remains opaque.

The upshot is that if Charlie wants to exchange Signal messages with Alice while pretending to be Bob, he has to either compromise Bob's phone or steal Bob's phone number. The options are much the same as if he wanted to steal money from Bob's bank account. They include hacking and stealing the phone; using SS7 exploits to steal Bob's SMS messages; and a SIM swap attack to take over Bob's phone number. The easiest attack for an individual to mount is probably SIM swapping, which we discussed in section 12.7.4. Signal now offers an additional PIN that you need to enter when recovering service on a phone number on which a different handset was previously active. But nation states have sophisticated hacking tools, and have SS7 access. So if the FSB's in your threat model, it's best to use a phone whose number they don't know, and don't carry it around switched on at the same time as a phone they do know is yours, or they might correlate the traces – as I described in section 2.2.1.10.

As we will discuss in section 26.2.2, much of the benefit of signals intelligence comes from metadata, from knowing who called whom and when (or who traveled with whom and when). So for a whistleblower, the game depends on how many other people will become suspects as well as you – the *anonymity set*. If you're a senior civil servant thinking of leaking an illegal policy to a newspaper, and you're one of ten people who knows the story, then you might be the only one of the ten who has ever used Signal.

However, if you're one of hundreds of low-level suspects (say you're a union organiser or NGO staffer) and might be on a long list of targets for thematic collection, then you may want to block the local police from systematically recording your patterns of contacts, and here Signal can indeed help. It offers the interesting innovation of *private contact discovery*.

Previous attempts to help ordinary people use end-to-end encryption, such as the email encryption program PGP, never got much traction outside specialist niches because key management was too much bother. Messaging apps solved the usability problem by demanding access to your address book, looking up all your contacts on their servers to see who else was a user and then flagging them so you know you can message them. However, giving service firms a copy of your address book is already a privacy compromise, and if you also let them keep a plaintext record of your social graph, profile name, location, group memberships and who is messaging whom, then investigators can get all this by subpoena. The original version of Signal compared hashes of the phone numbers in people's address books to discover who was using it; however, Christof Hagen and colleagues used 100 accounts over 25 days to scan all 505m phone numbers in the USA, discovering 2.5m Signal users [849]. Signal has now implemented private contact discovery; I will discuss it later in section 20.6 which discusses SGX, the mechanism it uses. However, even with private contact discovery, when you set up a Signal account on your phone it becomes visible to everyone in your address book who's also on Signal, so they might say – 'Hey, Fred's about to leak something'. (This effect may have been mitigated somewhat when lots of government employees started using Signal following the election and inauguration of President Trump, including people who had held Top Secret clearances for decades.)

A critical but less visible part of the system is the message server. This has to store encrypted messages that have not yet been delivered but how much else is kept and for how long[2]? Signal keeps records of group memberships, but there's now a proposal for anonymous group messaging, which would make group members known to each other but not to Signal's servers [411]. Again, technology can only do so much; if one member of your group is disloyal, they can betray others. However Signal has got real traction as the leading communications security tool available to the public. There was a significant uptick in usage in the USA after the 2016 election, and in 2020 the European Commission (Europe's civil service) ordered its staff to switch to Signal after the compromise of a server containing thousands of diplomatic cables [401].

There was an upset in July 2020, when a Signal update forced users to select a PIN, with a view to keeping each user's contact data encrypted in an enclave, so it could be recovered if the user got a new phone, and so that there could be some other way to make a Signal contact other than by sharing a phone number. This created a storm of protest as users assumed that Signal would also keep message content; other users didn't think a PIN gave enough protection, or didn't want to give Signal a PIN they used for banking, or just didn't like the idea of any centralised data at all. People started questioning the wisdom of relying on a secure communications app whose chief maintainer is someone who uses a pseudonym, who can hold millions of users hostage on a whim, and whose backing was partly from the government and partly from a billionaire[3]. What should the governance of public-interest critical infrastructure look like?

[2]There was a debate about how to handle undelivered messages when keys change, and the WhatsApp implementation was criticised for prioritising delivery over failing closed.
[3]Brian Acton, one of the founders of WhatsApp.

Signal claims to keep no records of traffic, but what if a FISA warrant from the NSA had forced them to do so and lie about it? This brings us to the harder question of how communications can be made anonymous.

20.4 Tor

The Onion Router (Tor) is the main system people use to get serious anonymity online, with about 2 million concurrent users in 2020. It began its life in 1998 at the US Naval Research Laboratory, and was called Onion Routing because messages in it are nested like the layers of an onion [1593]. If Alice wants to visit Eve's website without Eve or anyone else being able to identify her, she sets up a TLS connection to a Tor relay operated by Bob, which sets up a TLS connection to a Tor relay operated by Carol, which in turn sets up a TLS connection to a Tor relay operated by David – from whose 'exit node' Alice can now establish a connection to Eve's website [1362]. The idea is to separate routing from identity – anyone wanting to link Alice to Eve has to subvert Bob, Carol and Dave, or monitor the traffic in and out of Bob's and David's systems.

The inspiration had been a 1981 idea of David Chaum's, the *mix* or *anonymous remailer* [412]. This accepts encrypted messages, strips off the encryption, and then remails them to the address that it finds inside. People experimented with these in the 1990s and found that you need three more things to make it work properly. First, you need more than one mix; an opponent could compromise a single mix by coercing the operator, or simply correlating the traffic in and out. Second, you need to engineer it for the traffic you want to protect, be that email, web or messaging. Third, and hardest of all, you need scale.

The Navy opened Tor up to the world in 2003 because you can only be anonymous in a crowd. If Tor had been restricted to US intelligence agents, then anyone using it would be a target. It is now maintained by the Tor Project, a US nonprofit that maintains the Tor Browser, which has become the default Tor client. This not only handles circuit setup and encryption but manages cookies, JavaScript and other browser features that are hazardous to privacy. Similar functionality is also built into some other browsers, such as Brave. There's also software for Tor relays, which are run by volunteers with high-bandwidth connections; in 2020, about 6,000 active relays serve about 2 million users. When you turn on a Tor-enabled browser, it opens a circuit by finding three Tor relays through which it connects to the outside world.

Tor's cryptographic and software design has evolved over 20 years in the face of a variety of threats and abuse, and it is now used as a component in many applications. It's used to defeat censorship in countries like Iran and Pakistan so you can connect to Facebook and read American and European newspapers. The US State Department supports it, and Facebook is the biggest Tor destination. It can also be used to connect to underground dark markets where you can buy drugs and malware. It can be used to leak classified documents. It can be used to visit child sex abuse websites. The police also use it to visit such sites, so the operators don't know they're police.

The principal vulnerabilities were known from day one and documented in the 1998 paper that introduced onion routing to the world, six years before Tor itself appeared [1593]. But they have frequently been overlooked by careless users. First, a *malicious exit node* can monitor the traffic if Eve's website doesn't use encryption, or if she uses it in such a way that the exit node can do a man-in-the-middle attack. In September 2007, someone set up five Tor exit nodes, monitored the traffic that went through them, and published the interesting stuff [1361]. This included logons and passwords for a number of webmail accounts used by embassies, including missions from Iran, India, Japan and Russia[4]. Yet the Tor documentation made clear that exit traffic can be read, so more careful diplomats would have used a mail service that supported TLS encryption, as Gmail already did by then.

The second problem is the many tricks that web pages employ to track users. This was the main reason for the introduction in 2008 of the Tor Browser, which limits the tracking ability of cookies and other fingerprinting mechanisms. But many applications get users to identify themselves explicitly, or leak information without realising it. In section 11.2.4 I discussed how supposedly anonymous search histories from AOL identified users: a few local searches (that tell where you live) and a few special-interest searches (that reveal your hobbies) can be enough.

Third, low-latency, high-bandwidth systems such as Tor have some intrinsic exposure to traffic analysis [1365]. A global adversary such as the NSA, that taps traffic at many points in the Internet, need only tap a small number of exchange points to get a good enough sample to reconstruct circuits [1367]. In practice this is harder than it looks[5]. Tor has made clear since the start that it does not protect against traffic confirmation attacks, where the opponent controls both the entry and exit relays and correlates the timing, volume or other characteristics of the traffic to identify a particular circuit. Indeed, in 2014 it was discovered that someone (presumably an intelligence agency) had been doing just this, volunteering relays into the system that tinkered with protocol headers in order to make it easier [561]. Tor relays now have countermeasures against such tweaks, but traffic confirmation is still a threat.

Fourth, as Tor connects through a pool of some 6,000 relays, a firewall can simply block their IP addresses. This is done by some companies and also by some countries, most notably China. To circumvent such blocking, volunteers make available *Tor bridges* – Tor entry nodes not listed in the public directory.

[4]This gave an insight into password choice: Uzbekistan came top with passwords like 's1e7u0l7c' while Tunisia just used 'Tunisia' and an Indian embassy '1234'.

[5]The intelligence community paid a compliment to Tor, on a GCHQ slide deck leaked by Ed Snowden, saying "Tor stinks!"

Various games are played as Chinese and other censors try to find and block these too, and to characterise Tor traffic. China appears to prefer that people circumventing its national firewall use VPNs instead; these are not only more scalable but easier to shut down completely at times of crisis (such as in the early stages of the 2020 coronavirus outbreak).

Law-enforcement agencies have on a number of occasions managed to find and close down *Tor onion services*, websites that are available only through the Tor network; rather than a normal URL, they have a '.onion' address that is essentially a cryptographic key. The most famous such service was Silk Road, an underground marketplace where people bought and sold drugs; its operator was arrested because of poor operational security (the email address he used to announce his new service could be traced back to him). Other onion services have had their servers hacked, or supply chains traced. Many of them use cryptocurrencies, which we'll describe later and which can also be traced in various ways. There have also been attacks on the browsers of Tor users with techniques such as zero-days and sandbox escapes. And even in the absence of technical failures, anonymity is intrinsically hard; real-world transactions (and indeed real-world web traffic) can be very dirty, so unexpected inferences can often be drawn.

As with FDE, Tor has a significant entanglement with compliance, helping a variety of actors to evade surveillance and circumvent laws both good and bad. The engineering has become a lot more complex under the hood than it looks. It definitely imposes a performance penalty – websites can take a second to load rather than a few hundred milliseconds. And despite the robustness of the Tor system itself, it has intrinsic limitations that are not intuitively obvious and make anonymity systems built on it hazardous to use. Anonymity systems require careful operational security as well as just the right software.

The governance aspects are of interest. Tor is maintained by the Tor Project, a US nonprofit set up in 2006 to formalise a volunteer project that had started in 2002. Although it has many volunteers, a growing core of permanent staff have been funded from various sources over the years, from the EFF to the US State Department. It remains at heart an international community of people motivated by human rights. An ethnographic study by Ben Collier describes it as made up of three overlapping groups: a group of engineers who see Tor as a structure, and believe that political problems can be solved by doing engineering; a group of activists see it as a struggle, and are committed to specific political values such as anti-racism; while a third group of people largely maintain the Tor relays, are generally politically agnostic, and see what they do as providing infrastructure – "privacy as a service" [455]. Security at scale requires infrastructure, and to provide this largely by volunteer effort requires leaders who can translate between the different stakeholders' agendas and negotiate values rather than just contracts.

20.5 HSMs

In the chapter on banking and bookkeeping, we described how banks use HSMs to enforce a separation-of-duty policy: no single person at the bank should be able to get their hands on a customer's card details and PIN. HSMs are also used to protect the SSL/TLS keys for many websites; you don't want important live keys to be sitting on a developer's laptop, or to be easily extractable by a cloud provider through a memory dump. In the cryptocurrency industry, HSMs are used to protect keys that could sign away substantial assets. In the chapter on Tamper Resistance, we described the mechanisms used to make the HSM tamper-proof. But this isn't enough. You also have to ensure that when you split a computation between a more trusted component such as an HSM and a less trusted component, an attacker can't exploit the split.

Whenever a trusted computer talks to a less trusted one, you have to expect that the less trusted device will lie and cheat, and probe the boundaries by using unexpected combinations of commands, to trick the more trusted one. How can we analyse this systematically?

Banking HSMs have a lot to teach. In 1988, Longley and Rigby identified the importance of separating key types while doing work for security module vendor Eracom [1186]. In 1993, we reported a security flaw that arose from a custom transaction added to a security module [108]. However, we hit paydirt in 2000 when Mike Bond, Jolyon Clulow and I observed that HSM APIs had become immensely complex, with hundreds of different transactions involving complex combinations of cryptographic operations to support dozens of payment protocol variants, and started to think systematically about whether there might be a series of HSM transactions that would break it [72]. We asked: "How can you be sure that there isn't some chain of 17 transactions which will leak a clear key?' After we spent some time staring at the manuals, we started to discover lots of vulnerabilities of this kind.

20.5.1 The xor-to-null-key attack

HSMs are driven by transactions sent to them by servers at a bank or ATMs in the field. The HSM contains a number of master keys that are kept in tamper-responding memory. Most keys are stored outside the device, encrypted under one or more master keys. It's convenient to manage keys for ATMs and other terminals in the databases used to manage them; and nowadays many HSMs are located in the Azure and Amazon clouds where they serve multiple tenants.

The encrypted working keys have a type system that classifies them by function. For example, in the PCI standard for security modules, a PIN derivation key – the master key used to derive a PIN from an account number as described in section 12.4.1 – is stored encrypted under a particular pair of master DES keys to mark it as a non-exportable working key. The *Terminal Master Key* for an ATM is of the same type, and you'll recall from section 12.4.1 that ATM security policy is dual control, so the bank generates separate keys for two ATM custodians, say the branch manager and the branch accountant, who enter them at a keypad when the device is commissioned, or following a service visit. The HSM thus has a transaction to generate a key component and print it out on an attached security printer. It also returns its encrypted value to the calling program. There was another transaction that combines two components to produce the terminal master key: given two encrypted keys, it would decrypt them, exclusive-or them together, and return the result – encrypted in such a way as to mark it as a non-exportable working key.

The attack was to combine a key with itself, yielding a known key – the key of all zeros – marked as a non-exportable working key. As there was a further transaction, which would encrypt any non-exportable working key with any other, you were now home and dry. You could extract the crown jewels – the PIN derivation key – by encrypting it with your all-zero key. You can now decrypt the PIN derivation key and work out the PIN for any customer account. The HSM has been defeated.

The above attack went undiscovered for years. The documentation did not spell out what the various types of key in the device were supposed to do; non-exportable working keys were just described as *'keys supplied encrypted under master keys 14 and 15'*, and the implications of a transaction to encrypt one such key under another were not immediately obvious. In fact, the HSMs had simply evolved from earlier, simpler designs as ATM networking was introduced in the 1980s and banks asked for lots more features so they could make heterogeneous networks talk to each other.

So Mike Bond built a formal model of the key types used in the device and immediately discovered another flaw. You could supply the HSM with an account number, pretend it's a MAC key, and get it encrypted with the PIN verification key – which also gives you the customer PIN directly. Confused? Initially everyone was – modern APIs are way too complicated for bugs to be evident on casual inspection. Anyway, the full details are at [101]. The latest HSMs have strong typing to make it easier to reason formally about keys.

20.5.2 Attacks using backwards compatibility and time-memory tradeoffs

We worked with an HSM vendor, nCipher, who supplied us with samples of their competitors' products, so we could break them – not just to help their marketing, but to enable them to migrate customer key material to their own products. The top target at the time was the IBM product, the 4758 [953]. This was the only device certified to FIPS 140-1 level 4; in effect the US government had said it was unbreakable. It turned out to be vulnerable to an attack exploiting backwards compatibility [280].

As DES became vulnerable to keysearch during the 1980s, banks started migrating to two-key triple-DES: each block was encrypted with the left key, decrypted with the right key and then encrypted with the left key once more. This bright idea gave backward compatibility: if you set the left key equal to the right key, the encryption reverts to single-DES. The 4758 stored left keys and right keys separately, and encrypted them differently, giving them different types – but failed to bind together the two halves of a triple-DES key. You could take the 'left half' of a single-DES key plus the 'right half' of another, put them together into a true triple-DES key, and then use this to export other keys.

So all you had to do to break the 4758 was a single-DES keysearch. That's not too hard now, but was still a fair bit of work back in 2002. Fortunately there was another vulnerability – a time-memory tradeoff attack. That generation of HSMs had 'check values' for keys – one-way hashes of each key, calculated by encrypting a string of zeroes. Suppose you want a single DES key of a specific type. You precompute a table of (say) 2^{40} keys and their hashes. You get the HSM to generate keys of the desired type and output the hashes until you see a hash that's already in the table. This takes about 2^{16} hashes, which takes an hour or so [449]. The backwards-compatibility and time-memory tradeoff attacks are examples of an API attack on the HSM platform itself rather than on the PCI PIN management app.

20.5.3 Differential protocol attacks

The 4758 bugs got fixed, and recent models of ATM offer public-key mechanisms for automatic enrolment. But legacy key-management and PIN-management mechanisms persist at the app layer, as it's hard to change the architecture of a distributed system with hundreds of vendors and thousands of banks. And there was much more to come. The next wave of attacks on HSM APIs was initiated by Jolyon Clulow in 2003; they perform active manipulation of the application logic to leak information. Many HSMs support transactions tailored for specific applications; the largest market segment is to support card payments, though there are also HSMs for prepayment utility meters, for certification authorities and even for nuclear command and control.

Clulow's first attack exploited error messages [451]. I described in section 12.4.2 how banks who just wrote a customer's encrypted PIN to their bank card got attacked, as a customer could change the account number to another one and use their PIN to loot that account. In order to stop such attacks, Visa introduced an optional PIN block format that exclusive-ors the PIN with the account number before encrypting them. But if the wrong account number was sent along with the PIN block, the HSM would decrypt it, xor in the account number, and when the result was not a decimal number, it would return an error message. So by sending a few dozen transactions to the HSM with a variety of wrong account numbers, you could work out the PIN[6]. There are now special PCI rules for HSMs on PIN translation [979]. Complexity opens up new attacks, which need yet more complexity to patch them.

A further class of attacks was then found by Mike Bond and Piotr Zielinski. Recall the method used by IBM (and most of the industry) to generate PINs, as shown in Figure 12.3. The primary account number is encrypted using the PIN verification key, giving 16 hex digits. The first four are converted to decimal, and while most banks do this by taking the hex digits modulo 10, not all do. HSM vendors parametrised the operation by having a *decimalisation table*, of which the default is 0123456789012345, which just reduces the hex output modulo 10. This was a big mistake.

If we set the decimalisation table to all zeros (i.e., 0000000000000000) then the HSM will return a PIN of '0000', albeit in encrypted form. We then repeat the call using the table 1000000000000000. If the encrypted result changes, we know that the DES output contained a 0 in its first four digits. Given a few dozen queries, the PIN can be deduced. Attacks that compare repeated, but slightly modified, runs of the same protocol, we call *differential protocol analysis*. The only real solution was to pay your HSM vendor extra for a machine with your own bank's decimalisation table hard-coded. That may cause more problems when you want to move your bank to the cloud, and share HSMs maintained by Amazon or Azure[7].

At a philosophical level, this illustrates the difficulty of designing a robust *secure multiparty computation* – a computation that uses secret information from one party, but also some inputs that can be manipulated by a hostile party [100]. Even in this extremely simple case, it's so hard that you end up having to abandon the IBM method of PIN generation, or at least nail down its parameters so hard that you might as well not have made them tweakable in the first place.

At a practical level, it illustrates one of the main reasons APIs fail over time. They get made more and more complex, to accommodate the needs of more and more customers, until suddenly there's an attack.

[6]There are now four different PIN block formats for PIN transmission, three of which include the PAN as well; and there's a further format, the *PIN Verification Value* (PVV), which is a one-way encryption of the PIN and PAN that's sent by banks to switches such as VISA and Mastercard if they want the switch to do stand-in PIN verification when their own system is down.

[7]One vendor decreed that a table must have at least eight different values, with no value occurring more than four times. But this doesn't work: 0123456789012345, then 1123456789012345, and so on.

20.5.4 The EMV attack

You'd have thought that after the initial wave of API attacks were published in the early 2000s, HSM designers would have been more careful about adding new transactions. However, just as security researchers and HSM vendors found and fixed bugs, the banking industry mandated new ones.

For example, an HSM feature ordered by EMVCo to support secure messaging between a smartcard and a bank HSM introduced an exploitable vulnerability in all EMV compliant HSMs [22]. The goal was to enable a bank to order any EMV card it had issued to change some parameter, such as a key, the next time it did an online transaction. So EMVCo defined a transaction *Secure Messaging For Keys* whereby a server can command an HSM to encrypt a text message, followed by a key of a type for sharing with bank smartcards. The encryption can be in CBC or ECB mode, and the text message can be of variable length. The attack is to choose the message length so that just one byte of the target key crosses the boundary of an encryption block. That byte can then be determined by sending a series of messages that are one byte longer, and where the extra byte cycles through all 256 possible values until the key byte is found.

20.5.5 Hacking the HSMs in CAs and clouds

The most recent HSM break, in 2019, was by Jean-Baptiste Bédrune and Gabriel Campana, on a Gemalto HSM whose application supported the PKCS#11 standard for public-key cryptography so it could be used in certification authorities and as a TLS accelerator. (This standard is notoriously obscure and difficult to implement.) They got a software development kit for the HSM, which contained an emulator for the device, and fuzzed it until they found several vulnerabilities. They managed to patch the authentication function so they could login as admin into the HSM and install tools that read out the keys [204]. This is just one example of many where sophisticated cryptography was fatally undermined by careless software engineering.

20.5.6 Managing HSM risks

At one time or another, someone had found an attack on at least one version of every security module on the market. The root cause, as so often in security engineering, is featuritis. People make APIs more complex until they break.

Banks still have to use HSMs for compliance with PCI rules, but the crypto keys in them are not protected by the tamper responding enclosures alone. The configuration management has to be tight and vendor software patches have to be applied promptly, just like in other systems. But while most banks of any size have people who understand software security and the patching lifecycle, they are less likely to have serious HSM expertise.

Specialist firms offer HSM management systems, and we'll have to see if these get subsumed eventually by the big cloud service providers. Management of cloud HSMs is still a work in progress, and products such as Microsoft Cloud Key Vault allow keys to be moved back and forth between HSMs and enclaves that offer similar functionality. Of course, if a PIN management app has intrinsic API vulnerabilities, these will be independent of whether it's running on a traditional on-premises HSM, an HSM in a cloud data centre, or an enclave. Indeed, one selling point of the Microsoft offering is 'Removing the need for in-house knowledge of Hardware Security Modules' [1311].

With that warning, it's time to look at enclaves.

20.6 Enclaves

Enclaves are like HSMs in that they aim to provide a platform on which you can do some computation securely on a machine operated by someone you don't entirely trust. Early attempts involved mechanisms for *digital rights management* (DRM), which obfuscated code to make it hard to interfere with; I discuss this further in the chapter on copyright. They were followed by the 'trusted computing' initiative of the early 2000s, which proposed an architecture in which CPUs would execute encrypted code, with the keys stored in a separate Trusted Platform Module (TPM) chip. Arm duly produced TrustZone in 2004, as I described in section 6.3.2.

TrustZone is typically implemented in the System-on-Chip (SoC) at the heart of a modern Android phone, although its trust boundary is typically the whole motherboard; enclave data may be available in clear on the bus and in DRAM chips. The main application has been mobile phones, whose vendors wanted mechanisms to protect the baseband against user tampering (for regulatory reasons) and to enable the phone itself to be locked (so that mobile network operators who subsidise phones could tie them to a contract). In neither case are hardware attacks a real concern.

Could an enclave mechanism such as TrustZone be used to harden a phone-banking system against the kind of attacks we discussed in section 12.7.4? Attempts were made to market it for this purpose, but even firms that write banking apps were reluctant to adopt it. Up until 2015, it was a closed system, and you could only run code in TrustZone if you had it signed by the OEM. So a developer of a banking app who wanted a 'more secure' authentication component would have to get that signed by Samsung for Samsung phones, by Huawei for their products, and so on. What's more, the code would be different depending on which SoC the product used. Now it's hard enough to make an app run robustly on enough versions of Android without also having to cope with multiple customised versions of TrustZone running on different SoC offerings. It's also hard to assess security claims that vendors make about closed platforms. For the gory details, see Sandro Pinto and Nuno Santos [1512].

In 2015, Intel launched SGX, whose access-control aspects I discussed in section 6.3.1. SGX enclaves have aimed at a more ambitious use case, namely cloud computing. It's become cheaper to run systems on services such as AWS, Azure and Google: virtualisation lets resources be shared efficiently, so the costs of data centres, sysadmins and so on can be amortised over thousands of customers. But this raises many questions. How can you be sure that sensitive data isn't leaked to other tenants of the cloud service, for example via technical exploits of the hypervisor software? Such products have dozens of bugs patched every year [479]. And what protection do you have against a nation state using a warrant to get access to your data – in effect a legal exploit of the hypervisor? The cloud service providers themselves long for a technical mechanism that would save them the trouble of dealing with such warrants. Because of these concerns, the security perimeter of SGX is the boundary of the chip itself. Code and data are encrypted as they leave the chip, and decrypted as they're imported into the cache. The CPU's hardware protects both confidentiality and integrity.

The key cryptographic mechanism is *software attestation*, which enables the CPU to certify to the owner of the software that it is running without modification on top of trustworthy hardware. SGX enclaves run as applications, at ring 3, and the CPU machinery isolates their code and data from everything underneath, including both operating system and hypervisor[8]. The full details of enclave initialisation, address translation, page eviction, exception handling and so on are extremely complicated; for an explanation and analysis, see Victor Costan and Srini Devadas [479]. One concern they raise is that with the exception of memory encryption, SGX is implemented in microcode, which can be updated; the whole system is therefore changeable. There are also multiple side-channel attacks, particularly since Meltdown and Spectre introduced the transient execution family of side-channel attacks, which I discussed in section 19.4.5. Some have been patched, but the real scandal may be that Intel has said it won't fix the Membuster attack as a matter of policy[9].

Here my concern is the cryptography used to support the enclave and attest to the software running on it, and its suitability as a platform for other crypto or crypto support for applications.

[8]The earlier proposals of the Trusted Computing Group required that the whole software stack underneath the enclave be attested and trustworthy, which is incompatible with an untrusted hypervisor.

[9]SGX doesn't defend against cache timing attacks, so when writing enclave code, you can't use data-dependent jumps. More generally, it does not protect against software side-channel attacks that rely on performance counters, but doesn't give enough information for developers to model the possible leakage.

As the silicon processes used in high-end CPUs don't support nonvolatile memory, the first problem is to provide unique and persistent chip keys. Each chip has fuses into which the fab burns a seal secret and a provisioning secret, of which the former is not known to Intel but the latter is. This is used to generate the master derivation key (MDK), which in turn generates key material dependably across power cycles. Provisioning seal keys are persistent, so when a computer changes owners, Intel doesn't need to know. These keys enable the CPU to prove its authenticity to Intel, which supplies it with an attestation key – a member private key in Intel's *Enhanced Privacy ID* (EPID), a group signature scheme intended to preserve signer anonymity.

These operations are done in a privileged *launch enclave* (LE). Originally all SGX code had to be signed by Intel, but recent versions allow code signed by third parties. Each enclave author is now a CA and certifies each enclave, which has a public key, a product ID and a version number (migration of secrets is allowed only to higher version numbers to support patching but not rollback). The same ratchet applies to updates of the CPU microcode.

One issue is that the compromise of one chip's MDK – in any CPU, anywhere – breaks the attestation security of every CPU in the same group. This happened in 2019 for AMD's equivalent of SGX, when a bug in the microcode enabled such a key to be extracted [339]. Intel is vulnerable in the same way: given a clear value of MDK you can create an SGX enclave outside of SGX's protection mechanisms. If such a break were discovered, Intel would have to blacklist all the CPUs in the same EPID group. We have no idea how large these groups are, as all attestations are done opaquely by Intel and users must simply trust the results.

There are now some SGX systems doing real work. An example I mentioned earlier in this chapter is the messaging app Signal, which uses an enclave for private contact discovery. Its developers published the source code along with an extensive discussion of the difficulties of developing it on the Signal blog [1228]. The goal is to enable Signal clients to determine whether the contacts in their address book are also Signal users without revealing their address book to the Signal service. How can you build a large social graph without having any insight into it? The idea is that clients can contact the enclave, verify it's running the right software, and send their contacts in to see who's also a user. However, doing this within the memory limit of an SGX enclave (128Mb) needs careful organisation of hash tables of an inverted file of users' phone numbers.

There are many more things you have to do to prevent information leakage through memory access patterns: as branches might be observed through such patterns, critical sections of code must not contain branches. In short, blocking side channels is much like organising crypto code to run in constant time: fiddly, ad hoc, manual and prone to error. SGX is also slow: while the memory encryption itself adds little overhead, context switching is a killer. Checking contacts against others is really slow, so the process has to be batched for multiple joiners to make it acceptable.

Another example of an SGX app is Microsoft's Cloud Key Vault, which enables Azure tenants to store secrets such as keys, passwords and tokens separately from their code [1311]. There's an app to help you create and manage certificates for TLS; secrets and keys can also be stored in cloud HSMs at the top end, while routine applications can be both more secure and more manageable if you don't have to store database passwords inline in your code.

In short, writing good SGX code is hard. The toolchain is restricted, and things like antivirus are excluded. If you're smart, you can write trusted malware. You can even write malware that will run in one SGX enclave and do timing attacks on code in other enclaves in the same machine, using the SGX mechanisms to hide itself from detection [1692].

And even if you trust Intel completely; even if you believe that the NSA won't use a FISA warrant to force Intel to attest to an enclave in debug mode; even if you're not worried about an MDK compromise or the exploitation of side channels – then there's still the risk of app-layer exposure, just as with HSMs. If you write your enclave code in such a way that it can be used as an oracle by less trusted code, you're in trouble.

Intel (and Arm) are talking about successor versions of their enclave technology. Meantime Intel points crypto developers at their management engine (ME), a separate microcontroller shipped in the CPU chipset that starts the CPU and contains a firmware TPM to do secure boot. It can brick a CPU by erasing keys if the machine is reported stolen. Its code is proprietary, based on Minix, and is signed by Intel. It supports yet another enclave with a Java trusted execution environment, in which developers can do crypto; for example, in payment terminals you can engineer a hardware trusted path from the ME to a PIN pad [1701]. This enables crypto code to be shielded from malware on the CPU but brings issues of its own, such as attacks involving physical access. The ME has also had a whole series of vulnerabilities and exploits. It is considered by the EFF to be a backdoor, and at least one vendor has made machines available to governments where it is switched off after boot.

20.7 Blockchains

The previous sections on the uses and limits of cryptography, on how cryptography can be used to support anonymity, and how crypto apps can suffer flaws at various levels in the stack, set us up to discuss cryptocurrencies and smart contracts. During 2016–7, cryptocurrencies were 'the' thing, taking their place in the hype cycle after Big Data and the Internet of Things, alongside AI and quantum. To many people, the word 'crypto' now refers to bitcoins rather than to ciphers.

In 2008, Bitcoin was released quietly by someone using the pseudonym of Satoshi Nakamoto, with a white paper and an implementation [1377]. This system of anonymous digital cash circulated initially among hobbyists and activists on the cypherpunks mailing list, but within two years it had gone viral. In February 2011, a young libertarian called Ross Ulbricht set up Silk Road, an online marketplace outside government control. Buyers and sellers met on a Tor onion service and could pay for goods and services using Bitcoin. They could rate each other, as on eBay, and there was an escrow service so that a buyer could deposit bitcoins for release when goods were delivered. Silk Road rapidly became the market for the mail-order supply of controlled drugs, and over $1bn worth of trades went through it before the FBI arrested Ulbricht in October 2013 [423]. Other underground markets adopted Bitcoin too. While Silk Road was trading, the price had risen from about a dollar to over a hundred dollars, and the rising price attracted investors[10]. Further transaction demand came from people wanting to get their money out of countries with exchange controls, leading to investment demand from people seeing Bitcoin as an asset to be bought in times of crisis, like gold. By 2017 we had a bubble – with the price of a bitcoin rising steeply through the thousand-dollar mark to a peak in December 2017 of almost $20k.

Bitcoin has spawned multiple imitators – most of them scams, but some real innovations too. Boosters claimed that cryptocurrency would enable a new wave of innovation and automation as machines could negotiate smart contracts with each other without humans or banks getting in the way. At the time of writing (2020), the peak of enthusiasm has passed, but cryptocurrencies have become a new asset class for investors, as well as posing multiple problems for financial regulators and law enforcement.

All that said, Bitcoin is a fascinating construct of cryptography and economics which has led to the emergence of a payment system that is also a trusted computer, out of the distributed effort of millions of machines that attempt to mine bitcoins. There are no trusted parties other than the people who write the software, and no pre-assumed identities of participants. The mechanisms provide a new way of achieving consensus in distributed systems, quite distinct from the Byzantine fault-tolerance mechanisms we discussed in section 7.3.1. That is one reason to include cryptocurrencies as an example of advanced cryptographic engineering; another is the smart contracts and other second-layer protocols built on top of them, which are of technical interest although they have had little impact so far on business (the total capital of digital exchanges may be only about $1bn).

Here is a brief summary of the basic mechanisms.

1. The Bitcoin *blockchain* is an append-only file containing a series of *transactions*.

[10]When Ulbricht was busted, the Bitcoin price fell from $145.70 to $109.76, but as other drug markets got going, it quickly recovered.

2. Users appear on the blockchain as addresses – pseudonyms which are hashes of public keys.
3. Most transactions transfer currency from one address to another by taking an *unspent transaction output* (UTXO) from a previous transaction and transferring it to one or more addresses. Such a transaction must be signed by the private key corresponding to the UTXO address.
4. To make a payment, you sign a transaction and broadcast it via a peer-to-peer network to other users. Other users are free to select a set of requested transactions, check that they're valid, and mine them into a new block for the blockchain.
5. Each block of transactions is authenticated by a miner by means of a SHA256 hash of the block contents and a random salt. Miners try different salts until the hash output has enough leading zeros to make it a hard enough puzzle. Such a hash constitutes a *proof of work*, and finding them is a random process, so it's hard to predict which miner will find the next one. The blockchain consists of a chain of hashes and the blocks they authenticate. The difficulty of the puzzle is adjusted automatically so that a new block is *mined* about every ten minutes.
6. Miners are paid a *block reward* for each block they mine. This halves every 210,000 blocks; while I was writing this book in May 2020, it halved from 12.5 to 6.25 bitcoins per block[11].
7. Miners also get *transaction fees*, which are the amount by which the inputs of each transaction exceed the outputs. Users bid transaction fees to get priority for their transactions; they are usually in the tens of cents but can rise into the tens of dollars at times of congestion.
8. If two competing next blocks are mined then the conflict is resolved by the rule that miners mine the longest chain. As a result, transactions aren't really considered final until about half a dozen further blocks have been mined – about an hour for classic Bitcoin. Even so, a majority of miners could rewrite history by constructing a chain that reached even further back – a so-called *chain reorganisation*.
9. If the conflict isn't resolved then you can end up with a *fork* – the system spawns two incompatible successors. Bitcoin split in 2017 into Bitcoin and Bitcoin Cash over a policy dispute about block length, and users who owned bitcoins before the fork ended up owning bitcoins in both. But some forks have been

[11]This is about $60,000 as we go to press in September 2020, and a miner with a reasonably new rig who can buy electricity for 5c per kWh can still expect to mine Bitcoin for slightly less than the coins' market value, if you disregard the capital cost of the equipment. Up till May, the reward was about double the operating cost.

deliberate, and on top of that entrepreneurs have started several thousand Bitcoin clones – most of which were scams.

10. Transactions can also contain scripts, which make payments programmable.

For a detailed description, there are three standard references. The first two are technical expositions by a group of Princeton computer scientists: an 18-page systematisation-of-knowledge paper in 2015 by Joe Bonneau, Andrew Miller, Jeremy Clark, Arvind Narayanan, Joshua Kroll and Ed Felten [294] while at 308 pages there's a 2016 book by Arvind Narayanan, Joe Bonneau, Ed Felten, Andrew Miller and Steven Goldfeder [1385]. The third is a 2015 paper in the Journal of Economic Perspectives by Rainer Böhme, Nicolas Christin, Benjamin Edelman, and Tyler Moore [275]. At the time of writing, these are getting out of date, so in what follows I will concentrate on developments since then. I'll assume you know the detail, or can look it up, or are not too bothered.

To understand what can go wrong with cryptocurrencies, we have to look at a lot more than just the cryptomathematics. A common pattern has been that elegant cryptographic ideas are let down by shoddy software engineering, a lack of systems thinking and a near-total lack of concern for users.

20.7.1 Wallets

In the beginning, all Bitcoin users were peers: the full client software would mine Bitcoin and let you spend the coins you mined. But things soon started to specialise with custom rigs for miners, and light clients for ordinary users which don't do mining or store the whole blockchain, but make the process of buying and selling more manageable. There is no intrinsic concept of an account, as you own Bitcoin by knowing a private key that will unlock one or more UTXOs. *Wallets* initially stored one or more private keys and provided an interface so the user could see the UTXOs that these keys could spend ('my bitcoins'). Wallet security rapidly became a big deal. So-called 'brain wallets' that generated private keys from a user-selected passphrase were broken by attackers doing exhaustive search over the public keys visible on the blockchain; brain wallets with guessable passwords were typically emptied within 24 hours [1951].

Software wallets that keep your signing keys on your hard disk, protected by a passphrase, are an improvement, but vulnerable to malware and other attacks. Serious operators use hardware wallets, which are essentially small HSMs and which may be kept offline (so-called *cold wallets*). Even so it is not unknown for people who are known to own millions of dollars worth of Bitcoin to be held up by armed robbers in their homes and forced to transfer it. If you have sole physical custody of a Bitcoin wallet then you're just as vulnerable as when, centuries ago, people kept their savings in gold coins. By 2013 we'd seen the emergence of *hosted wallets* where an exchange or other online service provider does everything for you. That doesn't really solve the robbery problem, as the robber will just force you to log on and pay him. But hosted wallets have led to widespread other fraud and abuse as I'll describe below.

20.7.2 Miners

As bitcoins grew in popularity and value, more people joined in to mine them. Mining rigs appeared using FPGAs and then ASICs that run so much faster than software on general-purpose machines that within a few years they had taken over. Miners operate where electricity is naturally cheap, such as Iceland and Quebec, but are mostly in places like Russia or China where they can do deals with local officials. The total energy consumption of cryptocurrency mining during 2019 was about 75TWh, and the CO_2 emissions were over 35Mt – comparable to the carbon footprint of New Zealand. As of 2020, each bitcoin transaction consumes over half a MWh and emits over a quarter ton of CO_2.

Miners have organised themselves into a small number of mining pools that average their earnings. The control of these pools is opaque. Capacity can be rented and is sometimes used to attack cryptocurrencies in so-called 51% attacks. The whole point of the blockchain is to prevent double spending by creating a tamper-proof, public, append-only log of transactions; but if a majority of miners collude then they can rewrite history and spend coins multiple times. In the early days, people thought that such an attack would be instantly fatal to a currency's credibility, but reality turned out to be more complex. For example, in January 2019, attackers used this technique to steal over $1m from Ethereum Classic, a cryptocurrency with a market capitalisation of over $500m, with chain reorganisations dozens of blocks in length [1430]. Yet its market value was not significantly affected. Had they stolen most of it, the price would have collapsed and their loot would have been worthless. There were two further attacks in August 2020, in one of which the attackers spent $192,000 to buy the hash power required to steal $5.6m [1521]. So we need to think carefully about the game theory as well as the cryptography when reasoning blockchains; the simplistic arguments don't always align with reality.

20.7.3 Smart contracts

The scripting language in Bitcoin is simple, but a later cryptocurrency system, Ethereum, has a Turing-complete VM whose bytecode is usually compiled from a language called *Solidity*. Ethereum has become the second cryptocurrency by market cap as it holds out the prospect of *smart contracts* that can perform complex transactions automatically. During the bubble, many startups talked of using smart contracts to animate the Internet of Things, and to create new services such as distributed storage, where people might pay others for the use of their spare hard disk space for backup. The idea of such a *distributed autonomous organisation* was heavily promoted during the bubble. This is linked to the 'redecentralize' movement which seeks to move the online world away from the large service firms that came to dominate it during the 2000s; and while we have good tools to decentralize the distribution of static, read-only content, we lacked a good way to decentralize transactions [509]. As of 2020, the main applications seem to be around trading, where distributed exchanges (DEXs) enable people to trade one cryptocurrency for another without human intervention. (They still account for only a tiny fraction of the total trading volume.)

This has led to interesting new failure modes. Although the consensus mechanisms of the original Bitcoin blockchain are believed to be incentive compatible, this is not the case when the transactions on a blockchain represent extra value that a miner can extract by manipulating the consensus. There have now appeared *arbitrage bots* that exploit inefficiencies in DEXs by frontrunning (anticipating and exploiting) trades. The bots bid up transaction fees, called *gas* in Ethereum; there have been hundreds of millions of these *priority gas auctions* where traders hustle to get priority for their trades [508]. Bots might in theory take over the governance of a market and loot it if they could raise enough money [870]; they already make large profits by exploiting bugs in smart contracts [1509].

Fixing bugs can be expensive. In 2016, an investment fund called DAO was set up as a smart contract on the Ethereum blockchain, and attracted over $150m from over 10,000 investors. Attackers exploited a flaw in the contract to steal the money[12], and after some discussion the Ethereum software was changed to move the stolen money to a recovery account. This resulted in a hard fork of the blockchain, with holders of the original cryptocurrency acquiring units in both the modified currency and in 'Ethereum Classic', as the unmodified version became known.

A Danish study illustrates the further problems of using smart contracts in a real-world application context. There had been a proposal to use them to pay parents who have to take time off work to care for sick children, which has complex legal rules that clerks often miss, leading to appeals. The idea was to put hashes of the case documents on the Ethereum blockchain so that both parents and the appeals board can track them, in the hope that automating the

[12]An alternative view is that if the contract was to accept the output of the code, then the flaw was in the users' grasp of what the code did, and in that case nobody stole anything!

execution of decisions would cut bureaucratic foot-dragging. But what about insiders, hackers and mistakes? Local governments tend to get hacked a lot and end up paying ransomware. And who updates the contract when the law changes, or a bug is discovered? Blockchains are by design immutable, so can't be patched. But the real deal-breaker was local government fear of losing control of the process. Two further issues include the fact that people often have to bend the rules to get stuff done, and that programmers are more likely to write bugs in an unfamiliar language such as Solidity rather than a familiar one such as Python or even Cobol – a known problem with new languages, which I discussed in section 7.3.1.2.

20.7.4 Off-chain payment mechanisms

A standard Bitcoin transaction can take six blocks, or one hour, to become final, and even longer at times of congestion. This may be fast enough for paying ransoms or buying drugs online, but it's unimpressive compared with EMV. What's more, Bitcoin's throughput of about 5 transactions per second is no match for Visa's 50,000.

People are trying to fix this using side chains, an example of a *layer 2 protocol*; such protocols do transactions outside, but tethered to, a layer 1 protocol such as Bitcoin or Ethereum. Alice and Bob open a channel by locking coins on a layer 1 blockchain, and can now do rapid transactions between themselves. The key idea is that they commit some cryptocurrency to each other using a *hashed time-lock contract* (HTLC) made of two conditional transfers. In such a transfer, Bob sends Alice $h(R)$, where R is a random number, and Alice makes a commitment in the blockchain's scripting language to the effect that "if you show me R by time t I'll give you this coin." Bob makes a similar commitment. This opens a channel for them to trade signed transactions at speed, until they decide to settle up and close the channel.

Quite a bit more engineering is needed to turn this into a working payment system. You need a dispute resolution mechanism in case Alice and Bob disagree how much each of them should take from the proceeds. Then you build mechanisms for Alice to pay Charlie via Bob, and routing algorithms so you can get money to anybody. In theory this can be peer-to-peer but in practice such systems appear to organise themselves into hubs, with channels that are always open, like a banking network. Protocol security involves ensuring that honest users must not lose money even if others collude. Costs include the need for intermediate nodes to have enough liquidity to forward transactions, and the need for all active players to be online – whose implications range from the theft risks of hot wallets, to the risk of miners front-running Bob when he broadcasts R, to the risk of mass collapse following a network failure [832]. The leading such system in 2020 is the Lightning network, which makes payments final in seconds, enables people with the right phone app to pay to a

QR code as with WeChat Pay, and is now handling 1000 transactions per day. The limit here appears to be liquidity: although Lightning chains themselves are trust-free, they tie up capacity at the nodes, and the recipient has to decide whether or not to accept them. So a malicious user can set up hundreds of payments, leave them for hours and then cancel them at no cost. As Lightning's total capitalisation appears to be only a few million dollars, this may leave it somewhat fragile. It also appears very possible that regulators will crack down on forwarding nodes.

20.7.5 Exchanges, cryptocrime and regulation

Mining all your own coins is inconvenient, and by 2010 entrepreneurs had set up exchanges that would trade Bitcoin for conventional money. Most went bust, often because they were hacked, or because insiders stole the money and claimed to have been hacked. The leader by 2011 was Mt Gox in Japan which survived one hack in 2011 but went bust in 2014 claiming that it had been hacked for $460m. The court case continues; news coverage at the time reported that internal controls and software development processes were chaotic [1282].

That was not all. One of Mt Gox's innovations was to become a *custodial exchange* over the course of 2013. Instead of keeping customer bitcoins in separate wallets, for which the exchange might or might not have temporary access to the private key after the customer entered the correct password, Mt Gox started to keep all the Bitcoin in its own wallets, showing customers a notional account balance when they visited its website. It had made the transition we saw in eighteenth-century finance from being a gold merchant to being a bank: rather than owning a specific bag of gold coins in the vault, the customer now just had a claim on the bank's whole assets. Victims related how after their wallets were hosted, they started to see outgoing transactions they had not authorised. Analysis after the collapse of Mt Gox revealed that many of these transactions did not even appear on the blockchain. From mid-2013, when you bought a bitcoin from them, all they did was to show you a web page saying that you had a balance of one bitcoin. (And that's how many exchanges work to this day.)

The Bitcoin world has been full of scams, and it looks like the majority of victims of cryptocrime were ripped off by exchanges that went bust, or got hacked, or that claimed to have been hacked. Even in the first three years that exchanges existed, 2010–13, 18 of the 40 exchanges collapsed [1341].

A report by Chainalysis, a Bitcoin analytics firm, concluded that exchanges lost about $1bn to hackers in 2018, with most of the thefts perpetrated by two crime gangs; one of them has since been linked to North Korea. In addition to this, turnover on underground markets where drugs and other illicit goods are bought and sold was $600m, approximately double the value for 2017 [402]. There's also market manipulation. John Griffin and Amin Shams present evidence that Bitcoin's price was supported by insider trading involving Tether, a digital currency pegged to the U.S. dollar, during the 2017 boom [823], raising the prospect that the market price of many cryptocurrencies may often have been a result of unlawful manipulation. This has been borne out by subsequent studies showing that much of the spot trading is generated by unregulated exchanges [1618].

Market manipulation aside, the largest single cryptocurrency scam to date appears to have been a Ponzi scheme called PlusToken, which netted some $3bn from Chinese nationals before the organisers were arrested in 2019 [865]. But Bitcoin has affected many other crime types too. Ransomware went up from about $2–3m a year to maybe $8m a year between 2001 and 2015, as Bitcoin suddenly made ransoms easy to collect [92]; this crime type is growing steadily, although ransoms are also collected via gift cards [1192]. By 2018, bulletproof hosting sites, which provide services to cybercriminals, were moving to cryptocurrency as other payment mechanisms became more difficult [1454]. In that year, the world's largest darknet child pornography website, Welcome to Video, was closed down after its operators were traced via flows of Bitcoin on the blockchain, so the pseudonymous nature of cryptocurrency has its limits [551]. In total, scams and other abuse add up to something like 3% of cryptocurrency transaction volume directly; and in addition to the visible cryptocurrency exchanges, there are a number of over-the-counter brokers, some 100 of which have been identified as involved in money laundering [403]. The regular exchanges also make life difficult for law enforcement. Crime gangs may turn proceeds into Bitcoin through one channel, switch it into a different coin in a second country, and then send it to a third country where they get it out via bank transfer.

However, although Bitcoin uses pseudonyms, the blockchain contains a permanent record of all transactions. As we've discussed in a number of contexts – from our chapter on inference control to the section on Tor in this chapter – anonymity is hard. Real-world transactions and data have context and allow inferences to be made. Bitcoin users have tried all sorts of tricks to make transactions more anonymous, for example by splitting payments into many smaller ones, mixing them up, and then recombining them – a so-called 'tumbler' or 'mixer'. However, if you do that, you taint your bitcoins with attempted money laundering; and in total, perhaps 10% of Bitcoin have been stolen, or passed through a money-laundering service, at least once. (For an analysis, see [117].) As an example, an Ohio man was indicted in 2020 for operating just such a mixer that laundered $300m [553]. There are also cryptocurrencies that offer more privacy using further cryptographic techniques, notably Zcash and Monero. At present, Monero offers the strongest privacy and is designed so that coins can be mined using software; over 4% of its coins have been mined by malware running on other people's machines [1500].

Governments have been trying to push back using financial regulation. The US Treasury's Financial Crimes Enforcement Network (FinCEN) drives anti-money-laundering (AML) and know-your-customer (KYC) regulations worldwide, which get incorporated into local law, for example via the EU's 5th Anti-money-laundering Directive. Some governments go further. For example, Germany's regulator BaFin has used existing financial regulations to insist that all exchanges get licenses; as `localbitcoins.com`, a peer-to-peer exchange that enables individuals to buy and sell cryptocurrency from each other for cash, didn't apply for one, it is blocked there. But at the time of writing, the biggest push comes from a FinCEN advisory in 2019 that required cryptocurrency exchanges to implement the 'travel rule' whereby anyone handling a transaction over $10,000 has to identify both sender and recipient and file a suspicious activity report if relevant. The exchanges were given until June 2020 to come up with a solution; at least one individual exchanging sums over $10,000 has been fined [688].

Further regulation is on the agenda in Europe too. Mt Gox largely had Japanese clients while most Chinese appear to use Binance and many people in the UK and the USA use Coinbase. When one British or American user sends Bitcoin to another, there's a fair chance that the transaction never goes near the blockchain: if they're both Coinbase customers, then Coinbase can simply adjust the balances displayed in their Bitcoin wallet webpages. This immediately raises the question of why the exchanges are not regulated like any other money service business. In the EU, the E-money Directive might seem to apply, yet regulators in the UK and Germany only enforce it in respect of the traditional currency balances that customers have with the exchanges; the exchanges argued that as transaction demand is much less than investment demand, virtual currencies should be treated as assets rather than as payment mechanisms. But in that case, why does the regulator not require the exchanges to operate under the same rules as stockbrokers, so that a customer's bitcoins can't be used for transactions, but merely sold back to market with the proceeds being sent to the bank account used to purchase them?

In an analysis that colleagues and I produced of exchange operations and of the mechanics of tracing stolen Bitcoin, we also recommended applying the Payment Services Directive, which would give exchange customers consumer protection comparable to that with banks [117]. It is notable, for example, that while banks have shown a lot of interest in how to block SIM swap attacks on their customers' phones, most cryptocurrency exchanges have shown no interest at all – despite the fact that exchange credentials are one of the main targets of the SIM swap gangs [1451]. Consumer protection in the world of cryptocurrency is unfinished business, and regulatory agencies in Europe and elsewhere are working on it.

20.7.6 Permissioned blockchains

The hype around cryptocurrencies and blockchains piqued commercial interest, and from about 2015, CEOs coming back from Davos told their IT departments they needed a blockchain. The CIOs then had to explore whether blockchains could be created that could do useful work, without Bitcoin's environmental waste, illegal content and illegal actors. This led to initiatives such as Hyperledger and the Enterprise Ethereum Alliance, with corporate supporters developing a variety of blockchain tools and standards. Many involve a *permissioned blockchain* fabric that is based on Byzantine fault tolerance rather than proof-of-work and can still support smart contracts. A number of them use SGX as part of their consensus mechanism, such as Intel's own proof of elapsed time (PoET) proposal. There are many other proposed consensus mechanisms; for a survey, see Bano et al [166].

As an application example, JP Morgan worked on a system from 2015 that would enable participating banks to enter mortgages on a blockchain, so that its scripting language would allow traders to create futures and options of arbitrary complexity. They explored a number of design tradeoffs, such as between low latency and security in adversarial settings, and how transaction privacy can be extended to keep business logic private as well as the names of individual participants [1423]. One conclusion was that for the vast majority of applications, you don't need a blockchain; a forward-secure sealed log will do. And where a blockchain might help, you can't use a public one. Above all, blockchain apps must talk to legacy systems and must be no more likely to create application security mistakes or usability hazards. There have been enough screw-ups: for example, Argentina published its official gazette (Boletin Oficial) on a blockchain, and decreed it to be legally valid, whereupon someone hacked it to publish fake news about the coronavirus [499]. Such real-world experience appears to be taming the initial exuberance of the bubble.

Perhaps the most controversial project is Libra, a Facebook proposal to create a payment system with its value pegged against a basket of currencies. This was supposed to be run by a consortium of financial, tech and other firms, but has run into significant opposition from central banks, resulting in key financial players such as Visa, MasterCard and PayPal pulling out.

20.8 Crypto dreams that failed

A number of people have proposed electronic voting systems based on blockchains because they're supposedly immutable and you can build functionality on them using crypto. These proposals follow over thirty years of research into the possible use of cryptography in electronic elections to provide a system that is simultaneously anonymous and provably accurate.

In fact, during the Bitcoin boom of 2017–8, a common student project proposal was 'solving world peace by putting elections on the blockchain'.

Election systems claiming to use a blockchain have now been deployed in both Russia and America, with less than impressive results. In 2018 a system for three wards in the city of Moscow used an Ethereum blockchain for vote tallying, but the link between vote tallying and the blockchain was broken when two crypto vulnerabilities were fixed just before the election – and the blockchain vanished just afterwards [783]. Also in 2018, West Virginia became the first US state to allow some voters to cast their ballot using a mobile phone app. Michael Specter, James Koppel and Danny Weitzner from MIT reverse engineered it and found a number of vulnerabilities that would let an attacker expose or alter votes, despite the app's use of a blockchain, which was irrelevant to the attacks [1814]. According to the researchers, an attacker could create a tainted paper trail, making a reliable audit impossible – despite the selling points of blockchains including transparency and accountability.

The idea that blockchains can solve the problems of elections makes the experienced security engineer despair. You can't fix elections with this technology, because it doesn't tackle how they're stolen. Parties in power are constantly changing the rules and subverting the technology at all levels in the stack, from voter registration through campaign funding and advertising rules through media censorship, voter intimidation and voting schemes that can be manipulated. We'll discuss this at greater length in section 25.5.

20.9 Summary

Starting in the 1980s, many people have tried to use cryptography as a trusted platform for some aspect of system security. The original killer app for commercial cryptography was the protection of PINs in ATMs and then of card payments more generally, as we described in Chapter 12. Many cryptography researchers (including me) then started to hope that we could solve other economic and social problems with cryptography. Anonymous communications would stop censorship; anonymous digital cash would protect our privacy; digital voting would make elections harder to rig; threshold signatures would help us build robust internal control systems; and electronic auctions would push back on corruption. The research papers at the Crypto and Eurocrypt conferences of the period are brimming with ideas like these. A generation later, and with a techlash of scepticism about the effects of globalised technology, it may be time to take stock.

Our case studies teach a technical point, an economic one, and a policy one.

The technical point is that cryptographic systems aren't magic; they have bugs and have to be patched like anything else. Even the simplest applications, like FDE, get complex as they mature as products, and vary widely in implementation quality. HSMs are another example of cryptosystems that acquired ever more features until the features broke them, and now require other components to block targeted attacks. SGX runs on processors so complex that it's vulnerable to multiple side-channel attacks, and Intel doesn't even consider some of them to be within its threat model: if a capable motivated opponent can run their code on the same machine as you, you're basically toast. Much the same holds for blockchains, which have developed the most complex ecosystem of all. Even the basic assumption that rational miners are not motivated to rewrite history starts to fail when applications create the necessary incentives. Again, a cryptocurrency can go on acquiring features until they break it, and smart contracts can help the process along.

The economic point is that the advanced crypto mechanisms we've seen deployed all come with a significant cost. HSMs cost more than servers. SGX has memory limits and a real performance overhead on context switching. Bitcoin miners emit as much CO_2 as New Zealand. Smart contracts may be able to do some clever things but in practice are very restricted in size and scope compared with other software. There is a fine calculation about whether the cost is worth it; and this calculation may become more adverse over time as the maintenance costs mount and the system gets into technical debt.

The policy point is that advanced cryptographic mechanisms all get tangled up with liability. If successful they seem to acquire, as part of their core purpose, either the desire to satisfy some regulation or the desire to avoid regulation. So the decision to deploy them, or maintain them, may involve subtle externalities.

Hardware security modules are mandatory in card payment systems because of card scheme rules based, ultimately, on banks' desire to not be liable for fraud. SGX is seen as a way to assure customers of cloud computing services that they protect their most valuable assets against rogue sysadmins and against intelligence agencies. Bitcoin and its many clones have become a mechanism for circumventing everything from securities and payment law to anti-money-laundering regulations. Real systems get built for strategic reasons, and that tends to mean creating or entrenching power for their creators – be it market power or political power.

As for cryptocurrencies, they have so far had extreme volatility, limited capacity, unpredictable transaction costs, no governance, and limited transparency. The proof-of-work mechanisms used by most of them cause CO_2 emissions that reasonable people might consider unacceptable, and their use in practice is entangled with all sorts of criminality. While the law should defend the right of private firms and individuals to create value tokens such as coupons and air miles, once these start being used as currency and institutions emerge that behave like banks, it is reasonable for the lawgiver to treat them as such. It is also reasonable for the lawgiver to think about carbon taxes, or to require organisations that use blockchains to account for the CO_2 they produce.

If we had to sum up the experience of forty years of trying to apply the magic of mathematics to solve real-world problems, it would probably be TANSTAAFL: there ain't no such thing as a free lunch.

Research problems

There are deep problems around decentralisation that cross the boundary between cryptography and system security. Decentralised protocols tend to fossilise; we're still using email, DNS and BGP mechanisms from the early 1990s because of the difficulty of changing anything. End-to-end crypto could not be layered on top of SMTP email, despite the efforts of PGP, but needed to wait for a new platform like Signal that could impose it by fiat.

Bitcoin provides another example. The original cypherpunks ideal was a fully decentralised payment system providing a means of exchange and a store of value without the involvement of governments or other dominant players such as banks. Yet the production of mining rigs has become a monopoly, controlled by Bitmain, while the ASICs all come from TSMC. The great majority of Bitcoin users rely on custodial exchanges to hold their cryptocurrency, and these exchanges do most of the trading – DEXs are only 0.01% of it. The custodial exchanges have in effect become unregulated banks.

In systems such as Signal, Tor and Bitcoin, the real consensus is not cryptographic but social; it's the consensus of the developers. In Tor this is a community while in the world of cryptocurrency there are competing developer teams working for profit. The security economics may be expected to be more important than the cryptography, and we've already seen how smart contracts can create application-layer incentives that could break the underlying consensus layer.

What about the dependability of smart contracts in general? The computer science approach to the API security problem has been to try to adapt formal-methods tools to prove that interfaces are safe. There is a growing literature on this, and even a series of workshops, but the methods can still only tackle fairly simple APIs. Smart contracts are running into similar problems, complicated by the difficulty of changing them to fix bugs or to respond to changing circumstances. It is unsurprising that many of the smart contracts used to set up DEXs have hard-coded admin keys that enable human intervention if need be. This is just prudent engineering, but calls into question the ideological justification of such exchanges as 'trustless'.

Further reading

To get up to speed on Tor, a good starting point is the Tor Project's documentation page. For more detail on how Bitcoin works, read the Princeton book [1385] or the JEP paper [275], while for our more detailed view on tracing stolen Bitcoin and on cryptocurrency regulation, see [117]. For a discussion of the interaction between centralisation and privacy, see Carmela Troncoso and colleagues [1914]. A survey of the state of play in messaging apps in 2015 (the time when Signal came together from previous apps for messaging and VOIP) can be found at [1921].

CHAPTER

21

Network Attack and Defence

Simplicity is the ultimate sophistication.
– LEONARDO DA VINCI

There's no security here – keep moving!
– RICHARD CLAYTON

21.1 Introduction

In this chapter I'm going to try to draw together the network aspects of security in a coherent framework. This is not straightforward as much of network security is practical engineering; a purist from computer science might see the field as one bodge piled on top of another. And network security may not be that important to many developers: if you write apps for Androids and iPhones that talk to services on AWS or Azure, then you can leave much of the worry to Amazon or Microsoft.

But many organisations need to pay attention to network security, and there are some visible strategic trends. For twenty years, it was accepted that firms would have a trusted internal network or intranet, protected from the Internet by firewalls; while taken to extremes by defence and intelligence organisations with classified internal networks, milder versions were seen as best practice by most normal firms. And some industries have no viable alternatives. For example, the protocols used in industrial control systems – DNP3 and Modbus – don't support encryption or authentication, as they evolved in the days of leased lines and private radio links. By the late 1990s, control systems engineers were attaching sensors and actuators to IP networks, as they were cheaper – and then realising that anyone in the world who knew a sensor's IP address could read it, and anyone who knew an actuator's IP address could activate it. This led to the growth of specialist firms who sell firewalls that understand these protocols; energy companies have thousands of them.

A typical electricity substation might have two hundred devices from a multiplicity of vendors, on a LAN where performance is critical, so retrofitting crypto is impractical; but it has one connection to the outside world, so that's where you have to put the protection. This is known as *re-perimeterization*. The same approach is taken with vehicles, where the internal CANBUS cannot be protected, so the radio interfaces with the outside world have to be.

But in many firms the trend is firmly in the other direction, towards *deperimeterisation*. One thought leader is Google, promoting an architecture without firewalls that it calls a *zero-trust security model*: "By shifting access controls from the network perimeter to individual users and devices, BeyondCorp allows employees, contractors, and other users to work more securely from virtually any location without the need for a traditional VPN." Google's experience is that the move to mobile and cloud technology is making network perimeters ever harder to define, let alone police, and if a firm's large enough that some internal compromise is inevitable anyway then the perimeter is the wrong place to put the primary protection [1988]. There are still some perimeter defences, most notably against service-denial attacks, but internal networks are otherwise unprivileged and the emphasis is on tight authentication and authorisation of users and devices: each service has an Internet-facing access proxy. One might see this as a per-service firewall rather than a per-building firewall, but there is quite a lot more to it with tiers of sensitivity, a device inventory service and an access control engine [1481]. You also need really good HR data, so you can tie staff and contractors to devices and the services they're allowed to use. Much the same architecture is being adopted by other firms operating large-scale data centres, and zero-trust security is now the subject of draft standards activity by NIST [1621]. It will no doubt get a boost from the pandemic because of the huge increase in home working.

Other organisations may take a hybrid approach. The university where I work, for example, has some defences at the perimeter but largely lets departments do our own thing; a computer science department has quite different requirements from a humanities department or the finance office.

In order to explore the options and constraints, I'm first going to discuss networking protocols such as BGP, DNS and SMTP and the service-denial attacks that can result from their abuse. I'll then take a closer look at malware, and then at defensive technologies such as filtering and intrusion detection and how defenders can coordinate them. I'll then survey the limitations of widely-used crypto protocols such as TLS, SSH and IPsec, and the particularly tricky role of certification authorities. Finally I'll return to network architecture. Many issues are complex and interlinked, with some significant trade-offs. For example, various kinds of end-to-end crypto can bring benefits – particularly against bulk surveillance – but can get in the way of the surveillance we want for network security.

This chapter will deal with fixed networks, and I'll discuss what's different about mobile networks in the following chapter.

21.2 Network protocols and service denial

I'm going to assume some familiarity with basic network protocols. The telegraphic summary is as follows. The *Internet Protocol* (IP) is a stateless protocol that transfers packet data from one machine to another; IP version 4 uses 32-bit *IP addresses*, often written as four decimal numbers in the range 0–255, such as 172.16.8.93. ISPs are migrating to IP version 6, as the 4 billion possible IPv4 addresses are just about allocated; IPv6 uses 128-bit addresses. Some 10–15% of traffic is now IPv6; in many countries a new broadband subscription will get you an IPv6 address which works for all normal consumer purposes.

Local networks mostly use ethernet, in which devices have unique ethernet addresses (also called MAC addresses) that are mapped to IPv4 addresses using the *address resolution protocol* (ARP). The *Dynamic Host Configuration Protocol* (DHCP) is used to allocate IP addresses to machines as needed and to ensure that each IP address is unique. *Network address translation* (NAT) also enables multiple devices on a network to use the same Internet-facing IP address, typically with different port numbers; this is used by most mobile network operators and many ISPs. So if you want to track down a machine that has done something wicked, you will often have to get the logs that map MAC addresses of devices to IP addresses. There may be more than one log, and lots can go wrong – such as wrong timestamps, and failure to understand time zones.

One of the most basic concerns is the prevention and mitigation of *denial-of-service* (DoS) attacks. These have a number of flavours. An opponent can try to steal some of your IP address space, or one or more of your domains, in order to send spam; even when you get it back, you may find it's been extensively blacklisted. An opponent can send you huge floods of traffic from a botnet of many compromised machines; a *distributed denial-of-service* (DDoS) attack. They can abuse various online services such as DNS to send you floods of packet traffic. Let's work through these in turn.

21.2.1 BGP security

The Internet is an interconnected network of networks: its components are *Autonomous Systems* (ASes) such as ISPs, telcos and large organisations, each of which controls a range of IP addresses. The glue that holds them together, the core routing protocol of the Internet, is the *Border Gateway Protocol* (BGP).

Routers – the specialized computers that switch packets on networks – use BGP to exchange information about what routes are available to get to particular blocks of IP addresses, and to maintain routing tables so they can select efficient routes to use. ASes can route traffic to other ASes by buying service from large transit providers but typically cut the costs of this by peering with each other at a local *Internet interchange* (IX), of which most countries have at least one and large countries may have several.

Internet interconnectivity is a complex ecosystem with many interdependent layers. Its open and decentralised organisation has been essential to the success and resilience of the Internet, which has meant that the effects of natural disasters such as Hurricane Katrina and terrorist attacks such as 9/11 have been limited in time and space, as have assorted technical failures. However, the Internet is slowly becoming more centralised, as a result of the consolidation of Tier-1 providers, and is vulnerable to common-mode failures (such as electric power cuts) as well as to disruptive attacks.

About the worst attack we can reasonably foresee would involve an attacker planting malware on thousands of routers so they advertise large numbers of false routes, clogging the routing tables and tearing up the routing fabric. There have been several warnings already in the form of incidents and accidents. In 2008, YouTube became inaccessible for a few hours after the government of Pakistan tried to censor it locally by announcing false routes to it, which propagated globally; and in 2010 China Telecom advertised over 100,000 invalid routes, hijacking 15% of Internet addresses for 18 minutes. Some people ascribed that to accident, while others suggested that China had been testing a 'cyber-nuke', some of whose fallout escaped. Most routers now accept only a limited number of routes from each of their peers, be it a few dozen or a few hundred; so large-scale disruption would require thousands of subverted routers. Both China and (more recently) Russia have been working on making the Internet in their countries separable, so that major disruptive attacks could in theory be launched without inflicting unacceptable collateral damage on local services and facilities. There have been reports of BGP hijacking being used by China for intelligence collection; for example, traffic from Canada to Korean government websites was routed via China from February 2016 for six months [533]. There has also been criminal misuse, ranging from the hijacking of IP address space by spammers, to an eight-figure ad fraud in 2018 whose perpetrators hid in address space stolen from the US Air Force [792]. Finally, there is a growing political tussle in 2019–20 about whether Huawei should be allowed to sell routers at scale (or at all) in countries allied to the USA.

Taking a step backward, the resilience of the Internet is hard to define and to measure; it is in tension with efficiency and may be decreasing as a small number of very large networks come to dominate. These range from the dominant transit provider, Lumen (the company changed its name from Level 3 to Lumen), to content delivery networks (CDNs) operated by Google, Akamai,

Cloudflare and others. There are many complex interactions between resilience and efficiency, reachability and congestion, traffic prioritisation and commercial sensitivity, complexity and scale. There's no mechanism to check the validity of routing information distributed via BGP. The pervasive mistrust between ISPs and governments makes regulation difficult. The lack of good information about how the system works makes rational discussion difficult too. Resilience has so far depended on surplus capacity and rapid growth, but that cannot continue for ever. In 2011 colleagues and I wrote a major report for the European Network and Information Security Agency that explores these issues in detail [1910].

The main technical BGP security mechanism at present is the *Resource Public Key Infrastructure* (RPKI), which enables registries to certify that "Autonomous system X announces IP address range Y". This will not prevent capable attackers, as a malicious route announcement will just have the right AS at the end of the route following the attacker's in the middle; but it detects the fat-finger mistakes that cause most of the outages. Whether it will make an already fragile BGP system more robust to have lots of certificates in it remains to be seen; when RIPE's certificate expired in February 2020 there was a short outage until it was fixed. For the future, people are working on Peerlock, whereby the main ASes at an interchange share information about what routes they will and won't announce; this has the prospect of bringing enough local benefit to exchange members for it to be practically deployable.

21.2.2 DNS security

The *Domain Name System* (DNS) allows human-readable names such as `ross-anderson.com` to be mapped to IP addresses of either kind; there's a hierarchy of DNS servers that do this, ranging from several hundred top-level servers down through machines at ISPs and on local networks, which cache DNS records for performance and reliability. It does occasionally get attacked: the Mirai botnet attacked DynDNS in October 2016, taking out Twitter on the US eastern seaboard for five hours. But DNS has become a massively distributed system with a lot of very fast machines connected to very high-capacity networks, so service denial attacks on it are rare.

Hijacking does occur from time to time, and at various levels. Some states intercept and redirect DNS queries as a means of censorship; some ISPs have done so, as a means of replacing ads in web pages with ads from which they get a cut; and a DNS server at an ISP may be hacked to drive clients to a wicked website. This is known as *pharming*, and in a variant called *drive-by pharming*, the crooks lure you to a web page containing JavaScript that changes your home router's DNS server from the one at your ISP to one under their control [1819]. Next time you try to go to `www.citibank.com`, you may be directed to a phishing site that emulates it. That's one reason to change the default password on your home router – even if it's only accessible from inside your network.

In order to prevent DNS hijacking, DNSSEC adds digital signatures to DNS name records. By verifying such a signature you can check that the record came from the authoritative server and was not altered en route. Uptake is patchy: all US government domains in .gov are supposed to be signed, and most domains in Sweden are signed, as the registrar made signed domains cheaper. However, some major firms like Google don't sign their DNS records out of concern that cryptography makes systems more fragile; if anything goes wrong, you can just disappear. Other firms avoid DNSSEC because they don't want competitors to 'walk the zone' and enumerate all their subdomains; the NSEC3 extension enables firms to avoid this using hashes, but many firms (or their service providers) have not yet built the infrastructure.

Another problem with DNSSEC is that it gets abused in denial-of-service attacks. A common technique is that Alice attacks Bob by sending Charlie a message saying, "Hey, can you tell me the very large answer to this short question? Yours, Bob!" As signed DNS records are a lot larger, a DDoS-for-hire service can use DNSSEC as an amplifier, Alice can send packets that purport to come from Bob's IP address to many DNS servers, which then bombard the target with replies. (Cheeky criminals use the FBI as Charlie, as fbi.gov has two nice big keys.)

The controversial issue in 2020 is *DNS-over-https* (DoH). The main browser maintainers, Chrome and Mozilla, propose that rather than sending DNS traffic in the clear, it will go encrypted over https to a DoH resolver. This is claimed to be good for privacy, as your ISP will have less information about your browsing (but unless you use Tor, it will still have plenty). The downside is that many enterprise security products monitor DNS to detect abuse. If malware compromises a machine in your fleet, you may spot it when it tries to contact a command-and-control server, so enterprises buy threat intelligence feeds and monitor the domain names (and IP addresses) blacklisted on them. Sysadmins also like to monitor for DNS hijacking, and to block certain domains as inappropriate for work. DoH will make all this harder, and is questionable architecture as running a core network service over an application means it's 'not the Internet any more' [430]. On the commercial side, DoH may entrench Google's grip on the advertising market, while causing problems for content delivery networks like Akamai and Cloudflare over routing, load balancing and so on. It will also stop ISPs transcoding videos for mobile users to save bandwidth. Experts would have preferred to run DNS over TLS instead.

21.2.3 UDP, TCP, SYN floods and SYN reflection

On wide-area networks, most data move between machines using either the *User Datagram Protocol* (UDP), which is connectionless, or the *Transmission*

Control Protocol (TCP), which sets up persistent connections between endpoints. Let's start with the 3-way handshake used by Alice to initiate a TCP connection to Bob and set up sequence numbers for subsequent packet traffic (see Figure 21.1).

A ⟶ B:	SYN; my number is X
B ⟶ A:	CK; now X + 1
	SYN; my number is Y
A ⟶ B:	ACK; now Y + 1
	(start talking)

Figure 21.1: TCP/IP handshake

This protocol has been exploited in many ways. The classic service-denial attack is the *SYN flood.* Alice simply sends a lot of SYN packets and never acknowledges any of the replies. Bob accumulates more records of SYN packets than his software can handle. This was used in one of the first distributed denial-of-service attacks that brought down Panix, a New York ISP, for several days in 1996.

The technical fix was the 'SYNcookie': rather than keeping a copy of the incoming SYN packet, *B* simply sends out as *Y* an encrypted version of *X*. That way, Bob doesn't have to retain a lot of state about half-open sessions. Despite this, SYN floods persisted, albeit at a declining rate, for many years. The general principle is that when you're designing a protocol anyone can invoke, don't let malicious users force honest ones to do work.

The more common attack now is *SYN reflection*. Alice sends Bob a packet that purports to come from Charlie. Bob replies to Charlie, and in practice systems send up to five ACKs in response to each SYN as a robustness measure, so there's still a useful amplification effect.

21.2.4 Other amplifiers

Many other protocols have been used in service-denial attacks than DNS and TCP [1505]. An early favourite was *smurfing*; this exploited the *Internet control message protocol* (ICMP), which enables users to send an echo packet to a remote host to check whether it's alive. If Alice sent an ICMP packet purporting to come from Bob to a broadcast address, all the machines on the subnet would send him a response. The protocol was changed so that broadcast addresses didn't reply. The bad guys changed to use protocols such as NTP and DNS for which amplifiers could still be found.

More thorough fixes for attacks based on packet amplification were to follow. Most of the available amplifiers use UDP packets, including ICMP and NNTP but not SYN reflection; so starting from the mid-2000s, broadband ISPs started filtering out UDP packets with forged source addresses. Microsoft also changed their network stack to make it much harder for an infected machine to send a packet with a spoofed IP address; you now need to hack the operating system, not just any old application. So attacks that exploit UDP packet amplifiers have to be run from servers in hosting centres. In the late 2010s, such attacks have become increasingly the preserve of DDoS-for-hire operators, against whom the most effective countermeasure has been to raid them and arrest them.

21.2.5 Other denial-of-service attacks

As the clever ways of creating service-denial attacks have been closed off one by one, the bad guys have turned increasingly to brute force, by sending floods of packets from infected machines. The first *distributed denial-of-service* (DDoS) attack may have been the Morris worm in the 1980s, and the first deliberate one in the 1990s with the attack already mentioned on Panix. Nowadays, botnets are assembled using all sorts of vulnerabilities, and underground markets let some people specialise in hacking machines and selling them to others who extract value in various ways. Since 2016, the machines most used for DDoS have been IoT devices such as CCTV cameras, which are now connected in large numbers to home WiFi networks with reasonable bandwidth, but which tend to have known default passwords – and are often incapable of being patched. The Mirai botnet appeared in 2016 to exploit this opportunity, and there have been over a thousand variants of it since (its source code got posted to Hackforums).

There are various motives for service-denial attacks. Most are launched by schoolkids – typically gamers who want to take down an opposing crew's teamspeak server. There has for some years been a black market in DDoS-for-hire, which the authorities in the USA and elsewhere have been trying to close down. There have been some incidents of blackmail (e.g., of online bookmakers), and a growing use of the technique for suppressing political opponents – starting perhaps with attacks on the servers of an opposition party in Kyrgyzstan, even when these were relocated to North America [1616]. We discussed their use in conflict by states in Chapter 2.

That said, one mustn't forget online activism. If a hundred thousand people send email to the White House protesting against some policy or other, is this a DDoS attack? Protesters should not be treated as felons; but protest can easily shade over into abuse, and drawing legislative distinctions can be hard.

21.2.6 Email – from spies to spammers

The SMTP standard for email has particular issues around the prevention of bulk interception, and the prevention of bulk unwanted mail.

Email is by default neither encrypted nor authenticated, and was for decades available to anyone who could either monitor the network or access mail servers. It was possible to use programs such as PGP/GPG to encrypt mail, but this never caught on outside small communities. First, such programs can be a pain to use, and second, there are strong network effects: there's no point in using email encryption if none of your friends do. What's more, if only a small group of people use encryption, this may just bring them to the attention of the authorities; subversive groups, spies and so on really need anonymity rather than just confidentiality, as we discussed in section 20.4. So PGP/GPG tends to be used by specialists, such as sysadmins and anti-virus researchers.

There are two main countermeasures to bulk interception. First, most mail servers use `starttls` to set up encrypted communications with other mail servers as they exchange mail, especially since the Snowden revelations. Encrypted exchanges can be blocked by man-in-the-middle attacks, and these have been reported in some less-democratic countries. The current countermeasure to such attacks, *MTA Strict Transport Security* (MTA-STS), is supported by Microsoft, Google and Yahoo [1222]: it allows mail service providers to specify that mail should only be delivered to them via a TLS session authenticated by a proper certificate which you download from their website. This prevents downgrade or interception attacks on email to and from the big boys, and also allows opportunistic, trust-on-first-use encryption to other servers. MTA-STS has generally supplanted an earlier standard, *DNS-based Authentication of Named Entities* (DANE) which put a TLS certificate for starttls in the mail server's DNS record[1].

The second countermeasure is that some 95% of personal email accounts nowadays are at the big five webmail providers, and many corporates use them too. In this case, the confidentiality of email is assured by TLS, fortified with certificate pinning and certificate transparency which we'll discuss later. But although bulk access may be blocked, webmail is subject to warranted access, just like other services that corporates outsource.

Bulk unwanted mail, or spam, has two components. The first is entirely legal but unwanted marketing communication. As marketers can make it tiresome to opt out, users find it more convenient to press the 'report spam' button once an offer or supplier is no longer of interest.

The second consists of floods of generally unwanted traffic sent out for the most part by botnets, and often with clear criminal intent. This is in some respects similar to a DDoS attack: just as DDoS bots may forge IP addresses, spam bots may forge the sender's email address. This is fought by the big providers with four main mechanisms.

[1]DANE is still widely used in Germany, but Google refused to use it as it depends on DNSSEC, which Google considers to be insufficiently dependable.

1. *Domain Keys Identified Mail* (DKIM) ties email to the sending domain by signing it using a signature key whose public verification key is kept in the sending domain's DNS record. The signed material is selected to identify the message unambiguously despite the additions to headers that occur during transit, but to stop the bad guys adding an extra "From: PayPal" header. Mail that hasn't been altered too much can be forwarded. There's a replay attack in that the spammer sends his spam through Gmail, which signs it, and then forwards it afterwards; so mail servers cache DKIM signatures and discard mail carrying a signature that's already been seen a few times.
2. *Sender Policy Framework* (SPF) is similar but ties mail to the source IP address. Again, this is verifiable against a key in the domain DNS record. SPF doesn't allow mail forwarding; mailing list servers are supposed to use a related protocol called *Authenticated Received Chain* (ARC) to re-sign mail they forward.
3. A domain's DNS can also contain a *Domain-based Message Authentication, Reporting and Conformance* (DMARC) record, which enables its owner to recommend what a recipient should do with email that appears to come from the owner's domain but which fails authentication using both DKIM and SPF.
4. Machine-learning systems are used to filter mail against authentication results and other criteria, and take much of their ground truth from whether users report mail as spam. This is made more complicated by user preferences for marketing material, which vary by user and over time.

The illegal segment of spam is now a highly specialised business, run by several large gangs. Its statistics have been 'lumpy' since the mid-2000s, and this has been getting more pronounced. As of 2020, the gangs typically steal IP address space using malicious BGP route announcements, register thousands of domains, and send a few hundred spams from each before the machine-learning filters kick in and block them.

21.3 The malware menagerie – Trojans, worms and RATs

The first examples of malicious code were *Trojan Horses* – named after the horse the Greeks left for the Trojans, supposedly as a gift but which contained soldiers who opened the gates of Troy to the Greek army [1131]. There have been religious wars over nomenclature for years, which is why many people prefer to just use the term *malware*. My usage is that a Trojan is a program that does something malicious (such as capturing passwords) when run by an unsuspecting user. A *worm* is a malicious program that replicates itself on other systems, while one that does so by hooking itself into the code of other programs is a *virus*. A *remote access Trojan* (RAT) is software that may or may not run as root but that enables a remote party to access the device it runs on, while a *rootkit* is software installed as root on a device and that stealthily enables a third party to control it. *Potentially unwanted software* (PUS) may have been installed openly or by deception, but does something the user doesn't want (if they understand it at all).

These categories are not mutually exclusive and the boundaries can be context dependent. For example, stalkerware – software that enables one person to track another's mobile phone location and use – falls into different categories depending on whether it was installed covertly, or by a controlling man bullying his partner, or by a court ordering it as a condition of bail. Even stealthy malware isn't always illegal as it can be used by law-enforcement agencies to turn suspects' phones and laptops into listening devices, as well as by fraudsters to operate bank accounts by remote control[2].

Malware generally uses stealth techniques to hide, but eventually it's identified and tools to remove it are written. There's a whole ecosystem around malware: malware writers, botnets of infected machines, and a range of security firms offering everything from threat intelligence to antivirus software. (There are even firms selling malware – particularly to government agencies.) And in addition to the formal economy, there's an underground economy of cybercrooks selling everything from banking Trojans to DDoS-for-hire services.

21.3.1 Early history of malware

It the early 1960s, machines were slow and their CPU cycles were rationed – with students often at the tail of the queue. Students invented tricks such as writing computer games with a Trojan inside to check if the program is running as root, and if so to create a privileged account with a known password. By the 1970s, time-sharing systems at universities were the target of more and more pranks involving Trojans. All sorts of tricks were developed. In 1978, John Shoch and Jon Hupp of Xerox PARC wrote a program they called a *worm*, which replicated itself across a network looking for idle processors so it could assign them tasks [1727].

In 1984, Ken Thompson gave a classic paper "Reflections On Trusting Trust", when he accepted a Turing award, the top prize in computer science. He

[2]At the other end of the spectrum, some antivirus products behave like malware in various ways, including being very hard to remove after a 'free trial', or by introducing insecurities. In December 2019, one brand of AV software was removed by Chrome, Firefox and Opera for exfiltrating too much personal information [354].

showed that even if the source code for a system were carefully inspected and known to be free of vulnerabilities, a trapdoor could still be inserted [1887]. His trick was to build the trapdoor into the compiler. If this recognized that it was compiling the login program, it would insert a master password that would work on any account[3]. Of course, someone might examine the source code for the compiler, and then compile it again from scratch. So if the compiler recognizes that it's compiling itself, it inserts the vulnerability anyway, even if it's not present in the source. So even if you can buy a system with verifiably secure hardware, operating system and applications, the compiler binary can still contain a Trojan. The moral is that in order to trust a system completely, it is not enough to build all of it, in the sense that software engineers use the word 'build', namely compiling it from source code. You have to create all of it, including the tool chain, and the hardware too.

Malware next became mobile. The first-ever computer virus in the wild was written for the Apple II by a 9th-grader in 1981 [1218]. In 1984 Fred Cohen did a PhD on the topic; his experiments with different operating systems showed how code could propagate itself from one machine to another, and as I mentioned in Section 9.6.4, from one compartment of a multilevel system to another. Within about three years we started to see the first real live viruses in the wild: PC viruses which spread when users shared programs on diskettes or via bulletin boards[4].

One early innovation was the 'Christma' virus, which spread round IBM mainframes in December 1987. It was a program written in the mainframe command language REXX that had a header saying 'Don't read me, EXEC me' and code that, if executed, drew a Christmas tree on the screen – then sent itself to everyone in the user's contacts file. It was written as a prank, rather than out of malice; and by using the network (IBM's BITNET) to spread, and inviting users to run it, it was ahead of its time.

21.3.2 The Internet worm

The press and public became aware of malware in November 1988 with the Internet worm. This was a program written by Robert Morris Jr that exploited a number of vulnerabilities to spread from one machine to another in November 1988 [617]. It tried 432 common passwords in a guessing attack, looked for any machines trusted by the machine it infected, and also tried to exploit vulnerabilities in Unix (including the `fingerd` bug mentioned in

[3]This developed an idea first floated by Paul Karger and Robert Schell in the Multics evaluation in 1974 [1022].

[4]Before the Internet was opened up to the public, online services were mostly standalone; bulletin boards were typically operated by hobbyists and would let subscribers or even anonymous users dial in to share information and files.

section 6.4.1). It also took steps to camouflage itself: it was called `sh`, and it encrypted its data strings (albeit with a Caesar cipher).

Its author claimed that his code was not a deliberate attack on the Internet – merely an experiment to see whether code could replicate from one machine to another. But it had a bug. It should have recognised machines that were already infected, and not infected them again, but this feature didn't work. The result was a huge volume of traffic that completely clogged up the Internet (or more accurately, its predecessor the Arpanet) despite the fact that it only affected some 10% of the 60,000 machines on the Arpanet at the time. One lesson was that sites which kept their nerve and didn't pull their network connection recovered more quickly as they could find out what was happening and get the fixes.

21.3.3 Further malware evolution

By the early 1990s, PC viruses had become such a problem that they gave rise to a whole industry of anti-virus software. Through the 1990s, operating systems acquired better access controls, making the malware writer's job harder, but the spread of interpreted languages provided plenty of new opportunities. By the start of the 21st century, the main vector was the macro languages in products such as Word, and the main transmission mechanism had become the Internet [299].

The next phase of malware evolution was to enlist the user as the propagation mechanism. The 'Love Bug' in 2000 was a worm that sent itself to everyone in the victim's address book, with the subject line 'I love you' designed to get people to open it. Its author was Onel de Guzman, a poor computer science student in Manila who wanted to collect passwords so he could use other people's ISP accounts to get online without paying [2019]. This hack to save a few dollars ended up costing millions, and taught us about the difficulty of stopping such things by filtering: a Canadian company with 85,000 staff stripped out all Windows executables at the firewall, but many of their staff had personal webmail accounts, so the Love Bug got in anyway. The company had given each employee a copy of the corporate directory in their address book, and the result was meltdown as 85,000 mail clients each tried to say 'I love you' to each of 85,000 addresses. The Love Bug was followed by similar worms which persuaded people to click on them by offering pictures of celebs such as Britney Spears and Paris Hilton.

The next development was *flash worms* which propagate by scanning the whole Internet for machines vulnerable to some exploit or other, and taking them over; examples such as Code Red and Slammer infected all vulnerable machines within hours or even minutes, and drove research into what sort of automated defences might react in time [1824].

The early 2000s also saw the rise of *spyware* and *adware*. Spyware collects and forwards information from your computer (and now, your phone) without the owner's authorization, or with at best an obscure popup that doesn't really tell you what you're agreeing to. It may also be installed by someone else, such as a parent or partner; spyware is increasingly involved in intimate partner abuse. Adware may bombard the user with advertising popups and can be bundled with spyware. The vendors of such products have even sued antivirus companies who blacklisted their wares. Some spyware is installed deliberately, whether by companies who want to keep tabs on staff, by parents who want to see what their kids are up to, or by abusive men who want to monitor and control their partners. Boundaries are difficult and different people may have different views.

A sea-change came about in 2004–6. Until then, most malware writers did so for fun or to impress their friends – basically, they were amateurs. Since then, the emergence of underground markets and crime forums has made the whole business much more professional. Malware writers now get paid money for software to recruit machines that can be sold on for cash to botnet herders and for other exploits.

Back in the amateur era, most viruses were flaky; very few actually spread in the wild. If code isn't infectious enough it won't spread, but if you make it too infectious then within a few hours the world's anti-virus vendors are upgrading their products to detect and remove it. Now that malware writers focus on money rather than bragging rights, they tend to avoid self-replicating worms in favour of more controllable exploit campaigns. (The main exception is when exploiting IoT devices that can't be patched.)

By the late 2000s, the largest botnets were using professional online marketing techniques to grow their network. Various stories were used to get people to click on a link and run a Trojan that would drop a rootkit on to their machine. Victims had to click away several warnings to install software; but Windows pops up so many annoying dialog boxes that most people just click them away. One of the first really large ones, Storm, earned its living from pump-and-dump operators and pharmacy scammers [1092]. Security researchers tried to disable big botnets by finding and taking down their command-and-control server; Storm used a peer-to-peer architecture that removed this single point of failure [1839]. In the end, it was targeted by Microsoft for removal. The same game is still being played; in March 2020 Microsoft took down Necurs, a botnet with nine million machines that had been growing for eight years, distributing banking Trojans as well as ransomware and email spam [353].

Flash worms have made a comeback since October 2016 with the Mirai worm and its variants. Mirai initially took over WiFi-attached CCTV cameras that had a known root password and software that could not be upgraded; all such devices in the IPv4 address space could be found and recruited within an hour or so. Since then, there have been over a thousand Mirai variants attacking various IoT devices.

21.3.4 How malware works

Malware typically has two components – a replication mechanism or dropper, and a payload. A worm simply makes a copy of itself somewhere else when it's run, perhaps by breaking into another system by password guessing or using a remote code execution vulnerability (both of which were used by the Internet worm). Viruses spread in other software, perhaps as macros in documents, while Trojans are typically executed by the victim.

The second component of a virus is the payload. When activated, this may do one or more of a number of bad things:

- exfiltrate your confidential data;
- attack you directly using banking malware or spyware;
- encrypt your data and demand a ransom;
- attack others, such as when GCHQ's Operation Socialist described in section 2.2.1.9 subverted Belgacom and installed software in it to do surveillance of mobile-phone traffic passing through Belgium to other countries;
- perform some other nefarious task, such as using the CPU to mine cryptocurrency;
- install a rootkit or remote access Trojan to enable its controllers to do any of the above things, to coordinate attacks with malware on other machines, and to update itself in response to any countermeasures.

If the target is not an individual but a company – as in the Belgacom case – then the attack may involve weeks to months of work. Once attackers control a device on the target network, they will want to move sideways to map the network and find key assets such as authentication servers and mail servers so they can expand the compromise and install remote access Trojans to get a permanent presence. There are many possibilities.

1. In the old days, an attacker would install packet sniffer software to harvest passwords and compromise other accounts, eventually including a sysadmin's. Good practice nowadays is to block such attacks using two-factor authentication, or using a protocol such as Kerberos or SSH to ensure that clear text passwords don't go over the LAN.
2. Other techniques target shared resources such as file servers. For example, Linux servers may use the *Network File System* (NFS) protocol; when a volume is first mounted, the client gets a *root filehandle* from the server – an access ticket that doesn't depend on the time and can't be

revoked. We block this at our own lab using Kerberos to authenticate clients and servers. There are similar problems with Windows file shares, although the details are different; the EternalBlue vulnerability used by the WannaCry and NotPetya worm exploited such file shares.

3. Security mechanisms such as SSH bring further vulnerabilities in that machines in large organisations may have many thousands of SSH keys to communicate with each other, and intruders can exploit them and the trust structures they create to move around.

To get an idea of the range of tools available to a capable attacker nowadays, I'd suggest you browse the NSA papers released by Ed Snowden and the CIA toolkits leaked in the Vault 7 disclosure. Cyber warriors have a range of exploit kits, droppers, RATs and software for stealthy exfiltration of intelligence product.

The takeaway is that the ease with which an intruder on your network can take over other machines depends on how tightly you have the network locked down, and the damage that can follow any breach will depend on the extent to which other machines in your network trust, or are vulnerable to, the compromised machine. This is one of the arguments for not trusting local networks, but insisting on strong authentication between clients and servers at all times.

21.3.5 Countermeasures

Within a few months of the first PC viruses appearing in the wild in 1987, there were startups selling antivirus software. This led to an arms race in which virus and antivirus developers tried to outwit each other.

Early antivirus software came in basically two flavours – *scanners* and *checksummers*. Scanners search executable files for an *indicator of compromise* (IoC), typically a string of bytes from a specific virus. Malware developers responded in various ways, and the dominant technique became *polymorphism*. The idea is to change the code each time the malware replicates, to make it harder to find stable IoCs. The usual technique is to encrypt the code, and have a small header that contains decryption code. With each replication, the malware re-encrypts itself under a different key, and tweaks the decryption code by substituting equivalent sequences of instructions. Modern malware may be run through half-a-dozen such *packers* in turn, and recursively unpack itself when run. AV firms fight back by running the code in a virtual machine, so the malware devs include VM-detection code. The AV firms can at least use the unpacked code as an IoC so long as they can hack through to the last unpacking operation.

Checksummers keep a whitelist list of all the authorised executables on the system, together with checksums of the original versions, typically computed using a hash function. The malware devs' main countermeasure is *stealth*, which in this context means that the malware watches out for operating system calls of the kind used by the checksummer and hides itself whenever a check is being done.

To provide robust defences against malware, you have to combine tools, incentives and management. We learned in the old days of DOS-based file viruses to provide a central reporting point for all incidents, and to control all software loaded on an organisation's machines. The main risks were machines used at home both for work and for other things (such as kids playing games), and files coming in from other organisations. The same principles still apply. However, firms now need a more coordinated response than before. One of the reasons is that antivirus software has been getting steadily less effective. The commercialisation of botnets and of machine exploitation has meant that malware writers operate like companies, with research and test departments. Almost all exploits are undetectable by the current antivirus products when first launched (if their writers test them properly) and many of them recruit their target number of machines without coming to the attention of the antivirus industry. The net effect was that while antivirus software might have detected almost all of the exploits in circulation in the early 2000s, by 2010 the typical product might detect only a third of them, and by 2020 you expect to detect infection after the fact and have to clean up. That means having good tool support, logging network traffic and analysing it in the light of the latest threat intelligence. What's more, the rootkit vendors provide after-sales service; if a removal kit is shipped, the rootkit vendor will rapidly ship countermeasures. And nowadays many attackers – especially the competent ones – don't leave malware files lying around but 'live off the land'; they might just add their ssh key to a list of authorised keys on one of your servers so they can pop in when they feel like it, leaving nothing for legacy AV to find.

21.4 Defense against network attack

In defending against malware and network attack generally, the view from the second edition of this book in 2008 was that you needed three things: good enough management to keeping your systems patched up-to-date and configured properly; firewalls to stop known Trojans and network exploits; and intrusion detection to monitor your networks and machines for indicators of compromise so you can catch the stuff that got through and clean up afterwards.

The principles remain the same in 2020 but reality is much more complex now, because the scale and complexity of the task have made automation almost essential. A large Windows shop might have something like the following:

1. An agent running on each endpoint, reporting to a cloud service to give you full visibility of what software is running where and to enable you to push updates;
2. A vulnerability scanner that continually probes your network for known vulnerabilities;
3. Various boundary control devices which may include firewalls, a proxy server that filters all URLs of websites that staff visit, and proxies for critical applications;
4. An SSL gateway for staff working remotely;
5. A *bring-your-own-device* (BYOD) manager, to control laptops, phones and other devices that staff members use but that the firm doesn't own;
6. A *data leakage prevention* (DLP) system to identify staff who attempt to remove company documents or code;
7. A threat intelligence platform that integrates feeds from multiple providers, to alert you to various indicators of compromise including bad DNS names and IP addresses;
8. A log analysis tool that enables you to go back and work out when a compromise first happened, and how far it spread;
9. A *security orchestration and response* (SOAR) system that helps you respond quickly if you note that some devices in your network are communicating with bad addresses such as the command-and-control servers of known malware.

Making all this work together requires system integration, otherwise you'll have dozens of staff in your network security centre whose job is to copy lists of bad domains, bad IP addresses and other indicators of compromise from one tool to another.

That said, let's work our way down this list.

Organisations that are serious about IT security – because they are targets of state actors (like big service firms), or have demanding compliance requirements (like banks), or have a lot to lose (like the military) – aim to stop all vulnerabilities at source. This means keeping everything patched up to date, which in turn means automated patch management. But such a strategy is harder than it looks. It brings with it a number of hard subproblems, such as maintaining an accurate inventory of all the devices on your network. If you impose a rigid bureaucracy for registering new devices, people will have to find ways to circumvent it to get their work done. So you need to also scan your network to see what's there and whether it's vulnerable. And even diligent organisations may find it's just too expensive to fix all the security holes at once; patches may break critical applications, and an organisation's most critical systems often run on the least secure machines, as administrators have not dared to upgrade them for fear of losing service.

This interacts with operational security. In Chapter 2 and Chapter 8 we discussed the practice and limitations of training staff to not expose systems by foolish actions. By the mid-2000s, the main attack vector was spearphishing – getting people to click on links in email that download and install rootkits. We learned from Ed Snowden that this was the standard way for the NSA to attack a company in 2013: they would monitor external traffic to identify sysadmins, do some background research to identify individual targets, and craft a convincing phishing lure. Alternatively they would direct the target to a website they could spoof or where they could mount a man-in-the-middle protocol attack.

You may try to educate your staff to not click on links in suspicious mail, but competent attackers create mails that don't look suspicious. And so many businesses expect their customers and suppliers to click on links that your staff will have to do some clicking to get their work done. We discussed in Chapter 3 and elsewhere that victim blaming is maladaptive; if your security systems are not usable, you have to fix them rather than blaming the poor users.

Many firms mitigate the risk by opening all mail attachments in a cloud service rather than a local machine, giving staff non-Windows machines such as Chromebooks, iPads or Macs, or having a firewall or mail filter that strips out suspicious content.

21.4.1 Filtering: firewalls, censorware and wiretaps

A *firewall* is a machine that stands between a private network and the Internet, and filters out traffic that might be harmful. It's named after the metal bulkhead that separates the passenger compartment of a car or light plane from the engine compartment, to protect the occupants from a fuel fire. Firewalls were controversial when they appeared in the mid-1990s; purists said that all the machines in a company should be secured, while firewall advocates said this was impractical. The debate has swung back and forth since.

Firewalls are just one example of systems that examine streams of packets and perform filtering or logging operations. Bad packets may be thrown away, or modified in such a way as to make them harmless. They may also be copied to a log or audit trail. Very similar systems are also used for Internet censorship and for law-enforcement wiretapping; almost everything I'll discuss in this section goes across to those applications too. Developments in any of these fields potentially affect the others; and actual systems may have overlapping functions. For example, many corporate firewalls or mail filters screen out pornography, and some even block bad language, while ISP systems that censor child pornography or dissenting political speech may report the perpetrators automatically to the authorities. Many filters also keep logs, so that attacks can be investigated after the fact; and in parts of the financial sector, all staff communications are required to be logged so that regulators can investigate any suspicions of insider trading or money laundering.

Filters come in basically three flavours, depending on whether they operate at the IP packet level, at the TCP session level or at the application level.

21.4.1.1 Packet filtering

The simplest kind of filter merely inspects packet addresses and port numbers. This functionality is available as standard in routers, in Linux and in Windows. You can block IP spoofing by ensuring that only 'local' packets leave a network, and only 'foreign' ones enter. It's also easy to block traffic to or from 'known bad' IP addresses. For example, IP filtering is a major component of the censorship mechanisms in the Great Firewall of China; a list of bad IP addresses can be kept in router hardware, which enables packet filtering to be done at great speed.

Basic packet filtering is often used to block all traffic except that arriving on specific port numbers. You might initially allow the ports used by common services such as email and web traffic, and then open up further ports as needed. As we move to *software defined networks* (SDN), which replace expensive routers with cheap switches controlled by software on commodity servers, packet filtering rules become just the access-control rules in the SDN controller.

However, packet filters can be defeated by a number of tricks. For example, a packet can be fragmented in such a way that the initial fragment passes the firewall's inspection but is then overwritten by a subsequent fragment, replacing the source address with one that violates your security policy. Another limitation is that maintaining a blacklist is difficult, especially when it's not the IP address specifically you want to block, but something that resolves into an IP address, especially on a transient basis. For example, phishermen use tricks like fast-flux in which a site's IP address changes several times an hour.

21.4.1.2 Circuit gateways

The next step up is a *circuit gateway* that reassembles and examines all the packets in each TCP session. This is more expensive than simple packet filtering but can also provide the added functionality of a *virtual private network* (VPN) whereby corporate traffic passed over the Internet is encrypted from firewall to firewall. I'll discuss the IPSEC protocol that's used for this in the last section of this chapter.

TCP-level filtering can be used to do a few more things, such as DNS filtering. However, such a filter can't screen out bad things at the application level, from malicious code to child sex abuse material. Thus it may be programmed to direct certain types of traffic to application filters.

21.4.1.3 Application proxies

The third type of firewall is the *application proxy*, which understands one or more services. Examples are mail filters that try to weed out spam, and web proxies that block or remove undesirable content. The classic objective is stripping out code, be it straightforward executables, active content in web pages, or macros from incoming Word documents. The move to web-based mail services and the adoption of https have left significantly less work for mail filters to do, and as the service firms adopt technical measures such as certificate transparency to prevent proxying, filtering needs to shift to endpoints.

An application proxy can also be a bottleneck. An example is the Great Firewall of China, which tried through the 2000s to block mail and web content that refers to banned subjects [450]. Since the adoption of https by the major service providers, and the availability of services such as Google Docs that can also be used for communication, China simply stops most of its citizens from using services like Gmail and Facebook.

In the emerging BeyondCorp model promoted by Google, proxies sit in front of the application servers themselves so that the internal network does not need to be trusted.

21.4.1.4 Ingress versus egress filtering

Most firewalls look outwards and try to keep bad things out, but some look inwards and try to stop bad things leaving. The pioneers were military mail systems that monitor outgoing traffic to ensure that nothing classified goes out in the clear. Around 2005 some ISPs started looking at outgoing mail traffic to try to detect spam [444]; and by now most consumer ISPs prevent their customers sending packets with spoofed source addresses. This *source address validation* means that DDoS operators using UDP reflection attacks can no longer use botnets but need to rent servers in data centres.

The fastest-growing use of egress filtering in 2020 is for *data leakage prevention* (DLP). Software that 'phones home', whether for copyright enforcement or marketing purposes, can disclose highly sensitive material, and prudent organisations increasingly wish to monitor and control this kind of traffic. But the pervasive use of https means that DLP systems typically need to install software on endpoints rather than using middleboxes.

21.4.1.5 *Architecture*

For years, many firms bought a firewall to keep their auditors happy. If that's your pain point, a simple filtering router won't need much maintenance and won't get in the way too much. At the other extreme, a serious firewall system at a defence contractor might consist of a packet filter connecting the outside world to a screened subnet, also known as a *demilitarized zone* (DMZ), which in turn contains a number of application servers or proxies to filter mail, web and other services. You may also expect to find data diodes separating networks operating at different clearance levels, to ensure that classified information doesn't escape either outwards or downwards (Figure 21.2).

An alternative approach is to have more networks, but smaller ones. At our university, we have firewalls to separate departments, although we've got a shared network backbone and some shared central services such as logging. There's no reason why the students and the finance department should be on the same network, and a computer science department has got quite different requirements from a department of theology. Keeping each network small limits the scope of any compromise and helps incentivise system administrators to defend it.

Considerations in the design of a network security architecture include simplicity, usability, deperimeterisation versus re-perimterisation, underblocking versus overblocking, maintainability, and incentives.

First, since firewalls do only a small number of things, it's possible to make them simple to remove sources of vulnerability and error. If your organisation has a heterogeneous population of machines, then loading as much of the security task as possible on a small number of simple boxes makes sense. On

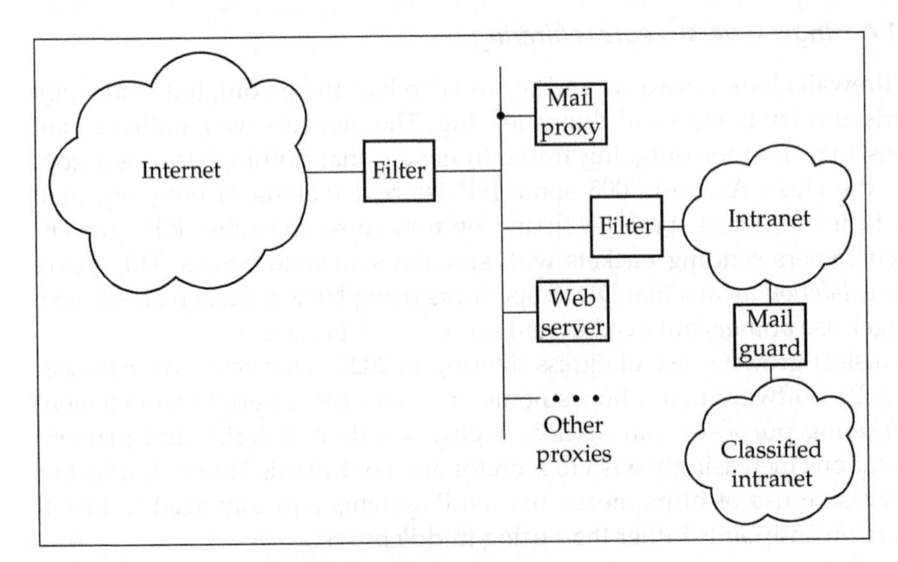

Figure 21.2: complex firewalls for an MLS network

the other hand, if you're running something like a call centre, with a thousand identically-configured PCs, it makes sense to put your effort into keeping this configuration tight. These are roughly the energy utility, and Google, models discussed in the introduction at the start of this chapter.

Second, elaborate central installations not only impose greater operational costs, but can get in the way so much that people install back doors, such as cable modems that bypass the firewall, to get their work done. I will discuss in section 20.4 how diplomats have come unstuck by using private email when their official systems were unusable. Many well-run firms have open guest networks, as does our department; there's always got to be something that works. And a prudent system administrator will monitor the actual network configuration rather than just relying on 'policy'.

Third, firewalls only work until people find ways round them. Early firewalls let only mail and web traffic through; so writers of applications from computer games to anonymity proxies redesigned their protocols to make the client-server traffic look as much like normal web traffic as possible. Then everything moved to Web 2.0 and such filters became largely ineffective.

Next, there's deperimeterisation – as Google's BeyondCorp notes, it's becoming steadily harder to put all the protection at the perimeter, thanks to the proliferation of phones and PDAs being used for functions that used to be done on desktop computers, and by changing business methods that involve more outsourcing of functions – whether formally to subcontractors or informally to advertising-supported web apps. If some parts of your organisation can't be controlled (e.g., the sales force and the R&D lab) while others must be (the finance office) then you may need separate architectures. The proliferation of web applications is complemented by a blunting of the incentive to do things at the perimeter, as useful things become harder to do. The difference between code and data is steadily eroded by new scripting languages. Many firms tried to block JavaScript in the early 2000s but were beaten by popular web sites that require it. Nowadays it may be impossible to prevent your staff attaching large numbers of IoT devices that just cannot be secured at all [1256].

And then there's our old friend the Receiver Operating Characteristic or ROC curve. No filtering mechanism has complete precision, so there's inevitably a trade-off between underblocking and overblocking. If you're running a censorship system to stop kids accessing pornography in public libraries, do you underblock, and annoy parents and churches when some pictures get through, or do you overblock and get sued for infringing free-speech rights? Things are made worse by the fact that the firewall systems used to filter web content for sex, violence and bad language also tend to block free-speech sites (as many of these criticise the firewall vendors – and some offer technical advice on how to circumvent blocking).

And as we've repeatedly pointed out, security depends at least as much on incentives as on technology. A sysadmin who looks after a departmental network used by a hundred people they know, and who will personally have to clear up any mess caused by an intrusion or a configuration error, is much more motivated than someone who's merely one member of a large team looking after thousands of machines.

21.4.2 Intrusion detection

Attacks will happen, and it's often cheaper to prevent some attacks and detect the rest than it is to try to prevent everything. The systems used to detect bad things happening are referred to generically as *intrusion detection systems* (IDS). The antivirus software products I discussed earlier are one example; but the term is most usually applied to boxes that sit on your network and look for signs of an attack in progress or a compromised machine [1639]. Examples include:

- a machine trying to contact a 'known bad' service such as an IRC channel that's used to control a botnet, or a known-bad IP address – or trying to resolve a known-bad DNS name;
- packets with forged source addresses – such as packets that claim to be from outside a subnet but that actually originate from it;
- spam coming from a machine in your network.

In cases like this, the IDS typically tells the sysadmin that a particular machine needs to be looked at. This may be just the first step in an investigation that involves staring at logs to see how it happened, and what else the attackers might have infected.

Other examples of intrusion detection, which we've seen in earlier chapters, include mechanisms for detecting payment card fraud and stock-market systems that look for insider trading, such as via increases in trading volume just before a price-sensitive announcement. This is now an active area of research: the boom in AI since 2012 has created lots of startups looking for pattern-matching problems.

21.4.2.1 Types of intrusion detection

The simplest intrusion detection method is to sound an alarm when a threshold is passed. Three or more failed logons, a credit card expenditure of more than twice the moving average of the last three months, or a mobile phone call lasting more than six hours, might all flag an account for attention. More sophisticated systems generally fall into two categories.

Misuse detection systems operate using a model of the likely behaviour of an intruder. A banking system may alarm if a user draws the maximum permitted amount from a cash machine on three successive days; and a Unix intrusion detection system may look for user account takeover by alarming if a previously naive user suddenly starts to use sophisticated tools like compilers. Simple misuse detection systems, such as antivirus scanners, look for a *signature* – a known characteristic of a specific attack. This can be either explicit in the data (such as a substring of an executable file that marks it as a specific piece of malware) or in behaviour (such as a machine contacting the IP address of a known botnet command-and-control server). More complex misuse detection systems treat a number of signatures as signals and then train a machine-learning classifier to make the decisions. As I discussed in section 12.5.4, the systems used to detect card fraud use dozens of signals, as they need low false alarm rates to be useful given the scale of modern payment systems.

Anomaly detection systems attempt the much harder job of looking for anomalous behaviour in the absence of a clear model of the attacker's modus operandi. The hope is to detect attacks that have not been previously recognized and cataloged. Systems of this type have used AI techniques since the 1990s, though some firms eschew them; Google policy, for example, is to avoid systems that try to learn thresholds or automatically detect causality, and instead have simple systems that detect changes in end-user request rates [237].

The dividing line between misuse and anomaly detection is somewhat blurred. A borderline case is Benford's law, which describes the distribution of digits in random numbers. One might expect that numbers beginning with the digits '1', '2', … '9' would be equally common. But when numbers come from random natural sources and span more than one order of magnitude, so that their distribution is independent of the number system in which they're expressed, the distribution is logarithmic: about 30% of decimal numbers start with '1'. Crooked clerks who think up numbers to cook the books, or even use random number generators without knowing Benford's law, are often caught this way [1249].

Another borderline case is the *honeypot* – something enticing left to attract attention. I mentioned, for example, that some hospitals have dummy records with celebrities' names in order to entrap staff who ignore patient confidentiality. In the network context, honeypots emulate many types of device so that attackers scanning the Internet looking for (say) a DSL modem of a particular upgrade status find one to attack; this may contain either a simple emulator, or with more recent designs, the actual modem firmware running in a VM [1959]. The upshot is that the honeypot operator gets to see who's attacking what, and how.

21.4.2.2 General limitations of intrusion detection

Some intrusions are obvious. If you're worried about activists vandalising your web site, then have a machine somewhere that fetches the page frequently and rings an alarm when it changes. But in the general case, intrusion detection is hard. The virus pioneer Fred Cohen proved that detecting viruses (in the sense of deciding whether a program is going to do something bad) is as hard as the halting problem, so we can't ever expect a complete solution [452].

There's also a matter of definitions. Some intrusion detection systems are configured to block some kinds of suspicious behaviour. But this turns the intrusion-detection system into an access control mechanism, as well as opening the door to service-denial attacks. I prefer to define an intrusion-detection system as one that monitors the logs and draws attention to suspicious occurrences.

Then there's the cost of false alarms. Academic machine-learning researchers often consider they've done well when they train a classifier to have a false alarm rate of 0.1%. But if you're on the Gmail team and dealing with a billion users authenticating themselves every day, that's way too much. Large-scale systems need really low false alarm rates.

Finally, there are three generic problems with machine-learning classifiers: the facts that they're not much good at detecting new attacks, that people game them, and that they inhale the prejudices of their training data. We will discuss these in more detail in section 25.3.

21.4.2.3 Specific problems detecting network attacks

Turning now to the specific problem of detecting network intrusion, it's harder to spot than payment fraud. Network intrusion detection products still have high missed alarm and false alarm rates. It's common to detect actual intrusions only afterwards. The reasons for the poor performance include the following, in no particular order.

- The Internet is a very noisy environment – not just at the level of content but also at the packet level. A lot of random crud arrives at any substantial site, and enough of it can be interpreted as hostile to provide a significant false alarm rate. Many bad packets result from software bugs; others are the fault of out-of-date or corrupt DNS data; and some are local packets that escaped, travelled the world and returned [214].
- There are 'too few attacks'. If there are ten real attacks per million sessions – which is almost certainly an overestimate – then even if the system has a false alarm rate as low as 0.1%, the ratio of false to real alarms will be 100. We talked about similar problems with burglar alarms; it's also a well-known problem for medics running

screening programs for diseases like HIV where the test error rate exceeds the disease prevalence. Where the signal is way below the noise, the guards get tired and the genuine alarms get missed.

- While a theft from a bank causes an incorrect state – money in the wrong place, and evidence on the audit trail – many network intrusions aim to avoid this, for example if their mission is to exfiltrate confidential data. It's easier to write software to detect errors than it is to detect slightly odd behaviour.
- Many network attacks are specific to particular versions of software, so you need a large and constantly-changing library of attack signatures. However, many firms buy intrusion detection systems in order to satisfy insurers or auditors, and the products aren't always kept up to date.
- As more and more traffic is encrypted, it can't easily be subjected to content analysis or filtered for malicious code. If DNS-over-https becomes the norm, tools that rely on analysing your DNS traffic will become much less effective.
- The issues we discussed in the context of firewalls largely apply to intrusion detection too. You can filter at the packet layer, which is fast but misses a lot; or you can proxy your applications, which is expensive – and needs to be constantly updated to cope with new applications and attacks.
- You may have to do intrusion detection both locally and globally. More and more things have to be done on local machines, thanks to encrypted web sessions; but some attacks are *stealthy* – the opponent sends 1–2 packets per day to each of maybe 100,000 hosts, and you need a central monitor that counts packets by source and destination address and by port.

Nowadays, intrusion detection systems involve the coordination of multiple monitoring mechanisms and products at different levels both in the network and on your fleet of endpoint devices. A large company with tens of thousands of staff using Windows will typically have several dozen products, as I discussed previously in section 21.4. Integrating and automating both monitoring and response makes up more and more of a CISO's job. The growth areas therefore include integration tools for *security incident and event management* (SIEM), *security orchestration and response* (SOAR), and metrics.

21.5 Cryptography: the ragged boundary

Network security interacts with cryptography in a number of ways. We already mentioned the debate about DNS over https; now I'm going to describe five other aspects of crypto briefly. They are SSH; the local link protection offered by WiFi, Bluetooth and HomePlug; the IPSec mechanisms used in VPNs; TLS; and the *public key infrastructures* (PKI) used to support many of these. In the previous chapter, we discussed how attempts to build more trustworthy components out of cryptography run up against many real-world engineering and economic constraints. The tools that we use to set boundaries on networks, and to translate trust within them, are no different.

The emerging themes are that the most distributed part of the problem is unmanageable because the vendors don't care; in particular the thousands of device types being marketed as part of the 'Internet of Things' have no remote management facility available to users, the vendor often doesn't upgrade the software, and the lack of a user interface means that authentication is haphazard at best. Meanwhile the most centralised part of the problem – PKI – is often subverted by government mandates.

21.5.1 SSH

When I use my laptop to access files on my desktop machine, or do anything with any other machine in our lab for that matter, I use *secure shell* (SSH) which provides encrypted links between Unix and Windows hosts. So when I work from home, my traffic is protected, and when I log on from the PC at my desk to another machine in the lab, the password I use doesn't go across the LAN in the clear.

SSH was initially written in 1995 by Tatu Ylönen, a researcher at Helsinki University of Technology, following a password-sniffing attack there [2061]. It sets up encrypted connections between machines, so that logon passwords don't travel across the network in the clear, and supports other useful features that led to its rapid adoption [1620].

There are various configuration options, but in the most straightforward one, each machine has a public-private keypair. The private key is protected by a passphrase that the user types at the keyboard. To connect from my laptop to a server at the lab, I install my laptop public key in a file on the relevant server. When I wish to log on to a server I'm prompted for my passphrase; the two machines set up a Diffie-Hellman key; the private keys are used to sign the transient public keys, to stop middleperson attacks; the subsequent traffic is thus both encrypted and authenticated. Manual key installation is intuitive, but doesn't scale particularly well. There are also options to use Kerberos, whether to authenticate the session key set up using Diffie-Hellman, or to set up the session key directly. (In the latter case, SSH falls back to being a variant of Kerberos in the sense that it is now a trusted third-party protocol, and the police can get the Kerberos server to decrypt the traffic.)

Possible problems include the fact that if you're typing at the keyboard one character at a time, then each character gets sent in its own packet, and the packet interarrival times can leak a lot of information about what you're typing [1807]. However, the worst is probably that most SSH keys used for server-to-server communication are stored in the clear, without being protected by a password at all. So if a server is compromised, the same can happen to every other machine that trusts an SSH key installed on it.

SSH is often used as a simple logon mechanism; many IoT devices run Linux and allow remote logon by anyone who knows an appropriate password. This opens them to password-guessing attacks, and where there are weak passwords or a known default password, to recruitment into botnets based on Mirai and similar tools. The countermeasure here is honeypots.

21.5.2 Wireless networking at the periphery

Many networks use wireless technology at the edge to go the last few feet from an access point to a device, or from one device to another. Protocols such as WiFi, Bluetooth and HomePlug all offer encryption to provide some protection against service abuse and perhaps against eavesdropping. However most are vulnerable to local attacks that are difficult to block completely because many devices don't get patched, lack user interfaces, or both.

21.5.2.1 WiFi

WiFi supports wireless local area networks, whether at home to connect phones and other devices to a home router, or by businesses to connect payment terminals and stock control devices as well as PCs. It has come with a series of encryption protocols since its launch in 1997. The first widely-used one, WEP (for *wired equivalent privacy*), was shown to be fairly easily broken because of the weak ciphers demanded by US export control and poor protocol design [300, 1876]. Since 2004, an improved system called WPA2 uses AES encryption. The key for each access point is typically printed on a card that fits into the back of the router.

Should WiFi networks be seen as untrusted? The reason to set a password is more to prevent third parties using your bandwidth or quota, rather than the risk of pharming. Many people in the UK or America find it convenient to have an open network for guests to use, and so that you and your neighbours can use each others' networks as backups. In countries where you pay for download bandwidth, home router passwords are mostly set. In some, like India, it's against the law to run an open WiFi access point (terrorists who mounted an attack in Bombay in 2008 used them to call home unobtrusively). Having the key on a card is a neat example of usable security design: the householder can make their network as open or as secure as needed by pinning the card on the wall or by locking it up.

WiFi security is still somewhat fragile. *Universal Plug and Play* (UPnP) lets any device in a network punch a hole through the router's firewall; DHS has been recommending since 2013 that people turn it off. However now that many devices and domestic appliances come with an attached cloud service, that's hard. It's used along with *WiFi Protected Setup* (WPS) which lets you enrol gadgets on your network with a simple button press. You can set a PIN but there have been a couple of attacks found on the mechanism.

Businesses may have to take a bit more care. In March 2007, retail chain TJ Maxx reported that some 45.7 million credit card numbers had been stolen from its systems; the Wall Street Journal reported that an insecure WiFi connection in St Paul, Mn., was to blame [1511]. Banks sued the company, and eventually settled for $41m [789].

Patching is an issue. For example, in March 2020 we learned of the Kr00k vulnerability in Broadcom WiFi chips which will get patched in Macs and iPhones but probably not in wireless routers or older Android phones [800]. As for the great majority of IoT devices, from toys through home appliances, they won't get patched, ever.

21.5.2.2 Bluetooth

Bluetooth is another short-range wireless protocol, aimed at *personal area networks*, such as linking a headset to a phone, or a phone in your pocket to a hands-free interface in your car. It's also used to connect cameras and phones to laptops, keyboards to PCs and so on. Like WiFi, the first versions of the protocol turned out to have flaws [1103, 1716]. From version 2.1 (released in 2007), Bluetooth has supported Secure Simple Pairing, which uses elliptic-curve Diffie-Hellman to thwart passive eavesdropping attacks. Man-in-the-middle attacks are dealt with by generating a six-digit number for numerical comparison. However, because one or both of the devices might lack a keyboard or screen (or both), it's also possible for the number to be generated at one device and entered as a passkey at another; and there's a 'just works' mode that's not protected against middleperson attack. What's more, the data may or may not be signed, giving a total of about ten different combinations of confidentiality, integrity and resistance to man-in-the-middle attack; and a number of attacks have been found, some inspired by NSA tools listed in the Snowden disclosures [1638]. Again, patching is an issue. In 2018, Eli Biham found that many implementations could be fooled by a man-in-the-middle supplying an invalid elliptic curve to the authentication protocol [245], and in 2020 Daniele Antonioli and colleagues discovered a variant of the mig-in-the-middle attack where you just reflect the challenge from a bluetooth device back to it, claiming that you're now the challenger and the target device is the responder [126]. So if you have a device with a bluetooth chip that hasn't been patched, it may be vulnerable.

21.5.2.3 HomePlug

HomePlug is a protocol used for communication over the mains power cables. HomePlug AV is widely used in WiFi extenders: you plug one station into your router or cable modem, and another gives a remote WiFi access point at the other end of your house. (Declaration of interest: I was one of the protocol's designers.) We were faced with the same design constraints as the Bluetooth team: not all devices have keyboards or screens, and we needed to keep costs low. We decided to offer only two modes of operation: secure mode, in which the user manually enters into their network controller a unique AES key that's printed on the device label, and 'simple connect' mode in which the keys are exchanged without authentication. The keys aren't even encrypted in this mode; its purpose is not to provide security but to prevent wrong associations, such as when a device wrongly mates with a network next door [1438]. However many vendors just support the 'simple connect' mode and end up with a policy of trust on first use, as already mentioned in section 4.7.1. Others sell extenders in pairs, with keys already installed. There are variants for smart meters to communicate with substations, and for electricity utilities to provide broadband to the home over the power line (though these are not widely used because of radio frequency interference). Vendors also customised the product in various ways to make it incompatible with competitors. As a result of this mess, little reliance can be placed on the key management.

21.5.2.4 VPNs

Virtual private networks (VPNs) typically do encryption and authentication at the IP layer using a protocol suite known as IPsec. This defines a *security association* as the combination of keys, algorithms and parameters used to protect a particular packet stream. Protected packets may be just authenticated, or encrypted too; in the former case, an authentication header is added that protects data integrity, while in the latter the packet is also encrypted and encapsulated in other packets. There's also an *Internet Key Exchange* (IKE) protocol to set up keys and negotiate parameters, and we may infer from Ed Snowden's disclosures that the standard default settings of this (with 1024-bit Diffie-Hellman) are insecure.

VPNs are offered by firewall vendors so that by installing one of their boxes in each branch between the local LAN and the router, all the internal traffic can pass encrypted over the Internet. Individual workers' laptops and home

PCs can also join a VPN given appropriate software. VPNs are also offered commercially, and are used for example by people and firms in countries like Iran and China to circumvent the national firewall.

21.6 CAs and PKI

As we discussed in section 5.7.4, the pioneers of public-key cryptography developed a vision of certificates that would bind public keys to the names or roles of the organisations, people or devices that controlled the corresponding private keys. Initially it was thought that governments or phone companies would do this, but they were too slow. During the dotcom boom, entrepreneurs set up *certificate authorities* (CAs) and software firms such as Microsoft and Netscape embedded their public keys into their browsers. There followed a gold rush as the CAs bought each other and consolidated; investors hoped that every device would need a public-key certificate, so you'd need to pay Verisign ten bucks every two years to renew the certificate on your toaster, or it wouldn't talk to your fridge.

Once that foolishness died down, the world's governments moved to get their own CAs' root certificates into the browsers for intelligence and surveillance purposes. As people moved to web services like Gmail, security agencies developed tools to do man-in-the-middle attacks, and as TLS was used to encrypt password entry (and later, the whole session), this meant having a CA that would produce a certificate on `www.gmail.com` for a security agency public key that the target's browser would accept. In fact, at a panel discussion at Financial Cryptography 2011, I asked the man from Mozilla how come, when I updated Firefox the previous day, it had put back a certificate I'd removed for Tubitak – a Turkish intelligence organisation. At this point a man stood up in the audience and shouted 'How dare you insult my country! Tubitak is not an intelligence agency – it is a research organisation!' The man from Mozilla shrugged and said wryly, 'Now you see how hard certificate governance is.'

Later that year came the DigiNotar scandal. DigiNotar was a Dutch CA which was found to have issued wildcard certificates for Gmail. Iranian agents had hacked it in order to monitor 300,000 Gmail users in Iran; sanctions meant that, unlike Turkey, they could not just have their government certificate installed in the major browsers. Mozilla and Google promptly put DigiNotar to death by removing its root certificates; Microsoft and Apple followed quickly. This caused real disruption in the Netherlands, many of whose online government services used DigiNotar certificates, and had to scramble to get others. It turned out that there had been earlier attacks on another CA, Comodo, but that company claimed to have revoked all its wrongly-issued certificates. Since then, there has been increasing pressure on CAs and auditors from the browsers' root stores.

There is frequent semantic confusion between 'public (key infrastructure)' and '(public key) infrastructure'. In the first, the infrastructure can be used by whatever new applications come along; I'll call this an *open PKI*. In the second, it can't; I'll call this a *closed PKI*. If you're building a service that government agencies are likely to attack, then it may be a good idea to keep your PKI closed, with a CA that runs on your own premises – so you get to know of any warrants. I advise firms who maintain software that's installed on many millions of machines to use a private CA for their code signing keys.

PKI has a number of intrinsic limitations, many of which we discussed in the chapter on distributed systems. Naming is difficult, and the more applications rely on a certificate, the shorter its useful life will be. You can sometimes simplify things by removing unnecessary names: rather than one certificate saying 'Ross Anderson's key is KR' and another saying 'Ross Anderson has the right to administer x.foo.com' you might just say 'KR has the right to administer x.foo.com.'

This is an aspect of the 'one key or many' debate. Should I expect to have a single digital credential to replace each of the metal keys, credit cards, swipe access cards and other tokens that I currently carry around? Or should each of them be replaced by a different credential? Multiple keys protect the customer: I don't want to have to use a key with which I can remortgage my house to buy my lunchtime sandwich. As we saw in the chapter on banking and bookkeeping, it's easy to dupe people into signing a message by having the equipment display another one.

Now the standard PKI machinery (the X.509 protocol suite) was developed to provide an electronic replacement for the telephone book, so it started off by assuming that everyone will have a unique name and a unique key in an open PKI architecture.

This in turn leads to issues of trust, of which there are many.

- If you remove one of the hundreds of root certificates from Firefox, then Mozilla silently replaces it; Windows comes with even more root certificates – but you can't delete them at all. In each case, you have to know how to mark a certificate as untrusted.
- There have been some interesting effects where a government that had its cert in Windows but not in other browsers (such as Thailand's, after the military coup in 2014) had to resort to different surveillance methods for Mac users [1557].
- Many firms use certs that are out-of-date, or that correspond to the wrong company, often because the firm's marketing department got a contractor to run some promotion or another. As a result, users have been trained to ignore security warnings, and only a small minority used to pay attention to them [842]. Recently browsers such as Firefox have made it harder to click past warnings.

- Certs bind a company name to a DNS name, but their vendors are usually not authorities on either; they hand out certificates after checking that the applicant can answer an email sent to that domain, or put up a web page with a CA challenge on it. Things are slightly better with 'extended validation' certificates[5], but even they aren't foolproof.
- On their 'certification practice statements' CAs go out of their way to deny all liability.
- Certificate revocation is an issue. The original idea was that anyone relying on a cert could download a *certificate revocation list* (CRL) from the CA and check any cert on which they were about to rely. However, this vitiated much of the benefit of public-key cryptography by requiring online operation for high assurance. In addition, users of some systems (particularly US government ones) had to download large CRLs every time they started up their systems, leading to delay and network congestion. Since about 2013, people have moved to the *Online Certificate Status Protocol* (OCSP), a more efficient protocol for online status checking.

Behind all this mess lies, as usual, security economics. During the dotcom boom in the 1990s, the SSL protocol (as TLS then was) won out over a more complex and heavyweight protocol called SET, because it placed less of a burden on developers [111]. The costs of compliance were dumped on the users – who are often unable to cope [524]. Much of the engineering around CAs and certs since then has been playing catchup.

The big issues at the time of writing are certificate lifetime; LetsEncrypt; and certificate transparency.

The maximum permitted lifetime of a certificate, if it's to be accepted by the main browsers, has steadily reduced from 8 years to 3 years to 27 months. Ballots in 2017 and 2019 proposed a cut to 13 months [1584] and in 2020 Apple forced the issue by declaring that from September, its devices would no longer accept any certs valid for longer than 398 days [1448]. This will force many websites to refresh their certificates; it will be interesting to see how firms flush out all the certs in DNS. (It will also widen the gap between systems with annual certs and some industrial and IoT systems where certs have to last for years because of the difficulty of software upgrade.)

Getting certs used to be difficult as you had to go shopping for one, prove you controlled your domain, get the cert, upload it to your server, change the configuration and then test it all. The change maker here has been a nonprofit, the Internet Security Research Group (ISRG) which provides certs for free and by February 2020 had issued a billion of them. Making certs free allowed full

[5]These used to bring up a green padlock in your browser, though this is being discontinued in Chromium from v 76 in 2020 after research showed that nobody paid any attention.

automation, which keeps costs down: their 'LetsEncrypt' CA supports 100m sites on a budget of $3m pa. LetsEncrypt set out to make deploying certs easy, and the impact has been real: 20% of browser connections are still in plaintext, but this is down from 60% four years ago. This service started in 2015, two years after the Snowden revelations. Their automated certificate management environment is now standardised as RFC8555, so commercial CAs are using it too. There's a transparency log and the system has no manual override, so there's some assurance that they have never been compelled to issue a cert. (In fact, the NSA uses their certs.) At November 2019, they were the largest CA, with 112m certs for 188m domains; they had 5% of the top hundred sites but 35% of the top million. Their scale means that mistakes affect lots of sites; in March 2020, a bug in their software meant that 3 million certificates covering 12 million server names had to be replaced [590].

Following the attacks on Comodo and DigiNotar, work started on mechanisms to block maliciously issued certificates. Certificate transparency sets out to do this by maintaining logs of all the certificates seen in the wild for each domain, so that domain owners can rapidly spot certs that should not have been issued for their domain. Google launched the first certificate transparency log in 2013 and Chrome started insisting on such logs for extended validation certificates in 2015. Google found that Symantec had issued certificates for a number of domains (including their own) without the domain owner's knowledge [1790], and made certificate transparency mandatory for all CAs in 2018.

21.7 Topology

The topology of a network is the pattern in which its nodes are connected, and this can be a significant component of the security architecture.

- A utility might have a number of islands, each containing a generator or substation with dozens to hundreds of devices on a trusted network, connected in turn via a specialised firewall and a VPN to a network control centre.
- A cloud service provider might have tens of thousands of machines in a data centre, with hierarchies of certificates issued both by the provider and its tenants determining which VMs or containers on which machines can communicate with each other. And while the internal network may be untrusted, in the sense that network location plays no role in access control decisions, it may be shielded from DDoS attacks by front-end systems.
- Classified systems used by governments may have quite large trusted networks operating at elevated levels, with separate LANs in buildings.

More complex topologies can be found where nodes are users and edges are their presence in each others' address books. Social-network analysis has been applied to disciplines from epidemiology through criminology and the study of how new technologies diffuse, to the study of harms transmitted directly between users, such as macro viruses [1435]. Social networks can be modelled by a graph with a power-law distribution of vertex order; a small number of well-connected nodes help make the network resilient against random failure, and easy to navigate. Yet they also make such networks vulnerable to targeted attack. Remove the well-connected nodes, and the network is easily disconnected [37]. Dictators have known this intuitively; Stalin consolidated his rule by killing the richer peasants, Pol Pot killed intellectuals, while William the Conqueror killed the Saxon gentry. Now we have quantitative models, they help explain why revolutionaries have tended to organise themselves in cells [1375]; by doing traffic analysis against just a few well-connected organisers, a police force can identify a surprising number of members of a dissident organisation – unless the dissidents organised in a cell structure in the first place [510].

21.8 Summary

Preventing and detecting attacks that are launched over networks is the core of a modern CISO's job. It's difficult because it involves a huge range of attack types and security technologies. It can lead to newsworthy failures. There is unlikely to be any magic solution, though a lot of things can help. Each new advance opens up new things to worry about; for example, cloud services may shift much of the network security task to a provider, but make configuration management more critical. Overall, the problems are so complex and messy that managing them needs a whole-system approach with automation.

Hacking techniques depend partly on the opportunistic exploitation of vulnerabilities introduced accidentally by the major vendors, and partly on techniques to social-engineer people into running untrustworthy code. However these have developed into a whole ecosystem of bad guys, which a security engineer also needs to study and understand.

Research problems

In 2000, the centre of gravity in network security research was technical: we were busy looking for new attacks on protocols and applications as the potential for denial-of-service attacks started to become clear. By 2010, there was much more discussion of economics and policy: of how changing liability rules might make things better [98]. By 2020, there is much more work on metrics: on measuring the actual wickedness that goes on, and feeding this not just into the policy debate but also into law enforcement. At the operational level, the game is about automation and integration – about enabling large firms to process large quantities of threat intelligence and network surveillance information, turn it into actionable intelligence, and measure how effectively the network security team is doing its job.

Further reading

The early classic on Internet security was written by Steve Bellovin and Bill Cheswick, with Avi Rubin joining them for the second edition [222]. The seminal work on viruses is by Fred Cohen [452], while Java security is discussed by Li Gong (who designed it) [784]. For BGP security, see our 2011 ENISA report: the full Monty is over two hundred pages, designed for people starting a PhD in network security, but there's a shorter executive summary too [1910].

For a more detailed overview of malware, I might suggest Wenke Lee's Cybok survey paper [1139]; and Sanjah Jha's Cybok survey of network security provides more detail of IPSEC as well as ethernet and port-based security [985].

I'm not aware of any good overview of the certification authority ecosystem. You might start with the 2004 oral history interview with Jim Bidzos, the founder of Verisign [241]. The initial goal of Microsoft and Netscape was to jump-start electronic commerce on the worldwide web; certificate use then spread to passwords and software updates, and when Javascript came along, the same origin principle shifted trust to websites. Many other players jumped in, with some government agencies trying to undermine the CA ecosystem and others trying to reinforce it. There's conflict between technical security goals and legal goals, as well as between auditors and regulators. So there are quite separate views on CA security from WebTrust (the American and Canadian accountants) and ETSI (the most relevant European standards body). For more detail, a presentation by Ryan Sleevi on what's wrong with the ecosystem [1789] has many pointers for those who want to dig into the current problems, both technical and operational, and their background.

CHAPTER

22

Phones

I rarely had to resort to a technical attack. Companies can spend millions of dollars toward technological protections and that's wasted if somebody can basically call someone on the telephone and either convince them to do something on the computer that lowers the computer's defenses or reveals the information they were seeking.

– KEVIN MITNICK

Privacy is not about hiding – privacy is about human growth and agency.

– CHRISTOPHER WYLIE

22.1 Introduction

The protection of phones, the app ecosystem they support, and the telecommunications networks on which they rely, is central to the modern world. First, in the decade after the launch of the iPhone, the world moved from accessing the Internet via PCs or laptops to using smartphones instead, and added billions of new users too. Whole business sectors are being revolutionised as they move to apps; of the 5.5bn adults on earth, 5bn have phones, and 4bn of them have smartphones. Second, the new generation of connected devices, from smart speakers to cars, are very much like phones, often using the same platforms and sharing the same vulnerabilities. Third, phones now provide the bedrock for authentication: if you forget your password, you get an SMS to recover it – so someone who can steal an SMS from you may be able to spend your money. Fourth, mobile networks are critical to other infrastructure: electricity companies rely on mobile phones to direct their engineers when repairing faults, so if the phone system goes down a few hours after the power does, there's a real problem. Finally, there's public policy. While smartphones have revolutionised the lives of the third-world poor by giving access to services such as banking, they also facilitate surveillance and control.

The phone ecosystem is mind-numbingly complex, and to master it the security engineer needs not just general security knowledge such as crypto and access controls, and knowledge of specific platforms such as Android and iOS, but of mobile and fixed-line networks too. The history of telecomms security is instructive. Early attacks were carried out on phone companies by enthusiasts ('phone phreaks') to get free calls; then the phone system's vulnerabilities were exploited by crooks to evade police wiretapping; then premium rate calls were introduced, which brought in large-scale fraud; then when telecomms markets were liberalized, some phone companies started conducting attacks on each other's customers; and some phone companies have even attacked each other. At each stage the defensive measures undertaken tended to be inadequate for various reasons. The same cycle of exploitation then repeated with the Internet – amateur hackers followed by debates about wiretaps followed by fraud and tussles between companies and users; and as the two came together we've seen lots of complex interactions. Now we see rapidly growing phone-based fraud against banking systems, bad apps stealing people's personal information and high policy debates on the national security implications of 5G infrastructure. How is the security engineer to navigate this?

The security of the phone as a platform depends on a number of things, which I'll deal with under two main headings.

1. First, there's whether the network to which it's attached has somehow been compromised, whether by some kind of wiretap or by a SIM swap attack which undermines the phone's network identity.
2. Second, there's the question of whether the device itself has been compromised, whether by malware rooting the operating system, or by the installation of a potentially hostile application or library.

Phone security used to be all about the first of these, but by now it's mostly about the second.

22.2 Attacks on phone networks

The abuse of communications goes back centuries. Before Sir Rowland Hill invented the postage stamp, postage was paid by the recipient. Unsolicited mail became a huge problem – especially for famous people – so recipients were allowed to inspect a letter and reject it rather than paying for it. People soon worked out schemes to send short messages on the covers of letters which their correspondents rejected. Regulations were brought in to stop this, but were never really effective [1462].

A second set of abuses developed with the telegraph. Early optical telegraphs worked using semaphores or heliographs; people would bribe operators, or 'hack the local loop' by observing the last heliograph station through a telescope, to learn which horse had won before the local bookmaker did. Here too, attempts to legislate the problem away were a failure [1821]. The problems got worse when the electric telegraph brought costs down; the greater volumes of communication, and the greater flexibility that got built into and on top of the service, led to more complexity and more abuse.

The telephone was to be no different.

22.2.1 Attacks on phone-call metering

Early phone-call metering systems were open to creative abuse.

- In the 1950s, the operator in some systems had to listen for the sound of coins dropping on a metal plate to tell that a callbox customer had paid, so people practised hitting the coinbox with a piece of metal that struck the right note.
- Initially, the operator had no way of knowing which phone a call had come from, so she had to ask the caller his number. He could give the number of someone else – who would then be charged. Operators started calling back to verify the number for international calls, so people worked out social engineering attacks ('This is IBM here, we'd like to book a call to San Francisco and because of the time difference can our Managing Director take it at home tonight? His number's xxx-yyyy'). So payphone lines had a warning to alert the operator. But the UK implementation had a bug: a customer who had called the operator from a payphone could depress the rest briefly, whereupon he'd be reconnected (often to different operator), with no warning this time that the call was from a payphone. He could then call anywhere and bill it to any local number.
- Early systems also signalled the entry of a coin by one or more pulses, each of which consisted of the insertion of a resistance in the line followed by a brief open circuit. At a number of colleges, enterprising students installed 'magic buttons' which could simulate this in a callbox in the student union so people could phone for free. (The bill in this case went to the student union, for which the magic button was not quite so amusing.)

Attacks on toll metering have continued for over a century now. Most countries moved their payphones from coins to chip cards in the 1990s to cut the costs of coin collection and vandalism, but as I remarked in section 18.5, the design was often poor at first and villains sold lots of bogus phone cards until it got fixed.

Other attacks involve what's called *clip-on*: physically attaching a phone to someone else's line to steal their service. In the 1970s through the 1990s, when international phone calls were very expensive, some foreign students would clip a phone on to a residential line in order to call home, and the unsuspecting homeowner could get a huge bill. The Norwegian phone company had customer premises equipment authenticate itself to the exchange before a dial tone was given [996].

The UK phone company was not as enlightened as its Norwegian counterpart, and had a policy of denying that wiretaps were possible, so it could just collect the call charges from victim households. This occasionally caused collateral damage, as a family in Cramlington was to find out. The first sign they had of trouble was hearing a conversation on their line. The next was a visit from the police who said there'd been complaints of nuisance phone calls. The complainants were three ladies, all of whom had a number one digit different from a number to which this family had supposedly made a huge number of calls. When the family's bill was examined, there were also calls to clusters of numbers that turned out to be payphones; these had started quite suddenly at the same time as the nuisance calls. When the family had complained later to the phone company about a fault, their connection was rerouted, and this had solved the problem.

A report from the phone company's maintenance engineer noted that the family's line had been tampered with at the distribution cabinet, but this was against doctrine and the company later claimed the report was in error. It turned out that a drug dealer had lived close by, and it seemed a reasonable inference that he'd tapped their line in order to call his couriers at the payphones. By using an innocent family's phone line instead of his own, he not only saved on the phone bill, but also had a better chance of evading police surveillance. But both the police and the local phone company refused to go into the house where the dealer had lived, claiming it was too dangerous – even though the dealer had by now got six years in jail. The Norwegian phone company declined an invitation to testify about clip-on for the defence. The upshot was that the subscriber was convicted of making harassing phone calls, in a case widely believed to have been a miscarriage of justice.

Stealing dial tone from cordless phones was another variant on the theme. In the 1990s, this became so widespread in Paris that France Telecom broke with phone company tradition and announced that it was happening, claiming that the victims were using illegally imported cordless phones which were easy to spoof [1099]. That was a bit cheeky, as most equipment seems to simply send a handset serial number to the base station rather than using the DECT security mechanisms, which use cryptography patented by the French company Alcatel. These mechanisms were proprietary but turned out to have multiple weaknesses, as Erik Tews documented in 2012 after reverse engineering them [1874]. DECT authentication is based on a weak block cipher; confidentiality uses a weak stream cipher (a slightly more complicated version of A5/1 which I describe below in section 22.3.1), which can be broken with typically 2^{34} effort; there are weak random number generators; while protocol failures include a man-in-the middle attack, and a replay attack where you make a silent call to collect keystream to decrypt a call you recorded earlier. It's said that the German intelligence services used DECT to train recruits in signal collection and cryptanalysis. Since Tews' work was published, the DECT standards body suggests using AES instead, but it's not clear how many vendors can be bothered. The takeaway is that a cordless phone gives you no security against a capable opponent nearby, and as the standard emerged during the Crypto Wars of the 1990s you should have expected nothing else. As for clip-on fraud, it has largely disappeared since services like Skype and WhatsApp made long-distance calls free.

Social engineering gives another way in. A crook calls you pretending to be from AT&T and asks whether you made a large number of calls to Peru on your calling card. When you deny this, they say that, in order to reverse out the charges, can you confirm that your card number is 123-456-7890-6543? No, you say (if you're not really alert), it's 123-456-7890-5678. Now 123-456-7890 is your phone number and 5678 your password, so that crook can now bill calls to you.

Premium-rate phone services grew rapidly during the 1990s, leading scamsters to develop all sorts of tricks to get people to call them: pager messages, job ads, fake emergency messages about relatives, 'low cost' calling cards with 0900 access numbers, you name it. Indeed the business of tricking people into calling premium numbers enabled crooks to hone the techniques they now use in phishing attacks. The 809 area code for the Caribbean used to be a favourite cover for crooks targeting US subscribers; many people weren't aware that 'domestic' numbers (numbers within the USA's +1 international direct dialling code) include countries other than the relatively cheap USA and Canada. Even though many people have now learned that +1 809 is 'foreign' and more expensive, the introduction of still more Caribbean area codes, such as +1 345 for the Cayman Islands, has made it even harder to spot such scams.

Phone companies advised their customers 'Do not return calls to unfamiliar telephone numbers' – but how practical is that? Just as banks now train their customers to click on links in marketing emails and thus make them vulnerable to phishing attacks, so I've had junk marketing calls from my phone company – even though I'm on the do-not-call list. Governments typically set up weak regulators who avoid trying to regulate premium-rate operators, claiming it's too hard; and from time to time it all blows up. In the late 2000s, all the major UK TV companies (including the state-owned BBC) ended up getting fined for getting viewers to phone in and vote, in all sorts of shows. Many of these are recorded, so the calls were futile [1325]. Phone scams by broadcast stations have been a recurring problem worldwide since radio broadcasting took off in the 1920s, and got worse when TV went mainstream in the 1950s [2052]. It's also a recurring pattern that the biggest scams are often run by 'respectable' companies rather than by Russian gangsters.

22.2.2 Attacks on signaling

The term 'phone phreaking' refers to attacks on signaling as well as pure toll fraud. Until the 1980s, phone companies used signalling systems that worked *in-band* by sending tone pulses in the same circuit that carried the speech. The first attack I've heard of dates back to 1952, and by the mid-to-late 1960s many enthusiasts in both America and Britain had worked out ways of rerouting calls. One of the pioneers, Joe Engresia, had perfect pitch and discovered as a child that he could make free phone calls by whistling a tone he'd heard in the background of a long-distance call. His less gifted colleagues used home-made tone generators, of which the most common were called *blue boxes*. The trick was to call an 0800 number and then send a 2600Hz tone that would *clear down* the line at the far end – that is, disconnect the called party while leaving the caller with a trunk line connected to the exchange. The caller could now enter the number he really wanted and be connected without paying. Phone phreaking was one of the roots of the computer hacker culture that took root in the Bay Area and was formative in the development and evolution of personal computers [1224]. Steve Jobs and Steve Wozniak first built blue boxes before they diversified into computers [722].

Phone phreaking started out with a strong ideological element. In those days most phone companies were monopolies – large, faceless and unresponsive. In America, AT&T was such an abusive monopoly that the courts eventually broke it up; most phone companies in Europe were government departments. People whose domestic phone lines had been involved in a service theft found they were stuck with the charges. If the young man who had courted your daughter was (unknown to you) a phone phreak who hadn't paid for the calls he made to her, you would suddenly find the company trying to extort either the young man's name or a payment. Phone companies were also aligned with state security. Phone phreaks in many countries discovered signalling codes or switch features that would enable the police or the spies to tap your phone from the comfort of their desks, without having to send out a lineman to clip on a wiretap. Back in the days of the Vietnam war and student protests, this was inflammatory stuff. Phone phreaks were counterculture heroes, while phone companies were hand-in-hand with the forces of darkness.

As there was no way to stop blue-box attacks so long as telephone signalling was carried in-band, the phone companies spent years and many billions of dollars moving to a signaling system called SS7, which is out-of-band – in effect on a private Internet to which normal subscribers had no easy access. Gradually, region by region, the world was closed off to blue-box attacks. This forced attackers to become insiders.

22.2.3 Attacks on switching and configuration

Once telephone exchange switches became programmable, a second wave of attacks targeted the computers. Typically these were Unix machines on a LAN in the exchange, which also had machines with administrative functions such as scheduling maintenance. By hacking one of these less well guarded machines, a phreak could go across the LAN and break into the switching equipment – or into other secondary systems such as subscriber databases. For a survey of PacBell's experience of this, see [390]; for Bellcore's, see [1061].

Using these techniques, unlisted phone numbers could be found, calls could be forwarded without a subscriber's knowledge, and all sorts of mischief became possible. A Californian phone phreak called Kevin Poulsen got root access to many of PacBel's switches and other systems in 1985–88: this apparently involved burglary as much as hacking (he was eventually convicted of conspiring to possess fifteen or more counterfeit, unauthorized and stolen access devices). He did petty things like obtaining unlisted phone numbers for celebrities and winning a Porsche from Los Angeles radio station KIIS-FM. Each week KIIS would give a Porsche to the 102nd caller, so Poulsen and his accomplices blocked out all calls to the radio station's 25 phone lines save their own, made the 102nd call and collected the Porsche. He was also accused of unlawful wiretapping and espionage; these charges were dismissed. In fact, the FBI came down on him so heavily that there were allegations of an improper relationship between the agency and the phone companies, along the lines of 'you scratch our backs with wiretaps when needed, and we'll investigate your hacker problems' [690].

The FBI's sensitivity does highlight the fact that attacks on phone company computers are used by foreign intelligence agencies to conduct remote wiretaps. Some of the attacks mentioned in [390] were from overseas, and the possibility that such tricks might be used to crash the whole phone system in the context of an information warfare attack worried the NSA [727, 1108]. Countries that import their telephone exchanges rather than building their own just have to assume that their telephone switchgear has vulnerabilities known to the supplier's government. (During the invasion of Afghanistan in 2001, Kabul had two exchanges: an old electromechanical one and a new electronic one. The USAF bombed only the first.)

Many real attacks involved insiders, who misconfigured systems to provide free calls through special numbers. This didn't matter much when the phone company's marginal cost of servicing an extra phone call was zero, but with the proliferation of value-added services in the 1990s, and with deregulation giving rise to cash payments between phone companies, it got serious [461]. In a hack reminiscent of Poulsen, two staff at British Telecom were dismissed after they each won ten tickets for Concorde from a phone-in offer at which only one randomly selected call in a thousand was supposed to get through [1918].

As for outsiders, the other 'arch-hacker' apart from Poulsen was Kevin Mitnick, who got arrested and convicted following a series of break-ins which made him too the target of an FBI manhunt. They initially thought he was a foreign agent who was abusing the US phone system to wiretap sensitive US targets. As I mentioned in Chapter 3, he testified after his release from prison that almost all of his exploits had involved social engineering. He wrote a book on deception that became a classic [1327]. In congressional testimony, he came up with the quote at the head of this chapter: "Companies can spend millions of dollars toward technological protections and that's wasted if somebody can basically call someone on the telephone and either convince them to do something on the computer that lowers the computer's defenses or reveals the information they were seeking". Phone companies, like other firms, are vulnerable to careless insiders as well as malicious insiders.

Fast-forward to 2020, and one worrying development is the growth of switching exploits. A number of telcos now give SS7 access to corporate customers, for example if they want to send bulk SMS messages to authenticate customers. Access to the switch fabric lets them play the kind of games that Poulsen and Mitnick got up to in the 1980s. For example, if I want to hack your Gmail account, I send a message to your mobile service provider saying that you've roamed into my network. I then start an account recovery at Google, which sends an SMS to reset your password. As I noted in sections 3.4.1 and 12.7.4, this is now in active use for bank fraud; the first instance of its use to steal money from bank customers was in Germany in 2016, when they were moved without their knowledge to another network; there was a similar fraud in London in 2019 [485]. SS7 has also been abused by Saudi Arabian MNOs to track Saudi dissidents in the USA [1056]. Most major telcos in developed countries now use some SS7 firewalling, and allow or deny remote access depending on their roaming agreements. If there is such an agreement, a firm given SS7 access by the remote telco can either steal a phone to get its SMS messages, or get it to do premium fraud. Forensics can be hard if there's a complaint from a single user; the best you can do may be to look for roaming charges. If there are a thousand cases the bank might be motivated to go to the operator. But banks and their bulk SMS contractors are paying operators for SS7 access, opening up the formerly closed system. In short, we used to think that attacks involving SS7 were the preserve of nation states, but that is no longer the case.

22.2.4 Insecure end systems

The next major vulnerabilities of modern phone networks were insecure terminal equipment and feature interaction.

There have been many exploits of voicemail, whether implemented as an answering machine on customer premises or, as common now, a cloud service. Exploits start with tricking someone into calling a premium-rate number, and escalate to journalists and others hacking voicemail via the default PINs that many people don't bother to change. The most notorious case was the murder, on the 21st of March 2002, of the English schoolgirl Millie Dowler. In 2011 it transpired that an investigator working for the News of the World, then the UK flagship of the Murdoch empire, had hacked Millie's voicemail, interfered with the police investigation in the process, and may have caused some of her messages to be deleted, giving Millie's family a false hope that she might still be alive. The resulting outrage led to the closure of the newspaper, several criminal convictions – including the imprisonment in 2014 of David Cameron's publicist Andy Coulson, a former News of the World editor – and a public inquiry into press standards.

But the really big frauds that exploit insecure end systems tend to target companies and government departments, as they have the ability to pay big phone bills. Attacks on corporate *private branch exchange* systems (PBXes) had become big business by the mid-1990s and cost business billions of dollars a year [468]. PBXes are usually supplied with facilities for *refiling* calls, also known as *direct inward system access* (DISA). The company's sales force could call in to an 0800 number, enter a PIN or password, and then call out again taking advantage of the low rates a large company can get for long-distance calls. As you'd expect, these PINs become known and get traded by villains [1354]. The result is known as *dial-through* fraud.

In many cases, the PINs are set to a default by the manufacturer, and never changed by the customer. Many PBX designs also have fixed engineering passwords that allow remote maintenance access, and prudent people reckon that any PBX will have at least one back door to give easy access to law enforcement and intelligence agencies (it's said, as a condition of export licensing). Such features get discovered and abused. In one case, the PBX at Scotland Yard was compromised and used by criminals to refile calls, costing the Yard a million pounds, for which they sued their telephone installer. The crooks were never caught [1871]. One of the criminals' motivations is to get access to communications that will not be tapped. Businesses who're the victims of such crimes find the police reluctant to investigate, and the phone companies aren't helpful – they don't like having their bills disputed [1627].

In a notorious case, Chinese gangsters involved in labour market racketeering – smuggling illegal immigrants from Fujian, China, into Britain – hacked the PBX of an English district council and used it to refile over a million pounds' worth of calls to China. The gang was tackled by the police after a number of its labourers died; they were picking shellfish in Morecambe Bay when the tide came in and drowned them. The council had by now discovered the discrepancy in its phone bills and sued the phone company for its money back. The phone company argued that it wasn't to blame, even though it had supplied the insecure PBX. Here, too, the gangsters were interested not just in saving money but in evading surveillance. (Indeed, they routed their calls to China via a compromised PBX in Albania, so the cross-border segment of the call, which is most likely to be monitored by the agencies, was between numbers their collection systems wouldn't touch; the same trick seems to have been used in the Scotland Yard case, where the crooks made their calls via the USA.)

Such cases apart, dial-through fraud is mostly driven by premium rate services and the crooks are in cahoots with premium line operators. Most companies don't understand the need to guard their 'dial tone' and don't know how to even if they wanted to. PBXes are typically run by company telecomms managers who know little about security, while the security manager often knows little about phones. This is changing as company phone networks adopt VOIP technologies and merge with the data network. Estimates of the losses from PBX fraud sustained by business worldwide fell from $4.96bn in 2011 to $3.88bn in 2017, with about half the latter figure now VOIP rather than classical PBX [92].

Exploits of insecure end-systems affect domestic subscribers too. Premium-rate mobile malware arrived in 2006, when the Red Browser worm cashed out by sending $5 SMSs to Russia [943]; this scaled up after Android came along, and we'll discuss mobile malware in section 22.4.1.4. And now that phones are used more and more for tasks such as voting, securing entry into apartment buildings, checking that offenders are observing their parole terms, and authenticating financial transactions, more motives are created for ever more creative kinds of mischief, and especially for hacks that defeat caller-line ID. Since the early 2000s, there have been warnings that caller-line ID hacks, SMS spoofing and attacks on the SS7 signaling could be used for fraud. This is now reality, and we'll discuss it in more detail later in this chapter.

22.2.5 Feature interaction

Phone manipulation often involves feature interaction.

- Inmates at the Clallam Bay Correctional Center in Washington state, who were only allowed to make collect calls, found an interesting exploit of a system that the phone company ('Fone America') introduced to handle collect calls automatically. The system would call the dialled number and a synthesised voice would say: "If you will accept a collect call from ... (name of caller) ... please press the number 3 on your telephone twice." Prisoners were supposed to state their name for the machine to record and insert. The system had, as an additional feature, the ability to have the greeting delivered in Spanish. Inmates did so, and when asked to identify themselves, said "If you want to hear this message in English, press 33." This worked often enough that they could get through to corporate PBXes and talk the operator into giving them an outside line. The University of Washington was hit several times by this scam [696].

- Many directory-enquiry services will connect you to the number they've just given you, as a premium service for motorists who can't dial while driving. It can also be used to defeat mechanisms that rely on endpoint identification. Naughty children use it to call sex lines despite call barring, while naughty grown-ups use it to prevent their spouses seeing lovers' numbers on the family phone bill [1458].
- Call forwarding is a source of many scams. In the old days, it was used for pranks, such as kids social-engineering a phone company operator to forward their teacher's calls to a sex line. Nowadays, it can be both professional and nasty. For example, a fraudster may tell a victim to confirm their phone number with the bank by dialing a sequence of digits – which forwards incoming calls to a number controlled by the attacker. So the bank's callback mechanisms are defeated.
- Conference calls can be exploited in all sorts of ways. For example, football hooligans in some countries are placed under a curfew that requires them to be at home during a match, and to prove this by calling the probation service, which verifies their caller ID. So you get your partner to set up a conference call with the probation service and your mobile. If the probation officer asks about the crowd noise, you tell him it's the TV and you can't turn it down or your mates will kill you. (And if he wants to call you back, you get your partner to forward the call.)

22.2.6 VOIP

In *voice over IP* (VOIP), voice traffic is digitised, compressed and routed over the Internet. This had experimental beginnings in the 1970s; products started appearing in the 1990s, and it became big business from the mid-2000s. Nowadays, most traditional phone calls are digitized and sent over IP networks belonging to the phone companies, so in a technical sense almost all phone calls are now 'VOIP'. But though my home phone pretends to be a plain old telephone, my lab phone is now a born-VOIP device that offers conference calling and all sorts of other complicated features that I don't understand.

The most popular VOIP protocol, the Session Initiation Protocol (SIP), has had its share of vulnerabilities [2072] but is mostly attacked through poor configurations, for which many actors are constantly scanning; a PBX can get over a million messages a day trying to register as an extension, and then attempting to call high-cost numbers in less developed countries [1273]. As I noted in section 22.2.4, the VOIP segment of frauds against corporate PBX systems was about $2bn a year by 2017 [92]. The broader interaction with security is complicated. Corporate security policies can result in firewalls refusing to pass VOIP traffic. The current political tussle is over robocalls, which can hide caller ID more easily if they go over VOIP. The FCC voted in 2020 to insist that telcos implement by the end of June 2021 a suite of protocols, STIR/SHAKEN, which authenticate callers over SIP [327]. Another regulatory issue is that governments want emergency calls made through VOIP services to work reliably, and provide information about the location of the caller. But an IP packet stream can come from anywhere, and no-one owns enough of the Internet to guarantee quality of service. And although a VOIP handset looks like a phone and works like a phone, if the power goes off, so does your service. Then you're forced to fall back on the mobile network. So now it's the mobile network rather than the traditional one that is the default emergency system.

22.2.7 Frauds by phone companies

Phone fraud is not just a story of crooked customers committing toll fraud against telcos, and defrauding other customers by exploiting mechanisms that the telcos have no real incentive to harden. There are many scams by unscrupulous telcos. The classic scam is *cramming*, where a rogue phone company bills lots of small sums to unwitting users. Billing was designed in the days when phone companies were monopolies, usually state-owned, and assumes that phone companies trust each other: if company A creates a *call data record* (CDR) saying that a customer of telco B called their subscriber, they just pass it on to telco B, which pays up. (It has no incentive to quibble, as it gets a cut.)

I was myself the victim of an attempt at cramming. On holiday in Barcelona, my wife's bag was snatched, so we called up and cancelled the phone that she'd had in it. Several months later, we got a demand to pay a few tens of dollars roaming charges recently incurred by that SIM card in Spain. In all probability, the Spanish phone company was simply cramming a few charges to a number that they'd seen previously, in the knowledge that they'd usually get away with it. My wife's former MNO insisted that even though she'd cancelled the number, she was still liable for calls billed to it months afterwards and had to pay up. We got out of the charges only because I'd met the company's CEO at an academic seminar and was able to get his private office to fix the problem. Customers without such access usually get the short end of the stick. Indeed, UK phone companies' response to complaints has been to offer customers 'insurance' against fraudulent charges. That they can get away with this is a clear regulatory failure. There are many variants: if you call an 800 number in the USA, the company may say "Can we call you right back?" and if you agree then you're deemed to have accepted the charges, which can be at a high premium rate. The same can happen if you respond to voice prompts as the call progresses.

Another problem is *slamming* – the unauthorized change of a subscriber's service provider without their consent. It would be a mistake to assume that cramming and slamming are just done by small fly-by-night operators. AT&T was one of the worst offenders, having been fined not only for slamming, but for forging signatures of subscribers to make it look as if they had agreed to switch to their service. They got caught when they forged a signature of the deceased spouse of a subscriber in Texas.

Yet another is the exploitation of international calls for premium-rate scams. The abuse of domestic premium-rate numbers led regulators in many countries to force phone companies to offer premium-rate number blocking to subscribers. The telcos got round this by disguising premium rate numbers as international ones. I mentioned scams with Caribbean numbers in section 22.2.1, and many other phone companies from small countries got into the act. Such scams benefit from an international agreement (the Nairobi Convention) that stops phone companies selectively blocking international destinations. Advisories from governments still warn of 'wangiri' scams where you get a call that rings once, in the hope you'll call back – to an international premium number. But these seem to have stopped; an extensive study of robocalls in 2020 found no evidence of them any more [1546]. There are many reasons why scams may be moving away from the telco platform to the app ecosystem, as the interaction between scams and regulation is complex.

By the time smartphones came along, the phone companies had got used to taking a cut of high-value service delivery, ranging from parking meters in London to ferry tickets in Finland. As malware became widespread on mobile phones, the botnet herders who control subverted phones could pay for goods and services by SMS. Many new services were made possible by the smartphone revolution and payment moved from SMS to payments via apps. SMS abuses have got to the point that neither Google nor Apple allows normal apps to send or receive text messages. We might pause to think of the industry's economics. Why have telcos never felt a duty of care towards their customers?

22.2.8 Security economics of telecomms

Phone and cable companies have extremely high fixed costs and very low marginal costs. Building a nationwide network costs billions and yet the cost of handling an additional phone call or movie download is essentially zero. As I discussed in the chapter on economics, this has a couple of implications.

First, there's a tendency towards dominant-firm markets. For many years telephone service was considered in most countries to be a 'natural monopoly' and operated by the government; the main exception was the USA where the old AT&T system was heavily regulated. After the breakup of AT&T following an antitrust case, and Margaret Thatcher's privatisation of BT in the UK, the world moved to a different model, of regulated competition. The details vary from one country to another but, in general, some sectors (such as mobile phones) had a fixed number of allowed competitors; others (such as long-distance provision) were free for companies to compete in; and others (such as local loop provision) remained monopolies but were regulated.

Second, the competitive sectors (such as long-distance calling) saw prices drop quickly to near zero. Some sectors were made competitive by apps: Skype and WhatsApp made international calls essentially free.

In many telecomms markets, the outcome is *confusion pricing* – products are continually churned, with new offerings giving generous introductory discounts to compete with the low-cost providers, but with rates sneakily raised afterwards. There is constant bundling of broadband access with mobile service and TV offerings. If you can be bothered to continually check prices, you can get good deals, but often at the cost of indifferent service. If you don't have the time to keep scrutinising your broadband and mobile phone bills, you can get some unpleasant surprises.

22.3 Going mobile

Since their beginnings as an expensive luxury in 1981, mobile phones have become one of the big technological success stories. By 2020, we now have over five billion subscribers; it's said that over a billion phones were sold in 2019 alone. In developed countries, most people have at least one mobile, and many new electronic services are being built on top of them. Growth has been rapid in developing countries too, where the wireline network is often dilapidated and people used to wait years for phone service. In many places it's the arrival of mobile networks that connected villages to the world. This has brought many benefits, and new crimes too. Both developed steadily as the technology was evolved and deployed.

Mobile phone security has developed as the abuse has. The first generation of mobile phones (1G) used analog signals and the handset simply sent its serial numbers in clear over the air link[1]. So villains built devices to capture these numbers from calls in the neighborhood, or reprogrammed phones to steal ID from other phones nearby. One of the main customers was the *call-sell operation* that would steal phone service and resell it cheaply, often to immigrants

[1]In the US system, there were two of them: one for the equipment, and one for the subscriber.

or students who wanted to call home. The call-sell operators would hang out at known pitches with cloned mobiles, and their customers would queue up to phone home for a few dollars. The call-sell market was complemented by the criminal market for anonymous communications: people hacked mobile phones to use a different identity for each call. Known as *tumblers*, these were particularly hard for the police to track [946]. 1G phones did not encrypt voice traffic, so anyone could casually eavesdrop on calls with a radio receiver, yet despite this the possibility of caller anonymity led to their use in crime. The demand for serial numbers grew rapidly and satisfying it was increasingly difficult, even by snooping at places like airports where lots of mobiles get turned on. So prices rose, and as well as passive listening, active methods started to get used.

Mobile phones are cellular: the operator divides the service area up into cells, each covered by a base station. The mobile uses the base station with the strongest signal, and there are protocols for handing off calls from one cell to another as the customer moves about. Early active attacks consisted of a fake base station, typically at a place with a lot of passing traffic such as a freeway bridge. As phones passed by, they heard a stronger signal and attempted to register by sending their serial numbers and passwords.

Various mechanisms were tried to cut the volume of fraud. Most operators ran intrusion-detection systems to watch out for suspicious patterns of activity, such as too-rapid movement or a rapid increase in call volume or duration. Vodafone also used RF fingerprinting, a military technology in which signal characteristics arising from manufacturing variability in the handset's radio transmitter are used to identify individual devices and tie them to the claimed serial numbers [777].

22.3.1 GSM

The second generation of mobile phones (2G) adopted digital technology. The *Global System for Mobile Communications* (GSM) was founded when 15 companies signed up to the GSM Association in 1987 and secured political support from the EU; service was launched in 1992. The designers of GSM set out to secure the system against cloning and other attacks: their goal was that GSM should be at least as secure as the wireline system. What they did, how they succeeded and where they failed, make an interesting case history.

The industry initially tried to keep secret the cryptographic and other protection mechanisms which form the core of the GSM protocols. This didn't work: some eventually leaked and the rest were discovered by reverse engineering. I'll describe them briefly here. Mobile networks consist of a *radio access network* (RAN) and a *core network* (CN), and each mobile network has two databases, a *home location register* (HLR) that contains the location of its own mobiles, and a *visitor location register* (VLR) for the location of mobiles which have roamed in from other networks. These databases enable incoming calls to be forwarded to the correct cell.

The handsets are commodity items, personalised using a *subscriber identity module* (SIM) – a smartcard you get when you sign up for a network service, and which you load into your handset. The SIM can be thought of as containing three numbers:

1. there may be a personal identification number that you use to unlock the card;
2. there's an *international mobile subscriber identification* (IMSI), a unique number that maps on to your mobile phone number;
3. finally there is a *subscriber authentication key* K_i, a 128-bit number that serves to authenticate that IMSI and is known to your home network.

There is also a handset serial number, the *international mobile equipment identification* (IMEI). The protocol used to authenticate the handset to the network runs as follows (see Figure 22.1). On power-up, the SIM emits the IMSI, which the handset sends to the nearest base station along with the IMEI. The IMSI is relayed to the subscriber's HLR, which generates five *triplets*. Each triplet consists of:

- RAND, a random challenge;
- SRES, a response; and
- K_c, a ciphering key.

The algorithm is that RAND is encrypted under the SIM's authentication key K_i, giving SRES concatenated with K_c:

$$\{RAND\}_{K_i} = (SRES|K_c)$$

The encryption method is up to the issuer; an early standard called Comp128 turned out to be insecure [1975, 1976], so issuers nowadays use hash functions or constructions using AES.

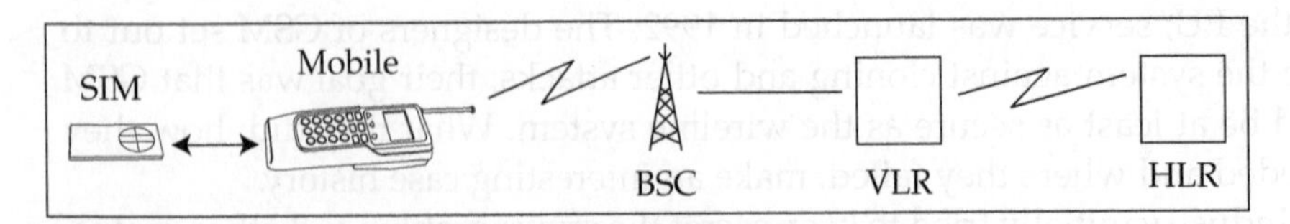

Figure 22.1: GSM authentication system components

Anyway, the triplets are sent to the *base station controller* (BSC), which now presents the first RAND to the mobile. It passes this to the SIM, which computes SRES. The mobile returns this to the base station and if it's correct the mobile and the base station can now communicate using the ciphering key K_c. So the whole authentication protocol runs as in Figure 22.2.

SIM⟶ HLR	IMSI
HLR⟶ BSC	(RAND, SRES, K_c), ...
BSC⟶ SIM	RAND
SIM⟶ BSC	SRES
BSC⟶ mobile	$\{\text{traffic}\}_{K_c}$

Figure 22.2: GSM authentication protocol

There are several vulnerabilities in this protocol. First, the base station isn't authenticated, so it's easy for a wiretapper to use a false base station to intercept calls. Such devices, known as *IMSI catchers* in Europe and *StingRays* in the USA, are now standard law-enforcement equipment[2]. Second, in most countries the communications between base stations and the VLR pass unencrypted on microwave links[3]. This allows bulk interception by intelligence agencies, and in many cases access to the triples needed to spoof or decrypt traffic.

The introduction of GSM caused significant shifts in patterns of crime. The authentication mechanisms made phone cloning difficult, so the villains switched to buying phones using stolen credit cards, using stolen identities or bribing insiders [2037]. Robbery was the next issue, with a spate of media stories about kids being mugged for their phones. Mobile phone crime did indeed increase 190% between 1995 and 2002, but to keep this in context, the number of subscribers went up 600% in the same period [866]. Some of the theft is bullying – kids taking smaller kids' phones; some is insurance fraud by subscribers who've dropped their phones in the toilet and report them as stolen as their insurance doesn't cover accidental damage; but there is a hard core of theft where muggers take phones and sell them to fences. Many of the fences either work at mobile phone shops that have authorised access to tools for reprogramming the IMEI, the serial number in the handset, or else have links to organised criminals who ship the handsets abroad[4].

Prepaid mobile phones appeared from about 1997, enabling the industry to expand rapidly to people without credit ratings, including both poor people in rich countries and everyone in poor countries. By 2008, prepaids made up 90% of the market in Mexico but 15% in the USA. During the 2010s, billions of people got access not just to calls and texts but to online information and payment services.

[2]When 2G was designed, a base station filled a whole room and cost $100k, so it might have seemed reasonable to ignore man-in-the-middle attacks. Nowadays all it takes is a low-cost software radio.

[3]The equipment can encrypt traffic, but the average phone company has no incentive to switch the cryptography on.

[4]In recent smartphone designs, the IMEI is supposed to be unalterable; some Android phones keep it in TrustZone.

Prepaid phones also made anonymous communication practical. The issues include not just evading police wiretapping but fraud, stalking, extortion, bullying and other kinds of harassment. However, prepaid phones only protect you from the police if they don't try very hard. Most criminals don't have any clue of the level of operational discipline needed to stop traffic analysis. As I already remarked, one alleged 9/11 mastermind was caught when he used a prepaid SIM from the same batch as one that had been used by another Al-Qaida member; and after the failed 21/7 London bombings, one would-be bomber fled to Rome, where he was promptly caught. He had changed the SIM in his mobile phone en route; but call records show not just the IMSI from the SIM, but also the IMEI from the handset. If you've got all the world's police after you, just changing the SIM isn't anything like enough. Operational security requires some understanding of how networks operate.

In addition to authentication, 2G was supposed to provide two further kinds of protection – location security and call content confidentiality.

The location security mechanism is that when a mobile is registered to a network, it is issued with a *temporary mobile subscriber identification* (TMSI), which acts as its address in that network. This is a lightweight mechanism; it is defeated trivially by IMSI catchers, which pretend to be a base station in a different network.

2G GSM also provides some call content confidentiality by encrypting the traffic between the handset and the base station once authentication and registration are completed. The speech is digitized, compressed and chopped into packets; each packet is encrypted by xor-ing it with a pseudorandom sequence generated from the ciphering key K_c and the packet number. The algorithm commonly used in Europe is A5/1. This is a stream cipher that, like Comp128, was originally secret; like Comp128, it was leaked and attacks were quickly found on it [249]. By the mid-2000s, law enforcement suppliers were selling devices that would break the key in under a second, enabling a surveillance team to hoover up all the GSM traffic and decrypt it, so they could then pick out conversations of interest. Phones also supported an even weaker algorithm called A5/2, which was licensed for export to non-EU countries[5] and which can be broken almost instantly. As I mentioned above in section 22.2.1, the DECT standard for cordless phones is somewhat similar, and also weak. The embassies of major powers round the world have roof structures that indicate antennas for capturing local telephone traffic, and the Snowden papers confirm that the NSA collects local phone traffic at US diplomatic missions.

In addition to passive bulk collection, targeted active collection can exploit protocol tricks.

GSM vendors introduced a third cipher, A5/3, which is based on a strong block cipher known as Kasumi and became standard in third-generation

[5]There was a row when it emerged that Australia was using A5/2.

mobile phones. But there's the *bidding-down attack*, which exploits the fact that the initial algorithm negotiation is in plaintext. The IMSI catcher simply tells the handset to use a weaker cipher. Elad Barkan, Eli Biham and Nathan Keller realised that this can be done retrospectively [172]. If you're following a suspect who uses his mobile, you record the call, including the initial protocol exchange of challenge and response. Once he's finished, you switch on your IMSI-catcher and cause him to register with your bogus base station. The IMSI-catcher tells his phone to use A5/2 rather than A5/1, and a key is duly set up – with the IMSI-catcher sending the challenge that was used before. So the mobile phone generates the same key K_c as before. As this is now being used in a weak cipher, it can be cracked quickly, giving access to the conversation already recorded. A5/2 has now been retired; handsets that cannot use A5/1 or A5/3 communicate in plaintext. However A5/1 is easy to break with modern equipment.

Phone companies, equipment vendors and ISPs are now compelled to provide for local law-enforcement access, but other countries often want access too and the wiretap facilities are often so poorly engineered that they can be abused [1710]. In 2004-5, persons unknown (but presumed to be from the NSA or CIA) tapped the mobile phones of the Greek Prime Minister and about a hundred of that country's political, law enforcement and military elite during the Athens Olympics, by subverting the wiretapping facilities built into Vodafone's Greek network. Both Vodafone, and their equipment supplier Ericsson, were heavily fined [1553]. Colleagues and I warned about this problem years ago [4] and the Snowden disclosures suggest that it has got steadily worse. I'll discuss it at greater length in Chapter 25.

Anyway, the net effect is while the 2G GSM security mechanisms were designed to provide slightly better protection than the wireline network in countries allowed to use A5/1, and somewhat worse protection elsewhere, they now provide slightly worse protection everywhere because of the range of exploits that can be industrialised by third parties.

22.3.2 3G

The third generation of digital mobile phones was initially known as the *Universal Mobile Telecommunications System* (UMTS) and now as the *Third Generation Partnership Project* (3gpp, or just 3G). The acronym 3gpp is still used for the standards body working on 4G, 5G and beyond. 3G entered service in 2003–2004 and is due to be retired in 2022, after which mobile devices that cannot use 4G or 5G are supposed to fall back to 2G. This may happen mostly in sparsely-populated rural areas where it is uneconomic to install the newer 4G and 5G technologies and the far greater backhaul transmission bandwidth they need. 3G uses spread-spectrum technology on the radio access network, and instead of the 9.6kb/s of standard 2G and the tens of kilobits per second of the 2.5G variant (GPRS), 3G data rates are in the hundreds of thousands of bits per second. 3G's vision was to enable all sorts of mobile services, from mobile TV to laptops that just go online anywhere. It laid the foundation for the smartphone revolution.

The overall security strategy is described in [1980], and the security architecture is at [1965]. The crypto algorithms A5/1 and A5/2 are replaced by A3, based on a block cipher called Kasumi [1024], which in turn is based on a design by Mitsuru Matsui called Misty, which has now withstood public scrutiny for two decades [1247]. All keys are now 128 bits. Cryptography is used to protect the integrity and confidentiality of both message content and signalling data, rather than just content confidentiality, and the protection runs from the handset to the core network, rather than simply to the local base station. So picking up the keys, or the plaintext, from the base station or microwave backhaul is no longer an attack. The authentication is now two-way rather than one-way. The theory was that this would end the vulnerability to rogue base stations, and IMSI catchers wouldn't work any more. In practice, they work fine as they just tell the target handset to fall back to 2G operation. 3G also has a proper interface for local interception [1966].

In the basic 3G *authentication and key agreement* (AKA) protocol, the authentication runs from the handset to the visitor location register. The home location register is now known as the *home environment* (HE) and the SIM as the *UMTS SIM* (USIM). The home environment chooses a random challenge RAND as before and enciphers it with the USIM authentication key K_i to generate a response RES, a confidentiality key CK, and integrity key IK, and an anonymity key AK.

$$\{RAND\}_K = (RES|CK|IK|AK)$$

There is also a sequence number SEQ known to the HE and the USIM. A MAC is computed on RAND and SEQ, and then the sequence number is masked by exclusive-or'ing it with the anonymity key. The challenge, the expected response, the confidentiality key, the integrity key, and the masked sequence number are made up into an *authentication vector AV*, which is sent from the HE to the VLR. The VLR then sends the USIM the challenge, the masked sequence number and the MAC; the USIM computes the response and the keys, unmasks the sequence number, verifies the MAC, and if it's correct returns the response to the VLR (see Figure 22.3).

The 3G standards set out many other features, including identity and location privacy mechanisms, backwards compatibility with 2G, mechanisms for encrypting authentication vectors in transit from HEs to VLRs, and negotiation of various optional cryptographic mechanisms.

As with 2G, its design goal was that security should be comparable with that of the wired network [924] and the net effect was a modest improvement:

USIM⟶ HE	IMSI (this can optionally be encrypted)
HE⟶ VLR	RAND, XRES, *CK*, *IK*, $SEQ \bigoplus AK$, *MAC*
VLR⟶ USIM	RAND, $SEQ \bigoplus AK$, *MAC*
USIM⟶ VLR	RES

Figure 22.3: 3gpp authentication protocol

bulk eavesdropping on the air link is prevented by higher-quality mechanisms, although targeted attacks by IMSI catchers still work by exploiting fallback. In a number of countries, third-generation mobiles were hard for the police to tap in the first few years, as they had to integrate their systems with those of the network operators to operate at any scale greater than tactically.

22.3.3 4G

Fourth-generation mobile networks were first rolled out in 2009, and accounted for most mobile subscriptions (4.2bn of the 8bn) by 2019 [983]. They use IP throughout, unlike 2G and 3G which had circuit-switched core networks. The radio access network changed from 3G's spread spectrum to *frequency-domain equalization* (FDE) schemes, making very high bit rates possible despite multi-path radio propagation (echoes). The higher data rates made apps such as Google Maps and Snapchat work much better, and made video streaming apps possible. There is actually a family of standards that has evolved during the 2010s, supporting bandwidths in the megabits up to tens of megabits per second. The 4G security standards rowed back from 3G by limiting encryption to the link between the handset and the base station, though to be fair most apps now encrypt data at the application layer. The authentication and key agreement (AKA) protocol is very similar to 3G, although the nomenclature has changed. The handset is now the UE or user equipment while the HE/HLR is now the *home subscriber server* (HSS). The base station functionality is split into an Evolved NodeB (eNodeB) base station and a smaller number of Mobility Management Entities (MMEs), which handle the AKA exchange, make admission decisions, supply session keys to the base stations and handle law enforcement access. The idea was that the MMEs can be housed in protected spaces or at least made tamper-resistant (people talked about TPMs, but no operator seems to have implemented them).

The three main weaknesses in 4G are that local traffic at a base station (or MME) can still be monitored by anyone who can take it over; that the user equipment's identity is sent to the network in the clear, or masked using a *Globally Unique Temporary Identity* (GUTI) that is fairly weak, like its predecessor the TMSI [920]; and that the home network delegates authentication to the serving network [364]. SS7 is replaced by a control protocol suite called Diameter, where messages can be optionally encrypted, but as the operators trust each other, it's vulnerable to many of the same types of attack [428]. It started off with fewer abusable functions, but they got put back in following business pressure.

Rich Communications Services (RCS) became widely available during 2019 thanks to support from Google in its Messages app. It is intended to replace SMS with richer chat features including geolocation exchange, social presence information and voice-over-IP. Also known as SMS+, +Message or joyn, it provides many of the same services as WhatsApp, but without the end-to-end encryption, as it's a telco hosted product. Many of the initial implementations are insecure as the telcos haven't configured them correctly [1699].

For decades, phone security has been kept weak at the behest of the security and intelligence community. Yet this strategy blew back when it turned out that Russian agents in the USA compromised the communications of FBI counterintelligence agents who used push-to-talk cellphones [579]. We haven't been told whether they were 3G or 4G, or what the specific exploits were, but it was so bad that in December 2016 the Obama administration kicked out three dozen Russian diplomats. They had also been obsessed with getting premises with line of sight to the CIA HQ at Langley, Virginia.

22.3.4 5G and beyond

Fifth-generation networks entered service in 2019, promising a further significant improvement over 4G in terms of bandwidth and latency. The main driver at present is bandwidth; mobile traffic grew by 68% between Q3 2018 and Q3 2019, mostly from video, and growth at over 25% is anticipated up till 2025, by which time almost half the traffic worldwide will be 5G [983]. Again, there's an evolving family of standards, with complexity increasing still further. Initial deployments use *non-standalone mode* (NSA), which reuse the 4G control plane (and even the 4G towers) but boost the data rate. The real excitement is about *standalone mode* (SA), which will follow. 5G makes it cheaper and easier for mobile network operators to build new capacity, not just at existing frequencies, but at millimeter-wave frequencies over 20GHz, which will mean much larger numbers of small base stations on lamp posts, bus stops and so on (this will also limit the time available to do authentication handshakes). Network energy efficiency and area traffic capacity could be up two orders of magnitude, while connection density, mobility and data rates could go up one order. Availability is a high priority; after the 2016 Brussels bombings, the police couldn't get network service on their phones because of congestion, and had to find wifi hotspots to talk to each other.

The terminology changes yet again. Each tiny base station is now a *distributed unit* (DU) and is controlled by a *centralised unit* (CU), which is also in the field but counted as part of the core network. The encryption goes from your device to the CU, and from there it's protected using IPSec to the *access management function* (AMF), which replaces the MME boxes. The authentication and key agreement protocols are much the same (XRES is renamed HXRES). One material improvement is that your device identity is sent to your home network encrypted under its public key, so location privacy will be harder to break; and we're told that IMSI catchers won't work any more[6]. Passive and active attacks by fake base stations seem still possible, including man-in-the-middle attacks that downgrade a device to a previous generation of technology, and could be used to deplete the batteries of energy-critical devices [1715].

However, the whole core network moves to the cloud, including all the law-enforcement access mechanisms. Instead of defending familiar technologies, mobile network operators will depend on new ones that they don't understand and which most will just buy from the cheapest vendor. One mistake in configuration, and things could be world readable; and unless something like SGX can be made to work, the cloud providers' governments may well be able to get access by serving warrants on them rather than on the operators. The use of SDN in the core cloud network opens up still more questions, of which the most troublesome long-term may be whether 5G becomes an end-run round net neutrality, enabling network operators to customise offerings to each application by performance (and price). Meanwhile the specifications are complex and the implementations are still flaky. As the standards evolve, one fight is between the big data carriers who want to manipulate traffic to break net neutrality and claw their way up the value chain, versus the big mobile network operators who want end-to-end trust. In theory traffic edits will be signed by the firm that does the editing, but nobody seems to know how that will work. Another is that the US government is trying to prevent Huawei getting a critical mass of installations outside China; the 2019 annual report of the UK National Cyber Security Centre (part of GCHQ) noted that significant supply-chain risks have developed over 2010–19, for which market drivers were insufficient to ensure an adequate response [1395]. In 2020, with anti-Chinese sentiment rising with the coronavirus pandemic and the end of 'one country two systems' in Hong Kong, the UK government decided to ban Huawei from selling 5G network equipment from the end of 2020 and remove its existing equipment by 2027. A longer-term resolution may depend on a third tussle, between the 'bellheads' and the 'netheads': between firms like Nokia and Huawei who take a phone-industry approach and culture, and insurgents such as Rakuten whose culture is from the computer industry and which will happily virtualise everything in sight once it's in the cloud [609].

[6]We heard that before with 3G: the wiretappers just forced fallback to 2G. We hear that the intelligence agencies are lobbying to break this, in alliance with the big data carriers.

What about 6G and 7G? Telecomms researchers talk about the former seeing evolution in the radio access network to support a diversity of apps with different requirements for peak bandwidth, latency, service quality and power consumption [1456]; and the latter having thousands of micro-satellites to deploy 200Mbps broadband over all the earth's surface. The arrival of streaming games, augmented reality and (perhaps) autonomous vehicles will create demand for ultra-low-latency cloud services, so rather than having our data shipped off to a few dozen data centres run by Google, Facebook, Microsoft and Amazon, we may see edge clouds with clusters of servers in each town, perhaps even in the buildings that used to house the old telephone exchanges. Then, just as the dotcom boom in the late 1990s forced us to partition web services into the active processes at the core and the rest that could be served more or less statically and thus cached locally in CDNs, we'll have to host some of the active stuff locally too.

22.3.5 General MNO failings

Regardless of the generation of radio link technology in use, there are some common failings of MNOs whose root causes lie in the economics and regulation of the industry. One is the rapidly growing attacks on authentication functions supported by mobile phones. In addition to the SS7 security issues we discussed in section 22.2.3, which apply also to wireline telcos, the mobile world has brought us SIM swapping, channel jacking and the theft of cookies from authenticator apps. Many of these have security economics at their root: there is some misalignment of incentives between the various principals in the system.

In section 3.4.1 we introduced SIM swap attacks, where the attacker persuades the victim's telco to issue a new SIM card on the victim's account. This can open the door to all sorts of mayhem; individuals can have their lives trashed by attackers who take over their online accounts. Celebrities are targets: in August 2019, Twitter CEO Jack Dorsey had his account taken over for an hour and used to send racist and antisemitic tweets, causing commentators to wonder whether someone who took over President Trump's twitter account might start World War 3 [1342]. As I mentioned in section 12.7.4, SIM-swap attacks are mostly used in 2020 against the customers of banks and bitcoin exchanges, and often involve phone company insiders. Yet the response of phone companies has been at best patchy. The only major US MNO making SIM swapping harder is Verizon [712]. But not all countermeasures help all users: if they are optional, then the company can more easily disclaim losses by the customers who don't opt to use them. The first MNO to take action was MTN in South Africa in 2003, which enabled users to designate a second SIM to authorise SIM replacement; curiously, this was the phone company involved in the first SIM-swap fraud case in 2007, which I described in section 12.7.4. Phone companies can also help relying parties detect SIM swaps by sending a hash of the IMSI as a response to the second-factor SMS; but few do so. We discussed the often adversarial attitude of phone companies toward their customers in section 22.2.8; MNOs are no different in this respect from legacy wireline phone companies. Indeed, they may be worse because most of their customers in most countries are prepayment customers.

Another example of MNOs and their suppliers feeling unable to do customer security properly is SIMjacking. In 2013, Karsten Nohl warned that many SIMs in use were easy to hijack, because of features built in to facilitate over-the air software update. The industry retorted that it wasn't a problem as SIM cards could run only signed software [1585]. In 2019, it emerged that governments had been using this for surveillance [1109]. MNOs' relationship with their customers has always been somewhat adversarial, and they are compelled in many countries to run middleperson attacks on demand. When a suspect's mobile phone browser visits an unencrypted URL, the MNO serves police malware instead. Such network injection attacks can be done tactically, with IMSI-catchers, but doing them at the MNO is more convenient. This practice started in less developed countries but has now spread as far as Germany [1445]. We will discuss government surveillance, and the tensions it has generated with security since the crypto wars, in section 26.2.7.3.

The real underlying problem for the MNOs is that they lost control of services. For various reasons, they were unable to engage with developers and promote an app ecosystem from which they could extract value. They ended up being commoditised – bit shifters who have to maintain the infrastructure, but who see the monopoly profits they used to enjoy being creamed off by others.

22.4 Platform security

The second part of the phone story is the app ecosystems. These fix some problems, and create others: the most acute security problem is whether the platform itself is trustworthy, or whether your phone might act against your interests. This has been a growing concern since programmable phones came along in the early 2000s. For the back story see the second edition of my book, which describes the state of play in 2007. Briefly, before the iPhone came along, security was fragmented along the supply chain, with chip designers, chip makers, OS vendors, handset OEMs and MNOs passing the buck while they tussled over DRM and over control. MNOs refused to allow OEMs to have any relationship with the customer. As I remarked in the chapter on access control, Arm launched TrustZone in 2004; by 2007, several hundred viruses and worms were being detected in Symbian phones each year, and vendors responded with access controls, code signing, and so on.

Apple changed the world in several ways at once. First, it broke the taboo on OEMs having a relationship with the customer. Second, it made it much easier for third party vendors to write apps. Third, it made the App Store central to a platform strategy, which it monetised by taking a share of both music downloads and software. This entailed a semi-closed platform. Devices could go online either through an MNO or via wifi, and could switch easily between the two as needed. The effect was to shift power from the MNO to Apple. Google launched Android the following year, with a strategy of making a similar platform as open as possible[7], allowing anyone to write apps for Android phones. They aimed to provide a minimum level of trust, to enable the ecosystem to grow. They remembered that Microsoft had grabbed most of the PC software market from Apple in the early 1980s by offering a more open platform that got the network effects going in their favour and hoped to do the same with phones, leaving the iPhone as a niche product for the rich. This did not in the end happen, and we now have two large ecosystems that have converged in a number of ways. But Apple's monetisation strategy does give it a better incentive to maintain its platforms, and iPhones are typically patched for at least five years while Android products are patched for three, and often less.

Both the iPhone and Android launched with security architectures I describe in the chapter on access control; both approaches aim to separate apps from each other and to prevent them from subverting the platform itself. The main processor is not the whole story, as phones contain dozens of other CPUs, and there have been vulnerabilities discovered in DSPs too, which can affect handsets from multiple OEMs [1214]. I also discussed in the chapter on side channels how a bad app could, for example, use the phone's accelerometer and gyro to work out a password or PIN being entered into another app, even if denied direct access to the screen. The combination of rich sensors and a huge range of applications makes security and privacy services at the platform level rather complex. Both the Android and iPhone security mechanisms have been refined over time, with more controls added to block or mitigate the more flagrant abuses. However, they can best be understood as an ecosystem, rather than as a list of protection options.

This ecosystem is truly immense. By 2019, 56% of all Internet access globally was from mobile devices, but 63% in the USA and 80% in India [1254]. It consists at the very least of the apps that run on the two families of mobile devices themselves, and the back-end services they rely on. The boundaries are hard to define. We probably have to include the ad ecosystems that app developers bundle with their products. Do we include the web services that mobile devices access from browser apps? Do we include voice telephony, now that

[7] subject to the regulators' insistence that the baseband software that controls the device's RF behaviour had to be locked down

this is migrating to apps like WhatsApp, Skype and Signal? What about other devices, from watches to cars, that run mobile operating systems and apps? It may be simplest to start with the app families.

22.4.1 The Android app ecosystem

Android is the most widely deployed end-user operating system, found not just in phones but in tablets, watches, TVs, cars and other devices – a total of over 2bn monthly active devices. Its platform security model is described by René Mayrhofer and colleagues from Google in [1254], and in section 6.2.8 I discussed the technical architecture. Actions are based on three-party consent: the user, the developer and Google should all agree. The implementation is that rather than giving a userid to the end user, as in a conventional *nix system, Android runs each app with a separate userid; data in private app directories is controlled by the app, while data in shared storage is controlled by the end user, and there are mandatory access control mechanisms to ensure that critical system data remain under the control by the platform, unless it's rooted. So long as this does not happen, the user cannot be tricked into letting a bad app access or overwrite the data of other apps. The threat model includes everything from physical attacks and wiretapping through the exploitation of vulnerabilities in the operating system, libraries and other apps; it's assumed that users will be tricked into installing malicious apps [1254]. Apps sold via Google's Play store are scanned for malware (though the scanning isn't perfect).

However, Google takes 30% of revenues from sales of apps, and refuses to host adult apps. This has driven many vendors of paid and adult apps to use less secure distribution channels such as OEM deals, third-party stores and their own websites [1826]. Since 2014 Google has offered to upload non-Play-store apps for scanning when they're first run, but the risk of evil apps is ever present. Many more apps are somewhat predatory, even if they're distributed by apparently respectable businesses such as hardware vendors, MNOs and security firms. The sad fact is that user data has become a major commodity; little else might have been expected given that most apps are free and the ecosystem is driven as much by ad revenue as anything else. One major consequence is that Android does not support the most critical permission for privacy – allowing the user to control Internet access for an app. (Blackberry allowed users to deny Internet access.) This pleases ad companies as otherwise many users would turn off internet access for the flashlight/game/compass app the moment they installed it. If this displeases you, you can get firewall apps that pretend to be VPNs and can block other apps' access to the Internet. But of course most users go with the default, of letting the ad ecosystems harvest just about everything.

22.4.1.1 *App markets and developers*

App markets mitigate some security problems while amplifying others. As the Android ecosystem is open, anyone can be a developer and distribute the software they write through the Play Store. This makes a huge market available to novice developers, who can get simple apps running with little effort. The fact you have to use the framework with the Android SDK constrains developers in potentially useful ways. Although fragmentation greatly impedes the update process for operating systems, app updates are easy if you use an app store that pushes updates.

However, the developer rapidly encounters both technical and business complexity. Some simple apps are little more than a customised browser for an online back end; others exercise a single feature of the phone in new ways, as flashlight apps do. But how uniform is that feature? How many versions of Android do you need to support? Do you need to test on hundreds of different handsets? There are now test frameworks to help, but fragmentation is a real issue if your app uses the rich hardware features on many modern phones. For example, people developing contact-tracing apps for coronavirus have struggled with the variation in bluetooth performance between different handsets. Another example is where developers want to protect really sensitive information, such as key material in banking apps. Arm hoped that developers would use TrustZone, but this turned out to be so hard given the variation between OEMs, handsets and software versions, that most turned to obfuscation instead. Android then provided KeyStore, which lets an app store its keys in TrustZone or a Secure Element or other cryptoprocessor if available, and block other apps from using them. Some developers prefer obfuscation in the hope of blocking malware that roots the phone and can thus pretend to be the app; as I mentioned in section 12.7.4, some banking regulators insist on this.

Business complexity can come from the application itself, or from the ecosystem's underlying economics: platform companies, device vendors, app developers, app publishers (who add all sorts of ads), ad networks, toolsmiths and end users all have different incentives. There are different rules for paid apps, apps allowing in-app purchases and free apps. The rules for identifying users are complex: the user's consent is needed to use some UIDs (IMEI, IMSI, phone number and ad ID) but not others such as MAC address and hardware fingerprint.

22.4.1.2 *Bad Android implementations*

The first bundle of systemic security problems to become obvious as Android became widespread around 2010 was the poor quality of the engineering work by many of the OEMs who licensed it. One example was factory reset. There's a thriving trade in second-hand phones, as rich users buy the latest models and their old phones end up being sold. You might think that when you do a factory reset on your phone, that clears all your personal information, not just from shared storage but from app storage as well. But it's hard to get this right because of all the interactions with how Flash memory is organised on a typical phone; there may be an embedded multimedia card (eMMC) and virtual SD card, with their own wear-levelling mechanisms. If the OEM's engineers don't take the trouble to implement secure deletion, then the all-too-common outcome is that someone who buys your phone second-hand can retrieve the Google master cookie and access the Gmail account associated with the phone [1761]. For several years I bought Google's own-brand Nexus and Pixel phones and never sold them after use, but many people get phones subsidised by a contract and locked to the MNO, which sells them in second-hand markets afterwards – often in less developed countries. (It is prudent to assume that Android phones in LDCs have been rooted and had remote access Trojans installed by local distributors.)

These quality problems extend to TrustZone and its Trusted Execution Environment (TEE), as implemented by various chipset vendors. For example, Qualcomm's TEE system lets a *trusted app* (TA) map in memory regions of the host OS, and as a result any insecure TA can let an adversary root the device. Other problems allow attacks on the TEEs of the other four vendors: the software security mechanisms used in trusted environments lag the state of the art by several years, with absent or weak ASLR, excessively large TCBs, information leaks through debugging channels, no execution prevention, multiple side channels and no good ways to revoke wicked or vulnerable TAs – of which there are plenty. See David Cerdeira and colleagues for a survey of these issues [405].

However, the biggest security problem with Android implementations is poor after-sales support. Many OEMs only support the version that's currently being actively marketed; they are reluctant to spend engineer time backporting fixes to old versions. A 2015 survey revealed that 87% of active devices were insecure, averaged over 2011–15, because they were running versions of the operating system that contained known vulnerabilities. In many cases, the OEM simply did not make fixes available [1883]. This had already been identified as a problem by Google by 2011; the company offered OEMs access to cut-price components if they undertook to patch their systems, but this got little traction. Google now offers certification programs for both vendors and apps, but the problems go deeper than just OEM engineering effort. If a vulnerability is found in, say, the OpenSSL or Bouncy Castle cryptographic library, this fix has to propagate to Linux, then to Android, then to each OEM, and then in many cases to each mobile network operator – as the MNOs control updates for phones that are locked to the network. Each of these steps can take several months, and each can be neglected for commercial reasons [1883]. This raises thorny issues around coordinated disclosure, which we'll discuss in section 27.5.7.2, and regulation, which we'll discuss in the last chapter of this book.

22.4.1.3 Permissions

Consent has been a wicked problem from the beginning, as we noted in the chapter on access control. In early versions of Android, an app's manifest specified the access rights it demanded and the user would have to approve them all on installation in order to run it. This led to widespread abuse, as most users would just click approval to get the installation done, and a lot of utility apps became machines for harvesting and reselling your address book, browser history and other personal data. Already in 2012, research showed that only 17% of users paid attention during installation, and only 3% could answer basic questions about what was going on [676]. In 2015, Android 6 moved to the Apple model of approving access to such resources on first use. Indeed, progressive restrictions of the more dangerous permissions have driven platform evolution more than anything else. Android 6 also made fine-grained location access a separate permission; Android 7 limited apps' access to the metadata of other apps; Android 8 randomised MAC addresses and mandated the use of a single Advertising ID for monetisation; Android 9 limited access to sensors when an app is in background mode and restricted access to the phone and call logs; and Android 10 restricted location access in background mode.

Google now provides several dozen permissions, and developers have always been able to define custom permissions when making services available to other apps; thousands of these are defined by hardware vendors, MNOs, security firms and Internet browsers [741]. These further balkanise the ecosystem and make it even harder for users (and developers) to understand.

An analysis of the consent problem by Yasemin Acar and colleagues breaks it up into comprehension of permissions, and attention to permissions, by both users and developers [10]. There are both usability and incentive failures on both sides. It's clear enough why a predatory flashlight app wants access to my address book; many failures are more subtle. Developers are just trying to make stuff work so they can ship it, while users are just trying to access some service or other. Developer usability is a significant source of bugs; we've noted this elsewhere (e.g., in section 5.5) but it looms larger in appified ecosystems as the developers have to drive the application framework APIs to get useful work done. A substantial minority of developers request more permission than they need out of ignorance or confusion, and this holds even for system apps whose developers should know better. Google failed to implement fail-safe defaults; the APIs are confusing and poorly documented. This drove developers to copy each others' code via fora such as stackexchange, to an even greater extent than with conventional development[8].

22.4.1.4 Android malware

As Android is an open platform, for which anyone can write apps, it has attracted a lot of harmful software. As we mentioned in section 22.2.4, premium-rate phone malware arrived in 2006 with the Red Browser worm; Android's arrival turned mobile malware from a niche activity into a mainstream problem. Definitions here are hard, as many apps are harmful in different ways to at least some people; here I focus on apps that act secretly against the interests of the user that installed them. I'll discuss bad programs installed by OEMs and MNOs later in section 22.4.1.6.

Malware can be bulk or targeted, and it can come from private-sector criminals or state actors. Most of it by volume is of the bulk private-sector variety, and most of that comes through regular distribution channels. As well as the millions of apps in the Play Store, alternative markets are widely used, especially in countries like China and Iran where the Play Store is censored. The largest single source of malware has been the Play Store, with a significant minority of apps being harmful at some times, while some alternative markets have on occasion removed most of their apps for being harmful. Apps may be born harmful, or libraries on which they rely may become bad, or the bad guys may buy failing app companies, just as they snap up domains of former banks. One of the biggest crime rings exposed recently did hundreds of millions of dollars of ad fraud by buying Android apps and using their user data to train bots that then clicked on ads [1741]; such scams exploit other kinds of malware too. The measurement problems are non-trivial, as over 60 anti-virus firms label apps using different criteria and classify them into different families. There are several hundred families active at any one time.

A 2018 survey by Guillermo Suarez-Tanguil and Gianluca Stringhini analysed 1.2m samples collected over 2010–17, and classified them into over a thousand families [1846]. Since 2012, most of them have involved repackaging, where the malware dev takes a legitimate app (the *carrier*) and adds harmful code (the *rider*). This is industrialised by repackaging many benign carriers with variants of the same malicious rider. The riders may try to root the phone for persistent access, and drop a remote access Trojan (RAT) that can earn money at the direction of a command-and-control server, just as with regular PC malware. Monetisation strategies have evolved; in 2010 the focus was on making premium-rate calls, but by 2018 it had shifted to ad fraud and the

[8]It also drove Acar and her colleagues to look at usability from the developers' viewpoint [11], creating an important new area of security research which I mentioned in the research problems section at the end of the chapter on access control.

exfiltration of personal information. The great majority of riders use obfuscation tricks such as encryption, while only a quarter of benign apps do this (Facebook's app uses obfuscation as a defence against user data and keys being stolen by malware, particularly RATs in less developed countries). Riders are mostly native code rather than Java (or Kotlin, which replaced it as the official Android language of choice in 2019).

Banking Trojans stand out among the more targeted varieties of private-sector malware. A common approach is the *overlay attack* where the malware tricks the user into allowing it to use Android Accessibility Services, which enables it to build an overlay over (for example) your banking app so it can capture the screen and input data, under the control of a remote command server [398]. Android malware has been stealing bank SMSes for some time, and Google has pushed back by allowing only approved apps the permission to read SMSes; the latest development in 2020 is that the Cerberus banking malware can now steal Google authenticator cookies too [433].

States already used targeted malware in intelligence and law-enforcement missions, and by 2012 vendors such as Gamma had produced mobile-phone versions of their products that were found in multiple jurisdictions [1233]. Such malware also seeks root access but implants spyware. Recent examples of bulk malware deployment come from Turkey, which in 2018 was using man-in-the-middle devices on the Türk Telekom network to deploy spyware [1220], and China, which sets website traps for Uighurs' phones [395]. Bulk state-actor malware can include mandating doctored versions of apps in some jurisdictions; Skype was available in China from 2005 only through a local distributor, Tom Online, which repackaged it to scan for words forbidden by Chinese censors. After Microsoft bought Skype, they took back control from 2013, but the app was banned from app stores accessible in China from 2017 [1349].

There are technical abuses where apps defeat the permission framework while stopping short of rooting your phone. Joel Reardon and colleagues ran 88,000 Android apps in an instrumented virtual environment to look for apps abusing side channels [1591]. They found two large Chinese companies, Baidu and Salmonads, using the SD card as a covert channel, so that ads which could read the phone's IMEI could store it for those which could not. They also found 42 apps getting the IMEI when they shouldn't, using `ioctl` system calls, and over 12,000 with the code to do so.

22.4.1.5 Ads and third-party services

Mobile phone apps typically incorporate third-party services to support ads, social network integration and analytics for a range of purposes from crash reporting to A/B testing. Such services can track users across multiple apps, even without their consent. An example of what can go wrong comes from CamScanner, an app downloaded by over 100m people for scanning and managing documents. At some point, the app was updated to add a new advertising network that contained a malicious module. Negative reviews led antivirus researchers to take a look, and it turned out that the module was dropping Trojans on to people's phones [797].

Third-party services are a fairly opaque part of the ecosystem, as they are not directly visible to the user. Some light has been shed by a survey carried out by Abbas Razaghpanah and colleagues, using a VPN app used by 11,000 volunteers to monitor traffic to and from their phones [1589]. They mapped over 2,000 *advertising and tracking services* (ATS), including hundreds that had not previously been reported, and found that a substantial minority (39%) did cross-device tracking; 17 of the top 20 had a presence on the web as well as in the app ecosystem. Eight of the top ten reserved the right, in their privacy policies, to share data with other organisations. The largest of all were Alphabet and Facebook, but firms whose whole business consists of ATS, such as Chartboost, Vungle and Adjust, have a significant share and are relatively unknown to users. App developers often use several such services simultaneously. Paid apps have the fewest trackers, free apps have more, and free apps that allow in-app purchases, often of premium services, tend to have the most.

Mutual trust issues are discussed by Yasemin Acar and colleagues [10]. App developers have to trust ad networks, as they execute in the app sandbox and inherit its permissions. Ad libraries exploit apps in various ways, such as loading insecure code from web services and stealing users' private information; app developers return the compliment by stealing money from the networks with fake click events, just like malware developers. (The boundaries are a bit fuzzy, as they were before in the world of the PC; there's predatory behaviour at just about every layer of the stack.)

There are many examples of children's apps collecting personal data without parental consent, contrary to the US Children's Online Privacy Protection Act (COPPA): Irwin Reyes and colleagues scanned 5,855 of the most popular free children's apps and found that most of them potentially violated COPPA because of the way they used third-party SDKs; these typically enable developers to disable third-party tracking and advertising but most developers don't bother. Worse, 19% of the apps were collecting personally identifiable information using SDKs that banned this in children's apps [1602]. This study led to legal action by state attorneys general, which might encourage app developers to take the law more seriously. There are other practices contrary to the EU GDPR and its ePrivacy Directive, but EU regulators seem reluctant to get engaged, as the ATS industry is overwhelmingly based in the USA, and amounts to a substantial invisible export. Even from the viewpoint of the US authorities, most of the ATS specialists don't even have a COPPA policy, leaving regulatory compliance to their customers.

Most people expect that if they pay for an app, they get more privacy. But given that developers rely on third-party services for analytics as well as ads, this costs effort, which many developers can't be bothered to make. Catherine Han and colleagues compared free and paid versions of the same app and found that a third of the paid versions were just as predatory in terms of data collection; another sixth collected at least some of the same data; three-quarters used the same permissions; and almost all had the same security policy. Looking at paid/free app pairs designed for families, she found that the majority of paid apps violated COPPA in the same way as the free versions [860].

22.4.1.6 Pre-installed apps

Julien Gamba and colleagues studied the firmware distributed by over 200 vendors worldwide [741]. Distributions typically reflect a partnership between a handset OEM and an MNO, with various affiliated developers, ad networks and distributors. They can be poorly controlled; there have been multiple cases of malware finding its way in, as well as software to do mass-scale data collection for commercial or regulatory reasons. Some phones also have diagnostic or support modes that could be exploited by wicked apps. Most of the pre-installed apps are not available in the Play Store and thus appear to fall outside the conventional framework. Some are from firms like Facebook and AccuWeather which are known to collect personal data aggressively; many of these are not the public versions of these firms' apps; and many pre-installed apps use mobile analytics or targeted advertisement libraries. What's more, 74% of the non-public apps do not seem to get updated, and 41% remained unpatched for 5 years or more [741]. Many have sensitive custom permissions in order to perform such tasks as mobile device management for enterprise customers, call blocking, and VPN services. Behavioral analysis showed that a significant proportion of pre-installed apps could access and disseminate user and device identifiers, configuration and current location. The domains most contacted by such apps were Alphabet, Facebook, Amazon, Microsoft and Adobe. Some pre-installed apps, particularly in cheaper phones, have components in the system partition that the user cannot easily remove, and which serve annoying ads or even act as loaders for Trojans [1111].

22.4.2 Apple's app ecosystem

Apple has led from the start on security usability, providing fine-grained access controls long before Android, but its ecosystem has always been more closed. When the Mac was competing with the PC it was one hardware platform against many OEMs; the same pattern followed with the iPod, where Apple demanded 30% of music sales, and it continued when Apple launched the iPhone. The business model was much the same as a gaming console. Apple is the only hardware vendor and demands 30% of software revenues, as well as 30% of in-app purchases of online goods and services. Now that Apple has half the market in developed countries (and three-quarters of teens) this is becoming an antitrust issue. Every developer has horror stories, and although Amazon was allowed in April 2020 to sell movies on Apple devices without giving Apple a cut [837], this just highlights the arbitrary nature of Apple's rules. Why should dating sites like `match.com` have to hand it 30% of their sales, while Uber does not? Apple treats dating as a digital good, but Uber tries to avoid taxi regulation by claiming it's the same, a mere matchmaking service between drivers and riders. The rules appear to hit smaller firms particularly hard, and imposed an 'Apple tax' on people like musicians, fitness instructors and yoga teachers who went online because of the pandemic, if people booked them via an iPhone app. All this has led to an antitrust lawsuit in the USA from Epic Games, and a competition policy investigation by the EU [890].

Apple also used its control of the hardware and the operating system to implement rights-management mechanisms to protect its aftermarket revenue; competing app stores are not allowed. The company does due diligence on developers, requiring them to pay $99 a year for a license. Its app vetting process is a lot tougher than Google's: there's extensive automated security testing, followed by manual review to ensure that apps follow Apple policy on matters such as payment, content and abuse. To support this, iOS apps submitted to the App Store are only allowed to use the publicly-documented APIs [1816]. Academic researchers have therefore dug into the iOS ecosystem a lot less, but nevertheless a few things can be said.

The overall protection against malware is the best of any mass-market system, with zero-day remote exploits of iOS trading for multiple millions of dollars and being patched as soon as they're used at scale. Indeed, when our own university's finance division has asked for advice on how to protect really high-value transactions against phishing, my advice has been simple: buy an iPad on which you run the bank's authenticator app to release payments, use it only for payments, and keep it in a safe the rest of the time.

However, the protection isn't entirely bulletproof, and various actors have found workarounds.

First, there's a long history of hobbyists and others 'jailbreaking' Apple devices, starting with people who objected to DRM or who wanted to sideload their own apps without paying Apple $99 tax, as they can with Android. As jailbreaks come out, Apple patches them; so at least the company has an incentive to patch its devices up to date, rather than abandon them after sale as the typical Android OEM does. Sometimes patching isn't possible, as when the exploit is of the device's boot ROM; for example, the 2019 Checkra1n jailbreak will liberate most devices sold before 2017 [799], and the forensics industry uses the Checkm8 jailbreak, which exploits the boot ROM of all iPhones from the 4S to the X [799]; this is used widely in the forensic 'kiosks' sold to the world's police forces, as I describe in section 26.5.1. Although ROM exploits cannot defeat the user PIN on devices later than the 5s, thanks to the secure element, they can access those user data that are made accessible after first unlock, as described in section 6.2.7. There's also a market for carrier unlocking, where you can also assume that the phone is in the physical custody of the attacker.

Attacks that can exploit iOS remotely are more valuable, as state actors are willing to pay millions of dollars for them. We described in section 2.2.4 how the UAE used such a tool to target dissidents, and how Saudi Arabia used one against Jeff Bezos, whose newspaper the Washington Post they detested; the Saudis also hacked their regional rival, the King of Qatar. Cybercriminals also do it: in 2019, Google's Project Zero revealed iOS exploits that were being used in the wild to infect iPhones [205]. Apple always patches such exploits quickly, so your millions only give you access to a handful of targets. If someone's likely to spend a million dollars to compromise your phone, you'd better have several and not tell your enemies the number of your private phone that contains the data you really care about[9].

Second, Apple sells large firms 'enterprise certificates' which let iOS developers bypass the app review process. This led to abuse and spats, with Facebook's enterprise cert being suspended until their app stopped infringing App store policy; Google's app on the iPhone had a similar experience, and suddenly lots of abuse by porn, gambling and spyware apps came to light. They had been abusing enterprise certificates and hiding in plain sight in the app store [1700]. Many of the bad actors had got their enterprise certs by pretending to be helpline apps from MNOs in less developed countries [1165].

Third, Apple is like Android in that it doesn't allow the user to block an app's access to the Internet. So we find firewall apps for iOS too, but this is one way in which the iOS privacy mechanisms get in the way of privacy. One app can't even see another let alone block it, so all the iOS firewalls can do on the iPhone is block access to ad servers.

Although the malware issues are less serious than with Android, the same market forces apply, and so ad abuse still happens. Many popular apps (including dating apps such as Grindr and OkCupid) share a lot of data with advertisers, and are still allowed in the Apple ecosystem [1766]. The same holds for apps you might expect to be more privacy conscious, such as VPNs and ad blockers – where the privacy exploits come in through embedded ad networks, as in the Android ecosystem [1742]. In one case, an advertising SDK let

[9]I know of one tycoon who would borrow the mobile phone of a different employee each day and get the switchboard to forward his calls. If that's your strategy you'd better assume it may occasionally double as a listening device and have your PA carry it for you. And against a state adversary, maintaining separation between a hot phone and a cold one is not straightforward: see the cotraveler system described in section 2.2.1.10.

its authors steal clicks from the 1,200 apps that used it and were installed on 300m iPhones; its code had stealth features that may have helped it past the app review process [1316]. And although more apps are paid for in the Apple App Store than in the Google Play Store (6% rather than 4.4%) and people assume that paid apps that don't show ads don't track you, such an expectation may be optimistic – in both ecosystems. In section 22.4.1.5 I mentioned research showing how the paid versions of Android apps often still track you. One might expect similar results for Apple, but the iPhone is a harder platform to do research on.

Apple, like Google, has been progressively tightening up the permissions apps need. For example, iOS13 refines geodata from 'allow' on installation to 'allow once' and 'allow while using app', and also curtails the use of wifi and Bluetooth to determine location – causing the same kind of complaints from developers [436]. From September 2020, iOS14 will turn *identification for advertisers* (IDFA) from opt-out to opt-in, essentially killing it, and undermining advertisers' ability to track the effectiveness of campaigns. This is supposedly for privacy, but it also looks set to promote Apple's ad business at the expense of Google, Facebook and third-party ad service firms [1075].

The two stores share some political problems, such as the fact that they both allowed an app used by men in Saudi Arabia to control the movements of their wives, daughters and servants, as I discussed in section 2.5.4. Occasionally, they do diverge. Apple is more aggressive than Google at removing 'bad' apps, though this can sometimes get them a bad press. During the 2019 protests in Hong Kong, Apple banned a crowdsourced protest safety app that demonstrators were using to avoid the police, claiming "Your app contains content – or facilitates, enables, and encourages an activity – that is not legal ... specifically, the app allowed users to evade law enforcement", while Google left the Android version up [1255].

Another political controversy arose with coronavirus contact tracing. In February 2020 the government of Singapore announced an app that would use Bluetooth to record which phones had been near each other, so that when someone tested positive for the virus, public health officials could trace possible contacts automatically rather than just asking the patient who they'd met over the past week. This turned out to not work very well, as Bluetooth isn't a good ranging technology. If you set the volume to be sure to see people 2m away, you see a fair number 10m away – which greatly increases the number of false alarms that contact tracers have to deal with. What's more, if the proportion of the population running the app is p, then the probability that both a patient and their contact were both running it is p^2 and the missed alarm rate is $1 - p^2$; for Singapore, p was 12% so over 98% of contacts were missed. By the time this was reported in April, a number of other countries, including the UK, France, Germany, Latvia and Australia, had started to develop contact tracing apps too. They discovered that the restrictions on Bluetooth use made such apps tricky to write for Android phones and essentially impossible for iPhones [439]. When they asked for better access Google and Apple refused, citing the privacy risk to their customers if all apps could do Bluetooth contact tracing. Google and Apple made available an API for anonymous contact tracing, but from the epidemiologists' point of view this is even less useful [1805]. This led to criticism of Google and especially Apple for taking policy decisions that are the job of elected politicians [957]. Germany switched to the Google/Apple API but started requiring pubs and restaurants to keep lists of customers' contact details, so that if one customer gets sick, people who sat nearby can be traced using traditional methods.

22.4.3 Cross-cutting issues

The convergence of the two ecosystems is leading to a growing number of cross-cutting issues. These apply not just to phones but to other IoT devices, many of which are either in the iOS ecosystem, such as Apple watches, or the Android one, including thermostats, doorbell cameras, building sensors and Google Home smart speakers. The other notable ecosystem is probably that of the Amazon Alexa, which kickstarted the smart speaker product category. This category has grown extremely quickly, taking four years to be adopted by half the US population rather than eight for the smartphone. Many of these devices are also designed to support an ecosystem of apps, although the number and usage varies by product.

In addition to the issues that stem from the MNOs, which we discussed in section 22.3.5, and the rapacious ad ecosystems, which we discussed in the above section, a major problem is poorly engineered apps.

Quite simply, when billions of people entrust their financial lives, their social lives and even their sex lives to apps, then poorly-written apps can cause real harm. Specific application issues have been discussed in many other chapters of this book. Here, one example may suffice to put things in context. It illustrates a problem that many app developers just don't think through – that of revocation. In fact, when assisting in the design of a payment app, we spent about half of the security-engineering time working out in detail how we'd cope with stolen phones: how payments could be blocked quickly when alerts came in from different stakeholders, what would happen when the crime victim walked into a shop the following day and bought a new phone, whether you'd rely on the phone shop to authenticate them or make them call a bank contractor, how you'd deal with phone OEMs who had their own backup and recovery services – an absolute mass of mind-numbing detail. That's what real engineering comes down to: working with your supply chain and thinking through both the customer experience and the possible abuse cases.

My example of what can happen when you don't pay enough attention is FordPass, an app that enables you to control a rental car so you can track it, lock and unlock it, and start the engine – even several months after you've returned it to the rental lot [795]. There are many more cases, but this is enough to illustrate that poorly designed apps can expose other systems, including safety-critical ones.

The threats from poorly written apps cover the whole spectrum of confidentiality, integrity and availability. The consequences of goods relying on apps that are no longer maintained are such that the EU passed the Sales of Goods Directive in 2019 requiring vendors of goods with digital components to maintain these components for at least two years and for longer if that is a reasonable expectation of the customer. From January 2022, phone apps supplied along with a durable good such as a car or washing machine will have to be maintained for ten years after the last of these products leaves the showroom. We'll discuss sustainability further in the last chapter of this book.

22.5 Summary

Phone security is a fascinating case study. People have been cheating phone companies for a century, and since deregulation the phone companies have been vigorously returning the compliment. To start off with, systems were not really protected at all, and it was easy to evade charges and redirect calls. The mechanism adopted to prevent this – out-of-band signalling – proved inadequate as the rapidly growing complexity of the system opened up many more vulnerabilities. These range from social engineering attacks on users through poor design and management of terminal equipment such as PBXes to the exploitation of various hard-to-predict feature interactions. The main disruptive force was the development of premium-rate services that enabled people to steal real money.

On the mobile front, the attempts to secure GSM and its third, fourth and fifth generation successors make an interesting case study. Their engineers concentrated on communications security threats rather than computer security threats, and on the phone companies' interests at the expense of the customers'. Their efforts were not entirely in vain but have led to an immensely complex global ecosystem that has become the subject of significant political tussles, particularly over the control of 5G infrastructure.

The dominating factor in 2020 is the mobile app ecosystems. The Android ecosystem has attracted hundreds of thousands of developers, ranging from firms like Uber that have built apps into major international businesses, through apps offered by many established businesses and a host of specialist tools, to a substantial criminal fringe. The Apple ecosystem is more regulated but similar in a number of respects. Many apparently innocuous apps in both ecosystems can be abused in interesting ways, and the ad networks they use are a pervasive threat to privacy. The ecosystems of mobile apps, apps on more traditional platforms such as laptops, and apps on devices such as watches and cars converge and overlap in various ways, but insofar as they are still distinct, mobile platforms protect apps from each other more robustly than laptops do and the platform operators make significant security efforts at the ecosystem level. Indeed, as most Android phones are not patched up to date and are therefore insecure, the heavy lifting isn't done at the level of technical platform security but at the level of the ecosystem.

Research problems

The interaction between communications, mobility, platforms, and apps continues to be fertile ground for both interesting research and expensive engineering errors. We have explored a lot of the issues over the past ten years in the mobile phone app ecosystem, mostly in the Android part of it where most of the problems occur. Mobility is now extending to all sorts of other devices, from your watch to your car, and many of the issues around app ecosystems are arising with smart speakers and other domestic devices. Given the sheer scale of these new emerging ecosystems, we will need innovative ways to automate the hunt for both threats and vulnerabilities. One approach is to build honeypots and look for attack traffic; a somewhat more forward defence may be to analyse the companion apps used to control IoT devices and infer vulnerabilities from them [1982].

Further reading

Information about the world's phone systems is scattered across a large number of standards documents that can be rather heavy going, while app platforms at least have official guides, white papers and developer communities. Keeping up with the latest exploits is a matter of following the security blogs and tech press. There are some good surveys of specific subproblems, which I've cited in the relevant sections, but I'm not aware of any good books or survey papers of the overall phone security scene. Perhaps that's inevitable; now that more people go online via mobile devices then from laptops or desktops, mobile security touches one way or another on much of the subject matter of this book.

CHAPTER

23

Electronic and Information Warfare

All warfare is based on deception ... hold out baits to entice the enemy. Feign disorder, and crush him.

– SUN TZU

Force, and Fraud, are in warre the two Cardinal Virtues.

– THOMAS HOBBES

23.1 Introduction

For decades, electronic warfare was a separate subject from computer security, even though they use some common technologies. This started to change in the last years of the twentieth century as the Pentagon started to fuse elements of the two disciplines into the new subject of *information warfare*, followed by Russia and China. The Russian denial-of-service attacks on Estonia in 2007 put it firmly on many policy agendas; Stuxnet moved it into prime time; and the Russian interference in two big political events of 2016, the UK Brexit referendum and the US election, taught legislators that it could cost them their jobs.

There are other reasons why some knowledge of electronic warfare is important to the security engineer. Many technologies originally developed for the warrior have been adapted for commercial use, and instructive parallels abound. The struggle for control of the electromagnetic spectrum was the first area of electronic security to have experienced a lengthy period of coevolution of attack and defense involving capable motivated opponents, giving rise to deception strategies and tactics of a unique depth and subtlety. Although the subject languished after the end of the Cold War in 1989, it has revived recently as China works to become a peer competitor to the USA, as Russia modernises its armed forces, and as AI finds its way into radar, sonar and related systems. Warfare is about to get hi-tech again, unlike in 2000-2020 with its emphasis on spies hacking people's phones and special forces then kicking down their doors.

Electronic warfare was also our first teacher about service-denial attacks, a topic that computer security people ignored for years, and about hybrid attacks that involve both direct and psychological factors. Finally, many of the techniques evolved to defeat enemy radars, including various kinds of decoys and jamming, have interesting parallels in the new 'information warfare' world of fake news, troll farms and postmodern propaganda.

23.2 Basics

While old-fashioned computer security was about confidentiality, integrity and availability, electronic warfare has this the other way round. The priorities are:

1. denial of service, which includes jamming, mimicry and physical attack;
2. deception, which may be targeted at automated systems or at people; and
3. exploitation, which includes not just eavesdropping but obtaining any operationally valuable information from the enemy's use of his electronic systems.

At the level of doctrine, electromagnetic warfare is generally considered to consist of

- *electronic attack*, such as jamming enemy communications or radar, and disrupting enemy equipment using high-power microwaves;
- *electronic protection*, which is about retaining some radar and communications capability in the face of attack. It ranges from designing systems resistant to jamming, through hardening equipment to resist high-power microwave attack, to the destruction of enemy jammers using anti-radiation missiles; and
- *electronic support*, which supplies the necessary intelligence and threat recognition to allow effective attack and protection. It allows commanders to search for, identify and locate sources of intentional and unintentional electromagnetic energy.

These definitions are taken from Schleher [1665]. The traditional topic of cryptography, namely *communications security* (Comsec), is only a small part of electronic protection, just as it is only a small part of information protection in modern civilian systems. Electronic support includes *signals intelligence*, or

Sigint, which consists of *communications intelligence* (Comint) and *electronic intelligence* (Elint). The former collects enemy communications, including both message content and traffic data about which units are communicating, while the latter concerns itself with recognizing hostile radars and other non-communicating sources of electromagnetic energy.

Deception is central to electronic attack. The goal is to mislead the enemy by manipulating their perceptions in order to degrade the accuracy of their intelligence and target acquisition. Its effective use depends on clarity about who (or what) is to be deceived, about what and how long, and – where the targets of deception are human – the exploitation of pride, greed, laziness and other vices. Deception can be extremely cost effective and is increasingly relevant to commercial systems.

Physical destruction is an important part of the mix; while some enemy sensors and communications links may be neutralized by jamming (so-called *soft kill*), others will be destroyed (*hard kill*). Successful electronic warfare depends on using the available tools in a coordinated way.

Electronic weapon systems are like other weapons in that there are *sensors*, such as radar, infrared and sonar; *communications* links that take sensor data to the command and control center; and output devices such as jammers, lasers, missiles, bombs and so on. I'll discuss the communications system issues first, as they are the most self-contained, then the sensors and associated jammers, and finally other devices such as electromagnetic pulse generators. Once we're done with electronic warfare, we'll look at the lessons we might take over to information warfare.

23.3 Communications systems

Military communications were dominated by physical dispatch until about 1860, then by the telegraph until 1915, and then by the telephone and radio until after the end of the Cold War [1382]. Nowadays, a typical command and control structure is made up of various tactical and strategic radio networks supporting data, voice and images, operating over point-to-point links and broadcast. There are also fixed links including the Internet and classified IP networks. Without situational awareness and the means to direct forces, the commander is likely to be ineffective. But the need to secure communications is pervasive, and the threats are very diverse.

- One obvious type of traffic is the communications between fixed sites such as army headquarters and the political leadership. A significant historical threat here was that the cipher security might be penetrated and the orders, situation reports and so on compromised, whether as a result of cryptanalysis or – more likely – equipment sabotage, subversion of personnel or theft of key material. The insertion of deceptive messages may also be a threat in some circumstances. Cipher security may include protection against traffic analysis (such as by constant bitrate encryption of some links) as well as of the transmitted message confidentiality and authenticity. The secondary threat is that the link might be disrupted, whether by destruction of cables or relay stations, or by traffic flooding where resources are shared.

- There are more stringent requirements for communications with covert assets such as agents in the field. Here, in addition to cipher security, location security is important. Agents have to take steps to minimize the risk of being caught as a result of communications monitoring. If they send messages using a medium the enemy can monitor, such as the Internet or radio, then some effort may go into frustrating traffic analysis and radio direction finding.
- Tactical communications, such as between HQ and a platoon in the field, also have more stringent (but slightly different) needs. Radio direction finding is still an issue, but jamming may be at least as important, and deliberately deceptive messages may also be a problem. By the 1980s, there was equipment that enabled an enemy air controller's voice commands to be captured, cut into phonemes and spliced back together into deceptive commands, in order to gain a tactical advantage in air combat [730]. As voice morphing techniques are developed using deepfake techniques from machine learning, the risk of spoofing attacks on communications will increase. So cipher security may increasingly include authenticity as well as confidentiality and covertness.
- Control and telemetry communications, such as signals sent from an aircraft to a missile it has just launched, should be protected against jamming and modification. It would also be nice if they could be covert (so as not to trigger a target's warning receiver) but that is in tension with the power levels needed to defeat defensive jamming systems. A common solution is to make the communications adaptive – to start off in a low-probability-of-intercept mode, but ramp up the power as needed in response to jamming.

So the protection of communications will require some mix, depending on the circumstances, of content secrecy, authenticity, resistance to traffic analysis and radio direction finding, and resistance to various kinds of jamming. These interact in some subtle ways. For example, one radio designed for use by dissident organizations in Eastern Europe in the early 1980s operated in the radio bands normally occupied by the Voice of America and the BBC World Service – which were routinely jammed by the Russians. The idea was that unless the Russians were prepared to turn off their jammers, they would have to work harder at direction finding.

Attack also generally requires a combination of techniques – even where the objective is not analysis or direction finding but simply denial of service. According to Soviet doctrine, a comprehensive and successful attack on a military communications infrastructure would involve destroying one third of it physically, denying effective use of a second third through techniques such as jamming, trojans or deception, and then allowing the adversary to disable the remaining third by attempting to pass all their traffic over a third of their installed capacity [1158]. This applies even in guerilla wars; in Malaya, Kenya and Cyprus the rebels managed to degrade the telephone system enough to force the police to set up radio nets [1382].

NATO developed a comparable doctrine, called *Counter-Command, Control and Communications* operations (C-C3, pronounced C C cubed), in the 80s. It achieved its first flowering in Gulf War 1. Of course, attacking an army's command structures is much older; it's basic common sense to shoot at an officer before shooting at his men.

23.3.1 Signals intelligence techniques

Before communications can be attacked, the enemy's network must be mapped. The most expensive and critical task in signals intelligence is identifying and extracting the interesting material from the cacophony of radio signals and the huge mass of traffic on systems such as phone networks and the Internet.

In the case of radio signals, communications intelligence agencies collect a huge variety of signal types and build extensive databases of which stations or services use which frequencies and how. It is often possible to identify individual equipment by signal analysis. The giveaways can include any unintentional frequency modulation, the shape of the transmitter turn-on transient, the precise center frequency and the final-stage amplifier harmonics. This *RF fingerprinting* (RFID) technology was declassified in the mid-1990s for use in identifying cloned cellphones [777, 1665]. It is the direct descendant of the World War 2 technique of recognizing a wireless operator by his *fist* – the way he used Morse Code [1226].

Radio Direction Finding (RDF) is also critical. In the old days, this involved triangulating the signal of interest using directional antennas at two monitoring stations. So spies might have several minutes to send a message home before having to move. Modern monitoring stations use *time difference of arrival* (TDOA) to locate a suspect signal accurately and automatically by comparing the phase of the signals received at two sites; nowadays, anything more than a second or so of transmission can be a giveaway.

Traffic analysis – looking at the number of messages by source and destination – can also give very valuable information. Imminent attacks were signalled in World War 1 by a greatly increased volume of radio messages, and more recently by increased pizza deliveries to the Pentagon. However, traffic analysis really comes into its own when sifting through traffic on public networks, where its importance (both for national intelligence and police purposes) is difficult to overstate. Until the late 1990s, traffic analysis was the domain of intelligence agencies – when NSA ops people referred to themselves as 'hunter-gatherers', traffic analysis was much of the 'hunting'. In this century, however, traffic analysis has come out of the shadows and become a major subject of study; I discuss this in the context of law-enforcement and intelligence surveillance in section 26.2.2.

One of the basic techniques is the *snowball search*. If you suspect Alice of espionage (or drug dealing, or whatever), you note everyone she calls, and everyone who calls her. This gives you a list of dozens of suspects. You eliminate the likes of banks and doctors, who receive calls from too many people to analyze, and repeat the procedure on each remaining number. Having done this procedure recursively two or three times, you amass thousands of contacts – they accumulate like a snowball rolling downhill. You now sift the snowball you've collected – for example, for people already on one of your blacklists, and for telephone numbers that appear more than once. So if Bob, Camilla and Donald are Alice's contacts, with Bob and Camilla in contact with Eve and Donald and Eve in touch with Farquhar, then all of these people may be considered suspects. You now draw a *friendship tree* which gives a first approximation to Alice's network, and refine it by collating it with other intelligence sources. *Covert community detection* became a very hot topic after 9/11, and researchers have tried all sorts of hierarchical clustering and graph partitioning methods to the problem. One leading algorithm is by Mark Newman [1436]; it uses spectral methods to partition a network into its natural communities so as to maximise modularity. The standard reference on such techniques is Easley and Kleinberg [599].

But even given good mathematical tools for analysing abstract networks, reality is messier. People can have several numbers, and they also share numbers. When conspirators take active countermeasures, it gets harder still; Bob might get a call from Alice at his work number and then call Eve from a phone box. (If you're running a terrorist cell, your signals officer should get a job at a dentist's or a doctor's or some other place that has too many active contacts to analyse effectively.) Also, you'll need some means of correlating telephone numbers to people. Even if you have access to the phone company's database of unlisted numbers, prepaid mobile phones can be a serious headache, as can hacked PBXs and encrypted messaging services such as Signal. Tying IP addresses to people is even harder; ISPs don't always keep the Radius logs for long. I discuss all these issues in more detail elsewhere, including Ed Snowden's revelations about what the NSA did in section 2.2.1 and the history of the Five Eyes intelligence sharing agreement in section 26.2.6. For now, I'll just remark that anonymous communications aren't new. There have been letter boxes and public phone booths for generations. But they're not a universal answer for the crook as the discipline needed to use anonymous communications properly is beyond most criminals. It was reported, for example, that one of the alleged 9/11 masterminds was caught after he used in his mobile phone in Pakistan a prepaid SIM card that had been bought in Switzerland in the same batch as a SIM that had been used in another Al-Qaida operation.

Signals collection is not restricted to getting phone companies to give access to the content of phone calls and the itemised billing records. It also involves a wide range of specialized facilities, as revealed by Ed Snowden in 2013 and described in section 2.2.1. Even before then, we knew the broad picture, thanks to a long series of leaks and work by investigative journalists. A 1996 book by Nicky Hager [850] described a Five Eyes collection network. Known as *Echelon*, this consisted of a number of fixed collection stations that monitored phone, fax and data traffic with computers called *dictionaries* that searched passing traffic for interesting phone numbers, network addresses and machine-readable content; this traffic selection was driven by search strings entered by intelligence analysts. Two years before Google was founded, Echelon was already a kind of Google for the world's phone system; the 2013 system described by Snowden extends this to IP networks and to the greater traffic volumes of today. It has become a massive distributed search engine with over a hundred nodes worldwide. Ingested traffic is first subject to massive data reduction – the video and the broadcast stuff gets thrown away – and then content is kept for a period of a few days in case anyone wants it. Traffic data is also kept, but for longer.

This fixed network is supplemented by tactical collection facilities as needed. Hager described, for example, the dispatch of Australian and New Zealand navy frigates to monitor domestic communications in Fiji during military coups in the 1980s. Koch and Sperber discuss US and German installations in Germany in the 1990s in [1064]; Fulghum describes airborne signals collection in [730]; satellites are also used to collect signals, and there are covert collection facilities too that are not known to the host country. For example, in section 2.2.1.9. I describe Operation Socialist, where GCHQ hacked the Belgian phone company to get access to third-party mobile-phone traffic routed through Belgium and also to the communications of EU institutions in Brussels.

Since the Snowden revelations, over half of IP traffic has been encrypted, which has shifted the focus of intelligence and law enforcement somewhat to collection from endpoints. This brings us to the topic of attacks.

23.3.2 Attacks on communications

Once you have mapped the enemy network, you may wish to attack it. People often talk in terms of 'codebreaking', but this is a gross oversimplification.

First, although some systems have been broken by pure cryptanalysis, this is fairly rare. Most production attacks have been on the supply or custody of equipment or key material. Examples include the theft of the State Department code book during World War II by the valet of the American ambassador to Rome [1003]; errors in the manufacture and distribution of one-time pads leading to the 'Venona' attacks on Soviet diplomatic traffic [1003]; and the covert ownership of the Swiss company Crypto AG by the CIA and Germany's Bundesnachrichtendienst (BND), which I discuss in section 26.2.7.1. Ed Snowden disclosed the theft by GCHQ of the card personalisation files from Gemplus, which compromised the keys in millions of SIM cards, giving the intelligence community access to the traffic of millions of mobile phones. Even where attacks based on cryptanalysis have happened, they have often been made much easier by operational errors, as with the attacks on the German Enigma traffic during World War 2 [1004], or by political interference with cryptography. This can be overt, as with export controls (see sections 4.3.1 and 26.2.8), or subtle, as with standards for random number generators (see section 2.2.1.5) and VPNs (section 2.2.1.7). Such activities are known by the agencies as 'crypto enabling' and their budgets are in nine figures. Other states play similar games: the history of Soviet intelligence during the Cold War reveals that the USA's technological advantage was largely nullified by Soviet skills in 'using Humint in Sigint support' – recruiting traitors who sold key material, such as the Walker family [119]. More recently, Chinese attacks on cloud service providers and on key assets such as the Office of Personnel Management – which got them the clearance data files on essentially all US government employees – were described in section 2.2.2.

Second, access to content is often not the desired result. In tactical situations, the goal is often to detect and destroy nodes, or to jam the traffic. Jamming can involve not just noise insertion but active deception. In World War 2, the Allies used German speakers as bogus controllers to send German nightfighters confusing instructions, and there was a battle of wits as authentication techniques were invented and defeated. I mentioned in an earlier chapter the tension between intelligence and operational units: the former want to listen to the other side's traffic, and the latter to deny them its use [151]. Compromises between these goals can be hard to find. It's not enough to jam the traffic you can't read as that tells the enemy what you can read!

Matters can be simplified if the opponent uses cryptography – especially if they're competent and you can't read their traffic. This removes the ops/intel tension, so you switch to RDF or the destruction of protected links as appropriate. This can involve the hard-kill approach of digging up cables or bombing telephone exchanges (both of which the Allies did during Gulf War 1), the soft-kill approach of jamming, or whatever combination is effective. Jamming is useful where a link is to be disrupted for a short period, but is often expensive; not only does it tie up facilities, but the jammer itself becomes a target. Cases where it is more effective than physical attack include satellite links, where the uplink can often be jammed using a tight beam from a hidden location using only a modest amount of power.

The increasing use of civilian infrastructure, and in particular the Internet, raises the question of whether systematic denial-of-service attacks might be used to jam traffic. (There were anecdotes during the Bosnian war of Serbian information warfare cells attempting to DDoS NATO web sites.) This threat is still considered real enough that many Western countries have separate intranets for government and military use.

23.3.3 Protection techniques

So communications security techniques involve not just protecting authenticity and confidentiality, but also preventing traffic analysis, direction finding, jamming and physical destruction. Encryption can stretch to the first of these if applied at the link layer, so that all links have a constant-rate pseudorandom bitstream on them at all times. But link-layer encryption is tricky over radio, because of the tradeoff between synchronisation and jamming; and on its own it is not always enough, as enemy capture of a single node might put the whole network at risk.

Encryption alone cannot protect against RDF, jamming, and the destruction of links or nodes. For this, different technologies are needed. The obvious solutions are:

- redundant dedicated lines or optical fibers;
- highly directional transmission links, such as optical links using infrared lasers or microwave links using highly directional antennas and extremely high frequencies;
- *low-probability-of-intercept* (LPI), *low-probability-of-position-fix* (LPPF) and anti-jam radio techniques.

The first two of these options are fairly straightforward, and where they're feasible they are usually the best. Cabled networks are very hard to destroy completely, unless the enemy knows where the cables are and has physical access to cut them. Even with massive artillery bombardment, the telephone network in Stalingrad remained in use (by both sides) all through the siege.

The third option is a substantial subject in itself, which I will now describe (briefly).

A number of LPI/LPPF/antijam techniques go under the generic name of *spread spectrum* communications. They include *frequency hoppers*, *direct sequence spread spectrum* (DSSS) and *burst transmission*. From beginnings around World War 2, spread spectrum has spawned a substantial industry and the technology (especially DSSS) has been applied to numerous other problems, ranging from high resolution ranging (in the GPS system) through radio protocols such as Bluetooth. I'll look at each of these three approaches in turn.

23.3.3.1 Frequency hopping

Frequency hoppers are the simplest spread spectrum systems to understand and to implement. They do exactly as their name suggests – they hop rapidly from one frequency to another, with the sequence of frequencies determined by a pseudorandom sequence known to the authorized principals. They were invented, famously, over dinner in 1940 by actress Hedy Lamarr and screenwriter George Antheil, who devised the technique as a means of controlling torpedos without the enemy detecting them or jamming their transmissions [1705]. A frequency-hopping radar was independently developed at about the same time by the Germans [1685].

Hoppers are resistant to jamming by an opponent who doesn't know the hop sequence. If the hopping is slow and a nearby opponent has capable equipment, then an option might be *follower jamming* – observing the signal and following it around the band, typically jamming each successive frequency with a single tone. However if the hopping is fast enough, or propagation delays are excessive, the opponent may have to jam much of the band, which requires much more power. The ratio of the input signal's bandwidth to that of the transmitted signal is called the *process gain* of the system; thus a 100 bit/sec signal spread over 10MHz has a process gain of $10^7/10^2 = 10^5 = 50$dB. The *jamming margin*, which is defined as the maximum tolerable ratio of jamming power to signal power, is essentially the process gain modulo implementation and other losses (strictly speaking, process gain divided by the minimum bit energy-to-noise density ratio). The optimal jamming strategy, for an opponent who can't predict or effectively follow the hop sequence, is *partial band jamming* – to jam enough of the band to introduce an unacceptable error rate in the signal.

Frequency hopping is used in some civilian applications, such as Bluetooth, where it gives a decent level of interference robustness at low cost. On the military side of things, although hoppers can give a large jamming margin, they give little protection against direction finding. A signal analysis receiver that sweeps across the frequency band of interest will usually intercept them (and depending on the relevant bandwidths, sweep rate and dwell time, it might intercept a hopping signal several times).

Since frequency hoppers are simple to implement and give a useful level of jam-resistance, they are often used in combat networks, such as man-pack radios, with hop rates of 50–500 per second. To disrupt these communications, the enemy will need a fast or powerful jammer, which is inconvenient for the battlefield. Fast hoppers (defined in theory as having hop rates exceeding the bit rate; in practice, with hop rates of 10,000 per second or more) can pass the limit of even large jammers. Hoppers are less 'LPI' than the techniques I'll describe next, as an opponent with a sweep receiver can detect the presence of a signal; and slow hoppers have some vulnerability to eavesdropping and direction finding, as an opponent with suitable wideband receiving equipment can often follow the signal.

23.3.3.2 DSSS

In direct-sequence spread spectrum, we multiply the information-bearing sequence by a much higher rate pseudorandom sequence, usually generated by some kind of stream cipher (see Figures 23.1 and 23.2). This spreads the spectrum by increasing the bandwidth. The technique was first described by a Swiss engineer, Gustav Guanella, in a 1938 patent application [1685], and developed extensively in the USA in the 1950s. Its first deployment in anger was in Berlin in 1959.

Like hopping, DSSS can give substantial jamming margin (the two systems have the same theoretical performance). But it can also make the signal significantly harder to intercept. The trick is to arrange things so that at the intercept location, the signal strength is so low that it is lost in the noise floor unless the opponent knows the spreading sequence with which to recover it. Of course, it's harder to do both at the same time, since an antijam signal should be high power and an LPI/LPPF signal low power; the usual tactic is to work in LPI mode until detected by the enemy (for example, when coming within radar range) and then boost transmitter power into antijam mode.

There is a large literature on DSSS, and the techniques have now been taken up by the commercial world as *code division multiple access* (CDMA) in various mobile radio and phone systems.

DSSS is sometimes referred to as "encrypting the RF", and it comes in a number of variants. For example, when the underlying modulation scheme is FM rather than AM it's called *chirp*. The classic introduction to the underlying mathematics and technology is [1528]; the engineering complexity is higher than with frequency hop for various reasons. For example, synchronization is particularly critical. One strategy is to have your users take turns at providing a reference signal. If your users have access to a reference time signal (such as GPS, or an atomic clock) you might rely on this; but if you don't control GPS, you may be open to synchronization attacks, and even if you do the GPS signal might be jammed. It was reported in 2000 that the French jammed GPS in

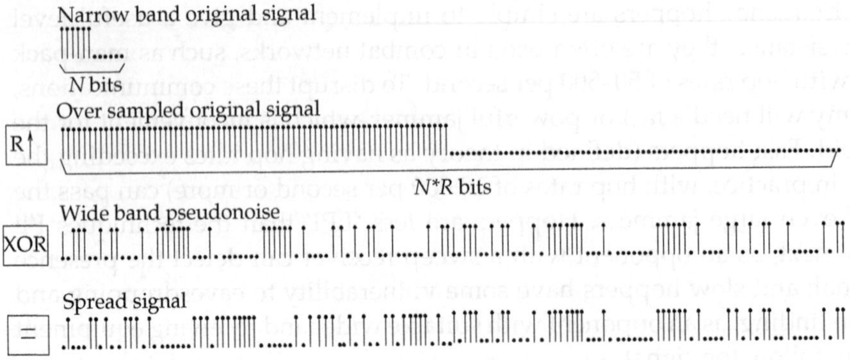

Narrow band original signal
N bits
Over sampled original signal
R↑
N*R bits
Wide band pseudonoise
XOR
Spread signal
=

Figure 23.1: Spreading in DSSS (courtesy of Roche and Dugelay)

Spread signal
Wide band pseudonoise
XOR
Demodulated signal
=
Restored signal
Σ

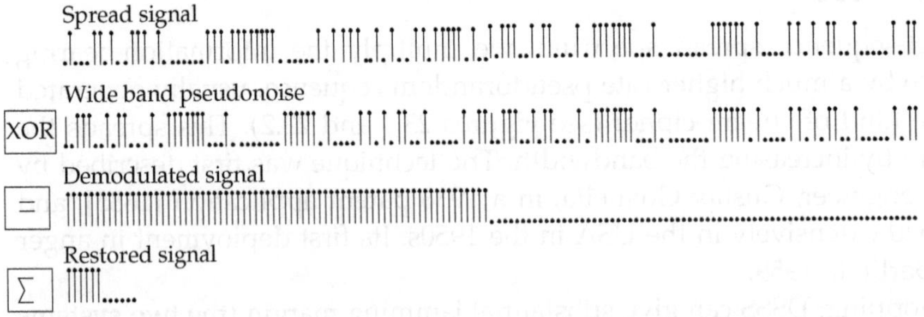

Figure 23.2: Unspreading in DSSS (courtesy of Roche and Dugelay)

Greece in an attempt to sabotage a British bid to sell 250 tanks to the Greek government, a deal for which France was a competitor. This caused the British tanks to get lost during trials. When the ruse was discovered, the Greeks found it all rather amusing [1922]. Now GPS jammers are commodity items and I'll discuss them in more detail a little later in this chapter.

23.3.3.3 Burst communications

Burst communications, as their name suggests, involve compressing the data and transmitting it in short bursts at times unpredictable by the enemy. They are also known as *time-hop*. They are usually not so jam-resistant (except insofar as the higher data rate spreads the spectrum) but can be even more difficult to detect than DSSS; if the duty cycle is low, a sweep receiver can easily miss them. They are often used in radios for special forces and intelligence agents. Really high-grade room bugs often use burst.

An interesting variant is *meteor burst* transmission (also known as *meteor scatter*). This relies on the billions of micrometeorites that strike the Earth's atmosphere each day, each leaving a long ionization trail that persists for typically a third of a second and provides a temporary transmission path between a mother station and an area of maybe a hundred miles long and a few miles wide. The mother station transmits continuously; whenever one of the daughters is within such an area, it hears mother and starts to send packets of data at high speed, to which mother replies. With the low power levels used in covert operations one can achieve an average data rate of about 50 bps, with an average latency of about 5 minutes and a range of 500–1500 miles. Meteor burst communications are used by special forces, and in civilian applications such as monitoring rainfall in remote parts of the third world. With higher power levels, and in higher latitudes, average data rates can rise into the tens of kilobits per second, and the USAF in Alaska uses such systems as backup communications for early warning radars. In niche markets where low bit rates and high latency can be tolerated, but where equipment size and cost are important, meteor scatter can be hard to beat. The technology is described in [1664].

23.3.3.4 Combining covertness and jam resistance

There are some rather complex tradeoffs between different LPI, LPPF and jam resistance features, and other aspects of performance such as resistance to fading and multipath, and the number of users that can be accommodated simultaneously. They also behave differently in the face of specialized jamming techniques such as *swept-frequency jamming* (where the jammer sweeps repeatedly through the target frequency band) and follower. Some types of jamming translate between different modes: for example, an opponent with insufficient power to block a signal completely can do *partial time jamming* on DSSS by emitting pulses that cover a part of the spectrum it uses, just like partial band jamming of frequency hop.

There are also engineering tradeoffs. For example, DSSS tends to be about twice as efficient as frequency hop in power terms, but frequency hop gives much more jamming margin for a given complexity of equipment. On the other hand, DSSS signals are much harder to locate using direction-finding techniques [673].

System survivability requirements can impose further constraints. It may be essential to prevent an opponent who has captured one radio and extracted its current key material from using this to jam a whole network. So a typical military system will use some combination of tight beams, DSSS, hopping and burst.

- Both DSSS and hopping are used with TDMA in *Link 16*, as it's known in NATO; it's also known to US forces as the *Tactical Digital Information Link* (TADIL), and was previously known as the *Joint Tactical Information Distribution System* (JTIDS) [1665]. TDMA separates transmission from reception and lets users know when to expect their slot. It has a DSSS signal with a 57.6KHz data rate and a 10MHz chip rate (and so a jamming margin of 36.5dB), which hops around in a 255MHz band with a minimum jump of 30 MHz. The hopping code is available to all users, while the spreading code is limited to individual circuits. The rationale is that if an equipment capture leads to the compromise of the spreading code, this would allow jamming of only a single 10MHz band, not the full 255MHz. Development started in 1967 with Gordon Welchman, who also broke German ciphers at Bletchley during World War 2; after pilot projects in the 1970s, serious development started in the 1980s and the system was fully deployed from about 2000, seeing use in Afghanistan and Iraq [1960].

- The US armed forces have been supported by a series of satellite communications systems (MILSTAR and DSCS) with 1 degree beams from a geostationary orbit. The effect of the narrow beam is that users can operate within three miles of the enemy without being detected. Jam protection is from hopping: its channels hop several thousand times a second in bands of 2GHz.
- French tactical radios have remote controls. The soldier can use the handset a hundred yards from the radio. This means that attacks on the high-power emitter don't have to endanger the troops so much [514].

There are also some system-level tricks, such as *interference cancellation* – where you communicate in a band which you're jamming with a waveform known to your own radios, so they can cancel it out or hop around it. This can make jamming harder for the enemy by forcing them to spread their available power over a larger bandwidth, and can make signals intelligence harder too [1604].

23.3.4 Interaction between civil and military uses

Civil and military communications are increasingly intertwined. Operation Desert Storm (Gulf War 1 against Iraq) made extensive use of the Gulf States' civilian infrastructure: a huge tactical communications network was created in a short space of time using satellites, radio links and leased lines, and experts from various US armed services claim that the effect of communications capability on the war was decisive [944].

Another example of growing interdependency is the Global Positioning System, GPS. This started off as a US military navigation system and had a *selective availability* feature that limited the accuracy to about a hundred yards unless the user had the relevant cryptographic key. This had to be turned off during Gulf War 1 as there weren't enough military GPS sets to go round and civilian equipment had to be used instead. As time went on, GPS turned out to be so useful in civil aviation that the FAA helped find ways to defeat selective availability and give an accuracy of about 3 yards compared with a claimed 8 yards for the standard military receiver [631]. Finally, in May 2000, President Clinton announced the end of selective availability.

The US government still reserves the right to switch off GPS, or to introduce errors, for example if terrorists are thought to be using it. But so many diverse systems now depend on GPS, from Google Maps to Uber, that responsible governments are unlikely to. However there are many applications with motivated opponents. Some countries use GPS to do road pricing, or to enforce parole terms on released prisoners via electronic ankle tags, as I discussed in section 14.4 As a result, GPS jammers appeared in car magazines in 2007 for $700, and now cost under $100; they're used by truck drivers to cheat road toll systems, company car drivers who want to stop their boss knowing where they're going, and car thieves. Cheap devices have short ranges, of typically 5–10m.

GPS spoofing takes slightly more work. An example is *meaconing*, where you sample the signals at location A and retransmit them at location B (this is also known as a *wormhole attack*). The result is that anyone near B thinks they're near A instead. This is used as a defensive mechanism in the limousines of some heads of government (a sophisticated assassin could use this to target a missile). Some countries engage in systematic GPS jamming, an example being Russia along its border with Norway. Spoofing can be largely detected using differential GPS, where you use another receiver at a known location as a reference point (the FAA's trick), and with interferometric GPS, also known as S-GPS, where you use the signals captured by successive readings by the same receiver to produce a synthetic aperture. This also increases sensitivity and deals with multipath in urban canyons, the main source of large errors in current equipment[1].

In addition to the US GPS system, Russia, China and Europe have separate navigation satellite systems using the same principles; collectively, such systems are known as GNSS.

23.4 Surveillance and target acquisition

Those aspects of electronic warfare that have to do with target acquisition and weapon guidance are where the arts of jamming and deception have been most highly developed. (In fact, although there is much more in the open literature on the application of electronic attack and defense to radar than to communications, much of the same science applies to both.)

[1]Full disclosure: the company that developed S-GPS, Focal Point Positioning, was started by one of my postdocs and I'm an investor in it.

The main methods used to detect hostile targets and guide weapons to them are sonar, radar and infrared. The first to be developed was sonar, which was invented and deployed in World War 1 (under the name of 'Asdic'), and still dominates submarine warfare [847]. Against other targets, such as surface ships, planes and tanks, the key sensor is radar. Although it was invented in 1904 as a maritime anti-collision device, its serious development only occurred in the 1930s and it was used by all major participants in World War 2 [856, 993]. The electronic attack and protection techniques developed for it tend to be better developed than, and often go over to, systems using other sensors.

23.4.1 Types of radar

The wide range of deployed systems includes search radars, fire-control radars, terrain-following radars, counter-bombardment radars and weather radars. They have a wide variety of signal characteristics. For example, radars with a low RF and a low *pulse repetition frequency* (PRF) are better for search while high-frequency, high-PRF devices are better for tracking. A classic textbook on the technology is by Schleher [1665].

Early radar designs for search applications may have a rotating antenna that emits a sequence of pulses and detects echos. In the days before digital electronics, the sweep in the display tube could be mechanically rotated in sync with the antenna. Fire control radars often used *conical scan*: the beam would be tracked in a circle around the target's position, and the amplitude of the returns could drive positioning servos (and weapon controls) directly. Now the beams are generated electronically using multiple antenna elements, but tracking loops remain central. Many radars have a *range gate*, circuitry which focuses on targets within a certain range of distances from the antenna; if the radar had to track all objects between (say) zero and 100 miles, then its pulse repetition frequency would be limited by the time it takes radio waves to travel 200 miles. This would have consequences for angular resolution and tracking performance generally.

Doppler radar measures the velocity of the target by the change in frequency in the return signal. It is very important in distinguishing moving targets from *clutter*, the returns reflected from the ground. Doppler radars may have *velocity gates* that restrict attention to targets whose radial speed with respect to the antenna is within certain limits.

An example of gating in a non-military application is adaptive cruise control in cars. This uses radar, gated to ignore vehicles whose relative speed is too great (so it doesn't panic at oncoming vehicles) as well as vehicles that are too near or too far. You may notice that if another car pushes in close in front of you, less than 20m away, your cruise control won't notice it and won't slow down.

23.4.2 Jamming techniques

Electronic attack can be passive or active.

The earliest countermeasure to be widely used was *chaff* – thin strips of conducting foil that are cut to half the wavelength of the target signal and then dispersed to provide a false return. Toward the end of World War 2, allied aircraft were dropping 2000 tons of chaff a day to degrade German air defenses. Chaff can be dropped directly by the aircraft attempting to penetrate the defenses (which isn't ideal as they will then be at the apex of an elongated signal), or by support aircraft, or fired forward into a suitable pattern using rockets or shells. The main counter-countermeasure against chaff is Doppler: as chaff is very light it comes to rest almost at once and can be distinguished fairly easily from moving targets.

Other techniques include small decoys with active repeaters that retransmit radar signals and larger decoys that simply reflect them; sometimes one vehicle (such as a helicopter) acts as a decoy for another more valuable one (such as an aircraft carrier). These principles are quite general. Weapons that home in on their targets using *radio direction finding* (RDF) are decoyed by special drones that emit seduction RF signals, while infrared guided missiles are diverted using flares.

The passive countermeasure in which the most money has been invested is *stealth* – reducing the *radar cross-section* (RCS) of a vehicle so that it can be detected only at very much shorter range. This forces the enemy to place their air defense radars closer together, so they have to buy a lot more of them. Stealth includes a wide range of techniques and a proper discussion is well beyond the scope of this book. Some people think of it as 'extremely expensive black paint', but there's more to it than that. As an aircraft's RCS is typically a function of its aspect, it may have a fly-by-wire system that continually exhibits a low-RCS aspect to identified hostile emitters (the F117 became known to its pilots as the 'wobbly goblin').

Active countermeasures are much more diverse. Early jammers simply generated a lot of noise in the range of frequencies used by the target radar; this is known as *noise jamming* or *barrage jamming*. Some systems used systematic frequency patterns, such as pulse jammers, or swept jammers that traversed the frequency range of interest (also known as *squidging oscillators*). But such a signal is fairly easy to block – one trick is to use a *guard band* receiver, a receiver on a frequency adjacent to the one in use, and to blank the signal when this receiver picks up a jamming signal. And jamming isn't restricted to one side; as well as being used by the target, the radar itself can also send spurious signals from an auxiliary antenna to mask the real signal or to simply overload the defenses.

At the other end of the scale lie hard-kill techniques such as *anti-radiation missiles* (ARMs), often fired by support aircraft, which home in on hostile signals.

Defenses against such weapons include the use of decoy transmitters, blinking transmitters on and off, and *passive radar* – which exploits the signals from existing transmitters such as TV and radio stations when they bounce off targets.

In the middle lies a large toolkit of *deception jamming* techniques. Most jammers used for self-protection are deception jammers of one kind or another; barrage and ARM techniques tend to be more suited to use by support vehicles.

The usual goal with a self-protection jammer is to deny range and bearing information to attackers. The basic trick is *inverse gain jamming* or *inverse gain amplitude modulation*. This is based on the observation that the directionality of the attacker's antenna is usually not perfect; as well as the main beam it has *sidelobes* through which energy is also transmitted and received, albeit much less efficiently. The sidelobe response can be mapped by observing the transmitted signal, and a jamming signal can be generated so that the net emission is the inverse of the antenna's directional response. The effect, as far as the attacker's radar is concerned, is that the signal seems to come from everywhere; instead of a 'blip' on the radar screen you see a circle centered on your own antenna. Inverse gain jamming is very effective against the older conical-scan fire-control systems.

More generally, the technique is to retransmit the radar signal with a systematic change in delay and/or frequency. This can be non-coherent, in which case the jammer's called a *transponder*, or coherent – that is, with the right waveform – when it's a *repeater*. Modern equipment stores received waveforms in *digital radio frequency memory* (DRFM) and manipulates them using signal processing.

An elementary countermeasure is *burn-through*. By lowering the pulse repetition frequency, the dwell time is increased and so the return signal is stronger – at the cost of less precision. A more sophisticated countermeasure is *range gate pull-off* (RGPO). Here, the jammer transmits a number of fake pulses that are stronger than the real ones, thus capturing the receiver, and then moving them out of phase so that the target is no longer in the receiver's range gate. Similarly, with Doppler radars the basic trick is *velocity gate pull-off* (VGPO). With older radars, successful RGPO would cause the radar to break lock and the target to disappear from the screen. Modern radars can reacquire lock very quickly, and so RGPO must either be performed repeatedly or combined with another technique – commonly, with inverse gain jamming to break angle tracking at the same time.

An elementary counter-countermeasure is to jitter the pulse repetition frequency. Each outgoing pulse is either delayed or not depending on a *lag sequence* generated by a random number generator, so the jammer cannot anticipate when the next pulse will arrive and has to follow it. Such *follower jamming* can only make false targets that appear to be further away. So the counter-counter-countermeasure, or (counter)^3-measure, is for the radar to have a *leading edge tracker*, which responds only to the first return pulse; and the (counter)^4-measures can include jamming at such a high power that the receiver's automatic gain control circuit is captured. An alternative is *cover jamming* in which the jamming pulse is long enough to cover the maximum jitter period.

The next twist of the screw may involve tactics. Chaff is often used to force a radar into Doppler mode, which makes PRF jitter difficult (as continuous waveforms are better than pulsed for Doppler), while leading edge trackers may be combined with frequency agility and smart signal processing. For example, true target returns fluctuate, and have realistic accelerations, while simple transponders and repeaters give out a more or less steady signal. Of course, it's always possible for designers to be too clever; the Mig-29 could decelerate more rapidly in level flight by a rapid pull-up than some radar designers had anticipated, so pilots could use this manoeuvre to break radar lock. And now CPUs are powerful enough to manufacture realistic false returns.

23.4.3 Advanced radars and countermeasures

A number of advanced techniques are used to defend against jamming.

Pulse compression was first developed in Germany in World War 2, and uses a kind of direct sequence spread spectrum pulse, filtered on return by a matched filter to compress it again. This can give processing gains of 10–1000. Pulse compression radars are resistant to transponder jammers, but are vulnerable to repeater jammers, especially those with digital radio frequency memory. However, the use of LPI waveforms is important if you don't wish the target to detect you long before you detect it.

Pulsed Doppler is much the same as Doppler, and sends a series of phase stable pulses. It has come to dominate many high-end markets, and is widely used, for example, in *look-down shoot-down* systems for air defense against low-flying intruders. As with elementary pulsed tracking radars, different RF and pulse repetition frequencies give different characteristics: we want low frequency/PRF for unambiguous range/velocity and also to reduce clutter – but this can leave many blind spots. Airborne radars that have to deal with many threats use high PRF and look only for velocities above some threshold, say 100 knots – but are weak in tail chases. The usual compromise is medium PRF – but this suffers from severe range ambiguities in airborne operations. Also, search radar requires long, diverse bursts but tracking needs only short, tuned ones. An advantage is that pulsed Doppler can discriminate some very specific signals, such as modulation provided by turbine blades in jet engines. The main deception strategy used against pulsed Doppler is velocity gate pull-off, although a modern variant is to excite multiple velocity gates with deceptive returns.

Monopulse became one of the most popular techniques. It was used, for example, in the Exocet missiles that proved so difficult to jam in the Falklands war. The idea is to have four linked antennas so that azimuth and elevation data can be computed from each return pulse using interferometric techniques. Monopulse radars are difficult and expensive to jam, unless a design defect can be exploited; the usual techniques involve tricks such as formation jamming and terrain bounce. Often the preferred defensive strategy is just to use towed decoys.

One powerful trick is *passive coherent location*. Lockheed's 'Silent Sentry' system has no emitters at all, but rather uses reflections of commercial radio and television broadcast signals to detect and track airborne objects [165]. The receivers, being passive, are hard to locate and attack; knocking out the system entails destroying major civilian infrastructure, which opponents will often prefer not to do for legal and propaganda reasons. Passive coherent location is effective against some kinds of stealth technology, particularly those that entail steering the aircraft so that it presents the nulls in its radar cross-section to visible emitters. Passive location actually goes back to the radar pioneer Robert Watson-Watt in the 1930s and appears to have been first used by the Germans from 1942 when their Klein Heidelberg station exploited British Chain Home radar signals to track RAF aircraft (in EW parlance, it was a 'hitchhiker'). When Britain realised this was happening in 1944, the Chain Home signals were jittered [825].

One research frontier in 2020 is *cognitive radar*. Attack and defence have become more complex since the arrival of digital radio frequency memory and other software radio techniques. Both radar and jammer waveforms may be adapted to the tactical situation with much greater flexibility than before. Simon Haykin and colleagues studied the strategies and tactics used by bats, who adapt their sonar intelligently while hunting insects, and applied this first to radio for the efficient use of spectrum, then to radar in a seminal 2006 paper [874]. From the moment a radar (or sonar) is switched on, it builds up knowledge of its environment, the interesting aspects of which are mostly dynamic. The basic idea is that a cognitive radar does a recursive update of a model of its environment and uses this to illuminate it intelligently, using learning mechanisms. This becomes adversarial with non-cooperative targets. There is now vigorous research into the fusion of ideas from the human visual system and from neural networks, Bayesian target tracking and signal processing.

23.4.4 Other sensors and multisensor issues

Much of what I've said about radar applies to sonar as well, and a fair amount to infrared. Passive decoys – flares – worked very well against early heat-seeking missiles which used a mechanically spun detector, but are less effective against modern detectors that incorporate signal processing. Flares are like chaff in that they decelerate rapidly with respect to the target, so the attacker can filter on velocity or acceleration. They are also like repeater jammers in that their signals are relatively strong and stable compared with real targets.

Active infrared jamming is less widespread than radar jamming because it's harder; it tends to exploit features of the hostile sensor by pulsing at a rate or in a pattern that causes confusion. Some infrared defense systems are starting to employ lasers to disable the sensors of incoming weapons; and it's emerged that a number of 'UFO' sightings have actually been due to various kinds of jamming (both radar and infrared) [176].

One growth area is *multisensor data fusion* whereby inputs from radars, infrared sensors, video cameras and even humans are combined to give better target identification and tracking than any could individually. The Rapier air defense missile, for example, used radar to acquire azimuth while tracking is carried out optically in visual conditions. Data fusion can be harder than it seems. As I discussed in section 17.8, combining two alarm systems will generally result in improving either the false alarm or the missed alarm rate, while making the other worse. If you scramble your fighters when you see a blip on either the radar or the infrared, you'll have more false alarms; but if you scramble only when you see both then it will be easier for the enemy to jam you or sneak through. Multisensor fusion is now in 2020 a hot research topic with self-driving cars, which fuse data from radar, lidar, ultransonics and video – as I'll describe in section 25.2.

Things become more complex where the attacker is on a platform that's itself vulnerable to counter-attack, such as a tank, a ship or an aircraft. It will have systems for threat recognition, direction finding and missile approach warning, whose receivers will be deafened by its jammer. The usual trick is to turn the jammer off for a short 'look-through' period at random times.

With multiple friendly and hostile platforms, things get more complex still. During the Cold War, you expected each side to have specialist support vehicles with high-power dedicated equipment, which makes it to some extent an energy battle – "he with the most watts wins". A SAM belt would have multiple radars at different frequencies to make jamming harder. The overall effect of jamming (as of stealth) is to reduce the effective range of radar. But jamming margin also matters, and who has the most vehicles, and the tactics employed; and the move to cognitive systems has changed doctrine to "subtly disrupt the enemy's communications and radar networks without their realizing they're being deceived" [721].

23.5 IFF systems

With multiple vehicles engaged, it's also necessary to have a reliable way of distinguishing friend from foe. *Identify-Friend-or-Foe* (IFF) systems are both critical and controversial, with a significant number of 'blue-on-blue' incidents in Iraq being due to equipment incompatibility between US and allied forces. Incidents in which US aircraft bombed British soldiers contributed to loss of UK public support for the war, especially after the authorities in both countries tried and failed to cover up such incidents out of a wish to both preserve technical security and also to minimise political embarrassment.

IFF goes back in its non-technical forms to antiquity. See for example Judges 12:5–6 (which I quote at the head of the chapter on biometrics): the Israelites identified enemy soldiers by their inability to pronounce 'Shibboleth'. World War 2 saw the French resistance asking people to pronounce 'grenouille', the French for 'frog', and anyone who couldn't was presumed German. In the early years of that conflict, air identification was procedural: allied bombers would be expected to cross the coast at particular times and places, while stragglers would announce their lack of hostile intent by a pre-arranged manoeuvre such as flying an equilateral triangle before crossing the coast. German planes would roll over when the radio operator challenged them, so as to create a 'blip' in their radar cross-section. There were then some early attempts at automation: when allied aircraft started to carry IFF beacons, the German air defence found they could detect the planes by triggering them [825].

The Korean war saw the arrival on both sides of jet aircraft and missiles, which made it impractical to identify targets visually. Early IFF systems simply used a serial number or 'code of the day', but this was wide open to spoofing, and the world's air forces started work on cryptographic authentication.

The legacy NATO system is the Mark XII, introduced in the 1960s and designed to solve the protocol problems discussed in section 4.3.3. The Mark XII secure mode uses a 32-bit challenge and a 4-bit response. If challenges or responses are too long, then the radar's pulse repetition frequency (and thus its accuracy) would be degraded. It sends 12–20 challenges in a series, and in the original implementation the responses were displayed on a screen at a position offset by the arithmetic difference between the actual response and the expected one. The effect was that while a foe had a null or random response, a 'friend' would have responses clustered near the center screen, which would light up. Reflection attacks are prevented, and MIG-in-the-middle attacks made much harder, because the challenge uses a focused antenna, while the receiver is omnidirectional. (The antenna used for the challenge is typically the fire control radar, which in older systems was conically scanned.)

This has been largely replaced by the Mark XIIA which has a backwards-compatible mode, but uses spread-spectrum waveforms in the new Mode 5, which has been the focus of development efforts by the US services and NATO armed forces during the 2010s. Such systems also have compatibility modes with the systems used by civil aircraft to 'squawk' their ID to secondary surveillance radar. However, the real problems are now air-to-ground. NATO's IFF systems evolved for a Cold War scenario of thousands of tactical aircraft on each side of the Iron Curtain; how do they fare in a modern conflict like Iraq or Afghanistan?

Historically, about 10–15% of casualties were due to 'friendly fire' but in Gulf War 1 this rose to 25%. Such casualties are more likely at the interfaces between air and land battle, and between sea and land, because of the different services' way of doing things; joint operations are thus particularly risky. Coalition operations also increase the risk because of different national systems. Following this experience, several experimental systems were developed to extend IFF to ground troops. But when Gulf War 2 came along, nothing decent had been deployed. A report from Britain's National Audit Office describes what went wrong [1391]. In a world where defence is purchased not just by nation states, and not just by services, but by factions within these services, and where legislators try to signal their 'patriotism' to less-educated voters by blocking technical collaboration with allies ('to stop them stealing our jobs and our secrets'), the institutional and political structures just aren't conducive to providing defense 'public goods' such as a decent IFF system that would work across NATO. And NATO is a broad alliance; as one insider told me, "Trying to evolve a solution that met the aspirations of both the US at one extreme and Greece (for example) at the other was a near hopeless task."

Project complexity is one issue: it's not too hard to stop your air force planes shooting each other, but it's a lot more complex to stop them shooting at your ships or tanks, and it's much harder still when a dozen nations are involved. There are some sexy systems used by a small number of units in Iraq that let all soldiers see each other's positions superimposed in real time on a map display on a helmet-mounted monocle. They greatly increase force capability in mobile warfare, allowing units to execute perilous maneuvers like driving through each other's kill zones, but are not a panacea in complex warfare such as Iraq in the late 2000s and early 2010s. There, the key networks were social, not electronic, and it's hard to automate networks with nodes of unknown trustworthiness [1662]. The big-bang approach was tried, but failed; the Joint Tactical Radio System (JTRS, pronounced 'jitters') set out to equip all the US services with radios that interoperate and do at least two IFF modes. However, it's one of the Pentagon's biggest procurement failures, as they spent a sum variously estimated as between \$6bn and almost \$16bn over 15 years without delivering a single usable radio [1987].

Experience has taught us that even with 'hard-core' IFF, where ships and planes identify each other, the hardest issues weren't technical but to do with economics, politics and doctrine. Over two decades of wrangling within NATO, America wanted an expensive high-tech system, for which its defense industry was lobbying hard, while European countries wanted something simpler and cheaper that they could also build themselves, for example by tracking units through the normal command-and-control system and having decent interfaces between nations. But the USA refused to release the location of its units to anyone else for 'security' reasons. America spends more on defense than its allies combined and believed it should lead; the allies didn't want their own capability further marginalised by yet more dependence on US suppliers.

Underlying doctrinal tensions added to this. US doctrine, the 'Revolution in Military Affairs' (RMA) promoted by Donald Rumsfeld and based on an electronic system-of-systems, was not only beyond the allies' budget but was distrusted, based as it is on minimising one's own casualties through vast material and technological supremacy. The Europeans argued that one shouldn't automatically react to sniper fire from a village by bombing the village; as well as killing ten insurgents, you kill a hundred civilians and recruit several hundred of their relatives to the other side. The American retort to this was that Europe was too weak and divided to even deal with genocide in Bosnia. The result was deadlock. Countries decided to pursue national solutions, and no real progress has been made on interoperability since the Cold War. Allied forces in Iraq and Afghanistan were reduced to painting large color patches on the roofs of their vehicles and hoping the air strikes would pass them by. US aircraft duly bombed and killed a number of allied servicemen, weakening the alliance. What will happen now, given deglobalisation and President Trump's impatience with foreign allies, is anyone's guess.

23.6 Improvised explosive devices

A significant effort was made in electronic-warfare measures to counter the improvised explosive devices (IEDs) that were the weapon of choice of insurgents in Iraq and Afghanistan. The first IED attack on US forces took place in March 2003, and they rose to a peak of 25,000 in 2007 with over 100,000 in total. These bombs became the 'signature weapon' of the Iraq war, like the machine-gun in World War 1 and the laser-guided bomb in Gulf War I. And now that unmanned aerial vehicles can be built by hobbyists for under $1000, we are starting to see improvised cruise missiles used in Syria and elsewhere, including an attempt to assassinate Venezuela's President Maduro.

Anyway, over 33,000 jammers were made and shipped to coalition forces. The Department of Defense spent over $1bn on them in 2006, in an operation that, according to insiders, "proved the largest technological challenge for DOD in the war, on a scale last experienced in World War 2" [141]. The effect was that the proportion of radio-controlled IEDs dropped from 70% to 10%, while the proportion triggered by command wires increased to 40%.

Rebels have been building IEDs since at least Guy Fawkes, who tried to blow up England's Houses of Parliament in 1605. Many other nationalist and insurgent groups have used IEDs, from anarchists through the Russian resistance in World War 2, the Irgun, ETA and the Viet Cong to Irish nationalists. The IRA got so expert at hiding IEDs in drains and culverts that the British Army had to use helicopters instead of road vehicles in the 'bandit country' near the Irish border in the 1980s and early 1990s. They also ran bombing campaigns against the UK on a number of occasions in the twentieth century. In the last of these, from 1970–94, they blew up the Grand Hotel in Brighton when Margaret Thatcher was staying there for a party conference, killing several of her colleagues. Later, London suffered two incidents in which the IRA set off truckloads of home-made explosive causing widespread devastation. The fight against the IRA involved a total of about 7,000 IEDs, and gave UK defense scientists much experience in jamming: barrage jammers were fitted in VIP cars that would cause IEDs to go off either too early or too late. These were made available to allies; such a jammer saved the life of President Musharraf of Pakistan when Al-Qaida tried to blow up his convoy in 2005.

The electronic environment in Iraq turned out to be much more difficult than either Belfast or Pakistan. Bombers can use any device that will flip a switch at a distance, and used everything from key fobs to cellphones. Meanwhile the RF environment in Iraq had become complex and chaotic. Millions of Iraqis used unregulated cellphones, walkie-talkies and satellite phones, as most of the optical-fibre and copper infrastructure had been destroyed in the 2003 war or looted afterwards. 150,000 coalition troops also sent out a huge variety of radio emissions, which changed all the time as units rotated. Over 80,000 radio frequencies were in use, and monitored using 300 databases – many of them not interoperable. Allied forces only started to get on top of the problem when hundreds of Navy electronic warfare specialists were deployed in Baghdad; after that, coalition jamming efforts were better coordinated and started to cut the proportion of IEDs detonated by radio.

But the 'success' in electronic warfare did not translate into a reduction in allied casualties. The IED makers simply switched from radio-controlled bombs to devices detonated by pressure plates, command wires, passive infrared or volunteers. The defence focus shifted to a mix of tactics: 'right of boom' measures such as better vehicle armor and autonomous vehicles, and 'left of boom' measures such as disrupting the bomb-making networks. Better armor made a difference: while in 2003 almost every IED caused a coalition casualty, by 2007 it took four devices on average [141]. Armored vehicles were also a key tactic in other insurgencies, while the DARPA investment in self-driving vehicles paid off a decade later in a surge of work on driver assistance systems, as I discuss in section 25.2. Network disruption, though, is a longer-term play as it depends on building good sources of human intelligence; Britain and Israel spent years targeting bombmakers in Ireland and Lebanon, respectively.

23.7 Directed energy weapons

In the late 1930s, there was panic in Britain and America on rumors that the Nazis had developed a high-power radio beam that would burn out vehicle ignition systems. British scientists studied the problem and concluded that it was infeasible [993]. They were correct – given the relatively low-powered radio transmitters, and the simple but robust vehicle electric systems, of the 1930s.

Things started to change with the arrival of the atomic bomb. The detonation of a nuclear device creates a large pulse of gamma-ray photons, which in turn displace electrons from air molecules by Compton scattering. The large induced currents give rise to an electromagnetic pulse (EMP), which may be thought of as a very high amplitude pulse of radio waves with a very short rise time.

Where a nuclear explosion occurs within the earth's atmosphere, the EMP energy is predominantly in the VHF and UHF bands, though there is enough energy at lower frequencies for a radio flash to be observable thousands of miles away. Within a few tens of miles of the explosion, the radio frequency energy may induce currents large enough to damage most electronic equipment that has not been hardened. The effects of a blast outside the earth's atmosphere are believed to be much worse (although there has never been a test). The gamma photons can travel thousands of miles before they strike the earth's atmosphere, which could ionize to form an antenna on a continental scale. It is reckoned that most electronic equipment in Northern Europe could be burned out by a one megaton blast at a height of 250 miles above the North Sea. For that matter, most electronic equipment on the US west coast, from Seattle to San Diego, could be wiped out by a blast 250 miles above Salt Lake City. Such an attack would kill no-one directly but could cause economic damage on the scale of the coronavirus pandemic [124]. A Carrington event – a massive solar flare, as observed by the astronomer Richard Carrington in 1859 – would cause similar disruption. That flare caused auroras as far south as the Caribbean, and telegraph systems failed all over Europe and North America, sometimes giving their operators electric shocks. Lloyd's of London later estimated that the cost of such an event to the USA alone could be in the low trillions of dollars, and that such an event is inevitable every generation or two [919]. Smaller geomagnetic storms happen regularly, for example in 1989 and 2003. For this reason, critical military systems are carefully shielded, big IT service firms disperse their data centres round the globe, we have warning satellites, and well-run utilities spend money to protect critical assets such as large transformers.

Western concern about EMP grew after the Soviet Union started a research program on non-nuclear EMP weapons in the mid-80s. At the time, the United States was deploying "neutron bombs" in Europe – enhanced radiation weapons that could kill people without demolishing buildings. The Soviets portrayed this as a 'capitalist bomb' that would destroy people while leaving property intact, and responded by threatening a 'socialist bomb' to destroy property (in the form of electronics) while leaving the surrounding people intact.

By the end of World War 2, the invention of the cavity magnetron had made it possible to build radars powerful enough to damage unprotected electronic circuitry at a range of several hundred yards. The move from valves to transistors and integrated circuits increased the vulnerability of most commercial electronic equipment. A terrorist group could in theory mount a radar in a truck and drive around a city's financial sector wiping out the banks. The banks' server farms might well be unaffected; the real damage would be to desktops, laptops and other everyday devices. Replacing the millions of gadgets on which a city's life depends would be tiresome.

For battlefield use, it's desirable for EMP weapons to fit into a standard bomb or shell casing rather than having to be truck-mounted. Their military use is however limited. The USA tried a device called Blow Torch in Iraq as a means of frying the electronics in IEDs, but it didn't work well [141]. There's a survey of usable technologies at [1084] that describes how power pulses in the Terawatt range can be generated using explosively-pumped flux compression generators and magnetohydrodynamic devices, as well as by high-power microwave transmitters. But EMP bombs dropped from aircraft need to deploy antennas before detonation in order to get decent coupling, and even so are lethal to ordinary electronic equipment for a radius of only a few hundred meters. Military command and control systems that are already hardened for nuclear EMP should be unaffected.

The real significance of EMP may be to give a blackmail weapon to countries such as Iran and North Korea with primitive nuclear technology. When North Korea fires a missile into the sea near Japan, it sends a signal: "We can switch off your economy any time we like, and without directly killing a single Japanese civilian either." Japan is now developing anti-missile defences. A massive attack on electronic communications is more of a threat to countries such as the USA and Japan that depend on them, than on countries such as North Korea (or Iran) that don't.

This observation goes across to attacks on the Internet as well, so let's now turn to 'information warfare'.

23.8 Information warfare

The phrase *Information warfare* came into use from about 1995. Its popularity was boosted by operational experience in Gulf War 1. There, air power was used to degrade the Iraqi defenses before the land attack was launched, and one goal of NSA personnel supporting the allies was to enable the initial attack to be made without casualties – even though the Iraqi air defenses were at that time intact and alert. The attack involved a mixture of standard e-war techniques such as jammers and anti-radiation missiles; cruise missile attacks on command centers; attacks by special forces who sneaked into Iraq and dug up lengths of communications cabling from the desert; and, allegedly, the use of hacking tricks to disable computers and telephone exchanges. (By 1990, the US Army was already calling for bids for virus production [1208].) The operation achieved its goal of ensuring zero allied casualties on the first night of the aerial bombardment. Military planners and think tanks started to consider how to build on the success.

In April 2007, information warfare was thrust back on the agenda by events in Estonia. There, the government had angered Russia by moving an old Soviet war memorial, and shortly afterwards the country was subjected to a number of distributed denial-of-service attacks that appeared to originate from Russia [525]. Estonia's computer emergency response team tackled the problem with cool professionalism, but their national leadership invoked the NATO treaty, calling for US military help against Russia. Russia had deniability: the packet storms were launched by Russian botnet herders, reacting to the news from Estonia and egging each other on via chat rooms; the one man convicted of the attacks was an ethnic Russian teenager in Estonia itself. There had been similar tussles between Israeli and Palestinian hackers, and between Indians and Pakistanis. Estonia also had some minor street disturbances caused by rowdy ethnic Russians objecting to the statue's removal. Nonetheless NATO did respond by setting up an information warfare centre in Tallinn, and as I described in section 2.2.3, one outcome was the Tallinn Manual, which sets out the military and international law applicable to online operations designed to have real-world effects in conflicts between states [1667].

States must act in self-defense or with some other lawful justification and in accordance with the law of armed conflict. Attacks are operations reasonably expected to cause injury to people or damage to property; they may only be directed at combatants and their logistics, not at civilians; attacks must be geographically limited, not indiscriminate; and some targets are off-limits, from hospitals and places of worship to nuclear power stations. Interpretation could keep the lawyers busy though. Infrastructure used by both military and civilian organisations is fair game, and although 'treachery' is prohibited, 'ruses of war' are not. It's worth noting that while these rules prohibit war crimes, they do not prohibit states from interfering with the privacy and other rights of each others' citizens, and this continues to happen at scale [31].

In section 2.2.3, I described how Estonia was just a warm-up for later Russian operations in Ukraine, where the Russians took down electricity infrastructure and did significant damage to companies operating there by the NotPetya worm, which inflicted significant collateral damage on some international companies with offices in that country.

But what's information warfare anyway? The conventional view from the mid-2000s, arising out of Gulf War 1, was expressed by Whitehead [1981]:

> *The strategist ... should employ (the information weapon) as a precursor weapon to blind the enemy prior to conventional attacks and operations.*

Cynics took the view that it was just a remarketing of the things the agencies have been doing for decades anyway, in an attempt to maintain their budgets post-Cold-War.

However, the most far-sighted analyst at the time was Dorothy Denning of the Naval Postgraduate School whose 1999 book on the topic defined information warfare as 'operations that target or exploit information media in order to win some advantage over an adversary' [539]. This was so broad that it includes not just hacking but all of electronic warfare and all existing intelligence gathering techniques (from Sigint through satellite imagery to spies), but propaganda too. In a later article she discussed the role of the net in the propaganda and activism surrounding the Kosovo war [540].

A similar view of information warfare, from a writer whose background was defense planning rather than computer security, was given by Edward Waltz [1981]. He defined *information superiority* as 'the capability to collect, process and disseminate an uninterrupted flow of information while exploiting or denying an adversary's ability to do the same'. The aim of such superiority is to conduct operations without effective opposition. The book has less technical detail on computer security matters than Denning but set forth a first attempt to formulate a military doctrine of information operations.

23.8.1 Attacks on control systems

If you want to use computer exploitation to do real damage to a rival nation, perhaps the first thing to look at is electricity generation and distribution. Taking down the grid is the cyber equivalent of a nuclear strike; once the electricity supply fails, then pretty well everything else in a modern economy shuts down too. For example, a five-week failure of the power supply to the central business district of Auckland, New Zealand, in 1996 led to 60,000 of the 74,000 employees having to work from home or from relocated offices, while most of the area's 6,000 apartment dwellers moved out for the duration [840]. And perhaps the worst terrorist 'near miss' in recent history was an IRA attempt in 1996 to blow up transformers at the big substations that supply London [232]. This failed because a senior IRA commander was a British agent; had it been successful it would have wrecked electricity supplies to much of London for many months, blacking out millions of people and businesses responsible for maybe a third of Britain's GDP. Finally, attacks on electricity transmission and distribution have been a standard US tactic in wars from Serbia to Iraq. (In fact, the Iraq insurgency after 2003 was fuelled by delays in restoring the power supply, which left millions of Iraqis sweltering in the summer heat with no air conditioning.)

Security researchers started paying attention to control systems in the mid-2000s once it was noticed that the protocols used to manage assets such as electricity grids and petrochemical plants, namely Modbus and DNP3, did not support authentication, as these systems had evolved in a world of private networks – with fixed LANs inside installations and leased lines linking them to control centres. Firms started moving to IP networks from the late 1990s because it was cheaper, but this meant that, without authentication, anyone who knew the IP address of a sensor could read it, and anyone who knew the address of an actuator could operate it. After one or two accidents caused by pranks, and an incident in 2000 where a disgruntled employee of a water company's IT contractor caused a spill of 800 tons of sewage in Maroochy, Australia [7], there started to emerge a control-systems security research community.

Governments tried to help with regulation. The US Departments of Energy and Homeland Security launched an initiative in 2006, and North American Electric Reliability Corporation (NERC), which sets standards for the bulk power system, ruled in its Critical Infrastructure Protection (CIP) standard that any generator with a black-start capability would need to have basic information security compliance. Black start is the ability to start up even if the grid is down; hydro power stations can do this, nuclear stations can't, and coal-fired stations can generally only do a black start if they have an auxiliary diesel generator. The industry's response was that some coal-fired plants scrapped their diesel plant, as information security could not be added to their regulated cost base and therefore came off the bottom line [105].

Attempts were also made to extend control-system protocols to support encryption and authentication, but this is seriously difficult. There are three main vendors of electricity substations, and if one becomes the prime contractor on a project it will typically buy components from the other two, so compatibility is essential. Substations have a design life of typically 40 years and come with maintenance contracts, so the rate of change is glacial. The threat model is also interesting. Anyone who can get physical access can switch off the power by pressing the red button; they can even destroy the transformer by causing an internal short-circuit, which takes only one bullet. It therefore makes little sense to encrypt or even just authenticate traffic on the substation LAN, and doing that is hard anyway as some of the control traffic has a 4ms latency requirement [731]. The only practical outcome was to secure the logical perimeter – the communications from the substation to the network control centre – just as one secures the asset physically by using a cage or a building. So one practical outcome of this research programme was startups whose focus was to enable energy companies and other utilities to protect their networks by re-perimeterising them. The specialist firewalls and gateways they designed have now become mainstream products and are widely used by energy companies.

A second outcome was increased awareness of indirect threats to national electricity supply. I described in section 14.2.4 how most European governments decided to install smart meters, following lobbying from the meter industry, and how we found that the proposed UK installation was insecure; it amounted to putting a remotely commandable off switch in every home in Britain, and not even protecting it with appropriate cryptographic authentication. GCHQ got involved in the design, but even seven years later only a minority of UK smart meters follow the 'improved' specification. As we discussed in section 14.2.4, the project has been a conspicuous failure in both financial and energy-saving terms.

A third outcome was a set of research tools. The Shodan search engine, launched in 2009, crawls the Internet to locate and index connected devices, enabling researchers to see which devices are vulnerable from their software update status; in 2011, Éireann Leverett used this to locate thousands of vulnerable control systems [1149]. A 2016 scan by Ariana Mirian and colleagues found some 60,000 vulnerable devices round the world, ranging from electricity substations to HVAC in government buildings; they also used honeypots to track the actors scanning for such devices, and although over half were from known security companies, a significant minority were in China or from shielded hosts [1323]. More recently our group has been involved in developing better honeypots to detect people doing scans and launching attacks on network-attached devices [1959]; by deploying realistic honeypots in realistic network locations, it's possible to provoke hostile action [573]. Our monitoring of underground crime forums, which goes back to the early days of control system security research, has detected no sustained competent interest in control system hacking by criminal groups, so it is reasonable to assume that the great majority of such activity is by state actors or their proxies.

The burst of research into control systems security ran in parallel with state actors' growing awareness of the potential. It's been reported that Idaho National Labs, which was involved in the US regulatory push and hosted some of the Scada security conferences at the time, helped the NSA and their Israeli counterparts develop the Stuxnet worm, which damaged Iran's uranium enrichment capacity over the period 2008–2010; I described this in section 2.2.1.11.

Finally, as I described in section 2.2.3, 2015 saw Russia responding to a conventional Ukrainian attack on power distribution in Crimea (a Ukrainian territory that Russia had annexed) by a cyber-attack that took down 30 Ukrainian substations, leaving 230,000 people in the dark for several hours [2070]. However, that seems to have been a warning rather than attempt to do serious economic damage, and since then there seem to have been no serious cyber-attacks on electricity distribution. There have been attacks on other control systems; notably, Iran tried to hack Israeli water distribution systems in April 2020 with a view to introducing toxic levels of chlorine into the rural water supply, but the Israelis detected and stopped this. They retaliated the following month by closing down one of the harbours at the Iranian port of Bandar Abbas, causing tailbacks of trucks that stretched for miles [230].

But the main action has moved elsewhere.

23.8.2 Attacks on other infrastructure

After the Stuxnet story broke there was a surge of interest among governments worldwide in cyber-conflict. The prices paid in underground markets for exploitable vulnerabilities skyrocketed, and in addition to the overt markets in vulnerabilites, there developed grey markets to which security researchers could take their ideas for resale to cyber-arms manufacturers. In addition to vulnerabilities that governments could use to exploit the PCs or phones of their foes, both foreign and domestic, there emerged concern about attacks on information infrastructure such as the Internet itself. The Russian attacks on Estonia in 2007 and Georgia in 2008 focused minds somewhat, as did an attack by Pakistan on YouTube in 2008 (Pakistan had planned to block the service only at home, but the BGP attack it mounted caused a global outage), and an incident in 2010 when China Telecom hijacked 15% of Internet addresses for 18 minutes, which some observers interpreted as a test of a 'cyber-nuke'.

The European Network and Information Security Agency (ENISA) commissioned us to write a report on the Internet's interconnect, which appeared in 2011 [1910]. I discussed the main findings in section 21.2.1 on BGP security. It is certainly possible to tear up the Internet's routing infrastructure by advertising lots of bogus routes; a number of incidents (including the Pakistani and Chinese ones) have taught us that. It is also true that if an opponent could take down the Internet for a few days in a developed country, the result would be chaos (and especially so since the coronavirus pandemic as even more human activities have been forced online). One of the main technical restraints on such action is that most capable opponents would themselves suffer tremendous harm, given that the online services used in most countries are globalised. However, China is largely immune, because of its policy of separating its infrastructure from the rest of the Internet using the Great Firewall, and excluding US service providers such as Google, Facebook and Twitter in favour of local champions. North Korea is even more isolated. Russia has been trying to follow China, and as its service providers such as Vkontakte are much more entangled with European and American infrastructure, President Putin passed a law in May 2019 requiring Russian ISPs to be able to operate independently of foreign Internet infrastructure by November. In December, a successful test was announced, though nobody noticed anything happening; a second test, due in March 2020, was apparently postponed because of the coronavirus [160]. If that were to be made to work, then Russia, like China, would be in a position to mount large-scale disruption attacks against the Internet in the rest of the world.

23.8.3 Attacks on elections and political stability

The period 2011–16 saw the emphasis in information operations shift from attacks on infrastructure to political conflict. The period started with the Arab Spring, which I will discuss in more detail in section 26.4.1. There, social media were used to fuel an uprising against autocratic regimes across the Arab world; although the Tunisians overthrew their dictator and achieved democracy, the results elsewhere ranged from civil war in Syria and the Yemen to state failure in Libya and crackdowns by rulers elsewhere. I described in section 2.2.4 how Arab governments splashed out on surveillance technology from the west and from Israel, and hired ex-NSA mercenaries, to track and harass their opponents both at home and abroad.

By 2016, we'd seen substantial Russian interference in both the Brexit referendum and the US presidential election. Russia has a long history of managed elections. I wrote sarcastically in the first edition in 2001: "I sincerely hope that the election of Vladimir Putin as the president of Russia had nothing to do with the fact that the national electoral reporting system is run by FAPSI, a Russian signals intelligence agency formed in 1991 as the successor to the KGB's 8th and 16th directorates. Its head, General Starovoitov, was reported to be an old KGB type; his agency reported directly to President Yeltsin, who chose Putin as his successor." [733, 1005] By the time Putin's party was re-elected in 2007, the cheating had become so blatant – with gross media bias and state employees ordered to vote for the ruling party – that the international community would not accept the result as free and fair.

By the 2012 election, as I noted in section 2.2.3, the Russian population was sufficiently restive that Putin felt the need for external enemies to rally public support. He invaded Ukraine in 2014, claiming simultaneously to be defending it against fascists, and against gays and Jews, and annexed the Crimea – bringing down international sanctions. This campaign involved 'hybrid warfare' tactics that combined 'little green men' – Russian soldiers in uniforms without insignia, claimed to be Ukrainian anti-fascists – with various cyber-attacks, propaganda and even an attack on Ukrainian media, reporting falsely that a pro-Russian candidate had won an election. After

Europe imposed sanctions on Russia as a punishment for invading Ukraine, the Kremlin became a major funder of far-right groups throughout Europe, supporting the Brexit campaigns in the UK and the rise of parties such as AfD in Germany. At the same time as openly promoting fascist ideas – including the ideology of Ivan Ilyin at home – Putin has managed to retain the sympathy of swathes of the anti-fascist left in Europe too. The overall strategy since sanctions has been to disrupt and weaken the USA and the EU by all available means.

The tactics used in such information warfare have a lot in common with electronic warfare. Putin, and other authoritarian leaders, often swamp target audiences, both at home and abroad, with fake news; this jamming undermines trust in more reliable media – who are in turn accused of being 'fake news'. If you can't stop your population from reading the New York Times, you just make sure they don't believe it [474]. There are bulk decoys, like chaff; after the Russians shot down Malaysia Airlines' flight MH17 over Ukraine in 2014, they pushed many different conspiracy theories in parallel [1596]. Many politicians use other decoys to distract the press from news that could damage them; Trump has used everything from the WHO to hydroxychloroquine [1713]. The equivalent of deceiving IFF may be triangulation – the art of stealing a key aspect of the opponent's brand (as when Boris Johnson made the NHS central to his pitch in the Brexit referendum). The equivalent of an anti-radiation missile might be blocking an opponent's website or choking off their funding. Corrupt leaders accuse their opponents of corruption, while authoritarians who blame gays and Jews for their country's plight will happily accuse their opponents of fascism.

Many people seem to think that the security of an election is limited to the anonymous but verifiable tallying of the vote itself. That is important, and I discuss it in section 25.5. However it is only a small piece of the picture. Just as an IED can be defeated before the boom (by intelligence or jamming) or afterwards (by armour), so also an election can be subverted before or after the vote. Even in mature democracies, politicians are forever trying to manipulate the franchise and the campaigning rules, such as campaign finance limits. For example, the Russians contributed money to both the 'Leave' campaigns in Britain's Brexit referendum, which was illegal, and both campaigns separately broke overall finance limits, for which they got fined [1267]. The disclosure of these offences did not lead to a rerun of the vote; it merely helped paralyse UK politics for three years. The UK Prime Minister David Cameron had earlier changed franchise rules to require all voters to register separately, rather than by households, to cut the number of young people on the electoral roll (this should have helped his Conservative party, but backfired in the referendum). The outcome was much more due to discontent among voters and to blunders by complacent pro-remain politicians than to enemy action, but the existence of an enemy actively promoting harmful outcomes did not help. To this day, many Remain supporters do not accept the referendum result as valid – a truly wonderful outcome from the Russians' point of view.

Similar comments can be made on the US presidential election later that year; I discuss the political scientist Yochai Benkler's analysis of the effect on that election of fake news in section 26.4.2. Again, the role played by the Russians was to exploit existing polarisation, throw petrol on the fire where possible (for example by leaking hacked emails from the Clinton camp, as discussed in section 2.2.3) and to buy influence where they could [387]. They also hacked into systems in Illinois and Florida (and probably some other states) and could have manipulated voter registration, but they opted not to pull the trigger on those attacks because they didn't need them; they hacked the electorate instead. Had Clinton won, then if either of those states had voted for her, evidence of 'fraud' could have emerged to undermine her presidency. The fact that there are 6,000 different voting systems across the USA makes the presidential ballot hard to steal outright by technical means, but exposes its credibility to challenge.

An election system is like an alarm; as we discussed in section 13.3, you can defeat an alarm by destroying confidence in it, so that alarms are ignored. The real customer for an election is the losing party, and if one of the parties isn't really prepared to accept defeat, then a pretext may be all they need. Whether Trump wins or loses in November 2020, we can expect an increase in polarisation among the US electorate and a decline in America's standing in the world – again, a win for Russia.

China has largely refrained from interfering in other countries' internal affairs; as I described in section 2.2.2, they have long taken the view that an uncensored Internet amounted to US subversion of communist party rule but their posture on that front has been defensive. Their focus has been on building their economic, technological and intelligence capacity while not conducting attacks, whether disruptive or political, on other countries. This capacity building has had political consequences, most notably in the US effort to prevent Huawei dominating 5G infrastructure, as I discuss in sections 2.2.2 and 22.3.4. This looks set to become a frontier in the new cold war that's emerging as China seeks to become the USA's peer competitor. There are signs in 2020 though of more aggressive diplomacy as China seeks to entrench its narrative around coronavirus and exploit the USA's chaotic response to the pandemic.

23.8.4 Doctrine

The inclusion by Denning and Waltz of propaganda and other psychological operations in information warfare back in 1999 was a minority view at the time, but has been borne out by events since. It does have historical precedent. From

Roman and Mongol efforts to promote a myth of invincibility, through the use of propaganda radio stations by both sides in World War 2 and the Cold War, to the bombing of Serbian TV during the Kosovo campaign and denial-of-service attacks on Chechen web sites by Russian agencies – the tools may change but the game remains the same.

In the intervening twenty years, the names have changed: the Pentagon adopted 'information warfare' in 1998, changed it to 'information operations' in 2006 and 'cyberspace operations' in 2013 [1167]. There have been some big blind spots: it wasn't anybody's job at the Pentagon in 2016 to worry about people in St Petersburg pretending to be from Black Lives Matter [1223]. Meanwhile a lot of wrong ideas have been gradually discarded. It used to be said that attribution would be too hard; that's not been borne out. Others used to suggest that information warfare provided a casualty-free way to win: 'just hack the Iranian power grid and watch them sue for peace'. Yet more developed countries are more exposed, and if a cyber-attack targets civilians to an even greater extent than the alternatives, then the attackers are likely to be portrayed as war criminals. What's more, if a NATO country is the aggressor, the Tallinn manual will bolster the prosecution.

In the second edition of this book, I wondered whether cyber-attacks would find their place in open conflict or in guerilla warfare. So far we've seen their development by Russia into a component of a hybrid warfare strategy honed in Georgia and Ukraine. We've seen attacks on democratic mechanisms not just in the UK and the USA but in Germany, France and elsewhere. Will this be the future for the next ten years too, as the USA, Russia and China continue to smile sweetly at the United Nations while kicking each other under the table? Or are there other possibilities? We've seen cyber tactics being used by peaceful demonstrators in the Arab spring, and by violent extremists in the Middle East, mostly without success. What else is there? Or will states continue to be the main actors?

23.9 Summary

Electronic warfare flourished during the Cold War, and developed a lot of interesting techniques, some of which have found their way into mainstream information security. After being starved of attention and money for years, it's starting to move back up the agenda as China aims to compete with the USA and the Russians also modernise their armed forces. The AI revolution may change how the game is played as cognitive radar and sonar, coupled with better techniques for multisensor data fusion, move the advantage from the platform with the most megawatts to the player with the smartest software. It is likely, though, that victory will require effective coordination of physical force and subtle deception.

A decade ago, people already talked of electronic warfare becoming information warfare. We have seen occasional use of cyber-weapons, from the 2010 Stuxnet attack on Iran's uranium enrichment facilities to the Russian NotPetya attack on Ukraine. And it is easily observable that nation state actors are making preparations to attack other nations' critical national infrastructure. However, the great majority of the information operations that have actually been carried out in 2010–20 have been psychological operations and propaganda, aimed at sowing discord, disrupting political institutions such as elections, and deepening political polarisation. There are some interesting similarities between the decoys, jamming and other techniques used to manipulate enemy radar, and the techniques used to manipulate public opinion.

Research problems

My own research group has two relevant interests. First, we've been looking at adversarial machine learning. For example, if a missile uses a neural network to seek its target, then can we approximate that model well enough from observations to determine whether there's an evasion strategy better than random maneuvering [2074]? Can we design camouflage that takes a lot of computational effort to understand? Can we add keys to neural networks so that different instances of them are vulnerable to different adversarial samples, thus limiting an opponent's ability to learn [1735]?

Second, via the Cambridge Cybercrime Centre, we collect large amounts of data on spam, phish, malware, botnet command-and-control traffic, and other online wickedness. We develop better honeypots for capturing attack traffic, including attacks aimed at embedded systems. We license our collections of data to over a hundred researchers worldwide. They are now starting to include scrapes of underground fora for political extremism as well as for cybercrime.

Further reading

The best all-round reference for the technical aspects of electronic warfare, from radar through stealth to EMP weapons, is by Curtis Schleher [1665]; a good summary was written by Doug Richardson [1604]. The classic introduction to the anti-jam properties of spread spectrum sequences is by Andrew Viterbi [1968]; the history of spread spectrum is ably told by Robert Scholtz [1685]; the classic introduction to the mathematics of spread spectrum is by Raymond Pickholtz, Donald Schilling and Lawrence Milstein [1528]; while the standard textbook is by Robert Dixon [567]. The most thorough reference on communications jamming is by Richard Poisel [1533]. Hugh Griffiths and Nicholas Willis describe the electronic war between the RAF and the Luftwaffe in World War 2 [825], while R. V. Jones' overall history of British electronic warfare and scientific intelligence gives a lot of insight not just into how the technology developed but also into strategic and tactical deception [993, 994]. The various protocols used in industrial control systems and surveyed, and their vulnerabilities discussed, by Santiago Figueroa-Lorenzo, Javier Añorga, and Saioa Arrizabalaga in [684]. The inadequacy of US power grid hardening against Carrington events and EMP are discussed by Matthew and Martin Weiss [2009]. For readings on information operations, I'd recommend the readings I list at the end of the chapters on psychology and on surveillance; for the Russian assault on democracy in the USA and Europe, one starting point is a report to the Committee on Foreign Relations of the U.S. Senate [387].

CHAPTER

24

Copyright and DRM

Be very glad that your PC is insecure – it means that after you buy it, you can break into it and install whatever software you want. What YOU want, not what Sony or Warner or AOL wants.

– JOHN GILMORE

24.1 Introduction

Copyright has been among the highly contentious issues of the digital age, and drove the development of *digital rights management* (DRM). The big fight was between Hollywood and the tech industry in the 1990s and 2000s; by 2010 it had essentially been resolved. We won; power in the music and film industry passed from firms like EMI and Universal to firms like Apple, Spotify, Amazon and Netflix, while Amazon cornered the market in books – first physically and then with ebooks. Technically, the world moved from enjoying music and video from local media such as CDs and DVDs (which many people used to share) and satellite broadcast TV (which some people used to hack), to broadband streaming services where subscription management is fairly straightforward. I thought seriously about dropping this chapter from the third edition and just referring you to the second edition chapter online, as there's not a lot more to say technically. On reflection I decided to edit it to give the context as seen from 2020. Just as the multilevel secure systems I describe in Chapter 9 are largely obsolete but drove the development of military computer security and influenced today's security landscape in many subtle ways, so also the copyright wars left their mark. DRM is still used: in ebooks, in the Fairplay system on your iPhone to make it harder to copy songs, and in HTML5 in your browser to make it harder for you to copy Netflix videos. Very similar techniques are used in gaming platforms to make it harder for players to use aimbots, in protecting user data on cloud platforms, and in mobile phone security where *Runtime Application Self-Protection* (RASP) is used to defend banking and other apps against malware that roots the phone. Accessory-control mechanisms that our industry adopted to protect game cartridges now use cryptography to support business models in dozens of business sectors. My final reason to spare this chapter is that the copyright wars became part of our shared security culture, and even if you're too young to have taken part, you may occasionally find it helpful to understand what we greybeards are blethering on about.

At the political level, the control of information has been near the centre of government concerns since before William Tyndale (one of the founders of the Cambridge University Press) was burned at the stake for printing the Bible in English. The sensitivity continued through the establishment of modern copyright law starting with the Statute of Anne in 1709, through eighteenth-century battles over press censorship, to the Enlightenment and the framing of the US Constitution. The link between copyright and censorship is obscured by technology from time to time, but has a habit of reappearing. Copyright mechanisms exist to keep information out of the hands of people who haven't paid for it, while censors keep information out of the hands of people who aren't trusted with it. Where ISPs are compelled to install filters that prevent their customers from downloading copyrighted material, these filters can often be used to block seditious material too.

Over the twentieth century, the great wealth accruing to the owners of literary copyright, films and music created a powerful interest in control. As the Internet took off, the music and film industries feared losing sales to digital copying, and lobbied for sweetheart laws – the DMCA in America in 1998, and a series of IP Directives in Europe – that give special legal protection to mechanisms that enforce copyright. These laws have since been used and abused for all sorts of other purposes, from taking down phishing websites to stopping people from refilling printer cartridges and even from repairing broken devices.

The ostensible target of these laws was the DRM used from the 1990s in products such as Windows Media Player, and since 2017 in browsers compliant with HTML5, to control the copying of music and videos. The basic idea in DRM is to make a file uncopiable by encrypting it, and then providing separately a 'license' which is the key to the media file encrypted using a key unique to the user, plus some statements in a 'rights management language' about what the user can do with the content. The app that renders the media content is trusted to abide by these. I'll also give a quick tour of the history and describe some interesting variants such as satellite TV encryption systems, copyright marking and traitor tracing. DRM is less relevant now than in 2008 when the second edition of this book came out, but there are still some applications, which I'll describe later.

Some serious policy issues are mixed up in all this. It's hard to make DRM compatible with open-source software unless you have either trustworthy hardware such as enclaves or TPMs, or closed-source sandboxes that are patched as soon as they are reverse engineered. The computer industry resisted DRM, but Hollywood and the music industry forced us to introduce it, saying that without it they'd be ruined. We warned them that DRM would ruin them, and they didn't listen. Music is no longer run by firms like Universal and EMI but by firms like Apple and Amazon – and the move to streaming let new firms like Spotify join the party. DRM introduced serious privacy issues, though, which have not gone away with streaming. Instead of a license management server in Microsoft knowing every music track you've ever listened to, and every movie you've ever watched, it's now streaming servers at Apple or Spotify or Netflix.

24.2 Copyright

The protection of copyright has for years been an obsession of the film, music and book publishing industries. There were long and acrimonious disputes in many countries about whether blank audiocasettes, and then videocassettes, should be subjected to a tax whose proceeds would be distributed to copyright owners. Going back to the nineteenth century, there was alarm that the invention of photography would destroy the book publishing trade; the eighteenth saw book publishers trying to close down public lending libraries, until they realised they were creating mass literacy and driving sales; while in the sixteenth, the invention of movable type printing was considered subversive by most of the powers of the day, from princes and bishops to craft guilds.

We'll come back to these historical examples later. But I'm going to start by looking at software protection – as most of the copyright issues that led to DRM played out in the PC and games software markets from the 1980s.

24.2.1 Software

Software for early computers was given away free by the hardware vendors or by users who'd written it. IBM even set up a scheme in the 1960s whereby its users could share programs they'd written. (Most business programs were too specialised, too poorly documented, or just too hard to adapt. But software used in research was widely shared.) So protecting software copyright was not an issue. Almost all organizations that owned computers were large and respectable; their software tended to require skilled maintenance. There were also computer bureau services – the forerunner of today's cloud computing – where the owner of a mainframe who used it to work out their own payroll would offer this as a service to other firms. There, you bought the service, not the software. The hardware costs were the dominant factor.

When minicomputers arrived in the 1960s, software costs became significant. Hardware vendors started to charge extra for their operating system, and third-party system houses sprang up. To begin with, they mostly sold you a complete bespoke system – hardware, software and maintenance – so piracy was still not much of an issue. By the mid-1970s, some of them had turned bespoke systems into packages: software originally written for one bakery would be parametrised and sold to many bakeries. The most common copyright dispute in those days was when a programmer left your company to join a competitor, and their code suddenly acquired a number of your features; the question then was whether he'd taken code with him, or reimplemented it.

One way to resolve such a problem is to look at *software birthmarks* – features of how a particular implementation was done. For example, litigation over whether people had copied software from the ROM of the early IBM PCs turned on the order in which registers are pushed and popped, as the software had been written in assembler. This merged with the field of *stylometry* in which humanities scholars try to attribute authorship by analysis of writing styles[1]. More recently, the natural-language processing community has written plagiarism detection tools, which typically recognise a passage of text by indexing it according to the least common words that appear in it [881]; by the 1990s this had led to tools that try to identify malware authors from their coding style [1101]. Code stylometry is still an active area of research [372].

With time, people invented lots of useful things to do with software. So a firm that had bought a minicomputer for stock control (or contracted for time on a bureau service) might be tempted to run a statistical program as well to prepare management reports. Meanwhile, the installed base of machines got large enough for software sharing to happen more than just occasionally. So some system houses started to design enforcement mechanisms. A common one was to check the processor serial number; another was the *time bomb*. When I worked in 1981 for a company selling retail stock control systems, we caused a message to come up every few months saying something like "Fault no. WXYZ – please call technical support". WXYZ was an encrypted version of the license serial number, and if the caller claimed to be from that customer we'd give them a password to re-enable the system for the next few months. (If not, we'd send round a sales person.) This mechanism could have been defeated easily if the 'customer' understood it, but in practice it worked fine: most of the time it was a low-level clerk who got the fault message and called our office.

Software copyright infringement really started to become an issue when the arrival of microcomputers in the late 1970s and early 80s created a mass market, and software houses started to ship products that didn't need technical support to install and run. Initial responses varied. There was a famous open letter from Bill Gates in 1976, a year after Microsoft was founded, in which he complained that less than 10% of all microcomputer users had paid them for BASIC [722].

[1] The cryptanalyst William Friedman and his wife Elizebeth were hired by an eccentric millionaire to figure out whether Bacon wrote Shakespeare. They concluded that he hadn't. [1003].

"Who cares if the people who worked on it get paid?" he asked. "Is this fair?" His letter concluded: "Nothing would please me more than being able to hire ten programmers and deluge the hobby market with good software."

Appeals to fair play only got so far, and the industry next tackled the main difference between minis and the early micros – the latter had no processor serial numbers. There were three general approaches tried: to add uniqueness on to the machine, to create uniqueness in it, or to use whatever uniqueness happened to exist already by chance.

1. The standard way to add hardware uniqueness was a *dongle* – a device attached to the PC that could be interrogated by the software. The simplest just had a serial number; the most common executed a simple challenge-response protocol; while some top-end devices actually performed some critical part of the computation.
2. A very common strategy in the early days was for the software to install itself on a PC's hard disk in a way that resisted naive copying. For example, a sector of the hard disk would be marked as bad, and a critical part of the code or data written there. Now if the product were copied from the hard disk using the standard utilities, the bad sector wouldn't be copied, and the copy wouldn't work. A variant on the same theme was to require the presence of a master diskette which had been customized in some way, such as by formatting it in a strange way or even burning holes in it with a laser. In general, though, a distinction should be drawn between protecting the copy and protecting the master; it's often a requirement that people should be able to make copies for backup if they wish, but not to make copies of the copies (this is called *copy generation control*).
3. 1988 saw the arrival of the *license server*, basically a machine programmed to act as a dongle shared by all the machines on a company network, which supported more complex business models such as enabling a company to buy the right to run a program on up to 20 machines at once, and enabling multiple software companies to license their products via the same license server.
4. A product I worked on in 1989 fingerprinted the PC – what extension cards were present, how much memory, what type of printer – and if this configuration changed too radically, it would ask the user to phone the helpline. It's quite surprising how many unique identifiers there are in the average PC; ethernet addresses and serial numbers of disk controllers are only the more obvious ones. So you can tie software to a given machine fingerprint; ad trackers use similar techniques to this day.

A generic attack that works against most of these defenses is to go through the software with a debugger and remove all the calls made to the copy protection routines. Many hobbyists did this for sport, and competed to put unprotected versions of software products online as soon as possible after their launch. Even people with licensed copies of the software often got hold of unprotected versions as they were easier to back up and often more reliable generally. You can stop this by having critical code somewhere uncopiable (such as in a dongle, a license server, or nowadays in the cloud), but this arms race taught everyone that if you don't do something like that then kids with debuggers will always break your scheme eventually. It's one reason why closed platforms, like games consoles and the iPhone, only run signed code.

The vendors also used psychological techniques.

- The installation routine for many business programs would embed the registered user's name and company on the screen, for example, in the toolbar. This wouldn't stop a pirate distributing copies registered in a false name, but it will discourage legitimate users from giving casual copies to colleagues. To this day, when I download papers from many academic journals, my university's name and a serial number are visible in the pdf. These are examples of *copyright marking* which I'll discuss in more detail later.
- Industry people delighted in telling tales of organizations that had come unstuck when they failed to get a critical upgrade they hadn't paid for.
- If early Microsoft software (Multiplan, Word or Chart) thought you were running it under a debugger, it would put up the message 'The tree of evil bears bitter fruit. Now trashing program disk.' It would then seek to track zero on the floppy disk and go 'rrnt, rrnt, rrnt'.

In the late-1980s, the market split. The games market moved to hardware protection, and ended up dominated by consoles with closed architectures whose software was sold in proprietary cartridges. As consumers are more sensitive about the sticker price of a product than about its total cost of ownership, it makes sense to subsidise the console out of later sales of software. This led to *accessory control* in which hardware protection is used to control aftermarkets; it was adopted by firms selling printers and much else. We'll discuss it in detail in section 24.6.

Business software vendors moved from dongles to license servers for high-value products such as the CAD software used to design everything from chips to ships. Technical support is often critical for such products, so they may be sold as a bundle of software and service. But vendors generally stopped trying to protect mass-market products using technical means, for several reasons.

- Unless you're prepared to spend money on dongle hardware to execute some of your critical code, the mechanisms in mass-market software will be defeated by people for whom it's an intellectual challenge, and unprotected code will be published anonymously.

- Protection was a nuisance. Multiple dongles get in the way or interfere with each other. Software protection techniques get in the way of backup and recovery; they also cause software from different vendors to be incompatible and in some cases unable to reside on the same machine. (The difficulty of doing this right is one reason why so many of the firms who use license management use Flexlm.)
- Many vendors preferred not to have to worry about whether the software was licensed to the user (in which case he could migrate it to a new machine) or to the machine (in which case he could sell the computer second-hand with the software installed). As both practices were common, mechanisms that made one or the other very much harder caused problems. Mechanisms that could deal with both (such as dongles and license servers) tended to be expensive.
- The arrival of computer viruses forced corporate customers to invest in software hygiene, so casual copying couldn't be condoned so easily. Within a few years, antivirus programs made life much harder for copy protection mechanisms in any case, as non-standard operating system usage tended to set off alarms.
- There was not much money to be made out of harassing personal users as they often made only casual use of the product and would throw it away rather than pay.
- A certain level of sharing was good for business. People who got a pirate copy of a tool and liked it would often buy a regular copy, or persuade their employer to buy one. In 1998 Bill Gates even said, "Although about three million computers get sold every year in China, people don't pay for the software. Someday they will, though. And as long as they're going to steal it, we want them to steal ours. They'll get sort of addicted, and then we'll somehow figure out how to collect sometime in the next decade" [755].
- Competition led to falling costs which made piracy less attractive. In the case of tools, for example, Borland shook up the industry with its launch of Turbo Pascal in 1983. Before then a typical language compiler cost about $500 and came with such poor documentation that you had to spend a further $50 on a book to tell you how to use it. Borland's product cost $49.95, was technically superior to Microsoft's, and came with a manual that was just as good as a third-party product. (So, like many other people, once I'd heard of it, borrowed a copy from a friend, tried it and liked it, I went out and bought it.) 'Pile it high and sell it cheap' simply proved to be a more profitable business model.

The industry then turned to the law. Software is mostly protected by copyright law; when you write software (or a book, or a tune) copyright comes into existence automatically nowadays and you have the right to sue people for damages if they make copies without your permission. The details vary by country but copyright infringement tends to be a crime only if done at commercial scale. So copyright owners can send unpleasant letters to individuals and small businesses, but actually suing them for a few dollars or pounds or euros in the small claims court is uneconomic. Against large-scale users, though, copyright enforcement can be worthwhile. In fact, when IBM separated its hardware and software businesses in 1969 – following a lawsuit from the US government which claimed that bundling software with hardware entrenched their market dominance – they took a strategic decision not to use any technical copyright enforcement mechanisms as they would be onerous to customers and not effective against clever thieves, so they'd rely on the law instead [1797].

In 1988, Microsoft led the industry in IBM's footsteps, and established trade organizations (such as the Business Software Alliance in the USA) that brought high-profile prosecutions of large companies that had been condoning widespread use of unlicensed software. This was followed up by harassing medium and even small businesses with threatening letters demanding details of the company's policy on enforcing copyright – basically demanding they sign up for an approved software audit scheme or risk a raid by an enforcement squad.

The industry discovered that the law not only provides tools for enforcement, but sets limits too. In 1993, a software company director in Scunthorpe, England, received a criminal conviction under Britain's Computer Misuse Act for 'making an unauthorized modification' to a system. Their customers had to enter unlock codes regularly into his software or it froze, denying access to data. But when he used this mechanism to enforce payment of a disputed invoice, the court decided he'd gone too far, and he ended up with a criminal record [459].

Thanks to the ubiquity of Office, Microsoft had by then become a tax on the corporate sector, making most of its revenue from customers with over 25,000 licenses. In addition to Office, it was selling many high-value products for network management and other tasks, so like the CAD firms it turned to license servers. Although these could still be defeated by disassembling the application code, this got harder as code became larger, and was unattractive to large firms after a few of them had been sued. Then the very idea of running on unlicensed software became crazy when Patch Tuesday arrived in 2003. With personal software, the emphasis shifted to online registration: you'd design your product to get customers to interact with your website – whether to download the tunes, latest exchange rates or security updates. Large-scale commercial counterfeiting can then be detected by monitoring product serial numbers registered online[2].

I wrote in the second edition of this book in 2008: "software-as-a-service may be the ultimate copyright protection or DRM for software (or any other content that can live online): you can't buy it, freeze the version you're running, or use it offline. You may also get to control all your customers' data too, giving you impressive lockin". That is precisely the model to which the software industry has converged since the early 2010s. Putting some or all of the functionality in the cloud can give real advantages of cost and reliability, which I will discuss in section 27.5.5. Software is then sold by subscription and the issue of copy protection goes away.

24.2.2 Free software, free culture?

In the old days, software was shared and this continued to be the case among academics and other research scientists, who evolved many communities of practice within which software was shared freely and adapted by successive contributors. This continued to support the dominant platforms of the time, which initially meant IBM. During the 1970s, for example, the UK government pushed British academics to buy ICL computers; ICL was Britain's champion, having been set up in the 1960s when the government nationalised the computer industry to 'save' it from IBM. However, we academics wanted IBM mainframes as other academics worldwide had written software that ran on their hardware, and even although most was written in high-level languages like FORTRAN, porting it was a hassle. The arrival of home computers in the 1970s and the PC in 1981 developed ever wider communities of software enthusiasts who shared our work, whether by physically passing diskettes around friends or in clubs, or via early bulletin-board systems and other dial-up networks.

In 1983 IBM stopped supplying the source code for its products, introducing a policy of 'object code only', and other vendors followed. This made it a lot harder to understand the platforms and tools on which we relied and led to pushback on a number of fronts. Two years later, Richard Stallman, an engineer at MIT, was annoyed when he could not integrate a new Xerox printer with the local maintenance arrangements as Xerox would not supply source code for the printer driver. He announced the GNU project to build a free operating system, and helped found the Free Software Foundation (FSF), which promoted the

[2]Once they got product registration sorted out, Microsoft found that a third of the copies of Office sold in Germany were counterfeit, and traced them to a small factory a few miles up the road from us in Cambridge. Almost all the factory's staff were unaware of the scam – they believed the company was a bona fide Microsoft supplier. They were proud of their product and their sales staff used it to try to get CD duplication business from other software houses.

idea of free software. Free software means that users should be able to run it for any purpose, study how it works and change it, and redistribute it – including improved or modified versions. One slogan was 'free as in free speech, not as in free beer', but free software comes in many flavours. The FSF promoted the GNU General Public License (GPL) which has the property that anyone adapting GPL licensed software and making it available must make the source code of their adaptation publicly available, under the same license – a viral property also known as 'copyleft'. In 1988, the University of California released the Berkeley distribution of Unix under the less restrictive BSD license that simply allows anyone to use the software for any purpose.

Such licensing arrangements are necessary because otherwise an operating system that had been written by 500 different people over 20 years would contain code that was their copyright, and so any of them could go to court to exercise their right to prevent some third party from using it. Proprietary software vendors can get the copyright in code written by engineers they employ[3], but what about projects maintained by volunteers? Open licenses help avoid thickets of conflicting claims.

There was much argument through the 1990s about their respective merits, but both approaches are in wide use. Linux was first released in 1991 under the GPL, while Berkeley Unix spawned FreeBSD and other variants that are available under the BSD license. As we noted in the chapter on access controls, Linux was the platform on which Android was built, while FreeBSD evolved into OSX and iOS. Other free software licenses were developed for Apache and in other communities, and public licenses spread quickly from software to other creative activities: for example, a variant of BSD was adapted for Wikipedia.

Software and culture both involve the adaptive and cumulative contributions of many individuals. Traditional musicians sometimes compose new tunes but more often change existing ones; even new compositions draw on phrases from the existing vocabulary. DJs rip tracks from others and mash them together into new compositions. Novelists reuse old storylines and character stereotypes, while comedians recycle old jokes. The law doesn't always deal with this very well as it tends to be written for large corporate interests rather than for communities. So music companies would press musicians to write entirely new tunes with clean copyrights rather than following tradition and adapting the best tunes of the older players.

Academia is also a place where we build on each other's work, and has the further twist that we get our recognition from the number of people who use our work rather than the number of people who pay for it. Mathematicians

[3]The law varies from one country to another. In some countries, such as the USA, you own copyright in a program written by an employee, while in others you have to make it a term in an employment contract; and contractors are another matter altogether. And since the pandemic lockdown, half my team are working from home in different countries. It really is prudent to have a written agreement.

become famous if lots of other mathematicians use their theorems in other results, and computer scientists get recognition if lots of people use our software. This creates real tensions with publishers. Indeed, starting in the 1970s, many computer scientists made both our code and our publications available freely online, using FTP servers and later, once they were invented, web pages. We tended to ignore the copyright agreements we had to sign with academic journals to get our papers published – or if we were careful we crossed out the 'exclusive' clause in the agreements, which back then were paper forms that the publishers never bothered to check.

1994 saw a couple of publications with real impact. Andrew Odlyzko calculated that the US government spent about $100M a year doing mathematics (by paying professors' salaries and the stipends of grad students) and a further $100M a year marketing mathematics (being the money that was spent in journals and conferences, plus the unpaid labour that mathematicians put in so journal publishers could make their profits) [1461]. If publication went fully online and all papers were available for all to read, perhaps the amount spent on actual mathematics could be increased. A quarter of a century and many tussles later, most government and charitable funders insist that the research they pay for is made available to all (though the journals have survived very comfortably by imposing page charges on authors, and also demanding that university libraries buy subscriptions for online access to their back catalogue).

The second, and better-known, was a paper by EFF founder John Perry Barlow, who was also a lyricist for the Grateful Dead. He pointed out that as the marginal cost of copying is zero with digital technology, 'information wants to be free' (which he ascribed to Stewart Brand). Both the physical containers of ideas (books, CDs) were vanishing, as was jurisdiction, as the Internet enabled people to swap files across national boundaries. He warned against corporate legal departments trying to protect by force what could no longer be protected by practical efficiency or general social consent, and about the USA writing copyright compliance into trade treaties: "Ideally, laws ratify already developed social consensus." He called for firms to develop business models that would work with the grain of the information age. His band, the Grateful Dead, let people tape their songs from the 1970s, and became one of the biggest stadium draws. He suggested that other industries explore models of live performance and service rather than selling bundles of bits [171].

There was vigorous debate and innovation on the copyright front during the dotcom boom of the later 1990s. Quite apart from arguments about books, journals, music and films – to which we will return shortly – there was a growing realisation of the need for shared infrastructure and tools. Many common components of the communications infrastructure, such as BGP, DNS and SMTP, had been first implemented at taxpayer expense and published, and firms often found they needed to add still more code to the commons. For example, after Netscape made available the first popular web browser in 1994, Microsoft killed them by giving away its own browser, Internet Explorer, free with Windows, and tried to create a monopoly at the server side with a product then called Internet Information Server which it launched in 1995. Other firms who were racing to establish a presence in the growing e-commerce industry were so alarmed at the prospect of Microsoft extracting all the value that they set up Apache, which became the leading web server the following year. This may have been one of the most important pieces of software ever written, as it meant that Microsoft could not control both ends of the link in the early days of the web, so they could not turn it into something proprietary from which they could extract rent. As a result, the web remained open for many years, and it was possible for companies such as Google and Facebook to get going. (We may now have a policy struggle with them instead, but a lot of innovation happened meantime.)

Moving from the policy to the mechanics, when software engineers – or book authors or musicians – place works in the public domain, we have a wide range of conditions we may want to attach. Some writers are happy for their work to be used by anyone, so opt for a BSD-style license; others want their work to remain in the commons rather than being incorporated into closed proprietary products, so prefer the GPL; academics generally want our stuff to be used provided we're acknowledged as the creators. In 2001 Larry Lessig founded the *Creative Commons* (CC) to bring some order to this; it makes available a set of licenses which parametrise this and enable you to specify how your work may be used. For example, you can specify whether a user can share your work with others; whether commercial uses are allowed; whether they must give you proper attribution; whether they can adapt and build on it, and if so whether they have to distribute their contributions under the same license as the original. These licenses are now used widely outside of software. In fact, most of my academic papers are available under CC licenses, and my agreement with the publishers of this book specifies that I may make all the chapters available freely online 42 months after the manuscript is sent for publication. I appreciate it if you pay for the book, but I want it to be available to everybody – even if the latest versions go online after a delay.

A critical development came in 1996 with section 230 of the US Communications Decency Act (CDA). This let the online service providers off the hook on copyright law by stating that 'No provider or user of an interactive computer service shall be treated as the publisher or speaker of any information provided by another information content provider' – making firms like Google and Facebook possible, and leaving the corporate lawyers to chase individual file sharers. The service firms are supposed to take down infringing content when they're notified of it; in practice, the boundaries are hard to police, and the incentives are perverse (section 230 shelters them when they run ads for counterfeiters [1833]). We'll return to this later, in this chapter and in Chapter 26.

So there are many alternative business models, both for software and for other products of human creativity. One is *freemium*: you give away a basic version of the product, and sell a premium version. (Even once this book is free online as PDF files, you'll have to pay money for a printed book.) Another is to give your software away free, and make your money from selling services, from advertising, or by acting as spyware and selling data about the user. You can combine them: get customers addicted to your free product, and then sell them more storage or an ad-free experience. The success of these models in software – with the Linux industry living from consulting and Google from ads – suggested a similar approach to other online businesses.

In the second edition of this book in 2008, I suggested then that "the solution for Hollywood's problem lies in a change of business model." As this third edition went to press in August 2020, the New York Times was lamenting the death of Hollywood [1795]. The studio that led Hollywood, Warner, had its executives fired, without the usual golden parachutes; no longer masters of the universe, they had become the employees of the video production arm of a phone company. The film industry had changed from a wholesale business that did deals with distributors over a handshake by the pool into a retail one where maximising subscription revenue is the core skill. The only studio to remain in recognisable form is Disney, which managed the transition to subscription early – helped perhaps by having Steve Jobs as its largest shareholder and as a main board director.

I will return to copyright policy later in section 24.5, but let's now take a quick historical tour at the world of protecting media content.

24.2.3 Books and music

In 1800, there were only 80,000 frequent readers in England; most of the books up till then were serious philosophical or theological tomes. After the invention of the novel, a mass market appeared for books, and circulating libraries sprang up to service it. The educated classes were appalled, and printers were frightened that the libraries would deprive them of sales. But the libraries so whetted people's appetite for books that the number of readers grew to 5,000,000 by 1850. Sales of books soared as people bought books they'd first borrowed from a library. The library movement turned out to have been the printers' greatest ally and helped create a whole new market for mass-market books [1721].

People have been copying music much longer than software. Paganini was so worried that people would copy his violin concertos that he distributed the scores himself to the orchestra just before rehearsals and performances, and collected them again afterwards. (As a result, many of his works were lost to posterity.)

Copyright *collecting societies* were established from the mid-19th century, starting in Paris; composers who were members would charge venues or bands a fee for performing their compositions. In many countries these have become monopolies backed by law; to perform at our university's concert hall, you have to pay the Performing Rights Society a levy. You can submit them a playlist, and if you play all your own compositions then some of the money may find its way back to you eventually. Many tunes are *orphan works* in that their composers' heirs are unknown, so the societies can either keep the money or share it among their known composers. The free culture movement and the pirate parties advocate restricting or abolishing copyright in order to erase such injustices; but while they've won a few parliamentary seats in some European countries, they always seem to be outgunned by the copyright lobbyists on the world stage (an issue to which I'll return later in section 24.5.1).

When the cassette recorder came along in the 1960s, the record industry lobbied for (and in some countries got) a tax on audiocassettes, to be distributed to copyright holders. Technical measures were also tried. The Beatles' record Sergeant Pepper contained a 20KHz spoiler tone that should in theory have combined with the 21KHz bias frequency of the tape to produce a 1KHz whistle that would spoil the sound. In practice it didn't work, as many record players didn't have the bandwidth to pick up the spoiler tone. But in practice this didn't matter. Cassettes turned out not to be a huge problem because sound quality is noticeably poorer on home equipment; people mostly used them to record music to listen to in their cars. Then, in the 1980s, the arrival of the Sony Walkman made cassettes into big business, and although there was some copying, there were huge sales of pre-recorded cassettes and the music industry cleaned up.

Audio copying became a headline concern again in the 1990s, thanks to the MP3 format for compressing audio. Previously, digital audio was protected by its size: a CD of uncompressed music can take 650Mb. However, MP3 enables people to squeeze an audio track into a few megabytes, and broadband enables files of this size to be shared easily. By 1998, some 40% of the network traffic at MIT was MP3 traffic.

The industry response was to push for technical fixes. This led to the growth of the rights-management industry. It had its origins in work on digital publishing and in the mechanisms used to protect pay-TV and DVDs, so let's take a quick look at those first.

24.2.4 Video and pay-TV

The early history of videocassettes was a replay of the history of audio cassettes. At first Hollywood was terrified, and refused to release movies for home viewing. Crude technical measures were taken to prevent copying – such as the Macrovision system which added spurious synchronization pulses to confuse the recording circuitry of domestic VCRs – which again turned out to be easy to defeat. Then Hollywood became paranoid about video rental stores, just as book publishers had been about libraries. Once more, libraries turned out to be the publisher's friend, as being able to rent videos got people to buy VCRs and whetted their desire to own their favorite movies. VCRs and videocassettes became mass-market products rather than rock stars' toys, and by 2000 sales of prerecorded cassettes made up most of the income of firms like Disney. The business model changed so that the cinema release was really just advertising for the sales of the video.

By then, many of the world's pre-teens demanded that their parents build them a collection of Disney cassettes, just like their friends had, so a videocassette pirate had to make the packaging look original. This reduced the problem to an industrial counterfeiting one. As with mass-market software before the onset of online registration, or with perfumes and Swiss watches today, enforcement involves sending out field agents to buy products, look for forgeries, trace the supply chain and bring prosecutions.

More interesting technical protection mechanisms were built into broadcast pay-TV equipment.

The advent of pay-TV, whether delivered by cable or satellite, created a need for *conditional access* mechanisms which would allow a station operator to restrict reception of a channel in various ways. If the operator had only bought the rights to screen a movie in Poland, they'd have to block German or Russian viewers within the satellite footprint from watching. Porn channel operators needed to prevent reception in countries like Ireland with strict censorship laws. Most operators also wanted to be able to charge extra for specific events such as boxing matches.

24.2.4.1 Typical system architecture

The evolution of early systems was determined largely by the hardware cost of deciphering video (for a history of set-top boxes, see [427]). The first generation of systems, available since the 1970s, were crude analog devices which used tricks such as inverting the video signal from time to time, interfering with the synchronization, and inserting spikes to confuse the TV's automatic gain control. They were easy enough to implement, but also easy to defeat; breaking them didn't involve cryptanalysis, just an oscilloscope and persistence.

The second generation of systems appeared in the late 1980s and employed a hybrid of analog and digital technologies: the broadcast was analog, but the subscriber control was digital. These included systems such as Videocrypt and Nagravision, and typically had three components:

- a subscription management service at the station enciphers the outgoing video, embeds various *entitlement management messages* (EMMs) and *entitlement control messages* (ECMs) in it, and issues access tokens such as smartcards to subscribers;

- a *set-top box* converts the cable or satellite signal into one the TV can deal with. This includes descrambling it;
- the subscriber smartcard personalises the device and controls what programmes the set-top box is allowed to descramble. It does this by interpreting the ECMs and providing keys to the descrambling circuit in the set-top box.

This architecture means that the complex, expensive processes such as bulk video scrambling could be done in a mass-produced custom chip with a long product life, while key-management functions that may need to be changed after a hack can be sold to the customer in a low-cost token that is easy to replace. If the set-top box itself had to be replaced every time the system was hacked, the economics would be much less attractive[4].

The basic mechanism is that the set-top box decodes the ECMs from the input datastream and passes them to the card. The card deciphers the ECMs to get both control messages (such as "smartcard number 123356, your subscriber hasn't paid, stop working until further notice") and keys, known as *control words*, that are passed to the set-top box. The set-top box then uses the control words to descramble the video and audio streams. There's a detailed description in [460].

24.2.4.2 Video scrambling techniques

Because of the limitations on the chips available at low cost in the early 1990s, hybrid systems typically scrambled video by applying a transposition cipher to picture elements. A typical scheme was the *cut-and-rotate* algorithm used in Videocrypt. This scrambles one line of video at a time by cutting it at a point determined by a control byte and swapping the left and right halves (Figure 24.1).

This involved analog-to-digital conversion of the video signal, storage in a buffer, and digital-to-analog conversion after rotation – a process which could just about be shoehorned into a low-cost custom VLSI chip by 1990. However, a systemic vulnerability of such systems is that video is highly redundant, so it may be possible to reconstruct the image using 'oscilloscope and persistence' techniques, enhanced by simple signal processing. This was first done by Markus Kuhn in 1995 and required the use of a university supercomputer to do in real time. Figure 24.2 shows a frame of enciphered video, and Figure 24.3 the

[4]Now that set-top boxes cost a few dollars, and the shipping costs dominate, the smartcard is often just soldered to the motherboard and the whole box is replaced if there's a hack.

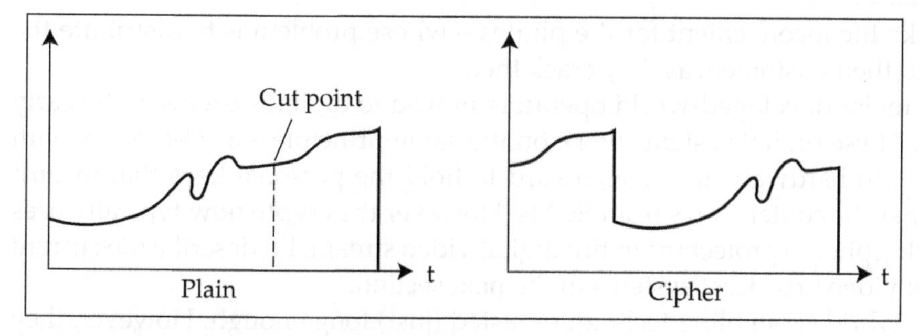

Figure 24.1: Cut-and-rotate scrambling

Figure 24.2: Scrambled video frame

Figure 24.3: Processed video frame

same frame after processing. By 2000, it was possible to do this on a PC [1827]. If this attack had been feasible earlier, it would have given a complete break of the system, as regardless of how well the smartcard managed the keys, the video signal could be retrieved without them. Hybrid systems are still used by some stations in less developed countries, together with frequent key changes to make life inconvenient for the pirates – whose problem is to distribute the keys to their customers as they crack them.

The major developed-world operators moved to digital systems in the early 2000s. These digital systems work on the same principle – a set-top box with the crypto hardware and a smartcard to hold the personal keys that in turn decipher the content keys from ECMs. However the crypto now typically uses a block cipher to protect the entire digital video stream. I'll describe the current digital video broadcast systems in the next section.

The hybrid scrambling techniques lasted (just) long enough. However, they have some interesting lessons to teach, as they were subjected to quite determined attack in the decade after 1995, so I'll go briefly through what went wrong.

24.2.4.3 Attacks on hybrid scrambling systems

Given a population of set-top boxes that can use a stream of control words to unscramble broadcast video, the next problem was to ensure that only paying customers could get the control words. In general, this could be done with allow and deny messages. But the bandwidth available was typically of the order of ten ECMs per second. So sending an allow message to each of five million subscribers would take over a week, and deny messages were mostly used instead.

The customer smartcard interprets the ECMs. If the current programme is one the subscriber is allowed to watch, then a keyed hash – essentially a message authentication code (MAC) – is computed on a series of ECMs using a master key held in the card and supplied to the set-top box as the control word:

$$CW = MAC(K; ECM_1, ECM_2, ECM_3, ECM_4)$$

So if a subscriber stops paying their subscription, their card can be inactivated by sending an ECM ordering it to stop issuing control words; and it needs access to the ECM stream in order to compute control words at all. Provided the cards can be made tamper-resistant, only compliant devices should have access to the master key K, and they should commit suicide on demand. So what could go wrong?

The first attacks were on the protocol. Since the control word sent from the smartcard is the same for every set-top box currently unscrambling the program, one person can record the stream of control words, by placing a PC between the smartcard and the set-top box, and post them online. Other people can video-record the scrambled program, and unscramble it later [1257]. Servers sprung up for this *key-log attack*, but were only a minor nuisance to the industry; not many viewers were prepared to buy or build a special adapter to connect their PC to their set-top box. Hobbyists with such equipment found other attacks including *blockers*, programs that would prevent ECMs addressed to your card from being delivered to it; this way, you could cancel your subscription without the operator being able to cancel your service [1257].

Cryptanalysis also gave some opportunities. Every half-second or so the smartcard supplies the set-top box with a new control word, and this is loaded into a keystream generator which works as follows. There are two linear feedback shift registers, of lengths 31 and 29 in the Eurocrypt system, which generate long linear sequences. Some of the bits of register 1 are used as address lines to a multiplexer, which selects a bit from register 2; this bit becomes the next bit of the keystream sequence. Each successive byte of output becomes a control byte for the scrambler (Figure 24.4).

The designers intended that breaking this cipher should involve guessing the key, and as this is 60 bits long a guess would take on average 2^{59} trials, which is uneconomic – as it has to be done about twice a second. But it turns out that the cipher has a shortcut attack. The trick is to guess the contents of register 1, use this address information to place bits of the observed keystream in register 2, and if this causes a clash, reject the current guess for register 1. (I discovered this attack in 1985 and it's what got me interested in cryptography.) The high-order four bits or so of each control word are easy to deduce from inter-line correlations – it's the least significant bits you really have to work hard for. So you can reconstruct the latter using cryptanalysis. But this computation is still of interest to hobbyists rather than the mass market.

Perhaps the most powerful of the 'amateur' attacks exploited a master-key leakage: someone who bought a second-hand PC, looked at the hard disk out of curiosity, and managed to undelete a complete subscriber management system for one pay-TV operator, including embedded master keys. This enabled enthusiasts to write software to emulate a subscriber smartcard completely – in fact, it could even be 'improved' so it would not turn itself off when ordered to do so by an ECM.

Anyway, the commercial pirates turned to reverse engineering smartcards using microprobing techniques, and in section 18.5 I described the arms race that followed. But hardware fixes were limited to new card issues, and the operators didn't want to issue a new card more than once a year as it cost

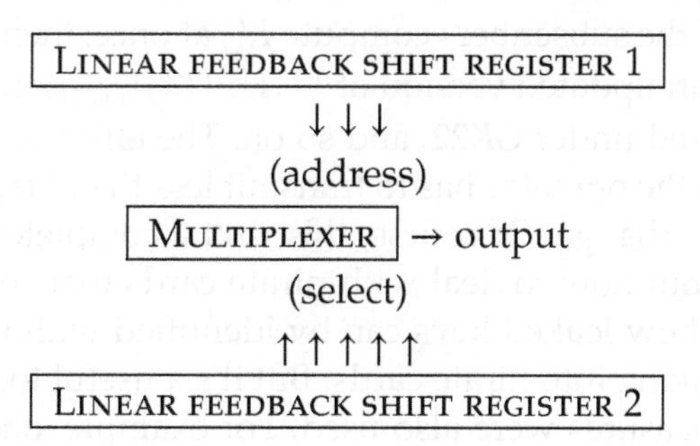

Figure 24.4: The multiplexer generator

several dollars per subscriber, and the subscriptions were usually less than $20 a month. So other defensive techniques were tried too.

Litigation was one route, but it took time. A lawsuit was lost against a pirate in Ireland, which for a while became a haven from which pirates sold cards by mail order all over Europe. The industry's lobbying muscle was deployed to bring in European law to override Dublin, but this took years. By the middle of 1995, the main UK satellite TV station (Sky-TV) was losing 5% of its revenue to pirate cards, mostly sold by mail order from Dublin.

So all through the mid-1990s, pirates and the operators engaged in a war of technical countermeasures and counter-countermeasures. The operators would ship a new card, and within months the pirates would have reversed it and be offering clones for sale. The operators would buy some, analyze them, and develop tricks to cause them to fail. The problem faced by the operators was this: when all the secrets in your system can be compromised within months, how can you still fight back against the pirates without having to reissue all the cards?

The operators came up with all sorts of cunning tricks. One of their more effective ones was an ECM whose packet contents were executed as code by the smartcard; in this way, the existing card base could be upgraded on the fly and implementation differences between the genuine and pirate cards could be exploited. Any computation that would give a different answer on the two platforms – even if only as a result of an unintentional timing condition – could be fed into the MAC algorithm to make the pirate cards deliver invalid control words.

One of the systems (Eurocrypt) had an efficient revocation scheme designed in from the start, and it's worth looking at briefly. Each of the subscriber smartcards contains a subscriber key k_i, and there is a binary tree of intermediate group keys *KGij* linking the subscriber keys to the currently active master key K_M. Each operational card knows all the group keys in the path between it and the master key, as in Figure 24.5.

In this scheme, if (say) key k_2 appears in pirate cards and has to be revoked, then the operator will send out a stream of packets that let all the other subscriber cards compute a new master key K_M. The first packet will be $\{K'_M\}_{KG12}$ which will let half the subscribers compute K'_M at once; then there will be a K'_M encrypted under an updated version of *KG*11: $\{K'_M\}_{KG'11}$; then this new group key *KG*′11 encrypted under *GK*22; and so on. The effect is that even with ten million customers the operator has to transmit less than fifty ECMs in order to do a complete key change. Of course, this isn't a complete solution: one also needs to think about how to deal with pirate cards that contain several subscriber keys, and how leaked keys can by identified without having to go to the trouble of breaking into pirate cards. But it's a useful tool in the box.

Psychological measures were also used. For example, one cable TV station broadcast a special offer for a free T-shirt, and stopped legitimate viewers from

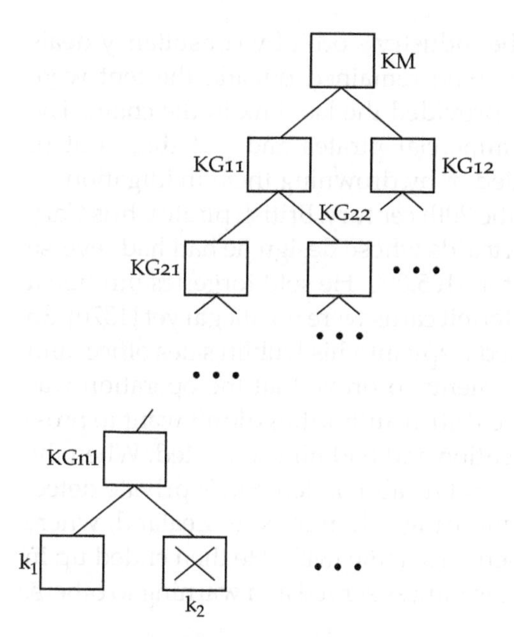

Figure 24.5: Binary revocation tree

seeing the 0800 number to call; this got them a list of the pirates' customers. Economic factors also matter here, as everywhere. Pay-TV pirates depend for their success on time-to-market as much as conventional software firms: a pirate who could produce a 99% correct forgery in three weeks would wipe out a competitor who produced a 99.9% forgery after three months. So pirates race to market just like legitimate vendors, and pirate cards have bugs too. An understanding of economics teaches that it's best to let a pirate build up a substantial user base before you pull the plug on him, as this gives him time to wipe out his competitors, and also as switching off his cards once he's established will destroy his credibility with more potential customers than an immediate response would. But if you leave him too long, he may acquire the financial and technical resources to become a persistent problem.

The pay-TV industry learned to plan in advance for security recovery, and to hide features in their products that weren't used initially but could be activated later[5].

Eventually, the smartcards were made much harder to forge by including proprietary encryption algorithms in the processor hardware. As the attacker couldn't simply read out the algorithm with a probing station but had to reverse engineer thousands of gates in the chip, they reduced to a handful the number of laboratories with the technical capability to do attacks. Many of

[5]We discussed in section 16.3.1 how banknote printers learned years ago to include a whole series of security printing features that could be disclosed one at a time as needed.

these laboratories were drawn into the industry's orbit by consultancy deals or other kinds of sponsorship. Those who remained outside the tent were watched. Vigorous legal enforcement provided the last link in the chain. The industry hunted down the main commercial pirates and put them out of business, whether by having them jailed or by drowning them in litigation.

In the last big pay-TV piracy case in the 20th century, British pirate Chris Cary was convicted of forging Sky-TV smartcards whose design he had had reverse engineered by a company in Canada for $105,000. He sold forgeries through a front company in Ireland, where counterfeit cards were not illegal yet [1370]. So Sky TV's security consultants infiltrated a spy into his Dublin sales office, and she quietly photocopied enough documents to prove that the operation was really being run from the UK [958]. The British authorities didn't want to prosecute, so Sky brought a private prosecution and had him convicted. When the authorities put him in an open prison and he absconded, Sky's private detectives relentlessly hunted him down and caught him in New Zealand, where he'd fled using a passport in a dead person's name [848]. He then ended up in a proper jail. Sky-TV's relentless unpleasantness served as a warning to others.

24.2.4.4 DVB

Digital video broadcasting (DVB) largely operates using a set of standards that have evolved over the years since 1996 and that are controlled by the DVB Consortium, an industry group of over 250 members. The standards are many and complex, relating to IPTV and digital terrestrial TV as well as satellite TV, and to free-to-air services as well as pay-TV. DVB has been replacing analog/hybrid systems, starting with the UK and Germany in 2003. The latest standards, DVB-T2, were promulgated by ETSI in 2009.

The protection mechanisms are complex, and some of them are covered by nondisclosure agreements, but here is a telegraphic summary. The conditional access mechanisms for DVB are similar to the hybrid system: the content encryption is digital, but the keys are generated by subscriber smartcards operating on EMMs and ECMs as before. The encryption uses the DVB Common Scrambling Algorithm, which was available only under NDA, but leaked in 2002. In 2011, an attack was found by Erik Tews, Julian Wälde and Michael Weiner, which was then barely practical as it requires an 8TB rainbow table [1875]. The smartcards are not standardised (except at the interface level) so each broadcaster can use his favorite crypto tricks and suppliers; the piracy to date seems to have involved smartcard cloning, and there have been various lawsuits where pay-TV operators have accused each other of hacking.

Pay-TV, whether cable or satellite, peaked in 2008 with 75% of US households. What dislodged it was Netflix, and more generally the move to online subscription services based on broadband.

24.2.5 DVD

The history of DVD was both a warning of trouble to come between Hollywood and the computer industry, and an object lesson on how not to do copy protection.

The consumer electronics industry introduced the *digital video disk* (DVD), later renamed the *digital versatile disk*, in 1996. As usual, Hollywood took fright and said that unless DVD had a decent copy protection mechanism, first-class movies wouldn't be released for it. So a mechanism called the *content scrambling system* (CSS) was built in at the last minute; arguments over this held up the launch of DVD and it was designed in a rush. (The story of how the DVD standards evolved is told in Jim Taylor's standard reference [1868], which also describes most of them.)

DVD had *region coding*: disks were supposed to run only on players from some designated list of regions, to support the traditional practice of releasing a movie in the USA first, then in Europe and so on, in order to minimise the cost of producing physical film prints, and the financial loss if the film bombs. But users preferred to buy DVD players in which region coding could be turned off. So every DVD vendor wanted to have the second most insecure player on the market; they didn't want to be the firm that Hollywood was beating up on, but they wanted prospective customers to be confident that their player's region coding could be hacked.

This left CSS, which was known to be vulnerable by the time that DVD was launched [1496]. It has a keylength of 40 bits so the equipment wouldn't fall foul of US export regulations, but the design was so poor that the effective keylength was only 16 bits. A Norwegian teenager, Jon Lech Johansen, reverse engineered the algorithm and wrote decryption software for it, DeCSS. Industry lawyers got injunctions against people who put it online, but these were seen as censorship, so it started appearing on websites outside the USA, on T-shirts, in songs, and in other forms of speech that traditionally enjoy constitutional protection[6]. This just got it distributed ever more widely, and made Hollywood look foolish [1129]. Their lawyers blundered on, persuading the government of Norway to prosecute Johansen. He was acquitted on appeal in 2003.

Another set of problems came from the fact that the PC is an open platform. The DVD consortium required people producing DVD player software to obfuscate their code so that it would be hard to reverse engineer. Papers duly appeared on tricks for systematic software obfuscation [142]. But this closed approach came into conflict with Linux, the open-source PC operating system that was already used by millions of people. The DVD consortium's philosophy was not consistent with making DVD drivers available to the Linux

[6]There was a full description of CSS and how to break it in the first and second editions of this book; as DVDs are going the way of the dinosaur, I've dropped it for this edition.

community. So as PCs with CD drives started being replaced in the shops with PCs fitted with DVD drives, the Linux user community either had to break CSS, or give up using Linux in favour of Windows. Under the circumstances, it was only a matter of time before someone figured out CSS and DeCSS appeared.

Anyway, DVD followed the usual pattern: Hollywood terrified, and refusing to release their best movies; technical measures taken to prevent copying, which quickly got broken; then litigation. I wrote in 2001: "A reasonable person might hope that once again the studios will see sense in the end, and make a lot of money from selling DVDs. There will be copying, of course, but it's not entirely trivial yet – even a DSL modem takes hours to send a 4Gb DVD movie to a friend, and PC disk space is also an issue." This came true; although some studios held out for a year or two, they all climbed on the DVD bandwagon, and by the second edition in 2008, Disney was making most of its money from DVD sales.

There was then an attempt to market higher-density optical media, with a format war in 2007 between HD-DVD and Blu-Ray, which both used shorter wavelength lasers to encode information more densely giving up to 50Gb per disk. Both used the Advanced Access Content System (AACS), which I described in the second edition of this book. However, only the PlayStation 3 did a full implementation of Blu-Ray, and HD-DVD never got real traction at all. They were destroyed, as distribution media, by the growth of broadband, and as storage media by the falling cost of USB memory sticks.

24.3 DRM on general-purpose computers

Victor Shear patented self-destruct software in the 1980s and his company became InterTrust [1797]; their DigiBox system is described by Olin Sibert, David Bernstein and David Van Wie in [1738]. This enabled a DRM mechanism to reflect real-world ownership, so that I could sell you a photo and you'd be able to decrypt it once you had the receipt; what's more, you could give it to somebody else after which you'd no longer have it.

InterTrust was the most successful of a number of firms who worked in the mid-90s on ways to control the sale and distribution of digital goods over the Internet to customers with personal computers[7]. The original applications included the distribution of newspapers and articles from scientific journals [316], although it was always understood that music and video would follow once networks had enough bandwidth.

The basic problem is that a PC, being a general-purpose computer, can in principle copy any file and send it to any other computer; unlike with

[7]The InterTrust patents were one of only four computer-related patents from the 20th century that caused a nine-figure sum to change hands, the others being the Harvard virtual memory patents, the RSA public-key patents and the Fraunhofer MP3 patents.

analog copying, copies are perfect, so millions of copies might be made from one original. The problem is compounded by the fact that, from the viewpoint of the content vendor, the PC owner is the 'enemy'. The music industry believed that unlimited copying would destroy their business; the computer industry told them that DRM was intrinsically impossible on a general-purpose computer, so they'd better get a new business model. The music and film industries, despite being a tenth of the computer industry's size, had much more clout in Congress (a Microsoft guy complained that the average Congressman was much keener to be photographed with Madonna than with Bill), and they still controlled access to the music and video that the computer industry wanted their PCs and phones to be able to play. The result was a push for DRM.

24.3.1 Windows media rights management

Windows Media Player (WMP) was an early deployment of DRM, replacing an earlier media player when Windows 98 was released. It enabled a user to play music, watch video and view photos, with features ranging from MP3 player support to synchronisation of lyrics for karaoke. It introduced *Windows Media Rights Management* (WMRM), which works as follows.

A store wanting to sell digital media encrypts each item using a content key and puts the encrypted files on a streaming media server linked to their website. In order to access a media object, the customer must get hold of a license, which consists of the object identifier, the license key seed, and a set of instructions in a *rights management language* which state what they can do with it; how many times they may play it, whether they can burn it to a CD, and so on. The license is generated by a license server and encrypted using a public key generated by the customer's WMP application. License acquisition may involve registration or payment, but it may also happen silently in the background [1561].

The architecture is similar to pay-TV conditional access, in that the bulk encryption task of protecting the music or video is separated from the personalised task of key management, so the video doesn't have to be encrypted anew for each customer. And just as pay-TV smartcards can be replaced when keys are leaked or the key management mechanism compromised, so the key management functions of WMRM are performed in an 'individualized blackbox' (IBX) component of the software, which gets replaced as needed during the Windows update process.

The IBX internals have been reverse-engineered from time to time [1696]. The customer's private key is obscured by the blackbox and hidden in a file; licenses the customer has previously acquired are kept in a license store; content keys are encrypted using the customer's public key; and the protocol gets tweaked from time to time as Microsoft has to recover from hacks. I described in section 6.2.5 how in the early 2000s Microsoft, Intel and some other big players formed the Trusted Computing Group to try to build DRM properly into the PC architecture. The attempt failed for both business and technical reasons, but led to TPM chips for trusted boot, to TrustZone enclaves in Arm processors, and eventually to SGX enclaves in Intel chips.

Microsoft launched *Information Rights Management* (IRM) with Windows Server 2003, which aimed to extend DRM to general users; the idea was that access controls over a document or other digital object would be retained by its creator. So DRM wouldn't just benefit Hollywood; I could send you an email that you could only read, and never copy, and that would vanish after a month. The vision was that this would be supported by Trusted Computing mechanisms across the entire Windows ecosystem, and conveniently fortify the ecosystem against challenges from the likes of Linux or Google docs. Corporate America didn't like the lock-in, though, and Microsoft couldn't get the operating system mechanisms to work. Nowadays, it's easy to implement such distributed use controls in cloud-based systems such as Office365 or Gmail, but it's too hard to work across such ecosystems; so we've ended up not too far from where we might have been had Trusted Computing been made to work.

WMRM was then replaced in Windows 10 by PlayReady, a newer Microsoft 'media file copy prevention technology'. WMP is used at its most basic to provide a streaming media service, to support music subscription services, and geographically-linked services, such as `MLB.com` which makes major league baseball games available everywhere except in the team's home area – for which the rights have usually been sold to local TV stations.

24.3.2 FairPlay, HTML5 and other DRM systems

The Microsoft offering was fairly typical of rights-management systems. Apple's FairPlay, which was launched in the iPod and in its media player QuickTime, also has tunes encrypted under master keys. When a tune is bought the customer is sent the master key encrypted under a random session key, plus the session key encrypted under his iTunes player's RSA public key. Session keys are backed up online on Apple's servers. As with Windows, a number of programs have appeared from time to time that unlocked protected content, and Apple duly upgraded iTunes. Apple iTunes was replaced with Apple Music in 2020.

Some firms' rights-management systems were downright abusive, and a particularly extreme case arose in 2005 with Sony's XCP system. The first time a user inserted a CD with this system into a PC, it presented an end-user license agreement; if the user declined, the CD was ejected, and if they accepted it loaded and hid a rootkit that intercepted all accesses to the CD drive and prevented Sony music being played by any other media player. Microsoft classified it as malware and had it removed by Windows Defender and the Malicious Software Removal Tool [1309]. It later turned out that Sony had even included in their rootkit some software that violated the copyrights of others.

There was significant controversy in 2012–14 when the World Wide Web Consortium (W3C) was debating whether to adopt HTML5 which provides for a sandbox in browsers to support multimedia content with DRM, and Encrypted Media Extensions (EME) as a means for the software in the sandbox to communicate with online license managers. When they eventually went ahead in 2014, W3C chair Tim Berners-Lee was fiercely criticised for adopting a standard that excludes open-source browsers in the future. Since 2017, browsers need to license 'Widevine' DRM software from Google to support services such as Netflix. Mozilla was the last major browser to switch, after they concluded that refusing would just cause most of their users to switch browsers. In 2020, Google stopped supplying this technology to open-source browsers; thereafter all new browsers will have to be proprietary; this had been predicted by EFF during the debate in 2012–4 [571].

The other development in 2020 is Microsoft's launch of "double encryption", a kind of DRM to make regulated industries like banking happier about keeping sensitive data in the Office365/Azure cloud: content keys are kept on the local device, but the whole thing is integrated with the Microsoft structure of access controls [434]. Whether DRM operated by Microsoft would stop an FBI agent armed with a FISA warrant getting access to data on a Microsoft cloud is an interesting question; I suppose we'll only know the answer when the next Snowden comes out.

24.3.3 Software obfuscation

As I already mentioned, early software protection mechanisms used software obscurity to hide keys and to check for the presence of machine fingerprints, dongles and license servers. Kids with disasssemblers and time on their hands tended to defeat such tricks, so where possible firms would move some critical functionality to the cloud, to trustworthy hardware, or both.

But that is not always possible, and in 2020 the critical applications include *runtime application self-protection* (RASP). As I discussed in section 12.7.4, this is a set of techniques used by some mobile app developers to protect apps on phones that may have been rooted or jailbroken by malware. It's used by Facebook to protect customers using its Android app in less developed countries where many Android phones are secondhand, out of patch support and rooted, often by local sales agents. And following a mandate from the European

Central Bank, RASP is becoming mandatory for banking apps in Europe, or for authenticator apps on which they rely. In both cases the objective is to protect cryptographic keys from an attacker who roots the device. This was also the threat model for 1990s products such as Windows Media Player.

There were early attempts to write obfuscating compilers that would produce tamper-resistant software; an early Intel project is described at [142] and led to tools used in early software DVD players. These were duly broken, as I described in section 24.2.5 earlier, and led Intel to move towards Trusted Computing and eventually SGX, as I described in section 6.3.1.

Theoretical computer scientists have written many papers on obfuscation and indistinguishability; a seminal result by Boaz Barak and colleagues in 2001 suggests that we can't write obfuscating compilers with strong and sustainable protection properties [167]. But – as with other impossibility results in security such as those on malware detection – the question then arises whether even if perfect obfuscation isn't possible in theory, practical obfuscation might be good enough for some purposes.

Microsoft moved to a philosophy of security renewal: the key-management code for Windows Media Player was hidden in IBX and moved around, so it might be in the Windows error handler one month and an obscure device driver the next. Malware writers took a similar trajectory. As I described in section 21.3.5, they often obfuscate their code by running it through a packer that contains a polymorphic header which in turn decrypts the malware body. Keys and headers are all different, making malware harder to recognise. Approaches like this can sometimes be made to work moderately well, provided the maintainers are capable and motivated. Very often, though, they aren't; naive firms buying RASP from salesy vendors should expect the worst.

The main security research conferences have tended not to accept papers on obfuscation as they see it as a tactical arms race rather than the accumulation of scientific knowledge. There is nonetheless a small research community working on obfuscation, and as of 2020 the state of the art when protecting an engine for authentication or decryption is to implement a virtual machine that has an odd instruction set, in which you implement the crypto, and then further obfuscate the virtual machine itself (custom opcodes had already been used in Sky-TV smartcards back in the 1990s). It is still a real problem though to evaluate such a scheme, or even guess how much effort it will take to break it [555]. If a RASP tester can't extract the crypto key despite trying for a fortnight, that doesn't give you any guarantee against someone who tries for a month[8]. Decompilation tools and techniques improve all the time, and many

[8]I bear the scars personally. Back in the 1990s, Intel paid us to spend a fortnight trying to hack a prototype DVD player binary that had been produced by Beelzebub, their internal obfuscating compiler. We only got about halfway through, and the company then boasted to its customers that 'Cambridge couldn't break this'. Jon Lech Johansen later spent a month staring at the code and broke it, making us look stupid – but at least Intel ended up looking stupider.

engineers spend much of our lives trying to figure out what other people's code actually does. Some people acquire a real knack for this, but they might not be working in your compliance testing lab! A lemons market is therefore to be expected.

All that said, there are some less heavyweight aspects to this. Some tools obfuscate Java bytecode as they shrink and optimise it; one such, ProGuard, is distributed as part of the Android SDK. And for entertainment, there's the International Obfuscated C Code Contest, where people have fun trying to hide functionality in plain sight.

24.3.4 Gaming, cheating, and DRM

Games were one of the first applications of all – pretty well as soon as the world's first proper computer, the EDSAC, was operational, research students were writing games for it. Computer games have been big business for decades. They drove the home-computer boom of the 1970s that in turn spawned the PC industry; games consoles have been a huge market for microprocessors and memory chips; and gaming – whether on consoles or PCs – has largely driven the development of computer graphics [2059]. Game sales in the USA surpassed movie box-office sales in 2001; and as games moved online, game firms started to sell subscriptions, not just one-off tickets [281].

When Nintendo moved console games into the home, they subsidised the consoles from later sales of software cartridges and other add-ons, so a lot of effort was put into controlling which accessories could be used, as I discuss later in section 24.6; copy-protection of game software for PCs was also a big deal. However the move to online computer games has mitigated these concerns. As a critical part of the game logic runs on a server, the client software can be given away, and the residual issue is whether players can get an unfair advantage.

There are very many ways in which gamers can cheat [2060]. Some games ban collusion, such as contract bridge, and it's hard to stop people playing on an online platform from using an entirely separate channel to cheat. In the real world, allegations of cheating are heard by a jury of experienced players, who take a view on whether the outcome was better than could have been expected in honest play. Even so, some decisions remain controversial for years: players may be lucky, and partners who've played together for years may communicate subconsciously without trying to. Online play can help as you can have online records for statistical analysis, online tournaments where many players use the same deal of cards, and new forms of play where people play with many partners rather than just one.

Other games require collusion, such as adventure games involving teams of people. As I discuss in section 8.6.9, these are currently, in 2020, the biggest market for DDoS-for-hire services. Players, who are often schoolkids, pay a few dollars for a service that will knock key members of the opposing team offline at a critical time.

The third type of cheating tactics are those that emerge from the nature of computer games. In tactical shooters, for example, success should depend on the player's tactics and shooting skill, not on the game mechanics. Yet there are always shortcomings in the game's physics model, often introduced by network latency and by the optimisations game designers use to deal with it. For example, you'd normally expect that in a shooting duel, you'd have an advantage if you have the lowest network latency, or if you move first. Yet the prediction algorithms used in many game clients cache information about nearby players, so if you leap round a corner, see your enemy and shoot, then the slower your network connection is, the longer it will take him to see you and respond. Mike Bond coined the term 'neo-tactic' to refer to players subliminally exploiting such anomalies [281]. That may not of itself be cheating, but in recent years players have started manipulating network connections deliberately to create artificial lag, whether of incoming packets to delay other players, or our outgoing ones in order to see what other players are about to do.

That brings us on to one of the classic game cheats, namely to have code of your own for automation and support. People have written a huge variety of tools, from simple routines that repeatedly click a fire button (to hack the games where the rate at which you can physically fire is a factor) through proxies that intercept the incoming network packets, identify the bad guys, examine your outgoing shots, and optimise their aim. These *aimbots* come with different levels of sophistication, from code that does all the target acquisition and shooting, to human-controlled versions that merely improve your aim. They can hook into the packet stream as proxies, into the graphics card, or even into the client code. Another variant on the same theme is the *wall hack*, where a player modifies his software to see through walls – for example, by changing the graphics software to make them translucent rather than opaque. Such hacks are possible because first-person shooters typically send out raw positional information to all players in the game, and leave it up to client software to render it according to the local physics model.

Game companies who sell first-person shooters reckon that aimbots and other client-side hacks seriously spoil other players' fun, so they use a variety of encryption, authentication and DRM mechanisms to reduce not only cheating, but also the perception of cheating – which is almost as damaging to the operator [282]. Guard software such as Punkbuster has been around since 2000, using anti-virus techniques to detect attempts to hook into game code or the drivers on which it relies. The large gaming platforms such as Steam have their own DRM mechanisms that attempt to block aimbots and other game cheats, as well as protecting their own revenue by making it harder for customers to resell games [1290]. This is a constant battle, and some techniques such as artificial lag are difficult to deal with completely. However, gaming is one of the applications in which trustworthy client software, whose protection involves DRM-like mechanisms, has become well entrenched, even though most modern games are locked to customer accounts and most of their logic now runs on a server. The server is also often fortified with analytics to detect cheating after the event, just like in a professional bridge tournament.

24.3.5 Peer-to-peer systems

From the late 1990s, peer-to-peer file-sharing became one of the main ways in which music was distributed online. Once people had CD drives on their computers and broadband connections, they could copy and share their favourite tracks. In 1999, Shawn Fanning, an 18-year-old drop-out, revolutionised the music business by creating the Napster service, which enabled people to share MP3 audio files with each other [1383]. Rather than keeping the files centrally, which would invite legal action, Napster just provided an index so that someone wanting a given track could find out who else had it and was prepared to share or trade. It attracted tens of millions of users, but lawsuits from Hollywood closed it down in September 2002. Systems such as Gnutella and Freenet then borrowed ideas from the world of censorship-resistant systems to set up networks without a central node that could be closed down by legal attacks [441]. These were followed by other systems such as Kazaa and BitTorrent.

I was the designer of an early censorship-resistant system, the Eternity Service. The motivation came when an early anonymous remailer, `anon.penet.fi`, was used to post a message that upset the Scientologists and was closed down after they got a court order forcing its operator to disclose the linkage between users' real email addresses and the pseudonyms they used on his system [883]. The messages that were the subject of the case contained an affidavit by a former minister of their church to the effect that once members had been fully initiated they were told that the rest of the human race was suffering from false consciousness; that, in reality, Jesus was the bad guy and Lucifer was the good guy. Well, history has many examples of religions that denounced their competitors as both deluded and wicked; the Scientologists' innovation was to claim that their scriptures were their copyright, so the whistleblower's leak was a breach of copyright. They got away with this argument in a number of jurisdictions until eventually a court in the Netherlands put a stop to it by allowing an NGO there to publish the 'Fishman affidavit', as it was called.

The Eternity Service was designed to provide long-term file storage by distributing file fragments across the net, encrypted so that the people hosting them would not be able to tell which fragments they had, and so that reconstruction could only be performed via remailer mechanisms [62]. A later version of this was Publius[9], which also provided a censorship-resistant anonymous publishing mechanism [1978].

The United States Copyright Office defines peer-to-peer networks as networks where computers are linked to one another directly rather than through a central server. The absence of a server that can be closed down by court order creates an interesting problem for music industry enforcers. The two tactics on which the music industry relied were suing uploaders and technical attacks on the systems.

One way to attack peer-to-peer systems is to 'walk the network' by introducing a modified peer, contacting as many other peers as possible, and then identifying them. During the mid-2000s, the music industry tried harassing users at scale, filing tens of thousands of lawsuits. In many cases people agreed to cease and desist and pay a small penalty rather than fight a case; but in October 2007 a federal jury in Duluth, MN., convicted 30-year-old Jammie Thomas of copyright infringement for sharing material on Kazaa and ordered her to pay $9,250 for each of the 24 songs involved in the case. Firms working for the music industry were also uploading damaged music files to spam out systems (which will usually be legal), and it was suspected that they were also conducting denial-of-service attacks (which in many jurisdictions isn't). In September 2007, a company called Media Defender that worked for the music industry on 'file-sharing mitigation' had several thousand of its internal emails leaked, after an employee forwarded his email to Gmail and his password was compromised. It turned out that Media Defender's business model was to charge $4,000 per album per month, and $2,000 per track per month, for 'protection' that involved attacks on twelve million users of fifteen P2P networks [1503]. Peer-to-peer systems have also allegedly been attacked by Comcast, which is said to have disrupted its customers' connections by sending forged reset packets to tear down Bittorrent connections. Comcast might prefer its customers to watch TV over its cable network, so they see its ads, but the allegations raise public policy issues if true: Comcast is not a law-enforcement agency [220].

The state of play in 2020 is that some jurisdictions suffer from this kind of extortion, from law firms sometimes referred to as Torrent trolls: in Sweden, for example, there have been tens of thousands of cases where lawyers demand large payments from families claiming that their kids uploaded some copyrighted material [1658]. This appears to be a function of local procedural law more than anything else; in many countries, lawyers can't be as crooked, or at least not in this particular way.

In the larger global ecosystem, the big service firms are now dominant and the deciding factor in copyright infringement is the notice-and-takedown

[9]For non-US readers: the revolutionaries Alexander Hamilton, John Jay, and James Madison used the pen name Publius when they wrote the Federalist Papers, a collection of 85 articles published in New York State newspapers in 1787–8 and which helped convince New York voters to ratify the United States constitution.

regime set up under the US DMCA, and followed by similar laws elsewhere. I will discuss this further in section 24.5.

24.3.6 Managing hardware design rights

Another rights-management ecosystem is the protection of designs licensed for use in hardware. Companies like Arm earn their living by licensing designs for processors and other components to firms who make custom chips, whether by designing application-specific integrated circuits (ASICs) or by using Field-Programmable Gate Arrays (FPGAs).

The first use case for hardware protection is when such devices are used to make it harder to counterfeit products, for example by overrun production. A camera company licenses a circuit that they integrate into a bitstream that's loaded into an FPGA, that then becomes a key component in a new camera that they have made in a factory in China. They pay for 100,000 licenses, yet 200,000 cameras arrive on the market. There are two failure modes: the camera company could have ordered the extra production and lied to the IP owner, or the Chinese factory could be cheating the camera company. In fact, they could both be cheating, each having decided to make an extra 50,000 units. Now there are technical mechanisms that the camera company could use to stop the factory cheating it, such as personalising each camera with a serial number and so on after manufacture – but these could make it harder to cheat the IP owner.

So the second problem is how the IP owner can tell whether a product contains a particular circuit. The camera company might have licensed a processor or a filter for one model, then built it into another cheaper model too without declaring it.

These risks cause some large IP vendors to prefer to license their best designs only to other large firms, so small startups can be disadvantaged. They also depress sales of FPGAs, whose manufacturers offer mechanisms to tackle the first problem by distributing encrypted bitstreams and updates for whole chips; the second problem is harder, because chip design tools come within the trust boundary. Customers need to be able to evaluate designs, and debug designs, which is in tension with controlling dissemination. There has been some use of side-channels for forensics. Owners of semiconductor IP can buy samples of suspect goods, then measure the chips' precise analog behaviour such as power consumption and timing, which can often reveal the presence of a given functional component. Components can even be deliberately designed to generate a suitable signal in their power trace. (Similar techniques are used by military contractors to look for hardware Trojans.)

This brings us to the question of copyright marking.

24.4 Information hiding

Hollywood's interest in finding new mechanisms for protecting copyright came together in the mid-1990s with the military's interest in unobtrusive communications and public concerns over government efforts to control cryptography, and started to drive rapid developments in the field of *information hiding*. This largely refers to techniques for hiding data in other data, such as when a secret message is hidden in an MP3 audio file, or a program's serial number is embedded in the order in which certain instructions are executed.

Hollywood sought salvation in *copyright marks* embedded unobtrusively in digital audio, video and artwork. These include *watermarks*, copyright messages that may or may not be hidden but are hard to remove, and *fingerprints* that are hidden serial numbers. For example, when you downloaded an mp3 from Apple's iTunes music store, it contained a fingerprint embedded in the audio that identified you. The idea was that if you then uploaded your copy to a file-sharing system, the copyright owner could sue you. (Some people believed that fingerprinting depressed sales overall because of the legal hazards it created for honest purchasers. Amazon, for example, did not mark MP3 downloads [853].)

The privacy interest is in *steganography* whose purpose is to embed a message in some cover medium in such a way that its very existence remains undetectable. The conceptual model, proposed by Gus Simmons [1749], is as follows. Alice and Bob are in jail and wish to hatch an escape plan; all their communications pass through the warden, Willie; and if Willie detects any encrypted messages, he will frustrate their plan by throwing them into solitary confinement. So they must find some way of hiding their secret messages in an innocuous covertext. As in the related field of cryptography, we assume that the mechanism in use is known to the warden, and so the security must depend solely on a secret key that Alice and Bob have somehow managed to share [1757].

There is some similarity with electronic warfare. First, if steganography is seen as a low-probability-of-intercept communication, then copyright marking is like jam-resistant communication: it may use much the same methods but in order to resist focused attacks it is likely to have a much lower bit rate. We can think of Willie as the pirate who tries to mangle the audio or video signal in such a way as to cause the copyright mark detector to fail. Second, techniques such as direct-sequence spread spectrum that were originally developed for electronic warfare found use in the information hiding community.

Copyright marks don't have to be hidden to be effective. Some TV stations embed their logo in a visible but unobtrusive manner in the corner of the picture, and as I noted, academic journal downloads do something similar. However, in what follows I'll concentrate on hidden copyright marks.

24.4.1 Watermarks and copy generation management

The DVD consortium became concerned that digital video or audio could be decoded to analog format and then redistributed (the so-called 'analog hole'). They set out to invent a *copy generation management system* that would work even with analog signals. The idea was that a video or music track might be unmarked, or marked 'never copy', or marked 'copy once only'; compliant players would not record a video marked 'never copy' and when recording one marked 'copy once only' would change its mark to 'never copy'. Commercially sold videos would be marked 'never copy', while TV broadcasts and similar material would be marked 'copy once only'. In this way, the DVD players available to consumers would allow unlimited copying of home videos and time-shifted viewing of TV programmes, but could not easily be abused for commercial piracy. The mechanisms depended on hiding copyright marks in the content, and are reviewed in [1170]. For each disk, choose a *ticket* X, which can be a random number, plus copy control information, plus possibly some information unique to the physical medium such as the wobble in the lead-in track. Use a one-way hash function h to compute $h(X)$ and then $h(h(X))$. Embed $h(h(X))$ in the video as a hidden copyright mark. Have compliant machines look for a watermark, and if they find one refuse to play a track unless they are supplied with $h(X)$ which they check by hashing it and comparing it with the mark. Compliant devices will only record a marked track if given X, in which case only $h(X)$ is written to the new disc. In this way, a 'copy once only' track in the original medium becomes a 'copy no more' track in the new medium. This ended up in Blu-ray, but that failed in the marketplace, as well as being a complete pain for developers to work with.

Robustness depends on many things including our old friend, the receiver operating characteristic or ROC, which sets the trade-off between false alarms and missed alarms. It's not enough for a marking mechanism to have a low missed alarm rate; it needs a low false alarm rate too [1320]. If your player were to detect a 'no-copy' mark by mistake in the video you made of your child's birthday party, then you'd have to buy a pirate player to watch it. So what sort of marks are possible, and how robust are they against forgery, spoofing and other attacks?

24.4.2 General information hiding techniques

Information hiding goes back even further than cryptology, having its roots in camouflage. Herodotus records tricks used during the wars between the Greeks and the Persians, including hiding a message in the belly of a hare carried by a hunter, tattooing it on the shaven head of a slave whose hair was then allowed to grow back, and writing it on the wooden base under the wax of a writing tablet [891]. Francis Bacon proposed a system that embedded a binary message in a book at one bit per letter by alternating between two different fonts [1515]. Until quite modern times, most writers considered hiding confidential information much more important than enciphering it [2025]. Military and intelligence organizations are keenly aware that traffic security is often more important than content confidentiality, and have used all sorts of technologies from the microdots used by spies to low-probability-of-intercept radios.

When it comes to hiding data in other data, the modern terminology of the subject is as follows [1523]. The copyright mark, or in the case of steganography, the *embedded text*, is hidden in the *cover-text* producing the *marked text* or in the case of steganography the *stego-text*. In most cases, additional secret information is used during this process; this is the *marking key* or *stego-key*, and some function of it is typically needed to recover the mark or embedded text. Here, the word 'text' can be replaced by 'audio', 'video' and so on, as appropriate.

A wide variety of embedding schemes has been proposed.

- Many people have proposed hiding a mark or secret message in the least significant bits of an audio or video signal. This isn't usually a very good strategy, as the hidden data is easy to detect statistically (the least significant bits are no longer correlated with the rest of the image), and it's trivial to remove or replace. It's also severely damaged by lossy compression techniques.
- A better technique is to hide the mark at one or more locations determined by a secret key. This was first invented in classical China. The sender and receiver had copies of a paper mask with holes cut out of it at random locations. The sender would place his mask over a blank sheet of paper, write his message in the holes, then remove it and compose a cover message including the characters of the secret embedded message. This trick was reinvented in the 16th century by the Italian mathematician Cardan and is now known to cryptographers as the Cardan grille [1003].
- A modern version of this hides a mark in a `.gif` format image as follows. A secret key is expanded to a keystream which selects an appropriate number of pixels. The embedded message is the parity of the color codes for these pixels. In practice even a quite large number of the pixels in an image can have their color changed to that of a similar one in the palette without any visible effects [974]. However, if all the pixels are tweaked in this way, then again the hidden data is easy to remove by just tweaking them again. A better result is obtained if the cover image and embedding method are such that 1% of the pixels can safely be tweaked. Then, if the warden repeats the process but with a different key, a different 1% of the pixels will be tweaked and only 1% of the bits of the hidden data will be corrupted. These can then be recovered using an error-correcting code.

- In general, the introduction of noise or distortion – as happens with lossy compression – will introduce errors into the hidden data almost regardless of the embedding method unless some kind of error correcting code is added. A system proposed for banknote marking, Patchwork, uses a repetition code – the key selects two subsets of pixels, one of which is marked by increasing the luminosity and the other by decreasing it. This embeds a single bit; the note is either watermarked using that key, or it isn't [226, 831]. This is reminiscent of differential power analysis: the key tells you how to sort your input data into two piles, and if the key was right they're noticeably different.
- In the general case, one may want to embed more than one bit, and have the embedded data survive very high levels of induced errors. So a common technique is to use direct-sequence spread-spectrum techniques borrowed from electronic warfare [1894]. You have a number of secret sequences, each coding a particular symbol, and you add one of them to the content to mark it.
- Spread spectrum encoding is often done in a transform space to make its effects less perceptible and more robust against common forms of compression. These techniques are also commonly used in conjunction with perceptual filtering, which emphasises the encoding in the noisiest or perceptually most significant parts of the image or music track, where it will be least obtrusive, and de-emphasises it in quiet passages of music or large expanses of color [289].
- Some schemes use the characteristics of particular media, such as a scheme for marking print media by moving text lines up or down by a three-hundredth of an inch [316], or adding extra echoes to music below the threshold of perception [226]. So far, such techniques don't seem to have become as robust, or as widely used, as generic techniques based on keyed embedding using transform spaces, spread spectrum and perceptual filtering.

Progress in copyright marking was very rapid in the late 1990s: people invented marking schemes which other people broke, until some systems were adopted in banknotes and in some tools such as Adobe's. From the mid-2000s, interest in copyright marking waned with the move to broadband, but research in steganography and steganalysis continued, merging with research in image forensics.

24.4.3 Attacks on copyright marking schemes

Throughout this book, we've seen attacks on cryptographic systems that occasionally involved cryptanalysis but more often relied on mistaken assumptions, protecting the wrong things, protocol failures and implementation bugs. And in the history of technology as a whole, inventions tend to end up being used to solve problems somewhat different from the problems the inventor was originally thinking about. Copyright marking has been no different on either count.

- In the beginning, many people tackled the problem of embedding hidden copyright messages so that ownership of a work could be proved in court. But this is a non-problem. Lawyers almost never have any difficulty in proving ownership of an exhibit; they don't rely on technical measures which might confuse a jury, but on documents such as contracts with bands and model release forms.
- As usual, many designers ignored Kerckhoffs' principle – that the security of a system should reside in the choice of key, not in the algorithm in use. But when marks are used to prove whether a particular digital object was licensed, this means disclosing them in court together with the marking keys, so it may be necessary to use multiple keys.
- As an example, color copiers sold in the USA hide a *Machine Identification Code* (MIC) in the bit patterns of copies as an extra means of detecting currency forgers [2006]. Introduced by Xerox and Canon in the 1980s, apparently following a secret agreement with one or more governments, its existence was disclosed in a court case in the Netherlands in 2004. The mechanism was then reverse engineered in a crowdsourced effort led by EFF. The MIC is a pattern of yellow dots 0.1mm in diameter that is barely visible to the human eye and repeated about 150 times on an A4 colour copy. There is now software to identify and remove it, so whistleblowers can sanitise sensitive documents before leaking them to the press [1605].
- Many marks simply add some noise to the signal. But if all the frames in a video carry the same mark, you can average them to get the mark and then subtract it out. Or you supply some known content to a marking system, and compare its input and output. Even if the mark is applied in a tamper-resistant process immediately after decryption, and every device adds a different mark, then if the mark consists of small signals added at discrete points in the content, an opponent can just decrypt the same ciphertext with several different devices and compare them to remove the marks.
- There have been attempts to develop a marking equivalent of public-key cryptography, so that (for example) anyone could insert a mark which only one principal could detect, or anyone could detect a mark that only one principal could have inserted. The former seems just about feasible if the mark can be inserted as the cover audio or video is being manufactured [494]. The latter seems a lot harder. First, you can't authenticate all

of an image by embedding a signature in it, as then you'd be modifying it in order to prove that it has not been modified. Second, if you try to authenticate just the high-order bits or the salient features, then there are robustness issues: given a device that will detect a mark, an attacker can remove it by applying small changes to the image until the decoder cannot find it anymore, then apply their own signature [1171,1513]. So the main effort was invested in mechanisms that put a different mark in each instance of the content as it is decrypted.

- Steganalysis techniques were developed to break most embedding schemes. For over a decade, people would propose new information hiding mechanisms at the Information Hiding Workshop, and the following year they'd be broken. The most prolific attack team was Jessica Fridrich and her students at Binghamton; her book on steganography is the starting point for serious work on the subject [724].
- The most successful marking startup – Digimarc – set up a service to track intellectual property on the web. They supplied tools to let picture owners embed invisible fingerprints, and had a bot that crawled the web looking for marked pictures and reported them to the copyright owner. There were various ways to defeat this. For example, a marked image could often be chopped up into smaller images that together look just like the original when rendered on a web page but in which a copyright mark won't be detected (Figure 24.6) [1518]. Digimarc worked for a while on monitoring broadcast streams; but over time, AI improved to

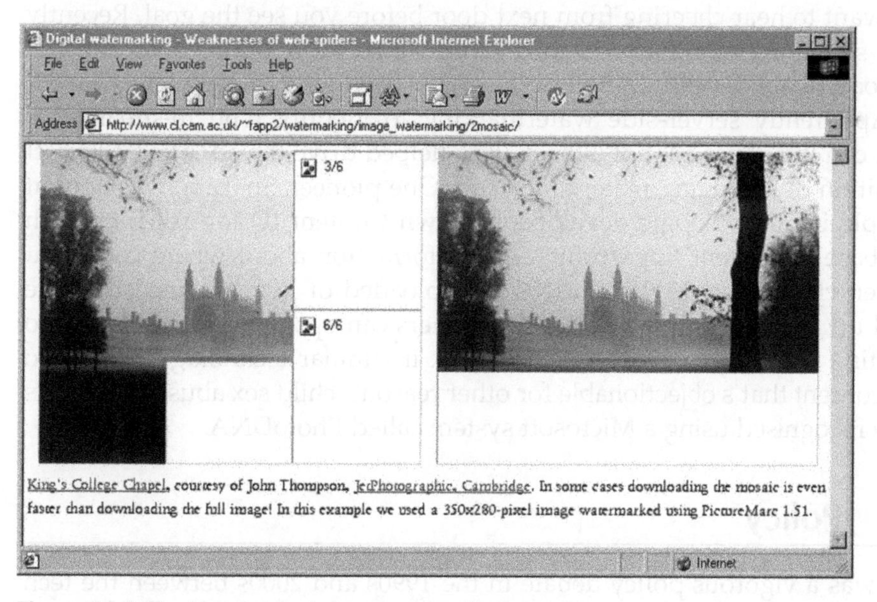

Figure 24.6: The Mosaic attack (courtesy Jet Photographic, www.jetphotographic.com)

the point that software can identify which song is being played directly. Digimarc moved into security printing, licensing their marking technology to central banks as a counterfeit detection measure. For example, it's found in Euro banknotes, which it prevents from being scanned or copied using the latest equipment [2064]. Software packages such as Photoshop and PaintShop Pro now refuse to handle marked images. Digimarc now monitors packaging and provides labeling systems.

- The most general attacks on imperceptible copyright marking schemes involve suitably chosen distortions. Audio marks can be removed by randomly duplicating or deleting sound samples to introduce inaudible jitter; techniques used for click removal and resampling are also powerful mark removers. For images, a tool my students developed, called Stirmark, introduces the same kind of errors into an image as printing it on a high-quality printer and then scanning it again with a high-quality scanner. It applies a minor geometric distortion: the image is slightly stretched, sheared, shifted, and/or rotated by an unnoticeable random amount This defeated almost all the marking schemes in existence when it was developed and is now a standard benchmark for copyright mark robustness [1518].

For a fuller account of attacks on copyright marking schemes, see [724]. It's still difficult to design marking schemes that remain robust once the mark detection algorithm is known.

Perhaps the key technical factor that killed copyright marking wasn't an attack but latency. This is really important for streamed sports events; you don't want to hear cheering from next door before you see the goal. Recently media streaming standards (DASH, HLS) have been updated to support downloading media chunks before they have been written completely to 'fix' this. Apparently server-side watermarking to identify who re-streamed a stream can introduce a lot of latency. This helped drive the adoption of direct recognition of infringing material instead. One pioneer, Shazam, was bought by Apple in 2017; Google developed its own Content ID for YouTube with a database of content fingerprints with information about where copyright has been claimed, and when videos are uploaded or live streamed they are looked up in this database. Copyright owners can opt to monetize the video by getting a share of ad revenue, or block it. Similar technology is used to block content that's objectionable for other reasons: child sex abuse material is mostly recognised using a Microsoft system called PhotoDNA.

24.5 Policy

There was a vigorous policy debate in the 1990s and 2000s between the tech industry and many of the owners of 'intellectual property' (IP) – copyright, patents and trademarks – as the opening up of the Internet made copying easy and threatened traditional music, book and film publishers[10]. The reaction included a series of laws from copyright term extension through America's Digital Millennium Copyright Act (DMCA) to an IP Enforcement Directive in Europe, which shifted power in ways that many people in tech and elsewhere felt to be threatening. The get-out for tech was section 230 of the US Communications Decency Act of 1996 (CDA) which states that 'No provider or user of an interactive computer service shall be treated as the publisher or speaker of any information provided by another information content provider' so platforms cannot be held liable for copyright infringement by users. This favoured the growth of information service firms in the USA rather than Europe.

The US DMCA does give copyright owners the power ('Notice and Take Down') to compel ISPs to take down websites with infringing material. Although there is also a provision ('Notice and Put Back') for the subscriber to file a counter notice and have his stuff put back within 14 days unless the copyright owner files suit, in practice many ISPs will just terminate a customer's service rather than get involved in litigation. This led not just to a lot of music copying using peer-to-peer systems, but to floods of takedown requests from music industry lawyers, as well as to the push for DRM that we discussed earlier.

Over half of the takedown requests to Google come from the top 16 copyright owners, with the top three generating over a billion a year – many of them to links that are not even on Google. Many complaining organisations get few or none of the links they complain about removed, as they are either not relevant or judged to be non-infringing; see Google's transparency reports for details [801]. This has real policy consequences: censoring a Chinese shop that pretends to be Nike is one thing, while censoring Black Lives Matter Peckham in response to a complaint from a white supremacist is quite another.

There are many side-effects: for example, the legal rules that allowed copying for personal use ('fair use' in the USA and 'fair dealing' in the UK) are being replaced by technical controls that don't. For example, when I applied for planning permission to extend my kitchen, I had to file four copies of a local plan; but the map software at our university library only lets you print three copies. This is an entirely deliberate act by the Ordnance Survey to maximise its revenue. Legal controls are supplemented by access controls, and the legal privilege given to those access controls by the DMCA and comparable EU laws creates a new bundle of rights, described by legal scholars as 'paracopyright' [532].

[10]The term 'intellectual property' is controversial. Many activists object to it as a propaganda term coined by corporate lobbyists who want people to start seeing patents and copyrights as permanent natural rights, like title to real estate or human rights, rather than as the temporary monopolies that they are in law.

In effect, copyright regulations are no longer made by lawmakers in Washington or Brussels, but by programmers working for Microsoft or Apple or Amazon. The result has been to erode the rights of copyright users. In one spectacular example, Amazon quietly removed from its customers' Kindles an edition of George Orwell's '1984' and 'Animal Farm' over which some dispute had arisen [1835]. This was a sobering reminder of the huge gap between owning a physical copy of a book, and 'owning' an ebook – in fact you just bought a license from a vendor who wrote the license so as to give you next to no rights at all.

At the same time, copyright law suddenly became relevant to millions of people. Whereas in the past it was only a concern of specialists such as publishers, it now touches the lives of everyone who downloads music, time-shifts movies, or maintains a personal web page. As the law has failed to keep up with technology, the gap between what it permits and what people actually do has become wider. In the UK, for example, it's technically illegal to rip a CD to listen to on your phone; yet as this is one of the main reasons that people still buy CDs, the British Phonographic Industry (the trade body) graciously says it won't sue anybody. But many of the minor infringements that used to take place in private, or unsurveilled public spaces (such as singing a song in a pub), now go online (as when a phone video clip of the song gets on someone's social-network page). John Tehranian calculates that a typical law professor commits over 80 copyright infringements a day, carrying statutory penalties of over $10m [1869]. In effect, we only tolerated copyright law because it wasn't enforced against private individuals. Technology makes enforcement possible, the consolidation of copyrights into an ever smaller number of corporate owners and collecting societies makes for a concentrated lobby, greed makes abuses happen, and the frictions increase.

The consolidation of copyrights also leads to injustice in the distribution of income. I already mentioned the problems with collecting societies, which in effect tax venues and distribute the proceeds in such a way that the rich get lots and the small fry not so much at all; this has become worse with streaming, whose payouts are a function of plays rather than users. So if my granddaughter pays £10 a month and listens to Ariana Grande four hours a day while I pay the same and listen to Kathryn Tickell two hours a week, then rather than giving them £10 each (less Apple's 30% commission), Ariana will get fourteen times what Kathryn gets [1556]. This means that most of your subscription – or at least of the money the tech firms don't take one way or another – goes to the megastars like Ariana, and Ed Sheeran and Lady Gaga.

There are also privacy concerns. In the old days, people would buy a book or a record for cash; the move to downloads means that servers run by firms such as Google, Spotify and Apple have a record of what people watch and listen to, and this can be subpoena'ed. (The move to online bookselling and then to Kindles has created similar records at Amazon.) These records are also used for marketing. A survey for the Privacy Commissioner of Canada found many examples of intrusive behavior, including ebook software profiling individuals, DoubleClick advertising in a library service, systems tracking individuals via IP addresses, and contradictions between vendors' stated privacy policies and observed behaviour – including undisclosed communications to third parties [682]. Why do copyright owners, or big tech firms claiming to act on their behalf, get away with so much? The answer lies in the dynamics of lobbying.

24.5.1 The IP lobby

The IP lobby has its modern origins in an effort by the drug company Pfizer to extend patent protection on its drugs from the USA to less developed countries like Brazil and India in the 1970s. The history is told by Peter Drahos and John Braithwaite [581]; in summary, Pfizer and the other drug companies allied themselves with the music and film industry (who wanted to cut bootlegging and copying), the luxury-goods industry (who wanted to reduce the number of cheap knock-offs), and a number of other US players (including the Business Software Alliance), and persuaded the US government to start applying pressure on other countries to bring their patent, copyright and trade-mark laws in line with America's. From the mid-1980s this was largely a matter of bullying less developed countries who wanted trade deals, but in 1995 a treaty on Trade-Related Aspects of Intellectual Property Rights (TRIPS) took effect for members of the World Trade Organisation (WTO), followed by two treaties of the World Intellectual Property Organisation (WIPO) in 1996. Essentially the USA and the EU got together and bullied holdouts like India and Brazil.

The implementation of these treaties stirred up opposition in developed countries as people began to realise how they might be affected. In the USA, the Digital Millennium Copyright Act of 1998 made it an offence to circumvent a copyright-protection mechanism, as required by WIPO, while in the European Union the Copyright Directive of 2001 had a similar effect. This was seen as enabling vendors to create closed platforms and control competition; it was also seen as a threat by the free and open source software movement, and by security researchers – especially after the Russian researcher Dmitri Sklyarov was arrested at a US conference at the request of Adobe, after his employer had sold tools circumventing password protection on PDF documents.

There were many other high-profile incidents; for example, I was on the program committee of the 2001 Information Hiding Workshop when an attempt was made by the Recording Industry Association of America (RIAA) to force the program chair to pull a paper by Ed Felten and his students describing vulnerabilities in a copyright marking scheme being touted for a digital music standard [495]. Ed then sued RIAA, in a landmark academic-freedom case [620]. The irony is that the promoters of this scheme had issued a public challenge to academics and others to break it. The next case was Bunnie Huang's book "Hacking the Xbox": this described how, as an MIT student, he'd overcome the protection mechanisms in the first version of Microsoft's games console [932]. The book he wrote caused his publisher to take fright, but he found another one. The encroachment on liberties threatened by rights-management mechanisms and anti-hacking laws led to the growth of digital-rights NGOs in a number of countries (others had them already as a result of the 'Crypto Wars'; I'll discuss all this in more detail in section 26.2.7).

One turning point came in 2003–4, as the IP lobby was trying to steer a further measure through Brussels, the IP Enforcement Directive. In its original form, this would have further ratcheted up the penalties on infringers and removed the prospects for public-interest defences based on free speech or fair use. This time opponents of the measure managed to assemble a sufficiently strong coalition of opposing interests that the measure was substantially amended. This opposition led to the establishment the following year of EDRi, an NGO that promotes European digital rights, and is supported by several dozen NGOs in Europe who realised that a lobbying presence in Brussels was essential.

The IP lobby's mistake was trying to compel every country in Europe to make patent infringement a crime, rather than just a civil matter. This was intended by Big Pharma to undermine firms who make low-cost generic versions of drugs once they have come off patent. At present, drug patent holders try to prolong their patents by 'evergreening' – filing subsidiary, later patents, with often dubious derivative claims – which the generic drugmakers deal with by offering their distributors indemnities against having to pay damages. Making infringement a criminal matter would have upset these arrangements. This caused the generic drugmakers to oppose the directive vigorously, along with supermarkets, car parts dealers and consumer groups. Even the software industry started to get nervous: we pointed out to Microsoft that thousands of companies believe that Microsoft is infringing their patents, but don't have the money to go the distance in a civil court. If patent infringement became a crime, surely they would take their grievances to the police? Would Bill risk arrest on some future trip to Europe? The attempt to criminalise patent infringement collapsed when tech firms withdrew their support. A rich, powerful lobby isn't stopped by fine words, or by outrage from university professors and free-software activists. It's stopped when it comes up against another rich, powerful lobby pushing in the opposite direction.

Some copyright activists hope that once copyright expires – or assuming that lots of material can be made available under a Creative Commons license – then everything will be hunky-dory. I doubt it. The theory behind both copyright and patent was to offer creators a temporary monopoly in order to increase the supply of creations. Initially copyright was for 18 years, then 35, then 50, then the creator's lifetime plus 70 years after that. Cynics noted that whenever Mickey Mouse was in danger of going out of copyright, the US government would step in to increase the copyright term, and bully other governments to fall in line. (Other cynics noted that the copyright term for musical performance was extended from 50 years to 70 after Sir Cliff Richard let the then Prime Minister Tony Blair holiday at his mansion in Barbados.) Some lawyers would like to extend copyright term indefinitely, but that violates the social contract on which copyright is based and it also doesn't solve the problem of preservation: many publishers have failed to look after their own back catalogue properly and had to retrieve copies from national deposit collections.

Curating old bits costs money, just as curating old manuscripts does; indeed the film industry has recently discovered that archiving digital productions actually costs more than they used to pay in the old days, when they just locked away the master copies in an old salt mine. There's just an awful lot of bits generated during digital production, and copying them to new disks every few years isn't cheap. In the long term, once bitstrings belong to nobody, who will pay for their upkeep? Might we extend the existing taxpayer-funded deposit library system to digital materials? But such organisations typically fail to make much progress with digital materials for a number of reasons, from lack of understanding to being too defensive about copyright law[11]. There has been a very creditable effort by the Internet Archive, a San Francisco NGO, to preserve online material for future generations, and it has run an open library project since 2006. Google scanned many books in university libraries, eventually getting a legal settlement with authors and other interested parties following a long court case[12]. As a result, Google Books can make millions of volumes searchable, and supply the full contents of books that are out of copyright. Where a book is still in copyright, it can let people search and see snippets as a fair use allowed under copyright law, but it cannot sell an electronic version without the publisher's agreement. (It had wanted to sell electronic versions of everything and simply pay the publishers a fixed royalty, so as to challenge Amazon's hold on the book market.) The latest development in 2020 is a lawsuit by book publishers (including Wiley, the publisher of this book) to stop the Internet Archive lending out electronic copies of books [1002]. The copyright wars drag on, even despite the pandemic.

24.5.2 Who benefits?

As I mentioned in section 8.6.4, a turning point in the copyright wars came in 2005. In January of that year, Google's chief economist Hal Varian addressed a

[11] When the British Library wanted to archive our NGO web page they wanted us to sign copyright release and indemnity forms, which we couldn't do for material from third parties or written by people who'd left or died. The only practical way forward is to just put stuff online and take it down if anyone makes a convincing objection. That's what tech firms do; legacy organisations often don't have the confidence.

[12] The Authors Guild, Inc. et al v. Google, Inc.; October 16, 2015 (2d Circuit); November 14, 2013 (SDNY).

DRM conference in Berlin and asked who would benefit from stronger DRM. He pointed out that, in classical economic theory, a technical link between two industries would usually benefit the more concentrated industry (for example, car makers and car parts). But the platform industry was concentrated (then it was Apple, Microsoft and Sony) while the music industry was less so (four majors and many independents): so why should the music industry expect to be the winners from better DRM? Economic theory says that platform vendors should win more. The music industry scoffed, and yet by the end of that year they were hurting – by the fall of that year, they were tearfully lobbying the UK government and the European Commission to 'do something' about Apple, such as forcing it to open its FairPlay DRM scheme.

Over the next few years, Hal's prediction came true. The music majors lost their market power to firms like Apple, Amazon and Spotify, while Netflix established a dominant position in distributing video. Music downloading – with or without DRM – changed the structure and dynamics of the music industry. Bands used to rely on the majors to promote them, but now they can do that themselves by giving away their albums on their websites; they always made most of their money from performances, and now they make more than ever – just as John Perry Barlow had predicted back in 1994. In fact, smart bands now go with an indie label, as then they'll get a bigger share of the streaming and other revenues. And thanks to the pandemic, there is now a rapidly-growing new sector of online concerts, where bands perform in empty venues and stream live to their fans, cutting out both the subscription streaming services and the big firms that own the big venues [1688].

24.6 Accessory control

One of the most important and rapidly-growing uses of cryptographic mechanisms and of rights-management technology generally is in accessory control.

The story starts in 1895 when King Camp Gillette invented the disposable razor blade, and subsidised razors from later sales of blades. Economists call this strategy *two-part pricing*, or even just the 'razors and blades' model, in Gillette's memory. The tech industry first adopted it for games consoles; it was then adopted by printer makers who subsidise the printers from the ink cartridges, starting in 1996 with the Xerox N24 (see [1825] for the history of cartridge chips). In a typical system, if the printer senses a third-party cartridge, or a refilled cartridge, it may silently downgrade from 1200 dpi to 300 dpi, or even refuse to work at all. In 2003, expiry dates and ink usage controls were added [1209]; and modern cartridges now limit the amount of ink dispensed electronically rather than waiting for it to run out physically. The latest development is region coding: you can't use US ink cartridges in a recently UK-purchased HP printer. Other industries are adopting this technology. For example, the amount of RAM you are allowed to use in our lab oscilloscope depends on how much you paid for it.

After some grumbling, European regulators decided to put up with this, but in the USA, the matter was decided in court. The printer maker Lexmark sued SCC, which had reverse-engineered their print-cartridge crypto, alleging violation of the Digital Millennium Copyright Act. Although they won at first instance, they lost on appeal in 2004 [1159]. In a similar case, Chamberlain (who make garage door openers) sued Skylink (who made compatible openers) and also lost, losing the appeal too in 2004. This settled US law in favour of a free market for cryptologists, which was the position before the DMCA came along [1650]. A firm wanting to control its aftermarket using crypto chips is free to hire the smartest cryptographers it can find to build authentication chips that are really hard to hack, while its competitors are free to hire the smartest cryptanalysts they can find to try to reverse-engineer them.

There are many, many more examples. Even things that never used to have electronics in them, and that don't need electronics for any purpose, have acquired chips to enforce predatory business models. There are hundreds of examples: one that came up in 2020 as I was revising this chapter is their use in water filters in GE fridges. Six months after he bought a 'smart' fridge, Jack Busch got a demand that he buy another water filter for $54.99. It turned out that the filtered water option would turn itself off unless you bought a new filter every six months, whether you needed it or not. Jack duly figured out a hack and published it [358].

Is accessory control objectionable? The view that I took in the second edition of this book was that of standard economics: depends on how competitive the markets are. If ink cartridges have a high profit margin but the market for printers is competitive, competition will push down the price of printers to compensate for the high-priced cartridges [1946]. But in many other industries it might be anticompetitive; it just depends on how concentrated the industry is, and in winner-take-all platform markets it could be particularly objectionable [74].

I have since changed my mind. Competition matters, and we're seeing less of it as one industry after another adopts software in its products and becomes more like the software industry, with the tendency to monopoly that we discussed in Chapter 8. For example, John Deere now fits its tractors with locks that limit repairs to authorised dealers, causing great resentment among farmers at having to pay a $230 call-out and $135 an hour for a technician to authorise a spare part [1072]. The use of cryptographic mechanisms for product tying and bundling is among the anti-competitive factors with which our policymakers are now realising they have to deal. In the case of tractors, a right-to-repair law may be one of the necessary mitigations.

Sustainability also matters, and technical tying mechanisms are often about shortening product lives, leading to unnecessary consumption. Forcing a six-monthly change of water filter cartridges is a good example; we use ours for about five years. Such mechanisms also lead to products that are fragile and difficult to maintain. Another common outcome if you buy a 'smart fridge' is that it will turn into a frosty brick a couple of years later, when the vendor stops maintaining the server that it speaks to. I will discuss this at greater length in section 28.5.

The covid pandemic has illustrated other side-effects of accessory control. Early in the lockdown, some hospitals didn't have enough batteries for the respirators used by their intensive-care clinicians, now they were being used 24 × 7 rather than occasionally. The market-leading 3M respirators and the batteries that powered them had authentication chips, so the company could sell batteries for over $200 that cost $5 to make. Hospitals would happily have bought more for $200, but China had nationalised the factory the previous month, and 3M wouldn't release the keys to other component suppliers. The fix in this case was indeed competition. Respirators from other suppliers are cheaper and don't insist on proprietary batteries, while in Southampton, Paul Elkington and colleagues at the medical school designed their own respirator, making the design open to everyone in the world who wants to make them [623]. With luck 3M will lose the dominant market position they abused, but there was a real cost to clinical staff who didn't have enough personal protective equipment in the early months of the pandemic. Market-control mechanisms can have implications not just for sustainability tomorrow, but for safety today.

24.7 Summary

The technical protection of digital content against unauthorised copying is a wicked problem both technically and politically. It's difficult technically because general-purpose computers can copy bitstrings at no cost, and it's difficult politically because rights-management technology has done a lot of collateral damage. That the music industry itself was one of the casualties may have been just, but doesn't solve the continuing problems. These are tied up with much broader and deeper problems of competition, consumer protection and sustainability.

Research problems

Many of the tough problems around copyright in 2020 are policy problems rather than technical ones. There may be more work to be done in the field of digital forensics with the advent of deepfake images generated using machine learning techniques. If you want to do technical work on that or on information hiding, you might find Jessica Fridrich's books a useful starting point [724]. For software obfuscation, you might start with the report of a 2019 Dagstuhl seminar on the subject organised by Bjorn De Sutter and colleagues [555]. One open problem that spans both technology and policy is the privacy of the anti-cheat engines used in computer games. What information do they collect from your PC, where do they send it, and is this reasonable? Is it even legal?

Further reading

David Kahn is, as usual, good historical background reading [1003]. The software copy protection techniques of the PC era are discussed in [830]; there's a history of pay-TV systems in [1257]. More accessible may be a 2016 talk by Chris Gerlinsky on how he broke VideoCipher [759]. As for information hiding, there are books by Stefan Katzenbeisser and Fabien Petitcolas [1026], as well as by Jessica Fridrich [724]. The standard reference on game security is by Greg Hoglund and Gary McGraw [914]; see also Jeff Yan and Brian Randell for the history of computer game cheating [2057, 2059].

For a principled discussion of the policy issues around copyright and open culture, you might start with Pam Samuelson [1649,1650] and Larry Lessig [1146,1147]. Then I'd suggest you read up on whatever application areas are relevant to you. If you're an academic, you ought to read up about the tragedy of Aaron Swartz – the founder of Reddit who killed himself after putting millions of scientific papers online and being hounded by publishers' lawyers – and the long-running battles around Sci-Hub, which makes scientific papers available to all in defiance of copyright. If you play music for money you may want to follow the tussles around streaming and the antitrust settlement between Live Nation and Ticketmaster. If you play music in pub sessions you might be interested in the controversy around the Irish Music Rights Organisation.

If you're a lawyer or policymaker, you would do well to talk to NGOs engaged on copyright issues. Here for example is the view of European Digital Rights (EDRi): "In the digital environment, citizens face disproportionate enforcement measures from states, arbitrary privatised enforcement measures from companies and a lack of innovative offers, all of which reinforce the impression of a failed and illegitimate legal framework that undermines the relationship between creators and the society they live in. Copyright needs to be fundamentally reformed to be fit for purpose, predictable for creators, flexible and credible."

CHAPTER

25

New Directions?

But: connecting the world meant that we also connected all the bad things and all the bad people, and now every social and political problem is expressed in software. We've had a horrible 'oh shit' moment of realisation, but we haven't remotely worked out what to do about it.

– BENEDICT EVANS

If you campaign for liberty you're likely to find yourself drinking in bad company at the wrong end of the bar.

– WHIT DIFFIE

25.1 Introduction

Our security group at Cambridge runs a blog, `www.lightbluetouchpaper.org`, where we discuss the latest hacks and cracks. Many of the attacks hinge on specific applications, as does much of the cool research. Not all applications are the same, though. If our blog software gets hacked it will just give a botnet one more server, but there are other apps from which money can be stolen, others that people rely on for privacy, others that mediate power, and others that can kill.

I've already discussed many apps from banking through alarms to prepayment meters. In this chapter I'm going to briefly describe four classes of application at the bleeding edge of security research. They are where we find innovative attacks, novel protection problems, and thorny policy issues. They are: autonomous and remotely-piloted vehicles; machine learning, from adversarial learning to more general issues of AI in society; privacy technologies; and finally, electronic elections. What these have in common is that while previously, security engineering was about managing complexity in technology with all its exploitable side-effects, we are now bumping up against complexity in human society. Autonomous cars are hard because of the people driving other cars on the same road. AI is hard because our cool new pattern-matching tools, such as deep neural networks, can pick out not just real patterns in human behaviour – sometimes unexpected ones – but false ones too. Privacy is hard because of the richness of human interaction in society. And elections are hard not just because of the technical difficulty of counting votes in a way that preserves both privacy and auditability, but because of the huge variety of dirty tricks used by political players, both upstream and downstream of the voting process itself. All of these problems explore, in various ways, the boundary between what humans can do and what machines can do.

25.2 Autonomous and remotely-piloted vehicles

The aviation pioneer Lawrence Sperry invented the first autopilot in 1912 and demonstrated it in 1914, flying past the judges in a 'safer aircraft' competition in Paris with his hands up. In the process he and his father Elmer invented the artificial horizon. A fixed-wing aircraft left to its own devices will eventually go into a spiral dive and crash; the pilot can keep it level with reference to the horizon, but when flying in cloud that external reference is missing. A gyroscope can provide the missing reference, and it can also drive the ailerons and elevators via servos.

In 1975, I got my first proper job re-engineering a fast-jet inertial navigation set to work on the midget submarines used in the oil industry. Engineers in the same building were working on early head-up displays and satellite navigation equipment. Each of these pieces of equipment weighed about 20 kg and cost £250,000 – about $3M in today's money. All three together left little change out of $10M and weighed as much as a person.

Now, in 2020, you have all three in your phone. Rather than three spinning mechanical gyros in a precision-engineered cage, your phone has a chip with MEMS accelerometers and gyros. It also has a GPS chip for satellite navigation and a Google or Apple Maps app to show you how to walk, cycle or drive to your destination. Over forty years, the cost has fallen by six orders of magnitude and the mass by four. This has driven rapid evolution of assistive technology on sea, air and land. Pioneering single-handed yachtsmen developed self-steering gear to cross oceans from the 1920s, to give them time to sleep, cook and repair sails; amateurs now have smarter autopilots for coastal cruising. Autonomous probes swim beneath the Antarctic ice to measure how quickly it's melting. The world's navies develop underwater mines, autonomous submersibles to find them, and much else.

25.2.1 Drones

In the air, early weapons such as the German V1 and V2 used twin-gyro autopilots, while the Cold War gave us the Tomahawk cruise missiles used to great effect in both Gulf Wars. In service since the early 1980s, these sneak under the enemy radar by flying close to the ground, and use terrain contour matching to update their inertial navigation. They were followed closely by a variety of unmanned aerial vehicles (UAVs), which saw their first large-scale use in the war between Israel and Syria in 1982; the Israeli Air Force used them for reconnaissance and as decoys, wiping out the Syrian air force with minimal losses. The best-known of the next generation of UAVs was the Predator. Initially designed as a reconnaissance vehicle, it could linger over a target area at medium altitude for many hours, and was adapted to carry Hellfire missiles to strike targets on the ground. In service from 1995–2018, it saw service in Iraq, Afghanistan, Libya and elsewhere. It was replaced by the larger, faster Reaper, which became a mainstay of the war in Syria against the Islamic State. The world's armed forces now have a large range of UAVs, right down to small drones that soldiers carry in their rucksacks and use to see what's round the next corner.

Through the 20th century, enthusiasts built small radio-controlled model aircraft, but the FAA only issued its first commercial drone permit in 2006. In 2010, Parrot unveiled its AR Drone, a quadcopter that could be controlled by wifi from a smartphone, and in 2013 Amazon announced it was considering drones for delivery. Interest took off rapidly; within a couple of years our students were building drones and soon you could buy low-cost models in hobby shops. The main application in 2020 is aerial photography. There have been both insurgent and criminal uses, though, with drones used to deliver both drugs and mobile phones to prisoners, while insurgents have fitted drones with improvised explosive devices for use as weapons.

25.2.2 Self-driving cars

Most of the recent surge in interest though has been in self-driving cars and trucks. In 2004, faced with mounting combat losses to improvised explosive devices in Afghanistan and Iraq, DARPA decided to push the development of self-driving vehicles, and announced a competition with a million-dollar prize for whoever built one that could cross 149 miles of the Mojave desert the fastest. The prize went unclaimed as no vehicle finished the course, but the following year a team from Stanford led by the roboticist Sebastian Thrun collected the prize, now two million. His robot, Stanley, used machine learning and probabilistic reasoning to cope with terrain perception, collision avoidance, and stable vehicle control on slippery and rugged terrain [1891]. This built on robotics research going back to the 1980s, much of which DARPA had also funded. Their next challenge in 2007 moved from the desert to a simulated urban environment; competitors had to detect and avoid other vehicles, and obey the rules of the road. This bootstrapped a research community and the technology started to improve quickly.

Previously, carmakers had been steadily adding assistive technology, starting with antilock braking systems (ABS) in the last century and progressing through adaptive cruise control (ACC), which I described in section 23.4.1, automatic emergency braking (AEB) and lane keeping assist (LKA). The industry vision was that these would eventually come together into a full autopilot. Inspired by the DARPA challenges, Google hired Sebastian Thrun to lead Project Chauffeur in 2009 with a goal of building a fully self-driving car. This was announced in 2010, stimulating a market race involving both the tech and auto industries. Tesla was the first to field a product in 2014, when its 'Autopilot' software was launched as an over-the-air upgrade that could take control on the freeway or in stop-start traffic. There was already a hype cycle underway for machine learning, which I'll discuss in the next section, and self-driving cars hitched a ride. Tesla's Elon Musk was predicting full autonomy by 2018, and Google's Sergey Brin by 2017, before the Google car project was spun off as Waymo in 2016. People talked excitedly about low-cost robotaxis causing personal car ownership to be replaced by mobility-as-a-service; the arrival of Uber added a further competitor, and the hype scared even auto industry execs who should have known better into predicting that by the mid-2020s people wouldn't own their own cars any more. The hype cycle passed, as it always does. As I write in 2020, Waymo is operating a limited self-driving car service in a 50-square-mile area of Phoenix [873]. The service isn't available when it's raining, or in dust storms, and is monitored in real-time by humans at a control centre. It had been announced several times, but problems kept on forcing the company to put safety drivers back in the cars. So what's going on?

A large part of the answer is that other road users are unpredictable. Automation can deal with some of the resulting hazards: if the car in front brakes suddenly, a robot can react faster. Adaptive cruise control cuts driver fatigue and even cuts congestion once enough vehicles use it, as it damps the propagation of shock waves through traffic. But even here there are limits. When engineers extended the technology to automatic emergency braking, the inability to infer the intentions of other drivers became a limiting factor. Suppose for example you're driving on an open country road when the car in front indicates a turn and starts to slow down. You maintain speed as you expect it'll have left the road by the time you get there, and if not you'll just overtake. But the AEB might not understand this, so as you get too close to the turning car it activates, throwing you forward on your seat belt. Consumer tests of AEB systems in 2020 still show quite some variability, both in the false alarm rate and in the ability to stop the car in time when a pedestrian dummy is pulled across the road. Some systems restrict activation to city rather than highway speeds, and in 2020 all tend to be options available on more expensive models. AEB should be in all new cars in about 2022. Since 2016 insurers have been happy that it reduces the overall risk; I'll discuss safety assurance in section 28.4.1.

But each new assistive technology takes years to optimise and debug, and it's not straightforward to combine a dozen of them into an autopilot. The paper that Sebastian Thrun and his team wrote to describe Stanley gives a useful insight into the overall technology [1891]. There are several dozen programs interacting loosely, reflecting our understanding of how humans do such tasks; your subconscious looks at all sorts of things and brings hazards to your attention. Simultaneous processes in Stanley handled path planning, steering control and obstacle avoidance; this used laser rangefinders up to 22m, a colour camera beyond that, and a radar beyond that (which was not used in the race, as Stanley was given over 2000 waypoints for a predetermined course). Each of these systems had to solve many subproblems; the vision system, for example, had to adapt to changing light conditions and road colour. Stanley then had to be optimised via extensive testing, where the objective function was to maximise the mean distance between catastrophic failures (defined as the human safety driver taking over).

Combining the subsystems means compromises, and while the main vendors hold their design details secret, we're starting to learn about the optimisations and what goes wrong with them from accidents. For example, when a self-driving Uber killed Elaine Herzberg in Arizona in March 2018, it emerged at the NTSB inquiry that Elaine had been pushing a bicycle and the vision system flapped between identifying her as a pedestrian and as something else, but ultimately she was not recognised as a pedestrian because she was not on a crosswalk. AEB might have stopped the car but it had been turned off "to reduce the potential for erratic vehicle behavior" – in other words, because the false alarm rate was annoying [454]. Ultimately, Uber relied on the safety driver – who was unfortunately watching TV at the time[1].

Now we've known for decades that relying on humans to take over in an emergency takes time: a human has to react to an alarm, analyse the alarm display on the console, scan the environment, acquire situational awareness, get into the optical flow, and take effective control. Even in commercial aviation, it takes a flight crew about eight seconds to regain control properly after an autopilot failure. You cannot expect a safety driver in a car to do much better.

25.2.3 The levels and limits of automation

For such reasons, the Society of Automotive Engineers sets out five levels of automation:

1. Driver assistance – the software controls either steering or speed, and the human driver does the rest of the work;
2. Partial automation – the software controls both steering and speed in some modes but the human driver is responsible for monitoring the

[1] In fact, the very first fatal crash involving a Tesla on autopilot claimed the life of a driver who appeared to be watching a movie on his laptop when his car ran under a truck [1396].

environment and assuming control at zero notice if the software gets confused;

3. Conditional automation – the software monitors the environment, and controls both steering and speed, but assumes the human can take over if it gets confused;
4. High automation – the software monitors the environment and drives the car, in some driving conditions, without assuming that a human can intervene. If it gets confused it stops at the side of the road;
5. Full automation – the software can do everything a human can.

As of 2020, vehicles available on the mass market only have *advanced driver assistance systems* (ADAS) levels one and two, and insurers consider words like 'autonomous' and 'autopilot' to be dangerous as they cause customers to assume that a vehicle is operating at Level 4, which can lead to accidents. The Arizona crash can be seen as a car operating at Level 2 while the safety driver operated at Level 3. Level 4 often assumes a backup driver sitting in a control centre, overseeing several dozen 'autonomous' cars, but they won't have the bandwidth to understand a hazard as quickly as a safety driver on the spot. They don't feel the road noise and accelerations, they can't use their peripheral vision, and above all, they are not immersed in the optical flow field that is critical to driving a car (or landing an aircraft) safely, as we discussed in section 3.2.1.

To what extent is Level 5 feasible at all, unless we invent artificial general intelligence? John Naughton remarked that a downtown delivery driver's job is pretty safe, as the work demands all sorts of judgment calls such as whether you can double-park or even block a narrow street for half a minute while you dash up to a doorway and drop a parcel, as the cars behind honk at you [1419]. Another hard case is the cluttered suburban street with cars parked either side, where you are forever negotiating who goes first with oncoming vehicles, using a wave, a nod or even just eye contact. Even the current Level 2 systems tend to have difficulty when turning across traffic because of their inability to do this tacit negotiation. They end up having to be much more cautious than a human driver and wait for a bigger gap, which annoys human drivers behind them. And if you've ever tried to ease a car through the hordes of students on bicycles in a college town like Cambridge, or any urban traffic in India, you know that dealing with human traffic complexity is hard in many other situations. Can your self-driving car even detect hand signals from police officers to stop, let alone cope with eight students carrying a bed, or with an Indian temple procession?

As of 2020, the Level 2 systems have lots of shortcomings. Tesla can't always detect stationary vehicles reliably; it uses vision, sonar and radar but no lidar. (One Tesla driver in North Carolina has been charged after running into the back of a stationary police car [1120].) A colleague's Range Rover can't always detect the boundary between a paved road and grass, but perhaps that wasn't a priority for a 4 x 4. Many cars have issues with little roundabouts, not to mention potholes and other rough surfaces; the first time I got a ride in one, my teeth were rattled as we went over speed bumps at almost 30mph. Roadworks play havoc with automatic lane-keeping systems, as old white lines that have been painted over can be shiny black and very prominent in some light conditions, leading cars to oscillate sickeningly back and forth between old and new markings [624]. There's a huge amount of research on such technical topics, from better algorithms for multi-sensor data fusion though driving algorithms that can provide an explanation for their decisions, to getting cars to learn routes as they travel them, just like humans do. Tesla even has a 'shadow mode' for its autopilot; when it's not in use, it still tries to predict what the driver will do next, and records its mispredictions for later analysis. This has enabled Tesla to collect billions of miles of training data across a vast range of road and weather conditions.

I'll discuss safety assurance in section 28.4.1, but the state of play in 2020 is that while Tesla and NHTSA claimed that there are fewer crashes after a Tesla customer activates Autosteer, an independent lab claimed there were more. Now as I discussed in section 14.3.1, falling asleep at the wheel is a major cause of accidents, accounting for 20% of the UK total. These tend to be at the serious end of the spectrum; they account for about 30% of fatal accidents and half of fatal accidents on freeways. (That's why we have laws to limit commercial drivers' hours.) So we ought to be able to save lives with a system that keeps your car in lane on the freeway, brakes to avoid collisions, and brings it to a stop at the side of the road if you don't respond to chimes. Why is this not happening?

I suspect we'll need to disentangle at least three different factors: the risk thermostat, the system's affordances, and the expectations created by marketing. First, the risk thermostat is the mechanism whereby people adapt to a perceived reduction in risk by adopting more risky behaviour; we noted in section 3.2.5.7 that mandatory seat-belt laws caused people to drive faster, so that the overall effect was merely to move casualties from vehicle occupants to pedestrians and cyclists, rather than to reduce their number overall. Second, affordances condition how we interact with technology, as we discussed in section 3.2.1, and if a driver assistance system makes driving easier, and apparently safer, people will relax and assume it is safer – disposing some of them to take more risks. Third, the industry's marketing minimises the risks in subtle ways. For Tesla to call its autosteer feature an autopilot misled drivers to think they could watch TV or have a nap. That is not the case with an autopilot on an airplane, but most non-pilots don't understand that.

25.2.4 How to hack a self-driving car

The electronic security of road vehicles started out in the last century with the truck tachographs and speed limiters we discussed in section 14.3 and the remote key entry systems we discussed in section 4.3.1. It has become a specialist discipline since about 2005, when the carmakers and tier-1 component vendors started to hire experts. By 2008, people were working on tamper resistance for engine control units: the industry had started using software to control engine power output, so whether your car had 120 horsepower or 150 was down to a software switch, which people naturally tried to hack. The makers tried to stop them. They claimed they were concerned about the environmental impact of improperly tuned cars, but if you believe that, I have a bridge I'd like to sell you.

In 2010, Karl Koscher and colleagues got the attention of academics by showing how to hack a late-model Ford. Cars' internal data communications use a CAN bus, which does not have strong authentication, so an attacker who gets control of (say) the radio can escalate this access to operate the door locks and the brakes [1087]. In 2015, Charlie Miller and Chris Valasek got the attention of the press when they hacked a Jeep Cherokee containing a volunteer journalist, over its mobile phone link, slowed the vehicle down and drove it off the road [1318]. This compelled Chrysler to recall 1.4m vehicles for a software patch, costing the company over $1bn. This finally got the industry's attention.

There's now a diverse community of people who hack cars and other vehicles. There are hobbyists who want to tune their cars; there are garages who also want to use third-party components and services; and there are farmers who want to repair their tractors despite John Deere's service monopoly, as I mentioned in section 24.6. There are open-source software activists and safety advocates who believe we're all safer if everything is documented [1796]. And there are the black hats too: intelligence agencies that want to spy on vehicle occupants and thieves who just want to steal cars.

Car theft is currently the main threat model, and we discussed the methods used to defeat remote key entry and alarm systems in section 4.3.1. State actors and others can take over the mobile phones embedded in cars, using the techniques discussed in section 2.2.1. The phones, navigation and infotainment systems are often poorly designed anyway – when you rent a car, or buy one secondhand, you often see a previous user's personal information, and we described in section 22.4.3 how an app that enables you to track and unlock a rental car let you continue to do this once the car had been rented to somebody else.

So what else might go wrong, especially as cars become more autonomous? A reasonable worst-case scenario might see a state actor, or perhaps an environmental activist group, trying to scare the public by causing thousands of simultaneous road traffic accidents. A remote exploit such as that on the Chrysler

Jeep might already do this. The CAN bus that most modern cars use for internal data communications trusts all its nodes. If one of them is subverted it might be reprogrammed to transmit continuously; such a 'blethering idiot', as it's called, makes the whole bus unusable. If this is the powertrain bus, the car becomes almost undriveable; the driver will still have some steering control but without power assistance to either steering or brakes. If the car is travelling at speed, there's a serious accident risk. The possibility that a malicious actor could hack millions of cars causing tens of thousands of road traffic accidents simultaneously is unacceptable, and such vulnerabilities therefore have to be patched. But patching is expensive. The average car might contain 50–100 electronic control units from 20 different vendors, and the integration testing needed to get them to all work together smoothly is expensive. I'll discuss this in more detail in section 27.5.4.

Attacks are not limited to the cars themselves. In 2017, Elon Musk told an audience, "In principle, if someone was able to say hack all the autonomous Teslas, they could say – I mean just as a prank – they could say 'send them all to Rhode Island' – across the United States ... and that would be the end of Tesla and there would be a lot of angry people in Rhode Island." His audience laughed, and three years later it emerged that he'd not been entirely joking. A few months previously, a hacker had gained control of the Tesla 'mothership' server, which controls its entire fleet; luckily he was a white hat and reported the hack to Tesla [1121]. At the other end of the scale, the performance artist Simon Weckert pulled a handcart containing 99 Android phones around Berlin in February 2020, causing Google Maps to register a traffic jam wherever he went [2001]. As advanced driver assistance systems rely ever more extensively on cloud facilities, the scope for such indirect attacks will increase.

And external attacks need not involve computers. If car systems start to slow down automatically for pedestrians and cyclists, some of them may exploit this. In India and some parts of southern Europe, pedestrians walk through congested traffic, flagging cars to stop, and they do; it will be interesting to see if this behaviour appears in London and New York as well.

Companies will exploit assistance systems if they can. Now that the initial dream of self-driving trucks seems some way off, and even the intermediate dream of multiple trucks driving in convoy between distribution hubs with a single driver seems ambitious, may we expect lobbying to relax the legal limits on drivers' hours? Trucking firms may argue that once the truck's on autopilot on the freeway, the driver only has to do real work on arrival and departure, so he should work ten hours a shift rather than eight. But if the net effect of the technology is to make truck drivers work more time for the same money, it will be resented and perhaps sabotaged.

Should Level 5 automation ever happen, even in restricted environments – so that we finally see the robotaxis Google hoped to invent – then we'll have to think about social hacking as a facet of safety. If your 12-year-old daughter calls a cab to get a ride home from school, then at present we have safeguards in the form of laws requiring taxi drivers to have background checks for criminal records. Uber tried to avoid these laws, claiming it wasn't a taxi company but a 'platform'; in London, the mayor had to ban them and fight them in court for years to get them to comply. So how will safeguarding work with robotaxis?

There will also be liability games. At present, car companies try to blame drivers for crashes, so each crash becomes a question of which driver was negligent. If the computer was driving the car, though, that's product liability, and the manufacturer has to pay. There have been some interesting tussles around the safety figures for assisted driving, and specifically whether the carmakers undercount crashes with autopilot activated, which we'll discuss in section 28.4.1.

So much is entirely predictable. But what about new attacks on the AI components of the systems themselves? For example, can you confuse a car by projecting a deceptive image on a bridge, or on the road, and cause it to crash? That's quite possible, and I've already seen a crash caused by visual confusion. On the road home from my lab, there was a house at a right-hand bend whose owner often parked his car facing oncoming traffic. At night, in a left-hand driving country like Britain, your driving reflex is to steer to the left of the facing car, but then you'd notice you were heading for his garden wall, and swerve right to pass to the right of his car instead. Eventually a large truck didn't swerve in time, and ended up in the wall.

So could clever software fool a machine vision system in new ways, or ways that might be easier for an attacker to scale? That brings us to the next topic, artificial intelligence, or to be more precise, machine learning.

25.3 AI / ML

The phrase *artificial intelligence* has meant different things at different times. For pioneers like Alan Turing, it ranged from the Turing test to attempts to teach a computer to play chess. By the 1960s it meant text processing, from Eliza to early machine translation, and programming in Lisp. In the 1980s there was a surge of research spurred by Japan's announcement of a huge research programme into 'Fifth generation computing', with which Western nations scrambled to keep up; much of that effort went into rule-based systems, and Prolog joined Lisp as one of the languages on the computer science curriculum.

From the 1990s, the emphasis changed from handcrafted systems with lots of rules to systems that learn from examples, now called *machine learning* (ML). Early mechanisms included logistic regressions, support vector machines (SVMs) and Bayesian classifiers; progress was driven by applications such as natural language processing (NLP) and search. While the NLP community developed custom methods, the typical approach to designing a payment fraud detector or spam filter was to collect large amounts of training data, write custom code to extract a number of signals, and just see empirically which type of classifier worked best on them. Search became intensely adversarial during the 2000s as search engine optimisation firms used all sorts of tricks to manipulate the signals on which search engines rely, and the engines fought back in turn, penalising or banning sites that use underhand tricks such as hidden text. Bing was an early user of ML, but Google avoided it for years; the engineer who ran search from 2000 until he retired in 2016, Amit Singhal, felt it was too hard to find out, for a given set of results, exactly which of the many inputs was most responsible for which result. This made it hard to debug machine-learning based algorithms for search ranking. If you detected a botnet clicking on restaurants in Istanbul and wanted to tweak the algorithm to exclude them, it was easier to change a few 'if' statements than retrain a classifier [1302].

A sea change started in 2011 when Dan Cireşan, Ueli Meier, Jonathan Masci and Jürgen Schmidhuber trained a deep convolutional neural network to do as well as humans on recognising handwritten digits and Chinese characters, and better than humans on traffic signs [437]. The following year, Alex Krizhevsky, Ilya Sutskever and Geoff Hinton used a similar *deep neural network* (DNN) to get record-breaking results at classifying 1.2 million images [1100]. The race was on, other researchers piled in, and 'deep learning' started to get serious traction at a variety of tasks. The most spectacular result came in 2016 when David Silver and colleagues at Google Deepmind produced AlphaGo, which defeated the world Go champion Lee Sedol [1740]. This got the attention of the world. Before then, few research students wanted to study machine learning; since then few want to study anything else. Undergraduates even pay attention in classes on probability and statistics, which were previously seen as a chore. Bayes' theorem remains the same, but the pedantically cautious stats profs of old are being replaced by AI evangelists. Some of the evangelists have exciting sales pitches: around artificial general intelligence making robots self-conscious, or a bright future in which we upload and become immortal. Others see a darker future in which the robots take over. Old-school AI researchers explained carefully to students that it's all just pattern matching and we have no idea at all about the nature of consciousness.

25.3.1 ML and security

The interaction between machine learning and security goes back to the mid-1990s. Malware writers started using tricks such as polymorphism to evade the classifiers in anti-virus software, as I described in section 21.3.5; banks and credit card companies started using machine learning to detect payment fraud, as I described in section 12.5.4; and phone companies also used it for first-generation mobiles, as I noted in section 22.3. The arrival of spam as the Internet opened up to the public in the mid-1990s created a market for spam filters. Hand-crafted rules didn't scale well enough for large mail service providers, especially once botnets appeared and spam became the majority of email, so spam filtering became a big application.

Alice Hutchings, Sergo Pastrana and Richard Clayton surveyed the use of machine-learning in such systems, and the tricks the bad guys have worked out to dupe them [941]. As spam filtering takes user feedback as its ground truth, spammers learned to send spam to accounts they control at the big webmail firms, and mark it 'not spam'; other statistical analysis mechanisms are now used to detect this. Poisoning a classifier's training data is a quite general attack. Another is to look for weak points in a value chain: airline ticket fraudsters buy an innocuous ticket such as from London to New York, pass the fraud checks, and then change it just before departure to a ticket to a high-risk destination such as Lagos, for which the fraud checks are stricter. There are vigorous discussions of such techniques on the underground forums where the bad actors trade not just services but boasts and tips. Battista Biggio and Fabio Rolli give more technical background: in 2004, spammers found they could confuse the early linear classifiers in spam filters by varying some of the words, and an arms race took off from there [242].

It turns out that these attack ideas generalise to other systems, and there are other attacks too.

25.3.2 Attacks on ML systems

There are at least four types of attack on a machine-learning system.

First, as I mentioned, you can poison the training data. If the model continues to train itself in use, then it can sometimes be simple to lead it astray. Tay was a chatbot released by Microsoft in March 2016 on Twitter; trolls immediately started teaching it to use racist and offensive language, and it was shut down after only 16 hours.

Second, you can attack the model's integrity in its inference phase, for example by causing it to give the wrong answer. In 2013, Christian Szegedy and colleagues found that the deep neural networks which had been found to classify images so well in 2012 were vulnerable to *adversarial samples* – images perturbed very slightly would be wildly misclassified [1860]. The idea is to choose a perturbation that maximises the model's prediction error. It turns out that neural networks have plenty of such blind spots, which are related to the training data in non-obvious ways. The decision space is high-dimensional, which makes blind spots mathematically inevitable [1709]; and with neural networks the decision boundaries are convoluted, making them non-obvious.

Researchers quickly came up with real-world adversarial examples, ranging from small stickers that would cause a car vision system to misread a 30mph speed sign as 60mph, to coloured spectacles that would cause a man wearing them to be misrecognised as a woman, or not recognised at all [1723]. In the world of malware detection, people found that non-linear classifiers such as SVM and deep neural networks were not actually harder to evade than linear classifiers provided you did it right [242].

Third, Florian Tramèr and colleagues showed that you can attack the model's confidentiality in the inference phase, by getting it to classify a number of probe inputs and building a successively better approximation. The result is often a good working imitation of the target model. As in the manufacture of real goods, a knock-off is often cheaper; big models can cost a lot to train from scratch. This approximation attack works not just with neural networks but also with other classifiers such as logistic regression and decision trees [1905].

What's more, many attacks turn out to be transferable, so an attacker doesn't need full access to the model (a so-called *white-box attack*) [1904]. Many attacks can be developed on one model and then launched against another that's been trained on the same data, or even just similar data (a *black-box attack*). The blind spots are a function of the training data, so in order to make attacks less transferable you have to make an effort. For example, Ilia Shumailov, Yiren Zhao, Robert Mullins and I have experimented with inserting keys in neural networks so that the blind spots appear in different places, and models with different keys are vulnerable to different adversarial samples [1736]. Kerckhoffs' principle applies in machine learning, as almost everywhere else in security.

A variant on the confidentiality attack is to extract sensitive training data. Large neural networks contain a lot of state, and the simplest way to deal with outliers is often just to memorise them. So if some business claims that a classifier trained on a million medical records is not personal data because it's "statistical machine learning", take care. Ways of mitigating the privacy risks to individual outliers by combining machine learning with differential privacy, which we discussed in section 11.3, are a subject of active research [1495].

Finally, you can deny service, and one way is to choose samples that will cause the classifier to take as long as possible. Ilia Shumailov and colleagues found that one can often deny service by posing a conundrum to a classifier. Given a straight-through pipeline, as in a typical image-processing task, a confusing image can take 20% more time, but in more complex tasks such as natural language processing you can invoke exception handling and slow things down hundreds of times [1733].

More complex attacks straddle these categories. For example, there's an arms race between online advertisers and the suppliers of ad-blocking software, and as the advertisers adopt ever more complicated ways of rendering web pages to confuse the blockers, the blockers are starting to use image processing techniques on the rendered page to spot ads. However this leaves them open to advertisers using adversarial samples either to escape the filter, or to cause it to wrongly block another part of the page [1903].

So how can one use machine learning safely in the real world? That's something we're still learning, but there are some things we can say. First, one has to take a systems security approach and look at the problem end-to-end. Just as we sanitise inputs to web services, do penetration testing, and have mechanisms for responsible disclosure and update, we need to do the same for ML systems [659].

Second, we need to pay attention to the experience of the last twenty years' work on topics like card fraud, spam and intrusion detection, where early ML systems were used in the field. As we mentioned in section 21.4.2.2, ML systems have been largely ineffective at real-world network intrusion detection; Robin Sommer and Vern Paxson were the first to give a good explanation why. They discuss the lack of training data, the distance between theory and practice, the difficulties in evaluation, the high cost of errors and above all the inability to deal with novel attacks [1806]. The problem of keeping capable opponents out of complex corporate networks just isn't one that artificial intelligence has ever been good at.

There may occasionally be a change in emphasis, though. If we want to lower the probability of a new adversarial attack causing real damage, there are various things we can do, depending on the context. One is simply to detune the classifier, which is the approach taken in at least one machine-vision system used in cars. By making it less sensitive, you make it less easy to spoof, and then you complement it with other sensors such as radar and ultrasonics so that the vision system on its own is less critical. An alternative strategy is to head in the other direction and make one ML component of your system so fragile that an attack triggers an alarm – whereupon you switch to a defensive mode of operation, such as a low-sensitivity limp-home mode or stopping and waiting for a human to drive. In other words, you build in situational awareness, in that your system is constantly asking itself "Am I under attack now?" This is how humans operate; as I discussed in section 3.2.5.1, the ancestral evolutionary environment taught us to take extra care when we sense triggers such as adversarial intent and violations of tribal taboos. So we've experimented with using neural networks trained so that a number of outputs and activations are considered to be taboo and avoided; if any of these taboos is broken, an attack can be suspected [1736].

One fundamental problem is that once we start letting machine learning blur the boundary between code and data, and systems become data-driven, people are going to game them. This brings us to the thorny problem of the interaction of machine learning and society.

25.3.3 ML and society

The surge of interest in machine learning since 2016, and its representation as 'artificial intelligence' in the popular press, has led to a lot of speculation about ethics. For example, the philosopher Dan Dennett objects on moral grounds to the existence of persons that are immortal and intelligent but not conscious. But companies already meet that definition! The history of corporate wrongdoing shows that corporations can behave very badly indeed (we discussed some examples in section 12.2.6). The most powerful ML systems belong to corporations such as Google, Amazon, Microsoft and IBM, all of which have had tussles with authority. The interplay between ML, big data and monopoly adds to the thicket of issues that governments need to navigate as they ponder how to regulate tech. One aspect is that the tech majors' ML offerings are now becoming platforms on their own, and used by lots of startups solving specific real-world problems [658].

One cross-cutting issue is prejudice. Aylin Caliskan, a Turkish research student at Princeton, noticed that machine translations from Turkish to English came out with gender bias; although Turkish has no grammatical gender, the English translations of Turkish sentences would assign doctors as 'he' and nurses as 'she'. On further investigation, she and her supervisors Joanna Bryson and Arvind Narayanan found that essentially all machine translation systems in use were not merely sexist, but racist too [371]. Natural-language systems based on machine learning inhale the prejudices of their training data. If the big platforms' ML engines then suffuse prejudice through the systems on which hundreds of downstream firms rely and which take decisions affecting billions of people, there is a real public-policy issue.

A related policy problem is *redlining*. When insurance companies used postcode-level claim statistics to decide the level of premiums, it was found that many minority areas suffered high premiums or were excluded from cover, breaking anti-discrimination laws. I wrote in the second edition of this book in 2008: "If you build an intrusion detection system based on data mining techniques, you are at serious risk of discriminating. If you use neural network techniques, you'll have no way of explaining to a court what the rules underlying your decisions are, so defending yourself could be hard. Opaque rules can also contravene European data protection law, which entitles citizens to know the algorithms used to process their personal data."

A second cross-cutting issue is snake oil, and the AI/ML gold rush has led to thousands of startups, many of them stronger on marketing than on product. Manish Raghavan and colleagues surveyed 'AI' systems used in employment screening and hiring, finding dozens of firms that claim their systems match new hires to the company's requirements. Most claim they don't discriminate, yet as few employers retain comprehensive and accessible data on employee performance, it's entirely unclear how such systems can even be trained, let alone how a firm that used such a system might defend a lawsuit for discrimination [1574]. Applicants quickly learn to game the system, such as by slipping the word 'Oxford' or 'Cambridge' into their CV in white text. A prudent employer would demand more transparent mechanisms, and devise independent metrics to validate their outcomes. Even that is nontrivial, as machine learning can discover correlations that we do not understand.

Arvind Narayanan has an interesting analysis of snake oil in AI [1384]. 'AI' and even 'ML' are generic terms for a whole grab-bag of technologies. Some of them have made real progress, like DNNs for face recognition, and indeed AlphaGo. So companies exploit this hype, slapping the 'AI' label on whatever they're selling, even if its mechanisms use statistical techniques from a century ago. Digging deeper, Arvind argues that machine-learning systems can be sorted into three categories:

1. ML has made real progress on tasks of *perception*, such as face recognition (see section 17.3), the recognition of songs by products like Shazam (see section 24.4.3), medical diagnosis from scans, and speech-to-text – at all of which it has acquired the competence of skilled humans;
2. ML has made some progress on tasks of *judgment*, such as content recommendation and the recognition of spam and hate speech. These have many difficult edge cases about which even skilled humans disagree. The systems that perform them often rely on substantial human input – from billions of email users clicking the 'report spam' button to the tens of thousands of content moderators employed by the big tech companies;
3. ML has made no progress on tasks of *social prediction*, such as predicting employee performance, school outcomes and future criminal behaviour. A very extensive study by Matthew Sagalnik and over 400 collaborators has concluded that insofar as life outcomes can be predicted at all, this can be done as well using simple linear regressions based on a handful of variables [1641].

This claim of Arvind's is falsifiable, so we'll see how accurate it is over time, and if there's a fourth edition of this book in 2030 we'll have a lot more data then. A major theme of research meanwhile will be to look for better ways for people and machines to work together. Intuitively, we want people to do the jobs involving judgment and machines to do the boring stuff; but making that actually work can be harder than it looks. Often people end up being the machine's servants, and according to one VC firm, 40% of 'AI' startups don't actually use ML in any material way; they're merely riding the wave of hype and employ people behind the scenes [1964]. One way or another, there will be lots of bumps in the road, and lots of debates about ethics and politics.

Perhaps the best way to approach the ethics is this. Many of the problems now being discussed in the context of AI ethics arose years ago for research done using traditional statistical methods on databases of personal information. (Indeed, linear regressions have been used continuously for about a century; they've just been rebranded as machine learning.) So our first port of call should be existing law and policy. When we discussed ethics in the context of records-based health and social-policy research in section 10.4.6, we observed that many of the issues arose because IT companies and their customers ignored the wisdom that doctors, teachers and others had accumulated over years of dealing with paper-based records. The same mistakes are now being repeated, and excused as before with sales hype around 'innovation' and 'disruption'.

In the case of predicting which children are likely to turn to crime, it's been known for years that such indicators can be deeply stigmatising. In section 10.4.7 we noted that if you tell teachers which kids have had contact with social services, then the teachers will have lower expectations of them. Both child welfare and privacy law argue against sharing such indicators. How much more harmful might it be if clueless administrators buy software that claims to be making predictions using the inscrutable magic that enabled AlphaGo to beat Lee Sedol? As for 'predictive policing', studies suggest that it might just be another way to get the computer to justify a policy of 'round up the usual suspects' [677]. (In section 14.4 we discussed how curfew tags also have this effect.) Similar issues arise with the use of ML techniques to advise judges in bail hearings about whether a suspect poses a flight risk or reoffending risk, and also in sentencing hearings about whether a suspect is dangerous. Such technologies are likely to propagate existing social biases and power structures, and provide lawmakers with an excuse to continue ineffective but populist policies, rather than nudging them to tackle the underlying problems.

ML is nonetheless likely to upset some of the equilibria that have emerged over the years on issues like surveillance, privacy and censorship, as it makes even more powerful tools available to already powerful actors, as well as creating new excuses to revive old abuses. Many countries already restrict the use of CCTV cameras; now that face-recognition systems enable pedestrians to be recognised, do we need to restrict them more? As we saw in section 17.3, a number of cities (including San Francisco) have decided the answer is 'yes'. In section 11.2.6 we discussed how location and social data can now make it very hard to be anonymous, and how people's Facebook data could be mined for political ad targeting. ML techniques make it easier to do traffic analysis, by spotting patterns of communication [1722]; in fact, police and intelligence agencies depend ever more on traffic and social-network analysis of the sort discussed in sections 21.7, 23.3.1 and 26.2.2.

In short, the charge sheet against machine learning is that it is one of the technologies helping entrench the power of the tech majors while pushing the balance between privacy and surveillance towards surveillance and facilitating authoritarian government in other ways. It may be telling that Google and Microsoft are funding big research programs to develop AI for social good. Time will tell whether this leads to results of consequence, or whether it is just PR.

So what can we do as a practical matter right now to get some privacy in this electronic village in which we now live?

25.4 PETS and operational security

Even if you don't blurt out all your thoughts on Facebook, social structure – who hangs out with whom – says an awful lot, and has become much more visible. In section 11.2.6 we discussed research which suggested that as few as four Facebook likes enable a careful observer to work out whether you're straight or gay most of the time, and how this observation led among other things to the Cambridge Analytica scandal, where voters' preferences were documented covertly and in detail.

Even if you don't use Facebook at all, the traffic data on who contacted whom gives a lot away to those who have access to it, as we discussed in section 11.4.1. This can cause problems for people who are in conflict with authority, such as whistleblowers. Anonymity can sometimes be a useful tool here. The abuse of academic authority is countered by anonymous student feedback on professors and anonymous refereeing of conference paper submissions. If your employer pays your health insurance, you might want to buy an HIV test kit for cash and get the results anonymously online, as the mere fact that you took a test says something, even if the result is negative. Privacy can also be a necessary precursor of free speech. People trying to innovate in politics or religion may need to develop their doctrine and build their numbers before going public. And then there are opposition politicians digging a bear trap for the government of the day, whose concerns are more tactical.

The importance of such activities to an open society is such that we consider privacy and freedom of speech to be interlinked human rights. We also enact laws to protect whistleblowers. But how can this work out in practice?

In pre-technological societies, two people could walk a short distance away from everyone else and have a conversation that left no hard evidence of what was said. If Alice claimed that Bob had criticised the king, then Bob could always claim the converse – that it was Alice who'd proposed a demonstration to increase the powers of parliament and he who'd refused out of loyalty.

In other words, many communications were *deniable*. Plausible deniability remains an important feature of some communications today, from everyday life up to the highest reaches of intelligence and diplomacy. It can sometimes be fixed by convention: for example, a litigant in England can write a letter marked 'without prejudice' to another proposing a settlement, and this letter cannot be used in evidence. But most circumstances lack such clear and convenient rules, and the electronic nature of communication often means that 'just stepping outside for a minute' isn't an option. What then?

A related issue is anonymity. Until the industrial revolution, most people lived in small villages, and it was a relief – in fact a revolution – to move into a town. You could change your religion, or vote for a land-reform candidate, without your landlord throwing you off your farm. In a number of ways, the effect of the Internet has been to take us back to an 'electronic village': electronic communications have not only shrunk distance, but in some ways our freedom too.

Can technology help? To make things a bit more concrete, let's consider some people with specific privacy problems.

1. Andrew is a missionary in Texas whose website has attracted a number of converts in Iran. That country executes Muslim citizens who change their religion. He suspects that some of the people who've contacted him aren't real converts, but religious policemen hunting for apostates. He can't tell a policeman apart from a real convert. What sort of technology should he use to communicate privately with converts?
2. Bella is your ten-year-old daughter, who's been warned by her teacher to remain anonymous online. What sort of training should you give her?
3. Charles is a psychoanalyst who sees private patients suffering from depression, anxiety and other problems. Previously he practised in a nondescript house that his patients could visit discreetly. Since lockdown, he's had to use tools like Skype and Zoom. What's prudent practice to protect patient privacy?
4. Dai is a human-rights worker in Vietnam, in contact with people trying to set up independent trade unions, microfinance cooperatives and the like. The police harass her frequently. How should she communicate with colleagues?
5. Elizabeth works as an analyst for an investment bank that's advising on a merger. She wants ways of investigating a takeover target without letting the target get wind of her interest – or even learn that anybody at all is interested. Her opponents are people like her at other firms.
6. Firoz is a gay man who lives in Tehran, where being gay is a capital offence. He'd like some way to download porn and perhaps contact other gay men without getting hanged.

7. Graziano is a magistrate in Palermo setting up a hotline to let people tip off the authorities about Mafia activity. He knows that some of the cops who staff the office in future will be in the Mafia's pay – and that potential informants know this too. How does he limit the damage that corrupt cops can do?
8. Hristo helps refugees enter the UK so they can claim asylum. Most of his clients are fleeing wars or bad government in the Middle East and North Africa. He operates from Belgium and gets clients into trucks or on to speedboats depending on the weather. He also gets clients across the land border from Ireland, and supplies creative documentation. He needs to coordinate with colleagues in France, Britain and elsewhere. How can they do this despite surveillance from assorted security and intelligence agencies?
9. Irene is an investigative journalist on a combative newspaper who invites whistleblowers to contact her. She dreams of landing the next Ed Snowden. What preparations should she make in case she does get contacted by a major source that the government would try hard to unmask?
10. Justin is running for elected office. Irene would happily dig the dirt on his family; and there are many other people who want to read his email, send a racist tweet from his social media account, or wire his campaign war chest to North Korea. How can he frustrate them?

Privacy isn't just about encrypting messages. If Andrew tells his converts to download and use Wickr, then the police spies pretending to be converts will get the national firewall to detect anyone who uses it. Andrew has to make his traffic look innocuous – so that the police can't spot converts even when they know what apostate traffic looks like. If only a few dozen people use Wickr, the police can just break all their doors down. So it's not just about whether Wickr is a more secure product than Signal or Skype, but how many people in that country use it.

And while technical measures may solve part of Andrew's problem, they won't be much use with Bella's. One risk to children is that they'll say something careless that may embarrass them later. Another is that political and media scaremongering about child safety gets in the way of their welfare. Most of your effort will go into educating her. As Bella grows up, she'll have to become adept with the tools the rest of her peer group use; and soon enough she'll adopt her security procedures from them more than from you. You have to impart understanding, not rituals.

The intensity of attacks will vary widely. Andrew and Firoz might face only sporadic interest, while Graziano, Hristo and Justin have capable motivated opponents. As for Dai, she's frequently put under surveillance. She's not using anonymous communications to protect herself, but to protect others who haven't come to the police's attention yet.

There are radically different incentives. Andrew, Charles, Dai, Graziano and Irene go to some trouble to protect vulnerable people they deal with, while the sites in which Firoz is interested don't care much about his safety. Andrew, Dai, Graziano and Hristo all have to think about dishonest insiders. In Justin's case it's careless insiders: the juicy stuff that the Russians would like to give to Irene lives in the personal accounts of his campaign volunteers, as well as in the personal accounts of friends and family who're hard to include in any organised defensive effort.

There are different thresholds for success and failure. Hristo can only be jailed if the police prove a case against him beyond reasonable doubt; Irene can take down Justin if she can defend a libel suit on the balance of the evidence; while mere suspicion could be bad news for Elizabeth or Firoz. And there are different costs of failure: Elizabeth might lose some money if she screws up, while Justin could lose his career and Firoz could lose his life.

We discussed in section 22.3.1 how people who don't want their phone calls traced buy prepaid mobile phones, use them for a while, and throw them away. But these *burners*, as they're sometimes called, are hard to use properly; even Al-Qaida couldn't do it right. So what's the state of play for hard privacy online?

25.4.1 Anonymous messaging devices

As we discussed in section 2.2.1.10, investigators often get much of their information from traffic analysis. Regardless of whether people use email, a messaging service or the plain old telephone service, access to the social graph lets policemen map out friendship networks – and the marketers do this too when they can get their hands on it [598]. In the old days, encrypting your email traffic could be dangerous; if you were one of only 20 people in the country using PGP, that made you a suspect. It's more complex now that most people use webmail services that are TLS encrypted by default, but the same principles apply.

People under government surveillance like Hristo learned that normal privacy apps like WhatsApp or Signal aren't enough on their own, even if lots of other people use them for innocuous purposes. Suppose Hristo uses Signal to arrange for Kevan to bring eight people across the English Channel in a speedboat. But if a Royal Navy cutter arrests Kevan and they find Hristo's messages on his phone, he faces extradition. If Kevan, or Hristo, also uses their phone to chat with their family, it might help the police to map their network using traffic analysis. There's not just an issue of making networks hard to trace, but about what evidence can be seized when people are caught. Similar problems are faced by Dai and by Graziano's undercover operatives.

So we've seen the development of a market for 'crypto phones' which not only provide encrypted messaging, but try to support *operational security* (opsec) as well. We discussed opsec in the corporate context in section 3.3.4, but it matters here too. Crypto phones enable a group of people to use phones that are locked down, to minimise the risk that one member is compromised by the carelessness of others. The first on general sale was probably Silent Circle's Blackphone in 2014, which was sold to government agencies, special forces, corporates and human-rights workers. There have since been a number of competing systems. Ed Caesar describes some of the people who promoted crypto phone businesses out of the Cyberbunker in Germany, which was the country's biggest hoster of illegal web sites until it was raided and shut down in September 2019 [366]. The handsets are typically modified so you can't run apps (which could spy on you); they may have the microphone and camera disabled so GCHQ can't turn them into monitoring devices; GPS may also be disabled; they can't be read out by standard police forensic kiosks; and they're part of a closed system consisting of both phones and messaging servers where you don't identify the other party by a phone number but by a user ID. Crypto phone firms found that some people were prepared to pay over a thousand dollars or Euros for a handset, and the same again for a six-monthly subscription to the associated service. The market includes all sorts of people, from cryptocurrency operators and spies through money launderers to drug dealers. Network effects apply in covert communities too; Hristo, Kevan and the rest of the gang all need to use the same system. And as some people smugglers also smuggle drugs, and some smugglers make enough money to need fancy tax accountants who also work for the cryptocurrency crowd, network effects can drag in all sorts of people who seek privacy from state surveillance for reasons both good and bad.

The established pattern is that, thanks to network effects, one crypto phone system gets used ever more widely, until enough of its users are police targets and the authorities bust it. For the benefit of non-UK readers, I might mention here that newspapers of the left and right see Hristo and his human cargo in somewhat different terms. While some immigrant communities see Hristo's operation as a family reunification service, the conservative press stigmatises refugees, and ministers have made immigration offences a higher priority for the agencies than organised acquisitive crime. So what can Hristo buy to keep GCHQ off his back?

Until 2016, the market leader was Ennetcom, a Dutch company which used a private network of messaging servers in Canada to support anonymous user IDs. In April of that year, the Dutch and Canadian authorities raided them and arrested the owner, who had been involved with CyberBunker. In 2017, it was the turn of PGP Safe; four Dutchmen were arrested [1083]. The following year, the Dutch police also claimed to have broken a cryptophone system called Iron Chat [793]. In 2018, the market leader was a company called Phantom Secure; the US, Australian and the Canadian authorities closed down that system [1135]. Its CEO Vincent Ramos pleaded guilty to supplying the phones to drug dealers worldwide, and at his sentencing hearing, prosecutors read out a message he sent to colleagues: "We are f–ing rich man … get the f–ing Range Rover brand new. Cuz I just closed a lot of business. This week man. Sinaloa cartel, that's what's up" [279]. He got nine years in jail. The next market leader, EncroChat, used modified Android phones. In 2020, the French and Dutch police hacked its main server and infected all 50,000 devices in use worldwide with law-enforcement malware that copied their messages in real time to the police. On June 13th, EncroChat realised they'd been hacked and advised their customers to get rid of their phones at once [1926]. Hundreds of arrests followed all over Europe [572].

So policemen like Graziano have a standard playbook for taking down crypto phone systems. But he may also use them to protect those of his sources who remain emplaced in the gangs and in the communities in which they swim. Indeed, when PGP first came out in the 1990s, it was adopted by the Provisional IRA in their insurgency against British rule in Northern Ireland. Up till then, a big headache for the police had been making unobtrusive regular contact with IRA informers, who lived in a nationalist community that hated the police and where informers were killed. PGP made contact easy. An informer simply had to tell his handler his private key, and the cops could collect all his traffic. He could even report in by sending an encrypted email to himself.

25.4.2 Social support

The journalist Irene probably has the hardest task. If she's approached by a senior civil servant who wants to spill the beans on the government's latest folly, then as soon as the story appears the 'mole hunt' will begin. Her informant – let's call her Liz – will now be hunted by the police and intelligence apparatus. How can Irene help Liz minimise the probability of being identified, fired, and prosecuted? We discussed whistleblowing briefly in section 2.3.6, where we saw that technical security is usually only one of the problems facing a whistleblower – and often not the most serious.

The big problem is establishing trust, and that is a two-sided process. Irene will need to assess Liz as a source. Does she have a real story to tell? Why's she telling it? Is it a semi-authorised leak, which she's offering with the tacit approval of her minister as part of a political game? Can her story be stood up with enough evidence, in case someone sues for libel? Is it a provocation, designed to discredit Irene or the newspaper she works for? Is Liz vulnerable, and in need of emotional support? When the story comes out, who else could have leaked it? If a hundred people could have leaked it, you can talk about anonymity; if the anonymity set size is only ten, you're talking more about plausible deniability, and Irene will want to talk to Liz about what happens when the PM's goons interrogate her. But in many cases the whistleblower will be completely exposed once the story comes out. For example, if Liz's complaint is that a minister tried to rape her, then the conversation with Irene will be about getting support and about whether people will believe her, rather than about how to use Signal.

So best practice is for Irene to meet Liz in person as soon as possible after Liz makes contact. If Liz may be targeted by state actors, but has a reasonable chance of staying anonymous, Irene can give her a burner phone to establish a chain of contact that's independent of her existing home and work devices. If Liz is one of ten suspects after the story breaks and the Prime Minister starts shouting at the Director of the Security Service, then she'd better assume that all ten of them will have all their known devices compromised by tea-time.

When Ed Snowden decided to blow the whistle on illegal surveillance, he initially had difficulty getting a journalist to use PGP encryption. Afterwards, many newspapers rushed to provide technical means for whistleblowers to contact them, publishing PGP keys, the mobile numbers of journalists who use Signal, and a facility called SecureDrop that enables people to upload files. Mansoor Ahmed-Rengers, Darija Halatova, Ilia Shumailov and I did a study of such mechanisms and found they suffer from two types of problem [32]. First, such mechanisms are hard to use. We discussed in section 3.2.1 how security usability research started from the difficulty of using PGP, and the problem is still there. Second, a whistleblower needs to understand the hazards in order to devise sensible operational security procedures, but a typical newspaper doesn't discuss them the way that, for example, this chapter does. So Irene might want to give Liz not just a burner phone but a training session on how to use tools like Tails and Tor to upload files to SecureDrop[2]. (A crypto phone would be more usable but Irene probably doesn't have the budget, and if Liz were caught with one, it could be a giveaway.)

It would be a mistake, though, to think of Liz as Irene's typical source. Most whistleblowers are in an anonymity set of size one, and their disclosures are not about state secrets but about fraud and abuse. In section 12.2.6 we saw that whistleblowers stopped more of the really serious fraud than either auditors or regulators. But often a decision to expose wrongdoing may carry some personal cost, such as getting fired or being stigmatised. Social support is often the key. It was only after several women who'd been raped by Harvey Weinstein found the courage to speak out that dozens of others came forward too.

Support is critical for many of our other users, too. Charles the psychoanalyst knows that the privacy he can offer his patient, whom we might call Mary, is essential to the therapeutic work. The move from an office to videoconferencing not only creates some (small) actual risks but makes privacy less

[2]Even then, there's lots more a journalist ought to be aware of, such as the machine identification codes that modern printers embed in documents and which we discussed in section 24.4.3. They were used to trace Reality Winner, an NSA whistleblower who leaked an NSA document describing Russian interference in the 2016 election and got 63 months jail [175].

comprehensible to both, undermining its role as a facilitator in therapy. Mary might be afraid that if her employer discovers she's having therapy, she might be stigmatised by colleagues or passed over for promotion. In most cases the fear will be much greater than the actual risk, but sometimes the risk could be real: she might be Dai, or Irene, or Liz. So the therapeutic environment must calm her and inspire confidence. Charles cannot start off the relationship with a detailed briefing on opsec of the kind that Irene might give Liz at their first meeting. Privacy advice, if any, may have to be drip-fed along with the rest of the support.

When dealing with children such as Bella, the priority is also providing a calm and reassuring environment in which they can learn and develop. Sensible parents will see through the scaremongering around child safety; the rate at which children are abducted and murdered by strangers is about one in ten million population per year, a rate so low that rational people will ignore it. Your mission as a parent is to help your children grow into empowered citizens, not to train them to cower from imaginary monsters.

Dai, the activist, is also a giver of support, to the people she's trying to recruit. Her case is much more tricky than Charles's because the authorities are trying to stop her being effective. I assume she's known to the authorities and under intermittent surveillance.

Human-rights workers such as Dai do indeed use common tools such as Skype, Tails, Tor and PGP to protect their traffic, but the attacks to which they're subjected are not just technical; they're the stuff of spy novels. The police enter their homes covertly to implant rootkits that sniff passwords, and room bugs to listen to conversations. When they encrypt a phone call, they have to wonder whether the secret police are getting one side of it (or both) from a hidden microphone. Sometimes the microphone isn't all that hidden; we've heard from activists of the police standing openly outside their house pointing a shotgun mike at the window.

Countering such attacks requires tradecraft in turn. Some of this is just like in spy movies: leaving telltales to detect covert entry, keeping your laptop with you at all times, and holding sensitive conversations in places that are hard to bug. Other aspects of it are different: human-rights workers (like journalists but unlike spies) need to avoid breaking the law, and they also need to nurture multiple support structures – not just giving covert support to recruits downstream, but receiving overt support from overseas NGOs and governments. And to make recruits, they also need – while under intermittent observation – to make covert contact with people who aren't themselves under suspicion. Dai's case is the reverse of Charles's, as when she acquires a new recruit, training them in tradecraft is part of the induction, socialisation and support process.

If you want to learn about what works and what doesn't in tradecraft, then human-rights workers are the people to talk to. (The spies and smugglers may know more but they're not talking.) The emerging picture is that the behaviour of both police and nonviolent government opponents is embedded in how a society operates, and evolves over time. There's a complex game where all but the most totalitarian rulers attempt to marginalise, tame or co-opt their opponents, while the opposition movements evolve in response. Any movement that starts being too nice to an unpopular ruler will lose credibility and be displaced by others. The groups with the best opsec will be able to grow fastest, and the most militant groups may have the greatest credibility. Pushed too hard, nonviolent opposition can spawn either open insurrection or violent terrorism (and rulers who denounce nonviolent opposition as 'terrorism' may invite just that). So a smart secret police chief will cut Dai some slack, watch what she gets up to, and play a long game; the Putin philosophy is to tolerate rebel movements until you can figure out how to lead them. Just in case things heat up later, he'll be sparing in the use of some of his capabilities, so he's got stuff in reserve for which she hasn't developed countermeasures.

25.4.3 Living off the land

Irene, Charles and Dai may find that their privacy tactics are influenced by the kind of support they have to give or receive, but they have something else in common – that they have to make the smartest use they can of what's available rather than buying or building special tools. We might perhaps call this *living off the land*[3].

In the old days, covertness could mean hiding in plain sight. Every country's elite has places to hang out, so if a senior civil servant wants to meet an eminent journalist, they can chat openly at a gentlemen's club in London or a country club in Virginia without anyone taking any notice. Such mechanisms allowed people to make contact discreetly, and establish trust at the same time.

So the first thing to ask when trying to improvise anonymous communications is what clubs or platforms you already share. One of the hard cases is China, which blocks most of the services familiar to us at the Great Firewall. Even there, we find platforms open to user content that have encrypted communications: three examples are Linkedin, GitHub and Amazon book reviews. In the case of Iran, Andrew will have to figure out whether messaging systems such as Skype and Signal are sufficiently widely used there for their use not to be suspicious.

The second thing you have to think through is the threat model. One thing many of our users have in common is intermittent threat: most of the time there's no threat at all, but just occasionally it may become severe. Even a large secret police force can only work so many files at once. Most of the time,

[3]This phrase is also used of hackers who attack systems by exploiting the target's vulnerabilities directly as they need to, and don't leave remote access Trojans behind. It seems appropriate in this context too.

nobody's interested in Mary, or in Firoz either. However, if Mary suddenly becomes a celebrity, people will get interested in her mental health quickly enough. If the government suddenly decides to go after Nur, then Skype might provide her with cover in Iran, but not in Saudi Arabia – because Skype belongs to Microsoft which generally complies with government warrants except in rogue states. Even in Iran, some opsec is needed. If Andrew uses Skype to talk to Nur then he'd better not use the same username (or IP address) to talk to all his other converts too, or the religious police will learn it from their bogus convert and come knocking.

A third factor is capability, including support, and motivation. Of all our users, Elizabeth the investment banker may be the simplest case. Her work is lawful and she has an IT team for support. Tor provides fairly good anonymity if used with care, and the stakes are low; if a target suspects her interest, she only loses some money, not her life. Graziano faces higher risks but has an experienced police organisation at his back. Justin is also playing for high stakes, but has a much less tractable management problem. An election campaign is a long slog of fundraising with dozens of volunteers who're hard to discipline and whose focus is victory rather than security. Liz faces significant risks and the quality of support available from Irene may vary. Dai, Firoz, Hristo and Nur all face extreme hazards without any capable technical support.

Finally there's the problem of forensics. I'll discuss this in detail later in section 26.5, but the main problem for the police is the sheer volume of data found when searching a house nowadays: there can be terabytes of data scattered over laptops, phones, tablets, cameras, TVs, memory sticks and all sorts of other devices. If you don't want a needle to be found, build a larger haystack. So Firoz might have a lot of electronic junk scattered around his apartment, as cover for the memory stick that has the contraband stashed in an encrypted volume. And there are many ad-hoc ways in which content can be made inaccessible to the casual searcher; he might damage the memory stick in some repairable way, or just hide it physically. The same approach might be taken by Nur, or anyone for whom a police raid might be bad news.

This all comes back to tradecraft. What works will vary from one place and time to another, as it depends on what the local opponents actually do. To defeat routine traffic analysis, it might be enough to get a day job as a receptionist: if everyone in town calls the doctors' surgery, then the fact that someone called the surgery conveys little information.

25.4.4 Putting it all together

Returning now to our list of users, how can we sum up what we've learned?

1. The missionary, Andrew, has one of the hardest secure communication tasks. He can't meet his converts to train them in opsec, and

needs to use something that's available and inconspicuous. Perhaps the simplest solution for him is to use Skype or WhatsApp.

2. In the case of your daughter Bella, the goal is to help her grow into a capable adult. I'd never dream of getting my grandkids to use Tor; that's just creepy. What I do is to talk about scams, phishing and other abuses from time to time round the dinner table. The kids enjoy this and slowly absorb the art of adversarial thinking. It's all in the same spirit as the board games we play.
3. The psychoanalyst, Charles, should have a basic awareness of the risks and the possible mitigations. As he gets to know his patient Mary he may occasionally make suggestions he thinks are relevant and needful, so long as they go with the flow and empower her rather than scaring her. But he may also be reluctant to make suggestions if this goes against the clinical method to which he is committed, by undermining her trust in the therapeutic environment. It may be too hard to negotiate this environment; informed consent is a difficult issue in therapy because of the asymmetric power relationship between the patient and the therapist. Both parties may lack relevant knowledge, and even if Mary knows more about the risks than Charles, she may feel unable to offer any suggestions.
4. The human-rights activist Dai has one of the hardest jobs of all, but as she's shaken down by the secret police from time to time and works with other activists with whom she can share experiences, she can evolve good tradecraft over time.
5. The M&A analyst Elizabeth may well find that Tor does pretty well what she needs. Her main problem will be using it properly and paying attention to the kind of queries she makes of target websites so as not to give the game away.
6. Firoz is in a bad way, and quite frankly were I in his situation I'd set out on the walk to Germany. If that's not possible then he should not just use Tor, but get a Mac or Linux box so he's less exposed to porn-site malware. He'll need to think through in advance what happens if he gets raided by the police. (Perhaps he should join the Revolutionary Guard so the police won't dare raid him in the first place.)
7. Graziano also has a hard job. It's bad enough defending a covert network against one or two traitors at the client end (as Andrew must); defending against occasional treachery at the server side is even harder. Part of his solution might be a compartmented police record keeping system, as we described in section 10.2, to stop bent cops getting access to everything, and refer to informers on police systems only by codenames. He might also chat to informers using whatever mechanisms they themselves use.

8. Hristo may see advantages in using a crypto phone, but when the cops crack it they may roll up his whole network. In his shoes I'd learn from Dai that in the long run the group with the best opsec wins out. So I'd focus on that, and educate my colleagues about traffic security. If we use a chat app such as Signal with ephemeral messages, and change phones and SIM cards regularly, then I can see which of my colleagues are disciplined, and decide who to trust with what.
9. Irene the journalist has one of the most challenging jobs of all. A journalist needs to be skilled not just at writing stories but at reading people, assessing truth and judging risk. An investigative journalist also needs tradecraft. Just as any journalist nowadays needs to know how to drive a search engine, a sleuth needs to know how to protect her sources. It's not enough to have some basic familiarity with privacy tech; she needs to know how to teach the right tactics to contacts who may be under extreme stress and at risk of their lives. That means understanding not just the people, but also the threats and the tools. (And just as this job becomes ever more critical and highly skilled, the budgets available to the press are collapsing, as Google and Facebook eat all their advertising.)
10. Justin also has a difficult problem. It's hard to protect short-lived high-consequence efforts staffed by enthusiastic volunteers who are hard to discipline and who may have unfixable bad technology habits. However he probably doesn't understand his vulnerability, and will just press on, hoping for the best.

Richard Clayton wrote a thesis on anonymity and traceability in cyberspace, which analysed how complicated network anonymity has become [444]. There are many ways in which even people who made no particular effort to hide themselves end up not being traceable. It's hard to establish responsibility when abusive traffic comes from a phone line in a multi-occupied student house, or a prepaid mobile phone. ISPs also often keep inadequate logs and can't trace traffic afterwards. But there are also many ways in which people who try to be anonymous, fail; eventually people make mistakes, regardless of how much effort they put into opsec. And technology is making opsec harder all the time. This even applies to government security and intelligence agencies.

25.4.5 The name's Bond. James Bond

We got a warning in January 2010 that traditional intelligence agency tradecraft, as described in the novels of Ian Fleming and John le Carré, was beginning to fray. The Israelis sent a team of 26 Mossad agents to Dubai to kill

Mahmoud al-Mabhouh, a senior Hamas official who was there to buy arms from Iran. In the past such killings had been covert, but this time the UAE authorities collected and examined all the CCTV footage, correlating it with the agents' hotel stays and border crossings. It turned out twelve of them used British passports – many of them issued to Brits who'd emigrated to Israel, but with the agents' photos on them – along with six Irish, four French, three Australian and one German. Britain and Australia expelled Israeli diplomats for passport offences [308]. In the modern world of pervasive surveillance, biometrics at border controls and online passport databases make it a lot harder to travel under a false name.

A second warning came in 2013, when a report analysed the kidnapping of a Muslim cleric called Abu Omar in Italy in 2003, and pinned it on the CIA, leading to a number of agents being charged by the Italian police in absentia [1276]. The third warning came in 2014, when the Chinese stole the entire US security clearance database from the Office of Personnel Management, as I described in section 2.2.2; this included not just the entire US intelligence community but 22 million current and former federal employees. The weaponisation of personal information continues; the 2016 Investigatory Powers Act enabled the UK government to demand bulk personal datasets from firms who have them, giving the agencies access to credit records, medical records and much else. By the end of the decade, the military were worried that the Chinese were collecting personal information on every single enlisted person for use in future information warfare, while intelligence agencies were starting to wonder whether the age of traditional spying was over [1276]. The defence and intelligence communities have responded in various ways, with the Pentagon telling staff not to use consumer DNA testing kits and the Chinese apparently favouring more low-tech stuff like dead drops, but it's not clear that there's any silver bullet. It's hard to run covert operations when so much is known about almost everybody.

In this context, China's bid for 'AI supremacy' is of concern. The country's political structure encourages, rather than restrains, this technology's worst uses: President Xi wants an all-seeing digital system of social control, patrolled by precog algorithms that identify potential dissenters in real time [49]. I discussed face recognition in section 17.3; as China's cities are straddled with CCTV systems, they can surely follow people about. But how well will this work overall? The use of machine learning in multisensor data fusion applications isn't straightforward, and it tends not to work well or at all at social prediction – as we discussed earlier in this chapter. In section 26.4.1 we discuss how the Chinese system appears to be using the dissident Uighur population of Sinkiang as the test case, with substantial human-rights abuses which have led to US and EU sanctions against the Chinese firms involved.

Meanwhile, in our somewhat more chaotic democracies, it's hard to secure political campaigns from attack, as our discussion of Justin's case brings out.

The resulting operational problems from the 2018 US election are discussed by Maciej Ceglowski [399], who also warns of the broader problems of securing elections. We turn to them next.

25.5 Elections

As I write in 2020, people are worried about the conduct and credibility of the forthcoming US elections, following the controversy about Russian interference in 2016 in both the UK Brexit referendum and the US elections later that year. Because of the huge diversity of voting systems, US elections have for years been a testbed for voting technology. There have been very many attempts to defeat the will of the people, first by candidates, and more recently by external actors. We also have significant experience from the Commonwealth, which contains most of the other former British colonies; all of its member states hold elections of some form or another [330].

The story of election technology and its security is one of the co-evolution of attack and defence over centuries. In school, we all learned some variant of the history of how we evolved modern constitutions. Participatory government has long been widespread at the level of small groups such as villages, where everyone knows everyone else and decisions can be taken by consensus or by a majority; the problem is scaling it up to larger units such as cities and states. The Greeks and Romans experimented with mechanisms for selecting representatives to sit in assemblies, councils and courts but found that, all too often, democracy degenerated into oligarchy, or a monarch seized power. They devised constitutional mechanisms to reduce the risk of such failures, including the separation of powers, voting by geographical constituencies rather than by tribe, selecting officeholders by lot rather than by ballot, and term limits. Although the Roman Empire ended these experiments, the ideal persisted through papal elections and medieval guilds via Swiss and Italian city-states. In the English Civil War, a parliament seized power from the king and cut his head off; the settlement of 1689 made England a constitutional monarchy. The seventeenth century also saw the first assemblies in the New World, leading to the American revolution in the eighteenth century, where the Founding Fathers were inspired by the Greek and Roman model.

Behind it lies another story of how the elites who enjoyed power kept manipulating the system so as to hang on to it. Early elections had no privacy; Roman electors lined up behind their candidate, and voting by open outcry remained the norm until the nineteenth century, leading to bribery and intimidation. The tension in England was about social class: barons acquired some rights in 1215, followed by other property-owners in a series of reforms. The first modern reform in 1832 introduced redistricting: few of the English cities that had sprung up in the industrial revolution had MPs, while other constituencies had few voters and the MP was selected by the local landowner. It took a whole series of reform bills to extend and equalise the franchise to men of successively lower wealth and income, but the high costs of campaigning limited political careers to the wealthy. Eventually, secret ballots were introduced in 1872. Meanwhile in America the story was more about race. The Civil War ended slavery and extended the franchise to all men; but after the failure of Reconstruction, former Confederate states devised literacy tests and other laws to stop black citizens voting. Only after World War I were women allowed to vote in either country. Abuses were rife: to this day, politicians in the UK, the USA and elsewhere try by fair means and foul to get their supporters to vote more than their opponents.

25.5.1 The history of voting machines

From the late 1800s there were waves of technological innovation that tried to push back on electoral abuses in America, a story told by Douglas Jones and Barbara Simons [992]. Many cities and states had political 'machines' that not only got out the vote but also manipulated it, exploiting the fact that elections in America are organised at state and county level rather than nationally as in Britain. In New York, Tammany Hall's Boss Tweed would sometimes stuff ballot boxes, and sometimes just have his precinct staff make up the results. To push back on this, inventors came up with everything from transparent ballot boxes to voting machines that clocked a mechanical counter when a lever was pulled.

Crooked politicians and officials adapted. In Louisiana, the Long brothers defeated the seals, set the count to the desired outcome and ran the state for years. Eventually people realised that the technicians in the county building who maintain and program the machines controlled the outcome. Mechanical voting machines had about 100 bits of programmability, typically in the form of cotter pins and other mechanical linkages, which nobody else understood. Wear and tear could also cover tampering; the technicians could cause an undercount for a candidate they didn't favour by knocking a few teeth off the relevant gearwheel.

25.5.2 Hanging chads

Inventors devised a competing type of machine that punched a hole in a paper roll, inspired by the player piano; once punched cards were popularised by tabulating machines and computers, they became widely used. The idea was that a vote punched as a hole in a card is both human-readable and capable of being counted quickly by machine. It's also anonymous once dropped into a ballot box (unless you worry about fingerprints).

In the 2000 US presidential election, the result turned on Florida, which used punched-card machines, and the recount involved arguing over chads – the little rectangles of cardboard that a voter punched out of the card. Was a 'hanging chad', still attached to the card, a valid vote? What about a dimple, where the punch hadn't penetrated? Vote-counting machines rejected over 100,000 votes while George Bush's majority over Al Gore was only 537. Eventually the Supreme Court halted a recount, giving the election to Bush. This created such controversy that in 2002 Congress passed the Help America Vote Act (HAVA) which allocated $3.8 billion for the purchase of newer election equipment.

A gold rush followed as companies scrambled to build and sell machines into this huge new market. This alarmed security engineers. In fact, as the Florida recount was underway, I was at the Applications Security conference in New Orleans, whose attendees included many NSA and defense contractor staff, and we organised a debate. Even though politicians thought that mechanical or paper voting systems should be replaced with electronics as quickly as possible, security experts didn't agree. A large majority voted, on an old-fashioned show of hands, that we didn't trust electronic elections. A 1988 report by Roy Saltman at the National Bureau of Standards had already spelled out most of what was likely to go wrong [1644].

Some of the new products were *direct recording electronic* (DRE) machines, the descendants of the lever machines of the 19th century, which typically presented the candidates and other ballot options on a screen, then recorded the voter's input. Later research showed that about a quarter of votes made with a DRE machine contained at least one error – defined as a vote different from voter intent. Such 'vote flipping' was widely reported in Sarasota, Florida, in 2006, and it was unclear whether the root cause was usability or technology (depending for example on how you classify insensitive touch screens). Either way, a third of voters ignored wrong votes on the review screen [992].

Many problems were reported in the 2002 elections [807]; the following summer, the leading voting-machine supplier Diebold left its source code on an open web site in a security lapse. Yoshi Kohno and colleagues analysed it and found that the equipment was "far below even the minimal standards of security expected in other contexts": voters could cast unlimited votes, insiders could identify voters, and outsiders could also hack the system [1077]. Almost on cue, Diebold CEO Walden O'Dell, who was active in the campaign to re-elect President Bush, wrote 'I am committed to helping Ohio deliver its electoral votes to the President next year' [1991]. This led to uproar, and calls for a law to implement Yoshi's key recommendation, that there should be a voter-verifiable audit trail. (The voting researcher Rebecca Mercuri had argued as early as 1992 that DRE equipment should display the voter's choice on a paper roll behind a window and get them to validate it prior to casting [1297].) In some DRE machines this is provided in the form of a nonvolatile memory cartridge that records all voter actions, but this creates a tension with privacy. Other DRE machines had no audit trail at all; all an auditor could do was ask them to print out the same result again.

25.5.3 Optical scan

Most of the non-DRE equipment consisted of *optical-scan* machines that would scan a ballot paper or card that the voter had completed, whether with a pen or a special ballot-marking device, and then dropped into a ballot box. Optical scan systems had been around since the 1980s, and had evolved from the mark-sense scanners used to score multiple-choice tests in schools.

In the following electoral cycle, Californian Secretary of State Debra Bowen authorized a large team of computer scientists, led by University of California professors David Wagner and Matt Bishop, to do a thorough evaluation of the state's voting systems. The reports made depressing reading [307]. All the DRE voting systems they examined had serious design flaws that led directly to specific vulnerabilities that attackers could exploit to affect election outcomes. All of the previously approved voting machines – by Diebold, Hart and Sequoia – had their certification withdrawn, and a late-submitted system from ES&S was also decertified. California could take such radical action, as perhaps three-quarters of the nine million people who voted in 2004 did so using a paper or optical-scan ballot.

A similar inspection of Florida equipment was carried out by scientists at Florida State University, who reported a bundle of new vulnerabilities in the Diebold equipment in July 2007 [749]. Ohio followed suit and came to similar conclusions. All the evaluated equipment had serious security failings: data that should have been encrypted wasn't; encryption done badly (for example, the key stored in the clear next to the ciphertext); buffer overflows; useless physical security; SQL injection; audit logs that could be tampered with; and undocumented back doors [1263].

But if you abandon DRE machines for optical scanning of paper ballots, as most US counties have since 2006, you can do a hand recount if a close result is challenged. But there are still lots of things to go wrong.

First, hundreds of counties use ballot-marking devices, so that the voter makes their choices on a touch screen, after which the machine prints out a voting form they can inspect visually and drop into a ballot box. But some machines make separate human-readable and machine-readable marks, and if such a machine can be hacked, it could print a ballot card where the text says 'Gore' but the barcode says 'Bush'. So there's a lot of detail around what you inspect, and how; best practice is to design for a *risk-limiting audit*. In the UK, the gold standard is still the hand-marked paper ballot, but in the USA the vendors of ballot-marking machines have enlisted disability rights campaigners to help sell their equipment.

Our experience in the UK is broadly comparable, although we never adopted voting machines. Tony Blair's government progressively expanded the use of postal and other absentee forms of ballot, which was criticised by opposition parties as it made vote-buying and intimidation easier. Party workers (of which Blair's Labour party had more) could pressure voters into opting for a postal ballot, then collect their ballot forms, fill them out, and submit them. Plans to extend voting from the post to email and text were criticised for making this existing low-grade abuse easier and potentially open to automation. Finally, in the May 2007 local government elections, electronic voting pilots were held in eleven areas around the UK. Two of my postdocs acted as scrutineers in the Bedford election, and observed the same kind of shambles that had been reported at various US elections. The counting was slower than with paper; the system (optical-scan software) had a high error rate, resulting in many more ballots than expected being sent to human adjudicators for decision. (The printers had changed the ink halfway through the print run, so half the ballot papers were 'the wrong shade of black'.) Even worse, the software sometimes sent the same ballot paper to multiple adjudicators, and it wasn't clear which of their decisions got counted. In the end, so that everyone could go home, the returning officer accepted a letter of assurance (written on the spot by the vendor) saying that no vote would have been miscounted as a result. Yet the exercise left the representatives from the various parties with serious misgivings. The Open Rights Group, which organised the volunteers, reported that it could not express confidence in the results for the areas observed [1474]. The Electoral Commission did not disagree, and this experience persuaded the UK to continue using hand-counted, hand-marked paper ballots to this day. (UK election abuses happen at other places in the kill chain, from voter registration through postal voting abuses to breaches of campaign finance limits: so fixing the computers won't be enough to fix the problems.)

25.5.4 Software independence

This experience brought home both the importance of, and the difficulty of achieving, *software independence* – the property that an undetected change or error in voting software cannot cause an undetectable change or error in an election outcome [1611]. We must assume that vote-counting software is buggy and it may be malicious, so we should not have to depend on it, and the possibility of a manual recount is a vital mitigation. But how do you do that in practice? In Bedford the candidates reckoned that a manual recount would have led to the same result but with a different majority, and didn't want to spend another 20 hours on a full manual recount.

The consensus view in 2020 is that systems must be designed to support a *risk-limiting audit* that can place strict bounds on the probability of fraud or error arising as a result of things going wrong with the software. For optical scan, this might mean keeping all the votes from each ballot box in a separate bundle, so that a candidate could challenge "let's do a hand count of boxes 17, 37 and 169" and this could be completed quickly. If the count is close, or discrepancies are found, you can hand-count more boxes. (In fact, an argument over partial versus state-wide recounts figured in the Bush v Gore lawsuit in 2000.)

Cryptographers have tried to make vote-tallying more verifiable. Research into cryptographic election mechanisms goes back to the early 1980s, when David Chaum proposed giving voters a digital ballot token constructed using the same general techniques as digital cash, which they can spend with the candidate of their choice. In section 5.7.7 I described the mechanism: it's an interesting crypto design problem as you need to support anonymity and auditability at the same time. The voter needs to be confident that their vote has been tallied properly but in order to prevent vote buying they must not be able to prove this to anybody else – the vote must be *receipt-free*.

After more than thirty years of research, there are now well-understood mechanisms for this. For example, the free Election Guard system from Josh Benaloh and colleagues at Microsoft Research allows digital ballots to be cast in a vote collection device such as a scanner or ballot-marker in such a way that the encrypted ballots can be counted – the homomorphic property of El-Gamal encryption is used so that multiplying two encrypted votes has the same effect as adding two plaintext ones. A bit more work is required to ensure that all the ballots are well-formed and the result is decrypted properly, but the outcome is a software-independent count [224]. This was piloted in Fulton, Wisconsin, in 2020 in a primary election for Wisconsin Supreme Court candidates.

Cryptographic vote-tallying is marketed as 'end-to-end verifiable' but this claim is somewhat ambitious. It solves only the vote-tallying part of the problem. As with the electronic signature devices discussed in section 18.6.1, you don't have a trustworthy user interface, so you still have to worry about bugs and Trojans in the ballot-marking device or scanner. You still need the audit. You still have to worry about attacks on voter registration, on pollbooks, on result aggregation, and on the announcement of results. And if the vote collection device is an app on the voter's phone, you have to worry about vote-buying and intimidation, as with postal ballots. Then you also have to worry about phone malware, and about the quality of the design and implementation. A detailed evaluation of such an app that has been used in some US elections found dozens of problems [615].

25.5.5 Why electronic elections are hard

Another interesting threat emerged in the Netherlands. DRE voting machines had been introduced progressively during the 1990s, and cyber-rights activists were worried. They ran some tests and discovered that the machines from the leading vendor, Nedap, were vulnerable to a Tempest attack: using simple equipment, an observer sitting outside the polling station could see what party a voter had selected [786]. From the security engineer's perspective this was useful, as it led to the declassification by the German intelligence folk of a lot of Cold War Tempest material, as I discussed in section 19.3.2 (the Nedap machines are also used in Germany). The activists got the political result they wanted: the District Court in Amsterdam decertified all the Nedap machines.

As for other countries, the picture is mixed. I described in the chapter on electronic and information warfare, in section 23.8.3, how the Russians have attacked other countries' elections not just at the vote itself, but before it and after it. We find the same abuses being perpetrated by local political elites trying to cling on to power in the face of opposition. In some elections in less-developed countries, the state has systematically censored opposition parties' websites and run denial-of-service attacks; in others (typically the most backward), elections are rigged by more traditional methods such as filing bogus criminal charges to get opposition candidates off the ballot, or just kidnapping and murdering them. The best survey of abuses worldwide may be the Commonwealth's 2020 report [330]. The news as I write this is of unrest following the election in Belarus where 'Europe's last dictator', Alexander Lukashenko, declared he'd won over 80% of the votes in an election at which exit polls suggested that his opponent Svetlana Tikhanovskaya had actually won 70% of the vote. His thugs compelled her to make a concession speech and drove her into exile in Lithuania, keeping her husband hostage. Lukashenko then put the resulting demonstrations down by force [611]. Another news story was the overthrow in a coup of the President of Mali, following allegations that he had stolen an election five months previously [1202].

In recent years there have also been many tussles over population registration; in section 7.4.2.2 I described how less developed countries rig elections by re-issuing the national ID card, and making cards harder to get for the ethnic groups less likely to support the president. Even where registration mechanisms are fairly robust, as in India with its Aadhaar biometric system mentioned in section 17.4, the authorities can attack voting rights directly: the government of Narendra Modi passed a law in 2019 to disenfranchise many Muslims, particularly those in border areas.

This is a very old playbook. As I already mentioned, right up until the twentieth century, electoral history in the UK was about whether poor people could vote, while in the USA it was about whether black people could vote. Even in Florida in 2000, more voters were disenfranchised as a result of registration abuses than there were ballots disputed because of hanging chads. And just as the government can bias an election by making it harder to vote if you haven't got a car, it could make it harder to vote if you haven't got a computer. There have also been lawsuits over whether the ballots, or the voting machines, were made so complex as to disenfranchise the less educated.

Several disputes over technical security have got to court. For example, the state of Georgia appears a complete mess as I write in 2020; after years of trying to make it harder to vote, failing to fix known flaws in Diebold machines and being targeted by the Russians, the state government was ordered by a court to replace its systems. The new systems were in meltdown during the June 2020 primaries, with insufficient capacity to meet voter demand [852].

However the main focus of attention has shifted to the use of social media in elections. Barack Obama used Facebook effectively in 2008 and 2012, prompting others to study social media; the 2016 election went to Donald Trump, who was not only much more skilful than Hilary Clinton at using Twitter, but ended up paying significantly less for his Facebook ads. As I explained in section 8.5, the ad auction mechanisms used by Google and Facebook multiply the amount that you bid by a factor called 'ad quality', which is the probability that people will click on the ad and, in the case of social media, share it. The outcome is extremism bias: inflammatory ads are cheaper.

Another factor in 2016 was Russian interference, as I describe in section 2.2.3. Russian agents not only campaigned for Trump, running troll farms and social-media advertising campaigns aimed at suppressing black votes among other things; they hacked the Gmail of Clinton campaign chair John Podesta. And as I describe in section 25.5.5, they also appear to have set things up so that, had Clinton won the election, evidence of hacked election systems could have emerged to enable Trump to refuse to accept defeat.

How might this all affect the election due in November 2020? As this book is due for release then, I will merely note that there's already been a fiasco over result aggregation in the Democratic primary in Iowa [637], and the Russians are once more running inflammatory pro-Republican campaigns online [1622]. Both Twitter and Facebook have removed postings by Trump and his associates containing false information about Covid [1033], and there is concern that he or others might use online media to undermine the electoral process, or confidence in the results. Trump prepared the ground at the Republican National Convention by claiming he could only lose if the election was stolen. There is anxiety within Facebook that although Zuckerberg has said he'll block attempts at voter suppression, he's been giving the right wing an easier ride [1743]. In August, the major tech companies announced an alliance to fight election manipulation [965]. But what about a dispute over the result afterwards? There's over a century of American political history to warn us against looking for technological solutions to political problems.

In the different political culture of Europe, we have a long tradition of campaign finance limits (as America also did before the Citizens' United decision of the Supreme Court turned it into a free-for-all). Parties can spend only so much per campaign, and per candidate; and most European countries forbid paid TV ads during campaigns. But enforcement has been getting steadily weaker. During the Brexit referendum, for example, both Leave campaigns exceeded the spending limit but just paid the £20,000 maximum fine. The Russian involvement in Brexit was largely in the form of financial contributions and further campaigning on social media. What might be done to block such abuses?

At the 2019 conference of the Open Rights Group, I argued that we should extend the advertising ban from TV ads to all ads on Facebook, Twitter, and YouTube. This is not just a matter of avoiding the worst of big-money politics of the USA, but also because political ads that are targeted at individuals rather than at everybody foster extremism and fragment political discourse. The politicians' job is to mediate conflicts between different stakeholders in society; if these groups end up in their own filter bubbles, then our politicians can be tempted to inflame conflicts instead. Banning ads will not be a panacea (India banned Facebook ads in 2019) but it will keep election contests more within the cultural and economic space with which Europeans are familiar.

Elections remain one of the tough security engineering problems. While the individual problems – such as voter registration, vote casting, vote counting, result aggregation and audit – all have reasonably robust solutions, putting them together into a robust system is nontrivial. Computer systems for registering electors, recording votes and tallying them have a number of properties which make them almost a pathological case for robust design, implementation, testing and deployment. First, the election date is immovable and, ready or not, the software must be deployed then. Second, different regions and countries have different requirements and they change over time. Third, in the long gap between elections, staff with experience move on and know-how is lost. Fourth, operating systems and other software must be updated to fix known vulnerabilities, and updates can also break security in unforeseen ways; a Windows update caused the EV2000 voting machine to highlight the last voter's choice to the next voter [992]. Yet most voting machines in use in the USA are no longer manufactured, so where are the updates to come from and how will they be tested? Finally, elections are high-stress events, which increases the likelihood of mistakes [1359].

Let's now look up from the engineering to the politics. In the event of attack, the winners don't want to investigate what might have gone wrong if they can possibly avoid it – as we saw in both the USA and the UK in 2016[4]. The 'customer' for an election is the losing side, and in the absence of any hope of redress – whether through the courts, or through the ballot box next time – trust in democracy's mechanisms can start to fail. But there is no 'designer' to ensure that the mechanisms and laws align all the way along the electoral cycle. On the

[4]As I write, litigation continues in an attempt to force the release of the redacted parts of the Mueller report into that election.

contrary, it's typically the incumbent who tweaks the laws, buys the voting machines, and creates as many advantages for their own side, small and large, as the local political culture will tolerate. And while voting mechanisms can support a democratic consensus, they cannot replace it: there are too many other ways to undermine the outcome. If the underlying social contract erodes, a hyper-partisan environment can lead incumbents to feel they do not dare to cede power. In the worst cases the outcome can be civil war and failed states.

25.6 Summary

Some of the most challenging security engineering problems in 2020 have to do with the fact that as software becomes pervasive in the services we use and the devices around us, the design of these services and devices comes up against the underlying complexity in human societies. We looked at four examples. Self-driving cars can cope with empty desert roads but find real traffic with human drivers very much harder. Machine-learning mechanisms can go only so far; they may be brilliant at pattern matching but lack understanding, which opens up new possibilities of abuse at all levels in the stack – especially as people rush to use them for social prediction tasks for which they are intrinsically unsuited. Privacy-enhancing tools and techniques are one way to explore the security consequences of human complexity, but however hard we work to encrypt and anonymise things, social structure tends to show through one way or another. And finally, we have elections; when incumbent rulers are prepared to do everything they think they can get away with – whether within or beyond the law – to stay in office, we can learn a lot about the limits of both technology and law.

As more and more of human life moves online, so the criticality and the complexity of online applications grow at the same time. Many of the familiar problems come back again and again, in ever less tractable forms. Traditional software engineering tools helped developers get ever further up the mountain of systems complexity before they fell off. What sort of tools, techniques, and governance processes are appropriate for dealing with the complexity of real societies? And how does this interact with politics? These are the topics we will try to tackle in the third part of this book.

Research problems

One bundle of research problems is around how to split responsibility between people and automation. HCI guru Ben Shneiderman argues that human control plus extensive automation is the sweet spot for systems to be reliable, safe and trustworthy [1726]. This is natural for flight-control systems and life-support machinery, but scaling it up to things like recommender systems and hate-speech detection is not trivial. How can humans do quality control on millions of filtering decisions being taken every second by a large tech company? And what should the governance on top of that look like? Underlying it all is a long debate about whether automation (including ML) is heading towards artificial intelligence or intelligence augmentation. I have long favoured the latter option [88].

As automation involving ML becomes more pervasive, the questions may become broader. Architects and city planners will have to wrestle with how we design living and working environments that have to take into account the interests of multiple stakeholders. Then there will be global social and political questions around the coevolution of mechanisms and societies. In the second edition I said that "one of the critical research problems between now and the third edition of this book … will be how protection mechanisms scale … how one goes about evolving 'security' (or any other emergent property) in a socio-technical system with billions of users." I noted that simple systems of rules, such as the multilevel security beloved of governments, were never natural, and people always had to break them to get their work done. So what lies beyond? We have more experience of that now; several large tech firms run systems with over a billion active users, and hundreds of firms have over a hundred million.

In such systems, the technology and the behaviour adapt to each other, but the system developers are much more powerful and have different incentives (they want data while users want privacy). The basic mechanisms that humans have for rule negotiation at scale are competition in the market and government regulation. Neither of these is adequate on its own, and the interaction between tech and politics may even undermine the machinery of selecting a government.

We engineers need to care about these issues, and try to understand them. In the third section of this book we'll try to tackle the broader policy and management questions (such as surveillance versus privacy), how the evolution of large complex systems can be managed and governed, and how technology can be regulated to meet social goals such as safety and privacy.

Further reading

For an introduction to car security, you might first look at Charlie Miller and Chris Valasek's account of how they hacked a Jeep [1318], then at Craig Smith's *Car Hacker's Handbook* if you want to dive into the technical detail [1796].

Nicolas Papernot's "Marauder's Map" may be the best introduction right now to the fast-moving field of adversarial machine learning [1495], while Gary

McGraw and colleagues offer design principles plus a list of things to think about when working on the security of systems with machine-learning components [1269]. Google's Jeff Dean, its SVP of machine learning, describes the company's research on AI fairness at [528]. My own philosophical position on the AI versus IA debate may be found at [88].

As for personal privacy in the face of hostile state actors, that's a moving conflict as the tools evolve on both sides. One starting point might be the "Surveillance Self-Defence" page on the EFF website [618]. There's an interesting account by Ben Collier of the organisational and social dynamics of the Tor project, which maintains the leading online anonymity service, at [455]. For more technical depth, see section 20.4 on Tor, or the anonymity bibliography at [123].

The history of US voting systems is told by Douglas Jones and Barbara Simons [992]. The US National Academies of Sciences, Engineering and Medicine produced an extensive report on election security in response to the events of 2016 [1390]. More recently, the Commonwealth produced a guide to the electronic security of elections based on its own member states' very diverse experiences, also covering the whole cycle from registration through vote casting, tallying and communication of the results [330].

PART III

In the final part of the book I cover three broad themes: politics, management and assurance. Given that we now have some idea how to provide protection, the three big questions are: what should you do? How do you go about organizing it? And how do you know when you're done?

The first two decades of the 21st century have seen the growth of a security-industrial complex that has consumed billions of dollars and eroded both our freedom and our privacy, for often negligible gains in actual protection. The coronavirus pandemic has brought home with some force that we spend much of our social resilience budget on surveillance systems, when we should have been spending it on public health instead. Pandemic flu was at the top of most countries' risk registers for years, yet it was the heads of the security and intelligence agencies that got to sit in the national security bodies that spent the money. Sustainability should probably take over, yet there too we see just lip service.

The mechanisms that lead to the misperception of risk and the misallocation of resources are fairly well understood. Politicians scare up the vote, and threats seen as personal or cultural make people more anxious. Our industry helps them along with systems that are often best described as 'security theater'. This gives rise to a number of ethical and political issues for the security engineer. Are our societies vulnerable to terrorism because we overreact, and if so, how can we avoid becoming part of the problem rather than part of the solution? Can we find ways to make more rational decisions about allocating protective resources, or at least stop security arguments being used to bolster bad policy? And how do we deal with the more traditional security policy issues we've been worrying about since the 1990s, such as the online abuse, censorship, privacy and digital evidence? And then there's the growing problem of how our societies can deal with the monopolies that our industry is so good at creating.

Next we turn to management. Leading a team of developers to create, maintain or enhance a complex system with critical security or safety properties is one of the more challenging things that humans do for a living. The move from top-down waterfall or V-model approaches to agile development has enabled us to build bigger systems and to patch them more quickly when they fail, but has made it harder to manage emergent system properties such as security and safety. Fixing this has different names at different firms, from DevSecOps to reliability engineering; it's a work in progress, with which we'll be busy for some time. There are useful things we can contribute by studying organisational and economic incentives, the statistics of failures, and the best practices of leading firms.

Our third chapter here is on assurance and sustainability. On the face of it, it's an engineering issue: how do you go about finding convincing answers to the questions of whether you're building the right system and whether you're building it right. These questions are familiar from software engineering (which can teach us a lot), but they acquire new meaning when systems are exposed to hostile attack. Also, most of the organisational structures within which assurance claims can be made, or certified, are conflicted one way or another. Claims about system security properties are often thinly veiled assertions of power and control, and vendors put a lot of effort into manipulating and capturing any certification processes for their offerings. So it should surprise no-one if the results of evaluation by vendors, insurers' laboratories, government agencies and academic attackers are very different.

What's more, as all sorts of goods acquire software and communications, they have to be patched. Up till now, vendors used the patching cycle as part of a planned obsolescence strategy: you'd get maybe three years' use out of your phone, and five years out of your laptop, before you had to buy a new one. That doesn't work for cars, though; although the car makers would love to have all cars scrapped after six years, the environmental costs would be horrendous. So now we have laws in Europe requiring durable consumer goods such as cars and fridges to be patched for ten years after the last one leaves the showroom. That means that engineers have to plan to maintain the security and safety of software for twenty years or more. This is one of the grand challenges facing us over the coming decade.

CHAPTER

26

Surveillance or Privacy?

Experience should teach us to be most on our guard to protect liberty when the government's purposes are beneficient ... The greatest dangers to liberty lurk in insidious encroachment by men of zeal, well meaning but without understanding.

– SUPREME COURT JUSTICE LOUIS BRANDEIS

Every thing secret degenerates, even the administration of justice; nothing is safe that does not show how it can bear discussion and publicity.

– LORD ACTON

The arguments of lawyers and engineers pass through one another like angry ghosts.

– Nick Bohm, Ian Brown and Brian Gladman

26.1 Introduction

Governments have ever more interests online, ranging from surveillance to censorship, from privacy to safety, and from market competition to fair elections. Their goals are often in tension with the reality of a globalised online world, and with each other too. They crystallise around a number of specific policy concerns, from terrorism and counterinsurgency, through national strategic and economic advantage, to the suppression of harmful or unpopular content and the maintenance of human rights. In this chapter we explore the nexus of surveillance, censorship, forensics and privacy.

The Internet has transformed the world in lots of complicated ways, like other big technologies before it – electricity, the steam engine, writing, agriculture and fire. The relationship between the citizen and the state has changed everywhere, with the state usually acquiring more power and control. In the early years, as the PC replaced the mainframe and the Internet opened up to all, many pioneers were utopians: we believed that free access to information would be liberating at the personal level, and would destabilise authoritarian governments too. Yet governments and large companies learned in time to use the new tools. The terrorist attacks of September 11, 2001, on New York and Washington had a real impact, by creating the incentive for mass surveillance and weakening political opposition to it. The move of business online created the tools, and a commercial market for personal information to pay for them. The Arab Spring of 2011 also mattered; while Tunisia escaped to democracy, most other countries in the region have become more authoritarian. Heads of government in China, Russia and elsewhere have become rulers for life, bolstered by new mechanisms for social control. The COVID-19 pandemic also looks set to increase state surveillance, with the trade-off being not privacy versus security but privacy versus health.

In short, the early twenty-first century has been a boom time for surveillance. It's not just the NSA capabilities revealed in 2013 by Ed Snowden; nation-state competitors like Russia and China also have serious capabilities, while there are more primitive but still effective systems in less developed countries like Syria.

The 2010s also saw growing cyber conflict and disruption with states interfering covertly in other states' affairs. The USA and Israel used the Stuxnet malware to damage and delay Iran's push to acquire nuclear weapons, and this caused a rush by other states to acquire cyber-weapons of various kinds. Since the Russian interference in the 2016 US election, legislators in a number of countries want to regulate social media: a lot of politicians have stopped ignoring technology once they realised their jobs were on the line.

There are many thorny issues. First, are open societies with democracy and a free press more vulnerable, because we're easier to exploit? And if so, what can we do about it? We face real challenges to our core values – expressed in the USA as the Constitution, and in Europe as the Convention on Human Rights. Since 9/11 we've seen one authoritarian measure after another, ranging from large-scale surveillance of communications to detention without trial and even torture. Many of these measures were not just illegal and immoral but ineffective or even counterproductive: torturing Iraqi secret policemen alongside al-Qaida terrorists in the Abu Ghraib prison was what forged the two groups into the core of the Islamic State. Can't we find better ways to defend freedom? And how can we reassert and defend our core values?

Second, there's the political economy of security. President Eisenhower warned in his valedictory speech that 'we must guard against the acquisition of unwarranted influence, whether sought or unsought, by the military industrial complex. The potential for the disastrous rise of misplaced power exists and will persist'. Since 9/11, we've seen a security-industrial complex capturing policy in the same ways that the defence industry did at the start of the Cold War. Politicians of left and right have stoked a culture of fear, abetted by security agencies and the press. This has been deepened since the financial crisis of 2008 by the rise of nationalism.

Security technology arguments are often used to bamboozle or intimidate legislators. For example, all through the Irish republican terrorist campaign from the 1970s through 1990s, the British police had to charge arrested terrorist suspects within four days. But after 9/11, this was quickly raised to 28 days; then the government said it needed 90 days, claiming they might have difficulty decrypting data on PCs seized from suspects. The real problem was police inefficiency at managing forensics. Now if the police had just said, 'We need to hold suspects for 90 days because we don't have enough Somali interpreters,' then common sense could have kicked in; Parliament might well have told them to use staff from commercial translation agencies. But talk of decryption seems a good way to turn legislators' brains to mush. People who understand cryptography have a duty to speak out.

The focus on terrorism starved the rest of law enforcement. About half of all crime is now online, and yet the resources devoted to fighting it are tiny. Many scammers operate with impunity.

There are further problems around censorship. Concerns about online abuse are real, but this is a difficult area. Abuses range in seriousness from videos of murder and child rape at the top end, down through hate speech, rape threats and cyber-bullying to news manipulation – which, at scale, can be toxic. Countries are starting to pass laws requiring firms like Facebook to do the censorship for them, which causes many tensions. The companies don't like the extra costs, so they often make only token efforts. Thoughtful citizens don't like the idea of censorship being in the hands of private monopolies – or the idea that everything we upload, from pictures and videos to private messages, is filtered. So the firms have an incentive to redesign their systems so that they're harder to abuse; Facebook, for example, claims to be rebuilding its systems to focus more on groups, which are harder for extremists to game, and to make more use of end-to-end encryption, so it can claim ignorance. Such arguments cut no ice in major incidents, such as when a shooter killed people at two mosques in Christchurch, New Zealand, in March 2019 and used Facebook to share live video of the crime. This forced the company to start censoring white supremacist groups, a politically sensitive task it had previously avoided [1917]. The COVID-19 pandemic led the company to rapidly do many things that the industry had previously denounced as impossible, undesirable or impractical: removing misinformation, banning exploitative ads and pushing official advice [986]. The tensions between privacy and censorship may continue to work out in unpredictable ways.

Privacy regulation is already complex. US laws are fragmented, with federal laws on specific topics such as health data and video rentals and the FTC punishing firms that violate their published privacy policies, while state laws drive security-breach disclosure. Europe is very different: the General Data Protection Regulation provides a comprehensive framework, backed up by human-rights law that has been used to strike down laws on surveillance. The overall effect, from the viewpoint of the IT industry, is that Europe is becoming the world's privacy regulator; Washington doesn't care, and nobody else is big enough to matter. (There are strong signs that this regulatory power will be extended steadily to safety as well, although we'll leave that to the chapter on assurance.)

In this chapter, I'm going to discuss the evolution of surveillance, then look at terrorism before discussing censorship and privacy regulation, and finally trying to put the whole thing in context.

26.2 Surveillance

The 2010s saw a huge increase in technical surveillance, not just by governments but also by commercial firms monitoring our clickstream and location history in order to target ads better – described by Shoshana Zuboff as 'Surveillance Capitalism' [2078]. The two interact in various ways. In some countries, like the USA, law enforcement and intelligence agencies don't just get information from their own collection systems but use warrants to get it from firms like Google and Facebook too. In others, like China, these firms are banned because they refused to give complete access to the authorities; in others, like Iran and Syria, the police agencies just beat people's passwords out of them, or phish their friends, or hack their phones.

This is a huge subject, and all I can reasonably provide is a helicopter tour: to place surveillance in its historical context, sketch what's going on, and provide pointers to primary sources.

26.2.1 The history of government wiretapping

Rulers have always tried to control communications. In classical times, couriers were checked at customs posts, and from the Middle Ages, many kings either operated a postal monopoly or granted it to a crony. The letter-opening and codebreaking facilities of early modern states, the so-called *Black Chambers*, are described in David Kahn's history, 'The Codebreakers' [1003].

When electronic communications came along, governments tried to keep control. In most of Europe, the telegraph service was set up as part of the post office and owned by the government; in Britain, the telegraph industry was nationalized by Gladstone in 1869. A profusion of national rules caused so much trouble that the *International Telegraph Union* (ITU) was set up in 1865 to standardise things [1821]. In the USA, Western Union was the first nationwide industrial monopoly and dominated the market through the nineteenth century. Union and Confederate soldiers tapped each others' telegraph lines, and the New York Police Department started wiretapping operations in 1895.

The invention of the telephone led to tussles over privacy. In the USA, the Supreme Court ruled in 1928 in *Olmstead v United States* that wiretapping didn't violate the fourth amendment provisions on search and seizure as there was no physical breach of a dwelling; Justice Brandeis famously dissented. In 1967, the Court reversed itself in *Katz v United States*, ruling that the amendment protects people, not places. The following year, Congress legalized Federal wiretapping (in 'title III' of the Omnibus Crime Control and Safe Streets Act) following testimony on the scale of organized crime. In 1978, following an investigation into the Nixon administration's abuses, Congress passed the Foreign Intelligence Surveillance Act (FISA), which controls wiretapping for national security. In 1986, the Electronic Communications Protection Act (ECPA) relaxed the Title III warrant provisions. By the early 1990s, the spread of deregulated services from mobile phones to call forwarding had started to undermine the authorities' ability to wiretap, as did technical developments such as adaptive echo cancellation in modems.

So the 1994 Communications Assistance for Law Enforcement Act (CALEA) required all communications companies to make their networks tappable in ways approved by the FBI. By 1999, over 2,450,000 telephone conversations were legally tapped following 1,350 court orders [634, 1259]; by 2017 the number of wiretap orders had almost tripled to 3,813, but 94% were against portable devices such as cellphones [1931][1]. A further 1,598 orders were granted in whole or in part by the Foreign Intelligence Surveillance Court (FISC) while 26 were denied.

Even before 9/11, some analysts believed that there were at least as many unauthorized wiretaps as authorized ones [558]. First was phone company collusion: while a phone company must give the police access if they present a warrant, in many countries they are also allowed to help – and there have been many reports over the years of phone companies being cosy with the government. Second, there's intelligence-agency arbitrage: if the NSA wants to wiretap an American citizen without a warrant they can get an ally to do it, and return the favour later. It was said, for example, that Margaret Thatcher used the Canadian intelligence services to wiretap ministers suspected of disloyalty [728]. Such practices were denied by the agencies for years, but the Snowden leaks showed them to be reality; for example, the NSA got GCHQ to tap the links between Google data centres, as I described in 2.2.1.3. Third, in some countries, wiretapping is uncontrolled if one of the subscribers consents – so calls from phone boxes are free to tap (the owner of the phone box is the legal subscriber). Companies may wiretap their staff to detect fraud and voluntarily pass the product to the police or security agencies; there was a scandal in the UK when it emerged that the security services were

[1]The relevant law is 18 USC (US Code) 2510–2521, while FISA's regulation of foreign intelligence gathering is now codified in US law as 50 USC 1801–1811.

involved in an unlawful, clandestine scheme to blacklist construction industry staff who had tried to organise unions [658]. Finally, in many countries, the police get hold of email and other stored communications by subpoena rather than warrant. They did this in America too before a court stopped the practice in 2007 [1163] – but the judgment didn't stop private actors such as bounty hunters and bail agents buying phone location histories from data aggregators [485].

But even if the official figures have to be doubled or tripled, democratic regimes use wiretapping very much less than authoritarian ones. The surveillance leader now is China, which uses pervasive technical monitoring in regions with minority populations such as Xinjiang and Tibet, with surveillance cameras mounted over street corners, mosques and schools hooked up via face-recognition software to databases recording who was seen where and when. There are also intrusive physical measures ranging from frequent street checkpoints, through billeting party members in the homes of minority families, to mass incarceration in labour camps [1112].

The incidence of wiretapping has also been highly variable within and between democracies. In the USA, for example, only about half the states use it, and for much of the 20th century most taps were in the 'Mafia' states of New York, New Jersey and Florida (though Nevada and California have now caught up) [1931]. There is similar variation in Europe. Wiretaps are very common in the Netherlands: they have up to 1,000 taps on the go at once with a tenth of America's population [350]. In a Dutch homicide investigation, it's routine to tap everyone in the victim's address book for a week to monitor how they react to the death. The developed country with the most wiretaps is Italy, thanks to its history of organised crime [1162]. In the UK, domestic wiretaps are supposed to need a ministerial warrant, and cannot be used in evidence; so the police use room bugs and computer exploits instead. If you can root a gangster's phone or laptop you can record, and mail home, everything said nearby, whether it's said to someone in the same room, or on a call. International calls have been routinely recorded for decades and stored for some days to weeks in case they turn out to be of interest, a model followed by many other countries; for example, after the Mumbai massacre in 2008, India could dig out recordings of phone calls the terrorists made to their controllers in Pakistan.

Automation is shifting the costs of wiretapping from per-call labour costs to one-off capital costs. Before CALEA was introduced, in 1993, US police agencies spent only $51.7 million on wiretaps – perhaps a good estimate of their value before the issue became politicised [863]. The implementation of CALEA cost over $500m, and that was before it was extended to VOIP in 2007. VOIP was harder: "The paradigm of VoIP intercept difficulty is a call between two road warriors who constantly change locations and who, for example, may call from a cafe in Boston to a hotel room in Paris and an hour later from an office in

Cambridge to a giftshop at the Louvre" [221]. During the 2010s things became harder still as people moved from physical platforms, such as their cellphone, to virtual platforms such as Facebook, Skype and Signal. So the trend for policymakers has been to make capital investments that cut the marginal costs of access. For example, ten years ago, if the UK police were investigating three similar rapes, they might have had to pay the phone companies thousands of pounds to assemble cellsite dumps so they could look for any mobile phones that were present at all three locations. Now, after spending hundreds of millions and getting several laws passed, they have access to databases of mobile phone locations, and all it takes is a database query. This changes the nature of both police and intelligence work.

The USA also changed its laws to facilitate bulk surveillance. 43 days after the 9/11 attacks, Congress passed the Patriot Act, which allowed increased access by law enforcement to stored records (including financial, medical and government records), 'sneak-and-peek' searches of homes and businesses without the owner's knowledge, and the use by the FBI of National Security Letters to get access to financial, email and telephone records.

But this was not enough for the agencies. In December 2005, the New York Times revealed that President Bush had signed a secret 2002 order mandating warrantless wiretapping of US residents suspected of terrorism, contrary to law [1609]. In 2006, USA Today revealed that the NSA had covertly obtained full call-data records (CDRs) for the 200m customers of AT&T, Verizon and BellSouth, the nation's three biggest phone companies. The CDR program had been started by the DEA in 1992 under the older President Bush, and targeted calls by Americans to and from certain countries; it was ramped up after 9/11, when his son authorised the collection of CDRs for all internal US calls too [879]. Qwest did not cooperate, because its CEO at the time, Joe Nacchio, maintained that the NSA needed a court order. The NSA put pressure on Qwest by threatening to withhold classified contracts, so Qwest's lawyers asked the NSA to take its proposal to the FISA court. They refused, saying the court might not agree with them. It's since emerged that they had put pressure on Qwest to hand over data even before 9/11 [769]. In October 2007, Verizon admitted to senators that it had given the FBI second-generation call data on its customers against national security letters on 720 occasions since 2005 [1378]. In November 2007, the Washington Post revealed that the NSA had tapped a lot of purely domestic phone calls and traffic data, and had also tapped AT&T's peering centre in San Francisco to get access to Internet traffic [1379]. After two years of debate, Congress amended FISA to grant retroactive immunity to phone companies who cooperated with unlawful wiretapping, and to change the law so that the NSA no longer needs even a FISA warrant to tap a call if one party's believed to be outside the USA or a non-US person. (This split both parties, with Senators Obama and Feinstein supporting the amendment while Senators McCain, Biden, Reid, Leahy and Clinton opposed it.)

26.2.2 Call data records (CDRs)

Historically, more police communications intelligence has come from the analysis of telephone call data records and other metadata rather than wiretaps. We discussed in the chapter on telecoms security how the police use such data to trace networks of criminal contacts, and how criminals respond by burying their signals in innocuous traffic using techniques such as pre-paid mobile phones and PBX hacking.

Again, this is nothing new. Rulers have long used their control over postal services to track the correspondents of suspects, even when the letters weren't opened. The introduction of postage stamps in 1840 was an advance for privacy as it made it much easier to send a letter anonymously. Some countries got so worried about the threat of sedition that they passed laws requiring a return address to be written on the back of the envelope. The development of the telegraph, on the other hand, was an advance for surveillance; as messages were logged by sender, receiver and word count, traffic totals could be compiled and were found to be an effective indicator of economic activity [1821]. The First World War taught the combatants how much intelligence could be gleaned from measuring the volume of enemy radio traffic, even when it couldn't conveniently be deciphered [1003, 1382]. Later twentieth-century conflicts reinforced this.

When I wrote the first edition of this book, I noted that the USA had 1,329 wiretap applications approved in 1998, while there were 4886 subpoenas (plus 4621 extensions) for *pen registers* (devices that record all the numbers dialed from a target phone line) and 2437 subpoenas (plus 2770 extensions) for *trap-and-trace* devices (which record the calling line ID of incoming calls, even if the caller tries to block it). Law-enforcement agencies were also starting to switch in the 1990s to using subpoenas for the call-detail records in the phone companies' databases. Bell Atlantic, for example, responded to 25,453 subpoenas or court orders for toll billing records of 213,821 of its customers in 1989–92, while NYNEX processed 25,510 subpoenas covering an unrecorded number of customers in 1992 alone [404]. Scaled up across the seven Baby Bells, this suggests that perhaps half a million customers were having their records seized every year in the 1990s, and that traffic data were collected on perhaps a hundred times as many people as were subjected to wiretapping.

Statistics went dark after 9/11, during the period of unlawful collection, although the NSA did reveal in 2006 that it wanted "to create a database of every call ever made within the nation's borders" so it could map the entire US social network for the War on Terror [397]. After Snowden revealed in 2013 that it had built databases of pretty well all traffic data for all communications worldwide, Congress passed the Freedom Act in 2015 and we started to get an annual Statistical Transparency Report from the Director of National Intelligence. The April 2018 report gives some figures for 2017; these relate only to national-security matters, but give some feel for the balance between content and traffic data. Wiretap warrants are stable at about 1,500 per year in the USA (targeting about 300 US persons and 1000 others), as well as a rising number of targets overseas – 106,469 in 2016 and 129,080 in 2017. In addition, there were 7,512 US residents whose communications content was retrieved (e.g. subpoenas for email) while 16,924 residents had non-content (such as traffic data) retrieved, along with 56,064 non-residents. There were also 87,834 collected business records, which might include records of which subscriber was using which IP address [1466].

Now the US intelligence community only considers a communication to be 'intercepted' when a human analyst looks at it; analysis by software doesn't count (UK law counts both). As I described in section 23.3.1, the usual procedure when hunting for suspects is contact chaining, also known as a 'snowball search'. If someone blows themselves up in a terror attack, analysts will use software that looks at all the people they communicated with, and then everyone these direct contacts communicated with, and exceptionally even out to a third degree of separation. The standard depth-two search typically gives some tens of thousands of indirect contacts. These contacts are then compared against millions of names on various suspect lists – religious extremists, right-wing hate groups, organised crime – and the analysts then home in on the links with any known suspects. (The analogy is rolling a snowball downhill, then melting it and seeing what dirt you find in the bottom of the bucket.) So the analyst may look at only half a dozen people who were in contact with the dead terrorist and also with members of some religious group, but tens of thousands of innocent people had their call data records looked at by the software. The DNI report estimates that in 2017, 534,396,285 call data records (CDRs) were examined automatically in this way – a huge increase from 151,230,968 in 2016.

Yet there was a long debate in Congress about allowing Section 215 of the Patriot Act (as amended by FISA) to lapse. This was the section that allows the bulk collection of CDRs [418]; the NSA has said that it doesn't want it. The bulk collection of communications data was one of the matters highlighted by Ed Snowden that sparked the most controversy. On June 8th 2013, the press disclosed Boundless Informant, an NSA visualisation tool that shows a heat map of where metadata are collected for both voice and computer communications; in a 30-day period ending in March 2013, 3 billion records were collected from 504 sources (or SIGADs). Although the most intensive collection was in the Middle East, Snowden said that more records were collected on Americans in America than on Russians in Russia [756]. On another reading of the material, Boundless Informant collected 3 billion phone records via US telecommunications providers, plus a further 97 billion emails and 124 billion phone calls round the world [817, p. 92]; overall, 20 billion events a day are collected [817, p. 98]. However, a declassified report revealed that while the NSA call-data record program in the USA cost over $100m, it produced only two leads and one significant investigation [1659]. In 2020, the clause was allowed to lapse in March but reinstated in May; the politics was messy. Susan Landau and Asaf Lubin explained that with 4G mobile networks, traditional CDRs don't identify both the caller and the called party reliably any more [1128]. In any case, the action is shifting from the plain old telephone system to messaging systems.

As for targeted collection in specific criminal investigations, under 18 USC 3123 [1929], the investigative officer merely has to certify to a magistrate 'that the information likely to be obtained by such installation and use is relevant to an ongoing criminal investigation'. This can be any crime – felony or misdemeanour – and under either Federal or State law. Since CALEA, warrants are still required for such communications data as the addresses to which a subscriber has sent e-mail messages, but basic toll records can be obtained under subpoena – the subscriber need not be notified, and there is no court supervision once the order has been made. The US Department of Justice is required by law to publish statistics for its non-national-security law-enforcement activities but appears reluctant to do so; the American Civil Liberties Union (ACLU) extracted figures for 2011–12 only after freedom-of-information (FOI) litigation, which revealed that the combined number of original orders for pen registers and trap and trace devices used to spy on phones increased by 60%, from 23,535 in 2009 to 37,616 in 2011 [766]. I've been unable to find anything more recent.

Bulk access to traffic data has also led to serious political tussles in Europe. The UK pushed through a Data Retention Directive in the European Union in 2006, under which member states had to store telecommunications data – including IP address and timing of every email, phone call and text message sent or received – for between 6 months and 24 months, and make all this available to law enforcement and intelligence agencies. The Directive was struck down in 2014 by the European Court of Justice after Digital Rights Ireland brought a lawsuit arguing that blanket data collection violated the EU Charter of Fundamental Rights.

In Britain, targeted access to communications data requires only a notice from a senior police officer to the phone company or ISP, not a warrant; and data can be provided to a wide range of public-sector bodies, just as in the USA. After its initial success with the Data Retention Directive, the Blair government wanted to centralise things; it argued that the police needed a 'communications database' and pushed a law to establish it. Fate intervened when some wicked person made a copy of all the expenses claims filed by Members of Parliament and sold it to the Daily Telegraph. It turned out that numerous ministers and others had been making embarrassing claims; several honourable members went to jail, and most of the well-known politicians in Britain had to make repayments. (I told the tragic tale of the Home Secretary, Jacqui Smith – who had been promoting the communications database – in section 8.6.6 above.) We heard nothing more of the communications database until Ed Snowden told us in 2013 that they'd just built it anyway, without parliamentary approval.

After the European Court struck down data retention, and Snowden revealed some highly objectionable activities by GCHQ, the UK passed the 2014 DRIP Act to assert that what GCHQ had been doing was legal after all. It was clear that the European Court would object eventually, but some breathing space was needed and the Act provided this (it had a two-year sunset clause; Prime Minister Cameron's liberal coalition partners wouldn't give him any more). Eventually, in the wake of the Brexit vote, Parliament passed the Investigatory Powers Act, which pretty well enables GCHQ to do as it pleases and compel any company in the jurisdiction to assist it. The interesting action in the future will be, first, the extent to which the large US firms will help, and second, the line to be taken by the European Court of Human Rights[2]. I'll return to these issues later.

26.2.3 Search terms and location data

It has become ever clearer over the past 20 years that the regulation of surveillance that evolved in the phone-company era is not really fit for purpose in the era of the Internet. Back then, you got either a full wiretap and recorded the content, or made do with traffic data from call data records. But as things moved online, communications data and content got all mixed up, as what's content at one level of abstraction is often communications data at the next. Some people might think of a URL as just the address of a page to be fetched, but a URL such as `http://www.google.com/search?q=marijuana+cultivation+UK` contains the terms entered into a search engine as well as the search engine's name. Clearly, some policemen would like a list of everyone who submitted such an enquiry. This became a live issue in 1999, when the UK government modernised its surveillance law; academics, NGOs and industry managed to get a 'Big Browser Amendment' into the resulting Regulation of Investigatory Powers Act of 2000 defining traffic data as the information necessary to identify the communicating machine. (For URLs, this means everything up to the first slash.)

In the USA, the Department of Justice issued a subpoena to a number of search engines to hand over two full months' worth of search queries, as well as all the URLs in their index, claiming it needed the data to bolster its claims that the Child Online Protection Act did not violate the constitution and that filtering could be effective against child pornography. (Recall we discussed

[2]Britain's departure from the EU will let it escape the European Court of Justice, which is an EU institution, but not the Court of Human Rights, as this is an institution of the Council of Europe, of which Britain remains a member.

in section 11.2.4 how when AOL released some search histories, a number of them were easily identifiable to individuals.) AOL, Microsoft and Yahoo quietly complied, but Google resisted. A judge finally ruled in 2006 that the Department would get no search queries, and only a random sample of 50,000 of the URLs it had originally sought [2038].

The next issue was mobile-phone location data, which ended up being treated differently in different jurisdictions. In Britain, all information about the location of mobile phones counts as traffic data, and officials get it easily; but in the USA, the Court of Appeals ruled in 2000 that when the police get a warrant for the location of a mobile, the cell in which it is active is sufficient, and that to require triangulation on the device (an interpretation the police had wanted) would invade privacy [1930]. Also, even cell-granularity location information would not be available under the lower standards applied to pen-register subpoenas. Yet despite these rules, there were massive leaks of information. It emerged in 2019 that AT&T and Sprint had both been selling their customers' location information to data brokers for years, including not just cellsite data but GPS; and this had routinely been bought by bounty hunters and bail agents to track defaulters [485]. Location data is now being collected by many governments with a view to tracing contacts of COVID-19 sufferers and epidemiology more generally. It's also collected by lots of apps: the 'Untappd' beer-rating app is run by millions of beer drinkers who record hundreds of time-stamped locations, which enabled journalists to track US military and intelligence personnel around the world [1541].

26.2.4 Algorithmic processing

The analysis of call data is only one aspect of a much wider issue: law-enforcement matching of bulk datasets. The earliest serious use of multiple-source data appears to have been in Germany in the late 1970s to track down safe houses used by the Baader-Meinhof terrorist group. Investigators looked for rented apartments with irregular peaks in utility usage, and for which the rent and electricity bills were paid by remote credit transfer from a series of different locations. This worked: it yielded a list of several hundred apartments among which were several safe houses. The tools to do this kind of analysis are now shipped with a number of the products used for traffic analysis and for managing major police investigations. The extent to which they're used depends on the local regulatory climate; there have been rows in the UK over police access to databases of the prescriptions filled by pharmacists, while in the USA doctors are alarmed at the frequency with which personal health information is subpoenaed from insurance companies by investigators. There are also practical limits imposed by the cost of understanding the many proprietary data formats used by commercial and government data processors. But it's common for police to have access at least to utility data, such as electricity bills that they trawl to find marijuana growers, and there's little to stop them using commercially available data such as feeds from credit reference agencies.

Since AlphaGo beat Lee Sedol in 2016, there's been a host of machine-learning startups, and quite a few aim to make law enforcement easier one way or another. But it's not as easy as it looks. Terrorists are so rare as a percentage of the population that any tests you use to 'detect' them would require extraordinary specificity if you're not to drown in false positives. Combining multiple sensors is hard, and if you're looking for a needle in a haystack, it's not always smart to build a bigger haystack. As Jeff Jonas, once the chief scientist at IBM's data-mining operation, put it, "techniques that look at people's behavior to predict terrorist intent are so far from reaching the level of accuracy that's necessary that I see them as nothing but civil liberty infringement engines" [757].

26.2.5 ISPs and CSPs

The 2000s saw rapid growth of intrusive surveillance at both Internet Service Providers (ISPs) and Communications Service Providers (CSPs – firms like Google and Yahoo). Tapping data traffic at an ISP is harder than voice used to be; there are many obstacles, such as transient IP addresses given to most customers and the increasingly distributed nature of traffic. In the old days (say 2002), an ISP might have had modem racks, and a LAN where a wiretap device could be located; nowadays many customers come in via DSL, and providers use switched networks that often don't have any obvious place to put a tap. The ISP simply became the natural control point.

Many countries now have laws requiring ISPs to help, and the usual way to do it at a large ISP is to have equipment already installed that will send copies of packets of interest (or NetFlow records) to a separate classified network. The FBI's system, DCSNet, is very slick – allowing agents point-and-click access to traffic and content from participating phone companies [1765]. (Information about which companies have been brought onboard is closely held, but smart bad guys use small ISPs.) And things often go wrong because the police don't understand ISPs; they subpoena the wrong things, or provide inaccurate timestamps so that the wrong user is associated with an IP address. For an analysis of failure modes, see Clayton [444].

The smartphone revolution has changed the natural control point from the ISP to the CSP. A modern criminal might get up, check his messages on Gmail or WhatsApp using his home wifi, then get on a bus into town and do the same using his 3G or 4G data connection, then perhaps use wifi at a Starbucks or a public library ... and in none of these cases does a wiretap at the ISP tell anything much beyond the fact that a particular service has been used. As the traffic to that communications service is encrypted, the police have to serve paperwork on the service to get anywhere. This is what led the FBI to set up the Prism system, whereby intelligence agencies can get customer data from Google, Yahoo, Apple, Microsoft, Facebook and others at the press of a button. It is also what led the UK, in its 2016 Investigatory Powers Act, to grant itself the power to order any company to do anything it physically can in order to assist law-enforcement of intelligence investigations. More and more countries are passing such laws, which put the service providers in conflict with other countries' laws.

One big flashpoint is the tension between EU privacy and data-protection law, which requires due process for privacy infringement, and US surveillance law which demands that US firms hand over foreigners' data on demand. But there are many more. Google left China rather than give the police unfettered access to all user data. And as a senior Google executive told me, 'If a family court in India orders you to hand over the Gmail of someone who lives in Canada and imposes a lifelong secrecy order, how do you simultaneously employ people in India, and give believable assurances of privacy to people in Canada?'

Finally, there are lots of issues around the much richer data available from CSPs like Facebook, which not only collect highly sensitive data at scale but enable sensitive facts to be deduced from traffic data in ways that were not previously possible. As I discussed in section 11.2.6, Michal Kosinski and colleagues figured out that he could tell whether someone was straight or gay from four Facebook likes [1088], after which some of his colleagues collected Facebook data at industrial scale and weaponised it for political campaigning, leading to the Cambridge Analytica scandal when it was discovered that social-network data had been used in 2016 to intervene unlawfully and at scale in both the Brexit referendum in the UK and the presidential election in the USA. What sort of controls should there be on the use of social analysis methods by law-enforcement and intelligence agencies, or for that matter by public-health agencies? (We'll return to the broader issues raised by these techniques later.)

26.2.6 The Five Eyes' system of systems

We discussed the technical meat of the Snowden revelations in 2.2.1. These did not come entirely from the blue; there had been many previous disclosures about signals intelligence collection. David Kahn's influential history of cryptography sets the scene by describing what happened up till the start of World War II [1003]. An anonymous former NSA analyst, later identified as Perry Fellwock, then revealed the scale of NSA operations in 1972 [674]. "Information gathering by NSA is complete," he wrote. "It covers what foreign governments are doing, planning to do, have done in the past: what armies are moving where and against whom; what air forces are moving where, and what their capabilities are. There really aren't any limits on NSA. Its mission goes all the way from calling in the B-52s in Vietnam to monitoring every aspect of the Soviet space program."

While Fellwock's motive was opposition to Vietnam, the next major whistleblower was a British wartime codebreaker, Frederick Winterbotham, who wanted to write a memoir of his wartime achievements and, as he was dying, was not bothered about prosecution. In 1974, he revealed the Allies' success in breaking German and Japanese cipher systems during that war [2034], which led to many further books on World War II signals intelligence (Sigint) [440, 1004, 2011]. Thereafter there was a slow drip of revelations by investigative journalists, quite a few of whose sources were concerned about corruption or abuse of the facilities by officials monitoring targets they should not have, such as domestic political groups. Whistleblower Peg Newsham revealed that the NSA had illegally tapped a phone call made by Senator Strom Thurmond [375, 376]. James Bamford pieced together a lot of information on the NSA from open sources and by talking to former employees [161], while New Zealand journalist Nicky Hager [850] dug up a lot of information following the New Zealand intelligence community's failure to obey an order from their Prime Minister to downgrade intelligence cooperation with the USA.

The first high-profile exposé of US economic espionage was made in a 1999 report to the European parliament [644], which was concerned that after the collapse of the USSR, European Union member nations were becoming the NSA's main targets [379]. By then, people who paid attention were aware that data, faxes and phone calls get collected at a large number of nodes ranging from where international communications cables land in friendly countries (or are tapped clandestinely underwater), through observation of traffic to and from commercial communications satellites and special Sigint satellites that collect traffic over hostile countries, to listening posts in member states' embassies [644].

During the Cold War, much of the effort was military, aimed at understanding Soviet radar and communications, and at gaining a decisive advantage in location, jamming and deception. Without an ability to conduct electronic warfare, a modern state is not competitive in air or naval warfare or even in tank battles. Most of the personnel at NSA were military, and its director has always been a serving general or admiral. A lot of effort still goes into understanding the signals of potential adversaries.

One might question whether this huge worldwide system of systems still gives value for money. Politicians have justified its budgets since 9/11 in terms of terrorism, and there have indeed been some successes against terrorists – notably the arrest of an alleged 9/11 terrorism planner after he used a mobile phone SIM from a batch bought by a known terrorist in

Switzerland. But electronic warfare against insurgents in Iraq proved less productive, as I discussed in Chapter 19. And it's clear that more effort should have been put into human intelligence. In an article published just before 9/11, an analyst wrote "The CIA probably doesn't have a single truly qualified Arabic-speaking officer of Middle Eastern background who can play a believable Muslim fundamentalist who would volunteer to spend years of his life with shitty food and no women in the mountains of Afghanistan. For Christ's sake, most case officers live in the suburbs of Virginia. We don't do that kind of thing." Another put it even more bluntly: "Operations that include diarrhea as a way of life don't happen" [758]. Nearly two decades after the start of the wars in Afghanistan, Iraq, Syria and North Africa, we haven't trained enough soldiers to carry a basic conversation in Arabic, Dari or Pushtu.

Although other countries may complain about US Sigint collection, for them to moralise about it is hypocritical. Other countries also run intelligence operations, and are often much more aggressive in conducting economic and other non-military espionage. The real difference between the Five Eyes countries and the others is that no-one else has built the 'system-of-systems'. Indeed, there are network effects in Sigint as elsewhere: while non-aligned countries like India were happy to buy their warplanes from the old Soviet Union, they nowadays tend to share intelligence with the USA, as it has a much bigger network than the Russians or the Chinese [85]. The Snowden documents reveal NSA information sharing with over 60 other countries.

My own view is that, like the armed forces of which they are often a part, signals intelligence agencies are both necessary but potentially dangerous. An army can be a good servant but is likely to be an intolerable master. The issue is not whether such resources should exist, but how they are held accountable. In the USA, hearings by Senator Church in 1975 detailed a number of abuses such as the illegal monitoring of US citizens [425]; this led to FISA. The Snowden revelations in turn led to action by all three arms of the US government, albeit of limited effect[3].

The structural problems remain, though. The NSA is responsible for both attack and defence, and defence tends to play second fiddle. Imagine that you're the Director of the NSA, and one of your engineers comes to you with a cool new zero-day exploit of Windows. Do you tell Microsoft, thereby protecting 300m Americans, or do you keep it secret, so you can attack 1.2bn Chinese? Stated in those terms, the answer is obvious. This *equities issue* is the one issue on which President Obama declined to follow the advice of the NSA review group. The group recommended that in almost all cases, vulnerabilities

[3]President Obama set up the NSA review group and accepted most of its recommendations, but his work was undone by President Trump. Congress passed the USA Freedom Act, which imposed some limits on the bulk collection of communications data on US residents by US agencies. Chief Justice Roberts made some changes to the FISA court.

that come to the attention of the NSA should be reported to vendors for fixing; the NSA prefers to stockpile them instead. Indeed it has a $100m a year budget for Bullrun, a program to insert them into commercial products by means fair and foul, as discussed in section 2.2.1.5. And when bugs occur naturally, the NSA uses them where it can; it was reported in 2014, for example, that the hugely disruptive Heartbleed bug in SSL had been exploited by the NSA for two years before it was discovered independently and fixed [2068].

In some countries things are cleaner: in both France and Germany, there are separate agencies for attack and defence. But in most countries, the oversight of intelligence isn't even discussed. In the UK, it's only the European courts that forced the government to admit to the scale of surveillance, and to legislate some controls on it. New cases continually highlight excessive collection, by both electronic and human methods. In 2019, the European Court of Human Rights ordered the UK police to delete from its 'extremism' database the records of some 60 demonstrations attended by John Catt, a 94-year-old protester with no criminal record – a verdict applauded even in the conservative press [2028].

That is the high-level picture of how surveillance has evolved over the past few decades. Another aspect is scale. Cross-border bandwidth increased from 11Tbit/sec in 2007, when the systems described by Ed Snowden were being built, to 704Tbit/sec in 2017; this firehose creates yet more pressure for the agencies to collect traffic from CSPs or other edge systems rather than from ISPs or the backbone, as they can target the collection much better. The resulting pressure for government access to data is remarkably similar to the pressure for government access to cryptographic keys in the 1990s, which was a formative experience for many governments (as well as for industry and civil society) on issues of surveillance and technology policy.

26.2.7 The crypto wars

Technology policy during the 1990s was dominated by acrimonious debates about *key escrow* – the Clinton administration doctrine that anyone who encrypted data should give the government a copy of the key, so that the civilian use of cryptography would not interfere with intelligence gathering.

I was involved as one of the academics whose research and teaching was under threat from the proposed controls, and in 1998 I was one of the people who set up the Foundation for Information Policy Research, a UK Internet-policy think-tank, which wrestled with crypto policy, export policy, copyright and related issues. In 2003 we set up European Digital Rights (EDRi) along with other European NGOs to campaign on these issues in Brussels. In the next few sections I'll lay out a brief background to the crypto wars, and then discuss how governments have failed to get to grips with the Internet.

26.2.7.1 The back story to crypto policy

Many countries made laws in the mid-19th century banning the use of cryptography in telegraph messages, and some even forbade the use of languages other than those on an approved list. Prussia went as far as to require telegraph operators to keep copies of the plaintext of all messages [1821]. Sometimes the excuse was law enforcement – preventing people obtaining horse race results or stock prices in advance of the 'official' transmissions – but the real concern was national security. This pattern was to repeat itself again in the twentieth century.

After the immense success that the Allies had during World War II with signals intelligence, the UK and US governments agreed in 1946 to continue intelligence cooperation. This 'BRUSA agreement' was joined by Canada in 1948 and by Australia and New Zealand in 1956, giving the 'Five Eyes' partnership in signals intelligence. They decided to prevent the proliferation of cryptographic equipment and know-how. Until the 1980s, about the only vendors were companies selling into government markets, who could mostly be trusted not to do anything overseas which would upset their major customers at home. This was reinforced by export controls that were operated "in as covert a way as possible, with the minimum of open guidance to anyone wanting, for example, an export licence. Most things were done in behind-the-scenes negotiation between the officials and a trusted representative of the would-be exporter." [207]

In these negotiations, the authorities would try to steer applicants towards using weak cryptography where possible, and where confronted with a more sophisticated user would try to see to it that systems had a 'back door' (known in the trade as a *red thread*) which would give access to traffic. Anyone who tried to sell decent crypto domestically could be dissuaded by various means. If they were a large company, they would be threatened with loss of government contracts; if a small one, they could be strangled with red tape as they tried to get licenses and product approvals. The upshot was that most governments used weak crypto, and the NSA could break it with ease. But this wasn't the whole story, as we learned in the Bühler case.

Hans Bühler worked as a salesman for the Swiss firm Crypto AG, a leading supplier of cryptographic equipment to governments without the technical capability to build their own. He was arrested in 1992 in Iran when the authorities figured out that the Iraqis had been reading their traffic during the Iran-Iraq war; they accused him of selling them cipher machines which had been tampered with so that the NSA could get at the plaintext. Crypto AG paid 1.44 billion Rials – then about a million US dollars – to bail him, but fired him once he got back to Switzerland. Bühler then alleged on Swiss radio and TV that the firm was secretly controlled by the German intelligence services and that it had been involved in intelligence work for years [337]. One story was that when the founder of Crypto AG, Boris Hagelin, decided to retire, he contacted William Friedman, the NSA's chief scientist; Friedman was a friend, and the US government had been a big customer, buying Hagelin machines during World War II. Hagelin sold his company secretly to the NSA, which had it secretly controlled by German nominees. The equipment it sold was routinely red threaded [1207]. Crypto AG's line was that these allegations were concocted by the NSA to undermine the company, as it was one of the third world's few sources of cryptographic equipment. Bühler's story was told in a book by Res Strehle [1841]. It is now known that Crypto AG was run by the German Bundesnachrichtendienst in collaboration with the agencies of Denmark, Sweden, the Netherlands and France, and with the CIA. The backdoors in their equipment were used, for example, by the UK to decipher Argentinian communications during the Falklands war in 1982 – the outcome of which was "materially influenced, if not decided" by this operation [972].

26.2.7.2 DES and crypto research

Despite the poor quality of early banking cryptosystems, the NSA still worried in the seventies that the banking sector might evolve good algorithms that would escape into the wild. Many countries were still using rotor machines or other equipment that could be broken using the techniques developed in World War II. How could the banking industry's thirst for a respectable cipher be slaked, not just in the USA but overseas, without this cipher being adopted by foreign governments and driving up the costs of intelligence collection?

The solution was the Data Encryption Standard (DES). At the time, as I mentioned in section 5.4.3.2, there was controversy about whether 56 bits were enough. We now know that this was deliberate. The NSA did not at the time have the machinery to do DES keysearch; that came later. But by giving the impression that they did, they managed to stop most foreign governments adopting it. The rotor machines continued in service, in many cases reimplemented using microcontrollers; Crypto AG and other biddable vendors continued to thrive; and the traffic continued to be harvested. Foreigners who encrypted their important data with such ciphers merely marked that traffic as worth collecting.

A second initiative was to undermine academic research in cryptology. In the 1970s this was done directly by harassing the people involved; by the 1980s it had evolved into a subtler strategy. While the Pentagon funded research into computer security, it tried to divert crypto research into theoretical channels and claimed that more practical published research work was all old hat: 'we did all that stuff thirty years ago; why should the taxpayer pay for it twice?' The insinuation that DES may have had a 'trapdoor' inserted into it fitted well with this playbook. A side effect we still live with is that the crypto and computer security communities got separated from each other in the early 1980s as the NSA worked to sideline one and build up the other.

By the mid-1990s this line had become exhausted. Agency blunders in the design of key escrow systems taught us that they were not way ahead of the rest of us in cryptology, and in any case the fight moved to a different battlefield.

26.2.7.3 *Crypto War 1 – the Clipper chip*

Crypto policy went mainstream in 1993 with the launch of the Clipper chip. After AT&T proposed the introduction to the US domestic market of an encrypting telephone that would have used Diffie-Hellman key exchange and triple-DES to protect traffic, the NSA persuaded the Clinton administration to promote a different standard. This would use a classified block cipher, Skipjack, implemented in a tamper-resistant chip and with a protocol that made a spare ('escrowed') key available to the agencies to decrypt traffic. This 'Escrowed Encryption Standard' led to a public outcry; an AT&T computer scientist, Matt Blaze, found a protocol vulnerability in Clipper that defeated the escrow mechanism [259] and the proposal was withdrawn.

Several more attempts were made through the 1990s to promote the use of cryptography with government access to keys. Key escrow acquired various new names, such as *key recovery*; certification authorities which kept copies of their clients' private decryption keys became known as *Trusted Third Parties* (TTPs) – somewhat emphasising the NSA definition of a trusted component as one which can break security. In the UK, a key escrow protocol was introduced for the public sector [982], and this was used to try to get the private sector to adopt it as well; but we found a number of vulnerabilities in it too [116].

The pro-escrow people said that as crypto provided confidentiality, and confidentiality could help criminals, there needed to be some way to defeat it. The anti-escrow lobby started out by arguing that since crypto was necessary for privacy, there must not be a way to defeat it. Reality was more complex [57]. Most crypto applications are about authentication rather than confidentiality, to help the police rather than hindering them. As for criminals, they mainly require unobtrusive communications – and back in the 1990s, encrypting a phone call was a good way to bring attention to yourself. If you wanted to be unobtrusive, it was better to just buy a prepaid phone. As for privacy, most violations result from abuse of authorized access by insiders. Finally, a much more severe problem for policemen is to find acceptable evidence, for which decent authentication can also be helpful.

The debate got rapidly tangled up with export controls on weapons, the means by which cryptography was traditionally controlled. US software firms were not allowed to export products containing cryptography that was too hard to break, and this was also used as a means of controlling cryptography at home; Americans who put cryptography software on their websites were liable to prosecution for making it available to foreigners. A US software author, Phil Zimmermann, was hauled up before a grand jury for arms trafficking after a program he wrote – PGP – 'escaped' on to the Internet. He became a folk hero and made a fortune as his product grabbed market leadership. Others, such as Bruce Schneier, printed cryptographic algorithms in books as a way of exercising their constitutional right to free speech [1670]. The conflict became international: the US State Department tried hard to persuade other countries to control cryptography too (I'll go into more detail in Section 26.2.8 on export control below). Imposing American policy worldwide became one of the missions of Vice-President Gore (a reason why many tech people contributed to the Bush campaign in 2000).

The apparent resolution of Crypto War 1 came in two phases. In 1999, the European Union's Commissioner for the Single Market, Martin Bangemann, pushed through the Electronic Signature Directive, a law that banned the compulsory licensing of certification authorities. This undermined the demand from the NSA and GCHQ that all private signing keys should be escrowed – not just decryption keys, but also signature verification keys. The Germans objected that escrowing signature keys would let the agencies not just read messages, but forge them too, undermining trust in electronic commerce and authentication generally. When the EU followed the German line rather than the British one, it followed that individuals could either use their signature keypairs for encryption, or to authenticate Diffie-Hellman keys and use those for encryption. European officials mollified the US administration by passing an export control regulation that extended EU export controls from physical goods to intangibles such as software, so that European firms faced the same export controls on cryptographic software as US firms [650].

Second, in 2000 when Al Gore was running for president and wanted to get Silicon Valley onside, the administration decided to call a halt. Meetings were held at the FBI offices in Quantico between the agencies and the tech majors, leading to an agreement that the agencies would no longer push for vulnerabilites to be inserted into products and systems. Instead, the agencies would exploit the many naturally-occurring vulnerabilities, and the NSA inveigled itself into the patching cycle. When a software vulnerability is reported to the CERT ecosystem, it finds its way to the CERT at the Software Engineering Institute in Pittsburgh, which is sponsored by the DoD. This shares it with the NSA and also reports it to the vendor for fixing. The patch cycle typically takes a month or two – sometimes more, if coordinating vulnerability disclosure and product testing is hard – giving the NSA a window to exploit the bug.

Those of us who were active in digital rights in Europe were generally pleased at the e-signature directive but appalled at intangible export controls; we set up European Digital Rights (EDRi) in 2003 to create a lobbying presence in Brussels, backed by dozens of individual NGOs in European countries. We thought that the surveillance issue had been largely settled and that future fight would be over issues like software copyright and data protection. In 2013, Ed Snowden showed us how wrong we'd been. The NSA and the other agencies had simply gone underground, and had been running a covert program called Bullrun with a budget of $100m a year to undermine commercial cryptography – interfering with standards, implementations, supply chains and much else. But that came later.

One of the engineering lessons from Crypto War 1 is that doing key escrow properly is hard. Making two-party security protocols into three-party protocols increases the complexity and the risk of serious design errors, and centralizing the escrow databases creates huge targets; I discussed this in a paper 'The Risks of Key Recovery, Key Escrow, and Trusted Third-Party Encryption' that I wrote with ten other cryptographers and that became the most highly-cited reference on the subject [4]. Where escrow is required it's usually better done with simple local mechanisms. In one army, every officer must write down his passphrase on a piece of paper, put it in an envelope, stamp it 'Secret' and hand it to his commanding officer, who puts it in his office safe. That way the keys are kept in the same place as the documents whose electronic versions they protect, and there's no central database for an airplane to bomb or a spy to steal. But trying to automate this and scale it up leads to trouble. The UK government idea was that everyone's private key would be generated from their email address using a super-secret master key generated by GCHQ and kept in equipment controlled by their departmental security officer, so that both the department and GCHQ could decrypt traffic if they had to. The result was a clunky system that couldn't easily deal with the frequent changes of name as government departments were reorganised and renamed. The demand for customised central control leads to vast IT projects that run years late and millions over budget, or just never work at all. Problems providing officials with working email systems led to them using private accounts instead, and eventually the Cameron government more or less gave up; routine email in the Cabinet Office (the stuff below Top Secret) started to use a branded version of G Suite, the paid-for version of Gmail. By the coronavirus pandemic, the cabinet was using Zoom for meetings, despite known insecurities; there did in fact exist a secure videoconferencing system, but as it was classified, ministers weren't allowed to take it home.

Crypto War 1 left a significant legacy, with both technical and political aspects. On the technical front, the mandated use of weak cryptography made DVDs easy to rip, made cars easier to steal, made Bluetooth easy to hack, and made millions of building locks easy to defeat – including the building where I work[4]. The business models of firms selling hotel door locks have

[4]See section 4.3.1 for car theft, section 5.7.2.2 for attacks on Bluetooth and section 13.2.5 for attacks on door locks.

been undermined as they can no longer lock in their customers to buying their proprietary card stock. As for policy, authoritarian governments such as Russia's passed harsh crypto control laws; Britain went from a laissez-faire policy under John Major in the mid-1990s to Tony Blair's Regulation of Investigatory Powers (RIP) Act of 2000 which enables the police to demand that I hand over a key or password in my possession, and the Export Control Act of 2002 instructs me to get an export licence if I send any cryptographic software outside Europe that uses keys longer than 56 bits[5]. I'll return to export control later.

26.2.7.4 Crypto War 2 – going spotty

The 2013 disclosures by Edward Snowden have led to a resumption, after a fashion, of the crypto wars. In fact, the NSA and its partners never stopped, but just took their 'crypto enabling' activities underground. They were not only harvesting everyone's SMSes and email from the backbone, and getting content from major service providers using warrants at much larger scale than we imagined. They were hacking allies, as when GCHQ hacked Belgacom [734] – an amazing story about how one EU member state attacked the critical infrastructure of another, and went on to wiretap the European Commission. Another example was New Zealand's contribution to the Five Eyes which includes spying on small neighbours such as Samoa, Tonga and French Polynesia [851]. The NSA had lied to Congress, for example about collecting call data records on US citizens. They were bypassing legal controls: GCHQ could get my Gmail from Google using Prism, as I'm not a US resident, and we'd always suspected this, but it had always been denied. They were also getting it from major services by covert means – by tapping the communications between Google's data centres. In 2015, a UK court ruled that for the UK to obtain mass surveillance data on UK residents via the USA had been unlawful, as it contravened the European Convention on Human Rights [305].

All this had a real effect on behaviour. First, the service providers cleaned up their act; Google had been starting to encrypt its internal network but accelerated the program to ensure that the only way to get their users' data was through the front door, by a warrant. Microsoft and Yahoo followed. Second, most messaging systems offered end-to-end encryption to reassure users (and also to save system operators the cost of complying with warrants). Third, the policy conversation started tackling more realistic problems, such as jurisdiction; given that most of the material of interest to the world's police

[5]Thankfully, the person who does the exporting is the person who clicks on the link – so if you're in Iran, you would be a very bad person if you clicked on the link on my website to download the Serpent block cipher. You have been warned!

forces is kept on servers belonging to US companies, who can get access to it, and on what terms? While countries like the UK worked at getting faster access to US data, others went for localisation. India had already insisted that all private Blackberry users keep their messages on servers in India; China banned Facebook and Google to ensure its residents used Chinese systems instead; and many countries have passed data-localisation laws to ensure that some kinds of personal data are kept within the jurisdiction. Most countries in Africa, for example, require financial data to be kept locally; I'll discuss the European Union's data-protection regulation and its interaction with US firms later.

Although the agencies no longer ask for access to all keys, the escrow arguments came back in new forms. GCHQ, along with the FBI, started to argue that providers of messaging services such as WhatsApp and FaceTime should be compelled to build in a facility whereby law enforcement can be added as a silent conference-call party (so-called 'ghost users') when they get a warrant. FBI Director James Comey led the charge along with GCHQ Director Robert Hannigan, who accused Facebook in 2014 of helping terrorism [1569] by requiring him to go through the procedures of the UK/USA Mutual Legal Assistance Treaty to get information. Facebook's response was that they were just obeying US and EU privacy laws; the relevant service centre was in Ireland, not the UK, so Hannigan couldn't simply use UK law to force them to help him. Hannigan and Comey were supported by UK Prime Minister David Cameron.

My cryptographer colleagues and I reconvened to write an update of our analysis, 'Keys Under Doormats', which explains how many of the problems with 1990s key escrow proposals simply come back in a new form if you mandate government access to data instead of to keys [5]. The effects if anything are likely to be worse, as we are now much more dependent on the Internet than in the 1990s. It would be a bad thing if governments were to force designers to abandon security mechanisms such as forward secrecy, authenticated encryption and strict transport security that have become widespread in the meantime; and because of the many interactions between systems that have been secured in different ways, the risk of mandated vulnerabilities having serious and unanticipated side-effects is now much greater. Building in exceptional access also creates huge targets in the wiretapping systems themselves, and extra complexity that can lead to further security failures. Indeed, the 2010 Chinese hack of Google's wiretapping system suggests that even the best-run companies cannot keep out state actors all the time – and that hack was aimed at the systems Google built to service wiretaps. The Chinese obviously wanted to know which of their agents in the USA was under suspicion. There are huge problems around jurisdiction. If Facebook carries a WhatsApp message from a user in France to a user in Argentina, do only these two governments get access, or does the NSA demand it too? Since Snowden, everyone knows they will, and nobody believes they could keep such a capability under control. Any demand for such systems raises a lot of questions of both law and engineering, some of which we spelled out in our analysis [5].

The next move came in 2016 when the FBI tried to force Apple to produce an operating system 'upgrade' for the iPhone that would unlock it, using as their test case a locked iPhone that had been used in a terrorist attack in San Bernardino. Apple's Tim Cook had resisted pressure to install back doors before, and saw the case as a serious threat to Apple users' privacy and to the Apple brand; he fought the FBI in court [1008]. Comey testified that the agency would not be able to get at such vital information without assistance from Apple. The case divided American opinion, with Republicans supporting the FBI (and candidate Trump, as he then was, calling for a boycott of Apple) while most Democrats, and the tech industry, supported Tim Cook. My colleague Sergei Skorobogatov worked out how to defeat the iPhone PIN retry counter [1781], as I discussed in 3.4.8.3. As for the FBI, they bought a commercial iPhone exploit from an Israeli firm, Cellebrite, and dropped the case.

In the chaos following the Brexit referendum, the new UK Prime Minister Theresa May (who as home secretary had been a surveillance hawk) pushed the Investigatory Powers Act through UK parliament. This law grants ministers the power to order any company to do anything physically possible to facilitate signals intelligence collection, and to keep quiet about it forever. In 2018, two senior GCHQ mathematicians, Ian Levy and Crispin Robinson, suggested how government access to messaging services might work [1155]; their idea was that when GCHQ presented Facebook with a warrant, they would add a GCHQ public key quietly to the target's keyring, so that they'd become a silent conference party to all his calls. My colleague Bruce Schneier responded in detail [1681]: the fact that such an approach would work with some systems (it would work with WhatsApp but not with Signal) is actually a bug that's being fixed by better transparency mechanisms, and mandating it would prevent the bugfix. In any case, such an access power is excessive; intelligence agencies should not have it because of their history of abusing such access, or simply losing it. In section 2.2.3 I described how the NSA tool EternalBlue was stolen and used by the Russians against Ukraine in the NotPetya worm, causing billions of dollars of collateral damage to US firms in 2016; by 2019 it was being used in ransomware that shut down email and other services in the city of Baltimore, just up the road from the NSA [1512].

In 2019, Mark Zuckerberg announced that Facebook will shift its emphasis from public posts to ephemeral, end-to-end encrypted messaging by unifying WhatsApp with Instagram and Messenger [1441]. Some cynics suggested that this would make it easier to hide fake news and hate speech from both the media and the law, and cut the costs of moderation as well as the PR damage from scandals; others that it was to prevent either the EU or the US government from ordering the breakup of the company [1915, 1935]. In

October, the US Attorney General joined the UK Home Secretary and the Australian Minister for Home Affairs in asking Zuck to think again, highlighting the risk of 'a single platform that would combine inaccessible messaging services with open profiles, providing unique routes for prospective offenders to identify and groom our children'. Time will tell whether Zuck can do abuse detection using metadata alone; we'll consider moderation and other forms of censorship below.

26.2.8 Export control

One spillover from the crypto wars was the imposition of more uniform export controls than before, particularly in Europe; here's a quick summary. International arms control agreements (COCOM and Wassenaar) bind most governments to implement export controls on cryptographic equipment, and the latter is implemented in the European Union by an EU regulation compelling Member States to control and license the export of *dual-use goods* – goods which have both civilian and military uses. Cryptanalytic products fall under the military regime, whereas software that just uses cryptography for protection falls under dual-use.

National policy used to vary more, and during the 1990s European researchers like me could write crypto software and publish it on our web pages, while our US colleagues were prevented from doing that by the US International Trafficking in Arms Regulations (ITAR). US firms complained and in 1997, Vice-President Al Gore persuaded the incoming British Prime Minister Tony Blair to extend export control to intangibles. He initially tried to sell this to the UK parliament, but the relevant committees weren't keen, so Blair had it pushed through as an EU regulation and his ministers then happily told us "Our hands are tied – we have to do this as it's EU law". (Such policy laundering, as it's called, has been endemic in Europe and is one of the factors that fuelled the movement to get Britain to leave the EU.)

Tens of thousands of academics and small software companies are now breaking the law without knowing it by exporting products (or even by giving away software) containing crypto with keys longer than 56 bits. There are open general export licenses (OGELs) that you can use, but you have to understand the mechanisms and file the paperwork. And it's not just cryptography. For example, in our hardware tamper-resistance research we use an ion beam workstation, which is like an electron microscope only it fires metal ions at the target rather than electrons, so you can modify a chip by cutting tracks and adding new ones. Like cryptography, this is on the dual-use list. In the old days, we had to get an export licence when we bought one, and another seven years later when we threw it in a skip. Now, we're in theory supposed to get a licence whenever we share a script we've written for the machine with someone who isn't an EU citizen or resident. The practical outcome is that tens of thousands of scientists happily break the law – which can make them vulnerable to pressure from the agencies. The number has surely shot up now that the pandemic has led to many people working from home, often from overseas, and that the UK has left the EU. How I deal with such issues personally is to be very careful that all such software and scripts are on my website, which enables me to use a public-domain exemption, and rely on the fact that it's the person who clicks on the link who performs the export.

The civil war in Syria exposed the dark side of export control in 2012. People from several digital rights NGOs lobbied the UK government, asking it to use export control law to prevent a UK company selling bulk surveillance equipment to the Assad government. UK NGOs argued that mass surveillance equipment should not just be on the dual-use list but the military list, that the intelligence community includes bulk collection in 'cryptanalysis' which is military; and its sale to a government involved in wholesale abuses was against human-rights law. The lady from GCHQ fought this tooth and nail; the sales were going through an arms dealer in Dubai so how could the vendor be sure of the destination; they came from a German subsidiary so it was the Germans' problem; Wassennaar was a forum for military issues rather than human rights ones; and even that mass surveillance is also used for marketing. The real issue was that GCHQ feared that UK troops would end up in Syria and they were determined that if President Assad was going to have black boxes on his network, they should be British black boxes rather than Ukrainian ones. Eventually the German chancellor Angela Merkel admitted in public that she had decided to allow surveillance equipment to be sold to Syria, and that it was one of the hardest decisions she'd taken. In August 2013, the UK Parliament voted against authorising military action in Syria, and President Obama decided not to go it alone. In due course, the export control issue was referred to European agencies and quietly forgotten.

One unpleasant side-effect of this fight lingers: a system of vetting foreign students at UK universities. GCHQ was opposed to Chinese students studying cryptography, and the security service briefed that an Iraqi woman who'd got a PhD in Britain had gone on to direct part of Saddam Hussein's alleged research programme into weapons of mass destruction. Briefers raised a scare about people from countries on the terrorist list, such as Sudan, being allowed to study medicine. Tony Minson, a professor of virology and Cambridge colleague, argued that nature can do much nastier things than people can, and if there were no competent public-health people in Khartoum when something like Ebola came down the Nile, we'd regret it. He was of course ignored. We got an 'Academic Technology Approval Scheme', and graduate students coming to the UK have to get an 'ATAS clearance' to get a visa.

26.3 Terrorism

Talk about terrorism has driven a lot of policy around surveillance and privacy, especially since 9/11. The tide is starting to recede, but it's still a card that politicians play when they want to scare us, and the media often play along. There has been talk of cyber-terrorism; that basically hasn't happened, but there are real concerns about encrypted chat services and social media being used to groom and recruit young people to criminal organisations ranging from right-wing hate groups to violent Islamists. So what can we say about terrorism?

Political violence is nothing new; anthropologists have found that tribal warfare was endemic among early humans, as indeed it is among chimpanzees [1134]. Terror has long been used to cow subject populations – by the Maya, by the Inca, by William the Conqueror. Terrorism of the 'modern' sort also goes back centuries. Guy Fawkes tried to blow up Britain's Houses of Parliament in 1605; his successors, the Irish Republican Army, ran a number of campaigns against the UK. In the latest, from 1969–97, some three thousand people died, and the IRA even blew up a hotel where the Prime Minister, Margaret Thatcher, was staying for a party conference, killing several of her colleagues. During the Cold War, the Russians supported not just the IRA but the Baader Meinhof Gang in Germany and many others; the West armed and supported jihadists fighting the Russians in Afghanistan. Some terrorists, like Baader and Meinhof, ended up in jail, while others – such as the IRA leaders Gerry Adams and Martin McGuinness, the Irgun leader Menachem Begin, the French resistance leader Charles de Gaulle and the African anti-colonial leaders Jomo Kenyatta, Robert Mugabe and Nelson Mandela – ended up in office.

What general lessons can be drawn from this history? Well, there's good news and bad news.

26.3.1 Causes of political violence

The biggest piece of good news is that the trend in terrorist violence has been steadily downward [1352]. There were many insurgencies in the 1960s and 70s, some ethnic, some anti-colonial, and some ideological. Many were financed by the Soviet Union or its allies as proxy conflicts in the Cold War, although a handful (notably the Nicaraguan Contras and the resistance to the Soviets in Afghanistan) were financed by the West. The end of the Cold War removed the motive and the money.

The second (and related) point is that the causes of civil conflict are partly economic. An influential study by Paul Collier and Anke Hoeffler for the World Bank looked at wars from 1960-1999 to see whether they were caused largely by grievances (such as high inequality, a lack of political rights, or ethnic and religious divisions), or by greed (some rebellions are more economically viable than others) [458]. The world has plenty of grievances, but the data show that the incidence of rebellion was more determined by whether it could be sustained. (Indeed, Cicero said two thousand years ago that "Endless money forms the sinews of war.") Thus the IRA campaign got significant support from the Soviet bloc and Libya; the Tamil revolt in Sri Lanka was sustained by funds from ethnic Tamils in the USA and India; and Al-Qaida was financed by rich donors in the Gulf states. So we know one way to tackle an insurgency: cut off their money supply. It's not entirely that simple, of course; the loss of Soviet support for the ANC (and Angola and Mozambique) reduced the pressure on the last white government of South Africa but gave them the space to do a historic peace deal with Nelson Mandela.

26.3.2 The psychology of political violence

Less encouraging findings come from scholars of psychology, politics and the media. Psychology gives a lot of insight into the underlying mechanisms. I mentioned the affect heuristic in Section 3.2.5: where people rely on affect, or emotion, calculations of probability tend to be disregarded. The prospect of a happy event, such as winning the lottery, will blind most people to the long odds and the low expected return; similarly, a dreadful event, such as a terrorist attack, will make most people disregard the fact that such events are exceedingly rare [1791]. Most of the Americans who died as a result of 9/11 probably did so since then in car crashes, after deciding to drive rather than fly: the shift from flying to driving led to about 1,000 extra fatalities in the following three months alone, and about 500 a year since then [1680].

There are other effects at the border between psychology and culture. A study of the psychology of terror by Tom Pyszczynski, Sheldon Solomon and Jeff Greenberg looked at how people cope with the fear of death [1567]. They got 22 municipal court judges in Tucson, Arizona, to participate in an experiment in which they were asked to set bail for a drug-addicted prostitute. They were all given a personality questionnaire first, in which half were asked questions such as 'Please briefly describe the emotions that the thought of your own death arouses in you" to remind them that we all die one day. The judges for whom mortality had been made salient set an average bail of $455 while the control group set an average bond of $50 – a huge effect for such an experiment. Further experiments showed that the mortality-salience group had not just become mean: they were also prepared to give larger rewards to citizens who performed some public act. It turns out that when you remind people of death, it makes them adhere more strongly to their cultural norms and defend their worldview more vigorously. This helps explain why cyber-terrorism just hasn't happened. Hacking a couple of substations and turning off a town's electricity can be mighty inconvenient, but it just doesn't have the same emotional effect as a bleeding child. The media analysis confirms this; coverage is strongly correlated with fatalities, and increases by 46% for each extra dead body [1029].

The 9/11 attacks brought mortality to the forefront of people's minds, and were also an assault on symbols of national and cultural pride. It was natural that the response included religion (the highest level of church attendance since the 1950s), patriotism (in the form of a high approval rating for the President), and for some people bigotry too. It was natural that, as the memory of the attacks receded, society would repolarise because of divergent core values. Curiously, when they're reminded that they're mortal, both conservatives and liberals take a more polarised view of an anti-American essay written by a foreign student – except in experiments where they are first reminded of the Constitution, in which case conservatives defend the student's right to free speech even more vigorously than liberals do [1567].

So a national leader trying to keep a country together following an attack should constantly remind people what they're fighting for. This is what the best leaders do, from Churchill's radio broadcasts to Roosevelt's fireside chats. In more recent years, some countries have taken a bipartisan approach to terrorism – as when Germany faced the Baader-Meinhof Gang, and Britain the IRA. In others, politicians have given in to the temptation to use fearmongering to get re-elected.

A study by the University of Alabama of over 200,000 articles on the 136 different attacks in the USA between 2005 and 2016 showed that attacks by Muslims get 357% more news coverage than other terrorist attacks [1029]. Islamic extremists were labelled terrorists 78.4% of the time, whereas far-right extremists were identified as terrorists only 23.6% of the time. Political leadership does matter. Perhaps the best recent response was that of New Zealand Prime Minister Jacinda Ardern to the Christchurch shooting; she not only described it immediately as terrorism but refused to name the shooter. On the other hand, the Pittsburgh synagogue shooting was simply described as a 'wicked act of mass murder' by the US President. In each case, the media followed [1337].

What are the dynamics here, and which approaches work best?

26.3.3 The role of institutions

There's a whole academic subject – *public-choice economics* – devoted to explaining why governments act the way they do, and for which one of its founders James Buchanan won the Nobel prize in 1986. As he put it in his prize lecture, "Economists should cease proffering policy advice as if they were employed by a benevolent despot, and they should look to the structure within which political decisions are made." Much government behaviour is explained by the incentives facing individual public-sector decision makers. It's natural for officials to build empires as they're ranked by their span of control rather than by the profits they generate. Similarly, politicians maximise their chances of reelection rather than the abstract welfare of the public. Understanding their decisions requires methodological individualism – analysis of the incentives facing individual presidents, congressmen, generals, police chiefs and newspaper editors, rather than the potential gains or losses of a nation. We know it's prudent to design institutions so that their leaders' incentives are aligned with its goals – we give company managers stock options to make them act like shareholders. But this is harder in a polity. What's the equivalent for presidents and prime ministers? How is the national interest even to be defined?

Public-choice scholars argue that both markets and politics are instruments of exchange. In the former we seek to optimise our utility individually, while in the latter we do the same but using collective actions to achieve goals that we cannot attain in markets because of externalities or other failures. The political process in turn is thus prone to specific types of failure. Intergenerational bargaining is hard: it's easy for politicians to borrow money to buy votes now, and leave the bill with the next generation, who can't vote yet. But then why do some countries have much worse public debt than others? The short answer is that institutions matter. Political results depend critically on the rules and norms that constrain political action.

Although public-choice economics emerged in response to problems in public finance in the 1960s, it has some clear lessons. Constitutions matter, as they set the ground rules of the political game. So do administrative structures, as officials are self-interested agents too. In the UK, for example, the initial response to 9/11 was to increase the budget for the security service; but this hundred million pounds or so didn't offer real pork to the security-industrial complex. So all the pet projects got dusted off, and the political beauty contest was won by a national ID card, a grandiose project that in its original form would have cost £20 billion [1184]. Washington insiders remarked that a similar dynamic was involved in the decision to invade Iraq: although the 2001 invasion of Afghanistan had been successful, it had not given much of a role to the Pentagon barons who'd spent careers assembling fleets of tanks, capital ships and fighter-bombers, or much of a payoff to the defense industry either. Indeed, USAF Colonel Karen Kwiatkowski retired at the start of the Iraq war, described how intelligence assessments were politically manipulated, and later ran for Congress [1115]. (Similar things were said in the aftermath of World War I, which some blamed on the 'merchants of death' such as Sir Hiram Maxim, whose machine gun was used by both sides.)

An institution in play here is the media, whether the old-fashioned press or the social media that are taking over some of their functions. 'If it bleeds, it leads', as the saying goes; bad news sells more papers than good. The self-interest of media owners combines with that of politicians who want to get re-elected, officials who want to build empires, and vendors who want to sell security stuff. They pick up on, and amplify, the temporary blip in patriotism and the need for heroes that terrorist attacks naturally instil. Fearmongering gets politicians on the front page and helps them control the agenda. And the recommender algorithms of many social media platforms learn to promote fear and outrage, as they increase the time people spend on the platform and the number of ads they click on.

26.3.4 The democratic response

Yet people also learn over time. The worldwide reaction to 9/11 was sharp; it was more muted four years later, in July 2005, when four suicide bombers killed 52 people on London's public transport and injured about 700. The initial response of the public was gritty resignation: 'Oh, well, we knew something like this was going to happen – bad luck if you were there, but life goes on.'[6]

And as populations learn, so might political elites. John Mueller has written a history of the attitudes to terrorism of successive US administrations [1352]. Presidents Kennedy, Johnson, Nixon and Ford ignored terrorism. President Carter made a big deal of the Iran hostage crisis, and like 9/11 it gave him a huge boost in the polls at the beginning, but later it ended his presidency. His Secretary of State Cyrus Vance later admitted they should have played down the crisis rather than giving undeserved credibility to the Iranian 'students' who'd kidnapped US diplomats. President Reagan mostly ignored provocations, but succumbed to temptation over the Lebanese hostages and shipped arms to Iran to secure their release. However, once he'd distanced himself from this error, his ratings recovered quickly. In America, people got fed up with President Bush's fear-based policies and elected President Obama whose line was "9/11 is not a way to scare up votes but a challenge that should unite America and the world against the common threats of the 21st century". Much the same happened in the UK, where Margaret Thatcher was re-elected twice after treating terrorists as common criminals. Later, Tony Blair played the fear game, and his departure from office was met with a sigh of relief; his successor Gordon Brown forbade ministers from using the phrase 'war on terror', and David Cameron's government continued that. Mature voters prefer politicians who stand up to terrorists rather than using them as props in their re-election campaigns.

[6]The press went along with this for a couple of days: then there was an explosion of fearmongering. It seems that ministers needed a day or two of meetings to sort out their shopping lists and decide what they would try to shake out of Parliament.

The harshest teacher may be the coronavirus. For years, a pandemic has been at the top of Britain's risk register, yet far less was spent preparing for one than on anti-terrorist measures, many of which were ostentatious rather than effective. This misallocation of resources looks set to cost far more of us our lives than any terrorist could have dreamed of. The US and UK governments justified torture in the 2000s by talking of an al-Qaida cell stealing a nuclear bomb and detonating it in New York or London. Yet a 10 kT atomic demolition munition set off in a major city might cost 50–100,000 lives, compared with the 50–100 million who died in the 1918–19 pandemic. The rhetoric of terror puffed up the security agencies at the expense of public health, predisposing governments in America, Europe, India and Africa to disregard the lesson of SARS in 2003 – unlike the governments of China, Singapore, Taiwan and South Korea.

26.4 Censorship

I wrote in the first edition that "the 1990s debate on crypto policy is likely to be a test run for an even bigger battle, which will be over anonymity, censorship and copyright." By the second edition, I noted that "copyright law has largely stabilised", and it was during 2008 that power over content distribution shifted from the music majors and Hollywood to tech firms like Apple and Amazon. I also noted that "censorship has become a much bigger issue over the past few years". Now, a decade later, censorship is front and centre. It has two faces: state censorship, and content filtering by service companies.

Rulers have long censored books, although the invention of the printing press made their job a whole lot harder. When John Wycliffe translated the Bible into English in 1380–1, the Lollard movement he started was suppressed along with the Peasants' Revolt. But when William Tyndale had another go in 1524–5, printing let him spread the word so widely that the princes and bishops could not suppress it. They had him burned at the stake, but by then over 50,000 copies of the New Testament had been printed, and the Reformation was under way. After that upset, printers were closely licensed and controlled; things only eased up in the eighteenth century.

Censorship nowadays is done for a variety of motives. Most countries block images of child sex abuse; during the 1990s, as the dotcom boom got underway, governments started looking for some handle on the Internet, and a view arose that images of child sex abuse were about the one thing that all states could agree should be banned. In due course the 2004 Cybercrime Convention obliged signatory states to ban sexual images of under-18s. Most governments go further and block some kinds of hate speech. Britain bans websites that 'radicalise' young people by glorifying terrorism. Finally, censorship is sometimes imposed by the courts.

The invention of the Internet has made the censors' job easier in some ways and harder in others. It's easier for the authorities to order changes in material that not many people care about: for example, courts that find a newspaper guilty of libel order the offending material to be removed. Changing the historical record wasn't possible when it consisted of physical copies in libraries, and the centralisation of human knowledge in the servers of a small number of firms – from Amazon's e-book system to the servers of the major news organisations – takes us, in some sense, back to the 15th century. It's also easier for the authorities to observe the transmission of disapproved material, as they can monitor electronic communications more easily than physical packages. On the other hand, nowadays everyone can be a publisher; much of the really unpleasant material online comes from millions of individuals posting sort-of anonymously to social media, to the comment pages of newspapers, and to individuals whom they wish to harass and intimidate. Censors have learned to harness this. While a decade ago China had tens of thousands of people who took down dissident speech, now they have millions of citizen volunteers who drown it out. Once, speech was scarce, and the censors tried to silence the speaker; now it's the listener's attention that's scarce, and so different tactics work.

To tease out the issues, let's look at some contexts.

26.4.1 Censorship by authoritarian regimes

When I wrote the second edition of this book, I was cautiously optimistic that the government of China would fail in its attempts to censor all online content. However the authorities there have become steadily more effective at suppressing any forms of organisation and human solidarity outside of party control.

By 2006, observers noted that online discussion of local news events had led to the emergence of 'public opinion' that for the first time was not in thrall to media managers [1472]. China had 137 million Internet users then, including a quarter of the population in the big cities, and 'the Great Firewall of China' was already a complex system of controls giving defence in depth against a range of material, from pornography to religious material to political dissent [1471]. The defences work at three levels.

First, there are the perimeter defences. China's border routers filter on IP addresses to block access to known 'bad' sites like the Voice of America and the BBC; they also use DNS cache poisoning. Deep packet inspection at the TCP level is used to identify emails and web pages containing forbidden words such as 'Falun Gong'; such connections are torn down. Ten years ago, much of the work was done at this level. Nowadays, since most traffic is encrypted, that's not so easy. In 2020, the firewall started dropping TLS 1.3 traffic using *Encrypted Server Name Indication* (ESNI) as this stops the censor telling which subdomain the traffic's going to; this amounted to over 30% of traffic by the beginning of July [435].

Second, there are application-level defences, which now do much of the work. Nowadays some services are blocked and some aren't, depending on whether the service provider is prepared to help the regime with both surveillance and censorship. Google and Facebook are largely blocked; China has promoted Tencent, Alibaba and Baidu instead. Now that the borders that matter most are those of firms rather than of nations, the Chinese government has aligned its industrial policy with its politics. This is the big change; we never believed ten years ago that China would build an entire ecosystem of Chinese-owned online service providers to keep western influence at bay. Language provides one barrier, but there are strong technical barriers too: the perimeter defences now focus on blocking Tor and VPNs that could be used by Chinese residents to use non-approved services.

Third, there are social defences. There were already 30,000 online police a decade ago; now many more citizens have been engaged in the process, and rather than trying to block all dissident speech the strategy is to swamp it. Loyal citizens are expected to post lots of pro-regime comments and to flame anybody who criticises authority, whether local or national. A social credit system gives people positive points for such pro-social behaviour, while they can lose points for anything considered antisocial. Online monitoring is being integrated with the monitoring of physical space, such as by CCTV cameras with face recognition and emotion recognition – which is particularly aggressive in areas with rebellious minority populations, such as the Tibetans and Uighurs. Since 2014, a system in Sinkiang for 're-education' has pioneered a fusion of techniques from the western 'war on terror' and Maoist social control, leading to the internment of hundreds of thousands of Muslims on the basis of a scoring system whose inputs include whether a suspect prays regularly or has a VPN on their phone. The U.S. Congress has denounced this regime for 'crimes against humanity': dozens of the contractor companies have been placed on the sanctions list [361].

So China appears to be winning the censorship battle, using populist but authoritarian techniques. Russia's Internet is fairly open, and although the government had an ally take over the main social network, and has organised armies of trolls to shout down its opponents, the opposition politician Alexei Navalny has his own YouTube channel with millions of viewers, and attempts to censor Telegram have been met with street protests. Putin has fought back with a 'digital sovereignty' law enabling him to order ISPs to install surveillance and censorship equipment.

The Arab Spring has also been significant. This series of uprisings started in Tunisia in December 2010 after a street vendor, Mohamed Bouazizi, set himself on fire after an official confiscated his wares and humiliated him. Protests were organised using Facebook and other social media, leading to the downfall of the government, and spreading to neighbouring countries too. The government of Egypt also fell, along with those of Libya and the Yemen; in Egypt's case a Google employee, Wael Ghonim, turned Internet activist after the police beat a man to death in Alexandria on suspicion that he had video evidence of their involvement in a drug deal. The government of Syria almost fell, but fought back in a civil war that killed hundreds of thousands and displaced millions. A number of other Arab countries, such as Bahrain, suffered significant unrest and cracked down. As I write in 2020, only Tunisia has managed the transition to democracy. In Egypt, one military dictator has been replaced by another; Libya is in chaos, and Yemen, like Syria, is racked by war. The lesson drawn by the world's autocrats is that, to stay in power, they'd better study the methods used by China. Arab countries do censor the Internet (as do many of the less-developed countries) but their infrastructure is still fairly easily defeated using VPNs or Tor. They also buy in kit for both bulk surveillance and targeted work; for a description of how the UAE hired US mercenaries to set up an equivalent of the NSA, see Bing and Schectman [248].

To what extent was the Arab Spring a function of technology, and to what extent was this just marketing hype put out in 2011 by companies like Facebook and Google while things seemed to be going well? It's unclear. Some of the populations that rose up made little use of the Internet, particularly those of Libya and the Yemen; on the other hand, a revolt in Burma in 2007 was catalysed by the Internet, even though only 1% of the population had access [1473]. In the Arab world, the Qatari TV station Al-Jazeera may have done more work than the Internet, by showing news videos of uprisings elsewhere in the region.

26.4.2 Filtering, hate speech and radicalisation

Democracies' laws on hate speech vary widely. At one end, the USA has constitutional protection for free speech; so do France and Germany. But interpretations differ. France and Germany both prohibit the sale of Nazi memorabilia, and hate speech ('Volksverhetzung') has been a crime in Germany for decades. In January 2018 the authorities started enforcing it against online service providers, with the threat of a fine of €50m if any service provider with more than 2m customers doesn't take down any such material within 24 hours. Whatever the service companies say about the cost of taking down bad stuff, the German example shows they can do it when they have to. Many countries now ban terrorist material and extreme violence, the definition of which is never straightforward. It might seem a good thing to ban not just beheading videos but all videos of murder, such as drug gangs shooting a customer who didn't pay his debts. But it gets complex quickly. Platforms that enforce such a policy end up deleting evidence, both of local killings and of human-rights violations overseas.

Already much of the material you put online gets filtered automatically to look for material that's forbidden by local laws, or by a platform's terms of service. Facebook's former CISO Alex Stamos described the tension between privacy and censorship as a spectrum: people expect end-to-end encrypted chat such as WhatsApp to be private rather than censored, and broadcast media to be censored rather than private, with the difficult stuff in the middle, like Facebook groups. By now, most social media are censored. The platforms vary widely; Facebook is perhaps the tightest, and bans even nudity[7]; though it is much more forgiving of hate speech from President Trump than from others, and in return appears to receive less attention on the antitrust front [1794]. Authoritarian countries are becoming more aggressive about forcing service firms to block content they deem to be illegal. For example, Facebook's service was slowed to a crawl in Vietnam in early 2020 until the company agreed to suppress dissent [1508].

Behind the AI systems that try to spot forbidden content are thousands of content moderators. Filtering is expensive, and the costs are not just financial, but human; we've seen an increasing number of news articles about the psychological toll on staff who have to spend all day looking at videos of gang murders and terrorist beheadings, animal cruelty, child abuse, and other unpleasantness [1440]. Many moderators are in less developed countries; just as we dump a lot of unpleasant refuse there, we also dump a lot of the Internet's nastiest trash [416]. It's also problematic to outsource censorship to large service monopolies. They act in a quasi-judicial manner, regulating the speech of billions of people but without the transparency and due process we expect of government decisions. The world sees them allowing abuse by the rich and powerful while ignoring the weak. Perhaps it was inevitable that firms would snuggle up to power and then try to direct political speech; this has become a factor in the backlash against the whole tech sector.

One focus of debate is section 230 of the US Communications Decency Act of 1996 (CDA) which states that 'No provider or user of an interactive computer service shall be treated as the publisher or speaker of any information provided by another information content provider' so platforms cannot be held liable for bad stuff provided by users; it also left platforms free to remove anything 'obscene, lewd, lascivious, filthy, excessively violent, harassing, or otherwise objectionable.' When it passed the CDA, Congress was concerned that firms that moderated content could be treated as publishers and held liable for all of it (including copyright infringement and libel) while firms that didn't would be treated as distributors and escape liability. How could we get a civil internet without killing innovation? Section 230 made firms like YouTube and Facebook possible, but protected sites whose business model is based on revenge

[7]Facebook bans photos of female nipples but not male ones, so dozens of naked women demonstrated in 2019 in New York holding pictures of men's nipples over their own; men and women demonstrated with pictures of female nipples [616].

porn, defamation, or getting a cut of illegal gun sales [1421]. It also enabled service firms to acquire some of the powers of states. Back then, the Internet had 10-20m users, mostly geeks; now most human activity is online, and it's not sustainable for a handful of American firms to act as censor, prosecutor and judge for 200-odd countries. As a result the CDA, and similar laws elsewhere, are starting to be trimmed: in the USA in 2018 with laws on sex trafficking and in Europe with a 2019 law on copyright [1601]. The tensions can only get worse.

When making laws to restrict speech, it's a good idea to stop and look at the historical context. Tim Wu's 'The Attention Merchants' [2052] is a history of propaganda since the 1830s when the first mass-market newspapers appeared, stuffed with grisly crime reports and adverts for patent medicines; this gave politicians their first industrial mass-market channel. Radio followed, and was used skilfully by Hitler. TV was next, and its nature was shaped by advertising; people invented quiz shows, soaps and much else to grab eyeballs. A second useful perspective is Yochai Benkler's 'Network Propaganda' which analyses the 2016 US election campaign. He traces the history of political polarisation and argues that the root cause of the outcome wasn't technology or Russian interference so much as the asymmetric media systems of right and left that have developed over the past 20 years; the left and centre-right are fact-based while the right is a propaganda feedback loop [228]. A third perspective is the critique of recommender systems by former Googler Tristan Harris: the platforms' algorithms learn that to maximise the time people spend on site, they should be fed articles that stoke fear, anxiety and outrage. A fourth comes from Sophie Zhang, who describes how Facebook left her alone to deal with governments of less-developed countries using the platform for political manipulation at scale. For a junior employee to wield such power with no oversight and little support was stressful, especially when unrest broke out in places she hadn't been able to prioritise for action. Eventually she concluded that Facebook cared more about spam than about civil wars, resigned, and spoke out [1744].

The reactions of governments to fake news are mostly ineffective. The most capable may be Finland, which has been a target of Russian propaganda since Tsarist times. Its government has been promoting critical thinking and media literacy in schools and elsewhere since 2014, making it every citizen's job to spot and counter information that's designed to sow division. In Britain we have laws designed to please tabloid newspapers rather than to push back against them. Schoolteachers and university professors are supposed to report students who seem at risk of being radicalised, and have procedures to figure out whether seminars or other talks could radicalise them; there are also laws against online material that might lead them astray. If such an approach were applied consistently it might lead to banning much of the literature produced or funded by religious institutions from Saudi Arabia [1265], but action against our largest arms export customer isn't going to happen anytime soon. White supremacists are at least as much of a threat, having murdered a member of the UK parliament during the Brexit campaign; but our government is much less keen on cracking down on them, and the people who broke the law by spending too much money on that campaign (including Russian money) did not end up in jail, but at the heart of government. In general, Internet censorship lets the government claim it's doing something, but doesn't really work well, and undermines whatever our diplomats might say about freedom of speech to the world's despots. I'd prefer to enforce existing laws on incitement to murder (and campaign finance), leave other political material in the open, let the police monitor the traffic to the worst of the sites, and train them to use the existing laws better [642]. In the longer term, the key is education, as Finland has shown.

As for targeting Muslim students, this runs directly against the criminological evidence. The few UK students who've signed up to extremist organisations have been those who experienced lack of respect socially, perhaps being rejected by their peers, were searching for identity but couldn't find it in the religion of their parents – then fell in with small groups of other disaffected youngsters. They came under the influence of radical preachers, who offered ideals, community, kinship, caring and brotherhood. The radicalisation of white boys into white supremacist groups is not hugely different. Research by Max Abrahms also shows that terrorists mostly joined their movement in a search for social solidarity; that's why they recruit from lonely young men rather than from among political activists. Their groups become institutions to which members cleave, rather than agents of change; that's why they can respond to sensible peace offers with increased violence, and indulge in fratricidal conflict with similar groups [6]. In fact, as Lydia Wilson pointed out after interviewing large numbers of young people who'd gone to Syria to join Islamic State and ended up in Kurdish jails, the process whereby young men (and occasionally women) find their identity by joining terror groups or crime gangs is no different from finding identity by joining religions, sports clubs or dance bands [2026]. Zoë Quinn's more recent experience of angry online mobs during the Gamergate drama, which we discussed in section 2.5.1, draws much the same conclusion [1570]. The people who join extreme organisations in search of social solidarity need to think of themselves as the good guys. To stop them, you need to undermine that, and you can't do it by excluding them.

For all these reasons, it is unwise to model terrorist groups as rational economic actors, and just as unwise to try to prevent radicalisation on similar assumptions. The best approach is to have an environment that doesn't exclude people – one in which students get to know others from different backgrounds on the staircase in their residence, in small teaching groups, and in project groups – and with hundreds of sports and student societies to choose from, so everyone can find a gang to belong to. That's how great universities have always worked anyway.

26.5 Forensics and rules of evidence

Our last main policing topic is how information can be recovered from computers, mobile phones and other electronic devices for use in evidence. This has been getting more problematic over the past twenty years because of first, the sheer volumes of data; and second, the fact that while much of it is seized from platforms such as mobile phones and laptops, more and more of it is held on cloud services that require paperwork and often quite substantial delays. The rising costs and operational difficulties lead to more selective law enforcement, with whole categories of online harms where states rarely intervene. As a result, many bad people, from cybercriminals to creeps, bullies and extremists, operate online with near-total impunity.

26.5.1 Forensics

Computer forensics has been a growing problem for the police since at least the 1980s; by the early 2000s both the facilities and the staff training were hopelessly behind. The move of everything online during the 2010s has made matters still worse. When the police raid even a small-time drug dealer nowadays, they can get half-a-dozen mobile phones, several laptops, and gadgets such as a navigator or a Fitbit that hold his location history. The suspect may also have dozens of accounts for webmail, social-networking sites and other services. We have all sorts of clever ways of extracting information from the data – for example, you can identify which camera took a picture from the pattern noise of the CCD array [1194], and even use this to figure out which parts of a photo might have been tampered with.

The use of digital material in evidence depends, however, on both law and economics. Material has to be lawfully collected, whether with a search warrant or equivalent powers; and the forensic officer has to maintain a *chain of custody*, which means being able to satisfy a court that evidence wasn't tampered with. That means using trustworthy tools to make evidential copies of data; to document everything that's done; and to have means of dealing appropriately with any private material that's found (such as privileged lawyer-client emails, or the trade secrets of a suspect's employer). The traditional approach to computer forensics is described in standard textbooks such as Sammes and Jenkinson [1647].

Since the world moved to smartphones and cloud services, the centre of gravity has shifted to a handful of companies that sell mobile forensics tools to police and intelligence agencies. They supply kiosks to police forces that enable unskilled officers to download mobile-phone contents, and to use the tokens on them to download data from suspects' accounts in the cloud. Some police forces are working hard to get the legal issues sorted out (such as Police

Scotland, who don't use 'cloud forensics' without a warrant) but many just grab and keep all the data.

At the more sophisticated end of the trade, there's an arms race between forensics and countermeasures. Police forces used to always turn PCs off, so that hard disks could be copied for prosecution and defence lawyers. Phishing gangs exploited this by making their phishing software memory-resident, so that the evidence would self-destruct. And since laptops started to ship with decent encryption, the risk is multiplied. By 2013, when the FBI arrested Ross Ulbricht – the creator of the Silk Road underground drugs market – one agent's mission was to put his hand in the laptop to stop Ulbricht closing it, and he was ready with the right kind of power cord for it [481].

In the old days, people – and small businesses – who got caught up in a police investigation and had their computers seized could wait years to get them back, even if they were just a bystander, or if they were charged but eventually acquitted. Nowadays, people have seizure-proof offsite backup thanks to cloud services. These services also make life harder for the police where suspects' material sits on servers overseas. The fight between Facebook and GCHQ to which I referred in Section 26.2.7.4 arose when two terrorists murdered a British soldier, Lee Rigby, near Woolwich barracks in March 2013 by running him over with a car and then stabbing him. While they were at the crime scene, facing off against the police, Facebook fed the police and security services data instantly, but once the two had been shot and were in custody in hospital, requests had to go through the UK/US mutual legal assistance treaty. This involves the police filing forms at the US Embassy in London that are then considered at length in the Department of Justice in Washington. The forms are often sent back as UK police staff don't understand US law and complete them incorrectly. Even where everything goes right, it can take six weeks for the FBI to serve the paperwork on Facebook in Menlo Park, California, and collect the data. So we found we'd gone from a world in which, after a raid, the police would have your data and you wouldn't, to one in which you still have your data but the police don't – unless you cooperate, or unless you're a serious enough bad guy to be worth the time and attention of diplomats.

Since about 2017, there's been a third option: cloud forensics. What this means in practice is that your phone is hacked by the police's forensic kiosk and gives up access tokens to your email, your photos, your Facebook and your other cloud services. Some UK police forces think this is wonderful; they treat the downloaded data as 'data at rest' as if it had been found on the phone itself and keep it forever. Others consider that it can only be obtained by consent or with a further warrant. The incentives to grab cloud data are strong, but the mechanisms involved (phone hacking followed by impersonation of the user) are likely to strike most citizens as unfair. And ever more devices are now acquiring an attached cloud service and an app. Will the police investigate traffic offences in future by seizing the driver's phone and using it to download the car's logs from the manufacturer's server? This is a current policy topic in 2020: for example, the UK privacy regulator called for a statutory code of practice to be developed [960]. As it happens, courts already have some rules about what evidence can be used.

26.5.2 Admissibility of evidence

When courts were first confronted with computer evidence in the 1960s there were many concerns about its reliability. There was not just the engineering issue of whether the data were accurate, but the legal issue of whether computer-generated data were inadmissible as hearsay. Different legislatures tackled this differently. In the US, most of the law is found in the Federal Rules of Evidence where 803(6) allows computer data to be introduced as records 'made at or near the time by, or from information transmitted by, a person with knowledge, if kept in the course of a regularly conducted business activity ... unless the source of information or the method or circumstances of preparation indicate lack of trustworthiness.' The UK is similar, and the rules of electronic evidence in the common-law countries (including Canada, Australia, South Africa and Singapore) are analysed by Stephen Mason [1238].

The definition of 'writing' and 'signature' is of interest, and varies by jurisdiction. In Britain, courts took the view that an email is writing just as a letter is: the essence of a signature is the signer's intent [2044, 2045]. The US approach was similarly pragmatic. In 2000, Congress enacted the Electronic Signatures in Global and National Commerce ('ESIGN') Act, which gives legal force to any 'sound, symbol, or process' by which a consumer assents to something. So pressing a telephone keypad ('press 0 to agree or 9 to terminate this transaction'), clicking a hyper-link to enter a web site, or clicking 'continue' on a software installer, the consumer consents to be bound to a contract [669]. This makes click-wrap licenses perfectly valid in America. Nonetheless, DocuSign has built a business offering digital signatures as a service for firms who want something a bit more showy.

In Europe the Electronic Signature Directive, which came into force in 2000, gave special force to an *advanced electronic signature*, which basically means a digital signature generated with a smartcard or hardware security module. Europe's smartcard industry thought this would earn them lots of money, but it languished for years. In many countries, the risk that a paper check will be forged is borne by the relying party: if someone forges a check on my account, then it's not my signature, and I have not given the bank my mandate to debit my account; so if they negligently rely on a forged signature and do so, that's their lookout. However, if I ever accept an advanced electronic signature device, then I become liable to anyone in the world for any signature that appears to have been made by this device, regardless of whether or not I actually made it! This, coupled with the facts that smartcards don't have a trusted user interface and that the PCs which most people would use as an interface are easily subverted, made such electronic signatures unattractive. Following further lobbying, Europe updated the law with the eIDAS Regulation (910/2014) which tries to improve the incentives for adoption, by requiring all organisations delivering public services to accept electronic signatures since 2018. A number of EU countries now insist that you use such a signature to file your taxes, rather than permitting it. There's a hierarchy whereby a signature can be 'advanced' or 'qualified' depending on the certification of the technology used, and a qualified electronic signature must be accepted for any purpose for which a handwritten signature was previously required. Dozens of signature creation products were duly certified and brought to market. The assurance mechanisms used to certify such products are defective in many ways, as I will discuss later in section 28.2.7.2. The European Commission duly made a reference implementation available to help governments get started with verifying all the signatures; in 2019 bugs were discovered in it that would let any citizen impersonate any other [431].

26.5.3 What goes wrong

Many things can go wrong with police investigations, and the computerised kind are no different. An old pitfall is relying on evidence extracted from the systems of one party to a dispute, without applying enough scepticism about its dependability. Recall the Munden case described in section 12.4.3. A man was falsely accused and wrongly convicted of attempted fraud after he complained of unauthorized withdrawals from his bank account. On appeal, his defence team got an order from the court that the bank open its systems to the defence expert as it had done to the prosecution. The bank refused, so the bank statements were ruled inadmissible and the case collapsed. The same has happened multiple times since then, including in two terror cases involving curfew tags which I discussed in section 14.4.

The worst failure of computer evidence of which I'm aware was Operation Ore. After the US Postal Service raided a porn site in Texas, they discovered hundreds of thousands of credit card numbers that they thought had been used to buy child sex abuse images, and some eight thousand of these were from UK cardholders. Some 3,000 homes got raided in the early 2000s, until the police finally realised that most of the cardholders were probably victims of card fraud. The vice squad used unskilled staff in their initial analysis of the seized material, and were slow to learn – because they were fixated on getting porn convictions, because they didn't have the forensic capacity to process all the seized computers quickly, because they didn't understand card fraud (they preferred to leave that to the banks) and because of politics (Prime Minister Tony Blair himself had ordered the raids). So several thousand men had their lives disrupted for months or even years, and the sad story of police bungling and cover-up is told by Duncan Campbell in [377, 378]. For some, the revelation that the police had screwed up came too late; over thirty men, faced with prosecution, killed themselves. At least one of them, Commodore David White, commander of British forces in Gibraltar, appears to have been innocent [888]. The gangsters in Indonesia and Brazil who organised and photographed the child abuse do not seem to have been seriously pursued. America handled this case much more carefully. Some 300,000 US credit card numbers were found on the same servers, but US police forces used the data for intelligence rather than evidence, identifying suspects of concern – such as people working with children – and quietly investigating them. Over a hundred convictions for actual child abuse followed.

Sometimes systems are deliberately designed to not provide evidence; an example is the policy adopted by Microsoft after embarrassing emails came out during their antitrust battles with the US government in the 1990s. The firm reacted with a policy that all emails are discarded after a fixed period of time unless someone takes positive action to save them, and many other firms followed suit. Another example is the move by service firms in the mid-2010s to adopt end-to-end encryption, so they don't have access to customer message traffic and don't have to employ hundreds of lawyers to deal with requests for it.

The biggest problem with computer forensics, though, has always been sheer lack of money. Despite all the cool tricks that intelligence agencies can use to extract information from computer systems, a county drugs squad often won't have the budget to do even basic computer forensics except for occasional big cases. They can't even afford to send every wrap of white powder off to the lab to see if it's illegal or not. In normal cases, they were only able to use digital material that was easily available, such as copies of messages on the phones of cooperative witnesses, until mobile-phone forensic kiosks came along around 2016–8 and made masses of data available from seized handsets at low marginal cost. Hence the huge pressure to use the kiosks, even before robust legal procedures could be developed. And, of course, the use of forensic tools by regular police officers with no specialist training raises the risk of miscarriages of justice. Judicial education is also an issue; few judges understand probability theory, and indeed the UK Court of Appeal has refused to accept analysis of evidence based on Bayes' theorem. Quite apart from the injustice of a court system that denies mathematics, there's the practical issue that defendants faced with computer evidence that's the result of bugs, or simply misrepresented, may have no practical way to prove their innocence[8].

[8]In one exception, the Horizon case we discussed in section 12.2.6.1, so many people were defrauded or wrongly prosecuted as a result of bugs in Post Office software that a hedge fund was prepared to bankroll a class action. But challenging the faulty computer evidence still cost millions and took years.

26.6 Privacy and data protection

Privacy and data protection are one subject on which the USA and Europe have taken separate paths. A concentrated interest (such as business wanting to use our personal information to exploit us) usually prevails over a diffuse interest (such as the desire of individuals to keep control of our personal information). Lawmakers set up regulators, but the concentrated interest will try to neuter any regulator, or even capture it outright. And Europe, for historical reasons regulates more than America does. The resulting gulf was highlighted powerfully in May 2014 when, in the USA, the Presidential Council of Advisers on Science and Technology (PCAST) published "Big Data: A Technological Perspective" [1549]. This report, whose authors included Google's Eric Schmidt and Microsoft's Craig Mundie, painted a picture of a world full of smart objects connected to cloud servers, with an ecology in which sensors reported to cloud analytics which in turn provided information to users, such as advertisers. PCAST warned that the spread of voice and gesture interfaces meant that pretty soon, every inhabited space on the planet would have microphones and cameras in it, whose output would be processed centrally for energy efficiency. They argued that privacy controls could not be imposed on the sensors, as they'll be too numerous; that they should not be imposed on the central service aggregators; and that the controls would therefore have to fall on how the information was used.

Less than two weeks later, the European Court of Justice disagreed. A Spanish lawyer, Mario Costeja Gonzàlez, had complained that searches for his name brought up two ancient press reports of an auction sale of his repossessed house. He asked the Spanish data protection authorities to order Google to stop serving these results as they were out of date and no longer relevant. Google argued that it was just reporting the contents of a newspaper. The case went to the ECJ, which found in Gonzàlez' favour, creating what the media colourfully if inaccurately called a 'right to be forgotten', later codified into Europe's General Data Protection Regulation from 2018. Google and other online service providers had to set up mechanisms whereby people could complain about search results that are 'inadequate, irrelevant or no longer relevant, or excessive in relation to the purposes for which they were processed' and have them removed. The mechanisms are contentious: Gonzàlez' results are removed from Google searches in Spain, but European regulators want them removed globally. Google's supporters claim that this would interfere with its right to free speech in the USA.

How did this rift come about?

26.6.1 European data protection

Fear of technology undermining privacy isn't a recent development. As early as 1890, Justices Warren and Brandeis warned of the threat to privacy posed by 'recent inventions and business methods' – specifically photography and investigative journalism [1992]. After banks, tax collectors and welfare agencies started using computers in the early 1960s, people started to worry about the privacy implications if all our transactions could be collated and analyzed. In Europe, business argued that only government could afford enough computers to be a serious privacy threat. This became a human-rights issue, given living memory of the Gestapo in most European countries and of communist secret police forces in the East[9].

A patchwork of data protection laws started to appear starting with the German state of Hesse in 1969. Because of the rate at which technology changes, the successful laws have been technology neutral. Their common theme was a regulator (whether at national or state level) to whom users of personal data had to report and who could instruct them to cease and desist from inappropriate processing. The practical effect was usually that the general law became expressed through a plethora of domain-specific codes of practice.

Over time, processing by multinational businesses became an issue too, and people realised that purely local or national initiatives were likely to be ineffective against them. Following a voluntary code of conduct promulgated by the OECD in 1980 [1478], data protection was entrenched by a Council of Europe convention in January 1981, which entered into force in October 1985 [475]. Although strictly speaking this convention was voluntary, many states signed up to it for fear of losing access to data-processing markets. It required certain minimum safeguards for *personal information*, which generally means any data kept on an identifiable human being, or *data subject*, such as bank account details and credit card purchasing patterns. Data subjects have the right to inspect personal data held on them, have records changed if inaccurate, understand how they're processed, and in many cases prevent them being passed on to other organizations without their consent. Almost all commercial data are covered. There are exemptions for national security, but they are not as complete as the spies would like: there was a big row when it turned out that data from SWIFT, which processes interbank payment instructions, were being copied to the Department of Homeland Security without the knowledge of data subjects; SWIFT eventually agreed to stop processing European data in the USA [1487, 1488].

The quality of implementation varied widely. In the UK, for example, Margaret Thatcher unashamedly did as little as possible to comply; a data protection body was established but starved of funds and technical expertise,

[9]In Germany, privacy is now entrenched in the constitution, and trumps even the 'war on terror'. The highest court found unconstitutional a 2001 police action to create a file on over 30,000 male students or former students from Muslim-majority countries – even though no-one was arrested as a result. It ruled that such exercises could be performed only in response to concrete threats, not as a precautionary measure [346].

and many exemptions were provided for both government and industry[10]. In Germany, which had written a right to privacy into its post-war constitution, the data protection bodies became proper law-enforcement agencies. Many other countries, such as Australia, Canada, New Zealand and Switzerland passed comparable privacy laws in the 1980s and early 1990s: some, like Switzerland, went for the German model while others, like Iceland and Ireland, followed the British one.

By the early 1990s the difference between national laws was creating barriers to trade. Some businesses avoided controls altogether by moving their data processing to the USA. So data protection was finally elevated to the status of European Union law in 1995 with a Data Protection Directive [647]. This set higher minimum standards than before, with particularly stringent controls on highly sensitive data such as health, religion, race and political affiliation. It also set out to prevent personal information being shipped to 'data havens' such as the USA in the absence of comparable controls enforced by contract or treaty.

The British implementation was again minimal, falling far short of European requirements [597]. For example, data controllers could pretend that lightly-anonymised information was no longer personal information, just so long as they themselves did not possess the auxiliary data needed to re-identify it. The Information Commissioner's Office was overwhelmed, and severely conflicted as a result of being simultaneously the public sector's adviser on privacy and the privacy enforcer; the enforcement arm was reluctant to take action against systems blessed by their colleagues in the advisory arm. Ireland's enforcement was even weaker – its industrial strategy for the past 50 years has been to attract US firms' European headquarters. So in addition to having low corporate taxes, the Dublin government located its data protection office in Portarlington, a town of less than 10,000 people, gave it only 30 staff, and did not allow it to publicise the results of investigations.

This so annoyed countries with tighter privacy laws such as France and Germany that they pushed for the General Data Protection Regulation (GDPR), which passed in 2016 and came into force in May 2018. This was the most heavily lobbied piece of European legislation ever, with over 3,000 amendments discussed in committee in the European Parliament [83]; it was helped over the line by the Snowden disclosures, although it had been cooking for some time before that[11]. GDPR took direct effect in all EU member states, removing the wriggle room for Britain or Ireland to introduce loopholes; but lobbyists got quite a few of those in the Regulation already (particularly for

[10]In one case where you'd expect there to be an exemption, there wasn't; journalists who kept notes on their laptops or PCs which identified people were formally liable to give copies of this information to the data subjects on demand.

[11]Snowden revealed some egregious abuses such as the large-scale collection of by GCHQ of Yahoo video chats in Operation Optic Nerve, including intimate video chats [14].

'research', whether of the scientific or marketing kind). The main effect on normal businesses is to force them to document all their uses of personal information and write down, in advance, what the legal basis is for each of them; it's not enough to try and figure things out once challenged. For information-intensive businesses, the implications could be more significant, and there have been fascinating disclosures of how Facebook executives lobbied to amend the regulation – effectively using the Irish prime minister, Enda Kenny, as their advocate in Brussels [1420].

Despite the many carve-outs inserted by the lobbyists, GDPR is still providing regulators with tools to push back. France fined Google €50m for failing to tell users enough about its data consent policies or give them enough control over how their information is used [1537]. The fact that consent can no longer be coerced or presumed may become a big deal, and there are many further cases in the pipeline. For example, the systems for real-time bidding for ads are clearly contrary to GDPR as they enable advertisers to target users based on sensitive personal data such as health, sexuality and political opinions, and broadcast such information to hundreds of firms that participate in auctions. The Irish authorities are trying hard to do nothing about this [1183].

26.6.2 Privacy regulation in the USA

In the USA, business has mostly managed to persuade government to leave privacy largely to 'self-regulation'. Although there's a patchwork of state and federal laws, they're sector-specific and fragmented. In general, privacy in federal government records and in communications is regulated, while business data are largely uncontrolled. The few islands of regulation include the Fair Credit Reporting Act of 1970, which governs disclosure of credit information and is broadly similar to European rules; the Video Privacy Protection Act or "Bork Bill", enacted after a Washington newspaper published Judge Robert Bork's video rental history, scuppering his nomination to the US Supreme Court; the Drivers' Privacy Protection Act, enacted to protect privacy of DMV records after the actress Rebecca Schaeffer was murdered by an obsessed fan who hired a private eye to find her address; and the Health Insurance Portability and Accountability Act which protects medical records and which I discussed in section 10.4.

Most states also have a breach disclosure law, which requires firms suffering any security failure that compromises residents' personal information to tell them about it. Several torts also provide a basis for civil action in a surprising number of circumstances; for a survey, see Daniel Solove [1804]. So if your firm has 10 million customers' personal data compromised, that might mean 10 million letters at $5 each and 3 million reissued credit cards at $10 each, even if you don't get claims from banks for actual fraud losses on those accounts. (But of 3 million accounts, a few tens of thousands would suffer some fraud each year anyway, and the banks might well sue you for all of it.) So the financial loss from a big breach can easily hit eight figures. Although most disclosed breaches are smaller – with the median cost around $200k – a firm that suffers more than one can expect to lose customers, and take a hit to its stock price; and firms that suffer the pain of one disclosure are less likely to have another [336]. So breach-disclosure laws are having an effect.

The first case that started to put privacy on CEOs' radar came in 2006, when Choicepoint paid $10m to settle a lawsuit brought by the FTC after it failed to vet subscribers properly and let crooks buy the personal information of over 160,000 Americans, leading to at least 800 cases of 'identity theft' [671]. In 2007, it came out that the store chain TJ Maxx had had 45.7 million customers' credit card details stolen [1161]; Albert Gonzales got 20 years in prison for this in 2010, and it's reckoned that the breach cost the company $800m. The FTC sued Facebook over deceptive changes to privacy settings and settled in 2011, just before its IPO, requiring it to get user consent for certain changes and subjecting it to 20 years of audits [182]. The real shock to CEO-land came when Target's CEO, Gregg Steinhafel, was fired in May 2014 following a hack of more than 100m credit card numbers the previous December; the CIO was also replaced [702]. The C-suite carnage has continued, both in the USA[12] and elsewhere[13] moving cybersecurity steadily up the corporate agenda.

In 2018, California passed a consumer privacy law, the California Consumer Privacy Act (CCPA). This followed a privacy ballot initiative which, if it had gone to a ballot and passed, would have entrenched an even tougher privacy law. The ballot in turn followed the Cambridge Analytica scandal where the Facebook data of 87 million users was harvested without their knowledge or consent and used to target behavioural advertising during the 2016 election campaign. The big tech companies' defence was to negotiate the new law instead of the ballot initiative, so they could have it amended later, or even trumped by a Federal law. CCPA is somewhat similar to European data-protection law: it empowers consumers to request the deletion of personal information, opt out of its sale, and access it in a format that enables its

[12]Amy Pascal of Sony in 2014, Walter Stephan of FACC in 2016, Richard Smith of Equifax in 2017; and maybe we can note Marissa Meyer of Yahoo who forfeited her bonus and stock in 2017, and perhaps even Travis Kavalnick of Uber whose successor publicised a hack that had been covered up.

[13]Dido Harding of TalkTalk, UK, in 2017; Bruce Liang of Integrated Health Information Systems, Singapore, in 2019; and maybe we can count Martin Winterkorn of VW and Rupert Stadler of Audi, who presided over the company hacking its car emissions.

transfer to third parties. The European right to be forgotten is a non-starter thanks to the US First Amendment. CCPA can be enforced by the state attorney general but also by private action. A really important policy question now is whether this law is progressively copied by other states, or whether Big Tech manages to emasculate it[14]. But the USA is not the only serious player here.

26.6.3 Fragmentation?

Since 1998, European law has forbidden companies from sending personal data to organizations in countries where the law does not provide comparable protection or other safeguards – which in practice means America and India. The first attempt to resolve this was the *Safe Harbour Agreement* whereby a data processor in America or India would promise their European customer to abide by European law. In 2000, the European Commission adopted an executive decision to the effect that this would give 'adequate protection'. However, it left no practical recourse for EU citizens who felt their rights had been violated.

The case that killed Safe Harbour was brought by Max Schrems, an Austrian lawyer, against Facebook. Following the Snowden revelations, he argued that for Facebook in Ireland (its EU headquarters) to pass his data to the USA for processing was unlawful, as the law and practice of the United States offer no protection against surveillance by the public authorities, specifically the NSA, which can collect it all via Prism. The European Court of Justice agreed and in 2015 it struck down the Safe Harbour principles. The USA and the EU then agreed to replace them with a fresh arrangement, called Privacy Shield, which adds an ombudsperson to whom an EU citizen can complain if they think the NSA might have spied on them [1476]; Max took this to the European Court of Justice, which duly struck it down in July 2020 [1686]. The defendant was the Irish Data Protection Commissioner, who spent almost €3M defending the position that she had the right to look the other way as US tech firms with their EU headquarters in Ireland ride roughshod over privacy law. The court also ruled that privacy authorities have a duty to take action when they receive a complaint. It also made clear that the NSA's right under US law to get free access to the data of people who are not US persons is not consistent with US firms keeping data on EU citizens under US custody and control[15].

[14]Their lobbyists are already attacking it, but as I write in 2020, there's a ballot initiative that would entrench it in California law and put it beyond the grasp of state legislators.

[15]There is also a case pending at the European Court of Human Rights, brought by Big Brother Watch against US mass surveillance [422], which has been granted an appeal to the Grand Chamber. If this goes the same way, the ECJ judgment will be extended to those countries that are members of the Council of Europe but not of the EU, such as the UK and Russia.

Many companies that process data in the USA had in the meantime fallen back on contract, forcing customers to agree to their personal data being shared before they do business with them. This has a long and sordid history (it's how medical insurers get away with selling your data to drug companies), and the ECJ allowed the continued use of *standard contractual clauses* (SCCs) to protect data. But this isn't straightforward. First, the data controller has to establish that there's an adequate level of protection in the country where the data will be held, and second, you can't simply impose such terms on consumers in the world of the GDPR as coercive consent is specifically disallowed. It is hard to see how US firms can establish adequacy when US law provides unfettered access to foreigners' data on US soil and the Snowden disclosures document the systematic use (and, from the EU law viewpoint, abuse) of this access.

So this is developing into a real fight, with real consequences for how and where the world's server farms are located and controlled. Some of the better-informed firms assume that they will eventually have to process European data in Europe and under European law; Microsoft put a data centre in Germany under the control of a German trustee for a couple of years, but then changed its mind, while Google has done its privacy research and development for some years in Munich. And public opinion in the USA isn't that different from Europe: most Americans think their personal data is less secure now, that the risks of surveillance capitalism outweigh the benefits, that they don't understand what's going on, that they have no control and neither companies nor government are accountable for abuse, but that they just don't have any alternative. Oh, and 20% suffered some kind of online fraud in the last twelve months [145].

Meanwhile, data-protection law is pushing into new areas where it gives a way of responding to abuses. For example, after the Brexit referendum, the UK Information Commissioner fined Facebook £500,000[16] after they let Cambridge Analytica harvest personal data on 87 million people worldwide, and used this to target election ads in both the Brexit referendum and the US 2016 presidential election [959]. As many modern practices in marketing and in political propaganda involve offences under data-protection law, this gives scope for regulatory innovation. The US equivalent is the FTC's use of truth-in-advertising law to punish firms that break their privacy policies or previous agreements about user privacy; and Facebook was in due course fined $5bn by the FTC. The Electronic Privacy Information Center[17] had been

[16]The UK fine was the maximum allowed under pre-GDPR data-protection law; since then the maximum is 4% of the defendant's turnover, which should bring European penalties into line with American ones.

[17]Full disclosure: I'm a member of their advisory board.

arguing ever since the Cambridge Analytica scandal broke that Facebook had violated the terms of its 2011 settlement with the FTC.

26.7 Freedom of information

Information tends to flow from the weak to the powerful, increasing their power and making it harder for others to hold them to account. As James Madison wrote:

> *A popular government without popular information or the means of acquiring it is but a prologue to a farce or a tragedy, or perhaps both. Knowledge will forever govern ignorance: And a people who mean to be their own Governors, must arm themselves with the power which knowledge gives.*

In the aftermath of Watergate, Congress passed the Freedom of Information Act, and other countries followed; Britain got one in 1997[18]. More radical versions have been tried: tax returns are published in Iceland and in some Swiss cantons, and the practice cuts evasion, as rich men fear the loss of social status that a low declared income would bring. The most radical version is proposed by David Brin, in 'The Transparent Society' [323]. He reasons that the falling costs of data acquisition, transmission and storage will make pervasive surveillance technologies available to the authorities, so the only real question is whether they are available to the rest of us too. He paints a choice between two futures – one in which the citizens live in fear of a Chinese–style policing system and one in which officials are held to account by public scrutiny. He argues that essentially all information should be open – including, for example, all our bank accounts. The cameras will exist: will they be surveillance cams or webcams? Social media often seem to be pushing us in that direction. In any case, Freedom of Information Acts typically let the citizen demand copies of information held by the state unless there's a good reason to withhold it, and help ensure that the flow of information between the citizen and the state isn't entirely one-way.

However, transparency leads to interesting tussles. Many European countries have clean-slate laws whereby most criminal convictions are expunged after a period of time that depends on the severity of the offence, and in 2019 Pennsylvania, Utah and California followed suit [607]. But how can such laws be enforced now that web search engines exist? Do you tag the names of offenders in newspaper accounts of trials with an expiration date, and pass laws compelling search and archive services to respect them? The Google Spain case gives us the answer: someone whose conviction has expired has a right to have

[18] Tony Blair later described it as his biggest mistake.

it suppressed in searches, although it may remain in the newspaper archive for those who know where to look.

That's one example of the shifting boundary between data protection and freedom of information. Another has been the monitoring of former child sex offenders, with laws in some states requiring that registers of offenders be publicly available, and riots in the UK following the naming of some former offenders by a Sunday newspaper and at least one innocent person being lynched. A third is the release of crime statistics: homeowners object to their neighbourhood being stigmatised, and if the data are too granular there may be some risk of individual victims being identified. For further examples, see Section 11.1 on inference security.

26.8 Summary

Public policy is increasingly entangled with the work of the security engineer. The largest single concern of governments, if we measure it in dollar terms, is intelligence; a typical government spends a hundred times more money collecting information on its enemies, real and potential, than it does on fighting cyber-crime. Intelligence collection is also in conflict with both defensive security and with privacy, both of which have historically come second. However, since the Snowden revelations made clear the scale of US data collection worldwide, and of Five Eyes operations against allied countries, the balance has started to shift, and the effects have propagated through privacy and data protection law, albeit slowly and with little effect so far on the agencies themselves. Perhaps when the analysis is done, Snowden's effect on the agencies' capabilities will be largely technical (through getting people to use cryptography more, and more intelligently) while the policy effect may be to curb some of the excesses of 'surveillance capitalism' by making privacy more salient to more people. The strains between the US and European ways of dealing with privacy are becoming more significant and in the medium term we may see more localisation – where US companies have to keep data on EU citizens on servers in Europe and perhaps even under the control of European trustees. Other countries are starting to follow suit.

Censorship is a real issue. Some countries, like China, ban many of the large US service firms outright, while more and more are demanding that they take down not just abusive material but also material that offends local political sensitivities. The Internet still makes it harder for countries that won't go as far as China to censor subversive content, but much of the optimism we had ten years ago has dissipated with the failure of the Arab Spring. Even the developed countries push the large service firms to moderate and filter user-generated content at scale, and despite the cost and complexity, it's becoming universal except on end-to-end encrypted services. It's now 25 years since AOL barred users living in Scunthorpe, and large-scale filtering still raises a host of policy issues whether we're talking about copyright, radicalisation, harassment or fake news.

The security-industrial complex, whose growth was fuelled by the climate of fear whipped up after the 9/11 attacks, has got a second wind from China and the Arab Spring, as the world's authoritarians buy surveillance systems to keep track of their populations. This has led to the proliferation of computer and network exploitation tools that erode our security, our liberty, and our quality of life. This proliferation is aided and abetted by Western governments who should know better, and is bound to be extended as social media firms and others are co-opted into ever more content screening as a condition of doing business. Understanding and pushing back on the surveillance ecosystem while mitigating online harms is the highest priority for security engineers who have the ability to get involved in public life – whether directly, or via our writing and teaching. And research also helps. Individual academics can't hope to compete with national leaders in the mass media, but the careful accumulation of data and knowledge over the years can and will undermine their excuses. I don't mean just knowledge about why extreme airport screening measures are a waste of money; we also must disseminate knowledge about the economics and psychology that underlie maladaptive government behaviour, and its terrible consequences in terms of spending money on security theatre that should have been spent on pandemic preparedness.

Research problems

Technology policy involves a complex interplay between science, engineering, psychology, law and economics. There is still too little serious cross-disciplinary research, and initiatives which speed up this process are almost certainly a good thing. Since 2002 I've worked to build up the security-economics research community; and since 2008 we've run an annual workshop on security and human behaviour to engage psychologists, anthropologists and philosophers too. But we need much, much more. Where are the historians, the sociologists and the political scientists?

Further reading

It's extraordinarily easy for technology policy arguments to get detached from reality, and many of the scares conjured up to get attention and money (such as 'cyberterrorism') are the modern equivalent of the monsters that appeared on medieval maps to cover up the cartographer's ignorance. An engineer should look for primary sources – from material written by experienced insiders such as R.V. Jones [994] to the thousands of documents leaked by Ed Snowden. As for the use of information warfare techniques in the Brexit referendum and the 2016 US election, Carole Cadwalladr's movie 'The Great Hack' is unmissable.

There's a good book on the history of wiretapping and crypto policy by Whit Diffie and Susan Landau, who had a long involvement in the policy process [558], and an NRC study on cryptography policy was also influential [1413]. There's a video on my website of the history of the crypto wars from a European perspective.

The history of export control is tied up with Soviet attempts to buy US computer, semiconductor and energy technology during the 1970s and 80s, and the US and French intelligence community's work to block them and feed them misleading information: see the memoir on Gus Weiss, a CIA maverick involved in this work [723].

Resources on online censorship include Reporters without Borders, who publish a 'Handbook for bloggers and cyber-dissidents' on how to circumvent censorship, with a number of case histories of how blogging has helped open up the media in less liberal countries [1597].

The standard work on computer forensics is by Tony Sammes and Brian Jenkinson [1647], while Privacy International has a survey of mobile phone forensics [1558] and the Department of Justice's "Guidelines for Searching and Seizing Computers" also bear some attention [550]. For early computer crime case histories, see Peter Neumann [1431] and Dorothy Denning [539]. The standard work on computer evidence in the common law countries is by Stephen Mason [1238].

On the topic of privacy versus data protection, there is a huge literature but no concise recent guide that I know of. Recent material can be found on the web sites of organizations such as EPIC [632], EFF [618], FIPR [708] and EDRi [643], and of Max Schrems [1686].

As for the policy problems around the filtering of inflammatory content and propaganda, the two most thought-provoking books for me are those by Tim Wu [2052] and Yochai Benkler [228], while Facebook's former CISO Alex Stamos now discusses the tech companies' view of filtering political ads [1001].

Finally, the definitive story of the Cambridge Analytica scandal is told in the book by the whistleblower Chris Wylie [2055], and in the journalism by Carole Cadwalladr based on information that he and others supplied [365].

CHAPTER

27

Secure Systems Development

My own experience is that developers with a clean, expressive set of specific security requirements can build a very tight machine. They don't have to be security gurus, but they have to understand what they're trying to build and how it should work.

– RICK SMITH

When it comes to being slaves to fashion, American managers make adolescent girls look like rugged individualists.

– GEOFF NUNBERG

The fox knows many things; the hedgehog one big thing.

– ARCHILOCHUS

27.1 Introduction

So far we've discussed a great variety of security applications, technologies and concerns. If you're a working engineer, manager or consultant, paid to build or maintain a system with some security assurance requirements, you will by now be looking for a systematic way to go about it. This brings us to such topics as risk analysis, system engineering methodology, and, finally, the secret sauce: how you manage a team to write secure code.

The secret is that there isn't actually a secret, whether sauce or anything else. Lots of people claim there is one and get religious fervour for the passion of the moment, from the Orange Book in the 1980s to Agile Development now. But the first take offered on this was the right one. In the 1960s Fred Brooks led the team on the world's first really large software project, the operating system for the IBM S/360 mainframe. In his classic book "The Mythical Man-Month" he describes all the problems they struggled with, and his conclusion is that "there is no silver bullet" [329]. There's no magic formula that makes an intrinsically hard job easy. There's also the famous line from Archilochus at the head of this chapter: the fox knows many things, while the hedgehog knows one big thing. Managing secure development is fox knowledge rather than hedgehog knowledge. An experienced security engineering manager has to know thousands of little things; that's why this book is so fat! And the security engineering manager's job is getting harder all the time as software gets everywhere and starts to interact with safety.

In 2017, I changed the way I teach undergraduates at Cambridge. Up till then we'd taught security courses separately from software engineering, with the latter focusing on safety. But most real-world systems require both, and they're entangled in complex ways. Both safety and security are emergent properties that really have to be baked in from the beginning. Both involve systematic thinking about what can go wrong, whether by accident or as a result of malice. Accidents can expose systems to attacks, and attacks can degrade systems so they become dangerous. The course was developed further by my colleague Alastair Beresford while I was on sabbatical in 2019, and the 2020 course on software and security engineering is now online as ten video lectures, thanks to the pandemic [90]. That course is designed to give our first-year undergraduates a solid foundation for later work in security, cryptography and software engineering. Like this book, it introduces the basics, from definitions through the basics of protocols and crypto, then the importance of human and organizational issues as well as technical ones, illustrated with case histories. It discusses how you set goals for safety and security, how you manage them as a system evolves, and how you instil suitable ways of thinking and working into your team. Success is about attitudes and work practices as well as skills.

The two questions you have to ask are, "Are we building the right system?" and "Are we building it right?" In the rest of this chapter I'm going to start with how we assess and manage risks – to both safety and security; and then go on to discuss how we build systems, once we've got a specification to work to. I'll then discuss some of the hazards that arise as a result of organisational behaviour – a real but often ignored kind of insider threat.

27.2 Risk management

At the heart of both safety engineering and security engineering lie decisions about priorities: how much to spend on protection against what. Risk management must be done within a broader framework of managing all the risks to an enterprise or indeed to a nation. That is often done badly. The coronavirus crisis should have made it obvious to everyone that although pandemics were at the top of the risk register of many countries, including the UK, most governments spent much more of their resilience budget on terrorism, which was several places down the list. Countries with recent experience of SARS or MERS, such as Taiwan and South Korea, did better: they were ready to test residents and trace contacts at scale, and responded quickly. Britain wasted two months before realising the disease was serious, at a cost of tens of thousands of lives.

So what actually is a *risk register*? A common methodology, as used by the governing body of my university, is to draw up a list of things that could go wrong, giving them scores of 1 to 5 for seriousness and for probability of occurrence, and multiplying these together to get a number between 1 and 25. For example, a university might rate 'loss of research contract income due to economic downturn' at 5/5 for seriousness if 20% of its income is from that source, and rate 'probability' at 4/5 as downturns happen frequently but not every year, giving a raw product of 20. You then write down the measures you take to mitigate each of these risks, and have an argument in a risk committee about how well each risk is mitigated. For example, you control the risk of variable research contract income by making a rule that it can be used to hire only contract staff, not tenured faculty; you might then agree that this rule cuts that risk from 20 to 16. You then rank all the risks in order and assign one senior officer to be the owner of each of them.

National risk assessments are somewhat similar: you rate each possible bad event (pandemic, earthquake, forest fire, terrorist attack, ...) by how many people it might kill (millions? thousands? dozens?) and then rate it for probability by how many you expect each century. The UK national risk register, for example, put pandemic influenza at the top, with a 5 for severity (could kill up to 750,000) and a 4 for likelihood, saying in 2017: "one or more major hazards can be expected to materialise in the UK in every five-year period. The most serious are pandemic influenza, national blackout and severe flooding" [363]. You then work out what's reasonably practical by way of mitigation, be it quarantine plans and PPE stockpiles for a pandemic, or building codes and zoning to limit the damage from floods and earthquakes. You do the cost-benefit analysis and turn priorities into policy. You can get things wrong in various ways. The UK largely ignored pandemics because the National Security Council had been captured by the security and intelligence agencies; they prioritised terrorism, and the health secretary was not a regular attendee [1852]. I already discussed terrorism in section 26.3; here I'll just add that another aspect of the failure was policy overshoot. When 9/11 taught the world that terrorist attacks can kill thousands rather than just dozens, and the agencies got a lot more of the resilience budget, it made them greedy: they started talking up the risk of terrorists getting hold of a nuke so they'd have an even scarier threat on the register to justify their budgets.

In business too you can find that both political behaviour and organisational behaviour get in the way of rational risk management. But you often have real data on the more common losses, so you can attempt a more quantitative approach. The standard method is to calculate the *annual loss expectancy* (ALE) for each possible loss scenario, as the expected loss multiplied by the number of incidents expected in an average year. A typical ALE analysis for a bank's

IT systems might have several hundred entries, including items such as we see in Figure 27.1.

Loss type	Amount	Incidence	ALE
SWIFT fraud	$50,000,000	.005	$250,000
ATM fraud (large)	$250,000	.2	$100,000
ATM fraud (small)	$20,000	.5	$10,000
Teller takes cash	$3,240	200	$648,000

Figure 27.1: Items of annualized loss expectancy (ALE)

Note that while accurate figures are likely to be available for common losses (such as 'teller takes cash'), the incidence of low-probability high-risk losses such as a large money-transfer fraud is largely guesswork – though you can sometimes get a rough sanity check by asking for insurance quotes.

ALEs have long been standardized by NIST as the technique to use in US government procurements. The UK government uses a tool called CRAMM for systematic analysis of information security risks, and the modern audit culture is spreading such tools everywhere. But the process of producing such a table for low-probability threats tends to be just iterative guesswork. The consultants list all the threats they can think of, attach notional probabilities, work out the ALEs, add them up, and find that the bank's ALE exceeds its income. They then tweak the total down to whatever will justify the largest security budget that their client the CISO has said is politically possible. I'm sorry if this sounds a bit cynical; but it's what often seems to happen. The point is, ALEs may be of some value, but you need to understand what parts are based on data, what parts on guesswork and what parts on office politics.

Product risks are different. Different industries do things differently because of the way they evolved and the history of regulation. The rules for each sector, whether cars or aircraft or medical devices or railway signals, have evolved in response to accidents and industry lobbying. Increasingly, the European Union is becoming the world's safety regulator as it's the biggest market, as Washington cares less about safety than Brussels does, and as it's simpler for OEMs to engineer to EU safety specifications than to have multiple products. I'll discuss safety and security certification in more detail in the next chapter. For present purposes, software for cars, planes and medical devices must be developed according to approved procedures, subjected to analyses we'll discuss later, and tested in specific ways.

Insurance can be of some help in managing large but unlikely risks. But the insurance business is not completely scientific either. Your insurance premiums used to give some signal of the risk your business was running, especially if you bought cover for losses of eight figures or above. But insurance is a cyclical industry, and since about 2017 a host of new companies have started offering insurance against cybercrime, squeezing the profits out of the market. As a result, customers will no longer put up with intrusive questionnaires, let alone site visits from assessors. So most insurers' ability to assess risk is now limited; I will discuss the mechanics of what they do further in section 28.2.9. They are also wary of correlated risks that give rise to many claims at once, as that would force them to hold greater reserves; as some cyber risks are correlated, policies tend to either exclude them or be relatively expensive [276]. (The coronavirus crisis is teaching firms about correlated risk as some insurers refuse to pay up on business-interruption risk policies – even those that explicitly mention the risk of staff not being able to get to the office because of epidemics; businesses are asking insurers in turn what the point of insurance is.)

Actuarial risks aside, a very important reason for large companies to take out insurance cover – and for much other corporate behaviour – is to protect executives, rather than shareholders. The risks that are being tackled may seem on the surface to be operational but are actually legal, regulatory and PR risks. Directors demand liability insurance, and under UK and US law, professional negligence occurs when a professional fails to perform their responsibilities to the level required of a reasonably competent person in their profession. So negligence claims are assessed by the current standards of the industry or profession, giving a strong incentive to follow the herd. This is one reason why management is such a fashion-driven business (as per the quote at the head of this chapter). This spills over into the discourse used to justify security budgets. During the mid 1980s, everyone talked about hackers (even if their numbers were tiny). From the late 80s, viruses took over the corporate imagination, and people got rich selling antivirus software. In the mid-1990s, the firewall became the star product. The late 1990s saw a frenzy over PKI. By 2017 it was blockchains. Amidst all this hoopla, the security professional must keep a level head and strive to understand what the real threats are.

We will return to organisational behaviour in a later section. First, let's see what we can learn from safety engineering.

27.3 Lessons from safety-critical systems

Critical computer systems are those in which a certain class of failure is to be avoided if at all possible. Depending on the class of failure, they may be safety-critical, business-critical, security-critical, or critical to the environment. Obvious examples of the safety-critical variety include flight controls and automatic braking systems. There's a large literature on this subject, and a lot of methodologies have been developed to help manage risk intelligently.

27.3.1 Safety engineering methodologies

Safety engineering methodologies, like classical security engineering, tend to work systematically from a safety analysis to a specification through to a product, and assume you're building safety in from the start rather than trying to retrofit it. The usual procedure is to identify hazards and assess risks; decide on a strategy to cope with them (avoidance, constraint, redundancy ...); trace the hazards to hardware and software components which are thereby identified as critical; identify the operator procedures which are also critical and study the various applied psychology and operations research issues; set out the safety functional requirements which specify what the safety mechanisms must do, and safety integrity requirements that specify the likelihood of a safety function being performed satisfactorily; and finally decide on a test plan. The outcome of testing is not just a system you're confident to run live, but an integrated part of a *safety case* to justify running it. The basic framework is set out in standards such as ISO 61508, a basic safety framework for relatively simple programmable electronics such as the control systems for chemical plants. This has been extended with more specialised standards for particular industries, such as ISO 26262 for road vehicles.

This safety case will provide the evidence, if something does go wrong, that you exercised due care. It will typically consist of the hazard analysis, the safety functional and integrity requirements, and the results of tests (both at component level and system level), which show that the required failure rates have been achieved. The testing may have to be done by an accredited third party; motor vehicles firms get away with the safety case being done by a different department in the same company, with independent management. Vehicles are a more complex case because of their supply chains. At the top is the brand, whose badge you see on the front of the car. Then there's the *original equipment manufacturer* (OEM), which in the case of cars is usually the same company, but not always; in other industries the brand and the OEM are quite separate. A modern car will have components from dozens of manufacturers, of which the Tier 1 suppliers who deal directly with the brand do much of the research and development work but get components from other firms in turn. In the car industry, the brand puts the car through type approval and carries the primary liability, but demands indemnities from component suppliers in case things go wrong (the law in most countries does not allow you to disclaim liability for death and injury). The brand relies on the supply chain for significant parts of the safety functionality and integrity and thus for the safety case. There are also tensions: as we already noted, safety certification can prevent the timely application of security patches. Let's now look at common safety engineering methods and what they can teach us.

27.3.2 Hazard analysis

In an ideal case, we might be able to design hazards out of a system completely. As an example, consider the motor reversing circuits in Figure 27.2. In the design on the left, a double-pole double-throw switch reverses the current passing from the battery through the motor. However, this has a potential problem: if only one of the two poles of the switch moves, the battery will be shorted, and a fire may result. The solution is to exchange the battery and the motor, as in the modified circuit on the right. Here, a switch failure will only short out the motor, not the battery. Safety engineering is not just about correct operation, but about correct failure too.

Hazard elimination is useful in security engineering too. We saw an example in the early design of SWIFT in section 12.3.2: there, the keys used to authenticate transactions between one bank and another were exchanged between the banks directly, so SWIFT did not have the means to forge a valid transaction, and its staff and systems had to be trusted less. In general, minimizing the trusted computing base is an exercise in hazard elimination. The same applies in privacy engineering too. For example, if you're designing a contact tracing app to monitor who might have infected whom in an epidemic, one approach is to have a central database of everyone's mobile phone location history. However, that has obvious privacy hazards, which can be reduced by keeping a Bluetooth contact history on everyone's mobile phone instead, and uploading the contact history of anyone who calls in sick. You then have a policy decision to take between better privacy and better tracing.

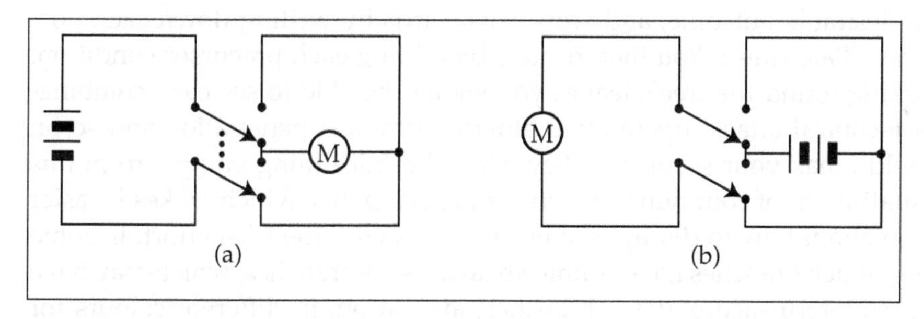

Figure 27.2: Hazard elimination in motor reversing circuit

27.3.3 Fault trees and threat trees

Once you have eliminated as many hazards as possible, the next step is to identify failures that could cause accidents. A common top-down way of identifying the things that can go wrong is *fault tree analysis* where a tree is constructed whose root is the undesired behavior and whose successive nodes are its possible causes. This top-down approach is natural where you have a complex system with a small number of well-known bad outcomes that you have to avoid. It carries over in a natural way to security engineering. Figure 27.3 shows an example of a fault tree (or *threat tree*, as it's often called in security engineering) for fraud from automatic teller machines.

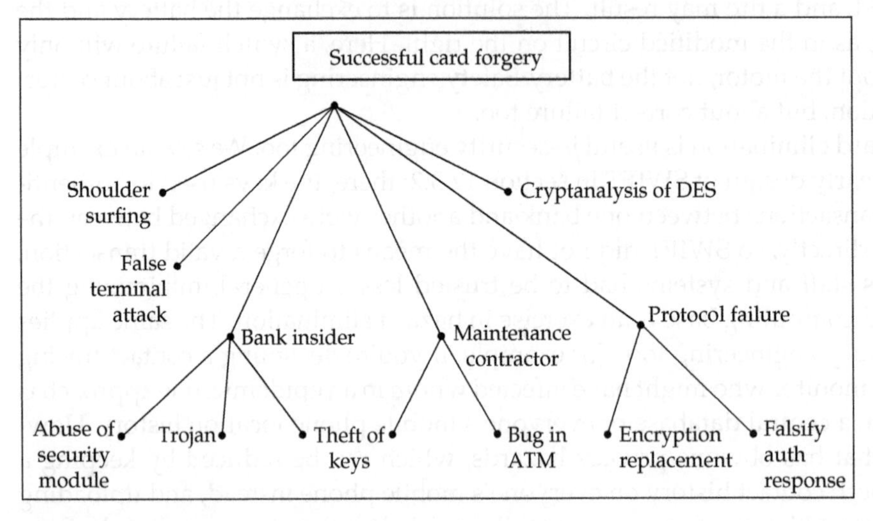

Figure 27.3: A threat tree

Threat trees are used in the US Department of Defense. You start out from each undesirable outcome, and work backwards by writing down each possible immediate cause. You then recurse by adding each precursor condition. By working round the tree's leaves you should be able to see each combination of technical attack, operational blunder, physical penetration and so on that could break your security policy. The other nice thing you get from this is a visualisation of commonality between attack paths, which makes it easier to reason about how to disrupt the most attacks with the least effort. In some variants, attack branches have countermeasure sub-branches, which may have counter-countermeasure attack branches, and so on, in different colours for emphasis. A threat tree can amount to an attack manual for the system, so it may be highly classified, but it's a DoD requirement – and if the system evaluators or accreditors can find significant extra attacks, they may fail the product.

27.3.4 Failure modes and effects analysis

Returning to the safety-critical world, another way of doing hazard analysis is *failure modes and effects analysis* (FMEA), pioneered by NASA, which is bottom-up rather than top-down[1]. This involves tracing the consequences of a failure of each of the system's components all the way up to the effect on the mission. This is the natural approach in systems with a small number of well-understood critical components or subsystems, such as aircraft. For example, if you're going to fly a plane over an ocean or mountains where you can't glide to an airport in the case of engine failure, then engine power is critical. You therefore study the mean time to failure of your powerplant and its failure modes, from a broken connecting rod to running out of fuel. You insist that single-engine aircraft use reliable engines and you regulate the maintenance schedules; planes have more than one fuel tank. When carrying a lot of passengers, you insist on multi-engine aircraft and drill the crews to deal with engine failure.

An aerospace example of people missing a failure mode that turned out to be critical is the 1986 loss of the space shuttle Challenger. The O-rings in the booster rockets were known to be a risk by the NASA project manager, and damage had been found on previous flights; meanwhile the contractor knew that low temperatures increased the risk; but the concerns did not come together or get through to NASA's top management. An O-ring, made brittle by the cold, failed – causing the loss of the shuttle and seven crew. On the resulting board of inquiry, the physicist Richard Feynman famously demonstrated this on TV by putting a sample of O-ring in a clamp, freezing it in iced water and then showing that when he released it, it remained dented and did not spring back [1615]. This illustrates that failures are often not just technical but also involve how people behave in organisations: when protection mechanisms cross institutional boundaries, as for example with cars, you need to think of the law and economics as well as just the engineering. Such problems will become much more complex as we move towards autonomous vehicles, which will rely on all sorts of third-party services and infrastructure.

27.3.5 Threat modelling

Both fault trees and FMEA depend on the analyst understanding the system really well; they are hard to automate, not fully repeatable and can be up-ended by a subtle change to a subsystem. So a thorough analysis of failure modes will often combine top-down and bottom-up approaches with some methods specific to the application that people have learned over time. Many industries now have to rethink their traditional safety analysis methods to incorporate security.

[1]FMEA is bottom-up in the technical sense that the analysis works up from individual components, but its actual management often has a top-down flavour as you start work on the safety case once you have an outline design and refine it progressively as the design is evolved into a product.

In car safety, complex supply chains mean we have to do multiple interlocking analyses of vehicles and their subsystems. A traditional subsystem analysis might work through the failure modes of headlamps, since losing them while driving at night can lead to an accident. As well as mitigating the risk of a lamp failure by having two or more lamps, you worry about switch failure, and when the switch becomes electronic you build a fault tree of possible hardware and software faults. When we extend this from safety to security, we think about whether an attacker might take over the entertainment system in a car, and use it to send a malicious 'lamp off' message on the CAN bus once the car is moving quickly enough for this to be dangerous. This analysis may lead to a design decision to have a firewall between the cabin CAN bus and the powertrain CAN bus. (This is the worked example in the new draft ISO 21434 standard for cybersecurity in road vehicles [964].)

More generally, the shift from safety to security means having to think systematically about insiders. Just as double-entry bookkeeping was designed to be resilient against a single dishonest clerk and has been re-engineered against the similar threat of a clerk with malware on their PC, so modern large-scale systems are typically designed to limit the damage if a single component is compromised. So how can you incorporate malicious insiders into a threat model? If you're using FMEA, you can just add an opponent at various locations, as with our malicious 'lamp off' message. As for more complex systems, the methodology adopted by Microsoft following its big push in 2003 to make Windows and Office more secure is described by Frank Swiderski and Window Snyder [1855]. Rather than being purely top-down or bottom-up, this is a meet-in-the-middle approach. The basic idea is that you list not just the assets you're trying to protect (ability to do transactions, access to confidential data, whatever) but also the assets available to an attacker (perhaps the ability to subscribe to your system, or to manipulate inputs to the smartcard you supply him, or to get a job at your call center). You then trace the attack paths through the system, from one module to another. You try to figure out what the trust levels might be; where the barriers are; and what techniques, such as spoofing, tampering, repudiation, information disclosure, service denial and elevation of privilege, might be used to overcome particular barriers. The threat model can be used for various purposes at different points in the security development lifecycle, from architecture reviews through targeting code reviews and penetration tests.

There are various ways to manage the resulting mass of data. An elementary approach is to construct a matrix of hazards against safety mechanisms, and if the safety policy is that each serious hazard must be constrained by at least two independent mechanisms, then you can check for two entries in each of the relevant columns. So you can demonstrate graphically that in the presence of the hazard in question, at least two failures will be required to cause an accident. An alternative approach, *system theoretic process analysis* (STPA), starts off with the hazards and then designs controls in a top-down process, leading to an architectural design for the system; this can be helpful in teasing apart interacting control loops [1152]. Such methodologies go across to security engineering [1559]. One way or another, in order to make the complexity manageable, you may have to organise a hierarchy of safety and security goals. The security policies discussed in Part 2 of this book may give you the beginnings of an answer for the applications we discussed there, and some inspiration for others. This hierarchy can then drive a risk matrix or risk treatment plan depending on the terminology in use in your industry.

27.3.6 Quantifying risks

The safety-critical systems community has a number of techniques for dealing with failure and error rates. Component failure rates can be measured statistically; the number of bugs in software can be tracked by techniques I'll discuss in the next chapter; and there is a lot of experience with the probability of operator error at different types of activity. The bible for human-factors engineering in safety-critical systems is James Reason's book *'Human Error'*; I discussed in Chapter 3 the rising tide of research in security usability through the 2010s as the lessons from the safety world have started to percolate into our field.

The error rate in a task depends on its familiarity and complexity, the amount of pressure and the number of cues to success. Where a task is simple, performed often and there are strong cues to success, the error rate might be 1 in 100,000 operations. However, when a task is performed for the first time in a confusing environment where logical thought is required and the operator is under pressure, then the odds can be against successful completion. Three Mile Island and Chernobyl taught nuclear engineers that no matter how many design walkthroughs you do, it's when the red lights go on for real that the worst mistakes get made. The same lesson has come out of one air accident investigation after another. When dozens of alarms go off at once, there's a fair chance that someone will push the wrong button. One guiding principle is to default to a safe state: to damp down a nuclear reaction, to return an aircraft to straight and level flight, or to bring an autonomous vehicle to a stop at the side of the road. No principle is foolproof, and a safe state may be hard to measure. A vehicle can find it hard to tell where the side of the road is if there's a grass verge; and in the Boeing 737Max crashes (which I describe in detail in section 28.2.4) the flight control computer tried to keep the plane level but was confused by a faulty angle-of-attack sensor and dived the plane into the ground instead.

Another principle of safety usability in an emergency is to keep the information given to operators, and the controls available for them to use, both simple and intuitive. In the old days, each feed went to a single gauge or dial and there was only so much space for them. The temptation nowadays is to give the operator everything, because you can. In the old days, designers knew that an emergency would give the pilots tunnel vision so they put the six instruments they really needed right in the middle. Nowadays there can be fifty alarms rather than two and pilots struggle to work out which screen on which menu of the electronic flight information system to look at. It is much broader than aviation. A naval example is the 2017 collision of the USS McCain in the Straits of Singapore, where UI confusion was a major factor. Steering control was shifted to the wrong helm station and an engine was not throttled back in time, resulting in an uncommanded turn to port across a busy shipping lane, impact with a chemical tanker, and the death of ten sailors [1933].

So systems that are not fully autonomous must remain controllable, and for that the likely human errors need to be understood. Quite a lot is known about the cognitive biases and other psychological factors that make particular types of error more common; we discussed them in Chapter 3, and a prudent engineer will study how they work out in their field. Errors are rare in frequently-performed tasks at which the operator has developed some skill, and are more likely when operators are stressed and surprised. This starts to get us out of the territory of risk, where the odds are known, and into that of uncertainty, where they're not.

In security systems, too, the most egregious blunders can be expected in important but rarely performed tasks. Security usability isn't just about presenting a nice intuitive interface to the end-user. It should present the risks in a way that accords with common mental models of threat and protection, and the likely user reactions to stress should lead to safe outcomes.

It is important to be realistic about the skill level of the people who will perform each critical task and any known estimates of the likelihood of error. An airplane designer can rely on a predictable skill level from anyone with a commercial pilot's license, and a shipbuilder knows the strengths and weaknesses of an officer in the merchant marine. Cars can and do get operated by drivers who are old and frail, young and inexperienced, distracted by passengers, or under the influence of alcohol. At the professional end of things, usability testing can be profitably integrated with staff training: when pilots go for their refresher courses in the simulator, instructors throw all sorts of combinations of equipment failure, bad weather, cabin crisis and air-traffic-control confusion at them. They observe what combinations of stress result in fatal accidents, and how these differ across cockpit types. Such data are valuable feedback to cockpit designers. In aviation, the incentives for safe operation are sufficiently strong and well aligned, and the scale is large enough, to support a learning system. Even so, there are expensive disasters, such as the Boeing 737Max flight control software. This not only had at least one serious bug, but escaped a proper failure modes and effects analysis because the engineers responsible – under pressure from their managers to complete the project on time – wrongly assumed that pilots would be able to cope with any failure [90]. As a result, the software relied on a single angle-of-attack sensor rather than using the two sensors with which the aircraft was fitted, and sensor failure led to fatal accidents[2].

When testing the usability of redundant systems, you need to pay attention to *fault masking*: if the output is determined by majority voting between three processors, and one of them fails, then the system will continue to work fine – but its safety margin will have been eroded, perhaps in ways the operators won't understand properly. Several air crashes have resulted from flying an airliner with one of the cockpit systems out of action; although pilots may be intellectually aware that one of the data feeds to the cockpit displays is unreliable, they may rely on it under pressure by reflex rather than checking with other instruments. So you have to think hard about how faults can remain visible and testable even when their immediate effects are mitigated.

Another lesson from safety-critical systems is that although a safety requirements specification and test criteria will be needed as part of the safety case for the lawyers and regulators, it is good practice to integrate both of them with the mainstream product documentation. If the safety case is separate, then it's easy to sideline it after approval and fail to maintain it properly. (This was a factor in the Boeing 737Max disaster as the usability assumptions underlying the safety case for the flight control software were not updated from the previous model of 737.) The move from project-based software management to agile methodologies, and via DevOps to DevSecOps, is finally starting to embed security management into the way products evolve. We will discuss this in the next section.

Finally, safety is like security in that it really has to be built in as a system is developed, rather than retrofitted. The main difference between the two is in the failure model. Safety deals with the effects of random failure, while in security we assume a hostile opponent who can cause some of the components of our system to fail at the least convenient time and in the most damaging way possible. People are naturally more risk-averse in the presence of an adversary; I will discuss this in section 28.4. A safety engineer will certify a critical flight-control system with an MTBF of 10^9 hours; a security engineer has to worry whether an adversary can force the preconditions for that one-in-a-billion failure and crash the plane on demand.

In effect, our task is to program a computer that gives answers that are subtly and maliciously wrong at the most inconvenient moment possible. I've described this as 'programming Satan's computer' to distinguish it from the more common problem of programming Murphy's [114]. This is one of the reasons security engineering is hard: Satan's computer is harder to test [1671].

[2]Aviation safety standards such as DO178 and DO254 generally require diversity in measurement type, physics, processing characteristics in addition to redundancy to mitigate common-mode failures.

27.4 Prioritising protection goals

If you've a project to create an entirely new product, or to radically change an existing one, it's an idea to spend some time thinking through the protection priorities from first principles. A careful safety analysis or threat modelling exercise can provide some numbers to inform this. When developing a safety case or a security policy in detail, it's essential to understand the context, and much of this book has been about the threat models relevant to a wide range of applications. You should try to refine numerical estimates of risk from the environment or context as well.

In the case of a business system, analysis will hinge on the tradeoff between risk and reward. Security people often focus too much on the former. If your firm has a turnover of $10m, gross profits of $1m and theft losses of $150,000, you might make a loss-reduction pitch about 'how to increase profits by 15% by stopping theft'; but if you could double the turnover to $20m, then the shareholders would prefer that even if it triples the losses to $450,000. Profit is now $1.55m, up 85%, rather than 15%. This is borne out by the experience of online fraud engines. When discussing fraud management strategies with a number of retailers, I noticed that the firms who got the best results were those where the fraud management team reported to sales rather than finance. A typical bricks-and-clicks retailer in the UK might decline something like 4% of offered shopping baskets because the fraud engine alerts at the combination of goods, delivery address and payment details. So if you can improve the fraud engine and reject only 3%, that's 1% more sales – a prospect to light up your Chief Marketing Officer's eyes. But if the fraud team reports instead to the Chief Financial Officer, they're likely to be seen as a cost rather than as an opportunity.

Similarly, the site reliability engineers of online services have learned not to make a system too reliable. If local Internet availability is only 99%, then a service that's up 99.9% of the time will be fine; there's no point spending millions more to hit 99.99% if none of your users will notice the difference. You're better off deliberately setting an 0.1% *error budget*, which you can use productively – such as by causing occasional deliberate failures to exercise your resilience mechanisms [237]. This brings me to one of the open debates in security management: should one aim at having no CVEs open in any of the software on which one relies? The tick-box approach is to say 'Of course there must be no open CVEs', but that may impose a rather high compliance cost. If you're Google, and wrote all your own infrastructure, maybe you can aim at that; many firms can't and have to prioritise. I'll discuss CVEs in more detail in section 27.5.7.1 later.

So don't trust people who can only talk about 'tightening security'. Often it's too tight already, and what you really need to do is just focus it slightly differently. In the first edition of this book, I presented a case study of self-service checkout at supermarkets. Twenty years ago, a number of supermarkets started to introduce self-checkout lanes. Some started to obsess about losses, and let security get in the way of usability by aggressively challenging customers about product weight. One of the stores that got an advantage started with a more forgiving approach that they tuned up gradually in the light of experience. Eventually the industry figured out how to operate self-checkout lanes, but the quality of the implementation still varies significantly. By early 2020, the pioneers are small convenience stores like Lifvs in Sweden that have no staff; you open the store's door with an app, scan your purchases and pay online. Amazon was also experimenting with fully self-service food stores. We saw the next 20 years of innovation crammed into the few months of the 2020 coronavirus lockdown; by June, other supermarkets have been urging us to download their scanning app, scan our purchases as we pick them, charge them to a card, and just go.

Many modern business models were once considered too risky, starting with the self-service supermarket itself back in the days when grocers kept all the goods behind the counter. Everyone thought Richard Sears would go bust when he adopted the slogan 'Satisfaction guaranteed or your money back' in the 1880s, yet he invented the modern mail-order business. In business, profit is the reward for risk. But entrepreneurs who succeed may have to improve security quickly. One recent example is the videoconferencing platform Zoom – which grew from 20 million users to 200 million in March 2020, and changed in the process from an enterprise platform into something more like a public utility – forcing them into a major security engineering effort [1767].

Trade-offs in safety are harder. Logically, the value of a human life in a developed country might be a few million dollars, that being an average person's lifetime earnings. However, our actual valuation of a human life as revealed by safety behaviour varies from about $50,000 for improvements to road junctions, up to over $500m for train protection systems – and that's just in the context of transport policy. The variance in health policy is even greater, with costs per life saved ranging from a few hundred dollars for flu jabs and some cancer screening to billions for the least effective interventions [1872]. In other safety contexts, domestic smoke alarms cost a few hundred dollars per life saved while the number for the "war on terror" is in the billions [1352]. The reasons for this irrationality are fairly well understood – I discussed the psychology in section 3.2.5 and the policy aspects in 26.3.3. Safety preferences can be changed very sharply by the threat of hostile action; people may shrug off a 1-in-10,000 risk of being killed by poorly-designed medical devices until there's a possibility that the devices might be hacked, at which point even a 1-in-10,000,000 risk becomes scary. I discuss this phenomenon in section 28.4.

27.5 Methodology

Software projects usually take longer than planned, cost more than budgeted and have more bugs than expected[3]. By the 1960s, this had become known as the *software crisis*, although the word 'crisis' may be inappropriate for a state of affairs that has now lasted, like computer insecurity, for two generations. Anyway, the term *software engineering* was proposed by Brian Randall in 1968 and defined to be:

> *Software engineering is the establishment and use of sound engineering principles in order to obtain economically software that is reliable and works efficiently on real machines.*

The pioneers hoped that the problem could be solved in the same way we build ships and aircraft, with a foundation in basic science and a framework of design rules [1422]. Since then there's been a lot of progress, but the results have been unexpected. Back in the late 1960s, people hoped that we'd cut the number of large software projects failing from the 30% or so that was observed at the time. But we still see about 30% of large projects failing – the difference is that the failures are much bigger. Modern tools get us farther up the complexity mountain before we fall off, but the rate of failure is set by company managers' appetite for risk. We'll discuss this further in section 27.5.8 at the end of this chapter.

Software engineering is about managing complexity, of which there are two kinds. There is the *incidental complexity* involved in programming using inappropriate tools, such as the assembly languages which were all that some early machines supported; programming a modern application with a graphical user interface in such a language would be impossibly tedious and error-prone. There is also the *intrinsic complexity* of dealing with large and complicated problems. A bank's core systems, for example, may involve tens of millions of lines of code that implement hundreds of different products sold through several different delivery channels, and are just too much for any one person to understand.

Incidental complexity is largely dealt with using technical tools. The most important are high-level languages that hide much of the drudgery of dealing with machine-specific detail and enable the programmer to develop code at an appropriate level of abstraction. They bring their own costs; many vulnerabilities are the result of the properties of the C language, and if we were rerunning history we'd surely use something like Rust instead. There are also formal methods such as static analysis tools, that enable particularly error-prone design and programming tasks to be checked.

[3]This is sometimes known as "Cheops' law" after the builder of the Great Pyramid.

Intrinsic complexity requires something subtly different: methodologies that help us divide up a problem into manageable subproblems and restrict the extent to which these subproblems can interact. These in turn are supported by their own sets of tools. There are basically two approaches – top-down and iterative.

27.5.1 Top-down design

The classical model of system development is the *waterfall model* formalised by Win Royce in the 1960s for the US Air Force [1631]. The idea is that you start from a concise statement of the system's requirements; elaborate this into a specification; implement and test the system's components; then integrate them together and test them as a system; then roll out the system for live operation (see Figure 27.4). From the 1970s until the mid-2000s, this was how all systems for the US Department of Defense were supposed to be developed, and their lead was followed by many governments worldwide, including not just in defence but in administration and healthcare. When I worked in banking in the 1980s, it was the approved process there too, promoted assiduously by IBM, by governments and by the big accountancy firms.

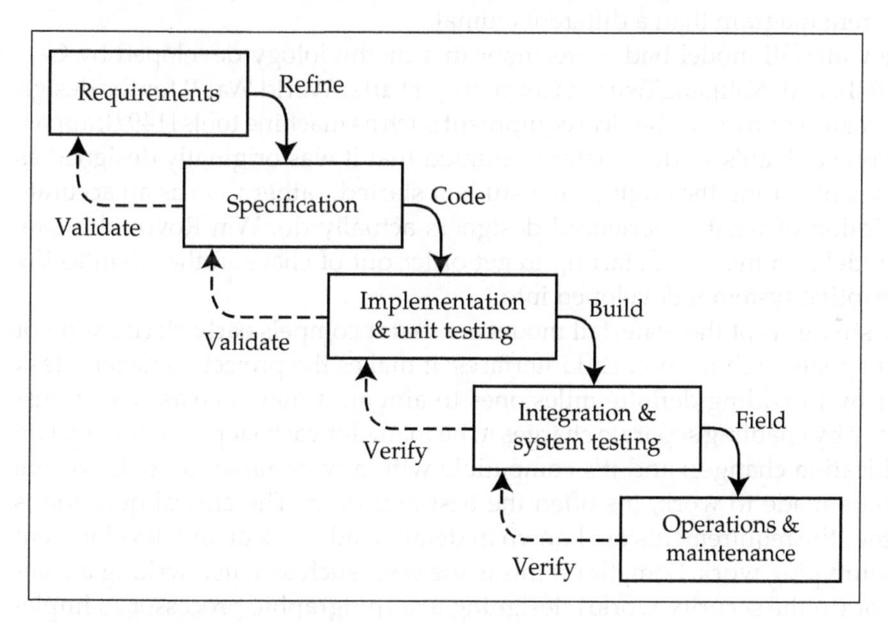

Figure 27.4: The waterfall model

The idea is that the requirements are written in the user language, the specification is written in technical language, the unit testing checks the units against the specification and the system testing checks whether the requirements are met. At the first two steps in this chain there is feedback on whether we're building the right system (*validation*) and at the next two on whether we're building it right (*verification*). There may be more than four steps: a common elaboration is to have a sequence of *refinement* steps as the requirements are developed into ever more detailed specifications. But that's by the way.

The defining feature of the waterfall model is that development flows inexorably downwards from the first statement of the requirements to the deployment of the system in the field. Although there is feedback from each stage to its predecessor, there is no system-level feedback from (say) system testing to the requirements.

There is a version used in safety-critical systems development called the V model, where the system flows down to implementation, then climbs back up a hill of verification and validation on the other side, where it's tested successively against the implementation, the specification and the requirements. This is a German government standard, and also used in the aerospace industry worldwide; it's found in the ISO 26262 standard for car software safety. But although it's written from left to right rather than top-down, it's still a one-way process where the requirements drive the system and the acceptance test ensures that the requirements were met, rather than a mechanism for evolving the requirements in the light of experience. It's more a different diagram than a different animal.

The waterfall model had a precursor in a methodology developed by Gerhard Pahl and Wolfgang Beitz in Germany just after World War II for the design and construction of mechanical equipment such as machine tools [1492]; apparently one of Pahl's students later recounted that it was originally designed as a means of getting the engineering student started, rather than as an accurate description of what experienced designers actually do. Win Royce also saw his model as a means of starting to get order out of chaos, rather than as the prescriptive system it developed into.

The strengths of the waterfall model are that it compels early clarification of system goals, architecture, and interfaces; it makes the project manager's task easier by providing definite milestones to aim at; it may increase cost transparency by enabling separate charges to be made for each step, and for any late specification changes; and it's compatible with a wide range of tools. Where it can be made to work, it's often the best approach. The critical question is whether the requirements are known in detail in advance of any development or prototyping work. Sometimes this is the case, such as when writing a compiler or (in the security world) designing a cryptographic processor to implement a known transaction set and pass a certain level of evaluation. Sometimes a top-down approach is necessary for external reasons, as with an interplanetary space probe where you'll only get one shot at it.

But very often the detailed requirements aren't known in advance and an iterative approach is necessary. The technology may be changing; the environment could be changing; or a critical part of the project may be the design of a human-computer interface, which will probably involve testing several prototypes. Very often the designer's most important task is to help the customer decide what they want, and although this can sometimes be done by discussion, there will often be a need for some prototyping.

Sometimes a formal project is just too slow. Reginald Jones attributes much of the UK's relative success in electronic warfare in World War II to the fact that British scientists hacked stuff together quickly, while the Germans used a rigid top-down development methodology, getting beautifully engineered equipment but always six months too late [993].

But the most common reason for using iterative development is that we're starting from an existing product that we want to improve. Even in the early days of computing, most programmer effort was always expended on maintaining and enhancing existing programs rather than developing new ones; surveys suggest that 70–80% of the total cost of ownership of a successful IT product is incurred after it first goes into service, even when a waterfall methodology was used [2063]. Nowadays, as software becomes a matter of embedded code, apps and cloud services–which all become ever more complex–the reality in many firms is that 'the maintenance is the product'.

Even in the late 1990s, when the most complex human artefacts were software packages such as Microsoft Office, the only way to write such a thing was to start off from the existing version and enhance it. That does not make the waterfall model obsolete; on the contrary, it is often used to manage a project to develop a major new feature, or to refactor existing code. However, the overall management of a major product nowadays is likely to be based on iteration.

27.5.2 Iterative design: from spiral to agile

There are different flavours of iterative development, ranging from a rapid prototyping exercise to firm up the specification of a new product, through to a managed process for fixing or enhancing an existing system.

In the first case, one approach is the *spiral model* in which development proceeds through a pre-agreed number of iterations in which a prototype is built and tested, with managers being able to evaluate the risk at each stage so they can decide whether to proceed with the next iteration or to cut their losses. Devised by Barry Boehm, it's called the spiral model because the process is often depicted as in Figure 27.5. There are many applications where an initial prototype is the key first step; from a startup aiming to produce a demo to show to investors, through a company building a mockup of a new product to show a focus group, to DARPA seedling projects that aim to establish that some proposed technology isn't completely impossible. Prototype applications for the security engineer range from security usability testbeds to proof-of-concept attack code. The key is to solve the worst problem you're facing, so as to reduce the project risk as much as possible.

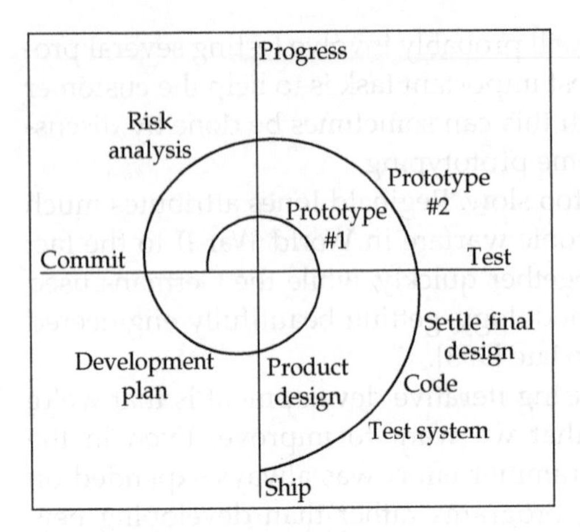

Figure 27.5: The spiral model

The second case we now describe as *agile development*, which may be summed up in the slogan: "Solve your worst problem. Repeat".

An early advocate for an evolutionary approach was Harlan Mills, who taught that you should build the smallest system that works, try it out on real users, and then add functionality in small increments. This is how the packaged software industry had learned to work by the 1990s: as PCs became more capable, software products became so complex that they could not be economically developed (or redeveloped) from scratch. Indeed, Microsoft tried more than once to rewrite Word, but gave up each time. A landmark early book on evolutionary development was 'Debugging the Development Process' by Steve Maguire of Microsoft in 1994 [1211]. In this view of the world, products aren't the result of a project but of a process that involves continually modifying previous versions. Microsoft contrasted its approach with that of IBM, then still the largest IT company; in the IBM ecosystem, the waterfall approach was dominant. (IBMers for their part decried Microsoft as a bunch of undisciplined hackers who produced buggy, unreliable code; but IBM's near-death experience after Microsoft stole their main business markets has been ascribed to the rigidity of the IBM approach to development [392].) Professional practice has evolved in the quarter century since then, and evolutionary development is now known as 'agile', but it is recognisably the same beast.

A key insight about evolutionary development is that just as each generation of a biological species has to be viable for the species to continue, so each generation of an evolving software product must be viable. The core technology is *regression testing*. At regular intervals – typically once a day – all the teams working on different features of a product check in their code, which gets compiled to a *build* that is then tested automatically against a large set of inputs. The regression test checks whether things that used to work still work, and that old bugs haven't found their way back. It's always possible that someone's code broke the build, so we consider the current 'generation' to be the last build that worked. Things are slightly more complex when systems have to work together, as when an app has to talk to a cloud service, or when several electronic components in a vehicle have to work together, or where a single vehicle component has to be customised to work in several different vehicles. You can end up with a hierarchy of builds and test regimes. But one way or another, we always have viable code that we can ship out for beta testing, or whatever the next stage of our process might be.

The technology of testing was probably the biggest practical improvement in software engineering during the 1990s and early 2000s. Before automated regression tests were widely used, IBM engineers used to reckon that 15% of bug fixes either introduced new bugs or reintroduced old ones [18]. The move to evolutionary development was associated with a number of other changes. For example, IBM had separated the roles of system analyst, programmer and tester; the analyst spoke to the customer and produced a design, which the programmer coded, and then the tester looked for bugs in the code. The incentives weren't quite right, as the programmer could throw lots of buggy code over the fence and hope that someone else would fix it. This was slow and led to bloated code. Microsoft abolished the distinction between analysts, programmers and testers; it had only developers, who spoke to the customer and were also responsible for fixing their own bugs. This held up the bad programmers who wrote lots of bugs, so that more of the code was produced by the more skilful and careful developers. According to Steve Maguire, this is what enabled Microsoft to win the battle to rule the world of 32-bit operating systems; their better development methodology let them take a $100bn business-software market from IBM [1211].

27.5.3 The secure development lifecycle

By the early 2000s, Microsoft had overtaken IBM as the leading tech company, but it was facing ever more criticism for security vulnerabilities in Windows and Office that led to more and more malware. Servers were moving to Linux and individual users were starting to buy Macs. Eventually in January 2002 Bill Gates sent all staff a 'trustworthy computing' memo ordering them to prioritise security over features, and stopping all development while engineers got security training. Their internal training materials became books and papers that helped drive change in the broader ecosystem. I already discussed their threat modelling in section 27.3.5; their first take on secure development appeared in 2002 in Michael Howard and David LeBlanc's '*Writing Secure Code*' [929], which sets out the early Microsoft approach to managing the security lifecycle, and which I discussed in the second edition of this book. More appeared over time and their *security development lifecycle* (SDL) appeared in 2008, being adopted widely by Windows developers.

The widely used 2010 'simplified implementation' of SDL is essentially a waterfall process [1310]. It 'aims to reduce the number and severity of vulnerabilities in software' and 'introduces security and privacy throughout all phases of the development process'. The 'pre-SDL' component is security training; it's assumed that all the developers get a basic course, the contents of which will depend on whether they're building operating systems, web services or whatever. There are then five SDL components.

1. Requirements: this involves a risk assessment and the establishment of quality gates or 'bug bars' that will prevent code getting to the next stage if it contains certain types of flaw. The requirements themselves are reviewed regularly; at Microsoft, the reviews are never more than six months apart.
2. Design: this stage requires threat modelling and establishment of the attack surface, to feed into the detailed design of the product.
3. Implementation: here, developers have to use approved tools, avoid or deprecate unsafe functions, and perform static analysis on the code to check this has been done.
4. Verification: this step involves dynamic analysis, fuzz testing, and a review of the attack surface.
5. Release: this is predicated on an incident response plan and a final security review.

As well as providing some basic security training to all developers, there are some further organisational aspects. First, security needs a subject-matter expert (SME) from outside the dev team, and a security or privacy champion within the team itself to check that everything gets done.

Second, there is a maturity model. Starting in 1989, Watts Humphrey developed the *Capability Maturity Model* (CMM) at the Software Engineering Institute at Carnegie-Mellon University (CMU), based on the idea that competence is a function of teams rather than just individual developers. There's more to a band than just throwing together half-a-dozen competent musicians, and the same holds for software. Developers start off with different coding styles, different conventions for commenting and formatting code, different ways of managing APIs, and even different workflow rhythms. The CMU research showed that newly-formed teams tended to underestimate the amount of work in a project, and also had a high variance in the amount of time they took; the teams that worked best together were much better able to predict how long they'd take, in terms of the mean development time, but reduced the variance as well [1941]. This requires the self-discipline to sacrifice some efficiency in resource allocation in order to provide continuity for individual engineers and to maintain the team's collective expertise. Microsoft adapted this and defines four levels of security maturity for developer teams.

27.5.4 Gated development

It's telling that the biggest firm pushing evolutionary development reverted to a waterfall approach for security. Many of the security engineering approaches of the time were tied up with waterfall assumptions, and automated testing on its own is less useful for the security engineer for a number of reasons. Security properties are both emergent and diverse, we security engineers are fewer in number, and there hasn't been as much investment in tools. Specific attack types often need specific remedies, and many security flaws cross a system's levels of abstraction, such as when specification errors interact with user interface features – the sort of problem for which it's difficult to devise automated tests. But although regression testing is not sufficient, it is necessary, as it finds functionality that's been affected by a change. It's particularly important when development sprints add lots of features that can interact with each other. For this reason, security patches to Windows are an example of *gated development*: at regular intervals, a pre-release version of the product is pushed through a whole series of additional tests and reviews and prepared for release. This is fairly common across systems with safety or security requirements. The preparation may involve testing with a wide variety of peripherals and applications in the case of Windows, or recertification in the case of software for a regulated product.

An issue many neglect is that security requirements evolve, and also have to be maintained and upgraded. They can be driven by changing environments, evolving threats, new dependencies on platforms old and new, and a bundle of other things. Some changes are implicit; for example, when you upgrade your static analysis tools you may find hundreds of 'new' bugs in your existing codebase, which you have to triage. Once more Microsoft was a pioneer here. When a vulnerability was found in Windows, it's not enough to just patch it; whoever wrote it might have written a dozen similar ones that are now scattered throughout the codebase, and once you publish a patch, the bad guys study it and understand it. So rather than just fixing a single bug, you update your toolchain so you find and eliminate all similar bugs across your products. In order to manage the costs, both for Microsoft and its customers, the company started bundling patches together into a monthly update, the now famous 'patch Tuesday', in 2003. From then until 2015, all customers – from enterprises to the users of home PCs and tablets – had their software updated on the second Tuesday every month. And such patching creates further dependencies. Modern quality tools can help you check that no code has a CVE open, so all your customers should have to patch too, if they live by such tools. But many don't: as many as 70% of apps on both phones and desktops have vulnerabilities in the open-source libraries they use, and which could usually be fixed by a simple update [1698]. Since 2015, Windows home users receive continuous updates[4].

Much the same considerations apply to safety-critical systems, which are similar in many respects to secure systems. Safety, like security, is an emergent property of whole systems, and it doesn't compose. Safety used to depend, in most applications, on extensive pre-market testing. But it's hard for a connected device to have safety without security, and now that devices such as cars are connected to the Internet, they are acquiring patch cycles too. Yet ensuring that the latest version of a safety-critical system satisfies the safety case may require extensive and expensive testing. For example, a car may contain dozens of *electronic control units* (ECUs) from different component suppliers, and in addition to testing the individual ECUs you have to test how they work together. Firms in the car industry are mutually suspicious and won't share source code with each other, even under NDA, so testing can be complex. The main test rig may be a 'lab car' containing all the electronics from a particular model of car, plus extra test systems that let you simulate various maneuvers and even accidents. These cost real money, and you also need to keep real vehicles for road testing. The cost of maintaining fleets of lab cars and real test cars is one of the reasons car companies dragged their heels when the EU decided to require them to patch car software for ten years after the last vehicle left the showroom.

This is one respect in which Tesla has a significant advantage; as a tech company with software at the core of its business, Tesla can test and ship changes in weeks that take the legacy car firms years, as they leave most of the software development to the component suppliers [406]. Traditionally, automotive software contracts involved ten years' support; now you need to support a product for three years' development, seven years in the showroom and a further ten after that. I'll discuss the sustainability aspects of this in the next chapter. Meanwhile, Tesla is forcing the legacy industry to raise its game, with VW announcing they've spent $8bn to create a proper software division, just as their main electric car project runs late [1689].

27.5.5 Software as a Service

Since the early 2010s, more and more software has been hosted on central servers, accessed by thin clients and paid for on a subscription basis, rather

[4]This also breaks things: we were once about to demonstrate an experiment using a body motion-capture suit to a TV crew when the Windows laptop we used to drive it updated itself, and suddenly the capture software wouldn't work any more. There followed frantic phone calls to the software developer in the Netherlands and thankfully we got their update a few hours later, just in time for the show.

than being sold and distributed to users. The typical customer has many costs for running software beyond the license fee, including not just the cost of servers and operators but of deploying it, upgrading it regularly and managing it. If the vendor can take over these tasks from all their customers, many duplicated costs are removed, and they can manage things better because of their specialised knowledge. Software can be instrumented so that developers can monitor all aspects of its performance on a dashboard.

The key technical innovations behind *Software as a Service* (SaaS) are *continuous integration* and *continuous deployment*. Rather than having thousands of customers managing dozens of different versions of the software, the vendor can migrate a few customers to a new version to test it, and then migrate the rest. Upgrades become much more controllable, as they can be tested in a dry run against a snapshot of the real customer data, called a *staging environment*. Some companies now deploy several times a day, as their experience is that frequent small changes can be safer and have less risk of breaking something than a larger deployment, such as Microsoft's Patch Tuesday.

Deployment itself is tentative. A SaaS company will typically run its software on a number of service instances running on VMs behind a load balancer, which provides a point of indirection for managing running services. The separate instances also provide separate *failure domains* to improve robustness. To do a *rolling deployment* we configure a load balancer to send say 1% of the traffic to an instance with the new version, often called the 'canary' after the caged bird used by miners to detect carbon monoxide leaks. If the canary survives, deployment can be rolled forward progressively to new service instances. If the logging system detects any problems, developers are alerted. Some care needs to be taken that things don't go wrong if users flap between old and new versions of a design between transactions. If you make a change that breaks backwards compatibility, you typically build an intermediate stage that will work with both old and new systems (we were doing this in the world of bank mainframes back in the 1980s anyway).

The ability to manage risks through phased release and rolling deployment changes the economics of testing. The fact that you can fix bugs extremely quickly mean that you can achieve a target quality level with much less testing. You can also see everything the users do, so for the first time you can really understand how usability fails from the point of view of security, safety – and revenue. Of course it's revenue that usually drives the exploitation of this. Analytics collectors write all behavioural events to a log, which is fed into a data pipeline for metrics, analytics and queries. This in turn supports experiment frameworks that can do extensive A/B testing of possible features. Ad-driven services can optimise by engagement metrics such as active users, time per user session and use of specific features. Controlled experiments are used to improve security too; for example, Google has tuned its browser warnings by measuring how millions of users react to different warnings of expired certificates. Such improvements are usually fairly small by themselves, so you really need controlled experiments to measure them; but when you do lots of them, they add up. The investment in building such frameworks into the phased deployment mechanisms gives an increasing return to scale; the more users you have, the faster you can achieve statistical significance. So large firms can optimise their products more quickly than their smaller competitors; SaaS, like a lot of other digital technology, not only cuts costs in the short term, but increases lock-in in the long term. Each time you access a service from a large SaaS firm, you may be an unwitting participant in tens or even hundreds of experiments. There are lots of fiddly details about running multiple concurrent experiments while also deploying system enhancements.

Things can get more complex still when you have services put together from multiple microservices. This brings us to the world of *infrastructure as code*, also known as cloud native development or DevOps, where everything is developed in containers, VMs etc., so all the infrastructure is based on code and can be replicated quickly. You can also use containers to simplify things, packaging as many security dependencies with the code as possible. New code can be deployed to a test infrastructure rapidly and tested realistically. You could if you wanted manage rolling deployment manually, but this is not scalable and prone to error. The solution is to write *deployment code*, as part of the application development process, that uses the cloud platform APIs to allow applications to deploy themselves and the associated infrastructure, and to hook into the monitoring mechanisms. In the last few years, some toolkits have become available that allow engineers to do this in a more declarative fashion.

The best guide to this I know is Google's 2013 book '*Site Reliability Engineering*'; SRE is their term for DevOps [237]. Google led the industry in the art of building large dependable systems out of large fleets of low-cost PCs, building the necessary engineering for load balancing, replication, sharding and redundancy. As they operated at a larger scale than anybody else through the 2000s and early 2010s, they had to automate more tasks and became good at it. The goals of SRE are availability, latency, performance, efficiency, change management, monitoring, emergency response, and capacity planning. The core strategy is to apply software engineering techniques to automate system administration tasks so as to balance rapid innovation with availability.

As we already noted, there's no point striving for 99.9999% availability if ISPs only let users get to your servers 99% or 99.9% of the time. If you set a realistic error budget, say 0.1% or 0.01% unavailability, you can use that to achieve a number of things. First, most outages are due to live system changes, so you monitor latency, traffic, errors and saturation well and roll back quickly whenever anything goes wrong. You use the rest of the error budget to support your experimental framework, and doing controlled outages to flush dependencies. (This was pioneered by Netflix whose 'chaos monkey' would occasionally take down routers, servers, load balancers and other components, to check that the resilience mechanisms worked as intended; such 'fire drills' are now an industry standard and involve taking down whole data centres.)

In section 12.2.6.2, we mentioned *technical debt*. This concept, due to Ward Cunningham, encapsulates the observation that development shortcuts are like debt. Whenever we skimp on documentation, fix a problem with a quick-and-dirty kludge, don't test a fix thoroughly, fail to build in security controls, or fail to work through the consequences of errors, we're storing up problems that may have to be repaid with interest in the future [42]. Technical debt may make sense for a startup, or a system nearing the end of its life, but it's more often a product of poor management or poorly-aligned incentives. Over time, systems can fall so deeply into debt that they become too hard to maintain or to use; they have to be refactored or replaced. For a bank to have to replace its core banking systems is hugely expensive and disruptive. So managing technical debt is really important; this is one of the changes in system management thinking since the second edition of this book. One important aspect of the philosophy of DevOps is to run debt-free.

27.5.6 From DevOps to DevSecOps

As I write, in 2020, the cutting edge is applying agile ideas and methodology not just to development and operations, but to security too. In theory this can mean a strategy of 'everything as code'; in practice it means not just maintaining an existing security rating (and safety case if relevant) but responding to new threats, environmental changes, and surprising vulnerabilities. Bringing the two together involves real work, and sometimes things need to be reinvented. I mentioned for example in section 12.2.2 that DevOps undermines the separation between development and production on which banks have relied for years; where separation of duties is necessary, we have to reimagine it.

We see several different approaches in the companies with which we work. In what follows I will give two examples, which we might roughly call the Microsoft world and the Google world. There are of course many others.

27.5.6.1 *The Azure ecosystem*

Most of the world's largest commercial firms from banks and insurers through retail to shipping and mining have built their enterprise systems on Windows over the past 25 years and are now migrating them to Azure, often using systems integration and facilities management firms to do the actual work. The typical client has a mixture of on-premises and cloud systems with new developments mostly migrating from the former to the latter. Here policy is largely set by the Big Four auditors who, in addition to their standard set of internal control features, follow Microsoft in requiring a secure development lifecycle. The several dozen tools used to do threat modelling, static analysis, dynamic analysis, fuzz testing, app and network monitoring, security orchestration and incident response impose a significant overhead with dozens of people copying data from one tool to another. The DevSecOps task here is to progressively integrate the tools by automating these administrative tasks.

To support this ecosystem, Microsoft has extended its SDL with further steps: defining metrics and compliance reporting; threat modelling; cryptography standards; managing the security risks of third-party components; penetration testing; and a standardised incident response. The firm now claims that 10% of its engineering investment is in cybersecurity. The capable system integration and facilities management firms have worked out ways of building these steps into their workflows; much of the actual work involves integrating the third-party security products that they or their customers have bought. Appropriate automation is vital for the security team to continue raising their game, extending their scope and increasing effectiveness; without it, they fall further and further behind, and burn out [1850].

The organising principles for DevSecOps in such a company will be to 'shift left', which can cover a number of things: the unifying theme is moving security, like software and infrastructure, into the codebase. One strategy is to cause things to 'fail fast' including engaging security experts early enough in the development process to avoid delays later: doing pre-commit static analysis of each developer's code to minimise failed builds; buying or building specialist tools to detect errors such as incorrect authentication, mistakes in using crypto functions, and injection opportunities; both automated and manual security testing of new versions; and automated testing of configuration and deployment including scanning of the staging network and checks on credentials, encryption keys and so on. And while, back in 2010, Microsoft considered operational security to be separate from software security, a modern Azure shop will close the loop by following up deployment with continuous monitoring, manual penetration tests and finally bug bounties for third parties who spot something wrong. We will discuss these in more detail later.

27.5.6.2 The Google ecosystem

A second view comes from engineers working on infrastructure, and the best reference I know is a 2020 book by six Google engineers, *'Building Secure and Reliable Systems'* [23]. Amazon's DevSecOps strategy is somewhat similar, but optimised for their product offerings; it is described by their CTO Werner Vogels at [1970]. However, the Google experience is described in much more detail. This section draws on their book, and on colleagues who have worked recently at the major service firms.

When building infrastructure systems on which hundreds of millions of people will rely, it is critical to automate support functions quickly, and to have really robust processes for threat identification, incident response, damage limitation and service recovery. So while a facilities-management firm might work at integrating support functions to save money and reduce errors, the emphasis at major service firms is reliability. I already mentioned the Google approach to site reliability engineering: set a realistic target, of say 99.9% availability, and then use the residual error budget of 0.1% downtime by apportioning it between failure recovery, upgrades and experiments.

This in turn drives further principles such as design for recoverability, design for understandability, and a desire to stop humans touching production systems wherever possible. It's not enough to have automation for the incremental deployment of new binaries; you also want to stop sysadmins having to type complicated command lines into routers to configure networks; this is where most of the network outages come from, as we noted in section 21.2.1. You manage such risks by building suitable tool proxies. This can involve quite a lot of work to align the update of binary and config files and work out how to allocate support and recovery effort between SRE and security engineering teams. Further complexity arises with secure testing. How do you build test infrastructures to exercise least privilege? How do you test systems that contain large amounts of personal information? How do you test the break-glass mechanisms that give SRE teams emergency human access to live systems? Most of these are questions we already had to deal with in the mainframe world of the 1980s, but they arose only occasionally and were dealt with by human ingenuity and by trusting some key staff. Scaling everything up from thousands of users to billions means that a lot more has to be automated.

There are still tensions. In site reliability engineering, alarms should be as simple, predictable and reliable as possible; but in security, some randomisation is often a good idea.

At the application level, systems are increasingly compartmentalised into microservice components with defensible security boundaries and tamper-resistant security contexts, so that if Alice compromises a shopping system's catalogue, she still can't spend money as Bob as the payment service is separate. Each component will typically be implemented as a number of parallel copies or shards, giving still smaller failure domains. Such domains enable you to limit the blast radius of any compromise; ideally, you want to be able to deal with an intrusion without taking your whole system offline. Compartmentalised systems can be engineered for resilience too, but this is not straightforward. When a failure domain fails, when do you just spin up a new one, and when do you do something different? What are the dependencies? Which components should fail open, and which should fail secure? What sort of degraded performance is acceptable under congestion, or under attack?

What's the role of load shedding and throttling? And what sort of pain can you rationally inflict on users, and on business models? Do you ditch some of the ads, require extra CAPTCHAs for logons, or both? And how do you test and validate all these resilience mechanisms?

Large firms invest a lot of engineering time in building application frameworks for such services. There are also standard frameworks for web pages, which should not only prevent SQL injection and cross-site scripting attacks in the first place, but also provide support for dozens of different languages. Having a single front end to terminate all http(s) and TLS traffic means that if you have to update your certificate management mechanisms or ciphersuites you only need to do it once, not in all your different services. A single front end can also provide a single location for load balancing and DDoS protection, as well as for many other functions such as supporting dozens of different languages.

Using type encapsulation to enforce properties of URLs, SQL and so on can reduce the amount of code you need to verify. If you have secure-by-construction APIs that are also understandable, that's best. Google has a crypto API called Tink that forces more correct use. It requires use of a key management service, whether in the Google cloud, AWS or the Android keystore. This fits into an overall framework for managing crypto termination, code provenance, integrity verification and workload isolation, called BeyondProd [1000].

27.5.6.3 Creating a learning system

Whether you follow the Microsoft approach, the Google approach or your own, to tune such a process you need metrics, and suitable candidates include the numbers of security tickets opened to dev teams, the number of security-failed builds, and the time it takes for a new application to achieve compliance under the relevant regulation (whether SOX, GDPR or HIPAA). As Dev, Sec and Ops converge, the metrics and management processes converge with the network defence mechanisms discussed in section 21.4, from network monitoring to security incident and event management. But all this needs to be managed intelligently. A well-run firm can make the security process more visible to all the dev/ops staff via the sprints that you do to work up a privacy impact assessment, improve access controls, extend logging or whatever. A badly-run firm will manage to the metrics, which will create tensions: their security staff can end up with conflicting goals of keeping the bad guys out, and also of 'feeding the beast' by hitting all the metrics used to justify the team's own existence [1850]. It's important to understand where conflicts naturally arise as a function of the organisation's management structure, and somehow keep them constructive.

One of the big drivers in either case, though, will be the vulnerability lifecycle. The processes whereby bugs become exploits and then attacks, and these attacks are noticed leading to vulnerability reports, interim defences using devices such as firewalls, then definitive patches that are rolled out not just to direct users but along complex supply chains, is ever more central to security management.

27.5.7 The vulnerability cycle

Back in the 1970s and 1980s, people sometimes described the evolutionary procedure of finding security bugs in systems and then fixing them dismissively as *penetrate-and-patch*. It was hoped that some combination of an architecture that limited the attack surface and the application of formal methods would enable us to escape. As we've seen, that didn't really work, except in a few edge cases such as cryptographic equipment. By the early 2000s, we had come to the conclusion that we just had to manage the patch cycle better, and the modern approach of security breach disclosure laws, CERTs and responsible disclosure bedded down during this period. I discussed the security economics of this in section 8.6.2; let's now look at the technical details.

The vulnerability cycle consists of the process whereby someone, the *researcher*, discovers a vulnerability in a system that is maintained by a *vendor*. The researcher may be a *customer*, an academic, a contractor for a national intelligence agency or even a criminal. They may sell it in a market. The idea of vulnerability markets was first suggested by Jean Camp and Catherine Wolfram in 2000 [373]; firms were set up to buy vulnerabilities, and over time several markets emerged. Most of the big software and service firms now offer bug bounties, which can range from thousands to hundreds of thousands of dollars; at the other extreme are operators who buy up exploits for sale to *exploiters* such as cyber-arms manufacturers (who sell to military and intelligence agencies) and forensic firms (who sell to law enforcement). Such operators now offer millions of dollars for persistent remote exploits of Android and iOS.

The researcher may also disclose the bug to the vendor directly – nowadays many vendors have a *bug bounty program* that pays rewards for disclosed vulnerabilities that attempt to match market prices, at least in order of magnitude. As market prices for zero-day exploits against popular platforms have headed into six and even seven figures, so have bug bounties. Apple, for example, offers $1M for anyone who can hack the iOS kernel without requiring any clicks by the user. In 2019, it emerged that at least six hackers have now earned over $1M through the bug bounty platform HackerOne alone [2033]. A downside of large bug bounties is that while bugs used to occur naturally, we now see them being introduced deliberately, for example by contributors to open-source projects whose code ends up in significant platforms. Such *supply-chain attacks* used to be the preserve of nation states; now they're opening up [892].

If an exploit is used in the wild before the vendor issues a patch, it is called a *zero day*, and is typically used for targeted attacks. If it's used enough, then eventually someone will notice; the attack gets reported, and then the vendor issues a patch, which may be reverse engineered so that many other actors now have exploit code. Customers who fail to patch their systems are now vulnerable to multiple exploits that can be deployed at scale by crime gangs.

Getting the patching cycle right is a problem in the economics of information security as much as anything else, because the interests of the various stakeholders can diverge quite radically.

1. The vendor would prefer that bugs weren't found at all, to spare the expense of patching. They'll patch if they have to but want to minimise the cost, which may include a lot of testing if their code appears in lots of product versions. Indeed, if their code is used in customer devices that now need patching (like cars) they may have to pay an indemnity to cover their customer's costs; so in such industries there's an even more acute incentive for foot-dragging and denial.
2. The average customer might prefer that bugs weren't found, to avoid the hassle of patching. Lazy customers may fail to patch, and get infected as a result. (If all the infected machines do is send a bit of spam, their owners may not notice or care.)
3. The typical security researcher wants some reward for their discoveries, whether fame, cash or getting a fix for a system they rely on.
4. The intelligence agencies want to learn of vulnerabilities quickly, so they can be used in zero-day exploits before a patch is shipped.
5. The security software firms benefit from unpatched vulnerabilities as their firewalls and AV software can look for their indicators of compromise to block attacks that exploit them.
6. Large companies don't like patches, and neither do government departments, as the process of testing a new patch against the enterprise's critical systems and rolling it out is expensive. The better ones have built automation to deal with regular events like Microsoft's Patch Tuesday, but updating or risk-assessing the zillions of IoT devices in their offices and factories will be a headache for years to come. Most firms just don't have a good enough asset inventory system to cope.

During the 1990s, the debate was driven by people who were frustrated at software vendors for leaving products unpatched for months or even years. The bugtraq mailing list was set up to provide a way for people to disclose bugs anonymously; but this meant that a product might be completely vulnerable for a month or two until a patch was written, tested and shipped, and until customer firms had tested it and installed it. This led to a debate on 'responsible disclosure' with various proposals about how long a breathing space the researcher should give the vendor [1575].

As we discussed in section 8.6.2, the consensus that emerged was responsible disclosure: that researchers should disclose vulnerabilities to a computer emergency response team (CERT)[5] and the global network of CERTs would inform the vendor, with a delay for a patch to be issued before the vulnerability was published. The threat of eventual disclosure got vendors off their butts; the delay gave them enough time to test a fix properly before releasing it; researchers got credit to put on their CVs; customers got bug fixes at the same time as bug reports; and the big companies organised regular updates for which their corporate customers can plan. Oh, and the agencies had a hot line into their local CERT, so they learned of naturally occurring exploits in advance and could exploit them. This was part of the deal described in section 26.2.7.3 that ended Crypto War 1 back in 2000.

27.5.7.1 The CVE system

An industrial aspect is the *Common Vulnerabilities and Exposures* (CVE) system, launched in 1999, which assigns numbers to reported vulnerabilities in publicly released software packages. This is maintained by Mitre, but it delegates the assignment of CVEs to large vendors. CVE IDs are commonly included in security advisories, enabling you to search for details of the reporting date, affected products, available remedies and other relevant information. There is a Common Vulnerability Scoring System (CVSS) that provides a numerical representation of the severity of a vulnerability. The method for calculating this has become steadily more complex over time and now depends on whether the attack requires local access, its complexity, the effort required, its effects, the availability of exploit code and of patches, the number of targets and the potential for damage.

NIST's *National Vulnerability Database* (NVD), described as a "comprehensive cybersecurity vulnerability database that integrates all publicly available US Government vulnerability resources and provides references to industry resources", is based on the CVE List. These resources are critical for automating the tracking of vulnerabilities and updates. There are now so many thousands of vulnerabilities reported, and so many hundreds of patches shipped, that automation is essential.

As the system was bedding down, it became a subject of study by security economists. Traditionalists argued that since bugs are many and uncorrelated, and since most exploits use vulnerabilities reverse-engineered from existing patches, there should be minimal disclosure. Pragmatists argued that,

[5] The EU is renaming these CSIRTs – computer security incident response teams.

from both theoretical and empirical perspectives, the threat of disclosure was needed to get vendors to patch. I discussed this argument in section 8.6.2. Since then we have seen the introduction of automatic upgrades for mass-market users, the establishment of firms that make markets in vulnerabilities, and empirical research on the extent to which bugs are correlated. Modulo some tuning, the current computer industry way of doing things has been stable for over a decade.

27.5.7.2 Coordinated disclosure

Yet some industries are lagging well behind. In section 4.3.1 I described how Volkswagen sued academics at Birmingham and Nijmegen universities after they discovered, and responsibly disclosed, vulnerabilities in Volkswagen's remote key entry system that were already being exploited in car-theft tools that were available online. This was Volkswagen's mistake; it drew attention to the vulnerability, and they also lost in court. Companies like Microsoft and Google have had twenty years to learn that running bug bounty programs and monthly patching works better than threatening to sue people, but a lot of firms in legacy industries still haven't worked this out even though their products contain more and more software.

One of the problems in the Volkswagen case was that the researchers initially disclosed the vulnerability to the supplier of its key entry system, which in turn told Volkswagen only at the last minute. As a result of supply chain problems like this, responsible disclosure has given way to *coordinated disclosure*. Few firms build all their own tools any more, and even a child's toy may have multiple software dependencies. If it does speech and gesture recognition, it probably contains an Arm chip running some flavour of Linux or FreeBSD, communicates with a cloud service running another flavour of Linux, and can be controlled by an app that may run on Android or iOS. The safety of the toy will depend on secure communications; for example, it was discovered in February 2019 that the communications between Enox's 'Safe-KID-One' toy watch and its back-end server were unencrypted, so that hackers could in theory track and call kids. The response was an immediate EU-wide safety recall [653]. Getting this sort of thing wrong can be sudden death for your product, and your company.

Now what happens when someone discovers an exploitable bug in a platform used in dozens of embedded products? This can be traumatic, as with the Shellshock bug in Linux and the Heartbleed bug in OpenSSL (which also affected Linux). If Linux gets an emergency patch, coordinating the disclosure is a nightmare: the Linux maintainers may be able to work in private with the main Linux distributions, and with derivatives like Android whose developers keep in close contact with them. But there are the thousands of products that incorporate Linux, from alarm clocks to TVs and from kids' toys to land mines. You may suddenly find that the CCTV cameras in your building security system have all become hackable, and the vendor can't fix them quickly or at all. Coordinating disclosure on platforms is one of the seriously hard problems. There is no silver bullet, but there are still many things you can do, ranging from documenting your upstream and downstream dependencies, through aggressive testing of software you depend on so you get to exercise and understand the bug reporting mechanisms, to becoming part of its developer community.

Dealing with such shocks is just one aspect of a process that in the late 2010s became a speciality of its own, namely security incident and event management.

27.5.7.3 Security incident and event management

You need an incident response plan for what you'll do when you learn of a vulnerability or an attack. In the old days, vendors could take months to respond with a new version of the product, and would often do nothing at all but issue a warning (or even a denial). Nowadays, breach-notification laws in both the USA and Europe oblige firms to disclose attacks where individuals' privacy could have been compromised, and people expect that problems will be fixed quickly. Your plan needs four components: monitoring, repair, distribution and reassurance.

First, make sure you learn of vulnerabilities as soon as you can – and preferably no later than the bad guys (or the press) do. This means building a threat intelligence team. In some applications you can just acquire threat intelligence data from specialist firms, while if you're an IoT vendor, it may be prudent to operate your own honeypots so you get immediate warning of people attacking your products. Listening to customers is important: you need an efficient way for them to report bugs. It may be an idea to provide some incentive, such as points towards their next upgrade, lottery tickets or even cash. You absolutely need to engage with the larger technical ecosystem of bug bounties, vulnerability markets, CERTs and CVEs described in section 27.5.7.

Second, you need to be able to repair the problem. Twenty years ago, that meant having one member of each product team 'on call' with a pager in case something needed fixing at three in the morning. Nowadays it means preparing an orchestrated response to anything from a vulnerability report to a major breach. This will extend from the intrusion-detection and network monitoring functions we discussed in section 21.4.2.3 and the threat intelligence team through to identifying the dev teams responsible and notifying both your suppliers upstream and your customers downstream. Responder teams may also need alternative means of communication. Did you ever stop to think whether you need satellite phones?

Third, you need to be able to deploy the patch rapidly: if all the software runs on your own servers, then it may be easy, but if it involves patching code in millions of consumer devices, then advance planning is needed. It may seem easy to get your customers to visit your website once a day and check for upgrades, but if their own systems depend on your devices and they need to test any dependencies, there's a tension [196]: pioneers who apply patches quickly can discover problems that break their systems, while people who take time to test will be more vulnerable to attack. The longer the supply chains get, the harder the conflicts of interest are to manage. Operations matter hugely: an emergency patch process that isn't tested may do more harm than good, and experience teaches that in an emergency you just run your normal patch process as fast as possible [23].

Finally, you need to educate your CEO and main board directors in advance about the need to deal quickly and honestly with a security breach in order to keep confidence and limit damage, by giving them compelling examples of firms that did well and others that did badly. You need to have a mechanism to get through to your CEO and brief them immediately so they can show the thing's under control and reassure your key customers. So you need to know the mobile and home phone numbers of everyone who might be needed urgently. And you need a plan to deal with the press. The last thing you need is for dozens of journalists to phone up and be stonewalled by your PR person or even your switchboard operator as you struggle madly to fix the bug. Have a set of press releases ready for incidents of varying severity, so that your CEO only has to pick the right one and fill in the details. This can then ship as soon as the first (or perhaps the second) journalist calls.

Remind your CEO that both the USA and Europe have security-breach disclosure laws, so if your systems are hacked and millions of customer card numbers compromised, you have to notify all current and former customers, which costs real money. As we discussed in section 26.6.2, you can expect to lose customers and take a hit to your stock price if you have a large breach or more than one small one; and if it's really bad your CEO can get fired. Information security is a CEO issue.

27.5.8 Organizational mismanagement of risk

Organizational issues are not just a contributory factor in system failure, as with the loss of organizational memory and the lack of mechanisms for monitoring changing environments. They can often be a primary cause. There's a large literature on how people behave in organisations, which I touched on in section 8.6.8, and I've given a number of further examples in various chapters. However, the importance of organisational factors increases as projects get bigger. Bezos' law says you can't run a dev project with more people than can be fed from two pizzas. A team of eight people is just about manageable, but you can't go six times as fast by having six such teams in parallel. If a project involves multiple teams the members can't talk to each other at random, or you get chaos; and they can't route all their communications through the lowest common manager as there isn't the bandwidth. As you scale up, the coordination will start to involve a proliferation of middle managers, staff departments and committees. The communications complexity of a clean military chain of command, for N people with no lateral interaction, is $\log N$; where everybody has to consult everybody else, it's N^2; and where any subset can form a committee to think about the problem, it can head towards 2^N. Business school people have written extensively about this, and their methodology is generally based on case studies.

Many large development projects have crashed and burned. The problems appear to be much the same whether the disaster is a matter of safety, of security or of the software simply never working at all; so security people can learn a lot from studying project failures documented in the general engineering literature.

A classic study of large software project disasters was written by Bill Curtis, Herb Krasner, and Neil Iscoe [504]. They found that failure to understand the requirements was mostly to blame: a thin spread of application domain knowledge typically led to fluctuating and conflicting requirements, which in turn caused a breakdown in communication. The example I give in my undergraduate lectures is the meltdown of a new dispatch system for the London Ambulance Service where a combination of an overly ambitious project, an inadequate specification and no real testing led to the city being without ambulance cover for a day. There are all too many such examples; I use the London Ambulance Service case because the subsequent inquiry documented the causes rather well [1809]. I also happened to be in London that day, so I remember it. If you haven't ever read the inquiry report, I recommend you do so. (In fact, I strongly recommend that you read lots of case studies of project failure.)

The millennium bug gives another useful data point. If one accepts that many large commercial and government systems needed extensive repair work to change two-digit dates into four-digit ones in preparation for the year 2000, and the conventional experience that a significant proportion of large development projects are late or never delivered at all, many people naturally assumed that a significant number of systems would fail at the end of 1999, and predicted widespread chaos. But this didn't happen. Certainly, the risks to the systems used by small and medium-sized firms were overstated; we did a thorough check of all our systems at the university, and found nothing much that couldn't be fixed fairly easily [70]. Nevertheless, the systems of some large firms whose operations are critical to the economy, such as banks and utilities, did need substantial repairs. Yet there were no reports of high-consequence failures. This appears to support Curtis, Krasner, and Iscoe's thesis. The requirement for Y2K bug fixes was known completely: "I want this system to keep on working, just as it is now, through into 2000 and beyond".

This is one of the reasons I chose the quote from Rick Smith to head this chapter: "My own experience is that developers with a clean, expressive set of specific security requirements can build a very tight machine. They don't have to be security gurus, but they have to understand what they're trying to build and how it should work."

Organisations have difficulty dealing with uncertainty, as it gets in the way of setting objectives and planning to meet them. So capable teams tackle the hard problem first, to reduce uncertainty; that was DARPA's mission, and the core of the spiral model. There's a significant business-school literature on how to manage uncertainty in projects [1180]. But it's easy to get this wrong, even in a fairly well-defined project. Faced with a hard problem, it is common for people to furiously attack a related but easier one; we've seen a number of examples, such as in section 26.2.7.4.

Risk management can be even worse in security where the problem is open-ended. We really have no idea where the next shitstorm will come from. In the late 1990s, we thought we'd got secure smartcards; then along came differential power analysis. In the mid-2010s we thought we had secure enough CPUs for competitor firms to run their workloads on the same machines in Amazon data centres; then along came Spectre. We also used to think that Apple products couldn't get malware and that face recognition would never be good enough to be a real privacy threat. Even though Moore's law is slowing down, there will be more surprises.

Middle managers prefer approaches that they can implement by box-ticking their way down a checklist, but to deal with uncertainties and open-ended risks, you need a process of open learning, with people paying attention to the alerts, or the frauds, or the safety incidents, or the customer complaints – whatever you can learn from. But checklists demand less management attention and effort, and the quality bureaucracy loves them. I noted in section 9.6.6 that certified processes had a strong tendency to displace critical thought; instead of constantly reviewing a system's protection requirements, designers just reach for their checklists. The result is often perverse. By not tackling the hard problem first, you hide the uncertainty and it's worse later[6]. Also, people rapidly learn how to game checklists. There is the eternal tension between us security experts telling firms to pay smart people to anticipate what might go wrong, and boards telling managers to deliver product faster using fewer and cheaper engineers.

[6] I will discuss ISO 27001 in the next chapter. The executive summary for now is that almost every firm hit by a big data breach had ISO 27001 certification, but it failed because their auditors said something was OK that wasn't.

When the threat model is politically sensitive, things get more complicated. The classic question is whether attacks come from insiders or outsiders. Insiders are often the biggest security risk, whether because some of them are malicious or because most of them are careless. But you can't just train all your staff to be unhelpful to each other and to customers, unless perhaps you are a government department or other monopoly. You have to find the sweet spot for control, and that often means working out how to embed it in the culture. For example, bank managers know that dual-control safe locks reduce the risk of their families being taken hostage, and requiring two signatures on large transactions means extra shoulders to take the burden when something goes wrong.

Getting the risk ecosystem right in an organisation can take both subtlety and persistence. The cultural embedding of controls and other protective measures is hard work; if you come into contact with multiple firms then it's interesting to observe how they manage their rules around everything from code audits (which the tech majors insist on) to tailgating (which semiconductor firms are at pains to prevent) and whether people are expected to keep one hand on a banister as they walk up and down the stairs (a favourite of energy companies). Where do these risk cultures come from, how are they promoted, and why do they cluster by sector? Their transactional internal control structures may be heavily influenced by their auditors, as we discussed in section 12.2.6.3, but the broader security culture varies a lot – and matters.

A further factor is that good CISOs are almost as rare as hens' teeth. There are some stars at the top tech and fintech firms, but being a CISO can be a thankless job. Good engineers often don't want it, or don't have the people skills to cope, while ambitious managers tend to avoid the job. In many organisations, promotions are a matter of seniority and contacts; so if you want to be the CEO you'll have to spend 20 years climbing up the hierarchy without offending too many people on the way. Being CISO will mean saying no to people all the time, and a generalist with no tech background can't hack it anyway. The job also brings a lot of stress, and the risk of burnout; a CISO's average tenure is about two years [432]. In any case, embedding an appropriate culture around risk and security is for the CEO and the board. If they don't think it's important, the CISO has no chance. But breaches have now led to enough CEOs being fired, or losing millions on their stock, that other members of that tribe are starting to pay attention.

One way the risk ecosystem can be skewed is that if a company manages to arrange things so that some of the risks of the systems it operates get dumped on third parties. This creates a moral hazard by removing the incentives to take care. We discussed this in section 12.5.2 in the context of banks trying to shift fraud liability in payment systems to cardholders, merchants or both. Staff can get lazy or even crooked if they know that customer complaints will be brushed off. Another example is Henry Ford, who took the view that if you were injured by one of his cars, you should sue the driver, not him; it took decades for courts and lawmakers to nail down product liability.

Companies may also swing from being risk takers to being too risk averse, and back again. The personality of key executives does matter. My own university has been gung-ho when we hired an engineer to be Vice-Chancellor, timorous when we hired a lawyer, and in the middle when we hired a medic.

Another source of problems is when system design decisions are taken by people who are unlikely to be held accountable for them. This can happen for many reasons. IT staff turnover could be high, with much reliance placed on contract staff; fear of redundancy can turn loyal staff into surreptitious job-seekers. This can be a particular problem in big public-sector IT projects: none of the ministers or civil servants involved expect to be around when the thing is delivered seven years from now. So when working on a big system project, don't forget to look round and ask yourself who'll take the blame later when things go wrong.

Yet another is that when hiring security or safety consultants to help with product design, firms have an incentive to go for a firm that is 'good enough' but will not be too demanding; a gentle review from a Big Four firm will be much more useful than a detailed review from an expert who might recommend much more expensive design changes. Indeed, if a firm was determined to get a completely secure product, then they should hire multiple experts. We described in section 14.2.3 how this helped with the design of prepayment electricity meters, and a later experiment with students confirmed that the more people you got to think about a proposed system design, the more potential hazards and vulnerabilities they could spot [69]. Of course, this rarely happens.

27.6 Managing the team

To develop secure and reliable code, you need to build a team with the right culture, the right mix of skills, and the right incentives.

Many modern systems are already so complex that few developers can cope with all aspects of them. So how do you build strong development teams with complementary skills? This has been a subject of vigorous debate for over fifty years now, with different writers reflecting their personal style or company culture. It has long been entangled with cultural issues such as diversity, although these have only got serious attention since the mid-2010s.

27.6.1 Elite engineers

Going back to the 1960s, Fred Brooks's famous book 'The Mythical Man-Month' describes the lessons learned from developing the world's first large software product, the operating system for the IBM S/360 mainframe [329]. He describes the 'chief programmer team', a concept evolved by his colleague Harlan Mills, in which a chief programmer – a development lead, in today's language – is supported by a toolsmith, a tester and a language lawyer. The thinking was that some programmers are much more productive than others, so rather than promoting them to management and 'losing' them you create posts for them with the salary and esteem of senior managers. The same approach was found in other tech companies in the 1960s through the 1980s, and even in bank IT departments where I worked in the late 1980s.

The view taken by more modern companies such as Microsoft, Google, Facebook and Netflix is that you only want to hire the ultra-productive engineers in the first place – especially if you get a million CVs a year but plan to hire only 20,000 new engineers. One approach is to hire people as contractors for a few months to see how they do. But that's harder with fresh graduates, as even bright students from elite schools can take a few months to become productive in a commercial team. Productivity is also a matter of culture; engineers who thrive at one company may do much less well at another. A related issue is that if you have each candidate interviewed by a number of your engineers, that's not just a drain on engineer time, but can also perpetuate a culture that's not very welcoming to women engineers. Elite universities are in a similar situation to the tech majors, with dozens of applicants for each place; over the years we've developed mechanisms to monitor diversity in hiring and admissions.

The two approaches are not in conflict. Modern tech firms employ multiple tech superstars from famous designers to Turing-award winning computer scientists. The view at one such firm is that you cannot expect to write good software if you don't have a career structure for programmers. People who want to spend their lives writing software, and are good at it, have to get respect, however your organisation signals that – whether it's salary, bonuses, stock or fripperies like access to the executive dining room. Universities get this; we professors run the place. Tech companies get it too, and one or two banks have started to. But governments are generally appalling. In the UK civil service, the motto is that "scientists should be on tap but not on top." And more than one car company I know of has real problems hiring and retaining decent software engineers. In one of them, software engineers are expected to become managers after five years or remain on a junior pay grade, while in another all engineers are expected to wear business suits to work (and still get lousy money). I'll return to this in section 27.6.6.

27.6.2 Diversity

At the beginning of computing, there were plenty of women programmers – they were the majority until the late 1960s, and included pioneers such as Grace Hopper and Dame Stephanie Shirley (who ran her company for years as 'Steve Shirley'). When I started in the early 1970s there was still a much better gender balance than today. There were minorities too; the orbital calculations for the Mercury, Gemini and Apollo missions were led by an African-American woman, Katharine Johnson. But things have become male-dominated in the USA and the UK. Since I became an academic in the 1990s, about a sixth of local computer science students have been women, despite significant efforts to recruit more women students. But in the formerly communist countries of Eastern Europe, the ratio is about a third. (We've improved our gender balance by admitting lots of students from southern and eastern Europe.) In India there's close to gender balance. So this is a cultural issue, and there's a lot of debate on how it came about. Is it a lack of role models, or is it the fault of careers advisers in schools, or are many IT shops just an unpleasant working environment for women? That has certainly been an issue: the Gamergate scandal, which I discussed in section 2.5.1, exposed deep misogyny in some gaming communities, while the `#MeToo` movement has highlighted many cases of sexism in Silicon Valley.

Even within computer science we see a lot of subcultural variation. The last time I went to a hardware conference – an Arm developer event – I saw about 500 men but only three women (all of them Indian). In the security field, we were overwhelmingly male in the 1990s when the emphasis was cryptology and operating system internals, but are much more balanced now we have embraced the importance of design, usability and psychology. Role models and history do matter. Research groups with a woman faculty member get more applications from able women[7].

More diverse teams are more effective, and the real change doesn't come with the first woman you hire, but when you have enough to change the team culture. That might mean three or more. It also means getting more enlightened managers. More subtly, if you want to attract more women and retain them, it can be an idea to manage the people rather than the work. You have to protect your staff and give them space to do what they're good at. Clearly it's a bad idea to hire misogynistic bullies, though it can be hard to spot them in advance. Bullies are often creeps too; as well as bossing the people under them they suck up to the people above them. Very often such people don't understand what's going on technically so they have no idea who's productive and have to judge people by timekeeping or by how much they ingratiate themselves. It's essential to identify such bullies and get rid of them, hard though firing can be. If this management style spreads through an organisation, smart people will go somewhere else.

[7]We have gender balance in our natural language processing group, started in the 1960s by the late Karen Spärck Jones.

27.6.3 Nurturing skills and attitudes

Modern development has a tension between the desire to keep teams together, so that they get more efficient and predictable, and moving people around to develop their skills, stop them going stale, and ensure that there's more than one person able to maintain everything that matters.

You will also need a diversity of skills. If you're writing an app, for example, you may want a couple of people to write the Android code, a couple for the Apple code and a couple for the server. Depending on the task, there may be a user advocate who leads usability testing, advocates for safety and security, an architect to keep the overall design clean and efficient, a language lawyer who worries about APIs, a test engineer who runs the regression testing machinery and a toolsmith who maintains the static and dynamic analysis tools. If you're doing continuous integration you'll have an engineer specialising in A/B testing while if you have a gated approach the test emphasis might be on compatibility with third-party products or with security certification. You'll need to give some thought to how many of these skills you try to get in each dev, and how many are subject-matter experts who work across teams or come in as consultants. And as you can't run a project with more people than you can feed from two pizzas, you want some of your people to have two or more of these skills. Good tech firms rotate engineers slowly through the company to acquire a range of skills that maximises their value to the firm (even though it also maximises their value to others, and makes it easier for them to leave) [1211].

But skills are not enough: you need to get people to work together. Here, too, working practices have evolved over the years. By about 2010, agile developers had adopted the 'scrum' where the whole dev team has a stand-up meeting for five minutes each day, at which the only people allowed to speak are the developers. They describe what they've done, what they're about to do and what the problems are. Some firms have moved teams to collaboration tools such as Jira. In our team we combined daily lunches together with a formal progress meeting once a week. (Since the coronavirus lockdown the formal meeting has become more important and we've worked to complement it with other online activities.)

It's bad practice if people who find bugs (even bugs that they coded themselves) just fix them quietly; as bugs are correlated, there are likely to be more. Bug tracking matters, and a ticketing system that enables good statistics to be kept is an important tool in improving quality. As an example of good practice, in air traffic control it's expected that controllers making an error should not only fix it but declare it at once by open outcry: "I have Speedbird 123 at flight level eight zero in the terminal control area by mistake, am instructing to descend to six zero." That way any other controller with potentially conflicting traffic can notice, shout out, and coordinate. Software is less dramatic, but is no different: you need to get your devs comfortable with sharing their experiences, including their errors.

Another factor in team building is the adoption of a standard style. One signal of a poorly-managed team is that the codebase is in a chaotic mixture of styles, with everybody doing their own thing. When a programmer checks out some code to work on it, they may spend half an hour formatting it and tweaking it into their own style. Apart from the wasted time, reformatted code can trip up your analysis tools. You also want comments in the code, as people typically spend more time reading code than writing it. You want to know what a programmer who wrote a vulnerability thought they were doing: was it a design error, or a coding blunder? But teams can easily fight about the 'right' quantity and style of comments. So when you start a project, sit everyone down and let them spend an afternoon hammering out what your house style will be. Provided it's enough for reading the code later and understanding bugs, it doesn't matter hugely what the style is: but it does matter that there is a consistent style that people accept and that is fit for purpose. Creating this style is a better team-building activity than spending the afternoon paintballing, or whatever the latest corporate team-building fad happens to be.

27.6.4 Emergent properties

One debate is whether you make everyone responsible for securing their own code, or have a security guru on whom everyone relies. The same question applies to safety in fields such as avionics. The answer, as the leading firms have discovered, is 'both'. We already noted that Microsoft found it more effective to have developers responsible for evolving their own designs and fixing their own bugs, rather than splitting these functions between analysts, programmers and testers, as IBM did in the last century. Both Microsoft and Google now put rookie engineers through a security 'boot camp', so that everyone knows the basics, and also have subject matter experts at a number of levels. These range from working security consultants with a masters degree or the equivalent internal qualification, to people with PhDs in the intricate details of cryptography or virtualisation.

The trick lies in managing the amount of specialisation in the team, and the way in which the specialists (such as the security architect and the testing guru) interact with the other developers.

27.6.5 Evolving your workflow

You also need to think hard about the tools you'll use. Professional development teams avoid a large number of the problems described in this book by using appropriate tools. You avoid buffer overflows by using a modern language such as Rust, or if you must use C or C++ then have strict coding conventions and enforce them using static-analysis tools such as SonarQube and Coverity. You avoid crypto problems, such as timing attacks and weak random number generators, by using well-maintained libraries. But you need to understand the limitations of your tools. In the case of Coverity, for example, its authors explain that while it's great if you use it from the start of a project, adopting it in midstream imposes real costs, as you suddenly have 20,000 more bug reports to triage, and your ship date slips by a few months [236]. Improvements in static analysis tools, say in response to a new kind of attack, can also throw up a lot of alarms in an existing codebase. In the case of crypto libraries, we discussed in Chapter 5 how they tend to offer weak modes of operation such as ECB as defaults, so you need to ensure your team uses GCM instead. (Crypto is one of the areas where you need to talk to a subject matter expert.)

You'll be constantly adding new tools, whether to avoid cross-site scripting vulnerabilities and SQL injection as you update your website, or to make sure you don't leave your client data world-readable in an S3 bucket. If you don't follow the security news you may not be aware of the latest exploits and attacks, so you may not realise when you have to either grow your own expertise or buy it in. But you can't just buy everything in; the security industry has lots of unscrupulous operators who exploit ignorant customers. You need to understand what you need to buy, and why, and then you will need to integrate it with your existing tools, or your security ops people will spend ever more of their time copying IP addresses from one tool to another. Doing some of your own automation helps empower your staff as well as saving time.

Your tools and libraries have to support your architecture. One critical thing here is that you need to be able to evolve APIs safely. A system's architecture is defined more than anything else by its interfaces, and it decays by a thousand small cuts: by a programmer needing a file handling routine that uses two more parameters than the existing one, and who therefore writes a new routine – which may be dangerous in itself, or may just add to complexity and thus contribute indirectly to an eventual failure. In an ideal world, you'd rely on your programming language to prevent API problems using type safety mechanisms.

But the cross-system fan-out of dependencies is a real hazard to safe APIs. We saw in section 20.5 how the APIs of cryptographic hardware security modules were extended to support hundreds of banks' legacy ATM systems until we suddenly realised that the resulting feature interactions made them completely insecure. There are similar tensions in many other application areas, from mobile phone baseband software used in over a hundred different models of phone, to vehicle components used in over a hundred different cars. There must be better ways of managing this; I expect that applications with high fan-out will move in the direction of a microservices architecture with a common core and pluggable proxies for different calling applications.

27.6.6 And finally …

You also need to understand how to manage people, and the HR department can't do this for you[8]. Tech management cannot be done by generalists as they're unlikely to win the trust of their staff[9]. It also cannot be done well by engineers who are too introverted to engage and motivate others. Far too many managers went for the job not because they thought they might be good at it, but because it was the only way to get a decent salary. Successful managers in tech have to love and understand tech; they also have to love and understand people.

For your star engineers, you need to create other leadership roles. They may be innovators who will be most productive in an R&D lab. They may be the custodians of your institutional memory: old-timers who know the thirty years of history behind your product and can stop people repeating the mistakes of the past. They may provide moral leadership to your engineering staff and reassurance to your customers. They can help attract bright young recruits who want to work with them. But the key, I feel, is this: that you have one or more engineering professions in your firm. What's their shape? Who leads them? How do they compare to those in your competitors? How do you grow and develop them? If you realise that all of a sudden you have to unify the safety engineering and security engineering professions in your company, who is going to do that, and how?

27.7 Summary

Managing a project to build, or enhance, a system that has to meet critical requirements for security, safety or both, is a hard problem. As more and more devices acquire CPUs and communications, we need to build things that do real work while keeping out any vulnerabilities that would make them a target for attack. In other words, you want software security – together with other functionality, and other emergent properties such as safety and real-time performance.

If you're building something entirely new, or a major functional enhancement of an existing system, then understanding the requirements is often the hardest part of the process. More gentle system evolution can involve subtler changes to requirements. Larger changes can be forced externally; systems that succeed and get popular, can expect to get attacked.

[8]The main job of HR is damage limitation – stopping leavers from suing you.

[9]As a math geek I always tended to see the MBA types and other corporate politicians much as the Earl of Rochester saw King Charles II: "Here lies our sovereign lord the king, Whose word no man relies on; He never says a foolish thing, Nor ever does a wise one."

Writing secure code is hard because of this dynamic context: the first problem is to figure out what you're trying to do. However, even given a tight specification, or constant feedback from people hacking your product, you're not home and dry. There are a number of challenges in hiring the right people, giving them the right tools, helping them develop the right ways of working, backing them up with expertise in the right way, and above all creating an environment in which they work to improve their security capability.

Research problems

The issues discussed in this chapter are among the hardest and the most important of any in our field. However, they receive little attention because they lie at the boundaries with software engineering, applied psychology, economics and management. Each of these interfaces could be a productive area of research. Security economics and security psychology have made great strides in the last few years, and we now know we need to do a lot more work on making security tools easier for developers to use. One logical next step is integrating what we know with safety economics and safe usability.

Yet many failures are due to organisational behaviour. Every experienced developer or security consultant has their share of horror stories about firms with perverse incentives, toxic cultures, high staff turnover, incompetent management and all the rest of the things we see in the Dilbert cartoons. It could be useful if someone were to collect a library of case histories of security failures caused by unsatisfactory incentives in organisations, such as [878]. What might follow given a decent empirical foundation?

The late Jack Hirshleifer took the view that we should try to design organizations in which managers were forced to learn from their mistakes: how could we do that? How might you set up institutional structures to monitor changes in the threat environment and feed them through into not just systems development but into supporting activities such as internal control? Maybe we need something like Management as Code? How can you design an organization that is 'safety-incentive-compatible' in the sense that staff behave with an appropriate level of care? And what might the cultural anthropology of organisations have to say? We saw in the last chapter how the response of governments to the apparently novel threats posed by Al-Qaida was maladaptive in many ways: far too much of our social resilience budget was spent on anti-terror theatre, at the expense of preparedness for other societal risks such as pandemics. Similarly, far too much of the typical firm's resilience budget has been captured by compliance, safety theatre and security theatre. As a result, too much of the security development effort is aimed at compliance rather than managing security and safety risks properly. How can we design feedback mechanisms that will enable us to put the right amount of effort in the right place? Or do we need broader structural change, such as the breakup of the Big Four accountancy firms?

Further reading

Managing the development of information systems has a large, diffuse and multidisciplinary literature. There are classics everyone should read, such as Fred Brooks's *'Mythical Man Month'* [329] and Nancy Leveson's *'Safeware'* [1151]. An influential modern classic is Reed Hastings' culture slide deck, describing his management policy when building Netflix [872]. The economics of the software life cycle are discussed by Brooks and by Barry Boehm [273]. The modern books everyone should read, as of 2020, are probably the Google books on *'Site Reliability Engineering'* [237] and on *'Building Secure and Reliable Systems'* [23]. The Microsoft approach to the security development lifecycle has many online resources; their doctrine on threat modelling is discussed by Frank Swiderski and Window Snyder [1855]; and their security VP Mike Nash describes the background to the big security push and the adoption of the security development lifecycle at [1387]. The most general set of standards on safety functional and integrity requirements, and the associated engineering processes, is IEC 61508; there are further sets of industry-specific standards. For example, there's IEC 61511 for process plant control systems, IEC 62061 for safety of machinery, and the EN 5012x series for railways. In aviation it's RTCA DO-254 for electronic hardware and RTCA DO-178C for software, while in the motor industry it's ISO 26262 for safety and ISO 21434 for security – though at the time of writing this is still just a draft. Standards for the Internet of Things are also a work in progress, and the current draft is ETSI EN 303 645 V2.1.

We can learn a lot from other engineering disciplines. Henry Petroski discusses the history of bridge building, why bridges fall down, and how civil engineers learned to learn from the collapses: what tends to happen is that an established design paradigm is stretched and stretched until it suddenly fails for some unforeseen reason [1520]. IT project failures are another necessary subject of study; there's a casebook on how to manage uncertainty in projects by Christoph Loch, Arnoud DeMeyer and Michael Pich [1180]. For security failures, it's important to follow the leading security blogs such as Schneier on Security, Krebs on Security and SANS, as well as the trade press.

Organizational aspects are discussed at length in the business school literature, but this can be bewildering to the outsider. Many business academics praise business, which is fine for selling airport books, but what we need is a more critical understanding of how organisations fail. If you're only going to read one book, make it Lewis Pinault's *'Consulting Demons'* – the confessions of a former insider about how the big consulting firms rip off their customers [1530]. Organisational theorists such as Charles Handy talk of firms having cultures based on power, roles, tasks or people, or some combination. It's not just who has access to whom, but who's prepared to listen to whom and who will just ignore orders from whom. Perhaps such insights might help us design more effective tools and workflows that support how people actually work best.

CHAPTER

28

Assurance and Sustainability

There are two ways of constructing a software design. One way is to make it so simple that there are obviously no deficiencies. And the other way is to make it so complicated that there are no obvious deficiencies.

– TONY HOARE

Security engineers are the litigation lawyers of tech. We only get paid when something is wrong and we can always find something wrong.

– DAVE WESTON

To improve is to change; to be perfect is to change often.

– WINSTON CHURCHILL

28.1 Introduction

I've covered a lot of material in this book, some of it quite tricky. But I've left the hardest parts to the last. First, there's the question of *assurance* – whether the system will work, and how you're sure of this. Next, there's its cousin *compliance* – how you satisfy other people about this. Finally, there's *sustainability* – how long it will keep on working. Many practical questions are linked to these. How do you decide to ship the product? How do you sell the security and safety case to your insurers? How long are you going to have to maintain it, and at what cost?

What's new in 2020 is *sustainability*. In the 2008 edition, I called this chapter 'Evaluation and Assurance', and ended up by remarking that sound processes for vulnerability disclosure and product update were beginning to be as important as pre-market testing. The emphasis back then was on testing and evaluation schemes like the Common Criteria. That world is now moribund: the idea that a device should be secure because someone spent $100,000 getting an evaluation lab to test it five years ago would strike most people nowadays as quaint. Assurance is no longer static.

Ten years ago, we knew how to make two types of secure system. We had things like phones and laptops, which contained software and were online, but were sort-of secure because the software got patched once a month. And we had things like cars and medical devices, which contained software but were not online; you tested them to death before they were put on sale, and then hoped for the best, as patching meant a physical recall. Now we've started to put cars and medical devices online, so they have to be patched online too.

The number of vulnerabilities reported in common platforms is so great that we have to automate the process. As we described in the previous chapter, the software development lifecycle has become DevOps and then DevSecOps; the online components of systems are maintained using continuous integration, while components in the field need regular upgrades.

With a new product, assurance can be measured roughly by whether capable motivated people have beat up on the system enough. But how do you define 'enough'? And how do you define the 'system'? How do you deal with people who protect the wrong thing? And how do you deal with usability? Too many systems are designed for use by alert experienced professionals, but are too tricky for ordinary folk or are intolerant of error. Once they get fielded, the injury claims or fraud disputes start to roll in.

In the security engineering of a decade ago, we often talked of assurance in terms of *evaluation*, which was about how you assembled the evidence to convince your boss, your clients, and (if need be) a jury, that it did indeed work (or that it did work at some particular time in the past). As we've seen again and again, things often fail because one principal carries the cost of protection while another carries the risk of failure. Third-party evaluation schemes such as the Common Criteria were supposed to make these risks more transparent and mitigate them, but ended up acting as a liability shield – particularly in the public sector and in regulated industries such as banking. Systems protecting classified information were subjected to extensive compliance requirements and had to use evaluated products at the attack surface; much the same held, with different details, for payment systems. Evaluation was driven by compliance.

Compliance is still the main driver of security design and investment, but it places much less emphasis on requiring evaluated products at specific trust boundaries. The details vary from one industry to another. When we look at medical systems, cars or aircraft we find regulatory regimes driven by safety that are starting to incorporate security. General business systems have policy set by the Big Four audit firms, and payment systems by PCI. We have touched on some of their specific requirements in previous chapters; there are some broader issues and principles that we'll try to pull together here.

Right at the start of this book, in Figure 1.1, I presented a framework for security engineering based on incentives, policy, mechanism and assurance.

- *Incentives* are critical, as we've seen time and again. They often fall outside a formal assurance process, but are the most critical part of the environment within which the security policy has to be defined.
- *Policy* is often neglected, as we've seen: people often end up protecting the wrong things, or protecting the right things in the wrong way. We spent much of Part 2 of the book exploring security policies for different applications.
- *Mechanisms* may be independent of policy, but can interact with it by making some policy options easier to implement.
- *Assurance* is our estimate of the likelihood that a system will not fail in a particular way. This estimate can be based on a number of factors, such as the process used to develop and maintain it; the people who develop and maintain it; and specific technical assessments, such as the statistics of failure rates, bug reports, breach reports and insurance claims. It was traditionally about *evaluation* – whether, given the agreed security policy and strength of mechanisms, a product had been implemented correctly. Had the bugs been found and fixed? Could you quantify the mean time to failure? Nowadays it's increasingly about the vendor's future commitment. For how long, and how diligently, will the system be patched?

By the second edition of this book in 2008, I noted that the big missing factor was usability. Most system failures have a significant human component. Usability is a cross-cutting issue in the above framework: if done properly, it has a subtle effect on policy, a large effect on choice of mechanisms, and a huge effect on how systems are tested. It cuts across individual products: a common reason for accidents is that different products have different user interfaces, an issue to which we'll return later. However, designers often saw assurance simply as an absence of obvious bugs, and designed technical protection mechanisms without stopping to consider human frailty. (There are some exceptions: bookkeeping systems are designed to cope with both error and fraud.)

Usability is not purely a matter for end-users, but for developers too. Many vulnerabilities arise because security mechanisms are too hard to understand or too fiddly to use. Developers often didn't use operating-system access controls, but just ran their code with administrator privilege instead; when mobile phones didn't allow this, they kept demanding too many permissions for their apps; and cryptography often uses ECB mode as it's the default with many crypto libraries.

Customers and vendors want different things at multiple points in the value chain. Regulation doesn't always help, because governments have multiple agendas of their own, often in conflict: intelligence agencies, safety regulators and competition authorities pull in different directions. It's in this treacherous landscape that the assurance game is played.

Assurance is thus a political and economic process. It is also a dynamic process, just like the development of code or of documents. Just as you have bugs in your code, and in your specification, you will also have things wrong with your security and safety policies, leading to omissions and errors in your test suite. So assurance is steadily turning from something done as a one-off project to another aspect of continuous evolution.

With that warning, it's helpful to start with the classic problem of evaluating a static product that is built in a single project.

28.2 Evaluation

Product evaluation tackles the problem of the lemons market we discussed in section 8.3.3: when customers can't measure quality, bad products drive out good ones. Security has been a lemons market for generations. An 1853 book on locksmithing justified disclosing the 'secrets' of the trade on the grounds that the burglars knew them already; it was just the locksmiths' customers who were ignorant [1899]. Modern consumer-grade products, from anti-virus software to mobile phone apps, are way beyond the ability of most consumers to assess technically. If they are just going to rely on the brand name, the vendor may as well buy ads rather than hiring security engineers. As for professional products, the tech majors may employ enough PhDs to do an assessment, but banks don't – not even money-centre banks[1]. In earlier chapters, we discussed a number of examples of static security standards against which various products get evaluated and certified. Banks and governments are among the keenest purchasers of certified security products.

That may have been where computer security got started fifty years ago, but as computers end up everywhere, we have to look at other industries too. Dozens of industries have their own safety standards, with which security mechanisms are increasingly intertwined. We already talked about electricity transmission and distribution in section 23.8.1. Safety standards for software in road vehicles have developed over decades; we talked about trucks in 14.3.3. Now that both trucks and cars have multiple systems for assisted driving and are connected to the Internet, they have critical security as well as safety requirements. The same is happening for medical equipment and much else.

[1]In my late 20s and early 30s I worked in banking, and when I went to an interbank security standards committee there were only about four of us in the room who knew what we were talking about – of whom one was from IBM. Fintech has become an order of magnitude more complex since then.

I'll explore this via a number of case studies. Two important questions are whether the evaluation is conducted by the relying party or by a third party, and whether the standards are static or dynamic.

28.2.1 Alarms and locks

The US insurance industry set up a joint testing lab in 1894, alarmed at the fire risks from electric lightbulbs; it was incorporated in 1901 as Underwriters' Laboratories, a nonprofit that develops fire safety and other standards, and started approving security products in 1913 [1920]. Other countries have similar bodies. An evaluator spends a fixed budget of effort looking for flaws and writes a report, after which the lab either approves a device, turns it down or demands some changes.

As the insurance industry bears much of the cost of fires and burglaries, incentives are somewhat aligned, although in practice these labs get much of their income from testing fees. One risk is inertia: the standards may not keep up with progress. In the case of high-security locks, a lab in 2000 might have demanded ten minutes' resistance to picking and say nothing about bumping. We described in section 13.2.4 how bumping tools had improved enough to be a major threat by 2010, and picks have got better too. We also described in section 13.2.3 how bank vaults certified to resist attack for ten minutes can be defeated in much less by a modern angle grinder or a burning bar. Insurance labs in some countries, such as Germany, have been prepared to withdraw certifications as attacks got better; in the USA, they appear reluctant to, perhaps for fear of being sued. The willingness of an industry to tolerate changing standards may depend on its structure: a mature industry with a handful of large players can drag its feet a lot more than a growing competitive one.

28.2.2 Safety evaluation regimes

Safety standards tend to emerge one industry at a time in response to major accidents or scandals. The safety of drugs and medical devices is regulated in the USA by the FDA, set up in 1906 by President Theodore Roosevelt after journalists exposed abuses in the patent medicine industry. It turned out that the top-selling medicine in America was just a dilute solution of sulphuric acid and turpentine – really cheap to manufacture, yet tasting nasty enough that people could believe it was good for them [2052]. As for air safety, the first step was in 1931, when America's top football coach Knute Rockne died in a plane crash caused by structural failure, causing a public outcry that led to the establishment of the National Transportation Safety Board. The FAA was set up later by President Eisenhower after a 1956 crash between two airliners over the Grand Canyon killed all 128 people aboard the two planes [666]. As for the car industry, it managed to disclaim liability for safety for decades. Vendors competed to decorate cars with chromium rather than fit them with seat belts, until Ralph Nader's book 'Unsafe at Any Speed' spurred Congress to set up National Highway Traffic Safety Administration (NHTSA) in 1970; its power and influence grew with successive safety scandals.

Europe harmonised a patchwork of national laws into the Product Liability Directive in 1985, adding further regulations and safety agencies by industry sector. Since then, the European Union has developed into the world's lead safety regulator, with its agencies setting safety standards in industries from aviation through railway signals to toys [1150]. With cars, for example, Europe generally requires safety testing by independent labs[2], while America doesn't; but most US vendors have their US models tested independently too, as Europe created the 'industry norm' by which US courts assess tort cases when things go wrong. In this sense, Europe has become a 'regulatory superpower'.

The EU's overall safety strategy is to evolve a set of standards by negotiation with industry working groups and lobbyists and update them every seven to ten years. Many products that cause serious harm, such as cars, have to get explicit approval, typically following testing in an independent laboratory. Less dangerous goods such as toys require self-certification: the vendor places a 'CE' mark on the product to assert that it complies with all relevant standards. This removes some of the excuses that vendors might use when non-compliant products cause accidents; it's also used for a wide range of components from car brakes to industrial pressure valves.

28.2.3 Medical device safety

Safety regulation is a complex ecosystem, imperfect in many ways. For example, there has long been controversy in both America and Europe over medical device safety. This came to prominence in the 1980s when bugs in the Therac 25 medical accelerator caused the death of three patients and injured three more. The cause was a software bug that surfaced as a usability issue: if the operator edited the machine's parameters too quickly, they could get the machine into a dangerous state where it delivered far too much radiation to the patient. The case study is set reading for my software engineering students even today [1151].

The most lethal medical devices nowadays are probably infusion pumps, used to administer intravenous drugs and other fluids to patients in hospital. Many of the fatal accidents are usability failures. Just look at Figure 28.1: each of these claims to be a 'BodyGuard 545' yet to increase the dose on the

[2]Europe delegates type approval to Member States, most of which have a Type Approval Authority which delegates testing to a specialist lab. In Germany, that's TÜV. Some smaller countries have a TAA that allows the manufacturer to do its own testing, with a TAA inspector present.

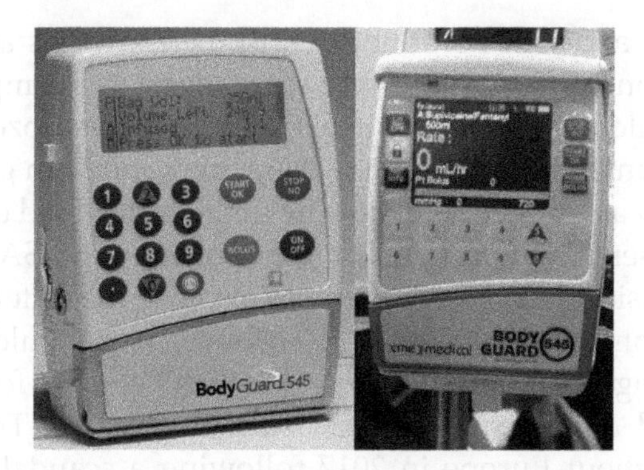

Figure 28.1: Two infusion pumps that are apparently of the same model (photo courtesy of Harold Thimbleby)

machine on the left, you press '2' while on the right you press '5'. An emergency room might have equipment from half-a-dozen different vendors, all with different user interfaces. Doctors and nurses occasionally press the wrong button, the wrong dose gets administered, or the dose for an eight-hour transfusion is given all in one bolus – and patients die. Infusion pumps kill about as many people as cars do, with the body count being in the low thousands in the UK and the low tens of thousands in the USA [1881].

Surely this could be fixed with standards? Well, there are standards. For example, 'litres' is supposed to be marked with a capital 'L' so it's not mistaken for a '1', but you can see on the right-hand image that although the '0L/h' complies with this, the '500ml' does not. So why is the standard not enforced? Well, the FDA budget of engineering effort is about half a day per device, and vendors don't give the engineers actual devices to play with. It's just a paperwork review[3]. In addition, usability falls outside the FDA's scope. This is, I hear, a result of lobbying by the industry to 'cut red tape'. The fact that two different devices are marketed as the same product is a common strategy to minimise compliance costs.

There has recently been international guidance for usability engineering of medical devices in the form of ISO/IEC 62366-2, which took effect in 2018. This is a significant advance that covers a lot of ground, but usability is a huge field. The new standard is very basic, and explains at length that manufacturers should not just list hazards in a legal warning leaflet, or even highlight them with notices on the equipment – they should actually try to mitigate them, and in the process understand how their equipment is likely to be used and abused. It describes a number of assessment techniques the engineer could use, but "insufficient experience with the type of medical device" is just one bullet point on its list of factors that might contribute to use errors. Manufacturers will find

[3]By way of comparison, when colleagues and I helped to evaluate a burglar alarm designed for low-consequence risks such as small shops and houses, our budget was two person-weeks.

all this expensive, and will no doubt talk to their lawyers about how much really has to be done. Safety in number entry alone is a complex field [1882]; every vendor should probably train an expert in it, and in dozens of other techniques too, but many will do as little as they think they can get away with. In the end, a usability assessment will now be in the trolleyload of paperwork the manufacturer presents to regulators, at least outside the USA. But it's unclear whether the confusion arising when nurses also use the different interfaces of competitors' equipment will be taken as seriously as it should be.

This is all teaching us that pre-market testing isn't enough for medical device safety – you need diligent post-market surveillance too. This started to be introduced throughout Europe in 2017 following a scandal about defective breast implants [234]. In the UK, a further scandal about teratogenic drugs and pelvic mesh implants led to an Independent Medicines and Medical Devices Safety Review, which in 2020 documented decades of indifference to safety and recommended among many other things that regulation 'needs substantial revision particularly in relation to adverse event reporting and medical device regulation' [503]. In May 2020, a new EU medical device regulation (2017/745) was supposed to require post-market surveillance systems and a public database of anonymised incident reports; implementation was postponed until May 2021. And in June 2020, the UK Parliament passed a Medicines and Medical Devices Act that will enable ministers to amend the existing regulations after Brexit. The mood music there, however, is to make Britain a more attractive place for drug companies and medical device makers, not a safer place for patients. Within Britain's National Health Service, it's hard to make a career as a safety specialist[4].

Now here's an interesting question. If infusion pumps kill as many people as cars or – in the USA – as guns, why aren't people more worked up, as they are about road safety and gun control? Well, the harm is both low-key and diffuse. At your local hospital, such accidents probably kill less than one person a month, and many of them won't be noticed, as people on infusion pumps tend to be fairly sick anyway. When they are noticed, they are more likely to be blamed on the nurse, rather than on the medical director who bought pumps from half a dozen different suppliers following nice lunches with the sales folks. As a cause of death in the hospital, recorded safety usability failures don't make it into the top twenty, and so don't get attention from politicians or the press. (The exception is when a safety failure has a security angle, as people are very sensitive indeed about hostile intent. I'll discuss this in section 28.4.2 below.)

The standardisation of user interfaces is managed better in industries where accidents and their causes are more visible. Road traffic accidents are fairly

[4]The UK NHS has a Healthcare Safety Investigations Branch, established in 2016, but it investigates what it's told to, often has to keep its findings confidential, and doesn't have or seek enforcement powers to require other healthcare organisations to make changes [877].

visible and most people drive, so car crashes and their causes are a topic of conversation. The controls in cars are now fairly standard, with the accelerator on the right, the brake in the middle and the clutch on the left. Things aren't perfect; if you're in a hurry, you might get in a rental car, drive off down the freeway, then struggle to find the light switch as night falls. But it used to be much worse. Some cars in the 1930s had the accelerator in the middle, while the first mass-produced car, the Model T Ford, had a hand throttle and a pedal gear-change, like a motorcycle. The average modern driver would have a hard time getting such a car out of the rental lot.

28.2.4 Aviation safety

Aviation has much stronger safety incentives still: airliners are worth eight or nine figures, crashes are front-page news, they cause pilots as well as passengers to lose their lives, and airline CEOs may even lose their bonuses. Pilots pay attention to accident reports, and are required to train on each type of plane they fly. This has led the vendors to standardise cockpit design, starting with the Boeing 757 and 767, which were designed from the start to be so similar that a pilot trained on one could fly the other. If nurses were similarly required to get a type rating for each infusion pump, that would cost real money; hospital executives would pay attention, the vendors would eventually follow Boeing, and a lot of lives could be saved.

Yet we find regulatory failure in aviation too, and an example was exposed with the Boeing 737Max crashes. Since Boeing had bought McDonnell Douglas in 1997 and become the only US firm making large aircraft, the Federal Aviation Administration had come to see its role as supporting Boeing. The company's engineers were allowed to take over much of the safety evaluation and certification work that the FAA had done in the past. An even more toxic effect of the takeover was that McDonnell Douglas executives took over, the company moved its headquarters from Seattle to Chicago, and was no longer run by engineers but by finance people – who had already destroyed one engineering company and whose goal now was to milk the maximum profits from the new monopoly. Boeing's traditional engineering culture was sidelined and corners were cut [729]. Two crashes followed, in Indonesia and Ethiopia, killing 346 people. The cause was reminiscent of the Therac case a generation earlier: a design error in software that surfaced as a life-threatening usability failure.

In order to compete with the latest model of Airbus, Boeing needed to make the 737 more fuel efficient quickly, and this meant larger engines, which had to be fitted further forward, or it would have required re-engineering the airframe to the point that it would have been a new plane for regulatory purposes, and would have taken much longer to certify. The new engine location made the aircraft harder to trim at high speeds, so Boeing added software called the

Maneuvering Characteristics Augmentation System (MCAS) to the flight control computer to compensate for this.

The MCAS software needed to know the aircraft's angle of attack, and the critical design error was to rely on one angle-of-attack sensor rather than two, although these are often damaged by ground handlers and bird strikes. The implementation error was that, with an incorrect angle-of-attack input, the plane could get into a regime where the pilots needed to pull about 50kg on the yoke to keep the plane level. This was compounded by an error in safety analysis: the unintended activation of the MCAS software was not anticipated. As a result, Boeing didn't do a proper failure modes and effects analysis and the software's behaviour was not even documented in the pilot manual. The pilots were not trained how to diagnose the problem or switch MCAS off. Boeing had become complacent about the ability of pilots to cope with the chaos of a cockpit emergency with many alarms going off at once [1057].

The company had also got away with bullying investigators over a similar previous crash in the Netherlands in 2009, and initially hoped that the Indonesia crash could be blamed on pilot error [858]. The FAA responded to the crash by sending an emergency airworthiness directive to all known U.S. operators of the airplane, which consisted of inserting a warning notice in the airplane flight manual [665]. However, the warning light that alerted pilots to disagreement between the two sensors had been made an airline option, like a sun roof in a car, and the operation of the switch that could disable MCAS was changed to make it less intuitive [156]. A number of US pilots logged complaints, with one describing the manual as 'almost criminally insufficient' [140]; but the FAA saw such complaints as only relevant to air carrier operations and did not analyse them for global safety hazards [664].

After the second crash in Ethiopia, other countries' regulators started grounding the 737Max, and the FAA could no longer protect them. Boeing had lost $18.7bn in sales by March 2020, when the coronavirus pandemic closed down commercial aviation sales, as well as $60bn in market capitalisation. This was by some distance the world's biggest ever software failure, in terms of both lives lost and economic damage. The fix, approved by the FAA in August 2020, involves not just a software change so that MCAS reads both angle-of-attack sensors and deploys only once per flight and with limited stick force; but a procedural change so that both sensors are checked pre-flight; an update to pilot training; and a regulatory change so that the FAA, rather than Boeing, checks each plane after manufacture [592]. Even so, pilots are worried that the Ethiopian crash might still be repeated, as the plane could be difficult to trim manually in some circumstances [482].

When analysing safety, it's not enough to think of it as a technical testing matter. Psychology, incentives, institutions and power matter too. The power of lobbyists, and the risk that regulators will be captured by the industry they're supposed to regulate, place real limits on what can be achieved by testing regimes. Over time, measures designed for risk assessment and risk reduction become industrialised and tend to become a matter of compliance, which firms then seek to pass at minimum cost. It's also important to stop thinking of problems as 'aerospace engineering' versus 'software engineering', or 'safety engineering' versus 'security engineering'. If you want to be a good engineer you need to try to understand every aspect of the whole system that might be relevant.

28.2.5 The Orange book

The first serious computer security testing regime was the *Orange Book* – the Trusted Computer Systems Evaluation Criteria [544]. We touched on this in section 9.4, where I described the multilevel security model that the US Department of Defense was trying to promote through it. Orange Book evaluations were done from 1985–2000 at the NSA on computer systems proposed for government use and on security products such as cryptographic devices. In incentive terms, it was a collective relying-party scheme, as with insurance.

The Orange Book and its supporting documents set out a number of evaluation classes, in three bands. C1 meant just that there was an access-control system; C2 corresponded to carefully configured commercial systems. In the next band, B1 meant mandatory access control; B2 added covert channel analysis, a trusted path to the TCB from the user, and severe penetration testing; while B3 required the TCB had to be minimal, tamper-resistant, and subject to formal analysis and testing. At the top band, A1 added a requirement for formal verification. (Very few systems made it to that level.)

The evaluation class of a system determined what spread of information could be processed on it. The example I gave in section 9.6.2 was that a system evaluated to B3 could process information at Unclassified, Confidential and Secret, or at Confidential, Secret and Top Secret.

When the Orange Book was written, the Department of Defense thought that they paid high prices for high-assurance computers because the markets were too small, and hoped that security standards would expand the market. But Orange Book evaluations followed government work practices. A government user would want some product evaluated; the NSA would allocate people to do it; given traditional civil service caution and delay, this could take two or three years; the product, if successful, would join the evaluated products list; and the bill was picked up by the taxpayer. Evaluated products were always obsolete, so the market stayed small, and prices stayed high[5].

[5]To this day, most governments are hopeless at buying technology and pay several times the market rate, if they make it work at all. The reasons are much broader and deeper than standards. See for example section 10.4.4 on the £11bn failure of a project to modernise Britain's National Health Service, and section 23.5 for the $6bn failure of the Pentagon's Joint Tactical Radio System.

Other governments had similar ideas. European countries developed the *Information Technology Security Evaluation Criteria* (ITSEC), a shared scheme to help their defense contractors compete against US suppliers. This introduced a pernicious innovation – that the evaluation was not arranged by the relying party (the government) but by the vendor. Vendors started to shop around for the lab that would give their product the easiest ride, whether by asking fewer questions, charging less money, taking the least time, or all of the above. Contractors could obtain approval as a *commercial licensed evaluation facility* (CLEF), and in theory the CLEF might have its license withdrawn if it cut corners. That never happened.

28.2.6 FIPS 140 and HSMs

The second evaluation scheme promoted by the US government in the 20th century was NIST's FIPS 140 scheme for assessing the tamper-resistance of cryptographic processors. This was aimed at helping the banking industry as well as the government, and as I described in section 18.4 it uses a number of independent laboratories as contractors. Launched in 1994, it is still going strong today, and is favoured by US customers of cryptographic equipment.

There are two main failure modes of FIPS 140. The first is that it covers the cryptographic device's hardware, not its software, and many FIPS 140 evaluated devices (even at the highest levels) run applications with intrinsic vulnerabilities. Weak algorithms, legacy modes of operation and vulnerable APIs are mandated by bank standards bodies for backwards compatibility, as described in section 20.5. The fix for this has been a growing emphasis on standards set by PCI, the payment industry's self-regulation scheme, which I describe in section 12.5.2.

The second is that the FIPS 140-1 standard has a big gap between level 3 and level 4 for historical reasons I discussed in section 18.4. FIPS 140 level 3 is easy to obtain (you just pot the circuit in epoxy to make it inaccessible to casual probing) and some level-3 devices are not too hard to break (you just scrape off the epoxy with a knife). Level 4 is really hard, and only a few devices ever made that grade. So many vendors aim at what the industry calls, informally, 'level 3.5'. As this doesn't have any formal expression in the FIPS standard, firms often rely on the Common Criteria instead when talking to customers outside the USA.

28.2.7 The common criteria

This sets the stage for the Common Criteria. Following the collapse of the Soviet Union in 1989, military budgets were cut, and it wasn't clear where the opponents of the future would come from. Eventually the USA and its allies agreed to scrap their national schemes and replace them with a single standard – the Common Criteria for Information Technology Security Evaluation [1398].

The work was substantially done in 1994–1995, and the European ITSEC model won out over the Orange Book approach. Evaluations at all but the highest levels are done by CLEFs, are supposed to be recognised in all participating countries, and vendors pay for them.

The innovation was support for multiple security policies. Rather than expecting all systems to conform to Bell-LaPadula, the Common Criteria evaluate a product against a *protection profile* (PP), which is a set of security functional requirements and assurance requirements for a class of product. You can think of it as a detailed security policy, but oriented at products rather than systems, and expanded into several dozen pages of detail. There are protection profiles for operating systems, access control systems, boundary control devices, intrusion detection systems, smartcards, key management systems, VPN clients, voting machines, and even transponders that identify when a domestic waste bin was last emptied. Anyone could propose a protection profile and have it evaluated by the lab of their choice. It's not that the defence community abandoned multilevel security, so much as tried to mainstream its own evaluation system by getting commercial firms to use it for other purposes too. But an evaluation depends entirely on what was measured and how. Some aspects of security were explicitly excluded, including cryptography, emission security (as the NATO standards were classified) and administrative procedures (which was bad news for usability testing).

The Common Criteria have enjoyed some limited success. Its evaluations are used in specialised markets, such as smartcards, hardware security modules, TPMs and electronic signature devices, where sectoral due-diligence rules (such as PCI) or regulation (such as electronic signature laws) create a compliance requirement. Evaluations of such devices were kept honest for a while by an informal cartel run by SOG-IS (the senior officials group – information security) – a committee of representatives of the intelligence agencies of EU countries. However, the operation of the CC outside Europe has been a bit of a joke, and even within Europe it has been undermined by both companies and countries gaming the system. The UK withdrew in 2019.

28.2.7.1 The gory details

To discuss the Common Criteria in detail, we need some jargon. The product under test is known as the *target of evaluation* (TOE). The rigor with which the examination is carried out is the *evaluation assurance level* (EAL) and can range from EAL1, for which functional testing is sufficient, all the way up to EAL7, which demands not only thorough testing but a formally verified design. The highest evaluation level commonly obtained for commercial products is EAL4, although in 2020 there are 85 products at EAL6 or above out of 1472 certified under CC, and many smartcards are evaluated to EAL4+, which means EAL4 plus one or more of the requirements set at higher levels.

When devising something from scratch, the idea is to first work out a threat model, then create a security policy, refine it to a *protection profile* (PP) and evaluate it (if a suitable one doesn't exist already), then do the same for the security target, then finally evaluate the actual product. A protection profile consists of security requirements, their rationale, and an EAL, all for a class of products. It's supposed to be expressed in an implementation-independent way to enable comparable evaluations across products and versions. A *security target* (ST) is a refinement of a protection profile for a specific product. One can evaluate a PP to ensure that it's complete, consistent and technically sound, and an ST too. The evaluations are filed with the national authority, which is typically the defensive arm of the local signals intelligence agency. The end result is a registry of protection profiles and a catalogue of certified products.

There is a stylized way of writing a PP or ST. For example, `FCO_NRO` is a functionality component (hence `F`) relating to communications (`CO`), and it refers to non-repudiation of origin (`NRO`). Other classes include `FAU` (audit) and `FCS` (crypto support).

There are also catalogues of:

- *threats*, such as `T.Load_Mal` – "Data loading malfunction: an attacker may maliciously generate errors in set-up data to compromise the security functions of the TOE;"
- *assumptions*, such as `A.Role_Man` – "Role management: management of roles for the TOE is performed in a secure manner" (in other words, the developers, operators and so on behave themselves);
- *organizational policies*, such as `P.Crypt_Std` – "Cryptographic standards: cryptographic entities, data authentication, and approval functions must be in accordance with ISO and associated industry or organizational standards;"
- *objectives*, such as `O.Flt_Ins` – "Fault insertion: the TOE must be resistant to repeated probing through insertion of erroneous data;"
- *assurance requirements*, such as `ADO_DEL.2` – "Detection of modification: the developer shall document procedures for delivery of the TOE or parts of it to the user."

A protection profile should now contain a *rationale*, which typically consists of tables showing how each threat is controlled by one or more objectives, and in the reverse direction how each objective is necessitated by some combination of threats and environmental assumptions. It will also justify the selection of an assurance level and requirements for strength of mechanism.

The fastest way to get the hang of this may be to read the core CC documentation itself, then a few profiles. The quality varies widely. For example, a protection profile for automatic cash dispensers, written in management-speak with clip art, 'has elected not to include any security policy' and misses many of the problems that were well known when it was written in 1999 [342]. A profile for voting machines from 2007 [563] was written more in politicians' language, but at least with reasonable clarity[6].

Protection profiles for smartcards emphasise maintaining confidentiality of the chip design by imposing NDAs on contractors, shredding waste and so on [656], while in practice most attacks on smartcards used probing or power-analysis attacks for which knowledge of the chip mask was irrelevant. This has developed into a political row, as I discussed in section 18.6.4: the smartcard vendors have pushed the evaluation labs into demanding that all cryptographic products be secure against 'advanced persistent threats'. The fight is over assurance requirement `AVA_VAN.5`, which essentially requires that the entire development environment should be air-gapped, like the Top Secret systems at an intelligence agency. An air gap in itself won't stop a capable opponent, as the Iranians found out with Stuxnet and the Americans with Snowden; but it causes real inconvenience to normal IT companies who rely on Github and other cloud-based systems. And that's entirely the point: the smartcard firms don't want HSMs or enclaves encroaching on their markets.

28.2.7.2 What goes wrong with the Common Criteria

By the time the second edition of this book came out in 2008, industry people had a lot of complaints about the Common Criteria, which I discussed there and which I update more briefly here.

- The biggest complaint for years has been the cost and bureaucracy of the process. A startup wanting to sell devices such as HSMs will nowadays have to spend several million Euros and several years of effort to navigate the process. In practice the CC have become a moat that defends established cartels.
- The next biggest is that, as well as avoiding 'technical physical' aspects such as Emsec or crypto algorithms, the CC ignore administrative security measures, which means in practice ignoring usability. In general, user interfaces are considered to be somebody else's problem.
- Protection profiles are designed by their sponsor firms to rig the market. I mentioned above how the smartcard firms demand that HSM vendors

[6]This appears designed to support French firms' drive to export population registration systems, and it is these rather than the actual voting machines that are often the real weak point in elections – as I discussed in section 7.4.2.2.

also use air-gapped systems to push their costs up. The gaming often leads to insecure products: vendors write their PPs to cover the things they can do easily. They might evaluate the boot code, but leave most of the operating system outside the scope. Recall the API attacks on HSMs described in section 20.5; some vulnerable HSMs were CC-certified, and similar failures are seen in other CC-certified products too.

- Sometimes the protection profiles might be sound, but the way they're mapped to the application isn't. In section 26.5.2 I discussed the European eIDAS regulation, which requires businesses to recognise digital signatures made using smartcards, and encouraged governments to demand them for interactions such as filing tax returns. The main problem in this application, as I discussed in section 18.6.1, is the lack of a trusted interface. As that problem's too hard, it's excluded, and the end result is a 'secure' signature on whatever the virus or Trojan in your PC sent to your smartcard. This hole was duly slathered with several layers of fudge. PPs were written for a smartcard to function as a 'Secure Signature-Creation Device'; other PPs appeared for HSMs, and for the *signature activation module* (SAM) – the server software that passes them digital objects to be signed. The HSM plus the SAM are evaluated as a *qualified signature creation device* (QSCD) [29]. But the front-end server software used by the service provider is only audited, not certified, and if you're lucky the app on your phone or tablet might have RASP on it as a malware countermeasure, as I discussed in section 12.7.4. That is what lobbyists can achieve: the whole certification machinery has been twisted to allow services like Docusign inside the tent, so long as they use a CC certified HSM to hold their signature keys.
- The CC claim not to assume any specific development methodology, but in practice assume a waterfall approach. There's a nod in the direction of policy evolving in response to experience but re-evaluation of PPs or products is declared to be outside the scope. So they're unable to cope with normal security development lifecycles, or with commercial products that get monthly security patches. (The same goes for FIPS; of the available standards, only PCI can cope with updates.)
- The Criteria are technology-driven, when in most applications it's the business processes that should drive protection decisions. We're learning the hard way that hand-marked paper ballots are way better than voting machines for all sorts of reasons. Security is a property of systems, not of products.
- The rigour of the evaluations varies widely between countries, with Germany generally considered to be almost impossibly difficult, the Netherlands in the middle, while Spain and Hungary let their

CLEFs give sponsors an easy ride. Nobody within the system can actually say this in public without causing a diplomatic incident, so it cannot be fixed. The costs also vary, with an evaluation in Germany costing perhaps three times what you pay in Hungary.

- The Common Criteria brand isn't well defended. I described in section 12.6.1.1 how PIN entry devices claimed by VISA to have been evaluated under the Common Criteria were insecure; GCHQ's response was that as the evaluation had not been registered with them, and the devices were not claimed to be 'CC certified' it wasn't their problem. So suppliers are free to continue describing a defective terminal as 'CC evaluated'. A business would not tolerate such abuse of its trademark.
- More generally, there's nothing on liability: 'The procedures for use of evaluation results in accreditation are outside the scope of the CC'.

In the second edition of this book, I took the view that Common Criteria evaluations were somewhat like a rubber crutch. Such a device has all sorts of uses, from winning a judge's sympathy through wheedling money out of a gullible government to whacking people round the head. Just don't try to put serious weight on it.

28.2.7.3 Collaborative protection profiles

In an attempt to deal with these criticisms, collaborative protection profiles (cPPs) started to appear in 2015. The idea was to move away from the EAL levels towards a single protection profile for each class of secure device, and to develop that profile as a collaborative effort among firms in an industry, with input from government and academics [463]. The hope was to stop security evaluations being abused in strategic games between competitor firms. The results of this can now be seen in 2020 by browsing the catalogue of evaluated products on the CC website. Vendors in France and Germany still offer many smartcards, and related products such as electronic signature creation devices, with certificates at EAL4+ or EAL6; that's the legacy of the SOG-IS cartel.

Outside Europe, though, the CC system has been completely captured by vendor interests. American firms offer many firewalls, routers and other networking products, evaluated according to industry cPPs; and Japanese firms offer a range of printers and fax machines. So what is a secure fax machine – does it encrypt faxes? Not at all; it just behaves as you'd expect a fax machine to (if you're old enough to remember them). In short, cPPs have become a marketing mechanism, and are now undermining the traditional CC core. Firms wanting to sell electronic signature systems can have them evaluated under a cPP that's considered EAL4, and most customers can't tell the difference between that and an EAL4+ evaluation done under the old rules.

28.2.8 The 'Principle of Maximum Complacency'

There's a substantial literature on the economics of standards, as there are many contexts in which people have to choose between them. If you're a bright teenager, do you apply to a top university and risk getting a second-class degree, or should you go to a local college and be a star? Should you worry about grade inflation eroding the value of your degree in either case? If you're raising money for a startup, should you get your money from business angels or try to get a big-name venture fund on board? An IT vendor wondering whether to go for some kind of certification faces somewhat similar choices. And even nations play certification games. The large service firms all have their EU headquarters in Ireland as it has long been Dublin's policy to have the most relaxed regime of privacy regulation in Europe, as well as the lowest corporate taxes. What options are there for dealing with such games?

The most influential model of such choices is a 2006 paper on forum shopping by Josh Lerner and Jean Tirole[7]. Their model is a three-stage game in which the sponsor selects a certifier, the certifier then studies the offering and perhaps demands some changes, and finally the end-users make decisions to buy or not [1145]. The big question is whether competition between certifiers will result in better standards, or in a race to the bottom. In most cases the *principle of maximum complacency* wins out: owners seek endorsement from a single certifier, and resist attempts to get them to improve the product. Only in certain circumstances can competition improve quality. One example is where NGOs compete to certify products as sustainable: there, the certifier cares more about the users' outcome than the sponsors do, and the desired property isn't strongly controlled by a single sponsor. Another is competition between elite universities: students have no market power, and enough employers will pay a premium for elite graduates that there's plenty of incentive for Cambridge to compete with Oxford, MIT and Berkeley.

Where there are more players than just the sponsor, the certifier and the users, things get more complicated.

Certification games take place in a much larger ecosystem. A company invents some new product and sells it to some customers. The customers then want a standard, and some tests to satisfy their auditors. They may want the inventor to license the product to their established suppliers, or at least to a second supplier. Other inventors pile in, and all of a sudden there's a patent pool. The firms negotiate long and hard to get their patents in to maximise their share of the royalties; this often results in horrible standards that are insecure and hard to fix (see section 14.2.4 on smart meters; there are many more examples). The patent pools may become cartels that prevent new market entrants; this complaint has been made of the GSMA standards

[7]Tirole won the 2014 Nobel for this and much other work in market power and regulation.

around 5G (see section 22.3.4). The GSMA has also been criticised for its *Network Equipment Security Assurance Scheme* (NESAS) where the vendor pays for a security assessment that only takes a few days (and now allows remote audits because of the pandemic). In short, industrial strategy doesn't optimise for great products so much as for monopolies or cartels.

Where a market is dominated by a monopoly, customer and political pressure may eventually cause the monopolist to pay attention to security, and it can even be rational for a monopolist to internalise some of the security externalities (see the Microsoft case in section 27.5.3). But in the general case, of complex supply chains with some steps dominated by cartels, it can be a lot harder. The complexities in security certification are roughly: (a) the relying parties – those at risk if the thing gets hacked – may be customers, third parties such as insurers, or the public; (b) the sponsors may be vendors, customers, relying parties or associations of any of these; (c) the testers may compete on price or on quality, and this means the lowest quality threshold they can get away with subject to not losing a license from an accreditation body, which may be a government entity or a trade association; (d) there may be more than one accreditation body, plus politics between them. So we can have multiple layers of indirection and we occasionally even get competition about "who certifies the certifiers". To make sense of things we have to look at actual cases in detail.

In the case of CC-evaluated products at EAL4 or above such as smartcards and HSMs, suppose Alice's company sells a product to Bob's Bank and gets Charlie the certifier to say it's secure, after which Bob's customer Dorothy defrauds another customer Eve and absconds. How does the evaluation change things when Eve now claims her money back from Bob in court? Bob will argue he wasn't negligent because he operated according to the standards of the industry, so isn't liable to reimburse Eve. This argument is even more powerful if Charlie signed off on his system. Charlie's role is not so much a technical authority as a liability shield. So Alice will work only as hard as she has to to satisfy Charlie. Charlie will compete with his competitors and a race to the bottom will ensue. The upshot in real life was that the payment card brands set up PCI to take over Charlie's role. We discussed in section 12.5.2 how such standards shift liability in banking: they protect the bank more than the merchant (surprise, surprise).

In the case of electronic signature devices, as we discussed in section 28.2.7.2 above, smartcard industry lobbying led Europe to pass signature laws that gives special force to signatures created with certified products, even when these are insecure. Lobbying by online service signature providers such as Docusign got them on board too. The ultimate effect is not security but a tax. (And to file a tax return in some EU countries you have to get it signed by such a service, adding an extra twenty Euros to your tax accountant's fee.)

So should certification be voluntary? An interesting case study was by Ben Edelman of the Trust-e scheme to certify websites. He discovered that certified websites were more likely to attempt to load malware on to your computer, rather than less. Adverse selection turned the scheme into a negative signal of quality: the weaker vendors certified their websites, while well-known consumer brands didn't bother [612]. The reason for this was that Trust-e certification, being voluntary, was cheap, and the technical barrier to certification was also low.

But although industry lobbies like to talk of 'cutting red tape', how many might be happy with the outright abolition of a government-backed safety or security standard or agency? In practice, lobbyists seek to capture regulators rather than abolish them. Many regulatory regimes function both as moats to prevent incumbents being challenged too easily by startups and also as liability shields. As an example, we discussed in section 17.3 how Amazon, Microsoft, Google and IBM have restricted sales of face-recognition software – among the most controversial of their products – until it's regulated.

28.2.9 Next steps

Since Brexit, the UK and Europe have diverged. Europe passed a Cybersecurity Act (regulation 2019/881) which strengthens the European Network and Information Security Agency (ENISA) and places it at the centre of its strategy. ENISA is to act as a centre of expertise and liaise with sectoral regulators in banking, aviation, energy and telecomms, as well as the data protection authorities. I expect this will be of major importance in the long run, as safety and security regulation are coming together and will inevitably be managed on a sectoral basis by the standards bodies for cars, aircraft, medical devices, railway signals and so on. I will return to this later.

As for the certification of information security products, its approach might be described as 'one more heave': it is setting up an *EU Cybersecurity Certification Framework* under ENISA, which will take over as the top-level certifier. It's supposed to "help avoid the multiplication of conflicting or overlapping national cybersecurity certification schemes and thus reduce costs for undertakings operating in the digital single market" [654]. It will apply to services and processes as well as products. As I write in 2020, the details are still being worked out, but the intention is that sponsoring bodies of EU member states will run certification at three levels, ranging from 'basic', which entails the vendor self-assessing conformance with standards and assuming responsibility for compliance, through 'substantial', which will involve verification of security functionality, to 'high', which will involve ENISA taking over from SOG-IS the supervision of the smartcard/HSM/e-signature kit currently evaluated at EAL4 and above.

The UK government was concerned about certification for many years and was involved in pushing cPPs in order to try to make certification more standardised. But by 2017 they had come to the conclusion that the Criteria were neither necessary nor sufficient for security, and GCHQ withdrew as a sponsor from 2019. It no longer licenses CLEFs or approves certifications, although UK organisations may continue to use certifications created elsewhere[8]. It has long had its own national product certification scheme, now known as *commercial products assurance* (CPA), but the only consumer product for which it currently maintains CPA certification is the smart meter discussed in section 14.2.4. Future legislation will require basic security for IoT devices, including a ban on default passwords and a requirement for a software update mechanism; this is being done in harness with ETSI, leading to a draft European standard ETSI EN 303 645 V2.1 [646].

The direction of travel is now to look at process rather than product, both for firms developing critical equipment for Britain's national infrastructure, and more generally. The general scheme, *Cyber Essentials*, is mandated for government contractors supplying IT services or handling personal information.

There was already the ISO 27001 standard for security management, which we mentioned in section 12.2.4: this is expensive, having been turned into an income stream by the big accountancy firms, and about as useless as CC. Almost all of the large security breaches happen at firms with ISO 27001 certification, where the auditor said something was OK that wasn't. The auditors have to rely on what the firms tell them, and a firm that doesn't know how to protect its systems will just say 'We have a great process for X' when they don't. Why should a small business owner cough up tens of thousands for that, unless they need it to bid for government contracts? And why should a government impose such a tax? So the Cyber Essentials scheme focuses on the very basic stuff and costs only £300 for a validated self-certification. Its target was small and medium enterprises, but the first firms to be actually certified under it were large firms like banks and phone companies who wanted to add every single tassel to their corporate due diligence.

As governments bicker, we've seen the emergence of a private sector standard, Bitsight. Recall how in the first chapter I remarked that in the corporate world, a trusted system often means one acceptable to insurers. Recall also how in section 2.2.1.6 we described how the NSA has a system called Mugshot that crawls the Internet looking for vulnerable systems, and another called Xkeyscore that enables cyber-warriors to find vulnerable systems near a target of interest? Well, Bitsight does Mugshot for the private sector, but instead of attacking companies' systems it rates firms for cybersecurity risk by counting how many of their servers are not patched up to date, and how many other indicators of compromise are visible. They have come to dominate insurance market assessments because they give a single numerical rating at a time when

[8]One of my spies in the Doughnut says 'We absolutely recognise any CC certificate from any producing nation as though it were our own and our assurance processes assign that certificate precisely the weight it deserves :-)'

the insurance industry, which is cyclical, is having its profits squeezed and can no longer get clients to fill out long questionnaires about their cybersecurity practices. This makes sense in the Lerner-Tirole model, as Bitsight is motivated to keep ahead of possible competitors, just like an elite university. Their ratings are bringing more honesty to the ecosystem than most of the schemes promoted by governments and audit firms, but have some interesting side-effects. For example, service firms are now less willing to sponsor capture-the-flag competitions for schools; if the Bitsight crawler sees a vulnerable system in your IP address space that you set up as a target for such an exercise, it can cut your Bitsight rating by more than 10%, which can cost you real business.

So much for certifying products and business processes. In the next section, we look more closely at dependability metrics from the viewpoints of failure analysis, bug tracking, cross-product dependencies, open-source software and the development team.

28.3 Metrics and dynamics of dependability

As dependability becomes a lifetime property we need better ways of measuring it. We know that it is often a function of the development team; we discussed the capability maturity model in section 27.5.3. To get secure code, you need to hire smart people with a suitable mix of skills and get them to work together on shared projects so they learn to work together. In the process, you measure how well they're doing and improve it by giving feedback and constantly improving the process and tools. But how do you do the measurement?

This has two main aspects: reliability growth, as systems become more dependable over time with testing and bug fixing, and vulnerability disclosure, as bugs are found and may or may not be fixed.

28.3.1 Reliability growth models

The growth of reliability as systems get more testing, both in the lab and in the field, is of interest to many more people than just software engineers; nuclear, electrical and aerospace engineers all depend on reliability models and metrics.

In the simplest possible case – where the tester is trying to find a single bug in a system – a reasonable model is the Poisson distribution: the probability p that the bug remains undetected after t statistically random tests is given by $p = e^{-Et}$ where E depends on the proportion of possible inputs that it affects [1176]. So where the reliability of a system is dominated by a single bug – say when we're looking for the first bug in a system, or the last one – reliability growth can be exponential.

But extensive empirical investigations have shown that in large and complex systems, the likelihood that the t-th test fails is not proportional to e^{-Et} but to k/t for some constant k. So reliability grows very much more slowly. This was first documented in the bug history of IBM mainframe operating systems [18], and has been confirmed in many other studies [1200]. As a failure probability of k/t means a mean time between failure (MTBF) of about t/k, reliability grows linearly with testing time. This result is often stated by the safety critical systems community as 'If you want a mean time between failure of a million hours, then you have to test for (at least) a million hours' [360]. This has been one of the main arguments against the development of complex, critical systems that can't be fully tested before use, such as President Reagan's 'Star Wars' ballistic missile defence program.

The reason for the k/t behaviour emerged in [250] and was proved under more general assumptions by observing that the Maxwell-Boltzmann statistics developed to model ideal gases apply to statistically independent bugs too [313]. This model gives a number of other interesting results. If you can assume that the bugs are statistically independent, then the k/t reliability growth is the best possible: the rule that you need a million hours of testing to get a million hours MTBF is inescapable, up to some constant multiple that depends on the initial quality of the code and the scope of the testing. This can be seen as a version of 'Murphy's Law': that the number of defects which survive a selection process is maximised.

These statistics give a neat link between evolutionary models of software and the evolution of a biological species under selective pressure, where the 'bugs' are genes that reduce fitness. Just as software testing removes the minimum possible number of bugs consistent with the tests applied, biological evolution enables a species to adapt to a changed environment at a minimum cost in early deaths while preserving as much diversity as possible to help the species survive future environmental shocks. For example, if a population of rabbits is preyed on by snakes, they will be selected for alertness rather than speed. Their variability in speed will remain, so if foxes arrive in the neighbourhood the rabbit population's average running speed can rise sharply under selective predation[9].

The evolutionary model also points to fundamental limits on the reliability gains to be had from reusable software components such as objects or libraries; well-tested libraries simply mean that overall failure rates will be dominated by new code. It also explains the safety-critical systems community's observation that test results are often a poor performance indicator [1176]. The failure time measured by a tester depends only on the initial quality of the program,

[9]More formally, the *fundamental theorem of natural selection* says that a species with a high genic variance can adapt to a changing environment more quickly [695].

the scope of the testing and the number of tests, so it gives virtually no further information about the program's likely performance in another environment. There are also some results that are unexpected, but obvious in retrospect: for example, each bug's contribution to the overall failure rate is independent of whether the code containing it is executed frequently or rarely – intuitively, code that is executed less is also tested less. Finally, different testers should work on a program in parallel rather than in series.

So complex systems only become reliable following prolonged testing by diverse testers. This gives the advantage to tried-and-tested designs for machinery, as we gain statistical knowledge of how it fails. Mass-market software started to be used at sufficient scale to enable thorough testing, especially once crash reports started to be sent to the vendor. The use of regression testing by development teams meant that billions of test cases can be exercised overnight with each new build. Services that move to the cloud can be monitored for failure all the time.

So what are the limits to reliability? First, new bugs are introduced by the new code in new versions dictated by platform business models, and second, adversarial action brings in a significant asymmetry between attack and defence.

Let's take a simplified example. Suppose a product such as Windows has 1,000,000 bugs each with an MTBF of 1,000,000,000 hours. Suppose that Ahmed works for the Iranian Revolutionary Guard to create tools to break into the US Army's network, while Brian is the NSA guy whose job is to stop Ahmed. So he must learn of the bugs before Ahmed does.

Ahmed has only half a dozen people, so he can only do 10,000 hours of testing a year. Brian has full Windows source code, dozens of PhDs, oversight of the commercial evaluation labs, an inside track on CERT, an information sharing deal with other Five Eyes member states, and also runs the government's scheme to send round consultants to critical industries such as power and telecomms to find out how to hack them (pardon me, to advise them how to protect their systems). This all adds up to the equivalent of 100,000,000 hours a year of testing.

After a year, Ahmed finds 10 bugs, while Brian has found 100,000. But the probability that Brian has found any one of Ahmed's bugs is only 10%, and the probability that he'll have found them all is negligible. And Brian's bug reports will have become such a firehose that Microsoft will have found some excuse to stop fixing them. In other words, the attacker has thermodynamics on his side.

In real life, vulnerabilities are correlated rather than independent; if 90% of your vulnerabilities are stack overflows, and you introduce compiler technology such as stack canaries and ASLR to trap them, then for modelling purposes there was perhaps only a single vulnerability. However, it's taken years to sort-of-not-quite fix that one, and new ones come along all the time. So if you are actually responsible for Army security, you can't just rely on some commercial off-the-shelf product you bought a few years ago. One way to escape the statistical trap is simplicity – which, as we saw in Chapter 9, steers you towards policies such as mandatory access controls, architecture such as multilevel secure mail guards, and much else besides. The more modern approach is a learning system that observes what's broken and fixes it quickly. That in turn means vigilant network monitoring, breach reporting, vulnerability disclosure and rapid patching – as we described in section 27.5.7.

28.3.2 Hostile review

When you really want a protection property to hold, it's vital that the design and implementation be subjected to hostile review. It will be eventually, and it's likely to be cheaper if it's done before the system is fielded. As we've seen in one case history after another, the motivation of the attacker is critical; friendly reviews, by people who want the system to pass, are essentially useless compared with contributions by people who are seriously trying to break it. That's the basic reason evaluations paid for by the vendor from one of a number of competing evaluators, as in the Common Criteria and ISO 27001, are fundamentally broken. (Recall our discussion in section 12.2.6 of auditors' chronic inability to detect fraud by the executives who hired them. One hedge fund manager who made $100M from shorting Wirecard, Jim Chanos, said, "When people ask us, who were the auditors, I always say 'Who cares?' Almost every fraud has been audited by a major accounting firm." [30].)

To do hostile review, you can motivate attackers with either money or honour. An example of the first was the Independent Validation and Verification (IV&V) program used by NASA for manned space flight; contractors were hired to trawl through the code and paid a bonus for every bug they found. An example of the second was in the evaluation of nuclear command and control, where Sandia National Laboratories and the NSA vied to find bugs in each others' designs. Another was at IBM, which maintained a leading position in cryptography for years by having two teams, one in New York and the other in North Carolina, who would try to break each others' work, like Cambridge and Oxford trying to win a boat race every year. Yet another is Google's Project Zero where the company devotes real engineering effort to finding vulnerabilities both in products that it relies on, such as Linux, and competitor products such as iOS, and aggressively discloses them after 90 days' notice in order to force them to be fixed. This gets over 97% of them fixed [589].

Review by academics is, at its best, in this category. We academics win our spurs by breaking stuff, and get the highest accolades by inventing new types of attack. We compete with each other – Cambridge against Berkeley against CMU against the Weizmann. The established best practice, though, is to motivate hostile review with money, and specifically via bug bounty programs where vendors offer big rewards for reports of vulnerabilities. As we noted in section 27.5.7 above, Apple offers $1m for anyone who can hack the iOS kernel without requiring any clicks by the user; this is one significant metric for iOS security[10].

One way to turbocharge either academic review or a bug bounty program is to open your design and implementation, so all the world can look for bugs.

28.3.3 Free and open-source software

Should security mechanisms be open to scrutiny? The historical consensus is that they should be. The first book in English on cryptography was written in 1641 by Oliver Cromwell's cryptographer John Wilkins. In *'Mercury, or the Secret and Swift Messenger'* he justified discussing cryptography with the remark 'If all those useful Inventions that are liable to abuse, should therefore be concealed, there is not any Art or Science which might be lawfully profest'. The first exposition of cryptographic engineering, Auguste Kerckhoffs *'La Cryptographie Militaire'* in 1883, recommended that cryptographic systems should be designed in such a way that they are not compromised if the opponent learns the technique being used: security must depend only on the key [1044]. In Victorian times, the debate also touched on whether locksmiths should discuss vulnerabilities in locks; as I noted in section 13.2.4, one book author pointed out that both locksmiths and burglars knew how to pick locks and it was only the customers who were ignorant. In section 15.8 I discussed the partial openness found even in nuclear security.

The free and open-source software (FOSS) movement extends this philosophy of openness from the algorithms and architecture to the implementation detail. Many security products have publicly-available source code, of which the first was probably the PGP email encryption program. The Linux and FreeBSD operating systems and the Apache web server are also open-source and are widely relied on: Android runs on Linux, which is also dominant in the world's data centres, while iOS is based on FreeBSD.

Open-source software is not entirely a recent invention; in the early days of computing, most system software vendors published their source code. This started to recede in the early 1980s when pressure of litigation led IBM to adopt an 'object-code-only' policy for its mainframe software, despite bitter criticism from its users. The pendulum has swung back since 2000, and IBM is one of the stalwarts of open source.

There are a number of strong arguments in favour of open software, and a few against. First, while many closed systems are developed in structured ways with waterfall or spiral models of the initial development and later

[10]On this metric the most secure system on earth might be Bitcoin, as anyone who could break the signature mechanism could steal billions.

upgrades, the world is moving towards more agile development styles, a tension described by Eric Raymond as "The Cathedral and the Bazaar" in an influential 1999 book of that name [1587]. Second, systems are getting so complex and toolchains so long that often the bug you're trying to bust isn't in the code you wrote but in an operating system or even a compiler on which you rely, so you want to be able to find bugs there quickly too, and either get them fixed or contribute a fix yourself. Third, if everyone in the world can inspect and play with the software, then bugs are more likely to be found and fixed; in Raymond's famous phrase, "To many eyes, all bugs are shallow". Fourth, it may also be more difficult to insert backdoors into such a product (though people have been caught trying, now that an exploit can sell for seven figures). Finally, for all these reasons, open source is great for confidence.

The proprietary software industry argues that while openness helps the defenders find bugs so they can fix them, it also helps the attackers find bugs so they can exploit them. There may not be enough defenders for many open products, as the typical volunteer finds developing code more rewarding than bug hunting (though bug bounties are starting to shift this). Second, as I noted in section 28.3.4, different testers find different bugs as their test focus is different. As volunteers will look at cool bits of code such as the crypto, smart cyber warriors or bug-bounty hunters will look at the boring bits such as the device drivers. In practice, major vulnerabilities lurk for years. For example, a programming bug in PGP versions 5 and 6 allowed an attacker to add an extra escrow key without the key holder's knowledge [1703].

So will the attackers or the defenders be helped more? Under the standard model of reliability growth, we can show that openness helps attack and defence equally [75]. Thus whether an open or proprietary approach works best in a given application will depend on whether and how that application departs from the standard assumptions, for example, of independent vulnerabilities. In the end, you have to go out and collect the data; as an example, a study of security bugs found in the OpenBSD operating system revealed that these bugs were significantly correlated, which suggests that openness there was a good thing [1490].

So where is the balance of benefit? Eric Raymond's influential analysis of the economics of open source software [1588] suggests five criteria for whether a product would be likely to benefit from an open source approach: where it is based on common engineering knowledge rather than trade secrets; where it is sensitive to failure; where it needs peer review for verification; where it is sufficiently business-critical that different users will cooperate in finding and removing bugs; and where its economics include strong network effects. Security passes all these tests.

The law-and-economics scholar Peter Swire has explained why governments are intrinsically less likely to embrace disclosure: although competitive forces drove even Microsoft to open up a lot of its software for interoperability and trust reasons, government agencies play different games, such as expanding their budgets and avoiding embarrassment [1857]. Yet even there, the security arguments have started to prevail: from tentative beginnings in about 1999, the US Department of Defense has started to embrace open source, notably through the SELinux project I discussed in section 9.5.2.

So while an open design is neither necessary nor sufficient, it is often going to be helpful. The important first-order questions are how much effort was expended by capable people in checking and testing what you built – and whether they tell you everything they find. The prudent thing to do here is to have a generous bug-bounty program. And there's a second-order question of growing importance: if your business depends on Linux, shouldn't some of your engineers be engaged in its developer community, so you know what's going on?

28.3.4 Process assurance

In recent years less emphasis has come to be placed on assurance measures focused on the product, such as testing, and more on process measures such as who developed it and how. As anyone who's done system development knows, some programmers produce code with an order of magnitude fewer bugs than others. There are also some organizations that produce much better code than others. Capable firms try to hire good people, while good people prefer to work for firms that value them and that hire kindred spirits.

While some of the differences between high-quality and low-quality developers are down to talent, many are conditioned by work culture. In my own experience, some IT departments are slow and bureaucratic while others are lively. Leadership matters; just as replacing Boeing's engineering leadership with money men contributed to the 737Max disaster, I've seen an IT department's morale collapse when its CIO was replaced by a bureaucrat. Another problem is that engineer quality has a tendency to decline over time. One factor is glamour: a lot of bright graduates want to work for startups rather than the big tech firms, or for racy fintechs and hedge funds rather than boring old money-centre banks. Another is demographics: the Microsoft of the early 1990s was full of young engineers working long hours, but a decade later many had cashed their stock options and left, while the rest had mostly acquired families and worked office hours. Once a company stops growing, promotion is slow; there was a saying in IBM that 'The only people who ever left were the good ones[11].' Banks and government agencies have similar problems. Some firms have tried to counter this by rating systems that require managers to fire the least productive 10% or so of their team each year, but the damage this does

[11] As a former IBM employee, I liked that one!

to morale is dreadful; people spend their time sucking up rather than writing code. Maintaining a productive work culture is one of the really hard problems and a surprising number of big-name firms are really bad at it. The capability maturity model, which we discussed in section 27.5.3, is one of the tools that can help good managers keep good teams together and improve them over time. But on its own it's not enough. The whole corporate environment matters, from the water-cooler chat to the top leadership. Is the mission to do great engineering, or just to make money for Wall Street? Of course every firm pretends to have a mission, but most are bogus and the staff see through them instantly.

Some old-fashioned companies swear by the ISO 9001 standard, which requires them to document their processes for design, development, testing, documentation, audit and management control generally. For more detail, see [1941]; a whole industry of consultants and auditors has got its snouts in this trough. Like ISO 27001 which we discussed in section 28.2.9 above, it's decorative rather than effective. At best it can provide a framework for incremental process improvement; but very often it's an exercise in box-ticking that merely replaces chaos by more bureaucratic chaos. Just as agile development methodologies displaced waterfall approaches, so ISO 9001 is being displaced by the capability maturity model. What that comes down to, in assurance terms, is trusted suppliers.

But trusted suppliers are hard to certify. Government certifiers cannot be seen to discriminate, so a program degenerates into box-ticking. Private certification schemes have a tendency to reinforce cartels, or to race to the bottom, as we discussed above in section 28.2.8. In both cases the consultancies and audit firms industrialise the process to maximise their fee income, and we get back to where we started. If you are good at your job, how do you get that across? Small businesses who do high-quality work generally do better when they sell to the most discriminating customers – to the few big players who're smart enough to appreciate what they do. In short, you usually have to be an expert yourself to really understand who the quality providers are.

So what about the dynamics? If quality is hard to measure, and the incentives for quality are mixed, and improving quality is hard, then what can usefully be said about the assurance level of evolving products? Will they be like milk, or like wine [1490]? Will they get better with age, or go off?

The simple answer is that you have to do real measurements. The quality of a system may improve, or decline. It may even find an equilibrium if the rate at which new bugs are introduced by product enhancements equals the rate at which old bugs are found and removed. There are several research communities measuring reliability, availability and maintainability of systems in various applications and contexts. Empirically, the reliability of new systems often improves for a while as the more energetic bugs are found and fixed, then stays in equilibrium for a number of years, and then deteriorates as the code gets complex and more difficult to maintain (which software engineers sometimes even refer to as *senescence*). However, if the firms that maintain the code are still making enough money from it, and are incentivised to care about quality, they can fix this by rewriting the parts that have become too messy – a process known as *refactoring*. In short, the real world is complicated. Models can take you only so far, and you have to study how a system behaves in actual use.

Measurement brings its own problems. Some vendors collect and analyse masses of data about how their products fail – examples being platform companies like Microsoft, Google and Apple – but make only selected data available to outsiders, creating a market for specialist third-party evaluators, from the tech press to academics. Other firms say much less, creating an opportunity for rating firms such as Bitsight. The healthcare sector is notoriously cagey about evidence of harm to patients, whose lawyers may have to work for years to build a negligence case. But in applications such as medical devices, there is enough of a public interest for regulators to intervene to increase transparency, and as we noted in section 28.2.3 above, the EU recently changed the law on medical device regulation to compel aftermarket surveillance. As most software nowadays is in applications rather than platforms, and very often in or supporting devices, this brings us to consider the regulation of safety.

28.4 The entanglement of safety and security

As we discussed in 28.2.2 governments regulate safety for many types of device from cars to railway signals and from medical devices to toys. As software finds its way into everything and everything gets connected to cloud services, the nature of safety regulation is changing, from simple pre-market safety testing to maintaining security and safety over a service lifetime of years during which software will be patched regularly. We've already seen how this is becoming entangled with security. We discussed smart grids in section 23.8.1, smart meters in section 14.2 and building alarms in section 13.3.

I believe that the increasing entanglement of safety and security is so significant for our field that since 2017 we've merged teaching on safety and security for our first-year undergraduates, as I mentioned in section 27.1. Safety is a much more diverse subject than security. While security engineering is a fairly coherent discipline, safety engineering has fragmented over time into separate disciplines for aircraft, road vehicles, ships, medical devices, railway signals and other applications. We can still learn a lot from safety engineers, as I discussed in section 27.3, and safety engineers are starting to have to learn about security too. This will be a long process. Thanks to the coronavirus lockdown, these lectures are now publicly available on video [90]; I now wish I'd put my lectures online years ago.

What spurred us to unite security and safety teaching was some work we did for the European Union in 2015–6 looking at what will happen to safety regulation once computers are embedded invisibly everywhere. The EU is the leading safety regulator worldwide for dozens of industries, as it's the largest market and cares more about safety than the US government does. Officials wanted to know how this ecosystem would have to adapt to the 'Internet of Things' where vulnerabilities (whether old or new) may be remotely exploited, and at scale. Many regulators who previously thought only in terms of safety will have to start thinking of security as well.

The problem facing the EU in 2015 was how to modernise safety regulation across dozens of industries from cars and planes to medical devices, railway signals and toys, and to introduce security regulation as appropriate. The regulatory goals are different. In this book, we have discussed how security fails in a number of different sectors and the nature of the underlying market failure. In different contexts, security regulators might want to drive up attackers' costs and reduce their income; to reduce the cost of defence; to reduce the impact of security failure; to enable insurers to price cyber-risks efficiently; and to reduce both the social cost of attacks and social vulnerability to them.

Safety regulators seem to be more straightforward. They tend to ignore the economic subtleties underlying each market failure and focus on injury and death, then on direct property damage. For deaths, at least, you'd think we have decent statistics, but priorities are modulated by public concern about different types of harm. As we've discussed, the public are much more alarmed at a hundred people dying all at once in a plane crash than a thousand people dying one at a time in medical device accidents. However, when hackers showed they could go in over wifi and change the dose delivered by several models of Hospira Symbiq infusion pump to a potentially fatal level, the FDA issued a safety advisory telling hospitals to stop using it [2069]. It did not issue advisories about the 300+ models that merely suffered from the safety issues we discussed in section 28.2.3. When you stop to think about it, that's rather striking. A safety regulator ignores a problem that kills several thousand Americans a year while panicking at a safety-plus-security issue that has so far killed nobody. Perhaps people intuitively grasp the principle we discussed in section 27.3.6: that a one-in-a-million chance of a fatal accident happening by chance doesn't give much assurance if an opponent can engineer the combination of inputs needed to trigger it.

The pattern continued the following year, when the FDA recalled 465,000 St Jude pacemakers in the USA for a firmware update after a report that the device could be hacked. The update involves a hospital visit because of a small risk of device failure. The report itself was controversial, as it was promoted by an investment firm that had shorted St Jude's stock [1842].

The EU already had work in progress on medical device safety and, the following year, updated its Medical Device Directives to require that medical device software be developed 'in accordance with the state of the art taking into account the principles of development life cycle, risk management, including information security, verification and validation', and 'designed and manufactured in such a way as to protect, as far as possible, against unauthorised access that could hamper the device from functioning as intended' [652]. This text doesn't cover all the bases but is a useful first step; it comes into force in 2021.

28.4.1 The electronic safety and security of cars

Road safety helped drive interest in the convergence of security and safety in the mid-2010s, thanks to the surge of interest in self-driving cars driven by Google and Tesla, among others. Following the breakthrough in computer vision using deep neural networks in 2012, there was rapid progress. The first news of early accidents with experimental vehicles arrived around 2015 at the same time as the breakthrough research on adversarial machine learning I described in section 25.3 and the high-profile hack of the Jeep Cherokee, which I described in section 25.2.4. Autonomous cars suddenly became a hot topic, not just for stock-market investors and security researchers, but for safety. Could terrorists hack them and drive them into crowds? Could they get the same result by projecting deceptive images on a building? And if kids could use their phone to hail a car home from school, could someone hack it to abduct them? And what about the ethics – if a self-driving car was about to crash and could choose between killing its one occupant or two pedestrians, what would it do? What should it do? Let's take the safety and assurance aspects one step at a time.

Road safety is a major success story for safety regulation. Following Ralph Nader's book *'Unsafe at any speed'* [1372], the US Congress created the National Highway Traffic Safety Administration (NHTSA). It started from a belief that crash testing of new models would be enough, but found it needed to force the recall of vehicles that were discovered later to be unsafe[12]. The effects can be seen starkly in a Consumer Reports video of a crash test between a 2009 Chevy Malibu and a 1959 Chevy Bel Air. The Bel Air's passenger compartment is crushed and the dummy driver impaled on the steering wheel; a human driver would have been killed. Thanks to 50 years of progress, the passenger compartment of the Malibu remains intact; the front crumple zone absorbs much of the energy, the seatbelt and airbag hold the dummy driver, and a human driver would have walked away [472]. I show this video to my first-year students to emphasise that safety engineering is not just about making mistakes less likely, but also about mitigating their effects. The decades of progress that the video illustrates involved not just engineering, lobbying and

[12]The story is told in *'The Struggle for Auto Safety'* [1237].

standard setting across multiple countries, but many tussles between safety campaigners and the industry. Within the industry, some carmakers tried to lead while others dragged their heels. Car safety also involves driver training, laws against drink driving and excessive driver working hours, changing social norms around such behaviour, steady improvements to road junction design and much else. It has grown into a large and complex ecosystem. This now has to evolve as cars become smarter and more connected.

During the 2010s, cars were steadily acquiring more assistive technology, from parking assist through adaptive cruise control to automatic emergency braking and automatic lane keeping. I described in section 25.2 how companies like Google and Tesla drove a research program to join these systems up together, giving autonomous driving. The assistive technology features themselves had various bugs; I discussed the blind spots of adaptive cruise control in section 23.4.1. Some were also open to exploitation: Charlie Miller and Chris Valasek had hacked the Jeep's park-assist feature to drive it off the road. Companies that sold limited autonomous driving features, such as Tesla, experienced accidents that began to undermine public confidence. I discussed some of the security implications of autonomous vehicles in section 25.2. We discussed the usability aspects of safety too. Tesla's 'Autopilot' required the driver to pay attention and keep a hand on the steering wheel, in order to remain in control and avoid accidents. But as it drove adequately much of the time, many drivers didn't, with consequences that were occasionally both fatal and newsworthy. Even in 2020, while the better autopilot systems can drive a car passably well on the motorway, they can be flaky on smaller roads, getting confused at round abouts and running over grass verges. So how should we test their safety?

Testing an *anti-lock braking system* (ABS) is fairly straightforward as we understand the physics of skidding and aquaplaning, and such systems have been around long enough for us to have a long accident history. We next had *emergency brake assist* (EBA), which applies full braking force if it thinks you're trying to do an emergency stop. The usual algorithm is that if you move your foot from the accelerator to the brake in under 300ms and then apply at least 2kg of force, it activates and stops the car as quickly as possible. This is a simple algorithm but is harder to evaluate, as it's trying to infer the driver's intent. (I once triggered mine unintentionally and thankfully there wasn't a car close behind me.)

A recent addition is automatic emergency braking (AEB), which is supposed to stop the car if a child or a dog runs in front of you. This is harder still, as you're trying to understand everything you see on the street ahead, with complex processing that uses both traditional logic and machine-vision systems based on deep neural networks. As we discussed in section 25.2, the current products are both limited and of variable quality. Add lane keeping assist and adaptive cruise control, and your car can pretty well drive itself on the freeway.

But how should you test that? And if we ever move to full autonomy, your risk and threat analysis must include a lot of the bad things that happen in human societies.

Tesla says in defence of its Autopilot feature that its cars are safer than others; of the 135 fatalities in crashes involving its vehicles up to June 23 2020, only 10 were attributed to Autopilot [1873]. The actual figures are controversial, though. An insurance forensics company brought a lawsuit against NHTSA to get the raw figures for accidents up till June 2016, studied them, and claimed that the analysis offered by Tesla and accepted by NHTSA had considered only 13% of the data. Rather than a 40% decrease in airbag deployments after the Autosteer feature of the vehicle was activated, as Tesla had claimed, the full data showed a 57% increase from 0.76 deployments per million miles of travel to 1.21 [1568].

The insurance industry accumulates good data over time across all car makers and worries about the cost of claims. It was concerned at AEB, worrying that if cars brake hard when a rabbit runs in front of them, there might be more rear-end collisions. But once the data started to arrive in 2016, insurers relaxed. When I check online how much it would cost me to insure a Tesla with Autopilot versus a plug-in hybrid Mercedes of similar value, I get about the same answer (though more insurers bid for the Mercedes).

But actuarial costs are not the only driver of public policy. Politicians started to worry about truck drivers' jobs. Philosophers started to worry about ethics: given a choice between killing a pedestrian and the driver, would an autopilot protect its driver? The industry worried about updates. Progress in machine vision is so rapid that you can imagine having to sell a whole new vision unit every five years, as the systems we have now won't run on the hardware of five years ago. Would the customers stand for having to pay several thousand Euros every few years for a new autopilot?

People also worry more about security threats, as we have evolved to be sensitive to adversarial activity. By 2020, we have a flurry of security standardisation, including the draft ISO 21434 standard on cybersecurity, which I mentioned in section 27.3.5; proposed amendments to the regulations of the UNECE[13] to deal with cybersecurity and software updates for connected vehicles [1925]; and in Japan, following cyber attacks on Toyota and Honda, baseline requirements for the whole car industry supply chain [1245]. That's all great, but the target is moving faster all the time.

In Brussels, officials started to worry about how the regulatory ecosystem could cope. Over 20 agencies are involved one way or another in vehicle safety (unlike in the USA, where NHTSA covers everything from car design to speed

[13]The UN Economic Commission for Europe was established by a 1958 treaty. It includes the car-making countries in Europe and Africa plus Japan, Korea and Australasia and is effectively one of three standardisation zones for cars, the others being the Americas and China.

limits). Would each agency have to hire a security engineer? Some of them don't have any engineers at all, just lawyers and economists. How should the ecosystem evolve to cope? Officials were suddenly less willing to trust the industry's assurances after the Dieselgate emissions scandal in 2015, when it turned out that Volkswagen had installed software in its cars to cheat on emissions tests. The Volkswagen and Audi CEOs lost their jobs and face criminal charges, along with about a dozen other executives; the companies paid billions in legal settlements. The threat model was no longer just the external hacker, but included the vendors themselves. Regulators wanted to get back in control. What did they need to do?

28.4.2 Modernising safety and security regulation

Our brief was to consider the policy problem generally across all sectors. It was clear that European institutions needed cybersecurity expertise to support safety, privacy, consumer protection and competition. But what would this mean in practice? In order to flesh this out, Éireann Leverett, Richard Clayton and I studied three industries of which we had some knowledge: medical devices, cars and electricity distribution. Our full report [158] was presented in 2016 and published the following year, along with a summary version for academic audiences [1150]. The full report has an extensive analysis of the existing patchwork of safety/security standards for embedded devices from ISO, IEC, NIST and others.

This exercise taught us a huge amount about subjects we didn't expect would be on the agenda. Usability is critical in a number of ways. The dominant safety paradigm used to be to analyse how limited or erratic human performance could degrade an otherwise well-designed system, and then work out how to mitigate the consequences. Some countries demand that drivers over 67 get a medical or re-sit their driving test, as well as insisting on seat belts and airbags. In security, malice comes into the equation: you worry about the widow in her eighties who's called up and persuaded to install an 'upgrade' on her PC. Car security is not just about whether a terrorist can take over your car remotely and drive it into some pedestrians. If a child can use her mobile phone to direct a car to take her to school, what new threats do we have to worry about? Might she be abducted, whether by a stranger or (more likely) in a custody dispute? And whose engineers need to worry about her safety – the car company's, the ride-hailing company's, or the government's?

The security engineer's task is to enable even vulnerable users to enjoy reasonable protection against a capable motivated opponent. How do you embed good practice in industries that have never had to think of distant adversaries before? That's not just a matter of setting minimum standards but also of embedding security thinking into standards bodies, regulatory agencies, testing facilities and many other places in the ecosystem. That will be a long and arduous process, just as car safety was. Getting test engineers who work by checking carefully whether the 'British standard finger' can be accidentally poked into an electrical appliance to think in terms of creative malice instead will be hard. Where do we start?

We came up with a number of recommendations. Some were considered by the Commission to be in the 'too hard' category, including extending product liability law to services, and requiring the reporting of breaches and vulnerabilities not just to security agencies and privacy regulators but to other stakeholders too. Eventually we'll need laws regulating the use of car data in investigating accidents, particularly if there are disputes over liability when car autopilots cause fatal crashes. (At present the vendors hold the data close and it takes vigorous litigation to get hold of it.) Without data we won't be able to build a learning system.

One of our recommendations was that vendors should have to self-certify, for their CE mark, that products can be patched if need be. This looks set to be partly achieved by means of a technical standard, ETSI EN 303 645 V2.1 [646], as I discussed in section 28.2.9 above. ETSI is a membership organisation of some 800 firms; it can move more quickly than governments but still has some clout; for example, it set up the standards bodies for mobile telephony. Failure to comply with an ETSI standard does not however empower a customs officer in Rotterdam to send a container of toys back to China. For that, we need to endow standards with the force of law.

28.4.3 The Cybersecurity Act 2019

Another recommendation was that Europe should create a European Security Engineering Agency to support policymakers. Europe already had the European Network and Information Security Agency (ENISA), which coordinated security breach reporting among EU government agencies. However, it had been exiled to Crete as a result of lobbying by the UK and French intelligence agencies, who did not want a peer competitor among the European institutions. The Brexit vote shifted the politics and made it feasible for ENISA to open a proper Brussels office so it could take on the security engineering advisory role.

The Cybersecurity Act 2019 formalised this [654]. It empowered ENISA to be the central agency for regulating security standards, as we described in section 28.2.9, and also to be the main agency for cybersecurity advice to other European bodies. It is to be hoped that ENISA will build its competence and clout over time, and see to it that new safety standards pay appropriate attention to security too, including at a minimum an appropriate development lifecycle (which was another of our recommendations).

For a security technology to really work, functionality isn't enough, and the same goes for testing and even incentives for learning. The right people have to trust it and it has to become embedded in social and organisational processes, which means alignment with wider systems and stable persistence over a long enough period of time. The implication is that regulators should shift from the testing of products to the assurance of whole systems (this was our final recommendation).

28.5 Sustainability

The problem our report identified as the most serious in the long term was that products are becoming much less static. As security and safety vulnerabilities are patched, regulators will have to deal with a moving target. Automobile mechanisms will need security testing as well as safety testing, and also means of dealing with updates. As we saw from the Volkswagen debacle, many legacy manufacturers haven't caught up with coordinated disclosure.

Most two-year old phones don't get patched because the OEM and the mobile network operator can't get their act together. So how on earth are we going to patch a 25-year-old Land Rover that spent 10 years in the Danish countryside and was then exported to Romania? This kicked off a political fight, as the car industry did not want to be liable for software patching for more than six years. (The typical European car dealer will sell you a 3-year lease on a new car if you're rich, and on an approved used car if you're not quite so rich.) However, the embedded carbon cost of a new car – the amount of CO_2 emitted during its manufacture – is about equal to its lifetime fuel burn. And it's predictable that, sooner or later, a car whose software isn't up-to-date won't be allowed on the roads. At present, the average age of a car at scrappage is about 15 years; if that were reduced to six, the environmental cost would be unacceptable. We would not even save CO_2 by moving from internal combustion engines to electric vehicles, because of the higher embedded carbon cost of electric vehicles; the whole energy transition is based on the assumption that they will last at least as long as the 150,000km average of our legacy fleet [614].

We found a very ready audience in European institutions. A number of other stakeholders had been complaining about the effects of software on the durability of consumer goods, with updates available only for a short period of time or not at all. Right-to-repair activists were campaigning for consumer electronic devices to be reusable in a circular economy, annoyed that tech firms try to prevent repair using 'security' mechanisms, or even abuse them in an attempt to make repair illegal. The self-regulation of the IoT market has been largely unsuccessful, thanks to a complex interplay of economic incentives and consumer expectations [1958]. Consumer-rights organisations were starting to warn of the shockingly short lifespan of smart devices: you could spend extra on a 'smart fridge' only to find that it turned into a frosty brick a year later when the vendor stopped maintaining the server [935]. Planned obsolescence was already a hot political topic as green parties increased their vote share across Europe. Lightbulbs used to last longer; the bicentennial light has been burning at Livermore since 1901. In 1924 a cartel of GE, Osram and Philips agreed to reduce average bulb lifetimes from 2500h to 1000h, and this behaviour has been followed by many industries since. Governments have pushed back; France made it illegal to shorten product life in 2015, and after Apple admitted in 2017 that it had used a software update to slow down older iPhones, prompting users to buy newer ones, it was prosecuted. In 2020 it received the highest-ever fine, €1.2B, for anti-competitive practices, although this also related to its treatment of its French distributors [1195]. (It settled a US class action for $500m [968].)

Security agencies were already warning us about the risks of the 'Internet of Things', including network-connected devices with default passwords and unpatchable software. In fact, I learned of the Mirai botnet taking down Twitter as I was on the Eurostar train back to London from giving the first presentation of our work, to an audience of about 100 security and IT policy people in Brussels. We soon found out that it exploited Xiaomi CCTV cameras that had default passwords and whose software could not be patched. It was a perfect illustration of the need for action.

Over the ensuing three years there was more than one initiative to try to create a legal means to push back on tech companies that failed like Xiaomi to support their products by patching vulnerabilities (or even making patching possible). The tech lobbyists blocked the first couple of attempts, but eventually in 2019 the European Parliament updated consumer law to cover software maintenance.

28.5.1 The Sales of goods directive

This Directive passed the European Parliament in May 2019 [655] and will take effect from 2021. Thereafter, firms selling goods 'with digital elements' must maintain those elements for a reasonable service life. The wording is designed to cover software in the goods themselves, online services to which the goods are connected, and apps that may communicate with the goods either via the services or directly. They must be maintained for a minimum of two years after sale, and for a longer period if that is a reasonable expectation of the customer. What might that mean in practice?

Existing regulations require vendors of durables such as cars and washing machines to keep supplying spares for at least ten years, so we can hope that the new regulatory regime will require at least as long. Indeed, the preamble to the Directive notes that "A consumer would normally expect to receive updates for at least as long as the period during which the seller is liable for a lack of conformity, while in some cases the consumer's reasonable expectation could extend beyond that period, as might be the case particularly with regard to security updates." Given that in many countries cars have to pass an annual roadworthiness test to remain in use, and that such a test is likely to include a check that software is patched up to date in the foreseeable future, we could well see a requirement for security patches to extend beyond ten years.

No doubt there will be all sorts of arguments as the lobbyists try to cut the costs of this, but it's a huge step in the right direction. American practice often follows Europe on safety matters.

28.5.2 New research directions

Now that there is not just a clear social need for long-term maintenance of the safety and security of software in durable goods, but a clear legal mandate, I urge my fellow computer scientists to adopt this as a grand challenge for research.

Since the 1960s we have come to see computers almost as consumables, thanks to Moore's law. This has conditioned our thinking from the lowest level of technical detail up to the highest levels of policy. We've crammed thousands, and then millions, more transistors into chips to support more elaborate pipelining and caching. We've put up with slow and inefficient software in the knowledge that next year's PC will run it faster. We've shrugged off monopolies, believing that the tech ten years from now will be quite different from today's, so we can replace competition in the market with competition for the market. We've been like a cruise ship, happily throwing the trash overboard in the expectation that we'll leave it far behind us.

Moore's law is now running out of steam. The analysis of CPU performance by Hennessy and Paterson shows that while this grew by 25% per annum from 1978 to 1986 and a whopping 52% from 1986 to 2003, it slowed to 23% in 2003–11, 12% in 2013–15 and 3.5% after that [884]. As the party winds down, we'll have to start clearing up the trash. That extends from the side-channel attacks like Spectre that were caused by the 12-stage CPU pipelines, through the technical debt accumulated in our bloatware, right up to the monopolistic business ecosystem that drives it all.

There is much, much more. The root certificates of a number of popular CAs are starting to expire, and if these are embedded in devices such as TVs whose software can't be upgraded, then the devices are essentially bricked [118]. (The most popular, Letsencrypt, rolls over in 2021.) When CA root certs expire you have to update clients, not servers, to fix them. In consumer devices, the trend is towards shorter lifetimes, to make crypto updateable; as I discussed in section 21.6, browsers such as Safari and Chrome are starting to enforce

398-day certificate expiry, and that's another strong incentive for frequent updates.

There are many environments with long-lived equipment where updates aren't usual, from petrochemical plants to electricity substations. Systems in buildings and civil engineering projects are somewhat of a hybrid; some vendors are working on versions of Linux that are expected to be as stable as possible and maintained for 25 years, while others are pushing for more aggressive regular updating of whole systems and telling us to 'put everything in the cloud'. This latter approach is associated with the 'smart buildings' meme, but has its own drawbacks. Once multiple contractors and subcontractors need online access to systems that contain full engineering information on buildings – from the electricity substations through the air-conditioning to the fire and burglar alarms – there are obvious risks. Some of these contractors operate at international scale, so a subverted employee or rooted machine there may have access to the critical national infrastructure of dozens of countries. Are we comfortable with that?

Adapting to the new normal will take years, as it will require behaviour change by millions of stakeholders. I suspect that the tensions created by this adaption will become significant in policy, entrepreneurship and research over the next decade.

So what might sustainable security research look like? As a first pilot project, Laurent Simon, David Chisnall and I tackled the maintenance of cryptography software. As I mentioned in section 19.4.1, TLS was proven secure twenty years ago, but there's been about one attack a year on it since, mostly via side channels. One of the problems is that the crypto implementation, such as OpenSSL, typically has code designed to perform cryptographic operations in constant time, so that the key in use won't leak to an outside observer, and also to zeroise memory locations containing key material or other sensitive data, so that the key can't be deduced by other users of the same machine either. But every so often, somebody improves a compiler so that it now understands that certain instructions don't do any real work. It optimises them away, and all of a sudden millions of machines have insecure crypto software. This is extremely annoying; you're out there fighting the bad guys and all of a sudden your compiler writer stabs you in the back, like a subversive fifth column in your rear. Our toolsmiths should be our allies rather than our enemies, and so we worked out what would be needed to fix this properly. Languages like C have no way of expressing programmer intent, so we figured out how to do this by means of code annotations. Getting a compiler to do constant-time code and secure object deletion properly turns out to be surprisingly tricky, but we eventually got a working proof of concept in the form of plugins for LLVM [1762].

Much, much more will be needed. Moving from the low level of compiler internals to the medium level of safety systems, a big challenge facing the car industry is getting accident data to the stakeholders who can learn from it.

In Europe, some fifty thousand people die in road traffic accidents each year, and another half a million are injured. Worldwide, there are something like a million deaths a year. As cars are starting to log both control inputs and sensor data, there are many megabytes of data about a typical accident, but at present these are mostly not analysed. Increasingly, the data are on the vendors' servers as well as in the damaged vehicles. But when the police investigate major road accidents, they do not at present have access to much information from data recorders or to most of the 100-million-plus lines of software in the vehicle – some of which will be from subsidiary suppliers, and of uncertain provenance, version and patch status. Where there is a closely-fought lawsuit, data may be demanded, but vendors are reluctant to share it and it typically takes a court order.

What should happen? We should aim at a learning system. We keep hearing reports of people getting killed by an autonomous car in a stupid accident – as when an Uber killed Elaine Herzberg in Tempe, Arizona, because she was pushing a bike on the road and its software detected pedestrians only on or near a crosswalk [1266]. We should expect to be able to push an update to stop that happening again. So what would the patch cycle look like? In aviation, accidents are monitored resulting in feedback not just to operators such as pilots and air traffic controllers but to the designers of aircraft and supporting ground systems. Work is starting on systems for monitoring accidents involving medical devices, though the vendors may well drag their feet. There, too, the key is mandatory systems for monitoring adverse events and collecting data. At present, we fix road junctions once there have been several accidents there; that's all the 'patch cycle' we have at present, because the only data available to the highways department is the location and severity of each accident, plus perhaps a couple of sentences in the report from the attending officer. A learning system for cars too is inevitable as vehicles become more autonomous, but they won't learn on their own.

Learning will involve analysing the causes of failures, accumulating engineering knowledge, and ultimately politics involving multiple stakeholder groups. For starters, we'll need the fine-grained data from what the cars sensed, what they decided to do, and why. The task of writing the laws to get these data from vendors to accident investigators, insurance assessors and other stakeholders lies ahead. At present, EU Member States are responsible for post-market surveillance of vehicle standards, so very little gets done, and there have been proposals to give the European Commission a surveillance power in the wake of Dieselgate. Then there will be the task of actually building these systems. They will be large and complex, because of the need to deal with multiple conflicting rights around safety, privacy and jurisdiction.

Moving still further up the stack to the level of policy, there's a growing consensus that tech needs to be better regulated. We could perhaps tolerate the various harms to privacy and competition while the technology was changing rapidly. If you didn't like the IBM monopoly in the 1980s you just had to wait until Microsoft came along; and by the time Microsoft had become the 'evil empire' in the late 1990s, Larry and Sergey were starting Google. Was Google+ too clunky for you? No matter, try Facebook or Twitter. But as Moore's law runs out of steam, the dominant firms we have now may remain dominant for some time – just like the railways dominated the second half of the nineteenth century and the first third of the twentieth. And there are many other sectors where technology has enabled some players to lock in market dominance; as I write in 2020, Amazon is the world's most valuable company. We need to refresh our thinking on antitrust law. There are some signs that this is happening [1046]. What would you hope the law to look like twenty years from now? How should the safety, security and antitrust pieces fit together?

28.6 Summary

In the old days, the big question in a security engineering project was how you know when you're done. All sorts of evaluation and assurance methodologies were devised to help. Now the world is different. We're never done, and nobody who says they are done should be trusted.

Security evaluation and assurance schemes grew up in a number of different ecosystems. The US military spawned the original Orange Book, and inspired both the FIPS 140 standards for cryptographic modules and the Common Criteria, both of which attempted to spread the gospel of trustworthy systems to businesses and to other countries. Safety certification schemes evolved separately in a number of industries – healthcare, aerospace and road vehicles to name just three. Vendors game these systems all the time, and work to capture the regulators where this is possible. Now that everything's acquiring connectivity, you can't have safety without security, and these ecosystems are merging.

In both safety and security, the emphasis will move from pre-market testing to monitoring and response, which will include updating both devices already in the field and the services that support them. This will move beyond software lifecycle standards towards the goal of a learning system that can recover quickly even from novel hazards and attacks.

Things are improving, slowly. Back in the 20th century, many vendors never got information security right. By 2010, the better ones were getting it more or less right at the third or fourth attempt. In the future, everyone will be expected to fix their products reasonably promptly when they break, and to do so for a reasonable period of time.

But the cost of all this, the entanglement of security with safety in all sorts of devices and services, and their interaction with issues from discrimination to globalisation and trade conflict, will make these issues increasingly the stuff of global politics. The safety and security costs inflicted on us by tech, in its broadest sense, will be in increasing tension with national ideas of sovereignty and, at a more practical level, people's ability to achieve by collective action those goals that cannot be achieved through individual action or market forces. Just as security economics was a hot topic in the 2000s and security psychology in the 2010s, I expect that the politics of security will be a growth topic in the 2020s and beyond.

Research problems

In addition to the grand challenge of sustainable security I discuss in section 28.5.2 above, there are many other open problems around assurance. We really don't know how to do assurance in complex ecosystems such as where cars talk to online services and mobile phone apps. A second bundle of problems comes from the fact that as the worlds of safety and security are slowly coming together, like a couple of galaxies slowly merging, we find that safety engineers and security engineers don't speak each others' languages, have incompatible sets of standards and even incompatible approaches to standardisation. Working this out in one industry after another will take years.

Another big opportunity may be for lightweight mechanisms to improve real deployed systems. Too many researchers take the view that 'If it's not perfect, it's no good.' We have large communities of academics writing papers about provable security, formal methods and about obscure attacks that aren't found in the wild because they don't scale. We have large numbers of real problems arising from companies corner-cutting on development. If programmers are going to steal as much code as they can from stackexchange, do we need a public-interest effort to clean up the examples there to get rid of the buffer overflows? And do we have any chance of setting security usability standards for tools such as crypto libraries and device permissions, so that (for example) libraries that default to ECB would be forcibly retired, just like MD5 and SHA1?

Yet another is likely to be the testing of AI/ML systems, both before deployment and for continuous assessment. We already know, for example, that deep neural networks and other ML mechanisms inhale prejudice along with their training data; because machine-vision systems are mostly trained on photos of white people, they are uniformly worse at spotting people with darker skin, leading to the concern that autonomous vehicles could be more likely to kill black pedestrians [2030]. What will a learning system look like when it touches a contentious social issue? How do you do continuous safety in a world where not all lives are valued equally? How do we ensure that the security, privacy and safety engineering decisions that firms take are open to public scrutiny and legal challenge?

Further reading

There's a whole industry devoted to promoting the security and safety assurance business, supported by mountains of your tax dollars. Their enthusiasm can even have the flavour of religion. Unfortunately, there are nowhere near enough people writing heresy.

CHAPTER

29

Beyond "Computer Says No"

At the start of this century, security technology was an archipelago of mutually suspicious islands – the cryptologists, the operating system protection people, the burglar alarm industry, right through to the chemists who did banknote inks. We all thought the world ended at our shore. By 2010, security engineering was an established and growing discipline; the islands were being joined up by bridges as practitioners realised we had to look beyond our comfort zones. The banknote ink chemist who didn't want to understand digital watermarks, and the cryptologist who could only talk about confidentiality, were steadily marginalised.

Now, in 2020, everyone needs to have a systems perspective in order to design components that can be integrated usefully into real products and services. And as these are used by real people, and often at global scale, our field is embracing the humanities and social sciences too.

Security engineering is about ensuring that systems are predictably dependable in the face of all sorts of malice, from bombers to botnets. And as attacks shift from the hard technology to the people who use it, systems must also be resilient to error, mischance and even coercion. So a realistic understanding of people – staff, customers, users and bystanders – is essential; human, institutional and economic factors are as important as technical ones. The ways in which real systems provide dependability are becoming ever more diverse, and protection goals are not just closer to the application, they can be subtle and complex. Conflicts between goals are common: where one principal wants accountability and another wants deniability, it's hard to please them both.

Starting in 2001, we began to realise that many persistent security failures are incentive failures at heart; if Alice guards a system while Bob pays the cost of failure, you can expect trouble. This led to the growth of security economics, which the first edition of this book helped to catalyse. The second edition in 2008 documented how failures were also increasingly about usability, and the decade after that saw a lot of research into security psychology.

So what next? By way of a conclusion to this book, I'd like to highlight three things.

First, complexity. Computer science has spent seventy years devising an impressive array of tools to manage technical complexity, but we're now coming up hard against social complexity. We can program cars to drive themselves fairly well on the freeway or in the desert, but we can't cope with cluttered city streets with all those unpredictable people. We can encrypt messages or strip people's names from databases but we can't stop social structure showing through. And bullying people has its limits; "computer says no" is a fast way to lose customers. It's not enough to study how a computer system can interact with a human; we need to figure out how it can work with many interacting humans.

Second, sustainability. As we put software in everything and connect everything online, we have to patch the software and maintain the servers. With durable goods like cars, pacemakers and electricity substations, we may have to maintain software for twenty or even forty years. We have no real idea how to do that, and if we don't crack it then our automation will be bad news for our planet's future. So-called 'smart' devices are often just things that have to be thrown away sooner, when "computer says no".

Third, politics. Security is not a scalar, but a relationship. It's not some kind of magic fairy dust you sprinkle on systems, but about how these systems exercise power. Who loses and who gains when "computer says no"? Does the social-network user get privacy, or does the advertiser get access? How is it used to turn money into political power? And if people want public goods such as a dependable Internet or a low rate of cybercrime, how can these be provided in a global world?

The stability of cybercrime over a decade in which the technology has changed completely suggests that it's not fundamentally about technology. The persistence of tech monopolies raises other questions about how tech and society can co-evolve, and about the nature of power. When Facebook becomes the arbiter of political speech, when Apple and Google can dictate policy on coronavirus contact tracing, and when Amazon, Microsoft and Google dictate policy on facial recognition (outside China), then I suspect that technology people should start reading up on political science, as well as on economics and psychology. The most intractable problems of the next ten years may be around governance.

Just as individuals can learn through experience, so our societies learn and adapt too. Democracy is the key mechanism for that. So a crucial way in which engineers can contribute is by taking part in the policy debate. The more we engage in the problems that technology poses around complexity, sustainability and the nature of power, the faster our societies will adapt to deal with them.

Bibliography

[1] M Aamir Ali, B Arief, M Emms, A van Moorsel, "Does the Online Card Payment Landscape Unwittingly Facilitate Fraud?" *IEEE Security & Privacy Magazine* (2017)

[2] M Abadi, RM Needham, "Prudent Engineering Practice for Cryptographic Protocols", *IEEE Transactions on Software Engineering* v 22 no 1 (Jan 96) pp 6–15; also as DEC SRC Research Report no 125 (June 1 1994)

[3] A Abbasi, HC Chen, "Visualizing Authorship for Identification", in *ISI 2006*, LNCS 3975 pp 60–71

[4] H Abelson, RJ Anderson, SM Bellovin, J Benaloh, M Blaze, W Diffie, J Gilmore, PG Neumann, RL Rivest, JI Schiller, B Schneier, "The Risks of Key Recovery, Key Escrow, and Trusted Third-Party Encryption", in *World Wide Web Journal* v 2 no 3 (Summer 1997) pp 241–257

[5] H Abelson, RJ Anderson, SM Bellovin, J Benaloh, M Blaze, W Diffie, J Gilmore, M Green, PG Neumann, RL Rivest, JI Schiller, B Schneier, M Specter, D Weizmann, "Keys Under Doormats: Mandating insecurity by requiring government access to all data and communications", MIT CSAIL Tech Report 2015-026 (July 6, 2015); abridged version in *Communications of the ACM* v 58 no 10 (Oct 2015)

[6] M Abrahms, "What Terrorists Really Want", *International Security* v 32 no 4 (2008) pp 78–105

[7] M Abrahms, J Weiss, "Malicious Control System Cyber Security Attack Case Study – Maroochy Water Services, Australia", *ACSAC 2008*

[8] A Abulafia, S Brown, S Abramovich-Bar, "A Fraudulent Case Involving Novel Ink Eradication Methods", in *Journal of Forensic Sciences* v 41 (1996) pp 300-302

[9] DG Abraham, GM Dolan, GP Double, JV Stevens, "Transaction Security System", in *IBM Systems Journal* v 30 no 2 (1991) pp 206–229

[10] Y Acar, M Backes, S Bugiel, S Fahl, PD McDaniel, M Smith, "SoK: Lessons Learned from Android Security Research for Appified Software Platforms", *IEEE S&P 2016* pp 433–451

[11] Y Acar, S Fahl, M Mazurek, "You Are Not Your Developer, Either: A Research Agenda for Usable Security and Privacy Research Beyond End Users", *IEEE SecDev 2016*

[12] N Achs, "VISA confronts the con men", *Cards International* (20 Oct 1992) pp 8–9

[13] O Acıiçmez, ÇK Koç, JP Seifert, "On the Power of Simple Branch Prediction Analysis" *2nd ACM symposium on Information, computer and communications security* (2007) pp 312–320

[14] S Ackerman, J Ball "Optic Nerve: millions of Yahoo webcam images intercepted by GCHQ" *The Guardian* Feb 28 2014

[15] A Acquisti, A Friedman, R Telang, "Is There a Cost to Privacy Breaches?", *Fifth Workshop on the Economics of Information Security* (2006)

[16] A Acquisti, G Loewenstein, L Brandimarte, "Secrets and Likes: The need for privacy and the difficulty of achieving it in the digital age", *Journal of Consumer Psychology* (2020)

[17] NR Adam, JC Wortmann, "Security-Control Methods for Statistical Databases: A Comparative Study", *ACM Computing Surveys* v 21 no 4 (1989) pp 515–556

[18] EN Adams, "Optimising preventive maintenance of software products", *IBM Journal of Research & Development*, v 28 no 1 (1984) pp 2–14

[19] J Adams, *'Risk'*, University College London Press 1995

[20] J Adams, "Cars, Cholera and Cows: the management of risk and uncertainty", *Policy Analysis* no 335, Cato Institute, Washington, 1999

[21] E Addley "Animal Liberation Front bomber jailed for 12 years", *The Guardian* Dec 6 2006

[22] B Adida, M Bond, J Clulow, A Lin, RJ Anderson, RL Rivest, "A Note on EMV Secure Messaging in the IBM 4758 CCA", at `www.ross-anderson.com`

[23] H Adkins, B Beyer, P Blankiship, P Lewandowski, A Oprea, A Stubblefield, *'Building Secure and Reliable Systems'*, Google 2020

[24] A Adler, "Sample images can be independently restored from face recognition templates", in *Proc. Can. Conf. Elec. Comp. Eng.* (2003) pp 1163–1166

[25] A Adler, "Vulnerabilities in biometric encryption systems", in *NATO RTA Workshop: Enhancing Information Systems Security – Biometrics* (IST-044-RWS-007)

[26] D Adrian, K Bhargavan, Z Durumeric, P Gaudry, M Green, JA Halderman, N Heninger, D Springall, E Thomé, L Valenta, B VanderSloot, E Wustrow, S Zanella-Bǵuelin, P Zimmermann, "Imperfect Forward Secrecy: How Diffie-Hellman Fails in Practice", *ACM CCS 2015*, `weakdh.org`

[27] Y Afina, C Inverarity, B Unal, *'Ensuring Cyber Resilience in NATO's Command, Control and Communication Systems'*, Chatham House, July 2020

[28] S Afroz, M Brennan, R Greenstadt, "Detecting hoaxes, frauds, and deception in writing style online", in *IEEE Symposium on Security and Privacy* (2012) pp 461–475

[29] *'Trustworthy Systems Supporting Server Signing Part 2: Protection Profile for QCSD for Server Signing'*, 419241-2, Agence nationale de la sécurité des systèmes d'information, 2018

[30] H Agnew, "Jim Chanos pockets $100m from Wirecard short", *Financial Times* Jul 24 2020

[31] E Ahmed-Rengers, M Ahmed-Rengers, "Democracy on the Margins of the Market: A Critical Look into the Privatisation of Cyber Norm Formation", *Hague Conference on Cyber Norms* 2020, at `https://ahmed-rengers.com/cybernorms/`

[32] M Ahmed-Rengers, R Anderson, D Halatova, I Shumailov, "Snitches Get Stitches: On The Difficulty of Whistleblowing", *Security Protocols Workshop* (2019); online as *arXiv:2006.14407* (2010)

[33] C Ajluni, "Two New Imaging Techniques Promise To Improve IC Defect Identification", in *Electronic Design* v 43 no 14 (10 July 1995) pp 37–38

[34] Y Akdeniz, "Regulation of Child Pornography on the Internet" (Dec 1999), at `http://www.cyber-rights.org/reports/child.htm`

[35] G Akerlof, "The Market for 'Lemons: Quality Uncertainty and the Market Mechanism", in *The Quarterly Journal of Economics* v 84 no 3 (1970) pp 488–500

[36] M Alagappan, JV Rajendran, M Doroslovački, G Venkataramani, "DFS Covert Channels on Multi-Core Platforms", *Visisoc 2017*

[37] R Albert, HW Jeong, AL Barabási, "Error and attack tolerance of complex networks", in *Nature* v 406 no 1 (2000) pp 387–482

[38] J Alfke, "Facebook and Decentralized Identifiers", in *Thought Palace* Dec 2 2007

[39] AM Algarni, YK Malaiya, "Software Vulnerability Markets: Discoverers and Buyers", *International Journal of Computer, Information Science and Engineering* v 8 no 3 (2014)

[40] M Ali, P Sapiezinski, M Bogen, A Korolova, A Mislove, A Rieke, "Discrimination through Optimization:How Facebook's Ad Delivery Can Lead to Biased Outcomes", *Proceedings of the ACM on Human-Computer Interaction* v 3 (2019)

[41] M Ali, P Sapiezinski, A Korolova, A Mislove, A Rieke, "Ad Delivery Algorithms:The Hidden Arbiters of Political Messaging", *arXiv:1912.04255*, Dev 17 2019

[42] E Allman, "Managing Technical Debt", *Communications of the ACM* v 55 no 5 (May 2012) pp 50–55

[43] M Allman, V Paxson, "Etiquette Concerning Use of Shared Measurement Data", in *Internet Measurement Conference* (IMC 2007), at `http://www.imconf.net/imc-2007/papers/imc80.pdf`

[44] F Almgren, G Andersson, T Granlund, L Ivansson, S Ulfberg, "How We Cracked the Code Book Ciphers", at `http://codebook.org`

[45] T Alves, D Felton, "TrustZone: Integrated Hardware and Software Security", *Information Quarterly* (2004)

[46] American Society for Industrial Security, `http://www.asisonline.org`

[47] *Amnesty International*, "Evolving Phishing Attacks Targeting Journalists and Human Rights Defenders from the Middle-East and North Africa", Aug 16 2019

[48] E Amoroso, *'Fundamentals of Computer Security Technology'*, Prentice Hall 1994

[49] R Andersen, "The Panopticon Is Already Here", *The Atlantic*, Sep 2020

[50] C Anderson, K Sadjadpour, "Iran's Cyber Threat: Espionage, Sabotage, and Revenge", *Carnegie Endowment* Jan 4 2018

[51] B Andersen, M Frenz, "The Impact of Music Downloads and P2P File-Sharing on the Purchase of Music: A Study for Industry Canada", 2007, at `http://strategis.ic.gc.ca/epic/site/ippd-dppi.nsf/en/h_ip01456e.html`

[52] J Anderson, *'Computer Security Technology Planning Study'*, ESD-TR-73-51, US Air Force Electronic Systems Division (1973) `http://csrc.nist.gov/publications/history/index.html`

[53] M Anderson, W Seltzer, *Official Statistics and Statistical Confidentiality: Recent Writings and Essential Documents*, at `http://www.uwm.edu/%7Emargo/govstat/integrity.htm`

[54] RJ Anderson, "Solving a Class of Stream Ciphers", in *Cryptologia* v XIV no 3 (July 1990) pp 285–288

[55] RJ Anderson, "Why Cryptosystems Fail" in *Communications of the ACM* vol 37 no 11 (November 1994) pp 32–40; earlier version at `http://www.cl.cam.ac.uk/users/rja14/wcf.html`

[56] RJ Anderson, "Liability and Computer Security: Nine Principles", in *Computer Security — ESORICS 94*, Springer LNCS v 875 pp 231–245

[57] RJ Anderson, "Crypto in Europe – Markets, Law and Policy", in *Cryptography: Policy and Algorithms*, Springer LNCS v 1029 pp 75–89

[58] RJ Anderson, "Clinical System Security – Interim Guidelines", in *British Medical Journal* v 312 no 7023 (13th January 1996) pp 109–111; `http://www.cl.cam.ac.uk/ftp/users/rja14/guidelines.txt`

[59] RJ Anderson, *'Security in Clinical Information Systems'*, British Medical Association 1996

[60] RJ Anderson, "A Security Policy Model for Clinical Information Systems", in *1996 IEEE Symposium on Security and Privacy* pp 30–43; at `http://www.cl.cam.ac.uk/users/rja14/policy11/policy11.html`

[61] RJ Anderson, "An Update on the BMA Security Policy", in [64] pp 233–250

[62] RJ Anderson, "The Eternity Service", in *Proceedings of Pragocrypt 96* pp 242–252

[63] RJ Anderson (ed), *Proceedings of the First International Workshop on Information Hiding* (1996), Springer LNCS v 1174

[64] RJ Anderson (ed), *'Personal Medical Information – Security, Engineering and Ethics'*, Springer-Verlag 1997

[65] RJ Anderson, "On the Security of Digital Tachographs", in *ESORICS 98*, Springer LNCS v 1485 pp 111–125

[66] RJ Anderson, "Safety and Privacy in Clinical Information Systems", in *'Rethinking IT and Health'*, J Lenaghan (ed), IPPR (Nov 98) pp 140–160

[67] RJ Anderson, "The DeCODE Proposal for an Icelandic Health Database"; *Læknabladhidh* (The Icelandic Medical Journal) v 84 no 11 (Nov 98) pp 874–5, `http://www.cl.cam.ac.uk/users/rja14/#Med`

[68] RJ Anderson, "The Formal Verification of a Payment System", chapter in *Industrial Strength Formal Methods: A Practitioners Handbook*, MG Hinchey and JP Bowen (editors), Springer Verlag (Sep 1999) pp 43–52

[69] RJ Anderson, "How to Cheat at the Lottery (or, Massively Parallel Requirements Engineering)", in *15th Annual Computer Security Application Conference* (1997); pp xix–xxvii; at `http://www.cl.cam.ac.uk/~1rja14/lottery/lottery.html`

[70] RJ Anderson, "The Millennium Bug – Reasons not to Panic", at `http://www.ftp.cl.cam.ac.uk/ftp/users/rja14/y2k.html`

[71] RJ Anderson, "Comments on the Security Targets for the Icelandic Health Database", at `http://www.cl.cam.ac.uk/ftp/users/rja14/iceland-admiral.pdf`

[72] RJ Anderson, "The Correctness of Crypto Transaction Sets", in *Proceedings of Security Protocols 2000*, Springer LNCS v 2133 pp 125–141

[73] RJ Anderson, "Why Information Security is Hard – An Economic Perspective", in *ACSAC 2001* pp 358–365; also given as a distinguished lecture at SOSP, 2001

[74] RJ Anderson, "Cryptography and Competition Policy – Issues with 'Trusted Computing' ", *Second Workshop on Economics and Information Security* (2003)

[75] RJ Anderson, "Open and Closed Systems are Equivalent (that is, in an ideal world)", in *Perspectives on Free and Open Source Software*, MIT Press 2005, pp 127–142

[76] RJ Anderson, "Closing the Phishing Hole – Fraud, Risk and Nonbanks", at *Nonbanks in the Payments System: Innovation, Competition, and Risk*, US Federal Reserve, Santa Fe, May 2–4 2007

[77] RJ Anderson, *'Security Economics Resource Page'*, at `http://www.cl.cam.ac.uk/~rja14/econsec.html`

[78] RJ Anderson, "A Merry Christmas to all Bankers", at `https://www.lightbluetouchpaper.org`, Dec 25 2010

[79] RJ Anderson, "Security Economics – A Personal Perspective", *ACSAC 2012*

[80] RJ Anderson, "Risk and Privacy Implications of Consumer Payment Innovation" *Consumer Payment Innovation in the Connected Age*, Kansas City Fed, March 2012

[81] RJ Anderson, "The privacy of our medical records is being sold off", The Guardian Aug 28 2012

[82] RJ Anderson, "Will the Information Commissioner be consistent?", *https://www.lightbluetouchpaper.org*, Nov 20 2012

[83] RJ Anderson, "How privacy is lost", at `https://lightbluetouchpaper.org`, April 28 2013

[84] RJ Anderson, "Offender tagging", at `https://lightbluetouchpaper.org`, Sep 2 2013

[85] RJ Anderson, "Privacy versus government surveillance: where network effects meet public choice", in *Workshop on the Economics of Information Security* (2014)

[86] RJ Anderson, "Curfew tags – the gory details" `https://lightbluetouchpaper.org` Dec 13 2014

[87] RJ Anderson, "Meeting Snowden in Princeton", at `https://lightbluetouchpaper.org` May 2 2015

[88] RJ Anderson, "He Who Pays The AI, Calls The Tune", *The Edge Question 2015: What do you think about machines that think?*, `https://www.edge.org/response-detail/26069`

[89] RJ Anderson, "Future ID", Mar 19 2019, at `https://www.lightbluetouchpaper.org/2019/03/19/future-id/`

[90] RJ Anderson, *Software and Security Engineering*, Cambridge University, 2020, at `https://www.cl.cam.ac.uk/teaching/1920/SWSecEng/materials.html`

[91] RJ Anderson, C Barton, R Böhme, R Clayton, M van Eeten, M Levi, T Moore, S Savage, "Measuring the Cost of Cybercrime", WEIS 2012

[92] RJ Anderson, C Barton, R Böhme, R Clayton, C Gañán, T Grasso, M Levi, T Moore, M Vasek, "Measuring the Changing Cost of Cybercrime", WEIS 2019

[93] RJ Anderson, T Berger-Wolf, "Privacy for Tigers", at *Usenix Security* 2018

[94] RJ Anderson, SJ Bezuidenhoudt, "On the Reliability of Electronic Payment Systems", in *IEEE Transactions on Software Engineering* v 22 no 5 (May 1996) pp 294–301

[95] RJ Anderson, E Biham, LR Knudsen, "Serpent: A Proposal for the Advanced Encryption Standard", submitted to NIST as an AES candidate; at [96]

[96] RJ Anderson, E Biham, L Knudsen, *'The Serpent Home Page'*, at `http://www.cl.cam.ac.uk/~rja14/serpent.html`

[97] RJ Anderson, N Bohm, T Dowty, F Fisher, D Korff, E Munro, M Thomas, "Consultation response on The Data Sharing Review", *FIPR* Feb 15 2008

[98] RJ Anderson, R Böhme, R Clayton, T Moore, *'Security Economics and the Internal Market'*, ENISA, 2008

[99] RJ Anderson, M Bond, "API-Level Attacks on Embedded Systems", in *IEEE Computer* v 34 no 10 (October 2001) pp 67–75

[100] RJ Anderson, M Bond, "Protocol Analysis, Composability and Computation" in *Computer Systems: Theory, Technology and Applications*, Springer 2003, pp 7–10

[101] RJ Anderson, M Bond, J Clulow, S Skorobogatov, *'Cryptographic processors – a survey'*, Cambridge University Computer Laboratory Technical Report no 641 (July 2005); shortened version in *Proc. IEEE* v 94 no 2 (Feb 2006) pp 357–369

[102] RJ Anderson, I Brown, R Clayton, T Dowty, D Korff, E Munro, *'Children's Databases – Safety and Privacy'*, Information Commissioner's Office, UK, Nov 2006

[103] RJ Anderson, I Brown, T Dowty, W Heath, P Inglesant, A Sasse, *Database State*, Joseph Rowntree Reform Trust, 2009

[104] RJ Anderson, B Crispo, JH Lee, C Manifavas, V Matyás, FAP Petitcolas, *'The Global Internet Trust Register'*, MIT Press 1999, and at `http://www.cl.cam.ac.uk/Research/Security/Trust-Register/`

[105] R Anderson, S Fuloria, "Security Economics and Critical National Infrastructure", at *WEIS 2009*; in *Economics of Information Security and Privacy* (2010) pp 55–66

[106] R Anderson, S Fuloria, "Who controls the off switch?" at *IEEE SmartGridComm* (2010)

[107] RJ Anderson, MG Kuhn, "Tamper Resistance – a Cautionary Note", in *Proceedings of the Second Usenix Workshop on Electronic Commerce* (Nov 96) pp 1–11

[108] RJ Anderson, MG Kuhn, "Low Cost Attacks on Tamper Resistant Devices", in *Security Protocols* (1997) pp 125–136

[109] RJ Anderson, MG Kuhn, "Soft Tempest – An Opportunity for NATO", at *Protecting NATO Information Systems In The 21st Century*, Washington DC, Oct 25–26, 1999

[110] RJ Anderson, JH Lee, "Jikzi: A New Framework for Secure Publishing", in *Security Protocols 99*, Springer LNCS v 1976 pp 21–36

[111] RJ Anderson, TW Moore, "Information Security Economics – and Beyond", in *Crypto 2007*, Springer LNCS 4622, pp 68–91

[112] RJ Anderson, TW Moore, "Economics and Internet Security: a Survey of Recent Analytical, Empirical and Behavioral Research", in *Oxford Handbook of the Digital Economy* (2011)

[113] RJ Anderson, RM Needham, "Robustness principles for public key protocols", in *Crypto 95* Springer LNCS v 963 pp 236–247

[114] RJ Anderson, RM Needham, "Programming Satan's Computer", in *'Computer Science Today'*, Springer Lecture Notes in Computer Science v 1000 (1995) pp 426–441

[115] RJ Anderson, RM Needham, A Shamir, "The Steganographic File System", in *Second International Workshop on Information Hiding*, Springer LNCS vol 1525 pp 74–84

[116] RJ Anderson, MR Roe, "The GCHQ Protocol and Its Problems", in *Eurocrypt 97*, Springer LNCS v 1233 pp 134–148

[117] RJ Anderson, I Shumailov, M Ahmed, A Rietmann, "Bitcoin Redux", *Workshop on the Economics of Information Security* (2018)

[118] T Anderson, "An Internet of Trouble lies ahead as root certificates begin to expire en masse, warns security researcher", *The Register* Jun 10 2020

[119] CM Andrew, V Mitrokhin, *'The Sword and the Shield: The Mitrokhin Archive and the Secret History of the KGB'*, Basic Books 1999

[120] M Andrews, JA Whitaker, *'How to Break Web Software'*, Addison-Wesley 2006

[121] `http://www.anonymizer.com`

[122] Anonymous, "I'm the Google whistleblower. The medical data of millions of Americans is at risk", *The Guardian* Nov 14 2019

[123] *Anonymity Bibliography*, 2007, at `http://freehaven.net/anonbib/`

[124] JC Anselmo, "US Seen More Vulnerable to Electromagnetic Attack", in *Aviation Week and Space Technology* v 146 no 4 (Jul 28 1997) p 67

[125] D Antonioli, NO Tippenhauer and KB Rasmussen, "The KNOB is Broken: Exploiting Low Entropy in the Encryption Key Negotiation Of Bluetooth BR/EDR", *Usenix 2019*

[126] D Antonioli, NO Tippenhauer and KB Rasmussen, "BIAS: Bluetooth Impersonation Attacks", *IEEE S&P 2020*

[127] APACS, "Fraud abroad drives up card fraud losses", October 3 2007; at `http://www.apacs.org.uk/media_centre/press/03.10.07.html`; see also *The Register*, `http://www.theregister.co.uk/2007/10/03/card_fraud_trends/`

[128] APACS, "Payment Advice – Protect Your PIN", Aug 16 2007; at `http://www.apacs.org.uk/media_centre/press/08_16_07.html`

[129] Apple, *'iOS Security'*, May 2019

[130] T Appleby, "Chilling debit-card scam uncovered", in *The Globe & Mail* (10/12/1999) p 1

[131] I Arghire, "Hardware-based Password Managers Store Credentials in Plaintext" *Security Week* Dec 9 2019

[132] Arm Inc., *'Cache Speculation Side-channels'* v 2.4, Oct 2018

[133] US Army, *'Electromagnetic Pulse (EMP) and Tempest Protection for Facilities'*, Corps of Engineers Publications Depot, Hyattsville (1990)

[134] A Arora, R Krishnan, A Nandkumar, R Telang, YB Yang, "Impact of Vulnerability Disclosure and Patch Availability – An Empirical Analysis", *Third Workshop on the Economics of Information Security* (2004)

[135] A Arora, CM Forman, A Nandkumar, R Telang, "Competitive and strategic effects in the timing of patch release", in *Workshop on the Economics of Information Security* (2006)

[136] SE Asch, *'Social Psychology'*, OUP 1952

[137] D Asonov, R Agrawal, "Keyboard Acoustic Emanations", IBM Almaden Research Center, 2004

[138] *'ASPECT – Advanced Security for Personal Communications Technologies'*, at http://www.esat.kuleuven.ac.be/cosic/aspect/index.html

[139] Associated Press, "Charges dropped against Ex-HP chairwoman – Three others charged in boardroom spying case receive no jail time", Mar 14 2007, at http://www.msnbc.msn.com/id/17611695/

[140] C Aspinwall, A Giorgi, D DiFurio, "Several Boeing 737 Max 8 pilots in U.S. complained about suspected safety flaw", *Dallas Morning News* Mar 12 2019

[141] R Atkinson, "The single most effective weapon against our deployed forces" and "The IED problem is getting out of control. We've got to stop the bleeding", in the *Washington Post*, Sep 30 2007; "There was a two-year learning curve... and a lot of people died in those two years", Oct 1 2007; "You can't armor your way out of this problem", Oct 2 2007; "If you don't go after the network, you're never going to stop these guys. Never", Oct 3 2007; all linked from https://web.archive.org/web/20080827220904/http://smallwarsjournal.com/blog/2007/09/print/weapon-of-choice/

[142] D Aucsmith, "Tamper-Resistant Software: An Implementation", in [63] pp 317–333

[143] D Aucsmith (editor), *Proceedings of the Second International Workshop on Information Hiding* (Portland, Apr 98), Springer LNCS 1525

[144] B Audone, F Bresciani, "Signal Processing in Active Shielding and Direction-Finding Techniques", *IEEE Transactions on Electromagnetic Compatibility* v 38 no 3 (August 1996) pp 334-340

[145] B Auxier, L Rainie, M Anderson, A Perrin, M Kumar, E Turner, "Americans and Privacy: Concerned, Confused and Feeling Lack of Control Over Their Personal Information", *Pew Research Center* Nov 15 2019

[146] A Aviv, *'Side channels enabled by smartphone interaction'*, PhD Thesis, University of Pennsylvania, 2012

[147] A Aviv, B Sapp, M Blaze, JM Smith, "Practicality of Accelerometer Side Channels on Smartphones" *ACSAC 2012*

[148] R Axelrod, *The Evolution of Cooperation*, Basic Books (1984)

[149] I Ayres, SD Levitt, "Measuring Positive Externalities from Unobservable Victim Precaution: An Empirical Analysis of Lojack", in *Quarterly Journal of Economics* v 108 no 1 (Feb 1998), http://www.nber.org/papers/w5928

[150] D Austin, "Flood warnings", in *Banking Technology* (Jul–Aug 1999) pp 28–31

[151] "Computer Combat Rules Frustrate the Pentagon", in *Aviation Week and Space Technology* v 147 no 11 (15/9/97) pp 67–68

[152] J Bacon, *'Concurrent Systems'*, Addison-Wesley 1997

[153] J Bacon, K Moody, J Bates, R Hayton, CY Ma, A McNeil, O Seidel, M Spiteri, "Generic Support for Distributed Applications", in *IEEE Computer* (March 2000) pp 68–76

[154] L Badger, DF Sterne, DL Sherman, KM Walker, SA Haghighat, "Practical Domain and Type Enforcement for UNIX," in *Proceedings of the 1995 IEEE Symposium on Security and Privacy* pp 66–77

[155] M Baggott, "The smart way to fight fraud", *Scottish Banker* (Nov 95) pp 32–33

[156] M Baker, D Gates, "Boeing altered key switches in 737 MAX cockpit, limiting ability to shut off MCAS ", *Seattle Times*, May 10 2019

[157] P Baker, "Five Takeaways From John Bolton's Memoir", *New York Times* Jun 18 2020

[158] G Baldini, E Leverett, R Clayton, R Anderson, "*Standardisation and Certification of Safety, Security and Privacy in the 'Internet of Things'* " European Commission Joint Research Centre, 2017

[159] D Balfanz, EW Felten, "Hand-Held Computers Can Be Better Smart Cards", in *Eighth USENIX Security Symposium* (1999), pp 15–23

[160] T Balmforth, "Russia postpones sovereign internet test over coronavirus", *Reuters* Mar 20 2020

[161] J Bamford, *'The Puzzle Palace: A Report on NSA, America's Most Secret Agency'*, Houghton, Mifflin 1982

[162] Bank for International Settlements, *'Security and Reliability in Electronic Systems for Payments'*, British Computer Society (1982)

[163] *'Enhancing cross-border payments: building blocks of a global roadmap – Stage 2 report to the G20'*, Bank for International Settlements, July 2020

[164] "Card Fraud: Banking's Boom Sector", in *Banking Automation Bulletin for Europe* (Mar 92) pp 1–5

[165] J Baniak, G Baker, AM Cunningham, L Martin, "Silent Sentry Passive Surveillance", *Lockheed Martin Mission Systems* (1999)

[166] S Bano, A Sonnino, M Al-Bassam, S Azouvi, P McCorry, S Meiklejohn, G Danezis, "SoK: Consensus in the Age of Blockchains", *arXiv:1711.03936*, Nov 10 2017

[167] B Barak, O Goldreich, R Impagliazzo, S Rudich, A Sahai, S Vadhan, K Yang, "On the (Im)possibility of Obfuscating Programs", *Crypto 2001*, `http://www.wisdom.weizmann.ac.il/~oded/p_obfuscate.html`

[168] M Barbaro, T Zeller, " A Face Is Exposed for AOL Searcher No. 4417749", in *New York Times* Aug 9 2006

[169] R Barbulescu, P Gaudry, A Joux, E Thomé, "A Heuristic Quasi-Polynomial Algorithm for Discrete Logarithm in Finite Fields of Small Characteristic", *Eurocrypt 2014* pp 1–16

[170] A Barisani, B Bianco, "Practical EMV PIN interception and fraud detection", `https://github.com/abarisani/`, 2017

[171] JP Barlow, "The Economy of Ideas", *Wired* Mar 1 1994

[172] E Barkan, E Biham, N Keller, "Instant Ciphertext-Only Cryptanalysis of GSM Encrypted Communication" Technion Technical Report CS-2006-07

[173] R Barkan, S Ayal, D Ariely, "Ethical dissonance, justifications and moral behaviour", *Current Opinion in Psychology* v 6 (2015) pp 157–161

[174] RL Barnard, *'Intrusion Detection Systems'*, Butterworths 1988

[175] T Barnes, "NSA Whistleblower Reality Winner Was Held in Isolation for a Week and No One Has Explained Why", *The Intercept* Sep 26 2018

[176] A Barnett, "Britain's UFO secrets revealed", in *The Observer* Jun 4 2000

[177] S Baron-Cohen, *The Essential Difference: Men, Women, and the Extreme Male Brain*, Penguin, 2003

[178] S Baron-Cohen, AM Leslie, U Frith, "Does the autistic child have a 'theory of mind'?" Cognition (Oct 1985) v 21 no 1 pp 37–46

[179] J Barr, "The Gates of Hades", in *Linux World* April 2000; at `http://www.linuxworld.com/linuxworld/lw-2000-04/lw-04-vcontrol_3.html`

[180] B Barrow, B Quinn, "Millions in danger from chip and pin fraudsters" in *Daily Mail* June 5th 2006

[181] B Bartholomew, JA Guerrero-Saade, "Wave your false flags! Deception tactics muddying attribution in targeted attacks, *Karpersky Labs*, Oct 6 2016

[182] D Bartz, A Oreskovic, "UPDATE 3-Facebook settles privacy case with U.S. FTC" *Reuters* Nov 30 2011

[183] D Basin, R Sasse, J Toro, "The EMV Standard: Break, Fix, Verify", *arXiv:2006.08249*, Jun 15 2020

[184] R Baskerville, "Information Systems Security Design Methods: Implications for Information Systems Development", in *ACM Computing Surveys* v 265 (1993) pp 375–414

[185] PJ Bass, "Telephone Cards and Technology Development as Experienced by GPT Telephone Systems", in *GEC Review* v 10 no 1 (95) pp 14–19

[186] *'Bates and others v Post Office group litigation,'* 2019, at `https://www.postofficetrial.com/`

[187] W Bax, V Dekker, "Met zijn allen meekijken in de medische kaartenbak", in *Trouw* Dec 11 2007

[188] S Baxter, "US hits panic button as air force 'loses' nuclear missiles", in *Sunday Times* Oct 21 2007

[189] BBC News Online, "Tax records 'for sale' scandal", Jan 16 2003, at `https://news.bbc.co.uk/1/hi/business/2662491.stm`

[190] BBC News Online, " 'Relief' over fingerprint verdict", Feb 7 2006, at https://news.bbc.co.uk/1/hi/scotland/4689218.stm

[191] BBC News Online, "Schools get rules on biometrics", July 23 2007, at https://news.bbc.co.uk/1/hi/education/6912232.stm

[192] BBC News Online, "PC stripper helps spam to spread", Oct 30 2007, at https://news.bbc.co.uk/1/hi/technology/7067962.stm

[193] BBC News Online, "The mystery of Ireland's worst driver", Feb 19 2009, at http://news.bbc.co.uk/1/hi/northern_ireland/7899171.stm

[194] BBC News Online, "G4S and Serco lose tagging contracts", Dec 12 2013, at https://www.bbc.co.uk/news/uk-25348086

[195] BBC News Online, "Citizenship Amendment Bill: India's new 'anti-Muslim' law explained", Dec 11 2019

[196] S Beattie, S Arnold, C Cowan, P Wagle, C Wright, "Timing the Application of Security Patches for Optimal Uptime", in *LISA XVI* (2002) pp 101–110

[197] A Beautement, MA Sasse, M Wonham, "The Compliance Budget: Managing Security Behaviour in Organisations", *NSPW 2008*

[198] F Beck, *'Integrated Circuit Failure Analysis – A Guide to Preparation Techniques'*, Wiley 1998

[199] J Beck, "Sources of Error in Forensic Handwriting Examination", in *Journal of Forensic Sciences* v 40 (1995) pp 78–87

[200] G De Becker, "Bezos Investigation Finds the Saudis Obtained His Private Data", *The Daily Beast* Mar 30 2019

[201] GS Becker, "Crime and Punishment: An Economic Approach", in *Journal of Political Economy* v 76 no 2 (March/April 1968) pp 169–217

[202] I Becker, A Hutchings, R Abu-Salma, RJ Anderson, N Bohm, SJ Murdoch, MA Sasse, G Stringhini, "International comparison of bank fraud reimbursement: customer perceptions and contractual terms", *Journal of Cybersecurity*, v 3 no 2 (2017) pp 109–125

[203] L Beckwith, C Kissinger, M Burnett, S Weidenbeck, J Lowrance, A Blackwell, C Cook, "Tinkering and Gender in End-User Programmers' Debugging", in *CHI '06*, Montreal, April 2006; at http://eusesconsortium.org/gender/

[204] JB Bédrune G Campana, "Everybody be cool, this is a robbery!", *Black Hat* 2019; at https://donjon.ledger.com/BlackHat2019-presentation/

[205] I Beer, "A very deep dive into iOS Exploit chains found in the wild", *Google Project Zero Blog* Aug 29 2019, at https://googleprojectzero.blogspot.com/2019/08/a-very-deep-dive-into-ios-exploit.html

[206] S Begley, "Fingerprint Matches Come Under More Fire As Potentially Fallible", *Wall Street Journal* Oct 7 2005 p B1; at http://online.wsj.com/article_print/SB112864132376462238.html

[207] HA Beker, C Amery, "Cryptography Policy", at https://www.cl.cam.ac.uk/~rja14/Papers/zergo_cryptographypolicy.html

[208] HJ Beker, JMK Friend, PW Halliden, "Simplifying key management in electronic fund transfer point of sale systems", in *Electronics Letters* v 19 (1983) pp 442–443

[209] H Beker, F Piper, *'Cipher Systems'*, Northwood 1982

[210] H Beker, M Walker, "Key management for secure electronic funds transfer in a retail environment", in *Advances in Cryptology – Crypto 84*, Springer LNCS v 196 pp 401–410

[211] DE Bell, L LaPadula, *'Secure Computer Systems'*, ESD-TR-73-278, Mitre Corporation; v I and II: November 1973, v III: Apr 1974

[212] M Bellare, J Kilian, P Rogaway, "The Security of Cipher Block Chaining" in *Advances in Cryptology – Crypto 94* Springer LNCS v 839 pp 341–358

[213] M Bellare, P Rogaway, "Optimal Asymmetric Encryption", in *Advances in Cryptology – Eurocrypt 94*, Springer LNCS v 950 pp 103–113; see also RFC 2437

[214] SM Bellovin, "Packets Found on an Internet", in *Computer Communications Review* v 23 no 3 (July 1993) pp 26–31

[215] SM Bellovin, "Defending Against Sequence Number Attacks", RFC 1948 (May 1996)

[216] SM Bellovin, "Problem Areas for the IP Security Protocols," in *Proceedings of the Sixth Usenix Unix Security Symposium* (1996); at `http://www.cs.columbia.edu/~smb/papers/badesp.pdf`

[217] SM Bellovin, "Debit-card fraud in Canada", in `comp.risks` v 20.69; at `http://catless.ncl.ac.uk/Risks/20.69.html`

[218] SM Bellovin, "Permissive Action Links", at `http://www.research.att.com/~smb/nsam-160/`

[219] SM Bellovin, *'ICMP Traceback Messages'*, Internet Draft, March 2000, at `http://search.ietf.org/internet-drafts/draft-bellovin-itrace-00.txt`

[220] SM Bellovin, "More on Comcast Blocking Peer-to-Peer Traffic", Oct 22 2007, at `http://www.cs.columbia.edu/~smb/blog/2007-10/2007-10-22.html`; and "Comcast Apparently Blocking Some Peer-to-Peer Traffic", Oct 19 2007, ibid.

[221] S Bellovin, M Blaze, E Brickell, C Brooks, V Cerf, W Diffie, S Landau, J Peterson, J Treichler, "Security Implications of Applying the Communications Assistance to Law Enforcement Act to Voice over IP", `http://www.itaa.org/news/docs/CALEAVOIPreport.pdf`

[222] SM Bellovin, WR Cheswick, A Rubin, *'Firewalls and Internet Security, Second Edition: Repelling the Wily Hacker'*, Addison-Wesley 2003

[223] SM Bellovin, M Merritt, "Encrypted Key Exchange: Password-Based Protocols Secure Against Dictionary Attacks", in *Proceedings of the IEEE Symposium on Security and Privacy* (1992) pp 72–84

[224] J Benaloh, "ElectionGuard Preliminary Specification v0.85", *Microsoft Research*, 2020

[225] M Benantar, R Guski, KM Triodle, "Access control systems: From host-centric to network-centric computing", in *IBM Systems Journal* v 35 no 1 (96) pp 94–112

[226] W Bender, D Gruhl, N Morimoto, A Lu, "Techniques for Data Hiding", in *IBM Systems Journal* v 35 no 3–4 (96) pp 313–336

[227] T Benkart, D Bitzer, "BFE Applicability to LAN Environments", in *Seventeenth National Computer Security Conference* (1994); proceedings published by NIST, pp 227–236

[228] Y Benkler, *'Network Propaganda – Manipulation, Disinformation, and Radicalization in American Politics'*, Oxford 2018

[229] Y Berger, A Wool, A Yeredor, "Dictionary Attacks Using Keyboard Acoustic Emanations", *ACM CCS 2006*

[230] R Bergman, DM Halbfinger, "Israel Hack of Iran Port Is Latest Salvo in Exchange of Cyberattacks", *New York Times* May 19 2020

[231] M Bernhard, J Benaloh, JA Halderman, RL Rivest, PYA Ryan, PB Stark, V Teague, PL Vora, DS Wallach, "Public Evidence from Secret Ballots", *arXiv:1707.08619*, Aug 4 2017

[232] J Bennetto, "How IRA plotted to switch off London", *The Independent*, Apr 12 1997

[233] DJ Bernstein, *'Cache-Timing Attacks on AES'*, preprint, 2005

[234] I Berres 2018, "Was Patienten jetzt wissen müssen", *Der Spiegel* Nov 26 2018

[235] J Bessen, "Industry Concentration and Information Technology", *SSRN 3044730*, 2019

[236] A Bessey, K Block, B Chelf, A Chou, B Fulton, S Hallem, C Henri-Gros, A Kamsky, S McPeak, D Engler, "A few billion lines of code later: using static analysis to find bugs in the real world", in *Communications of the ACM* v 53 no 2, Feb 2010

[237] B Beyer, C Jones, J Petoff, NR Murphy, *'Site Reliability Engineering'*, Google Books 2013

[238] K Biba, *'Integrity Considerations for Secure Computer Systems'*, Mitre Corporation MTR-3153 (1975)

[239] S Biddle, "The NSA Leak Is Real, Snowden Documents Confirm", *The Intercept* Aug 19 2016

[240] AD Biderman, H Zimmer, *'The Manipulation of Human Behavior'*, Wiley 1961; at `http://www.archive.org/details/TheManipulationOfHumanBehavior`

[241] J Bidzos, "Oral History Interview with James Bidzos", *Charles Babbage Institute* Dec 11 2004

[242] B Biggio, F Rolli, "Wild Patterns: Ten Years After the Rise of Adversarial Machine Learning", *arXiv:1712.03141*, Jul 19 2018

[243] E Biham, A Biryukov, A Shamir, "Cryptanalysis of Skipjack Reduced to 31 Rounds Using Impossible Differentials", in *Advances in Cryptology – Eurocrypt 97*, Springer LNCS v 1592 pp 12–23

[244] E Biham, O Dunkelman, S Indesteege, N Keller, B Preneel, "How To Steal Cars – A Practical Attack on KeeLoq", 2007, at `http://www.cosic.esat.kuleuven.be/keeloq/`

[245] E Biham, L Neumann, "Breaking the Bluetooth Pairing: Fixed Coordinate Invalid Curve Attack", *SAC 2019* pp 250–273

[246] E Biham, A Shamir, *'Differential Cryptanalysis of the Data Encryption Standard'*, Springer 1993

[247] E Biham, A Shamir, "Differential Fault Analysis of Secret Key Cryptosystems", in *Advances in Cryptology – Crypto 97*, Springer LNCS v 1294 pp 513–525

[248] C Bing, J Schectman, "Special Report: Inside the UAE's secret hacking team of U.S. mercenaries" *Reuters* Jan 30 2019

[249] A Biryukov, A Shamir, D Wagner, "Real Time Cryptanalysis of A5/1 on a PC", in *Fast Software Encryption* (2000)

[250] R Bishop, R Bloomfield, "A Conservative Theory for Long-Term Reliability-Growth Prediction", in *IEEE Transactions on Reliability* v 45 no 4 (Dec 96) pp 550–560

[251] DM Bishop, "Applying COMPUSEC to the battlefield", in *17th Annual National Computer Security Conference* (1994) pp 318–326

[252] M Bishop, M Dilger, "Checking for Race Conditions in File Accesses", in *Computing Systems Usenix* v 9 no 2 (Spring 1996) pp 131–152

[253] Wolfgang Bitzer, Joachim Opfer *'Schaltungsanordnung zum Messen der Korrelationsfunktion zwischen zwei vorgegebenen Signalen'* [Circuit arrangement for measuring the correlation function between two provided signals]. German Patent DE 3911155 C2, Deutsches Patentamt, November 11, 1993

[254] J Blackledge, "Making Money from Fractals and Chaos: Microbar", in *Mathematics Today* v 35 no 6 (Dec 99) pp 170–173

[255] RD Blackledge, "DNA versus fingerprints", in *Journal of Forensic Sciences* v 40 (1995) p 534

[256] B Blair, "Keeping Presidents in the Nuclear Dark", in *Bruce Blair's Nuclear Column*, Feb 11 2004, at `https://web.archive.org/web/20120511191600/http://www.cdi.org/blair/permissive-action-links.cfm`

[257] GR Blakley, "Safeguarding cryptographic keys", in *Proceedings of NCC AFIPS* (1979), pp 313–317

[258] B Blakley, R Blakley, RM Soley, *'CORBA Security: An Introduction to Safe Computing with Objects'*, Addison-Wesley 1999

[259] MA Blaze, "Protocol Failure in the Escrowed Encryption Standard", in *Second ACM Conference on Computer and Communications Security* pp 59–67

[260] Matt Blaze, "Cryptology and Physical Security: Rights Amplification in Master-Keyed Mechanical Locks", at *IEEE Symposium on Security & Privacy* 2003

[261] MA Blaze, "Toward a Broader View of Security Protocols", in *Security Protocols 2004*, Springer LNCS v 3957, pp 106–132

[262] MA Blaze, "Safecracking for the computer scientist", U. Penn Technical Report (2004), at `http://www.crypto.com/papers/`

[263] MA Blaze, SM Bellovin, "Tapping, Tapping On My Network Door", in *Communications of the ACM* (Oct 2000), Inside Risks 124

[264] MA Blaze, J Feigenbaum, J Lacy, "Decentralized Trust Management", in *Proceedings of the 1996 IEEE Symposium on Security and Privacy* pp 164–173

[265] D Bleichenbacher, "Chosen Ciphertext Attacks against Protocols Based on the RSA Encryption Standard PKCS #1", in *Advances in Cryptology – Crypto 98* Springer LNCS v 1462 pp 1–12

[266] G Bleumer, *'Electronic Postage Systems – Technology, Security, Economics'*, Springer 2006

[267] B Blobel, "Clinical record Systems in Oncology. Experiences and Developments on Cancer Registers in Eastern Germany", in [64] pp 39–56

[268] JA Bloom, IJ Cox, T Kalker, JPMG Linnartz, ML Miller, CBS Traw, "Copy Protection for DVD Video", in *Proceedings of the IEEE* v 87 no 7 (July 1999) pp 1267–1276

[269] P Bloom, *'Descartes' Baby: How Child Development Explains What Makes Us Human'*, Arrow (2005)

[270] S Blythe, B Fraboni, S Lall, H Ahmed, U de Riu, "Layout Reconstruction of Complex Silicon Chips", in *IEEE Journal of Solid-State Circuits* v 28 no 2 (Feb 93) pp 138–145

[271] WE Boebert, "Some Thoughts on the Occasion of the NSA Linux Release", in *Linux Journal*, Jan 24 2001; at `http://www.linuxjournal.com/article/4963`

[272] WE Boebert, RY Kain, "A Practical Alternative to Hierarchical Integrity Policies", in *8th National Computer Security Conference* NIST (1985) p 18

[273] BW Boehm, *'Software Engineering Economics'*, Prentice Hall 1981

[274] A Bogdanov, D Khovratovich, C Rechberger, "Biclique Cryptanalysis of the Full AES", *Asiacrypt 2011*, and IACR preprint no. 2011-449

[275] R Böhme, N Christin, B Edelman, T Moore, "Bitcoin: Economics, Technology, and Governance", *Journal of Economic Perspectives* v 29 no 2 (Spring 2015) pp 213–238

[276] R Böhme, G Kataria, "Models and Measures for Correlation in Cyber-Insurance", at *WEIS 2006*

[277] R Böhme, T Moore, "The Iterated Weakest Link—A Model of Adaptive Security Investment", at *WEIS 2009*

[278] N Bohm, I Brown, B Gladman, *'Electronic Commerce – Who Carries the Risk of Fraud?'*, Foundation for Information Policy Research 2000

[279] K Bolan, "Richmond IT expert sentenced to 9 years in U.S. prison for helping violent criminal organizations", *Vancouver Sun*, May 29 2019

[280] M Bond, *'Understanding Security APIs'*, PhD Thesis, Cambridge, 2004

[281] M Bond, "BOOM! HEADSHOT! (Building Neo-Tactics on Network-Level Anomalies in Online Tactical First-Person Shooters)" (2006), at `http://www.lightbluetouchpaper.org/2006/10/02/`

[282] M Bond, "Action Replay Justice", Nov 22 2007, at `http://www.lightbluetouchpaper.org/2007/11/22/action-replay-justice/`

[283] M Bond, O Choudary, SJ Murdoch, S Skorobogatov, RJ Anderson, "Chip and Skim: cloning EMV cards with the pre-play attack", *IEEE Symposium on Security and Privacy* (2014)

[284] M Bond, D Cvrček, S Murdoch, *'Unwrapping the Chrysalis'*, Cambridge Computer Lab Tech Report no. 592, 2004

[285] M Bond, SJ Murdoch, J Clulow, *'Laser-printed PIN Mailer Vulnerability Report'*, 2005, at `https://murdoch.is/papers/cl05pinmailer-vuln.pdf`

[286] D Boneh, RA Demillo, RJ Lipton, "On the Importance of Checking Cryptographic Protocols for Faults", in *Advances in Cryptology – Eurocrypt 97*, Springer LNCS v 1233 pp 37–51

[287] D Boneh, M Franklin, "Identity-Based Encryption from the Weil Pairing", in *Advances in Cryptology – Proceedings of CRYPTO 2001*, Springer LNCS 2139 pp 213–29

[288] D Boneh, V Shoup, *'A Graduate Course in Applied Cryptography'*, `https://cryptobook.us`, 2017

[289] L Boney, AH Tewfik, KN Hamdy, "Digital Watermarks for Audio Signals", in *Proceedings of the 1996 IEEE International Conference on Multimedia Computing and Systems*, pp 473–480

[290] J Bonneau, "Guessing human-chosen secrets", PhD thesis, *Cambridge University Computer Laboratory Tech Report 819*, 2012

[291] J Bonneau, "Deep Dive: EFF's New Wordlists for Random Passphrases" *EFF* July 19 2016

[292] J Bonneau, E Bursztein, I Caron, R Jackson, M Williamson, "Secrets, lies, and account recovery: Lessons from the use of personal knowledge questions at google", *WWW 2015*

[293] J Bonneau, C Herley, PC van Oorschot, F Stajano, "The Quest to Replace Passwords: A Framework for Comparative Evaluation of Web Authentication Schemes", *IEEE Security & Privacy 2012*, and full-length version as technical report

[294] J Bonneau, A Miller, J Clark, A Narayanan, JA Kroll, EW Felten, "SoK: Research Perspectives and Challenges for Bitcoin and Cryptocurrencies" *IEEE Security & Privacy* (2015)

[295] J Bonneau, S Preibusch, "The password thicket: technical and market failures in human authentication on the web", *WEIS 2010*

[296] J Bonneau, S Preibusch, R Anderson, "A birthday present every eleven wallets? The security of customer-chosen banking PINs", *Financial Cryptography 2012*

[297] J Bonneau, E Shutova, "Linguistic properties of multi-word passphrases," *USEC 2012*

[298] SC Bono, M Green, A Stubblefield, A Juels, AD Rubin, M Szydlo, "Security Analysis of a Cryptographically-Enabled RFID Device", *Usenix 2005*

[299] V Bontchev, "Possible macro virus attacks and how to prevent them", in *Computers and Security* v 15 no 7 (96) pp 595–626

[300] N Borisov, I Goldberg, D Wagner, "Intercepting Mobile Communications: The Insecurity of 802.11", at *Mobicom 2001*

[301] NS Borenstein, "Perils and Pitfalls of Practical Cybercommerce", in *Communications of the ACM* v 39 no 6 (June 96) pp 36–44

[302] F Boudot, P Gaudry, A Guillevic, N Heninger, E Thomé, P Zimmermann, "Factorization of RSA-250", *Cado-nfs-discuss mailing list* Feb 28 2020

[303] E Bovenlander, invited talk on smartcard security, *Eurocrypt 97*, reported in [108]

[304] E Bovenlander, RL van Renesse, "Smartcards and Biometrics: An Overview", in *Computer Fraud and Security Bulletin* (Dec 95) pp 8–12

[305] O Bowcott, "UK-US surveillance regime was unlawful 'for seven years'", *The Guardian* Feb 6 2015

[306] C Bowden, Y Akdeniz, "Cryptography and Democracy: Dilemmas of Freedom", in *Liberating Cyberspace: Civil Liberties, Human Rights, and the Internet* Pluto Press (1999) pp 81–125

[307] D Bowen, *'Top-to-Bottom Review'*, Aug 2007, at `http://www.sos.ca.gov/elections/elections_vsr.htm`

[308] J Bowen, "Expulsion of diplomat sends a strong signal to Israel", *BBC News*, Mar 23 2011

[309] M Brader, "Car-door lock remote control activates another car's alarm", in `comp.risks` 21.56 (Jul 2001)

[310] M Brader, "How to lose 10,000,000 pounds", in `comp.risks` v 24 no 25, Apr 19 2006

[311] T Bradshaw, "Uber loses licence to operate in London", *Financial Times* Nov 25 2019

[312] RM Brady, RJ Anderson, "Maxwell's fluid model of magnetism", *arXiv 1502.05926* Feb 20 2015

[313] RM Brady, RJ Anderson, RC Ball, *'Murphy's law, the fitness of evolving species, and the limits of software reliability'*, Cambridge University Computer Laboratory Technical Report no. 471, 1999

[314] R Brandom, "Your phone's biggest vulnerability is your fingerprint", *The Verge* May 2, 2016

[315] S Brands, *'Rethinking Public Key Infrastructures and Digital Certificates – Building in Privacy'*, MIT Press 2000

[316] JT Brassil, S Low, NF Maxemchuk, "Copyright Protection for the Electronic Distribution of Text Documents", in *Proceedings of the IEEE* v 87 no 7 (July 1999) pp 1181–1196

[317] H Bray, " 'Face testing' at Logan is found lacking", in *Boston Globe* July 17 2002

[318] M Brelis, "Patients' files allegedly used for obscene calls", in *Boston Globe* April 11, 1995; also in `comp.risks` v 17 no 7

[319] M Brennan, S Afroz, R Greenstadt, "Adversarial stylometry: Circumventing authorship recogition to preserve privacy and anonymity", *ACM Transactions on Information System Security* v 15 no 3 (Nov 2012)

[320] DFC Brewer, MJ Nash, "Chinese Wall model", in *Proceedings of the 1989 IEEE Computer Society Symposium on Security and Privacy* pp 215–228

[321] B Brewin, "CAC use nearly halves DOD network intrusions, Croom says", in *fcw.com*, Jan 25 2007, at `http://www.fcw.com/article97480-01-25-07`

[322] T Brewster, "Inside America's Secretive Research Hub: Collecting Fingerprints from Facebook, Hacking Smartwatches and Fighting COVID-19", *Forbes* Jul 13 2020

[323] D Brin, *'The Transparent Society: Will Technology Force Us to Choose Between Privacy and Freedom?'* Perseus Press (1999) magazine version in *Wired*, Dec 1996, at `http://www.wired.com/wired/archive/4.12/fftransparent.html`

[324] R Briol "Emanation: How to keep your data confidential", in *Symposium on Electromagnetic Security For Information Protection, SEPI 91*, Rome, 1991

[325] British Standard 8220-1.2000, *'Guide for Security of Buildings Against Crime – part 1: Dwellings'*

[326] WJ Broad, J Markoff, DE Sanger, "Israeli Test on Worm Called Crucial in Iran Nuclear Delay", *New York Times* Jan 15 2011

[327] J Brodkin, "FCC requires anti-robocall tech after 'voluntary' plan didn't work out", *Ars Technica* Apr 1 2020

[328] M Broersma, "Printer makers rapped over refill restrictions", *ZDnet*, Dec 20 2002, at `http://news.zdnet.co.uk/story/0,,t269-s2127877,00.html`

[329] F Brooks, *'The Mythical Man-Month: Essays on Software Engineering'*, Addison-Wesley (1995 Anniversary Edition)

[330] I Brown, CT Marsden, J Lee, M Veale, *'Cybersecurity for Elections – a Commonwealth Guide to Best Practice'*, Commonwealth Secretariat, 2020

[331] D Brumley, D Boneh, "Remote timing attacks are practical", in *Computer Networks* v 48 no 5 (Aug 2005) pp 701–716

[332] D Brown, "Unprovable Security of RSA-OAEP in the Standard Model", IACR eprint no 2006/223, at `http://eprint.iacr.org/2006/223`

[333] JDR Buchanan, RP Cowburn, AV Jausovec, D Petit, P Seem, XO Gang, D Atkinson, K Fenton, DA Allwood, MT Bryan, "Fingerprinting documents and packaging", in *Nature* v 436 no 28 (July 2005) p 475

[334] JM Buchanan, "The Constitution of Economic Policy", 1986 Nobel Prize Lecture, at `http://nobelprize.org/nobel_prizes/economics/laureates/1986/buchanan-lecture.html`

[335] RT Buchanan, "Stag party member claims he was 'grossly exploited' by lap dancing club Spearmint Rhino after spending third of his salary in single evening", *The Independent* Nov 11 2014

[336] J Buckman, MJ Hashim, T Woutersen, J Bockstedt, "Fool Me Twice? Data Breach Reductions Through Stricter Sanctions", *SSRN 3258599* Oct 31 2018

[337] H Buehler, interview with Swiss Radio International, July 4 1994. at `http://www.funet.fi/pub/crypt/mirrors/idea.sec.dsi.unimi.it/rpub.cl.msu.edu/crypt/docs/hans-buehler-crypto-spy.txt`

[338] http://archives.neohapsis.com/archives/bugtraq/

[339] R Buhren, C Werling, JP Seifert, "Insecure Until Proven Updated: Analyzing AMD SEV's Remote Attestation", *CCS 2019*

[340] J Van Bulck, M Minkin, O Weisse, D Genkin, B Kasikci, F Piessens, M Silberstein, TF Wenisch, Y Yarom, R Strackx, "Foreshadow: Extracting the Keys to the Intel SGX Kingdom with Transient Out-of-Order Execution", *Usenix Security 2018*

[341] J Van Bulck, D Moghimi, M Schwarz, M Lipp, M Minkin, D Genkin, Y Yarom, B Sunar, D Gruss, F Piessens, "Lvi: Hijacking Transient Execution through Microarchitectural Load Value Injection", *IEEE Symposium on Security and Privacy* (2020)

[342] Bull, Dassault, Diebold, NCR, Siemens Nixdorf and Wang Global, *'Protection Profile: Automatic Cash Dispensers / Teller Machines'*, version 1.0 (1999), at `http://www.commoncriteriaportal.org/`

[343] DB Bulloch, "Tracking terrorist finances: The SWIFT program and the American Anti-Terrorist Finance Regime", *Amsterdam Law Forum v 3* (2011), SSRN 1964531

[344] Bundesamt für Sicherheit in der Informationstechnik (German Information Security Agency), *'Schutzmaßnahmen gegen Lauschangriffe'* [Protection against bugs], Faltblätter des BSI v 5, Bonn, 1997; `http://www.bsi.bund.de/literat/faltbl/laus005.htm`

[345] Bundesamt für Sicherheit in der Informationstechnik (German Information Security Agency), *'Elektromagnetische Schirmung von Gebäuden'*, 2007, BSI TR-03209

[346] Bundesverfassungsgericht, "Beschluss des Ersten Senats", Apr 4 2006, 1 BvR 518/02 Absatz-Nr. (1–184), at `http://www.bverfg.de/entscheidungen/rs20060404_1bvr051802.html`

[347] J Bunnell, J Podd, R Henderson, R Napier, J Kennedy-Moffatt, "Cognitive, associative and conventional passwords: Recall and guessing rates", in *Computers and Security* v 16 no 7 (1997) pp 645–657

[348] M Burgess, "North Korea's elite hackers are funding nukes with crypto raids", *Wired* Apr 3 2019

[349] J Burke, P Warren, "How mobile phones let spies see our every move", in *The Observer* Oct 13 2002; at `http://observer.guardian.co.uk/uk_news/story/0,6903,811027,00.html`

[350] Buro Jansen & Janssen, *'Making up the rules: interception versus privacy'*, Aug 8 2000, at `http://www.statewatch.org/news/2002/nov/11jj.htm`

[351] N Burow, SA Carr, J Nash, P Larsen, M Franz, S Brunthaler, M Payer, "Control-Flow Integrity: Precision, Security, and Performance", *ACM Computing Surveys, 2017*

[352] M Burrows, M Abadi, RM Needham, "A Logic of Authentication", in *Proceedings of the Royal Society of London A* v 426 (1989) pp 233–271; earlier version published as DEC SRC Research Report 39

[353] T Burt, "New action to disrupt world's largest online criminal network", *Microsoft on the issues,* Mar 10 2020

[354] G Burton "Equifax used default 'admin' user name and password to secure hacked portal", *Computing* Oct 21 2019

[355] G Burton, "IT security specialists need to look at IoT security in buildings in a completely different way, says Cundall director Chris Grundy", *Computing* July 12 2019

[356] G Burton, "More than 600 US government entities hit with ransomware so far this year – and it's only going to get worse", *Computing* Oct 1 2019

[357] G Burton, "Google removes Avast and AVG extensions from Chrome web store over 'unnecessary' data collection", *Computing* Dec 18 2019

[358] J Busch, "How to Hack RWPFE Water Filters for Your GE Fridge", *Groovypost* May 7 2020

[359] L Butler, "Post Office boss receives 7% pay rise as postmaster salaries cut", *The Guardian* Oct 19 2018

[360] RW Butler, GB Finelli, "The infeasibility of experimental quantification of life-critical software reliability", in *ACM Symposium on Software for Critical Systems* (1991) pp 66–76

[361] D Byler, "The Global Implications of 'Re-education' Technologies in Northwest China", *Center for Global Policy* Jun 8 2020

[362] RW Byrne, A Whiten, *'Machiavellian Intelligence – Social Expertise and the Evolution of Intellect in Monkeys, Apes and Humans'*, Oxford, 1988; see also A Whiten, RW Byrne, *'Machiavellian Intelligence II – Extensions and Evaluations'*, Cambridge 1997

[363] Cabinet Office, *'National Risk Register Of Civil Emergencies'*, 2017

[364] *'A Comparative Introduction to 4G and 5G Authentication'*, Cable Labs, Winter 2019

[365] C Cadwalladr, "Facebook's role in brexit – and the threat to democracy", *TED2019*

[366] E Caesar, "The Cold War Bunker That Became Home to a Dark-Web Empire", *New Yorker*, July 27 2020

[367] L Cai, H Chen, "On the practicality of motion based keystroke inference attack", *Proceedings of the 5th International Conference on Trust and Trustworthy Computing, TRUST'12* pp 273–290

[368] A Cain, "Before Envelopes, People Protected Messages With Letterlocking", *Atlas Obscura* Nov 9 2018, at `https://www.atlasobscura.com/articles/what-did-people-do-before-envelopes-letterlocking`

[369] F Caldicott, *'Report on the review of patient-identifiable information'*, Department of Health, 1997

[370] RE Calem, "New York's Panix Service Is Crippled by Hacker Attack", *New York Times* Sep 14 1996

[371] A Caliskan, JJ Bryson, A Narayanan, "Semantics derived automatically from language corpora contain human-like biases", *Science* v 356 no 6334 pp 183–186

[372] A Caliskan-Islam, R Harang, A Liu, A Narayanan, C Voss, F Yamaguchi, R Greenstadt, "De-anonymizing programmers via code stylometry", *USENIX Security* (2015) pp 255-270

[373] J Camp, C Wolfram, "Pricing Security", in *Proceedings of the CERT Information Survivability Workshop* (Oct 24-26 2000) pp 31–39

[374] J Camp, S Lewis, *'Economics of Information Security'*, Springer 2004

[375] D Campbell, "Somebody's listening", in *The New Statesman* (12 August 1988) pp 1, 10–12; at `http://jya.com/echelon-dc.htm`

[376] D Campbell, "Making history: the original source for the 1988 first Echelon report steps forward", (25 February 2000), at `http://cryptome.org/echelon-mndc.htm`

[377] D Campbell, "Operation Ore Exposed", *PC Pro*, Jul 2005, archived at `https://www.duncancampbell.org/content/operation-ore`

[378] D Campbell, "Sex, Lies and the Missing Videotape", *PC Pro*, Apr 2007, archived at `https://www.duncancampbell.org/content/operation-ore`

[379] D Campbell, P Lashmar, "The new Cold War: How America spies on us for its oldest friend – the Dollar", in *The Independent* (2 July 2000)

[380] K Campbell, L Gordon, M Loeb, L Zhou, "The economic cost of publicly announced information security breaches: empirical evidence from the stock market", in *Journal of Computer Security* v 11 no 3 (2003) pp 431–448

[381] O Campion-Awwad, A Hayton, L Smith, M Vuaran, "The National Programme for IT in the NHS", Cambridge 2014, at `https://www.lightbluetouchpaper.org/2014/08/13/largest-ever-civil-government-it-disaster/`

[382] C Canella, J Van Bulck, M Schwarz, M Lipp, B von Berg, P Ortner, F Piessens, D Evtyushkin, D Gruss, "A Systematic Evaluation of Transient Execution Attacks and Defenses", *USENIX Security Symposium* 2019

[383] C Canella, M Schwarz, M Haubenwallner, M Schwarzl, D Gruss, "KASLR: Break it, Fix it, Repeat", *ACM CCS* (2020)

[384] C Cant, S Wiseman, "Simple Assured Bastion Hosts", in *13th Annual Computer Security Application Conference* (1997) pp 24–33

[385] "Dark horse in lead for fingerprint ID card", *Card World Independent* (May 94) p 2

[386] "German A555 takes its toll", in *Card World International* (12/94–1/95) p 6

[387] BL Cardin, *'Putin's Asymmetric Assault on Democracy in Russia and Europe – Implications for U.S. National Security'* Minority Staff Report, Committee on Foreign Relations, U.S. Senate, Jan 10 2018

[388] "High tech helps card fraud decline", in *Cards International* no 117 (29 Sep 94)

[389] "Visa beefs up its anti-fraud technology", in *Cards International* no 189 (12/12/97) p 5

[390] JM Carlin, "UNIX Security Update", at *Usenix Security 93* pp 119–130

[391] M Carr, SF Shahandashti, "Revisiting Security Vulnerabilities in Commercial Password Managers", *arXiv 2003.01985* Mar 17 2020

[392] J Carroll, *'Big Blues: The Unmaking of IBM'*, Crown Publishers 1993

[393] H Carter, "Car clock fixer jailed for nine months", in *The Guardian* Feb 15 2000

[394] R Carter, "What You Are ... Not What You Have", in *International Security Review* Access Control Special Issue (Winter 93/94) pp 14-16

[395] A Case, M Meltzer, S Adair, "Digital Crackdown: Large-Scale Surveillance and Exploitation of Uyghurs", *Volexity* Sep 2 2019

[396] M Castro, B Liskov, "Practical Byzantine Fault Tolerance", *Symposium on Operating Systems Design and Implementation* (1999)

[397] L Cauley, "NSA has massive database of Americans' phone calls", in *USA Today* Nov 11 2005, at `http://www.usatoday.com/news/washington/2006-05-10-nsa:x.htm`

[398] E Cebuc, "How are we doing with Android's overlay attacks in 2020?" *F-secure Labs* Mar 27 2020

[399] M Ceglowski, "What I Learned Trying To Secure Congressional Campaigns", *Idlewords*, May 26 2019, at `https://idlewords.com/2019/05/what_i_learned_trying_to_secure_congressional_campaigns.htm`

[400] Center for Democracy and Technology, `http://www.cdt.org/`

[401] L Cerulus, "EU Commission to staff: Switch to Signal messaging app", *Politico Pro* Feb 20 2020

[402] Chainalysis *'Crypto Crime Report'*, January 2019

[403] Chainalysis *'The 2020 State of Crypto Crime'*, January 2020

[404] "The Nature and Scope of Governmental Electronic Surveillance Activity", Center for Democracy and Technology, July 2006

[405] D Cerdeira, N Santos, P Fonseca, S Pinto, "SoK: Understanding the Prevailing Security Vulnerabilities in TrustZone-assisted TEE Systems", *IEEE Symposium on Security and Privacy* 2020

[406] P Chain, F Filloux, "Code, on wheels: Reinventing the car, episode 5" *Mondaynote*, Aug 9 2020

[407] A Chakraborty, "How Boots went rogue", *The Guardian* Apr 13 2016

[408] Chaos Computer Club, *'How to fake fingerprints?'* at `https://web.archive.org/web/20090327044558/http://www.ccc.de/biometrie/fingerabdruck_kopieren.xml?language=en` (2004)

[409] L Chapman, *'Your disobedient servant'*, Penguin Books 1979

[410] Chartered Institute of Building Services Engineers, *'Security Engineering'*, Applications Manual AM4 (1991)

[411] M Chase, T Perrin, G Zaverucha, "The Signal Private Group System and Anonymous Credentials Supporting Efficient Verifiable Encryption", *Cryptology ePrint 2019/1416* Dec 10 2019

[412] D Chaum, "Untraceable electronic mail, return addresses, and digital pseudonyms", in *Communications of the ACM* v 24 no 2 (Feb 1981)

[413] D Chaum, "Blind signatures for untraceable payments", in *Crypto 82*, Plenum Press (1983) pp 199–203

[414] D Chaum, A Fiat, M Naor, "Untraceable Electronic Cash", in *CRYPTO '88*, Springer LNCS v 403 pp 319–327

[415] S Checkoway, J Maskiewicz, C Garman, J Fried, S Cohney, M Green, N Heninger, R-P Weinmann, E Rescorla, H Shacham, "A Systematic Analysis of the Juniper Dual EC Incident", *CCS 2016*

[416] A Chen, "The Laborers Who Keep Dick Pics and Beheadings Out of Your Facebook Feed", *Wired* Oct 23 2014

[417] YS Cheng, XY Ji, TY Lu, WY Xu, "DeWiCam: Detecting Hidden Wireless Cameras via Smartphones" *AsiaCCS* 2018

[418] R Chesney, "Telephony Metadata: Is the Contact-Chaining Program Unsalvageable?" *Lawfare Blog* March 6 2019

[419] K Chiu, "The world's biggest online population is staying home and China's internet can't cope", *Abacus News* Feb 17 2020

[420] " 'Trial by Internet' Casts Spotlight on Korean Cyber Mobs", *Chosun Ilbo* July 8 2005

[421] MO Choudary, MG Kuhn, "Efficient, portable template attacks", *IEEE Transactions on Information Forensics and Security* v 13 no 2 (Feb 2018)

[422] T Christakis, "A fragmentation of EU / ECHR law on mass surveillance: initial thoughts on the Big Brother Watch judgment", *European Law blog* Sep 20 2018

[423] N Christin, " Traveling the Silk Road: A measurement analysis of a large anonymous online marketplace", *WWW* 2013

[424] KH Chuang, E Bury, R Degraeve, B Kaczer, G Groeseneken, I Verbauwhede, D Linten, "Physically unclonable function using CMOS breakdown position", *IEEE International Reliability Physics Symposium (IRPS)* (2017)

[425] F Church (chairman), *'Intelligence Activities – Senate Resolution 21'*, US Senate, 94 Congress, First Session, at `http://cryptome.org/nsa-4th.htm`

[426] RB Cialdini, *'Influence: Science and Practice'*, Pearson 2009

[427] WS Ciciora, "Inside the set-top box", in *IEEE Spectrum* v 12 no 4 (Apr 95) pp 70–75

[428] C Cimpanu, "Newer Diameter Telephony Protocol Just As Vulnerable As SS7", *Bleeping Computer* July 2 2018

[429] C Cimpanu, "Backdoor found in Ruby library for checking for strong passwords", *ZDNet* July 8 2019

[430] C Cimpanu, "DNS-over-HTTPS causes more problems than it solves, experts say", *ZDNet* Oct 6 2019

[431] C Cimpanu, "Major vulnerability patched in the EU's eIDAS authentication system", *ZDNet* Oct 29 2019

[432] C Cimpanu, "Average tenure of a CISO is just 26 months due to high stress and burnout", *ZDNet* Feb 12 2020

[433] C Cimpanu, "Android malware can steal Google Authenticator 2FA codes", *ZDNet* Feb 27 2020

[434] C Cimpanu, "Microsoft Double Key Encryption enters public preview", *ZDNet* Jul 21 2020

[435] C Cimpanu, "China is now blocking all encrypted HTTPS traffic that uses TLS 1.3 and ESNI", *ZDNet* Aug 8 2020

[436] J Cipriani, "iOS 13: Top 5 new security and privacy features for your iPhone", *CNet* Sep 22 2019

[437] D Cireşan, U Meier, J Schmidhuber, "Multi-column deep neural networks for image classification", *arXiv:1202.2745* Feb 13 2012

[438] D Clark, D Wilson, "A Comparison of Commercial and Military Computer Security Policies", in *Proceedings of the 1987 IEEE Symposium on Security and Privacy* pp 184–194

[439] P Clark, H Warrell, T Bradshaw, S Neville "The rise and fall of Hancock's homegrown tracing app", *Financial Times* Jun 26 2020

[440] R Clark, *'The man who broke Purple'*, Little, Brown 1977

[441] I Clarke, *'The Free Network Project Homepage'*, at `http://freenet.sourceforge.net/`

[442] RW Clarke, "The Theory of Crime prevention Though Environmental Design"; see also *'Situational Crime Prevention: successful case studies'*, Harrow and Heston 1997

[443] R Clayton, "Techno-Risk", at *Cambridge International Symposium on Economic Crime* (2003), at `http://www.cl.cam.ac.uk/~rnc1/talks/030910-TechnoRisk.pdf`

[444] R Clayton, *'Anonymity and traceability in cyberspace'*, PhD Thesis; Cambridge University Technical Report UCAM-CL-TR-653, 2005

[445] R Clayton, "Insecure Real-Word Authentication Protocols (or Why Phishing is so Profitable)", at *Cambridge Security Protocols Workshop* 2005

[446] R Clayton, *private conversation*, 2006

[447] R Clayton, "When firmware attacks! (DDoS by D-Link)", *Light Blue Touchpaper*, Apr 7 2006

[448] R Clayton, "ClimateGate Email 'Hacking' ", 2009, at `https://www.cl.cam.ac.uk/~rnc1/climategate-20091215.pdf`

[449] R Clayton, M Bond, "Experience Using a Low-Cost FPGA Design to Crack DES Keys", *CHES Workshop* (2002), Springer LNCS 2523 pp 579–592

[450] R Clayton, SJ Murdoch, R Watson, "Ignoring the Great Firewall of China", at *6th Workshop on Privacy Enhancing Technologies* (2006)

[451] J Clulow, *'The Design and Analysis of Cryptographic APIs for Security Devices'*, MSc Thesis, University of Natal 2003

[452] FB Cohen, *'A Short Course on Computer Viruses'*, Wiley 1994

[453] K Cohn-Gordon, C Cremers, L Garratt, "Post-Compromise Security", *IACR preprint*, v 1.4 Oct 2019

[454] D Coldewey, "Uber in fatal crash detected pedestrian but had emergency braking disabled", *TechCrunch* May 24 2018

[455] B Collier, "The power to structure: exploring social worlds of technology, privacy and power in the Tor project", *Information, Communication and Society* (2020), `https://www.cl.cam.ac.uk/~bjc63/power_to_structure.pdf`

[456] B Collier, R Clayton, A Hutchings, D Thomas, "Cybercrime is (often) boring: maintaining the infrastructure of cybercrime economies", *Workshop on the Economics of Information Security* (2020)

[457] B Collier, D Thomas, R Clayton, A Hutchings, "Booting the booters: measuring the impact of law enforcement interventions on DoS markets", Internet Measurement Conference 2019

[458] P Collier, A Hoeffler, "Greed and grievance in civil war", in *Oxford Economic Papers* v 56 (2004) pp 563–595

[459] A Collins, "Court decides software time-locks are illegal", in *Computer Weekly* (19 August 93) p 1

[460] D Cohen, J Hashkes, "A system for controlling access to broadcast transmissions", European Patent no EP0428252

[461] "Telecomms Fraud in the Cellular Market: How Much is Hype and How Much is Real?' in *Computer Fraud and Security Bulletin* (Jun 97) pp 11–14

[462] Committee of Sponsoring Organizations of the Treadway Commission (CSOTC), *'Internal Control – Integrated Framework'* (COSO Report, 1992); from `http://www.coso.org/`

[463] Common Criteria, 'Collaborative Protection Profiles – The Benefits of an Evolved Common Criteria Implementation', Sep 2014

[464] *'Communicating Britain's Future'*, at `http://www.fipr.org/polarch/labour.html`

[465] A Compagno, M Conti, D Lain, G Tsudik, "Don't Skype & Type! Acoustic Eavesdropping in Voice-Over-IP", *arXiv:1609.09359* (2016); later *ASIA CCS* 2017 pp 703–715

[466] Computer Emergency Response Team Coordination Center, at `http://www.cert.org/`

[467] "Samsung rushes out fix for Galaxy S10 fingerprint security flaw", *Computing News* Oct 24 2019

[468] JB Condat, "Toll fraud on French PBX systems", in *Computer Law and Security Report* v 10 no 2 (Mar/April 94) pp 89–91

[469] D Conner, "Cryptographic techniques — secure your wireless designs", in *EDN* (18/1/96) pp 57–68

[470] K Connolly, "Treasures worth 'up to a billion euros' stolen from Dresden museum", *The Guardian* Nov 25 2019

[471] L Constantin, "One year after DigiNotar breach, Fox-IT details extent of compromise", *PC World* Oct 31 2012

[472] US Consumer Reports, *'2009 Chevy Malibu vs 1959 Bel Air Crash Test'*, 2009, at `https://www.youtube.com/watch?v=fPF4fBGNK0U`

[473] D Coppersmith, *'The Data Encryption Standard (DES) and its Strength Against Attacks'*, IBM report RC 18613 (81421)

[474] M Coppins, "The Billion-Dollar Disinformation Campaign to Reelect the President", *The Atlantic* Feb 10 2020

[475] Council of Europe, *'Convention For the Protection of Individuals with Regard to Automatic Processing of Personal Data'*, European Treaty Series no 108 (January 28, 1981)

[476] FJ Corbató, "On building systems that will fail", *Communications of the ACM* v 4 no 9, (1991) pp 72–81

[477] R Cordery, L Pintsov, "History and Role of Information Security in Postage Evidencing and Payment", in *Cryptologia* v XXIX no 3 (Jul 2005) pp 257–271

[478] S Cordier, "Bracelet électronique, ordonnance de protection, TGD… Ce que contient la loi sur les violences conjugales", *Le Monde* Dec 18 2019

[479] V Costan, S Devadas, "Intel SGX Explained", *IACR Cryptology ePrint 2016/086* (2016)

[480] F Courbon, SP Skorobogatov, C Woods, "Reverse engineering Flash EEPROM memories using scanning electron microscopy", *International Conference on Smart Card Research and Advanced Applications* (2016) pp 57–72

[481] G Corfield, "I helped catch Silk Road boss Ross Ulbricht: Undercover agent tells all" *The Register* Jan 29 2019

[482] G Corfield, "Proposed US fix for Boeing 737 Max software woes does not address Ethiopian crash scenario, UK pilot union warns" *The Register* Sep 23 2020

[483] L Cosmides, J Tooby, "Cognitive adaptations for social exchange", in *The Adapted Mind: Evolutionary psychology and the generation of culture* (1992)

[484] C Cowan, C Pu, D Maier, H Hinton, J Walpole, P Bakke, S Beattie, A Grier, P Wagle, Q Zhang, "StackGuard: Automatic Adaptive Detection and Prevention of Buffer-Overflow Attacks", *7th Usenix Security Conference* (1998) pp 63–77

[485] J Cox, "Criminals Are Tapping into the Phone Network Backbone to Empty Bank Accounts", *Vice* Jan 31 2019

[486] J Cox, "Hackers Are Breaking Directly Into Telecom Companies to Take Over Customer Phone Numbers", *Vice* Jan 10 2020

[487] J Cox, "Hundreds of Bounty Hunters Had Access to AT&T, T-Mobile, and Sprint Customer Location Data for Years", *Vice* Feb 6 2019

[488] J Cox, "Malware That Spits Cash Out of ATMs Has Spread Across the World", *Vice* Oct 15 2019

[489] J Cox, "The Companies That Will Track Any Phone on the Planet", *The Daily Beast* Aug 28 2017

[490] LH Cox, JP Kelly, R Patil, "Balancing quality and confidentiality for multivariate tabular data" in *Privacy in Statistical Data Bases* (2004) Springer LNCS v 3050 pp 87–98

[491] J Cradden, "Printer-makers hit by new EU law", in *Electricnews.net* December 19 2002, at `http://www.electricnews.net/news.html?code=8859027`

[492] L Cranor, "Time to rethink mandatory password changes", *Tech@FTC blog* Mar 2 2016

[493] L Cranor, S Garfinkel, *'Security Usability'*, O'Reilly 2005

[494] S Craver, "On Public-key Steganography in the Presence of an Active Warden", in *Second International Workshop on Information Hiding* (1998), Springer LNCS v 1525 pp 355–368

[495] SA Craver, M Wu, BD Liu, A Stubblefield, B Swartzlander, DS Wallach, D Dean, EW Felten, "Reading Between the Lines: Lessons from the SDMI Challenge", in *Usenix Security Symposium* (2000)

[496] RJ Creasy, "The origin of the VM/370 time-sharing system", in *IBM Journal of Research & Development* v 25 no 5 (Sep 1981) pp 483–490

[497] J Crémer, YA de Montjoye, H Schweizter, *'Competition Policy for the digital era'*, European Commission DG Competition, 2019

[498] C Criado Perez, *'Invisible Women'*, Chatto & Windus 2019

[499] "El Gobierno dice que le hackearon el Boletín Official con falsas resoluciones sobre coronavirus", EL Cronista, Mar 15 2020

[500] H Crouch, "Two NHS trusts sign agreements with Sensyne Health", *DigitalHealth* Feb 4 2019

[501] Cryptome.org, Deepwater documents, May 2007; at `http://cryptome.org/deepwater/deepwater.htm`

[502] C Culnane, BIP Rubinstein, V Teague, "Stop the Open Data Bus, We Want to Get Off", *arXiv:1908.05004* Aug 15 2019

[503] J Cumberledge, *'First Do No Harm – The report of the Independent Medicines and Medical Devices Review'*, UK Department for Health and Social Care, July 2020

[504] W Curtis, H Krasner, N Iscoe, "A Field Study of the Software Design Process for Large Systems", in *Communications of the ACM* v 31 no 11 (Nov 88) pp 1268–87

[505] F D'Addario, "Testing Security's Effectiveness", in *Security Management Online* October 2001

[506] T Dafoe, "A Hacker Posing as a Venerable British Art Dealer Swindled a Dutch Museum Out of $3.1 Million", *Artnet News*, Jan 30 2020

[507] J Daemen, V Rijmen, *'The Design of Rijndael: AES – The Advanced Encryption Standard'*, Springer (2002)

[508] P Daian, S Goldfeder, T Kell, YQ Li, XY Zhao, I Bentov, L Breidenbach, A Juels, "Flash Boys 2.0: Frontrunning, Transaction Reordering, and Consensus Instability in Decentralized Exchanges", *arXiv:1904.05234* Apr 10 2019

[509] G Danezis, "Distributed Ledgers: what is so interesting about them?" *Conspicuous Chatter* Sep 27 2018

[510] G Danezis, B Wittneben, "The Economics of Mass Surveillance", *Fifth Workshop on the Economics of Information Security* (2006)

[511] G Danezis, RJ Anderson, "The Economics of Resisting Censorship", in *IEEE Security and Privacy* v 3 no 1 (2005) pp 45–50

[512] G Danezis, C Diaz, "Survey of Privacy Technology", 2007, at `http://homes.esat.kuleuven.be/~gdanezis/anonSurvey.pdf`

[513] JM Darley, B Latané, "Bystander Intervention in Emergencies: Diffusion of Responsibility", *Journal of Personality and Social Psychology* v 8 no 4 Pt 1 pp 377–383

[514] M Darman, E le Roux, "A new generation of terrestrial and satellite microwave communication products for military networks", in *Electrical Communication* (Q4 94) pp 359–364

[515] Two statements, made by the Data Protection Commissioners of EU and EES countries and Switzerland, *20th International Conference on Data Protection*, Santiago de Compostela, 16-18 September 1998

[516] Daubert v. Merrell Dow Pharmaceuticals, 113 S. Ct. 2786 (1993)

[517] J Daugman, "High Confidence Visual Recognition of Persons by a Test of Statistical Independence", in *IEEE Transactions on Pattern Analysis and Machine Intelligence* v 15 no 11 (Nov 93) pp 1148–1161

[518] J Daugman, *'Biometric decision landscapes'*, Technical Report no TR482, University of Cambridge Computer Laboratory.

[519] J Daugman, C Downing "Searching for doppelgängers: assessing the universality of the IrisCode impostors distribution," IET Biometrics (2015)

[520] G Davidson, "Scottish Government to scrap Named Person scheme, John Swinney confirms", *The Scotsman* Sep 19 2019

[521] DW Davies, WL Price, *'Security for Computer Networks'* Wiley 1984

[522] G Davies, *'A history of money from ancient times to the present day'*, University of Wales Press 1996

[523] W Davies, "What's wrong with WhatsApp", *The Guardian* Jul 2 2020

[524] D Davis, "Compliance Defects in Public-Key Cryptography", in *Sixth Usenix Security Symposium Proceedings* (July 1996) pp 171–178

[525] J Davis, "Hackers Take Down the Most Wired Country in Europe", in *Wired*, Aug 21 2007

[526] D Deahl, "This 10-year-old was able to unlock his mom's iPhone using Face ID", *The Verge* Nov 14 2017

[527] D Dean, EW Felten, DS Wallach, "Java Security: From HotJava to Netscape and Beyond", in *Proceedings of the 1996 IEEE Symposium on Security and Privacy* pp 190–200

[528] J Dean, "Google Research: Looking Back at 2019, and Forward to 2020 and Beyond ", *Google AI Blog*, Jan 9 2020

[529] C Deavours, D Kahn, L Kruh, G Mellen, B Winkel, *'Cryptology – Yesterday, Today and Tomorrow'*, Artech House (1987)

[530] C Deavours, D Kahn, L Kruh, G Mellen, B Winkel, *'Selections from Cryptologia – History, People and Technology'*, Artech House (1997)

[531] C Deavours, L Kruh, *'Machine Cryptography and Modern Cryptanalysis'*, Artech House 1985

[532] JF de Beer, "Constitutional Jurisdiction Over Paracopyright Laws", in *'The Public Interest: The Future of Canadian Copyright Law'*, Irwin Law (2005)

[533] CC Demchak, Y Shavitt, "China's Maxim – Leave No Access Point Unexploited: The Hidden Story of China Telecom's BGP Hijacking", *Military Cyber Affairs* v 3 no 1 `https://scholarcommons.usf.edu/mca/vol3/iss1/7`

[534] B Demoulin, L Kone, C Poudroux, P Degauque, "Electromagnetic Radiation of Shielded Data Transmission Lines", in [701] pp 163–173

[535] I Denley, S Weston-Smith, "Implementing access control to protect the confidentiality of patient information in clinical information systems in the acute hospital", in *Health Informatics Journal* v 4 nos 3–4 (Dec 1998) pp 174–178

[536] I Denley, S Weston-Smith, "Privacy in clinical information systems in secondary care" in *British Medical Journal* v 318 (15 May 1999) pp 1328–1331

[537] DE Denning, "The Lattice Model of Secure Information Flow", in *Communications of the ACM* v 19 no 5 pp 236–248

[538] DE Denning, *'Cryptography and Data Security'*, Addison-Wesley 1982

[539] DE Denning, *'Information Warfare and Security'*, Addison-Wesley 1999

[540] DE Denning, "Activism, Hacktivism, and Cyberterrorism: The Internet as a Tool for Influencing Foreign Policy", InfowarCon 2000

[541] DE Denning, PJ Denning, M Schwartz, "The tracker: a threat to statistical database security", in *ACM Transactions on Database Systems* v 4 no 1 (1979) pp 76–96

[542] DE Denning, PH MacDoran, "Location-Based Authentication: Grounding Cyberspace for Better Security", in *Computer Fraud and Security Bulletin* (Feb 96) pp 12–16

[543] DE Denning, J Schlorer, "Inference Controls for Statistical Databases", in *IEEE Computer* v 16 no 7 (July 1983) pp 69–82

[544] Department of Defense, *'Department of Defense Trusted Computer System Evaluation Criteria'*, DoD 5200.28-STD, December 1985

[545] Department of Defense, *'A Guide to Understanding Covert Channel Analysis of Trusted Systems'*, NCSC-TG-030 (Nov 1993)

[546] Department of Defense, *'Password Management Guideline'*, CSC-STD-002-85 (1985)

[547] Department of Defense, *'A Guide to Understanding Data Remanence in Automated Information Systems'*, NCSC-TG-025 (1991)

[548] Department of Defense, *'Technical Rationale behind CSC-STD-003-85: computer security requirements'*, CSC-STD-004-85 (1985)

[549] Department of Defense, News Transcript, Oct 20 2007, at `http://cryptome.org/af-squirm/af-squirm.htm`

[550] Department of Justice, *'Guidelines for Searching and Seizing Computers'*, 1994; at `http://www.epic.org/security/computer_search_guidelines.txt`

[551] Department of Justice, "South Korean National and Hundreds of Others Charged Worldwide in the Takedown of the Largest Darknet Child Pornography Website, Which was Funded by Bitcoin" Oct 16 2019

[552] Department of Justice, "Chinese Military Personnel Charged with Computer Fraud, Economic Espionage and Wire Fraud for Hacking into Credit Reporting Agency Equifax", Feb 10 2020

[553] Department of Justice, "Ohio Resident Charged with Operating Darknet-Based Bitcoin 'Mixer,' which Laundered Over $300 Million" Feb 13 2020

[554] Y Desmedt, Y Frankel, "Threshold cryptosystems", in *Advances in Cryptology – Proceedings of Crypto 89*, Springer LNCS v 435 pp 307–315

[555] B De Sutter, C Collberg, M Dalla Preda, B Wyseur, "Software protection Decision Support and Evaluation Methodologies", *Report from Dagstuhl Seminar 19331* (2019)

[556] W Diffie, ME Hellman, "New Directions in Cryptography", in *IEEE Transactions on information theory* v 22 no 6 (Nov 76) pp 644–654

[557] W Diffie, ME Hellman, "Exhaustive cryptanalysis of the NBS Data Encryption Standard", in *Computer* v 10 no 6 (June 77) pp 74–84

[558] W Diffie, S Landau, *'Privacy on the Line – The Politics of Wiretapping and Encryption'*, MIT Press 1998

[559] M van Dijk, A Juels, A Oprea, RL Rivest, "F L I P I T : The Game of 'Stealthy Takeover' ", *Journal of Cryptology* v 26 no 4 (Oct 2013) pp 655–713; given as the Crypto 2011 distinguished lecture by Ron Rivest

[560] E Dijkstra, "Solution of a problem in concurrent programming control", in *Communications of the ACM* v 8 no 9 (1965) p 569

[561] R Dingledine, "Tor security advisory: 'relay early' traffic confirmation attack", *Tor Blog*, July 30 2014

[562] I Dinur, K Nissim, "Revealing information while preserving privacy", *Principles of database systems* (2003) pp 202–210

[563] 'Profil de Protection – Machine á Voter', Direction centrale de la sécurité de systèmes d'information (2007)

[564] R Diresta, C Miller, V Molter, J Pomfret, G Tiffert, *'Telling China's Story: The Chinese Communist Party's Campaign to Shape Global Narratives'*, Stanford Internet Observatory, July 2020

[565] *'The Annual Bullying Survey 2018'*, Ditch the Label

[566] AK Dixit, *'Lawlessness and Economics'*, Princeton University Press, 2003

[567] RC Dixon, *'Spread Spectrum Systems with Commercial Applications'*, Wiley 1994

[568] H Dobbertin, "Cryptanalysis of MD4", *Journal of Cryptology* v 11 no 4 (1998) pp 253–270

[569] T Docan-Morgan, *'The Palgrave Handbook of Deceptive Communication'*, 2019

[570] C Doctorow, "SAMBA versus SMB: Adversarial interoperability is judo for network effects", *Boing Boing* July 17 2019

[571] C Doctorow, "Three years after the W3C approved a DRM standard, it's no longer possible to make a functional indie browser", *BoingBoing* Jun 29 2020

[572] V Dodd, "Hundreds arrested as UK organised crime network is cracked", *The Guardian*, Jul 2 2020

[573] M Dodson, M Vingaard, AR Beresford. "Using Global Honeypot Networks to Detect Targeted ICS Attacks", *International Conference on Cyber Conflict (CyCon)* 2020

[574] P Doerfler, M Marincenko, J Ranieri, J Yu, A Moscicki, D McCoy, K Thomas, "Evaluating Login Challenges and a Defense Against Accout Takeover", *IW3C2* 2019

[575] Z Doffman, "New SIM Card Spyware Attack Puts 1 Billion Mobile Phones At Risk", *Forbes* Sep 12 2019

[576] B Dole, S Lodin, E Spafford, "Misplaced Trust: Kerberos 4 Session Keys", in *Internet Society Symposium on Network and Distributed System Security*, IEEE, pp 60–70

[577] L Donnelly, "Security breach fears over 26 million NHS patients", *Daily Telegraph* Mar 17 2017

[578] Z Dorfman, J McLaughlin, "The CIA's communications suffered a catastrophic compromise. It started in Iran", *Yahoo News*, Nov 2 2018

[579] Z Dorfman, J McLaughlin, SD Naylor, "Exclusive: Russia carried out a 'stunning' breach of FBI communications system, escalating the spy game on U.S. soil", *Yahoo News* Sep 16 2019

[580] JR Douceur, "The Sybil Attack", IPTPS 2002, `http://www.divms.uiowa.edu/~ghosh/sybil.pdf`

[581] P Drahos, J Braithwaite, *'Information Feudalism – Who Owns the Knowledge Economy?'*, Earthscan 2002

[582] S Drimer, "Banks don't help fight phishing", *Light Blue Touchpaper*, Mar 10 2006

[583] S Drimer, *'Volatile FPGA design security – a survey'*, 2007

[584] S Drimer, SJ Murdoch, "Keep your enemies close: Distance bounding against smartcard relay attacks", in *16th USENIX Security Symposium* (2007)

[585] S Drimer, SJ Murdoch, RJ Anderson, "Optimised to Fail: Card Readers for Online Banking", *Financial Cryptography 2009*

[586] IE Dror, D Charlton, AE Péron, "Contextual information renders experts vulnerable to making erroneous identifications", in *Forensic Science International* 156 (2006) 74–78

[587] IE Dror, D Charlton, "Why Experts Make Errors", in *Journal of Forensic Identification* v 56 no 4 (2006) pp 600–616

[588] I Drury, "Pointing the finger", in *Security Surveyor* v 27 no 5 (Jan 97) pp 15–17

[589] C Duckett, "Google Project Zero shifts to full 90-day disclosures to improve patch uptake", *ZDNet* Jan 8 2020

[590] P Ducklin, "Why 3 million Let's Encrypt certificates are being killed off today", *Naked security by Sophos*, Mar 4 2020

[591] C Duhigg, "Is Amazon Unstoppable?" *New Yorker* (Oct 21 2019)

[592] I Duncan, L Aratani, "FAA gives preliminary approval on design fixes for 737 Max", *Washington Post*, Aug 3 2020

[593] JM Dutertre, V Beroulle, P Candelier, S De Castro, LB Faber, ML Flottes, P Gendrier, D Hély, R Leveugle, P Maistri, G Di Natale, A Papadimitriou, B Rouzeyre, "Laser Fault Injection at the CMOS 28 nm Technology Node: an Analysis of the Fault Model", *Workshop on Fault Diagnosis and Tolerance in Cryptography* (2018)

[594] C Dwork, A Roth, "The Algorithmic Foundations of Differential Privacy", *Foundations and Trends in Theoretical Computer Science* v 9 nos 3–4 (2014) pp 211–407

[595] C Dwork, F McSherry, K Nissim, A Smith, "Calibrating noise to sensitivity in private data analysis", *Third conference on Theory of Cryptography* (2006)

[596] A Dyck, A Morse, L Zingales, "Who Blows the Whistle on Corporate Fraud?", *Journal of Finance* Nov 9 2010; first published as NBER Working paper 12882, Feb 2007

[597] C Dyer, "Europe's concern over UK data protection 'defects' revealed", in *The Guardian* Oct 1 2007

[598] N Eagle, A Pentland, D Lazer, "Inferring Social Network Structure using Mobile Phone Data", 2007, at `http://reality.media.mit.edu/pdfs/network_structure.pdf`

[599] D Easley, J Kleinberg, "Networks, Crowds, and Markets: Reasoning About a Highly Connected World", *Cambridge University Press* (2010)

[600] D Easter, "The impact of 'Tempest' on Anglo-American communications security and intelligence, 1945–1970", *Intelligence and National Security* (2020)

[601] W van Eck, "Electromagnetic Radiation from Video Display Units: An Eavesdropping Risk?" in *Computers & Security* v 4 (1985) pp 269–286, at `https://cryptome.org/emr.pdf`

[602] *The Economist*, "Living in the global goldfish bowl ", 18-24 Dec 1999, Christmas special

[603] *The Economist*, "A price worth paying?", May 19 2005

[604] *The Economist*, "Getting the message, at last", Dec 13 2007

[605] *The Economist*, "Russians are shunning state-controlled TV for YouTube", March 7 2019

[606] *The Economist*, "In genetic disease, who has the right to know—or not know—what?" ("A not-so-merry dance" in the print edition), Sep 28 2019

[607] *The Economist*, "Why states are rushing to seal tens of millions of old criminal records" Nov 14 2019

[608] *The Economist*, "The financial world's nervous system is being rewired", May 7 2020

[609] *The Economist*, "America does not want China to dominate 5G mobile networks", Apr 8 2020

[610] *The Economist*, "How Wirecard fooled most of the people all of the time", Jun 25 2020

[611] *The Economist*, "After rigging an election, Belarus's regime beats protesters" Aug 16 2020

[612] B Edelman, "Adverse Selection in Online 'Trust' Certificates", at *Fifth Workshop on the Economics of Information Security* (2006); at `http://weis2006.econinfosec.org/`

[613] A Edwards, "BOLERO, a TTP project for the Shipping Industry", in *Information Security Technical Report* v 1 no 1 (1996) pp 40–45

[614] C Edwards, "The EV life-cycle conundrum", *Engineering and Technology (E&T)* v 18 no 8 (Aug/Sep 2020) p 26–29

[615] S Edwards, D Guido, JP Smith, E Sultanik, "Voatz Security Assessment Vol I of II: Technical Findings", *Trail of Bits*, Mar 12 2020

[616] V Edwards, "Controversial artist Spencer Tunick protests the Facebook and Instagram ban on female nipples with a gathering of nude models in New York City", *Daily Mail* June 2 2019

[617] M Eichin, J Rochlis, "With Microscope and Tweezers: An Analysis of the Internet Virus of November 1988", in *Proceedings of the 1989 IEEE Symposium on Security and Privacy* pp 326–343

[618] Electronic Frontier Foundation, `http://www.eff.org`

[619] Electronic Frontier Foundation, *'Cracking DES: Secrets of Encryption Research, Wiretap Politics, and Chip Design'*, EFF (1998); `http://cryptome.org/cracking-des.htm`

[620] Electronic Frontier Foundation, *Felten, et al., v. RIAA, et al.* at `http://www.eff.org/IP/DMCA/Felten_v_RIAA/`

[621] Electronic Frontier Foundation, "DocuColor Tracking Dot Decoding Guide", at `http://w2.eff.org/Privacy/printers/docucolor/`

[622] G Elich, "North Korea And The Supernote Enigma", *Korea Policy Institute* Ap 14 2008

[623] P Elkington, A Dickinson, M Mavrogordato, D Spencer, R Gillams, A De Grazia, S Rosini, D Garay Baquero, L Diment, N Mahobia, H Morgan "A Personal Respirator Specification for Health-care Workers Treating COVID-19 (PeRSo)" `https://engrxiv.org/rvcs3/`, spec and videos at `https://www.southampton.ac.uk/publicpolicy/support-for-policymakers/policy-projects/perso.page`

[624] M Ellims, J Botham, "Issues with Rules for Autonomous Vehicle Safety", *Safety Critical Systems Club Symposium*, 2020

[625] M Ellims, "Is Security Necessary for Safety?", in *ESCAR 2006*

[626] JH Ellis, *The History of Non-secret Encryption*, 1987, at `http://www.jya.com/ellisdoc.htm`

[627] M Elliott, E MacKey, K O'Hara, C Tudor, *'The Anonymisation Decision-Making Framework'*, Manchester University, 2016; at `https://ukanon.net/ukan-resources/ukan-decision-making-framework/`

[628] C Ellison, B Schneier, "Ten Risks of PKI: What You're Not Being Told About Public Key Infrastructure", in *Computer Security Journal* v XIII no 1 (2000); also at `http://www.counterpane.com/pki-risks.html`

[629] M Emms, B Arief, N Little, A van Moorsel, "Risks of Offline Verify PIN on Contactless Cards", *Financial Cryptography* (2013) pp 313–321

[630] EMV documents available from EMVCo LLP at `http://www.emvco.com/`

[631] P Enge, T Walter, S Pullen, CD Kee, YC Chao, YJ Tsai, "Wide Area Augmentation of the Global Positioning System", in *Proceedings of the IEEE* v 84 no 8 (Aug 96) pp 1063–1088

[632] EPIC – Electronic Privacy Information Center, `http://www.epic.org`

[633] EPIC, *'Approvals for Federal Pen Registers and Trap and Trace Devices 1987–1998'*, at `http://www.epic.org/privacy/wiretap/stats/penreg.html`

[634] EPIC, *'Report of the Director of the Administrative Office of the United States Courts'*, at `http://www.epic.org/privacy/wiretap/stats/1999-report/wiretap99.pdf`

[635] J Epstein, H Orman, J McHugh, R Pascale, M Branstad, A Marmor-Squires, "A High Assurance Window System Prototype", in *Journal of Computer Security* v 2 no 2–3 (1993) pp 159–190

[636] J Epstein, R Pascale, "User Interface for a High Assurance Windowing System", in *Ninth Annual Computer Security Applications Conference* (1993), pp 256–264

[637] RG Epstein, S Ember, T Gabriel, M Baker, "How the Iowa Caucuses Became an Epic Fiasco for Democrats", *New York Times* Feb 11 2020

[638] T Escamilla, *'Intrusion Detection – Network Security beyond the Firewall'*, Wiley (1998)

[639] J Essinger, *'ATM Networks – Their Organisation, Security and Future'*, Elsevier 1987

[640] *'CYBER; Cyber Security for Consumer Internet of Things'*, ETSI EN 303 645 v 2.0.0, Nov 26 2019

[641] A Etzioni, *'The Limits of Privacy'*, Basic Books 1999

[642] European Commission, *'Impact assessment – amending Framework Decision 2002/475/JHA on combating terrorism'*, Brussels, Nov 6 2007, SEC(2007) 1424

[643] European Digital Rights, at `https://www.edri.org`

[644] European Parliament, *'Development of surveillance technology and risk of abuse of economic information'*, Luxembourg (April 1999) PE 166.184 / Part 3/4, at `http://www.gn.apc.org/duncan/stoa.htm`

[645] European Parliament and Council, *'Directive 2009/72/EC concerning common rules for the internal market in electricity and repealing Directive 2003/54/EC'*

[646] European Telecommunications Standards Institute, *'CYBER; Cyber Security for Consumer Internet of Things: Baseline Requirements'*, ETSI EN 303 645 V2.1.0 (2020–04)

[647] European Union, *'Directive on the protection of individuals with regard to the processing of personal data and on the free movement of such data'*, Directive 95/46/EC

[648] European Union, *'Directive on the retention of data generated or processed in connection with the provision of publicly available electronic communications services or of public communications networks'*, 2006/24/EC

[649] European Union, "Promoting Data Protection by Privacy Enhancing Technologies (PETs)", COM(2007) 228 final, Brussels, May 2nd 2007

[650] European Union, *'Council Regulation (EC) No 1334/2000 of 22 June 2000 setting up a Community regime for the control of exports of dual-use items and technology'*

[651] European Union, *'COMMISSION DIRECTIVE 2009/4/EC – counter measures to prevent and detect manipulation of records of tachographs'* Jan 23 2009

[652] European Union, *'Regulation (EU) 2017/745 of the European Parliament and of the Council'* 2017

[653] European Union, *RAPEX A12/0157/19*, Safety Gate Rapid Alert System for dangerous non-food products, Feb 2019

[654] European Union, *'ENISA (the European Union Agency for Cybersecurity) and on information and communications technology cybersecurity certification and repealing Regulation (EU) No 526/2013 (Cybersecurity Act)'*, Apr 17 2019

[655] European Union, *'Directive (EU) 2019/771 of the European Parliament and of the Council on certain aspects concerning contracts for the sale of goods, amending Regulation (EU) 2017/2394 and Directive 2009/22/EC, and repealing Directive 1999/44/EC'*, May 20 2019

[656] Eurosmart, *'Protection Profile – Smart Card Integrated Circuit With Embedded Software'*, 1999, at `http://www.commoncriteriaportal.org/`

[657] R Evans, D Leigh, "GM subsidiary paid conman for 'blagged' private data, court told", *The Guardian* Apr 24, 2007

[658] R Evans, "Trade unionist was refused job after police gave details to blacklist" *The Guardian* Mar 7 2019

[659] I Evtimov, WD Cui, E Kamar, E Kiciman, Ti Kohno, J Li, "Security and Machine Learning in the Real World", *arXiv:2007.07205*, Jul 3 2020

[660] M Fairhurst, "Signature verification revisited: promoting practical exploitation of biometric technology", in *Electronics and Communication Engineering Journal* v 9 no 6 (Dec 97) pp 273–280

[661] C Farivar, "Russian man pleads guilty, admits he ran notorious Kelihos botnet" *Ars Technica* Sep 13 2018

[662] K Faulkner, P Bentley, L Osborne, "Your secrets for sale: Now the NHS is in the dock after it's revealed details of patients who bought prescriptions online are sold off", *Daily Mail*

[663] B Feder, "Face-Recognition Technology Improves", *New York Times* Mar 14 2003

[664] Federal Aviation Administration, "Further Actions are Needed to Improve FAA's Oversight of the Voluntary Disclosure Reporting Program", Office of Inspector General Audit Report no. AV-2014-036, Apr 10 2014

[665] Federal Aviation Administration, "Airworthiness Directives; The Boeing Company Airplanes", *Federal Register* v 83 no 237 (Dec 11 2018) pp 63561–5

[666] Federal Aviation Administration, *'A Brief History of the FAA'*, `https://www.faa.gov/about/history/brief_history/`, June 2020

[667] Federal Committee on Statistical Methodology, *' Statistical Policy Working Paper 22 (Revised 2005) – Report on Statistical Disclosure Limitation Methodology'*

[668] Federal Trade Commission v Audiotex Connection, Inc., and others, at `http://www.ftc.gov/os/1997/9711/Adtxamdfcmp.htm`

[669] Federal Trade Commission and Department of Commerce, *'Electronic Signatures in Global and National Commerce Act – The Consumer Consent Provision in Section 101(c)(1)(C)(ii) '*, June 2001

[670] Federal Trade Commission, *'ID Theft: When Bad Things Happen to Your Good Name'*, at `http://www.consumer.gov/idtheft/`

[671] Federal Trade Commission, *'ChoicePoint Settles Data Security Breach Charges; to Pay $10 Million in Civil Penalties, $5 Million for Consumer Redress'*, Jan 26 2006 `http://www.ftc.gov/opa/2006/01/choicepoint.shtm`

[672] Federation of American Scientists, `http://www.fas.org`

[673] H Federrath, J Thees, "Schutz der Vertraulichkeit des Aufenthaltsorts von Mobilfunkteilnehmern", in *Datenschutz und Datensicherheit* (June 1995) pp 338–348

[674] P Fellwock (using pseudonym 'Winslow Peck'), "U.S. Electronic Espionage: A Memoir", in *Ramparts* v 11 no 2 (August 1972) pp 35–50; at `http://jya.com/nsa-elint.htm`

[675] AP Felt, A Ainslie, RW Reeder, S Consolvo, S Thyagaraja, A Bettes, H Harris, J Grimes, "Improving SSL Warnings: Comprehension and Adherence", CHI 2015

[676] AP Felt, E Ha, S Egelman, A Haney, E Chin, D Wagner, "Android Permissions: User Attention, Comprehension, and Behavior", *SOUPS 2012*

[677] AG Ferguson, "Policing Predictive Policing", *Washington University Law Review* v 94 no 5 (2017)

[678] D Ferraiolo, R Kuhn, "Role-Based Access Control", in *15th National Computer Security Conference*, NIST (1992) pp 554–563

[679] D Ferraiolo, R Kuhn, R Chandramouli, *'Role-Based Access Control'*, Artech House 2007

[680] H Ferradi, R Géraud, D Naccache, A Tria, "When Organized Crime Applies Academic Results – A Forensic Analysis of an In-Card Listening Device", *IACR Cryptology ePrint Archive Report 2015/963*, Oct 5, 2015

[681] J Ferrigno, M Hlaváč, "When AES blinks: introducing optical side channel", *IET Information Security* v 2 no 3 (2008) pp 94–98

[682] D Fewer, P Gauvin, A Cameron, "Digital Rights Management Technologies and Consumer Privacy – An Assessment of DRM Applications Under Canadian Privacy Law", *Canadian Internet Policy and Public Interest Clinic*, September 2007

[683] A Fiat, M Naor, "Broadcast Encryption", in *Crypto '93*, Springer LNCS v 773 pp 480–491

[684] S Figueroa-Lorenzo, J Añorga, S Arrizabalaga, "A Survey of IIoT Protocols: A Measure of Vulnerability Risk Analysis Based on CVSS", *ACM Computing Surveys* v 55 no 2 (Apr 2020)

[685] PFJ Fillery, AN Chandler, "Is lack of quality software a password to information security problems?", in *IFIP SEC 94* paper C8

[686] "FCA fines RBS, NatWest and Ulster Bank Ltd £42 million for IT failures", *Financial Conduct Authority*, Nov 20 2014

[687] "Final Notice, Tesco Personal Finance plc, Reference Number 186022", *Financial Conduct Authority*, Oct 1 2018

[688] "Application of FinCEN's Regulations to Certain Business Models Involving Convertible Virtual Currencies", *US Financial Crimes Enforcement Network* May 9 2019

[689] "Psychologists and banks clash over merits of photographs on cards", in *Financial Technology International Bulletin* v 13 no 5 (Jan 96) pp 2–3

[690] D Fine, "Why is Kevin Lee Poulsen Really in Jail?", at `http://www.well.com/user/fine/journalism/jail.html`

[691] A Finkelstein, M Shattuck, "CAPSA and its implementation: Report to the Audit Committee and the Board of Scrutiny, University of Cambridge", *Cambridge University Reporter* No 5861, Nov 2 2001

[692] P Finn, "Cyber Assaults on Estonia Typify a New Battle Tactic" *Washington Post* May 19 2007

[693] ML Finucane, P Slovic, CK Mertz, J Flynn, TA Satterfield, "Gender, race, and perceived risk: the 'white male' effect", *Health, risk & society* v 2 no 2 (2000) pp 159–172

[694] G Fiorentini, S Pelzman, *'The Economics of Organised Crime'*, Cambridge University Press 1995

[695] RA Fisher, *'The Genetical Theory of Natural Selection'*, Clarendon Press, Oxford (1930); 2nd ed. Dover 1958

[696] J Flanagan, "Prison Phone Phraud (or The RISKS of Spanish)", reporting *University of Washington staff newspaper*, in `comp.risks` v 12.47 (Oct 10 1991); at `http://catless.ncl.ac.uk/Risks/12.47.html`

[697] M Fleet, "Five face sentence over notes that passed ultraviolet tests", in *The Daily Telegraph* (23/12/1999), available at `http://www.telegraph.co.uk:80/`

[698] N Fletcher, "Barclays boss Jes Staley fined £642,000 over whistleblower scandal", *The Guardian* May 11 2018

[699] E Flitter, "The Price of Wells Fargo's Fake Account Scandal Grows by $3 Billion", *New York Times* Feb 21 2020

[700] SN Foley, "Aggregation and separation as noninterference properties", in *Journal of Computer Security* v 1 no 2 (1992) pp 158–188

[701] Fondazione Ugo Bordoni, *'Symposium on Electromagnetic Security for Information Protection'*, Rome, Italy, 21–22 November 1991

[702] "Target's CEO Steps Down Following The Massive Data Breach And Canadian Debacle", *Forbes*, May 8 2014

[703] J Ford, T Kinder, "After Wirecard: is it time to audit the auditors?", *Financial Times* Jul 3 2020

[704] "The New China Scare – Why America Shouldn't Panic About Its Latest Challenger", *Foreign Affairs* Dec 6 2019

[705] S Forrest, SA Hofmeyr, A Somayaji, "Computer Immunology", in *Communications of the ACM* v 40 no 10 (Oct 97) pp 88–96

[706] DS Fortney, JJ Lim, "A technical approach for determining the importance of information in computerised alarm systems", in *Seventeenth National Computer Security Conference* (1994), proceedings published by NIST; pp 348–357

[707] K Foster, C Greene, J Stavins, "The 2018 Survey of Consumer Payment Choice: Summary results", *Federal Reserve Bank of Atlanta* (2019)

[708] The Foundation for Information Policy Research, `http://www.fipr.org`

[709] B Fox, "Do not adjust your set . . . we have assumed radio control", in *New Scientist* 8 Jan 2000

[710] LJ Fraim, "SCOMP: A Solution to the Multilevel Security Problem", in *IEEE Computer* v 16 no 7 (July 83) pp 26–34

[711] L Franceschi-Bicchierai, "AT&T Contractors and a Verizon Employee Charged With Helping SIM Swapping Criminal Ring", *Vice* May 31 2019

[712] L Franceschi-Bicchierai, "Verizon Makes SIM Swapping Hard. Why Doesn't AT&T, Sprint, and T-Mobile?" *Vice* Sep 19 2019

[713] T Frank, "Tougher TSA bomb tests raise stakes for screeners", in *USA Today* Oct 18 2007

[714] J Franklin, V Paxson, A Perrig, S Savage, "An Inquiry into the Nature and Causes of the Wealth of Internet Miscreants", *ACM CCS* (2007)

[715] J Franks, P Hallam-Baker, J Hostetler, S Lawrence, P Leach, A Luotonen, L Stewart, "HTTP Authentication: Basic and Digest Access Authentication", RFC 2617

[716] "Banks fingerprint customers to cut cheque fraud", in *Fraud Watch* (1997) no 1 p 9

[717] "Chip cards reduce fraud in France", in *Fraud Watch* (1996) no 1 p 8

[718] "Counterfeit and cross border fraud on increase warning', in *Fraud Watch* (1996) no 1 pp 6–7

[719] "Finger minutiae system leaps the 1:100,000 false refusal barrier", in *Fraud Watch* (1996) no 2 pp 6–9

[720] "Widespread card skimming causes European concern", in *Fraud Watch* (1997) v 3 pp 1–2

[721] SJ Freedberg, "Army Awards Lockheed $75M For AI Cyber/Jamming Pod", *Breaking Defense* Apr 29 2020

[722] P Freiberger, M Swaine, *'Fire in the Valley - the Making of the Personal Computer'*, McGraw-Hill (1999)

[723] A French, "The Secret History of a Cold War Mastermind" *Wired* Mar 11 2020

[724] J Fridrich, *'Steganography in Digital Media: Principles, Algorithms, and Applications'*, Cambridge University Press 2009

[725] P Frigo, E Vannacci, H Hassan, V van der Veen, O Mutlu, C Giuffrida, H Bos, K Razavi "TRRespass: Exploiting the Many Sides of Target Row Refresh", *arXiv:2004.01807* Apr 3 2020

[726] A Frik, N Malkin, M Harbach, E Peer, S Egelman, "A Promise Is A Promise – The Effect Of Commitment Devices On Computer Security Intentions", *CHI 2019*

[727] J Frizell, T Phillips, T Groover, "The electronic intrusion threat to national security and emergency preparedness telecommunications: an awareness document", *NCSC* (NIST, 1994) pp 378–399

[728] M Frost, *'Spyworld: Inside the Canadian & American Intelligence Establishments'*, Diane Publishing Co (1994)

[729] N Frost, "How the McDonnell Douglas-Boeing merger led to the 737 Max crisis", *Quartz*, Jan 3 2020

[730] DA Fulghum, "Communications Intercepts Pace EP-3s", in *Aviation Week and Space Technology* v 146 no 19 (5/5/97) pp 53–54

[731] S Fuloria, R Anderson, F Alvarez, K McGrath, "Key Management for Substations: Symmetric Keys, Public Keys or No Keys?" at *IEEE Power Systems Conference and Exhibition (PSCE 2010)*

[732] P Fussey, D Murphy, *'Independent Report on the London Metropolitan Police's Trial of of Live Facial Recognition Technology'*, Human Rights Centre, University of Essex (2019)

[733] M Galecotti, "Russia's eavesdroppers come out of the shadows", in *Jane's Intelligence Review* v 9 no 12 (Dec 97) pp 531–535

[734] R Gallagher, "The Inside Story of How British Spies Hacked Belgium's Largest Telco", *The Intercept* Dec 13 2014

[735] R Gallagher, "How U.K. Spies Hacked a European Ally and Got Away With It" *The Intercept* Feb 17 2018

[736] LA Galloway, T Yunusov, "First Contact: New Vulnerabilities in Contactless Payments", *https://leigh-annegalloway.com/presentation-materials/* Dec 4 2019

[737] E Galperin, M Marquis-Boire, J Scott-Railton, "Quantum of Surveillance: Familiar Actors and Possible False Flags in Syrian Malware Campaigns", *EFF and Citizen Lab*

[738] Sir, F Galton, "Personal identification and description," in *Nature* (21/6/1888) pp 173-177

[739] Sir, F Galton, *'Finger Prints'*, Macmillan, 1892

[740] HF Gaines, *'Cryptanalysis – a study of ciphers and their solution'*, Dover (1939, 1956)

[741] J Gamba, M Rashed, A Razaghpanah, J Tapiador, N Vallina-Rodriguez, "An Analysis of Pre-installed Android Software", *IEEE S&P 2020*

[742] D Gambetta, *'Codes of the Underworld: How Criminals Communicate'*, Princeton (2009)

[743] J Gamblin, "Nearly 20% of the 1000 Most Popular Docker Containers Have No Root Password", *Kenna Security Blog* May 20 2019

[744] T Gandy, "Brainwaves in fraud busting", *Banking Technology* (Dec 95/Jan 96) pp 20–24

[745] F Ganji, S Tajik, JP Seifert, "Why Attackers Win: On the Learnability of XOR Arbiter PUFs', *Trust and Trustworthy Computing* 2015 pp 22–39

[746] HC Gao, JX Yan, F Cao, ZY Zhang, L Lei, MY Tang, P Zhang, X Zhou, XQ Wang, JW Li, "A Simple Generic Attack on Text Captchas", *NDSS 2016*

[747] FD Garcia, G de Koning Gans, R Muijrers, P van Rossum, R Verdult, R Wickers Schreur, B Jacobs, "Dismantling MIFARE Classic", *ESORICS 2008*, Springer LNCS v 5283 pp 97–114

[748] FD Garcia, D Oswald, T Kasper, P Pavlidés, "Lock It and Still Lose It – On the (In)Security of Automotive Remote Keyless Entry Systems", *Usenix 2016*

[749] R Gardner, A Yasinsac, M Bishop, T Kohno, Z Hartley, J Kerski, D Gainey, R Walega, E Hollander, M Gerke, *'Software Review and Security Analysis of the Diebold Voting Machine Software'*, Florida State University, Jul 27 2007

[750] S Garfinkel, *'Database Nation'*, O'Reilly and Associates 2000

[751] S Garfinkel, *'Design Principles and Patterns for Computer Systems That Are Simultaneously Secure and Usable'*, PhD Thesis, MIT 2005, at `http://www.simson.net/thesis/`

[752] S Garfinkel, JM Abowd, C Martindale, "Understanding Database Reconstruction Attacks on Public Data", *ACM Queue* v 16 no 5, Nov 28 2018

[753] S Garfinkel, G Spafford, *'Practical Unix and Internet Security'*, O'Reilly and Associates (1996)

[754] B Gassend, D Clarke, M van Dijk, S Devadas, "Silicon Physical Random Functions", *ACM CCS 2002*

[755] W Gates, W Buffett, "The Bill & Warren Show", in *Fortune*, 20/7/1998

[756] B Gellman, "Edward Snowden, after months of NSA revelations, says his mission's accomplished", *Washington Post* Dec 23 2013

[757] B Gellman, D Linzer, CD Leonnig, "Surveillance Net Yields Few Suspects", *Washington Post* Feb 5 2006 p A01

[758] RM Gerecht, "The Counterterrorist Myth", in *Atlantic Monthly*, Jul-Aug 2001

[759] C Gerlinsky, "How do I Crack Satellite and Cable Pay TV?"*Chaos Communications Congress – CC33* (2016), at `https://media.ccc.de/v/33c3-8127-how_do_i_crack_satellite_and_cable_pay_tv`

[760] J Germain, "And we return to Munich's migration back to Windows – it's going to cost what now?! €100m!" *The Register* Jan 4 2018

[761] E German, "Problem Idents", at `http://onin.com/fp/problemidents.html`

[762] E German, "Legal Challenges to Fingerprints", at `http://www.onin.com/fp/daubert_links.html`

[763] JJ Gibson, *'The Ecological Approach to Visual Perception'*, Houghton Mifflin 1979

[764] D Gifford, A Spector, "The CIRRUS Banking Network", in *Communications of the ACM* v 28 no 8 (Aug 1985) pp 797–807

[765] D Gilbert, "If only gay sex caused global warming", *LA Times*, July 2 2006

[766] N Gilens, "New Justice Department Documents Show Huge Increase in Warrantless Electronic Surveillance", *ACLU blog*, Sep 27 2012

[767] M Gill, A Spriggs, *'Assessing the impact of CCTV'*, UK Home Office Research Study 292

[768] J Gillum, J Kao, J Larson, "Millions of Americans' Medical Images and Data Are Available on the Internet. Anyone Can Take a Peek." *ProPublica* Sep 17 2019

[769] J Gilmore, "Nacchio affects spy probe", in *Denver Post* Oct 20 2007; cited in "NSA solicited illegal Qwest mass wiretaps right after Bush inauguration", *Cryptography List* Oct 20 2007

[770] T Gilovich, D Griffin, D Kahneman, *'Heuristics and Biases – The Psychology of Intuitive Judgment'*, Cambridge University Press 2002

[771] AA Giordano, HA Sunkenberg, HE de Pdero, P Stynes, DW Brown, SC Lee, "A Spread-Spectrum Simulcast MF Radio Network", in *IEEE Transactions on Communications* v TC-30 no 5 (May 1982) pp 1057–1070

[772] V Goel, "Verizon will pay $350 million less for Yahoo", *New York Times* Feb 21 2017

[773] WN Goetzmann, *'Financing Civilization'*, `http://viking.som.yale.edu/will/finciv/chapter1.htm`

[774] J Goguen, J Meseguer, "Security Policies and Security Models", in *Proceedings of the 1982 IEEE Computer Society Symposium on Research in Security and Privacy* pp 11–20

[775] B Goldacre, "Care.data is in chaos. It breaks my heart", *The Guardian* Feb 28 2014

[776] I Goldberg, D Wagner, "Randomness and the Netscape browser", in *Dr Dobbs Journal* no 243 (Jan 96) pp 66–70

[777] L Goldberg, "Recycled Cold-War Electronics Battle Cellular Telephone Thieves", in *Electronic Design* v 44 no 18 (3 September 1996) pp 41–42

[778] S Goldwasser, S Micali, "Probabilistic encryption", in *J Comp Sys Sci* v 28 (1984) pp 270–299

[779] G Goller, G Sigl, "Side channel attacks on smartphones and embedded devices using standard radio equipment", *COSADE 2015* pp 255–270

[780] D Gollmann, *'Computer Security'*, Third edition, Wiley 2010

[781] D Gollmann, "What Is Authentication?" in *Security Protocols* (2000), Springer LNCS 1796 pp 65–72

[782] R Golman, D Hagman, G Loewenstein, "Information Avoidance", *Journal of Economic Literature* v LV (Mar 2017)

[783] S Golovnev, P Gaudry, "Breaking the encryption scheme of the Moscow internet voting system", *Financial Cryptography 2020*

[784] L Gong, *'Inside Java 2 Platform Security: Architecture, API Design, and Implementation'*, Addison-Wesley (1999)

[785] L Gong, DJ Wheeler, "A matrix key-distribution scheme", in *Journal of Cryptology* v 2 no 1 (1990) pp 51–59

[786] R Gonggrijp, WJ Hengeveld, A Bogk, D Engling, H Mehnert, F Rieger, P Scheffers, B Wels, "Nedap/Groenendaal ES3B voting computer – a security analysis", Oct 2006, at `http://www.wijvertrouwenstemcomputersniet.nl/Nedap-en`

[787] D Goodin, "Anatomy of an eBay scam", in *The Register*, Mar 21 2007; at `http://www.theregister.co.uk/2007/03/21/ebay_fraud_anatomy/`

[788] D Goodin, "Firefox leak could divulge sensitive info", in *The Register*, Aug 13 2007

[789] D Goodin, "TJX agrees to pay banks $41m to cover Visa losses", in *The Channel Register*, Dec 3 2007

[790] D Goodin, "Ukrainian eBay scam turns Down Syndrome man into cash machine", in *The Register* Nov 8 2007

[791] D Goodin, "How Soviets used IBM Selectric keyloggers to spy on US diplomats", *The Register* Oct 13 2015

[792] D Goodin, "How 3ve's BGP hijackers eluded the Internet—and made $29M", *Ars Technica*, Dec 21 2018

[793] D Goodin, "Police decrypt 258,000 messages after breaking pricey IronChat crypto app", *Ars Technica*, Jul 11 2018

[794] D Goodin, "Developer of Checkm8 explains why iDevice jailbreak exploit is a game changer", *Ars Technica* Sep 28 2019

[795] D Goodin, "Five months after returning rental car, man still has remote control", *Ars Technica*, Oct 28 2019

[796] D Goodin, "Forum cracks the vintage passwords of Ken Thompson and other Unix pioneers", *Ars Technica* Oct 10 2019

[797] D Goodin, "Google Play app with 100 million downloads executed secret payloads", *Ars Technica* Aug 27 2019

[798] D Goodin, "Kingpin of Evil Corp lived large. Now there's a $5 million bounty on his head", *Ars Technica* Dec 5 2019

[799] D Goodin, "What the newly released Checkra1n jailbreak means for iDevice security", *Ars Technica* Nov 15 2019

[800] D Goodin, "A Flaw in Billions of Wi-Fi Chips Let Attackers Decrypt Data", *Wired* Feb 27 2020

[801] "Content delistings due to copyright", *Google Transparency Report* (2018), at `https://transparencyreport.google.com/copyright/overview`

[802] KE Gordon, RJ Wong, "Conducting Filament of the Programmed Metal Electrode Amorphous Silicon Antifuse", in *Proceedings of International Electron Devices Meeting*, Dec 93; reprinted as pp 6-3 to 6-10, *QuickLogic Data Book* (1994)

[803] HM Government, *'Collection – Government security'*, at `https://www.gov.uk/government/collections/government-security` (2019)

[804] MF Grady, F Parisi, *'The Law and economics of Cybersecurity'*, Cambridge University Press, 2006

[805] RM Graham, "Protection in an Information Processing Utility," in *Communications of the ACM* v 11 no 5 (May 1968) pp 365-369

[806] FT Grampp, RH Morris, "UNIX Operating System Security", *AT&T Bell Laboratories Technical Journal* v 63 no 8 (Oct 84) pp 1649–1672

[807] S Granneman, "Electronic Voting Debacle", in *The Register* Nov 18 2003

[808] RD Graubart, JL Berger, JPL Woodward, *'Compartmented Mode, Workstation Evaluation Criteria, Version 1'*, Mitre MTR 10953, 1991 (also published by the Defense Intelligence Agency as document DDS-2600-6243-91)

[809] J Gray, P Syverson, "A Logical Approach to Mulilevel Security of Probabilistic Systems," in *Distributed Computing* v 11 no 2 (1988)

[810] A Greenberg, "A 'Blockchain Bandit' Is Guessing Private Keys and Scoring Millions", *Wired* Apr 23, 2019

[811] A Greenberg, "A Mysterious Hacker Group Is On a Supply Chain Hijacking Spree", *Wired* Mar 3, 2019

[812] A Greenberg, "The Confessions of Marcus Hutchins, the Hacker Who Saved the Internet", *Wired* May 12, 2020

[813] T Greening, "Ask and Ye Shall Receive: A Study in Social Engineering", in *SIGSAC Review* v 14 no 2 (Apr 96) pp 9–14

[814] A Greenberg, "The Untold Story of NotPetya, the Most Devastating Cyberattack in History", *Wired* Aug 22 2018

[815] G Greenwald, "NSA collecting phone records of millions of Verizon customers daily", *The Guardian* June 7 2013

[816] G Greenwald, "XKeyscore: NSA tool collects 'nearly everything a user does on the internet' ", *The Guardian* July 13 2013

[817] G Greenwald, *'No Place to Hide'*, Penguin 2015

[818] G Greenwald, E MacAskill, "NSA Prism program taps in to user data of Apple, Google and others", *The Guardian* June 9 2013

[819] G Greenwald, E MacAskill, L Poitras, "Edward Snowden: the whistleblower behind the NSA surveillance revelations", *The Guardian* June 11 2013

[820] M Gregory, P Losocco, "Using the Flask Security Architecture to Facilitate Risk Adaptable Access Controls", in *2007 Security Enhanced Linux Symposium*, at `http://selinux-symposium.org/2007/agenda.php`

[821] J Grierson, "Ringleader of gang responsible for £113m fraud jailed for 11 years", *The Guardian* Sep 21 2016

[822] A Griew, R Currell, *'A Strategy for Security of the Electronic Patient Record'*, Institute for Health Informatics, University of Wales, Aberystwyth, March 1995

[823] JM Griffin, A Shams, "Is Bitcoin Really Un-Tethered?" *SSRN 3195066* 2018

[824] H Griffiths, "Car crime rises again with 113,000 vehicles stolen last year", *Auto Express* Apr 25 2019

[825] H Griffiths, N Willis, "Klein Heidleberg – a WW2 bistatic radar system that was decades ahead of its time", (2010), at `https://www.cdvandt.org/k-h.htm`

[826] V Groebner, J Peck, M Kyburz, *'Who Are You?: Identification, Deception, and Surveillance in Early Modern Europe'*, Zone Books, 2007

[827] E Groll, " 'Obama's General' Pleads Guilty to Leaking Stuxnet Operation", *Foreign Policy* Oct 16 2016

[828] J Gross, "Keeping Patients' Details Private, Even From Kin", in *New York Times* July 3 2007

[829] P Grother, M Ngan, K Hanaoka, *'Face Recognition Vendor Test (FRVT)'* NIST IR 2871, Sep 11 2019

[830] D Grover, *'The protection of computer software – its technology and applications'*, British Computer Society / Cambridge University Press 1992

[831] D Gruhl, W Bender, "Information Hiding to Foil the Casual Counterfeiter", in *Proceedings of the Second International Workshop on Information Hiding* (Portland, Apr 98), Springer LNCS v 1525 pp 1–15

[832] L Gudgeon, P Moreno-Sanchez, S Roos, P McCorry, A Gervais, "SoK: Layer-Two Blockchain Protocols", *Financial Cryptography 2020*

[833] LC Guillou, M Ugon, JJ Quisquater, "The Smart Card – A Standardised Security Device Dedicated to Public Cryptology", in [1752] pp 561–613

[834] U Guin, K Huang, D DiMase, JM Carulli, M Tehranipoor, Y Makris, "Counterfeit Integrated Circuits: A Rising Threat in the Global Semiconductor Supply Chain", *Proc IEEE* v 102 no 8 (Aug 2014)

[835] GD Guo, N Zhang, "A survey on deep learning based face recognition", *Computer Vision and Image Understanding* 189 (2019) 102805

[836] R Gupta, SA Smolka, S Bhaskar, "On Randomization in Sequential and Distributed Algorithms", in *ACM Computing Surveys* v 26 no 1 (March 94) pp 7–86

[837] M Gurman, "Apple Lets Some Video Apps Sell Shows Without Taking 30% Cut", *Bloomberg*, Apr 1 2020

[838] P Gutmann, "Secure Deletion of Data from Magnetic and Solid-State Memory", in *Sixth USENIX Security Symposium Proceedings* (July 1996) pp 77–89

[839] P Gutmann, "Software Generation of Practically Strong Random Numbers", in *Seventh Usenix Security Symposium Proceedings* (Jan 1998) pp 243–257

[840] P Gutmann, "Auckland's Power Outage, or Auckland – Your Y2K Beta Test Site", `https://www.cs.auckland.ac.nz/~pgut001/misc/mercury.txt` May 24 1998

[841] P Gutmann, "Data Remanence in Semiconductor Devices", in *Usenix Security Symposium* (2001)

[842] P Gutmann, "Invalid banking cert spooks only one user in 300", *Cryptography List* May 16 2005

[843] P Gutmann, "A Cost Analysis of Windows Vista Content Protection", April 2007, at `http://www.cs.auckland.ac.nz/~pgut001/pubs/vista_cost.html`

[844] P Gutmann, "Commercial CAPTCHA-breakers for sale", *Cryptogaphy List* Oct 22 2007

[845] S Haber, WS Stornetta, "How to time-stamp a digital document", in *Journal of Cryptology* v 3 no 2 (1991) pp 99–111

[846] S Haber, WS Stornetta, "Secure Names for Bit-Strings", in *4th ACM Conference on Computer and Communications Security* (1997) pp 28–35

[847] W Hackmann, "Asdics at war", in *IEE Review* v 46 no 3 (May 2000) pp 15–19

[848] "Chris Carey Arrested In New Zealand", in *Hack Watch News* (9/1/1999)

[849] C Hagen, C Weinert, S Sendner, A Dimitrienko, T Schneider, "All the Numbers are US: Large-scale Abuse of Contact Discovery in Mobile Messengers", University of Würzburg, 2020

[850] N Hager, *'Secret Power – New Zealand's Role in the International Spy Network'*, Craig Potton Publishing (1996), at `http://www.nickyhager.info/Secret_Power.pdf`

[851] N Hager, R Gallagher, "Snowden revelations / The price of the Five Eyes club: Mass spying on friendly nations", *New Zealand Herald* and *Seemorerocks* Mar 5 2015

[852] D Hakim, RJ Epstein, S Saul, "Anatomy of an Election 'Meltdown' in Georgia", *New York Times* Jul 25 2020

[853] JA Halderman, "Amazon's MP3 Store Wisely Forgoes Watermarks", Oct 2 2007, at `http://www.freedom-to-tinker.com/?p=1207`

[854] JA Halderman, N Heninger, "How is NSA breaking so much crypto?" Oct 14 2015, *Freedom to Tinker*

[855] JA Halderman, SD Schoen, N Heninger, W Clarkson, W Paul, JA Calandrino, AJ Feldman, J Appelbaum, EW Felten, "Lest we remember: cold-boot attacks on encryption keys", Communications of the ACM v 52 no 5 (2009) pp 91–98

[856] PS Hall, TK Garland-Collins, RS Picton, RG Lee, *'Radar'*, Brassey's New Battlefield Weapons Systems and Technology Series (v 9), ISBN 0-08-037711-4

[857] M Hamburg, "Understanding Intel's Ivy Bridge Random Number Generator", *Electronic Design* Dec 11 2012

[858] C Hamby, C Moses, "Boeing Refuses to Cooperate With New Inquiry Into Deadly Crash", *New York Times* Feb 6 2020

[859] J Hammer, "The Billion-dollar Bank Job", *New York Times* May 13 2018

[860] C Han, I Reyes, Á Feal, J Reardon, P Wijesekera, N Vallina-Rodriguez, A Elazari, KA Bamberger, S Egelman, "The Price is (Not) Right: Comparing Privacy in Free and Paid Apps", *PoPETS* (2020)

[861] H Handschuh, P Paillier, J Stern, "Probing attacks on tamper-resistant devices", in *Cryptographic Hardware and Embedded Systems – CHES 99* pp 303–315

[862] R Hanley, "Millions in thefts plague New Jersey area", in *New York Times*, Feb 9, 1981, lc A; p 1

[863] R Hanson, "Can wiretaps remain cost-effective?", in *Communications of the ACM v 37 no 12 (Dec 94)* pp 13–15

[864] D Hardt, "The OAuth 2.0 Authorization Framework", *IETF RFC 6749* Oct 2012

[865] C Harper, "How the PlusToken Scam Absconded With Over 1 Percent of the Bitcoin Supply", *Botcoin Magazine* Aug 19 2019

[866] V Harrington, P Mayhew, *'Mobile Phone Theft'*, UK Home Office Research Study 235, January 2002

[867] K Harris, *'The State of Human Trafficking in California'*, California Department of Justice, 2012

[868] T Harris, "How Technology is Hijacking Your Mind – from a Magician and Google Design Ethicist", *Medium* May 18 2016

[869] MA Harrison, ML Ruzzo, JD Ullman, "Protection in Operating Systems", in *Communications of the ACM* v 19 no 8 (Aug 1976) pp 461–471

[870] D Harz, "Stealing All of Maker's Collateral", *Medium* Feb 20 2020

[871] A Hassey, M Wells, "Clinical Systems Security – Implementing the BMA Policy and Guidelines", in [64] pp 79–94

[872] R Hastings, "Freedom & Responsibility Culture", 2009, published 2011; archived at `https://www.slideshare.net/reed2001/culture-2009`; updated in 2017 as "Netflix Culture", at `https://jobs.netflix.com/culture`

[873] AJ Hawkins, "Waymo's driverless car: ghost-riding in the back seat of a robot taxi", *The Verge*, Dec 9 2019

[874] S Haykin, "Cognitive Radar: A Way of the Future" *IEEE Journal of Signal Processing* Feb 2006

[875] Health and Human Services, 'Standards for Privacy of Individually Identifiable Health Information', HHS 45 CFR parts 160–164, 65 *Federal Register* at 82461–82,510; see also 82,777–82,779

[876] *'HSE Team Inspection of the Control and Supervision of Operations at BNFL's Sellafield Site'*, Health and Safety Executive, 2000

[877] *'Annual Review 2018–9'*, Healthcare Safety Investigation Branch, NHS

[878] LJ Heath, *'An Analysis of the Systemic Security Weaknesses of the US Navy Fleet Broadcasting System 1967–1974, as Exploited by CWO John Walker'*, MSc Thesis, Georgia Tech, at `http://www.fas.org/irp/eprint/heath.pdf`

[879] B Heath, "U.S. secretly tracked billions of calls for decades", *USA Today* Apr 8 2015

[880] T Heim, "Outrage at 500,000 DNA database mistakes", *Daily Telegraph*, Aug 28 2007

[881] N Heintze, "Scalable Document Fingerprinting", in *Second USENIX Workshop on Electronic Commerce* (1996) pp 191–200

[882] P Helland, "Identity by any other name", *Communications of the ACM* April 2019 pp 80–87

[883] S Helmers, "A Brief History of anon.penet.fi – The Legendary Anonymous Remailer", *CMC Magazine*, Sep 1997; at `http://www.december.com/cmc/mag/1997/sep/helmers.html`

[884] JL Hennessy, DA Patterson, *'Computer Architecture: A Quantitative Approach'*, Morgan Kaufmann 2017

[885] A Henney, R Anderson, "Smart Metering – Ed Milliband's Poisoned Chalice", *Lightbluetouchpaper* Feb 8 2012

[886] E Henning, "The Stamp of Incompetence", *c't magazine*, Sep 3 2007; at `http://www.heise-security.co.uk/articles/95341`

[887] ER Henry, *'Classification and Uses of Finger Prints'* George Rutledge & Sons, London, 1900

[888] I Herbert, "No evidence against man in child porn inquiry who 'killed himself' ", in *The Independent* Oct 1 2005

[889] C Herley, "The Plight of the Targeted Attacker in a World of Scale", *WEIS* 2010

[890] A Hern, "Microsoft president's criticism of app stores puts pressure on Apple", *The Guardian* June 21 2020

[891] Herodotus, *'Histories'*; Book 1 123.4, Book 5 35.3 and Book 7 239.3

[892] T Herr, J Lee, W Loomis, S Scott, "Breaking Trust: Shades of Crisis Across an Insecure Software Supply Chain", *Atlantic Council* Jul 2020

[893] J Van den Herrewegen, FD Garcia, "Beneath the Bonnet: a Breakdown of Diagnostic Security", *ESORICS 2018*

[894] A Herzberg, M Jakobsson, S Jarecki, H Krawczyk, M Yung, "Proactive Public Key and Signature Systems", *4th ACM CCS* (1997) pp 100–110

[895] *'IA-64 Instruction Set Architecture Guide'*, Hewlett-Packard 2000

[896] TS Heydt-Benjamin, DV Bailey, K Fu, A Juels, T O'Hare, "Vulnerabilities in First-Generation RFID-enabled Credit Cards", in *Eleventh International Conference on Financial Cryptography and Data Security*, 2007

[897] HM Heys, "A Tutorial on Linear and Differential Cryptanalysis", in *Cryptologia* v XXVI no 3 (Jul 2002) pp 189–221

[898] HJ Highland "Electromagnetic Radiation Revisited", in *Computers & Security* v5 (1986) 85–93 and 181–184

[899] K Hill, "The Secretive Company That Might End Privacy as We Know It", *New York Times* Jan 18 2020

[900] K Hill, A Krolik, "How Photos of Your Kids Are Powering Surveillance Technology", *New York Times* Oct 11 2019

[901] K Hill, H Murphy, "Your DNA Profile is Private? A Florida Judge Just Said Otherwise", *New York Times* Nov 5 2019

[902] K Hill, S Mattu, "The House That Spied on Me", *Gizmodo* Feb 7 2018

[903] R Hill, "European Commission orders mass recall of creepy, leaky child-tracking smartwatch", *The Register* Feb 4 2019

[904] TF Himdi, RS Sandhu, "Lattice-Based Models for Controlled Sharing of Confidential Information in the Saudi Hajj System", in *13th Annual Computer Security Applications Conference* pp 164–174

[905] E von Hippel, "Open Source Software Projects as User Innovation Networks", Open Source Software Economics 2002

[906] W von Hippel, R Trivers, "The evolution and psychology of self-deception", T*Behavioral and Brain Sciences* v 34 (2011) pp 1–16

[907] J Hirshleifer, "Privacy: its Origin, Function and Future", in *Journal of Legal Studies* v 9 (Dec 1980) pp 649–664

[908] J Hirshleifer, "From weakest-link to best-shot: the voluntary provision of public goods", in *Public Choice* v 41, (1983) pp 371–386

[909] J Hirshleifer, *'Economic behaviour in Adversity'*, University of Chicago Press, 1987

[910] T Hobbes, *'Leviathan, or The Matter, Forme and Power of a Common Wealth Ecclesiasticall and Civil, commonly called Leviathan'*, 1651

[911] H Hodson, "DeepMind and Google: the battle to control artificial intelligence", *The Economist 1848* April/May 2019

[912] J Hoffman, "Implementing RBAC on a Type Enforced System", in *13th Annual Computer Security Applications Conference* (1997) pp 158–163

[913] G Hoglund, G McGraw, *'Exploiting Software – How to Break Code'*, Addison Wesley 2004

[914] G Hoglund, G McGraw, *'Exploiting Online Games – Cheating Massively Distributed Systems'*, Addison-Wesley 2007

[915] R Holiday, *'Trust me, I'm lying – Confessions of a media manipulator'*, Profile Books 2018

[916] P Hollinger, "Single language for barcode Babel", in *Financial Times* Jul 25 2000

[917] C Holloway, "Controlling the Use of Cryptographic Keys", in *Computers and Security* v 14 no 7 (95) pp 587–598

[918] G 't Hooft, "The cellular automaton interpretation of quantum mechanics", *arXiv 1405.1548*, 2014

[919] N Homeier, R Horne, M Maran, D Wade, "Solar storm risk to the north American electric grid" *Lloyd's of London* 2013

[920] BD Hong, SW Bae, YD Kim, "GUTI Reallocation Demystified: Cellular Location Tracking with Changing Temporary Identifier", *NDSS 2018*

[921] N Hopkins, "Ofgem exploited national security law to silence us, whistleblowers claim", *The Guardian* Sep 17 2018

[922] AL Hopkins, TB Smith, JH Lala, "FTMP – A Highly Reliable Fault-Tolerant Multiprocessor for Aircraft", *Proceedings of the IEEE* v 66 no 10 (Oct 1978) pp 1221–1240

[923] DI Hopper, "Authorities Sue Adult Web Sites", in *Washington Post* Aug 23 2000

[924] G Horn, B Preneel, "Authentication and Payment in Future Mobile Systems", in *ESORICS 98*, Springer LNCS v 1485, pp 277–293; journal version in *Journal of Computer Security* v 8 no 2–3 (2000) pp 183–207

[925] JD Horton, R Harland, E Ashby, RH Cooper, WF Hyslop, DG Nickerson, WM Stewart, OK Ward, "The Cascade Vulnerability Problem", in *Journal of Computer Security* v 2 no 4 (93) pp 279–290

[926] M Horton, "Historical drivers' hours offences: 1 year on", *Moving On* Mar 20 2019

[927] House of Commons Health Committee, *'The Electronic Patient Record'*, 6th Report of Session 2006–7, at `http://www.publications.parliament.uk/pa/cm200607/cmselect/cmhealth/422/422.pdf`

[928] JD Howard, *'An Analysis Of Security Incidents On The Internet 1989–1995'*, PhD thesis (1997), Carnegie Mellon University, at `http://www.cert.org/research/JHThesis/Start.html`

[929] M Howard, D LeBlanc, *'Writing Secure Code'*, (second edition), Microsoft Press 2002

[930] J Hsu, M Gaboardi, A Haeberlen, S Khanna, A Narayan, BC Pierce, A Roth, "Differential Privacy: An Economic Method for Choosing Epsilon", *CSF* (2014)

[931] Q Hu, JY Yang, Q Zhang, K Liu, XJ Shen, "An automatic seal imprint verification approach", in *Pattern Recognition* v 28 no 8 (Aug 95) pp 251–266

[932] A Huang, *'Hacking the Xbox – An Introduction to Reverse Engineering'*, No Starch Press 2003

[933] Huawei Cyber Security Evauation Centre Oversight Board, *Annual Report* (2019)

[934] G Huber, "CMW Introduction", in *ACM SIGSAC* v 12 no 4 (Oct 94) pp 6–10

[935] M Hughes, "Smart fridges are cool, but after a few short years you could be stuck with a big frosty brick in the kitchen", *The Register* Jun 8 2020

[936] N Humphrey, "The social function of intellect", in *Growing Points in Ethology* (1976) pp 303–317

[937] D Hurst 2020, "Cyber-attack Australia: sophisticated attacks from 'state-based actor', PM says" *The Guardian* Jun 19 2020

[938] A Hutchings, "Flying in Cyberspace: Policing Global Travel Fraud", *Policing: A Journal of Policy and Practice* Sep 10 2018

[939] A Hutchings, "Leaving on a jet plane: the trade in fraudulently obtained airline tickets" *Crime, law, and social change* v 70 no 4, pp 461–487

[940] A Hutchings, R Clayton, R Anderson, "Taking down websites to prevent crime", *eCrime 2016*

[941] A Hutchings, S Pastrana, R Clayton, "Displacing Big Data", in *The Human Factor of Cybercrime*, Rutger Leukfeldt and Thomas J Holt (eds) Routledge, 2020

[942] N Htoo-Mosher, R Nasser, N Zunic, J Straw, "E4 ITSEC Evaluation of PRISM on ES/9000 Processors", in *19th National Information Systems Security Conference* (1996), proceedings published by NIST, pp 1–11

[943] M Hypponen, "Malware goes mobile", in *Scientific American* Nov 2006 pp 70–77

[944] "Role of Communications in Operation Desert Storm", in *IEEE Communications Magazine* (Special Issue) v 30 no 1 (Jan 92)

[945] "New England shopping mall ATM scam copied in UK", in *Information Security Monitor* v 9 no 7 (June 94) pp 1–2

[946] "Pink Death Strikes at US West Cellular", in *Information Security Monitor* v 9 no 2 (Jan 94) pp 1–2

[947] Independent Security Evaluators Inc., "Content Protection for Optical Media", May 2005

[948] Information Systems Audit and Control Association, *'Control Objectives for Information and related Technology'*, at `http://www.isaca.org/cobit.htm`

[949] Information Systems Audit and Control Association, *'Exam Preparation Materials available from ISACA'*, at `http://www.isaca.org/cert1.htm`

[950] "Feds Praise Open Data Health Cloud Launch", *InformationWeek* Nov 12 2013

[951] International Atomic Energy Authority (IAEA), *'The Physical Protection of Nuclear Material and Nuclear Facilities'*, INFCIRC/225/Rev.4 (1999)

[952] *'International Standard on Auditing 315 (Revised 2019)'*, International Auditing and Assurance Standard Board, Dec 2019

[953] IBM, *'IBM 4758 PCI Cryptographic Coprocessor – CCA Basic Services Reference and Guide*, Release 1.31 for the IBM 4758-001

[954] *IEEE Carnahan Conference*, `http://www.carnahanconference.com/`

[955] *IEEE Spectrum*, special issue on nuclear safekeeping, v 37 no 3 (Mar 2000)

[956] CC Ife, Y Shen, SJ Murdoch, G Stringhini, "Waves of Malice: A Longitudinal Measurement of the Malicious File Delivery Ecosystem on the Web", *AsiaCCS 2019*

[957] I Ilves, "Why are Google and Apple dictating how European democracies fight coronavirus?" *The Guardian* June 16 2020

[958] "Ex-radio chief 'masterminded' TV cards scam", in *The Independent* Feb 17 1998; see also "The Sinking of a Pirate", Sunday Independent, Mar 1 1998

[959] Information Commissioner's Office, *'Investigation into the use of data analytics in political campaigns'*, July 11 2018

[960] Information Commissioner's Office, *'Mobile phone data extraction by police forces in England and Wales'*, June 2020

[961] Intel Corporation, *'Intel Architecture Software Developer's Manual – Volume 1: Basic Architecture'*, Order number 243190 (1997)

[962] Intel Corporation and others, *'Advanced Access Content System (AACS) – Technical Overview (informative)'*, July 21 2004

[963] International Electrotechnical Commission, *'Digital Audio Interface'*, IEC 60958, Geneva, February 1989

[964] International Organization for Standardization, *'Road Vehicles – Cybersecurity Engineering'*, ISO/SAE DIS 21434, 2020

[965] M Isaac, K Conger, "Google, Facebook and Others Broaden Group to Secure U.S. Election", *New York Times*, Aug 12 2020

[966] KK Ispoglu, B AlBassam, T Jaeger, M Payer, "Block Oriented Programming: Automating Data-Oriented Attacks", *CCS 2018*

[967] T Iwata, K Kurosawa, "OMAC: One-Key CBC MAC", in *Fast Software Encryption* (2003) Springer LNCS v 2887 pp 129–153

[968] R Iyengar, "Apple will pay up to $500 million to settle lawsuit over slowing down older iPhones", *CNN* Mar 2 2020

[969] C Jackson, DR Simon, DS Tan, A Barth, "An Evaluation of Extended Validation and Picture-in-Picture Phishing Attacks", *USEC 2007*

[970] I Jackson, *personal communication*

[971] L Jackson, "BT forced to pay out refunds after free calls fraud", in *The Sunday Telegraph* Feb 9 1997

[972] B Jacobs, "Maximator: European signals intelligence cooperation, from a Dutch perspective", *Journal of Intelligence and National Security* Apr 7 2020

[973] TN Jagatic, NA Johnson, M Jakobsson, F Menczer, "Social Phishing", in *Communications of the ACM* v 50 no 10 (Oct 2007) pp 94–100

[974] G Jagpal, *'Steganography in Digital Images'*, undergraduate thesis, Cambridge University, 1995

[975] AK Jain, L Hong, S Pankanti, R Bolle, "An Identity-Authentication System Using Fingerprints", in *Proceedings of the IEEE* v 85 no 9 (Sep 97) pp 1365–1388

[976] S Jajodia, W List, G McGregor, L Strous (editors), *'Integrity and Internal Control in Information Systems – Volume 1: Increasing the confidence in information systems'*, Chapman & Hall (1997)

[977] M Jakobsson, "Modeling and Preventing Phishing Attacks", *Financial Cryptography 2005*

[978] M Jakobsson, S Myers, *'Phishing and Countermeasures'*, Wiley 2007

[979] A Jamieson, "Securing digital payments – Transformation of the payments industry", *Underwriters' Laboratories* (2019)

[980] *'Horizontal Integration: Broader Access Models for Realizing Information Dominance'*, JASON Program Office report JSR-04-132, 2004

[981] M Jay, "ACPO's intruder policy — underwritten?", in *Security Surveyor* v 26 no 3 (Sep 95) pp 10–15

[982] N Jefferies, C Mitchell, M Walker, "A Proposed Architecture for Trusted Third Party Services", in *Cryptography: Policy and Algorithms*, Springer LNCS v 1029 pp 98–104

[983] F Jejdling, *'Ericsson Mobile Report'*, Nov 2019

[984] R Jenkins, "Hole-in-wall thief used MP3 player", in *The Times* Nov 15 2006

[985] S Jha, "Network Security Knowledge Area", *Cyber Security Body of Knowledge* v 1.0 Oct 2019

[986] KX Jin, "Keeping People Safe and Informed About the Coronavirus", *Facebook*, Mar 26 2020, at `https://about.fb.com/news/2020/03/coronavirus/`

[987] D Joel, Z Berman, I Tavor, N Wexler, O Gaber, Y Stein, N Shefi, J Pool, S Urchs, DS Margulies, F Liem, J Hänggi, L Jäncke, Y Assaf, "Sex beyond the genitalia: The human brain mosaic" *PNAS* Dec 2015 v 112 no 50 pp 15468–15473; first published November 30, 2015

[988] John Young Architect, `http://www.jya.com`

[989] LK John, A Acquisti, G Loewenstein, "Strangers on a plane: Context-dependent willingness to divulge sensitive information", *Journal of consumer research* v 37 no 5 (2011) pp 858–873

[990] K Johnson, "One Less Thing to Believe In: Fraud at Fake Cash Machine", in *New York Times* 13 May 1993 p 1

[991] RG Johnston, ARE Garcia, "Vulnerability Assessment of Security Seals", in *Journal of Security Administration* v 20 no 1 (June 97) pp 15–27; backed up at `http://www.cl.cam.ac.uk/~rja14/preprints/Johnston/`

[992] DW Jones, B Simons, "Broken Ballots – Will Your Vote Count in the Electronic Age?" *Stanford* (2012)

[993] RV Jones, *'Most Secret War'*, Wordsworth Editions (1978, 1998)

[994] RV Jones, *'Reflections on Intelligence'*, Octopus 1989

[995] J Jonsson, B Kaliski, "Public-Key Cryptography Standards (PKCS) #1: RSA Cryptography Specifications Version 2.1", RFC 3447

[996] A Jøsang, K Johannesen, "Authentication in Analogue Telephone Access Networks", in *Pragocrypt 96*, CTU Publishing, pp 324–336

[997] Dorothy Judd v Citibank, *435 NYS, 2d series*, pp 210–212, 107 Misc.2d 526

[998] A Juels, RL Rivest, "Honeywords: Making Password-Cracking Detectable", *IEEE SIGSAC* 2013

[999] MY Jung, "Biometric Market and Industry Overview", IBG, Dec 8 2005

[1000] M Kaczorowski, B Baker, "BeyondProd: How Google moved from perimeter-based to cloud-native security", *Google Cloud Blog* Dec 17 2019

[1001] P Kafka, "Facebook's political ad problem, explained by an expert" *Vox*, Dec 10 2019

[1002] B Kahle, "Libraries have been bringing older books to digital learners: Four publishers sue to stop it", *Internet Archive Blogs*, July 22 2020

[1003] D Kahn, *'The Codebreakers'*, Macmillan 1967

[1004] D Kahn, *'Seizing the Enigma'*, Houghton Mifflin 1991

[1005] D Kahn, "Soviet Comint in the Cold War", in *Cryptologia* v XXII no 1 (Jan 98) pp 1–24

[1006] D Kahneman, "Maps of Bounded Rationality: a Perspective on Intuitive Judgment and Choice", *Nobel Prize Lecture*, 2002

[1007] D Kahneman, *'Thinking, Fast and Slow'*, Penguin 2012

[1008] L Kahney, "The FBI Wanted a Backdoor to the iPhone. Tim Cook Said No", *Wired* Apr 16 2019

[1009] AM Kakhki, S Jero, D Choffnes, C Nita-Rotaru, A Mislove, "Taking a Long Look at QUIC", *IMC 2017*

[1010] B Kaliski, "PKCS #7: Cryptographic Message Syntax Version 1.5", RFC 2315

[1011] JB Kam, GI Davida, "A Structured Design of Substitution-Permutation Encryption Network", in *Foundations of Secure Computation*, Academic Press (1978)

[1012] M Kam, G Fielding, R Conn, "Writer Identification by Professional Document Examiners", in *Journal of Forensic Sciences* v 42 (1997) pp 778–786

[1013] M Kam, G Fielding, R Conn, "Effects of Monetary Incentives on Performance of Nonprofessionals in Document Examination Proficiency Tests", in *Journal of Forensic Sciences* v 43 (1998) pp 1000–1004

[1014] MH Kang, IS Moskowitz, "A Pump for Rapid, Reliable, Secure Communications", in *1st ACM CCS*, 1993, pp 118–129

[1015] MH Kang, JN Froscher, J McDermott, O Costich, R Peyton, "Achieving Database Security through Data Replication: The SINTRA Prototype", in *17th National Computer Security Conference* (1994) pp 77–87

[1016] MH Kang, IS Moskowitz, DC Lee, "A Network Pump", in *IEEE Transactions on Software Engineering* v 22 no 5 (May 96) pp 329–338

[1017] MH Kang, IS Moskowitz, B Montrose, J Parsonese, "A Case Study of Two NRL Pump Prototypes", in *12th ACSAC*, 1996, pp 32–43

[1018] MH Kang, IS Moskowitz, S Chincheck, "The Pump: A Decade of Covert Fun", at *21st ACSAC* (2005)

[1019] CS Kaplan, "Privacy Plan Likely to Kick Off Debate", in *New York Times*, July 28 2000

[1020] ED Kaplan, C Hegarty, *'Understanding GPS – Principles and Applications'*, Artech House 2006

[1021] PA Karger, VA Austell, DC Toll, "A New Mandatory Security Policy Combining Secrecy and Integrity", *IBM Research Report* RC 21717 (97406) Mar 15 2000

[1022] PA Karger, RR Schell, "Thirty Years Later': Lessons from the Multics Security Evaluation", at *ACSAC 2002* pp 119–126

[1023] F Kasiski, *'Die Geheimschriften und die Dechiffrier-Kunst'*, Mittler & Sohn, Berlin (1863)

[1024] *'KASUMI Specification'*, ETSI/SAGE v 1 (23/12/1999), at `http://www.etsi.org/dvbandca/`

[1025] J Katz, Y Lindell, *'Introduction to Modern Cryptography'*, CRC Press 2015

[1026] S Katzenbeisser, FAP Petitcolas, *'Information hiding – Techniques for steganography and digital watermarking'*, Artech House 2000

[1027] A Katwala, "The race to create a perfect lie detector – and the dangers of succeeding" *The Guardian* Sep 5 2019

[1028] C Kaufman, R Perlman, M Speciner, *'Network Security – Private Communication in a Public World'*, Prentice Hall 1995

[1029] EM Kearns, AE Betus, AF Lemieux, "Why Do Some Terrorist Attacks Receive More Media Attention Than Others?" Justice Quarterly, 2018

[1030] DT Keitkemper, SF Platek, KA Wolnik, "DNA versus fingerprints, in *Journal of Forensic Sciences* v 40 (1995) p 534

[1031] MB Kelley, "Obama Administration Admits Cyberattacks Against Iran Are Part Of Joint US-Israeli Offensive", *Business Insider* June 1 2012

[1032] GC Kelling, C Coles, *'Fixing Broken Windows: Restoring Order and Reducing Crime in Our Communities'*, Martin Kessler Books 1996

[1033] H Kelly, "Facebook, Twitter penalize Trump for posts containing coronavirus misinformation", *Washington Post*, Aug 7 2020

[1034] J Kelsey, B Schneier, D Wagner, "Protocol Interactions and the Chosen Protocol Attack", in *Security Protocols – Proceedings of the 5th International Workshop* (1997) Springer LNCS v 1361 pp 91–104

[1035] J Kelsey, B Schneier, D Wagner, C Hall, "Cryptanalytic Attacks on Pseudorandom Number Generators", in *Fifth International Workshop on Fast Software Encryption* (1998), Springer LNCS v 1372 pp 168–188

[1036] J Kelsey, B Schneier, D Wagner, C Hall, "Side Channel Cryptanalysis of Product Ciphers," in *ESORICS 98*, Springer LNCS v 1485 pp 97–110

[1037] R Kemp, N Towell, G Pike, "When seeing should not be believing: Photographs, credit cards and fraud", in *Applied Cognitive Psychology* v 11 no 3 (1997) pp 211–222

[1038] R Kemmerer, "Shared Resource Matrix Methodology: An Approach to Identifying Storage and Timing Channels", in *IEEE Transactions on Computer Systems* v 1 no 3 (1983) pp 256–277

[1039] MG Kendall, B Babington-Smith, "Randomness and Random Sampling Numbers", part 1 in *Journal of the Royal Statistical Society* v 101 pp 147–166; part 2 in *Supplement to the Journal of the Royal Statistical Society*, v 6 no 1 pp 51–61

[1040] T Kendall, "Pornography, Rape, and the Internet", at *The Economics of the Software and Internet Industries* (Softint 2007)

[1041] ST Kent, MI Millett, *'Who Goes There? Authentication Through the Lens of Privacy'*, National Research Council 2003; at `http://www.nap.edu/catalog.php?record_id=10656`

[1042] JO Kephardt, SR White, "Measuring and Modeling Computer Virus Prevalence", in *Proceedings of the 1993 IEEE Symposium on Security and Privacy* pp 2–15

[1043] JO Kephardt, SR White, DM Chess, "Epidemiology of computer viruses", in *IEEE Spectrum* v 30 no 5 (May 93) pp 27–29

[1044] A Kerckhoffs, "La Cryptographie Militaire", in *Journal des Sciences Militaires*, 9 Jan 1883, pp 5–38; `http://www.cl.cam.ac.uk/users/fapp2/kerckhoffs/`

[1045] D Kesdogan, H Federrath, A Jerichow, "Location Management Strategies Increasing Privacy in Mobile Communication", in *12th International Information Security Conference* (1996) pp 39–48

[1046] LM Khan, "Amazon's antitrust paradox", *Yale Law Journal* v 126 pp 710–805 (2017)

[1047] J Kieselbach, JP Ziegler, "Mit der Axt", *Der Spiegel* Nov 25 2019

[1048] JD Kilgallin, "Securing RSA Keys & Certificates for IoT Devices", `https://info.keyfactor.com/factoring-rsa-keys-in-the-iot-era`, Dec 18 2020

[1049] J Kilian, P Rogaway, "How to protect DES Against Exhaustive Key Search", in *Advances in Cryptology – Crypto 96* Springer LNCS v 1109 pp 252–267

[1050] YG Kim, R Daly, Jeremie Kim, C Fallin, JH Lee, DH Lee, C Wilkerson, K Lai O Mutlu, "Flipping Bits in Memory Without Accessing Them: An Experimental Study of DRAM Disturbance Errors", *ISCA 2014*

[1051] T Kinder, "Regulator outlines plans to break up Big Four accounting firms", *Financial Times* Feb 27 2020

[1052] T Kinder, "Big Four told to outline plans for audit split by October", *Financial Times* Jul 6 2020

[1053] T Kinder, D McCrum, "EY fights fires on three audit cases that threaten its global reputation", *Financial Times* Jun 8 2020

[1054] J King, "Bolero — a practical application of trusted third party services", in *Computer Fraud and Security Bulletin* (July 95) pp 12–15

[1055] S Kirchgaessner, "Jeff Bezos hack: Amazon boss's phone 'hacked by Saudi crown prince' ", *The Guardian* Jan 22 2020

[1056] S Kirchgaessner, "Revealed: Saudis suspected of phone spying campaign in US", *The Guardian* Mar 29 2020

[1057] N Kitroeff, "Boeing Underestimated Cockpit Chaos on 737 Max, N.T.S.B. Says", *New York Times*, Sep 26 2019

[1058] DV Klein, "Foiling the Cracker; A Survey of, and Improvements to Unix Password Security", *Proceedings of the USENIX Security Workshop* (1990)

[1059] P Klemperer, *'Auctions: Theory and Practice – The Toulouse Lectures in Economics'*, Princeton 2004; at `http://www.nuffield.ox.ac.uk/users/klemperer/VirtualBook/VBCrevisedv2.asp`

[1060] RL Klevans, RD Rodman, *'Voice Recognition'*, Artech House 1997

[1061] HM Kluepfel, "Securing a Global Village and its Resources: Baseline Security for Interconnected Signaling System # 7 Telecommunications Networks", in *First ACM CCS* (1993) pp 195–212; later version in *IEEE Communications Magazine* v 32 no 9 (Sep 94) pp 82–89

[1062] N Koblitz, *'A Course in Number Theory and Cryptography'*, Springer Graduate Texts in Mathematics no 114 (1987)

[1063] N Koblitz, A Menezes, "Another Look at 'Provable Security'", in *Journal of Cryptology* v 20 no 1 (2007) pp 3–37

[1064] ER Koch, J Sperber, *'Die Datenmafia'*, Rohwolt Verlag (1995)

[1065] M Kochanski, "A Survey of Data Insecurity Devices", in *Cryptologia* v IX no 1 (1987) pp 1–15

[1066] P Kocher, "Timing Attacks on Implementations of Diffie-Hellman, RSA, DSS, and Other Systems", in *Advances in Cryptology – Crypto 96* Springer LNCS v 1109 pp 104–113

[1067] P Kocher, "Differential Power Analysis", in *Advances in Cryptology – Crypto 99* Springer LNCS v 1666 pp 388–397

[1068] P Kocher, "Design and Validation Strategies for Obtaining Assurance in Countermeasures to Power Analysis and Related Attacks", at *FIPS Physical Security Workshop*, Hawaii 2005; at `http://csrc.nist.gov/groups/STM/cmvp/documents/fips140-3/physec/papers/physecpaper09.pdf`

[1069] P Kocher, J Jaffe, B Jun, P Rohatgi, "Introduction to differential power analysis", *Journal of Cryptographic Engineering* (2011) v 1 pp 5–27

[1070] P Kocher, D Genkin, D Gruss, W Haas, M Hamburg, M Lipp, S Mangard, T Prescher, M Schwarz, Y Yarom, "Spectre Attacks: Exploiting Speculative Execution", *arXiv:1801.01203* Jan 3 2018

[1071] P Kocher, J Horn, A Fogh, D Genkin, D Gruss, W Haas, M Hamburg, M Lipp, S Mangard, T Prescher, M Schwarz, Yuval Yarom, "Spectre Attacks: Exploiting Speculative Execution", IEEE Symposium on Security and Privacy 2019

[1072] J Koebler, "Why American Farmers Are Hacking Their Tractors With Ukrainian Firmware", *Vice*, Mar 21 2017

[1073] J Koebler, "Hacker Bypasses GE's Ridiculous Refrigerator DRM", *Vice* Jul 12 2020

[1074] BI Koerner, "Inside the Cyberattack That Shocked the US Government", *Wired* Oct 23 2016

[1075] J Koetsier, "Apple Just Crippled IDFA, Sending An $80 Billion Industry Into Upheaval", *Forbes* Jun 24 2020

[1076] A Kofman, "Digital Jail: How Electronic Monitoring Drives Defendants Into Debt", *New York Times Magazine*, July 3, 2019

[1077] T Kohno, A Stubblefield, AD Rubin, DS Wallach, "Analysis of an Electronic Voting System", Johns Hopkins TR 2003-19; also published in *IEEE Symposium on Security and Privacy* (2004)

[1078] S Kokolakis, "Privacy attitudes and privacy behaviour", *Computers and Security* v 64 (2017)

[1079] S Kokolakis, D Gritzalis, S Katsikas, "Generic Security Policies for Health Information Systems", in *Health Informatics Journal* v 4 nos 3–4 (Dec 1998) pp 184–195

[1080] O Kömmerling, MG Kuhn, "Design Principles for Tamper-Resistant Smartcard Processors", in *Usenix Workshop on Smartcard Technology*, (1999) pp 9–20

[1081] O Kömmerling, F Kömmerling, "Anti tamper encapsulation for an integrated circuit", US Patent 7,005,733, Dec 26 2000

[1082] A Kondi, R Davis, "Software Encryption in the DoD", in *20th National Information Systems Security Conference* NIST (1997) pp 543–554

[1083] MR Koot, "After Ennetcom, Dutch police makes arrests re: PGP Safe, another Dutch company, for allegedly providing crypto phones to (primarily?) the underworld", *Mattijs R. Koot's Notebook*, May 14 2017

[1084] C Kopp, "Electromagnetic Bomb – Weapon of Electronic Mass Destruction", at `https://web.archive.org/web/20120218213215/http://www.abovetopsecret.com/forum/thread59555/pg1`

[1085] DP Kormann, AD Rubin, "Risks of the Passport Single Signon Protocol", in *Computer Networks* (July 2000); at `http://avirubin.com/vita.html`

[1086] K Korosec, "VW fires jailed Audi CEO Rupert Stadler" *Techcrunch* Oct 2 2018

[1087] K Koscher, A Czeskis, F Roesner, S Patel, T Kohno, S Checkoway, D McCoy, B Kantor, D Anderson, H Shacham, S Savage, "Experimental security analysis of a modern automobile" *2010 IEEE Symposium on Security and Privacy* pp 447–462

[1088] M Kosinski, D Stillwell, T Graepel, "Private traits and attributes are predictable from digital records of human behavior", PNAS April 9, 2013 v 110 no 15 pp 5802–5805

[1089] M Kotadia, "Citibank e-mail looks phishy: Consultants", *Zdnet* Nov 9 2006

[1090] KPHO, "Sodomized Ex-McDonald's Employee Wins $6.1M", KPHO, Oct 6 2007

[1091] H Krawczyk, M Bellare, R Canetti, *'HMAC: Keyed-Hashing for Message Authentication'*, RFC 2104 (Feb 1997)

[1092] B Krebs, "Just How Bad Is the Storm Worm?" in *The Washington Post* Oct 1 2007

[1093] B Krebs, "Salesforce.com Acknowledges Data Loss", in *The Washington Post* Nov 6 2007

[1094] B Krebs, "Busting SIM Swappers and SIM Swap Myths" *Krebs on Security* Nov 7 2018

[1095] B Krebs, "Experts: Breach at IT Outsourcing Giant Wipro" *Krebs on Security* Apr 15 2019

[1096] B Krebs, "Romanian Skimmer Gang in Mexico Outed by KrebsOnSecurity Stole $1.2 Billion" *Krebs on Security* Jun 3 2020

[1097] S Krempl, "Lauschangriff am Geldautomaten", in *Der Spiegel* Jan 8 1999; at `http://web.archive.org/web/20001031024042/http://www.spiegel.de/netzwelt/technologie/0,1518,13731,00.html`

[1098] S Krishna, "The man who put us through password hell regrets everything", *Engadget* Aug 8 2017

[1099] HM Kriz, "Phreaking recognised by Directorate General of France Telecom", in *Chaos Digest* 1.03 (Jan 93)

[1100] A Krizhevsky, I Sutskever, GE Hinton, "ImageNet classification with deep convolutional neural networks", *NIPS 2012* pp 1097–1105

[1101] I Krsul, EH Spafford, "Authorship analysis: identifying the author of a program", in *Computers and Security* v 16 no 3 (1996) pp 233–257

[1102] H Kuchler, "Can we ever trust Google with our health data?" *Financial Times* Jan 20 2020

[1103] D Kügler, " 'Man in the Middle' Attacks on Bluetooth", in *Financial Cryptography 2004*, Springer LNCS v 2742 pp 149–161

[1104] MG Kuhn, "Cipher Instruction Search Attack on the Bus-Encryption Security Microcontroller DS5002FP", in *IEEE Transactions on Computers* v 47 no 10 (Oct 1998) pp 1153–1157

[1105] MG Kuhn, "Optical Time-Domain Eavesdropping Risks of CRT Displays", in *IEEE Symposium on Security and Privacy* (2002)

[1106] MG Kuhn, "Electromagnetic Eavesdropping Risks of Flat-Panel Displays", in *PET 2004*, at `http://www.cl.cam.ac.uk/~mgk25/pet2004-fpd.pdf`

[1107] MG Kuhn, RJ Anderson, "Soft Tempest: Hidden Data Transmission Using Electromagnetic Emanations", in *Information Hiding* (1998), Springer LNCS v 1525 pp 126–143

[1108] R Kuhn, P Edfors, V Howard, C Caputo, TS Philips, "Improving Public Switched Network Security in an Open Environment", in *Computer*, August 1993, pp 32–35

[1109] M Kumar, "New SIM Card Flaw Lets Hackers Hijack Any Phone Just By Sending SMS", *Hacker News* Sep 12 2019

[1110] S Kumar, C Paar, J Pelzl, G Pfeiffer, M Schimmler, "Breaking Ciphers with COPACOBANA – A Cost-Optimized Parallel Code Breaker", in *CHES 2006*

[1111] D Kundaliya, "Android devices are being increasingly targeted by undeletable adware, researchers warn", *Computing* July 7 2020

[1112] L Kuo, "Chinese surveillance company tracking 2.5m Xinjiang residents", in The Guardian Feb 18 2019

[1113] J Kuo, "Storm Drain", in *Anti-Malware Engineering Team blog*, Sep 20 2007, at `http://blogs.technet.com/antimalware/default.aspx`

[1114] GD Kutz, G Aloise, JW Cooney, *'NUCLEAR SECURITY – Actions Taken by NRC to Strengthen Its Licensing Process for Sealed Radioactive Sources Are Not Effective'*, GAO Report GAO-07-1038T, July 12, 2007

[1115] K Kwiatkowski, "The New Pentagon Papers – A High-Ranking Military Officer Reveals how Defense Department Extremists Suppressed Information and Twisted the Truth to Drive the Country to War", *Salon* Mar 10 2004

[1116] A Kwong, D Genkin, D Gruss, Y Yarom, "RAMBleed: Reading Bits in Memory Without Accessing Them", *IEEE Symposium on Security & Privacy* (2020)

[1117] *'LophtCrack 2.52 for Win95/NT'*, at `http://www.l0pht.com/l0phtcrack/`

[1118] J Lacy, SR Quackenbush, A Reibman, JH Snyder, "Intellectual Property Protection Systems and Digital Watermarking", in *Information Hiding* (1998), Springer LNCS v 1525 pp 158–168

[1119] RJ Lackey, DW Upmal, "Speakeasy: The Military Software Radio", in *IEEE Communications Magazine* v 33 no 5 (May 95) pp 56–61

[1120] F Lambert, "Tesla driver on Autopilot admits to watching a movie when crashing into police car" *Elektrek*, Aug 26 2020

[1121] F Lambert, "The Big Tesla Hack: A hacker gained control over the entire fleet, but fortunately he's a good guy", *Elektrek*, Aug 27 2020

[1122] G Lambourne, *'The Fingerprint Story'*, Harrap 1984

[1123] L Lamont, "And the real Lotto winner is … that man at the cash register", *Sydney Morning Herald*, May 3 2007

[1124] L Lamport, "Time, Clocks and the Ordering of Events in a Distributed System", in *Communications of the ACM* v 21 no 7 (July 1978) pp 558–565

[1125] L Lamport, Email message sent to a DEC SRC bulletin board at 12:23:29 PDT on 28 May 1987, link No. 75

[1126] L Lamport, R Shostak, M Pease, "The Byzantine Generals Problem", in *ACM Transactions on Programming Languages and Systems* v 4 no 3 (1982) pp 382–401

[1127] B Lampson, "A Note on the Confinement Problem", in *Communications of the ACM* v 16 no 10 (Oct 1973) pp 613–615

[1128] S Landau, A Lubin, "Examining the Anomalies, Explaining the Value: Should the USA FREEDOM Act's Metadata Program be Extended?" *Harvard National Security Journal* v 11 pp 308–358 (2020)

[1129] R Landley, "Son of DIVX: DVD Copy Control", *Motley Fool*, `http://www.fool.com/portfolios/rulemaker/2000/rulemaker000127.htm`

[1130] P Landrock, "Roles and Responsibilities in BOLERO", in *TEDIS EDI trusted third parties workshop* (1995)

[1131] CE Landwehr, AR Bull, JP McDermott, WS Choi, *'A Taxonomy of Computer Program Security Flaws, with Examples'*, US Navy Report NRL/FR/5542–93-9591 Nov 19 1993

[1132] T Lavin, "The Fetid, Right-Wing Origins of 'Learn to Code' " *The New Republic* Feb 1 2019

[1133] J Leake, "Workers used forged passes at Sellafield", in *Sunday Times* Apr 2 2000

[1134] S LeBlanc, KE Register, *'Constant Battles: Why We Fight'*, St Martin's (2003)

[1135] D Lee, "Blackberry modified to 'help drug cartels' ", *BBC News*, Mar 16 2018

[1136] DY Lee, DH Jung, IT Fang, CC Tsai, RA Popa, "An Off-Chip Attack on Hardware Memory Enclaves Using the Memory Bus", *IEEE Symposium on Security and Privacy* (2000)

[1137] HC Lee, RE Guesslen (eds), *'Advances in Fingerprint Technology'*, Elsevier 1991

[1138] K Lee, B Kaiser, J Meyer, A Nayaranan, "An Empirical Study of Wireless Carrier Authentication for SIM Swaps", *CITP, Princeton*, Jan 10 2020

[1139] W Lee, "Malware and Attack Technologies Knowledge Area", *Cyber Security Body of Knowledge*, v 1.0 October 2019

[1140] D Leigh, "Crackdown on firms stealing personal data", in *The Guardian* Nov 15 2006

[1141] D Leloup, M Untersinger, "Comment les services de renseignement font la chasse aux employés des télécoms", *Le Monde* Dec 8 2016

[1142] AK Lenstra, JP Hughes, M Augier, JW Bos, T Kleinjung, C Wachter, "Ron was wrong, Whit is right", *IACR ePrint 2012/064*

[1143] AK Lenstra, HW Lenstra, *'The development of the number field sieve'*, Springer Lecture Notes in Mathematics v 1554 (1993)

[1144] D Leppard, P Nuki, "BA staff sell fake duty-free goods", in *Sunday Times* Sep 12 1999

[1145] J Lerner, J Tirole, "A Model of Forum Shopping", *American Economic Review* v 96 no 4 pp 1091–1113 (2006)

[1146] L Lessig, *'Code and Other Laws of Cyberspace'*, Basic Books 2000; *'Code: Version 2.0'*, Basic Books 2006; at `https://www.lessig.org/`

[1147] L Lessig, *'Free Culture: The Nature and Future of Creativity'*, Penguin (2005); at `https://www.lessig.org/`

[1148] G Leurant, T Peyrin, "SHA-1 is a Shambles: First Chosen-prefix Collision and Application to the PGP Web of Trust", *IACR Preprint 2020-014*, Jan 7 2020

[1149] É Leverett, *'Quantitatively Assessing and Visualising Control System Attack Surfaces'*, MPhil Thesis, University of Cambridge, 2011

[1150] É Leverett, R Clayton, R Anderson "Standardisation and Certification of Safety, Security and Privacy in the Internet of Things", European Commission 2017

[1151] NG Leveson, *'Safeware – System Safety and Computers'*, Addison-Wesley (1995), and in particular the appendix, "Medical Devices – The Therac-25"

[1152] NG Leveson, "An Improved Design Process for Complex, Control-Based Systems Using STPA and a Conceptual Architecture", *MIT*, Jan 11 2020

[1153] S Levitt, SJ Dubner, *'Freakonomics: A Rogue Economist Explores the Hidden Side of Everything'*, William Morrow 2005

[1154] HM Levy, *'Capability-Based Computer Systems'*, Digital Press 1984

[1155] I Levy, C Robinson, "Principles for a More Informed Exceptional Access Debate", *Lawfare blog* Nov 29 2018

[1156] K Levy, B Schneier, "Privacy threats in intimate relationships", *Journal of Cybersecurity* v 6 no 1 (2020)

[1157] A Lewcock, "Bodily Power", in *Computer Business Review* v 6 no 2 (Feb 98) pp 24–27

[1158] O Lewis, "Re: News: London nailbomber used the Net", post to `ukcrypto` mailing list, Jun 5 2000, archived at `http://www.chiark.greenend.org.uk/mailman/listinfo/ukcrypto`

[1159] Lexmark International, Inc., vs Static Control Components, Inc., US Court of Appeals (6th Circuit), Oct 26 2004, at `www.eff.org/legal/cases/Lexmark_v_Static_Control/20041026_Ruling.pdf`

[1160] J Leyden, "Thai police crack credit card wiretap scam", in *The Register* Aug 4 2006

[1161] J Leyden, "Hacked to the TK Maxx", in *The Register* Jan 19 2007

[1162] J Leyden, "Italy tops global wiretap league", in *The Register*, Mar 7 2007

[1163] J Leyden, "Feds told they need warrants for webmail", in *The Register* June 19 2007

[1164] MY Li, Y Meng, JY Liu, HJ Zhu, XH Liang, Y Liu, N Ruan, "When csi meets public wifi: Inferring your mobile phone password via wifi signals", *CCS 2016* pp 1068–1079

[1165] S Liao "Spyware app abused iOS enterprise certificate to track targets", *The Verge*, Apr 8 2019

[1166] LS Liebst, R Philpot, P Poder, MR Lindegaard, "The Helpful Bystander: Current Evidence from CCTV-Captured Public Conflicts", *Discover Society* June 5 2019

[1167] H Lin, "Doctrinal Confusion and Cultural Dysfunction in the Pentagon Over Information and Cyber Operations", *Lawfare Blog* Mar 27 2020

[1168] R Linde, "Operating Systems Penetration," *National Computer Conference*, AFIPS (1975) pp 361–368

[1169] David Lindenmayer, Ben Scheele "Do Not Publish", *Science Magazine* v 356 no 6340 (May 26 2017) pp 800–801

[1170] JPMG Linnartz, "The 'Ticket' Concept for Copy Control Based on Embedded Signalling", *ESORICS 98*, Springer LNCS 1485 pp 257–274

[1171] JPMG Linnartz, M van Dijk, "Analysis of the Sensitivity Attack Against Electronic Watermarks in Images", in [143] pp 258–272

[1172] SB Lipner, "The Birth and Death of the Orange Book", *Annals of the History of Computing* (2015)

[1173] M Lipp, M Schwarz, D Gruss, T Prescher, W Haas, S Mangard, P Kocher, D Genkin, Y Yarom, M Hamburg, "Meltdown", *arXiv:1801.01207* Jan 3 2018

[1174] A Liptak, "Hackers reportedly used a tool developed by the NSA to attack Baltimore's computer systems", *The Verge* May 25 2019

[1175] D Litchfield, C Anley, J Heasman, B Grindlay, *'The Database Hacker's Handbook: Defending Database Servers'*, Wiley 2005

[1176] B Littlewood, "Predicting software reliability", in *Philosophical Transactions of the Royal Society of London* A327 (1989), pp 513–527

[1177] FF Liu, Y Yarom, Q Ge, G Heiser, RB Lee, "Last-Level Cache Side-Channel Attacks are Practical", *IEEE Symposium on Security and Privacy* 2015

[1178] XY Liu, Z Zhou, WR Diao, Z Li, KH Zhang, "When good becomes evil: Keystroke inference with smartwatch", *ACM CCS 2015* pp 1273–1285

[1179] WF Lloyd, *'Two Lectures on the Checks to Population'*, Oxford University Press (1833)

[1180] C Loch, A DeMeyer, MT Pich, *'Managing the Unknown'*, Wiley 2006

[1181] L Loeb, *'Secure Electronic Transactions – Introduction and technical Reference'*, Artech House 1998

[1182] N Lomas, "Targeted ads offer little extra value for online publishers, study suggests", *Techcrunch* May 31 2019

[1183] N Lomas, "Ireland's data watchdog slammed for letting adtech carry on 'biggest breach of all time' ", *Techcrunch* Sep 21 2020

[1184] London School of Economics & Political Science, *'The Identity Project – An assessment of the UK Identity Cards Bill & its implications'*, 2005, at `http://eprints.lse.ac.uk/id/eprint/29117`

[1185] J Long, *Google Hacking Database*, at `http://johnny.ihackstuff.com/ghdb.php`

[1186] D Longley, S Rigby, "An Automatic Search for Security Flaws in Key Management", *Computers & Security* v 11 (March 1992) pp 75–89

[1187] HC Longuet-Higgins, K Prazdny, "The interpretation of a moving retinal image", *Proc Roy Soc B* v 208 (1980) pp 385–397

[1188] PA Loscocco, SD Smalley, PA Muckelbauer, RC Taylor, SJ Turner, JF Farrell, "The Inevitability of Failure: The Flawed Assumption of Security in Modern Computing Environments", in *20th National Information Systems Security Conference* (1998) pp 303–314

[1189] PA Loscocco, SD Smalley, "Integrating Flexible Support for Security Policies into the Linux Operating System", in *Proceedings of the FREENIX Track: 2001 USENIX Annual Technical Conference (FREENIX '01)* (June 2001). See also NSA SELinux site: `http://www.nsa.gov/selinux`

[1190] JR Lott, *'More Guns, Less Crime: Understanding Crime and Gun-Control Laws'*, University of Chicago Press 2000

[1191] J Loughry, DA Umphress, "Information leakage from optical emanations", in *ACM Transactions on Information and System Security* v 5 no 3 (Aug 2002) pp 262–289

[1192] B Lovejoy, "Apple being sued for refusing to help iTunes gift card scam victims", *9to5Mac* Jul 20 2020

[1193] WW Lowrance, *'Privacy and Health Research'*, Report to the US Secretary of Health and Human Services (May 1997)

[1194] J Lukàš, J Fridrich, M Goljan, "Digital 'bullet scratches' for images", in *ICIP 05*

[1195] I Lunden, "Apple fined record $1.2B in France over anti-competitive sales practices", *TechCrunch* Mar 16 2020

[1196] JM Luo, Y Cao, R Barzilay, "Neural Decipherment via Minimum-Cost Flow: from Ugaritic to Linear B", *arXiv* 1906.06718 (June 16 2019)

[1197] HT Luong, HD Phan, DV Chu, VQ Nguyen, KT Le, Luc, LT Hoang, "Understanding Cybercrimes in Vietnam: From Leading-Point Provisions to Legislative System and Law Enforcement", *International Journal of Cyber Criminology* (2019) pp 290–308

[1198] J Lynch, "HART: Homeland Security's Massive New Database Will Include Face Recognition, DNA, and Peoples' 'Non-Obvious Relationships' ", *EFF* June 7 2018

[1199] B Lysyk, *'Annual report of the Auditor General of Ontario'*, 2014

[1200] M Lyu, *'Software Reliability Engineering'*, IEEE Computer Society Press 1995

[1201] E MacAskill, J Borger, N Hopkins, N Davies, J Ball, "GCHQ taps fibre-optic cables for secret access to world's communications", June 21 2013

[1202] R Maclean, "Mali's President Resigns After Being Arrested in Military Coup", *New York Times*, Aug 18 2020

[1203] D Mackenzie, *'Mechanising Proof – Computing, Risk and Trust'*, MIT Press 2001

[1204] D Mackett, "A Pilot on Airline Security", in *Hot Air*, July 16 2007, at http://hotair.com/archives/2007/07/16/a-pilot-on-airline-security/

[1205] B Macq, *'Special Issue – Identification and protection of Multimedia Information'*, *Proceedings of the IEEE* v 87 no 7 (July 1999)

[1206] M Madden, L Rainie, "Americans' Attitudes About Privacy, Security and Surveillance", *Pew Research Center* May 20 2015

[1207] W Madsen, "Crypto AG: The NSA's Trojan Whore?" in *Covert Action Quarterly* (Winter 1998), at http://www.mediafilter.org/caq/cryptogate/

[1208] W Madsen, "Government-Sponsored Computer Warfare and Sabotage", in *Computers and Security* v 11 (1991) pp 233–236

[1209] M Magee, "HP inkjet cartridges have built-in expiry dates – Carly's cunning consumable plan", *The Inquirer*, 29 April 2003, at http://www.theinquirer.net/?article=9220

[1210] K Maguire, "Muckraker who feeds off bins of the famous", in *The Guardian* Jul 27 2000

[1211] S Maguire, *'Debugging the Development Process'*, Microsoft Press 1994

[1212] F Main, "Your phone records are for sale", *Chicago Sun-Times*, Jan 5 2006

[1213] D Maio, D Maltoni, "Direct Gray-Scale Minutiae Detection in Fingerprints", in *IEEE Transactions on Pattern Analysis and Machine Intelligence* v 19 no 1 (Jan 97) pp 27–40

[1214] S Makkaveev, "Pwn2Own Qualcomm compute DSP for fun and profit", *DefCon 2020*; also on CheckPoint Blog as "Over 400 vulnerabilities on Qualcomm's Snapdragon chip threaten mobile phones' usability worldwide", Aug 7 2020

[1215] D Maltoni, D Maio, AK Jain, S Prabhakar, *'Handbook of Fingerprint Recognition'*, Springer-Verlag New York, 2003

[1216] S Mangard, E Oswald, T Popp, *'Power Analysis Attacks – Revealing the Secrets of Smartcards'*, Springer 2007

[1217] G Manaugh, "The Rise and Fall of an All-Star Crew of Jewel Thieves", *The Atlantic* Dec 17 2019

[1218] F Manjoo, "The computer virus turns 25", *Salon*, Jul 12 2007

[1219] T Mansfield, G Kelly, D Chandler, J Kane, *'Biometric Product Testing Final Report*, Issue 1.0, 19 March 2001, National Physical Laboratory

[1220] W Marczak, J Dalek, S McKune, A Senft, J Scott-Railton, R Deibert, "BAD TRAFFIC: Sandvine's PacketLogic Devices Used to Deploy Government Spyware in Turkey and Redirect Egyptian Users to Affiliate Ads?" *Munk School, Toronto* Mar 9 2018

[1221] W Marczak, J Scott-Railton, "The Million Dollar Dissident NSO Group's iPhone Zero-Days used against a UAE Human Rights Defender", University of Toronto Aug 24 2016

[1222] D Margolis, M Risher, B Ramakrishnan, A Brotman, J Jones, "SMTP MTA Strict Transport Security (MTA-STS)" *RFC 8461* (Sep 2018)

[1223] A Marino, "Vergecast: Is Facebook ready for 2020?" *The Verge* Aug 27 2019

[1224] J Markoff, *'What the Dormouse Said: How the 60s Counterculture Shaped the Personal Computer'*, Viking Adult (2005)

[1225] J Markoff, "Vast Spy System Loots Computers in 103 Countries", *New York Times* Mar 28 2009

[1226] L Marks, *'Between Silk and Cyanide – a Codemaker's War 1941–1945'*, Harper Collins 1998

[1227] P Marks, "Picking Locks with Audio Technology", *Communications of the ACM*, Aug 13 2020

[1228] M Marlinspike, "Technology preview: Private contact discovery for Signal", *Signal Blog*, Sep 26 2017

[1229] M Marlinspike, T Perrin, "The X3DH Key Agreement Protocol", https://signal.org/docs/specifications/ Nov 4 2016

[1230] V Marotta, V Abhishek, A Acquisti, "Online Tracking and Publishers' Revenues: An Empirical Analysis", *WEIS 2019*

[1231] P Marquardt, A Verma, H Carter, P Traynor, "(sp)iphone: Decoding vibrations from nearby keyboards using mobile phone accelerometers", *CCS 2011* pp 551–562

[1232] M Marquis-Boire, G Greenwald, M Lee, "XKEYSCORE – NSA's Google for the World's Private Communications", *The Intercept* July 1 2015

[1233] M Marquis-Boire, B Marczak, C Guarnieri, J Scott-Railton, "You Only Click Twice – FinFisher's Global Proliferation" *Munk School, Toronto*, Mar 13 2013

[1234] S Marsh, "US joins UK in blaming Russia for NotPetya cyber-attack", *The Guardian* Feb 15 2018

[1235] L Martin, "Using Semiconductor Failure Analysis Tools for Security Analysis", FIPS Physical Security Workshop, Hawaii 2005

[1236] AG Martínez, "How Trump Conquered Facebook—Without Russian Ads", *Wired* Feb 23 2018

[1237] JL Mashaw, DL Harfst, *'The struggle for auto safety'*, Harvard 1990

[1238] S Mason, *'Electronic Evidence – Disclosure, Discovery and Admissibility'*, LexisNexis Butterworths 2007

[1239] S Masondo, "Postbank Forced to Replace 12-Million Bank Cards after Employees Steal 'Master Key' ", *Sunday Times* Jun 14 2020

[1240] M Mastanduno, "Economics and Security in Statecraft and Scholarship", *International Organization* v 52 no 4 (Autumn 1998)

[1241] S Matala, T Nyman, N Asokan, "Historical insight into the development of Mobile TEEs", *Aalto University Secure Systems Group blog*, June 20 2019

[1242] JM Matey, O Naroditsky, K Hanna, R Kolczynski, DJ LoIacono, S Mangru, M Tinker, TM Zappia, WY Zhao, "Iris on the Move: Acquisition of Images for Iris recognition in Less Constrained Environments", in *Proc IEEE* v 94 no 11 (Nov 2006) pp 1936–1947

[1243] SA Mathieson. "Gone phishing in Halifax – UK bank sends out marketing email which its own staff identify as a fake", in *Infosecurity News*, Oct 7 2005

[1244] A Mathur, G Acar, M Friedman, E Lucherini, J Mayer, M Chetty, A Narayanan, "Dark Patterns at Scale: Findings from a Crawl of 11K Shopping Websites", *arxiv:1907.07032* July 16 2019

[1245] M Matsubara, "The Japanese Automobile Industry Is Taking Next Steps for Cybersecurity Collaboration", *Lawfare* Jul 7 2020

[1246] M Matsui, "Linear Cryptanalysis Method for DES Cipher", in *Eurocrypt 93*, Springer LNCS v 765 pp 386–397

[1247] M Matsui, "New Block Encryption Algorithm MISTY", in *Fourth International Workshop on Fast Software Encryption* (1997), Springer LNCS v 1267 pp 54–68

[1248] T Matsumoto, H Matsumoto, K Yamada, S Hoshino, "Impact of Artificial 'Gummy' Fingers on Fingerprint Systems" *Proceedings of SPIE* v 4677, Optical Security and Counterfeit Deterrence Techniques IV, 2002

[1249] R Matthews, "The power of one", in *New Scientist* Jul 10 1999 pp 26–30

[1250] T Matthews, K O'Leary, A Turner, M Sleeper, J Palzkill Woelfer, M Shelton, C Manthorne, EF Churchill, S Consolvo, "Stories from Survivors: Privacy & Security Practices when Coping with Intimate Partner Abuse" *CHI 2017*

[1251] V Matyás, "Protecting the identity of doctors in drug prescription analysis", in *Health Informatics Journal* v 4 nos 3–4 (Dec 1998) pp 205–209

[1252] V Mavroudis, P Svenda, "JavaCard: The execution environment you didn't know you were using", *Software Sustainability Institute* July 13 2018

[1253] J Maynard Smith, G Price, "The Logic of Animal Conflict", in *Nature* v 146 (1973) pp 15–18

[1254] R Mayrhofer, J Vander Stoep, C Brubaker, N Kralevich, "The Android Platform Security Model", *arXiv:1904.05572*, Apr 11 2019

[1255] K McCarthy, "Here's that hippie, pro-privacy, pro-freedom Apple y'all so love: Hong Kong protest safety app banned from iOS store", *The Register*, Oct 2 2019

[1256] K McCarthy, "The Internet of Things is a security nightmare reveals latest real-world analysis: unencrypted traffic, network crossover, vulnerable OSes", *The Register*, Mar 11 2020

[1257] J McCormac. *'European Scrambling Systems – The Black Book'*, version 5, Waterford University Press 1996

[1258] D McCrum, "Wirecard: the timeline", *Financial Times* Jun 25 2020

[1259] D McCullagh, "U.S. to Track Crypto Trails", in *Wired*, May 4 2000; statistics at `http://www.uscourts.gov/wiretap99/contents.html`

[1260] D McCullagh, R Zarate, "Scanning Tech a Blurry Picture", in *Wired*, Feb 16 2002

[1261] K McCurley, Remarks at IACR General Meeting. *Crypto 98*, Santa Barbara, Ca., Aug 1998

[1262] D McCullough, "A Hook-up Theorem for Multi-Level Security", in *IEEE Transactions on Software Engineering* v 16 no 6 (June 1990) pp 563–568

[1263] P McDaniel, K Butler, W Enck, H Hursti, S McLaughlin, P Traynor, MA Blaze, A Aviv, P Černý, S Clark, E Cronin, G Shah, M Sherr, A Vigna, R Kemmerer, D Balzarotti, G Banks, M Cova, V Felmetsger, W Robertson, F Valeur, JL Hall, L Quilter, *'EVEREST: Evaluation and Validation of Election-Related Equipment, Standards and Testing'*, Final Report, Dec 7, 2007

[1264] AD McDonald, MG Kuhn, "StegFS: A Steganographic File System for Linux", in [1522] pp 463–477

[1265] D MacEoin, *'The hijacking of British Islam – How extremist literature is subverting mosques in the UK'*, Policy Exchange (2007)

[1266] M McFarland, "Feds blame distracted test driver in Uber self-driving car death", *CNN* Nov 20 2019

[1267] E McGaughey, "The extent of Russian-backed fraud means the referendum is invalid", *LSE* Nov 14 2018

[1268] G McGraw, *'Software Security – Building Security In'*, Addison-Wesley 2006

[1269] G McGraw, H Figueroa, V Shepardson, R Bonett, *'An architectural risk analysis of machine learning systems: Towards more secure machine learning'*, BIML, 2020

[1270] D McGrew, J Viega, "The Galois/Counter Mode of Operation (GCM)", Submission to NIST Modes of Operation Process, January 2004; updated May 2005

[1271] J McGroddy, HS Lin, *'A Review of the FBI's Trilogy Information Technology Modernization Program'*, National Academies Press, 2004

[1272] J McHugh, "An EMACS Based Downgrader for the SAT" in *Computer and Network Security*, IEEE Computer Society Press (1986) pp 228–237

[1273] N McInnes, G Wills, E Zaluska, "Analysis of threats on a VoIP based PBX honeypot", *Infonomics Society* (2019) pp 113–118

[1274] I McKie, "Total Vindication for Shirley McKie!" Jun 23 2000, at `http://onin.com/fp/mckievindication.html`

[1275] I McKie, M Russell, *'Shirley McKie – The Price of Innocence'*, Birlinn 2007

[1276] J McLaughlin, Z Dorfman, " 'Shattered': Inside the secret battle to save America's undercover spies in the digital age", *Yahoo News* Dec 30 2019

[1277] J McLean, "The Specification and Modeling of Computer Security", in *Computer* v 23 no 1 (Jan 1990) pp 9–16

[1278] J McLean, "Security Models," in *Encyclopedia of Software Engineering*, Wiley 1994

[1279] J McLean, "A General Theory of Composition for a Class of 'Possibilistic' Properties,", in *IEEE Transactions on Software Engineering* v 22 no 1 (Jan 1996) pp 53–67

[1280] D McLeod, "FNB backs down on password decision after backlash", *Tech Central* Aug 20 2019

[1281] J McMillan, "Mobile Phones Help Secure Online Banking", in *PC World*, Sep 11 2007

[1282] R McMillan, "The Inside Story of Mt. Gox, Bitcoin's $460 Million Disaster", *Wired* Mar 3 2014

[1283] "Health data, AI, and Google DeepMind", MedConfidential, 2018, at `https://medconfidential.org/whats-the-story/health-data-ai-and-google-deepmind/`

[1284] J Meek, "Robo Cop", in *The Guardian*, June 13 2002

[1285] N Megaw, "UK consumers dragged into Wirecard's collapse", *Financial Times* Jun 29 2020

[1286] C Meijer, R Verdult, "Ciphertext-only Cryptanalysis on Hardened Mifare Classic Cards", *ACM CCS* (2015)

[1287] C Meijer, B van Gastel, "Self-encrypting deception: weaknesses in the encryption of solid-state drives", *IEEE Security & Privacy* (2019)

[1288] J Meikle, "G4S and Serco hand over offender tagging contracts over fraud claims", *The Guardian*, Dec 12 2013

[1289] M Mehrnezhad, M Aamir Ali, F Hao, A van Moorsel, "NFC payment spy: a privacy attack on contactless payments", *International Conference on Research in Security Standardisation* (2016) pp 92–111

[1290] J Mendez, "How Steam Employs DRM & What That Means For Your Game", *Black Shell Media*, Jun 28 2017

[1291] AJ Menezes, PC van Oorschot, SA Vanstone, *'Handbook of Applied cryptography'*, CRC Press (1997); available online at `http://www.cacr.math.uwaterloo.ca/hac/`

[1292] J Menn, "Exclusive: Secret contract tied NSA and security industry pioneer", *Reuters* Dec 20 2013

[1293] J Menn, "Exclusive: High-security locks for government and banks hacked by researcher", *Reuters* Aug 6 2019

[1294] J Menn, K Paul, R Satter, "Exclusive: More than 1,000 people at Twitter had ability to aid hack of accounts", *Reuters* Jul 23 2020

[1295] J Mercer, "Document Fraud Deterrent Strategies: Four Case Studies", in *Optical Security and Counterfeit Deterrence Techniques II* (1998), IS&T and SPIE v 3314, pp 39–51

[1296] H Mercier, D Sperber, "Why Do Humans Reason? Arguments for an Argumentative Theory", *Behavioral and Brain Sciences* v 34 no 2 pp 57–74, 2011, and at SSRN 1698090

[1297] R Mercuri, "Physical Verifiability of Computer Systems", *5th International Computer Virus and Security Conference* (March 1992); see also R Mercuri, *'Electronic Vote Tabulation Checks & Balances'*, PhD Thesis, U Penn, 2000, at `http://www.notablesoftware.com/evote.html`

[1298] R Merkle, "Protocols for public key cryptosystems", *IEEE Symposium on Security and Privacy* 1980

[1299] M Mesa, "Phish Scales: Malicious Actor Combines Personalized Email, Variety of Malware To Target Execs", *ProofPoint* Apr 5 2016

[1300] TS Messergues, EA Dabish, RH Sloan, "Investigations of Power Analysis Attacks on Smartcards", in *Usenix Workshop on Smartcard Technology* (1999) pp 151–161

[1301] E Messmer, "DOD looks to put pizzazz back in PKI", *Network World* Aug 15 2005

[1302] C Metz, "AI Is Transforming Google Search. The Rest of the Web Is Next", *Wired* Feb 4 2016

[1303] CH Meyer, SM Matyas, *'Cryptography: A New Dimension in Computer Data Security'*, Wiley 1982

[1304] C Meyer, J Schwenk, "SoK: Lessons Learned From SSL/TLS Attacks", *WISA 2013* pp 189–209

[1305] R Meyer-Sommer, "Smartly analyzing the simplicity and the power of simple power analysis on Smartcards", in *Workshop on Cryptographic Hardware and Embedded Systems* (2000); Springer LNCS v 1965 pp 78–92

[1306] A Michael, "Cyber Probing: The Politicisation of Virtual Attack", *Defence Academy of the United Kingdom* Oct 2012

[1307] J Micklethwait, A Wooldridge, *'The Witch Doctors – What the management gurus are saying, why it matters and how to make sense of it'*, Random House 1997

[1308] Microsoft Inc, *'Architecture of Windows Media Rights Manager'*, May 2004

[1309] Microsoft Inc, "Sony DRM Rootkit", Nov 12 2005

[1310] Microsoft Inc, "Security Development Lifecycle – Simplified Implementation of the Microsoft SDL" Nov 4 2010

[1311] Microsoft Azure, "What is Azure Key Vault?" Jan 7 2019

[1312] A Midgley, "R.I.P. and NHSNet", `ukcrypto` mailing list, Jul 1 2000

[1313] S Mihm, *'A Nation of Counterfeiters'*, Harvard 2007

[1314] S Milgram, *'Obedience to Authority: An Experimental View'*, HarperCollins, (1974, reprinted 2004)

[1315] J Millen, "A Resource Allocation Model for Denial of Service Protection", in *Journal of Computer Security* v 2 no 2–3 (1993) pp 89–106

[1316] A Miller, "SourMint: malicious code, ad fraud, and data leak in iOS", *Synk*, Aug 26 2020

[1317] B Miller, "Vital Signs of Security", in *IEEE Spectrum* (Feb 94) pp 22–30

[1318] C Miller, C Valasek, "Remote Exploitation of an Unaltered Passenger Vehicle", `https://www.illmatics.com` Aug 10 2015

[1319] GA Miller, "The Magical Number Seven, Plus or Minus Two: Some Limits on our Capacity for Processing Information", in *Psychological Review* v 63 (1956) pp 81–97

[1320] ML Miller, IJ Cox, JA Bloom, "Watermarking in the Real World: An Application to DVD", in *Sixth ACM International Multimedia Conference* (1998); v 41 of *GMD Report*, pp 71–76

[1321] JR Minkel, "Confirmed: The U.S. Census Bureau Gave Up Names of Japanese-Americans in WW II", in *Scientific American* Mar 30 2007

[1322] SF Mires, "Production, Distribution, and Use of Postal Security Devices and Information-Based Indicia", *Federal Register* v 65 no 191 Oct 2, 2000 pp 58682–58698

[1323] A Mirian, Z Ma, D Adrian, M Tischer, T Chuenchujit, T Yardley, R Berthier, J Mason, Z Durumeric, JA Halderman, M Bailey, "An Internet-Wide View of ICS Devices", *Conference on Privacy, Security and Trust* 2016

[1324] A Mirian, J DeBlasio, S Savage, GM Voelker, K Thomas, "Hack for Hire: Exploring the Emerging Market for Account Hijacking", *The World Wide Web Conference* 2019 pp 1279–1289

[1325] "BBC fined £400,000 by Ofcom for fake competitions", *Daily Mirror* July 30 2008

[1326] Mitchell and Webb, "Identity Theft", *YouTube* (2007)

[1327] KD Mitnick, *'The Art of Deception: Controlling the Human Element of Security'*, Wiley (2002)

[1328] V Mladenov, C Mainka, K Mayer zu Selhausen, M Grothe, J Schwenk "1 trillion Dollar Refund – How to Spoof PDF Signatures", *CCS 2019*

[1329] D Modic, RJ Anderson, "Reading This May Harm Your Computer: The Psychology of Malware Warnings", *Computers in Human Behavior* v 41 pp 71–79 and SSRN 2374379

[1330] A Moghimi, G Irazoqui, T Eisenbarth, "CacheZoom: How SGX Amplifies The Power of Cache Attacks" *CHES 2017* pp 69–90

[1331] D Moghimi, B Sunar, T Eisenbarth, N Heninger, "TPM-FAIL: TPM meets Timing and Lattice Attacks", *arXiv:1911.05673* Nov 13 2019

[1332] "Card fraud nets Esc6 billion', F Mollet, *Cards International* Sep 22 1995 p 3

[1333] JV Monaco, "SoK: Keylogging Side Channels", *IEEE Symposium on Security and Privacy* (2018)

[1334] "Démantèlement d'un réseau de téléphonie cryptée, utilisé par des organisations criminelles", *Le Monde* Jul 2 2020

[1335] YA de Montjoye, CA Hidalgo, M Verleysen, VD Blondel, "Unique in the Crowd: The privacy bounds of human mobility", *Scientific Reports* v 3 no 1376 (2013)

[1336] YA de Montjoye, J Quoidbach, F Robic, A Pentland, "Predicting Personality Using Novel Mobile Phone-Based Metrics", *2013 International Conference on Social Computing, Behavioral-Cultural Modeling, and Prediction* (SBP 2013) pp 48–55

[1337] B Moore, "Lessons from Christchurch: How the media finally acknowledged far-right terrorism", *Signal* April 3 2019

[1338] SW Moore, RJ Anderson, R Mullins, G Taylor, J Fournier, "Balanced Self-Checking Asynchronous Logic for Smart Card Applications", in *Microprocessors and Microsystems Journal* v 27 no 9 (Oct 2003) pp 421–430

[1339] T Moore, R Anderson, "How brain type influences online safety", *Security and Human Behaviour* (2008)

[1340] T Moore, A Friedman, A Procaccia, "Would a 'Cyber Warrior' Protect Us? Exploring Trade-offs Between Attack and Defense of Information Systems", *New Security Paradigms Workshop* (2010) pp 85–94.

[1341] T Moore, N Christin, "Beware the middleman: Empirical analysis of Bitcoin-exchange risk", *Financial Cryptography* 2013 pp 25–33

[1342] L Moran, "Tweeters Make Chilling Point About Jack Dorsey's Account Being Compromised", *Huffington Post*, Aug 31 2019

[1343] B Morgan, "Strip club which gave client £50k bill loses license", *Evening Standard* Jan 31 2020

[1344] R Morris, "A Weakness in the 4.2BSD Unix TCP/IP Software", Bell Labs Computer Science Technical Report no. 117, February 25, 1985; at `http://www.cs.berkeley.edu/~daw/security/seq-attack.html`

[1345] R Morris, Invited talk, *Crypto 95*

[1346] R Morris, K Thompson, "Password security: A case history", in *Communications of the ACM* v 22 no 11 (November 1979) pp 594–597

[1347] M Motoyama, D McCoy, K Levchenko, S Savage, GM Voelker, "An Analysis of Underground Forums", *IMC* (2011)

[1348] DP Moynihan, *'Secrecy – The American Experience'*, Yale University Press (1999)

[1349] P Mozur, "Skype Vanishes From App Stores in China, Including Apple's", *New York Times*, Nov 21 2017

[1350] P Mozur, "With Hacks and Cameras, Beijing's Electronic Dragnet Closes on Hong Kong", *New York Times*, Aug 25 2020

[1351] C Mueller, S Spray, J Grear, "The Unique Signal Concept for Detonation Safety in Nuclear Weapons", Sand91-1269, UC-706

[1352] J Mueller, *'Overblown – How Politicians and the Terrorism Industry Inflate National Security Threats, and Why we Believe Them'*, Simon and Schuster 2006

[1353] S Mukherjee, "What the Coronavirus Crisis Reveals About American Medicine", *New Yorker* 27 April 2020

[1354] T Mulhall, "Where Have All The Hackers Gone? A Study in Motivation, Deterrence and Crime Displacement", in *Computers and Security* v 16 no 4 (1997) pp 277–315

[1355] S Mullender (ed), *'Distributed Systems'*, Addison-Wesley 1993

[1356] E Munro, "Munro review of child protection: final report – a child-centred system", *Department for Education* May 10 2011

[1357] SJ Murdoch, "Browser storage of passwords: a risk or opportunity?" *Light Blue Touchpaper* Apr 18 2006

[1358] SJ Murdoch, "Hot or Not: Revealing Hidden Services by their Clock Skew", in *13th ACM Conference on Computer and Communications Security*, 2006

[1359] SJ Murdoch, "The role of software engineering in electronic elections", *Light Blue Touchpaper* Jul 13 2007

[1360] SJ Murdoch, *'Covert channel vulnerabilities in anonymity systems'*, PhD Thesis, Cambridge 2007

[1361] SJ Murdoch, "Embassy email accounts breached by unencrypted passwords", *Light Blue Touchpaper* Sep 10 2007

[1362] SJ Murdoch, "Comparison of Tor Datagram Designs", *Tor Tech Report 2011-11-001*, Nov 7 2011

[1363] SJ Murdoch, "UK Parliament on protecting consumers from economic crime", *Bentham's Gaze* Nov 5 2019

[1364] SJ Murdoch, RJ Anderson, "Verified by Visa and MasterCard SecureCode, or How Not to Design Authentication", *Financial Cryptography* (2010)

[1365] SJ Murdoch, G Danezis, "Low-Cost Traffic Analysis of Tor", in *IEEE Symposium on Security and Privacy* (2005)

[1366] SJ Murdoch, S Drimer, RJ Anderson, M Bond, "Chip and PIN is Broken", *IEEE Symposium on Security and Privacy* (2010)

[1367] SJ Murdoch, Piotr Zieliński, "Sampled Traffic Analysis by Internet-Exchange-Level Adversaries", at PETS 2007

[1368] K Murdock, D Oswald, FD Garcia, J Van Bulck, D Gruss, F Piessens, "Plundervolt: Software-based Fault Injection Attacks against Intel SGX", at `https://www.plundervolt.com` (2019)

[1369] JC Murphy, D Dubbel, R Benson, "Technology Approaches to Currency Security", in *Optical Security and Counterfeit Deterrence Techniques II* (1998), IS&T and SPIE v 3314 pp 21–28

[1370] K Murray, "Protection of computer programs in Ireland", in *Computer Law and Security Report* v 12 no 3 (May/June 96) pp 57–59

[1371] O Mutlu, JS Kim, "RowHammer: A Retrospective", *arXiv:1904.09724* Apr 22 2019

[1372] R Nader, *'Unsafe at Any Speed: The Designed-In Dangers of The American Automobile'*, Grossman 1965

[1373] A Nadler, A Aminov, A Shabtai, "Detection of Malicious and Low Throughput Data Exfiltration Over the DNS Protocol", *arXiv 1709.08395*

[1374] A Nadkarni, B Andow, W Enck, S Jha, "Practical DIFC Enforcement on Android", *Usenix Security* (2016)

[1375] S Nagaraja, RJ Anderson, "The Topology of Covert Conflict", *Fifth Workshop on the Economics of Information Security* (2006)

[1376] S Nagaraja, RJ Anderson, "The snooping dragon: social-malware surveillance of the Tibetan movement", *University of Cambridge Computer Laboratory Technical Report 746* (2009)

[1377] S Nakamoto, "Bitcoin: A Peer-to-Peer Electronic Cash System", `http://bitcoin.org/bitcoin.pdf` (2008)

[1378] E Nakashima, "Verizon Says It Turned Over Data Without Court Orders", in *The Washington Post* Oct 16 2007

[1379] E Nakashima, "A Story of Surveillance – Former Technician 'Turning In' AT&T Over NSA Program", in *The Washington Post* Nov 7 2007

[1380] E Nakashima, "FBI Prepares Vast Database Of Biometrics – $1 Billion Project to Include Images of Irises and Faces", in *The Washington Post* Dec 22 2007

[1381] E Nakashima, "Confidential report lists U.S. weapons system designs compromised by Chinese cyber-spies" in *The Washington Post* May 27 2013

[1382] Major General RFH Nalder, *'History of the Royal Corps of Signals'*, published by the Royal Signals Institution (1958)

[1383] *Napster*, `http://en.wikipedia.org/wiki/Napster`

[1384] A Narayanan, "How to recognize AI snake oil", *Arthur Miller lecture on science and ethics, Massachusetts Institute of Technology*, Nov 18 2019

[1385] A Narayanan, J Bonneau, E Felten, A Miller, S Goldfeder, *'Bitcoin and Cryptocurrency Technologies'*, Princeton University Press, 2016

[1386] A Narayanan, V Shmatikov, "How To Break Anonymity of the Netflix Prize Dataset", (Nov 2007) at `http://arxiv.org/abs/cs/0610105`

[1387] M Nash, "MS Security VP Mike Nash Replies", on *Slashdot* Jan 26 2006, at `http://interviews.slashdot.org/interviews/06/01/26/131246.shtml`

[1388] M Nash, R Kennett, "Implementing Security policy in a Large Defence Procurement", in *12th ACSAC*, 1996, pp 15–23

[1389] B Nassi, Y Pirutin, A Shamir Y Elovici, B Zadov, "Lamphone – Real-Time Passive Sound Recovery from Light Bulb Vibrations", *BlackHat USA* (2020)

[1390] National Academies of Sciences, Engineering and Medicine, *'Securing the Vote: Protecting American Democracy'*, National Academies Press (2018)

[1391] National Audit Office, *'Ministry of Defence: Combat Identification'*, 2002

[1392] National Audit Office, *'The National Programme for IT in the NHS: an update on the delivery of detailed care records systems'* May 18 2011

[1393] National Audit Office, *'Rolling out smart meters'*, Nov 23 2018

[1394] National Audit Office, *'Investigation into Verify'*, Mar 5 2019

[1395] National Cyber Security Centre, *'Annual Review 2019'*

[1396] National Highway Traffic Safety Administration, *'Special Crash Investigations: On-Site Automated Driver Assistance System Crash Investigation of the 2015 Tesla Model S 70D'*, Report No. DOT HS 812 481, 2018

[1397] National Institute of Standards and Technology, archive of publications on computer security, `http://csrc.nist.gov/publications/history/index.html`

[1398] National Institute of Standards and Technology, *'Common Criteria for Information Technology Security Evaluation'*, Version 2.0 / ISO IS 15408 (May 1998); Version 3.1 (Sep 2006–Sep 2007), at `http://www.commoncriteriaportal.org`

[1399] National Institute of Standards and Technology, *'Data Encryption Standard (DES)'* FIPS 46-3, Nov 1999 incorporating upgrade to triple DES

[1400] National Institute of Standards and Technology, *'Escrowed Encryption Standard'*, FIPS 185, Feb 1994

[1401] National Institute of Standards and Technology, *'Security Requirements for Cryptographic Modules'* (11/1/1994)

[1402] National Institute of Standards and Technology, *'SKIPJACK and KEA Algorithms'*, Jun 23 1998, `http://csrc.nist.gov/encryption/skipjack-kea.htm`

[1403] National Institute of Standards and Technology, *'Advanced Encryption Standard'*, FIPS 197, Nov 26, 2001

[1404] National Institute of Standards and Technology, *'Digital Signature Standard (DSS)'*, FIPS 186-2, Jan 2000, with change notice Oct 2001

[1405] National Institute of Standards and Technology, *'Digital Signature Standard (DSS)'*, FIPS 186-3, draft, Mar 2006

[1406] National Institute of Standards and Technology, *'Recommendation for Block Cipher Modes of Operation'*, Special Publication 800-38A 2001 Edition

[1407] National Institute of Standards and Technology, *'Recommendation for Block Cipher Modes of Operation: The CMAC Mode for Authentication'*, Special Publication 800–38B, May 2005

[1408] National Institute of Standards and Technology, *'Recommendation for Block Cipher Modes of Operation: The CCM Mode for Authentication and Confidentiality'*, Special Publication 800–38C, May 2004

[1409] National Institute of Standards and Technology, *'Recommendation for Block Cipher Modes of Operation: Galois/Counter Mode (GCM) and GMAC'*, NIST Special Publication 800–38D, November 2007

[1410] National Institute of Standards and Technology, *'Recommendation for Key Management – Part 1: General (Revised)*, Special Publication 800-57, May 2006

[1411] National Institute of Standards and Technology, *'Announcing request for Candidate Algorithm Nominations for a New Cryptographic Hash Algorithm (SHA-3) Family'*, in *Federal Register* v 72 no 212, Nov 2 2007, pp 62212–20

[1412] National Institute of Standards and Technology, "Comments received on NIST's Request for Information regarding 'Government use of standards for security and conformance requirements for cryptographic algorithm and cryptographic module testing and validation programs", *Federal Register Notice 2015-19743* (2018)

[1413] National Research Council, *'Cryptography's Role in Securing the Information Society'*, National Academies Press (1996)

[1414] National Research Council, *'For the Record: Protecting Electronic Health Information'*, National Academies Press (1997)

[1415] National Research Council, *'Strengthening Forensic Science in the United States: A Path Forward'* (2009)

[1416] National Security Agency, *'The NSA Security Manual'*, leaked at `http://www.cl.cam.ac.uk/ftp/users/rja14/nsaman.tex.gz`

[1417] "Interim report", *National Security Commission on Artificial Intelligence*, Nov 2019

[1418] National Statistics, "Protocol on Data Access and Confidentiality", at `http://www.statistics.gov.uk`

[1419] J Naughton, "Forget driverless tech – white-van man will keep on trucking", *The Guardian* Apr 16 2017

[1420] J Naughton, "Facebook's Vassal State", in *Memex 1.1* March 5, 2019

[1421] J Naughton, "The law that helped the internet flourish now undermines democracy", *The Guardian* Dec 21 2019

[1422] P Naur, B Randell, *'Software Engineering – Report on a Conference'*, NATO Scientific Affairs Division, Garmisch 1968

[1423] Y Nawaz, "Blockchain and Cryptography at JPMorgan Chase", *Financial Cryptography 2018*, at `https://www.lightbluetouchpaper.org/2018/02/26/financial-cryptography-2018/`

[1424] R Neame, "Managing Health Data Privacy and Security", in [64] pp 225–232

[1425] RM Needham, "Denial of Service: An Example", in *Communications of the ACM* v 37 no 11 (Nov 94) pp 42–46

[1426] RM Needham, "Naming", in [1355], pp 318–127

[1427] RM Needham, "The Hardware Environment", in *Proceedings of the 1999 IEEE Symposium on Security and Privacy* p 236

[1428] RM Needham, MD Schroeder, "Using Encryption for Authentication in Large Networks of Computers", in *Communications of the ACM* v 21 no 12 (Dec 78) pp 993–999

[1429] U Neisser, *'Cognition and reality: Principles and implications of cognitive psychology'*, Freeman, 1976

[1430] M Nesbitt, "Deep Chain Reorganization Detected on Ethereum Classic (ETC)", *Coinbase blog* Jan 7 2019

[1431] P Neumann, *'Computer Related Risks'*, Addison-Wesley 1995

[1432] P Neumann, *'Principled Assuredly Trustworthy Composable Architectures'*, CHATS Project final report (2004), at `http://www.csl.sri.com/users/neumann/`

[1433] J Neumann, "A Taxonomy of Moats", *Reaction Wheel* Sep 19, 2019

[1434] New South Wales Supreme Court, RTA v. Mitchell, New South Wales Supreme Court, Mar 24 2006, reported in "Australia: NSW Supreme Court Backs Away from Camera Decision", `http://www.thenewspaper.com/news/10/1037.asp`

[1435] MEJ Newman, "The structure and function of complex networks", in *SIAM Review* v 45 no 2 (2003) pp 167–256

[1436] MEJ Newman, "Modularity and community structure in networks", in *Proc. Natl. Acad. Sci. USA* v 103 pp 8577–8582 (2006); at `http://arxiv.org/abs/physics/0602124`

[1437] O Newman, *'Defensible Space: People and Design in the Violent City'*, MacMillan 1972

[1438] R Newman, S Gavette, L Yonge, RJ Anderson, "Protecting Domestic Power-line Communications", in *SOUPS* 2006 pp 122–132

[1439] R Newman, S Gavette, L Yonge, RJ Anderson, "HomePlug AV Security Mechanisms", *2007 IEEE International Symposium on Power Line Communications and Its Applications*

[1440] C Newton, "The Trauma Floor", *The Verge*, Feb 25, 2019

[1441] C Newton, "Mark Zuckerberg says Facebook will shift to emphasize encrypted ephemeral messages", *The Verge*, Mar 6 2019

[1442] J Newton, "Countering the counterfeiters", in *Cards International* (21/12/94) p 12

[1443] J Newton, *'Organised Plastic Counterfeiting'*, HMSO 1996

[1444] "The Vanishing Salad Oil: A $100 Million Mystery", *New York Times* Jan 6 1964

[1445] Nex, "The New Old Frontier of Interception", *Newsletter blog* Jul 28 2020

[1446] Andrew Ng, "How the Equifax hack happened, and what still needs to be done", *Cnet* Sep 7 2018

[1447] S Nichols "Silence of the WANs: FBI DDoS-for-hire greaseball takedowns slash web flood attacks 'by 11%'" *The Register* 19 Mar 2019

[1448] S Nichols "Apple drops a bomb on long-life HTTPS certificates: Safari to snub new security certs valid for more than 13 months", *The Register* Feb 20 2019

[1449] SJ Nightingale, H Farid, "Assessing the reliability of a clothing-based forensic identification", *PNAS* Jan 15 2020

[1450] N Nisan, T Roughgarden, E Tardos, VV Vazirani, *'Algorithmic Mechanism Design'*, CUP 2007

[1451] A Nixon, "Fraudsters Taught Us that Identity is Broken", *Financial Cryptography 2020* Feb 2 2020, at `https://www.lightbluetouchpaper.org/2020/02/10/fc-2020/`

[1452] K Nohl, D Evans, H Plötz, "Reverse-Engineering a Cryptographic RFID Tag", *Usenix Security 2008*; earlier version at Chaos Computer Congress 2007

[1453] DA Norman, "Cautious Cars and Cantankerous Kitchens: How Machines Take Control", chapter 1 of *The Design of Future Things* (2009)

[1454] A Noroozian, J Koenders, E Van Veldhuizen, CH Ganan, S Alrwais, D McCoy, M Van Eeten, "Platforms in everything: analyzing ground-truth data on the anatomy and economics of bullet-proof hosting", *USENIX Security 2019* pp 1341–1356

[1455] R v Ipswich Crown Court ex parte NTL Ltd, [2002] EWHC 1585 (Admin), at `http://www.cyber-rights.org/documents/ntl_case.htm`

[1456] *'White Paper – 5G Evolution and 6G'*, NTT Docomo, January 2020

[1457] Nuclear Regulatory Commission, US Government, `www.nrc.gov`

[1458] H Nugent, "Adulterers who call 118 118 for an affair", in *The Times*, May 27 2006

[1459] F Oberholzer, K Strumpf, "The Effect of File Sharing on Record Sales – An Empirical Analysis", June 2004; journal version F Oberholzer-Gee, K Strumpf, "The Effect of File Sharing on Record Sales: An Empirical Analysis, *Journal of Political Economy* v 115 (2007) pp 1–42

[1460] *'Victimation et Perceptions de la Sûreté'*, Observatoire National de la Délinquance et de Responses Pénales (2017)

[1461] AM Odlyzko, "Tragic loss or good riddance? The impending demise of traditional scholarly journals", *Notices Amer. Math. Soc.*, Jan 1995

[1462] AM Odlyzko, *'The history of communications and its implications for the Internet'*, at `http://www.dtc.umn.edu/~odlyzko/doc/networks.html`

[1463] AM Odlyzko, "Smart and stupid networks: Why the Internet is like Microsoft", *ACM netWorker*, Dec 1998, pp 38–46

[1464] AM Odlyzko, "Privacy, economics, and price discrimination on the Internet", in *ICEC '03: Proceedings of the 5th international conference on electronic commerce*, pp 355–366

[1465] AM Odlyzko, "Pricing and Architecture of the Internet: Historical Perspectives from Telecommunications and Transportation", *TPRC 2004*

[1466] Office of the Director of National Intelligence, *'Statistical Transparency Report Regarding Use of National Security Authorities – Calendar Year 2017'*

[1467] P Ohm, "Broken Promises of Privacy: Responding to the Surprising Failure of Anonymization", *UCLA Law Review* v 57 (2010) pp 1701–77

[1468] S O'Kane, "Daimler fined nearly $1 billion for selling cars that cheated emissions tests", *The Verge*, Sep 24 2019

[1469] N Okuntsev, *'Windows NT Security'*, R&D Books 1999

[1470] *"Nicht nachmachen: Dieser Vignetten-Trick kostet Sie 300 Euro"*, *Online Focus*, June 12 2015

[1471] Open Net Initiative, *'Internet Filtering in China in 2004-2005: A Country Study'*, April 14, 2005, at `https://opennet.net/`

[1472] Open Net Initiative, *'China (including Hong Kong)'*, Country report 2006, at `https://opennet.net/`

[1473] Open Net Initiative, *'Pulling the Plug'*, Oct 2007, at `https://opennet.net/research/bulletins/013`

[1474] Open Rights Group, *'May 2007 Election Report – Findings of the Open Rights Group Election Observation Mission in Scotland and England'*, at `http://www.openrightsgroup.org/e-voting-main`

[1475] A Orben, T Dienlin, AK Przybylski, "Social media's enduring effect on adolescent life satisfaction", *PNAS* April 16 2019

[1476] A Orlowski, "Schrems busts Privacy Shield wide open", *The Register*, Oct 3 2017

[1477] A Orlowski, "UK spy agency warns Brit telcos to flee from ZTE gear", *The Register* April 16 2018

[1478] Organization for Economic Cooperation & Development, *'Guidelines for the Protections of Privacy and Transborder Flow of Personal Data'*, OECD Doc No C(80)58 (1981)

[1479] Organization for Economic Cooperation & Development, *'CO4.4: Teenage suicides (15-19 years old)'* OECD Family Database (2017)

[1480] M Orozco, Y Asfaw, A Adler, S Shirmohammadi, A El Saddik, "Automatic Identification of Participants in Haptic Systems", in *IEEE Instrumentation and Measurement Technology Conference* (2005) pp 888–892

[1481] B Osborn, J McWilliams, B Beyer, M Saltonstall, "BeyondCorp – Design to Deployment at Google", *;login:* (Spring 2016) v 41 no 1

[1482] C Osborne, "University of California SF pays ransomware hackers $1.14 million to salvage research", *ZDNet*, Jun 30 2020

[1483] C Osborne, "In one click: Amazon Alexa could be exploited for theft of voice history, PII, skill tampering", *ZDNet*, Aug 13 2020

[1484] J Osen, "The Cream of Other Men's Wit: Plagiarism and Misappropriation in Cyberspace", in *Computer Fraud and Security Bulletin* (11/97) pp 13–19

[1485] DA Osvik, A Shamir, E Tromer, "Cache attacks and countermeasures: the case of AES," in *RSA Conference Cryptographers Track* 2006, LNCS 3860, pp 1–20

[1486] D Oswald, C Paar, "Breaking Mifare DESFire MF3ICD40: Power Analysis and Templates in the Real World", *CHes 2011* pp 207–222

[1487] *Out-law News*, "SWIFT broke data protection law, says Working Party", Nov 27 2006, at `http://www.out-law.com/page-7518`

[1488] *Out-law News*, "SWIFT will stop some US processing in 2009", Oct 15 2007, at `http://www.out-law.com/page-8548`

[1489] A Ozment, S Schechter, "Bootstrapping the Adoption of Internet Security Protocols", at *Workshop on the Economics of Information Security*, 2006

[1490] A Ozment, S Schechter, "Milk or Wine: Does Software Security Improve with Age?" in *15th Usenix Security Symposium* (2006)

[1491] D Page, *'Theoretical Use of Cache Memory as a Cryptanalytic Side-Channel'*, Technical Report CSTR-02-003, University of Bristol, June 2002

[1492] G Pahl, W Beitz, *'Konstruktionslehre'*; translated as *'Engineering Design: A Systematic Approach'*, Springer 1999

[1493] S Pancho, "Paradigm shifts in protocol analysis", in *Proceedings of the 1999 New Security Paradigms Workshop*, ACM (2000), pp 70–79

[1494] A Papadimoulis, "Wish-It-Was Two-Factor", Sep 20 2007, at `http://worsethanfailure.com/Articles/WishItWas-TwoFactor-.aspx`

[1495] N Papernot, "A Marauder's Map of Security and Privacy in Machine Learning", *arXiv 1811.01134* Nov 3 2018

[1496] DJ Parker, "DVD Copy Protection: An Agreement At Last? – Protecting Intellectual Property Rights In The Age Of Technology", in *Tape/Disc Magazine* (Oct 96)

[1497] C Parsons, A Molnar, J Dalek, J Knockel, M Kenyon, B Haselton, C Khoo, R Deibert, *'The Predator in Your Pocket: A Multidisciplinary Assessment of the Stalkerware Application Industry'*, Munk School, June 12 2019

[1498] N Partridge, *'Data Release review'*, Department of Health, June 2014

[1499] J Pastor,"CRYPTOPOST – A cryptographic application to mail processing", in *Journal of Cryptology* v 3 no 2 (Jan 1991) pp 137–146

[1500] S Pastrana, G Suarez-Tangil, "A First Look at the Crypto-Mining Malware Ecosystem: A Decade of Unrestricted Wealth", *arXiv:1901.00846* Jan 3 2019

[1501] S Pastrana, DR Thomas, A Hutchings, R Clayton, "CrimeBB: Enabling Cybercrime Research on Underground Forums at Scale", World Wide Web Conference (2018) pp 1845–1854

[1502] K Paul, "Twitter employees charged with spying for Saudi Arabia", *The Guardian* Nov 6 2019

[1503] R Paul, "Leaked Media Defender e-mails reveal secret government project", *Ars Technica* Sep 16 2007

[1504] LC Paulson, "Inductive analysis of the Internet protocol TLS", in *Security Protocols 1998* and *ACM Transactions on Computer and System Security* v 2 no 3 (1999) pp 332–351

[1505] V Paxson, "An Analysis of Using Reflectors for Distributed Denial-of-Service Attacks", in *Computer Communication Review* v 31 no 3, July 2001

[1506] M Payer, *'Software Security – Principles, Policies and Protection'* 2019

[1507] S Pearman, J Thomas, P Emani Naeini, H Habib, L Bauer, N Christin, L Faith Cranor, S Egelman, A Forget, "Let's go in for a closer look: Observing passwords in their natural habitat", *CCS 2017*

[1508] J Pearson 2020, "Exclusive: Facebook agreed to censor posts after Vietnam slowed traffic – sources", *Thnomson Reuters* Apr 21 2020

[1509] PeckShield, "bZx Hack Full Disclosure (With Detailed Profit Analysis)", *Medium* Feb 17 2020

[1510] C Percival, "Cache Missing for Fun and Profit", *BSDCan* 2005

[1511] J Pereira, "Breaking the Code: How Credit-Card Data Went Out Wireless Door", in *The Wall Street Journal*, May 4 2007, p A1

[1512] N Perlroth, S Shane, "In Baltimore and Beyond, a Stolen N.S.A. Tool Wreaks Havoc", in *New York Times* May 25 2019

[1513] A Perrig, *'A Copyright Protection Environment for Digital Images'*, Diploma thesis, École Polytechnique Fédérale de Lausanne (1997)

[1514] T Perrin, M Marlinspike, "The Double Ratchet Algorithm", `https://signal.org/docs/specifications/` Nov 20 2016

[1515] P Pesic, "The Clue to the Labyrinth: Francis Bacon and the Decryption of Nature", in *Cryptologia* v XXIV no 3 (July 2000) pp 193–211

[1516] M Peters, "MTN moves to prevent SIM card swap fraud", *IOL*, Dec 30 2007

[1517] I Peterson, "From Counting to Writing", MathLand Archives, `http://www.maa.org/mathland/mathland_2_24.html`

[1518] FAP Petitcolas, RJ Anderson, MG Kuhn, "Attacks on Copyright Marking Systems", in *Information Hiding* (1998) Springer LNCS v 1525 pp 219–239

[1519] FAP Petitcolas, RJ Anderson, MG Kuhn, "Information Hiding – A Survey", in *Proceedings of the IEEE* v 87 no 7 (July 1999) pp 1062–1078

[1520] H Petroski, *'To Engineer is Human'*, Barnes and Noble Books (1994)

[1521] A Peyton, "Ethereum Classic hit by another 51% hack", *Fintech Direct*, Aug 6 2020

[1522] A Pfitzmann, *Proceedings of the Third International Workshop on Information Hiding* (1999), Springer LNCS v 1768

[1523] B Pfitzmann, "Information Hiding Terminology", in *Information Hiding* (1996) Springer LNCS v 1174 pp 347–350

[1524] T Philippon, *'The Great Reversal – How America Gave up on Free Markets'*, Harvard 2019

[1525] PJ Phillips, AN Yates, Y Hu, CA Hahn, E Noyes, K Jackson, JG Cavazos, G Jeckeln, R Ranjan, S Sankaranarayanan, JC Chen, CD Castillo, R Chellappa, D White, AJ O'Toole, "Face recognition accuracy of forensic examiners, superrecognizers, and face recognition algorithms", *PNAS* June 12 2018 v 115 no 24 pp 6171–6176

[1526] Z Phillips, "Security Theater", in *Government Executive* Aug 1, 2007, at `http://www.govexec.com/features/0807-01/0807-01s3.htm`

[1527] GE Pickett, "How do you select the 'right' security feature(s) for your company's products?", in *Optical Security and Counterfeit Deterrence Techniques II* (1998), IS&T (The Society for Imaging Science and Technology) and SPIE (The International Society for Optical Engineering) v 3314

[1528] RL Pickholtz, DL Schilling, LB Milstein, "Theory of Spread Spectrum Communications – A Tutorial", in *IEEE Transactions on Communications* v TC-30 no 5 (May 1982) pp 855–884

[1529] RL Pickholtz, DB Newman, YQ Zhang, M Tatebayashi, "Security Analysis of the INTELSAT VI and VII Command Network", in *IEEE Proceedings on Selected Areas in Communications* v 11 no 5 (June 1993) pp 663–672

[1530] L Pinault, *'Consulting Demons'*, Collins 2000

[1531] S Pinto, N Santos, "Demystifying Arm TrustZone: A Comprehensive Survey", *ACM Computing Surveys* v 51 no 6 (Feb 2019)

[1532] JC Plantin, G de Seta, "WeChat as infrastructure: the techno-nationalist shaping of Chinese digital platforms", *Chinese Journal of Communication* v 12 no 3 (2019) pp 257–273

[1533] RA Poisel, *'Modern Communications Jamming Principles and Techniques'*, Artech House 2003

[1534] *Politech* mailing list, was at `http://www.politechbot.com/`

[1535] GJ Popek, RP Goldberg, "Formal Requirements for Virtualizable Third Generation Architectures", in *Communications of the ACM* v 17 no 7 (July 1974) pp 412–421

[1536] E Porter, "The Facebook Fallacy: Privacy Is Up to You", *New York Times* Apr 24 2018

[1537] R Porter, "Google fined €50 million for GDPR violation in France", *The Verge* Jan 21 2019

[1538] B Poser, "The Provenzano Code", in *Language Log*, Apr 21, 2006; at `http://itre.cis.upenn.edu/~myl/languagelog/archives/003049.html`

[1539] Richard Posner, "An Economic Theory of Privacy", in *Regulation* (1978) pp 19–26

[1540] Richard Posner, "Privacy, Secrecy and Reputation", in *Buffalo Law Review* v 28 no 1 (1979)

[1541] F Postma, "Military And Intelligence Personnel Can Be Tracked With The Untappd Beer App", *Bellingcat* May 18, 2020

[1542] K Poulsen, "ATM Reprogramming Caper Hits Pennsylvania", in *Wired*, July 12 2007

[1543] S Poulter, "Phone firm's whistleblower says his life has been made a misery", in *The Daily Mail* Jun 21 2007

[1544] J Powles, "DeepMind's Latest A.I. Health Breakthrough Has Some Problems", *Medium* Aug 8 2019

[1545] J Powles, H Hodson, "Google DeepMind and healthcare in an age of algorithms", *Health and Technology* v 7 no 4 (Dec 2017) pp 351–367

[1546] S Prasad, E Bouma-Sims, AK Mylappan, B Reaves, "Who's Calling? Characterising Robocalls thorugh Audio and Metadata Analysis", *Usenix Security 2020*

[1547] J Preece, H Sharp, Y Rogers, *'Interaction design: beyond human-computer interaction'*, Wiley 2002

[1548] B Preneel, PC van Oorschot, "MDx-MAC and Building Fast MACs from Hash Functions", in *Advances in Cryptology – Crypto 95*, Springer LNCS v 963 pp 1–14

[1549] President's Council of Advisers on Science and Technology, *'Big Data and Privacy: A technological perspective'*, May 1 2014

[1550] Press Association, "Hatton Garden ringleader 'Basil' found guilty over £14m heist", *The Guardian* Mar 15 2019

[1551] L Presser, M Hruskova, H Rowbottom, J Kancir, "Care.data and access to UK health records: patient privacy and public trust", *Journal of Technology Science* Aug 8 2015

[1552] RS Pressman, *'Software Engineering: A Practitioner's Approach'*, McGraw-Hill 2000

[1553] V Prevelakis, D Spinellis, "The Athens Affair", *IEEE Spectrum*, July 2007

[1554] H Pringle, "The Cradle of Cash", in *Discover* v 19 no 10 (Oct 1998)

[1555] C Prins, "Biometric Technology Law", in *The Computer Law and Security Report* v 14 no 3 (May/Jun 98) pp 159–165

[1556] W Pritchard, "Lockdown was a boon for Spotify. Now musicians are fighting back", *Wired*, Jul 19 2020

[1557] Privacy International, *'Who's That Knocking at My Door? Understanding Surveillance in Thailand'*, 2017

[1558] Privacy International, *'A technical look at Phone Extraction'* 2019

[1559] S Proctor, EY Wassermann, J Hatcliff, "SAFE and Secure: Deeply Integrating Security in a New Hazard Analysis", *SAW 2017*

[1560] S Protière, A Boudaoud, Y Couder, "Particle-wave association on a fluid interface", in *Journal of Fluid Mechanics* v 554 no 10 (2006) pp 85–108

[1561] A Pruneda, "Windows Media Technologies: Using Windows Media Rights Manager to Protect and Distribute Digital Media", *MSDN Magazine*, Dec 2001, at `http://msdn.microsoft.com/msdnmag/issues/01/12/DRM/`

[1562] Public Accounts Committee, *'Public Accounts Committee – Nineteenth Report: The dismantled National Programme for IT in the NHS'*, July 2013

[1563] Public Accounts Committee, *'Ministry of Defence nuclear programme'*, Sep 2018

[1564] *Public Lending Right* (PLR), at `http://www.writers.org.uk/guild/Crafts/Books/PLRBody.html`

[1565] Public Record Office, *'Functional Requirements for Electronic Record Management Systems'*, November 1999

[1566] RD Putnam, *'Bowling Alone: the Collapse and Revival of American Community'*, Simon & Schuster, 2000

[1567] T Pyszczynski, S Solomon, J Greenberg, *'In the Wake of 9/11 – the Psychology of Terror'*, American Psychological Association 2003

[1568] Quality Control Systems Corporation, *'NHTSA's Implausible Safety Claim for Tesla's Autosteer Driver Assistance System'*, Feb 8 2019

[1569] B Quinn, J Ball, Rushe, "GCHQ chief accuses US tech giants of becoming terrorists' 'networks of choice' ", *The Guardian* Nov 3 2014

[1570] Z Quinn, *'Crash Override'*, Hachette 2017

[1571] JJ Quisquater, D Samyde, "ElectroMagnetic Analysis (EMA): Measures and Counter-Measures for Smart Cards", in *International Conference on Research in Smart Cards*, Springer LNCS v 2140 pp 200–210

[1572] R v Paul Matthew Stubbs, [2006] EWCA Crim 2312 (12 October 2006), at `http://www.bailii.org/cgi-bin/markup.cgi?doc=/ew/cases/EWCA/Crim/2006/2312.html`

[1573] H Ragab, A Milburn, K Razavi, H Bos, C Giuffrida, "CrossTalk: Speculative Data Leaks Across Cores Are Real", *IEEE symposium on Security & Privacy* (2021)

[1574] M Raghavan, S Barocas, J Kleinberg, K Levy, "Mitigating Bias in Algorithmic Hiring: Evaluating Claims and Practices", *arXiv:1906.09208* Jun 21 2019

[1575] Rain Forest Puppy, "Issue disclosure policy v1.1", at `http://www.wiretrip.net/rfp/policy.html`

[1576] R Ramesh, "NHS England patient data 'uploaded to Google servers', Tory MP says" *The Guardian* Mar 3 2014

[1577] R Ramesh, "Online tool could be used to identify public figures' medical care, say critics" *The Guardian* Mar 17 2014

[1578] A Randal, "The Ideal Versus the Real: Revisiting the History of Virtual Machines and Containers", arXiv:1904.12226, Apr 27 2019

[1579] M Randolph, W Diehl, "Power Side-Channel Attack Analysis: A Review of 20 Years of Study for the Layman", *Cryptography* v 4 no 15 (2020)

[1580] J Rankin, "EU says China behind 'huge wave' of Covid-19 disinformation", *The Guardian* Jun 10 2020

[1581] W Rankl, W Effing, *'Smartcard Handbook'*, Wiley (1997); translated from *'Handbuch der Chpkarten'*, Carl Hanser Verlag (1995)

[1582] S Ransbotham, "An Empirical Analysis of Exploitation Attempts based on Vulnerabilities in Open Source Software", WEIS 2010

[1583] S Rashid, "Breaking the Ledger Security Model", *https://saleemrashid.com/* Mar 20, 2018

[1584] FY Rashid, "Proposal to make https certificate expire yearly back on the table", *Decipher* Aug 15 2019

[1585] B Ray, "How I hacked SIM cards with a single text – and the networks DON'T CARE", *The Register* Sep 23 2013

[1586] ES Raymond, "The Case of the Quake Cheats", 27/12/1999, at `http://www.catb.org/~esr/writings/quake-cheats.html`

[1587] ES Raymond, *'The Cathedral and the Bazaar'*, at `http://www.catb.org/~esr/writings/cathedral-bazaar/`

[1588] ES Raymond, *'The Magic Cauldron'*, June 1999, at `http://www.catb.org/~esr/writings/magic-cauldron/magic-cauldron.html`

[1589] A Razaghpanah, R Nithyanand, N Vallina-Rodriguez, S Sundaresan, M Allman, C Kreibich, P Gill, "Apps, Trackers, Privacy, and Regulators: A Global Study of the Mobile Tracking Ecosystem", *NDSS 2018*

[1590] K Razavi, B Gras, E Bosman, B Preneel, C Giuffrida, H Bos, "Flip Feng Shui: Hammering a Needle in the Software Stack", *USENIX Security* 2016

[1591] J Reardon, Á Feal, AE Bar On, N Valina-Rodriguez, S Egelman, "50 Ways to Leak Your Data: An Exploration of Apps' Circumvention of the Android Permissions System", *Usenix Security 2019*

[1592] J Reason, *'Human Error'*, Cambridge University Press 1990

[1593] MG Reed, PF Syverson, DM Goldschlag, "Anonymous Connections and Onion Routing", in *IEEE Journal on Special Areas in Communications* v 16 no 4 (May 98) pp 482–494

[1594] EM Redmiles, "Quality and Inequity in Digital Security Education", PhD Thesis, University of Maryland, 2019

[1595] J Rees, "Facial recognition use by South Wales Police ruled unlawful", *BBC News*, Aug 11 2020

[1596] P Reidy, "MH17: five of the most bizarre conspiracy theories", *The Guardian* Jul 22 2014

[1597] Reporters without Borders, *'Handbook for Bloggers and Cyber-dissidents'*, 2005, at `http://www.rsf.org/rubrique.php3?id_rubrique=542`

[1598] E Rescorla, *'SSL and TLS – Designing and Building Secure Systems'*, Addison-Wesley 2000

[1599] E Rescorla, "Is Finding Security Holes a Good Idea?", *Third Workshop on the Economics of Information Security* (2004)

[1600] *Reuters*, "No Surveillance Tech for Tampa", in *Wired* Aug 21 2003, at `http://www.wired.com/politics/law/news/2003/08/60140`

[1601] M Reynolds, "The strange story of Section 230, the obscure law that created our flawed, broken internet", *Wired* Mar 24 2019

[1602] I Reyes, P Wijesekera, J Reardon, A Elazari Bar On, A Razaghpanah, N Vallina-Rodriguez, S Egelman, "'Won't Somebody Think of the Children?' Examining COPPA Compliance at Scale", *Proceedings on Privacy Enhancing Technologies* (2018) pp 63–83

[1603] M Richards, R Anderson, S Hinde, J Kaye, A Lucassen, P Matthews, M Parker, M Shotter, G Watts, S Wallace, J Wise, *'The collection, linking and use of data in biomedical research and health care: ethical issues'*, Nuffield Bioethics Council, Feb 2015

[1604] D Richardson, *'Techniques and Equipment of Electronic Warfare'*, Salamander Books 1985

[1605] T Richter, S Escher, D Schönfeld, T Strufe, "Forensic Analysis and Anonymisation of Printed Documents", *IH&MMSec '18* pp 127–138

[1606] LW Ricketts, JE Bridges, J Miletta, *'EMP Radiation and Protection Techniques'*, Wiley 1975

[1607] M Ridley, *'The Red Queen: Sex and the Evolution of Human Nature'*, Viking Books 1993

[1608] G Rippon, *'The Gendered Brain'*, Bodley Head 2019

[1609] J Risen, E Lichtblau, "Bush Lets U.S. Spy on Callers Without Courts", *New York Times* Dec 16, 2005

[1610] RL Rivest, A Shamir, L Adleman, "A Method for Obtaining Digital Signatures and Public-Key Cryptosystems", in *Communications of the ACM* v 21 no 2 (Feb 1978) pp 120–126

[1611] RL Rivest, J Wack, "On the notion of 'software independence' in voting systems", *Philosophical Transactions of The Royal Society A* v 366 no 1881 pp 3759–67 (Nov 2008)

[1612] MB Robinson, "The Theoretical Development of 'CPTED': 25 years of Responses to C. Ray Jeffery", in *Advances in Criminological Theory* v 8; at `http://www.acs.appstate.edu/dept/ps-cj/vitacpted2.html`

[1613] AR Roddy, JD Stosz, "Fingerprint Features – Statistical Analysis and System Performance Estimates", in *Proceedings of the IEEE* v 85 no 9 (Sep 97) pp 1390–1421

[1614] J Rogers, "FAKE FIVER: Shopper's warning after being handed this fake £5 note – but is it counterfeit?", *The Sun* May 13 2018

[1615] WP Rogers, NA Armstrong, DC Acheson, EE Covert, RP Feynman, RB Hotz, DJ Kutyna, SK Ride, RW Rummel, JF Sutter, ABC Walker, AD Wheelon, CB Yeager, AG Keel, *'Report to the President by the Presidential Commission on the Space Shuttle Challenger Accident'* June 6 1986

[1616] R Rohozinski, M Mambetalieva, "Election Monitoring in Kyrgyzstan", 2005, *Open Net Initiative*, at `http://opennet.net/special/kg/`

[1617] E Ronen, C O'Flynn, A Shamir, AO Weingarten, "IoT Goes Nuclear: Creating a ZigBee Chain Reaction", *IACR Eprint 1047* (2016)

[1618] K Rooney, "Majority of bitcoin trading is a hoax, new study finds" *CNBC* Mar 22 2019

[1619] SJ Root, *'Beyond COSO – Internal Control to Enhance Corporate Governance'*, Wiley 1998

[1620] N Rosasco, D Larochelle, "How and Why More Secure Technologies Succeed in Legacy Markets: Lessons from the Success of SSH", in *WEIS 2003*

[1621] S Rose, O Borchert, S Mitchell, S Connelly, "Zero Trust Architecture (2nd Draft)", *SP 800-207(Draft)*, Feb 2020

[1622] M Rosenberg, JE Barnes, "A Bible Burning, a Russian News Agency and a Story Too Good to Check Out", *New York Times*, Aug 11 2020

[1623] B Ross, C Jackson, N Miyake, D Boneh, JC Mitchell, "Stronger Password Authentication Using Browser Extensions", in *Usenix Security 2005*; at `http://crypto.stanford.edu/PwdHash/`

[1624] DE Ross, "Two Signatures", in `comp.risks` v 20.81: `http://catless.ncl.ac.uk/Risks/20.81.html`

[1625] A Roth, "US charges Russian 'Evil Corp' hackers with $100m banking scheme", *The Guardian* Dec 5 2019

[1626] "Card fraud plummets in France", M Rowe, *Banking Technology* (May 94) p 10

[1627] T Rowland, "Ringing up the wrong numbers", in *The Guardian* May 18 2006; at `http://www.guardian.co.uk/media/2006/may/18/newmedia.technology`

[1628] A Roy, N Memon, A Ross "MasterPrint: Exploring the Vulnerability of Partial Fingerprint-Based Authentication Systems", *IEEE Transactions on Information Forensics and Security* v 12 no 9 (Sep 2017) 2013–25

[1629] The Royal Society, *'Strategy options for the UK's separated plutonium'*, Sep 27 2007

[1630] The Royal Society, *'Science as an open enterprise'* June 21 2012

[1631] WW Royce, "Managing the development of Large Software Systems: Concepts and Techniques", in *Proceedings IEEE WESCON* (1970) pp 1–9

[1632] HH Rubinovitz, "Issues Associated with Porting Applications to the Compartmented Mode Workstation", in *ACM SIGSAC* v 12 no 4 (Oct 94) pp 2–5

[1633] RA Rueppel, *'Analysis and Design of Stream Ciphers'*, Springer-Verlag 1986

[1634] RA Rueppel, "Criticism of ISO CD 11166 Banking: Key Management by Means of Asymmetric Algorithms", in *Proceedings of 3rd Symposium of State and Progress of Research in Cryptography*, Fondazione Ugo Bordoni, Rome 1993, pp 191–198

[1635] J Rushby, B Randell, "A Distributed Secure System", in *IEEE Computer* v 16 no 7 (July 83) pp 55–67

[1636] B Russell, Answer to parliamentary question, *Hansard* 10 Jun 2003 column 762W

[1637] J Rutkowska, "Running Vista Every Day!", *Invisible Things Blog*, Feb 2007

[1638] M Ryan, "The NSA Playset: Bluetooth Smart Attack Tools", at *Bluetooth Smart Security*, `http://lacklustre.net/bluetooth/`, 2015

[1639] DR Safford, DL Schales, DK Hess, "The TAMU Security Package: An Ongoing Response to Internet Intruders in an Academic Environment", in *Usenix Security* (1993) pp 91–118

[1640] M Safi, "India's ruling party ordered online abuse of opponents, claims book", *The Guardian* Dec 27 2016

[1641] MJ Salganik, I Lundberg, AT Kindel and others, "Measuring the predictability of life outcomes with a scientific mass collaboration", *Proceedings of the National Academy of Sciences* v 117 no 15 pp 8398–8403, Mar 30 2020

[1642] JH Saltzer, MD Schroeder, "The Protection of Information in Computer Systems", in *Proceedings of the IEEE* v 63 no 9 (Mar 1975) pp 1278–1308

[1643] JH Saltzer, MF Kaashoek, *'Principles of Computer System Design'*, Morgan Kaufman 2009

[1644] RG Saltman, *'Accuracy, Integrity and Security in Computerized Vote-Tallying'*, NBS Special Publication 500–158 (1988)

[1645] J Saltzman, M Daniel, "Man freed in 1997 shooting of officer – Judge gives ruling after fingerprint revelation", in *The Boston Globe* Jan 24 2004

[1646] P Samarati, L Sweeney, "Protecting Privacy when Disclosing Information: k-Anonymity and its Enforcement through Generalization and Suppression", *SRI Tech Report SRI-CSL-98-04* (1998)

[1647] T Sammes, B Jenkinson, *'Forensic Computing – A Practitioner's Guide'*, Springer 2007

[1648] I Sample, "NHS patient records to revolutionise medical research in Britain" *The Guardian* Aug 28 2012

[1649] P Samuelson, "Intellectual Property Rights and the Global Information Economy", in *Communications of the ACM* v 39 no 1 (Jan 96) pp 23–28

[1650] P Samuelson, S Scotchmer, "The Law and Economics of Reverse Engineering", *Yale Law Journal* (2002)

[1651] D Samyde, SP Skorobogatov, RJ Anderson, JJ Quisquater, "On a New Way to Read Data from Memory", in *IEEE Security in Storage Workshop* (2002) pp 65–69

[1652] RS Sandhu, S Jajodia, "Polyinstantiation for Cover Stories", in *Computer Security — ESORICS 92*, LNCS v 648 pp 307–328

[1653] G Sandoval, "Glitches let Net shoppers get free goods", in *CNET News.com*, July 5 2000

[1654] P Sankar, S Mora, JF Merz, NL Jones, "Patient Perspectives of Medical Confidentiality – A Review of the Literature", *J Gen Intern Med* 2003 August vol 18 no 8 pp 659–669

[1655] SANS Institute, "Consensus List of The Top Ten Internet Security Threats", at `http://www.sans.org/`, Version 1.22 June 19, 2000

[1656] DE Sanger, K Benner, "U.S. Accuses North Korea of Plot to Hurt Economy as Spy Is Charged in Sony Hack" *New York Times* Sep 6 2018

[1657] PF Sass, L Gorr, "Communications for the Digitized Battlefield of the 21st Century", in *IEEE Communications* v 33 no 10 (Oct 95) pp 86–95

[1658] E Van der Sar, "BitTorrent 'Copyright Troll' Lawsuits Skyrocket In Sweden", *Torrentfreak* Feb 14 2020

[1659] C Savage, "N.S.A. Phone Program Cost $100 Million, but Produced Only Two Unique Leads", *New York Times* Feb 25 2020

[1660] S Saulny, "118 Charged in A.T.M. Thefts After 9/11", *New York Times*, June 19 2003

[1661] J Scahill, J Begley, "How spies stole the keys to the encryption castle", *The Intercept* Feb 15 2015

[1662] W Schachtman, "How Technology Almost Lost the War: In Iraq, the Critical Networks Are Social – Not Electronic", in *Wired*, Dec 15 2007, at `http://www.wired.com/politics/security/magazine/15-12/ff_futurewar?currentPage=all`

[1663] M Schaefer, "Symbol Security Condition Considered Harmful", in *Proceedings of the 1989 IEEE Symposium on Security and Privacy*, pp 20–46

[1664] DL Schilling, *'Meteor Burst Communications: Theory and Practice'*, Wiley 1993

[1665] DC Schleher, *'Electronic Warfare in the Information Age'*, Artech House 1999

[1666] D Schmandt-Besserat, *'How Writing Came About'*, University of Texas Press 1996

[1667] MN Schmitt, *'Tallinn Manual on the International Law Applicable to Cyber Warfare'*, Cambridge University Press, first edition 2013; second edition 2017

[1668] ZE Schnabel, "The estimation of the total fish population in a lake", in *American Mathematical Monthly* v 45 (1938) pp 348–352

[1669] PM Schneider, "Datenbanken mit genetischen Merkmalen von Straftätern", in *Datenschutz und Datensicherheit* v 22 (6/1998) pp 330–333

[1670] B Schneier, *'Applied Cryptography'*, Wiley (1996)

[1671] B Schneier, "Why Computers are Insecure", in `comp.risks` v 20.67

[1672] B Schneier, *'Secrets and Lies : Digital Security in a Networked World'*, Wiley 2000

[1673] B Schneier, "Semantic Attacks: The Third Wave of Network Attacks", in *Crypto-Gram Newsletter* October 15 2000

[1674] B Schneier, *'Beyond Fear: Thinking Sensibly about Security in an Uncertain World'*, Copernicus Books (2003)

[1675] B Schneier, "Real-World Passwords", in *Crypto-Gram Newsletter* Dec 14, 2006

[1676] B Schneier, "Choosing Secure Passwords", in *Crypto-Gram Newsletter* Aug 7 2007

[1677] B Schneier, "Secure Passwords Keep You Safer, in *Crypto-Gram Newsletter* Jan 11, 2007

[1678] B Schneier, "The Psychology of Security", *RSA Conference* (2007), at `http://www.schneier.com/essay-155.html`

[1679] B Schneier, "Random Number Bug in Debian Linux", May 19 2020

[1680] B Schneier, "Excess Automobile Deaths as a Result of 9/11", Sep 9 2013

[1681] B Schneier, "Evaluating the GCHQ Exceptional Access Proposal", *Lawfare Blog* Jan 17 2019

[1682] B Schneier, *'The Originality Engine – How Hacking Changes the World, for Better and for Worse'*, to appear in 2021; Bruce announced this book at the 2020 Workshop on Security and Human Behaviour, liveblogged at `https://www.lightbluetouchpaper.org/2020/06/18/security-and-human-behaviour-2020/`

[1683] B Schneier, A Shostack, "Breaking up is Hard to Do: Modeling Security Threats for Smart Cards," in *USENIX Workshop on Smart Card Technology* 1999, pp 175–185

[1684] M Schnyder, "Datenfluesse im Gesundheitswesen", in *in Symposium für Datenschutz und Informationssicherheit*, Zuerich, Oct 98

[1685] RA Scholtz, "Origins of Spread-Spectrum Communications", in *IEEE Transactions on Communications* v TC-30 no 5 (May 1982) pp 822–854

[1686] M Schrems, "CJEU Judgment – First Statement", `https://noyb.eu` July 16 2020

[1687] MD Schroeder, *'Cooperation of Mutually Suspicious Subsystems in a Computer Utility'*, MIT PhD Thesis, September 1972, Project MAC Technical Report MAC TR-104 `http://hdl.handle.net/ncstrl.mit_lcs/MIT/LCS/TR-104`

[1688] Schumpeter, "Live-streaming will change rock 'n' roll for the better", *The Economist*, Jun 17 2020

[1689] Schumpeter, "Why companies struggle with recalcitrant IT", *The Economist*, Jul 18 2020

[1690] K Schwab, "How googly eyes solved one of today's trickiest UX problems" *Fast Company* Aug 27 2019

[1691] M Schwarz, S Weiser, D Gruss, "Practical Enclave Malware with Intel SGX", *arXiv:1902.03256* Feb 8, 2019

[1692] M Schwarz, S Weiser, D Gruss, C Maurice, S Mangard, "Malware Guard Extension: abusing Intel SGX to conceal cache attacks", *Cybersecurity* v 3 (2020)

[1693] N Scola. "Kamala Harris' Crusade Against 'Revenge Porn' ", *Politico* Feb 1 2019

[1694] M Scorgie, "Untapped sources for accountants" in *Genizah Fragments* (The Newsletter of Cambridge University's Taylor-Schechter Genizah Research Unit) no 29 (April 1995), at `http://www.lib.cam.ac.uk/Taylor-Schechter/GF/GF29.html`

[1695] J Scott-Railton, A Hulcoop, B Abdul Razzak, B Marczak, S Anstis, R Deibert, "Dark Basin – Uncovering a Massive Hack-For-Hire Operation", *Citizen Lab* June 9 2020

[1696] Beale Screamer, "Microsoft DRM – Technical description" and supporting documents, on *Cryptome.org*, Oct 23 2001; at `http://cryptome.org/beale-sci-crypt.htm`

[1697] M Seaborn, T Dullien, "Exploiting the DRAM rowhammer bug to gain kernel privileges", *Google project zero blog* Mar 9 2015

[1698] T Seals 2020, "70 Percent of Mobile, Desktop Apps Contain Open-Source Bugs", *Threatpost* May 25 2020

[1699] "New RCS technology exposes most mobile users to hacking", Security Research Labs, Nov 29 2019, `https://www.srlanbs.de/bites/rcs-hacking/`

[1700] E Selleck, "Apple's App Store is Populated With Gambling and Other Apps That Abuse Enterprise Certificates", *iPhone Hacks*, Feb 12 2019

[1701] L Seltzer, "New Intel tech protects point-of-sale data", *ZDNet* Oct 15 2014

[1702] W Seltzer, M Anderson, "Census Confidentiality under the Second War Powers Act (1942-1947)," Annual Meeting of the Population Association of America, Mar 30 2007, New York; at *Official Statistics and Statistical Confidentiality: Recent Writings and Essential Documents*, at `http://www.uwm.edu/~margo/govstat/integrity.htm`

[1703] R Senderek, *'Key-Experiments – How PGP Deals With Manipulated Keys'*, 2000, at `http://senderek.de/security/key-experiments.html`

[1704] Chandak Sengoopta, *'Imprint of the Raj'*, Pan Macmillan 2004

[1705] R Severo, "Hedy Lamarr, Sultry Star Who Reigned in Hollywood Of 30's and 40's, Dies at 86", *New York Times* Jan 20 2000; US patent no 2,292,387 (HK Markey et al., Aug 11 1942)

[1706] A Shamir, "How to share a secret", in *Communications of the ACM* v 22 no 11 (Nov 1979) pp 612–613

[1707] A Shamir, "Identity-based cryptosystems and signature schemes", in *Proceedings of Crypto 1984*, Springer LNCS v 196, pp 47–53

[1708] A Shamir, "Research Announcement: Microprocessor Bugs Can Be Security Disasters", Nov 2007, at `http://cryptome.org/bug-attack.htm`

[1709] A Shamir, I Safran, E Ronen, O Dunkelman, "A Simple Explanation for the Existence of Adversarial Examples with Small Hamming Distance", *arXiv 1901.10861*, Jan 30 2019

[1710] M Sherr, E Cronin, S Clark, M Blaze, "Signaling vulnerabilities in wiretapping systems", *IEEE Security and Privacy* v 3 no 6 (Nov/Dec 2005) pp 13–25

[1711] H Shacham, "The geometry of innocent flesh on the bone: return-into-libc without function calls (on the x86)" *ACM CCS* 2007 pp 552–561.

[1712] Y Shachmurove, G Fishman, S Hakim, "The burglar as a rational economic agent", Technical Report CARESS Working Paper 97-07, U Penn University of Pennsylvania Center for Analytic Research in Economics and the Social Sciences, June 1997

[1713] J Shafer, "Trump's Daily Dose of Distraction", *Politico* May 19 2020

[1714] G Shah, A Molina, M Blaze, "Keyboards and Covert Channels", in *15th USENIX Security Symposium* 2006, at `http://www.crypto.com/papers/`

[1715] A Shaik, R Borgaonkar, SJ Park, JP Seifert, "New vulnerabilities in 4G and 5G cellular access network protocols: exposing device capabilities", *WiSec 2019* pp 221–231

[1716] Y Shaked, A Wool, "Cracking the Bluetooth PIN", *Mobisys 2005*

[1717] CE Shannon, "A Mathematical Theory of Communication", in *Bell Systems Technical Journal* v 27 (1948) pp 379–423, 623–656

[1718] CE Shannon, "Communication theory of secrecy systems", in *Bell Systems Technical Journal* v 28 (1949) pp 656–715

[1719] C Shapiro, "Antitrust in a time of populism", *SSRN 3058345*, 2017

[1720] C Shapiro, "Protecting Competition in the American Economy: Merger Control, Tech Titans, Labor Markets", *Journal of Economic Perspectives* v 33 no 3 (2019) pp 69–93

[1721] C Shapiro, H Varian, *'Information Rules'*, Harvard Business School Press 1998

[1722] K Sharad, G Danezis, "An Automated Social Graph De-anonymization Technique", *WPES '14 – Workshop on Privacy in the Electronic Society* (2014) pp 47–58

[1723] M Sharif, S Bhagavatula, L Bauer, M Reiter, "Accessorize to a Crime: Real and Stealthy Attacks on State-Of-The-Art Face Recognition", *ACM CCS* (2016)

[1724] D Sherwin, "Fraud – the Unmanaged Risk", in *Financial Crime Review* v 1 no 1 (Fall 2000) pp 67–69

[1725] S Sheye, "SSL Client Certificates – Not Securing the Web", in *Cryptomathic NewsOnInk Quarterly Newsletter* (Nov 2006)

[1726] B Shneiderman, "Human-Centred Artificial Intelligence: Reliable, Safe and Trustworthy", *International Journal of Computer-Human Interaction* v 36 no 6 (2020) pp 495–504

[1727] JF Shoch, JA Hupp, "The 'Worm' Programs – Early Experience with a Distributed Computation", *Comm ACM* v 25 no 3 (1982) pp 172–180

[1728] PW Shor, "Algorithms for Quantum Computers", in *35th FOCS* (1994), IEEE, pp 124–134

[1729] A Short, *'Response to FOI request to Driver and vehicle Standards Agency'*, Jan 13 2020, at `https://www.whatdotheyknow.com/request/tachograph_offence_statistics`

[1730] A Shostack, P Syverson, "What Price Privacy? (and why identity theft is about neither identity nor theft)", in *Economics of Information Security*, Kluwer Academic Publishers, 2004, Chapter 11

[1731] V Shoup, "OAEP Reconsidered", IBM Zürich, Switzerland, September 18, 2001

[1732] JL Shreeve, "Chip and Pain: A Financial Fiasco", *The Independent* April 22 2009

[1733] I Shumailov, YR Zhao, D Bates, N Papernot, R Mullins, R Anderson, "Sponge Examples: Energy-Latency Attacks on Neural Networks", *arXiv 2006.03463* Jun 5 2020

[1734] I Shumailov, L Simon, J Yan, R Anderson, "Hearing your touch: A new acoustic side channel on smartphones", *arXiv:1903.11137* (2019), based on first author's MPhil thesis of 2017

[1735] I Shumailov, YR Zhao, R Mullins, R Anderson, "The taboo trap: Behavioural detection of adversarial samples", *arXiv:1811.07375* Nov 18 2018

[1736] I Shumailov, YR Zhao, R Mullins, R Anderson, "Towards Certifiable Adversarial Sample Detection", *arXiv:2002.08740*, Feb 20 2020

[1737] D Shumow, N Ferguson, "On the Possibility of a Back Door in the NIST SP800-90 Dual Ec Prng", *Crypto rump session* (2007)

[1738] O Sibert, D Bernstein, D Van Wie, "The DigiBox: A Self-Protecting Container for Information Commerce", *Usenix Security* (1995)

[1739] O Sibert, PA Porras, R Lindell, "An Analysis of the Intel 80x86 Security Architecture and Implementations", in *IEEE Transactions on Software Engineering* v 22 no 5 (May 96) pp 283–293

[1740] D Silver, A Huang, CJ Maddison, A Guez, L Sifre, G van den Driessche, J Schrittwieser, I Antonoglou, V Panneershelvam, M Lanctot, S Dieleman, D Grewe, J Nham, N Kalchbrenner, I Sutskever, T Lillicrap, M Leach, K Kavukcuoglu, T Graepel, D Hassabis, "Mastering the game of Go with deep neural networks and tree search" *Nature* v 529 (2016) pp 484–489

[1741] C Silverman, "Apps Installed On Millions Of Android Phones Tracked User Behavior To Execute A Multimillion-Dollar Ad Fraud Scheme", *BuzzFeed News*, Oct 23 2018

[1742] C Silverman, "Popular VPN And Ad-Blocking Apps Are Secretly Harvesting User Data", *BuzzFeed News*, Mar 9 2020

[1743] C Silverman, R Mac, "Facebook Fired An Employee Who Collected Evidence Of Right-Wing Pages Getting Preferential Treatment", *BuzzFeed News*, Aug 6 2020

[1744] C Silverman, R Mac, P Dixit, " 'I Have Blood on My Hands': A Whistleblower Says Facebook Ignored Global Political Manipulation", *BuzzFeed News*, Sep 14 2020

[1745] N Silvester, "Doctor who hacked into Prime Minister's health records escapes prosecution", *Daily Record* Jan 10 2012

[1746] C Simoiu, C Gates, J Bonneau, S Goel, " 'I was told to buy a software or lose my computer. I ignored it': A study of ransomware", *SOUPS 2019*

[1747] *Luther Simjian – Inventor of the Week*, at `https://lemelson.mit.edu/resources/luther-george-simjian`

[1748] D Simmons, "BBC fools HSBC voice recognition security system", *BBC* May 19 2017

[1749] GJ Simmons, "The Prisoners' Problem and the Subliminal Channel", in *Proceedings of CRYPTO '83*, Plenum Press (1984) pp 51–67

[1750] GJ Simmons, "A system for verifying user identity and authorization at the point-of sale or access," *Cryptologia* v 8 no 1 (1984) pp 1–21

[1751] GJ Simmons, "How to Insure that Data Acquired to Verify Treaty Compliance are Trustworthy", GJ Simmons, *Proceedings of the IEEE* v 76 no 5 (1988; reprinted as a chapter in [1752])

[1752] GJ Simmons (ed) *'Contemporary Cryptology – The Science of Information Integrity'*, IEEE Press (1992)

[1753] GJ Simmons, "A Survey of Information Authentication", in [1752] pp 379–439

[1754] GJ Simmons, "An Introduction to Shared Secret and/or Shared Control Schemes and Their Application", in [1752] pp 441–497

[1755] GJ Simmons, invited talk at the *1993 ACM Conference on Computer and Communications Security*, Fairfax, Virginia, Nov 3–5, 1993

[1756] GJ Simmons, "Subliminal Channels; Past and Present", *European Transactions on Telecommunications* v 5 no 4 (Jul/Aug 94) pp 459–473

[1757] GJ Simmons, "The History of Subliminal Channels", in *IEEE Journal on Selcted Areas in Communications* v 16 no 4 (April 1998) pp 452–462

[1758] H Simon, *'Administrative Behavior'*, 4th ed., Free Press 1997

[1759] H Simon, *'The Sciences of the Artificial'*, 3rd ed., MIT Press 1996

[1760] L Simon, RJ Anderson, "PIN Skimmer: Inferring PINs Through The Camera and Microphone", *Third ACM workshop on Security and Privacy in Smartphones & mobile devices (SPSM 2013)* pp 67–78

[1761] L Simon, RJ Anderson, "Security Analysis of Android Factory Resets", *Mobile Security Technologies (MoST) 2015*

[1762] L Simon, D Chisnall, RJ Anderson, "What you get is what you C: Controlling side effects in mainstream C compilers", *IEEE European Symposium on Security and Privacy (EUro S&P)* 2018, `https://sites.google.com/view/laurent-simon`

[1763] L Simon, WD Xu, RJ Anderson, "Don't interrupt me while I type: Inferring text entered through gesture typing on android keyboards", *PoPETs* 2016 v 3 pp 136–154

[1764] R Singel, "Yahoo Outed Chinese Dissident Knowing Investigation Was Political, Documents Show – UPDATED", in *Wired* July 31 2007

[1765] R Singel, "Point, Click … Eavesdrop: How the FBI Wiretap Net Operates", in *Wired* Aug 29 2007

[1766] N Singer, A Krolik, "Grindr and OkCupid Spread Personal Details, Study Says", *EarthInfo Now* Jan 14 2019

[1767] N Singer, N Perlroth, A Krolik, "Zoom Rushes to Improve Privacy for Consumers Flooding Its Service", *New York Times* Apr 8 2020

[1768] M Singh, P Leu, S Capkun, "UWB with Pulse reordering: Securing Ranging Against Relay and Physical-Layer Attacks", *NDSS 2019*

[1769] A Sipress, "Tracking Traffic by Cell Phone; Md., Va. to Use Transmissions to Pinpoint Congestion", in *Washington Post* (22/12/1999) p A01

[1770] KS Siyan, J Casad, J Millecan, D Yarashus, P Tso, J Shoults, *'Windows NT Server 4 – Professional Reference'*, New Riders Publishing (1996)

[1771] SP Skorobogatov, "Copy Protection in Modern Microcontrollers", at `http://www.cl.cam.ac.uk/~sps32/mcu_lock.html`

[1772] SP Skorobogatov, *'Low temperature data remanence in static RAM'*, Cambridge University Technical Report UCAM-CL-TR-536 (June 2002)

[1773] SP Skorobogatov, *'Semi-invasive attacks – A new approach to hardware security analysis'*, PhD Thesis, 2004; University of Cambridge Technical Report 630, 2005

[1774] SP Skorobogatov, "Data Remanence in Flash Memory Devices", in *CHES 2005* pp 339–353

[1775] SP Skorobogatov, "Optically Enhanced Position-Locked Power Analysis", in *CHES 2006* pp 61–75

[1776] SP Skorobogatov, "Tamper resistance and physical attacks", at *Summer School on Cryptographic Hardware, Side-Channel and Fault Attacks*, June 12–15, 2006, Louvain-la-Neuve, Belgium; slides at `http://www.cl.cam.ac.uk/~sps32`

[1777] SP Skorobogatov, "Optical surveillance on silicon chips: your crypto keys are visible", Security group seminar Oct 13 2009, slides at `https://www.cl.cam.ac.uk/~sps32/`

[1778] SP Skorobogatov, "Flash Memory 'Bumping' Attacks", *CHES 2010*

[1779] SP Skorobogatov, C Woods, "Breakthrough silicon scanning discovers backdoors in military chip", *CHES 2012*

[1780] SP Skorobogatov, "Security, reliability and back doors", Security group seminar May 13 2013, slides at `https://www.cl.cam.ac.uk/~sps32/`

[1781] SP Skorobogatov, "The bumpy road towards iPhone 5c NAND mirroring", arXiv:1609.04327, Sep 14 2016; project page at `https://www.cl.cam.ac.uk/~sps32/5c_proj.html`

[1782] SP Skorobogatov, "Deep dip teardown of tubeless insulin pump", *arXiv:1709.06026*, Sep 18 2017

[1783] SP Skorobogatov, "How microprobing can attack encrypted memory", *Proceedings of Euromicro Conference on Digital System Design, AHSA 2017 Special Session* (2017)

[1784] SP Skorobogatov, "Hardware Security: Present challenges and Future directions", *IC Hardware Analysis Workshop, NTU, Singapore 2018* at `http://www.cl.cam.ac.uk/~sps32`

[1785] SP Skorobogatov, "Is Hardware Security prepared for unexpected discoveries?", *2018 IEEE International Symposium on the Physical and Failure Analysis of Integrated Circuits* pp 1–4

[1786] SP Skorobogatov, RJ Anderson, "Optical Fault Induction Attacks", in *Cryptographic Hardware and Embedded Systems Workshop* (CHES 2002), Springer LNCS v 2523 pp 2–12

[1787] SP Skorobogatov, C Woods. "In the blink of an eye: There goes your AES key" *IACR Preprint 2012/296*

[1788] B Skyrms, *'Evolution of the Social Contract'*, Cambridge University Press (1996)

[1789] R Sleevi, "What's wrong with the ecosystem", *CA Browser Forum* (2014), `https://cabforum.org/wp-content/uploads/CABF45-Sleevi-Whats-Wrong-With-the-Ecosystem.pdf`

[1790] R Sleevi, "Sustaining Digital Certificate Security", *Google Security Blog* Oct 28 2015

[1791] P Slovic, ML Finucane, E Peters, DG MacGregor, "Rational Actors or Rational Fools? Implications of the Affect Heuristic for Behavioral Economics"; revised version as "The Affect Heuristic" in *Heuristics and Biases: The Psychology of Intuitive Judgment*, CUP (2002) pp 397–420

[1792] A Smith, *'An Inquiry into the Nature and Causes of the Wealth of Nations'*, 1776

[1793] A Smith, "New fake £20 notes 'trick shop assistants then peel off within a week' ", *Metro* Nov 15 2018

[1794] B Smith, "What's Facebook's Deal With Donald Trump?" *New York Times* June 21 2020

[1795] B Smith, "The Week Old Hollywood Finally, Actually Died" *New York Times* Aug 16 2020

[1796] C Smith, *'The Car Hacker's Handbook'*, No Starch Press, 2016

[1797] E Smith, "The Incredibly Technical History of Digital Rights Management", *Vice* Oct 19 2017

[1798] RE Smith, "Constructing a high assurance mail guard", in *Seventeenth National Computer Security Conference* (1994) pp 247–253

[1799] SW Smith, SH Weingart, "Building a High-Performance, Programmable Secure Coprocessor", IBM Technical report RC 21102, also in *Computer Networks (Special Issue on Computer Network Security)* v 31 (Apr 1999) pp 831–860

[1800] P Smulders, "The Threat of Information Theft by Reception of Electromagnetic Radiation from RS-232 Cables", in *Computers & Security* v 9 (1990) pp 53–58

[1801] T Snoke, "Best Practices for NTP Services", *SEI Blog* April 3 2017

[1802] T Snyder, *'The Road to Unfreedom'*, Bodley Head 2018

[1803] O Solon, "NHS patient data made publicly available online", *Wired* Mar 3 2014

[1804] D Solove, "A Taxonomy of Privacy", in *University of Pennsylvania Law Review* v 154 no 3 (2006) pp 477–560; at `http://papers.ssrn.com/abstract_id=667622`

[1805] A Soltani, R Calo, C Bergstrom, "Contact-tracing apps are not a solution to the COVID-19 crisis", *TechStream* April 27, 2020

[1806] R Sommer, V Paxson, "Outside the Closed World: On Using Machine Learning for Network Intrusion Detection", *IEEE Symposium on Security and Privacy* (2010)

[1807] DX Song, D Wagner, XQ Tian, "Timing analysis of keystrokes and SSH timing attacks", in *Proceedings of 10th USENIX Security Symposium* (2001)

[1808] R v Department of Health, ex parte Source Informatics: [2000] 2 WLR 940

[1809] South West Thames Regional Health Authority, *'Report of the Inquiry into the London Ambulance Service'* (1993), at `http://www.cs.ucl.ac.uk/staff/A.Finkelstein/las.html`

[1810] E Spafford, "The Internet worm program: an analysis", in *Computer Communications Review* v 19 no 1 (Jan 89) pp 17–57

[1811] A Sparrow, "NHS patient records may be shared with private companies", The Guardian Dec 4 2011

[1812] J Specht, "The price of plenty: how beef changed America", *The Guardian* 7 May 2019, and *'Red Meat Republic'*, Princeton University Press (2019)

[1813] M Specter, "Do fingerprints lie? The gold standard of forensic evidence is now being challenged", *New York Times*, May 27, 2002

[1814] MA Specter, J Koppel, D Weitzner, "The Ballot is Busted Before the Blockchain: A Security Analysis of Voatz, the First Internet Voting Application Used in U.S. Federal Elections", Feb 13 2020

[1815] R Spencer, S Smalley, P Loscocco, M Hibler, D Andersen, J Lepreau, "The Flask Security Architecture: System Support for Diverse Security Policies," in *Proceedings of the 8th USENIX Security Symposium* (1999) pp 123–139

[1816] C Spensky, J Stewart, A Yerukhimov, R Shay, A Trachtenberg, R Housley, RK Cunningham, "SoK: Privacy on Mobile Devices – It's Complicated", *Proceedings on Privacy Enhancing Technologies* vol 2016 no 3

[1817] "Tip von Urmel", in *Der Spiegel*, Sep 11 1995

[1818] N Springer, "When Apps Get Your Medical Data, Your Privacy May Go With It", *New York Times* Sep 3 2019

[1819] S Stamm, Z Ramzan, M Jakobsson, "Drive-By Pharming", *Indiana University Department of Computer Science Technical Report TR641*, 2006

[1820] M Stamp, RM Low, *'Applied Cryptanalysis'*, Wiley 2007

[1821] T Standage, *'The Victorian Internet'*, Phoenix Press 1999

[1822] F Stajano, RJ Anderson, "The Resurrecting Duckling: Security Issues in Ad-Hoc Wireless Networks", in *'Security Protocols – 7th International Workshop'*, Springer LNCS 1796 pp 172–182

[1823] F Stajano, P Wilson, "Understanding scam victims: seven principles for systems security", *Cambridge University Computer Lab tech report no 754* (2009)

[1824] S Staniford, D Moore, V Paxson, N Weaver, "The Top Speed of Flash Worms", in *WORM04*, 2004

[1825] "Computer Chip Usage in Toner Cartridges and Impact on the Aftermarket: Past, Current and Future", Static Control, Inc., formerly at `http://www.scc-inc.com/special/oemwarfare/whitepaper/default.htm`, retrieved via `www.archive.org`

[1826] N Statt, "Fortnite for Android will ditch Google Play Store for Epic's website", *The Verge* Aug 3 2018

[1827] WA Steer, "VideoDeCrypt", at `http://www.ucl.ac.uk/~ucapwas/vdc/`

[1828] P Stein, P Feaver, *'Assuring Control of Nuclear Weapons'*, CSIA occasional paper number 2, Harvard University 1987

[1829] J Steiner, BC Neuman, JI Schiller, "Kerberos: An Authentication Service for Open Network Systems", in *USENIX (Winter 1988)*; version 5 in *'RFC 1510: The Kerberos Network Authentication Service (V5)'*

[1830] N Stephenson, *'Snow Crash'*, Bantam Doubleday Dell (1992)

[1831] M Stevens, E Bursztein, P Karpman, A Albertini, Y Markov, A Petit Bianco, C Baisse, "Announcing the first SHA1 collision", Google security blog (Feb 23 2017)

[1832] DR Stinson, *'Cryptography – Theory and Practice'*, CRC Press 1995

[1833] M Stoller, "Absentee Ownership: How Amazon, Facebook, and Google Ruin Commerce Without Noticing", *BIG by Matt Stoller* Jul 28 2020

[1834] M Stoller, "Warren Buffett: America's Folksiest Predator", *BIG by Matt Stoller* Aug 10 2020

[1835] B Stone, "Amazon Erases Orwell Books From Kindle", *New York Times* Jul 17 2009

[1836] B Stone-Gross, T Holz, G Stringhini, G Vigna, "The Underground Economy of Spam: A Botmaster's Perspective of Coordinating Large-Scale Spam Campaigns", *USENIX Workshop on Large-Scale Exploits and Emerging Threats (LEET)* (2011)

[1837] PO Stoutland, S Pitts-Kiefer, *'Nuclear Weapons in the New Cyber Age'*, Nuclear Threat Initiative 2018

[1838] O Storbeck, T Kinder, S Palma, "EY failed to check Wirecard bank statements for 3 years", *Financial Times* Jun 26 2020

[1839] S Stover, D Dittrich, J Hernandez, S Dittrich, "Analysis of the Storm and Nugache trojans: P2P is here", *;login* Dec 2007

[1840] J van der Straaten, "So You Think Digital is the Future? Your Internet Data is Rotting", *Researchgate* May 2019

[1841] R Strehle, *'Verschlüsselt – Der Fall Hans Bühler'*, Werd Verlag 1994

[1842] E Strickland, "Expert Questions Claim That St. Jude Pacemaker Was Hacked", *IEEE Spectrum* Sep 2 2016

[1843] DH Strobel, B Driessen, T Kasper, G Leander, D Oswald, F Schellenberg, C Paar, "Fuming Acid and Cryptanalysis: Handy Tools for Overcoming a Digital Locking and Access Control System", *Crypto 2013* pp 147–164

[1844] A Stubblefield, J Ioannidis, A Rubin, "Using the Fluhrer, Mantin, and Shamir Attack to Break WEP", in *ISOC 2002*

[1845] C Stupp, "Fraudsters Used AI to Mimic CEO's Voice in Unusual Cybercrime Case", *Wall Street Journal*, Aug 30 2019

[1846] G Suarez-Tanguil, G Stringhini, "Eight Years of Rider Measurement in the Android Malware Ecosystem", *IEEE Transactions on Dependable and Secure Computing* (2018)

[1847] Suetonius (Gaius Suetonius Tranquillus), *'Vitae XII Caesarum'*, translated into English as *'History of twelve Caesars'* by Philemon Holland, 1606; Nutt 1899

[1848] T Sugawara, B Cyr, S Rampazzi, D Genkin, K Fu, "Light Commands: Laser-Based Audio Injection Attacks on Voice-Controllable Systems", at *https://lightcommands.com* Nov 11 2019

[1849] J Suler, "The Online Disinhibition Effect", *CyberPsychology & Behavior* (July 2004)

[1850] SC Sundaramurthy, M Wesch, XM Ou, J McHugh, SR Rajagopalan, AG Bardas, "Humans Are Dynamic - Our Tools Should Be Too", *IEEE Internet Computing* v 21 (May-June 2017) pp 40–46

[1851] D Sutherland, "A Model of Information", in *9th National Computer Security Conference* (1986)

[1852] T Swarbrick, "Our National Security Council is a joke", *Unherd* May 20 2020

[1853] L Sweeney, "Weaving Technology and Policy Together to Maintain Confidentiality", in *Journal of Law, Medicine and Ethics* v 25 no 2–3 (1997) pp 98–110

[1854] L Sweeney, JS Yoo, L Perovich, KE Boronow, P Brown, JG Brody, " Re-identification Risks in HIPAA Safe Harbor Data: A study of data from one environmental health study", *Technology Science* 2017082801 (2017)

[1855] F Swiderski, W Snyder, *'Threat Modeling'*, Microsoft Press 2004

[1856] P Swire, "Efficient Confidentiality for Privacy, Security, and Confidential Business Information", Brookings-Wharton Papers on Financial Services (2003), at `http://ssrn.com/abstract=383180`

[1857] P Swire, "A Theory of Disclosure for Security and Competitive Reasons: Open Source, Proprietary Software, and Government Agencies", in *Houston Law Review* v 42 no 5 (Jan 2006) pp 101–148; at `http://ssrn.com/abstract_id=842228`

[1858] *Symposium On Usable Privacy and Security*, `http://cups.cs.cmu.edu/soups/2007/`

[1859] J Szczesny, "Daimler Agrees to Multi-Billion Dollar Diesel Settlement for U.S. Company paying out more than $2.2 billion", *The Detroit Bureau*, Aug 14 2020

[1860] C Szegedy, W Zaremba, I Sutskever, J Bruna, D Erhan, IJ Goodfellow, R Fergus, "Intriguing properties of neural networks", *arXiv 1312.6199* (2013)

[1861] A Tang, S Sethumadhavan, S Stolfo, "CLKSCREW: Exposing the Perils of Security-Oblivious Energy Management", *Usenix Security* (2017)

[1862] S Tajik, F Ganji, JP Seifert, H Lohrke, C Boit, "Laser Fault Attack on Physically Unclonable Functions", *FDTC 2015*

[1863] AS Tanenbaum, M van Steen *'Distributed systems'*, Prentice Hall 2002

[1864] T Tanielian, LH Jaycox, "Invisible Wounds of War", *Rand Corporation*, 2008; p 128, 436

[1865] C Tarnovsky, "Sophisticated Million Dollar Hack To Discover Weaknesses In A Series Of Smartcards", `https://youtu.be/2td3-sWsiKg`; and "Exposing The Deep-Secure Elements Of Smartcards", `https://youtu.be/-vnik_iUuUs`, both at *hardwear.io* (2019)

[1866] C Tavris, E Aronson, *'Mistakes were made – but not by me'*, Harcourt 2007

[1867] J Taylor, "Major breach found in biometrics system used by banks, UK police and defence firms", *The Guardian* Aug 14 2019

[1868] J Taylor, MR Johnson, CG Crawford, *'DVD Demystified'*, Third edition, McGraw-Hill 2006

[1869] J Tehranian, "An Unhurried View of Copyright Reform: Bridging the Law/Norm Gap", *Utah Law Review* (2007)

[1870] J Temperton, "Inside Sellafield: how the UK's most dangerous nuclear site is cleaning up its act", *Wired*, 17 September 2016

[1871] S Tendler, N Nuttall, "Hackers run up £1m bill on Yard's phones", in *The Times*, 5 Aug 1996

[1872] T Tengs, M Adams, J Pliskin, D Safran, J Siegel, M Weinstein, J Graham, "Five-hundred life-saving interventions and their cost-effectiveness", *Risk Analysis* v 15 no 3 (1995) pp 369–390

[1873] *'Tesla deaths'*, at `https://www.tesladeaths.com/`, June 23 2020

[1874] E Tews, *'DECT Security Analysis'*, PhD Thesis, Darmstadt, 2012

[1875] E Tews, J Wälde, M Weiner, "Breaking DVB-CSA", in *Western European Workshop, WEWoRC 2011*

[1876] E Tews, RP Weinmann, A Pyshkin, "Breaking 104 bit WEP in less than 60 seconds", *Cryptology ePrint archive*, Apr 2007

[1877] RH Thaler, *'Misbehaving: The Making of Behavioural Economics'*, Penguin 2016

[1878] RH Thaler, "Nudge, not sludge", *Science* v 361 no 6401 (2018) p 431

[1879] R Thaler, C Sunstein, *'Nudge'*, Penguin 2009

[1880] L Thalheim, J Krissler, PM Ziegler, "Body Check – Biometric Access Protection Devices and their Programs Put to the Test", *c't magazine*, Nov 2002 p 114

[1881] H Thimbleby, "Improving safety in medical devices and systems", *IEEE International Conference on Healthcare Informatics* (2013)

[1882] H Thimbleby, "Safer user interfaces: A case study in improving number entry", *IEEE Transactions on Software Engineering* v 41 no 7 (2015) pp 711–729

[1883] DR Thomas, AR Beresford, A Rice, "Security Metrics for the Android Ecosystem", *Workshop on Security and Privacy in Smartphones and Mobile Devices, 2015* pp 87–98

[1884] TL Thomas, "Dragon Bytes: Chinese Information-War Theory and Practice", Foreign Military Studies Office, Fort Leavenworth, Kansas, 2004

[1885] K Thomas, A Moscicki, "New research: How effective is basic account hygiene at preventing hijacking", *Google Security Blog* May 17 2019

[1886] C Thompson, "YouTube's Plot to Silence Conspiracy Theories", *Wired* Sep 18 2020

[1887] K Thompson, "Reflections on Trusting Trust", in *Communications of the ACM* v 27 no 8 (Aug 84) pp 761–763

[1888] R Thompson, "Google Sponsored Links Not Safe", Exploit Prevention Labs Apr 24 2007, at `http://explabs.blogspot.com/2007/04/google-sponsored-links-not-safe.html`; see also J Richards, "Hackers hijack Google AdWords", *The Times*, Apr 27 2007

[1889] SA Thompson, C Warzel, "Twelve Million Phones, One Dataset, Zero Privacy", *New York Times* Dec 19, 2019

[1890] I Thomson, "Talk about unintended consequences: GDPR is an identity thief's dream ticket to Europeans' data", in *The Register* Aug 9 2019

[1891] S Thrun, M Montemerlo, H Dahlkamp, D Stavens, A Aron, J Diebel, P Fong, J Gale, M Halpenny, G Hoffmann, KL Oakley, M Palatucci, V Pratt, P Stang, S Strohband, C Dupont, LE Jendrossek, C Koelen, C Markey, C Rummel, J van Niekerk, E Jensen, P Alessandrini, G Bradski, B Davies, S Ettinger, A Kaehler, A Nefian, P Mahoney, "Stanley: The Robot That Won the DARPA Grand Challenge", *Journal of Field Robotics*, Springer Texts in Advanced Robotics v 36, pp 1–43; at `https://robots.stanford.edu/papers/thrun.stanley05.pdf`

[1892] Y Tian, C Herley, S Schechter, "StopGuessing: Using Guessed Passwords to Thwart Online Guessing", *EuroS&P* (2019)

[1893] TimeWarner, "Carmine Caridi, Motion Picture Academy Member Who Handed Over His Awards Screeners for Illegal Duplication, Ordered to Pay $300,000 to Warner Bros. Entertainment Inc.", Nov 23 2004, at `http://www.timewarner.com/corp/newsroom/pr/0,20812,832500,00.html`

[1894] AZ Tirkel, GA Rankin, RM van Schyndel, WJ Ho, NRA Mee, CF Osborne, "Electronic Watermark", in *Digital Image Computing, Technology and Applications* (DICTA 93) McQuarie University (1993) pp 666–673

[1895] MW Tobias, *'Locks, Safes and Security – An International Police Reference'*, at `https://www.securitylaboratories.org/`

[1896] MW Tobias, "Opening locks by bumping in five seconds or less: is it really a threat to physical security?", 2006, at `https://www.securitylaboratories.org/`

[1897] MW Tobias, "Bumping of locks – legal issues in the United States", at `https://www.securitylaboratories.org/`

[1898] MW Tobias, "The Medeco M3 Meets the Paper Clip: Is the security of this lock at risk?" (2007), at `https://www.securitylaboratories.org/`

[1899] C Tomlinson, *'Rudimentary Treatise on the Construction of Locks'*, 1853 (excerpt), at `http://www.deter.com/unix/papers/treatise_locks.html`

[1900] TT Tool, *'The MIT Lock Picking Manual'*, 1991; at `http://people.csail.mit.edu/custo/MITLockGuide.pdf`

[1901] R Torrance, D James, "The State-of-the-Art in IC Reverse Engineering", *CHES 2009* pp 363–381; also at *DAC '11* pp 333–338

[1902] MA Toy, "Chinese hack into film festival site", *Sydney Morning Herald* July 26 2009

[1903] F Tramèr, P Dupré, G Rusak, G Pellegrino, D Boneh, "AdVersarial: Perceptual Ad Blocking Meets Adversarial Machine Learning", *arXiv:1811.03194*, Aug 26 2019

[1904] F Tramèr, N Papernot, I Goodfellow, D Boneh, P McDaniel, "The Space of Transferable Adversarial Examples", *arXiv 1704.03453* Apr 11 2017

[1905] F Tramèr, F Zhang, A Juels, MK Reiter, T Ristenpart, "Stealing Machine Learning Models via Prediction APIs", *arXiv 1609.02943* Oct 3 2016

[1906] A Travis, "Voice ID device to track failed asylum seekers", in *The Guardian* Mar 10 2006

[1907] A Travis, "Terror suspects cleared of tampering with 'faulty' tags", in *The Guardian* Nov 1 2013

[1908] A Travis, "Man who escaped mosque in burqa was under counter-terror restrictions", in *The Guardian* Nov 5 2013

[1909] I Traynor, "DNA database agreed for police across EU", in *The Guardian*, Jun 13 2007

[1910] P Trimintzios, C Hall, R Clayton, R Anderson, E Ouzounis, *'Resilience of the Internet Interconnection Ecosystem'*, ENISA, April 11 2011; abridged version published at WEIS 2011

[1911] A Troianovski, "Not Just a Crisis: Coronavirus Is a Test for Putin's Security State", *New York Times*, Mar 19 2020

[1912] E Tromer, *'Hardware-Based Cryptanalysis'*, PhD Thesis, Weizmann Institute of Science (2007)

[1913] C Troncoso, G Danezis, E Kosta, B Preneel, "PriPAYD: Privacy Friendly Pay-As-You-Drive Insurance", in *Workshop on Privacy in the Electronic Society* (2007)

[1914] C Troncoso, M Isaakidis, G Danezis, H Halpin "Systematizing Decentralization and Privacy: Lessons from 15 Years of Research and Deployments" *Proceedings of Privacy Enhancing Technologies* 2017 v 4 307–329

[1915] Z Tufekci, "Zuckerberg's So-Called Shift Toward Privacy", *New York Times* March 7 2019

[1916] JD Tygar, BS Yee, N Heintze, "Cryptographic Postage Indicia", in *ASIAN 96* (Springer-Verlag LNCS v 1179) pp 378–391, CMU tech report CMU-CS-96-113

[1917] D Uberti, "Facebook Went to War Against White Supremacist Terror After Christchurch. Will It Work?" *Vice* Oct 3 2019

[1918] R Uhlig, "BT admits staff could have fiddled system to win Concorde trip", in *The Daily Telegraph* July 23 1997

[1919] ukcrypto mailing list, at `http://www.chiark.greenend.org.uk/mailman/listinfo/ukcrypto`

[1920] Underwriters' Laboratories company history, at `https://www.company-histories.com/`

[1921] N Unger, S Dechand, J Bonneau, S Fahl, Hg Perl, I Goldberg, M Smith, "SoK: Secure Messaging", *IEEE Security & Privacy*, 2015

[1922] J Ungoed-Thomas, A Lorenz, "French play dirty for £1bn tank deal", in *Sunday Times* Aug 6 2000

[1923] United Kingdom Government, *'e-commerce@its.best.uk'*, 2000

[1924] United Kingdom Passport Service, *'Biometrics Enrolment Trial Report'*, May 2005

[1925] United Nations Economic Commission for Europe, *'Proposal for a new UN regulation on uniform provisions concerning the approval of vehicles with regards to cyber security and cyber security management system'*, ECE/TRANS/WP.29/2020/REVISED

[1926] M Untersinger, J Follorou, "EncroChat, cette mystérieuse société technologique prisée par le crime organisé", *Le Monde*, Aug 3 2020

[1927] UPI newswire item, Oklahoma distribution, November 26, 1983, Tulsa, Oklahoma

[1928] US Army, *'TM 31-210 Improvised Munitions Handbook'*, 1969, at `http://cryptome.org/tm-31-210.htm`

[1929] *'United States Code'* – online at `http://www4.law.cornell.edu/uscode/`

[1930] United States Court of Appeals, District of Columbia Circuit, *United States Telecom Association v. Federal Communications Commission and United States of America*, no 99-1442, 15/8/2000, at `http://pacer.cadc.uscourts.gov/common/opinions/200008/99-1442a.txt`

[1931] United States Courts, *'Wiretap Report 2017'*, at `https://www.uscourts.gov/statistics-reports/wiretap-report-2017`

[1932] US Immigration and Customs Enforcement, *'Russian national pleads guilty for role in transnational cybercrime organization responsible for more than $568 million in losses'*, Jun 29 2020

[1933] US Navy, " Navy Releases Collision Report for USS Fitzgerald and USS John S McCain Collisions" NNS171101-07 Nov 1 2017

[1934] S Usborne, "How did Tesla make some of its cars travel further during Hurricane Irma?", *The Guardian* Sep 11 2017

[1935] S Vaidhyanathan, "Facebook's new move isn't about privacy. It's about domination", *The Guardian* March 7 2019

[1936] J Valenti, "Anita Sarkeesian interview: 'The word "troll" feels too childish. This is abuse' ", The Guardian Aug 29 2015

[1937] L van Hove, "Electronic Purses: (Which) Way to Go?", in *First Monday* v 5 no 7 (June 2000)

[1938] P Van Oorschot, M Wiener, "Parallel Collision Search with Application to Hash Functions and Discrete Logarithms", *Second ACM Conference on Computer and Communications Security* pp 210–218

[1939] R van Renesse, *'Optical Document Security'* (second edition), Artech House 1997

[1940] R van Renesse, "Verifying versus falsifying banknotes", in *Optical Security and Counterfeit Deterrence Techniques II* (1998), IS&T (The Society for Imaging Science and Technology) and SPIE (The International Society for Optical Engineering) v 3314, pp 71–85

[1941] H van Vliet, *'Software Engineering – Principles and Practice'*, Wiley (second edition), 2000

[1942] R van Voris, "Black Box Car Idea Opens Can of Worms", in *Law News Network* Jun 4 1999

[1943] V Varadharajan, N Kumar, Y Mu, "Security Agent Based Distributed Authorization: An Approach", in *20th National Information Systems Security Conference*, proceedings published by NIST (1998) pp 315–328

[1944] H Varian, "Economic Aspects of Personal Privacy", in *Privacy and Self-Regulation in the Information Age*, National Telecommunications and Information Administration report, 1996

[1945] HR Varian, *'Intermediate Microeconomics – A Modern Approach'*, Norton 1999

[1946] HR Varian, "New Chips Can Keep a Tight Rein on Customers", *The New York Times* July 4 2002

[1947] H Varian, "Managing Online Security Risks", Economic Science Column, The New York Times, June 1, 2000

[1948] H Varian, "New chips and keep a tight rein on consumers, even after they buy a product", New York Times, July 4 2002

[1949] H Varian, "System Reliability and Free Riding", in *Economics of Information Security*, Kluwer 2004 pp 1–15

[1950] H Varian, Keynote address to the Third Digital Rights Management Conference, Berlin, Germany, January 13, 2005

[1951] M Vasek, J Bonneau, R Castellucci, C Keith, T Moore, "The Bitcoin Brain Drain: Examining the Use and Abuse of Bitcoin Brain Wallets", *Financial Cryptography* (2016)

[1952] M Vass, " 'Spearmint Rhino took my teen son's money while he was at home in bed' – more complain about lap dancing club" *Bournemouth Daily Echo* Nov 15 2014

[1953] S Vaudenay, "Security Flaws Induced by CBC Padding", *Eurocrypt 2002*

[1954] A Vaughan, "UK launched passport photo checker it knew would fail with dark skin", *New Scientist* Oct 9 2019

[1955] W Venema, "Murphy's Law and Computer Security", in *Usenix Security 96* pp 187–193

[1956] R Verdult, F Garcia, B Ege, "Dismantling Megamos Crypto: Wirelessly Lockpicking a Vehicle Immobilizer", *Usenix 2013*

[1957] R Verdult, F Garcia, "Cryptanalysis of the Megamos Crypto automotive immobilizer" *USENIX; login* v 40 no 6 pp 17–22

[1958] A Vetterl, "Three Paper Thursday: Will we ever get IoT security right?", `www.lightbluetouchpaper.org` May 14 2020

[1959] A Vetterl, R Clayton, "Honware: A Virtual Honeypot Framework for Capturing CPE and IoT Zero Days" *APWG Symposium on Electronic Crime Research (eCrime)*, Nov 2019

[1960] "Link 16/MIDS Frequently Asked Questions", *Viasat*, at `https://www.viasat.com/support/data-links/faq`

[1961] J Vijayan, "Retail group takes a swipe at PCI, puts card companies 'on notice' ", *Computerworld* Oct 4 2007

[1962] N Villeneuve, "DNS tampering in China", Jul 10 2007

[1963] N Villeneuve, "Breaching Trust: An analysis of surveillance and security practices on China's TOM-Skype platform", *Information Warfare Monitor* Oct 1 2008

[1964] J Vincent, "Forty percent of 'AI startups' in Europe don't actually use AI, claims report", *The Verge* Mar 5 2019

[1965] B Vinck, "Security Architecture" (3G TS 33.102 v 3.2.0), from *Third Generation Partnership Project*, at `http://www.3gpp.org/TSG/Oct_status_list.htm`

[1966] B Vinck, "Lawful Interception Requirements" (3G TS 33.106 v 3.0.0), from *Third Generation Partnership Project*, at `http://www.3gpp.org/TSG/Oct_status_list.htm`

[1967] VISA International, *'Integrated Circuit Chip Card – Security Guidelines Summary*, version 2 draft 1, November 1997

[1968] A Viterbi, "Spread spectrum communications – myths and realities", in *IEEE Communications Magazine* v 17 no 3 (May 1979) pp 11–18

[1969] PR Vizcaya, LA Gerhardt, "A Nonlinear Orientation Model for Global Description of Fingerprints", in *Pattern Recognition* v 29 no 7 (July 96) pp 1221–1231

[1970] W Vogels, "Modern applications at AWS", *All Things Distributed*, Aug 28 2019

[1971] G Volovik, *'The Universe in a Helium Droplet'*, Clarendon Press, Oxford 2003

[1972] L von Ahn, *personal communication*, 2006

[1973] L von Ahn, M Blum, NJ Hopper, J Langford, "CAPTCHA: Using Hard AI Problems For Security", *Advances in Cryptology – Eurocrypt 2003*, Springer LNCS v 2656 pp 294–311

[1974] A Vrij, *'Detecting Lies and Deceit: Pitfalls and Opportunities'*, Wiley 2008

[1975] D Wagner, "Cryptanalysis of Some Recently-Proposed Multiple Modes of Operation", in *Fifth International Workshop on Fast Software Encryption* (1998), Springer LNCS v 1372 pp 254–269

[1976] D Wagner, I Goldberg, M Briceno, "GSM Cloning", at `http://www.isaac.cs.berkeley.edu/isaac/gsm-faq.html`; see also `http://www.scard.org/gsm/`

[1977] D Wagner, B Schneier, "Analysis of the SSL 3.0 Protocol", in *Second USENIX Workshop on Electronic Commerce* (1996), pp 29–40

[1978] M Waldman, AD Rubin, LF Cranor, "Publius: A robust, tamper-evident, censorship-resistant, web publishing system", in *9th USENIX Security Symposium* (2000) pp 59–72

[1979] J Walker, "IC Surgery: getting to the heart of the problem with the smallest scalpel" *HardwearIO* (2019) at `https://youtu.be/o1We1o3tMWc`

[1980] M Walker, "On the Security of 3GPP Networks", Invited talk at Eurocrypt 2000, at `http://www.ieee-security.org/Cipher/ConfReports/2000/CR2000-Eurocrypt.html`

[1981] E Waltz, *'Information Warfare – Principles and Operations'*, Artech House (1998)

[1982] XQ Wang, YQ Sun, S Nanda, XF Wang, "Looking from the Mirror: Evaluating IoT Device Security through Mobile Companion Apps" *Usenix 2019*

[1983] XY Wang, DG Feng, XJ Lai, HB Yu, "Collisions for Hash Functions MD4, MD5, HAVAL-128 and RIPEMD", *IACR Cryptology ePrint Archive* Report 2004/199

[1984] XY Wang, YQL Yin, HB Yu, " Collision Search Attacks on SHA1", Feb 13 2005; refined to "Finding Collisions in the Full SHA-1", *Crypto 2005*

[1985] XY Wang, HB Yu, "How to Break MD5 and Other Hash Functions", in *Advances in Cryptology – Eurocrypt 2005*

[1986] R Want, A Hopper, V Falcao, J Gibbons, "The Active Badge Location System", in *ACM Transactions on Information Systems* v 10 no 1 (Jan 92) pp 91–102; at `http://www.cl.cam.ac.uk/research/dtg/attarchive/ab.html`

[1987] D Ward, "JTRS: A Cautionary Tale For Today", *Mitre Disrupting Acquisition Blog* Apr 1, 2020

[1988] R Ward, B Beyer, "BeyondCorp: A New Approach to Enterprise Security" *;login:* v 39 no 6 (2014) pp 6–11

[1989] WH Ware, "Security and Privacy in Computer Systems", *Spring Joint Computer Conference, 1967* pp 279–282, at `https://www.rand.org/pubs/papers/P3544.html`

[1990] WH Ware, *'Security Controls for Computer Systems: Report of Defense Science Board Task Force on Computer Security'*, Rand Report R609-1 (Feb 1970), at `https://www.rand.org/pubs/reports/R609-1.html`

[1991] M Warner, "Machine Politics In the Digital Age", in *The New York Times* November 9, 2003

[1992] SD Warren, LD Brandeis, "The Right To Privacy", Harvard Law Review series 4 (1890) pp 193–195

[1993] *'Waste Electrical and Electronic Equipment (WEEE) regulations*, UK Health and Safety Executive 2006, updated 2014, transposing Directive 2012/19/EU

[1994] S Waterman, "Analysis: Russia-Georgia cyberwar doubted", *Space War* Aug 18 2008

[1995] M Watson, "Sat-nav 'jammer' threatens to sink road pricing scheme", in *Auto Express* Aug 8th 2007

[1996] RNM Watson, "Exploiting Concurrency Vulnerabilities in Kernel System Call Wrappers", in *First USENIX Workshop on Offensive Technologies* (WOOT 07), at `http://www.watson.org/~robert/2007woot/`

[1997] RNM Watson, "A decade of OS access-control extensibility", *Communications of the ACM* v 56 no 2 (Feb 2013)

[1998] DJ Watts, *'Six Degrees – The Science of a Connected Age'*, Heinemann 2003

[1999] N Weaver, "Our Government Has Weaponized the Internet. Here's How They Did It", *Wired* Nov 13 2013

[2000] W Webb, "High-tech Security: The Eyes Have It", in *EDN* (18/12/97) pp 75–78

[2001] S Weckert, "Google Maps Hacks – Performance & Installation, 2020", `http://www.simonweckert.com/googlemapshacks.html`, Feb 2020

[2002] SH Weingart, "Physical Security for the μABYSS System", in *Proceedings of the 1987 IEEE Symposium on Security and Privacy*, pp 52–58

[2003] SH Weingart, "A Survey of Attacks and Defenses", *CHES* 2000

[2004] SH Weingart, "Mind the Gap: Updating FIPS 140", at *FIPS Physical Security Workshop*, Hawaii 2005

[2005] SH Weingart, SR White, WC Arnold, GP Double, "An Evaluation System for the Physical Security of Computing Systems", in *Sixth Annual Computer Security Applications Conference* IEEE (1990) pp 232–243

[2006] L Weinstein, "IDs in Color Copies—A PRIVACY Forum Special Report" in *Privacy Forum Digest*, v 8 no 18 (6 Dec 1999), at `http://www.vortex.com/privacy/priv.08.18`

[2007] L Weinstein, "The Online Medical Records Trap", *Lauren Weinstein's Blog* Oct 4 2007, at `http://lauren.vortex.com/archive/000306.html`

[2008] K Weise, N Singer, "Amazon Pauses Police Use of Its Facial Recognition Software", *New York Times* Jun 10 2020

[2009] M Weiss, M Weiss, "An assessment of threats to the US power grid", *Energy, Sustainability and Society* v 9 no 18 (2019)

[2010] C Weissman, "Security Controls in the ADEPT–50 Time Sharing System", in *AFIPS Conference Proceedings, v 35, 1969 Fall Joint Computer Conference* pp 119–133

[2011] G Welchman, *'The Hut Six Story'*, McGraw Hill 1982

[2012] B Wels, R Gonggrijp, "Bumping locks", 2006, at `http://www.toool.nl/bumping.pdf`

[2013] A Welz, "Unnatural Surveillance: How Online Data Is Putting Species at Risk," *Yale Environment 360*, Sep 6 2017

[2014] J Werner, J Mason, M Antonakakis, M Polychronakis, F Monrose, "The SEVerESt Of Them All: Inference Attacks Against Secure Virtual Enclaves," *ACM Asia CCS* July 2019

[2015] *'Smart Metering – Obtaining and Using Consumption Data Relating to Domestic Premises – Data Privacy Plan*, Western Power Distribution, May 2018

[2016] A Westfeld, A Pfitzmann, "Attacks on Steganographic Systems", in *Information Hiding* (1999), Springer LNCS v 1768 pp 61–76

[2017] L Whateley, "Somebody stole £16,000 from my account but Barclays won't refund me", *The Times* Aug 20 2011; see also comments at `https://www.lightbluetouchpaper.org/2011/12/25/bankers-christmas-present/`

[2018] E Whitaker, "At SBC, It's All About 'Scale and Scope' ", in *Business Week* Nov 7 2005

[2019] G White, "The 20-Year Hunt for the Man Behind the Love Bug Virus", *Wired* Sep 12 2020

[2020] Z Whittaker, "Meet 'Muscular': NSA accused of tapping links between Yahoo, Google datacenters", *ZDnet* Oct 30 2013

[2021] Z Whittaker, "Hackers are stealing years of call records from hacked cell operators", *Techcrunch*, June 25 2019

[2022] A Whitten, JD Tygar, "Why Johnny Can't Encrypt: A Usability Evaluation of PGP 5.0", in *Eighth USENIX Security Symposium* (1999) pp 169–183

[2023] Wikileaks, *'Vault 7: CIA Hacking Tools Revealed'*, Mar 7 2017

[2024] MV Wilkes, RM Needham, *'The Cambridge CAP computer and its Operating System'*, Elsevier North Holland 1979

[2025] J Wilkins, *'Mercury; or the Secret and Swift Messenger: Shewing, How a Man May with Privacy and Speed Communicate his Thoughts to a Friend at Any Distance'*, London, Rich Baldwin 1694

[2026] L Wilson, "Understanding the Appeal of ISIS", *New England Journal of Public Policy* v 29 no 1 (2017)

[2027] C Williams, "Surge in encrypted torrents blindsides record biz", in *The Register* Nov 8 2007, at `http://www.theregister.co.uk/2007/11/08/bittorrent_encryption_explosion/`

[2028] TA Williams, "Peaceful left-wing activist, 94, with no criminal record wins eight-year battle to wipe details of his 66 anti-war, poll tax and tuition fees protests from police 'extremism' database", *Daily Mail* Jan 24 2019

[2029] E Williamson, AJ Walker, KJ Bhaskaran, S Bacon, Chris Bates, CE Morton, HJ Curtis, A Mehrkar, D Evans, P Inglesby, J Cockburn, HI Mcdonald, B MacKenna, L Tomlinson, IJ Douglas, CT Rentsch, R Mathur, A Wong, R Grieve, D Harrison, H Forbes, A Schultze, RT Croker, J Parry, F Hester, S Harper, R Perera, S Evans, L Smeeth, B Goldacre, "OpenSAFELY: factors associated with COVID-19-related hospital death in the linked electronic health records of 17 million adult NHS patients" *medRxiv* `https://doi.org/10.1101/2020.05.06.20092999` May 7 2020

[2030] B Wilson, J Hoffman, J Morgenstern, "Predictive Inequity in Object Detection", *arXiv 1902.11097* Feb 21 2019

[2031] CL Wilson, MD Garris and CI Watson, "Matching Performance for the US-VISIT IDENT System Using Flat Fingerprints", NIST IR 7110 (May 2004)

[2032] H Wimmer, J Perner, "Beliefs about beliefs: representation and constraining function of wrong beliefs in young children's understanding of deception", *Cognition* v 13 no 1 (1983) pp 103–28

[2033] D Winder, "How To Make $1 Million From Hacking: Meet Six Hacker Millionaires", *Forbes*, Aug 29 2019

[2034] FW Winterbotham, *'The Ultra Secret'*, Harper & Row 1974

[2035] P Woit, *'Not Even Wrong: The Failure of String Theory and the Continuing Challenge to Unify the Laws of Physics'*, Vintage 2007

[2036] A Wolfson, "A hoax most cruel", in *The Courier-Journal* Oct 9, 2005

[2037] K Wong, "Mobile Phone Fraud – Are GSM Networks Secure?", in *Computer Fraud and Security Bulletin* (Nov 96) pp 11–18

[2038] N Wong, "Judge tells DoJ 'No' on search queries", Google blog Mar 17 2006

[2039] E Wood, *'Housing Design, A Social Theory'*, Citizens' Housing and Planning Council of New York, 1961

[2040] L Wood, "Global Biometric System Market Report 2019: Size is Expected to Grow from USD 33.0 Billion in 2019 to USD 65.3 Billion by 2024", *BusinessWire* Nov 7 2019

[2041] Z Wood, "Dixons Carphone fined £500,000 for massive data breach", *The Guardian* Jan 9 2020

[2042] JPL Woodward, *'Security Requirements for System High and Compartmented Mode Workstations'* Mitre MTR 9992, Revision 1, 1987 (also published by the Defense Intelligence Agency as document DDS-2600-5502-87)

[2043] "Automated teller machines (ATMs) (per 100,000 adults)", *World Bank*, `https://data.worldbank.org/indicator/FB.ATM.TOTL.P5`

[2044] B Wright, "The Verdict on Plaintext Signatures: They're Legal", in *Computer Law and Security Report* v 14 no 6 (Nov/Dec 94) pp 311–312

[2045] B Wright, *'The Law of Electronic Commerce: EDI, Fax and Email'*, Little, Brown 1994

[2046] DB Wright, AT McDaid, "Comparing system and estimator variables using data from real line-ups", in *Applied Cognitive Psychology* v 10 no 1 pp 75–84

[2047] JB Wright, *'Report of the Weaponization and Weapons Production and Military Use Working Group –Appendix F to the Report of the Fundamental Classification Policy Review Group'*, US Department of Energy Office of Scientific and Technical Information 1997

[2048] MA Wright, "Security Controls in ATM Systems", in *Computer Fraud and Security Bulletin*, November 1991, pp 11–14

[2049] P Wright, *'Spycatcher – The Candid Autobiography of a Senior Intelligence Officer'*, William Heinemann Australia, 1987

[2050] L Wouters, J Van den Herreweghen, FD Garcia, D Oswald, B Gierlichs, B Preneel, "Dismantling DST-80 Based Immobiliser Systems", *IACR Transactions on Cryptographic Hardware and Embedded Systems* v 2 (2020) pp 99–127

[2051] T Wu, *'The Master Switch: The Rise and Fall of Information Empires'*, Knopf 2010

[2052] T Wu, *'The Attention Merchants: The Epic Scramble to Get Inside Our Heads'*, Penguin Random House 2016

[2053] T Wu, *'The Curse of Bigness'*, Atlantic 2018

[2054] R Wyden, *Letter to John Ratcliffe*, June 16 2020; linked from S Nicholls, "If you're despairing at staff sharing admin passwords, look on the bright side. That's CIA-grade security", *The Register* June 16 2020

[2055] C Wylie, *'Mindf*ck'*, Profile Books 2019

[2056] K Xiao, D Forte, Y Jin, R Karri, S Bhunia, M Tehranipoor, "Hardware Trojans: Lessons Learned after One Decade of Research", *ACM Transactions on Design Automation of Electronic Systems* v 22 no 1 (May 2016)

[2057] JX Yan, *'Security for Online Games'*, PhD thesis, University of Cambridge 2003

[2058] JX Yan, A Blackwell, RJ Anderson, A Grant, "The Memorability and Security of Passwords – Some Empirical Results", University of Cambridge Computer Laboratory Technical Report no 500; also in *IEEE Security & Privacy*, Sep–Oct 2004 pp 25–29

[2059] JX Yan, B Randell, *'Security in Computer Games: from Pong to Online Poker'*, University of Newcastle Tech Report CS-TR-889 (2005)

[2060] JX Yan, B Randell, "A systematic classification of cheating in online games", at *Proceedings of 4th ACM SIGCOMM workshop on Network and system support for games* (2005)

[2061] T Ylönen, "SSH – Secure Login Connections over the Internet", in *Usenix Security 96* pp 37–42

[2062] G Yuval, "Reinventing the Travois: Encryption/MAC in 30 ROM Bytes", in *Fast Software Encryption* (1997), Springer LNCS v 1267 pp 205–209

[2063] R Zarnekow, W Brenner, "Distribution of cost over the application lifecycle – A multi-case study", *European Conference on Information Systems (ECIS)*, (2005)

[2064] *ZDnet*, "Software blocks images of money", Jan 12 2004

[2065] S van der Zee, R Clayton, RJ Anderson, "The gift of the gab: Are rental scammers skilled at the art of persuasion?" *arXiv:1911.08253* Nov 19 2019

[2066] S van der Zee, R Poppe, PJ Taylor, RJ Anderson, "To freeze or not to freeze: A culture-sensitive motion capture approach to detecting deceit", *PLOS One* April 12 2019

[2067] K Zetter, "From the Eye of a Legal Storm, Murdoch's Satellite-TV Hacker Tells All", in *Wired*, May 30 2008

[2068] K Zetter, "Report: NSA Exploited Heartbleed to Siphon Passwords for Two Years", in *Wired*, Apr 11 2014

[2069] K Zetter, "Hacker Can Send Fatal Dose to Hospital Drug Pumps", in *Wired*, Jun 8 2015

[2070] K Zetter, "Inside the Cunning, Unprecedented Hack of Ukraine's Power Grid", in *Wired*, Mar 3 2016

[2071] K Zetter, "Researchers Uncover New Version of the Infamous Flame Malware", in *Wired*, Apr 9 2019

[2072] RS Zhang, XY Wang, XH Yan, XX Jiang, "Billing Attacks on SIP-Based VOIP Systems", in *WOOT 2007*

[2073] YQ Zhang, F Monrose, M Reiter, "The security of modern password expiration: An algorithmic framework and empirical analysis", *ACM CCS* (2010)

[2074] YR Zhao, I Shumailov, H Cui, XT Gao, R Mullins, R Anderson, "Blackbox Attacks on Reinforcement Learning Agents Using Approximated Temporal Information", *DSN-DSML* 2020; also *arXiv:1909.02918* (2019)

[2075] L Zhuang, F Zhou, JD Tygar, "Keyboard Acoustic Emanations Revisited" in *12th ACM CCS* (2005)

[2076] P Zimbardo, *'The Lucifer Effect'*, Random House 2007

[2077] Ellie Zolfagharifard, "How poachers use INSTAGRAM to find their prey: Geo-tagged photos help hunters track and kill tigers and rhinos," *Daily Mail* 8 May 2014

[2078] S Zuboff, *'The Age of Surveillance Capitalism – The fight for a human future at the new frontier of power'*, Profile Books 2019

[2079] M Zviran, WJ Haga, "A Comparison of Password Techniques for Multilevel Authentication Mechanisms", in *The Computer Journal* v 36 no 3 (1993) pp 227–237

Index

B

E

electronic support, 778
Comint (communications intelligence), 778
Comsec (communications security), 778
Elint (electronic intelligence), 778
Sigint (signals intelligence), 778–779

I

M

O

P

Q

R

S

T

U

V

W

X–Y–Z